Nineteenth-Century
Literature Criticism

Guide to Gale Literary Criticism Series

When you need to review criticism of literary works, these are the Gale series to use:

If the author's death date is: **You should turn to:**

After Dec. 31, 1959
(or author is still living)

CONTEMPORARY LITERARY CRITICISM

for example: Jorge Luis Borges, Anthony Burgess,
William Faulkner, Mary Gordon,
Ernest Hemingway, Iris Murdoch

1900 through 1959

TWENTIETH-CENTURY LITERARY CRITICISM

for example: Willa Cather, F. Scott Fitzgerald,
Henry James, Mark Twain, Virginia Woolf

1800 through 1899

NINETEENTH-CENTURY LITERATURE CRITICISM

for example: Fyodor Dostoevsky, Nathaniel Hawthorne,
George Sand, William Wordsworth

1400 through 1799

LITERATURE CRITICISM FROM 1400 TO 1800
(excluding Shakespeare)

for example: Anne Bradstreet, Daniel Defoe,
Alexander Pope, François Rabelais,
Jonathan Swift, Phillis Wheatley

SHAKESPEAREAN CRITICISM

Shakespeare's plays and poetry

Antiquity through 1399

CLASSICAL AND MEDIEVAL LITERATURE CRITICISM

for example: Dante, Homer, Plato, Sophocles, Vergil,
the Beowulf Poet

Gale also publishes related criticism series:

CHILDREN'S LITERATURE REVIEW

This series covers authors of all eras who have written for the
preschool through high school audience.

SHORT STORY CRITICISM

This series covers the major short fiction writers of all
nationalities and periods of literary history.

POETRY CRITICISM

This series covers poets of all nationalities and periods of literary
history.

DRAMA CRITICISM

This series covers dramatists of all nationalities and periods of
literary history.

ISSN 0732-1864

Volume 33

Nineteenth-Century Literature Criticism

Excerpts from Criticism of the
Works of Novelists, Poets, Playwrights,
Short Story Writers, Philosophers, and Other
Creative Writers Who Died between 1800
and 1899, from the First Published Critical
Appraisals to Current Evaluations

Paula Kepos

Editor

Tina Grant
Jelena O. Krstovic'
Thomas Ligotti
Joann Prosyniuk
Lawrence J. Trudeau

Associate Editors

Gale Research Inc. · DETROIT · LONDON

STAFF

Paula Kepos, *Editor*

Tina Grant, Jelena O. Krstović, Thomas Ligotti, Joann Prosyniuk, Lawrence J. Trudeau,
Associate Editors

David Engleman, Judy Galens, Alan Hedblad, Andrew M. Kalasky, Linda M. Ross, Mark
Swartz, Debra A. Wells, *Assistant Editors*

Jeanne A. Gough, *Permissions & Production Manager*
Linda M. Pugliese, *Production Supervisor*
Paul Lewon, Lorna Mabunda, Maureen Puhl, Camille Robinson, Jennifer VanSickle,
Editorial Associates
Donna Craft, Brandy C. Johnson, Sheila Walencewicz, *Editorial Assistants*

Maureen Richards, *Research Supervisor*
Mary Beth McElmeel, *Editorial Associate*
Kathleen Jozwiak, Amy Kaechele, Julie Karmazin, Tamara C. Nott, Julie Synkonis,
Editorial Assistants

Sandra C. Davis, *Permissions Supervisor (Text)*
Maria L. Franklin, Josephine M. Keene, Denise Singleton, Kimberly F. Smilay,
Permissions Associates
Michele Lonoconus, Shelly Rakoczy, Shalice Shah, Rebecca A. Stanko,
Permissions Assistants

Margaret A. Chamberlain, *Permissions Supervisor (Pictures)*
Pamela A. Hayes, *Permissions Associate*
Nancy M. Rattenbury, Karla Kulkis, Keith Reed, *Permissions Assistants*

Mary Beth Trimper, *Production Manager*
Mary Winterhalter, *Production Assistant*

Arthur Chartow, *Art Director*
C. J. Jonik, *Keyliner*

Since this page cannot legibly accommodate all the copyright notices, the acknowledgments constitute an extension of the copyright notice.

While every effort has been made to ensure the reliability of the information presented in this publication, Gale Research Inc. neither guarantees the accuracy of the data contained herein nor assumes any responsibility for errors, omissions, or discrepancies. Gale accepts no payment for listing; and inclusion in the publication of any organization, agency, institution, publication, service, or individual does not imply endorsement of the editors or publisher. Errors brought to the attention of the publisher and verified to the satisfaction of the publisher will be corrected in future editions.

Contents

Preface

Since its inception in 1981, *Nineteenth-Century Literature Criticism* has been a valuable resource for students and librarians seeking critical commentary on writers of this transitional period in world history. Designated an "Outstanding Reference Source" by the American Library Association with the publication of its first volume, *NCLC* has since been purchased by over 6,000 school, public, and university libraries. The series has covered more than 300 authors representing 22 nationalities and over 15,000 titles. No other reference source has surveyed the critical reaction to nineteenth-century authors and literature as thoroughly as *NCLC*.

Scope of the Series

NCLC is designed to serve as an introduction for students and advanced readers to the authors of the nineteenth century, and to the most significant interpretations of these authors' works. The great poets, novelists, short story writers, dramatists, and philosophers of this period are frequently studied in high school and college literature courses. By organizing and reprinting the enormous amount of commentary written on these authors, *NCLC* helps students develop valuable insight into literary history, promotes a better understanding of the texts, and sparks ideas for papers and assignments. Each entry in *NCLC* presents a comprehensive survey of an author's career or an individual work of literature and provides the user with a multiplicity of interpretations and assessments. Such variety allows students to pursue their own interests; furthermore, it fosters an awareness that literature is dynamic and responsive to many different opinions.

Every fourth volume of *NCLC* is devoted to literary topics that cannot be covered under the author approach used in the rest of the series. Such topics include literary movements, prominent themes in nineteenth-century literature, literary reaction to political and historical events, significant eras in literary history, prominent literary anniversaries, and the literatures of cultures that are often overlooked by English-speaking readers.

NCLC continues the survey of criticism of world literature begun by Gale's *Contemporary Literary Criticism (CLC)* and *Twentieth-Century Literary Criticism (TCLC)*, both of which excerpt and reprint commentary on authors of the twentieth century. For additional information about *TCLC, CLC,* and Gale's other criticism series, users should consult the Guide to Gale Literary Criticism Series preceding the title page in this volume.

Coverage

Each volume of *NCLC* is carefully compiled to present:

- criticism of authors, or literary topics, representing a variety of genres and nationalities
- both major and lesser-known writers and literary works of the period
- 8-12 authors or 4-6 topics per volume
- individual entries that survey critical response to each author's work or each topic in literary history, including early criticism to reflect initial reactions; later criticism to represent any rise or decline in reputation; and current retrospective analyses.

Organization of This Book

An author entry consists of the following elements: author heading, biographical and critical introduction, list of principal works, excerpts of criticism (each preceded by an annotation and followed by a bibliographic citation), and a bibliography of further reading.

- The **author heading** consists of the name under which the author most commonly wrote, followed by birth and death dates. If an author wrote consistently under a pseudonym, the pseudonym will be listed in the author heading and the real name given in parentheses on the first line of the biographical and critical introduction. Also located at the beginning of the introduction to the author entry are any name variations under which an author wrote, including transliterated forms for authors whose languages use nonroman alphabets.

- The **biographical and critical introduction** outlines the author's life and career, as well as the critical issues surrounding his or her work. References are provided to past volumes of *NCLC* and to other biographical and critical references series published by Gale, including *Short Story Criticism, Poetry Criticism, Children's Literature Review, Contemporary Authors, Dictionary of Literary Biography,* and *Something about the Author.*

• Most *NCLC* entries include **portraits** of the author. Many entries also contain reproductions of materials pertinent to an author's career, including manuscript pages, title pages, dust jackets, letters, and drawings, as well as photographs of important people, places, and events in an author's life.

• The list of **principal works** is chronological by date of first book publication and identifies the genre of each work. In the case of foreign authors with both foreign-language publications and English translations, the title and date of the first English-language edition are given in brackets. Unless otherwise indicated, dramas are dated by first performance, not first publication.

• **Criticism** is arranged chronologically in each author entry to provide a perspective on changes in critical evaluation over the years. All titles of works by the author featured in the entry are printed in boldface type to enable the user to easily locate discussion of particular works. Also for purposes of easier identification, the critic's name and the publication date of the essay are given at the beginning of each piece of criticism. Unsigned criticism is preceded by the title of the journal in which it appeared. Publication information (such as publisher names and book prices) and parenthetical numerical references (such as footnotes or page and line references to specific editions of works) have been deleted at the editors' discretion to provide smoother reading of the text.

• Critical excerpts are prefaced by **annotations** providing the reader with information about both the critic and the criticism that follows. Included are the critic's reputation, individual approach to literary criticism, and particular expertise in an author's works. Also noted are the relative importance of a work of criticism, the scope of the excerpt, and the growth of critical controversy or changes in critical trends regarding an author. In some cases, these annotations cross-reference excerpts by critics who discuss each other's commentary.

• A complete **bibliographic citation** designed to facilitate location of the original essay or book follows each piece of criticism.

• An annotated list of **further reading** appearing at the end of each author entry suggests secondary sources on the author. In some cases it includes essays for which the editors could not obtain reprint rights.

Cumulative Indexes

• Each volume of *NCLC* contains a cumulative **author index** listing all authors who have appeared in the following Gale series: *Contemporary Literary Criticism, Twentieth-Century Literary Criticism, Nineteenth-Century Literature Criticism, Literature Criticism from 1400 to 1800,* and *Classical and Medieval Literature Criticism.* Topic entries devoted to a single author, such as the entry on the textual reconstruction of James Joyce's *Ulysses* in *TCLC* 26, are listed in this index. Also included are cross-references to the Gale series *Poetry Criticism, Drama Criticism, Short Story Criticism, Children's Literature Review, Authors in the News, Contemporary Authors, Contemporary Authors Autobiography Series, Dictionary of Literary Biography, Concise Dictionary of American Literary Biography, Something about the Author, Something about the Author Autobiography Series,* and *Yesterday's Authors of Books for Children.* Useful for locating authors within the various series, this index is particularly valuable for those authors who are identified by a certain period but who, because of their death dates, are placed in another, or for those authors whose careers span two periods. For example, Fyodor Dostoevsky is found in *NCLC,* yet Leo Tolstoy, another major nineteenth-century Russian novelist, is found in *TCLC* because he died after 1899.

• Each *NCLC* volume includes a cumulative **nationality index** which lists all authors who have appeared in *NCLC* volumes, arranged alphabetically under their respective nationalities, as well as Topics volume entries devoted to particular national literatures.

• Each new volume in Gale's Literary Criticism Series includes a cumulative **topic index,** which lists all literary topics treated in *NCLC, TCLC, LC 1400-1800,* and the *CLC* Yearbook.

• Each new volume of *NCLC,* with the exception of the Topics volumes, contains a **title index** listing the titles of all literary works discussed in the volume. The first volume of *NCLC* published each year contains an index listing all titles discussed in the series since its inception. Titles discussed in the Topics volume entries are not included in the *NCLC* cumulative index.

A Note to the Reader

When writing papers, students who quote directly from any volume in Gale's Literary Criticism Series may use the following general forms to footnote reprinted criticism. The first example pertains to material drawn from periodicals, the second to material reprinted from books.

[1] T. S. Eliot, "John Donne," *The Nation and the Athenaeum,* 33 (9 June 1923), 321-32; excerpted and reprinted in *Literature Criticism from 1400 to 1800,* Vol. 10, ed. James E. Person, Jr. (Detroit: Gale Research, 1989), pp. 28-9.

[2] Clara G. Stillman, *Samuel Butler: A Mid-Victorian Modern* (Viking Press, 1932); excerpted and reprinted in *Twentieth-Century Literary Criticism,* Vol. 33, ed. Paula Kepos (Detroit: Gale Research, 1989), pp. 43-5.

Suggestions Are Welcome

In response to suggestions, several features have been added to *NCLC* since the series began, including annotations to excerpted criticism, a cumulative index to authors in all Gale literary criticism series, entries devoted to criticism on a single work by a major author, more extensive illustrations, and a title index listing all literary works discussed in the series since its inception.

Readers who wish to suggest authors or topics to appear in future volumes, or who have other suggestions, are cordially invited to write the editors.

ACKNOWLEDGMENTS

The editors wish to thank the copyright holders of the excerpted criticism included in this volume, the permissions managers of many book and magazine publishing companies for assisting us in securing reprint rights, and Anthony Bogucki for assistance with copyright research. We are also grateful to the staffs of the Detroit Public Library Complex, and University of Michigan Libraries for making their resources available to us. Following is a list of copyright holders who have granted us permission to reprint material in this volume of *NCLC*. Every effort has been made to trace copyright, but if omissions have been made, please let us know.

COPYRIGHTED EXCERPTS in *NCLC*, VOLUME 33, WERE REPRINTED FROM THE FOLLOWING PERIODICALS:

Eire-Ireland, v. VI, Spring, 1971 for "Ferguson and the Idea of an Irish National Literature" by Robert O'Driscoll. Copyright © 1971 Irish American Cultural Institute, 2115 Summit Ave., No. 5026, St. Paul, MN 55105. Reprinted by permission of the publisher and the author.—*ELH,* v. 32, June, 1965; v. 37, December, 1970; v. 39, March, 1972; v. 46, Summer, 1979. Copyright © 1965, 1970, 1972, 1979 by The Johns Hopkins University Press. All rights reserved. All reprinted by permission of the publisher.—*Essays in Criticism,* v. XVI, April, 1966 for "On Not Being Persuaded" by Andor Gomme; v. XVIII, October, 1968 for " 'Persuasion' Again" by Malcolm Bradbury. Both reprinted by permission of the Editors of *Essays in Criticism* and the respective authors.—*Essays in Studies,* v. 20, 1967. © The English Association 1967. All rights reserved. Reprinted by permission of the publisher.—*Grand Street,* v. 6, Winter, 1987 for a review of "Villette" by Steven Millhauser. Copyright © 1987 by Grand Street Publications, Inc. All rights reserved. Reprinted by permission of the author.—*Historical Studies,* v. 15, October, 1972 for "Francis Adams: The Arnoldian as Socialist" by I. M. Britain. Reprinted by permission of the author.—*Journal of Popular Culture,* v. IX, Winter, 1975. Copyright © 1975 by Ray B. Browne. Reprinted by permission of the publisher.—*Modern Fiction Studies,* v. 18, Winter, 1972-73. Copyright © 1973 by Purdue Research Foundation, West Lafayette, IN 47907. All rights reserved. Reprinted with permission.—*Nineteenth-Century Fiction,* v. VIII, March, 1954. Copyright 1954, renewed 1982 by The Regents of the University of California. Reprinted by permission of The Regents—*PMLA,* v. 88, May, 1973. Copyright © 1973 by the Modern Language Association of America. Reprinted by permission of the Modern Language Association of America.—*Rice University Studies,* v. 61, Winter, 1975. Copyright 1975 by Rice University. Reprinted by permission of the publisher.—*Romanian Review,* v. 30, 1976; v. 41, 1987; v. 43, 1989. All reprinted by permission of the publisher.—*The Sewanee Review,* v. LXIX, Winter, 1961. © 1961 by The University of the South. Reprinted by permission of the editor of The Sewanee Review.—*Slavic and East-European Journal,* n.s. v. 28, Fall, 1984. © 1984 by AATSEEL of the U.S., Inc. Reprinted by permission of the publisher.—*Studies in English Literature, 1500-1900,* v. XI, Autumn, 1971 for "Achievement of 'Persuasion' " by Thomas P. Wolfe. © 1971 William Marsh Rice University. Reprinted by permission of the publisher and the author.—*Studies in the Novel,* v. XVII, Spring, 1985; v. XVIII, Winter, 1986. Copyright 1985, 1986 by North Texas State University. Both reprinted by permission of the publisher.—*Texas Studies in Literature and Language,* v. V, Winter, 1964 for "Character and the Mock Heroic in 'Barchester Towers' " by William Cadbury; v. XIV, Fall, 1972 for "Dostoyevsky's 'Notes from Underground': The Form of Fiction" by Thomas M. Kavanagh. Copyright © 1964, 1972 by the University of Texas Press. Both reprinted by permission of the publisher and the respective authors.—*The Times Literary Supplement,* n. 4172, March 18, 1983. © The Times Supplements Limited 1983. Reproduced from *The Times Literary Supplement* by permission.

COPYRIGHTED EXCERPTS IN *NCLC*, VOLUME 33, WERE REPRINTED FROM THE FOLLOWING BOOKS:

Bakhtin, Mikhail. From *Problems of Dostoevsky's Poetics: Theory and History of Literature, Vol. 8.* Edited and translated by Caryl Emerson. University of Minnesota Press, 1984. Copyright © 1984 by the University of Minnesota. All rights reserved. Reprinted by permission of the publisher.—Bălan, Ion Dodu. From *A Concise History of Romanian Literature.* Translated by Andrei Bantas. Academy of Social and Political Sciences, 1981.—Brontë, Charlotte. From a letter in *The Brontës: Their Lives, Friendships and Correspondence, 1852-1928, Vol. IV.* Edited by Thomas J. Wise and J. Alexander Symington. Basil Blackwell, 1933. Reprinted by permission of Basil Blackwell Limited.—Brown, Terence. From *Northern Voices: Poets from Ulster.* Rowman and Littlefield, 1975. © Terence Brown, 1975. Reprinted by permission of the author.—Colum, Padraic. From an introduction to *The Poems of Samuel Ferguson.* Edited by Padraic Colum. Allen Figgis, 1963. Introduction and Selection © Allen Figgis & Co., Ltd., 1963. Reprinted by permission of the Literary Estate of Padraic Colum.—Deering, Arthur. From *Samuel Ferguson, Poet and Antiquarian.* N.p., 1931.—Epperly, Elizabeth R. From *Patterns of Repetition in Trollope.* The

PHOTOGRAPHS AND ILLUSTRATIONS APPEARING IN *NCLC,* **VOLUME 33, WERE RECEIVED FROM THE FOLLOWING SOURCES:**

Camera Press-PHOTO TRENDS: **p. 158;** Mansell Collection: **p. 360.**

Francis Adams

1862-1893

(Full name Francis William Lauderdale Adams) Anglo-Australian poet, critic, novelist, and dramatist.

Adams has been called one of the leading literary figures of nineteenth-century Australia. Primarily a poet and social critic, he is best known for his *Songs of the Army of the Night* (1888), a collection of poems and dramatic sketches inspired by Adams's sympathy with the radical socialist party in Australia. He also wrote essays, novels, and a posthumously published drama, *Tiberius* (1894), all of which attest to his disappointment with social oppression in England and his passionate support of the working class in Australia.

Adams was born on Malta to Andrew Leith Adams, a Scottish army surgeon and author of science and travel books, and Bertha Jane Grundy Adams, a novelist. He attended private school in Shrewsbury, England, and in Paris from 1878 to 1880, where he wrote poetry and a semiautobiographical novel entitled *Leicester* (published in 1884 and reprinted in 1894 as *A Child of the Age*). Adams was strongly influenced by the ideas of English poet and literary critic Matthew Arnold; though the two writers never met, their correspondence helped shape the young poet's beliefs concerning culture, education, religion, and literature. By 1880 he had begun to write a long series of interconnected novels and poems beginning with *Leicester,* hoping to become, in his own words, as "big as Balzac." When Adams returned to England as a schoolmaster at Ventnor College in the early 1880s, critics were already comparing him to the young Percy Bysshe Shelley, due to his sympathy with the poor and to what Henry S. Salt termed his "fiery . . . hatred of injustice." Adams moved to Australia in 1884, disappointed with the social and political systems of England and searching for a healthier climate to treat his chronic tuberculosis. He arrived in Australia just as new labor unions began showing increased socialist activity and immediately lent his support to the workers' cause through his journalistic writings. Adams spent his time between Sydney and Brisbane, earning modest wages as a writer and slowly building a literary reputation. Making a living by writing articles for various reviews and quarterlies, Adams eventually became a writer for the *Brisbane Courier* in 1885. He later made contributions to the *Boomerang,* a radical socialist weekly, and his poems, critical articles, and short stories appeared in the *Sydney Bulletin.* His *Poetical Works,* published in 1887, brought him into public prominence and were followed a year later by his most respected work, *Songs of the Army of the Night,* a collection that some critics deemed anarchist for Adams's advocacy of a violent overthrow of the capitalist system. Dissatisfied with Australian life, Adams returned to England in 1890. His health steadily declining, he worked furiously for three months on *The New Egypt,* a posthumously published essay criticizing British imperialism. Suffering from a consumptive seizure, Adams took his own life in 1893; his wife, by her own account, handed him the revolver. He is believed to have written the following lines as his epitaph:

> Bury me with clenched hands
> And eyes open wide,
> For in storm and struggle I lived
> And in struggle and storm I died.

Adams's *Poetical Works* received scathing reviews from his contemporaries, including the *Courier* critic who called the work "filthy," due partly to a reference to "full-peaked breasts" and sexually explicit characterizations. Reviewers also pointed out that the abundance of literary allusions in the poems made them inaccessible to many readers. Adams followed this disappointment with his *Songs,* in which he attempted to capture a vision of modern society from the viewpoint of the working class. As Clive Turnbull has written, the poems were "addressed to a new audience, to the mass of people, unread in the masterpieces of the past, and unskilled in literary allusion, direct, passionate and moving." Adams divided the *Songs* into three parts: "England" declares his despair at the rotting values of the old world; "Here and There" records his trip to the Orient and denounces the voracious imperialism he found there; and "Australia" expresses his hopes for a bright Australian future. In this collection, Adams violated many poetic conventions; some reviewers found the collection's unorthodox rhymes and meter a complement to its radical themes of opposition to oppression and support of the Australian worker in his fight against the injustices of the privileged classes. In this respect, critics have perceived a resemblance between the *Songs* and the visionary poetry of Walt Whitman's *Leaves of Grass.* As Henry S. Salt stated in an introduction to the *Songs,* "The new wine of revolutionary thought [could not] be put in the old bottles of academical versification."

In his *Songs,* Adams attacked capitalism and praised socialism in France, Russia, England, and Ireland, advocating the same system for Australia. The harsh, powerful invective of the poems was inflammatory for its day, and the work was received with disapproval and even contempt by Australian and English critics alike. Though some reviewers acknowledged the force and sincerity of the *Songs,* others ridiculed Adams's treatment of socialist themes as banal, immature, and overconfident. Adams nevertheless inspired and influenced many young Australian journalists and authors of his day (among them A. G. Stephens, J. F. Archibald, Sydney Jephcott, and John Farrell) by providing "a liaison," as Vance Palmer contended, "between the world of European culture and the national [Australian] impulses that were seeking expression."

In addition to poetry, Adams also published *Australian Essays* (1886), a collection of essays in social criticism; *The Melbournians* (1892), a novel about the Australian struggle for a new, equal society; *Australian Life* (1892), a collection of short stories about urban and bush life; and *The Australians* (1893), a series of social sketches contrasting the country's coastal regions with its arid interior. *Tiberius,* a tragedy portraying a severe Roman emperor as a defender of the common man, was completed during Adams's lifetime but not published until 1894. However, Adams's poetry is considered his greatest achievement. Contemporary scholars generally agree that because of his passionate, controversial poetry, and his biting social criticism, Adams deserves to be recognized as an author who helped shape Australia's culture during a formative period in its history.

PRINCIPAL WORKS

Henry, and Other Tales (poetry) 1884

Leicester (novel) 1884; also published as *A Child of the Age,* 1894

Australian Essays (essays) 1886

Madeline Brown's Murderer (novel) 1887

Poetical Works of Francis W. L. Adams (poetry) 1887

Songs of the Army of the Night (poetry) 1888

John Webb's End: A Story of Bush Life (novel) 1891

Australian Life (short stories) 1892

The Melbournians (novel) 1892

The Australians: A Social Sketch (prose) 1893

The New Egypt: A Social Sketch (prose) 1893

Tiberius: A Drama (drama) 1894

Lady Lovan (novel) 1895

Essays in Modernity: Criticisms and Dialogues (essays) 1899

Francis Adams (essay date 1887)

[*In the following excerpt from his preface to* Songs of the Army of the Night, *Adams briefly explains the general ideological framework of the collection.*]

A few words of preface seem necessary in sending out [**Songs of the Army of the Night**]. It is to be looked on as the product of the life of a social worker in England, on his Travels, and in Australia. The key-note of the First Part—"England"—is desperation, or, if any hope, then "desperate hope." A friend once reported to me a saying of Matthew Arnold's, that he did not believe in any man of intelligence taking a desperate view of the social problem in England. I am afraid that saying relegates me to the ranks of the fools, but I am content to remain there. I believe that never since 1381, which is the date of the Peasant's Revolt, has England presented such a spectacle of the happiness of the tens, of the misery of the millions. It is not by any means the artisan, or the general or the agricultural labourer, who is the only sufferer. All society groans under the slavery of stupendous toil and a pittance wage. The negro slavery of the Southern States of America was better than the white slavery of to-day all over the earth, but more particularly in Europe and in America. The vast edifice of our Civilization is built on the essential

wrong of recompensing Labour, not according to the worth of its work, but according to the worth of its members in the market of unlimited competition, and that soon comes to mean the payment of what will hold body and soul together when in the enjoyment of health and strength. Landlordism shares with Capitalism the plunder of Labour . . . Capitalism and Landlordism, like good Christian Institutions, leave the living to keep alive their living, and the dead to bury their dead. This cannot continue forever. At least all the intelligent portion of the community will grow to see the injustice and attempt to abolish it. But when will the great mass of unintelligent people who have won a large enough share of the plunder of their fellows to minister to their own comforts—when will these, also, awake and see? England will realize the desperation of her social problem when its desperation is shown her by fire and blood—then, and not till then! What shall teach her her sins to herself is what is even now teaching her her sins to Ireland.

I make no apology for several poems in the First Part which are fierce, which are even blood-thirsty. As I felt I wrote, and I will not lessen the truth of what inspired those feelings by eliminating or suppressing the record of them. Rather, let me ask you, whoever you be, to imagine what the cause was, from the effect in one who was (unhappily) born and bred into the dominant class, and whose chief care and joy in life was in the pursuit of a culture which draws back instinctively from the violent and the terrible. I will go further. I will arraign my country and my day, because their iniquity would not let me follow out the laws of my nature, which were for luminosity and quiet for the wide and genial view, but made me "take arms against a sea of troubles," hoping only too often "by opposing to end them." No, we make no apology for bloody sweat and for tears of fire wrung out of us in the Gethsemane and on the Calvary of our country; we make no apology to those whom we have the right to curse.

In the Second Part—"Here and There," the record of a short trip in the East—the sight of the sin which England has committed not only against herself, against Ireland, against Scotland, but against India, against China, against the sweetest and gentlest people in the earth, the Japanese—the sight of this, and of the signs of England's doom, the punishment for the abuse of the greatest trust any modern nation has had given to her, inspires a hatred which only that punishment can appease.

In the Third Part—"Australia"—there is neither ferocity nor blood-thirstiness. Its key-note is hope, hope that dreads but does not despair. (pp. 11-13)

> *Francis Adams, in a preface to his* Songs of the Army of the Night, *William Reeves, 1894, pp. 11-14.*

The Bookman, London (essay date 1893)

[*In the following excerpt, the reviewer praises* The Australians *for its effective style and description of town and bush life.*]

[In *The Australians*] Mr. Adams has written a very vigorous account of the social life and the prospects of a people he has lived amongst, whom he has sharply criticised, and who have been his very good friends. His always marked and decisive style is still more decisive here, probably with a purpose. The travesties of Australia have been so absurd, that the facts, as Mr. Adams conceives them, have to be stated in a very downright and perhaps exaggerated fashion—especially when they are addressed to an unimaginative people "ruled by fogs and a middle class." The statements look all the more dogmatic that as a rule each one is given a paragraph to itself. Politicians will find much to interest them in the vigorous and unconventional sketches of Australian statesmen, and a good deal to ponder over, to contradict, or to verify in the political statistics and prophecies. One valuable feature of Mr. Adams' book is the combative effect it has even on admiring and interested readers. It does not always convince, but it cannot leave any indifferent. It will possibly lead to a new kind of inquiry into Colonial matters.

Never before were the differences in temperament and ideals between ourselves and the Australians set so vividly before us. But he leaves on our minds a very uncertain impression as to what will be the future of this "lean and high-strung" people. In the description of town life, of Melbourne, for instance, with its vigour and earnestness and "nothing worth being eager or earnest about," which has not digested European culture, and has none of its own, practically pagan, materialist, and with social problems staring it in the face, there are pictures black and sordid enough. It is to the Bush people Mr. Adams evidently looks for the supply of health and manhood and intellect that will fertilize the continent; and there are some charming pictures of the dwellers away from the big cities. "The absolute fearless friendliness of the children, their innate feeling of the kindly respect due to themselves as to others, their simple and expansive intelligence, their unaffected modesty and self-control—I have found intercourse with bush children one of the most charming things in life!"

A review of "The Australians," in The Bookman, *London, Vol. 4, No. 20, May, 1893, p. 55.*

H. S. Salt   (essay date 1894)

[*Salt was an English critic and friend of Adams. In the following excerpt from his introduction to* Songs of the Army of the Night, *Salt notes the emotional power of Adams's poetry and defends the collection from the charge that Adams's style is "unbalanced."*]

The general intention and object of the ***Songs of the Army of the Night*** are sufficiently indicated in the author's Preface [see excerpt dated 1887] and Proem. The title itself is a suggestive one—a reminiscence perhaps of that "City of Dreadful Night" which another great democratic poet has depicted; but with the striking difference that the despondent fortitude of the pessimist is here quickened and energised into the fierce resolution of the reformer. The ***Songs,*** taken individually, will best speak for themselves; it is not necessary or desirable, in this brief Introduction, to attempt an estimate of their comparative merits or shortcomings. But it is highly important, for a full and just ap-

preciation of these most characteristic and impassioned products of Adams' genius, that something should be said of the very singular personality which everywhere underlies the poems, and is intimately connected with their mingled strength and weakness. In these lyrics, if anywhere, the writer spoke his soul; they are an absolutely faithful and unreserved expression of a certain portion of his feelings.

When Francis Adams died in the autumn of 1893, he was but thirty years old, yet during that short lifetime he had amassed an extraordinary record of poignant and heart-stirring experiences. . . . [One of his Australian friends, Sydney Jephcott, wrote:]

> I only heard of Adams' death two days ago. . . . I cannot tell how much smaller and poorer the world seems to me now he has gone. He was the truest comrade, with all his inward loneliness. The very light of *camaraderie* shone from his soul. Except that he might accomplish the work laid upon him by his destiny and his hour, there was no care for self in him. And the tragedy of his life and sufferings was, I calmly and firmly believe, the greatest and most dreadful in our literary history. For what the wrongs of the oppressed and dispossessed were to him, let the ***Songs of the Army of the Night*** bear witness, but what he suffered from physical disease and personal sorrows, let only oblivion keep the knowledge of—what he endured from the tortures of frustrate ambition, we can guess.

It will be readily understood how the natural sensitiveness of an intensely high-strung temperament was accentuated by such suffering and disappointment, until it left its mark both in the exacting fastidiousness of his literary judgments and in the scathing severity of his denunciation of social hypocrisies. This fact will account for much that were else unaccountable, and perhaps in some cases repellent, in the occasionally pitiless invective of these ***Songs of the Army of the Night;*** on the other hand, the poems bear unmistakable testimony to the passionate tenderness and humanity of the heart which inspired them. Was there ever, since Shelley died, so fiery a hatred of injustice, so eager a sympathy with the cause of the poor and oppressed? In this respect also, Francis Adams' writings are the exact counterpart of his personality. No memory of him will dwell more abidingly in the minds of those who knew him than the occasions when, with magnetic eloquence, he would dilate on the people's wrongs—his beautiful expressive features and large flashing eyes lit up with the glow of a single-hearted life-long enthusiasm.

But the poems are so "unbalanced," says the literary critic, who, with the caution of his kind, is always on his guard against militant writers who "mean business," who have got something to say, and are determined to say it at whatever hazard to delicate academical proprieties. The poems undoubtedly *are* unbalanced; that is an incidental defect which is accounted for by the circumstances to which I have already alluded. But on the other hand it should be remarked that there is a danger in too much intellectual balance, no less than in too little. We have already far too many balanced literary gentlemen sitting comfortably on the stile, with an equipoise which might move the envy of a Blondin; it is their æsthetic indifferentism, far more than any emotional excess, which is the bane of our present literature. It is therefore not to be regretted that a writer should appear who can voice the passionate resentment of sham philanthropy and sham religion, which is undoubtedly felt by a section, and an increasing section, of English workers,

> With its threat to the robber rich, the proud,
> The respectable free. . . .

It may be that there is exaggeration, unwisdom, injustice even, in the personal references of some of these poems; but in their general indictment of a pharisaical and selfish class-supremacy, they are essentially true and valuable. The *Songs,* as their author once told me, are an attempt to do what has never been done before—to express what might be the feelings of a member of the working classes, as he finds out the hollowness (to him, at any rate) of our "culture" and "respectability."

Still less valid, I think, is the technical criticism which would set aside the *Songs of the Army of the Night* as bad poetry and doggerel, because the book contains numerous violations of the customary "laws" of metre and rhyme-sound. The author's omission to conform with these supposed obligations was evidently deliberate, and in harmony with the whole purpose which he had in view; he felt, and felt rightly, that a work which was in substance a direct defiance of orthodox culture must similarly emancipate itself, in expression, from the trammels of orthodox rhyming. The new wine of revolutionary thought cannot be put in the old bottles of academical versification, and those readers who wish to form a fair judgment of the literary value of the poems must have the courage to regard them not from the standpoint of the conventional critic (who invariably fails to appreciate the true significance of any new and genuine poetry), but from that of the author himself, who knew exactly what he had to say, and how he could say it with most effect.

In the case of writings of this sort, the measure of the critic's antipathy is often the measure of the poet's success. It is not surprising that these revolutionary songs have aroused, and will continue to arouse, misunderstanding and reprobation, for they have an incisive and trenchant quality which seldom fails to make itself felt; whatever else they do, or fail to do, they strike home. The hilt of the dagger may not be carved in the most approved method of ornamentation; but the blade is keen and deadly, and its mark will not be easily concealed. Viewed in this light, many of the phrases and cadences, which according to ordinary canons of art are certainly formless and unmusical, are seen to be appropriate and inevitable; and the reader who turns away from the book on account of these peculiarities will be simply repeating the errors of those literary purists who have been successively unable to read Shelley, unable to read Whitman, unable to read [Edward] Carpenter—in a word, unable to read any new great writer whose style was as novel and unfamiliar as his ideas.

Yet, all such disabilities being allowed for, it is difficult to believe that any candid reader, who has a true love of poetry in his heart, can fail to appreciate the great literary mer-

its which distinguish the best, if the best only, of these remarkable lyrics, remarkable in all cases for their vigour and audacity, in a considerable number of cases for the highest qualities of song. If anyone cannot see the power and beauty of such poems as **"In Trafalgar Square," "One among So Many," "To England," "A South-Sea Islander,"** and **"A Death at Sea,"** it would be useless to multiply words on the subject. Time will show whether these and other of their author's productions are worthy or unworthy to live.

I have said that the *Songs of the Army of the Night* were a faithful expression of "a certain portion" of their author's feelings. It is necessary to make this limitation, because it would be an injustice to Francis Adams to let it be assumed, by those who may not be acquainted with his other writings, that his fiery zeal for social emancipation represents more than one side—albeit a most important one—of his many-sided labours. "I am but a poor devil who tries to touch life at several artistic points," He writes in one of his letters of 1892, "and if I give this one pleasure as a lyrist, and that as a dramatist, and that as a storyteller, and that as a critic, I am content." When quite a boy he had planned a vast cycle of character-sketches, a life-work which was to be realized in a series of poems and tales. "It was my modest little scheme" he continues "to draw types of all the social life of the day. *Leicester* is the first of the series of novels and tales. Oh, I was going to do as big as Balzac that way! Fancy what a pretty scheme for a jackanapes of eighteen, and to have sweated at it all these years! I finished the last but one of the novels (chronologically) on my way out to Australia. There are three novels to do yet, and about eight short tales."

It may be seen from [a] list of Adams' published writings how great was the amount, and how wide the scope, of the literary effort (not to mention the journalistic work) put forth by him during the last twelve years of his life. . . . It is as a critic that he has received from his fellow-critics the largest share of praise, doubtless because there is of necessity a more cautious tone in that class of his writings, which gives satisfaction to the "balanced" literary mind. I venture, however, to think that the reviewers are wrong in this estimate of Francis Adams' powers; for his temperament was essentially of the emotional, and not the judicial order, and in spite of the singular brilliancy of certain of his judgments his keenly sensitive and subtle instinct was more often, and more fatally, at fault in his critical than in his poetical productions. On the value of his works as a whole, or of his complete poetical works, so unequal in their merit, it is perhaps too early to express an opinion; for some of his writings on which he himself set most store still remain to be published. But for my own part, I believe that it is in his more impassioned and unrestrained work, such as *Leicester, an Autobiography* and *The Songs of the Army of the Night,* that we must look for his real masterpieces; for it is there alone that he wields the great imaginative quality, and the heart of fire, that can triumph over all superficial blemishes and defects.

At any rate we have here a volume of people's poems which deserves to rank with the memorable achievements of democratic literature. Once more, amidst the multitudinous parrot-cries of elegant versifying, comes the arresting call of one who has seen, and suffered, and sympathised—a veritable human voice, which speaks direct to the heart of the listener as no "mere literature" has ever spoken. Whatever place may be ultimately assigned him among English authors, it is through these *Songs of the Army of the Night* that the name of Francis Adams will be best loved and longest remembered by the friends of social freedom. (pp. 17-23)

> *H. S. Salt, in an introduction to* Songs of the Army of the Night *by Francis Adams, William Reeves, 1894, pp. 17-23.*

W. M. Rossetti   (essay date 1894)

[*Rossetti, the brother of Christina and Dante Gabriel Rossetti, was an important British critic and biographer. His works include a verse translation of Dante's* Inferno *(1865), a* Life of Keats *(1887), and memoirs of both his brother* (D. G. Rossetti, his family letters, with a memoir, *1895) and his sister* (memoir in Family Letters of Christina Rossetti, *1908). In the following excerpt, he offers a detailed positive assessment of Adams's* Tiberius, *emphasizing that the Roman emperor is portrayed as a "conscious avenger of the misdeeds" of the "tyrant aristocrat."*]

Of Mr. Adams personally I knew very little. It may have been towards the middle of 1888 that he sent me by post from Australia the Australian edition of his *Songs of the Army of the Night,* with an inscription showing that he had paid attention to some of my writings, and was in sympathy with their tone upon certain points. Such a message from a man of whom I had never heard was a surprise to me, and a pleasant surprise. I at once read the book, and was genuinely astonished at its intensity and fierceness of tone, its depth of emotion, and its splendid instantaneousness of poetic perception, suggestion, and expression—an instantaneousness as of lightning at twilight, revealing at one moment every corner and cranny of the scene, and at the next moment plunging all into a more sombre obscurity than before: the inarticulate things of passion and of poetry hurtled upon the mind through the articulate. Though far from blind to the excesses of opinion and of feeling in the volume, or to its defects as well as excesses of diction, I thought it one of the most remarkable and moving of recent poetic productions, and I wrote at once to the author to say as much. We then exchanged one or two further letters, and I looked through his earlier book named *Poetical Works.* When he came to London in September 1890, I saw him once, and regretted that it should be only once. I found him to be a young man of engaging and beautiful presence, and some appearance (though not at that date very marked) of delicate constitution; of amiable refined manners, and of mild, though certainly very self-resolved, tone in conversation. I had hoped to see a good deal of him, but his early departure from London—to which, so far as I am aware, he never returned—prevented this. He soon afterwards sent to me the MS. of his *Tiberius,* which I read, and returned to him with some observations.

Having now, since Mr. Adams's death, been invited to write a few words by way of introduction to the *Tiberius,* I readily assent. I am informed by Mr. J. W. Longsdon, the intimate friend to whom Mr. Adams confided the MS. of this play, that the author "quite recognised that, in order to ensure acceptance, Mr. Longsdon might be obliged to make considerable alterations." The same power has now been entrusted to me, and I have used it so far as I conceived to be really requisite. This I do with the less hesitation because I am also informed that in 1889, when there had been some idea of asking me to attend to an English edition of the *Songs of the Army of the Night,* Mr. Adams, writing to Mr. Longsdon and mentioning my name, said, "I would trust implicitly to his judgment in any repressions." However, that edition came out without my exercising any leading control over it, whether by means of "repressions" or otherwise.

I am not closely acquainted with the details of Adams's career, but I know that he saw much in many countries; felt much and intensely; suffered (even if we leave out of count his chronic and tormenting ill-health) much and intensely. The *Songs of the Army of the Night* are the record of his extreme opinions—which might with equal truth be called his extreme sentiments—in social, political, and religious matters; and, whatever may be the deduction which we make from them on the ground of over-vehemence in the estimate of things, and tameless fury of utterance, they are a momentous record, and will be increasingly recognised as such. They touch us too nearly at the present day to be regarded with either dispassionate calmness or indulgent allowance, but their time will assuredly come, and must in some quarters have come already. No doubt fierce sympathy and the response of hungry and shattered or outlawed hearts has greeted them here and there; and, looking along the perspective of years, the *Songs* will be found to have dwarfed many of the pleasant proprieties and well-accepted sleeknesses of our days and hours.

The deliberately planned and executed drama of *Tiberius* is, of course, a very different sort of production from the rapid outpouring of lyrical rage, the clench of fierce hand to hand, the cry of flaming spirit to spirit, which we discern in the *Songs of the Army of the Night;* and yet the essential and innermost core of it is by no means unrelated to these. The same abhorrence of dull oppression, of stolid self-indulgence sanctioned by usage, of egotistic self-applause drowning the call of human fellowship, speaks out as loudly in the antique drama as in the contemporary lyrics. But it is not on the man and emperor Tiberius that Adams, who might herein have followed the lead of Tacitus and many other historians, fastens these anti-social offences; he fastens them, on the contrary, on the Roman aristocracy, and regards Tiberius as the destined and conscious avenger of the misdeeds. Tiberius, according to his dramatist, accepts power and administers government with the express purpose of rooting out the tyrant aristocrats in the interest of the suffering populations, and is so far a public benefactor, though a ruthless sovereign. He labours to effect from above an upheaval of social forces, such as the "Army of the Night" are now, as by a clarion-cry, incited to battle . . . from below. That the general drift of recent historical investigation has been to take a much less dark and indignant view of the character of Tiberius than of old is a fact sufficiently well known. I am not aware, however, that Adams had been forestalled in the precise point of view which he adopts—that of a rooted hatred of Tiberius against the magnates, based on a strong sense of their public and private wickedness, and of the danger hence arising to the state, and the damage inflicted on those classes most needing imperial protection. Tiberius is generally admitted to be one of the most problematic characters in history—to some of us, one of the most fascinating. He comes down to us from Tacitus, a colossal figure of a truly portentous kind; either portrayed accurately, or, if this is not the case, then created magnificently. Suetonius, in his inferior but still very vivid and emphatic way, tells the same tale. Not only, however, in the interest of truth and equity, but as an exercise of independent intellectual perception, it is perfectly open to any thinking man at the present day to part company with Tacitus and Suetonius, and to set forth to us a very different sort of Tiberius. Adams has done this, and I for one feel grateful to him for the enterprising spirit in which he has worked.

I have endeavoured to learn what may have been the sources from which Mr. Adams derived his conception of Tiberius, but in this I have not succeeded. Mr. Longsdon, whom I consulted, informs me that the conception had certainly been already formed before 1884, though the play had probably not by that time been written, nor perhaps even begun. The proem-verses refer to "seven long years" preceding New Year 1889; thus amply confirming, or even going beyond, Mr. Longsdon's estimate. "Adams," says this gentleman, "never cared to talk of a thing he was writing or going to write. He said the story, once told even in conversation, lost its interest to him, and he wrote afterwards with less vigour. He was a classical man, with a leaning to scholarship, and an exceedingly patient and careful student." He regarded this drama as his best work from a literary point of view, and in his later days he only cared about this and the *Songs of the Army of the Night,* and thought they would live. He looked upon the *Tiberius* as a play not unsuited for the stage, and was fain to think that the principal personage would be well adapted for Mr. Irving—and indeed I am not sure but that he had in some way or other brought the matter under the consideration of that distinguished tragedian. That Mr. Irving might make a great deal out of the *rôle* of Tiberius is clear enough; but in other respects Mr. Adams may have been somewhat too sanguine in these opinions, not allowing sufficient weight to two considerations which make *Tiberius* a very difficult play to be put on the stage,—namely, the great lapse of years which its action covers, and the large element in it of mere dialogue, apart from striking action on the boards or strong scenic situation. Not, indeed, that the play is *destitute* of scenic situation, and in dramatic situation it has some truly powerful points. As to the lapse of time, some readers may perhaps like to be reminded that no less than forty-seven years pass between Act I. and Act V. In Act I., the divorce of Vipsania, the date is 11 B.C., the age of Tiberius 31; in Act II., closing with the return from Rhodes, 1 A. D., age 43; in Act III., the death of Augustus, 14 A.D., age 55; in Act IV., the fall of Sejanus, 31 A.D., age 72; in Act V., the death of Tiberius, 37 A.D., age 78. Minor references throughout the play are constantly historical, and also most of the minor personages—not, I think, that of Electra: she appears to be an invention, and one of which Adams might reasonably be proud.

I find the character of Tiberius in this play to be decidedly interesting, although as a historical portrait it is, of course, disputable in a high degree. He begins as a successful and indefatigable general returned home to domestic life; the firmest prop of the world-wide Roman state, finding home still sweeter than command and glory. He is in the fullest sense a great public man and a virtuous private man. By order of Augustus he is summoned to abandon his dearest domestic tie, and to contract a new marriage of the most distasteful kind, for purposes of state. He ponders, and, in the public interest alone and for the greatness of Rome, he assents. He even goes beyond the conception of Rome at her grandest: he hopes to aid in "the last creation, Man." We find him next degraded by an intolerable union to an intolerable woman, incapable for the present of further struggle, throwing up all public life and retiring to Rhodes, yet still resolved to be the true servant of the Roman world when the time shall come. In Rhodes he lives the life of a retired, much-cogitating philosopher, still hankering after some joy in domestic life and love. In the dialogue here between Tiberius and the soothsayer Thrasyllus there is something which reminds us in a remote way—certainly without the faintest touch of imitation—of the dialogue between Paracelsus and Aprile, in Browning's drama of *Paracelsus.* Attaining to empire, Tiberius devotes himself to the public weal by general beneficence, mingled with a purpose of quenchless severity to the "insolence of office," the luxurious and oppressive magnates. Confiding his policy to his minister Sejanus for practical development, he is betrayed by his ambitious subordinate, whom at last he unmasks and delivers over to condign punishment. Finally, in extreme old age, everything palls upon him—power, the exercise of will, the rule of right, the standard of justice, the lifetime's work—and, in combating tyranny, he has himself become a tyrant, reckless of the means, if still not unconscious of a purpose tenaciously conceived, unflinchingly upheld.

Mr. Adams's vindication of Tiberius proceeds in the main (as I have already suggested) on grounds different from those of others. The apologists generally have aimed at showing that, upon close and well-advised investigation, the severities of the emperor were by no means so numerous or so rigid as the reader of Tacitus is led to suppose. Adams works on a different principle. He says substantially: "Tiberius *was* severe, and he meant to be severe: but why? For the necessary and laudable purpose of extirpating a 'generation of vipers.' "

Most of the secondary characters are also imagined with vigour and presented with skill: but among these I could hardly include Sejanus, who appears to be the weakest personage in the drama; the tangled web of treachery and criminality being woven by the greed of power upon a character which appears to be originally sentimental, impressible, and well-meaning, rather than anything else. Chærea is an arch-traitor of a still more offensive sort, but

consistent enough in his meanness. Augustus is a sufficiently imposing figure; Thrasyllus and Artaxerxes well-
sustained; Caligula (which may or may not be historically
correct) a buffoon and a craven, with a touch of penetration, and full of all wicked machinations. Julia is delineated with extreme force, not stopping short at coarseness;
and the winsome Greek slave-girl Electra, who runs to
seed as a cynical and willful voluptuary, is invented with
steady insight and firm literary and poetic touch. I must
spare a word also to the proem-lines written by Adams in
Australia, in a sort of dithyrambic prose-verse: they seem
to me super-excellent of their kind, unsurpassed by anything of the same class. (pp. 10-22)

In *Tiberius* the weakest act, in point of writing, seems to
be the fourth, occupied with the conspiracy of Sejanus,
and its discovery and punishment. Yet, as regards scenic
situation, this is the strongest of all, and the most suitable
for acting purposes. It may deserve remark that, in the
original draft of the drama, the "Secretary in White," who
takes a leading part in exhibiting the details of the conspiracy, was Tiberius himself in a temporary disguise, which
at the right moment he throws off. This was certainly an
incident of some dramatic force and opportunity; but
Adams must have felt that it verged overmuch on melodrama, and he altered the scene into its present more sober
form. I need hardly point out that Adams's version of the
fall of Sejanus is not, in detail, historically true. Some incidents, such as that of Macro suddenly superseding Sejanus
as commander of the Prætorian Guards, are accurate; but
all about Tiberius appearing personally on the scene is a
playwright's fiction—perhaps a permissible one. Yet the
real fact was not a jot less dramatic: Sejanus presenting
himself in the Senate in full confidence of ever-increasing
honours, greeted with cringing adulation, denounced for
arrest by the written order of Tiberius, then at once hooted
and execrated, and hurried off to summary execution. (pp.
23-4)

"Spoiled by power" seems to be the ruling idea in the
drama of *Tiberius.* Tiberius himself is certainly spoiled to
some extent, though I do not understand that Mr. Adams
intended, even in the final act, to represent him as bereft
of some sense of public duty and justifiable policy. He dies
with the words "Rome, Rome!" upon his lips. Augustus
is in fuller degree exempted from the ban: the author of
the *Songs of the Army of the Night* was not likely to regard his imperium with entire sympathy, but nothing in
the play indicates disapproval of its general scope and aim.
Julia is spoiled by power in one way; Caligula, by the hope
or expectation of power, in another; Sejanus and Electra,
not to speak of Chærea and Macro, each in their several
ways. This is one of the lessons stamped on the front of
imperial Rome, and from of old legible to all men.

"Spoiled by power." It is an awful doom, and an awful
subject for tragic drama. Adams has treated it with
breadth and force, with deep human sympathy, with due
dignity and unstinted realism, and with a large measure
of poetic strength and handling. There is brain in his purpose and life-blood in his work, and the noble army of
dramatists may, in virtue of this posthumous tragedy,
enrol him in their ranks. (pp. 25-7)

W. M. Rossetti, in an introduction to Tiberius:
A Drama, *by Francis Adams, T. Fisher
Unwin, 1894, pp. 9-27.*

The Saturday Review, London   (essay date 1894)

[*In the following excerpt, the reviewer strongly criticizes
several works by Adams, labeling them immature and
lacking in permanence.*]

[Adams's] *Poetical Works* consist of 151 large quarto
pages printed in double columns and rather small type, so
that there is a considerable amount of matter in them. A
considerable amount of matter in one sense—in another
how little, and what a considerable absence of art! Mr.
Adams, as the mere sub-titles tell us, had read Heine; the
text soon tells us that he had read Mr. Swinburne, Whitman, and others. A friend in one of the prefaces tells us
that he was a "classical man," which is good. But unfortunately his classicality chiefly displays itself as of the kind
which carefully writes "Anagke," "Kalupso," and so
forth, which is equally careful not to defraud (P)sappho
of her Psi, but which does not otherwise betray a very intimate acquaintance with "Aischulos" and "Ovidius" (why
not "Ouidivs?"). There are all the proper things—verses
to Emily Brontë, translations of Villon's "Ballade des
dames" and of the "Vanneur." There are refrains in italics
and brackets just as there ought to be. Some of the Swin-
burnian *pastiches* are quite excellent for a line or so; and
the thing is full of other, though unconscious, reminiscences which are most engaging. Thus

> Day and night, Day and night Thy quenchless
>   thought Returning
> *owns me* quite

irresistibly suggests Mr. Hoolan's inquiry to Mr. Doolan,
"And how's the lady that owns ye?" In short, except that
the utterance is rather more guilelessly uncritical, but also
rather more spontaneously imitative, than that of most
youthful bards, it only wants a "tut! tut!" and a good-
humoured smile. Mr. Adams seems to say that when it
first appeared, or some of it, we called it "impious and obscene;" but he makes the imputation jointly upon us and
a respected contemporary, and we hope it was the contemporary. If we did call it impious and obscene we retract.
It was only foolish.

In the other three deliverances we hear Mr. Adams' *ma-
jora canentem.* . . . The Tennyson essay is almost shocking in its immaturity, for its author was all but thirty when
he died, and this was posthumous. Mr. Adams, about to
pronounce Tennyson "superficially picturesque," "shockingly wanting in self-knowledge and self-respect," a "half-
hearted dilettante," and a poet from whom a little volume
of beauties will some day be finally gathered, is almost
touchingly anxious not to do the deed too roughly. He
"hopes he will not be misunderstood," and pleads for "seriousness." And when we come to his treatment we find,
of course, that the truth of the matter is only the old one.
The critic cannot see what is in the poet—namely, poetical
beauty—and therefore pooh-poohs it; he does not see what
he wants to find—namely, political rant and "modern"
cant—and thunders at its absence. Such a criticism is sim-

ply *non avenu.* It is not merely that Tennyson stands where he did as a poet—there was not much danger of anything else happening; it is only that Mr. Francis Adams disappears as a critic.

Then we have *The New Egypt.* Here, again, Mr. Adams takes infinite pains to impress on us that he went out beautifully unprejudiced, that he actually gave Lord Cromer a fair hearing in speech as between man and man, that he patiently investigated the problem, and so forth, and so forth. Unhasting and unresting, we proceed to hear his solution of that problem. And lo! putting aside the interviewing, and the appropriate picture of the Khedive's boots, and the guide-book local-colour, it is just the downtrodden but aspiring fellah, the intrusive Englishman, the rights of nations, and all the other gabble and jargon which anybody who knew anything about the matter could have written in Fleet Street, and which many worthy Radical journalists who knew nothing of the matter have written in Fleet Street or its immediate neighbourhood, without going to Egypt, without taking up long-suffering Lord Cromer's time, without discovering by actual vision and possible cigarette-consumption that Abbas Pasha is a Heaven-born ruler.

And, lastly, we have the drama, even this *Tiberius.* Mr. [W. M.] Rossetti, who has edited it with some omissions and castigations, sees in it "extreme force, steady insight, literary form, and poetic touch." . . . That almost any man who has read the poetry of the nineteenth century, and who has any retentiveness of ear and any fluency of pen, could write it till half the papermakers in Kent and half the penmakers in Birmingham made their fortunes by his patronage will probably be the opinion of others.

To do Mr. Adams justice, his text is rather better, though not much better, than his proem. . . . The truth is that there is no dramatic connexion of any kind between the various acts or scenes representing Tiberius as forced to give up Vipsania, his finding Julia impossible, his long and enigmatic sojourn at Rhodes, his subjection to Sejanus, his emancipation therefrom, and his final apotheosis at the hands of Caligula and Macro. Even Shakespeare never made repeated jumps of this kind, and Shakespeare had a certain gift of bridging what he did make by the continuity of character-drawing which we must frankly say we do not find in Mr. Adams. A few *tirades* are not without merit—though it is merit not much greater than may be found in one out of every four or five of the scores of books of minor verse published every year. Of the character in which Mr. Adams has given himself scope unfettered by history—that of a Greek slave whom Tiberius buys at Rhodes, and makes his mistress—even Mr. Rossetti does not think that the creator need be more than "reasonably proud," and we have seen something of Mr. Rossetti's scale of praise. (pp. 75-6)

[In] this "momentous record," as Mr. Rossetti calls the most violent and flashy of Mr. Adams's work, the *Songs of the Army of the Night,* this record that is to be "increasingly recognizable," there is, to our impartial thinking, no sign of permanence whatever. There is nothing that the world will not willingly let die, if only for the very simple reason that the thing is always with the world—to wit, the

yeasty self-confidence and the vacuum of self-knowledge and knowledge of other things proper to youth. The more books people read, the easier it is for them to write books of a kind, especially in the rank journalese which is Mr. Adams's style; the more papers and the more publishers there are, the easier it is for them to get printed and published. The more Board schools there are, the easier it is for them to get uncritically read. But everything (even that which makes for its instantaneous toleration) is against such stuff as this lasting; and, while it does last, there is certainly no reason why rational people should pay any attention to it. There must be, at any given moment, between Highgate and the Crystal Palace, between Shepherd's Bush and the Tower Bridge, hundreds of young men with as much literary knowledge and as much literary power—if sometimes a little less forward and less articulate, sometimes, also, we trust, incapable of writing such vile English as "replete *in* blunders"—as were possessed by Francis Adams. And we sincerely trust that, to that knowledge and that power, at least ninety-nine out of every hundred can add far better sense and far better taste. (p. 76)

"The Prose and Poetry of Francis Adams," in The Saturday Review, *London, Vol. 78, No. 2021, July 21, 1894, pp. 75-6.*

The Athenaeum   (essay date 1894)

[*In the following excerpt from a review of Adams's play* Tiberius, *the critic evaluates the strengths of several characters and episodes in the work, concluding that the play is, as Adams considered it, the author's "highest achievement."*]

What liberties Mr. Francis Adams took with the character of Tiberius is to us matter of indifference; but in assigning as the motive of his hero in the murders he committed the desire to put down capitalists who fed upon the poor, and in establishing a Roman emperor as a leader of "the army of the night," the author is true to the promise of his morbid, bloodthirsty, and impetuous youth. When, as Mr. [W. M.] Rossetti holds, in unbearable anguish and in perfect sanity, he took his wretched life, the most capable laureate whom the forces of destruction and disorder have found expired. His death may be regarded as a possible loss. He was very young and unusually able, and there is a chance that his moral leprosy might have been cured. In reading *Tiberius* it is necessary to recall the mischievous and wild breathings of the *Songs of the Army of the Night* to find out the secret of its teaching. Rugged, uncouth, and shapeless as is much of Adams's verse, it furnishes proof of lyrical possession. With the author's permission, Mr. Rossetti excised some of the crudest utterances, and has made an attempt at added shapeliness. Shapely the drama is not, but it displays remarkable gifts of observation, poetry, and passion, and approaches, although it does not attain, greatness . . . Not wholly unsuited is it to the stage, and there are parts that would prove impressive in representation. The whole is, however, in some degree a chronicle play, the action of which extends over close upon half a century, and is necessarily carried on by a succession of different characters. In the opening act, in which, at the bidding of Augustus, Tiberius divorces Vipsania and marries Julia, he is thirty-one; when he expires, assassinated by the Prætorian guards, he is seventy-eight. A period such as this is too long for dramatic action; the flickering out of the life of a man senile and almost helpless cannot be accepted as tragic; and the decay of Tiberius has the added disadvantage of seeming a repetition of that of his predecessor in the purple.

Adams might almost be a belated descendant of the spasmodic school. We are reminded in reading him of Beddoes, of Sydney Dobell, and of Alexander Smith, the last-named especially, whose locutions are recalled. In many respects history is followed, the character of the first Julia being taken in the main from Suetonius and Dion Cassius. A scene in which she returns from banishment, derides Augustus and Tiberius, and, after a vain attempt to obtain forgiveness, inveighs fiercely against the entire court, is, we fancy, wholly imaginary. It is the strongest in the play. The chief charm of the piece is, however, in Electra, a Greek slave, whom Tiberius purchases at Rhodes, and promotes to quasiconjugal honours. This creature is a sort of prose or earthly Undine, and is one of the most fantastic and attractive characters in the modern drama. Frivolous, vain, pleasure-loving, soft, wanton, saucy, she is a pleasing type of alluring, delightful, deadly womanhood. To her are assigned snatches of song or entire lyrics, in which Adams's metrical gifts are exhibited at their best. The song concerning Phœbus is almost good enough for a Jacobean or Carolinian poet:—

> Phœbus is lord of the sea, he rises in light,
> His horses of gold, his chariot of gold, and his
>   face so bright.
> O that the god of day, the lord of the sea,
> Would bend down his eyes but one moment
> To me, even me!
>
> Phœbus is lord of the sea; and all day long
> The chaunt of his praise goes up, radiant and
>   strong!
> O that the god of day, the lord of the sea,
> Would speak with his lips but one word
> To me, even me!

Asked by Tiberius, who hears her for the first time, where she had heard that song she says:—

> O, that song is a wonderful, beautiful song!
> The ladies in white sing it in the temple there
> Among the marble pillars. I crept up
> And listened to them. There was one who sang
>   it,
> A great, tall lady with red burnished hair
> And a pale beautiful face. The others sang
> Together the first lines again, but she
> Sang by herself. She'd a deep voice like water.
> I had to shut mine eyes and open my mouth
> When *she* sang. I was hidden by a shrub.
> I went there twice on holiday mornings. Now
> I'll never hear her sing again, I fear.

This is delightful prattle. One more specimen of her talk after her promotion may be given:—

> There! Are not those notes pretty? Listen again.
> La, la, la, la, la, la! I learn so quick!
> The rain and clouds are gone! I am so glad!

> When I can play, I'll play and sing together,
> For I have many tunes here in my head,
> But when I make and sing them, I forget.
> Those silly birds shriek so in the vestibules.

The same hand that can supply idyls and pictures like these can also gloat over destruction and murder. The utterance in the following lines is, of course, dramatic, and must be accepted as such. A perusal of other works of Adams leaves little doubt as to the application he would give. Speaking of the nobles, Tiberius says:—

> Sejanus, there is but one word for them.
> That word's extermination! Man by man
> Calmly and coldly we will call them out
> As we would weeds—unwearied trap and slay
>   them
> As we would vermin. They are the world's curse.

Adams regarded this drama as his highest achievement. He was justified in so doing. (pp. 233-34)

> *A review of "Tiberius: A Drama," in* The Athenaeum, *No. 3486, August 18, 1894, pp. 233-34.*

The Bookman, London   (essay date 1899)

[*In the following review of* Essays in Modernity, *the critic questions Adams's literary judgement, contending that his assessments are immature and arrogant.*]

"Modernity" is an ugly word, and it stands for a crude and clumsy and chaotic thing. It does not mean the theory of the new forces that are to shape the coming age. It means rather the consciousness that new forces are about, that the odds are with their being beneficent, that at any rate they are very interesting. So long as the bias towards modernity is modified by even an occasional exercise of judgment, it is wholesome, as wholesome and refreshing as callow, vigorous youth, and as blundering. The essays in [Adams's *Essays in Modernity: Criticisms and Dialogues*] are rightly named. They were written by a man of great talent, who was keenly conscious of the new forces, and who was a stout fighter against old schools and old fogeys. Before his regretted death he was beginning to show signs of mature thought, and of a sense that the problems of the world were deeper and harder than fighting youth can ever guess. His papers did not all deserve reprinting and even the best deserve hearty castigation. Mr. Adams had some of the elements of a critic in him. He was a lover of truth in no conventional sense of the word. His culture was fairly wide. His ideals were high and generous. Names did not frighten him. He never mistook popular favourites for the prophets of the coming day. But he had some handicapping limitations for a critic of literature. Life in the actual world, imperfect and crude, interested him more than life nearer an ideal expression in letters—which explains why his remarks on the visionary poet are merely foolish. His opinions on social questions affected his opinions on literature not only unduly, but crabbedly. This is quite forgiveable, of course, but ruinous to fair judgment. He pardons a writer for being nothing save an artist, but woe be unto him if he try to be an active humanitarian as well, and fail in the attempt. Keats he thought sensible for keeping out of the coil of the world. But on Shelley's vague efforts at regeneration he pours infinite scorn. Jeanne d'Arc is his model of the serious visionary sincerely concerned with the affairs of the world. But what did the military tacticians of her own day—not of ours—think of her? And he is entirely and very far wrong in denying the practical influence of Shelley in reforms. The poet's own fingers were fumbling, perhaps, but he has armed a thousand hands. The truth is, Mr. Adams disliked nothing so much as those things he had done with himself, that were no longer inspirations to him. And this is the secret of a vast deal of the adverse criticism in the world. The essay on Tennyson, if one omits the impudence and the bad taste, amounts to nothing more than that the late laureate was not a profound thinker. Perhaps it was not superfluous to say so, for the general mind, to whom Tennyson presented just as hard problems as it was fit for, thought he was very deep. But the attack should have been directed to the general. It is not true to say Tennyson made bids for popularity. He spoke with his magic tongue, sincerely, out of his serious, limited, and very conventional mind. And it is not merely a fault against taste the critic commits, but a stupid blunder in psychology, and in the instinctive understanding of inspiration, when he attacks Arthur Hallam for not being literally, and to the world, all that he was spiritually to a loving friend. Mr. Kipling is placed only a little lower than most persons with a sound literary sense have by this time placed him; but the details of the judgment are not very careful. Mr. Adams was perfectly right in denouncing Mr. Swinburne's lack of mastery over style, and, indeed, it is not his standing up to the big ones that is offensive. His attempt to measure them was quite honest, and sometimes respectful. But the regret that this is a posthumous volume is made more poignant by the retention of such impertinences as calling Blake "the inspired Cockney," and Godwin "the most sordid of mediocrities." These are not even suggestive exaggerations.

A review of "Essays in Modernity," in The Bookman, London, Vol. XVI, No. 96, September, 1899, p. 166.

Henry S. Salt   (essay date 1930)

[*In the following excerpt, Salt examines contradictions in Adams's character and writings, praising the revolutionary* Songs *and the "extraordinarily fascinating"* A Child of the Age.]

There were two seeming contradictions in Adams, both in his character and in his writings, which struck me at the time of my first acquaintance with him, and must have been noticed by many of his readers. I refer in the first place to his strange mixture of sweetness and bitterness. He was at one moment, and in one aspect, the most simple, affectionate, and lovable of human beings; at another, the most aggressively critical and fastidious. His power of pitiless invective shows itself in many of the *Songs of the Army of the Night,* as in those addressed to Ruskin and Swinburne, and his conversation in this respect was fully as incisive as his poetry. I well remember the savage delight expressed by him at the thought that Herbert Spencer's ponderous philosophical structure was destined to

tumble asunder like a pack of cards, and the zest with which he denounced George Eliot for having *preached* a respectability which she herself was too advanced to practise. There can be no doubt, I think, that suffering and disappointment had aggravated and embittered the extreme sensitiveness of his disposition; but under this irritable surface the true warmth and lovingness of his nature lay unchangeable to the last. As one of his Australian friends has said of him, the very light of comradeship shone from his soul.

The other contradiction was that which stood apparent between the academic and the democratic sides of his character. In his early life a follower of Goethe in his devotion to culture, he has recorded, in the last of his *Songs,* the terrible struggle that shook him when he realized that the claims of Labour were more to him than the claims of Art. "Yes, let Art go", is the watchword of another of his poems; nevertheless, the purely artistic impulse was never wholly subordinated, and he did not live long enough to adjust and reconcile the two warring moods. Hence he spoke and wrote at different times like two different men; and this is the reason why the literary folk, by an instinctive preference, know him mostly by his essays, while to social reformers his name is more closely associated with the *Songs.*

Francis Adams's *Songs of the Army of the Night* are among our notable revolutionary poems, and even the literary critics must eventually become aware of them. As surely as Elliott's *Corn Law Rhymes* and Brough's *Songs of the Governing Classes* spoke the troubled spirit of their age, so do these fierce, keen lyrics, on fire alike with love and hate, express the passionate sympathies and deep resentments of the Socialist movement in its revolt from a sham philanthropy and a sham patriotism; and, unequal as the poems are, when judged by the usual literary standards—in parts so tender and melodious, and again, in other parts, harsh and formless to the verge of mere doggerel—few intelligent readers can be unmoved by their force and impressiveness. What rebel poet has ever "arraigned his country and his day" in more burning words than those of the stanzas **"To England"**?

> I whom you fed with shame and starved with
>   woe,
>   I wheel above you,
> Your fatal Vulture, for I hate you so,
>   I almost love you.

It is my belief, in spite of the verdict of the critics, who knew him mostly by his prose essays, that Francis Adams's name will in future be remembered through the *Songs of the Army of the Night*—through the *Songs* in the first place, and perhaps also through that extraordinarily fascinating, if somewhat morbid, story, *A Child of the Age,* which I would rank in the same category as *Wuthering Heights* and *The Story of an African Farm,* among the great works of immature imagination. I cannot believe that his criticism, much praised though it has been by some of those who knew him, will survive the test of time. (pp. 73-6)

Henry S. Salt, "Two Singers of Revolt," in his

Company I Have Kept, *George Allen & Unwin Ltd., 1930, pp. 70-80.*

Clive Turnbull (essay date 1949)

[*In the following excerpt from a biography of Adams that was later included as a chapter of a larger work, Turnbull defends the importance of Adams's poetry and fiction.*]

Perhaps [Francis Adams] was not the best but he was the most significant poet we in Australia have had. He was a great man. He ought to be remembered. He belonged to the most significant period in our history, the last quarter of the last century, when all that we are and shall be finally took shape. Francis Adams had a hand in the shaping. He was a man to weep for, brave in adversity, faithful in distress, and kindly toward all men of goodwill. Sometimes he was wrong in his judgments, but more often he was right; he was never wrong in his sentiments. When we look back upon him we see a figure of extraordinary charm who delighted all whom he met, racked by the then most relentless of all illnesses, tuberculosis, often in straitest poverty, often angry, with the savage indignation that lacerates the heart, but never soured—a man of such quality that you could find old men who, after half a century, would say, "Yes, I knew Francis Adams", with the air of one who once saw Shelley plain. I have said that Adams, perhaps, was not the best of our poets, thinking that Shaw Neilson was the greatest of them; but it may be that is not so. Neilson (a Scot likewise) sang the sweetest songs we have, warm with the tears of the great of heart, but his was too kindly and gentle a nature for whole greatness. Adams could hate as well as love; his tears were sometimes fire. He had the world-comprehending mind, the flame of which genius is born. Out of all that he wrote, and he wrote much, feeling death ever at his heels, not a great deal will survive—but of what survives, is there anything better? (pp. 97-8)

In the **Poetical Works** he had written to please himself and for a limited public, familiar with classical literature. Toward the end of 1887 he sent to the printers in Sydney the manuscript of the work on which his fame chiefly rests, **Songs of the Army of the Night**. It included a few poems in the old manner, but it was addressed to a new audience, to the mass of people, unread in the masterpieces of the past, and unskilled in literary allusion, direct, passionate and moving. Henry S. Salt, a friendly admirer, bred in the older tradition, felt the verse often "harsh, and formless to the verge of doggerel" [see excerpt dated 1930]. To us it does not seem so; Adams was one of the first to cast verse in what is now a familiar mould. He belonged to his new age as well as to the old. It is for these poems that we find most sympathy, not only for what they have to say but for the manner in which it is said. It is possible that D. H. Lawrence, for one, was influenced by Adams; at least in some of Lawrence there are the same cadences as in Adams.

To the **Songs** Adams attached a preface in which he described something of his spiritual pilgrimage [see excerpt dated 1888]. "The key-note of the First Part—

'England'—is desperation, or if any hope, then 'desperate hope'," he says. In the Second Part—"Here and There"—the record of a short trip in the East, there is expressed Adams's hatred of the results of a rapacious Imperialism. In the Third Part—"Australia"—"there is neither ferocity nor bloodthirstiness. Its key-note is hope, hope that dreads but does not despair."

Adams felt that his plea for comprehension would be too often idle—that what are now the commonplaces of democratic thought would be so wild and strange that little note would be taken of them, except perhaps as crankery. "None the less we make it, for the sake of those who are willing to attempt to realize the social problem and to seek within themselves what they can do for its solution." Against social injustices Adams protested with all his power. He saw, for an England which would not remedy these abuses, a future of violent resolution—"England will realize the desperation of her social problem when its desperation is shown here by fire and blood—then, and not till then! What shall teach her her sins to herself is what is even now teaching her her sins in Ireland." It was such references to fire and blood that so alarmed the gentler Socialists of the time, Fabians and others, many of whom were puzzled by what seemed to them the contradiction between Adams's religious feeling and his love for his fellow creatures on the one hand and his talk of violence and bloodletting on the other. To Salt, . . . Adams seemed "anarchist rather than socialist in tone", both simple and tender, vindictive and vitriolic in his writings. By anarchist here Salt presumably meant violent—not possessing a philosophy of anarchism. Adams's violence will scarcely startle us today. In England in 1883, or thereabouts, he had been connected for a short time with the Social Democratic Federation and "enrolled himself a member under the Regent's Park trees one Sunday afternoon, after a Socialist address from his friend Frank Harris". He afterwards dedicated one of his Australian works, oddly enough, to Harris—"to the friend all things friendly"—oddly because, to us, the subsequent career of Harris seems to reveal him as anything but a worthy person, although by his own account he was a good friend. Of his London politics, however, Adams afterwards said in a letter to Salt, "I find I was far too deeply absorbed in the personal emotions to have noticed much else." Adams's hatred was the complement of his love—a love expressed in the exordium to the **Songs** with such passion and eloquence as must indeed have embarrassed his audience:

> Brothers all over the earth, Brothers and Sisters, you of that silent company whose speech is only in the unknown deeds of love, the unknown devotions, the unknown heroisms, it is to you we speak! Our heart is against your heart; you can feel it beat. Soul speaks to soul through lips whose utterance is a need. In your room alone, in your lonely walks, in the still hours of day and night we will be with you. We will speak with you, we will plead with you, for these piteous ones. In the evening trees you shall hear the sound of our weeping. Our sobs shall shake in the wind of wintry nights. We are the spirit of those piteous ones, the wronged, the oppressed, the robbed, the murdered, and we bid you to

open your warm heart, your light-lit soul to us!
We will thrill you with the clarion of hate and
defiance and despair in the tempest of land and
sea. You shall listen to us there also. We will
touch your eyes and lips with fire. No, we will
never let you go, till you are ours and theirs! And
you too, O Sufferers, you too shall stay with us,
and shall have comfort. Look, we have suffered,
we have organized, we have longed to hasten the
hour of rest. But beyond the darkness there is
light, beyond the turbulence peace. "Courage
and be true to one another." *"We bid you hope."*

The *Songs* begin with a proem of which the first verse
reads:

> In the black night, along the mud-deep roads,
> Amid the threatening boughs and ghastly
>   streams,
> Hark! sounds that gird the darknesses like
>   goads,
> Murmurs and rumours and reverberant dreams,
> Trampling, breaths, movements, and a little
>   light—
> The marching of the Army of the Night!

The first section is the section of Adams's "desperate
hope". Here in **"Evening Hymn in the Hovels"**, and in
anathemas against Lord Leitrim and others, we see the
bitterness and violence which affronted his friends. But
even this is not all bitter; there are verses "on reading some
Greek lyrics after several toilsome months during which
he had not opened a Greek book" and the infinitely compassionate story of an encounter with a London street girl:

> . . . . In a dark street she met and spoke to me,
> Importuning, one wet and wild March night,
> one of the "vast flock that perishes alone . . . "
> O hopeless Wanderer that would not stay,
> ("It is too late, I cannot rise again!")
> O saint of faith in love behind the veils,
> ("You must believe in God, for you are good!")
> O Sister who made holy with your kiss,
> Your kiss in that wet dark wild night of March,
> There in the hideous infamous London streets,
> My cheek, and made my soul a sacred place,
> O my poor Darling, O my little lost Sheep!

The second part of the *Songs* is mostly in a quieter mood.
"England in Egypt" (actually first printed in a posthumous edition) reflects the poet's joy in the spectacle of the
red-coats on the march and the stirrings of his blood to
the sound of fife and drum, and his anger that these men
should be, as he sees it, "tools for pious swindlers" in the
unsavoury adventures of the Imperialism which he hated:

> But O, I knew, that hour,
>   Standing sick and dying there
> As I heard the fifes and drums
> As I heard the fifes and drums,
> The fifes and drums of England
>   Thrilling all the alien air!
> And "Tommy, Tommy, Tommy,"
>   I heard the wild fifes cry,
> "It is time to cease your fooling;
>   "It is time to do or die!"
> And "Johnnie, Johnnie, Johnnie,"
>   I heard the fierce drums roar,
> "It is time to break your fetters

> And be free for evermore!"

Others, again, some plaintive melodies in a minor key,
deal with the wrongs of oppressed peoples, among them
the Japanese, "the sweetest and gentlest people on earth",
a curious misjudgment, due to looking too long at the Dai-
butsu at Kamakura and too little to the code of the samurai, for in our calmer moments we may believe the code
of the samurai.

In the third part of the *Songs* we have Adams's hope "that
dreads but does not despair". He sees in Melbourne "the
outcasts", like "weary wounded animals" in the parks, but
he sees also, in Sydney, the "man of the nation", the common man that is, lying on the grass smoking his pipe, the
anonymous worker and soldier who, "when all the rest is
rotten", rises "and cuts and cures". In a bookshop in Melbourne he notes the adoration of Henry George; and in
Ballarat the statue of William Wallace. He writes poems
to Karl Marx and Abraham Lincoln and some dedicatory
verses to John Farrell (author of "How He Died"), and
others of an extremely hostile character to Algernon Swinburne and Queen Victoria (in her jubilee year):

> But what to you were our bravest and best, man
>   of science
> and poet,
> Struggling for Light and Truth, or the Women
>   who would be free?
> Carlyle, Darwin, Huxley, Spencer, Arnold? We
>   know it—
> Tennyson slavers your hand; Burdett-Coutts
>   fawns at your kneel

Much of this was reminiscence of old times, but in **"Fling
out the Flag"** (the flag of Eureka), written for the Australian Labour Federation, Adams sang in his new hope:

> Fling out the Flag! Let her flap and rise in the
>   rush of the eager air
> With the ring of the wild swan's wings as she
>   soars from the swamp and her reedy lair.
> Fling out the Flag! And let friend and foe be-
>   hold, for gain or loss,
> The sign of our faith and the faith we fight, the
>   Stars of the Southern Cross!
> Oh! Blue's for the sky that is fair for all, whoev-
>   er, whatever he be,
> And Silver's the light that shines on all for hope
>   and for liberty,
> And that's the desire that burns in our hearts,
>   for ever quenchless and bright,
> And that's the sign of our flawless faith and the
>   glorious fight we fight!

In the Epode of the book Adams turns again to his renunciation of literature as a career for socialism as he saw it:

> Darling, 'tis nothing that I shed and weep
> These tears of fire that wither all the heart,
> These bloody sweats that drain and sear and
>   smart.
> I love you, and you'll kiss me when I sleep!

(pp. 113-18)

Adams was twenty-six. His [*Songs* were] a remarkable
achievement. Even those parts of it which are mere denunciation are so alive with feeling, so fiery and often with
such a singing note that they will live; and the best pas-

sages are superb. Only a man of extraordinary insight, courage and ability could have produced, in the circumstances of his life and time, such work. And although it is in a sense fragmentary, it is on the other hand the greatest work we have, for these are fragments from the rock of genius, and none the less authentic for being fragments. Adams spent his life energy lavishly. Poems, novels, plays and the bread-and-butter work to keep himself alive were poured out in a turbulent stream. He had so much to say, and so little time to say it in. The great schemes, the schemes to be as big as Balzac, were never accomplished; but in this little work published in colonial Sydney he surely achieved, in fitful and blinding flashes perhaps, that illumination of life of which he dreamed.

In Australia *Songs of the Army of the Night* are forgotten except by such few people as cherish the early history of the Labour movement or of our literature. The judgments passed upon Adams are fantastic. H. A. Kellow says, "The influence of Adams on the poetry of Queensland is negligible . . . he was too much of a minor poet." Morris Miller says, "Adams's poetry leaves one cold. . . . " The English critics of the time received the *Songs* with "tacit contempt or open hostility". But there were other people whom Adams did not leave cold. He took a copy of his precious book and wrote on the flyleaf: *"To Walt Whitman—To the poet of the first generation of Democracy, the noble pioneer of a new Civilization, to the splendid singer of the health and freedom of man—with admiration, affection, reverence."* Old Walt was at first rather startled when he received this peculiar book, "written by an anarchist, or some such fellow", though even at a casual glance, Horace Traubel tells us, he found it "superior in its class". But one evening, about three weeks later, he came round to the subject again by way of Henry George. With his hand on the book he said to Traubel, "And do you know, Horace, there's poetry in that book—poetry after all—fire—strong places, passages without any tricky art, but natural, sustained. After all, if a fellow is to write poetry the secret is—get in touch with humanity—know what the people are thinking about: retire to the very deepest sources of life—back, back, till there is no farther point to retire to"; and the old poet was pleased by the inscription—it was "genuine, hearty and interesting".

As it proved there were others who were with Whitman rather than with the unmoved academics. (p. 120)

Adams's life in Australia gave him material for a quantity of other work, some published after his death. Of the works of fiction perhaps the most noteworthy is *Australian Life,* a collection of short stories, some of which had appeared in the *Boomerang.* These demonstrate not only Adams's gifts as a story-teller, as in the ghost story, **"The Hut by the Tanks"**, and in the devastating criticism of an English attitude in **"A Bush Girl"**, but his feeling for the Australian "up country" scene and the peculiar qualities of an old, hard and often mysterious continent. "The monotony of the plains ceases at night," he says in the story **"Flowers for the Dead"**.

> The ground wind becomes a person and raises its head towards the crowding stars. The carcases and skeletons seem agitated with a fitful

breath of being. The dry bones do not veritably live, but they seem to feel once more the electric currents of life thrilling through and through them. Why should the evil odour of dead animal matter be so appalling at night? The ghosts of wistful bullocks, aware of the greed and tyranny of mankind, standing impotently hostile to me as a member of the dominant race made me laugh, and yet I recognized a certain reality that was disquieting. . . .

This concern with the strangeness of the land reaches its height in the story **"The Red Snake"**. *Australian Life* is a book that deserves to be resurrected. . . .

In *The Australians,* based on a series of articles in the *Fortnightly Review,* Adams continued the social criticism of *Australian Essays* with the same objurgations against philistinism. He was now able to draw also upon his up-country experience and the book contains many sound observations on the circumstances of the time. (p. 121)

In 1890 Adams returned to England. He was not yet thirty, but already tubercular beyond hope, at least by the standards of those days. Such of the philistines as deigned to remember him at all remembered him as what seemed to them a disaffected misanthropic person in an age of evident progress. But to others, the men of goodwill, the ardent spirits of the Australian springtime, he was almost a being from another world, looking like a Greek god, talking with an exquisite felicity and a fire and an enthusiasm which remain vivid memories to this day, full of passion against injustice and kindliness toward decent people, poor, half-starved, "sick and dying" as he said, but yet more alive than any, a man of saintly and heroic spirit.

Adams was not only poet and novelist; he was critic as well, and an extremely discerning critic. Just as he was able to perceive the meretricious elements in Kipling and Tennyson at a time when those writers appeared to a majority to represent all that was admirable in the English spirit, so he was able to assess at his true value a neglected Byron. Here again Adams anticipated the verdict of a generation fifty years after him. He had an unerring sense in the discovery of the bogus. Of Kipling he remarks, "Into the mouth of Mulvaney, who gives us most of the military criticism, is put the ancient and stock abuse of the short-service system, backed up with the stock and ancient chauvinism about the glory and gain of the good old gentleman officer, all of the olden time, the individual with the courage of a mastiff and the brains of a rabbit"—Colonel Blimp, in other words.

Adams appreciates what is good in Kipling but castigates his reaction and snobbery; Gordon, he remarks, "never ranted and raved like a frenzied parvenu concerning the superhuman virtues and glories of caste". Nor was he favourably impressed by Kipling's pictures of Anglo-Indian life: "Duty and red-tape tempered by picnics and adultery." All this at a time when Kipling was so bemusing the sentimentalists of the Empire that Kipling Societies were set up, some of which endure in backwaters even to this day. The shallowness, snobbery and retreats from reality of Tennyson likewise came in for his scorn.

Adams, however, was no "debunker". He conceded these

men their due, and when that due was not given by society at large he was quick to point to the omission, as "Byron's glory is this: that at the darkest hour which the cause of liberty and progress has known in the century, when the furtherance of that cause was utterly hopeless in the domain of action, he asserted it with irresistible power in the domain of literature. . . .Civilization must refuse to forget the honour due to the man who, at the crisis of life and death, imperiously declared for life, and struggle and the claims of victory." (pp. 122-23)

> Clive Turnbull, "These Tears of Fire: The Story of Francis Adams," in his Australian Lives, F. W. Cheshire, 1965, pp. 97-125.

Vance Palmer   (essay date 1954)

[Palmer was an Australian novelist, playwright, and literary critic. In the following excerpt, he explores several aspects of Adams's poetry and critical observations in the context of Australian life in the mid to late 1880s.]

A really significant visitor [to Australia] was Francis W. L. Adams, who appeared, in 1884, in the disguise of a youthful migrant rather than a distinguished observer. Adams was a disciple of Matthew Arnold, a devotee of culture, but this critical side of his mind was occasionally swamped by eruptive, revolutionary moods in which he expressed intense hatred for the bourgeois civilization of Europe. The creative spark in him was reflected chiefly in his poems; these did not seem to come from the same fount as his cool, sardonic prose. Unlike Trollope and George Augustus Sala he had not yet found himself, and he had more to find than they had. In an immature English novel, **Leicester: an Autobiography** he had already proved his mettle.

But in his first contacts with the society of Sydney and Melbourne, it was the critical side of his mind that was uppermost. He was the cultured European looking for civilized values and not discovering them in any satisfying quantity. With one eye always on Matthew Arnold, he glanced at the educational systems of Victoria and New South Wales and was unimpressed. There was little that was either novel or inspiriting in them, he concluded, merely the slavish following of an exhausted tradition. He surveyed [Australian] attempts at literature and was chiefly attracted by Gordon and Marcus Clarke, these being exiles like himself. With Clarke, in particular, he had affinities. Clarke's sophistication in a society that was essentially crude, his easy independence of the opinions of drapers and bankers, the dry detachment of his preface to Gordon's poems—these were all things that struck a sympathetic chord in Adams. He was disgusted when an editor (probably David Syme of the *Age*) told him he had half a dozen young men on his staff who could write as well as Clarke.

Altogether, this young Englishman was inclined to be contemptuous of a society that was so brash in its self-assurance, yet imitated the worst features of the one he had left behind—a society dominated, as he said, by a Puritanism that had only begun to attain power when its sincerity was souring into cant. The young people of the well-to-do classes seemed animated and robust, but there was nothing inside them. They chattered about personalities and the form of horses; sport and dancing were the great things in their lives. How heart-rending to find all this brightness and intelligence wasted on the mere accidents and incidents of everyday existence!

As for politics, it was a mere squabble of mediocrities who represented the conflicting interests of land and capital. There were the pastoralists, clutching at the remnants of their dwindling powers, the traders and importers trying to establish themselves as the dominant class. He looked at the struggle going on between these groups in New South Wales and turned away.

"Political life in Europe," he wrote, "can scarcely be called noble, but here in Australia it is positively so base that there is danger of it becoming the monopoly of those whose verbose incompetence is only equalled by their jovial corruption."

All these reactions were such as one would expect from a young observer of some sensibility, fastidious in matters of taste and manners and extremely conscious of his European background—conscious, particularly, of the pedagogic figure of Arnold, to whom he dedicated his first book of essays. There was a slightly exaggerated stiffness in his attitudes. It was as if he had to keep up the prestige of the school's staff in the presence of the inspector.

But Adams was not merely the essayist and detached observer. There was the poet and rebel in him, always urging him to come to grips with life and take a hand in shaping it. Something in this new country, as he came to know it better, touched his spirit; beneath the complacent surface of its society, he felt, there might be creative forces waiting to be released. Weren't they, in fact, beginning to show themselves already in the sardonic belligerence of the small journals coming into being, in the clubs springing up to spread the ideas of Bellamy and Henry George, in the way unionism was preparing to take a hand in shaping the country's future? He travelled up and down the country, penetrating even the Western areas, where he was charmed with the friendly, forthcoming children who were so much at ease with their elders: he savoured the rough hospitality of wayside camps and bush homes. In the cities he mingled with ordinary workmen and began to ponder on the possibility of their forming the basis of a new society. [Adams wrote:]

> The People in Australia breathes free. . . . It does not feel the weight of the two great divisions of the middle class that are above it: the well-to-do and the gentle-folk. Workmen here do not go slouching down the streets as they do in England, crushed under the sense of their inferiority. This is a true republic; the truest, I take it, in the world. In England, the average man feels he is an inferior; in America he feels he is a superior; in Australia he feels he is an equal. This is indeed delightful. It is the first thing that strikes a new arrival in the country, and though Australia's sins—sins against true civilization, I mean—are as many as they are heinous, still a multitude of them is covered by this; namely that here the People is neither servile nor inso-

lent, but only shows its respect for itself by its respect for others.

This discovery of a people in Australia, with its own character and social habits, made Adams turn to the political movements in which it was involved. He began to associate with the obscure agitators, journalists, and organizers who were building up a labour movement and to take part in their discussions and activities. He followed every clue that might seem to prove that here, in this last continent, a new and energetic nation was coming into being. He constituted himself an advocate of that nationality, a supporter of any policies that might lead to its full emergence, a devout sharer of its mystique. In his novel, *The Melbournians,* we find him describing the conversion of his heroine, Susie, who had been discontented with the meagreness of the social life of Melbourne and had dreamed of the tempered richness of Europe. For a while she had played with the temptation to marry a wealthy peer who was in love with her, but in the end she decides to throw in her lot with the Australian young man she loves and the country that has a hold on her deepest loyalties. Speaking of their children to be, she says with the air of a religieuse who has seen a vision: 'I will bring them up to be proud of their country, and hate to prefer any other to it, but to give all their lives to making it better and happier than any other country.'

There can be no doubt that there must have been something in the climate of the late eighties to infect the loyal disciple of Matthew Arnold with this active enthusiasm. What he drew from the air about him could have been nothing less than the conviction that Australia was capable of building a society that would give new hope to mankind. This fervent, almost fanatical belief in the Australian future that he began to share with the people he had come to live among did not arise from any deep attachment to the soil. There had been no time for that to grow, and even the most patriotic spirits thought of Australia as a lean, unlovely mother, denied the teeming richness of happier lands. In the writing of the period the natural background was an enemy to be fought: you had the dauntless selector trying to wrest a living from the hostile earth, the shepherd watching the crows hang round his starving flocks, the drover battling through with his mob of cattle in the face of flood or drought. (pp. 26-9)

And there was little in the past to build on, little but the movement against transportation and the brief conflict at Eureka. Looking behind, there were great empty spaces, filled with episodes of pioneering and exploration that, no matter how spectacular, seemed like the sporadic ventures of individuals rather than the concerted projects of a people with a creative purpose. Whatever was heroic in the effort to plant a civilization in a new continent had lost face in the struggles over land-ownership: it could not serve as a tradition.

But there was always the future to provide substance for dreams. Most of the people who spread over the country in the days after the gold rush did have some vision of the just and perfect State at the back of their minds. There were the immediate problems, of course, of earning a living and getting a roof over their heads, but it was the pros-

pect of writing, on a virgin page, a new chapter in the history of humanity that touched their feelings and quickened their imaginations. (pp. 29-30)

Vance Palmer, "The Legend," in his The Legend of the Nineties, *1954. Reprint by Melbourne University Press, 1963, pp. 9-30.*

Cecil Hadgraft   (essay date 1960)

[*In the following excerpt, Hadgraft evaluates the strengths and weaknesses of Adams's poetic style.*]

In 1884 an ailing bird of paradise alighted in Australia, fluttered from one capital city to another, and left these shores in 1889. A few brilliant feathers remained to tell of his visitation. This was Francis Adams, talker, novelist, critic, journalist, essayist, dramatist. To fill all these rôles with distinction would hardly lie within human compass; but Adams during his brief stay was one of the most competent all-rounders in the country.

He was in addition one of the few poets of revolution. In the Preface to his *Songs of the Army of the Night* [see excerpt dated 1887] he says: "I make no apology for several poems in the First Part which are fierce, which are even bloodthirsty. As I felt I wrote." He goes on to say that he "was (unhappily) born and bred into the dominant class". The injustice that he saw prevailing in England and in the other lands he visited, including Australia, forms the staple of these poems.

The consumption from which Adams suffered exacerbated this bitter sensitiveness. His poems in consequence are filled with vituperation, only occasionally sweetened with a sort of desperate hope. He is a very uneven craftsman. Some of his non-political poems are maudlin, trite, and extremely ineffective. The prose writer, with standards of technique and a contempt for the trivial, and the poet who perpetrated absurdities hardly seem to be one and the same person. Even at his best Adams is, as he has been called, a minor poet; on the other hand it is not always true that he leaves us cold. **"London"**, for example, has its effect:

> Cruel City, London, London,
> Where, duped slaves of devils' creeds,
> Men and women desperate, undone,
> Dream such dreams, and do such deeds:
>
> London, London, cruel city,
> By day serpent, by night vampire—
> God, in thy great pity, pity,
> Give us light—though it be fire!

This little poem contains in brief some of the qualities of Adams—his occasional pointed force, his obvious sincerity, his infrequent felicity of phrase; but on the other hand it does not adequately illustrate his recurrent vices—banality, the blandly confident ludicrous, and the stridency of the man writing at the top of his voice. Adams is best in short poems and then when they are couched in the Landorian epigram mould. (pp. 63-4)

Cecil Hadgraft, "Turn of the Century: Poetry," in his Australian Literature: A Critical

Account to 1955, *Heinemann, 1960, pp. 57-83.*

H. M. Green   (essay date 1961)

[*An Australian poet and critic, Green is the author of the comprehensive critical study* A History of Australian Literature: Pure and Applied. *In the following excerpt from that work, Green discusses Adams's influence on Australia's poetry of revolt and contrasts the author's "naïve and rather watery love poems" in the* Poetical Works *with the "angry revolutionary fire" in the* Songs.]

The first in point of time among the Poets of Revolt was Francis Adams. He spent in Australia five or six out of his thirty-one years, and returned to England in the year before the Period opens, so that it might reasonably be contended that he did not belong to it; on the other hand both Adams and his work are part of the renascence of the English nineties and earlier, which, as has been pointed out, corresponds with the nascence of the Australian nineties and later. It might also be contended that Adams ought to be treated not as an Australian, but as a visiting writer: so far as his prose is concerned this is true enough, for his critical work is written from an obviously English point of view, and his novels and short stories are those of a visitor who has seen something of the country of which he writes, but has never become really naturalized; but though his verse is also un-Australian in tone, it has a definite place in the Australian poetry of revolt, which indeed it ushered in and to some extent influenced: Adams's verse therefore, but not his prose, is here treated as Australian. . . . There were several Adamses, and even as a verse-writer he is two different men. Most of the contents of the ***Poetical Works*** are naïve and rather watery love poems addressed to a number of women, and thin, outmoded playlets in verse: he writes about Sheep-shearers, the Kangaroo Hunt, the Swagsman, and refers to the "sun-scorched bank", the "intense clear light", the "wizened face of this Australian land", and so on, but he never really enters into an Australian subject; it never becomes part of him. The ***Songs*** are an extraordinary contrast to this sort of thing. Most of them are filled with angry revolutionary fire, with a passionate sympathy for the poor and oppressed, and with a fiery ungoverned arraignment of the rich, their tyrants, as exemplified by England, "The foul sea-harlot" with her "husk-hearted gentlemen" and "mud-hearted bourgeois". Adams was consumptive, and like some other consumptives he crammed what life he had with furious energy, determined to realize himself to the utmost within the short time left to him; his work is individual and exceedingly vigorous, but there is something not quite healthy about it: there are no bounds and no proportion to his invective; it has the lack of balance that characterized one aspect of the English nineties, and also a touch of its eroticism; [Henry Arthur] Kellow has pointed out that this is "the leitmotif of most of his poetical compositions", but the same tendency shows in his terms of abuse, which are often sexual, and among which "harlot" is a favourite. The motive that inspired Adams's verses was thus the exact opposite of [Henry] Lawson's, being hate rather than love; also, unlike Lawson, though

democratic in sympathy he was aristocratic in temperament, so that he seems to stand apart from those with whom he sympathizes, and his verses, in spite of their vigour and compelling sincerity, are not so human as Lawson's and have a quality of bookishness. But he is a poet as Lawson is not, and, turgid and hysterical as are so many of his outbursts, often as they lapse into prose propaganda or even sheer doggerel, their underlying emotion is sincere and compelling: several of the ***Songs,*** in particular **"At the West India Docks"**, are impressive in their power, and in the Proem revolutionary becomes poetic fire. The subject of this poem is that of Lawson's "Faces in the Street", but it lacks Lawson's human intimacy, as it is the product of a far greater poetic talent; here is the first verse:

> In the black night along the mud-deep roads,
>   amid the threatening boughs and ghastly
>   streams,
> hark! sounds that gird the darknesses like goads,
>   murmurs and rumours and reverberant
>   dreams,
> tramplings, breaths, movements, and a little
>   light.—
> *The marching of the Army of the Night!*
>
> (pp. 498-500)

H. M. Green, "Verse," in his A History of Australian Literature: Pure and Applied, 1789-1923, Vol. I, *Angus and Robertson, 1961, pp. 498-527.*

Edgar Jones   (essay date 1967)

[*In the following excerpt, Jones examines the theme of anarchy in Adams's* Songs *and explores his* A Child of the Age *as a debate between two questions central to late-nineteenth-century writers: "the first concerning the existence of God; the second the position of the artist in society."*]

Now and again works of art are created which are the quintessence of the age in which they appear. Just as Theodore Watts-Dunton's *Aylwin* is pure distillation of an earlier, less harsh and more romantic decade, so Francis Adams's *A Child of the Age* is the 1890's.

There is much in that tortured decade besides *fin de siècle* ennui,the posturing before outlandish and exotic altars, and the Religion of Beauty; something for which one may search the poems of Dowson and the works of Richard Le Gallienne almost (but not quite) in vain. *Cynara* and *The Quest of the Golden Girl* sound with echoes of this elusive quantity. It is an aspect of the 1890's we hear but little of, conditioned as we have long been to the moonlight face of the golden legend which the invincibly romantic of that generation, and the nostalgically romantic of the following, have handed down to us.

Yet we meet it often enough, and often enough without understanding how different, how essentially unromantic, it is, in that awful account by Beardsley of his own last agonies among the blood-splashed sheets. 'In these naked letters,' as Arthur Symons says, 'we see a man die. And the man dies inch by inch, like one who slips inch by inch over a precipice, and knows that the grasses at which his fingers tear, clutching their feeble roots, are but delaying him for so many instants, and that he must soon fall.' And again of the *Letters:* 'The whole book is a study in fear.'

We come upon this quantity somewhere in the procession of Dorian Gray's nightmare excesses—fleetingly, not untouched by affectation and pretence—and solidly enough in *De Profundis.* In the melancholy John Davidson's suicide; and Dowson's passion for a common—or uncommon—waitress before he guttered out in a café in Dieppe. Very strongly it shows in much that Hubert Crackanthorpe wrote. It is to be seen most clearly in the brief life of Francis Adams, one of the least known, as one of the best, writers of the 90's, in one savage novel, **A Child of the Age,** and in the racing vituperative poems that form his **Songs of the Army of the Night.**

If Adams is like anyone he is like Crackanthorpe. One may look in vain in him for the often exasperating affectations which are the stigmata of the Decadence, and which find perhaps their most perfect expression in *Under the Hill,* where Fanfreluche, yawning among the frilled silk pillows, thought among 'a hundred other things' of Rossini's 'Stabat Mater (that delightful *demodé* piece of decadence, with a quality in its music like the bloom upon wax fruit.)'

Little enough is known of Adams himself. Scottish by extraction, the son of Professor Leith Adams, a scientist and Army surgeon, he was born at Malta, where his father's regiment was stationed, on 27 September 1862. His childhood was spent adrift—now in England, now in New Brunswick, now in Ireland. He was educated at Shrewsbury School, which is the 'Glastonbury' described in his novel **A Child of the Age.** Leaving here in 1879, when he was seventeen, he went—as so many literary figures of the period seem to have done—to Paris; but his stay here was a short one only, of less than two years. Paris, like London, represented *Usuria* to him; it was the glittering scab on the decaying body of civilization.

> I stood in Père-la-Chaise. The putrid City,
> Paris, the harlot of the nations, lay,
> The bug-bright thing that knows not love nor
>   pity,
> Flashing her bare shame to the summer's day,

he writes, celebrating in his poem **"Père-la-Chaise"** the stand made by Parisian Communists, appropriately enough considering the outcome, in the famous cemetery. Such sentiments are in marked contrast to those implied or expressed by more conventionally 1890-ish literary figures; Arthur Symons, for instance:

> My Paris is a land where twilight days
> Merge into violent nights of black and gold;
> Where, it may be, the flower of dawn is cold:
> Ah, but the gold nights, and the scented ways!

or J. M. Synge, who only turned his back on Paris, where he had settled to become a critic of French art and literature, on Yeats's advice:

> I said 'Give up Paris, you will never create anything by reading Racine, and Arthur Symons will always be a better critic of French literature. Go to the Aran Islands. Live there as if you were

one of the people themselves; express a life that has never found expression.'

For this urban element, this love for the city, is characteristic of the period. It is as much characteristic as a love, in literature at least, of wild nature is a mark of the Romantic Movement of the beginning of the nineteenth century. The 'iron lilies' of Arthur Symons's Strand, and the 'Golden City' of William Ernest Henley; the impressionistic sketches in different media of J. T. Grein and Sir William Nicholson; the *Vignettes* of Hubert Crackanthorpe and the *Impression De Nuit: London* of Lord Alfred Douglas, have their counterpart in Adams's work, which is shot through with his awareness of urban life.

It drew him because, as much as—or more than—any of his contemporaries, he was a child of his age; it repelled him because he found the answer to his urgent questioning not before erotic altars, as did Symons and the early Wilde, or in the Mass, as did Beardsley, Dowson, and the ruined Wilde, but in a political ideal—Socialism; and it was in the cities that Adams felt the insistent pulse of human degradation throbbing fiercest, and heard loudest the cry of the dispossessed for succour.

All cities are the same to him. He tries to express his distaste for Paris and London, which he execrates as the 'City of Wealth and Woe' in **Songs of the Army of the Night.** But his poems are too personal, owe too little to the crucible, to rise above the incidental. His hatred is expressed far better, because universalized, in **A Child of the Age.** In his short poem **"London,"** for instance, this weakness is clearly enough seen.

> Cruel City, London, London,
>   Where, duped slaves of devils' creeds,
> Men and women desperate, undone,
>   Dream such dreams, and do such deeds:
>
> London, London, cruel city,
>   By day serpent, by night vampire—
> God, in thy great pity, pity,
>   Give us light—though it be fire.

Sydney, where 'the harlot's curse rings' in the streets, comes in for as bitter strictures. Here he apostrophises:

>   the groan
> Of out-worn men, the stabbed and plundered
>   slaves
> Of ever-growing Greed, these are your own!

The truth was that in any great city Francis Adams found thrusting in upon him on all hands evidence of the unbridgeable gulf that separated the haves and the have-nots; and his hunger for equality, a hunger sharpened, perhaps, by his agonizing consciousness of his own mortal sickness, consumption, not only made him incapable of shutting his eyes to social injustice but impelled him to dedicate what talents he had without respite to its removal. The *Epode* to the **Songs** makes his position quite clear, and differentiates Adams markedly from the Aesthetes:

> When I was young, the Muse I worshipped
>   took me,
> Fearless, a lonely heart, to look on men.
> "Tis yours,' said she, 'to paint this show of them
> Even as they are.' Then smiling she forsook me.

Wherefore with passionate patience I withdrew,
With eyes from which all loves, hates, hopes and
    fears,
Joy's aureole and the blinding sheen of tears,
Were purged away. And what I saw I drew.

The decision was no easy one for him. Of the Child, 'the Soul of this sad day,' whose

    lips were pale, her limbs were weak,
Her eyes had thirst's desire and hunger's moan,

he asks:

    how shall I leave my songs,
My songs and tales, the warp and subtle woof
Of this great work and web, in your behoof
To strive and passionately sing of wrongs?

Child, is it nothing that I here fulfil
My heart and soul?

But the whole tenor of Adams's life and work was struggle; and the restless energy, which joined with his hereditary consumption to destroy him, left the issue never for long in doubt.

Thus it would be truer to think of Adams as an anarchist, if a politically uncommitted one, than the committed Socialist he was. **"Anarchism," "An Assassin,"** and **"Holy Russia"** are clear evidence of this. And Adams's 'singing revolt' is very different from Henry James's mannered and self-conscious treatment of contemporary social problems as we find them in *The Princess Casamassima*.

It was in 1882, while Adams was teaching at Ventnor School, after spending between two and three years in Paris and London, that he wrote his verse attack on the Poet Laureate, **"The New Locksley Hall: 'Forty Years After' "**, an attack made more bitter from affection turned sour.

    Farewell, then, whom once I loved so, whom a
      boy I thrilled to hear
Urging courage and reliance, loathing acquies-
    cent fear.

Adams's appraisal of Tennyson in this poem is an interestingly accurate one, foreshadowing much later criticism.

    O half-hearted, pusillanimous, faltering heart
      and fuddled brain
That remembered Egypt's flesh-pots, and turned
      back and dreamed again—
Left the plain of blood and battle for the quiet
      of the hills,
And the sunny soft contentment that the woody
      homestead fills.

Indeed, Adams, who was a better critic than a poet, but a better novelist than a critic, has in his appreciation of the Laureate made a classic contribution to Tennyson criticism. (pp. 76-81)

A voyage to China and Japan [in 1887] elicited some few poems from him, dull things for the most part, less vignettes of fresh woods and pastures new—something that Adams does with penetrating skill in prose in a novel, *The Melbournians,* and a masterly piece of reportage, *The New Egypt*—than sudden glimpses into a mind so tor-

tured that it saw whole countries only as the masks of an obsessive foe—England,

        that land
    I loathe and hate.

Adams is a master of essentials. Even under the compulsion of his obsession he can still, on occasion, in this weaker medium, strike the poetic note. In **"New Guinea Converts,"** for instance, he shows a Hardy's sureness of touch with the simple portrait:

    I saw them as they were born,
      Erect and fearless and free,
    Facing the sun and the wind
      Of the hills and the sea.
    I saw them naked, superb,
      Like the Greeks long ago,
    With shield and spear and arrow
      Ready to strike and throw.
    I saw them as they were made
      By the Christianizing crows,
    Blinking, stupid, clumsy,
      In their greasy ill-cut clothes.

The same confident deftness we see again in **"Farewell to the Market: 'Susannah and Mary Jane' "**. Here the touching simplicity of his excursion with two small children, strangers of four and three, along the Edgware Road on a Saturday night

    And we bought some sweets, and a monkey
    That climbed up a stick 'quite nice'.
    And then last we adjourned for refreshments
    And the ladies had each an ice

etches deeper the sombre ending:

    And then we went home to Mother,
      And we found her upon the floor,
    And Father was trying to balance
      His shoulders against the door . . .

      And
    We kissed one another and parted,
    And they stole in hand in hand.

William Michael Rossetti, writing of the *Songs,* [see excerpt dated 1894], while 'far from blind to the excesses of opinion and of feeling in the volume, or to its defects as well as excesses of diction,' was

    genuinely astonished at its intensity and fierceness of tone, its depth of emotion, and its splendid instantaneousness of poetic perception, suggestion and expression—an instantaneousness as of lightning at twilight, revealing at one moment every corner and cranny of the scene, and at the next moment plunging all into a more sombre obscurity than before: the inarticulate things of passion and of poetry hurtled upon the mind through the articulate.

                        (pp. 81-3)

An outstanding inclusion, omitted from the earlier volumes [of the *Songs*] but assigned a place in the copies revised by Adams, was **"The Mass of Christ,"** a remarkable poem in the dream convention which elucidates Adams's position in regard to organized religion. Says Adams:

    The name of Christ has been the sovereign curse,

The opium drug that kept us slaves to wrong.

Yet in thus attacking organized religion Adams, as may be expected, stands firmly at the side of Jesus the Man, whom he clearly distinguishes from Jesus the Christ. It is one of Adams's representatives of abused mankind who speaks:

> 'O Christ, O you who found the drug of heaven,
> To keep consoled an earth that grew to hell,
> That else to cleanse and cure its sores had striv-
>   en,
> We curse that name!' A fierce hard silence fell,
> And Jesus whispered, 'Oh, and I as well!'

Two years after his return from England, on 4 September 1893, Adams killed himself; thus joining the not inconsiderable company of his contemporaries who were of their age and at the same time so out of tune with it that they could no longer bear to fill a place in it. He was thirty years old: 'a young man of engaging and beautiful presence, and some appearance . . . of delicate constitution.'

But it is in his novel *A Child of the Age* that Adams not only fully expresses himself but also stills for a moment the shifting chiaroscuro of the nineties: this latter although the first published version of the book antedates the historical decade by between eight and ten years, while even its final, revised and to a great extent rewritten form belongs to no later than the first two years of the decade. The explanation of this apparent pre-cognition seems to be twofold. A significant prefatory note, unsigned, in the 1894—the *Keynotes*—edition, states that Adams was surprised 'on reading his novel critically as the work of another writer . . . to find how truly he had depicted experiences which at the time of writing he had still to undergo.' Secondly, all Adams's work was conceived as falling into place on a giant canvas, the aim no less than to re-create, in all its complexity, the substance of the Age. In an untraced letter of March 1892, quoted in the same note to the 1894 edition, Adams wrote:

> It was my modest little scheme to draw types of all the social life of the day. *A Child of the Age,* is the first of a series of novels and tales. Oh, I was going to do as big as Balzac that way! Fancy what a pretty scheme for a jackanapes of eighteen, and to have sweated at it all these years! I finished the last but one of the novels (chronologically) on my way back from Australia [1890]. There are three novels to do yet and about eight short tales.

But even if the grand design, the Balzacian canvas, failed of execution, in the novel *A Child of the Age* Adams achieved a distillate of the spirit of the Age, a concentrate of the *Zeitgeist,* all the more remarkable because of the limits within which it was conceived.

This odyssey, in first-person narrative, of Bertram Leicester, a minor literary figure as unremarkable, save for curiosity value, as the scores of silver poets and prose-writers the nineties is distinguished for having thrust up for the briefest of flowerings is, in a very real sense, the odyssey of them all. Leicester, a solitary, is rootless and cosmopolitan, romantic and tragic. His path is dark with the shadows of sickness. Death coughs at every corner. There is nothing to hope for in this world; and only an ugly dissolution after death.

Leicester leaves Glastonbury (Adams's own Shrewsbury) after the crash of his finances, managed by a shadowy Colonel James, his dead father's friend and his own unseen guardian. Some secret clouds his birth. Once only, while on holiday from Glastonbury, he meets a relative: a dying Greek scholar, Cholmeley, his mother's only brother. It is an ominous meeting, for the boy Leicester first sets eyes on Rayne, the cousin who is destined to be his *princesse lointaine.*

A terrible Hellenic frustration before the inexorable approach of unalterable things runs through the odyssey. Again and again one cannot but be conscious of the consumption that was eating Adams away even as he wrote. This frustration is seen at its most poignant, because its most vulnerable, in the child Leicester's prayer on the eve of his being sent away, for the first time, to school:

> And I pray that you won't let me die till I am very old and have done all the things I want to do. But please help me to be a great man. Through Jesus Christ our blesséd Lord, Amen.

Adams's picture of these early years, every day tainted with the melancholy that accompanies increasing knowledge of their transitoriness, is etched with that minute accuracy that is characteristic of him:

> Whittaker is an old beast. He's fond of caning us I'm sure. When you go into the library on Saturdays after school, to get three strokes if you've had more than twelve mistakes in dictation, he won't let you kneel down loose, as if you were praying, but he makes you bend up over till you're quite tight. It's very nasty going tight again after the first one.

The innocence of childhood that saddens the account of Leicester's schooldays was an innocence that Adams carried with him to his death: a necessary concomitant to it was his hatred of the injustice and cruelty of life. But Adams is less concerned in *A Child of the Age* with the injustice and cruelty that derive from man, those twin forces which form the driving-power of the *Songs:* here his concern is rather with transcendent reality, with the irrational tyranny imposed on man by the *prima causa* of existence.

Anticipation of death is never very far away from young Leicester, as it was never very far away from Adams himself. Its shadow darkens his every encounter. Significantly, for Adams is no Aesthete, mutability holds no terrors for him. He is no Synge who broods on through play after play until, in *Deirdre of the Sorrows,* he comes to make his final statement on the transitoriness of human beauty. Death only is Adams's concern; and the finality implicit in dissolution.

While Adams returns again and again to this theme in the novel, we must look to his Wildean dialogue *The Hunt for Happiness* for the comprehensive and thoroughly objective statement. The dialogue is between Randal, a middle-aged cynic, and his young friend, the enthusiast Wilson.

'Then you don't believe,' he [Randal] said,
    'that death must be
Like all the rest, a mockery'?
Wilson shook his head.
    'Not in the least,' he said. 'If it is not the ex-
tinction of the ego, then it is nothing, and that
is the one—the great desideratum . . . I retain
unimpaired my belief in Death. It is the one certainty—the one need—the one consolation. This
is the love of Nature, that the same peace awaits
us all.'

It is an argument that finally convinces Randal:

    '. . . forgive [he implores his friend] an old and
worn-out huntsman of the foolish hunt for happiness. I will admit that I wish at times I had
been accidentally shot—by some one else or by
myself. It would have been better for me. Ah, the
women I have loved! the men I have loved! Ah,
beautiful and beneficent death!' . . .

    And as they went, Randal murmured again to
himself, but so softly that his friend did not hear
him:
    'O beautiful and beneficent Death!'

Death at least brings release from suffering. Leicester—
and Adams—know two kinds: the physical, and the spiritual that comes from that godlike identification with suffering humanity. Leicester makes acquaintance with the
first immediately on leaving Glastonbury when, lodging in
Kilburn, he tries to earn a living writing poetry. Adams's
account of the pathology of hunger bears all the authenticity of the experimental, paralleling in miniature Knut
Hamsun's *Hunger,* But his identification of Leicester with
the rest of suffering humanity leads Adams to pose two
fundamental questions: the first concerning the existence
of God; the second the position of the artist in society—
two questions at the very heart of the age.

Each is debated again and again throughout Adams's
work. For the young Leicester, however, the only possible
answer to the question of the existence of God is that one
does not know; more, one can never know. Bare existence
suffices to teach him, like Lear, only the worthlessness of
all things. The ambition of his early childhood—to be a
great man—vanishes in the face of this ultimate truth:

    Fools are great. When they die they rot and are
eaten. We shall all die some day, and rot, and be
eaten.

Yet Adams's tragedy—and it is the tragedy of the nineteenth century doubter—is that he cannot altogether satisfactorily dispense with the concept God; and even if he
were able to, he would have nothing to put in God's place:

    I ask You, God, if You are, to have pity on me
if I am blindly wandering, and to lead me to
know You some day before I die. I don't know
how I am going, but I know where I desire to go:
and yet I don't know more than that it is somewhere.

As to the second question, that of the position of the artist
in society, Adams has long been committed. Like Henry
James, only for different reasons, Adams repudiates Aestheticism as an answer to the unpleasant realities of the
age. Before Leicester comes face to face with human suffering we hear Adams's repudiation, as vehement as that
of Tennyson and, one suspects, owing its existence to the
same reason: that the lilies and languors of Aestheticism
offered an asylum only too inviting, only too real—we
hear it through Clayton, the missionary schoolfellow of
Leicester who has to give up his dream of future service
at the bidding of harsh reality. For Adams, fate treads
heavy on dreams and dreamers:

    Can't you see by the shore of what flood we are
standing? Can't you read the signs of the times?
Can't you see an Art that becomes day by day
more and more of a drug, less and less of a food
for men's souls? A misty dream floating around
it, a faint reek of the east and strange unnatural
scents breathing from it; but underneath mud,
filth, the abomination of desolation, the horror
of sin and of death.

                            (pp. 84-9)

Adams's development of the relationship between Leicester and Rosy [in *A Child of the Age*] is sure, and is marked
by a meticulous attention to psychological detail that parallels the detail of his descriptive vignettes. Its realism
takes it far beyond the limits set by the *vie de Bohème* convention, to which it owes little beyond the simple facts of
its existence, the rupture between lover and mistress, and
the deathbed conclusion. Adams indeed presents a fine
psychological study of Rosy. His own spiritual simplicity,
the mildness and 'amiable refined manners' noted by William Michael Rossetti, enable him to give authentic life to
this working-class girl of touching simplicity and integrity. Rosy's sensitivity, sharpened by her incipient tubercular condition; her moods of light and shadow; her jealousies; are posed for ever in uneasy equilibrium against Leicester's egoism, his essentially male romanticism; calling
out of her brooding childish silences, and out of him fleeting cruelties that only serve to emphasize Leicester's fatal
incapacity for communication:

    I remember that, as we sat together that evening,
    I looked across to her sitting with far-off eyes
    with her book, and thought how impossible it
    was to *know* anything about anyone else,

and illuminate above all Leicester's tortured rejection of
the age of which he is so clearly part. Leicester's is, in fact,
a rejection not merely of the spiritual poverties of the age
but of something far deeper. It is total rejection of an age
sapped by a spiritual malaise; an age which, after eliminating belief, succeeded only in substituting a nihilism which
offered man no possibility of happiness. Leicester can
sleep no more. On the brink of his estrangement from
Rosy,

    not only the general poorness, but also the gen-
    eral, and also the particular purposelessness of
    all life and of my own life came over me. I did
    not care to go to bed, I did not care to do any-
    thing. My eyes fell on my easy-chair: I went and
    lay back in it, in a state that kept, every now and
    then, rising to a level, over the edge of which lay
    disgust, and even despair. At last I rose, with an
    impatient curse. Was there *never* to be an end to
    this foolery? Was I *never* to have rest, peace,

comfort, self-sufficiency, call it what you please,—that spiritual sailing with spread canvas before a full and unvarying wind? *Why* was it, *why?* Was it really because the strange shadow of Purposelessness played the perpetual-rising Banquo at Life's feast for me? Or was it that I was one who could not lack the Personal Deity with impunity? I didn't know, I didn't know. I wished that I were dead. I wished that I had never been born.

The inevitable outcome is the disintegration of personality.

A letter from Rayne, who believes herself to be dying in childbed, precipitates the breach with Rosy. Yet Leicester, hurrying to London after the inevitable scene and as inevitable reconciliation, cruelly conducted on his part, suffers a sudden reversal of intention at the *Gare du Nord* and returns, telegraphing Rayne Gwatkin that he cannot come. Rosy, however, has fled; anticipating his final rejection of her, has she not told him all along: 'I would go away when it came'?

Leicester's moment of truth has come. If he is capable of love at all—and it is an open question—he loves Rosy. He is sure—now that it is too late—that he does so. Back in London, where he is certain she must be, he interrupts his search for her to call at the Gwatkins'; and hears from a servant that Rayne is not dead, has indeed recovered, and is gone with her husband into the country.

> It was enough. Further words I did not hear. I went away almost joyfully. She could be dead to me henceforth without a troubling thought.

But Rosy, when he finds her, is dying of pneumonia. Leicester, like the 'poor scribe' in Swinburne's *The Leper,* tends her who is now become his new *princesse lointaine* to the end; and at the end, like the scribe again, cradles her empty body in his arms.

But the old pattern, though complete, is shot through with a new and disquieting thread—forming a figure which is distinctly Adams's own, and therefore which belongs wholly to the age itself. For Adams, like Stephen Dedalus in a later time, is possessed by his vision of the truth; and like him is prepared to make no concession. It is a position at the heart of the modern spiritual dilemma, and that finds its clearer statement in an age which, having cast off its anchor of belief, contemplated with a kind of proud despair a future holding—nothing.

Rosy, like Stephen's mother, seeks out of another's charity some last fortification:

> 'Where do people *go* to when they die?' she said.
> I looked at her dear child's eyes, but did not answer her.
> 'Do *tell* me,' she said, in a child's aggrieved tone, rumpling her
> brow, 'Don't *tease* me! Tell me true!'
> After a pause, I answered her:
> 'I believe that they go into the earth and the air from which
> they came.'
> 'Yes,' she said, 'but that's not their *spirits.* What do their

spirits do?'
> 'Their spirits, too, go into the earth and the air.'
> She shook her head.
> 'No,' she said, 'their spirits go up'—(looking up)—'up into
> heaven!'
> I lifted her hand, and bent my head, and kissed her hand
> softly.
> 'But don't *you* think so too?' she said.
> 'No,' I said, still bent over her hand. 'But' (looking up at her
> and smiling), 'what does it matter *what* I think, dear?'

For Adams, then, truth has become the only belief that a man can hold to—even so, it is not one conducive to human happiness, either now or in some unforeseeable future.

Says Leicester:

> I ought to go out into the world and see its ways, so as to prepare myself for my work; that work which was nothing else than, having by self-culture and observation got an impression of things generally, to put down that impression on paper. Truth was the object of my work, and, by the very fact that I was a quite unprejudiced viewer of the phenomena of what is called Life, I did not see why I should not produce such an impression of things generally 'as posterity should not willingly let die.' The idea of telling the truth about things was a pleasing one. I could almost believe that some day that idea might be of itself a sufficient incentive to a love of existence.

Almost. Even the fundamental optimism of the evolutionist disintegrates in the cooling crucible that is the final decade of the nineteenth century. And Adams rejects the Religion of Beauty, to which so many of his contemporaries cling with all the passion of those already once dispossessed. 'Self's the man' at once his only anchor and epitaph, he faces alone into the unenviable future; so that, 'not in the least mad, but determined and deliberate, he can find no acceptable alternative but to put an end to his own life and 'the fully pondered train of thought' that had become intolerable to him. (pp. 99-103)

> *Edgar Jones, "Francis Adams, 1862-1893: A Forgotten Child of His Age," in* Essays and Studies, *Vol. 20, 1967, pp. 76-103.*

I. M. Britain   (essay date 1972)

[*Britain is an Indian-born Australian history professor and author of* Fabianism and Culture: A Study of British Socialism and the Arts, 1884-1918 *(1982). In the following excerpt, he evaluates the impact of Matthew Arnold's "ideal of Culture" on Adams's political beliefs and writings.*]

It is no wonder that [Adams,] a writer of such precocious and wide-ranging talent should have commanded, at one stage or another, the respect of many of his contemporaries in the literary and political circles in which he moved. Browning and Tennyson, Matthew Arnold and Oscar Wilde, George Moore and William Archer, W. M. Rossetti and Walt Whitman, were among the most celebrated literary figures who spoke favourably of his work. In Australia, . . . Adams became a well-known figure in socialist circles, especially in Queensland; and his book of revolutionary verse, *Songs of the Army of the Night,* made a considerable impact on a number of prominent figures on the 'Left' at that time: William Lane and his brother, Ernest, for example; and fellow 'rebel poets' like Bernard O'Dowd and Sydney Jephcott. (p. 401)

[The] fact that his work had gained the attention or admiration, however momentary, of so many of his more celebrated contemporaries, suggests that it was not deserving of the virtual oblivion to which most of it had been consigned by the time [P. I.] O'Leary wrote. The sheer volume of this work, and its enormous range and diversity, as well as its influence, would justify a closer examination of his achievement and thought. So far, however, such an examination has not been attempted by any political or literary historian of the period. In most of the studies of his age which happen to refer to Adams, only one or two aspects of his career or his writings are ever mentioned. A slim monograph on him was published in 1949; but it is little more than an evocative sketch [see excerpt dated 1949] of his life, giving some flesh and body to the bare bones of information presented in most biographical dictionaries and encyclopedias. The author of the recent short article on Adams in the *Australian Dictionary of Biography* has shown signs of a more exhaustive interest, but as yet no full-scale study has emerged in the manner of those on a score of other minor British writers at the time.

Perhaps the most serious reflection of the neglect Adams has suffered can be seen in the confusions which have arisen over the origins of his thought. Some of these date back even to his own lifetime. At one stage or another, he has been presented as an 'anarchist' in his political views; as an atheist in his religious outlook; as a Marxist in his economic thinking; and, in his attitude to literature, education and the general state of Victorian culture and society, as an almost unremitting devotee of Matthew Arnold. Such unintegrated images of the man only exaggerate the inconsistencies and paradoxes in his thought. Each of them, in fact, has been built up from a fairly superficial reading of the evidence. There has been no attempt to make a cohesive analysis of the disparate influences working on Adams's mind, and of the effect of these on the development of his ideas.

Such an analysis cannot effectively be undertaken here. It seems more useful, therefore, to concentrate on that aspect of the question which has been touched upon most frequently but still never examined in depth: the impact on Adams of Matthew Arnold and his ideal of Culture. By probing the image of Adams as a bearer of the Arnoldian gospel, it may be possible to gain some insights into his thought as a whole, and to clarify the other images of him which have been fostered by his contemporaries and later writers.

In the context of later nineteenth century intellectual and literary history Matthew Arnold has recently been described as 'everybody's parent'. Judging from the dedication in the *Australian Essays,* penned by Adams when he was in his early twenties, Arnold was a particularly dominant father-figure for the precocious young critic and man of letters. In the form of a poem addressed specifically to Arnold, the dedication reads:

> Poet, with this I send you—as a child
> that watches from below some cross-bow bird
> swoop on his quarry carried up aloft
> and cries a cry of victory to his flight
> with sheer joy of achievement: So to you
> I send my voice across the sundering sea,
> weak, lost within the winds and surfy waves,
> but with all glad acknowledgment fulfilled
> and honour to you and to sovran Truth.

A number of writers, in discussing Adams, have briefly noted the impact on him of Arnold's ideas; and some have implied, in their references to a master/disciple relationship between the two men, that Arnold was by far the most pervasive influence on Adams's thought. The nature of this influence has not been defined in any detail, however; and its precise extent at various stages of Adams's career has never been assessed.

The above passage from the *Australian Essays* suggests, on the face of it, an unmitigated devotion to Arnold on Adams's part, a sense of deep, if not total, indebtedness. Such an allegiance may seem puzzling in a man who had already been flirting with socialist ideas before he departed for Australia, and who was to publish only two years later a book of militant revolutionary songs which exhorted the working classes to overthrow contemporary society by violent means. Even such an isolated, and comparatively mild, outbreak of mass violence as the pulling-down of the Hyde Park railings in 1866 had seemed to Arnold an instance of the 'anarchy' which was to be resisted at all costs by 'lovers of Culture'. Moreover, he had designated all socialist and communist schemes for solving contemporary social ills as 'content with too low and material a standard of well being' and as ultimately coarsening in their effect on humanity.

How are we to explain these sharp contradictions in Adams's position? First, analysis reveals that they are not really as sharp as they appear. The adulatory comments which Adams made from time to time concerning Arnold cannot be taken at face value, as they seem to have been by certain writers who have commented on the relationship between the two men. Second, these contradictions are symptomatic of a basic duality in Adams's thinking, which was rooted in his upper middle class, social and intellectual background. Third, there was a kind of duality in Arnold's own ideas which gave them a significance for Adams that was never intended and was perhaps never consciously recognized by either man. In this [essay], I propose to deal with each of these points in turn.

An analysis of Adams's writings as a whole, including his *Australian Essays,* suggests that the almost fulsome tone of the dedicatory poem which precedes these essays was merely a literary convention. Adams later maintained that he owed more to Arnold than to anyone else; but he expressed the hope that this would not prevent him from viewing the man and his work 'without illusion'. 'Certainly,' he continued, 'on many questions I find myself on lines wholly different from him.' Adams's admiration for Arnold, then, was checked at a number of important points. These divergencies in thought between the so-called 'master' and so-called 'disciple' became increasingly evident as the 'disciple' matured, though there were continual fluctuations in the degree of Adams's allegiance to Arnold and no clear-cut process by which he broke away from it.

In all his writings (early or late) Adams made liberal use of typically Arnoldian vocabulary and turns of phrase: 'Culture', 'Philistine', 'Jew and Greek' (which in the context was the equivalent of Arnold's 'Hebrew and Hellene'), 'right living', 'sweet reasonableness', 'best possible self', 'the claims of conduct, intellect, knowledge, beauty and manners', and so on. Most of these terms and phrases were used in the original Arnoldian sense or spirit, and some as naturally as if they were of Adams's own coinage. It is probably not unusual for a budding young writer to take over, consciously or unconsciously, the diction of one older and much revered, and to assimilate it into his own style.

Over the definition of 'Culture', however, (the most fundamental of these terms from Arnold's point of view) Adams quibbled with the master from early on. In the preface to his *Literature and Dogma* Arnold had tried to sum up precisely what he meant by this perilously loose, all-embracing term. 'Culture', he declared, entailed 'acquainting ourselves with the best that has been known and said in the world, and thus with the history of the human spirit.' It was 'knowing the best that has been thought and known in the world' and 'getting the power, through reading, to estimate the proportion and relation in what we read'. But 'true culture' did not stop here. It involved 'not only knowledge, but right tact and justness of judgment forming themselves by and with knowledge'; and it entailed 'not only reading but reading with a purpose and a system to guide it'. By its very nature, this summing-up could give no sense of the richness and subtlety with which Arnold had invested the terms 'Culture' in his previous writings. But it was a fairly faithful résumé.

In an appreciation of Arnold which was written soon after the latter's death in 1888, Adams briefly referred to this capsule definition of the term, and implied his complete satisfaction with it. But in his much longer article on 'Culture' in the *Australian Essays,* published about three years earlier, he went to some lengths to point out the limitations of Arnold's definition in comparison to Goethe's. The German poet, he claimed, had been the originator of the whole 'Idea of Culture' in modern thought, implicitly prescribing its requisite components and procedures in his attempt to wean himself 'from halves' and to 'live for the Whole, the Good, the Beautiful'. Arnold's conception of Culture, according to Adams, envisaged perfectly what Goethe meant by 'the Whole, the Good and the Beautiful', but it was deficient on the question of procedure, placing as it did too much emphasis on mere reading and not any at all on personal experience of the world:

> If Faust could have achieved truth in his study,
> why does Goethe show us his achievement of it

by taking him away from his reading, and flinging him in the arms first of Love and then of Life? . . . To achieve a knowledge of the best that the world has thought and known, two things are necessary—reading and experience. No amount of reading will compensate for want of experience. It is useless for me to think I have attained to Truth, if I have never felt her absolute presence. No man who has not himself lived and loved can tell us the truth of love and life.

This detection of what he saw as a lacuna in Arnold's argument led Adams to formulate his own definition. Culture, he concluded, was

> the combination of reading with experience, of thought with knowledge. The one thing acts as a check on the other, the one is the spirit and the other the body . . . and in their commingling is found the perfect man. . . . Culture is reading and experience, but reading and experience with a purpose and a system.

All that Adams was really doing here was to inject a more overtly Romanticist element into the Arnoldian definition by giving explicit emphasis to the role of emotional and intuitive factors in perceiving reality. The departure from Arnold on this point was by no means fundamental, therefore. It nonetheless reflected the constant critical scrutiny to which Adams apparently subjected the work and thought of his mentor.

Adams's passionate concern for 'Culture' (whether in the precise Arnoldian sense or otherwise) was obviously a major impelling force behind his attacks on the mediocrity of popular fiction and of the commercial theatre of his day. The years Adams spent, immediately after leaving school, mixing in the literary and artistic circles of London and Paris, were also important, no doubt, in shaping his attitude to the state of the arts. During these years he became an habitué of the salons, studios and theatres of both cities; he struck up a warm friendship with Sarah Bernhardt; and he was invited to the 'bachelor "at homes"' of Oscar Wilde, where (in Adams's words) ' "society" met "Bohemia" and both had a good time'. It is possible that his contact with writers like Wilde and those in other semi-Bohemian groups was instrumental in introducing Adams to the ideas of Goethe, Arnold and the other 'modern men' in the field of letters. It is more likely, however, that he had already imbibed some of these ideas from the intellectual atmosphere of his family home—his father and his grandfather were both academics—and that his attitudes developed through a combination of these two streams of influence.

Despite the outward insouciance, levity and self-absorption of Wilde and his circle, they were engaged in as passionate a crusade against Victorian conventions in literature and the arts as Arnold himself. Their methods were perhaps more outrageous; and their ultimate aesthetic goals were in some cases completely at odds with Arnold's. But there was an inescapable flow of sympathy between him and them. That Oscar Wilde should have presented Arnold with a copy of his first book, *Poems,* is a testimony to the respect he felt. Walter Pater went so far as to claim that Wilde's literary criticism carried on 'more perhaps than any other writer, the brilliant critical work of Matthew Arnold'. There is some evidence, therefore, of an intellectual link joining Arnold with the leaders of the 'aesthetic revolt', and joining Adams with both.

One must be chary of overstressing this link. H. A. Kellow, who lays particularly heavy emphasis on Adams's dependence on Arnold, involves himself in something of a contradiction when he goes on to suggest that Adams's participation in the aesthetic revolt of his times was so total as to make him champion such (essentially non-Arnoldian) notions as 'art for art's sake'. This contention will not bear scrutiny in the face of disavowals from Adams himself, who referred explicitly to the 'Devil' of 'Art for itself' and demonstrated throughout his writings that true Art, as distinct from this 'tempting' distortion, contains a 'spiritual element', moral import and specific social purpose which no mere beauty or form of brilliance of technique can hope to provide. Such a position, of course, in this age-old debate about the bases of art, was by no means a peculiarly Arnoldian one. (pp. 402-08)

In an article he published in 1885 Adams lavished warm praise on Arnold as a poet, viewing him as the most 'representative' writer of his age in this capacity and therefore, if not the greatest among his contemporaries, the most likely to endure in the minds of men. This generally laudatory view of Arnold's poetry was balanced even at this stage by a candid criticism of its tendency on occasions to become 'bald, stale, conventional, not quite fused'. Later Adams was to comment on Arnold's 'emaciate early sonnets', and on the sickly, stultifying elements which his poems in general shared with those of a number of his contemporaries.

In the field of literary criticism Adams credited Arnold with being the pioneer of modern techniques, and contrasted the discrimination and balance implicit in his 'Scientific' approach to literature with the 'myopic assertiveness' and 'crude dogmatism' of a critic like Carlyle. Arnold's *Essays in Criticism* he held to be the poet's 'best prose memorial'. These claims were made in the article on Arnold which Adams published a few months after the former's death. . . . [A] certain disenchantment with his mentor had already begun to set in. Less than three years later, this had become so marked that Adams could be found referring to Arnold as one of those 'jejune critics' whose appreciation of the varieties of literary style was at once severely limited and remarkably undiscriminating.

This *volte-face* was not as sudden as it may appear. Numerous examples have already been cited of Adams's divergence from Arnold's line of thinking, and of his unhesitating criticism of the 'master' on a number of fundamental and subsidiary issues. Adams's mind was too independent, was cast in too critical a mould, and was subjected to too many disparate influences for him ever to remain— or even become—the unquestioning disciple of one master. (p. 414)

Because of Adams's militant stance in his revolutionary verse, some contemporaries (including Walt Whitman, to whom Adams had sent a copy of his *Songs*) went so far as to call him an anarchist; others, including Adams's own friends, Frederick Broomfield and Henry Salt, perceived distinct 'anarchist' strains in the *Songs*. It seems fairly clear that in most cases this epithet was used in the purely popular sense of 'violently disruptive'. This was much the same sense as Adams himself intended in his own poem **"Anarchism"**, and it corresponds partly with the Arnoldian conception of what 'tends to anarchy'.

Imprecision and confusion in the use of terms like 'anarchist' or 'socialist' were, naturally enough, quite common in the early days of the modern socialist movement in Britain. Even when avowedly 'Anarchist-Communist' journals like *Freedom* and the *Commonweal* claimed, in their obituaries of him, that Adams had preached anarchism, it seems clear from the context that they meant nothing more by this term than a sort of revolutionary iconoclasm. If, in fact, they intended to imply by this that Adams had looked to the complete and immediate destruction of the State *qua* State, of all political government as such, they were misguided. The concession which he had made to reformism in discussing the Australian political situation shows clearly that, when he diverged at all from a Marxist path, it was in a direction completely opposed to that of the anarchists.

The compulsive militancy of Adams's *Songs of the Army of the Night* was one of the most conspicuous symptoms of his gradual disillusionment with Matthew Arnold, of the essentially limited nature of his allegiance to the man who has been designated his intellectual master. But Adams's militancy was also limited, and these limitations reflected in part the hold which certain Arnoldian ideas (and associated influences) still managed to maintain over his mind. Adams's inability to commit himself fairly firmly either to Arnoldian ideas or to revolutionary socialist ideas indicates the dangers involved in attaching any specific label to the various aspects of his thought. It reflects, moreover, the central duality which lies at the base of his social and political outlook. (pp. 420-21)

> I. M. Britain, *"Francis Adams: The Arnoldian as Socialist,"* in Historical Studies, *Vol. 15, No. 59, October, 1972, pp. 401-23.*

Joseph Jones   (essay date 1976)

[*In the following excerpt, Jones discusses Adams's* Songs *in the context of the author's admiration of Walt Whitman and the analogies Adams saw between American history and contemporary Australian problems.*]

Adams's *Songs of the Army of the Night* . . . was his most passionate utterance. Sympathetic with outcasts and wage-slaves everywhere, who were seen as the great unregarded army of the night, the verse attacks capitalism and praises socialism in France, Russia, England, and Ireland, in addition to implying that Australia is more than ready for it. The book divides into three sections: "England", "Here and There" (especially the Orient), and "Australia". Adams's preface [see essay dated 1888] asserts that "The negro slavery of the Southern States of America was better than the white slavery of today all over the earth, but more particularly in Europe and America." By analogy, the struggle to eliminate American slavery is found instructive; in **"To John Ruskin"** the heroism of the North during the Civil War receives high praise; Ruskin, condemned as a "vain prophet", is bidden to

> Hark to the shout of those who cleared
>   The Missionary Ridge!
> Look on those dead who never feared
>   The battle's bloody bridge!
>
> Watch the stern swarm at that last breach
>   March up that came not thence—
> And learn Democracy can teach
>   Divine obedience.
>
> Pass through that South at last brought low
>   Where loyal freemen live,
> And learn Democracy knows how
>   To utterly forgive.

"To the Sons of Labor" links General U.S. Grant with Cromwell, mentioning the battles of the Wilderness and Petersburgh with Marston, Naseby, and Whitehall and offering them as models for militant labour. Closer home, **"Henry George"** (which appeared first in William Lane's Brisbane *Boomerang,* late in 1887) describes a young Australian girl in a bookshop gazing upon a picture of George as upon a saint; and there is a sonnet of praise addressed **"To Henry George in America"**.

It should come as no surprise that Adams had found so much to admire in Whitman that he dispatched to Camden a copy of his *Songs* with an inscription: "To Walt Whitman—To the poet of the first generation of Democracy, the noble pioneer of a new Civilization, to the splendid singer of the health and freedom of man—with admiration, affection, reverence." In *Australian Essays* two years previously, he had praised the Salvation Army for its "Religious Socialism", pointing out that it "proclaimed the spiritual equality of all men" even as Whitman was willing to accept the common prostitute. Bernard O'Dowd, writing as "Gavah" in *The Tocsin* (23 June 1898) some years after Adams's death, quoted part of the preface to *Songs* and remarked: "The student of Walt Whitman will recognise in such passages as this, as well as in the fact that after reading *Leaves of Grass* our author's old horror of irregular metres disappeared, the great influence of the sublime old bard of Democracy on the subject of this sketch." O'Dowd was accurate in making what, to him, was hardly even a shrewd guess.

Quite evidently a student of American history, Adams defined clearly the areas of American thought and experience he felt were pertinent to Australian problems and was ready to draw parallels, especially as related to the Civil War. The American West—"the heart of the country, the genuine America"—was the prototype of the Australian Outback: "the Interior", he declared in *The Australians,* "is the heart of the genuine Australia". And just as the West had been the decisive factor in the Civil War, the Bushman (whom he very much admired) could—and should, nay must—become the champion of socialism. Historically, his argument ran, Americans had long been anxious to have the road west kept clear—that was why the "duel between Montcalm and Wolfe" was fought. England at that time responded to American needs; would she do as much for Australia, seeing the necessity of keep-

ing foreign influence out of the Pacific? Considering the Australian land question, Adams thought there was an "acute parallelism" with the American West, accounting for "Henry George's passionate advocacy of Land Nationalisation and his singular mental obliquity with regard to other forms of social monopoly which tyrannise over and must ultimately enslave us".

There was, moreover, an analogy to be drawn between the curse of slavery that American democracy had to overcome, and the "white slavery" imposed by capitalism that could be eradicated only by an aroused labour. Adams did not believe that the Civil War had brought a final solution, for America was as deeply sunk in her economic mire as Europe. It was still interesting, however, to contemplate possible similarities. Fearing that the degraded small farmers, "selectors", would serve the squatters against the unionists—the "petty intermediate classes" were already "fordoomed to failure and ultimate extinction" because "the trend of things is relentlessly towards huge monopolies of capital and labour"—he reasoned:

> People are beginning to talk now of the possibilities of "civil war" between capital and labour, and some such eventuality might be possible where capital had a sufficient rank and file to draw from.
>
> The "mean whites" supplied that rank and file to Jefferson Davis and Lee, and another ten or twelve years may give the capitalistic squatters of Australia an organised body of selectors intensely hostile to the unionists.

In another connection, he wondered whether the Queenslanders would develop the "bilious and fiery genius of the Southern States of America, and prepare the explosive factor in yet another great problem of North and South, democrat and aristocrat".

Adams was not exaggerating the situation very much when he envisioned the threat, or promise, of industrial civil war in Australia during the early 1890s. The lines had been drawn, and the shearers together with their urban "mates" on the waterfront were inflamed; not since the early gold mining days had such climactic issues been raised. As it worked out, however, no clash of arms took place; and at the time of Adams's death, in 1893, his former colleague on the Brisbane *Boomerang,* William Lane, had already admitted defeat.

Except for Whitman, Adams paid less attention to the literature of America than to its history. Special phases of that history had their lessons to teach as part of the usable past, and he was convinced that the "army of the night" would have to rise against its overlords everywhere, with Australia offering perhaps the most likely theatre in which it could expect early success. Working in the urban centres but casting about for a malleable proletariat among the bushmen, he was one of the quickest and most aggressive observers to recognize and apply what he saw as the available parallels between American and Australian experience, most notably that of the frontier. (pp. 98-100)

Joseph Jones, "Socialism Rampant: Adams, Furphy," in his Radical Cousins: Nineteenth

Century American & Australian Writers, *University of Queensland Press, 1976, pp. 96-107.*

FURTHER READING

"Tiberius." The Bookman VI, No. 35 (August 1894): 150-51.
A favorable review of Adams's drama praising the author's intentions, sincerity, and artistic vision.

Hadgraft, Cecil. "Lyrics" and "Short Stories." In his *Queensland and Its Writers: 100 Years—100 Authors,* pp. 44, 108-09. Brisbane: University of Queensland Press, 1959.

Comments briefly on Adams's vision of Australia as seen in the style and themes of his poetry and short stories.

Harris, Frank. "Friends of the 'Nineties." In his *Frank Harris: His Life and Adventures—An Autobiography,* pp. 308-09. London: Richard's Press, 1947.
Short account of Harris's friendship with Adams.

Palmer, Vance. "Life and Death of Francis Adams." *Southerly* 15, No. 2 (1954): 102-07.
Critical evaluation of Adams including a memorial by the Australian poet Sydney Jephcott and Mrs. Adams's brief account of her husband's suicide.

"The New Egypt." The Spectator 72, No. 3424 (10 February 1894): 204-05.
Objects to Adam's anti-English stance in *The New Egypt.*

Jane Austen

1775-1817

English novelist.

The following entry presents criticism of Austen's novel *Persuasion* (1818). For discussion of Austen's complete career, see *NCLC,* Volume 1; for discussion of the novel *Pride and Prejudice,* see *NCLC,* Volume 13; for discussion of the novel *Emma,* see *NCLC,* Volume 19.

Persuasion, Austen's last completed work, is regarded as the author's most unconventional and complex novel. Its uncharacteristically romantic treatment of the relationship between protagonists Anne Elliot and Captain Wentworth was once thought to signal the dissipation of Austen's talent but has more recently been praised as an intentional departure from the author's extensive analyses of propriety in English society, offering an insightful and more realistic examination of human nature and relationships. In comparisons of *Persuasion* with Austen's previous writings, critics focus on characterization, the influence of Romanticism, social and political commentary, and narrative technique in the novel, often concluding that *Persuasion* is Austen's most perceptive and mature work.

Austen began writing *Persuasion* in 1815 while living with her sister and mother at Chawton Cottage in Hampshire. Suffering ill health during the year of its composition, she died in 1817, and the following year her brother and literary executor, Henry Austen, published the novel together with an earlier work, *Northanger Abbey.* Although *Pride and Prejudice, Mansfield Park,* and *Emma* received many favorable reviews in the years preceding Austen's death, *Persuasion* and *Northanger Abbey* attracted little critical notice, perhaps due to the growing preference for gothic romance among English readers at the time. The popularity of *Persuasion* has grown during the twentieth century, especially among literary scholars. Of special interest is the fact that autographs of the work's last two chapters exist and represent the only extant manuscript from any of Austen's novels. The manuscript includes significant revisions in the form of addenda and marginal notes, providing valuable insight into the author's creative process.

Like Austen's previous works, *Persuasion* examines life among English landed gentry, focusing particularly on the events leading up to the marriage of the novel's heroine. Anne Elliot, whose moral character Austen described in a letter as "almost too good for me," resides in Kellynch Hall with her widowed father and her two sisters, who exemplify the selfishness and vanity commonly satirized in Austen's novels. Austen's approach to Anne's story is unique, however, in that she begins the novel *in medias res:* Anne is, at the narration's commencement, in her late twenties and unmarried, having ten years earlier refused the marriage proposal of Wentworth, a young naval officer. Although in love with Wentworth, Anne had been persuaded by her father and Lady Russell, a neighbor and

family friend, that to marry him would be imprudent, given his impulsive personality and his lack of financial security and social standing. Upon hearing of Anne's decision, Wentworth had left the area, convinced that her submission to the will of others bespoke a weakness in her character. Soon after the novel opens, Wentworth returns, a prominent and prosperous captain in the naval services, and he and Anne become reacquainted through a series of coincidental meetings, during which each privately assesses the character of the other and gradually discovers that each still loves the other. At the novel's conclusion, Anne and Wentworth are reunited. Wentworth explains that he has forgiven Anne for rejecting his proposal and that he finally understands the nature of his affection for her as well as the superiority of her character. In turn, Anne defends her rejection, suggesting that it was an act of discretion rather than submission in that she was not afraid to contradict her father and Lady Russell, but, rather, doubted Wentworth's devotion to her and was unwilling to risk an unhappy marriage. Typical of Austen's fiction, the novel concludes with the marriage of the two main characters.

Most criticism of *Persuasion* focuses on Austen's characterization of Anne and Wentworth. Some commentators consider Anne a static character, contending that, in the words of Andor Gomme, her "motives, principles and perceptions remain essentially the same" throughout the novel. These critics, in unfavorable comparisons of *Persuasion* with Austen's previous works, argue that the process of self-discovery common among Austen's protagonists is experienced by Wentworth, who comes to acknowledge the importance of propriety, and that *Persuasion* is therefore considerably weakened by its narrative focus on Anne. More recent assessments, however, suggest that Austen intended to emphasize Anne's emotional maturation, her acquisition of romantic knowledge, and her rejection of the moral sensibility promoted in Austen's earlier novels. Lawrence Lerner, for example, has discussed *Persuasion* as "the one book in which Jane Austen ceased to see any contrast between sense and passion, and in which what distinguishes the heroine from the other characters—what makes her the heroine almost—is the intensity of her emotions." Joseph M. Duffy, Jr., and Malcolm Bradbury have also attributed Anne's unique role among Austen's heroines to the fuller examination of her emotional life afforded by Austen.

Austen's emphasis on emotional enlightenment as integral to personal achievement and happiness is considered by most critics to reflect a change in the author's perspective. Many commentators attribute this shift to Austen's developing interest in the philosophical tenets of Romanticism and Romantic poetry's particular focus on the interaction between humanity and nature. Grahame Smith has suggested that in *Persuasion* Austen "is beginning to discover that the world is larger, more mysterious, and more romantic than she had supposed." More specifically, A. Walton Litz has observed that "in the opening chapters of *Persuasion*, Jane Austen is most 'poetic,' most Wordsworthian, when she is willing to abandon the literary allusion and give herself to a direct passionate rendering of nature's changing face." Paul N. Zietlow and others have noted the recurring role of circumstance, coincidence, and fate in determining the events of *Persuasion*, speculating that toward the end of her life Austen discovered the limitations of a philosophy based on propriety, and espoused the Romantic concept of fate and circumstance as natural and often fortuitous.

While early critics found Austen's novels to be both socially and politically noncommittal, more recent critics have argued that *Persuasion* in particular reflects Austen's concern for the breakdown of the English class system and other social issues. Alistair M. Duckworth, for example, has detected in Austen's later novels "an authentic commitment to a social morality and a continuous awareness and exposure of attitudes destructive of social continuity," and has examined ways in which *Persuasion* demonstrates the moral and economic instability of the aristocracy during Austen's time. Similarly, David Monaghan has argued that Austen's censure of the landed gentry's moral convictions and her defense of the English seafarer's character in *Persuasion* communicates "the painful realisation that the social order which it has been the business of [Austen's] literary career to explore and vindicate is finally falling apart." Further, in his essay "Fiction and the 'Analog-

ical Matrix' " (1949), an influential linguistic study of the English novel, Mark Schorer has noted a proliferation of modern economic terminology in *Persuasion*, which, he suggests, may be interpreted as ironic commentary on the collapse of the English aristocracy's moral system.

Finally, stylistic studies of *Persuasion* indicate that Austen may have been among the first English novelists to employ "free indirect discourse," a technique fusing the narrator's voice with that of a character; *Persuasion* features the synthesis of the third-person omniscient narrative voice with Anne's idiomatic language and has prompted several studies of point of view in the novel. Louise Flavin has suggested that Austen used this technique "in a conscious effort to control the empathy or distance between the reader and the character." Norman Page, however, has demonstrated ways in which free indirect speech functions on several levels in *Persuasion*, establishing a conversational tone and heightening the dramatic effect of certain events in the novel.

Considered atypical in Austen's oeuvre, the departure in *Persuasion* from the style and content uniformly and masterfully handled in *Emma, Pride and Prejudice*, and *Mansfield Park* has incited more thematically diverse critical debates between Austen scholars than any of her previous works and explains why *Persuasion* is, in the words of David Daiches, "the novel which in the end the experienced reader of Jane Austen puts at the head of the list."

William Dean Howells   (essay date 1900)

[*Howells was the chief progenitor of American Realism and one of the most influential American literary critics of the late nineteenth century. Through Realism, a theory central to his fiction and criticism, he aimed to disperse "the conventional acceptations by which men live on easy terms with themselves" so that they might "examine the grounds of their social and moral opinions." In the following excerpt, he comments favorably on the characterization of Anne Elliot.*]

People will prefer Anne Elliot to Elizabeth Bennet [of ***Pride and Prejudice***] according as they enjoy a gentle sufferance in women more than a lively rebellion; and it would not be profitable to try converting the worshippers of one to the cult of the other. But without offence to either following, it may be maintained that ***Persuasion*** is imagined with as great novelty and daring as ***Pride and Prejudice***, and that Anne is as genuinely a heroine as Elizabeth.

In ***Persuasion*** Jane Austen made bold to take the case of a girl, neither weak nor ambitious, who lets the doubts and dislikes of her family and friends prevail with her, and gives up the man she loves because they think him beneath her in family and fortune. She yields because she is gentle and diffident of herself, and her indignant lover resents and despises her submission if he does not despise her. He is a young officer of the navy, rising to prominence in the service which was then giving England the supremacy of the seas, but he is not thought the equal of a daughter of such a baronet as Sir Walter Elliot. It is quite possible that in her portrayal of the odious situation Jane Austen avenges with personal satisfaction the new order against the old, for her brothers were of the navy, and the family hope and pride of the Austens were bound up with its glories. At any rate, when Sir Walter's debts oblige him to let Kellynch Hall, and live on a simple scale in Bath, it is a newly made admiral who becomes his tenant; and it is the brother of the admiral's wife who is Anne's rejected lover, and who now comes to visit his sister, full of victory and prize-money, with the avowed purpose of marrying and settling in life. (pp. 453-54)

For her part, [Anne] has merely to own again the affection which has been a dull ache in her heart for seven years. Her father's pride is reconciled to her marriage, which is now with a somebody instead of the nobody Captain Wentworth once was. Sir Walter "was much struck with his personal claims, and felt that his superiority of appearance might not be unfairly balanced against her superiority of rank. . . . He was now esteemed quite worthy to address the daughter of a foolish, spendthrift baronet who had not principle or sense enough to maintain himself in the situation in which Providence had placed him." As for Anne's mischievous, well-meaning friend who had urged her to break with Wentworth before, "there was nothing less for Lady Russell to do than to admit that she had been completely wrong, and to take up a new set of opinions and hopes."

This outline of the story gives no just sense of its quality, which resides mainly in its constancy to nature; and it gives no sufficient notion of the variety of character involved in the uneventful, quiet action. Anne's arrogant and selfish father, her cold-hearted, selfish elder sister, and her mean, foolish, empty-headed younger sister, with the simple, kindly Musgrove family, form rather the witnesses than the persons of the drama, which transacts itself with the connivance rather than the participation of Sir Walter's heir-at-law, the clever, depraved and unscrupulous cousin, William Walter Elliot; Lady Russell, the ill-advised adviser of the broken engagement; the low-born, manœuvring Mrs. Clay, who all but captures the unwary Sir Walter; the frank, warm-hearted Admiral Croft and his wife, and the whole sympathetic naval contingent at Lyme Regis. They brighten the reality of the picture, and form its atmosphere; they could not be spared, and yet, with the exception of Louisa Musgrove, who jumps from the sea-wall at Regis, and by her happy accident brings about the final understanding of the lovers, none of them actively contributes to the event, which for the most part accomplishes itself subjectively through the nature of Anne and Wentworth.

Of the two Anne is by far the more interesting and important personage; her story is distinctly the story of a heroine; yet never was there a heroine so little self-assertive, so far from forth-putting. When the book opens we find her neglected and contemned by her father and elder sister, and sunken passively if not willingly into mere aunthood to her younger sister's children, with no friend who feels her value but that Lady Russell who has helped her to spoil her life. She goes to pay a long visit to her sister as

soon as Kellynch Hall is taken by the Crofts, and it is in a characteristic moment of her usefulness there that Wentworth happens upon her, after their first cold and distant meeting before others.

The mother, as usual, had left a sick child to Anne's care, when

> Captain Wentworth walked into the drawing-room at the Cottage, where were only herself and the little invalid Charles, who was lying on the sofa. . . . He started, and could only say, 'I thought the Miss Musgroves had been here; Mrs. Musgrove told me I should find them here,' before he walked to the window to recollect himself, and feel how he ought to behave. 'They are upstairs with my sister; they will be down in a few minutes, I dare say,' had been Anne's reply in all the confusion that was natural; and if the child had not called to her to come and do something for him, she would have been out of the room the next moment, and released Captain Wentworth as well as herself. He continued at the window, and after calmly and politely saying, 'I hope the little boy is better,' was silent. She was obliged to kneel by the sofa, and remain there to satisfy her patient, and thus they continued a few minutes, when, to her very great satisfaction, she heard some other person crossing the vestibule. It proved to be Charles Hayter,

who supposes Wentworth to be his rival for one of the Miss Musgroves. He seats himself, and takes up a newspaper, ignoring Wentworth's willingness to talk.

> Another minute brought another addition. The younger boy, a remarkably stout, forward child of two years old, having got the door opened, made his determined appearance among them, and went straight to the sofa to see what was going on, and put in his claim to anything good that might be given away. There being nothing to eat, he could only have some play, and as his aunt would not let him tease his sick brother, he began to fasten himself upon her, as she knelt, in a way that, busy as she was about Charles, she could not shake him off. She spoke to him, ordered, insisted, and entreated in vain. Once she did contrive to push him away, but the boy had the greater pleasure in getting upon her back again directly. 'Walter,' said she, 'get down this moment. You are extremely troublesome. I am very angry with you.' 'Walter,' cried Charles Hayter, 'why do you not do as you are bid? . . . . Come to me, Walter.' But not a bit did Walter stir. In another moment she found herself in the state of being released from him; some one was taking him from her, though he had bent down her head so much that his sturdy little hands were unfastened from around her neck and he was resolutely borne away, before she knew that Captain Wentworth had done it. . . . She could not even thank him. She could only hang over little Charles with most disordered feelings. . . . with the conviction soon forced upon her by the noise he was studiously making with the child, that he meant to avoid hearing her thanks. . . . till enabled by the entrance of Mary and the Miss Musgroves to make

over her patient to their care and leave the room. She could not stay. . . . She was ashamed of herself, quite ashamed of being so nervous, and of being overcome by such a trifle; but so it was, and it required a long application of solitude and reflection to recover her.

As any practised reader of fiction could easily demonstrate, this is not the sort of rescue to bring about a reconciliation between lovers in a *true* novel. There it must be something more formidable than a naughty little boy that the heroine is saved from: it must be a deadly miscreant, or a mad bull, or a frightened horse, or an express train, or a sinking ship. Still it cannot be denied that this simple, this homely scene, is very pretty, and is very like things that happen in life, where there is reason to think love is oftener shown in quality than quantity, and does its effect as perfectly in the little as in the great events. Even the most tremendous incident of the book, the famous passage which made Tennyson, when he visited Lyme Regis, wish to see first of all the place where Louisa Musgrove fell from the Cobb, has hardly heroic proportions, though it is of greater intensity in its lifelikeness, and it reverses the relations of Anne and Wentworth in the characters of helper and helped.

> There was too much wind to make the high part of the new Cobb pleasant for the ladies, and they agreed to get down the steps to the lower, and all were contented to pass quietly and safely down the steep steps excepting Louisa; she must be jumped down them by Captain Wentworth. . . . She was safely down, and instantly to shew her enjoyment, ran up the steps to be jumped down again. He advised her against it, thought the jar too great; but no, he reasoned and talked in vain, she smiled and said, 'I am determined I will': he put out his hands; she was too precipitate by half a second; she fell on the pavement on the Lower Cobb, and was taken up lifeless! There was no wound, no visible bruise; but her eyes were closed, she breathed not, her face was like death. . . . Captain Wentworth, who had caught her up, knelt with her in his arms, looking on her with a face as pallid as her own in an agony of silence. 'She is dead!' screamed Mary, catching hold of her husband, and contributing with her own horror to make him immovable; and in the same moment, Henrietta, sinking under the conviction, lost her senses, too, and would have fallen on the steps, but for Captain Benwick and Anne, who supported her between them. 'Is there no one to help me?' were the first words that burst from Captain Wentworth. 'Go to him; go to him,' cried Anne, 'for Heaven's sake, go to him. Leave me and go to him. Rub her hands, rub her temples; here are salts; take them, take them.' Louisa was raised up and supported between them. Everything was done that Anne had prompted, but in vain; while Captain Wentworth, staggering against the wall for his support, exclaimed in the bitterest agony, 'Oh, God! Her father and mother!' 'A surgeon!' said Anne. He caught at the word; it seemed to rouse him at once; and saying only, 'True, true; a surgeon this

instant.'. . . . Anne, attending with all the strength and zeal and thought, which instinct supplied, to Henrietta, still tried, at intervals, to suggest comfort to the others, tried to quiet Mary, to animate Charles, to assuage the feelings of Captain Wentworth. Both seemed to look to her for direction. 'Anne, Anne,' cried Charles, 'what in Heaven's name is to be done next?' Captain Wentworth's eyes were also turned towards her. 'Had she not better be carried to the inn? Yes, I am sure; carry her to the inn.' 'Yes, yes, to the inn,' repeated Wentworth. . . . 'I will carry her myself.'

Anne has to show, with all this presence of mind, a greatness of mind superior to the misery of imagining that Wentworth is in love with Louisa, and that his impassioned remorse is an expression of his love. Only when they are going home together, to tell Louisa's parents of the accident, does she make one meek little tacit reflection in her own behalf.

> 'Don't talk of it, don't talk of it,' he cried. 'Oh God, that I had not given way to her at that fatal moment! Had I done as I ought! But so eager and so resolute! Dear, sweet Louisa!' Anne wondered whether it ever occurred to him now to question the justness of his own previous opinion as to the universal felicity and advantage of firmness of character. . . . She thought it could scarcely escape him to feel that a persuadable temper might sometimes be as much in favor of happiness as a very resolute character.

(pp. 454-57)

William Dean Howells, "Heroines of Nineteenth-Century Fiction," in Harper's Bazaar, *Vol. XXXIII, No. 25, June 23, 1900, pp. 453-60.*

Virginia Woolf (essay date 1925)

[*An English novelist, essayist, and critic, and one of the founders of the literary coterie known as the Bloomsbury Group, Woolf is one of the most prominent figures of twentieth-century literature. Like her contemporary, James Joyce, with whom she is often compared, Woolf employed the stream-of-consciousness technique in the novel. Concerned primarily with depicting the life of the mind, she rebelled against traditional narrative techniques and developed a highly individualized style. Woolf's works, noted for their subjective explorations of characters' inner lives and their delicate poetic quality, have had a lasting effect on the art of the novel. Her critical essays, which cover almost the entire range of English literature, contain some of her finest prose and are praised for their insight. In the following excerpt, originally published in* The Common Reader *(1925), she detects a heightened concern for emotions and romance in* Persuasion *and speculates on the content and style of ensuing works had Austen lived longer and continued to write.*]

The balance of [Austen's] gifts was singularly perfect. Among her finished novels there are no failures, and among her many chapters few that sink markedly below the level of the others. But, after all, she died at the age of forty-two. She died at the height of her powers. She was still subject to those changes which often make the final period of a writer's career the most interesting of all. Vivacious, irrepressible, gifted with an invention of great vitality, there can be no doubt that she would have written more, had she lived, and it is tempting to consider whether she would not have written differently. The boundaries were marked; moons, mountains, and castles lay on the other side. But was she not sometimes tempted to trespass for a minute? Was she not beginning, in her own gay and brilliant manner, to contemplate a little voyage of discovery?

Let us take *Persuasion,* the last completed novel, and look by its light at the books she might have written had she lived. There is a peculiar beauty and a peculiar dullness in *Persuasion.* The dullness is that which so often marks the transition stage between two different periods. The writer is a little bored. She has grown too familiar with the ways of her world; she no longer notes them freshly. There is an asperity in her comedy which suggests that she has almost ceased to be amused by the vanities of a Sir Walter or the snobbery of a Miss Elliott. The satire is harsh, and the comedy crude. She is no longer so freshly aware of the amusements of daily life. Her mind is not altogether on her object. But, while we feel that Jane Austen has done this before, and done it better, we also feel that she is trying to do something which she has never yet attempted. There is a new element in *Persuasion,* the quality, perhaps, that made Dr. Whewell fire up and insist that it was 'the most beautiful of her works'. She is beginning to discover that the world is larger, more mysterious, and more romantic than she had supposed. We feel it to be true of herself when she says of Anne: 'She had been forced into prudence in her youth, she learned romance as she grew older—the natural sequel of an unnatural beginning'. She dwells frequently upon the beauty and the melancholy of nature, upon the autumn where she had been wont to dwell upon the spring. She talks of the 'influence so sweet and so sad of autumnal months in the country'. She marks 'the tawny leaves and withered hedges'. 'One does not love a place the less because one has suffered in it', she observes. But it is not only in a new sensibility to nature that we detect the change. Her attitude to life itself is altered. She is seeing it, for the greater part of the book, through the eyes of a woman who, unhappy herself, has a special sympathy for the happiness and unhappiness of others, which, until the very end, she is forced to comment upon in silence. Therefore the observation is less of facts and more of feelings than is usual. There is an expressed emotion in the scene at the concert and in the famous talk about woman's constancy which proves not merely the biographical fact that Jane Austen had loved, but the aesthetic fact that she was no longer afraid to say so. Experience, when it was of a serious kind, had to sink very deep, and to be thoroughly disinfected by the passage of time, before she allowed herself to deal with it in fiction. But now, in 1817, she was ready. Outwardly, too, in her circumstances, a change was imminent. Her fame had grown very slowly. 'I doubt', wrote Mr. Austen Leigh, 'whether it would be possible to mention any other author of note whose personal obscurity was so complete.' Had she lived a few more years only, all that would have been altered.

She would have stayed in London, dined out, lunched out, met famous people, made new friends, read, travelled, and carried back to the quiet country cottage a hoard of observations to feast upon at leisure.

And what effect would all this have had upon the six novels that Jane Austen did not write? She would not have written of crime, of passion, or of adventure. She would not have been rushed by the importunity of publishers or the flattery of friends into slovenliness or insincerity. But she would have known more. Her sense of security would have been shaken. Her comedy would have suffered. She would have trusted less (this is already perceptible in *Persuasion*) to dialogue and more to reflection to give us a knowledge of her characters. Those marvellous little speeches which sum up, in a few minutes' chatter, all that we need in order to know an Admiral Croft or a Mrs. Musgrove for ever, that shorthand, hit-or-miss method which contains chapters of analysis and psychology, would have become too crude to hold all that she now perceived of the complexity of human nature. She would have devised a method, clear and composed as ever, but deeper and more suggestive, for conveying not only what people say, but what they leave unsaid; not only what they are, but what life is. She would have stood farther away from her characters, and seen them more as a group, less as individuals. Her satire, while it played less incessantly, would have been more stringent and severe. She would have been the forerunner of Henry James and of Proust— but enough. Vain are these speculations: the most perfect artist among women, the writer whose books are immortal, died 'just as she was beginning to feel confidence in her own success'. (pp. 151-54)

Virginia Woolf, "Jane Austen," in her Collected Essays, Vol. I, *Harcourt, Brace & World, Inc., 1967, pp. 144-54.*

Desmond MacCarthy   (essay date 1928)

[MacCarthy was one of the foremost English literary and dramatic critics of the twentieth century. He served for many years on the staff of the New Statesman *and edited* Life and Letters. *A member of the Bloomsbury group, which also included Leonard and Virginia Woolf, John Maynard Keynes, E. M. Forster, and Lytton Strachey, he was guided by the conviction that "one's prime objects in life were love, the creation and enjoyment of aesthetic experience, and the pursuit of knowledge." According to his critics, MacCarthy brought to his work a wide range of reading, serious and sensitive judgment, an interest in the works of new writers, and high critical standards. In the following excerpt from an essay originally published in the* New Statesman *in 1928, he praises the plot construction and narrative technique of* Persuasion.]

Anyone in search of an example in the art of conducting a story to its proper and foreseen close could not do better than study the construction of *Persuasion,* though such unity of effect presupposes something else not necessarily within the reach of other writers, however eager they may be to profit by Jane Austen's example. The consistency and confidence of her attitude towards every character, every event and every detail in her stories, cannot be imitated. Moreover such confidence must ever be as much the product of a period as of individual effort. It is the fruit of corroboration. Private conviction does not produce an equal stability, for human beings cannot possess the unself-conscious calm of complete assurance unless their judgments are confirmed by others. Here and there some passionate solitary may succeed in asserting consistently his own sense of proportion in the face of surrounding dissent, but inevitably in doing so he will feel a need to defend his views. He will be explanatory, and, almost inevitably, explanatory with that over-insistence which is liable to upset at any moment the subtle spiritual balance upon which so much depends in art. How distressing—and in the end how unconvincing—it is to find oneself catching continually the compelling but strained glance of the novelist's eye as one turns his pages! How blest, on the other hand, the writer of fiction who, if his reader should stop to ask, What is your point of view? can reply with mild surprise, "Why, of course, that of all sensible men!" But it stands to reason that such writers can only exist when sensible people do as a matter of fact agree; and it follows that works which possess the solid, restful quality of Jane Austen's must be the product, in a sense, of many minds and not of one. *Daphnis and Chloe* could only have been written at a time when all sensible men conceived the pleasures of sensuality to be one of the blessings of life; when they felt no need to dress up or disguise young desire to make it charming. But when, in an age in which all sensible people are not agreed on this point, Mr. George Moore, for instance, attempts to write in the same vein, consciousness of being naughty or daring inevitably creeps into his work. The benign and careful lubricity of Anatole France is not free from a taint of malicious awareness; he may have been sure that he was right to be on the side of Venus, but he was all too conscious that there was another. *Securus judicat orbis terrarum;* and it is a huge help to the artist to feel that "the verdict of the world is conclusive"—and on his side. It is hard for a rebel to attain the peace of assurance.

This complete harmony and confidence contributes enormously to our pleasure in reading Jane Austen; but since it comes by grace and fortune, let us consider her imitable qualities. *Persuasion* is, in my opinion, the most perfectly constructed of her novels. The theme is definite, and limited with great discretion: it is the story of the re-engagement of two lovers after a parting which took place seven years before. The reader anticipates their reunion and there are no external obstacles to it: Captain Wentworth is still unmarried—even heart-free; and he is now well-off; Anne still loves him, and she has no obligations of loyalty or duty elsewhere which could prevent her from becoming his wife. In the heart of such a straightforward situation, how then does the author manage to create the suspense and complication so important in exciting intense interest in the happy ending to a love story? She does so by telling it from the point of view of the one who is compelled to be entirely passive throughout, partly owing to her sex, but above all, owing to her previous conduct. It was Anne who broke off the engagement. It is only Anne's feelings that we follow; every other character is seen from outside. We watch Wentworth only through her

eyes (he is never on the scene unless she is there), and his behaviour in her presence, until near the end, is so adjusted to the purpose of creating suspense that it never conveys more than that his resentment may possibly be changing into temperate good will. Anne cannot hope for more than that. The reader is made to identify himself entirely with Anne, so far as Wentworth's behaviour is concerned, and to her each stage in their relations is full of pain, perplexity, and suspense, which the reader shares.

Henry James had a theory that it was necessary to get rid of the omniscient observer; that everything recounted in a novel should be seen through the eyes of some character in it; not necessarily the same, and perhaps through one character after another. *The Golden Bowl* was written on these lines. It seems to me a fallacious general principle. Let us test it by seeing what we should have lost had **Persuasion** been constructed in obedience to it. Let us suppose that everything, all the incidents, all the characters, Sir Walter Elliot, the Musgroves, Admiral Croft and his wife and Wentworth had been seen through Anne's eyes alone. Well, either Jane Austen's own delightful view of them would have been lost to us, or Anne would have become Jane Austen herself, with her intellect, irony and critical detachment; in which case we could never have felt the same poignant sympathy for Anne and her predicament. Suppose, on the other hand, that the business of reporting had been transferred later on to the brain of Wentworth; we should then have known every stage of his affections, and consequently followed Anne's misreading of them with indifference. Henry James would probably have then turned, say, Lady Russell and Charles Musgrove into a pair of gossips of genius who would, by exhibiting at once an extraordinary clairvoyance and an odd blindness to obvious probabilities, have complicated considerably the situation. But what a loss such a transfiguration would have been! Charles Musgrove, while doubtless keeping his gun, his riding-breeches and his good temper, would have been endowed with his creator's restless analytical curiosity—in short, have become unrecognizable as a normal young English squire. Here lies the fatal flaw in Henry James's theory. If the narrator is abolished, the characters who narrate in his place become inevitably endowed with the novelist's own peculiar faculties and intellectual temper. This happened in his own later novels, in which the characters were often so steeped in the colours of their creator's mind, that their individual tints barely showed through the permeating dye.

Contrast this method with the instinctive tact of Jane Austen in such matters. Her characters are introduced briefly and objectively. At first her heroine is a mere background figure, a member of the Elliot family: "Anne Elliot had been a very pretty girl, but her bloom had vanished early"; that is all we hear about her in the first chapter, which is devoted to exposing so amusingly the vanity of her father and sister, and those financial family embarrassments, incidentally the initial causes of bringing Anne and Wentworth together again. How quietly and inevitably it is done! The letting of Kellynch Hall is the first step in the love-story, yet we are not aware of it as such, but only as part of the comedy of Sir Walter. This is the art of construction. Gradually Anne comes to the front as the most sensible and honourable member of the family. The novelist continues to present scenes, to describe thoughts, and feelings, and characters objectively. She uses the privilege of omniscience only in the case of Anne's emotions; and that these are centred upon her old lover gives him a special prominence in the eyes also of the reader. Although Wentworth says and does very little, that little has peculiar weight because it reaches us through Anne's feelings about it. He alone is seen subjectively, emotionally; and this gives him a unique position among the other characters. Thus he need not do much or say much to make an impression on us; he is a man who is loved, moving among other men and women who are observed. This gives an intensity to all the scenes in which Wentworth appears which links them together in the reader's mind, so that the surrounding comedy never for a moment destroys, though it may suspend, the continuity of the love-interest. (pp. 230-34)

Desmond MacCarthy, *"Unity of Effect," in his* Criticism, *Putnam, 1932, pp. 230-34.*

Mark Schorer   (essay date 1949)

[*Schorer was an American critic and biographer who demanded that fiction receive the same attention to diction and metaphor afforded by critics to poetry. In the following excerpt from an essay originally published in the* Kenyon Review *in 1949, he cites examples in* Persuasion *of language pertaining to commerce, suggesting that Austen achieves irony and comical effects by relating domestic concerns in economic terminology.*]

Persuasion is a novel of courtship and marriage with a patina of sentimental scruple and moral punctilio and a stylistic base derived from commerce and property, the counting house and the inherited estate. The first is the expression of the characters, the second is the perception of the author. And whether we should decide that a persistent reliance on commerce and property for concepts of value is the habit of Jane Austen's mind, the very grain of her imagination, or that it is a special novelistic intention, is for the moment irrelevant. It is probably that the essence of her comedy resides, in either case, in the discrepancy between social sentiment and social fact, and the social fact is to be discovered not so much in the professions of her characters as in the texture of her style.

We are told at once that the mother of the three Elliot girls felt in dying that in them she left "an awful *legacy . . .* an awful *charge* rather"; that Sir Walter Elliot is devoted to his eldest daughter, Elizabeth (who opens "every ball *of credit*" and is waiting to be "properly *solicited* by baronet-blood"), but feels that his two younger daughters, Mary and Anne, are "of very inferior *value*"—indeed, "Anne's word had no *weight.*" Anne is befriended by Lady Russell, who "had a *value* for rank and consequence," and even though it was Lady Russell no less than Sir Walter who discouraged Anne's marriage, seven years before, to the property-less Captain Wentworth, Anne "*rated* Lady Russell's influence highly." "Consequence," we are told, "has its *tax,*" and for seven years Anne has been paying

it. The problem of the novel is to relieve her of the necessity of paying it and at the same time to increase her value.

We are in a world of substance, a peculiarly material world. Here, indeed, changes are usually named "*material alterings*"—for example, in "style of living" and "degree of consequence." Perhaps the word is used most tellingly in the phrases "a face not materially *disfigured*" and "a material difference in the *discredit* of it"; for *figure* and *credit* suggest the two large areas of metaphorical interest—arithmetic and business.

Time is *divided,* troubles *multiply,* weeks are *calculated,* and even a woman's prettiness is *reckoned.* Thus, one's independence is *purchased;* one is *rendered* happy or unhappy; one is on *terms,* friendly or unfriendly, with others. Young Mr. Elliot has "nothing to *gain* by being on *terms* with Sir Walter," but Lady Russell is convinced that he hopes "to *gain* Anne" even though Anne cannot "know herself to be so *highly rated.*" We are asked to "take all the charms and perfections of Edward's wife upon *credit,*" and "to judge of the general *credit due.*" Captain Wentworth thought that he had *earned* "every blessing." "I have *valued* myself on honourable toils and just *rewards.*" So Mary is in the habit of *claiming* Anne's energies, and Anne does not feel herself "*entitled*" to reward." Young ladies have a "*stock* of accomplishments." "Here were *funds* of enjoyment!" Anne does not wish "for the possibility of *exchange.*" Experience is thought of as *venture, reversal, prospect, fortune,* and *allowance.* Anne "*ventured* to recommend a larger *allowance* of prose in" Captain Benwick's "daily study." The death of a wife leaves a man with "*prospects . . .* blighted," and Anne contemplates "the *prospect* of *spending*" two months at Uppercross. In this metaphorical context, even the landscape takes on a special shimmer: "all the *precious* rooms and furniture, groves, and *prospects.*" An "arrangement" is *prudent* or *imprudent,* and feelings must be *arranged* as prudently as accounts: no one's "feelings could *interest* her, till she had a little better *arranged* her own." One *pays* addresses, of course, but one is also *repaid* for the "trouble of exertion." "It had *cost* her something to encounter Lady Russell's surprise." A town has *worth,* a song is not *worth* staying for, and Anne "had the full *worth* of" tenderness in "Captain Wentworth's affection." Captain Wentworth's account of Captain Benwick ("whom he had always *valued highly*") "*stamped him* well in the esteem of every listener." "Ten minutes were enough to *certify* that" Mr. Elliot was a sensible man. Stamped, certified; and at last Anne's character is "*fixed* on his mind as perfection itself," which is to say that, like a currency, it has been stabilized.

Moral qualities are persistently put in economic figures: Mary "had no *resources* for solitude" and she had *inherited* "a considerable *share* of the Elliot self-importance." Love, likewise: if Elizabeth is hoping to be *solicited* by baronet-blood, Anne has had to reject the "declarations and proposals" of an improvident sailor. "Alliance" is a peculiarly appropriate word for such prudential arrangements as these, and at the end of the novel, when "the engagement" is "*renewed,*" one sees bonded documents. Anne need no longer suffer those fits of dejection in which she contemplates others' "*prosperous* love," for hers at last has prospered, too.

In this context certain colorless words, words of the lightest intention, take on a special weight. The words *account* and *interest* are used hundreds of times in their homeliest sense, yet when we begin to observe that every narration is an *account,* and at least once "an *account . . .* of the *negotiation,*" we are reminded that they have more special meanings. When Anne's blighted romance is called "this little history of sorrowful *interest,*" we hardly forget that a lack of money was the blight. Is "a man of principle" by any chance a man of substance?

The significance of this metaphorical substructure is clearest, perhaps, not when Jane Austen substitutes material for moral or sentimental values, but when she juxtaposes them. "He had . . . been nothing better than a thick-headed, *unfeeling, unprofitable* Dick Musgrove, who had never done anything to entitle himself to more than the abbreviation of his name, living or dead." More simply, these three from a single paragraph: "a *fund* of good *sense,*" "*leisure* to *bestow,*" "something that is *entertaining* and *profitable.*" "I must endeavour," says Captain Wentworth, in another such juxtaposition near the end of the novel, "I must endeavour to subdue my *mind* to my *fortune.*"

Persuasion is a novel in which sensibility—and I am not now raising the question whether it is the sensibility of the author or of her characters or of her characters except for her heroes—a novel in which sensibility is subdued to property.

The novel explicitly asks, what is "the value of an Anne Elliot" and where is the man who will "understand" it? Anne herself feels that her value has sunk:

> A few months hence, and the room now so deserted, occupied by her silent, pensive self, might be filled again with all that was happy and gay, all that was *glowing and bright* in *prosperous love,* all that was most unlike Anne Elliot.

> . . . Anne felt her spirits not likely to be benefited by an increasing acquaintance among his brother-officers. "These would have been all my friends," was her thought; and she had to struggle against a great tendency to lowness.

"A great *tendency to lowness.*" The phrase clarifies her situation, for Anne's is finally the problem of a stock that has a debased value, and when she thinks of doing good in such a further phrase as "good of a lower standard," we can hardly escape the recognition that this is a novel about marriage as a market, and about the female as marketable, and that the novel makes the observation that to sentimental scruple and moral fastidiousness, as they are revealed to us in the drama, much property is not necessary but *some* is essential—and this is shown us primarily in the style. The basis of the comedy lies in the difference between the two orders of value which the metaphors, like the characters, are all the while busily equating. At the end, in the last sentence, a prosperous sailor's wife, Anne has been relieved of "the tax of consequence," but now "she must *pay the tax* of quick alarm for belonging to that

profession which is, if possible, more distinguished in its domestic virtues than in its national importance." (pp. 25-8)

Mark Schorer, "Fiction and the 'Analogical Matrix'," *in his* The World We Imagine: Selected Essays, *Chatto & Windus, 1969, pp. 24-45.*

Joseph M. Duffy, Jr.   (essay date 1954)

[*In the following excerpt, Duffy analyzes characterization in* Persuasion, *particularly "the complex figure of Anne Elliot."*]

Once upon a time there lived at Kellynch Hall in Somersetshire a vain and handsome knight, a widower, Sir Walter Elliot, who had three daughters. Two of the daughters, like their father, were vain and selfish. But one, the middle daughter, Anne, was, like her mother had been, kind and candid and good. Without complaint she suffered the ill temper, neglect, and impositions of her family. But in her goodness she was also lonely and dispirited. For almost eight years, while her father and older sister fed each other's vanity and selfishly pursued their own trivial pleasures and her younger sister married and became a querulous, valetudinarian wife and mother, Anne Elliot existed in a state of "desolate tranquillity," growing older, unloved and loving in memory only and without hope. Eight years previously, when she was twenty, Anne, on the advice of her middle-aged friend and counselor, Lady Russell, had rejected a vigorous, confident young naval officer whose sanguineness and ardor Lady Russell considered dangerous to a conservative society and whose financial resourcelessness and undistinguished family connections made him an unsuitable candidate, Lady Russell felt, for the hand of the daughter of Sir Walter Elliot of Kellynch Hall. Anne was persuaded of the propriety of Lady Russell's advice: the match was broken off, the young officer was sent away, and Anne was given up to living what was not life but a dull and spiritless routine. Astonishingly, however, in the eighth year after this rebuff, Anne and her former lover found themselves in the same company. Lately returned from the victory over Napoleon, Captain Wentworth had become a figure of heroic and expensive quality, esteemed even by those who had previously ignored him. In spite of initial misunderstanding, the two ultimately discovered that their love still endured and they were reunited—permanently this time. Her lover's return touched Anne's beauty to new life; she was freed of the enchantment which had enclosed her life; and with her superior husband she left her heartless father and older sister to pass their mean lives in each other's company.

The aim of this simple-minded synopsis of *Persuasion* is to underscore the simplicity of the story. No English novel of comparable importance has a plot which so basically—and, from a certain point of view, so unimaginatively—is the familiar one of a fairy tale. Here is the virtuous, self-effacing young woman contrasted with a selfish parent and sisters who form a community of pride in which she has no standing; she is properly motherless, and in this case her loss is ironically compensated for by a fairy godmother manqué, Lady Russell, who does not possess magical powers, who is myopic, and whose advice leads not to the heroine's deliverance but to her dreary enchantment; she undergoes a long period of withdrawal from life, and her return—rather her rescue—parallels the return of her heroic lover whose noble proportions all the world, except herself, had failed at first to acknowledge. Yet this tale, in outline so unsophisticated, is for comic effect distorted with brilliant irony, is in its love scenes rendered poignant and tender by the skillful indirection of its writing, and is sunk in a cultural and moral setting as complicated and ambiguous in its ramifications as that of a late play of Shakespeare. *Persuasion,* appearing when it did, is a miraculous event in the history of English fiction.

The fictional world in which this story operates is different from the world of the fairy tale on that level where the fairy tale, like a daydream, provides a dispensation from the pressure of the real world of time and change. The world that the novelist sets in motion here resembles the real world, for in it life is precarious, the consequences of apparently reasonable choice are sometimes unreasonable, benign forces do not lavish on the well-intentioned person fabulous and fortuitous rewards, and history is subversive to tradition without always providing an alternative to traditional ideals. The fairy tale is the vestigial element in *Persuasion.* Out of it Jane Austen has created a little novel of profound dimension. *Persuasion* is a comedy of personal and social relationships which subjects to ironical scrutiny some of the most portentous facts of human existence. In particular the novel describes the efforts of a young woman to retain personal control when the established society shows signs of fundamental weakness, when blood and friendship are caught in the general decay, when love is repressed, when life fails and death menaces.

The forces in *Persuasion* that move all the characters to action or reaction may be represented by three concentric circles, and the involvement of the characters with these forces constitutes the thematic movement of the novel. In their effect on the lives of individuals, these forces have an interdependent activity and they must be interpreted with reference to each other. Time, the outer circle, is the cosmic force, the sad burden to be accepted or the enemy to be opposed, the ultimate repository of human activity and feelings, the catalyst of society. It is given palpable existence throughout the novel by pervasive symbols of decay—the circuit of the seasons and the crumbling of cliffs in nature and the withering of youth and beauty in man; by reports of death and illness (the book's toll of dead and of victims of illness and accident would provide a mournful set of statistics on human mortality); and by the manner in which the characters face its effects on their own life and the lives of others. The decline of the hereditary landed aristocracy and the ascendency of the energetic naval class is the second circle, the social force. It is represented by such a symbolic—and functional—device as the renting (abdication) of Kellynch Hall by Sir Walter and its occupation (usurpation) by the Crofts; by Anne's ambiguous position of piety toward the authority of the old order and appreciation of the virtues of the new; and by the gallery of characters who are not only themselves as personalities but are also reflections of the debility and

power of their particular social class. The personal force, the inner smallest circle, provides the field in which Anne develops with immaculate splendor. It cannot be described so simply as the others, for it is the circumambience of a number of factors pressing in upon the young woman and presenting her with problems which she must resolve or at least face. It is composed of tensions within her, between conscience and love, between respect for authority and feeling for life, between constancy and carelessness. Subjectively these tensions are stated through a description of what goes on in her mind and objectively through a series of conversations with other characters, both of which devices advance the dialectic of the novel.

The significance of the time theme in *Persuasion* is indicated by the recurrence of the word "autumnal" in discussions of the work. From the early reviews to modern lectures, its "autumnal quality" has been most often commented upon. Often the reviewers are led to go further and, referring the tone and the setting of the novel to the facts of Miss Austen's biography, discover an increased pathos in the knowledge that the artist was undoubtedly dying while she composed this fictional commemoration of life's deciduousness. However interesting such speculations may be, the object of a work of art is not to provide a gloss on the life of the author, and the "autumnal quality"—the phrase is inevitable—of sections of *Persuasion* must be read in terms of the novel not as testimony about the novelist's personal condition.

In general the preoccupation with the effects of time is related to the novel's over-all attempt to resolve here a more formidable dichotomy between art and nature than occurs in Miss Austen's other fiction. On the level of society art is represented by an established order, the lesser aristocracy with all its appurtenances of manners, attitudes, and beliefs hardened to inflexible doctrine. In nature are found the threats to such a society with its excessively fixed standards, for nature implies freedom, flexibility, and change. At almost every point in the novel, any significant development in the social or human condition is tied to a metaphorical correspondence in external nature. The choice of autumn as the time setting for the first part of the book dramatizes the social and human problems with which it is to be concerned. The autumnal countryside in the vicinity of Kellynch Hall mirrors the autumn of the aristocracy. In addition, "that season of peculiar and inexhaustible influence on the mind of taste and tenderness" provides an exact commentary on Anne's personal situation: later we shall examine more closely the manifold use of images from nature to describe her fading and her rejuvenation.

More decisively than any of Miss Austen's other novels including *Mansfield Park,* which seems to have been written under the cloying halo of evangelical piety, *Persuasion* belongs to the later transition period between the influence of neoclassic and romantic ideas. One of the forms of opposition to the neoclassic discreet restraint of feeling in the novel is the elevation of that aspect of the romantic sensibility which celebrated the emotive power of external nature, not as it is artificially controlled and contrived but in its freedom and ruggedness and as it indicates a continuum of life more meaningful than the elements of decay that contribute to it. It is impossible to imagine the occurrence in Jane Austen's earlier fiction, with its vague and perfunctory descriptions of landscape, a passage such as the following.

> Charmouth, with its high grounds and extensive sweeps of country, and still more, its sweet, retired bay, backed by dark cliffs, where fragments of low rock among the sands make it the happiest spot for watching the flow of the tide, for sitting in unwearied contemplation; . . . and, above all, Plinny, with its green chasms between romantic rocks, where the scattered forest trees and orchards of luxuriant growth declare that many a generation must have passed away since the first partial falling of the cliff prepared the ground for such a state, where a scene so wonderful and so lovely is exhibited. . . .

The second part of this quotation gives a microcosmic account of the time theme of the novel: the sadness over the mutability of all natural things and the quiet exultation in the knowledge of the eternal re-creation of life out of decay. Jane Austen is renowned as the self-styled worker on bits of ivory, but the spaciousness of her vision contradicts both her own self-evaluation and the opinions of those critics who are more comfortable with the genteel wit than with the great artist who, without the reader's always suspecting it, comes face to face with what James called the mysteries abysmal.

By their attitude toward life as a majestically vacuous ceremony rather than the laborious process of blossoming and decay, the members of the aristocracy are distinguished from the representatives of the navy. Sir Walter Elliot is, of course, the sublime conserver of youth and energy. One of the great products in English literature of a sophisticated and ironic style, Sir Walter belongs in a class with some of the comic figures of Chaucer and Shakespeare, the creatures of their author's observation, the creations of their author's consummate art. He is in the paradoxical position of being time's captive and time's antagonist. On the one hand, his existence is the gift of history insofar as history is responsible for the aristocratic class to which he belongs; on the other hand, his existence is threatened by the present moment of history insofar as time daily undermines his own life and new social forces are set in motion which challenge the position of his class.

But Sir Walter is a deranged and comic individual whose fatuousness blinds him to his own dilemma. His concept of history is so simple that he is never perplexed by the possibility of his class being displaced. He does not foresee the portents of disaster in his selfish carelessness. He does not recognize his moral failure because he cannot conceive of the obligations of his rank, only of its existence and its privileges. Like another famous sophist, Ulysses, Sir Walter subscribes wholeheartedly to the notion of degree, and to him, too, degree in human society is as universally appointed as the position of the planets.

Furthermore, Sir Walter is too vain to disbelieve in his own permanence. He is the platonic ideal of himself: he exists in form only—as a name in the Baronetage, as an image the many mirrors in his room give back, as the admiration of himself another's eyes reflect. Similarly what he regards in others is the appearance they present of beauty and rank. He complains about the absence of beautiful women in Bath; he comments on the ill appearance of his daughter, Mary; he compliments Anne on the improvement in her appearance; for a while he is considered impervious to the wiles of Mrs. Clay because of her disfiguring freckles; and in a judgment on the navy, he summarizes his rejection of character as a standard of distinction and his horror of the ravages of time and expended energy on the human figure.

> "Yes; it [the navy] is in two points offensive to me; I have two strong grounds of objection to it. First, as being the means of bringing persons of obscure birth into undue distinction, and raising men to honours which their fathers and grandfathers never dreamed of; and, secondly, as it cuts up a man's youth and vigour most horribly; a sailor grows old sooner than any other man. A man is in greater danger in the navy of being insulted by the rise of one whose father his father might have disdained to speak to, and of becoming prematurely an object of disgust himself, than in any other line."

This quotation gives rich evidence of Miss Austen's method of ironic characterization through speeches, where the diction and structure of the sentences as well as the ideas turn back upon the speaker and wittily perform a double job of analysis and statement.

To exist as an ideal—in that principle Sir Walter may indeed have discovered the secret of eternal youth. One can quite easily imagine him never growing old and worn out and one day, at last, effecting his own apotheosis, ascending to a heavenly hierarchy of similar forms where the blissful tedium of prestige and beauty stretches out endlessly as the changeless routine of the blessed. But if Sir Walter may never die, he also cannot possibly have lived. One of the points of the novel is that participation in life wastes the individual. Mrs. Clay means to flatter Sir Walter when she contrasts his life with that of a "professional" man:

> "The sea is no beautifier, certainly; sailors do grow old betimes; I have often observed it; they soon lose the look of youth. But then, is not it the same with many other professions, perhaps most others? Soldiers, in active service, are not at all better off; and even in the quieter professions, there is a toil and a labour of the mind, if not of the body, which seldom leaves a man's looks to the natural effect of time. The lawyer plods, quite careworn: the physician is up at all hours, and the clergyman—" she stopt a moment to consider what might do for the clergyman—"and even the clergyman, you know, is obliged to go into infected rooms, and expose his health and looks to all the injury of a poisonous atmosphere. In fact, as I have long been convinced, though every profession is necessary and honourable in its turn, it is only the lot of those who are not obliged to follow any, who can live in a regular way, in the county, chusing their own hours, following their own pursuits, and living on their own property, without the torment of trying for more; it is only *their* lot, I say, to

hold the blessings of health and good appearance
to the utmost; I know no other set of men but
what lose something of their personableness
when they cease to be quite young."

But in this wonderfully inhuman celebration of a life of leisure, Mrs. Clay removes from Sir Walter and others like
him the possibility of ever becoming real simply by absolv-
ing them from even the quotidian responsibilities that
daily wear away the pristine comeliness of the human
form. The whole moral direction of the novel is toward an
embracing of the energetic life and a rejection of the life
of leisure. The attractions of leisure are considerable—
Mrs. Clay's rhetoric has a convincing basis in fact—but
its pitfalls are greater: Lady Bertram's permanently supine
position in **Mansfield Park,** from which she is unable to
make the most elementary responses to life around her, is
the true believer's application of this doctrine of leisure.
Instead, "the torment of trying for more" seems to be the
force by which individuals are raised to great heights of
satisfaction even while they exhaust themselves in the effort. Time's burden lies not upon the otiose Sir Walter and
Elizabeth Elliot, whose handsome exteriors do not give
way, but upon the naval officers and their wives, who always look older than their years, whose complexions are
rough, and who, in spite of their heartiness and vigor, are
frequently subject to various bodily infirmities; and upon
Anne whose peculiar plight is that she—until the end of
the novel—has undergone the pain of experience without
the fulfillment of experience.

"How can we know the dancer from the dance?" A century after Jane Austen, Yeats, rejecting in the poem any system of philosophical or religious idealism, asked the question and used a symbol from nature—the chestnut tree,
the "great-rooted blossomer"—as affirmative evidence of
life's growth, decay, and renewal. There can be no separate knowledge: the unuttered reply is a theme of **Persuasion.** Time is a thief and man the victim; but life endures.
When man and nature are in harmony, the general order
of existence is being carried out. Just as the season of autumn is cherished in the novel because it shows external
nature as it is passing in the eternal repetition of its immense cycle of bloom and decay, so life is to be cherished
as it is passing in the individual, and it is to be respected
as it endures in the race. The idols of the aristocracy are
another, lesser species of those presences that Yeats deplores in the poem because they deny life in favor of some
abstract chimera of belief. Anne Elliot is not only a victim
of time; she is also a self-immolated victim sacrificed to the
idols of the aristocracy.

Order, regularity, propriety—these are some of the characteristics of the landed aristocracy at its best, but they
had become a form simply, a thin abstraction of life, and
they were no longer vitalized by other, more practical and
human values. What was wanting was élan, straightfor-
wardness, humor, a capacity for deep feeling—lively qualities that would give meaning to the form. We have seen
the personification in Sir Walter of a way of life where the
ritualistic form is everything and the content nothing. His
life is a dry artistic performance brutally cut off from the
sources in nature that had originally made the role meaningful. Even his pride is a snobbish and self-conscious in-

sistence on status, vacant of any real sense of his own or
any one else's worth: he is not too proud to humiliate himself before Lady Dalrymple simply because her title is superior to his. Nor has he sufficient love—the kind of love
true pride would breed—for his ancestral home to regret
more than the personal inconvenience of leaving it. The
reality at Kellynch Hall, while Sir Walter dwells there, is
not a vital tradition charging the atmosphere in which the
inhabitants move; it is a code of manners concealing a cold
indifference to morals. The reality is blindness and illusion: it is a set of statistics—names and dates in a book;
it is the multiplicity of mirrors in Sir Walter's chamber;
it is the mortgaged condition of the land.

The entire Elliot family—Anne alone excluded—suffers
from this derangement of values. Elizabeth resembles her
father—heartlessly elegant, chill, and superficial—save
that with the passing of too many years she no longer enjoys looking into the Baronetage and finding no spouse
listed beside her name. Mary is a self-centered and irritable woman, whose triviality of character is responsible for
the submergence of useful qualities in her husband,
Charles Musgrove, and for the inconsequence of his life.
William Elliot's respect for "rank and connexion" are excessive. He possesses certain superficial virtues—
reasonableness, discretion, polish—but Anne suspects
him because he is not open: "She prized the frank, the
open-hearted, the eager character before all others." And
Lady Russell, for all her honorableness, is described with
tactful understatement as having a "value for rank and
consequence, which blinded her a little to the faults of
those who possessed them." Not until the end of the novel,
guided by her former protégée, does Lady Russell come
to realize that her most valued equipment, sense and good
judgement, are sometimes inadequate for distinguishing
between appearance and reality. Atrophy has indeed set
in among these people. They are suffering from a paralysis
of the imagination which renders them incapable of grasping life unless life is idealized to a stately and elaborate
paradigm.

The Elliots are homeless—this is the terrible joke which
symbolizes the derangement of the society. The representatives of the stable order, they are dispossessed; preferrers
of the prudent routine, they are forced by their imprudence to live in a rented house. The most palpable claim
that the Crofts have to succeed the Elliots at Kellynch
Hall is their wealth. Money has become an element in society as much to be reckoned with—to be feared and sought
for—as rank, and it takes a place in fiction that it is to hold
through the century. Nevertheless there have been other
groups—merchants, for example—in Miss Austen's novels who are rich: through wealth alone they do not become
protagonists in the conflict of classes. Some of them are
content to mimic the aristocracy, others have not yet
formed a character of their own. In **Persuasion** the "Musgroves, like their houses, were in a state of alteration, perhaps of improvement." Clearly, however, they have neither the resiliency nor the forcefulness to present an auspicious challenge.

In the navy Miss Austen found a group which, in addition
to being wealthy, possessed other desirable qualities. Be-

sides the natural logic of her choosing a class toward which she was so favorably disposed through family connections, there is a special appropriateness in her selection, as foils to an effete aristocracy, of national heroes who were enthusiastically received in England after the defeat of Napoleon. That "profession which is, if possible, more distinguished in its domestic virtues than in its national importance" had all the qualities of boldness, liberality, and candor that those about Kellynch Hall lacked—indeed abhorred. Lady Russell's early unfavorable judgment of Wentworth was based on her fear of precisely those characteristics in him, the want of which had immobilized the aristocracy.

> Lady Russell saw it very differently. His sanguine temper, and fearlessness of mind, operated very differently on her. . . . It only added a dangerous character to himself. . . . Lady Russell had little taste for wit, of anything approaching to imprudence a horror.

The Crofts are unceremonious and robust. They are committed to the business of life—war is a most profitable part of life's business—and have no time for idle narcissism. Sir Walter's mirrors unnerve Admiral Croft.

> "Such a number of looking glasses! Oh Lord! There was no getting away from one's self. So I got Sophy to lend me a hand, and we soon shifted their quarters. . . ."

As completely as the aristocracy are idealists and are self-contemplative and static, the navy are realists: they embody life's power and are uncontemplative and active. On the national level, they are their country's heroic adventurers; on the local scene they are the good-humored usurpers of the land, cheerfully paying for the right to live in houses their owners cannot afford to maintain. Like all great works of fiction, *Persuasion* is a radical novel and Anne is a radical heroine who welcomes the light-hearted invaders of her home: "she could not but in conscience feel that they were gone who deserved not to stay, and that Kellynch Hall had passed into better hands than its owners."

Anne's position in the conflict of classes is the most difficult one of all, for she is on the middle ground where most of the skirmishes take place. Although she may have ambivalent feelings toward her class, Anne does not betray it by an act of absolute rejection. Earlier she was called a sacrificial victim to the idols of the aristocracy. Remarkably—and paradoxically—however, this sacrifice is a waste only in the temporal sense: *sub specie aeternitas*—and here Yeats and Miss Austen part company—in the spirit in which it is given, Anne's loyalty and submission to a code of behavior represent the finest gesture of the aristocratic mind. Her radicalism and that of the novel do not stand for a coarse break with tradition but a critical acquiescence to it as a context in which the force of life may have somewhat less than unlimited play. She pays tribute to a tradition by living up to it not with a token performance but at the expense of all that she has to give.

At the center of the novel is the consciousness of Anne Elliot, and at the center of her consciousness is her love for Captain Wentworth. At this point the pressure of other factors in the book combine to create the climate under which Anne performs her role. And her role is to encounter again her still beloved Wentworth and to face the ambiguous possibilities of his reaction to her after so many years and after such treatment at her hands. The effects of time, the decline of her class, her devotion to Lady Russell as the authoritarian representative of that class are all significant insofar as they touch upon her relationship with the naval officer.

The low pressure of Anne's spirit during the first part of the novel ought not to be confused with mere passivity of character. Her bereaved and enervated condition is the deliberately emphasized effect of the loss of her lover, and its manifestations are internal and spiritual as well as external and physical. The reader is constantly reminded that Anne is no longer beautiful and that she faces the world with joyless tranquillity: "her bloom had vanished early . . . "; "her attachment and regrets had, for a long time, clouded every enjoyment of youth, and an early loss of bloom and spirits had been their lasting effect"; her "spirits were not high"; "the years . . . had destroyed her youth and bloom." Her pained awareness of her condition is intensified when she overhears Captain Wentworth describe her as "altered beyond his knowledge." She repeats the phrase to herself and she is bitterly reminded of it one evening as she plays the piano at a party at the Musgroves: "*Once* she felt that he was looking at herself, observing her altered features, perhaps, trying to trace in them the ruins of the face which had once charmed him. . . . "

The notable repetition of "bloom" in these descriptions underscores the parallel of human life with the natural cycle that Miss Austen develops in the novel and prepares the reader for at least the imagery of the recrudescence of Anne's beauty. Anne is like the sleeping beauty who is awakened by a kiss. In her case, however, the liberation is more subtle. The reader's first information of a break in her grieved enchantment occurs when her cousin, William Elliot (then a stranger to her), looks at her on the beach at Lyme with "a degree of earnest admiration." Anne is described: "She was looking remarkably well; her very regular, very pretty features, having the bloom and freshness of youth restored by the fine wind which had been blowing on her complexion, and by the animation of eye which it had also produced." Later the improvement in Anne's appearance is confirmed by Lady Russell.

> But happily, either Anne was improved in plumpness and looks, or Lady Russell fancied her so; and Anne, in receiving her compliments on the occasion, had the amusement of connecting them with the silent admiration of her cousin, and of hoping that she was to be blessed with a second spring of youth and beauty.

Sir Walter, that severe arbiter of beauty, pays the ultimate compliment:

> In the course of the same morning, Anne and her father chancing to be alone together, he began to compliment her on her improved looks; he thought her "less thin in her person, in her cheeks; her skin, her complexion, greatly improved; clearer, fresher."

In a further respect the scene at Lyme is crucial, for it is through the reflected admiration in William Elliot's eyes that Captain Wentworth observes the signs of "a second spring of youth and beauty" in Anne. This mirror device by which feelings and ideas are refracted rather than expressed directly is used through the novel to record the progress of the relationship between Anne and Wentworth. By handling her material so indirectly, Miss Austen avoids the danger of sentimentality latent in such a love problem. The lovers are shown scenically in a tangential rather than a direct relationship to each other. Since they are almost always together in company, their emotions are part of a community of emotion, and the two draw close to each other in sympathetic feeling away from the community, or one merges with the common emotion and leaves the other isolated. Through dramatic visualization their feelings, which may be simple, awakened, or changed, are immediately comprehended. These scenes are part of the technical equipment of the novel, which attains in its portrayal of character a high degree of objectivity combined with intimate knowledge.

Because of their obvious ironic possibilities, such scenes may also provide a commentary on all the characters through a contrast of reactions. The excess of Anne's love, which diminishes all within her view except the object of her love, is brilliantly contrasted with Lady Russell's blindness to what is most dear to her friend when Captain Wentworth passes near the two women as they walk down a Bath street. Anne watches Lady Russell peering intently in Wentworth's direction, and she "could thoroughly comprehend the sort of fascination he must possess over Lady Russell's mind. . . ." But when at last Lady Russell speaks, she informs Anne:

> "You will wonder . . . what has been fixing my eye so long; but I was looking after some window-curtains, which Lady Alicia and Mrs. Frankland were telling me of last night."

The smile of "pity and disdain" which Anne gives immediately afterward is either for "her friend or herself." The reader, caught up in the complex irony which deflates the two figures, feels something of each for both women.

The major conversations of the novel function in similar indirect fashion. They may take place between Anne or Wentworth and a third party and be overheard by the other—as the talk between Louisa Musgrove and Wentworth in the hedgerow near Uppercross or that between Anne and Admiral Harville; or between either of them and a third party in which news of the other is given that may affect their relationship—as Admiral Croft's report to Anne of the engagement of Louisa Musgrove and Captain Benwick and the consequent freedom of Wentworth; or directly between Anne and Wentworth where they hover about a subject on which each wishes to speak and on which neither quite fixes—as their discussion of the engagement of Louisa Musgrove and Benwick, where parallels to their own situation are sighted but turned away from. Together with Anne's interior observations, the conversations open up for analysis some of the principal ideas of the novel: the error of "over-anxious caution" as a guide to action; the value of the open-hearted character;

the conflict between "steadiness of principle and the obstinancy of self-will."

The dramatic climax of *Persuasion* centers about a conversation between Anne and Admiral Harville, whose dead sister had been engaged to Benwick, on the relative constancy of men and women. Here the nexus of the dialogue is ostensibly between the two conversationalists; actually it is between Anne and Wentworth, who sits nearby listening. Not until they are reunited after this scene do Anne and Wentworth directly address each other on the subject of her obedience to Lady Russell in rejecting Wentworth's earlier proposal to her. Anne upholds the propriety of her submission even though the advice was erroneous: "But I mean, that I was right in submitting to her, and that if I had done otherwise, I should have suffered more in continuing this engagement than I did even in giving it up, because I would have suffered in my conscience." In reply to a question from Wentworth, Anne admits that she would have renewed their engagement had Wentworth later persisted.

Conscience as the devotion to an apparently unreasonable ideal is as old in fiction as Quixote's chivalric folly and as recent as Gatsby's sacrifice to his exalted vision of Daisy. The argument in *Persuasion* seems heavily weighted on the side of the eager, liberal naval class against the fossilized aristocracy. Anne's defense is that if she were wrong in yielding to persuasion, it was on the side of safety not risk. There is something paradoxical in this assertion when safety evidently means a rejection of life and risk an affirmation of its possibilities. It is a contradiction of the mute eloquence of her earlier observation on the value of a "cheerful confidence in futurity" and "a trust in Providence."

Contradiction, however, is as much a part of the created world as it is of the real world, and irony is the attitude with which Jane Austen faces it. Miss Austen is far enough away from Anne Elliot to view her heroine's total situation not alone with tenderness but with a feeling for the absurd in it as well. Perhaps we might say that the absurdity accounts in part for the tenderness. After Louisa Musgrove's disastrous fall, the result of her obstinacy, Anne reflects on the "universal felicity and advantage" which Wentworth had ascribed to firmness of character; she wonders "whether it might not strike him that, like all other qualities of the mind, it should have its proportions and limits." The irony here is deceptive: it touches Anne's wistful yearnings toward Wentworth. But the statement also provides a warrant for all her deeds. Proportion is a key word in Jane Austen's vocabulary: it implies a philosophy of life, a prudent way of stability, security, continuity. It is a fortification against the unknown. In *Persuasion* a serious breach has been made in the concept of order and control which so rigidly sustains a novel like *Emma;* but no subversion has been effected. Now feelings are admitted to an extent which strain the structure to its limits. Because the novel is so literally concerned with life and death, *Persuasion* of all Jane Austen's fiction poses a condition of extreme ideological tension in the opposition between proportion and profound carelessness as principles of action. Existence between these two poles rests on a precarious equilibrium and inevitably results in paradoxical act and idea. One cannot urge cheerful confidence in futurity and trust in Providence and approve obedience to advice that distrusts Providence and undermines all confidence in futurity without seeming to contradict oneself.

Is not, therefore, the scrupulous recognition of contradiction a basis on which Anne's character develops? In the face of all the facts at hand, she does not conclude with a crude positive or negative judgment on her personal situation or on the world in which she is involved. She admits the immobility of the society in which she was raised, its inhuman addiction to forms and ceremonies—its concern with appearance; and she esteems the vigorous optimism of the society into which she marries—its grasp of reality. Nevertheless, whatever Anne is as a person rests in substantial measure on the training she received at Kellynch Hall—her mother, whom she resembles, lived until Anne was fourteen. What she becomes is due to an absorption of new ideas, new feelings, new energy from life outside Kellynch. In her evaluation of her obedience, Anne asseverates the virtue of proportion, of a sense of what is fitting for her as an individual to do: she at least could not have been unreasonable even in the face of unreasonable demands made upon her. Having proved to her own satisfaction her responsibility, at the end of the novel she chooses further and creates her own life. But she is not content simply to marry Wentworth. She cannot bear the hostility of Lady Russell and Wentworth to each other. Wentworth of course she would not give up, but she wants also the justification of her choice confirmed by that authority-figure, Lady Russell. The reconciliation between Lady Russell and Wentworth is insisted upon at the close of *Persuasion.* Where previously paradox had been inferred from life, Anne in bringing about this reconciliation creates life out of paradox: the compromise between the most loved representative of the aristocracy and the most loved representative of the navy is effected not without a realignment of ideas on both sides. The result appears then to have been worth Anne's practice over so many years of so much resignation.

In this examination of the complex figure of Anne Elliot, we have come a long way from the heroine of the fairy tale. And in creating her, Jane Austen came a long way from the Sophias, Amelias, Clarissas, and Evelinas of eighteenth-century fiction. Anne is an archetypal figure, the forerunner of a line of nineteenth-century heroines of fiction; it is a line which passes from Lizzie Hexam through Dorothea Brooke to Isabel Archer and culminates in Milly Theale. These are the large-souled intelligent women, living in a world of fundamental social dislocation, whose capacity for life is vast but whose devotion to a perhaps impossible ideal is more vast, who end with their ideals held aloft and shining but who usually achieve less of life than they deserve. The reassuring fact about Anne Elliot—and this *is* possibly the fairy tale after all—is that she is not only faithful to her ideals but she also attains, at last, as much of life as she deserves. (pp. 272-89)

Joseph M. Duffy, Jr., "Structure and Idea in Jane Austen's 'Persuasion'," in Nineteenth-Century Fiction, *Vol. VIII, No. 4, March, 1954, pp. 272-89.*

Elizabeth Bowen   (essay date 1957)

[*Bowen was an Anglo-Irish fiction writer and critic. Her novels and short stories, often compared with the fiction of Virginia Woolf, display stylistic control and subtle insight into the portrayal of human relationships. In the following excerpt, she traces the development of Anne Elliot's emotional fulfillment.*]

Jane Austen is, in the main, delighted in as a smiling satirist—a person most herself in the comic vein. Her art could seem drawn to the sparkling shallows rather than to the greater depths of emotion. Extreme grief, turbulence or despair are banished from her pages, where not shown as the penalties of excessive romanticism. All but one of her heroines are youthful, capable of feeling, but still untouched by the more searching experiences of life. We observe that, throughout most of her writing years, Jane Austen deliberately chose restraint—she had, it is true, a warning in the absurd contortions of sensibility to which some of her fellow-novelists could go, but we may be certain that for her choice there was also some compelling personal reason. Not till she came to write *Persuasion* did she break with her self-set limitations. Did something in her demand release, expression, before it was too late? This was, whether or not she knew it, the last book she was to live to complete.

Persuasion strikes a note unheard hitherto. It is a masterpiece of delicate strength, suggesting far more than is put on paper. For it was not that the author abandoned or turned against restraint: on the contrary, she made it her study—its hard cost and no less its painful causes are shown. *Persuasion,* whose lonely heroine, young no longer, seems committed to all but silence, is in fact a novel about restraint. It is, too, a novel about maturity.

Somebody, discussing fiction, remarked that whereas men write better about a first love, women write better about a second. For our sex, do the original raptures tend to evaporate from the later memory? . . . In *Persuasion,* Jane Austen does not, admittedly, deal with a second love—but she is concerned with a young love which has grown up, which has steadied, lasted, felt the stress of reality, woven itself into the fabric of a life. Anne Elliott is not a girl but a woman—though a woman doomed, it would seem, to unfulfilment. Because of a mistake she cannot retrieve, the future is to be empty for her. In Jane Austen's day, a spinster of twenty-seven was to all intents and purposes a nobody—a seat in the background, an anxious place on the margin of other people's activities were the most such an unfortunate might aspire to. When we first meet Anne Elliot, this is her lot. And worse, it is her lot by her own fault.

Tormentedly yielding to persuasion on the part of a worldlier older friend, Anne, at nineteen, had broken off her engagement to Frederick Wentworth, the then young, penniless naval officer. Nor had the love affair ended only thus: Anne has the additional pain of knowing that her weakmindedness (as it seemed to him) aroused Frederick Wentworth's contempt and anger—utterly she had failed and disappointed him. Now, for eight years, intense self-reproach has mingled with her regret. For his sake, the best she feels she can hope is that Wentworth by now has forgotten her—she has spoiled her own life: is that not enough?

There is present, in that early history of Anne's, everything that could have made a warped creature. Do we not all know women with poisoned temperaments, in whom some grievance or disappointment seems to fester like an embedded thorn? Today, with a hundred careers open, it is or should be easier to forget—but Anne, condemned to the idleness of her time and class, has not an interest or an ambition to distract her. Endlessly, if she so willed, she could fret and brood. But no: she shows an unbroken though gentle spirit and, with that, a calm which does not fail. From what inner source does her courage spring? Love, although lost to her, still inspires her. Her undying feeling for Frederick Wentworth, the unshadowed nobility of his image, still lights up for her the entire world. For Anne Elliot to love, to have loved, is a tremendous thing. Somehow, therefore, she is set apart from those whose easier longings have been satisfied.

Hence, I think, this reticent woman's hold on the reader—one is drawn to her as to no other more outwardly striking Jane Austen heroine; one feels honoured by being in her confidence; she is sympathetic rather than coldly 'admirable'. Her slender beauty is thrown into more relief by the bumptious, apple-cheeked charms of the young Miss Musgroves. Playing the piano while her juniors dance, listening to the long and imagined woes of a series of discontented matrons, Anne Elliot remains in her quiet way the mistress of any situation. Unlike the blameless Fanny of *Mansfield Park,* she never is over-meek, subservient or mousey. She never pities herself: who dare pity her? The dull young squire Charles Musgrove, now her brother-in-law, had been, we learn, Anne's unsuccessful suitor; in the course of the story she is to attract the eye of a jaded, roving man-of-the-world. If life *is* 'over' for Anne, it is so by force of her own decision—she can contemplate no form of the second-best.

Persuasion's heroine, when we first meet her, owes her poise to a sort of sad inner peace, the peace which comes with the end of hope. She does not expect, and she cannot wish, ever again to see Frederick Wentworth.

Yet, she must! And we watch her through that ordeal.

Frederick, now Captain Wentworth, a naval war hero enriched by prize-money, reappears in the Elliots' Westcountry neighbourhood. Here, in these same places, these rooms and gardens charged with so many associations, the former lovers are forced to meet face to face. Forced?—yes, for Anne it amounts to that. She hears the news of his coming with apprehension. He, by all signs, does not any more feel anything; she must conceal the fact that she feels so much. Nor is this all—she is to look on at Captain Wentworth's flirtation with and apparent courtship of her sprightly young neighbour Louisa Musgrove. For Frederick, Anne seems to be hardly there. Is it, for him, as though she had never been?

No. His formal good manners to her have a touch of ice: he has not forgotten, for he has not forgiven. Meet as they may as strangers, he and she cannot be strangers truly. Always, they are in the presence of crowds of people; there are walking-parties, dances, country house merrymakings, and there is the expedition to Lyme Regis which so nearly has a tragic end. One thing Anne *is* spared—prying or mocking eyes. For that eight-years-ago engagement had been kept secret: no outside person other than Lady Russell (whose advice had wrecked it) had ever known of it. Now, Lady Russell is elsewhere. Nobody, therefore, suspects either Anne's anguish or its cause.

All through *Persuasion,* the scenes in the country, at the seaside, the later episodes in Bath, we react to the tension of speechless feeling. Yet somehow the novel is not a thing of stress; it has the harmony of its autumnal setting. The landscape, the changing season, are part of the texture of the story. Here, as nowhere else in Jane Austen's work, brims over the poetry of Nature—uplands, woods and sea. We are tuned in to a mood, to a sensibility which (being at once Anne's and her creator's) rings beautifully true. And, as the plot of *Persuasion* unfolds itself, we follow each development through Anne's eyes. Or sometimes, we keep watch on her behalf. Is Frederick Wentworth relenting?—or, had his coldness, from the first, been a matter of self-protection? Has his indifference to this older Anne been less than she had imagined, or he had thought? So we suspect, some time before Anne herself has dared to envisage the possibility. We begin to be impatient for the *dénouement*—of its kind, the suspense set up by *Persuasion* is as keen as any I know in fiction.

Then it comes—that extraordinary scene in the Bath parlour when, while Anne is talking to other people, Frederick sits absorbed in writing a letter. Then, rising, he leaves the room hurriedly, 'without so much as a look'. But next:

> Footsteps were heard returning; the door opened; it was himself. He begged their pardon, but he had forgotten his gloves, and instantly crossing the room to the writing table, and standing with his back to Mrs Musgrove, he drew out a letter from under the scattered paper, placed it before Anne with eyes of glowing entreaty fixed on her for a moment, and hastily collecting his gloves, was again out of the room, almost before Mrs Musgrove was aware of his being in it—the work of an instant!

> The revolution which one instant had made in Anne was almost beyond expression. . . . On the contents of that letter depended all which the world could do for her!

There are, I know, those who find in *Persuasion* one fundamental improbability. *Would* Anne, even when very young, have let herself be persuaded by Lady Russell into making a break with her true love? The weakness, the lack of faith—the cowardice, almost—seem out of accord with the heroine whom we later know. One must recollect that Lady Russell's argument had been a wily one—she had represented to Anne that a penniless youthful marriage would be a fatal drag on Frederick's career. Anne had given up Frederick for (as she thought) his sake—though mistaken, her decision had been selfless. Also, at nineteen, repressed and young for her age, she was unaccustomed to trusting her own judgement. Ignored by an arrogant father and elder sister, she had found in the worldly-wise Lady Russell her first friend—whose word, accordingly, carried undue weight. The time, moreover, was long ago: girls deferred, instinctively, to adult authority. But should we not, before either decrying Anne or declaring her weakness to be 'impossible', think again about this question of influence? Dare we say that a friend's opinion, forcefully put, never has affected our own decisions? And is it not in regard to what matter most—for instance, some vital question of love—that we are most at the mercy of what is told us? Caught in a tempest of feeling, we lose our bearings: it may not be easy to know what is right or wrong. The truth, we may only perceive later—not, it is to be hoped, too late.

Jane Austen's otherwise open life contains one mystery: her love affair. Nobody but her sister Cassandra knew of it; and Cassandra, who outlived Jane, kept silence—it is known that, before Cassandra's death, she destroyed revealing letters written by Jane. The probable scene and time of the love affair have been pieced together; no more can be established with any certainty. It is understood that the love was mutual, wholly happy, tender and full of promise, and that there would have been marriage had not the young man died. Had Jane Austen married, it seems likely that the world would never have had her greater later novels—fate, by dealing that blow to her, has enriched us. Balanced, wise and adorable are her comedies, but her true depth was not to be felt till this final book. This, I think, is her testimony to the valour, the enduringness of the human spirit. She believed, and she was to show, that love for another can be the light of a life—can rise above egotism, accept hardship, outlive hope of reward. Out of a hard-won knowledge she wrote *Persuasion.* (pp. 47-51)

> *Elizabeth Bowen, "Persuasion," in* London Magazine, *Vol. 4, No. 4, April, 1957, pp. 47-51.*

Marvin Mudrick   (essay date 1964)

[*Mudrick is an American educator and critic perhaps best known for the wide range of his literary interests, his lively, informal style, his incisive and often controversial analyses, and the zeal with which he administers his criticism, prompting the observation that "the weight of his praise is hoisted by the tonnage of his blame." In the following excerpt from Mudrick's afterword to a 1964 edition of* Persuasion, *he discusses Austen's concept of propriety as exemplified in the novel.*]

"Propriety," wrote William Hazlitt, Jane Austen's contemporary, "is one great matter in the conduct of life; which, though like a graceful carriage of the body it is neither definable nor striking at first sight, is the result of finely balanced feelings and lends a secret strength and charm to the whole character." There's no evidence that Hazlitt ever read *Persuasion* (or, indeed, anything by its author, of whom only Sir Walter Scott among the literary figures of her time took serious notice); yet, describing this civilized virtue, he might have been beautifully describing its incarnation in the heroine of Jane Austen's last novel.

Propriety, in a more neutral sense than Hazlitt's, has of course always been Jane Austen's subject. In her novels, society—"three or four families in a country village"—is the unevadable basis, the decorum to which eventually one accommodates oneself. Character exercises and proves itself among the circumscribed social opportunities, most particularly in courtship and marriage. But her heroines have always been too high-spirited (Marianne Dashwood, Elizabeth Bennet), or too ingenuous (Catherine Morland), or too calculating (Elinor Dashwood, Emma Woodhouse), or too humble (Fanny Price), to make of propriety the virtue and fulfillment that Hazlitt celebrates. The guardians and exemplars of propriety in her earlier novels are likely to be fools, snobs, stuffed shirts: Mr. Collins, Mrs. Elton, Sir Thomas Bertram; as if the author deliberately separates herself by a margin of distaste from the society to which neither she nor her heroines have any prudent alternative. *Persuasion* is different: an epilogue of acceptance, a reconciliation. The proper parochial society that for a quarter of a century Jane Austen had been laughing at and amusing, despising and

Chawton Cottage, where Austen wrote Persuasion.

defending, at all events copiously memorializing, comes to its late flower in the unassuming grace, the finely balanced feelings, the secret strength and charm of character, of Anne Elliot.

Appearance nevertheless challenges and postpones reality. Though Anne is the heart, the vital breath, the crown of propriety, she merely is what numerous others, by the warrant of privilege and custom, plume themselves on being—nobody so much as her very silly father:

> Sir Walter Elliot, of Kellynch Hall, in Somersetshire, was a man who, for his own amusement, never took up any book but the Baronetage; there he found occupation for an idle hour, and consolation on a distressed one; there his faculties were roused into admiration and respect, by contemplating the limited remnant of the earliest patents; there any unwelcome sensations, arising from domestic affairs, changed naturally into pity and contempt. As he turned over the almost endless creations of the last century—and there, if every other leaf were powerless, he could read his own history with an interest which never failed—this was the page at which the favourite volume always opened. . . .

Sir Walter, besides, has been specially favored by nature in his role as the protagonist of this comedy of appearance:

> Vanity was the beginning and the end of Sir Walter Elliot's character; vanity of person and of situation. He had been remarkably handsome in his youth; and, at fifty-four, was still a very fine man. Few women could think more of their personal appearance than he did; nor could the valet of any new-made lord be more delighted with the place he held in society. He considered the blessing of beauty as inferior only to the blessing of a baronetcy; and the Sir Walter Elliot, who united these gifts, was the constant object of his warmest respect and devotion.

The comedy has a leading lady in his daughter Elizabeth (and even, back in the scullery, Anne as Cinderella):

> Sir Walter's continuing in singleness [after his wife's death] requires explanation.—Be it known, then, that Sir Walter, like a good father (having met with one or two private disappointments in very unreasonable applications), prided himself on remaining single for his dear daughter's sake. For one daughter, his eldest, he would really have given up anything, which he had not been very much tempted to do. Elizabeth had succeeded, at sixteen, to all that was possible, of her mother's rights and consequence; and being very handsome, and very like himself, her influence had always been great, and they had gone on together most happily. His two other children were of very inferior value. Mary had acquired a little artificial importance, by becoming Mrs. Charles Musgrove; but Anne, with an elegance of mind and sweetness of character, which must have placed her high with any people of real understanding, was nobody with either father or sister: her work had no weight; her convenience was always to give way—she was only Anne.

The comedy has, finally, a superb scheming toady, Mrs. Clay, who winds herself into the tangled narcissisms of Sir Walter and Miss Elliot by judiciously affirming their right to be stupid. Anne having ventured to speak well of the navy, Sir Walter states his objections to it:

> " . . . . First, as being the means of bringing persons of obscure birth into undue distinction, and raising men to honours which their fathers and grandfathers never dreamt of; and secondly, as it cuts up a man's youth and vigour most horribly; a sailor grows old sooner than any other man. . . . they are all knocked about, and exposed to every climate, and every weather, till they are not fit to be seen. . . . "

Whereupon Mrs. Clay rushes in to make her corroborative qualifications:

> "Nay, Sir Walter," cried Mrs. Clay, "this is being severe indeed. Have a little mercy on the poor men. We are not all born to be handsome. The sea is no beautifier, certainly; sailors do grow old betimes; I have often observed it; they soon lose the look of youth. But then, is it not the same with many other professions, perhaps most other? Soldiers, in active service, are not at all better off; and even in the quieter professions, there is a toil and a labour of the mind, if not of the body, which seldom leaves a man's looks to the natural effect of time. The lawyer plods, quite care-worn; the physician is up at all hours, and travelling in all weather . . . "

And so she eliminates, one by one, all the professions till she has proved by default that only the mild obligations of a country baronet are not hostile to "the blessings of health and a good appearance."

Propriety—modest public currency—can be easily counterfeited. Sir Walter and Elizabeth, imagining themselves models of propriety, have debased it into snobbery, name-worship, the sloth of self-love. Low-bred and penniless Mrs. Clay, who scrupulously cultivates the vices of others till she will be allowed to humor her own, takes the good name of propriety for her sycophancy and social-climbing. Mr. Elliot, as cunning as Mrs. Clay, uses his face, family, and manner to practice an opportunism that Anne is able to identify long before she has all the evidence of it:

> who could answer for the true sentiments of a clever, cautious man, grown old enough to appreciate a fair character? . . .

> Mr. Elliot was rational, discreet, polished—but he was not open. There was never any burst of feeling, any warmth of indignation or delight, at the evil or good of others. This, to Anne, was a decided imperfection. Her early impressions were incurable. She prized the frank, the open-hearted, the eager character beyond all others. Warmth and enthusiasm did captivate her still. She felt that she could so much more depend upon the sincerity of those who sometimes looked or said a careless or a hasty thing, than of those whose presence of mind never varied, whose tongue never slipped.

> Mr. Elliot was too generally agreeable. Various

as were the tempers in her father's house, he pleased them all.

False propriety may infect a nature neither vicious nor frivolous, even one as inclined to kindness and disinterested affection as Lady Russell's; for if Sir Walter's self-infatuation is the worst form of snobbery, Lady Russell's immoderate respect for name and family is snobbery enough to make her doubt and distrust merely personal virtues, and thus to effect Anne's disastrous refusal of Wentworth:

> Captain Wentworth had no fortune. He had been lucky in his profession, but spending freely what had come freely; had realized nothing. But, he was confident that he should soon be rich— full of life and ardour, he knew that he should soon have a ship, and soon be on a station that would lead to everything he wanted. He had always been lucky; he knew he should be so still.— Such confidence, powerful in its own warmth, and bewitching in the wit which often expressed it, must have been enough for Anne; but Lady Russell saw it very differently—His sanguine temper, and fearlessness of mind, operated very differently on her. She saw in it but an aggravation of the evil. It only added a dangerous character to himself. He was brilliant, he was headstrong.—Lady Russell had little taste for wit; and of anything approaching to imprudence a horror. She deprecated the connexion in every light.

Consistently with her social predispositions, Lady Russell is as blind to Sir Walter's silliness, Elizabeth's mean vanity, and Mr. Elliot's guile as she is to Wentworth's energy and Admiral Croft's shrewd benevolence. She is a good woman whose judgment is almost fatally incapacitated by the proper assumptions that she accepts without question from her class and time. Sure of being in the right, she is at the mercy of every façade.

Not that everyone is enlisted in this war of appearance versus reality: not the children, of whatever age, the amiable golden children (like Bingley and Jane Bennet in *Pride and Prejudice*) whose only motive is to be quickly pleased, and whom their author always treats with parental indulgence; the Musgrove girls, for example—

> like thousands of other young ladies, living to be fashionable, happy, and merry. Their dress had every advantage, their faces were rather pretty, their spirits extremely good, their manners unembarrassed and pleasant; they were of consequence at home, and favourites abroad. Anne always contemplated them as some of the happiest creatures of her acquaintance; but still, saved as we all are by some comfortable feeling of superiority from wishing for the possibility of exchange, she would not have given up her own more elegant and cultivated mind for all their enjoyment. . . .

Or, as the observant Admiral Croft sums them up, "very nice young ladies they both are; I hardly know one from the other."

Captain Benwick, another innocent, by his extravagant responsiveness to Romantic poetry provokes Anne to a rare pitch of moral admonition:

> he repeated, with such tremulous feeling, the various lines which imaged a broken heart, or a mind destroyed by wretchedness, and looked so entirely as if he meant to be understood, that she ventured to hope he did not always read only poetry, and to say that she thought it was the misfortune of poetry to be seldom safely enjoyed by those who enjoyed it completely; and that the strong feelings which alone could estimate it truly were the very feelings which ought to taste it but sparingly.

And when Benwick's heart, supposed to have been broken by his fiancée's recent death, recomposes itself and turns with butterfly lightness to one of the Musgrove girls, Anne accurately concludes: "He had an affectionate heart. He must love somebody."

Charles Musgrove, who must have been not quite so simple to begin with, has by this time declined into simplicity. Having first aspired to Anne and having had to make do with her querulous sister Mary, he sinks any prospects of maturity into the unthinking diversions that keep his marriage tolerable:

> he did nothing with much zeal, but sport; and his time was otherwise trifled away, without benefit from books, or anything else. He had very good spirits, which never seemed much affected by his wife's occasional lowness; bore with her unreasonableness sometimes to Anne's admiration; and upon the whole, though there was very often a little disagreement . . . they might pass for a happy couple.

If Charles isn't lucky enough to be as childlike and unfallen as the Musgrove girls and Captain Benwick, he's at least artless and good-natured, and only now and then childish.

As for Jane Austen's representatives of true propriety in *Persuasion,* it's no wonder that even for the well-intentioned Lady Russell they are—with the exception of Anne herself—so difficult to recognize and credit. Any conventional society is liable to mistake ceremoniousness for propriety; and Jane Austen's new exemplars (again, except for Anne) are about as vigorous and unceremonious as Lady Russell is slow and solemn. They are, after all, sailors. The personal hero of *Persuasion* is named Wentworth, and a very likable and dashing fellow he is; but the collective hero of *Persuasion* is the British Navy, at its zenith of power and reputation, just after the final defeat of Napoleon—Jane Austen's beloved navy, in which two of her brothers rose to the rank of admiral.

Her view of the navy man may not have been altogether unprejudiced. It seems improbable that every British ship's captain was either a sentimental admirer of Scott and Byron like Benwick, or a pattern of conjugal felicity like Admiral Croft or Captain Harville, or, like Wentworth, the soul of unaffected manliness. Yet if Jane Austen had been critically seeking out a profession in which every sort of social duty and ambition was compatible with enthusiasm and physical grace, she could hardly have chosen better. The navy was, as Sir Walter remarks, "the means of bringing persons of obscure birth into undue distinction," i.e. of gratifying their honorable ambition for rank and money. Jane Austen lived in a pre-Marxian, almost a pre-industrial, society, still unencumbered by a sense of guilt about rank and money, in an epoch when war at sea was a patriotic and personal adventure, a double opportunity in which a ship's master could simultaneously serve his country and make his fortune by the straightforward means of capturing enemy ships. So Wentworth exclaims in fond remembrance:

> "Ah! those were pleasant days when I had the *Laconia!* How fast I made money in her.—A friend of mine, and I, had such a lovely cruise together off the Western Islands.—Poor Harville, sister! You know how much he wanted money—worse than myself. He had a wife.—Excellent fellow! I shall never forget his happiness. He felt it all, so much for her sake.—I wished for him again the next summer, when I had still the same luck in the Mediterranean."

And sensible Admiral Croft makes casually explicit the indispensable condition for another set of such blissful reminiscences: " '. . . if we have the good luck to live to another war. . . . ' " No sensible person in Jane Austen's novels ever deludes himself against the authority and usefulness of money. A ship's captain has the advantage of being able to make his fortune rapidly, and the disadvantage that he can make it only in time of war. He must seize his chance, or renounce his hope of money and position, perhaps even his hope of a good marriage. Certainly, without money and the leisure it provides, Anne could not have become what she is; money is the foundation of true as of false propriety, and without it Wentworth doesn't deserve Anne. Her error was to let Lady Russell persuade her against Wentworth's destiny, against the temper and ambition that virtually guaranteed it. The sailor's life quite suits Jane Austen's purposes because his attitude toward money is the right one: direct, unpretending; as toward sails and keels, lifeboats and yardarms—whatever a sensible man would much rather not do without.

True propriety is, then, discretion still, for discretion and judgment have nothing to do with mere caution, conformity, moral sluggishness. One sort of propriety is the sailor's manliness, which is not rashness for its own sake, but passion and energy for the sake of the rewards that a man attains, if unassisted by birth, only by his own directed passion and energy. Jane Austen's attitude toward rank and money isn't that of, say, Dickens, an urban poor boy who grew up in the lengthening shadows of industrialism's satanic mills, and for whom money is rubbish or magic. Jane Austen is neither enthralled nor repelled (of course she spent her life among the rural gentry, and some years before industrialism had decisively asserted itself); she isn't sentimental: Anne is Anne, the jewel of a particular setting, and Wentworth will deserve her if, socially as well as personally, he can bring what will maintain and enhance her very nature. Lady Russell thinks as well of Anne as every reader must; but Lady Russell confuses propriety with obliquity and ceremoniousness, with Anne's gentle reserve; she is unaccustomed to the manners

of unevasive manliness, as when Admiral Croft comments on Miss Musgrove's fall:

> "Ay, a very bad business indeed.—A new sort of way this, for a young fellow to be making love, by breaking his mistress's head!—is not it, Miss Elliot?—This is breaking a head and giving a plaister truly!"

> Admiral Croft's manners were not quite of the tone to suit Lady Russell, but they delighted Anne. His goodness of heart and simplicity of character were irresistible.

Moreover, as war is the unarguable condition for a sailor's advancement, so in **Persuasion** manliness is the condition for a happy marriage. Only in **Persuasion** does Jane Austen offer images of conjugal happiness; and, not content with one couple, she offers two: the Crofts and the Harvilles. Anne is always pleased to see the Crofts out for a stroll because they are so plainly and justifiably pleased with each other:

> She always watched them as long as she could; delighted to fancy she understood what they might be talking of, as they walked along in happy independence, or equally delighted to see the Admiral's hearty shake of the hand when he encountered an old friend, and observe their eagerness of conversation when occasionally forming into a little knot of the navy, Mrs. Croft looking as intelligent and keen as any of the officers around her.

And "the picture of repose and domestic happiness" at the Harvilles' is almost too much for Anne—feeling her own chance gone by—to contemplate without pain, even as it incites one of the Musgrove girls, in love with Wentworth, to rhapsodize on the sailor's monopoly of the manly virtues:

> Louisa . . . burst forth into raptures of admiration and delight on the character of the navy—their friendliness, their brotherliness, their openness, their uprightness; protesting that she was convinced of sailors having more worth and warmth than any other set of men in England; that they only knew how to live, and they only deserved to be respected and loved.

It isn't surprising that such qualities—though Louisa's partiality may overestimate their prevalence among sailors—seek out and attract admirable women, and make for better marriages than those of which Lady Russell would be likely to approve.

Anne, if she didn't have reasons for keeping her counsel, could speak even more rapturously than Louisa; but the decision she made seven years ago excludes her, so she must believe, from the hope that Louisa can entertain. Anne is a Cinderella who long ago, at the behest of her fairy godmother, rejected her prince. The coach has since been permanently retranslated into a pumpkin, the footmen into mice; the heartless sister triumphs at the ball; and the angry prince returns, irreconcilable, with eyes for any girl except the one who spurned him. If ever gentleness, sweetness of temper, kindness of heart, the charm of quiet spontaneous feeling, the unsounded depth of passion—if propriety, in a word, is ever to be tested, it will be by Anne; for Anne's ordeal is so private and unconfessable that it bereaves her of even the world's pity; it's so vivid and absolute that it leaves her no resource beyond the womanliness which her state of being defines.

Propriety, in *Persuasion,* is like the original bisexual humanity in Plato's parable. Once there was a "male-female sex . . . sharing both male and female." Humanity, having in this union of capacities "terrible strength and force," challenged the very gods, who thereupon sliced them "through the middle, as you slice your serviceberries through the middle for pickle, or as you slice hardboiled eggs with a hair." Ever since, each half has sought and yearned for its complementary other. "So you see how ancient is the mutual love implanted in mankind, bringing together the parts of the original body, and trying to make one out of two, and to heal the natural structure of man."

The two halves of propriety are manliness and womanliness. They seek each other out, through the thickets of circumstance and misunderstanding; their natural and sufficient end is marriage. Anne's consummation is deferred, forever she believes; but her womanliness was the lodestar to Wentworth's manliness once. By seven years of regret and perfect fidelity she has proved his title as her fated complement, and her own claim to the last, undemanding privilege of womanliness. So she replies to Captain Harville's exclamation on the emotional trials of a sailor-husband:

> "Oh!" cried Anne eagerly, "I hope I do justice to all that is felt by you, and by those who resemble you. God forbid that I should undervalue the warm and faithful feelings of any of my fellow-creatures. I should deserve utter contempt if I dared to suppose that true attachment and constancy were known only by woman. No, I believe you capable of everything great and good in your married lives. I believe you equal to every important exertion, and to every domestic forbearance, so long as—if I may be allowed the expression, so long as you have an object. I mean, while the woman you love lives, and lives for you. All the privilege I claim for my own sex (it is not a very enviable one, you need not covet it), is that of loving longest, when existence or when hope is gone."

The plot of *Persuasion* could scarcely be more unitary. Its instigation is the return of Wentworth; its events are the stages of Anne's emotion, from despair to "joy, senseless joy": the inner agitation of a presence that never, in its bleakest moments, loses touch with the freshness of common reality—with Sir Walter's embarrassing fatuity, or Benwick's harmless sentimentality, or the Musgrove girls' vivacity, or Admiral Croft's unillusioned good nature. Anne, living her public life with open eyes and serviceable grace, is compelled to live her private life, painfully, at the center of a web of memory and speculation: what life was like when she and Wentworth were together; whether his feeling for her can now be—must it not be, in view of his attachment to Louisa?—entirely dead. The most trivial actions assume the proportions of hallucination and nightmare. At her sister's, one of Anne's nephews persists in

clinging to her "as she knelt, in such a way that . . . she could not shake him off":

> In another moment . . . she found herself in the state of being released from him; some one was taking him from her, though he had bent down her head so much that his little sturdy hands were unfastened from around her neck; and he was resolutely borne away before she knew that Captain Wentworth had done it.
>
> Her sensations on the discovery made her perfectly speechless. She could not even thank him. She could only hang over little Charles, with most disordered feelings. His kindness in stepping forward to her relief—the manner—the silence in which it had passed—the little particulars of the circumstance—with the conviction soon forced on her, by the noise he was studiously making with the child, that he meant to avoid hearing her thanks, and rather sought to testify that her conversation was the last of his wants, produced such a confusion of varying, but very painful agitation, as she could not recover from, till enabled by the entrance of Mary and the Miss Musgroves to make over her little patient to their cares, and leave the room.

From the stunning fact of his mere proximity till the great scene of lovers' reconciliation at the White Hart Inn, Anne sustains the numberless shocks of her ordeal, the trial and vindication of her passionate fidelity. Only once before has Jane Austen considered such intensity of feeling—in Marianne Dashwood; and only to betray Marianne, at last, into an insipid match that is supposed to subdue sensibility to sense. If Marianne is Jane Austen's Juliet (without a true Romeo), Anne is her Penelope, the tender wife to a husband who will not yet acknowledge himself, the goal of the sailor's long journey, the radiance of conjugal love after years of battle and wandering. "Propriety is one great matter in the conduct of life"—Hazlitt's maxim is what Anne's life illustrates, and what she believes in even to extremity:

> I have been thinking over the past, and trying impartially to judge of the right and wrong, I mean with regard to myself; and I must believe that I was right, much as I suffered from it, that I was perfectly right in being guided by the friend whom you will love better than you do now. To me, she was in the place of a parent. Do not mistake me, however. I am not saying that she did not err in her advice. It was, perhaps, one of those cases in which advice is good or bad only as the event decides; and for myself, I certainly never should, in any circumstance of tolerable similarity, give such advice. But I mean that I was right in submitting to her, and that if I had done otherwise, I should have suffered more in continuing the engagement than I did even in giving it up, because I should have suffered in my conscience. I have now, as far as such a sentiment is allowable in human nature, nothing to reproach myself with; and if I mistake not, a strong sense of duty is no bad part of a woman's portion.

Wentworth is not yet quite so devout a believer as Anne:

He looked at her, looked at Lady Russell, and looking again at her, replied, as if in cool deliberation, "Not yet. But there are hopes of her being forgiven in time. I trust to being in charity with her soon. . . ."

Still, Wentworth is less grudging than he appears. Odysseus has never objected to a Penelope with loftier notions of fidelity and duty than his own. (pp. 323-36)

> *Marvin Mudrick, "Good and Proper (II)," in his* Books Are Not Life But Then What Is? *Oxford University Press, 1979, pp. 323-36.*

Paul N. Zietlow   (essay date 1965)

[*Zietlow is an American educator and critic. In the following excerpt, he speculates on the function of fortuitous circumstance in* Persuasion, *suggesting that it either signifies an act of Providence in the novel or serves as a device used by Austen in order to facilitate the novel's conclusion.*]

A striking feature of Jane Austen's *Persuasion* is the way the action so frequently leads to the brink of disaster. Often the characters face situations whose only results, seemingly, can be misery, waste, and suffering. Other commentators of course have noticed this dark, menacing quality of the novel. Joseph Duffy, for example [see excerpt dated 1954], points out the frequency of symbols of death and decay, asserts that the heroine, Anne Elliot, "comes face to face with what James called the mysteries abysmal," and defines the novel's world as one in which "life is precarious, the consequences of apparently reasonable choice are sometimes unreasonable, [and] benign forces do not lavish on the well-intentioned person fabulous and fortuitous rewards." Yet, though the novel borders on tragedy, the events invariably take a happy turn, and Jane Austen leads the reader eventually to the felicitous conclusion he expected all along. It is true that the ending does not result from the reasoned and well-intentioned choices of the characters; yet, by the end of the novel, everyone is appropriately "rewarded," and the rewards seem, to a great extent, to be fortuitous. Andrew Wright [in his *Jane Austen's Novels: A Study in Structure,* 1957] emphasizes this point in his discussions of *Persuasion:* "Anne almost loses him [Captain Wentworth] forever [the dark possibility]; it is a set of very fortunate (and fortuitous) circumstances—the renting of Kellynch to his sister's husband, his own remarkable success in the Navy, the fall of Miss Musgrove at Lyme—that finally brings them together again." Wright, however, never analyzes thoroughly these fortuitous circumstances, nor does he attempt to interpret their larger meaning. Such analysis and interpretation, it seems to me, is necessary to an understanding of the total effect of *Persuasion.*

One must beware of finding too much meaning in chance occurrences. In fictional plots, as in real life, chance, good fortune, and events which reverse the expected course of things often play essential parts so unobtrusive and so utterly ordinary as to be hardly worth noticing. The normal and predictably abnormal patterns of everyday life, for example, provide many occasions for an eligible young woman to meet a suitable young man. Such occasions seem providential or lucky (or unlucky) only in retrospect, and only from narrowly limited points of view; in a novel, they are parts of the "given" which no reader ever questions and no critic ever comments on. Anne Elliot and Captain Wentworth, one learns early in *Persuasion,* met sometime in the past. The happy convergence of their lives undoubtedly resulted from a concatenation of events which *could* have been presented as a kind of remarkable, providential conspiracy. Jane Austen's scanty treatment of the circumstances surrounding this first chance meeting indicates that we are to find no such meaning in it. Likewise, unexpected though the death of Anne's mother must have been, one accepts it merely as a fact in the background out of which the novel's action arises. Had she lived, Anne might have accepted Wentworth's first offer; yet speculation of this sort on this event is irrelevant. Such circumstances as Anne's and Wentworth's meeting, and Anne's mother's death, readers accept without question; they require no special notice.

There is a second sort of fortuitous circumstance, however, which might elicit relevant comment. In order for the action of *Persuasion* to occur, Wentworth must return to Anne's neighborhood. He does so because his brother-in-law, Admiral Croft, happens, quite by chance, to take Sir Walter Elliot's house. That Andrew Wright includes "the renting of Kellynch" in his list of "fortunate circumstances" indicates that at least one careful reader has noticed Jane Austen's emphasis on the accidental quality of the event: Admiral Croft, "accidentally hearing—(it was just as he had foretold, Mr. Shepherd observed, Sir Walter's concerns could not be kept a secret,)—accidentally hearing of the possibility of Kellynch Hall. . . ." In one sense his hearing of Kellynch Hall is clearly no accident: Mr. Shepherd is an all too calculating informant. But in a larger sense, that Admiral Croft happened to be looking for an estate to rent at the very time Kellynch became available seems almost too good to be true. Similarly, in order that the novel progress, Anne must remain nearby, even though her family moves to Bath. At first she was to stay with Lady Russell, but other engagements call Lady Russell from the neighborhood. Anne resigns herself to Bath. "Something occurred, however, to give her a different duty." Mary feigns illness, and Anne remains with her. One wonders why Jane Austen did not leave out Lady Russell's plans altogether, and use Mary's illness in the first place. Perhaps she wished to provide a plausible reason for disposing of Lady Russell for the next seven chapters; but it is equally likely that she wished to emphasize the precariousness of Anne's plans, and the fortuitous nature of the circumstances which kept her near Kellynch. Again, Wright finds the situation worth noticing: "Luckily, she stays behind at Uppercross Cottage with her sister." And yet these events do not reverse the reader's expectations. The renting of Kellynch seems quite unremarkable at first reading, because one does not learn of Anne's and Wentworth's history until after the Crofts take the house. We have not been prepared to see it as unusually good luck for the two lovers. On the other hand, we *have* been prepared by our knowledge of Anne's distaste for Bath, for her efforts to stay behind her father and sister. It seems entirely likely that she would resort to some expedient to keep her in the country, and hence one tolerates Mary's felicitous illness. Events such as these the reader accepts as at least plausible, though not highly probable. If there were no more remarkable circumstances in the chain of fortuitous occurrences in **Persuasion,** Andrew Wright most likely would not have mentioned these.

In fictional plots, as in real life, chance, good fortune, and events which reverse the expected course of things often play essential parts so obtrusive and so utterly abnormal as to require special attention. The circumstances attending President Kennedy's death were so wildly improbable as to cause many observers, even the most sober and rational, to suspect conspiracy. Reading about the assassination, one can hardly resist exclaiming at every link in the chain, "If only this one, tiny event had not happened!" Likewise in **Persuasion** there are a number of circumstances which appear to be so unexpected, so felicitous, so contrary to the apparently inevitable course of things that they require interpretation, and lead the reader to speculate, "But what would have happened *if*! . . ." A number of such occurrences Jane Austen emphasizes, either through explicit statement, or by preparing her characters (and readers) so thoroughly for the contrary, that they find the actuality almost unbelievable. The main turning point in the novel, occurring exactly at the middle, is Louisa's *accident.* Even though it is an appropriate result of Louisa's stubbornness and Wentworth's heedlessness, Jane Austen calls it an accident, and insists that we accept it as such; it is an unexpected catastrophe, for which neither characters nor readers are prepared. And had this accident not occurred, events would have taken a different course—a course which both readers and characters have become quite ready to accept. Nor has anyone expected Benwick's happy engagement to Louisa—another crucial event, which frees Wentworth to propose to Anne. Anne's initial reaction to the news is exactly the same as ours. "She had never in her life been more astonished. Captain Benwick and Louisa Musgrove! It was almost too wonderful for belief." Louisa's accident and Benwick's engagement are more than a part of the novel's "given," and more than plausible though highly improbable circumstances; Jane Austen presents them as dramatic reversals of the normal course of things, as entirely unexpected chance occurrences, as bits of amazingly good luck. As an examination of the plot shows, incidents of this kind are crucial in this novel, and they demand interpretation.

The major action of **Persuasion** can be seen as the rectification of an almost tragic mistake made eight years before the novel takes place. Anne Elliot, intelligent, sensitive, considerate, has, at the age of nineteen, allowed herself to be persuaded by the only other sensible person in her confined world, Lady Russell, to reject an offer of marriage. One learns as the book progresses that her suitor, Captain Wentworth, a naval officer, was in most important ways her moral and intellectual equal, and therefore a fit match for her. Hence one's initial reaction is to regard as a bad argument Lady Russell's insistence that his lack of fortune and family name made him unsuitable for Anne; indeed, Jane Austen tells us that Lady Russell's respect for rank is her weakness: "She had a cultivated mind, and was, generally speaking, rational and consistent—but she had prej-

udices on the side of ancestry; she had a value for rank and consequence, which blinded her a little to the faults of those who possessed them." Many critics of the novel have been very hard on Anne's friend. Elizabeth Bowen describes a "worldly wise Lady Russell" with her "wily" arguments [see excerpt dated 1957], and W. R. Martin, after claiming that her values are "essentially the same" as Sir Walter's, goes so far as to say that "Lady Russell, who wears the disguise of virtue, is baneful" [see Further Reading]. But the situation is more complicated. Jane Austen herself, by having Lady Russell enter "thoroughly into [Anne's] sentiments" about the unfortunate Mrs. Smith, contrasts her values explicitly with those of Sir Walter, who says, only four pages later, " 'And who is Miss Anne Elliot to be visiting in Westgate buildings?—A Mrs. Smith. A widow Mrs. Smith,—and who was her husband? One of five thousand Mr. Smiths whose names are to be met with everywhere'." Clearly, unlike Sir Walter, Lady Russell has a core of warmth and human understanding which her prejudices may impair, but not destroy. She may be blind to the faults of those who possess rank, but she is not insensitive to the virtues of the lowly born.

Furthermore, Jane Austen provides ample justification for Lady Russell's judgment of Wentworth, despite the suffering which resulted from it. Anne suggests as much at the end of the novel in her remarkable evaluation of her own actions:

> "I have been thinking over the past, and trying impartially to judge of the right and wrong, I mean with regard to myself; and I must believe that I was right, much as I suffered from it, that I was perfectly right in being guided by the friend whom you will love better than you do now. To me, she was in the place of a parent. Do not mistake me, however. I am not saying that she did not err in her advice. *It was, perhaps, one of those cases in which advice is good or bad only as the event decides*" (italics mine).

If one examines how things looked to Lady Russell before the event decided, and the reasons for the event's turning out as it did, one can see that Lady Russell had a strong case. What she distrusted most about Wentworth was his impetuosity:

> He was confident that he should soon be rich;— full of life and ardour, he knew that he should soon have a ship, and soon be on a station that would lead to everything he wanted. *He had always been lucky; he knew he should be so still.*— Such confidence, powerful in its own warmth, and bewitching in the wit which often expressed it, must have been enough for Anne; but Lady Russell saw it very differently.—His sanguine temper, and fearlessness of mind, operated very differently on her. She saw in it but an aggravation of the evil. It only added a dangerous character to himself. He was brilliant, he was headstrong (italics mine).

A girl of nineteen could be bowled over—in a way a middle-aged widow could not—by a dashing young man's confidence that he would enjoy the favor of fortune. Anne had the sense to respect her older friend; in her acceptance of Lady Russell's advice, as Anne herself implies, she was merely acknowledging the obvious superiority of maturity to immaturity, of experience to inexperience, of age's wisdom to youth's ardent spirits. Jane Austen underlines this point by presenting the contrasting history of another sensible woman, who, at the age of nineteen, put her confidence in a dashing, handsome, high-spirited young man. " 'I, too, became excessively pleased with Mr. Elliot,' " says Mrs. Smith; " 'and entertained the highest opinion of him. *At nineteen, you know, one does not think very seriously,* but Mr. Elliot appeared to me quite as good as others, and much more agreeable than most others, and we were always together' " (italics mine). And it was her and her husband's excessive faith in Mr. Elliot that led to their downfall: "Mr. Elliot had led his friend into expenses much beyond his fortune. . . . And the Smiths accordingly had been ruined."

As the event decides, Wentworth's luck vindicates Anne's confidence in him. But Jane Austen constantly emphasizes that his rise to wealth and social prominence resulted from luck alone, and she leads the reader again and again to speculate, "Yes, but what would have happened *if?*. . . " Clearly, Wentworth's success exceeded rational expectations: "The actual results of their case, . . . as it happened, would have bestowed earlier prosperity than could be reasonably calculated upon." This Wentworth himself thoroughly understands. The role of good fortune provides him with his principal thesis when he describes his naval career to Anne's friends, the Musgroves. His gaining command of his first ship, the *Asp,* was a matter of sheer luck, as his brother-in-law, Admiral Croft, points out:

> "Lucky fellow to get her!—He knows there must have been twenty better men than himself applying for her at the same time. Lucky fellow to get anything so soon, with no more interest than his."

> "I felt my luck, Admiral, I assure you;" replied Captain Wentworth, seriously.

Wentworth points out that the *Asp,* a leaky old tub, could not have survived a storm at sea, yet there were only two unquiet days the whole time he commanded her. Then, on his return to England, after, as he puts it, " 'I had the good luck . . . to fall in with the very French frigate I wanted,' " there was " 'another instance of luck. We had not been six hours in the Sound, when a gale came on, which lasted four days and nights, which would have done for poor old *Asp,* in half the time. . . . Four-and-twenty hours later, and I should only have been a gallant Captain Wentworth, in a small paragraph at one corner of the newspapers'." Anne shudders as she imagines the grim possibility. His luck being different, Wentworth would be dead. As he describes his career, Wentworth compares it with that of Captain Harville, whose merits of character, one learns later in the book, would seem to make him worthy of a more fortunate fate. " 'Poor Harville, sister! You know how much he wanted money—worse than myself. *He had a wife.* . . . I wished for him again the next summer when I had still the same luck in the Mediterranean' " (italics mine). The reference to Harville might well lead the reader to speculate on the probabilities if Wentworth,

too, had had a wife; what if Anne had married him, and the *Asp* had gone down in a storm? Probably she could not have returned to her father, who had professed the resolution "of doing nothing for his daughter" if she went through with the "degrading alliance." And what could she have expected from Lady Russell, once she had rebelled against her prudent authority? Had Anne married Wentworth, only providential circumstance and the good will of people she had offended would have separated her from the condition of Mrs. Smith, a young widow, by accident a cripple, almost penniless, and with literally no one to rely on for help or protection. Mrs. Smith serves as a kind of metaphor for one of the possible extreme consequences of Anne's and Wentworth's alliance. Wentworth's luck being different, the event could as easily have vindicated Lady Russell.

Furthermore, the Wentworth we see in action as the story progresses reveals the very headstrong impetuosity which so frightened Lady Russell. Near the end of the novel he describes his history to Anne, and just as Anne's judgment of herself becomes ours, we also accept his evaluation of his behavior. Still loving Anne "unconsciously, nay unintentionally," but deeply hurt by her refusal of him, and motivated by the angry pride which resulted, he had paid attentions to willful, heedless Louisa Musgrove. The two of them, along with Anne, had made part of the larger party which visited the seaside town of Lyme, where Louisa, as a result of her stubbornness and Wentworth's neglect of his responsibility to be firm and resolute, suffered her almost fatal fall: "She fell on the pavement of the Lower Cobb, and was taken up lifeless! There was no wound, no blood, no visible bruise; but her eyes were closed, she breathed not, her face was like death.—The horror of that moment to all who stood around!" In this horrible moment, only Anne behaved calmly and sensibly, and Wentworth, as he later tells us, suddenly saw what he had done: "There, he had seen everything to exalt in his estimation the woman he had lost, and there begun to deplore *the pride, the folly, the madness of resentment,* which had kept him from trying to regain her when thrown in his way" (italics mine). Wentworth later asks Anne if she would have married him had he proposed after his triumphant return from war, and she implies that she would have. " 'Good God!' he cried, 'you would! It is not that I did not think of it, or desire it, as what could alone crown all my other success. But I was too proud, too proud to ask again. I did not understand you. I shut my eyes, and would not understand you, or do you justice'." Lady Russell's estimation of Wentworth, then, was not altogether wrong. His own evaluation of himself corroborates her judgment. There *was* something "dangerous" in his character. He *was* "brilliant," he *was* "headstrong."

What Jane Austen presents here is the material for domestic tragedy. Lady Russell's advice to Anne is based as much on sound judgment of character as on prejudice, and only the events which follow, brought about by unpredictable luck, prove her wrong. Anne had to choose between two conflicting "goods": her love—her heart's confidence in Wentworth—on the one hand, and on the other, her obligation to respect the one sensitive, loving, mature person in her acquainceship. She makes the just and prudent choice, the choice which will leave her conscience free from stain; but, as events turn out, she makes the wrong choice, for it results in almost tragic suffering, waste, and isolation. Anne Elliot is the person in this book most deserving of what makes life meaningful: human love, based on respect and understanding, and fulfilled through marriage. Yet she is the person who at the beginning seems destined to the least love. Her vain and foolish father and sister ignore her, and virtually throw her out of the family to make room for the unscrupulous Mrs. Clay. Her sister Mary and the Musgrove clan treat her with the respect and affection which we all have for competent and selfless human beings whom we can exploit; none has the power to love her as she deserves. Even Lady Russell lacks the full imaginative sympathy to feel what Anne feels, and the discernment to see what Anne sees.

The drawing-room scene in Chapter VI (Vol. I) provides a moving image of Anne's isolation. As usual, she is being exploited. She plays the piano as the others dance, and she plays with a grace and delicacy which she alone is capable of properly evaluating. While the others engage in a conventional form of amorous play, the member of the group who is, in the highest sense, the most eligible to be a participant, makes the music without which there could be no dancing. No one present is able to appreciate that the intrinsic value of her playing exceeds the value of the rather trivial function which has brought it about. "Excepting one short period of her life, she had never, since the age of fourteen, never since the loss of her dear mother, known the happiness of being listened to, or encouraged by any just appreciation of real taste. In music she had been always used to feel alone in the world." The key words in this passage describe what appears to be the inevitable pattern of her future: ". . . never . . . never . . . known the happiness. . . . always . . . alone in the world. . . . " The "one short period," of course, was Wentworth's courtship. Only Wentworth, precisely because of his wit, his ardor, and the magnitude of his personality revealed through his pride, has the power to understand and love an Anne Elliot—has the ability to save her from her tragic isolation. Jane Austen underlines the point in Chapter VIII (Vol. I), while describing Anne's and Wentworth's cold, polite drawing-room conversations at the Musgroves:

> They had no conversation together, no intercourse but what the commonest civility required. Once so much to each other! Now nothing. There *had* been a time, when of all the large party now filling the drawing-room at Uppercross, they would have found it most difficult to cease to speak to one another. With the exception, perhaps, of Admiral and Mrs. Croft, who seemed particularly attached and happy, (Anne could allow no other exception even among the married couples) there could have been no two hearts so open, no tastes so similar, no feelings so in unison, no countenances so beloved. Now they were as strangers; nay, worse than strangers, for they could never become acquainted. It was a perpetual estrangement.

It is important to note the emphasis on the precariousness of marriage. The slim chances of discovering strong, lasting love, based on compatibility of character and equality of intellectual and moral worth, make Anne's rejection of Wentworth seem all the more devastating and wasteful. She had her one chance, and she chose—she *wisely chose*—perpetual estrangement.

Wentworth's return eventually averts this tragedy, but in the meantime chance alone prevents his pride and foolishness from making matters worse. Louisa's accident causes him to realize that he still loves Anne; but it also brings him up abruptly to the chilling awareness that his attentions to Louisa make him honor-bound to marry her, even though he had not proposed. " 'I was no longer at my own disposal. I was hers in honour if she wished it. I had been unguarded. I had not thought seriously on this subject before. I had not considered that my excessive intimacy must have its danger of ill consequences in many ways'." One asks, what were the possible ill consequences which Wentworth failed to foresee? Most obviously there would have been misery and frustration for both Wentworth and Louisa as a result of their very real disparity of character. Certainly Anne's dreadful isolation would have been perpetuated—or would it? Jane Austen raises the possibility of a worse consequence: Anne might have submitted to the terrible mismatch with the scoundrel William Elliot, as she herself realizes. "Anne could just acknowledge within herself such a possibility of having been induced to marry him, as made her shudder at the idea of the misery which must have followed. It was just possible that she might have been persuaded by Lady Russell! And under such a supposition, which would have been most miserable, when time had disclosed all, too late?" However, Mrs. Smith, and not time, disclosed all before it was too late. But would Mrs. Smith have exposed Elliot had she not been convinced by Anne's behavior of her interest in another man? Probably not. " 'My dear,' was Mrs. Smith's reply, 'there was nothing else to be done. I considered your marrying him as certain, . . . and I could no more speak the truth of him, than if he had been your husband'." Jane Austen continually leads her readers to speculations on the possibilities of ill consequences. Yet the evils are always averted. Wentworth is "released from Louisa by the astonishing and felicitous intelligence of her engagement with Benwick," he proposes to Anne, she accepts him, and we are to understand that they will live happily ever after—or are we? Do not the last sentences of the book raise another dark possibility? "Anne was tenderness itself, and she had the full worth of it in Captain Wentworth's affection. His profession was all that could ever make her friends wish that tenderness less; the dread of future war all that could dim her sunshine."

Luck, then, is the prime instrument for averting disaster in this novel. Only Wentworth's good fortune puts him in the position of wealth and social prominence that enables him to court Anne a second time. It takes Louisa's accident to bring home to him the foolishness and stubbornness of his pride. Benwick's "astonishing and felicitous" proposal comes almost as a miracle to free him from his bonds to Louisa, so that he can pay his attentions to Anne, and prevent her possible alliance with William Elliot. But how is one to interpret this luck? What final effects does it have on the reader?

It seems to me there are two ways of looking at it. The first is to see **Persuasion** as an affirmation of Providence, of the notion that the very nature of things is permeated with value and so structured as to serve out to each individual the rewards and punishments which are his due. For example, the three marriages and one shady liaison which result from the novel's action illustrate an almost providential justice. In each case, the couple represents a just union of equals. The Henrietta Musgrove-Charles Hayter match, though seriously threatened by Wentworth's heedless toying with both Musgrove sisters, does finally occur, and in it one sees social, and, as far as one can infer from scanty information, moral and intellectual equals unite. The case of Louisa and Benwick is more interesting. At first their marriage seems incongruous. "The high-spirited, joyous, talking Louisa Musgrove, and the dejected, thinking, feeling, reading Captain Benwick, seemed each of them everything that would not suit the other. Their minds most dissimilar!" Yet Anne quickly comes to understand the affair: "Louisa, just recovering from illness, had been in an interesting state, and Captain Benwick was not inconsolable." In fact, Louisa's capricious high spirits are equitably matched by a trait in Benwick's character: his inconstancy. Saddened by Benwick's ability to rebound so quickly from the death of his fiancée, the good Captain Harville puts his finger on the weakness: "'Poor Fanny! she would not have forgotten him so soon!'" Benwick quickly forgets the past, as do the Elliots, for whom "the past was nothing," although, ironically, their only claim to distinction is hereditary title. Benwick forgets his Fanny and Louisa forgets her Wentworth just as Sir Walter and Elizabeth forget the pain caused them by William Elliot (who contemplates marriage too soon after the death of his wife), and the pain they have caused to Captain Wentworth. It is only Anne and Wentworth for whom the past lives in the present—who find they cannot change their natures as quickly as they would like: they cannot forget one another. Benwick, then, in every way socially qualified to be a fit match for Louisa, also shares with her a weakness in moral fiber. Little need be said about Mrs. Clay and William Elliot. It seems only proper that the novel's two corrupt, black-hearted scoundrels, shrewd and discerning though they are, should wind up in one another's clutches.

The fitness of Anne and Wentworth for each other raises two important questions. One must first ask, How it is that Wentworth, after foolishly almost causing such suffering to so many people, can be said to deserve Anne? The answer suggested by the book is that through his own suffering Wentworth does penance for his errors, comes to see himself and his actions in their true light, and purges himself of his pride and anger. He points out at the end of the book that after Louisa's accident "his penance had become severe"; he suffered "horror and remorse." He has had an experience, he says, "'which ought to make me forgive everyone sooner than myself'." He comes to the realization, in fact, that he does *not* deserve Anne, and this he explains with characteristic wit and irony: "'I have valued myself on honourable toils and just rewards. Like other great men under reverses . . . I must endeavour to subdue my mind to fortune. I must learn to brook being happier than I deserve'." Tragic heroes undergo reverses which bring them partially underserved suffering. In contrast, Providence seems to be rewarding Wentworth with an only partially earned happiness, and his awareness of this fact makes him the more deserving. After being convinced of his sin, and after having purged himself of his anger, Wentworth goes through something akin to Christian salvation—which no man fully deserves. The salvation provided for Wentworth, of course, is Anne; and now one must face another question: What justifies Anne's eight years of suffering between Wentworth's first and second proposals? We already know part of the answer: she gets a better Wentworth. Eight years previous he was, indeed, "dangerous," "brilliant," "headstrong"; but, because of his experience with Louisa, he is now more flexible, malleable, humble—more mature. Furthermore, Wentworth gets a better Anne. Instead of a young girl swept off her feet by ardent confidence in a dashing, handsome naval officer, he gets a mature, experienced woman, who is fully able to see and feel all the reasons that he is the fit agent of her worldly happiness. Jane Austen herself justifies the eight years of suffering in her description of the first meeting between the two after Wentworth, in a desperate and humiliating act, poured forth his heart in the letter to Anne: "There they exchanged again those feelings and those promises which had once before seemed to secure every thing, but which had been followed by so many, many years of division and estrangement. There they returned again into the past, more exquisitely happy, perhaps, in their re-union, than when it had been first projected; more tender, more tried, more fixed in a knowledge of each other's character, truth, and attachment; more equal to act, more justified in acting." "More justified in acting"! Justice has held back in order to strengthen itself.

In the beginning of the last chapter, there is a discussion of Elizabeth Elliot's change in attitude towards her brother-in-law-to-be: "Captain Wentworth, with five-and-twenty thousand pounds, and as high in his profession as merit and activity could place him, was no longer nobody. He was now esteemed quite worthy to address the daughter of a foolish, spendthrift baronet, who had not had the principle or sense enough to maintain himself in the situation in which Providence had placed him." It is true that the primary intent of this passage is to contrast Wentworth's "merit and activity" with Sir Walter's wastefulness. Yet it also includes the implication that Providence has had its part in putting Wentworth where he is, too, and that because he is aware that his rewards exceed his just deserts, he will have the principle and sense to guard his blessings with great care. It would seem at least partially valid to claim that behind what appears to be blind luck is the hand of Providence, dealing out just rewards and punishments, bringing good out of apparent evil, and happiness out of suffering.

And yet this view is not entirely satisfying. The frequency with which the novel leads to the brink of disaster, and the blatancy with which chance occurrences save the day suggest another interpretation. The way Jane Austen salvages Mrs. Smith from a life of perpetually straitened circumstances through the device of the West Indies property illustrates a larger effect of the book—an almost *deus ex machina* effect. Mrs. Smith herself is a case in point. Almost every commentator has found her to be mechanical and flat. O. W. Firkins [in his *Jane Austen,* 1920] sees her as playing a "perfunctory rôle . . . adumbrated in the name of Smith." Mary Lascelles [in her *Jane Austen and Her Art,* 1939] points out that, although the other characters of the book are appropriately integrated into the action, Mrs. Smith's entrance is entirely unexpected: "The episode of Mrs. Smith . . . is not neatly joined *at the end* of the narrative. . . . Mr. Elliot had been well prepared for; Mrs. Smith had omitted even to leave her washing-bills in an earlier chapter." Marvin Mudrick [see Further Reading] notices the same weakness: "Mrs. Smith does nothing but provide the facts of his [Elliot's] perfidy. Her presence is too useful, her story too pat in its corroboration of Anne." Elizabeth Jenkins [in her *Jane Austen,* 1949] finally, finds Mrs. Smith's narrative to be "a piece of machinery which has not been softened into life." Probably most readers will react similarly. Yet it is difficult to believe that a writer as skillful as Jane Austen, who, even in a first draft, could create characters as lively and convincing as the Elliots, the Musgroves, the Crofts and the Harvilles, did not *intend* to achieve the effect produced in Mrs. Smith. Why choose the name Smith, and have a character expatiate on its commonness at such length as Sir Walter does, if not to "adumbrate" the perfunctory quality of her appearance? Jane Austen has conceived of Mrs. Smith with considerable care; as my earlier comments suggest, her career contains important parallels and contrasts with Anne's. It seems odd that Jane Austen would have omitted devoting equal care to preparing for Mrs. Smith if she had not wanted to. Already in the second chapter she mentions Anne's unpleasant school career in Bath; it would have been easy to mention the childhood friend who had made it almost endurable for her. Elizabeth Jenkins, after describing Jane Austen's general practices in revising, claims that "it would require alterations of a much more radical nature than these [minor changes in style to add polish and luster] to bring up the story of Mrs. Smith to the level of Jane Austen's characteristic writing." Jane Austen *did* make a thorough revision—"alterations of a radical nature"—of the ending of the novel: *of that part immediately following Mrs. Smith's narration.* Yet she did nothing to enliven that narration, and she left Mrs. Smith unprepared for. It is not altogether unlikely that Jane Austen was aware of the somewhat contrived, mechanical effect Mrs. Smith makes, and that she was willing to let it stand; possibly, she intended it.

For the effect of Mrs. Smith's appearance is entirely consistent with the effects of other fortuitous circumstances in the book. Mrs. Smith is something like a goddess who descends on stage at a crucial moment to avert catastrophe. Likewise, the French frigate which so felicitously crosses Wentworth's path, the useful Captain Benwick, the happy circumstance of the West Indies property—all have the quality of convenient machinery lowered from above to bring about the happy ending to a bad situation. And as in skillfully handled *deus ex machina* endings, the effect is to drive home to the audience that the pleasing results are only the products of the writer's fantasy, designed to fulfill unrealistic human wishes. In the end of Gay's *Beggar's Opera,* the Player objects, "The catastrophe is manifestly wrong, for an opera must end happily." The Beggar replies,

> Your objection, sir, is very just and is easily removed. For you must allow that in this kind of drama 'tis no matter how absurdly things are brought about.—So—you rabble there—run and cry a reprieve!—let the prisoner be brought back to his wives in triumph.
>
> PLAYER. All this we must do, to comply with the taste of the town.

In order to preserve the expected comic form of the opera, Gay uses theatrical gimmickry to save his hero, whose inevitable destiny, by realistic standards, is defeat and death. He can end the story the way people want it to end, for he knows that his audience understands his work to be art, not life. Furthermore, the writer who lowers gods from the flies commits such absurdities to elucidate what Brecht makes explicit in his version of Gay's opera: *"Die reitenden Boten des Königs kommen sehr selten."* By bringing messengers from the king so arbitrarily and unexpectedly on stage, the writer emphasizes that in the normal course of things they probably would not come. Likewise, by pointing out that the storm providentially held back while Wentworth was at sea in the *Asp,* Jane Austen makes us see that in the normal course of things Wentworth might very well have drowned. The felicitous French frigate reminds us of how infrequently such strokes of luck occur. By contriving unexpected circumstances to save a man who has behaved like a fool from marrying the woman he has recklessly involved himself with, Jane Austen emphasizes an even more likely consequence of such a situation without bringing it about; very seldom does a love-sick Benwick show up in precisely the right place at precisely the right time. The surprising appearance of the West Indies property serves to remind us that only good luck can prevent the Mrs. Smiths of this world, whose improvident, short-sighted husbands leave them penniless, from spending the rest of their lives in poverty; and yet Mrs. Smith gets the reward she deserves. Finally, this whole chain of fortuitous events helps dramatize that the Anne Elliots, once having refused the offers of the men they love, may very likely not get a second chance, no matter how virtuous, loving, or constant they are; yet *our* Anne Elliot marries her Wentworth after all. The disparity between the phenomenal good luck of the characters of *Persuasion*—they seem almost to be protected by the gods—and what their destinies would be if events took their normal course, serves to emphasize the dark possibilities of human life—to emphasize them without actually bringing them about. Chance and fortuitous circumstance in *Persuasion* can be seen as Jane Austen's means for creating tragic effect while preserving comic form.

The two interpretations suggested here are not, however, irreconcilable. *Persuasion* is not a work *either* of triumphant affirmation *or* of dark questioning; it is both. It gives us long, fearful looks at the possible ill consequences of human pride and folly—nay, of even the best-intentioned, clearest-sighted human judgments—long, fearful looks which make us shudder as Anne so often does; for we know that these "possibilities" are what in real life would be the probabilities—such probabilities as only good fortune or Providence could prevent. And on the other hand, it helps us know that no matter how fearfully complex and precarious our world can be, evil is evil, and good is good; that Anne deserves her Wentworth and Wentworth deserves his Anne, despite the slim likelihood that in reality they would ever get one another. In itself, this knowledge is affirmation. (pp. 179-95)

Paul N. Zietlow, "Luck and Fortuitous Circumstance in 'Persuasion': Two Interpretations," in ELH, *Vol. 32, No. 2, June, 1965, pp. 179-95.*

Andor Gomme   (essay date 1966)

[*In the following excerpt, Gomme seeks to demonstrate that* Persuasion *is flawed by inconsistencies in plot and characterization.*]

Persuasion was not published in Jane Austen's lifetime. Though the existing manuscripts of the last chapters show that she did some careful revision, and indeed rewrote one chapter completely, there is evidence that the book we have is not quite the book she would have finally preferred to give us, and it may well have endured the attentions of Gifford, the rather too eager publisher's reader. Yet it seems to be pretty generally agreed that, had Jane Austen lived to give it more attention herself, she would have done little to it apart from some polishing here and there: she might—to take one example—have reduced the evidently overlong and repetitive list of conflicting confidences which Anne receives from various members of the Musgrove family in Chapter 6, a collection which seems to have been hastily gathered together so that later a selection could be made. This and a few other passages would have been refined, one or two comments sharpened perhaps, but the book would have remained substantially as we have it now.

This is the commonly accepted view: it has the support of the revisions—extensive, yet closely attentive to detail—which can be followed in the surviving manuscripts, though we need not take Jane Austen's 'Finis' too seriously (she certainly made substantial alterations after writing the word once). In his recent study of the literary manuscripts, B. C. Southam has shown how much the conclusion of the book was improved by the almost total rewriting of the penultimate chapter [see Further Reading]. The tone of this chapter, Mr. Southam claims, is now much more in harmony with that of the rest of the book: the suggestion inevitably seems to be that a nearly perfect book has now been given its perfect conclusion. And the very high valuation of the novel implied by Mr. Southam's account is also common form. Thus (on the cover of the edition I have to hand) Professor Daiches [see Further Reading] is quoted as calling **Persuasion** 'the novel which in the end the experienced reader of Jane Austen puts at the head of the list'. Experienced readers are of course of many kinds: I believe that **Persuasion** has been a particular favourite with the Janeites, but it is doubtful how much comfort it should bring to *them*. It has, for instance, what is surely the most unpleasant episode in all Jane Austen's

writings—the early link between Captain Wentworth and the Musgroves, of which this summary is representative:

> The real circumstances of this pathetic piece of family history were, that the Musgroves had had the ill fortune of a very troublesome, hopeless son; and the good fortune to lose him before he reached his twentieth year; that he had been sent to sea, because he was stupid and unmanageable on shore; that he had been very little cared for at any time by his family, though quite as much as he deserved; seldom heard of, and scarcely at all regretted, when the intelligence of his death abroad had worked its way to Uppercross, two years before.

> He had, in fact, though his sisters were now doing all they could for him, by calling him 'poor Richard', been nothing better than a thick-headed, unfeeling, unprofitable Dick Musgrove, who had never done anything to entitle himself to more than the abbreviation of his name, living or dead. (Chapter 6)

So Dick Musgrove was unfeeling; and what more, in the circumstances, can be said for his author? For sheer callousness I know no parallel in Jane Austen. Moreover it seems to be calculated, for the mockery rubs off on Wentworth, who allows himself the indulgence of a 'curl of his handsome mouth' at the absurdity of Mrs. Musgrove's wishing that Dick had never left his ship. (Of course, he is gentleman enough not to let anyone but Anne and the reader see it: but then the others were all 'unobservant and incurious'.) And Jane Austen makes sure that we register this offensive little piece by ending it with a relishing sneer at Mrs. Musgrove's fatness:

> Personal size and mental sorrow have certainly no necessary proportions. A large bulky figure has as good a right to be in deep affliction, as the most graceful set of limbs in the world. But, fair or not fair, there are unbecoming conjunctions, which reason will patronise in vain,—which taste cannot tolerate,—which ridicule will seize. (Chapter 8)

This lack of 'tolerance' is a failure of taste which can only be compared with Emma's heartless joke at Miss Bates's dullness—a joke for which Jane Austen (in the person of Mr. Knightley) fiercely reproves her.

A novel which contains such things as this beneath its bland surface cannot be altogether plain sailing. But though I find **Persuasion** a disturbing novel, this is not in a particularly profitable sense of the word. It is in fact a peculiarly delicate subject for literary analysis, calling upon the reader to exercise the utmost sensitivity in judgment, which nevertheless it often contrives to affront. The novel is in parts so fine, seems constantly to offer so much and finally to realise something so at variance with what appears to be its chief intention that a single all-encompassing judgment seems to me out of the question. I believe that as high a valuation as that of Professor Daiches is indefensible: **Persuasion** is badly flawed; but the weakness is the weakness of a sketch in which Jane Austen has not found the opportunity to develop her own most serious interests. In calling it a sketch, I do not want to be taken as holding that, had she lived, she would in fact have entirely rewritten the book: the detailed revisions we can see do not make this very plausible. I use the word simply to indicate the character that the published version seems to me to have.

Incomplete as it is, however, it is at times a work of characteristic genius: no-one but Jane Austen could have written it. I shall take these qualities of genius largely for granted, but some instances have a direct bearing on the peculiarities of the book that interest me here: what it is that makes it in the end so worrying and even frustrating. There is, for example, the expert precision with which in a few lines Jane Austen establishes the essential qualities of Charles Musgrove, while at the same time making plain not only how decisively he demonstrates Anne's superiority to Mary (why, that is, Charles would not have done for *her*) but also Anne's unconceited recognition of her superiority:

> Charles Musgrove was civil and agreeable; in sense and temper he was undoubtedly superior to his wife, but not of powers, or conversation, or grace to make the past, as they were connected together, at all a dangerous contemplation; though, at the same time, Anne could believe, with Lady Russell, that a more equal match might have greatly improved him; and that a woman of real understanding might have given more consequence to his character, and more usefulness, rationality, and elegance to his habits and pursuits. (Chapter 6)

Each word here is chosen with wonderful justness and precision, its meaning exactly weighed so that the total effect is extraordinarily telling: so much is done so simply and so entirely without redundancies. Charles is, in fact, extremely well done throughout, one of the book's clear successes: we are given, with complete clarity and directness not only what such a person counts for in himself, but how he stands to be affected and limited by the people with whom he associates.

Again, in the scenes at Lyme, there is the superb economy and delicacy with which we are shown just how much finer Anne is than all the others present: we recognise that this excellence, which reveals itself in her being the only one able to think or act coherently after Louisa's accident, is the natural gift of one who is both so intelligent and characteristically so spontaneous and open in her sympathy. Self-centredness and self-pity choke the others and prevent their acting when action is most needed; but Anne is perfectly capable just because she is completely unselfish. She agrees to stay and nurse Louisa partly at least because she knows she will do it better than anyone else; and we accept without scruple her right to feel so. The quietness with which Anne's fineness of character is revealed, both to us and to Wentworth, may conceal for a time the importance of these scenes in showing Wentworth what Anne really is like and what she means to him; but if we return to them from Wentworth's own self-examination at the end of the book, we find that his sudden realisation of her qualities is the mark of a marvellously clear (though unostentatious) psychological discrimination on Jane Austen's part.

Anne, attending with all the strength, and zeal, and thought, which instinct supplied, to Henrietta, still tried, at intervals, to suggest comfort to the others, tried to quiet Mary, to animate Charles, to assuage the feelings of Captain Wentworth. Both seemed to look to her for directions.

'Anne, Anne', cried Charles, 'what is to be done next? What, in Heaven's name, is to be done next?'

Captain Wentworth's eyes were also turned towards her.

'Had not she better be carried to the inn? Yes, I am sure: carry her gently to the inn.'

'Yes, yes, to the inn', repeated Captain Wentworth, comparatively collected, and eager to be doing something. (Chapter 12)

That the appeal should come *to* Anne, *from* Charles could not fail to make its mark on Wentworth (who already knows that she had refused Charles's proposal) and should not fail to make it on the reader.

In these scenes Anne seems to me a wonderful creation. But in the book as a whole she is a much less telling figure than she might be, because the social—and to some extent the personal—setting in which her story is played out is little more than roughed in, and sometimes crudely at that. There are, I think, clear signs of haste—it is hardly fair to call it carelessness—in the mechanics of the plot, most obviously, no doubt, in the invention of Mrs. Smith. Admittedly she has an important and well-realised function in providing the occasion for a display of the vicious side of Sir Walter's snobbery (Chapter 17); and her own excellence makes an interesting (though not fully explored) reflexion on certain other attitudes in the book: she had 'that elasticity of mind, that disposition to be comforted, that power of turning readily from evil to good, and of finding employment which carried her out of herself, which was from Nature alone' (Chapter 17). One thinks of Anne herself, who accepts her friend's courage a little too glibly. But the coincidence of Mrs. Smith's previous relationship with Mr. Elliot is altogether too clumsily handled—it is a mere convenience for giving us information about him which the author needs us to have but which, to make its proper effect, ought to be revealed within the action of the book. As it is, the two sides of Elliot's character are no more than asserted, and we have scarcely any good reason for believing that they belong to the same man. It is not that there is necessarily a conflict between what we *see* of him in the present and what we are *told* of him in the past: there is no difficulty in interpreting his plausible conversation as that of a clever and designing hypocrite (and Anne, we know, has had her suspicions all along). But the interpretation does not compel itself, and it is not enough that we should simply be informed that that is how things are. It is part of the essential evidence for Anne's shrewdness and her superior moral intelligence (in contrast to the willingness to follow and accept appearances which characterises not only the rest of her family but Lady Russell as well) that she should not be taken in by Elliot's superficial charm; and so it is important that we should know what makes her see what she does. In her case, clear-sightedness is little more than caution deriving from the presence of Wentworth and her own disinclination to discount the past: she is one of the very few people in the book who allow themselves to be guided by past experience; but with regard to Elliot's present appearance, the explanation of *his* past is arbitrary.

The case of Mrs. Clay is similar: in what we see of her she is perhaps more obviously a hypocrite than Elliot, but we still have to take her wickedness very much on trust. This is especially unfortunate since an accurate reading of Mrs. Clay's character and intentions is one of the few unambiguous signs we are given of the wisdom of Lady Russell on which so much hangs. Lady Russell's severity is not quite single-minded: she thinks the friendship between Mrs. Clay and Elizabeth 'quite out of place', but this is due at least as much to her exaggerated respect for situation as to her understanding of character, for which, again, the evidence is wanting in Mrs. Clay. The eventual unmasking of her collusion with Elliot is scarcely prepared for by that one glimpse that Anne has, and it looks too much like a hurried attempt to get rid of two inconvenient figures (giving us, of course, another—not very convincing—demonstration of how bad he is). It is an important difference between their elopement and Henry Crawford's running off with Maria Rushworth in **Mansfield Park** that we see Henry's unsteadiness—and Maria's headstrong selfishness—affecting their character and actions throughout.

Likewise, though Jane Austen's keen observation and keen wit make admirable use of it (see Mary's letter in Chapter 18 and Anne's subsequent musing), Benwick's sudden engagement to Louisa is surely a confession that she can think of no more satisfactory way to get Wentworth out of a hole. The point is not very important, for Wentworth's and the reader's registration of Anne's complete superiority to Louisa is already made; but the novelist with more time at her disposal might have made more of it. To place Wentworth in the position of having to decide between making an unequal (and inevitably unhappy) match and having to undeceive Louisa himself might have led to a moral probing almost more searching than any in the book. One would indeed have liked to see him made more uncomfortable through his carelessness than in fact he is. At the same time, while there is nothing in the least wrong with Jane Austen's surprising us (as she surprises her other people), if she could have made us feel later that the engagement had, after all, a kind of inevitability, that it was the natural outcome of such affections as Louisa and Benwick would share (for Anne's meditations are not quite enough to give us this sense), the real distinction of Anne's and Wentworth's feelings might have been more incisively brought home: it is these, after all, that really matter.

These faults are relatively minor: they could be eliminated without dislocation of the book. A miscalculation, if it could be proved, over Sir Walter or Lady Russell would be a more serious matter. On Sir Walter I find it hard to make up my mind. He is presented in something very near caricature—as, in different ways, are Mr. Woodhouse or Mrs. Norris. Yet, except on the opening page and fitfully

in the first two or three chapters, he does not live as they do: he seems much more than they just a target set up for Jane Austen's scorn. She places him with a brilliance that drives her withering contempt quite home: 'Few women could think more of their personal appearance than he did, nor could the valet of any new-made lord be more delighted with the place he held in society.' (Chapter I)

Such a phrase reveals just *how* contemptible is his fawning on his titled cousins, so vividly and with such penetration that no later elaborations add anything essential to our understanding of him. There are times when the sarcasm appears too easy and when what we have is virtually a lampoon; but it seems that Sir Walter is a man with no redeeming features at all: he is vain, conceited and ridiculous; and his faults lead him easily into the peculiarly spiteful cruelty which characterises the lower reaches of moral blindness and stupidity. What can be said in favour of such a man? Yet it is surely of some importance that he should not be merely an object to scoff at. For we find that, after his very nasty outburst about Mrs. Smith (Chapter 17), Anne is kept from speaking her mind by 'her sense of personal respect for her father'. That Anne should stop short of telling her father what she thinks of him is understandable; that by this time she should feel a *respect* which is *personal* for the man he has been shown to be is not. Moreover, he is the chief—very nearly the only—representative in the book of a sense of social standing which Jane Austen by no means found simply contemptible. She gently mocks Lady Russell's inflated respect for the dignity of a baronet; but we cannot dismiss altogether Lady Russell's sense of what is due, if not to Sir Walter's person, at least to what he represents: she was, we are told (Chapter 2), 'as solicitous for the credit of the family and as aristocratic in her ideas of what was due to them, as anybody of sense and honesty could well be'. But she remains to her author a woman of sense and honesty, and her opinions are always to be taken seriously. What then can we say of her respect for an institution whose sole representative in the action presented to us is a specimen as silly, as abject, as Sir Walter, at whose own subservience to the even higher dignity of a peerage Anne herself can only feel ashamed?

The miscalculation here is closely connected with a more serious one affecting Lady Russell, against whom the case that can be made is, I think, clear and damaging. Though she plays so small a part in the action, Lady Russell is in a sense the fulcrum of **Persuasion.** She has a place in each of the worlds of Anne and of her father without belonging wholly to either, having more respect for form and position than the one, and a great deal more discernment than the other; the whole action of the book depends from a decision and recommendation which she made eight years before, and much of the moral interest of the later part centres on whether it was right that Anne should have submitted her judgment to that of her older friend. She represents—impressively, we are to feel—the virtues of restraint and good sense, virtues very much at the heart of the author's concern. Any uncertainty here, then is likely to have grave effects on the coherence of attitude that one may reasonably look for in the book as a whole. I think it can be demonstrated that Jane Austen's attitude to Lady

Russell is in fact ambiguous, and I believe this is a result of her not having, in this unfinished state of the novel, made up her own mind on the exact part which Lady Russell was to play.

To take a small issue first: Lady Russell thinks that Mrs. Clay's 'situation' makes her a very unequal companion for Elizabeth, while the situation—the not very dissimilar situation (as Anne notes)—of Mrs. Smith hasn't the same effect on *her* suitability as a companion for Anne. True, Mrs. Smith hasn't Mrs. Clay's dangerous character, but Lady Russell would have disapproved of an association even with a blameless Mrs. Clay: it is situation which makes for inequality. The point is perhaps insignificant in itself, but less so when related to other uncertainties in Jane Austen's approach to this person who is unlike a character in the conventional sense of the word and yet seems to play so important a part in settling the author's comparative judgments of actions and characters within her story.

Jane Austen does not, of course, present Lady Russell's judgment as by any means wholly correct—or indeed without its rather absurd side. Her self-confidence is given an ominous note when we hear of her, three years after the decision which seemed to have settled Anne's fortunes for good, 'as satisfied as ever with her own discretion' (Chapter 4). Her reaction to the spontaneous good nature of Admiral Croft, whose manners delighted Anne but 'were not quite of the tone to suit Lady Russell' is obviously not Jane Austen's nor meant to be that of the reader, who is clearly invited throughout the story to identify his judgment with Anne's. But there can be no doubt that Lady Russell has her author's *general* approval: she stands for a restricted view of character and its relation to social forms, which, nevertheless, within its limits, is substantially sound: she was, indeed, 'rather of sound than quick abilities'—which suggests adequate power of generalisation without keen perception of particulars. It remains to the end Anne's belief, and (I am sure) Jane Austen's, that though Lady Russell's advice turned out to be bad advice, and though Anne herself would not, in similar circumstances, give the same advice, Anne was nevertheless right to take it when she did; and there can be no doubt about how, upon the whole, we are meant to regard Lady Russell. Unlike Sir Walter, who is very stupid as well as entirely self-centred, Lady Russell is the kind of person to whom Anne *should* go for guidance. Well, no doubt she was the best that Kellynch had to offer (and young ladies of nineteen were perhaps unused, in Anne's day, to making their own momentous decisions); but her understanding of character is far *too* restricted and her own deference for more or less arbitrary forms too strong to make her a safe guide, so that Anne's respect for her judgment seems out of proportion. Her opinion of character is in fact regularly formed on superficial evidence. And the great result is that she is twice disastrously wrong, about Wentworth and about William Elliot, in circumstances which very nearly bring her protégée to a state of permanent misery. Anne is generous enough to say that the first mistake was of the kind which could only be shown by its effects, but there seems no excuse possible for the relish with which Lady Russell, on quite insufficient knowledge, enters into the general acclamation of Elliot. 'There was nothing less for Lady Russell to do', we read at the end, 'than to admit that she had been pretty completely wrong, and to take up a new set of opinions and of hopes' (Chapter 24). The gesture is bland and disarming; and Anne is obviously far too happy and too generous to reflect on how things very nearly turned out as a result of Lady Russell's advice and complacency. The reader ought to have a keener memory and a more disinterested judgment, and in short is likely to show a good deal less condescension to Lady Russell's errors than she seems to meet from her author.

Perhaps, however, it would be possible to answer that I am here missing the whole point—which, it might on the contrary be claimed, is to establish Lady Russell's deficiencies so decisively that we see Anne's superior intelligence to the point where that intelligence has to be questioned as to its motives in bowing to the advice of such a person. How, for example, about the superb passage (Chapter 19), when Anne, walking with Lady Russell, sees Wentworth on the other side of the street and is 'perfectly conscious of Lady Russell's eyes being turned exactly in the direction for him, of her being, in short, intently observing him'? Anne analyses to herself all the awkward, even humiliating, sensations that Lady Russell must be going through, only to find that what she has been intent on is a set of curtains and that she hasn't been aware of Wentworth at all. The neatness of psychological observation is delightful: one wonders whom to laugh at most—Anne for assuming that everyone must see through her own eyes, or Lady Russell for simply not seeing at all. Jane Austen herself doesn't seem quite sure: 'Anne sighed and blushed and smiled, in pity and disdain, either at her friend or herself'. But if there is something ridiculous in Lady Russell's performance, it would be surely off the author's point to find her standards altogether deplorable: the new opinions that she has now to take up are opinions of particular characters and situations, not fresh general views about propriety, on which she must keep substantially her old position. It is Anne's own experience—so different, we assume, from Lady Russell's—which now moves *her* to say that she will never give such advice as she received. But she still claims that it was right for her to take it when she did.

The effect of this, it seems to me, is to cast doubt on Anne's own judgment of herself and her past actions. Anne has her moments of primness: she is in fact a little too quick to think herself right (though of course she normally is); but it is not really possible to believe that, inexperienced as she was at nineteen, she could convince herself that she broke her engagement for Wentworth's good. Her decision to turn him down is hardly shown in a creditable light by her admitting that she would have married him a year later when he returned to England with 'a few thousand pounds'. Obviously it isn't to be said that in the end Anne was much swayed by Wentworth's money; but the speech in which she explains to him why she would not yield to persuasion in her relations with Elliot comes uncomfortably near to being disingenuous:

> You should have distinguished. . . . You should not have suspected me now; the case so different, and my age so different. If I was wrong

in yielding to persuasion once, remember that it was persuasion exerted on the side of safety, not of risk. When I yielded, I thought it was to duty, but no duty could be called in aid here. In marrying a man indifferent to me, all risk would have been incurred, and all duty violated. (Chapter 23)

This is not the risk she would have incurred eight years before in marrying Wentworth: *then* his uncertain prospects were the risk—for indeed her age was not so very different when his 'few thousand pounds' would apparently have settled everything. Why should Wentworth not suppose now that a settled income, together with an apparent inclination towards Elliot which he had no means of disproving and which he saw encouraged by the person who had so effectively influenced her before, were capable enough now of moving Anne? There are times when she has gone a long way towards capitulating to Lady Russell's standards of judgment.

But the important thing, at the close of the book, is that we should be sure, not of course that Lady Russell gave good advice, but that it was at least sensible, if not entirely right of Anne to submit as she did. The whole must be more than a ridiculous and wearisome mistake. It is very well to say that events proved the advice wrong: what Lady Russell's appearances in the book do not give is enough indication that Anne had good reason to expect that, coming from her, it would be right. To say (as, a little complacently, Anne does) that she now has nothing to reproach herself with implies that all her duty then lay away from the man she loved and towards obeying a person for whose judgment and discretion the reader is by this time likely to have scant respect. And it is one thing to take such advice at nineteen, quite another to congratulate oneself on it at twenty-seven. Wentworth's 'own good' has been entirely dismissed.

The great strength of *Persuasion* is undoubtedly in Anne herself, who is one of Jane Austen's most appealing heroines. It is her association with Lady Russell which makes for its most obvious weakness—an uncertainty, perhaps, in the original intention, which affects our view of all the characters whose actions derive their significance for us from one decision made eight years before the book opens. It seems to me possible to conceive a treatment of the theme in which this uncertainty would have been resolved, and the moral issues made less ambiguous. Even so I cannot believe that *Persuasion* would ever have had the depth of moral interest that there is in *Emma* or in *Mansfield Park.* For while unfortunate effects, like the tendency to smugness observable near the end or the triviality of some of the action, need suggest no more than temporary tiredness or inattention to detail, the general design of the book is simply incapable of allowing for the moral development of character, the discovery and growth of conscience, that make *Emma* so impressive, or for the gradual unfolding of the complexities of involved human relationships, the working out of the effects of human weaknesses, which are the special concern of *Mansfield Park.* The human situation in *Persuasion* is in fact not at all involved; human weaknesses display themselves very much according to predictable pattern; and the only conscience and under-

standing that can be said in any way to grow are Wentworth's—as we hear related in that rather breathless walk up Milsom Street and into the gardens after his final reconciliation with Anne.

Wentworth indeed seems to be nearer than Anne to the centre of moral action in *Persuasion.* So far as there is any process of growth and discovery it is his; yet we are in truth given extremely little of it, though in a more completely worked out novel it might well have been the core of Jane Austen's interest (though it would in that case have been the only instance of her putting a man's consciousness at the centre of a novel). In the book as it is—and short as it is—Wentworth's part is presented in little more than summary: this (very briefly) is how things were with him, this (not much more wholeheartedly) is how they are and how they will become. The story, which seems designed round him, gives little chance for any great evaluation of moral forces through Anne, whose motives, principles and perceptions remain essentially the same throughout; yet it is she whom we see in depth, Wentworth in no more than outline. Correspondingly the action, even for him, is nearly limited to the mere clearing away of misapprehensions; and the events of the second half of the book are made up almost entirely of these. One accident or another reveals a truth which had been hidden or half-hidden (sometimes, as in the case of William Elliot, by a deliberate and unconvincing device of the author's); the net of misunderstandings is removed, and people's eyes are opened to old habits of feeling or new moral impostures. Yet, for all the derangements which upset a too complacently accepted view of the world, there is no-one (with the curiously played-down exception of Wentworth) whose moral character or understanding is more than momentarily affected by what he sees and learns. Nearly all see little and learn less; and in fact there is no other novel of Jane Austen's in which what movement there is is so largely mechanical or haphazard: character is virtually frozen on each first appearance, and human relations either perfectly predictable or quite arbitrary. The whole action takes place under conditions of nearly complete moral stasis: hence perhaps the sense of smugness. It is the kind of thing that might well occur in a blocked-in sketch waiting for detailed working out into something more recognisably human. But many large changes would have been needed before Jane Austen could realise those very different conditions in which her distinctive preoccupation with the morality of character and situation makes its richest return. (pp. 170-83)

Andor Gomme, "On Not Being Persuaded," in Essays in Criticism, *Vol. XVI, No. 2, April, 1966, pp. 170-84.*

Malcolm Bradbury   (essay date 1968)

[*An English novelist and critic, Bradbury is best known as the author of such satiric novels as* Eating People Is Wrong *(1959) and* Stepping Westward *(1965). As a literary critic, he has also written extensively on English and American literature, especially the works of E. M. Forster. In the following excerpt, Bradbury responds to criticism by Andor Gomme (see excerpt above) and oth-*

ers concerning the lack of moral introspection and growth experienced by the protagonists in Persuasion, *arguing that Austen intended to expand her exploration of personal development to include emotional maturation and the role of luck in her characters' lives.*]

Persuasion may indeed be, as Professor Daiches [see Further Reading] has said, 'the novel which in the end the experienced reader of Jane Austen puts at the head of the list', but if this is so it has never really had the kind of critical analysis commensurate with that status. Indeed, Andor Gomme's complaints against the novel in 'On Not Being Persuaded' [see excerpt dated 1966] seem a good deal more typical of critical opinion. Undergraduates generally seem not to like the novel in comparison with Jane Austen's other books, and commonly on the sort of grounds that Andor Gomme invokes: its movement is largely mechanical or haphazard; 'character is frozen on each first appearance, and human relations [are] either perfectly predictable or quite arbitrary'; the whole action takes place under conditions of nearly complete moral stasis, and of the characters only Wentworth (and in an oddly played down way) is more than momentarily affected by what he sees and learns. Thus, it is complained, the central character, Anne Elliot, does not change, and nor really does the hero, Captain Wentworth; this makes it less interesting and genuinely exploratory than, say, **Emma,** where the heroine changes in her moral attitude, or **Pride and Prejudice,** where she is rewarded for her moral quality by changing socially, rising in rank. The result of this absence of change is (at least according to many of my students) that a large part of the book seems simply diversionary, a succession of delaying events holding back the incident we too predictably expect, the marriage of Wentworth and Anne. Further, since the characters develop very little in moral or psychological terms, this conclusion is not brought about by any discovery at any internalized, psychological level—by, say, an inner revelation—but simply by externally artificial means that do no more than provide each party with the real information they need about the feelings of the other. In short, the novel seems to lack the structure which they and other critics in some way suppose necessary to sustain interest in a novel of this sort; certain features of the logical requirements of this kind of structure appear to be missing. Further, **Persuasion** is a book often said to be less convincing than the others in another respect—a novelist whose field is domestic attempts mistakenly to deal with scenes more violent (the scene at Lyme) and more dramatic (Mrs. Smith's story) than is appropriate, and comes off very badly at it. And so if we take as our measure of the worth of a novel of this sort the degree to which the characters alter in attitude or sentiments, discover themselves or suffer radical changes of fortune, or if we regard the full rendering of every event as the measure of a book's interest, **Persuasion** would in each case appear to have something missing.

What happens? An engagement and a love-relationship that has existed in the past has been broken, by interference from outside. It is finally renewed, by luck. A mature heroine grows, perhaps, a few faint gradations in maturity; but we are mostly concerned with misapprehension and suffering that could easily be resolved at almost any point in the action. The very fact that Anne is so stable and sensible means that the incidents that happen to her seem to have little import. She is not upset by losing the family home; why, then, that incident? She is not even upset or changed by the accident at Lyme; it seems to be an unnecessarily violent incident composed by the author to convince us that a person who is strong willed is liable to get into more trouble than one who is, like Anne, persuadable and held within right proportions and limits. She *is* attracted to a dishonest man, but this does not take the action very far, since she is so cautious. Jane Austen's description of Anne as a heroine almost too good for her may itself suggest why the book seems, by this view, thin, since there are few grounds for positive conflict and this tends in turn to create an abstractness of rendering and cause the action to appear as a collection of chance incidents stretching out until all the various mechanical confusions have been put right, and the predictable can happen. Andor Gomme's article, and the discussion of **Persuasion** in Mark Schorer's 'Fiction and the "Analogical Matrix" ' [see excerpt dated 1949], which suggests that there is in the very rhetorical base of the book an attitude and manner of discourse mechanical and calculated (he argues that **Persuasion** has a discourse derived from commerce and property: 'Time is divided, troubles multiply, weeks are calculated, and even a woman's prettiness is reckoned'), thus tend to crystallize a significant order of objection to the book.

In short, the book can be seen as having a compositional structure that is deficient, the standard of success here deriving from a notion either about what kind of fictional development is most effective and convincing for this kind of novel, or, more pragmatically, about what constitutes success in Jane Austen's other novels. But it is clearly possible to propose—and I believe this to be true—that Jane Austen is here trying to create effects that differ from those other novels. Certainly, as in most of the previous novels, she is quite evidently seeking to persuade us that marriage is in various terms the ideal reward for two persons whose maturity as people, whose capacity to act and value, has been shown to us at length and, in this case, over a considerable period of time. Here, as before, marriage is regarded both as an affectionate relationship involving the moral regard of both partners for the other, a recognition of some difference in function and sensibility between male and female, and as a form of stewardship, involving the tending of a household or estate. In previous novels, this view is developed by distinguishing the heroine in numerous details from others who fail to show the appropriate maturity, or else by showing her growing toward that maturity through a succession of events in which she reveals relative success or failure; the events and incidents seem largely to be selected by the novelist with such ends in view. Often, though not necessarily, marriage involves the heroine, who is often, though not necessarily, the point of consciousness from which we survey a considerable part of the action, rising in class. One reason why the choice of events in **Persuasion** seems to us less controlled and consistent seems therefore to be, first, that the heroine does not learn very much or alter in character, so that her 'maturity' can appear rather a species of old age, and, second, that the marriage involves what the sociologists would call

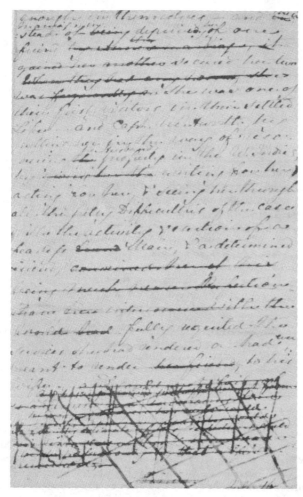

A page from the original manuscript of Persuasion.

downward mobility, so that the fascination of the movement toward social stewardship seems diminished. These two aspects are very much connected, and the connection lies, I think, in Jane Austen's desire to explore two salient forces in her society, two classes in interaction, in a way that she has never chosen to do before. She does this, throughout, within the framework of the domestic novel of marriage, but as each of her novels differs from one another, so this one differs from the rest and moves into dimensions much more elaborate than those we usually associate with her work. This, in turn, leads her into striking differences of narrative method and moral implication, and I think it is only if we grant this that we can effectively question the kind of critique that Andor Gomme makes.

Some of the differences can be suggested by briefly describing the action of **Persuasion.** A young sea-captain, Wentworth, who has no ship and no fortune, and a girl of nineteen, Anne Elliot, from an aristocratic family which has in fact little fortune either, fall in love and wish to get engaged. Anne is dissuaded from this by her father, a man vain and self-conscious about his class, on the grounds that the marriage is degrading; and, more influentially, by a friend of the family, indeed a mother-substitute, Lady Russell, on the grounds that her suitor's expectations are based primarily on his confidence in his future (which seems to her excessive). The suitor departs, and Anne remains at home for six years, somewhat regretting her prudence in being so persuaded, and fading in her looks. The family fortunes deteriorate and Anne's sensible suggestions about retrenchment are ignored. After six years—at a point which coincides with Jane Austen's opening of the 'narrative present', earlier events being told as recollection—the suitor returns at the moment when the family has to let its house and estate to an Admiral who has become wealthy from his profession, though he is without inherited social rank. And Anne's suitor's confidence has been justified; his luck has been good; he is now a Captain in the Navy—and rich. The two move together through a society interlinked both by family connection and by the letting of the house; they meet from time to time, though without seeking to do so. But both have retained their original love, though neither knows that the other has, and Wentworth does not entirely know that he has; so they become more and more divided. But at the same time Anne is growing further and further away from her own family, because of its extravagance in poverty. When Wentworth is drawn towards another woman whose striking characteristic is her strong will, Anne is drawn towards another man who is one of the family and can solve its problems. But circumstances enable Anne and Wentworth to discover that they are still in love, and the action concludes with their marriage and Anne's effective severance from the bonds of her family. So described, with the emphases I have given it, the action seems coherent; it also has elements strikingly different from the other novels, elements which involve Jane Austen as a conscious artist in all sorts of differences of treatment. These differences are, I think, clearly involved in the entire conception of the book, being fundamental to the structure (as one describes it in this abstract way) and in the kind of presentational choices she has in communicating it to us. I will list some of the most important features; Andrew Wright has observed [in his *Jane Austen's Novels: A Study in Structure,* 1957] that the book is marked by a faith in society, and that in Jane Austen's world the measure of a man is not isolation but integration; more recently Richard Poirier has developed a similar point, though with regard primarily to **Emma.** But this is only true of **Persuasion** in a certain sense. For the landowning virtues and responsibilities are not to be had among the class that should embody them, that is, among the Elliots themselves. They are not, however, to be had in a direct sense among the second main group of agents in the novel, the seafarers, with their luck and pluck. Andrew Wright says that Jane Austen is untouched by any awareness of radical social transformation; about this novel, the remark is wrong. For the tension that Anne embodies is, in my view, precisely that of a 'revolutionary' situation, or rather a situation of social transformation. It is in accommodating the new complex of values raised by that—raised by, to put it at its grandest, the question of who shall inherit England—that Anne is the necessary focus of the action (hence, I think, Andor Gomme's well-put argument that the focus of any process of growth and discovery lies in Wentworth, and it might therefore be more apposite for us to see the action through his eyes, is probably finally incorrect).

What I am suggesting, then, is that in this book Jane Austen seems to want to persuade us that the moral life and the life of the classes are intimately connected, and in a way that she has not so regarded the matter before. For here she is interested in exploring the ways in which the co-existence of two quite carefully defined social groupings—the world of the inherited aristocracy and the world of the seafarers—extends our notion of what the moral life is, and creates contrasting areas of value. In order to engage our interest in this, I would propose, she has employed certain new methods of deploying her materials to make these connections urgent, and has in fact altered her actual scope. She creates, as she always does, a very full social world, with its elaborate conventions of manners, a world whose probabilities we are led into with elaborate caution, through ironical tones of narrative voice and overt statements and a kind of implicit recognition of the constituted barriers—methods familiar enough in her work. But the ironies, statements, and conventions are always ordered somewhat differently from novel to novel, and there are numerous new intonations here. They are perhaps most evident of all in the larger blocks of presentation, the structural elements of the novel. For instance, she chooses to show us several representatives of each of the two groupings I have mentioned, and to do this, by comment and less direct methods of presentation, in such a way as to make the groupings significant. Because she does it here on this scale, there seems a strong case for our supposing that there is something more crucial to these differences than just to provide a division of background and therefore of values between the hero and the heroine, which at first separate them but which can finally be overcome. It is not just that Wentworth has insufficient appreciation of the role of caution and prudence, and that Anne has not sufficient of Wentworth's confidence to take a risk in marrying. We are also persuaded that there is a significant set of moral and social relationships and implications to be found in the way the other characters are socially and morally grouped. The grouping we see first is that of the Elliot family, which is aristocratic, landowning, ancient and respectable, of distinction and service in the past but now in different ways inclined to vanity, extravagance and social irresponsibility. The other group is composed around Admiral Croft, who becomes the tenant of Kellynch, and consists of a number of high-ranking professional sailors and their wives and friends. They are not, by Sir Walter Elliot's view, gentlemen; they are represented as a varied, intelligent and up to a point cultured group of people, who have risen rapidly in society as a result of having served it and defended it; their wealth comes from capturing sea-prizes, particularly in their battles with the French. Certain effective distinctions are made by the author between the two groups as groups; one instance is when Mrs. Clay, to flatter Sir Walter, comments on the value of not having a profession, and he finds himself making a double complaint against the seafarers:

> 'The profession has its utility, but I should be sorry to see any friend of mine belonging to it . . . it is in two points offensive to me: I have strong grounds of objection to it. First, as being the means of bringing persons of obscure birth into undue distinction, and raising men to hon-

> ours which their fathers and grandfathers never dreamt of; and secondly, as it cuts up a man's youth and vigour most horribly; a sailor grows old sooner than any other man . . . '.

Equally for Anne, who is effectively the central consciousness in the story, the sailors are a force of change, and she sees the difference between the two groups in social and moral terms. Not only are they freer and easier, but they can actually keep up estates better; and Anne's severance from her family is conducted by means largely of this sort of insight and her realization that here, in this group, there are much more supportable values, values basic to the moral level of persuasion in the book. The significant movement in the moral action is therefore the moment when Anne returns from Lyme Regis to see the Crofts at Kellynch, having already learned more about the lives and attitudes of the sailors, and realizes that they have more right to be there than her own family:

> She could have said more on the subject; for she had in fact so high an opinion of the Crofts, and considered her father so very fortunate in his tenants, felt the parish to be so sure of a good example, and the poor of the best attention and relief, that however sorry and ashamed for the necessity of the removal, she could not but in conscience feel that they were gone who deserved not to stay; and that Kellynch had passed into better hands than its owners.

And since one of the things that the novel persuades us towards is that, in this social world she has introduced to us and mediated for us, the social pattern is squirearchical, a world of rural gentry in which the administration of estates is a social and a moral duty, the Crofts now represent values for which her own family once stood but in which they have now failed. Hence Jane Austen's pattern here, as in the other novels, is to bestow the favours she can bestow in a domestic rural universe—a good marriage, a good home—on those who have deserved them.

And there are other moral reasons why the sailors deserve the favour of history which the action of the novel rewards them with. For if we go on to examine the moral values toward which the action persuades us, we must then see that these have sufficiently close analogies with this theme of supersession, of reappraising the relationship between the classes and the way in which the aristocratic duty can well devolve elsewhere. The sailors are carefully shown to have a more open, freer set of values, a demonstration which is encompassed within the moral stretch of the novel and given an important, in some ways a conclusive, place in the moral equilibrium of the ending. The difference between the two groupings is presented in many ways; in Captain Benwick, with his romantic reading, and Captain Harville with his fitted-up house at Lyme, showing both the effect of his profession and his own labours. Generally the sailors are presented to us as members of a profession shaped by their life of duty and yet making the most of their chances. 'These would have been all my friends', thinks Anne; finally they are. The play given to values associated with energy, steadfastness, and even luck (when it takes the form of 'honourable toils and just rewards') is here crucial. Because the action is about mistaken persuasion, we find a stress on the will (but not wilfulness). Because it is about status unearned, it is about the importance of luck that has been earned. But, though the testing place of these values is rural-domestic and genteel, they are also seen as in some sense heroic virtues and are given a place in the broader world, so suggesting, in a way unusual in Jane Austen, that there are other fields of action than the country and Bath; there is the question of social and national importance, the question of the very claims that the professions have on society, the sense, indeed, of an evolving need for moral virtue in an evolving society. This touch is of the greatest importance, and it is enforced right to the end; the concluding sentences enforce it again:

> His profession was all that could ever make her friends wish that tenderness [which Anne and Wentworth, married, have for each other] less; the dread of a future war all that could dim her sunshine. She gloried in being a sailor's wife, but she must pay the tax of quick alarm for belonging to that profession which is, if possible, more distinguished in its domestic virtues than in its national importance.

Anne now belongs in effect to the profession: it is, for Jane Austen, an unusual ending; and she associates herself with and so vindicates its domestic in addition to its heroic virtues. In consequence the moral universe, the scale of approved and unvalidated values, is in this novel different from the others (though in this matter all differ one from another) and answers to broader social necessities.

To say that in some sense the moral values of the novel are affected by a concern with the values of a new and emergent class is not, of course, to say that in this book they yield to a more primary interest; this is hardly a novel of social symbolism in the manner of, say, *Howards End.* The point is rather that Anne, originally persuaded towards a caution appropriate to rank and security, comes to question the values associated with these for those of energetic uncertainty and promise. Security proves to be false, morally and financially; the promise justifies itself, morally and financially. Anne's development in the novel is more substantial than most critics allow. She accepts as a given standard of her social world the dangers of lowering herself, and it is necessary that we realize this if the persuasion of Lady Russell is to seem to us rightly accepted by her. It is the subsequent events which show Lady Russell wrong, not the grounds on which she persuaded Anne; Anne comes to an understanding more radical than even a good woman like her can conceive of. If those events do have any order and meaning for a novelist with the controlling exactness that we know Jane Austen to have had, then surely their pattern takes its order from her development in her understanding of her situation. Anne's essential temptation is Kellynch, and it is a meaningful temptation. In the early part of the novel she shows, by her concern, her worthiness for it; in the latter part it is shown to be unworthy of her, for it is to be inherited by Walter Elliot; by the end of the action therefore Anne has moved out of the world of stewardship we are familiar with in Jane Austen ('Anne had no Uppercross-Hall before her, no landed estate, no headship of a family . . . '),

and the reader is now persuaded that this is to the good. But substantively this must be a moral rather than a social good, since it is in marriage and really in marriage alone that it is to be realised. Two essential lines of possible development of a sort that we are familiar with in the novels—the progress of a heroine towards social status and to self-awareness—must diverge in such a way as to show that self-awareness is incompatible with a social inheritance. The rewards that time can bring are thus, in this novel, of an unusual kind, and the real effort of literary management must be toward persuading us that Anne does, significantly, grow—does extend in moral and social awareness, does advance from a biddable acceptance of duty and 'persuasion exerted on the side of safety' to a conscientious appreciation of the proper obligations of risk-taking, this movement being justified by a revelation about the nature of the social and family world to which she belongs, and by an increased understanding not so much of Wentworth's character as of the environment in which it takes on its moral force.

This is, I think, the thread that takes us through ***Persuasion,*** and despite certain local failures (on which Andor Gomme pounces very effectively) it seems in general a triumph of management. One of the most obvious ways in which this theme is handled is the way in which the narrative present of the book is employed. A large part of the action, including the original engagement and the act of persuasion, is told to us in short compass and in retrospect. This leaves the present of the novel to deal with a relatively short period of time in which the complications deriving from that earlier action are worked out with close attention, in such a way as to follow out a real growth in Anne. These complications take us two ways—first, towards the theme of the separation of the lovers and their final reconciliation, and, second, towards the theme of the divorcing of Anne from her family. The novel begins at a point where the latter can only be the primary point of attention, since there are few direct grounds for supposing that she can regain Wentworth. At this point the real significance of the persuasion is that it has committed Anne to exploring life from within the family, and it is only when the moral and social weaknesses here have been fully exposed that she can have real grounds for judging Lady Russell to have been wrong. In fact, then, the main action is concerned not with Anne falling in love or feeling new emotions, but with recreating old emotions under the stimulus of Wentworth's presence and with showing how Anne, with no expectation whatever of getting back Wentworth's love, is growing away from her family. Hence, too, the meaning of presenting most of the action 'through' Anne, for if we were to know at just what point after the occasion in Chapter Seven when the author intervenes to indicate that Anne's power with Wentworth has gone forever the situation changes, we should not continue to regard Anne's discarding of her family as a disinterested moral progression. Nor would we appreciate in the same way those crucial virtues of steadfastness and constancy which are part of the moral meaning of the final alliance. The steadfastness, the constancy, the evident maturity of Anne are, of course, elements of her character when the action commences and give meaning to Wentworth's final sense that she has not altered, but the restoration of her energies and spirits through making mature free choices do form an essential advance. In the later scenes at Bath, Anne's capacities are severely tested, not only through the complications of the Walter Elliot episode, but through numerous other choices; and here we have a refiguring of the initial act of persuasion in a situation in which Anne is now capable of realizing all her actions and values and so of regaining the final 'warmth of heart' with which the novel ends.

Clearly, the ending of the novel complies with Richard Poirier's description of Jane Austen's culminating marriages—they are not only meaningful acts of choice but unions of 'social and natural inclinations'—and, as I have said, the direction of the literary persuasion is towards convincing us that two people have made a good marriage, in terms of a complex of social and moral discoveries, illuminating experiences of persons and events. But the nature of the persuasion, as we witness it and appreciate it through the basic dispositions of the action and the working decisions about what is to be told and how to tell it, is surely one that has a full development best defined through the way in which Anne's constancy enforces discoveries she could not have made had she sustained the engagement at the beginning (and hence can be measured by the distance Anne moves from her initial view of Lady Russell's assessment). The novel is a good deal more than a demonstration of the triumph of constancy, then, as the scene where Wentworth and Anne restore their engagement indicates:

> There they exchanged again those feelings and those promises which had once before seemed to secure every thing, but which had been followed by so many, many years of division and estrangement. There they returned again into the past, more exquisitely happy, perhaps, in their re-union, than when it had been first projected; more tender, more tried, more fixed in a knowledge of each other's character, truth, and attachment; more equal to act, more justified in acting.

And because there is, through the action as given, a demonstrable meaning in the claim that both are 'more equal to act, more justified in acting', and since this is very specifically true of Anne, from whose point of view most of the significant perceptions are realized, there are real grounds for judging the passage where Anne justifies her previous yielding to persuasion ('You should have distinguished. . . . You should not have suspected me now: the case so different, and my age so different') as other than what Mr. Gomme says it is—'disingenuous'. For only now, and because she has altered in a way that makes her more equal to act, more justified in acting, can the limitations of the persuasion be seen; and we are surely meant to perceive that there have been real benefits in it, since through it we have an Anne now who is not the original Anne. Jane Austen's proper qualifications ('. . . more exquisitely happy, *perhaps,* in their re-union . . . ') shouldn't, surely, be taken as lessening the point; they are emotionally logical in view of the initial joy felt by Anne in her first love. Equally, the way in which Wentworth varies between suggesting that Anne has altered and that Anne has remained the same should not be mistaken; for

one thing, his judgments refer now to personal appearance, now to character, now to her attitude toward him, her constancy, and for another they are in any case offered with a mild and amused irony, in which Anne partakes, with regard to what can now be regarded as his own mild inconstancy, which he now plays down. But the significant fact is that he does realize that Anne has acquired new extensions of character, as well as re-realizing her virtues, which are now thrown before him in a new light (mainly through the comparison with Louisa), and this explains his long pursuit of Anne, which is his real reason for being in Bath. Anne has acquired a new conception of duty, a new species of moral energy derived from social independence, which is associated, in turn, with the restoration of her looks and the new resources of her tenderness.

Far, then, from having created a novel in which the two major characters do not see and learn, Jane Austen has, in my view, created one in which a remarkable growth in moral resource and energy does occur in a heroine already distinguished from other Austen heroines by her relative maturity when the action of the book commences, a growth which occurs through the exploration of values having to do with luck, spirited energy and emotional resource that are made available to men by changes in society and by new conceptions of 'national importance'. Without wanting to overstate this element, I think we shall not see the moral radicalism of *Persuasion* without taking account of it and of the degree of interest Jane Austen exerts in it. And so, far from regarding the novel as one in which the action takes place under conditions of 'nearly complete moral stasis', I would hold it to cover moral and social dimensions on a scale that justifies our seeing it as a classic of its author's maturity; on a scale, in fact, that might let us put it near 'the head of the list'. (pp. 383-96)

> *Malcolm Bradbury, " 'Persuasion' Again," in* Essays in Criticism, *Vol. XVIII, No. 4, October, 1968, pp. 383-96.*

Thomas P. Wolfe   (essay date 1971)

[*In the following excerpt, Wolfe discusses point of view, narrative voice, and thematic unity in* Persuasion.]

There is something fitting, something that pleases our imaginations, in the fact that *Persuasion* was Jane Austen's last work. As Lionel Trilling has said [in *Beyond Culture: Essays on Literature and Learning,* 1965] it has "a charm that is traditionally, and accurately, called 'autumnal,' " and he further remarks that it "is beyond question a beautiful book." Since his writings on Jane Austen are among the very best there are, one wishes that Mr. Trilling had had occasion to say more about the peculiar effect of *Persuasion.* Its autumnal beauty is pleasing, not only in itself, but also as we remember it as the product of the autumnal season of Jane Austen's powers. One thinks of the "light and bright and sparkling" *Pride and Prejudice* as a book for spring, written in the delight of the writer's youthful energy; and *Emma* perhaps as the summer novel, coming at the time of the greatest unfolding of the imagination; and then there is *Persuasion,* more matured, and somehow more relaxed—one might say more seasoned— yet from which we can also say of its author, as she says of the heroine, that "the images of youth and hope, and spring, all gone together, blessed her memory."

It is through its dimension of remembrance, the sense of the past, that we can largely define the book's beauty. Yet I doubt that the words "beauty" and "charm" can sufficiently suggest the achievement of *Persuasion.* In the context in which Mr. Trilling uses them, they are even slightly negative in implication, indicating a somewhat lesser accomplishment than the "substantiality" or "difficulty" of *Emma* and *Mansfield Park.* I said that *Persuasion* seems more "relaxed"; and coming as it does, after *Mansfield Park* and *Emma,* we may feel that it does not offer quite the same intense demands on the moral imagination that these two earlier novels do, that it allows us a certain relaxation of moral vigilance. Indeed, one might speculate that the unrepentant sinner under His scrutiny would feel less uneasy than, say, the newcomer at table under the scrutiny of the narrator in the secular world of *Emma.* But the tone of *Persuasion* has something quite like a Jamesian generosity, characterized by the writer's mingled affection and amusement in regard to her creations. There is nothing "difficult" in the material of *Persuasion,* moreover, like that in *Mansfield Park* which has offended many readers. Yet "inoffensive" as *Persuasion* is, I find that, in a curious way, it unsettles; for I would locate in it new departures that radically disturb the notions of the limits of artistic concern usually ascribed to its author. To indicate in part what I think these new departures are, is the purpose of this essay.

I have never been wholly convinced by F. R. Leavis's assertion about *Emma* that "everything is presented through Emma's dramatized consciousness." Or perhaps I should say that to the degree that this is true, it seems to me more completely and significantly true of Anne Elliot in *Persuasion,* particularly in Book I. It is with Book I that I shall be primarily concerned, since Jane Austen is here doing something of a more distinctive nature than in the second half of the novel. The extent to which the consciousness of Anne will control the novel is hinted to us very early, when we find her own sense of the past pervading the language presumably describing another:

> Elizabeth did not quite equal her father in personal contentment. Thirteen years had seen her mistress of Kellynch Hall, presiding and directing with a self-possession and decision which could never have given the idea of her being younger than she was. For thirteen years had she been doing the honours, and laying down the domestic law at home, and leading the way to the chaise and four, and walking immediately after Lady Russell out of all the drawing-rooms and dining rooms in the country. Thirteen winters' revolving frosts had seen her opening every ball of credit which a scanty neighbourhood afforded; and thirteen springs shewn their blossoms, as she travelled up to London with her father, for a few weeks annual enjoyment of the great world. She had the remembrance of all this; she had the consciousness of being nine-and-twenty,

to give her some regrets and some apprehensions. She was fully satisfied of being still quite as handsome as ever; but she felt her approach to the years of danger, and would have rejoiced to be certain of being properly solicited by baronet-blood within the next twelvemonth or two. Then might she again take up the book of books with as much enjoyment as in her early youth; but now she liked it not.

The repetitions of "thirteen years . . . thirteen years . . . thirteen winters . . . thirteen springs," the rhythms of the cycles of the seasons, mixed with the monotony of the life they encompass, evoke beautifully a past that lingers as a determining force in the present. It is a prose that invests a great deal of sympathy in its object. But we are skeptical when we are told that Elizabeth "had a remembrance of all this"; we are inclined to deny to her this *kind* of involvement in remembrance, for it seems to be belied by the sentences that follow. Somehow the rich melancholy of that evoked consciousness does not reside well along with the rather vulgar connotations of such satisfaction with one's handsomeness, and the joy of "being properly solicited by baronet-blood within the next twelvemonth or two." We suspect rather that she had merely "the consciousness of being nine-and-twenty." This sense of the past is really not Elizabeth's—surely not the Elizabeth of the pages that follow—but the narrator's, or, we find, Anne's.

Something of a similar nature happens shortly after this, in Book I, Chapter 2, where we are able to infer that what we assent to in a speech of Lady Russell's is really the voice of Anne. We are told that in Lady Russell there is an "opposition of two leading principles": "She had a cultivated mind, and was, generally speaking, rational and consistent—but she had prejudices on the side of ancestry." Shortly after this description we find her reading over plans for economizing that Anne has revised:

> Every emendation of Anne's had been on the side of honesty against importance. She wanted more vigorous measures, a more complete reformation, a quicker release from debt, a much higher tone of indifference for every thing but justice and equity.

> "If we can persuade your father to all this," said Lady Russell, looking over her paper, "much may be done. If he will adopt these regulations, in seven years he will be clear; and I hope we may be able to convince him and Elizabeth that Kellynch-hall has a respectability in itself, which cannot be affected by these reductions; and that the true dignity of Sir Walter Elliot will be very far from lessened, in the eyes of sensible people, by his acting like a man of principle. What will he be doing, in fact, but what very many of our first families have done—or ought to do?— There will be nothing singular in his case; and it is singularity which often makes the worst part of our suffering, as it always does of our conduct. I have great hope of our prevailing. We must be serious and decided—for, after all, the person who has contracted debts must pay them; and though a great deal is due to the feelings of the gentleman, and head of a house, like your father,

there is still more due to the character of an honest man."

While Lady Russell reads and thinks, she has appropriated Anne's voice; she believes herself to be in complete agreement with Anne, restating her ideas. That there are two minds present in this speech, however, is made clear when we get to the question, "What will he be doing in fact . . . ?" There is a foreign voice, and a foreign sense of value, obtruding here, with its attention to "first families," and its apprehensiveness about "singularity." Jane Austen is here able to subtly dramatize the conflict between Anne and her father, to embody in Lady Russell's speech that "opposition of two leading principles." For this latter voice we recognize as a manifestation of that aspect of Lady Russell's character which shares Sir Walter's values.

The pervasiveness of Anne's consciousness is suggested further by what seems to be a relatively small proportion of dialogue in the novel, particularly an absence of dramatic dialogue of the kind that Reuben Brower has analyzed in his illuminating essay on *Pride and Prejudice* ["Light and Bright and Sparkling: Irony and Fiction in *Pride and Prejudice*,"]. In *Persuasion* we find that where there is a large body of conversation, it is often used for a different purpose from that in the earlier novels; it is not dialogue so much as mere "talking" that exists for the sake of supplying Anne with material for feeling. For example, Book I, Chapter 8, is largely "talk," but we hear it wholly through Anne's ear. The chatter about the navy is more or less irrelevant to the tones we catch through Anne, who, "When [Wentworth] talked, . . . heard the same voice, and discerned the same mind." It is a consciousness that lends to our own a sense of the past, with intimations of private, deeper significances unshared by others present. The technique is continued through Chapter 10, in the walk to Winthrop, where our awareness is identical with Anne's, as she evokes images from "autumn" poetry, and from the past, that emphasize her separateness from the conversation of the others—which conversation, through Anne's ear, we occasionally *overhear*.

As the talk is often "overheard," and consequently what is factually related often seems dissolved in the more significant overtones of the speech, so too, the solid outlines of the characters are displaced by Anne's consciousness of the immediately felt significance of what they say and do. Thus, in the scene in which Wentworth releases the Musgrove child from Anne's neck, what we feel is the "state of being released from him"; Wentworth is only a *presence, "some one"* who was "taking him from her." What so profoundly affects Anne, when she knows who did it, is something like a sense of having had physical contact with Wentworth. Such renderings of experience are surely unprecedented in Jane Austen, in the degree to which she allows an autonomy to "sensibility."

A reflection we attribute to Anne—which appears in a passage I quoted earlier—that "Kellynch-hall has a respectability in itself, which cannot be affected by these reductions," hints at a distinctiveness in the author's method of identifying Anne's selfhood. The truly relevant question is not so much whether Kellynch will or won't be af-

fected, but whether or not the identities of those attached to the hall will suffer a commensurate "reduction" by the changes. To emphasize the fact that Kellynch won't be reduced implies that for Anne there is no essential connection between its identity and her own. This has a significance perhaps enhanced by our recollection of the earlier novels. It is the moment of Elizabeth Bennet's first viewing Darcy's estate in *Pride and Prejudice* that ultimately completes the conversion in her attitude toward him; and we are then aware of the large extent to which his identity is bound up with the estate. It is somewhat the same, though to a less striking degree, with Knightley in *Emma.* Our sense of the solidity of Knightley's character is never so strong as on the visit to Donwell, in the walk about the grounds, with that sweet English verdure in view. This is not to say that Darcy and Knightley haven't individual selves apart from these more "socially" definitive aspects of identity; rather, this kind of division between the "social" and "individual" doesn't even occur to us in reading those books; the two kinds of identity are inextricable. There is something tending toward this dissociation in *Mansfield Park,* in the attempt to endorse Fanny's humble virtue at the expense of official public valuations of social status and character. But I think that in *Persuasion* we find for the first time in Jane Austen a deep sense of this split in the "modern" consciousness. In fact it seems to lie at the center of the novel. Sir Walter and Elizabeth have, as D. H. Lawrence said of Galsworthy's people, sunk to the level of wholly "social beings."

On first arriving at Bath, Anne finds that

> Sir Walter had taken a very good house in Camden-place, a lofty, dignified situation, such as becomes a man of consequence; and both he and Elizabeth were settled there, much to their satisfaction. . . .

> They had the pleasure of assuring her that Bath more than answered their expectations in every respect. Their house was undoubtedly the best in Camden-place, their drawing rooms had many decided advantages over all the others which they had either seen or heard of; and the superiority was not less in the style of the fitting-up, or the taste of the furniture. Their acquaintance was exceedingly sought after. Every body was wanting to visit them.

Anne wonders that they do not sense the change from Kellynch. But there are no "selves" there to sense that change. They *are* the house at Camden-place; and since it is the "best" house, the difficulty of their identity, so far as they can conceive it, is solved.

When Anne first visits the Musgroves, we are told that it was necessary for her to "clothe her imagination, her memory, and all her ideas in as much of Uppercross as possible." Her language takes on accents that carry the values of those whom she is visiting, as in her question to Mary, "How are your neighbours at the Great House?", implying that, to Mary, the identity of the elder Musgroves is somehow equivalent to Those-who-inhabit-the-Great-House. And a few pages later, the image is reinforced with the simile, "The Musgroves, like their houses, were in a state of alteration. . . ."

This necessity for clothing and unclothing the imagination is a very different matter from the fate of the elder Elliots. This flexibility of Anne's involves only what we might call her "social self." Anne can variously accommodate this social self to each "removal from one set of people to another," which means "a total change of conversation, opinion, and idea." Yet in doing this, she retains what we sense to be a private integrity, some inviolable core of self that almost defies analysis. It has to do with "poetry," with her relation to landscape and to the sea and to "autumn," and most importantly with what the author calls her constancy. Jane Austen locates it primarily in a "constancy to Wentworth," which, I think, gives inadequate expression to the quality Anne possesses.

Although Anne suffers perhaps as much as those two earlier suffering heroines, Elinor Dashwood and Fanny Price, there is always something present in the image of Anne that mitigates the painfulness, something that calls one's attention away from the immediate threats and always saves her from lapsing into a consciousness of martyrdom. Thus, when Anne performs at the piano for the Musgroves:

> She knew that when she played she was giving pleasure only to herself; but this was no new sensation: excepting one short period of her life, she had never, since the age of fourteen, never since the loss of her dear mother, known the happiness of being listened to, or encouraged by any just appreciation or real taste. In music she had been always used to feel alone in the world; and Mr. and Mrs. Musgrove's fond partiality for their own daughter's performance, and total indifference to any other person's, gave her more pleasure for their sakes, than mortification for her own.

As it seems often to occur, there is in the present situation a sense of the past that alleviates the feeling of suffering in the present. We are aware that she has continually experienced similar suffering, and the most immediate reaction to this fact would be an added sense of sympathy, or outrage at the mistreatment of Anne. But the "past" works another way; it builds immunity. That this was "no new sensation," that she had "been always used" to such treatment, has given her a persisting center of self that remains unhurt, that can channel what should be painful into an identity that is secure.

Anne, like Elizabeth Bennet and Emma, finds herself in a society in which the full extent of her intellectual and moral qualities cannot find expression. We are aware that the characters possess what we might call a superfluous or unutilizable knowledge; the movement of the three novels can be understood as the heroines' attempts to find a society or sub-society that can appreciate their better selves. In Anne, more than in Elizabeth or Emma, we find a capacity for transforming this "excess" knowledge into generosity. This unutilizable self in Emma, which is finally transformed into cruelty in the Box Hill scene, had, we feel, been latent for some time. We might compare this brutality to that which comes out in the paragraph on the "large fat sighings" of Mrs. Musgrove:

> Personal size and mental sorrow have certainly

no necessary proportions. A large bulky figure has as good a right to be in deep affliction, as the most graceful set of limbs in the world. But, fair or not fair, there are unbecoming conjunctions, which reason will patronize in vain,—which taste cannot tolerate,—which ridicule will seize.

What is interesting here, apart from the moralizing about Jane Austen that one might be inclined to make in connection with the passage, is that it is so unmistakably a voice unconnected with Anne's—it is wholly the author's. In *Emma*, the "ridicule" that "seized" on Miss Bates came from an impulse in the narrative voice that was shared by the heroine. But Anne's consciousness cannot share in such an inclination. It would be to misplace the point I wish to make to say that Anne has some moral superiority to Emma; rather, what I want to indicate is the presence of a different kind of self, a core of self built up out of its own past and persisting in the present, that invests Anne with a solidarity, an assurance, that *resists* such an impulse. Fanny Price, also, could not so "seize" on Mrs. Musgrove; but we feel it is because she, unlike Anne and Emma, has not that kind of "reason" or "taste" from which such ridicule could issue.

This sense of an inviolable past self persisting in the present finds metaphorical expression in what is perhaps the most beautiful moment in Jane Austen's fiction:

> When they came to the steps, leading upwards from the beach, a gentleman at the same moment preparing to come down, politely drew back, and stopped to give them way. They ascended and passed him; and as they passed, Anne's face caught his eye, and he looked at her with a degree of earnest admiration, which she could not be insensible of. She was looking remarkably well; her very regular, very pretty features, having the bloom and freshness of youth restored by the fine wind which had been blowing on her complexion, and by the animation of eye which it had also produced. It was evident that the gentleman, (completely a gentleman in manner) admired her exceedingly. Captain Wentworth looked round at her instantly in a way which shewed his noticing of it. He gave her a momentary glance,—a glance of brightness, which seemed to say, "That man is struck with you,—and even I, at this moment, see something like Anne Elliot again."

This seems to me the finest suggestion of those deeper overtones of what Jane Austen means by "constancy"— this shock of revelation in the momentary emergence of an abiding integrity that had disappeared only from the "surface." The incident is much more moving and significantly suggestive, than what is intended to be the climax of Book I, Anne's action following Louisa Musgrove's accident. Anne takes charge in the scene by remaining self-possessed amidst the hysteria of everyone else, by calming the women, finally by suggesting that a surgeon be fetched and seeing that Louisa is carried to the inn. It strikes me, however, that her behavior here is not capable of doing justice to the strength of mind that it is supposed to represent. This is made clear in the next few pages where the quality of the action is awkwardly translated into terms of mere "usefulness"; "The usefulness of her staying!"; and " 'no one so proper, so capable as Anne!' "; and "Why was not she to be as useful as Anne?" This reflecting on Anne's action in terms so insistent on utility undermines Jane Austen's surer intuition of its significance: Anne's grace under pressure approaches, in the sphere of action, something dramatically analogous to the unfaltering grace of her imagination when threatened by the present or by images that evoke a painful past. The discrepancy involved here might better be understood as less a local failure in Jane Austen's art, than as an unavoidable result of undertaking to render a consciousness that perhaps no "public activity" available to her could adequately express.

As Anne's public activities are incapable of expressing her "mind," so Wentworth, the hero, is never quite able to fulfill the vision of him imaged in Book I, Chapter 4:

> But, he was confident that he should soon be rich;—full of life and ardour, he knew that he should soon have a ship, and soon be on a station that would lead to everything he wanted. He had always been lucky; he knew he should be so still.—Such confidence, powerful in its own warmth. . . .
>
> . . . . .
>
> His genius and ardour had seemed to foresee and to command his prosperous path.
>
> . . . . .
>
> How eloquent could Anne Elliot have been,— how eloquent at least, were her wishes on the side of early warm attachment, and a cheerful confidence in futurity, against that over-anxious caution which seems to insult exertion and distrust Providence!—She had been forced into prudence in her youth, she learned romance as she grew older—the natural sequence of an unnatural beginning.

The vocabulary here cannot but strike us as a new note in Jane Austen's fiction. I would guess, for example, that the movement away from the classical sense of the word "genius" as a tutelary spirit, toward the more "romantic" sense of extraordinary intellectual and imaginative powers, appears nowhere else in her work. Here are overtones that have nothing in common with the insipid, self-conscious revelling of Marianne Dashwood in *Sense and Sensibility.* Our sense of this distinctiveness is furthered later, by Anne's "romantic" relation to uncultivated landscape, and also in Book I, Chapter 12, where Henrietta's insistence on the characteristically eighteenth-century conjunction of the "beautiful" and "useful" is shown up as vulgar and out of place. The terms in which Anne remembers Wentworth offer a conception of a hero in touch with some forces larger than social forces, some determining energy that suggests a connection between "Providence," "futurity," and the self—personal energy, "confidence," "genius." This is more striking for its coming after the image of Sir Walter and his Baronetage, a defining of self in purely social terms. But Jane Austen is at some pains to sustain this imagination of Wentworth when she must bring him within contexts more familiar to her. The

search for a wife, at least in the *English* novel around 1818, scarcely affords the best opportunity for dramatizing the "genius" that "commands" its own path.

Yet Wentworth brings with him the idea of the navy, a conception of a life characterized significantly by its disconnection from the larger societies encompassed by the book. Anne's admiration for the Crofts' little society of two, for their indifference to the social world of her father, is indicated in such a passage as this:

> She always watched them as long as she could; delighted to fancy she understood what they might be talking of, as they walked along in happy independence, or equally delighted to see the Admiral's hearty shake of the hand when he encountered an old friend, and to observe their eagerness of conversation when occasionally forming into a little knot of the navy. . . .

The "happy independence," and the "little knot of the navy," suggest the possibility of a sub-society, or a *new* society, into which a self like Anne's might move. In **Mansfield Park,** by contrast, the navy affords to Fanny's brother the possibility for distinction in the larger social world, rather than an environment offering freedom to superior selves.

Book II is unfortunately not able to sustain the full, rich texture of the first book. The central problem lies in the narrative relation to Anne. This changes as Anne herself changes, as she begins to participate more actively in the present, as the meanings the past held for her become transformed in the novel's movement toward its conclusion. But the attending faults may be exemplified by such losses of narrative poise as: "and Anne—but it would be an insult to the nature of Anne's felicity, to draw any comparison between it and her sister's; the origin of the one all selfish vanity, of the other all generous attachment." This provides a measure of the degree to which, in Book II, the narrative consciousness has disconnected itself from Anne; and it here unhappily indulges in the kind of moralizing unmistakably reminiscent of the Elinor-Marianne comparison in *Sense and Sensibility.* This is dangerous ground for Jane Austen. So too is the disruption of the narrative texture by the intrusion of melodramatic evil in the person of young Elliot, revealed in the scenes with Mrs. Smith. The Anne-Wentworth-Elliot configuration is similar in kind to the Elizabeth-Darcy-Wickham triangle in *Pride and Prejudice.* In each novel the heroine, confronted by two very engaging suitors, is faced with the problem of choice; and Jane Austen, consequently, is faced with the problem of helping her heroine make that choice—which results, in each instance, in resorting to melodrama to reveal the viciousness that exists behind the attractions of stylish manners appearing as virtue. It is true that Anne has had intimations of moral frailty in Elliot, but the bad notes he has struck are only matched by the factitious quality of "She saw that there had been bad habits; that Sunday-travelling had been a common thing," where Jane Austen rather peremptorily injects moral intonations of a kind that have little relevance to the values that generally define the moral tone of the book.

The episodes centering around Mrs. Smith, apart from their function of revealing Elliot, have, apparently, the further function of lending themselves to a fuller definition of Anne's moral character. We are to admire in Mrs. Smith something similar to what we do in Anne.

> A submissive spirit might be patient, a strong understanding would supply resolution, but here was something more; here was that elasticity of mind, that disposition to be comforted, that power of turning readily from evil to good, and of finding employment which carried her out of herself, which was from Nature alone. It was the choicest gift of Heaven. . . .

Such a statement, so clearly intended to enhance Anne's own qualities, seems, in being a mere *statement,* to insist on too much, to diminish rather than enlarge what in Anne has previously been dramatized. There is, finally, that sweet-sour odor of disinfectant lingering around the sickbed of Mrs. Smith, however much Jane Austen would like to escape it—such that when we hear Mrs. Smith say

> Call it gossip if you will; but when Nurse Rooke has half an hour's leisure to bestow on me, she is sure to have something to relate that is entertaining and profitable, something that makes one know one's species better. One likes to hear what is going on, to be *au fait* as to the newest modes of being trifling and silly . . . ,

we assent, we *do* call it gossip, and gossip of the mean and nursy sort that often enough thrives in the petty circumstances surrounding one in ill health. I point this out only because it is interesting to observe that the episodes with Mrs. Smith are the ones predominant in "news"; but to anyone mindful of the dramatic resources that Jane Austen can exploit in her "art of gossip," these in *Persuasion* appear peculiarly unsatisfactory.

But *Persuasion* comes finally to a brilliant close. There is no need to dwell on the particular excellences of Book II, Chapter 11, most of which are similar in kind to those I have analyzed from Book I. It is enough to note that in Anne's conversation with Harville, Jane Austen reverts to the earlier mode of suggestively rendering the extraordinarily vivid presence of a separate and silent figure. And the climactic reunion of the lovers, wherein the moment is prepared "for all the immortality which the happiest recollection of their own future lives could bestow," is a most fitting crescendo to Jane Austen's sense of the variously tender and painful past that the self can summon up to inform and enrich the life of the present. (pp. 687-700)

> *Thomas P. Wolfe, "The Achievement of 'Persuasion',"* in *Studies in English Literature, 1500-1900, Vol. XI, No. 4, Autumn, 1971, pp. 687-700.*

Nina Auerbach   (essay date 1972)

[*Auerbach is an American educator and critic known primarily for her feminist interpretations of the literary canon. In the following excerpt from an essay originally published in* ELH *in 1972, she argues that motifs and symbols in* Persuasion, *not present in any of Austen's prior works, indicate the author's increasing knowledge and acceptance of the philosophical, political, and artistic tenets gaining prominence during the Romantic period.*]

An analysis of the symbolism in Jane Austen's *Persuasion* may lead us to discover stirrings of revolution underneath the quiet surface of the novel. To define the revolution of *Persuasion,* we should begin by examining the laws of its created world in relation to those governing Jane Austen's earlier novels.

It may be helpful in this connection to think of *Persuasion* as Jane Austen's *Tempest,* another final work that reprises and transforms themes and motifs introduced earlier in the author's canon. The plots of both are determined to a great extent by the movements of the sea. Written during Jane Austen's last illness and not published until after her death, *Persuasion* is defined by its blended tone of elegiac departure and the "senseless joy" of renewal and reconciliation. Its action touches extremes of loss and desloation, but out of each desolation comes the grace of recovery and enrichment of what was lost.

Like *The Tempest, Persuasion* is brooded over by the threat of loss and death. Seen in these terms, the marriage of Louisa and Benwick is more than a mechanical contrivance to free Wentworth for Anne Elliot. It is a lighthearted exemplification of the law that governs *Persuasion,* a law oriented to the fulfillment of human desire, in close association with nature and natural rhythms.

The union of Louisa and Benwick comes only after each has been brought close to loss and death. Benwick is suffering after the death of his fiancée, "a very superior creature"; Louisa's fall on the Cobb threatens her for a time with death or derangement. Wentworth defines the rhythm of the union clearly: " 'It was a frightful hour,' said he [speaking of Louisa's fall], 'a frightful day!' and he passed his hand across his eyes, as if the remembrance were still too painful; but in a moment half smiling again, added, 'The day has produced some effects however—has had some consequences which must be considered as the very reverse of frightful.' "

The iron law of consequences is suspended in *Persuasion;* the seeds of apparent tragedy produce unexpected joy. The surprising union of Benwick and Louisa is a half-parodic repetition of the central reconciliation of Wentworth and Anne after "so many, many years of division and estrangement"; they are "more exquisitely happy, perhaps, in their re-union, than when it had been first projected."

Like *The Tempest, Persuasion* transforms tragedy into the profoundest comedy, and, also like *The Tempest,* it closes with a glimpse of a sea voyage, which will be explored more fully later on. At this point, we should examine some of the tragic motifs more closely, because almost all of them are reprises of events in Jane Austen's earlier novels. This transformation of material from earlier works relates *Persuasion* most intimately to *The Tempest:* it introduces for the last time motifs and events that have furnished the author's universe from the beginning, but which are joyfully transformed in the crucible of a brave new world.

In one important sense, *Persuasion* looks back as far as *Northanger Abbey,* which Jane Austen may have been revising during its composition: there is another journey to Bath. In *Northanger Abbey,* we regarded Bath with double vision. The inexperienced heroine, Catherine Morland, was dazzled by its excitement, but Henry Tilney's monologues subtly equated it with an oppressively inhuman spiritual climate. Phrases and incidents recurred in the narrative which associated Bath with imprisonment, further undermining Catherine's early innocent vision of it. When the Tilneys liberated Catherine from Bath, she found herself enclosed in the more obvious, if more genteel, prison of Northanger Abbey, which was governed by the same unnatural values that presided over the world of Bath. The apparent alternative to Bath provided by the Tilneys melted into a more insidious extension of it, and the disillusioned Catherine was cast out of both worlds after her journey of initiation into "actual and natural evil."

But Anne Elliot has no such lesson to learn. She knows from the beginning that she cannot endure "the white glare of Bath" (as Jane Austen could not). There are no subtle undercurrents needed to modulate our responses: Bath is equated from the beginning with the inhuman ostentation of Sir Walter and Elizabeth Elliot, and explicitly defined by Anne as a prison: "Anne entered [Bath] with a sinking heart, anticipating an imprisonment of many months, and anxiously saying to herself, 'Oh! when shall I leave you again?'"

But Wentworth and the naval group arrive in Bath almost immediately, and the alternative they provide is genuine. The Elliots have no power to oppress their joyful fellowship, although at first they may appear to: "The door was thrown open for Sir Walter and Miss Elliot, whose entrance seemed to give a general chill. Anne felt an instant oppression, and, wherever she looked, saw symptoms of the same. The comfort, the freedom, the gaiety of the room was over, hushed into cold composure, determined silence, or insipid talk, to meet the heartless elegance of her father and sister."

The Tilneys in *Northanger Abbey* were, like the Elliots, a motherless family presided over by a cold father; General Tilney was able to oppress his children's gaiety and freedom much as the Elliots do momentarily here. But in *Persuasion,* the world of heartless elegance is defeated on its own terms by the world of feeling. The new power of the navy forces Elizabeth Elliot to invite Wentworth to a select evening party, and Anne's knowledge of her secret engagement thaws her vision even of her father's house in Bath:

> It was but a card-party, it was but a mixture of those who had never met before, and those who met too often—a common-place business, too numerous for intimacy, too small for variety; but Anne had never found an evening shorter. Glowing and lovely in sensibility and happiness, and more generally admired than she thought about or cared for, she had cheerful or forbearing feelings for every creature around her. Mr. Elliot was there; she avoided, but she could pity him. The Wallises; she had amusement in under-

standing them. Lady Dalrymple and Miss Carteret; they would soon be innoxious cousins to her. She cared not for Mrs. Clay, and had nothing to blush for in the public manners of her father and sister. With the Musgroves, there was the happy chat of perfect ease; with Captain Harville, the kind-hearted intercourse of brother and sister; with Lady Russell, attempts at conversation, which a delicious consciousness cut short; with Admiral and Mrs. Croft, every thing of particular cordiality and fervent interest, which the same consciousness sought to conceal;—and with Captain Wentworth, some moments of communication continually occurring, and always the hope of more, and always the knowledge of his being there!

The infiltration of the naval group into Sir Walter's exclusive Bath soirée is able to nullify the power of Sir Walter's society, in Anne's eyes at least, and she is our guiding consciousness. When Anne is liberated from Bath, there is no imprisonment in an imperfectly restored medieval abbey: she is carried into the world of the future, and to sea.

It has often been noticed that *Persuasion* is an inverted *Sense and Sensibility.* In many ways, Anne Elliot is a mellowed and fully accepted variant of Marianne Dashwood with the world restored. Marianne's solitary walks and bursts of poetry were cruelly parodied at the beginning of *Sense and Sensibility,* and in the last volume of her story, they almost led to her death by bringing on an attack of putrid fever. Anne also escapes into solitary walks and poetic musings, but hers are sanctified. Their potential preciosity and affectation are drawn off into Jane Austen's parody of Benwick, just as the potential danger of Anne's abandonment to feeling is contained in Louisa Musgrove's fall on the Cobb. Mrs Musgrove's "large fat sighings" over the death of her unworthy son contain all the potential insincerity and ludicrousness of Anne's protracted mourning over the death of feeling. These flat, comic characters siphon off our subversive impulses toward the romantic heroine, and probably Jane Austen's subversive impulses as well. They allow a full acceptance of Anne's emotional world, and they allow Jane Austen to posit an ethic of feeling purified of "sensibility": "How eloquent could Anne Elliot have been,—how eloquent, at least, were her wishes on the side of early warm attachment, and a cheerful confidence in futurity, against that over-anxious caution which seems to insult exertion and distrust Providence!— She had been forced into prudence in her youth, she learned romance as she grew older—the natural sequel of an unnatural beginning."

Jane Austen's final admonition to Lady Russell is an unequivocal repudiation of the attempt of "sense" to counsel feeling:

> [Lady Russell] must learn to feel that she had been mistaken . . . ; that she had been unfairly influenced by appearances . . . ; that because Captain Wentworth's manners had not suited her own ideas, she had been too quick in suspecting them to indicate a character of dangerous impetuosity; and that because Mr. Elliot's manners had precisely pleased her in their propriety and correctness, their general politeness and

suavity, she had been too quick in receiving them as the certain result of the most correct opinions and well regulated mind. There was nothing less for Lady Russell to do, than to admit that she had been pretty completely wrong, and to take up a new set of opinions and of hopes.

In *Sense and Sensibility,* nature and feeling were dangerous and productive of disease; one could survive in a chilled society only by avoiding both. The passages cited seem to be clear and conscious signposts, indicating how far Jane Austen has traveled since then. In *Persuasion,* prudent accommodation gives way in a world guided by emotion and vision. A contrast of the villains in each novel seems to be another signpost:

> Elinor saw nothing to censure in [Willoughby] but a propensity, in which he strongly resembled and peculiarly delighted her sister, of saying too much what he thought on every occasion without attention to persons or circumstances. In *hastily* forming and giving his opinion of other people, in sacrificing general politeness to the enjoyment of undivided attention where his heart was engaged, and in slighting too easily the forms of worldly propriety, he displayed a want of caution which Elinor could not approve in spite of all that he and Marianne could say in its support.
>
> Mr. Elliot was rational, discreet, polished,—but he was not open. There was never any burst of feeling, any warmth of indignation or delight, at the evil or good of others. This, to Anne, was a decided imperfection. Her early impressions were incurable. She prized the frank, the openhearted, the eager character beyond all others. Warmth and enthusiasm did captivate her still. She felt that she could so much more depend upon the sincerity of those who sometimes looked or said a careless or a *hasty* thing, than of those whose presence of mind never varied, whose tongue never slipped. (my italics)

The contrast is clear. But the point is not simply that Jane Austen has discarded an ethic of prudence and repression for an ethic of emotional release: she has shifted the axis of her created world. The characters in *Persuasion* must accommodate themselves to a different set of laws. Its world is governed by nature and by human desire, and characters who cannot accommodate themselves to these laws, like the Elliots and Lady Russell, are threatened and deprived of power as unequivocally as Marianne Dashwood was in Jane Austen's earlier world.

When we open *Persuasion* we see staring at us from the first page in capital letters: ELLIOT OF KELLYNCH HALL. Sir Walter's identity is inseparable from his title, from his crest, above all from Kellynch Hall; he is identified with the apparatus and accoutrements that encompass him. This apparatus of identity lends resonance to the early description of Anne: "She was only Anne."

But the power of Kellynch Hall is no longer supported by the power of money: the Elliots cannot keep their house, just as the Bennets in *Pride and Prejudice* could not. Elizabeth was forced out of her childhood home by Mr. Col-

lins, a horrible embodiment of the power of form to stifle humanity, and her problem in the book was to find a house she could live in. Wickham's "unhoused free condition," his world of impulse and feeling, was an illusion, easily dissolved by the power of money. Nature, growth, freedom, could survive only in the heavily fortified atmosphere of Pemberley, presided over by the equivocal figure of Mr. Darcy.

Admiral Croft and his wife, Wentworth's sister, encroach upon Anne's home in a similar way, but unlike the threat of Mr. Collins, their encroachment is a liberation. The navy in *Persuasion* is associated with nature, openness, hospitality, romance; but, as Marvin Mudrick points out in *Jane Austen: Irony as Defense and Discovery* [see Further Reading], it is also associated with income, Jane Austen's central symbol of social power. Power has passed from those who oppress and chill feeling to those who represent it, and this is symbolized by the dispossession of the Elliots. If there has been a revolution of values in Jane Austen's mind, she depicts a similar revolution in her society. Only *Persuasion* endows the representatives of nature and feeling with the superior social power income symbolizes and bestows. Anne, our moral and emotional barometer, recognizes the justice of the change: "She could have said more on the subject; for she had in fact so high an opinion of the Crofts, and considered her father so very fortunate in his tenants, felt the parish to be so sure of a good example, and the poor of the best attention and relief, that however sorry and ashamed for the necessity of the removal, she could not but in conscience feel that they were gone who deserved not to stay, and that Kellynch Hall had passed into better hands than its owners." Admiral Croft symbolically strips away Sir Walter's mirrors, thus purifying Kellynch of its stagnant self-enclosure:

> "I have done very little besides sending away some of the large looking-glasses from my dressing-room, which was your father's. A very good man, and very much the gentleman I am sure—but I should think, Miss Elliot" (looking with serious reflection) "I should think he must be rather a dressy man for his time of life.—Such a number of looking-glasses! Oh Lord! there was no getting away from oneself . . . now I am quite snug, with my little shaving-glass in one corner, and another great thing that I never go near."

In *Pride and Prejudice,* the threat of dispossession was an additional threat to Elizabeth's security and independence. An influx of liberating energy might be indicated at the end of *Emma,* when Mr. Knightley moved into Hartfield, but the implications of this move were ambiguous; perhaps his own energy was boxed in. In *Persuasion,* the implications of the move are unshadowed: a decaying sector of the petty aristocracy is dislodged from its sanctuary by the purifying force of a new world.

Mansfield Park and *Persuasion* are often grouped together as Jane Austen's "Cinderella novels," but Fanny Price's alienation at Mansfield was the result of her social inferiority; she was removed from the Bertram family by her lower social and financial status. Anne, on the other hand, is an Elliot in all but spirit. It is her "elegance of mind and sweetness of character" that isolate her among the Elliots of Kellynch Hall: "She was only Anne." As her isolation is interiorized into a quality of mind and feeling, so are her silent observations of the world around her. Fanny's moralizing judgments are transformed into Anne's sympathetic emotional projection. She defines a situation not by its propriety, but by the emotional vibrations it contains. Furthermore, her own emotional life is so rich and constant that it often interferes with her role as spectator, as here, for instance: "[Wentworth's action] produced such a confusion of varying, but very painful agitation, as she could not recover from, till enabled by the entrance of Mary and the Miss Musgroves to make over her little patient to their cares, and leave the room. She could not stay. It might have been an opportunity of watching the loves and jealousies of the four; they were now all together, but she could stay for none of it."

Fanny had little to distract her from observing the sword dance of other peoples' loves and jealousies. Only Anne is provided with a significant and autonomous inner world, which is strong enough to pull her from the incessant conflicts around her.

When William Price entered Mansfield, the sea wind blew through Jane Austen's world for the first time, but it was not strong enough in *Mansfield Park* to provide an alternative to Fanny's oppressive existence at Mansfield; William sailed off again, and the sea became associated in Fanny's mind with the "noise, disorder, and impropriety" of her father's house at Portsmouth. This new element in Jane Austen's novels shrinks into a dirty puddle in *Mansfield Park.* Only in *Persuasion* do we become aware of the enormous revolutionary potential it contains, as it brings mobility to a static society and emotional release to a suppressed heroine. Wentworth is William Price transformed into a lover and able to offer the dispossessed heroine citizenship in a fresh community, full of vitality and promise.

The role of the sea in Jane Austen's last three novels, and perhaps in *Sanditon* as well, is a subject which has not been sufficiently examined. With the growth of her sailor brothers, a new world and new possibilities come into Jane Austen's novels. When William Price enters, there is a new emotional excitement in *Mansfield Park,* and the relationship between Fanny and her sailor brother is the vivid heart of the book. But later on, the sea becomes equated with a world in which Fanny cannot live, and she shrinks back into the bosom of Mansfield. Emma, Jane Austen's most powerful heroine, has never seen the sea: her father is afraid of it. Her honeymoon will be two weeks at the seashore under Mr. Knightley's protection, but then she will move back to Hartfield, where there will now be two fathers instead of one. Only in *Persuasion* is the sea world allowed to dominate and take control of the book and carry off the heroine, with all its romantic excitement, and all its attendant danger.

In *Persuasion,* Jane Austen's world is transformed, in its details as well as its larger structure and tone, by the influx of a revolutionary force: the world symbolized in the sea, which for the first time gives a home to values that had to struggle for survival on land. The passage of money from land to sea guarantees the power of these values. This sea change, symbolized by the transfer of Kellynch Hall at the beginning and the transfer of Anne Elliot at the end, suggests a hope that a purified community will be able to flourish in the "real" world. In freeing the navy of any trace of incompetence or corruption—even the incorrigible Dick Musgrove conveniently dies soon after his induction—Jane Austen is not simply echoing her brothers' probable chauvinism: she is symbolizing utopian hopes suggesting peculiar affinities to Shelley's in *Prometheus Unbound,* begun in 1818, the year of *Persuasion*'s publication.

The role of Wentworth as hero is interesting in relation to Jane Austen's new utopianism. Wentworth has been called the first of Jane Austen's heroes who is a self-made man, and he is also the first hero to represent the world of the future rather than the past. As Anne's lover, Wentworth can initiate her into the brave new world that is so radically transforming the structure of the old. The warmth and generosity that were chilled by the old society can flourish in the new. Before her reconciliation with Wentworth, Anne attends a naval officer's dinner party, and becomes aware that naval society thrives on everything aristocratic society suppresses: "There was so much attachment to Captain Wentworth in all this, and such a bewitching charm in a degree of hospitality so uncommon, so unlike the usual style of give-and-take invitations, and dinners of formality and display, that Anne felt her spirits not likely to be benefited by an increasing acquaintance among his brother-officers. 'These would have been all my friends,' was her thought; and she had to struggle against a great tendency to lowness."

To find this generosity of feeling, Elizabeth Bennet, Fanny Price, and Emma Woodhouse retreated into the past: Elizabeth ensconced herself in Pemberley, Fanny in Mansfield, and Emma was protected by the sheltering values of Mr. Knightley, whose relation to an older tradition of English life was symbolized in part by his name. But there were oppressive and equivocal elements in this protective world of tradition. Darcy's resemblance to his aunt, Lady Catherine de Bourgh, pointed to elements in his character of the antihuman pride of his class, although at times Jane Austen ignored Darcy's unpleasant side with skillful sophistry in order to maintain the light and bright and sparkling tone of the book. Mansfield was the home of vanity and oppression throughout most of *Mansfield Park:* only when the greater cruelty of the new was made apparent did it begin to loom large as a refuge. Even Emma and Mr. Knightley were not able to share the rich fruitfulness of Donwell. They had to move into Hartfield, another home of constriction and oppression, governed by Mr. Woodhouse's fear of marriage, procreation, food, and the elements. It is significant that in *Persuasion* we are placed on the fringes of the aristocracy from the beginning. The hero of this book breaks into the equivocal shelter of England's past, and links the heroine with forces of future hope and change.

In an interesting article, "Luck and Fortuitous Circumstance in *Persuasion:* Two Interpretations" [see excerpt dated 1965], Paul Zietlow provocatively discusses the role of fortune in the novel, which is associated particularly with Wentworth's rise. I would disagree only with Ziet-low's "darker" interpretation, which argues that the role of luck places the characters in a contingent universe. The world of **Persuasion** operates according to a coherent pattern, to which each instance of luck contributes: the novel becomes contingent only if we insist on comparing its autonomous laws with those of our own universe. The "providential" interpretation does not seem incompatible with intimations of tragedy; in fact, like the providential structure of *The Tempest*, it depends on them. The element of chance in Wentworth's career, particularly the favorable weather without which he would have been drowned on his first sea voyage, suggests an equation between his life and the rhythms of the elements: he is a man in harmony with the spirit of the sea, who lives in conjunction with the elements and their motions.

Wentworth's career brings us to another important element in **Persuasion** which has been merely hinted at in Jane Austen's earlier novels: the new importance of productive labor as fulfillment in itself. The importance of natural rhythms in the book, and the idealization of the navy as a life conjoined with them, are never equated with a passive yielding to external ebbs and flows. The relation between nature and human exertion is embodied in a beautiful emblem near the beginning of the novel, during the Uppercross party's walk to Winthrop: "After another half mile of gradual ascent through large enclosures, *where the ploughs at work, and the fresh-made path spoke the farmer, counteracting the sweets of poetical despondence, and meaning to have spring again,* they gained the summit" (italics mine).

The labor of the farmer harmonizes with and even anticipates the natural processes. As the farmer works with the rhythm of the seasons, so the sailors work with the rhythm of the sea. The luck guiding Wentworth's career indicates a healthy kinship to natural processes and laws similar to that of the farmer. The ideal of labor in harmony with nature is especially important if we compare it to the fear of the weather shown by so many of Jane Austen's earlier characters, a fear which many patronizing critics have attributed to Jane Austen herself. Moreover, this ideal is not limited to obviously "outdoor" professions such as farming and sailing: the social-climbing Mrs. Clay, of all people, makes a useful extension when she connects the idea of exposure with *all* the professions:

> "Soldiers, in active service, are not at all better off; and even in the quieter professions, there is a toil and a labour of the mind, if not of the body, which seldom leaves a man's looks to the natural effect of time. The lawyer plods, quite care-worn; the physician is up at all hours, and travelling in all weather; and even the clergyman;—" she stopt a moment to consider what might do for the clergyman—"and even the clergyman, you know, is obliged to go into infected rooms, and expose his health and looks to all the injury of a poisonous atmosphere."

With simple irony, Jane Austen invites us to reverse Mrs. Clay's meaning by linking work to wholesome exposure to the weather, even to a "poisonous atmosphere" of the kind Marianne Dashwood so rashly ventured into years

before. The opposite of the man who labors is the beautiful and youthful Sir Walter, says Mrs. Clay; and Sir Walter, says Jane Austen, represents the death-in-life of a man who escapes into his own mirrors. In **Emma,** Mr. Knightley the gentleman-farmer was permitted to stand as an ideal because we were always aware of William Larkins' and Mr. Knightley's own activities in attending to the business of the estate. But in **Persuasion,** this compromise is no longer possible. The world of gentlemen and fine ladies shrinks into the symbol of Sir Walter Elliot's mirror, and although there is some talk at the end of a reconciliation between Wentworth and Lady Russell, the landed world of the gentry is shown to be pretty much unredeemable and decaying. Money and the world of the future lie in work, of which the sea is the chief emblem.

But ideas of exertion and exposure are not linked exclusively to men. The first chapter of **Persuasion** describes Elizabeth Elliot's barren existence, "the prosperity and the nothingness" of her life. She is not barren only, or even primarily, because she is still unmarried at twenty-nine. She is barren because she has nothing to do: "Such were Elizabeth Elliot's sentiments and sensations; such the cares to alloy, the agitations to vary, the sameness and the elegance, the prosperity and the nothingness, of her scene of life—such the feelings to give interest to a long uneventful residence in one country circle, to fill the vacancies which there were *no habits of utility abroad, no talents or accomplishments for home, to occupy*" (my emphasis).

Her married sister Mary, whose attachment to her imaginary illnesses is as profound as Sir Walter's to his mirrors, is scarcely better off. Mrs. Croft, the first wholly admirable and likable married woman in Jane Austen's novels, makes a remark that casts an indirect light on Mary's illnesses:

> Thank God! I have always been blessed with excellent health, and no climate disagrees with me. . . . The only time that I ever really suffered in body or mind, the only time that I ever fancied myself unwell, or had any ideas of danger, was the winter that I passed by myself at Deal, when the Admiral . . . was in the North Seas. I lived in perpetual fright at that time, and had all manner of imaginary complaints *from not knowing what to do with myself, or when I should hear from him next.* (my emphasis)

If the navy is Jane Austen's vision of a brave new world, Mrs. Croft is her tactful and subtle portrait of the "new woman." The Crofts are the first happily married couple in Jane Austen's novels to receive more than peripheral treatment. But this does not mean that Jane Austen was mellowing in a sentimental way toward marriage as she had seen it on land. Their marriage is a naval marriage, different in kind from any other in Jane Austen's books, and it will set a hopeful pattern for Anne and Wentworth's.

"[Mrs. Croft] had bright dark eyes, good teeth, and altogether an agreeable face; though her *reddened and weather-beaten complexion, the consequence of her having been almost as much at sea as her husband,* made her seem to have lived some years longer in the world than her real eight-and-thirty'' (my emphasis). Although Jane Austen never trumpets on about "fulfilling careers for women," in the Crofts' exemplary marriage, the wife shares her husband's life of exertion and exposure; she no longer lives in a woman's world, and she has no children. Later on in the book, we see Mrs. Croft "looking as intelligent and keen as any of the officers around her." As an emblem of this good marriage, Jane Austen inserts a slyly feminist note:

> "My dear Admiral, that post!—we shall certainly take that post" [says Mrs. Croft].
>
> But by coolly giving the reins a better direction herself, they happily passed the danger; and by once afterwards judiciously putting out her hand, they neither fell into a rut, nor ran foul of a dung-cart; and Anne, with some amusement at their style of driving, which she imagined no bad representation of the general guidance of their affairs, found herself safely deposited by them at the cottage.

Mrs. Croft's view of women, which her life gives her freedom to practice, is summed up in her cry to Wentworth: "But I hate to hear you talking so, like a fine gentleman, and as if women were all *fine ladies,* instead of *rational creatures.* We none of us expect to be in smooth water all our days" (my emphasis).

To appreciate the triumph of this assertion, we must turn back to Mr. Collins' proposal in *Pride and Prejudice,* and to Elizabeth's truly desperate plea: "Do not consider me now as an *elegant female* intending to plague you, but as a *rational creature* speaking the truth from her heart." Mr. Collins' and his society's disjunction between the elegant female and the rational creature was perhaps the most severe threat to Elizabeth's life, and this disjunction has persisted as an undercurrent throughout Jane Austen's novels. In the quiet urgency of its insistence, we may even hear echoes of voices like Mary Wollstonecraft's: "My own sex, I hope, will excuse me, if I treat them like rational creatures, instead of flattering their *fascinating* graces, and viewing them as if they were in a state of perpetual childhood, unable to stand alone." In Jane Austen's canon, only the heroine of *Persuasion* is able to achieve the freedom to be rational, and therefore human, that Mary Wollstonecraft had envisioned twenty-five years before.

For the gentle Anne herself is not immune from such a topic. It arises in what is perhaps the most consistently misread scene in all of Jane Austen's novels: the dialogue with Captain Harville at the White Hart Inn, which Jane Austen substituted for a more conventionally contrived love scene after she had finished the novel. Therefore, if we define *Sanditon* as a sketch and a fragment, we may regard this scene as Jane Austen's last fully realized piece of writing. In the undercurrents of Anne's romantic lyric, Jane Austen's vaunted "realism" is given its fullest expression. If, in one side of the mirror, Anne's speeches are a simple lyric cry, a nineteenth-century provincial version of the "patience-on-a-monument" motif, a glance through the looking-glass shows us their unromantic foundation. Women feel, quite simply, because they are given nothing else to do: "We certainly do not forget you, so soon as you forget us. *It is, perhaps, our fate rather than our merit.* We cannot help ourselves. *We live at home, quiet, confined, and our feelings prey upon us. You are forced on exertion.* You have always a profession, pursuits, business of some sort or other, to take you back into the world immediately, and continual occupation and change soon weaken impressions" (my emphasis).

Only a rather cruel male supremacist would define intense suffering as the "merit" of women rather than their "fate." But many critics have done so, both in their reading of this scene and in their sentimentalization of one side of Anne Elliot's character. She does not sentimentalize herself, and she is right not to. Her modest and simple tone should not blind us to what she is saying: women do not pine for love and suffer over men because they are by nature more sensitive and emotionally refined, and thus, as it were, "created to suffer." They suffer because their social role creates for them a life without exertion, in which state one's feelings become a torment. Once again, Mary Wollstonecraft may help us to read Jane Austen, by defining a similar condition, though less sympathetically: "Their senses are inflamed, and their understandings neglected, consequently they become the prey of their senses, delicately termed sensibility, and are blown about by every momentary gust of feeling. . . . Ever restless and anxious, their over-exercised sensibility not only renders them uncomfortable themselves, but troublesome, to use a soft phrase, to others. . . . Miserable, indeed, must be that being whose cultivation of mind has only tended to inflame its passions!" (*Vindication*).

Anne shifts this theme into another key in her next speech: " 'You have difficulties, and privations, and dangers enough to struggle with. You are always labouring and toiling, exposed to every risk and hardship. Your home, country, friends, all quitted. Neither time, nor health, nor life, to be called your own. It would be too hard indeed' (with a faltering voice) 'if woman's feelings were to be added to all this'." Anne's own emotional situation is leading her to take an elegiac, even a tragic, view of all human affairs, men's doing as well as women's suffering. Her characteristic richness of sympathy may also obscure her basic statement: the life that women are expected to live is conducive primarily to anguish. We do not expect a radical definition of woman's nature from Anne Elliot, and putting such words in her mouth is a supreme example of Jane Austen's ability to bury her most significant statements in contexts that allow complacent readers to accept her without dismay.

But readers who want Jane Austen to be a defender of the status quo will have to skip Anne's next speech entirely. Harville has substituted for his initial interpretation of her words another male cliché about woman as "la belle dame sans merci." He supports his statement by citing poetry, songs, and proverbs, to which Anne replies, "If you please, no references to examples in books. Men have had every advantage of us in telling their own story. Education has been theirs in so much higher a degree; the pen has been in their hands. I will not allow books to prove anything."

This is Anne's only complaint that is directed specifically against society. It is mild, but telling. Society's conventional view of women is dictated by men, because better education allows men to write all the books. Only unequal education prevents women from writing as many books as men do, and presumably, books that are as good; if they were allowed to make themselves heard, the conventional view of women would be radically altered. This emphasis upon unequal education rather than inherent inequality once again recalls Mary Wollstonecraft's central thesis in *Vindication of the Rights of Woman;* and in fact, Jane Austen did write the books whose lack Anne Elliot deplores. How profoundly they subvert the conventional picture of the "elegant female," of the "fine lady," is something that only our own century has begun to see. In Jane Austen's most famous and emotionally charged love scene, the heroine speaks obliquely for her right to exist in something more than love. These speeches reveal Anne as worthy not only of Wentworth, but of Mrs. Croft as well.

Anne's life after her marriage seems to be forecast for us in the dialogue between the Crofts and Wentworth which has been cited above. Wentworth is holding forth vehemently on the evils of women at sea: "I hate to hear of women on board, or to see them on board; and no ship, under my command, shall ever convey . . . ladies anywhere, if I can help it." "Women . . . have no *right* to be comfortable on board" (Jane Austen's emphasis). Admiral Croft reminds Wentworth that once he marries, his feelings will change, and his sister berates him for seeing women only as "fine ladies." The irony is simple and cheerful. Once exposed to the sea air at Lyme, Anne will begin to "bloom" again. This word, which is applied to Anne throughout the novel, hints at her renewed conjunc-

Illustration from an 1897 edition of Persuasion, *depicting Wentworth and Anne Elliot.*

tion with the processes of nature. Like Mrs. Croft, Anne will be "liberated" after her marriage. She will go to sea.

To end a discussion of ***Persuasion*** on a note of triumph and cheer, however, is to falsify another side of the sea world. Death is not associated only with the land. It is a continual presence on the sea, and the book is always reminding us that great disaster is the other side of great achievement. Wentworth's description of his triumphant voyage on the *Asp* strikes a note that is sounded throughout: "I knew that we should either go to the bottom together, or that she would be the making of me."

Like *The Tempest* again, ***Persuasion*** does not end with a chorus of reconciliation and joy, but with a glimpse of "quick alarm." As in *The Tempest,* the sea is threatening as well as merciful. "His profession was all that could ever make [Anne's] friends wish [her] tenderness less; the dread of a future war all that could dim her sunshine. She gloried in being a sailor's wife, but she must pay the tax of quick alarm for belonging to that profession which is, if possible, more distinguished in its domestic virtues than in its national importance." Danger is the other side of romance. The sense of liberation does not nullify the sense of fear: it contains it. As in Tennyson's "Ulysses," the triumph of the sea over the land contains the possibility of violent death, but to die violently is better than to rust away on land in stagnant enclosure.

This final union of fear and joy strikes the emotional heart of the book. The pervasive tone of ***Persuasion*** is a tone of neither triumph nor tragedy; it is a paradoxical mixture of pleasure and pain. A description of a paradox of intense contrasting emotions is repeated over and over again. It is almost savored. "[Anne was] grieving to forego all the influence so sweet and so sad of the autumnal months in the country." "Anne walked up at the same time, in a sort of desolate tranquility." "It was a proof of his own warm and amiable heart, which she could not contemplate without emotions so compounded of pleasure and pain, that she knew not which prevailed." "Internally [Lady Russell's] heart revelled in angry pleasure, in pleased contempt." "All the overpowering, blinding, bewildering, first effects of strong surprise were over with her. Still, however, she had enough to feel! It was agitation, pain, pleasure, a something between delight and misery." "When pain is over, the remembrance of it often becomes a pleasure." "There was no delay, no waste of time. She was deep in the happiness of such misery, or the misery of such happiness, instantly." And so on. Emotional extremes meet and marry in an intensity of feeling.

This blended tone of ***Persuasion*** brings us close to the elegiac lyrics of Jane Austen's contemporaries, Shelley and Keats, whose poetry dwells on the inward complexities that accompany a release of passion and vision. The revolutionary vision of ***Persuasion*** encompasses both the polemics of a Mary Wollstonecraft and the subtleties of later Romantic art. Jane Austen was a provincial spinster who did, perhaps, spend most of her life indoors, but she was not encased in the eighteenth century; she felt and recorded the vibrations of her age as the Romantic poets and prophets did, but, like the lady that she was, she spoke more softly. (pp. 38-54)

Nina Auerbach, "O Brave New World: Evolution and Revolution in 'Persuasion'," in her *Romantic Imprisonment: Women and Other Glorified Outcasts, Columbia University Press, 1985, pp. 38-54.*

A. Walton Litz (essay date 1975)

[*Litz is an American educator and critic specializing in literature of the Modernist period. In the following excerpt, he examines the influence of English Romantic poetry on the content and style of* Persuasion.]

Persuasion has received highly intelligent criticism in recent years, after a long period of comparative neglect, and the lines of investigation have followed Virginia Woolf's suggestive comments [see excerpt dated 1925]. Critics have been concerned with the 'personal' quality of the novel and the problems it poses for biographical interpretation; with the obvious unevenness in narrative structure; with the 'poetic' use of landscape, and the hovering influence of Romantic poetry; with the pervasive presence of Anne Elliot's consciousness; with new effects in style and syntax; with the 'modernity' of Anne Elliot, an isolated personality in a rapidly changing society. Many of these problems were discussed in my own earlier study [*Jane Austen: A Study of Her Artistic Development,* 1965] but I would like to consider them again, I hope with greater tact and particularity. Of all Jane Austen's major works, **Persuasion** suffers the most from easy generalizations, and requires the most minute discriminations. For example, my own remark that 'more than has been generally realized or acknowledged, [Jane Austen] was influenced by the Romantic poetry of the early nineteenth century' has been frequently quoted with approval, but I now feel that it needs severe definition: What are the qualities of Romantic poetry reflected in Jane Austen's new attitudes toward nature and 'feeling'? How do these new effects in **Persuasion** differ from those in the earlier novels? The following pages offer no startlingly new perspectives, but rather a refinement of several familiar points of view.

In spite of Jane Austen's warning to a friend 'that it was her desire to create, not to reproduce,' readers from her own day to the present have delighted in identifying Anne Elliot with Jane Austen. Anne is twenty-seven years old, a dangerous age for Jane Austen's young women; Charlotte Lucas is 'about twenty-seven' when she accepts the foolish Mr Collins, and Marianne in *Sense and Sensibility* laments that a 'woman of seven and twenty . . . can never hope to feel or inspire affection again.' Jane Austen's own broken 'romance,' the details of which are hopelessly obscure, seems to have taken place around 1802, when she was twenty-seven, and Virginia Woolf was probably justified in her belief that **Persuasion** confirms 'the biographical fact that Jane Austen had loved.' Other passages from Jane Austen's life are obviously driven deep into the life of the novel: the careers of her sailor brothers, and the pleasant days at Lyme Regis in the summer of 1804, when she explored the area with Cassandra and her brother Henry. These facts give a certain sanction to biographical speculation, if one cares for that sort of thing, but they do not explain the intensity with which readers have pursued

the 'personal' element in **Persuasion.** That intensity comes from the fiction, not from a curiosity about the writer's life, and has to do with the lost 'bloom' of Anne Elliot.

If asked to summarize Jane Austen's last three novels in three phrases, one might say that **Mansfield Park** is about the loss and return of principles, **Emma** about the loss and return of reason, **Persuasion** about the loss and return of 'bloom.' To make these formulations, however crude they may be, is to appreciate the deeply *physical* impact of **Persuasion.** The motif words of the earlier novels are the value terms of the eighteenth century–sense, taste, genius, judgment, understanding, and so forth–and their constant repetition is a sign of Jane Austen's rational vision. But there is something idiosyncratic and almost obsessive about the recurrence of 'bloom' in the first volume of **Persuasion.** 'Anne Elliot had been a very pretty girl, but her bloom had vanished early,' while Elizabeth and Sir Walter remained 'as blooming as ever,' at least in their own eyes. The word occurs six times in the first volume, culminating in the scene on the steps at Lyme where Anne, 'the bloom and freshness of youth restored by the fine wind,' attracts the admiration of Wentworth and Mr Elliot. It then disappears from the novel, only to return in the 'blushes' which mark Anne's repossession of her lost love: 'Glowing and lovely in sensibility and happiness, and more generally admired than she thought about or cared for, she had cheerful or forebearing feelings for every creature around her.'

But 'bloom' is only one of many physical metaphors which make the first half of **Persuasion** Jane Austen's most deeply felt fiction. A sense of the earth's unchanging rhythms, confined in earlier works to an occasional scene and usually presented in the 'picturesque' manner, provides a ground-rhythm for the first half of **Persuasion.**

> Thirteen years had seen [Elizabeth] the mistress of Kellynch Hall, presiding and directing with a self-possession and decision which could never have given the idea of her being younger than she was. For thirteen years had she been doing the honours, and laying down the domestic law at home, and leading the way to the chaise and four, and walking immediately after Lady Russell out of all the drawing-rooms and dining-rooms in the country. Thirteen winters' revolving frosts had seen her opening every ball of credit which a scanty neighbourhood afforded; and thirteen springs shewn their blossom, as she travelled up to London with her father, for a few weeks annual enjoyment of the great world.

This marvellous passage, which acts out the progress of time and exposes the static lives of Kellynch Hall, would have been cast in a very different form in the earlier fictions. Narrative summary and authorial commentary have given way to a poetic sense of time's changes that commands the first volume of **Persuasion.** The chapters set in Somerset are pervaded with references to the autumnal landscape, which dominates Anne's emotions as she waits with little hope for 'a second spring of youth and beauty'; while the scenes at Lyme are softened by the romantic landscape and the freshening 'flow of the tide.' This poetic use of nature as a structure of feeling, which not only offers metaphors for our emotions but controls them with its unchanging rhythms and changing moods, comes to a climax in the scene where Anne's mind, depressed by the recent events at Lyme and her imminent departure for Bath, becomes part of the dark November landscape.

> An hour's complete leisure for such reflections as these, on a dark November day, a small thick rain almost blotting out the very few objects ever to be discerned from the windows, was enough to make the sound of Lady Russell's carriage exceedingly welcome; and yet, though desirous to be gone, she could not quit the mansion-house, or look an adieu to the cottage, with its black, dripping, and comfortless veranda, or even notice through the misty glasses the last humble tenements of the village, without a saddened heart.—Scenes had passed in Uppercross, which made it precious. It stood the record of many sensations of pain, once severe, but now softened . . . She left it all behind her; all but the recollection that such things had been.

Such a passage fully justifies Angus Wilson's reply to those who say 'that there is no poetry in Jane Austen' ["The Neighborhood of Tombuctoo" in *Critical Essays on Jane Austen,* edited by B. C. Southam, 1968]. The poetry is there in 'the essential atmosphere of her novels–an instinctive response to those basic realities of nature, the weather and the seasons.' All of Jane Austen's heroines, whether declining like Fanny and Anne, or flourishing like Emma and Elizabeth, are acutely conscious of their physical lives. The fact of 'being alive,' as Wilson says, 'is never absent from the texture of the thoughts of her heroines.'

Most readers of Jane Austen would agree with Wilson's claims, and would also agree that *Persuasion* represents her most successful effort to build this sense of physical life into the language and structure of a novel. If asked for proof, they would point to the frequent allusions to the Romantic poets, especially Byron and Scott, and to the famous passage where Anne's autumnal walk is permeated with poetic 'musings and quotations.' But here they would be, I think, demonstrably wrong. Most of Jane Austen's direct references to the Romantic poets in *Persuasion* are associated with Captain Benwick, and have the same satiric intent—although they are gentler in manner—as the references to contemporary poetry in *Sanditon.* When Anne and Captain Benwick talk of 'poetry, the richness of the present age,' his enthusiasm for Scott and Byron is so emotional that Anne ventures to 'recommend a larger allowance of prose in his daily study,' and her caution is confirmed when Benwick's raptures on Byron's *The Corsair* are interrupted by Louisa's rash jump to the Lower Cobb. Jane Austen has no place in her world for the Byronic hero, and Wentworth is not—as one recent critic has claimed—a successful recreation of Byron's Corsair.

Surely Angus Wilson is right in implying that Jane Austen's assimilation of the new poetry is most profound when least obtrusive. 'If we seek for any conscious concern for nature, we get either the Gilpin textbook stuff of *Northanger Abbey* or the "thoughts from the poets" of Fanny or Anne Elliot.' A good example of Jane Austen's conscious concern for nature would be the scene in *Mansfield Park* where Edmund joins Fanny at the window to view the stars:

> his eyes soon turned like her's towards the scene without, where all that was solemn and soothing, and lovely, appeared in the brilliancy of an unclouded night, and the contrast of the deep shade of the woods. Fanny spoke her feelings. 'Here's harmony!' said she, 'Here's repose! Here's what may leave all painting and all music behind, and what poetry only can attempt to describe. Here's what may tranquillize every care, and lift the heart to rapture! When I look out on such a night as this, I feel as if there could be neither wickedness nor sorrow in the world; and there certainly would be less of both if the sublimity of Nature were more attended to, and people were carried more out of themselves by contemplating such a scene.'

This is a set-piece out of eighteenth-century aesthetics, in which Fanny responds to the natural landscape with appropriate emotions of 'sublimity' and transport. Even the descriptive details are heavily literary, drawn from Shakespeare and Ann Radcliffe. A different and more intimate sense of landscape is displayed by the famous autumnal walk in *Persuasion:*

> Her *pleasure* in the walk must arise from the exercise and the day, from the view of the last smiles of the year upon the tawny leaves and withered hedges, and from repeating to herself some few of the thousand poetical descriptions extant of autumn, that season of peculiar and inexhaustible influence on the mind of taste and tenderness . . . After one of the many praises of the day, which were continually bursting forth, Captain Wentworth added:

> 'What glorious weather for the Admiral and my sister! They meant to take a long drive this morning; perhaps we may hail them from some of these hills. They talked of coming into this side of the country. I wonder whereabouts they will upset to-day. Oh! it does happen very often, I assure you—but my sister makes nothing of it—she would as lieve be tossed out as not.'

> 'Ah! You make the most of it, I know,' cried Louisa, 'but if it were really so, I should do just the same in her place. If I loved a man, as she loves the Admiral, I would be always with him, nothing should ever separate us, and I would rather be overturned by him, than driven safely by anybody else.'

> . . . Anne could not immediately fall into a quotation again. The sweet scenes of autumn were for a while put by–unless some tender sonnet, fraught with the apt analogy of the declining year, with declining happiness, and the images of youth and hope, and spring, all gone together, blessed her memory. She roused herself to say, as they struck by order into another path, 'Is not this one of the ways to Winthrop?' But nobody heard, or, at least, nobody answered her.

> Winthrop . . . was their destination; and after another half mile of gradual ascent through large enclosures, where the ploughs at work, and

the fresh-made path spoke the farmer, counteracting the sweets of poetical despondence, and
meaning to have spring again, they gained the
summit of the most considerable hill, which
parted Uppercross and Winthrop, and soon
commanded a full view of the latter, at the foot
of the hill on the other side.

Fanny Price has three transparencies on the panes of her
window, depicting Tintern Abbey, a cave in Italy, and a
moonlit lake in Cumberland; the subjects may suggest
Wordsworth, but her tastes are strictly for the picturesque
and the academic sublime. The presentation of Anne Elliot's autumnal walk is much closer to a Wordsworthian
view of nature, emphasizing as it does the responsive ego,
yet it would be a mistake to identify Anne's thoughts on
autumn with the powerful reactions of the great Romantic
poets. Her 'poetical descriptions' are, most likely, culled
from the popular magazine poets, and her literary taste is
not necessarily superior to that of Fanny Price. What is
different in **Persuasion** is the way in which two views of
nature, both conventional, have been internalized to provide a complex and original impression. Whereas in **Sense
and Sensibility** Marianne's sentimental effusions on nature are dramatically counterpointed to Edward's practical view, her sense of the picturesque set against his sense
of the ordinary, the autumnal scene from **Persuasion** locates both responses within Anne's mind. After she has
fallen sentimentally and self-indulgently into quotation,
the sight of the farmer ploughing, 'meaning to have spring
again,' rescues Anne from 'poetical despondence,' and restores her emotional composure. This passage is infused
with a sense of immediate feeling absent from the description of Fanny's rapture, but it remains a consciously 'literary' construction, closer to Cowper than to Wordsworth.
In the final scene at Uppercross already quoted, however,
the effects are truly Wordsworthian. The cottage viewed
on a 'dark November day' is a stockpiece of the picturesque, with its irregular shape and misty appearance, yet
it is transformed by memory, by 'reflection' and 'recollection,' into a complex symbol of what 'had been.' In the
opening chapters of **Persuasion** Jane Austen is most 'poetic,' most Wordsworthian, when she is willing to abandon
the literary allusion and give herself to a direct passionate
rendering of nature's changing face.

Our discussion of the romantic dimensions of **Persuasion**
has been confined to the first half of the novel, the opening
twelve chapters, and for good reason: the latter half of the
novel is radically different in style and narrative method.
Any census of the metaphors of natural change will find
that they are concentrated in the first half, suggesting that
Persuasion has a deliberate two-part structure that has
been often overlooked. **Northanger Abbey,** its companion
in the posthumous four-volume edition, was always intended as a two-part romance: the original version sold to
the publisher Crosby in 1803 was described as 'a MS.
Novel in 2 vol. entitled Susan.' All of Jane Austen's other
novels were published in three parts, and designed to fit
that pattern. Thus the three-part division of **Pride and
Prejudice** follows the three-act structure of a stage comedy, and the three parts of **Emma** correspond to three successive stages in a process of self-discovery. But Jane Austen deliberately chose to construct **Persuasion** in two parts

(the numbering of the cancelled last chapters proves this),
and much of the apparent unevenness or 'dullness' of the
novel is explained by this artistic decision.

The first half of **Persuasion** portrays Anne Elliot against
a natural landscape, and it is there that Jane Austen's newfound Romanticism is concentrated. Once the action has
moved to Bath a claustrophobic atmosphere descends,
and the external world becomes insubstantial: Anne, without a human confidante but sustained by nature in the first
volume, is left terribly alone in the second volume–only
the reconciliation with Wentworth can save her from anonymity. The language of the second volume, although less
satisfying to our modern taste, is deliberately fashioned to
express this sense of personalities moving in a vacuum.
The rich metaphors of Volume One are replaced by the
eighteenth-century value terms of earlier novels, but—as
Virginia Woolf noted—with a sense of perfunctory ritual.
It is as if Jane Austen, hurrying to the final reunion, were
at long last impatient with those weighty terms of judgment and admonition that had served her so well in earlier
years. In a space of seven pages the word 'sensible' occurs
six times along with 'pride,' 'understanding,' 'decorum,'
'candid,' 'amiable,' 'sensibility,' and 'imaginations.' This
is an aggressive return to the abstract language of the earlier fictions, but it is difficult to tell whether Jane Austen
does so out of boredom—as Virginia Woolf seems to
imply—or out of a desire to convey the eighteenth-century
stasis of Bath. In any case, the contrast between the first
and second volumes of **Persuasion** is profound in the
realm of language and metaphor, reflecting the radical dislocation of Anne Elliot. And there are differences in narrative method as well. The first half of the novel presents
Anne as the commanding center. As Norman Page has
shown [in his *The Language of Jane Austen,* 1972], the
'slanting of the narrative through the mental life of the
principal character,' already developed in **Emma,** is the
dominant mode in **Persuasion;** narrative, authorial comment, dialogue, and interior monologue merge into one
another. 'Free indirect speech,' in which lengthy dialogue
is compressed and located within the central consciousness, is combined with more conventional narrative methods to give a sense of the entire novel taking place within
the mind of the heroine. But this complex method of internalized presentation is most evident in the first volume,
and in Volume Two—as Anne Elliot enters the alien environment of Bath—Jane Austen reverts to earlier and more
objective methods. It is a sign of Anne's isolation that the
revelation of William Elliot's true nature, and even of
Wentworth's love, must come to her through letters, one
of the most 'external' of fictional devices.

Another aspect of style in **Persuasion,** present in both volumes but more characteristic of the first, is a rapid and
nervous syntax designed to imitate the bombardment of
impressions upon the mind. A fine example occurs when
Anne, a victim of the rambunctious child Walter, is rescued by Captain Wentworth.

> In another moment, however, she found herself
> in the state of being released from him; some one
> was taking him from her, though he had bent
> down her head so much, that his little sturdy
> hands were unfastened from around her neck,

and he was resolutely borne away, before she knew that Captain Wentworth had done it.

Here the passive construction, the indefinite pronouns, and the staccato syntax all imitate the effect of the incident upon Anne's mind. Page is certainly right when he says that such passages, common in **Persuasion,** do not make statements about an emotional situation but suggest the quality of the experience through the movement of the prose.

When we examine these details of sentence structure and punctuation, however, a certain caution is necessary. The sentences of **Persuasion** do, for the most part, move away from the Johnsonian norm, and in the revisions of the cancelled chapters one can see Jane Austen struggling toward a more expressive form. But one should remember that all of Jane Austen's manuscripts display a greater flexibility of sentence structure than her printed works, and although the cancelled chapters of **Persuasion** and the manuscript of **Sanditon** exhibit an extraordinary freedom, many of the same qualities are present in the manuscript of *The Watsons* (c. 1803-4). The printer of Jane Austen's day had great license with punctuation, paragraphing, and even sentence structure, and part of the 'flowing' quality of **Persuasion** may derive from a printer (T. Davison) whose standards and tastes differed from those of the printers who handled the earlier manuscripts. This does not affect the general import of Page's argument, but the dangers of relying too heavily on details of punctuation and sentence structure are evident in Page's comparison of a passage in the cancelled Chapter Ten with the revised version:

> He found that he was considered by his friend Harville an engaged man. The Harvilles entertained not a doubt of a mutual attachment between him and Louisa; and though this to a degree was contradicted instantly, it yet made him feel that perhaps by *her* family, by everybody, by *herself* even, the same idea might be held, and that he was not *free* in honour, though if such were to be the conclusion, too free alas! in heart. He had never thought justly on this subject before, and he had not sufficiently considered that his excessive intimacy at Uppercross must have its danger of ill consequence in many ways; and that while trying whether he could attach himself to either of the girls, he might be exciting unpleasant reports if not raising unrequited regard.
>
> He found too late that he had entangled himself [cancelled version].
>
> 'I found,' said he, 'that I was considered by Harville an engaged man! That neither Harville nor his wife entertained a doubt of our mutual attachment. I was startled and shocked. To a degree, I could contradict this instantly; but, when I began to reflect that others might have felt the same—her own family, nay, perhaps herself, I was no longer at my own disposal. I was hers in honour if she wished it. I had been unguarded. I had not thought seriously on this subject before. I had not considered that my excessive intimacy must have its danger of ill consequence in many ways; and that I had no right to be trying

whether I could attach myself to either of the girls, at the risk of raising even an unpleasant report, were there no other ill effects. I had been grossly wrong, and must abide the consequences.'

> He found too late, in short, that he had entangled himself . . . [final version].

Page's comments upon the improved 'personal and dramatic form' of the revised version are just, but his observation that three long sentences have been broken up into nine shorter sentences falls away when we realize that the cancelled version, as Page quotes it, is actually reprinted from the 1870 *Memoir,* where Jane Austen's lively manuscript had been 'regularized' by the Victorian editor and printer. The actual passage from the manuscript, reproduced below, shows the nervous energy of Jane Austen's first draft, and reminds us that the relationship between Jane Austen's first drafts and the printed texts must often have been that of sketch to varnished canvas.

> He found that he was considered by his friend Harville, as an engaged Man. The Harvilles entertained not a doubt of a mutual attachment between him & Louisa—and though this to *a degree,* was contradicted instantly—it yet made him feel that perhaps by *her* family, by everybody, by *herself* even, the same idea might be held—and that he was not *free* in honour—though, if such were to be the conclusion, too free alas! in Heart.—He had never thought justly on this subject before—he had not sufficiently considered that his excessive Intimacy at Uppercross must have it's danger of ill consequence in many ways, and that while trying whether he could attach himself to either of the Girls, he might be exciting unpleasant reports, if not, raising unrequited regard!—He found, too late, that he had entangled himself—

Persuasion reveals an author who is unusually sensitive to the forces of her time. Of all the novels, it is the only one where the action is precisely dated, and that date is 'the present' (1814-15). The other novels are slightly retrospective in their treatments of manners and events, but **Persuasion** is filled with references to contemporary history ('This peace will be turning all our rich Navy Officers ashore') and the most recent publications of the Romantic poets. These topical references are matched by certain passages in the novel which seem to reflect the events of 1815-16, when **Persuasion** was a work-in-progress. The description of the 'green chasms between romantic rocks' near Lyme may echo *Kubla Khan,* first published in 1816, although the chronology is doubtful and the whole passage strikes me as more picturesque than Coleridgean; more likely is the influence of Scott's famous review in the *Quarterly* upon Jane Austen's retreat from 'prudence.' In Scott's review, which Jane Austen had read by 1 April 1816 (**Persuasion** was not completed until the summer), Jane Austen was characterized as anti-sentimental and anti-romantic, her novels bearing the same relation to those of the 'sentimental and romantic cast, that cornfields and cottages and meadows bear to . . . the rugged sublimities of a mountain landscape.' Scott then went on to deplore the neglect of Cupid and romantic feelings, implying that Jane Austen coupled 'Cupid indivisibly with calculating prudence.' This must have stung the creator of Anne Elliot, and we may take her passionate statement on 'romance' as a covert reply.

> How eloquent could Anne Elliot have been,—how eloquent, at least, were her wishes on the side of early warm attachment, and a cheerful confidence in futurity, against that over-anxious caution which seems to insult exertion and distrust Providence!–She had been forced into prudence in her youth, she learned romance as she grew older–the natural sequel of an unnatural beginning.

Unlike Jane Austen's other major works, *Persuasion* is filled with a sense of the moment–both historical and personal–at which it was written.

It is not these particular signs of contemporaneity, however, but Jane Austen's powerful response to a changing relationship between society and the self that gives *Persuasion* its hold on the modern reader. In *Pride and Prejudice* the old order of Darcy and Pemberley can be accommodated to the new forces represented by the middle-class Gardiners; in *Persuasion* there seems little hope of accommodation between stasis and unpredictable change. 'The Musgroves, like their houses, were in a state of alteration, perhaps of improvement,' and this tension between old ways and 'more modern minds and manners' divides the novel. Sir Walter has retreated into a wilderness of mirrors, the Baronetage his favorite looking-glass, and Jane Austen's sympathies are firmly on the side of the new natural aristocracy represented by the Navy; but in giving her allegiance to them Jane Austen knows that Anne must 'pay the tax of quick alarm'. The ending of *Persuasion,* unlike that of the other novels, is open and problematic. One could glean from *Persuasion* a list of terms which would make it sound like a textbook in modern sociology: 'estrangement,' 'imprisonment,' 'alienations,' 'removals.' The heroine is 'only Anne,' and the word 'alone' echoes through the novel. *Persuasion* is filled with a sense of what time can do, with its 'changes, alienations, removals': it can lead to 'oblivion of the past' and even annihilation of the self. Anne has painfully learned 'the art of knowing our own nothingness beyond our own circle,' and at the end of the novel that circle, so lovingly restored and enlarged, has no permanence beyond the moment. Virginia Woolf might have said that *Persuasion* is marked by a peculiar terror as well as a peculiar beauty. (pp. 222-32)

> *A. Walton Litz, " 'Persuasion': Forms of Estrangement," in* Jane Austen: Bicentenary Essays, *edited by John Halperin, Cambridge University Press, 1975, pp. 221-32.*

Sandra M. Gilbert and Susan Gubar   (essay date 1979)

[*Gilbert and Gubar are American educators and critics best known for their* The Madwoman in the Attic: The Woman Writer and the Nineteenth-Century Literary Imagination, *which offers revisionist readings of the social and political history of women as reflected in fiction by women. In the following excerpt from that study, they demonstrate ways in which Anne Elliot becomes meta-phorically invisible in her family and community, indicating, the critics contend, Austen's dissatisfaction with the passivity and perceived unimportance of women in her society.*]

[Austen's] last completed novel, *Persuasion,* focuses on an angelically quiet heroine who has given up her search for a story and has thereby effectively killed herself off. Almost as if she were reviewing the implications of her own plots, Austen explores in *Persuasion* the effects on women of submission to authority and the renunciation of one's life story. Eight years before the novel begins, Anne Elliot had been persuaded to renounce her romance with Captain Wentworth, but this decision sickened her by turning her into a nonentity. Forced into "knowing [her] own nothingness," Anne is a "nobody with either father or sister" so her word has "no weight." An invisible observer who tends to fade into the background, she is frequently afraid to move lest she should be seen. Having lost the "bloom" of her youth, she is but a pale vestige of what she had been and realizes that her lover "should not have known [her] again," their relationship being "now nothing!" Anne Elliot is the ghost of her own dead self; through her, Austen presents a personality haunted with a sense of menace.

At least one reason why Anne has deteriorated into a ghostly insubstantiality is that she is a dependent female in a world symbolized by her vain and selfish aristocratic father, who inhabits the mirrored dressing room of Kellynch Hall. It is significant that *Persuasion* begins with her father's book, the *Baronetage,* which is described as "the book of books" because it symbolizes male authority, patriarchal history in general, and her father's family history in particular. Existing in it as a first name and birth date in a family line that concludes with the male heir presumptive, William Walter Elliot, Esq., Anne has no reality until a husband's name can be affixed to her own. But Anne's name is a new one in the *Baronetage:* the history of this ancient, respectable line of heirs records "all the Marys and Elizabeths they had married," as if calling our attention to the hopeful fact that, unlike her sisters Mary and Elizabeth, Anne may not be forced to remain a character within this "book of books." And, in fact, Anne will reject the economic and social standards represented by the *Baronetage,* deciding, by the end of her process of personal development, that not she but the Dowager Viscountess Dalrymple and her daughter the Honourable Miss Carteret are "nothing." She will also discover that Captain Wentworth is "no longer nobody," and, even more significantly, she will insist on her ability to seek and find "at least the comfort of telling the whole story her own way."

But before Anne can become somebody, she must confront what being a nobody means: "I'm Nobody!" Emily Dickinson could occasionally avow, and certainly, by choosing not to have a story of her own, Anne seems to have decided to dwell in Dickinson's realm of "Possibility," for what Austen demonstrates through her is that the person who has not become anybody is haunted by everybody. Living in a world of her father's mirrors, Anne confronts the several selves she might have become and discovers that they all reveal the same story of the female fall from authority and autonomy.

As a motherless girl, Anne is tempted to become her own mother, although she realizes that her mother lived invisibly, unloved, within Sir Walter's house. Since Anne could marry Mr. Elliot and become the future Lady Elliot, she has to confront her mother's unhappy marriage as a potential life story not very different from that of Catherine Morland's Mrs. Tilney. At the same time, however, since serviceable Mrs. Clay is an unattached female who aspires to her mother's place in the family as her father's companion and her sister Elizabeth's intimate, Anne realizes that she could also become patient Penelope Clay, for she too understands "the art of pleasing," of making herself useful. When Anne goes to Uppercross, moreover, she functions something like Mrs. Clay, "being too much in the secret of the complaints" of each of the tenants of both households, and trying to flatter or placate each and all into good humor. The danger exists, then, that Anne's sensitivity and selflessness could degenerate into Mrs. Clay's ingratiating, hypocritical service.

Of course, Mary Musgrove's situation is also a potential identity for Anne, since Charles had actually asked for Anne's hand in marriage before he settled on her younger sister, and since Mary resembles Anne in being one of Sir Walter's unfavored daughters. Indeed, Mary's complaint that she is "always the last of my family to be noticed" could easily be voiced by Anne. Bitter about being nobody, Mary responds to domestic drudgery with "feminine" invalidism that is an extension of Anne's sickening self-doubt, as well as the only means at Mary's disposal of using her imagination to add some drama and importance to her life. Mary's hypochondria reminds us that Louisa Musgrove provides a kind of paradigm for all these women when she literally falls from the Cobb and suffers from a head injury resulting in exceedingly weak nerves. Because incapacitated Louisa is first attracted to Captain Wentworth and finally marries Captain Benwick, whose first attentions had been given to Anne, she too is clearly an image of what Anne might have become.

Through both Mary and Louisa, then, Austen illustrates how growing up female constitutes a fall from freedom, autonomy, and strength into debilitating, degrading, ladylike dependency. In direct contradiction to Captain Wentworth's sermon in the hedgerow, Louisa discovers that even firmness cannot save her from such a fall. Indeed, it actually precipitates it, and she discovers that her fate is not to jump from the stiles down the steep flight of seaside stairs but to read love poetry quietly in the parlor with a suitor suitably solicitous for her sensitive nerves. While Louisa's physical fall and subsequent illness reinforce Anne's belief that female assertion and impetuosity must be fatal, they also return us to the elegiac autumnal landscape that reflects Anne's sense of her own diminishment, the loss she experiences since her story is "now nothing."

Anne lives in a world of mirrors both because she could have become most of the women in the novel and, as the title suggests, because all the characters present her with their personal preferences rationalized into principles by which they attempt to persuade her. She is surrounded by other people's versions of her story and offered coercive advice by Sir Walter, Captain Wentworth, Charles Musgrove, Mrs. Musgrove, Lady Russell, and Mrs. Smith. Eventually, indeed, the very presence of another person becomes oppressive for Anne, since everyone but she is convinced that his or her version of reality is the only valid one. Only Anne has a sense of the different, if equally valid, perspectives of the various families and individuals among which she moves. Like Catherine Morland, she struggles against other people's fictional use and image of her; and finally she penetrates to the secret of patriarchy through absolutely no skill of detection on her own part. Just as Catherine blunders on the secret of the ancestral mansion to understand the arbitrary power of General Tilney, who does not mean what he says, Anne stumbles fortuitously on the secret of the heir to Kellynch Hall, William Elliot, who had married for money and was very unkind to his first wife. Mr. Elliot's "manoevres of selfishness and duplicity must ever be revolting" to Anne, who comes to believe that "the evil" of this suitor could easily result in "irremediable mischief."

For all of Austen's heroines, as Mr. Darcy explains, "detection could not be in [their] power, and suspicion certainly not in [their] inclination." Yet Anne does quietly and attentively watch and listen and judge the members of her world and, as Stuart Tave has shown [in *Some Words of Jane Austen*, 1973], she increasingly exerts herself to speak out, only gradually to discover that she is being heard. Furthermore, in her pilgrimage from Kellynch Hall to Upper Cross and Lyme to Bath, the landscapes she encounters function as a kind of psychic geography of her development so that, when the withered hedgerows and tawny autumnal meadows are replaced by the invigorating breezes and flowing tides of Lyme, we are hardly surprised that Anne's bloom is restored. Similarly, when Anne gets to Bath, this woman who has heard and overheard others has trouble listening because she is filled with her own feelings, and she decides that "one half of her should not be always so much wiser than the other half, or always suspecting the other half of being worse than it was." Therefore, in a room crowded with talking people, Anne manages to signal to Captain Wentworth her lack of interest in Mr. Elliot through her assertion that she has no pleasure in parties at her father's house. "She had spoken it," the narrator emphasizes; if "she trembled when it was done, conscious that her words were listened to," this is because Anne has actually "never since the loss of her dear mother, known the happiness of being listened to, or encouraged."

The fact that her mother's loss initiated her invisibility and silence is important in a book that so closely associates the heroine's felicity with her ability to articulate her sense of herself as a woman. Like Elinor Tilney [in *Northanger Abbey*], who feels that "A mother could have been always present. A mother would have been a constant friend; her influence would have been beyond all others," Anne misses the support of a loving female influence. It is then fitting that the powerful whispers of well-meaning Mrs. Musgrove and Mrs. Croft furnish Anne with the cover—the opportunity and the encouragement—to discuss with Captain Harville her sense of exclusion from patriarchal culture: "Men have had every advantage of us in telling their own story. . . . The pen has been in their hands." Anne Elliot will "not allow books to prove anything" because they "were all written by men"; her contention that women love longest because their feelings are more tender directly contradicts the authorities on women's "fickleness" that Captain Harville cites. As we have already seen, her speech reminds us that the male charge of "inconstancy" is an attack on the irrepressible interiority of women who cannot be contained within the images provided by patriarchal culture. Though Anne remains inalterably inhibited by these images since she cannot express her sense of herself by "saying what should not be said" and though she can only replace the *Baronetage* with the *Navy Lists*—a book in which women are conspicuously absent—still she is the best example of her own belief in female subjectivity. She has both deconstructed the dead selves created by all her friends to remain true to her own feelings, and she has continually reexamined and reassessed herself and her past.

Finally, Anne's fate seems to be a response to Austen's earlier stories in which girls are forced to renounce their romantic ambitions: Anne "had been forced into prudence in her youth, she learned romance as she grew older—the natural sequel of an unnatural beginning." It is she who teaches Captain Wentworth the limits of masculine assertiveness. Placed in Anne's usual situation of silently overhearing, he discovers her true, strong feelings. Significantly, his first response is to drop his pen. Then, quietly, under the cover of doing some business for Captain Harville, Captain Wentworth writes her his proposal, which he can only silently hand to her before leaving the room. At work in the common sitting-room of the White Hart Inn, alert for inauspicious interruptions, using his other letter as a kind of blotter to camouflage his designs, Captain Wentworth reminds us of Austen herself. While Anne's rebirth into "a second spring of youth and beauty" takes place within the same corrupt city that fails to fulfill its baptismal promise of purification in **Northanger Abbey,** we are led to believe that her life with this man will escape the empty elegance of Bath society.

That the sea breezes of Lyme and the watery cures of Bath have revived Anne from her ghostly passivity furnishes some evidence that naval life may be an alternative to and an escape from the corruption of the land so closely associated with patrilineal descent. Sir Walter Elliot dismisses the navy because it raises "men to honours which their fathers and grandfathers never dreamt of." And certainly Captain Wentworth seems almost miraculously to evade the hypocrisies and inequities of a rigid class system by making money on the water. But it is also true that naval life seems to justify Sir Walter's second objection that "it cuts up a man's youth and vigour most horribly." While he is thinking in his vanity only about the rapidity with which sailors lose their looks, we are given an instance of the sea cutting up a man's youth, a singularly unprepossessing man at that: when worthless Dick Musgrove is created by Austen only to be destroyed at sea, we are further reminded of her trust in the beneficence of nature, for only her anger against the unjust adulation of sons (over daughters) can explain the otherwise gratuitous cruelty of her

remarks about Mrs. Musgrove's "large fat sighings over the destiny of a son, whom alive nobody had cared for." Significantly, this happily lost son was recognized as a fool by Captain Wentworth, whose naval success closely associates him with a vocation that does not as entirely exclude women as most landlocked vocations do: his sister, Mrs. Croft, knows that the difference between "a fine gentleman" and a navy man is that the former treats women as if they were "all fine ladies, instead of rational creatures." She herself believes that "any reasonable woman may be perfectly happy" on board ship, as she was when she crossed the Atlantic four times and traveled to and from the East Indies, more comfortably (she admits) than when she settled at Kellynch Hall, although her husband *did* take down Sir Walter's mirrors.

Naval men like Captain Wentworth and Admiral Croft are also closely associated, as is Captain Harville, with the ability to create "ingenious contrivances and nice arrangements . . . to turn the actual space to the best possible account," a skill not unrelated to a "profession which is, if possible, more distinguished in its domestic virtue than in its national importance." While Austen's dowagers try to gain power by exploiting traditionally male prerogatives, the heroine of the last novel discovers an egalitarian society in which men value and participate in domestic life, while women contribute to public events, a complementary ideal that presages the emergence of an egalitarian sexual ideology. No longer confined to a female community of childbearing and childrearing, activities portrayed as dreary and dangerous in both Austen's novels and her letters, Anne triumphs in a marriage that represents the union of traditionally male and female spheres. If such a consummation can only be envisioned in the future, on the water, amid imminent threats of war, Austen nonetheless celebrates friendship between the sexes as her lovers progress down Bath streets with "smiles reined in and spirits dancing in private rapture."

When Captain Wentworth accepts Anne's account of their story, he agrees with her highly ambivalent assessment of the woman who advised her to break off their engagement. Lady Russell is one of Austen's last pushy widows, but, in this novel which revises Austen's earlier endorsement of the necessity of taming the shrew, the cautionary monster is one of effacement rather than assertion. If the powerful origin of **Emma** is the psychologically coercive model of the woman as lady, in **Persuasion** Austen describes a heroine who refuses to become a lady. Anne Elliot listened to the persuasions of the powerful, wealthy, proper Lady Russell when she refrained from marrying the man she loved. But finally she rejects Lady Russell, who is shown to value rank and class over the dictates of the heart, in part because her own heart is perverted, capable of revelling "in angry pleasure, in pleased contempt" at events sure to hurt Anne. Anne replaces this cruel stepmother with a different kind of mother surrogate, another widow, Mrs. Smith. Poor, confined, crippled by rheumatic fever, Mrs. Smith serves as an emblem of the dispossession of women in a patriarchal society, and she is, as Paul Zietlow has shown [see excerpt dated 1965], also the embodiment of what Anne's future could have been under less fortunate circumstances.

While Lady Russell persuaded Anne not to marry a poor man, Mrs. Smith explains why she should not marry a rich one. Robbed of all physical and economic liberty, with "no child . . . no relatives . . . no health . . . no possibility of moving," Mrs. Smith is paralyzed, and, although she exerts herself to maintain good humor in her tight place, she is also maddened. She expresses her rage at the false forms of civility, specifically at the corrupt and selfish double-dealings of Mr. Elliot, the heir apparent and the epitome of patriarchal society. With fierce delight in her revengeful revelations, Mrs. Smith proclaims herself an "injured, angry woman" and she articulates Anne's—and Austen's—unacknowledged fury at her own unnecessary and unrecognized paralysis and suffering. But although this widow is a voice of angry female revolt against the injustices of patriarchy, she is as much a resident of Bath as Lady Russell. This fashionable place for cures reminds us that society *is* sick. And Mrs. Smith participates in the moral degeneration of the place when she selfishly lies to Anne, placing her own advancement over Anne's potential marital happiness by withholding the truth about Mr. Elliot until she is quite sure Anne does not mean to marry him. Like Lady Russell, then, this other voice within Anne's psyche can also potentially victimize her.

It is Mrs. Smith's curious source of knowledge, her informant or her muse, who best reveals the corruption that has permeated and informs the social conventions of English society. A woman who nurses sick people back to health, wonderfully named nurse Rooke resembles in her absence from the novel many of Austen's most important avatars. Pictured perched on the side of a sickbed, nurse Rooke seems as much a vulture as a savior of the afflicted. Her freedom of movement in society resembles the movement of a chess piece which moves parallel to the edge of the board, thereby defining the limits of the game. And she "rooks" her patients, discovering their hidden hoards.

Providing ears and eyes for the confined Mrs. Smith, this seemingly ubiquitous, omniscient nurse is privy to all the secrets of the sickbed. She has taught Mrs. Smith how to knit, and she sells "little threadcases, pin-cushions and cardracks" not unlike Austen's "little bit (two Inches wide) of Ivory." What she brings as part of her services are volumes furnished from the sick chamber, stories of weakness and selfishness and impatience. A historian of private life, nurse Rooke communicates in typically female fashion as a gossip engaged in the seemingly trivial, charitable office of selling feminine handcrafts to the fashionable world. This and her gossip are, of course, a disguise for her subversive interest in uncovering the sordid realities behind the decorous appearances of high life. In this regard she is a wonderful portrait of Austen herself. While seemingly unreliable, dependent (as she is) for information upon many interactions which are subject to errors of misconception and ignorance, this uniquely female historian turns out to be accurate and revolutionary as she reveals "the manoevers of selfishness and duplicity" of one class to another. Finally, sensible nurse Rooke also resembles Austen in that, despite all her knowledge, she does not withdraw from society. Instead, acknowledging herself a member of the community she nurses, she is a "favourer of matrimony" who has her own "flying visions" of social success. Although many of Austen's female characters seem inalterably locked inside Mr. Elton's riddle, nurse Rooke resembles the successful heroines of the author's works in making the best of this tight place. (pp. 174-83)

> *Sandra M. Gilbert and Susan Gubar, "Jane Austen's Cover Story (and Its Secret Agents)," in their* The Madwoman in the Attic: The Woman Writer and the Nineteenth-Century Literary Imagination, *Yale University Press, 1979, pp. 146-83.*

Tony Tanner   (essay date 1981)

[*Tanner is an American critic and editor. In the following excerpt, he discusses the restrictions that Anne Elliot's age and marital status place on her social acceptability in rural England.*]

The figure of the young girl who does not have a secure or defined position in society is familiar in Jane Austen's work, in which her heroines tend to be either overprivileged like Emma, or underprivileged like Fanny Price. The overprivileged think that they know their place, as we say, but they have to learn to redefine it; the underprivileged know that they do not have a place and they have to find one. This figure we may call the girl on the threshold, existing in that limboid space between the house of the father which has to be left and the house of the husband which was yet to be found. No longer a child and not yet a wife this threshold heroine is, precisely, in between, and she lives in betweenness. In this, I think, for Jane Austen these girls incorporated or reflected on the level of individual biography some problematical aspects of the England of her day as she perceived it, which was not what it was, nor yet what it was to become, as it were. You will remember the Musgroves in **Persuasion**: 'The Musgroves, like their houses, were in a state of alteration, perhaps of improvement. The father and mother were in the old English style, and the young people in the new.' Note the hesitation in that 'perhaps'; Jane Austen is not taking sides. There is no malice in the text directed against the new young people: 'Their dress had every advantage, their faces were rather pretty, their spirits extremely good, their manners unembarrassed and pleasant; they were of consequence at home, and favourites abroad.' They live to be 'fashionable, happy, and merry' and this frankly hedonistic commitment is not attacked by Jane Austen, for just as she knew there was a stability which preserved and transmitted values, so she knew there was an empty repetition of habit which was stagnation, and while she showed very clearly that there was a self-gratifying appetite which led to dissoluteness and destruction (as in the figures and fates of the Crawfords), so she recognised that there was a frankly self-delighting energy which engendered those innovations and renovations—those *differences,* as we say—which keep society alive. But Anne Elliot is no longer of the old nor yet does she belong to the new. She does not disapprove of the Musgrove children but 'she would not have given up her own more elegant and cultivated mind for all their enjoyments.' Nor can she find self-realisation in her father's house. She is in between.

Her position is in many ways exemplary and I want to look at it a little more closely—I will be coming back to her father's house later. *Persuasion* opens in a rather remarkable way:

> Sir Walter Elliot, of Kellynch-hall, in Somersetshire, was a man who, for his own amusement, never took up any book but the Baronetage; there he found occupation for an idle hour, and consolation in a distressed one; there his faculties were roused into admiration and respect, by contemplating the limited remnant of earliest patents; there any unwelcome sensations, arising from domestic affairs, changed naturally into pity and contempt, as he turned over the almost endless creations of the last century—and there, if every other leaf were powerless, he could read his own history with an interest which never failed—this was the page at which the favourite volume always opened:
>
> 'ELLIOT OF KELLYNCH-HALL'.

Jane Austen opens her book with the description of a man looking at a book in which he reads the same words as her book opens with—'Elliot, of Kellynch-hall'. This is the kind of teasing regression which we have become accustomed to in contemporary writers but which no-one associates with the work of Jane Austen. It alerts us to at least two important considerations—the dangers involved in seeking validation and self-justification in book as opposed to life, in record rather than in action, in name as opposed to function, and the absolutely negative 'vanity' (her key word for Sir Walter) in looking for and finding one's familial and social position, one's reality, in an inscription rather than in a pattern of behaviour, in a sign rather than the range of responsibilities which it implicitly signifies. We know how fond Sir Walter is of mirrors and how hopelessly and hurtfully unaware of the real needs and feelings of his dependents he is. This opening situation poses someone fixed in an ultimate solipsism gazing with inexhaustible pleasure into the textual mirror which simply gives him back his name. The opening of Jane Austen's text—a title, a name, a domicile, a geographic location—implies a whole series of unwritten obligations and responsibilities related to rank, family, society and the very land itself, none of which Sir Walter Elliot, book-bound and self-mesmerised, either keeps or recognises. He is only interested in himself and what reflects him—mirrors or daughters. Thus he likes Elizabeth because she is 'very like himself'—this is parenthood as narcissism—and Mary has 'acquired a little artificial importance' because she has married into a tolerably respectable family—'but Anne, with an elegance of mind and sweetness of character, which must have placed her high with any people of real understanding, was nobody with either father or sister: her word had no weight; her convenience was always to give way;—she was only Anne.' Only Anne—no rank, no effective surname, no house, no location; her words are weightless, and physically speaking she always has to 'give way'—that is, accept perpetual displacement. She is a speaker who is unheard; she is a body who is a 'nobody'. I emphasise this because the problems of the body who is, socially speaking, a nobody, were to engage many of the great nineteenth-century writers. We might recall here

that in one of the seminal eighteenth-century novels, *La Nouvelle Heloise,* Julie's father refuses even to listen to the idea of her marrying Saint-Preux because Saint-Preux is what he calls 'un quidam' which means an unnamed individual or in dictionary terms 'Person (name unknown)'. This is to say that as far as the father is concerned, Saint-Preux exists in a state of 'quidamity'. As far as her father is concerned Anne also exists in that state of quidamity—she was nobody, she was only Anne: 'He had never indulged much hope, he had now none, of ever reading her name in any other page of his favourite work.' Until she is, as it were, reborn in terms of writing in the Baronetage she does not exist—not to be in the book is thus not to *be*. We may laugh at Sir Walter but Jane Austen makes it very clear what kind of perversity is involved in such a radical confusion or inversion of values whereby script and name take absolute precedence over offspring and dependents: or, to put it another way, when you cannot see the body for the book.

Anne, then, is perpetually displaced, always 'giving way' as opposed to having her *own* way—it is worth emphasising the metaphor. The story of her life consists precisely in having had her own way blocked, refused, negated. One might almost think of the book as being about dissuasion, for she is not urged or forced into doing something which she does not want to do, but into *not* doing something which her whole emotional being tells her is the right way (that is, marry Captain Wentworth at a time when he had no fortune). Her words carry no weight. So when it comes to their early engagement (and they are said to fall 'rapidly and deeply in love') Sir Walter—and Jane Austen could not have chosen her words better—'gave it all the negative', the negative of 'great astonishment, great coldness, great silence' but the important point is in the generic 'negative'. He is a father who in every way negates his daughter—gives her all the negative. Now I am not here going into the whole matter of to what extent Jane Austen might seem to approve or disapprove of the 'persuasion' exercised by Lady Russell; there is rich ambiguity there, hesitation as I called it, and phrases like the 'fair interference of friendship' in their poised ambivalence indicate that Jane Austen knew all about the multiple motivations which are at work in the impulse to exert some apparently beneficent control over a person in a weaker position. There is no point at which you can clearly distinguish persuasion from constraint or constraint from coercion, and quite properly she leaves it a blur, a confusion if you will—for it is out of just that confusion that Anne the nobody has somehow to remake her life. What Jane Austen does say is this: 'She had been forced into prudence in her youth, she learned romance as she grew older—the natural sequence of an unnatural beginning.' Most of Jane Austen's heroines have to learn some kind of prudence (not Fanny Price who has suffered for her undeviating dedication to prudentiality!). Anne, born into repression and non-recognition, has to learn romance, a deliberate oxymoron surely, for romance is associated with spontaneous feelings. But in Anne's case these had been blocked; her father gave it all the negative. To find her own positive she has, as it were, to diseducate herself from the tutoring authorities who, whether by silence or disapproval or forceful opposition, dominated that early part of her life when she was—in relation to Captain Wentworth—becoming somebody. I want to stress the rather unusual process that Jane Austen is embarking on in starting her novel in this way. The whole story of Anne's first romance with Mr Wentworth is recounted in the first paragraph of Chapter 4—that is to say, what could and did make up the basic lineaments of her other novels—how the unattached young girl finally finds the most appropriate man who proposes because of her personal qualities and not for reasons of social advancement or whatever—is here reduced to a summary paragraph. It is a novel in brief. But the marriage is blocked by the father and others so Anne has to start on a long and arduous second life, which is based on loss, denial, deprivation. This is the 'unnatural beginning' to her life, and to Jane Austen's novel which differs quite radically from her previous works in which, as I said, her heroines tend to graduate from romance to prudence. And because of what she has lost and regretted losing (again an unusual condition for the Jane Austen heroine, who has usually not yet had any significant romance when the book opens) Anne undergoes a new kind of trial and tribulation since any reference to Captain Wentworth offers 'a new sort of trial to Anne's nerves' so that she has to 'teach herself to be insensible on such points.' Among other things Anne Elliot has to combine sense and *in*sensibility, again a change from Jane Austen's earlier work.

In all this I believe it is worth thinking a little more about Captain Wentworth's profession. If we recall the husbands of previous Jane Austen heroines—Knightley, Darcy, Edmund Bertram and so on—we are usually confronted with responsible landowners or an intending clergyman. But Captain Wentworth is of course a sailor and in writing about sailors Jane Austen identifies in that brotherhood a range of values which obtain there more obviously and sincerely than they seemed to do in society. Thus, when Anne is in the party with Captain Harville and Captain Benwick and their friends, she experiences 'a bewitching charm in a degree of hospitality so uncommon, so unlike the usual style of give-and-take invitations and dinners of formality and display.' And Louisa is allowed to expound 'on the character of the navy—their friendliness, their brotherliness, their openness, their uprightness' and warmth and so on. Society in the form of Sir Walter Elliot is all empty self-regarding form and display—he has no sense of responsibility to his position, to the land, and it is significant that he rents his house to go and participate in the meaningless frivolities in Bath. This matter of renting his house is worth pausing over for a moment. The notion—'Quit Kellynch-hall'—is initially horrendous to Sir Walter. But he would as he says 'sooner quit Kellynch-hall' than undertake any economies or constraints on his unrestricted pursuit of pleasure. His relation to his house is not a responsible one—he does not see his house as part of a larger context, an interrelated rural society, an ecology, if you will; it is more like a pleasure dome or a three-dimensional mirror which flatters his vanity. So he agrees to quit it if he cannot have those pleasures. But note that 'Sir Walter could not have borne the degradation of being known to design letting his house—Mr. Shepherd had once mentioned the word "advertise"—but never dared approach it again.' . . . [Here] again we note that Sir Walter wants the profits of 'renting' while still pretending to

belong to an aristocracy which did not contaminate itself with contact with any kind of 'trade' or commerce. This is the self-deception of a figure no longer sensible of the significance of his social rank. When he does consider renting it he thinks of it in terms of 'a prize' for the fortunate tenant—'a prize'; he has no appreciation of the real value of his inherited house. And I will just note the areas to which he does not really want the new tenant to have access: 'The park would be open to him of course . . . , but what restrictions I might impose on the use of the pleasure-grounds, is another thing. I am not fond of the idea of my shrubberies being always approachable.' Funny of course—but again there is no sense of the importance and significance of the house of his fathers, the house in which he so signally fails in *his* paternal duties. To abandon it in exchange for money for mere pleasure rather than 'economise' is a very notable dereliction of his duties. This is an alteration which is most definitely not 'perhaps an improvement' but indisputably a degradation.

If society in the form of Sir Walter has sacrificed responsibility to egoism, vanity and pleasure, society in the form of Mr Elliot the cousin is unmitigatedly evil. Hence the importance of the testimony of poor Mrs Smith, a victim of the inequities of the social system and again a rather new kind of character for Jane Austen to introduce into her world. She tells Anne that 'Mr. Elliot is a man without heart or conscience; . . . who, for his own interest or ease, would be guilty of any cruelty, or any treachery, that could be perpetrated without risk of his general character.' This description is not challenged but endorsed by the book.

It would seem then, that to find a locus and image of true values Jane Austen was turning from the landed society to a group whose responsibilities are to each other and to the country but not to the existing social structure (thus the naval figures may not have exquisite manners, they may lack 'polish', but they are authentic, open, generous, loyal and so on). In Sir Walter's world of mere rank and mirrors Anne is nobody; she gains her identity by marrying effectively *out* of society. You will remember that at the end her one regret is that she has 'no relations to bestow on him which a man of sense could value . . . no family to receive and estimate him properly.' Her new family is precisely the brotherhood of the sea and for a brief moment one is oddly close to Conrad and his sense of the hypocrisies of society on land and the values of fidelity within the ranks in the navy. The conclusion of the book is worth quoting as it is quite unlike the conclusions to her previous novels: 'His profession was all that could ever make her friends wish that tenderness less; the dread of a future war all that could dim her sunshine. She gloried in being a sailor's wife, but she must pay the tax of quick alarm from belonging to that profession which is, if possible, more distinguished in its domestic virtues than in its national importance.' The possibility of war introduces a note of potential insecurity and uncertainty into the usual concluding felicities, and, perhaps even more interesting, the new location for the true practice of the 'domestic virtues' has been moved out of conventional society into a group whose commitment is to the nation rather than this or that parish or village, and whose character values are developed not out of devotion to the land but engagement with the sea. We have come a long way from Mansfield Park and Pemberley.

I want to return briefly to Anne's situation as what I have called a threshold figure, the nobody in the house who always has to 'give way'. One consequence of this position is that she is literally moved about or displaced quite frequently and in the course of this she learns something which indicates once again Jane Austen's uncanny alertness to the operations of society: 'Anne had not wanted this visit to Uppercross, to learn that a removal from one set of people to another, though at a distance of only three miles, will often include a total change of conversation, opinion, and idea. . . . She acknowledged it to be very fitting, that every little social commonwealth should dictate its own matters of discourse.' This awareness that within the one common language—English—there can be innumerable discourses according to group, place and so on is a very crucial one. It is not the same thing as a dialect but what the French critic Roland Barthes [in his *Elements of Semiology*, 1967] calls an 'idiolect'—'the language of a linguistic community, that is of a group of persons who all interpret in the same way all linguistic statements'. This is not the arid point it may sound since a great many problems in Jane Austen's world, or our own come to that, stem from the fact that people within the same language can very often not really hear each other because they are operating within different discourses—an awareness which is an aspect of their sense and very often a consequence of their detachment or isolation. If you are 'in between' then you have no settled discourse of your own and are made aware of differences in the discourses around you. No one is more aware of this than Anne Elliot and it teaches her another painful but salutary lesson—'the art of knowing our own nothingness beyond our own circle, was become necessary for her.' Just as the one language is in fact made up of many discourses, so the one society is made up of many 'circles' and in many of these circles one is a nothing just as in some discourses one is inaudible. Anne's word carried no weight precisely because she is a nobody within the circle of her own family. Her speech can take on its full value only when she is taken into a new circle—the navy. In between she is, well—in between. (pp. 180-87)

> *Tony Tanner, "In Between—Anne Elliot Marries a Sailor and Charlotte Heywood Goes to the Seaside," in* Jane Austen in a Social Context, *edited by David Monaghan, Barnes & Noble Books, 1981, pp. 180-94.*

Mary Poovey (essay date 1983)

[*In the following excerpt, Poovey discusses ways in which Austen's reaction to nineteenth-century ideology informs the plot and characterization of* Persuasion.]

In the last decade, several critics have made significant inroads into the old critical commonplace that Jane Austen's novels occupy a special aesthetic domain, that they constitute unassailable proof not only that their author was serenely oblivious to the French Revolution, Napo-

leon, and the political and ethical debates of her society but also that art can simply be free of politics and, even more important, of ideology. But despite the eloquent arguments of such critics as Marilyn Butler and Alistair Duckworth [see Further Reading], we still need more expeditions into the ideological hinterland of Austen's novels, not least because her artistry *has* so skillfully effaced all but the most subtle ideological trails. In this paper I want to describe some of the ways in which the form of Austen's novels is shaped by the ideological tensions that characterized early-nineteenth-century English society. And in the process, I'll also suggest some of the reasons why generations of Austen admirers have been so anxious to overlook the disturbing implications raised by even her most aesthetically satisfying novels.

For the purposes of clarity, I'll focus my discussion on *Persuasion,* but my observations about Austen's moral premises and aesthetic strategies are based on (and should illuminate) all six of her major novels. My most fundamental assumption here is that each of Austen's novels is a symbolic response to a real social situation, or, more precisely, that each novel attempts to resolve a fundamental contradiction within the ideology that governed English society in the first decades of the nineteenth century. In Austen's novels, as in her society, the most pressing contradictions emerged from the challenge posed to the traditional vertical alliances of patriarchal society by the values and practices associated with bourgeois individualism. (p. 152)

The moral ambiguities of individualism and propriety play a central role in all of Jane Austen's major novels. But nowhere are the complexities of these two ideologies more clearly set out than in *Persuasion,* Austen's last completed work. In *Persuasion* the fact that the social and ethical hierarchy superintended by the landed gentry is in a state of total collapse is clear not only from the fiscal and moral bankruptcy of Sir Walter Elliot but also from the epistemological relativity which is emphasized both thematically and formally. On the one hand, this individualism is granted narrative and even moral authority by the very quality of the narration: the centralizing narrative authority taken for granted in Austen's earlier novels has almost completely disappeared from *Persuasion,* and in its place, we find a style inflected at nearly every level by the subjectivity of the heroine. But on the other hand, at the level of the novel's action, we repeatedly see the personal and social consequences of this epistemological relativism. In direct contrast to *Emma,* Austen's previous novel, *Persuasion* is punctuated by dramatic changes of locale, and each time Anne Elliot is forced to move, she experiences the vertiginous realization that "a removal from one set of people to another, though at a distance of only three miles, will often include a total change of conversation, opinion, and idea." For Anne, whose twenty-seven years have been scarred by more losses than just of place, the first lesson of relativity is inescapable and painful, for it involves "knowing our own nothingness beyond our own circle." The second lesson, as the action of *Persuasion* proves, is that no judgment is absolute and that even such "objective" principles as "duty" may be susceptible to personal interpretation and abuse. Finally, the complexities of individualism are duplicated in the character of the hero, for the self-confidence, "ardour," and even "imprudence" that make Frederick Wentworth a "dangerous character" in Lady Russell's terms are the very qualities that make him attractive, facilitate his personal success, and help defend England against Napoleon.

In *Persuasion* Austen uncovers the ideological complexities of this problem by exploring the relationship among "manners," "duty," and feeling. The first implication of their conjunction is obvious—and obviously problematic. Given the subjectivity of perception upon which the novel insists, it is clear that each individual's experience is personal and unique. It follows from this both that ethical judgment will be based at least initially upon appearances and that all moral evaluation will be at least implicitly subjective. The reader is exposed to the moral vertigo which results from these twin facts in the presentation of William Walter Elliot. Anne's early evaluation of Mr. Elliot is based upon the appeal of his "manners": "his manners were so exactly what they ought to be," Anne muses, "so polished, so easy, so particularly agreeable." But it is difficult for the reader to know whether Anne's assessment is morally authoritative or whether her response is simply colored by the admiration with which Mr. Elliot so frankly flatters her. Our judgment is further perplexed when, in the next chapter, Lady Russell's response endorses Anne's.

> Every thing united in him; good understanding, correct opinions, knowledge of the world, and a warm heart. He had strong feelings of family-attachment and family-honour, without pride or weakness; he lived with the liberality of a man of fortune, without display; he judged for himself in every thing essential, without defying public opinion in any point of worldly decorum. He was steady, observant, moderate, candid; never run away with by spirits or by selfishness, which fancied itself strong feeling; and yet, with a sensibility to what was amiable and lovely, and a value for all the felicities of domestic life, which characters of fancied enthusiasm and violent agitation seldom really possess.

The problem for Anne, Lady Russell, and the reader is that Mr. Elliot has completely detached the superficial niceties of manners from any ethical underpinnings. In the absence of both an objective, authoritative standard by which to judge such behavior and access to Mr. Elliot's hidden motivation, how are we to know what to make of such a character?

It is at least partly to avoid the implications of this dilemma that Austen never allows Anne to become seriously interested in Mr. Elliot; indeed, she almost immediately informs the reader why Anne does not succumb: "Mr. Elliot was rational, discreet, polished,—but he was not open. There was never any burst of feeling, any warmth of indignation or delight, at the evil or good of others. This, to Anne, was a decided imperfection." The problem with this narrative ruse, of course, is that it privileges the very subjectivity whose moral relativity we have just been led to identify. Before long, Mr. Elliot will be betrayed by Mrs. Smith, who *can* expose his secret design. But it is impor-

tant to keep in mind that our first and lasting evaluation of him is influenced not by reference to an objective or absolute assessment of "manners" but simply by Anne's subjective preference for "feeling" and "warmth."

In order to resolve the problems introduced by yoking feeling to judgment, Austen relies upon the fact that by the time Mr. Elliot becomes an issue, the reader will recognize that Anne's intuitions are meant to be morally responsible and hence authoritative. Certainly Anne Elliot comes closer to being educated in both principles and feelings when the novel opens than is any other Austen heroine at that point. Like Elinor and Fanny, Anne has from her youth internalized sound moral principles, but more surely than either of them, she has also experienced and fully acknowledged the demands of her heart. Austen's opening description of Anne Elliot's maturity summarizes her unusual career: "She had been forced into prudence in her youth, she learned romance as she grew older: the natural sequel of an unnatural beginning." But while this statement effectively suspends our estimation of Lady Russell's original admonition to "prudence," it does not really explain how even Anne's belated "romance" has acquired moral authority. Especially given both the vanity with which the desires of Sir Walter, Elizabeth, and William Elliot are inflected and the instability typical of the romantic inclinations of Benwick and Louisa Musgrove, the reader must wonder why Anne's desires are more reliable.

This question of the authority of Anne's intuitions and inclinations introduces a second facet of the dilemma of propriety. As in *Mansfield Park,* Austen suggests in *Persuasion* that "proper" behavior may have a psychological dimension which eighteenth-century moralists rarely described. This, she implies, may be the most significant paradox of propriety: not that manners can be manipulated to express and accommodate desire but that fidelity to "objective" principles may actually answer personal needs, that doing one's "duty" may protect one against both pain and unreasonable desire, and that virtuous behavior may even provide rewards to substitute for the gratifications it denies. Because the reader does not directly witness Anne's first—and, in many ways, most important—conflict, that struggle between her first love for Wentworth and Lady Russell's "prudence," we are encouraged to accept Anne's decision as one of the premises of the action and to evaluate it more by its consequences than by the principle it originally involved. Instead of focusing on the correctness of Anne's first decision, in other words, we are asked to understand *how,* given that decision, Anne was able to discipline her desire. Lady Russell's argument—that marriage to Wentworth was "a wrong thing . . . hardly capable of success, and not deserving it"—finally influenced Anne less than her confidence that in denying Wentworth she was actually "consulting his good, even more than her own." "The belief of being prudent and self-denying principally for *his* advantage, was her chief consolation, under the misery of a parting—a final parting." Anne has essentially been able to displace her own desire not simply by reference to an objective principle but by convincing herself that her love for Wentworth would be more adequately expressed by denying what they both so badly want.

One practical difficulty with this fundamental Christian truism is that in the world of *Persuasion* no one but Anne adheres to the morality of which it is a part. But a second, closely related problem is that if, in the absence of both an objective standard of moral absolutes and a communal consensus about ethical norms, an individual can identify "duty" only by the personal satisfaction it yields, then "principle" may easily shade over into unrecognized self-interest or self-defense. Austen raises the specter of this ethical chaos when she discusses the psychological function Anne's other exercises of "duty" play. When Mary asks Anne to Uppercross Cottage, for example, Anne leaps at the chance to act in compliance with the wishes of anyone else, to act according to any rule that seems to exist outside herself, and hence to be authoritative and reliable; Anne is simply "glad to be thought of some use, glad to have any thing marked out as a duty."

But as Austen describes Anne's situation, it becomes clear that one reason why Anne is so anxious to be dutiful is that the approbation which ideally attends selflessness is the only recognition which Anne is likely to receive. Repeatedly Austen points out that, except for the compassion of Lady Russell, Anne enjoys almost no domestic encouragement or support. "Excepting one short period of her life," the narrator tells us, "she had never, since the age of fourteen, never since the loss of her dear mother, known the happiness of being listened to, or encouraged by any just appreciation or real taste." Left behind by the Musgroves to nurse their child, Anne experiences "as many sensations of comfort, as were, perhaps, ever likely to be hers. She knew herself to be of the first utility to the child." The problem with this fusion of "duty" and "happiness" is twofold. On the one hand, because the "satisfaction of knowing herself extremely useful" is virtually the only happiness Anne has, she is driven to Christian virtue at least partly out of personal need. On the other hand, because this "satisfaction" is virtually her only assurance that what she does is right, Anne will be prone to identify "duty" primarily by the pleasure it brings. Austen never calls into question the authority of Anne's "satisfaction," but by showing us Mary, who happily tempers "duty" with personal convenience, and Mr. Elliot, for whom " 'to do the best for himself' passe[s] as a duty," Austen does provoke us to ask how the selfless definition of duty is to be distinguished from its self-serving twin.

But because these questions simply cannot be answered without calling into question the moral authority of both feeling and duty, Austen substitutes for an examination of feeling a conflict focused on romantic love, for *this* conflict is certain to engage her readers' sympathy instead of arousing their judgment. With consummate narrative skill, Austen completely displaces the problem of the basis and nature of Anne's moral discrimination by foregrounding the difficulty with which she exercises her moral intuition in the service of love. Because Anne's situation and her feelings are both given as premises of the plot, Austen can focus on the inevitable confrontation between repressive social conventions and the desires of an individual heart—a confrontation which, unlike the ideologically charged question of duty, *can* be resolved realistically and in the terms of traditional values. Austen never actually

examines the process by which Anne's feelings become moral, but because she does focus briefly on the emotional and psychological complexities of self-denial, she conveys the impression that Anne's first acquiescence to "duty" must have entailed soul-searching and a difficult weighing of alternatives. As in *Mansfield Park,* Austen asks us to sympathize with (although *not* to experience vicariously) the principle of self-denial. But unlike the earlier novel, *Persuasion* takes us beyond the subduing of desire to its struggle against social restraint. In so doing, Austen dramatizes the *power* of principled feeling and thus gives us an idea not only of what ideally should be but of how that triumph might actually come about.

So intent is Austen upon foregrounding the conflict between social conventions and moral desire that she dramatizes it not only at the level of content but also at the level of the narrative development itself. At this formal level Austen provides two narrative strains. The "private" plot of the novel corresponds to—and contains the story of—Anne's love for Wentworth. The "public" plot corresponds to repressive social conventions and contains the accounts of the interactions between the Elliots and Lady Russell, the Musgroves and their friends, Mr. Elliot and his relatives, and so on. Typically, we are imaginatively engaged in the private plot but must repeatedly experience a version of Anne's frustration when the public plot usurps center stage. The overall narrative action of *Persuasion* involves the gradual emergence of the private plot into the public sphere and its eventual triumph, just as the overall content involves the ultimate victory of personal needs and desires over social conventions. Thus the first three chapters of the novel confine the reader to the public plot, that domain of social intercourse which originally stifled Anne's emotions and into which her feelings will soon surface again. Even these chapters contain allusions to the hidden, private plot, but that plot does not emerge into visibility for the reader until the end of chapter 3, when we are suddenly exposed to Anne's turbulent consciousness: "A few months more, and *he,* perhaps, may be walking here." Only at this point do we begin to understand why Anne so intensely dislikes Bath and why she knows not only who Admiral Croft is but where he has seen action. And only at this point do we recognize that Anne is not a secondary character but the heroine and that it is *her* plot—as it is *her* desire—that is being repressed by the bustling vanity of her loquacious relatives.

What we are seeing here is Jane Austen's most sophisticated version of that narrative technique she employed at least as early as the conclusion of *Lady Susan.* Essentially, it consists of a shifting of different levels or planes of the fiction so that problems or contradictions raised at one level can be symbolically "resolved" by foregrounding another, nonproblematic level. In *Lady Susan* this "resolution," which is actually only a displacement, consists in the complete repression of the principal character, the thematic tensions, and the epistolary form itself. In *Pride and Prejudice,* just to give another example, it consists in the foregrounding of romance conventions in order to displace complexities raised by the introduction of realistic social and psychological details. And in *Persuasion* it consists in the double movement whereby the thematic contradictions raised by the problems of individualism and morality are displaced both by the foregrounding of other, apparently equivalent thematic complexities and by the shift of the reader's imaginative engagement to the conflict between the public and the private plots by way of the interest aroused by romantic love.

Austen makes this twin conflict seem as important as the epistemological conundrum it displaces by emphasizing the odds against Anne's happiness. Nearly all of the events of the first part of the public plot reinforce the anxiety we share with Anne that her love for Wentworth will be frustrated a second time. Louisa Musgrove actively pursues Wentworth, circumstances rarely bring the two old lovers together, Wentworth seems determined to misunderstand Anne, and Anne repeatedly retreats from exposure by defining her "duty" as self-effacement. She wants, she says repeatedly, only "to be unobserved," "not to be in the way of any body." Austen further underscores the likelihood that Anne's romantic hopes will be denied by giving us one revealing glimpse into Wentworth's consciousness. This passage constitutes one of the very few departures from the narrative's participation in Anne's point of view; and even though we eventually recognize its defensive tenor, it immediately serves to convince the reader that any struggle between Anne's sense of propriety and her feelings would inevitably lead to frustration and pain. "He had not forgiven Anne Elliot," the narrator tells us. "She had given him up to oblige others. It had been the effect of over-persuasion. It had been weakness and timidity. . . . Her power with him was gone for ever."

The turning point in **Persuasion**—both in Captain Wentworth's feelings and, as a consequence, in the dilemma which is foregrounded for the reader—occurs in the episode at Lyme. Before this episode, Wentworth has insisted that he does not love Anne, and thus the reader—confined, largely, to Anne's subjectivity—has remained engaged in the heroine's attempts to master her still active desire, not so much in the name of some authoritative principle but because circumstances—reality—make such self-discipline necessary. In order for the critical shift in the narrative to take place, two things must happen: Wentworth must realize that he still loves Anne, and this recognition must be conveyed to the reader. Only then will the primary conflict be between the private and the public plots instead of either between selfish and moral desire or between feeling and necessity; for only then will both lovers struggle to make social conventions express and accommodate their feelings. The delicate handling of this series of revelations generates the tension and the power of *Persuasion.*

Two illuminations are necessary for Wentworth to realize that his well-mannered consideration for Anne is actually the stirring of his old love: he must be reminded of Anne's powerful physical attractions, and he must learn to distinguish between simple selfishness in the name of principle and the genuine self-command which Anne can place in the service of others. Wentworth learns each of these lessons at Lyme. His desire for Anne is reawakened by the open admiration of Mr. Elliot, whom Wentworth suddenly sees as a rival. And his appreciation for Anne is given new meaning when Louisa, taking Wentworth's own ideal of "firmness" to its destructive extreme, jumps precipitously from the stile.

Eventually we discover that Anne's selfless and competent attendance upon the stricken Louisa had been instrumental in reanimating Wentworth's love, but we cannot immediately be sure of his feeling for Anne because Austen removes the heroine—and with her the reader—to Bath. But even though we are still basically confined to Anne's perspective, the two episodes immediately preceding Louisa's accident provide the reader with vantage points that materially enhance our appreciation of Anne. In doing so, these episodes settle once and for all any lingering questions about the moral authority of Anne's feelings; and thus they reinforce our hopes (if not our expectations) that her altogether admirable desire will ultimately be rewarded. Each of these episodes means something slightly different to Anne than to the reader. In the first, Wentworth's dialogue with Louisa about the nut, Anne understands only that the man she loves is rejecting her more "persuadable" character for Louisa's greater "firmness." The attentive reader, however, will hear that Wentworth's endorsement of "firmness" actually has a very personal stress. "It is the worst evil of too yielding and indecisive a character," he explains, "that no influence over it can be depended upon." From this statement it is clear that Wentworth does not really want "firmness"; he merely wants to be the one whose "influence" is longest felt. The second episode involves Anne's conversation with Captain Benwick. In his nourished grief Anne sees only a mirror-image of her own lingering sorrow, and in the "allowance of prose" she recommends, she sees only the medicine she has ineffectively administered to herself. But contrasting Anne's public self-command with Benwick's demonstrative and even occasionally eloquent suffering, we recognize how far Anne Elliot really is from indulging the pain she cannot help but feel. These two events reduce Anne to her lowest emotional state, for just as the first convinces her that Wentworth will never love her, the second shows her unequivocally that her love for Wentworth is not yet dead. For the reader, however, they establish the context in which Anne's self-command at Louisa's side can properly be appreciated.

In contrast to the emotional turmoil liberated in Lyme, Bath seems stultifying, claustrophobic. Its occupants and its formalities are artificial and repressive: Mr. Elliot's careful manners are of a piece with the "white glare of Bath," and, significantly, the only truth eventually emanates from Mrs. Smith's "dark bedroom," where Anne finally discovers Mr. Elliot's secret history. Anne's immediate problem in Bath is simply to stifle her feelings once again and to correct her first impression of William Walter Elliot. But Austen makes the month-long "imprisonment" in Bath occupy only three short chapters before she lets Anne know what the reader has already begun to suspect: that Wentworth will not marry Louisa, that he is "unshackled and free." Suddenly, emissaries from the country begin to pour into Bath, and, as Wentworth himself arrives, Austen sets in motion that intricate, almost musical movement through which, point counterpoint, Anne gradually discovers and elicits Wentworth's love.

In order to effect the resolution which will finally bring the private plot into public view, Austen forces Anne to take the initiative, to act upon her own feelings and her intuition of Wentworth's answering desires. Just as her ministrations in Lyme were completely in keeping with the behavior proper to a lady, so Anne's self-assertion is gentle, almost shy: she acts only indirectly, in other words, and only as opportunity allows. "Making yet a little advance," Anne greets Wentworth warmly at the Rooms, and she uses their polite conversation to voice heartfelt emotions whose significance only he will fully understand: "One does not love a place the less for having suffered in it," she says, referring to Lyme. From Wentworth's response, Anne realizes that "he must love her"; and she sets out to dispel the only remaining impediment to their happiness—Wentworth's misinterpretation of her relationship with Mr. Elliot. Fortified by the information Mrs. Smith gives her, Anne resolves to be "more direct" with Mr. Elliot and more assertive with Captain Wentworth. She seizes an "opportunity" to "decidedly" voice her disinclination to accompany Mr. Elliot; she openly alludes to her former relationship with Wentworth ("I am not yet so much changed"); and in her conversation with Captain Harville, after she becomes aware that Wentworth is listening, Anne "eagerly" claims the "privilege" for her sex of "loving longest, when existence or when hope is gone."

Even as Anne struggles to make social conventions accommodate and communicate her feelings, Captain Wentworth tries to do the same. Significantly, Austen makes the final reconciliation between Anne and Wentworth depend upon this self-reliant commander's accepting the "penance" and the anguish of the typical feminine situation. Discovering that others assume he is courting Louisa, Wentworth is hemmed in by social conventions, forced to wait passively while circumstances dictate his fate. Even after Louisa's turn to Benwick permits him once more to "exert" himself and follow Anne to Bath, Wentworth is still restricted to the feminine position of helpless onlooker and overhearer, and when he finally takes decisive action he does so indirectly, writing to Anne under the cover of another letter, even as she communicates with him under the cover of her conversation with Harville.

More than any previous Austen novel, *Persuasion* dwells on the reciprocity of love between man and woman. Wentworth's "agitation" is at least as frequently noted as Darcy's, and here this agitation is the counterpart to Anne's agitation, not its illustrative opposite. Perhaps even more important, however, is the fact that in *Persuasion* Austen is more attentive than ever before to the "situation" of women; placing Wentworth in that situation is a means both of making him do "penance" for his unthinking flirtation and of alerting the reader to the frustration such restriction can generate for anyone. Through the character of Mrs. Croft and Anne's conversation with Captain Harville, Austen addresses the implications of woman's social situation more explicitly than in any of her other novels. Recognizing that women are "rational creatures," Austen acknowledges that they are not always treated as such—either because of the patriarchal prerogatives which relegate "all the Marys and Elizabeths" to the single category of "wife" or because of the superficial dictates of propriety which insist that "fine ladies" have "no *right*" to comfortably endure hardships, that all women with ruddy faces are "frights," and that the "model of female excellence" should take no initiative and have no desires of her own. As Austen depicts them in this novel, women are imprisoned, confined, "surrounded and shut in," legally and sometimes physically crippled by the actions of men. While the obtrusive artifices of society make such restriction inevitable for every sensitive individual, Austen does not let us forget that women's position is especially cruel. Acknowledging that women love with special force, Anne will *not* grant Captain Harville's point that such fidelity is in woman's "nature." "It is, perhaps, our fate rather than our merit," she explains. "We cannot help ourselves. We live at home, quiet, confined, and our feelings prey upon us. You are forced on exertion. You have always a profession, pursuits, business of some sort or other, to take you back into the world immediately, and continual occupation and change soon weaken impressions." Jane Austen does not sound so very different from Mary Wollstonecraft here; if she does not aggressively agitate for reform, she nevertheless rejects both the determinist argument from nature and the definition of propriety which makes women psychologically and emotionally one-dimensional.

In *Persuasion* Mrs. Smith exists to remind us both how restrictive a woman's situation can be and, no matter how severe that restriction, how resilient a woman's emotions potentially are. "Here was that elasticity of mind," Anne remarks to herself, "that disposition to be comforted, that power of turning readily from evil to good, and of finding employment which carried her out of herself, which was from Nature alone." Significantly, Mrs. Smith's "power" epitomizes female indirection; through Nurse Rooke she learns the secrets of the most private rooms of Bath, and she takes advantage of the momentary incapacities of others to lighten the burden of her own physical affliction. As unsavory as some critics have found her, Mrs. Smith serves as the necessary secret agent of *Persuasion,* analogous to Mrs. Norris in *Mansfield Park* and Miss Bates in *Emma.* Because of Mrs. Smith, the novel's private plot surfaces and finally shatters the complacent round of evening parties and formal concerts. Mrs. Clay and Mr. Elliot are flushed, temporarily, from Sir Walter's home, and more satisfying, the romantic first love of Anne and Wentworth, now proved worthy through endurance and trial, moves the lovers into the prominence they have long held for the reader.

The conclusion of *Persuasion,* as many critics have noted, does not promise general social reform, an authoritative system of values, or even "happiness ever after" for one loving couple. Kellynch will still eventually descend to Mr. Elliot, Mrs. Clay may even preside over the great hall, and the "dread of a future war" is as much Anne's legacy as is domestic affection. For Austen, despite the gratification of romance, Anne's happiness is less complete than was Elizabeth's, Fanny's, or Emma's: "Anne had no Uppercross-hall before her, no landed estate, no headship of a family." And because she will not attain these offices, her society can look forward to no reform from within. Captain Wentworth can restore Mrs. Smith's West Indian property, but he cannot put Anne in her mother's place. For Austen, individual education no longer seems powerful enough to initiate reform; when she celebrates the culminating happiness of Anne Elliot and Frederick Wentworth, it is in the context of the present—and, implicitly, the future—disarray of family and class.

Yet in some respects, because *Persuasion* promises less, it achieves more. As Nina Auerbach has pointed out, *Persuasion* endorses possibilities never before valorized in Austen's novels. Instead of attempting primarily to reform the landed gentry, Austen shows that money—and, along with it, power—is passing from this class to those who actively labor (and, not incidentally, whose labor defends England). Significantly, the naval officers in *Persuasion* are "associated with nature, openness, hospitality, romance," and as they gain social prominence, Austen lends a new practical power to individual feeling. And because the question of the *moral* authority of feeling is not so pressing as in *Mansfield Park* or even *Emma,* empowering this quality seems to presage general social reform, if only through the gradual erosion of the mannered repression epitomized in William and Elizabeth Elliot. In *Persuasion,* Austen also devotes more attention to those social groups whose absence is so conspicuous—and essential—in her earlier novels. Not only do Mrs. Smith and Nurse Rooke make more than a token appearance here, but at least twice Austen alludes to anonymous groups of workers going about their ordinary business or only briefly interrupted by their social superiors. When Louisa falls, for example, there suddenly appear "workmen and boatmen" who have gathered "to be useful if wanted; at any rate, to enjoy the sight of a dead young lady, nay, two dead young ladies, for it proved twice as fine as the first report." What is startling about this passage is not its proof that Austen was aware of the lower classes but its demonstration, at least momentarily, of the validity of the workmen's point of view ("nay, two dead young ladies"). Near the beginning of the novel, Austen's allusion to the lower classes is more stylized, but again—here as so seldom before—we glimpse a group of people who are not defined by their relation to the upper classes, who are neither agents of the central characters nor even particularly interested in them. Walking from Uppercross to Winthrop, Anne and her friends make the "gradual ascent through large enclosures, where the ploughs at work, and the fresh-made path spoke the farmer, counteracting the sweets of poetical despondence, and meaning to have spring again."

Such brief asides do not, of course, significantly widen the focus of Jane Austen's art, although they do generate that illusion of realistic depth also apparent in *Emma.* But in *Persuasion* these receding depths do not simply expand the sphere of influence of the upper classes. Instead, they are the subtle reminders of the limitations of that influence; in some fundamental sense, the vanity of Sir Walter Elliot is not only foolish but irrelevant, for his preening arrogance no more affects the behavior of his social inferiors than poetic pretensions alter the inexorable rhythms of nature. In *Persuasion* Austen suggests that the landed classes have forfeited their moral authority partly through extravagance and a failure in social responsibility. But their gradual displacement is also partly the consequence of the

more general challenge to the stable system of values they ideally represented. This challenge is both political and epistemological; that the lower classes not only exist in their own right but have a distinct point of view provides a social context and content for the epistemological relativity implicit in the very title of *Persuasion.*

But even as it is important to appreciate the direction of Austen's last novel, it is also important to look closely at the inherent contradictions of the resolution she proposes. For even if the conclusion of *Persuasion* promises only temporary peace and limited happiness, its fundamental predication of a private sphere that can accommodate personal desire and yield personal fulfillment perpetuates many of the problems raised by her earlier works. And here we need to remember that these problems are not the stigmata of aesthetic failure but indices of contradictions within ideology itself. Essentially, *Persuasion* advances the argument, proposed as early as *Pride and Prejudice,* that personal feeling can be a moral force within society. Whereas in the earlier novel the way of life eventually ratified by desire was that of the landed gentry, in *Persuasion* feeling is put in the service of—and is gratified by—the much less certain lifestyle of those who earn their social position by ongoing personal effort. And whereas in *Pride and Prejudice* the aggressive energy of Elizabeth Bennet had to be chastened into love by circumstances and Fitzwilliam Darcy, in the later novel Anne Elliot's persistent love prevails, finally triumphing over both the pride of her lover and the institutional inhibitors that would disguise or deny it altogether. But by using individual feeling to inaugurate moral reform and by rewarding that desire with the conventional prizes of bourgeois society—marriage and (implicitly) a family—Austen is finally reproducing an unresolved (and in these terms unresolvable) contradiction inherent in her culture's values. This contradiction centers in the promise which is invariably fused to the demands of propriety; it centers, that is, in the concept of romantic love.

In Austen's society as today, romantic love purports to be completely "outside" ideology. It claims to be an inexplicable, irresistible, and possibly even biological drive which, in choosing its object, flaunts the hierarchy, the priorities, the inequalities of class society. Romantic love seems to defy self-interest and calculation as merrily as it ignores income and rank; as a consequence, if it articulates (or can be educated to do so) an essentially unselfish, generous urge toward another person, it may serve as an agent of moral reform: Louisa Musgrove might become a more serious person through loving Benwick, just as Henry Crawford seems launched on a significant course of moral improvement by his love for Fanny Price. But it is crucial to recognize that the moral regeneration ideally promised by romantic love is as individual and as private as its agent. In fact, the fundamental assumption of romantic love—and the reason it is so compatible with bourgeois society—is that the personal can be kept separate from the social, that one's "self" can be fulfilled in spite of—and in isolation from—the demands of the marketplace. Once one accepts this division of society into separate spheres, it is possible to argue that the gratification of personal desire will inaugurate social reform only if one assumes a social organization which structurally accommodates influence—at the smallest level, the nuclear family or, at a more general level, the patriarchal society modeled upon the family. If this concentric arrangement of "spheres" (which is, of course, actually a hierarchy of power) is disrupted or even seriously challenged—as it was during Jane Austen's lifetime—then the movement from individual fulfillment to social improvement becomes problematic. Ironically, even as the importance of imagining some program for social reform increases, the gap between the private and the public seems to widen and, completing the circle, the more necessary it becomes to believe that at least in the privacy of one's own home, the comfort of one's own family, and the personal gratification of one's own love, there can be deeply felt and hence "substantial" satisfaction.

In her realistic portrayal of the inevitable connections between the public and the private spheres and in her allusions to that complex society beyond the personal interests of her characters, Jane Austen exposes the fallacy of this claim for personal autonomy. Given the fact that living together in society necessarily requires dependence and compromise, the belief that one can withdraw or simply gratify oneself is morally irresponsible and, finally, practically untrue. Even Mrs. Smith has Nurse Rooke to connect her to the public world of Bath, and as Anne's prolonged and problematic courtship of Wentworth proves, even the most adamant personal desire must be defined within other social relations which are also configurations of power.

But in retaining the premises and promises of romantic love even as she makes this point, Jane Austen also perpetuates one of the fundamental myths of bourgeois society. For the model of private gratification which romantic love proposes is able to disguise the inescapable system of economic and political domination only by foregrounding those few relationships which flatter our desire for personal autonomy and power. But the notion that romantic relationships actually have the kind of social power this emotional prominence suggests is actually an illusion: in the absence of institutions that actually link the private and the public spheres, romantic relationships, by their very nature, cannot materially affect society. And even more distressing, they cannot even provide women more than the kind of temporary, imaginative consolation which serves to defuse criticism of the very institutions that make such consolation necessary. For by focusing on courtship, the myth of romantic love tends to freeze the relationship between a man and a woman at its moment of greatest intensity, when both partners are seen (and see themselves) in the most flattering light and, perhaps most important, when women exercise their greatest power. Romantic love, in other words, seems to promise women in particular ongoing emotional intensity which ideally compensates for all the practical opportunities they are denied. But all it can actually yield is the immediate gratification of believing that this single moment of woman's power will endure, that the fact that a woman seems most desirable when she is most powerful will have an afterlife in marriage and in society. In Jane Austen's society, of course, romantic love did not alter the institutions of marriage or property or female dependence. And even the private gratification available in the domestic sphere could not live up to the intensity and power promised by romantic love, for as a wife and mother, a woman could at best act indirectly, through her children, through sacrifice, through duty. Romantic love, finally, had its most vital, most satisfying existence not in society but in art.

The problems these ideological contradictions generate in Jane Austen's novels are clear in *Persuasion.* In order to give individual feeling moral authority—in order, that is, to place romance in the service of propriety, social reform, and realism—Austen must posit the existence of separate spheres within her fiction. These separate spheres exist at the levels of content and form, and at each level the "private" sphere is theoretically linked to the "public" sphere by the influence bred of contiguity. But these private spheres are actually qualitatively different from the public spheres. Whereas the public spheres activate expectations generated by her readers' actual experiences in class society, whereas they are governed by psychological and social realism and the iron law of cause and effect, the private spheres open out onto romance: they activate and feed off expectations generated by reading other romantic novels; they arouse and satisfy desire. Each of Jane Austen's novels contains these special pockets of romance, not just in their most obtrusive form—those fairy-tale marriages that stop realism dead in its tracks—but in unexpected, out-of-the-way places as well. Thus in *Persuasion* Mrs. Smith remains miraculously, inexplicably cheerful against all the odds her social situation dictates—and even though in the same novel Elizabeth Elliot withers in much less barren soil. And in *Mansfield Park* Fanny and William Price keep domestic affection alive even though we see it atrophy and die in both squalid Portsmouth and immaculate Mansfield Park. At the level of form this division of the fiction into public and private spheres dictates the relegation of all the potentially subversive content to a marginal position or a carefully delimited arena. Paradoxically, the "private," romantic spheres of her novels—Marianne's passion for Willoughby, Darcy's love for Elizabeth, Fanny's yearning for Edmund, Emma's capacity to love, and Anne's fidelity to Wentworth—must all be rigorously contained, whether by the narrative distancing of *Sense and Sensibility,* the circumstantial frustration of *Mansfield Park* and *Persuasion,* or the encrustation of other, less admirable traits, such as we see in *Pride and Prejudice* and *Emma.* This separation is essential to protect romance from the necessarily deflating power of reality. But it is also essential, finally, in order to ensure that the demands of reality will be taken seriously, not merely repressed or imaginatively escaped. For even though the private sphere is the location and source of the greatest fulfillment Austen can imagine, so, too, does this sphere nourish the very subjectivity which is potentially fatal to the claims of other people, to morality, and, implicitly, to society itself.

In the absence of institutional opportunities for power, then, Jane Austen can effect the aesthetic resolution she desires only by *asserting* that the private sphere of domestic relationships can remain autonomous yet retain a unique and powerful moral dimension. Such resolution is only symbolic, of course, and as we have seen, it can be achieved only by repressing or displacing those questions which might jeopardize it. The fact that Jane Austen's novels contain almost no examples of happy marriages despite their inevitable culmination in a happy marriage summarizes both the price of such symbolic resolution and its attractions. For, on the one hand, for Austen to move chronologically, realistically, from the suspended promise of romantic love to a dramatization of the power relations inherent in marriage (dynamics which she portrays elsewhere with such ruthless wit) would be to risk depriving romantic love of its capacity to engage our imaginations by offering us flattering images of socially acceptable (if unavailable) power. And even more damaging, it would be implicitly to call into question both the consoling assumption that the emotional gratification of love makes up for the absence of other forms of self-expression and the enabling belief that the self-denial which society demands can yield the fulfillment that every person desires. But, on the other hand, freezing the narratives precisely at the height of emotional intensity endorses the promises of romantic love and, in so doing, enjoins the reader to imitate the moral love which the hero and heroine promise to bring to fruition in society. And equally important, the model of female power inherent in the premises of romantic love provides Jane Austen the artist a legitimate paradigm for the self-assertion with which she not only expresses her own desires but works in the service of moral reform.

The division of society and morality into separate public and private spheres was a solution particularly attractive to women. Because bourgeois society defined women in terms of their relationships—specifically, their conjugal or familial relationships—because they were granted power within the "proper sphere" of the home, and because the theory of "influence" postulated a model for the dissemination of domestic virtues throughout society, women had a particular investment in conceptualizing their space as special and as containing special moral authority. More generally, however, we should remember that the cultural ideology of which romantic love was but a part had at its heart the same separation of spheres we see in Austen's novel. For bourgeois ideology held out the promise that every individual would have an equal opportunity to work for equal material rewards, a promise which the limitations of natural resources and the inherent inequalities of class society rendered patently false. The existence of a private sphere, replete with the resources of boundless love and uncritical sympathy, essentially promised a compensatory substitute for other kinds of unavailable gratification—for men as well as women. Not incidentally, of course, the home further reinforced bourgeois ideology through this very compensatory gratification, for it provided competitive labor both an end and a means—a goal to defend and, within the patriarchal family, a nursery for the habits of propriety and the promises of romantic love. To the extent that we still defend these goals and seek these promises, we are still anxious to acquiesce in those resolutions which make them seem not only right but possible. (pp. 156-77)

Mary Poovey, " 'Persuasion' and the Promises of Love," in The Representation of Women in

Fiction, *No. 7, new series, edited by Carolyn G. Heilbrun and Margaret R. Higonnet, The Johns Hopkins University Press, 1983, pp. 152-79.*

John Vernon (essay date 1984)

[*In the following excerpt from his study of economic issues in nineteenth-century fiction, Vernon argues that narrative events in* Persuasion *communicate Austen's observations on the decline in status and power of the English gentry.*]

The manifest themes of **Persuasion** are typical of Jane Austen: prudence versus love, persuasion versus fixity of purpose, woman's versus man's faithfulness (which branches out to include the differing estates of women and men). The story of love diverted, deflected, misunderstood, but eventually regained and the resolution (marriage) are also typical. But **Persuasion** is about none of these things. Of all Austen's novels, it is the one that most invites us to read through (or misread) its apparent intentions. In the first place, by comparison with her others the novel is clipped, abbreviated. Of course she was ill while writing it, already dying of Addison's disease. One senses that she may have grown tired of her old strategies and that her chief interest now lay in subverting them—not by irony (as many, led by Mark Schorer have asserted about her earlier work), but by the accumulated weight of seemingly peripheral matters, of subplots and minor characters, and the accompanying shrinkage, even disappearance (until the obligatory marriage), of her main character, Anne, her most self-effacing heroine since Fanny in **Mansfield Park.**

The novel begins when Anne's father, Sir Walter Elliot, finds himself forced to rent out Kellynch Hall because he is embarrassed by debt. To this point in Jane Austen's novels money has certainly been a factor, but not money in its various volatile states, not debt or speculation or sudden losses or gains of money. Neither have there been the extremes of character made possible for subsequent novelists by money: no spendthrifts (though some firstborn sons are injudicious), no misers (though a few characters are tightfisted), no profligates driven to distraction by debt, no thieves, speculators, or families made suddenly wealthy by a lucky inheritance. It is true that some of this is present as though at the edge of Austen's world; Margaret in **Sense and Sensibility** says, "I wish that somebody would give us all a large fortune apiece!" and Miss Crawford in **Mansfield Park** plays the card game Speculation with reckless abandon ("No cold prudence for me"). But Margaret's wish isn't granted (as it is, say, in *Great Expectations, Little Dorrit, The Portrait of a Lady,* or *The Wings of the Dove*), and Speculation remains a card game. For the most part, money in Jane Austen is what it has been for centuries, a medium of exchange, not capital. Edmund Bertram in **Mansfield Park** is forced to be content "only not to be poor" because he is a gentleman—therefore work and trade are out of the question—and a second-born son—therefore no inheritance. His only option is to enter the clergy and obtain a living. In Edmund's world, money is passed through families, inherited, tied to estates, and any other means of obtaining it except through a living—itself tied to land—is out of the question. Again, however, there are hints of a different world. Mary Crawford tells Edmund, "Be honest and poor, by all means—but I shall not envy you; I do not think that I shall even respect you. I have a much greater respect for those that are honest and rich." But until *Persuasion* these are only hints.

In *Persuasion,* Sir Walter has mortgaged his estate but still cannot afford to pay his debts, and now must rent it and find someplace else to live. He is even referred to at one point as a spendthrift, though his character is too subdued by vanity and the obligation to appear respectable to remind us of those wild, manic spendthrifts in Balzac and Dostoevsky. Still, the fall from land into money is clear, and Austen doesn't dwell on its horrors, simply because she regards them as self-evident. But the precedence of land in her world may be verified by a look at several other novels. In *Pride and Prejudice* the distinction between the Bingleys and Mr. Darcy is in a sense a distinction between money and land. "I am astonished," Miss Bingley says, "that my father should have left so small a collection of books. What a delightful library you have at Pemberley, Mr. Darcy!" His reply: "It ought to be good; it has been the work of many generations." In other words, money buys books, but only taste and good judgment, which are "the work of many generations" because they are tied to the stability of a place, a landed estate, can build libraries. Miss Bingley then turns to her brother, and this exchange follows:

> "Charles, when you build *your* house, I wish it may be half as delightful as Pemberley."
>
> "I wish it may."
>
> "But I would really advise you to make your purchase in that neighborhood, and take Pemberley for a kind of model. There is not a finer county in England than Derbyshire."
>
> "With all my heart; I will buy Pemberley itself if Darcy will sell it."
>
> "I am talking of possibilities, Charles."
>
> "Upon my word, Caroline, I should think it more possible to get Pemberley by purchase than by imitation."

Bingley is no fool (unlike his sister), and the point of his compliment is, of course, that neither is possible; if Pemberley could be purchased it could be imitated too, for both courses flow from the power of money. But if Pemberley could be purchased it would not be Pemberley, and everyone in the room knows that.

In Jane Austen's world the chief characteristic of land is that it cannot be purchased. Land *already* exists. It spreads its continuity into the past and (presumably) into the future as well. Money, by contrast, comes to the fore as an object of desire and imagination. In *Sense and Sensibility,* when Marianne imagines that just enough money (a "competence") will buy her "a proper establishment of servants, a carriage, perhaps two, and hunters," she is of course imagining the right sort of marriage, but in an embryonic way she is contemplating the power of money, and

in the very act she has ensured that such a world is lost to her—it has become an object of desire. The repeated lesson of nineteenth-century fiction (its clearest formulation is in *Great Expectations*) is foreseen here by Austen: that money will buy anything except what money has come to supplant, well-being.

Thus, land in Jane Austen has something of the flavor of a recent unfallen state that can be regained only through marriage. Marianne wants to imagine a "competence" because in fact her mother and sisters have been dispossessed of their estate. Ideally, marriage should have always already occurred, like being born into a "proper establishment," but then Austen would have nothing to write about. Her heroines must get married for the same reason that they have been dispossessed: because they are women. Though land is always prior in Austen, its title can never be possessed by her women, who must marry to enjoy its advantages. Thus they are forced to desire in order not to desire. "It is only the lot of those who are not obliged to follow any [profession], who can live in a regular way, in the country, choosing their own hours, following their own pursuits, and living on their own property, without the torment of trying for more; it is only *their* lot, I say, to hold the blessings of health and a good appearance to the utmost." This is said at the end of a long speech in *Persuasion* about the disadvantages of the various professions, made by Mrs. Clay, a widow herself engaged in one of the two professions open to women in nineteenth-century England: seeking to become married. The irony here is that the object of her intentions, Sir Walter, is embarrassed by debt, but she doesn't give up until she discovers (beyond the boundaries of the text, of course) that other profession for which only Jane Austen could find a term of consummate politeness: at the novel's end she is said to be living in London under the younger Mr. Elliot's "protection."

The key phrase in Mrs. Clay's statement is "without the torment of trying for more." Land, like marriage, means release from desire. So marriage *into* land contains a double guarantee of that release. Money on the other hand means enslavement to desire, to the necessity of always needing or wanting more, a necessity Sir Walter has lately been prey to. But land means release from necessity. In a sense, novels cannot be written in a world where land is the sole reality and something like money doesn't exist (only poems and masques can), because novels unfold through desire and necessity. Novels cannot be set in Paradise. In this one respect, *Persuasion* is similar to Austen's other novels, most of which enact a fall from Paradise. As we've seen, *Sense and Sensibility* opens when Mrs. Dashwood and her daughters are forced to move from Norland Park because the late Mr. Dashwood's son by a previous marriage has inherited it. Similarly in *Pride and Prejudice,* the fall at least threatens, since Mr. Bennet's property is entailed "in default of heirs male, on a distant relation." In *Mansfield Park,* in a variation of this theme, the heroine is dispossessed of her parents and home and brought to live in a "proper establishment," though initially at least this is felt as a fall. Only *Emma* begins without such a fall, though Jane Austen finds an ingenious way to suggest the regaining of Paradise at the novel's end: the

Lyme Regis, the seaside resort visited by the Elliot family in Persuasion.

marriage of Emma and Mr. Knightly restores Donwell Abbey to its original wholeness, because Hartfield was "a sort of notch" in Donwell.

When a heroine in Austen is expelled from the Garden, she is also decentered. She no longer occupies the nucleus of her existence, unlike, say, Mr. Woodhouse in *Emma,* who "from his fortune, his house, and his daughter . . . could command the visits of his own little circle." Repeatedly, the words "circle" and "center" appear in the novels. "Their estate was large, and their residence was at Norland Park, in the centre of their property" (*Sense and Sensibility*). "Their homes were so distant, and the circles in which they moved so distinct . . ." (*Mansfield Park*). "Marrying early and having a very numerous Family, their movements had been long limited to one small circle" (*Sanditon,* her unfinished novel). All these circles are made to be broken, but the one in *Persuasion* is ruptured several times over: by the loss of Anne's mother, the loss of Captain Wentworth, and finally the loss of Kellynch Hall. Of those decentered in Austen's novels, Anne thus seems the blankest, the one most emptied. In talking with the Musgroves, she learns "another lesson, in the art of knowing our own nothingness beyond our own circle." This is a conventional Austen observation, but applied to

Anne it seems curious, since up to this point in the novel— her visit to Uppercross—she has clearly been shown to be someone who in fact is nothing *within* her own circle. She possesses an elegant mind and a sweet disposition (a generic heroine), but she "was nobody with either father or sister; her word had no weight, her convenience was always to give away—she was only Anne." *Her word had no weight.* Repeatedly, Anne's reluctance or inability to speak is mentioned. "How eloquent could Anne have been!" "Anne longed for the power of representing to them all what they were about." "Anne said what was proper." For the first two-thirds of the novel, her responses in conversation are more often than not summarized instead of presented, and we cannot resist feeling that this represents Jane Austen's own devaluation of her heroine; that is, she treats Anne as those in her family do, who "had no inclination to listen to her." Indeed, Anne treats herself this way: "Anne's object was not to be in the way of anybody."

Of course, the presumed intention of all this is to demonstrate that what appears to be weakness and timidity is really strength, as evidenced by the steadfastness of Anne's love over eight and a half years. But the theme is a tired one and is undercut by too many other considerations. The first sign of Anne's weakness had occurred before the novel began when she caved in to her father's and Lady Russell's persuasion not to marry Captain Wentworth. Their compelling argument is that Captain Wentworth lacks means—that is, either money or property—a lack that by the novel's end has been rectified. One senses that by then Anne's strength is all in retrospect. In fact, it is she who now lacks means, her family's income having been reduced by debt. Love conquers all, but in this case love can afford to; Captain Wentworth now possesses a fortune of twenty-five thousand pounds. "Captain Wentworth, with five-and-twenty thousand pounds, and as high in his profession as merit and activity could place him, was no longer nobody. He was now esteemed quite worthy to address the daughter of a foolish, spendthrift baronet, who had not had principle or sense to maintain himself in the situation in which Providence had placed him, and who could give his daughter at present but a small part of the share of ten thousand pounds which must be hers hereafter." Sir Walter is of course an easy and deserving target, but Anne is by no means an innocent bystander in all this. Indeed, she comes to exist in the novel at the intersection of conflicting social codes by means of which true value (or love) sheds or dons the protective covering of financial considerations according to the situation.

Thus her initial choice—to accept or reject Wentworth—represents a double bind. To accept him would be to ignore the social code by which a nineteen-year-old is expected to respect the advice of her elders. It would also be to accept reduced circumstances. To reject him, however, is to equate that social code with financial survival, to accept the linkage of moral worth and money. The source of the problem, then, is the social code itself, which is ambiguous, in flux. As Raymond Williams says [in *The English Novel from Dickens to Lawrence,* 1970] Jane Austen's world "is indeed that most difficult world to describe, in English social history: an acquisitive high bourgeois society at the point of its most evident interlocking with an agrarian capitalism that is itself mediated by inherited titles and by the making of family names." Thus, "an openly acquisitive society, which is concerned also with the *transmission* of wealth, is trying to judge itself by an inherited code and the morality of improvement." Anne's blankness as a character—indeed, her near invisibility to some of the other characters—may be due to her functioning as a mediator between these conflicting codes. Austen gives her the nearly impossible task of reconciling the morality of self-sacrifice with that of self-interest. She may even be termed (in Max Weber's phrase) a "vanishing mediator," one whose purpose in the novel is to form a bridge not merely between changing social codes but between all the intolerable antinomies of her world: the vanity of her father and the love of Captain Wentworth, the good manners of the Captain and the false ones of Mr. Elliot (or the boorish ones of her family), the only slightly tarnished respectability of her name and the sheer poverty—the nothingness—of Mrs. Smith's ("a mere Mrs. Smith, an everyday Mrs. Smith, of all people and all names in the world," rants her father), the lofty world of marriage and the sordid one of debt and dishonor, the feudal world of the titled nobility and the bourgeois one of economic security (her father's baronetcy is itself a kind of mediating title between the nobility and gentry). The impossibility of forming such links and at the same time becoming a "character" as we usually understand that term in fiction is demonstrated by her strange emptiness, her sense of being hollowed out. She is a vanishing mediator because she enables a new kind of character, a new type, to come into existence, one whose status will always be crippled by economic considerations (as so many characters in this novel are literally crippled). Thus she marries Wentworth, and the novel proves to be (like all of Austen's) a social comedy—but the evil Mr. Elliot will still inherit Kellynch Hall and may very well still "bring it with best advantage to the hammer," as he had intended when younger. In other words, the marriage restores no Paradise; unlike her sister, "Anne had no Uppercross Hall before her, no landed estate, no headship of a family."

As a mediator, Anne occupies the center of the novel, the intersection of its various characters. She is the only one whose inner life is visible to us, and thus the only one we cannot see right through. But to the others she is repeatedly a substitute, someone who must care for her nephew so her sister can go to dinner at the big house, someone indeed who nurses others throughout the novel. At Uppercross she is literally the social medium, the go-between, "treated with too much confidence by all parties, and being too much in the secrets of the complaints of each house." The others speak *through* her. "She could do little more than listen patiently, soften every grievance, and excuse each to the other." For the reader she possesses a dense inner life—in fact, Jane Austen may insist too much upon her feelings, in the absence of anything else to insist upon—but for her fellow characters she is patronized, ignored, used, talked through. She acts as umpire, sounding board, servant, nurse. One senses that for Anne to act for herself would be to send out ripples entirely unreciprocated by the world, to find herself with a shoreless existence. Of course, this isn't entirely true. She does act for herself by approaching Captain Wentworth at the concert, but we sense in this that Captain Wentworth is precisely the device she requires to enable her to fold back upon herself, to become substantial. There is, incidently, one other mediator in the novel who serves both as a parody of Anne and as a warning: Mrs. Smith's Nurse Rooke, who tells her mistress the secrets of Bath society, from which the crippled Mrs. Smith in her squalid quarters is excluded. Like Anne, Nurse Rooke (who never actually appears in the novel) nurses others, listens to their complaints, and passes along their secrets, but unlike Anne—except by association—she has more than a touch of slime to her, as is clear from her function as a gossip, a disseminator of salacious information, and from her name, more characteristic of Dickens than Austen. Furthermore, through the agency of Nurse Rooke, at Bath Anne is still the repository of secrets (including the central one of the novel, regarding Mr. Elliot). . . . Nurse Rooke and Mrs. Smith are in a sense disruptions in this narrative, reminders of the thin ice Anne Elliot treads. Anne may not herself be sordid, but she is far from being untouched by sordid things—they threaten her at every step.

Indeed, the threatening presence of the sordid in this novel—sordid because of economic associations—is what is new for Jane Austen. . . . It is as though a trapdoor has revealed for an instant the cloacal cellar beneath a fine country house. The novel is interrupted by a series of falls, or near falls, which of course are not interruptions but part of its strategy. Still, they *function* as interruptions, as eruptions of contingency in the normal, seemingly timeless flow of events in English country life. Sir Walter's metaphoric fall is the first, the fall that echoes Austen's continuing preoccupation with the fall from Paradise. But there are also the literal falls of young Charles Musgrove and of Louisa, the former resulting in a dislocated collarbone, the latter in a severe concussion. Furthermore, the Admiral and Mrs. Crofts, Captain Wentworth says, often take spills in their carriage. And Anne herself, reeling from the emotions of Captain Wentworth's second proposal, appears to Mrs. Musgrove to have fallen. It takes the latter some time to assure herself "that there had been no fall in the case; that Anne had not at any time lately slipped down, and got a blow on her head; that she was perfectly convinced of having had no fall." Of course, Anne *has* fallen—in love—another kind of disruption with its own barely suggested sordid associations. We sense in all these falls, both metaphoric and literal, a fall of the human body from grace. Someone who falls finds that her body has become a weapon turned against her. The earth rears up, solid and unredeemed. The world becomes known as a material world. The same when one's body is crippled; one becomes immobile, often supine, more subject to gravity. Cripples abound in this novel as well: Captain Harville is lame and Mrs. Smith crippled. Louisa's mobility is reduced by her fall, as though she were crippled too; "there is no running or jumping about, no laughing or dancing."

Mrs. Smith is the text's most sedentary cripple, though—one who never moves, a kind of immobile secret herself at the heart of the novel. Her secret of course is financial disaster, much more severe than that experienced by Sir Walter, and her crippled state is obviously allegorical. In this little allegory we see, however, another conflation of the moral and financial in *Persuasion;* as a youth, she had "lived for enjoyment," suggesting that her downfall is perhaps deserved. "We were a thoughtless, gay set, without any strict rules of conduct." It is at least clear that if a base existence did not result in her fall, her fall resulted in a base existence. Of course Mr. Elliot materially contributed to it too, by leading her husband into ruinous expenses, expenses that, if they resembled his own, were "disposed to every gratification of pleasure and vanity." Mr. Elliot's conduct flows from a social code obviously appalling to Anne, a code unattached to history and one whose chief motivation is self-interest. "I have often heard him declare," says Mrs. Smith, "that if baronetcies were saleable, anybody should have his for fifty pounds, arms and motto, name and livery included." Yet Mr. Elliot's conduct makes a telling comment upon that of Anne, for whom social codes are in conflict. Anne may very well marry Captain Wentworth for love, but her conscience is surely eased by the money he now conveniently possesses. To assert, as Alistair Duckworth does about Jane Austen [see Further Reading], that "it is a consistent mark of moral integrity in her novels that solely financial considerations be excluded from personal decisions" may be stretching a point, particularly with regard to *Persuasion.*

One way of understanding all this may be to say that Mr. Elliot's conduct—echoed in Mrs. Smith's and Sir Walter's and faintly echoed in Anne's—is not conduct at all, in the way Jane Austen would understand the word. "Conduct" implies guidance, self-regulation. Conduct is behavior conscious of its past and future, of its antecedents and consequences. Mr. Elliot, however, behaves without regard to consequences, and we sense in Mrs. Smith's report of him the suggestion that he simply *acts,* perhaps for immediate gratification, a suggestion whose moral horror for Austen would approach that raised by Ivan Karamazov when he says that everything is lawful. But this is precisely the horror buried in *Persuasion*—that the solution to conflicting social codes is no code at all, but pure contingency. With no code, all acts become accidents, and novels are no longer possible. When Louisa falls, "she was too precipitate by half a second" in jumping down into Captain Wentworth's arms, and although this obviously begins as an act, it becomes an accident, an act displaced from the past and the future, a dislocated act.

For all its deliberateness, Mr. Elliot's plan to sell Kellynch Hall suggests the same threat of contingency as Louisa's accident. "My first visit to Kellynch," he says in the letter Mrs. Smith reveals to Anne, "will be with a surveyor, to tell me how to bring it with best advantage to the hammer." The hammer here is the auctioneer's hammer: Mr. Elliot will divide and sell the estate, which is thus for him merely a commodity. But the hammer also conjures up images of a more brutal division, of the reduction of all that an estate represents—tranquillity, security, the conservation of the past—to mere raw material, to wood, stone, and dirt. Mr. Elliot's hammer threatens to knock Kellynch Hall from the feudal world into the world of high capitalism: out of society—at least society as Jane Austen knew it—into the world of matter. (pp. 52-64)

> John Vernon, "The Breaking Up of the Estate: 'Persuasion'," in his Money and Fiction: Literary Realism in the Nineteenth and Early Twentieth Centuries, *Cornell University Press, 1984, pp. 42-64.*

Judith Weissman   (essay date 1987)

[*In the following excerpt, Weissman characterizes* Persuasion *as a radical departure from conventional nineteenth-century depictions of the woman's role in agricultural England.*]

Jane Austen's work has not been a source for radicals or for feminists. Her famous families in their country villages seem so tame, so decorous, so much emblems of the quiet and polite life of the privileged classes that would-be radical women from Charlotte Brontë to Sandra Gilbert have called her an enemy. She, the common story goes, did not write about the Napoleonic Wars; she lived through the same crises that stirred the Romantic poets to such passion and nevertheless kept her serene style, her cool composure, her unruffled view of the world. But the common story is wrong. Jane Austen lived through both the time of revolutionary hopes that the Romantic poets shared and the time of repression that embittered the poets; she explored both hopes and repression, not in the surfaces of her novels but in their underlying assumptions.

Austen perfected her form in her early novels, **Northanger Abbey, Sense and Sensibility, Pride and Prejudice.** In her last three, **Mansfield Park, Emma,** and **Persuasion,** she explored three dominant philosophical views of her time and invented three different types of heroines through whom she could offer hope to women. A feminist of the Charlotte Brontë type she is not, but a radical she is, in both **Emma** and **Persuasion.** She does not reflect historical change in any simple way; she makes ideas her own, traveling a path that defies anything that could be called the national temper. She makes the repressive ideas of the postrevolutionary years intellectually plausible in **Mansfield Park,** celebrates the threatened life of agricultural England in **Emma,** and ends with the single soul in **Persuasion.** As she says of her own last heroine [Anne Elliot], "she learned romance as she grew older." (pp. 47-8)

Love leads Emma to her position of the presiding woman in the rural economy; in Austen's last novel, **Persuasion,** there is nothing left for the heroine to preside over. It is impossible to say whether Austen actually thought that the economic situation of rural England had changed so much between 1816 and 1817 that she had to cast her lot, as a fiction writer, with an unexplored future; perhaps **Persuasion** is simply an intellectual experiment with the side of Romanticism that celebrates the power of the individual soul to live joyfully in virtual independence, apart from the social world.

Country life goes on in **Persuasion**—the Musgrove and Hayter families are pleasant enough. But Austen does not show us daily visits, exchanges of food, loving connections as she does in **Emma.** What we see and care about is Anne Elliot, who wanders through her world as a lovely rural landscape, feeling "the influence so sweet and sad of the autumnal months in the country," instead of presiding over the living community of an agricultural economy. We do not hear of any sensible intelligent farmers, like Robert Martin or William Larkin, in **Persuasion;** Sir Walter Elliot's tenant farmers are nameless. The only working farm belongs to the family of Charles Hayter, who is engaged to Henrietta Musgrove. The existence of all these persons is relegated to the edges of Austen's fiction.

The greatest social change in **Persuasion,** however, is the fact that the class of the country landowners has degenerated and has lost its vitality. Sir Walter Elliot, the negligent father and negligent landowner, is hardly worth Austen's attention, or ours: "Vanity was the beginning and the end of Sir Walter Elliot's character; vanity of person and of situation." This single trait precipitates the economic catastrophe with which **Persuasion** begins. Sir Walter refuses to curtail the conspicuous expenditure—horses, dinners, servants, luxuries—he considers incumbent upon a man of his greatness, even though he cannot pay his debts. And so he decides to rent his estate, his ancestral home, Kellynch Hall, to a tenant and to move with his family to lodgings in the resort town of Bath. He is simply giving up economic power; he has never had any moral power. And Austen gives us other evidence that his class is finished: he leaves no son; his oldest daughter, Elizabeth, remains unmarried; his daughters Mary and, eventually, Anne, marry below their class; their noble relatives, the Dalrymples and Cartarets, are entirely shallow and inconsequential; Lady Russell is a childless widow. The class is truly withering away. There is nothing in it for Anne to save, except her friendship with Lady Russell.

Anne's relationship with Lady Russell, her dead mother's friend, is at the heart of **Persuasion;** this relationship keeps the novel from being a callously cheerful vision of the death of an old order, like that in Shelley's "England in 1819." Lady Russell is old and childless; she has caused Anne great grief by persuading her not to marry the brash young sailor Frederick Wentworth, eight years earlier. Her values are essentially those of **Mansfield Park,** order and rank, quiet and propriety. She tries to persuade Anne to marry an immoral man, William Elliot; yet Anne loves her. Austen demands we share Anne's love and her grief for everything that was once good among the rural gentry and that is now dying. In this novel that goodness will die with Lady Russell; the death is a cause for sorrow. Anne cannot save the social and agricultural world Lady Russell ideally represents, but she cannot let it go lightly.

Sir Walter's class cannot be saved; in fact, the person who seems to offer Anne the opportunity to regenerate the old order is the single source of real evil in the book, William Elliot, Sir Walter's heir. Anne is tempted to marry him—tempted by his charm, by her loneliness, by the wish to return to Kellynch Hall and the old life, and by the pressure brought by Lady Russell. As a character he is as tempting as Henry Crawford, and as evil; as a part of a fictional world he is neither as interesting, nor as dangerous. In **Mansfield Park** the representative of a new, mercenary, immoral, urban class is truly threatening to the shaky remains of aristocratic life; in **Persuasion** the last scion of the aristocratic class is almost laughably powerless against the good characters. Austen does not bother to reveal him by stages, in an elegant plot. He does not seduce characters we like; we do not have to discern clues to his true nature. Austen simply allows Mrs. Smith, Anne's crippled friend, to blast his character open for Anne and for us. "Mr. Elliot is a man without heart or conscience; a designing, wary, cold-blooded being, who thinks only of himself; who, for his own interest or ease, would be guilty of any cruelty, or any treachery, that could be perpetrated without risk of his general character." When he turns out to have been in collusion with Mrs. Clay, who is trying to seduce Sir Walter into marriage, while he is pursuing Anne, we feel only that he and Mrs. Clay deserve each other. Austen actually treats their subsequent cohabitation with amusement rather than horror; "it is now a doubtful point whether his cunning, or hers, may finally carry the day; whether, after preventing her from being the wife of Sir Walter, he may not be wheedled and caressed at last into making her the wife of Sir William." She does not bother to punish the bad characters in **Persuasion;** they are not worth her trouble. In **Persuasion** Austen creates a new fictional world, different from that of **Mansfield Park** or that of **Emma,** where evil again exists, but has no power.

Evil does not have to be punished or purged because the characters Austen loves can escape from it. Anne, her husband, and their sailor friends can escape because they can move more freely than any of Austen's other characters. The very form of *Persuasion*—loose, sketchy, breathless, impressionistic—allows the reader to feel and share this new possibility of freedom, mystery, and change. No *place* is dominant in *Persuasion;* as readers we move with Anne from Kellynch Hall, to her sister Mary's home at Uppercross, to Lady Russell's home at Kellynch Lodge, to friends' lodgings in Lyme, back to Uppercross, and then to her father's rented home at Bath. And in spite of the traditions in the English novel that lead us to expect to know where a hero and heroine will settle when they marry, Anne's final destination, as a sailor's wife, is left unknown. The world is all before her as it has been before no earlier heroine in the English novel.

Anne's new liberty is part of Austen's new vision of humanity. *Persuasion* is not populated by fictional characters who must be on guard against corruption or who can govern themselves with a combination of kindness and rationality; the central characters in *Persuasion* live by and are protected by the human faculties celebrated by Wordsworth and Shelley—spontaneous cheerfulness, love, and joy. As a heroine Anne is not a central figure in a community; she is a free-floating priestess of joy. Her own emotions have protected her from William Elliot even before Mrs. Smith blasts him: "Mr. Elliot was rational, discreet, polished,—but he was not open. There was never any burst of feeling, any warmth of indignation or delight, at the evil or good of others. This, to Anne, was a decided imperfection. Her early impressions were incurable. She prized the frank, the openhearted, the eager character beyond all others. Warmth and enthusiasm did captivate her still. She felt that she could so much more depend upon the sincerity of those who sometimes looked or said a careless or a hasty thing, than of those whose presence of mind never varied, whose tongue never slipped." Openness, frankness, warmth, enthusiasm are new values in Austen's fiction; this is a new form of Romanticism for her, a celebration of the natural impulses of the heart.

These new emotional qualities belong to all the characters in *Persuasion* to whom Austen gives England's future. They have the same basic good nature as the characters in *Emma,* but Austen shows us less of their capacity for thought and more of their playfulness, more even of their carelessness. Both Mary's son Charles and her sister-in-law Louisa are careless enough to injure themselves seriously in falls—yet they recover easily enough. The characters in *Persuasion* are free in a new way, free in their behavior, free in their actions, even free from the elegance and order of Austen's usual plots. As characters they are free to play before us. For the first time in her fiction Austen actually shows us children playing, as at the Musgroves' Christmas party. "On one side was a table, occupied by some chattering girls, cutting up silk and gold paper; and on the other were tressels and trays, bending under the weight of brawn and cold pies, where riotous boys were holding high revel." For the first time, Austen abandons her sternness toward spoiled, noisy children and celebrates them as Wordsworth does, for their irrationality, their playfulness, their joyfulness. The young Musgrove women are playful too, more childish than the good women of Austen's earlier fiction. When Captain Wentworth is carelessly flirting with both of them they can fall carelessly in and out of love without being morally culpable. Unlike the Bertram sisters, both survive without a scar: Henrietta returns to Charles Hayter, and Louisa soon falls in love with Captain Benwick. In *Persuasion* love can be part of a world of play, not a world of danger.

The virtues of carelessness are even clearer in the sailors, the representatives of the new middle class into which Austen's heroine marries. The sailors come into the country neither to corrupt nor to join the community; the Crofts, who rent Kellynch Hall, simply replace the sterile snobbery of Sir Walter with their own vitality, their "heartiness . . . warmth . . . sincerity . . . comfort . . . freedom . . . gaiety." They cheerfully admit to Anne that they married very quickly and without the kind of self-examination Austen usually requires of her characters. "We had better not talk about it, my dear. . . . for if Miss Elliot were to hear how soon we came to an understanding, she would never be persuaded that we could be happy together." They continue to live hopefully and carelessly, continually risking accidents. " 'My dear admiral, that post!—we shall certainly take that post.' But by coolly giving the reins a better direction herself, they happily passed the danger, and by once afterwards judiciously putting out her hand, they neither fell into a rut, nor ran foul of a dung-cart; and Anne, with some amusement at their style of driving, which she imagined no bad representation of the general guidance of their affairs, found herself safely deposited by them at the cottage." The Crofts go gaily through the world, doing their work, meeting their friends, but always *moving.* They are true representatives of the middle classes who will gain the ascendancy in England, the class Anne will join when she leaves the country community.

The sailors' slang, like their movement, comes from a new world that offers liberty to Anne. Their slang does not indicate vulgarity, moral laxity, or inappropriate familiarity, as the slang of characters in earlier novels does. " 'Ay, a very bad business indeed.—A new sort of way this, for a young fellow to be making love, by breaking his mistress's head!—is not it, Miss Elliot? This is breaking a head and giving a plaister truly.' Admiral Croft's manners were not quite of the tone to suit Lady Russell, but they delighted Anne. His goodness of heart and simplicity of character were irresistible." In this novel Anne's response is right. The sailors' slang is not the degenerate, affected language of ill-bred people; it is the spontaneous, earthy, imagistic language of people who do perform honest labor. Their rough and active life has generated the kind of vital language Wordsworth attributes to rural people in his preface to the second edition of *The Lyrical Ballads:* "the essential passions of the heart find a better soil in which they can attain their maturity, are less under restraint, and speak a plainer and more emphatic language, because in that condition of life our elementary feelings co-exist in a state of greater simplicity." Austen has come to a similar theory of language in *Persuasion* and has expressed it with one of Wordsworth's key words—simplicity. The sailors offer Anne liberty of feeling, liberty of movement, and even a new liberty of speech.

Still, Anne has her own superior worth; she has her own spiritual values and remains the single true heroine of this novel. Because of the depth and strength of their love, Anne and Wentworth are superior to the other couples in the novel. Austen prevents us from categorizing them as the sort of excessive, sentimental Romantics she has always attacked in her fiction by playing them off against Louisa and Benwick. Benwick claims a love of the kind Anne and Wentworth have; he ostentatiously quotes Byron to demonstrate the depth of his grief over Fanny Harville. "He repeated, with such tremulous feeling, the various lines which imaged a broken heart, or a mind destroyed by wretchedness, and looked so entirely as if he meant to be understood, that she [Anne] ventured to hope he did not always read only poetry." He soon reveals that he is a quite ordinary man, when he recovers quickly in the company of Louisa Musgrove. They love easily and well, but without a depth of joy.

Joy belongs to Anne and Wentworth, joy and sorrow and memory. Still grieving, still in love, still possessed by memory even after a separation of eight years, they are the first characters in the nineteenth-century novel who have mysterious, loving souls like the soul Wordsworth celebrates in *The Prelude*. Their original love was different from love in Austen's other novels, where it is made up of admiration and gratitude, shared morality and intelligence, sexual attraction and kindness. Here Austen does not try to explain or anatomize love; her narrator describes it with a new vocabulary, which resists paraphrase or analysis. "They were gradually acquainted, and when acquainted, rapidly and deeply in love. . . . A short period of exquisite felicity followed." In no other novel does Austen ask us to value a character who falls rapidly and deeply in love; in *Persuasion* passionate, irrational love is the highest of human experiences.

The marriage between Anne and Wentworth was prevented not by flaws in their characters, but by pride on the part of Sir Walter, and by prudence on the part of Lady Russell; the reconciliation, therefore, has nothing to do with moral correction. Lady Russell, the family friend who has acted as Anne's mother, truly and honorably believes that Anne Elliot at nineteen would have been wrong to marry a man without family or fortune. Time has shown her to be wrong, but not morally wrong. And she would not have been wrong in Austen's other novels, where the good are prudent. She is wrong only because she does not share the new Romanticism of *Persuasion,* the Romanticism Anne Elliot has discovered through suffering. "How eloquent could Anne Elliot have been,—how eloquent, at least, were her wishes on the side of early warm attachment, and a cheerful confidence in futurity, against that over-anxious caution which seems to insult exertion and distrust Providence!—She had been forced into prudence in her youth, she learned romance as she grew older—the natural sequel of an unnatural beginning." Anne thinks Lady Russell has been wrong but does not blame her and does not stop loving her; as a narrator Austen asks us, too, to forgive her. "She was a very good woman, and if her second object was to be sensible and well-judging, her first was to see Anne happy. She loved Anne better than she loved her own abil-

ities." In *Persuasion* the loving heart is more important than anything else.

And though we sympathize with Anne's eight years of sorrow, and share the regret she and Wentworth feel when he discovers she would have accepted him if he had returned sooner, we still marvel and rejoice in our understanding of the effect of solitude on the loving heart. Though Austen tells us Wentworth has suffered deeply, she illuminates only Anne's heart for us, and illuminates it as no English novelist had illuminated a heroine's heart before. In most earlier English novels a character as solitary as Anne would be suspect, since solitude comes from broken social bonds; Anne Elliot is different, and *Persuasion* is different. Anne's solitude and grief began long before her separation from Wentworth, as Austen tells us late in *Persuasion;* "Anne had gone unhappy to school, grieving for the loss of a mother whom she had dearly loved, feeling her separation from home, and suffering as a girl of fourteen, of strong sensibility and not high spirits, must suffer at such a time." Though this information is unobtrusive in the narration, it is unusual; neither Austen nor earlier novelists have revealed before the secret griefs their characters felt in their youth. Grief, memory, solitude, all are the experiences given value by Romantic poetry.

Solitude has given Anne many strengths. She loves nature and loves music as a source of private pleasure, not as a means of entertaining guests. She has a rare capacity to love other women, for example, Lady Russell and Mrs. Smith, her former governess. And above all, she has gained the power to keep on loving Frederick Wentworth through the years of separation. Austen devotes most of the text of *Persuasion* to Anne's gradual discovery that her love is returned; she does not have to change her character, but has only to learn a joyful truth.

The language in which Austen reveals Anne's happiness is entirely Romantic. She concentrates on the intensity of the emotion, not on any moral or intellectual revelations to which the emotion may be attached. In earlier novels she gives only a few paragraphs to the happiness her heroines feel when they discover they are loved; here she develops Anne's happiness in subtle stages and exuberant language. First, she thinks Wentworth's apparent forgiveness when he meets her again will be a precious memory: Uppercross "stood the record of many sensations of pain, once severe, but now softened; and of some instances of relenting feeling, some breathings of friendship and reconciliation, which could never be looked for again, and which could never cease to be dear. She left it all behind her; all but the recollection that such things had been." When she discovers Wentworth is not disturbed by Louisa's engagement, she feels something more: "No, it was not regret which made Anne's heart beat in spite of herself, and brought the colour into her cheeks when she thought of Captain Wentworth unshackled and free. She had some feelings which she was ashamed to investigate. They were too much like joy, senseless joy."

Joy is the great new emotion of both Wordsworth and Shelley, the brief, transfiguring exaltation that transcends the rational powers of the mind. When Anne and Wentworth meet again at Bath, she has another burst of intense feeling: "it was agitation, pain, pleasure, a something between delight and misery." At the play, when Wentworth has hinted he still loves her, she is physically transfigured, above self-consciousness. "Anne saw nothing, thought nothing of the brilliancy of the room. Her happiness was from within. Her eyes were bright, and her cheeks glowed, but she knew nothing about it." And when they finally come to an understanding, they walk together with "smiles reined in and spirits dancing in private rapture." These spirits are new in the novel; they are the spirits of Romantic poetry. Austen has truly created a new and Romantic heroine in Anne Elliot.

Love and joy, not order, elegance, rationality, or morality, are the final values of *Persuasion.* Anne and Wentworth are not an absolutely isolated couple, alone in their happiness; they are bound to a mobile community of friends—the Crofts and the Harvilles and the Benwicks. The only stationary friends they have are Mrs. Smith and Lady Russell. Austen has set her characters free into a world of wandering, almost like the world Shelley created for himself. In Anne Elliot, Austen has given one side of Romanticism a beautiful and moving form; Anne Elliot truly possesses the spiritual powers of imagination and memory, grief and love; she floats before our sight, a luminous individual woman, self-sufficient, almost self-creating in her loveliness.

Yet there is a price. As readers we cannot grieve to lose Sir Walter Elliot, Elizabeth, William Elliot, Mrs. Clay; but Lady Russell, the Musgroves, the Hayters remain in the country, unblest by the company of Anne and Wentworth. Anne's freedom, her radical liberation from the old bonds, is a loss both to the community of rural England and to herself. She is right to grieve that she will never be mistress of Kellynch Hall; Austen has been honest enough to admit that there is something to grieve for. The kind of protection and comfort that an agricultural village, the village ideally presented in Highbury, offers to the old and sick and silly is not available to wanderers. Anne, of course, is leaving a sterile and worthless world; but her grief reminds us of what the country community ideally was and could be. In *Emma* and *Persuasion* Austen shows us the best a woman can get from Romantic radicalism: in *Emma* the precious moral economy for which rural workers were fighting in the early nineteenth century, the economy threatened by industrial capitalism; in *Persuasion* the joyful power of the loving heart and soul, isolated and at liberty. Austen never found a way to combine them; the two roads of Romanticism remain separate. Both are radical, for both declare that human goodness does not depend on the external repression Austen the experimental reactionary praised in *Mansfield Park,* and both oppose a corrupt economic order. In *Emma* the corrupt economic power is the new world of the Eltons; in *Persuasion* it is the old world of Sir Walter.

When Anne Elliot casts her lot with what will, in fact, be the new, competitive, capitalistic middle class, she has given up economic power. Though she might keep her sailor husband company on board ship as Mrs. Croft does, she can have no economic connection with Wentworth's

life. She has given up the kind of life available to women in agricultural England, a life with powers and duties like those Emma assumes in marrying Mr. Knightley. We must imagine what her world will be without her, as we imagine the abandoned village when we read Keats's "Ode on a Grecian Urn"; we must remember old Lady Russell and crippled Mrs. Smith. Realizing that the women of the centuries that follow *Persuasion* have more often chosen Anne's road than Emma's, we must also remember who has been left behind. The victims in our culture are the weak, the Miss Bateses of the world, the women who most need to know that other women, powerful women, feel a duty to them. (pp. 66-75)

> *Judith Weissman, "Jane Austen: Loving and Leaving," in her* Half Savage and Hardy and Free: Women and Rural Radicalism in the Nineteenth-Century Novel, *Wesleyan University Press, 1987, pp. 47-75.*

FURTHER READING

Astell, Ann W. "Anne Elliot's Education: The Learning of Romance in *Persuasion.*" *Renascence* XL, No. 1 (Fall 1987): 2-14.

> Examines ways in which the theme of self-discovery and education in *Persuasion* applies more directly to the character of Anne Elliot than Captain Wentworth.

Babb, Howard S. "*Persuasion:* In Defense of Sensibility." In his *Jane Austen's Novels: The Fabric of Dialogue,* pp. 203-41. 1962. Reprint. Hamden, Conn.: Archon Books, 1967.

> Contends that "the theme of *Persuasion*—as of [Austen's] previous novels—is essentially moral, the only difference being that feeling, suspect in the earlier works that vindicated 'sense,' is here the trustworthy agent of moral perception."

Barfoot, C. C. "*Persuasion:* Time's Change and Fate." In his *The Thread of Connection: Aspects of Fate in the Novels of Jane Austen and Others,* pp. 85-111. Amsterdam: Rodopi, 1982.

> Discusses *Persuasion* in terms of Austen's attitude toward fate, exploring the effects of time and circumstance on the characters' happiness.

Brown, Julia Prewitt. "The Radical Pessimism of *Persuasion.*" In her *Jane Austen's Novels: Social Change and Literary Form,* pp. 127-50. Cambridge, Mass.: Harvard University Press, 1979.

> Suggests that *Persuasion* is characterized by a sense of isolation and disillusionment often associated with literary Modernism.

Butler, Marilyn. "*Persuasion and Sanditon.*" In her *Jane Austen and the War of Ideas,* pp. 275-91. Oxford: Clarendon Press, 1975.

> Includes a discussion of *Persuasion* as a departure from Austen's previous works on both technical and philosophical levels.

Chapman, R. W. "A Reply to Mr. Duffy on *Persuasion*." *Nineteenth-Century Fiction* 9, No. 2 (September 1954): 154.

Responds to an essay by Joseph M. Duffy (see excerpt dated 1954), finding fault with Duffy's demarcation of social classes in the novel.

———, ed. *The Manuscript Chapters of "Persuasion."* London: Athlone Press, 1985, n.p.

Includes facsimile pages and a transcription of the last two chapters of *Persuasion,* which, of all Austen's novels, represent the only extant manuscript. Also provided are textual notes analyzing Austen's revisions to the novel's conclusion.

Craik, W. A. *"Persuasion."* In his *Jane Austen: The Six Novels,* pp. 166-200. London: Methuen & Co., 1965.

Examines *Persuasion* as Austen's last completed novel, finding that it contains "a more introspective kind of writing" and demonstrates more concern for "the individual and . . . his moral growth within himself, rather than within his society."

Crane, R. S. "Jane Austen: *Persuasion.*" In his *The Idea of the Humanities and Other Essays Critical and Historical,* Vol. 2, pp. 283-302. Chicago: University of Chicago Press, 1967.

Offers a general critical reading of *Persuasion*'s plot, characterization, and themes.

Daiches, David. Introduction to *Persuasion,* by Jane Austen, pp. v-xix. New York: W. W. Norton, 1958.

Offers introductory commentary on *Persuasion,* citing it as "the novel which the experienced reader of Jane Austen puts at the head of the list."

Davison, Trevor. "Jane Austen and the 'Process' of *Persuasion.*" *The Durham University Journal* LXXVII, No. 1 (December 1984): 43-7.

Traces the development of Austen's style and her sense of irony in *Persuasion.*

Duckworth, Alistair M. "*Persuasion:* The Estate Abandoned." In his *The Improvement of the Estate: A Study of Jane Austen's Novels,* pp. 179-208. Baltimore: Johns Hopkins Press, 1971.

Influential study of social and political issues in Austen's novels which includes a discussion of Austen's commentary on the individual's changing role in society as represented in *Persuasion.*

Flavin, Louise. "Austen's *Persuasion.*" *The Explicator* 47, No. 4 (Summer 1989): 20-3.

Suggests that *Persuasion* is one of the earliest examples in English fiction of "free indirect discourse," the infusion of the speech and thoughts of the novel's characters with the narrative voice.

Gunn, Daniel P. "In the Vicinity of Winthrop: Ideological Rhetoric in *Persuasion.*" *Nineteenth-Century Fiction* 41, No. 4 (March 1987): 403-18.

Proposes to "disentangle and clarify some of the socially resonant fragments in *Persuasion* by tracing them back to their class roots and examining Austen's complicated and ambiguous rhetorical presentation of them."

Harris, Jocelyn. "Anne Elliot, the Wife of Bath, and Other Friends." In *Jane Austen: New Perspectives,* edited by Janet Todd, pp. 273-93. New York: Holmes & Meier Publishers, 1983.

Speculates on Austen's familiarity with Geoffrey Chaucer's *Canterbury Tales* in a comparison of the social behavior and political thought of *Persuasion*'s Anne Elliot with Chaucer's Wife of Bath.

Ireland, K. R. "Future Recollections of Immortality: Temporal Articulation in Jane Austen's *Persuasion.*" *Novel* 13, No. 2 (Winter 1980): 204-20.

Proposes to "examine how far the climax of *Persuasion* and the novel as a whole can be articulated according to the development of its temporal elements."

Johnson, Judy van Sickle. "The Bodily Frame: Learning Romance in *Persuasion.*" *Nineteenth-Century Fiction* 38, No. 1 (June 1983): 43-61.

Examines Austen's portrayal of Anne Elliot's acquisition of romantic knowledge, as well as her descriptions of physical and emotional sensations, as the most candid of her characterizations of love relationships.

Lerner, Lawrence. "*Persuasion:* A Novel by the Anti-Jane." In his *The Truthtellers: Jane Austen, George Eliot, D. H. Lawrence,* pp. 166-72. New York: Schocken Books, 1967.

Detects in *Persuasion* a subversive attitude toward the moral propriety advocated in Austen's previous novels, which, the critic contends, allows for a richer examination of Anne Elliot's character.

Liddell, Robert. *"Persuasion."* In his *The Novels of Jane Austen,* pp. 118-37. London: Longmans, Green, and Co., 1963.

Provides character analyses of Mrs. Smith, Mr. Elliot, and Lady Russell, as well as a discussion of irony in the novel.

Lockwood, Thomas. "Divided Attention in *Persuasion.*" *Nineteenth-Century Fiction* 33, No. 3 (December 1978): 309-23.

Suggests that in *Persuasion* Austen's stance on moral issues is less definitive and her exploration of her characters' emotional lives more developed than in her previous works.

Martin, W. R. "Sensibility and Sense: A Reading of *Persuasion.*" *English Studies in Africa* 3, No. 2 (September 1960): 119-30.

Offers an interpretation of *Persuasion* based on analysis of Lady Russell's character.

Molan, Ann. "Persuasion in *Persuasion.*" *The Critical Review,* No. 24 (1982): 16-29.

Discusses various manifestations of persuasion in the novel, claiming that Austen "penetrates the intrinsic doubleness of persuasion, its ability to destroy and fashion, its ineradicable presence in all human dealings, and the riskiness of deciding one's lot by something uncertifiable."

Monaghan, David. *"Persuasion."* In his *Jane Austen: Structure and Social Vision,* pp. 143-62. New York: Harper & Row Publishers, 1980.

Examines parallels between the collapse of the English social order reflected in *Persuasion* and flaws in the structure of the novel itself.

Moon, E. B. " 'A Model of Excellence': Anne Elliot, *Persuasion,* and the Vindication of a Richardsonian Ideal of the Female Character." *AUMLA,* No. 67 (May 1987): 25-42.

Explores the influence of fiction by Samuel Richardson, particularly that of his novel *The History of Sir Charles Grandison,* on Austen's characterization of Anne Elliot.

Morgan, Susan. "The Nature of Character in *Persuasion.*" In her *In the Meantime: Character and Perception in Jane Austen's Fiction,* pp. 166-98. Chicago: University of Chicago Press, 1980.

Focuses on Anne Elliot in an examination of the relationship between the emotional lives of Austen's characters and their conceptions of reality.

Mudrick, Marvin. "The Liberation of Feeling: *Persuasion.*" In his *Jane Austen: Irony as Defense and Discovery,* pp. 207-40. Princeton, N.J.: Princeton University Press, 1952.

Suggests that in *Persuasion* Austen was able to use irony for purposes other than comedy and moral instruction, achieving "a new impulse, feeling; and a new climax, self-fulfillment" for both Austen and Anne Elliot.

Nardin, Jane. "Christianity and the Structure of *Persuasion.*" *Renascence* XXX, No. 1 (Autumn 1978): 43-55.

Examines ways in which Austen's Christian beliefs permeate the characterization and plot structure of *Persuasion.*

Page, Norman. "Categories of Speech in *Persuasion.*" *The Modern Language Review* 64, No. 4 (October 1969): 734-41.

Analyzes Austen's skill as a stylist in *Persuasion,* focusing on her presentation of dialogue.

Rackin, Donald. "Jane Austen's Anatomy of Persuasion." In *The English Novel in the Nineteenth Century: Essays on the Literary Mediation of Human Values,* edited by George Goodin, pp. 52-80. Urbana: University of Illinois Press, 1972.

Contends that "*Persuasion* is not so much a novel of moral development as it is an elaborate fictional anatomy of an achieved moral virtue in which that virtue is tested, refined, and rewarded, but above all in which that virtue is elegantly defined."

Sieferman, Sylvia. "*Persuasion:* The Motive for Metaphor." *Studies in the Novel* XI, No. 3 (Fall 1979): 283-301.

Examines Austen's use of figurative language in *Persuasion,* exploring its role in the characterization of Anne Elliot.

Smith, Grahame. "*Persuasion.*" In his *The Novel & Society: Defoe to George Eliot,* pp. 116-46. Totowa, N.J.: Barnes & Noble Books, 1984.

Studies *Persuasion* as a stylistic and substantive innovation in the history of the English novel.

Southam, B. C. "The Two Chapters of *Persuasion.*" In his *Jane Austen's Literary Manuscripts,* pp. 86-99. London: Oxford University Press, 1964.

Compares the manuscript pages of the last two chapters of *Persuasion* with the final revised edition of the novel in an examination of Austen's imaginative process.

Spence, Jon. "The Abiding Possibilities of Nature in *Persuasion.*" *Studies in English Literature* XXI, No. 4 (Autumn 1981): 625-36.

Explores the roles of accident and chance in *Persuasion.*

Swanson, Janice Bowman. "Toward a Rhetoric of Self: The Art of *Persuasion.*" *Nineteenth-Century Fiction* 36, No. 1 (June 1981): 1-21.

Argues that Anne Elliot's eventual mastery of rhetoric assists in her attainment of self-fulfillment and independence at the novel's conclusion.

Thomas, Keith G. "Jane Austen and the Romantic Lyric: *Persuasion* and Coleridge's Conversation Poems." *ELH* 54, No. 4 (Winter 1987): 893-924.

Compares "lyrical moments" in *Persuasion* with the Romantic poetry of Samuel Taylor Coleridge, finding similarities in structure and strategy.

Weissman, Cheryl Ann. "Doubleness and Refrain in Jane Austen's *Persuasion.*" *The Kenyon Review* n.s. X, No. 4 (Fall 1988): 87-91.

Demonstrates ways in which "the wistful tone of *Persuasion* is informed by a bizarre and implacable emphasis on doubleness and refrains in diction, plot, themes, and even syntax."

Whatley, Richard. Review of *Northanger Abbey* and *Persuasion. The Quarterly Review* XXIV, No. XLVIII (January 1821): 352-76.

Originally unsigned, favorable review of *Persuasion* praising the balance of passion and prudence achieved in the character of Anne Elliot.

Wiesenfarth, Joseph. "*Persuasion:* History and Myth." *The Wordsworth Circle* II, No. 4 (Autumn 1971): 160-68.

Discusses *Persuasion* from a historical perspective, focusing on Austen's representation of the social and economic changes in English society during the time in which she lived.

Wilhelm, Cherry. "*Persuasion:* Time Redeemed." *English Studies in Africa* 22, No. 22 (1979): 91-8.

Examines Austen's portrayal of the time frame involved in the development of romance between Anne Elliot and Captain Wentworth.

Charlotte Brontë

1816-1855

(Also wrote under pseudonym of Currer Bell) English novelist and poet.

The following entry presents criticism of Brontë's novel *Villette* (1853). For information on Brontë's complete career, see *NCLC*, Vol. 3; for a discussion of the novel *Jane Eyre: An Autobiography* (1847), see *NCLC*, Vol. 8.

Brontë's last completed novel endures as a key to understanding her art and anticipates many of the preoccupations of Victorian novels that followed it, including psychology, the role of women in society, and the relationship between narrator and reader. Told by Lucy Snowe, an imaginative and passionate woman who suppresses her emotions beneath a reserved exterior, *Villette* presents a highly subjective version of her experiences as a teacher in a French school for girls. Lucy's uncharismatic personality and her deliberately misleading narrative rendered her a perplexing character to many nineteenth-century critics, but recently she has come to be appreciated as an intriguingly complex narrator and an early opponent of patriarchal ideology.

In the years preceding the writing of *Villette*, Brontë experienced the loss of her brother Branwell and her sisters Emily and Anne. In their youths, the Brontë siblings had collaborated on a series of imaginative stories set in the fictional land of Angria, and, once they developed their own literary careers, they exchanged manuscripts and solicited counsel from each other. After their deaths Brontë found it very trying to write in solitude. Eventually taking for inspiration the general plot of *The Professor*—her first, unpublished novel about a torrid teacher-pupil relationship—and greatly expanding its themes and characterizations, she wrote *Villette* between March and November of 1852. She modified the ending slightly at the behest of her father, who felt it was too unhappy, and, believing that *The Professor* had been rejected by publishers because it lacked the supernatural elements common to the Gothic novels of the period, incorporated into the plot a ghostly nun. *Villette* was published in the conventional three-volume format in January of 1853. In 1854 Brontë married Arthur Bell Nicholls; she died the following year from complications resulting from pregnancy.

Villette begins in England where fourteen-year-old Lucy lives with her godparents the Brettons, their son Graham, and Paulina Home, a dramatic and affectionate girl also placed in the Brettons' care. Paulina develops a crush on Graham Bretton and confesses her fondness to Lucy, who comments unsympathetically on the situation, hiding her own amorous feelings for Graham. The narrative skips ahead eight years to tell of Lucy's service to Miss Marchmont, an elderly woman whose despairing account of her youthful love prefigures Lucy's tragic life and whose promise to include Lucy in her will goes unfulfilled.

Lucy travels to the French town of Villette, where she gains employment as a teacher, re-encounters Paulina, and develops a friendship with Dr. John, the local physician. Her feelings for him deepen, soon amounting to an obsession, impelling her to irrational—but symbolically important—actions: entering the confessional of a Catholic priest despite her virulent anti-Catholicism, imagining the ghostly nun, and burying letters from Dr. John. Critics see Lucy's behavior as one of the first nervous breakdowns in literature to be rendered in realistic psychological detail. Lucy discloses to the reader the information that Dr. John and Graham Bretton are one and the same. Dr. John, however, oblivious to Lucy's affection, becomes romantically involved with Paulina. Lucy begins a stormy relationship with Paul Emanuel, a brilliant and idiosyncratic professor who, before embarking on a journey overseas, pledges to marry her. At the novel's end, Lucy implies that Paul has died in a shipwreck.

Early appraisals of *Villette* were mixed. Many reviewers commended Brontë's realistic characterizations and powerful imagery. On the other hand, Matthew Arnold accused Brontë of having a mind containing "nothing but hunger, rebellion and rage, and therefore that is all she can, in fact put into her book," and William Thackeray, one of Brontë's literary idols, equated Lucy's unfulfilled romantic yearnings with those of her inventor. The tendency to view Brontë's writings as strictly autobiographical has since been discredited as reductive and ignorant of her imaginative powers. Some critics faulted Lucy for lacking the charisma of Jane Eyre, a circumstance which Brontë anticipated in a letter to her publisher W. S. Williams: "I consider that she *is* both morbid and weak at times; her character sets up no pretensions to unmixed strength, and anybody living her life would necessarily become morbid." Although the novel's depiction of what Steven Millhauser has called "a soul in anguish" has been admired as a compelling rendition of a character type rarely found in Victorian literature, scholars believe that the emotional demands placed on the reader by this portrait account for readers neglecting *Villette* in favor of *Jane Eyre,* a relatively simpler and lighter tale.

In his influential essay, "*Villette* and the Life of the Mind" (1960), Robert A. Colby sought to revitalize discussion of the work. "To read *Villette* as carefully as it deserves to be read," he asserted, "is to follow the curve of Charlotte Brontë's literary development to its completion—and at the same time to follow the direction of the nineteenth-century novel." Subsequently, critics began to approach *Villette* from fresh perspectives, unearthing new complexities and debating aspects of the novel that had been previously dismissed as flaws and contradictions. The narrative structure, for example, is now considered remarkable for the ways in which Lucy, haunted by memories of the misfortunes that befell her as a youth, provides a radically distorted account of those events. Information pertinent to the novel's opening scenes is volunteered much later in the text, forcing readers to return to earlier passages or at least reassess their meaning; scenes presented as fact turn out to be hallucination; and reports of emotional states, including the frequent refrain "I, Lucy Snowe, was calm," are revealed to be misrepresentations. Some critics now contend that the narrator's deliberate manipulation of the story, once criticized as unfair to readers, constitutes Brontë's means of investing her largely powerless protagonist with control over her own life. Others focus on Lucy's evasive treatment of the past as a manifestation of her repressed emotional life.

In the 1970s and 1980s, much of the criticism of *Villette* was informed by feminist thought. In her *Sexual Politics* (1970), Kate Millett described *Villette* as "a book too subversive to be popular" and characterized Lucy Snowe as a revolutionary disgusted by women's status in society as mere objects to be viewed by men, and by the punishment and servitude women inflicted upon themselves in order to be attractive to men. According to Millett, Lucy's heroism lies in her avoidance of the traps of patriarchal society, especially the Victorian conception of marriage. In exploring this area of inquiry, critics have examined other aspects of what Mary Jacobus called "Charlotte Brontë's double quest for literary form and for female emancipation," citing instances in which Lucy ridicules patriarchal prejudices in religion, aesthetics, and science, and interpreting the novel's unconventional narrative strategies as a challenge to traditional modes of storytelling. According

to this argument, Lucy's irrationality represents a conscious departure from the rigidity and logic of the male-dominated literary tradition. Such assessments have altered perceptions of Lucy Snowe, once seen as an ill-tempered manifestation of Charlotte Brontë's troubled psyche but presently recognized as one of the most original creations in the Victorian novel.

(See also *Dictionary of Literary Biography,* Vol. 21.)

Charlotte Brontë   (letter date 1852)

[*In the following letter to the publisher George Smith, Brontë remarks on her feelings about writing* Villette.]

October 30th, 1852.

MY DEAR SIR,—You must notify honestly what you think of *Villette* when you have read it. I can hardly tell you how I hunger to hear some opinion beside my own, and how I have sometimes desponded, and almost despaired, because there was no one to whom to read a line, or of whom to ask a counsel. *Jane Eyre* was not written under such circumstances, nor were two-thirds of *Shirley.* I got so miserable about it, I could bear no allusion to the book. It is not finished yet; but now I hope. As to the anonymous publication, I have this to say: If the withholding of the author's name should tend materially to injure the publisher's interest, to interfere with booksellers' orders, etc., I would not press the point; but if no such detriment is contingent I should be much thankful for the sheltering shadow of an incognito. I seem to dread the advertisements—the large-lettered 'Currer Bell's New Novel,' or 'New Work by the Author of *Jane Eyre.*' These, however, I feel well enough, are the transcendentalisms of a retired wretch; so you must speak frankly.

You will see that *Villette* touches on no matter of public interest. I cannot write books handling the topics of the day; it is of no use trying. Nor can I write a book for its moral. Nor can I take up a philanthropic scheme, though I honour philanthropy; and voluntarily and sincerely veil my face before such a mighty subject as that handled in Mrs Beecher Stowe's work, *Uncle Tom's Cabin.* To manage these great matters rightly they must be long and practically studied—their bearings known intimately, and their evils felt genuinely; they must not be taken up as a business matter and a trading speculation. I doubt not Mrs Stowe had felt the iron of slavery enter into her heart, from childhood upwards, long before she ever thought of writing books. The feeling throughout her work is sincere and not got up. Remember to be an honest critic of *Villette,* and tell Mr Williams to be unsparing: not that I am likely to alter anything, but I want to know his impressions and yours. (pp. 13-14)

Charlotte Brontë, in a letter to George Smith on October 30, 1852, in The Brontës: Their Lives, Friendships and Correspondence, 1852-1928, Vol. IV, *edited by Thomas J. Wise and J. Alexander Symington, 1933. Reprint by Basil Blackwell, 1980, pp. 13-14.*

Charlotte Brontë   (letter date 1852)

[*In the following letter to W. S. Williams, the reader for Smith, Elder publishers, Brontë discusses the emotional content of* Villette *and the nature of its protagonist, Lucy Snowe.*]

November 6th, 1852.

MY DEAR SIR,—I must not delay thanking you for your kind letter, with its candid and able commentary on· **Villette.** With many of your strictures I concur. The third volume may, perhaps, do away with some of the objections; others still remain in force. I do not think the interest culminates anywhere to the degree you would wish. What climax there is does not come on till near the conclusion; and even then I doubt whether the regular novel-reader will consider the 'agony piled sufficiently high' (as the Americans say), or the colours dashed on to the canvas with the proper amount of daring. Still, I fear, they must be satisfied with what is offered; my palette affords no brighter tints; were I to attempt to deepen the reds, or burnish the yellows, I should but botch.

Unless I am mistaken the emotion of the book will be found to be kept throughout in tolerable subjection. As to the name of the heroine, I can hardly express what subtlety of thought made me decide upon giving her a cold name; but at first I called her 'Lucy Snowe' (spelt with an 'e'), which Snowe I afterwards changed to 'Frost.' Subsequently I rather regretted the change, and wished it 'Snowe' again. If not too late I should like the alteration to be made now throughout the MS. A *cold* name she must have; partly, perhaps, on the *'lucus a non lucendo'* princi-ple—partly on that of the 'fitness of things,' for she has about her an external coldness.

You say that she may be thought morbid and weak, unless the history of her life be more fully given. I consider that she *is* both morbid and weak at times; her character sets up no pretensions to unmixed strength, and anybody living her life would necessarily become morbid. It was no impetus of healthy feeling which urged her to the confessional, for instance; it was the semi-delirium of solitary grief and sickness. If, however, the book does not express all this, there must be a great fault somewhere. I might explain away a few other points, but it would be too much like drawing a picture and then writing underneath the name of the object intended to be represented. We know what sort of a pencil that is which needs an ally in the pen.

Thanking you again for the clearness and fulness with which you have responded to my request for a statement of impressions, I am, my dear sir, yours very sincerely,

C. BRONTE.

I trust the work will be seen in MS. by no one except Mr Smith and yourself. (pp. 17-18)

Charlotte Brontë, in a letter to W. S. Williams on November 6, 1852, in The Brontës: Their Lives, Friendships and Correspondence, 1852-1928, Vol. IV, *edited by Thomas J. Wise and J. Alexander Symington, 1933. Reprint by Basil Blackwell, 1980, pp. 17-18.*

The Leader   (essay date 1853)

[*In the following excerpt, the critic concedes that* Villette *is a flawed novel by conventional standards, but argues that its appeal lies in its originality of style and thought.*]

In Passion and Power—those noble twins of Genius—Currer Bell has no living rival, except George Sand. Hers is the passionate heart to feel, and the powerful brain to give feeling shape; and that is why she is so original, so fascinating. Faults she has, in abundance; they are so obvious, they lie so legible on the surface, that to notice them with more insistence than a passing allusion is the very wantonness of criticism. On a former occasion, and in another place, we remonstrated with her on these said faults, but we now feel that the lecture was idle. Why wander delighted among the craggy clefts and snowy solitudes of the Alps, complaining at the want of verdure and of flowers? In the presence of real Power why object to its not having the quiet lineaments of Grace? There is a Strength clothed with Gentleness, but there may also be Strength rugged, vehement—careless of Beauty. Goethe, indeed (who was "himself the great sublime he drew") has somewhere said,—

> *Nur die gesattigte Kraft kehrel zur Aumuth*
> *zurück—*
> Only the fulness of Power moves with the calmness of Grace,

which is true of perfect Grace; yet there are few in whom

The publisher George Smith, after whom Brontë modeled the character Graham Bretton.

Power reaches this fulness, and of the few Currer Bell is not. Is it not enough for us to accept her *as* she is?

One may say of Currer Bell that her genius finds a fitting illustration in her heroes and heroines—her Rochesters and Jane Eyres. They are men and women of deep feeling, clear intellects, vehement tempers, bad manners, ungraceful, yet loveable persons. Their address is brusque, unpleasant, yet individual, direct, free from shams and conventions of all kinds. They outrage "good taste," yet they fascinate. You dislike them at first, yet you learn to love them. The power that is in them makes its vehement way right to your heart. Propriety, ideal outline, good manners, good features, ordinary thought, ordinary speech, are not to be demanded of them. They are the Mirabeaus of romance; and the idolatry of a nation follows the great gifts of a Mirabeau, let "Propriety" look never so "shocked." It is the triumph of what is sterling over what is tinsel, of what is essential to human worth over what is collateral. Place a perfectly well-bred, well-featured, graceful considerate gentleman—a hero of romance, vague and ideal—beside one who is imperious, coarse, ill-tempered, ill-featured, but who, under this husk of manner and of temper contains the kernel of what is noble, generous, loving, powerful, and see how in the long run human sympathies will detach themselves from the unsatisfying hero, and cling to the man whose brain and heart are powerful! It is like placing a clever agreeable novel beside *Jane Eyre.* Jane captured all our hearts; not because she was lovely, ladylike, good, but because she was direct, clear, upright, capable of deep affections, and of bravely enduring great affliction. If any one pointed out her faults, we admitted them, but never swerved a line from our admiration. We never thought her perfect, we loved her for what was loveable, and left the rest to be set down to human imperfection.

And so of this story we have just read. *Villette* has assuredly many faults, and novel readers, no less than critics, will have much to say thereon. More adroit "construction," more breathless suspense, more thrilling incidents, and a more moving story, might easily have been manufactured by a far less active, inventive, passionate writer; but not such a book. Here, at any rate, is an *original book.* Every page, every paragraph, is sharp with *individuality.* It is Currer Bell speaking to you, not the Circulating Library reverberating echos. How *she* has looked at life, with a saddened, yet not vanquished soul; what *she* has thought, and felt, not what she thinks others will expect her to have thought and felt; *this* it is we read of here, and this it is which makes her writing welcome above almost every other writing. It has held us spell-bound.

Descending from generals to particulars, let us say that, considered in the light of a novel, it is a less interesting story than even *Shirley.* It wants the unity and progression of interest which made *Jane Eyre* so fascinating; but it is the book of a mind more conscious of its power. *Villette* is meant for Brussels. The greater part of the scenes pass in the Netherlands, not unhappily designated as *Labassecour.* People will wonder why this transparent disguise was adopted. We conjecture that it was to prevent personal applications on the reader's part, and also to allow the writer a greater freedom as to details. The point is, however, very unimportant.

The story begins in England. Charming, indeed, is the picture of Mrs. Bretton's house, and the little love affair between Polly, a quaint child of six, and Graham, a youth of sixteen, who pets her as boys sometimes pet children. We hear this child objected to, and called "unnatural." To our experience, the child's character is perfectly consonant, and the only thing we could wish in the delineation is that which we miss in *all* portraits of quaint precocious children,—viz., a more vivid recollection on the artist's part of the childlike nonsense and whimsicality which *accompany* the demonstrations of feeling and intelligence. Children do frequently think and say things, the wisdom and maturity of which are startling—children constantly rival genius in the bright originality of their remarks—but these very children *also* say childish foolish things, and to convey a true picture of the child, both the foolishness and the "old fashioned" remarks must be contemporaneous. There is no true pudding made only of plums. (p. 163)

> *"Currer Bell's New Novel," in* The Leader, *Vol. 4, No. 151, February 12, 1853, pp. 163-64.*

W. Robertson Nicoll   (essay date 1900)

[*In the following excerpt, Nicoll presents a review of* Villette *from the* Christian Remembrancer *and a response by Brontë in which she protests the reviewer's judgments of her character.*]

The *Christian Remembrancer,* a Church of England quarterly, contained in its number for April, 1853, an article entitled "New Novels by Lady G. Fullerton and Currer Bell." The Currer Bell novel, it is needless to say, was *Villette.* The reviewer began his notice of *Villette* with the following paragraph:

> After threading the maze of harrowing perplexities thus set forth by Lady Georgiana, having followed her characters through their course of fatal mistakes and hairbreadth perils, witnessed their bursts of tragic passion, listened to their turgid sentiments, and felt the whole to be the offspring of a lively imagination, confined within too narrow a sphere of observation—a society removed so high above many of the real troubles of life that they must needs allow idleness and luxury to coin some for them—it is, we own, a relief to turn to the work-day world of *Villette.* The rough winds of common life make a better atmosphere for fiction than the stove heat of the "higher circles." Currer Bell, by hardly *earning* her experience, has, at least, won her knowledge in a field of action where more can sympathise; though we cannot speak of sympathy, or of ourselves as in any sense sharing in it, without a protest against the outrages on decorum, the moral perversity, the toleration of, nay, indifference to vice which deform her first powerful picture of a desolate woman's trials and sufferings—faults which make *Jane Eyre* a dangerous book, and which must leave a permanent mistrust of the author on all thoughtful and scrupulous minds. But however alloyed with blame this sympathy

has necessarily been, there are indications of its having cheered her and done her good. Perhaps, as it was argued of Gertrude, she has been the better for a little happiness and success, for in many important moral points *Villette* is an improvement on its predecessors. The author has gained both in amiability and propriety since she first presented herself to the world—soured, coarse and grumbling; an alien, it might seem, from society, and amenable to none of its laws.

In the *Christian Remembrancer* for October, 1853, under the heading "Notices," the following paragraph appears:

> A letter from the author of *Villette,* which claims at once our respect and sympathy, complains of a passage in our recent review of that work (April, 1853), which she says has been interpreted by some persons—not by herself, for this was not her own unbiassed impression—in a sense the remotest possible from our thoughts. We wrote in entire ignorance of the author's private history, and with no wish to pry into it. But her keen and vivid style, and her original and somewhat warped mode of viewing things, must excite speculation in her readers as to the circumstances of education and position which have formed both mind and style. Some grave faults in her earliest work we thought most easily accounted for by the supposition of a mind of remarkable power and great capabilities for happiness exposed to early and long trial of some kind, and in some degree embittered by the want of congenial employment. We refer our readers to the article in question, where not only is there no insinuation of "a disadvantageous occult motive for a retired life," but such a supposition is at variance with the whole line of suggestion, which tends to attribute what we must differ from in her writings to adverse circumstances, not to conduct. We will, however, distinctly state that we had no idea in our mind, and therefore could not desire to express any suspicion, of an unfavourable cause for a life of seclusion. We now learn with pleasure, but not with surprise, that the main motive for this seclusion is devotion to the purest and most sacred of domestic ties.

It is some time since I made note of this, but I had little hope of being able to recover the actual letter. However, in the *Christian Remembrancer* for July, 1857, there is printed a long and very able article on the life of Charlotte Brontë. In that article the letter in question is given in full as follows:

> TO THE EDITOR OF THE *Christian Remembrancer.*
>
> HAWORTH, NEAR KEIGHLEY, YORKSHIRE,
>
> July 18, 1853.
>
> SIR: I think I cannot be doing wrong in addressing you a few remarks respecting an article which appeared in the *Christian Remembrancer* for last April. I mean an article noticing *Villette.*
>
> When first I read that article I thought only of its ability, which seemed to me considerable, of

its acumen, which I felt to be penetrating; an occasional misconception passed scarce noticed, and I smiled at certain passages from which evils have since risen so heavy as to oblige me to revert seriously to their origin. Conscious myself that the import of these insinuations was far indeed from truth, I forgot to calculate how they might appear to that great public which personally did not know me.

The passage to which I particularly allude characterises me by a strong expression. I am spoken of as *an alien—it might seem from society, and amenable to none of its laws.*

The *G—* newspaper gave a notice in the same spirit. The *E—* culled isolated extracts from your review, and presented them in a concentrated form as one paragraph of unqualified condemnation.

The result of these combined attacks, all to one effect—all insinuating some disadvantageous occult motive for a retired life—has been such that at length I feel it advisable to speak a few words of temperate explanation in the quarter that seems to me most worthy to be thus addressed, and the most likely to understand rightly my intention. Who my reviewer may be I know not, but I am convinced he is no narrow-minded or naturally unjust thinker.

To him I would say no cause of seclusion such as he would imply has ever come near my thoughts, deeds or life. It has not entered my experience. It has not crossed my observation.

Providence so regulated my destiny that I was born and have been reared in the seclusion of a country parsonage. I have never been rich enough to go out into the world as a participator in its gaieties, though it early became my duty to leave home in order partly to diminish the many calls on a limited income. That income is lightened of claims in another sense now, for of a family of six I am the only survivor.

My father is now in his seventy-seventh year; his mind is clear as it ever was, and he is not infirm, but he suffers from partial privation and threatened loss of sight; and his general health is also delicate, he cannot be left often or long: my place consequently is at home. These are reasons which make retirement a plain duty; but were no such reasons in existence, were I bound by no such ties, it is very possible that seclusion might still appear to me, on the whole, more congenial than publicity; the brief and rare glimpses I have had of the world do not incline me to think I should seek its circles with very keen zest—nor can I consider such disinclination a just subject for reproach.

This is the truth. The careless, rather than malevolent insinuations of reviewers have, it seems, widely spread another impression. It would be weak to complain, but I feel that it is only right to place the real in opposition to the unreal.

Will you kindly show this note to my reviewer? Perhaps he cannot now find an antidote for the poison into which he dipped that shaft he shot at "Currer Bell," but when again tempted to take aim at other prey—let him refrain his hand a moment till he has considered consequences to the wounded, and recalled the "golden rule."

I am, Sir, yours respectfully,

C. BRONTE.

The critic goes on to say:

> Though criticism was never more needed than in the case of Currer Bell, yet this is inevitably a sad book for critics. We do not blame ourselves for what has been said in our pages of the author of *Jane Eyre.* We could not do otherwise than censure what was censurable. Where would books get their deserts, how could judgment be given, if private considerations had weight to restrain independent public opinion? Critics would then be no better than partial friends. But such revelations as this book gives us are a lesson to weigh words. We should never forget that the unknown author has a known side; that he is not an abstraction. And here we are taught that the private side of a character may be in strong contrast to its public manifestation; that it needs rare discernment to form a true estimate of a writer from his works; and that the boldest, most fearless style, may emanate from a nature which has its sensitive, shrinking, timid side. We believe that all the critics thought they had a tolerably tough nature to deal with, that there was no need to sugar the bitter draught in this instance; and when a woman assumed a masculine tone, wrote as well or better than any man among them, and showed herself afraid of nothing, that gallantry and patronising tenderness which is commonly bestowed upon women was changed to gall. And now the administrators of the potion have to reflect on the private most feminine sorrows of this Amazon; of a patient life of monotonous duty; of the passionate hold the purest domestic affections had on her character; and which among them, if he could rewrite his criticism, would not now and then erase an epithet, spare a sarcasm, modify a sweeping condemnation? We own it wounds our tenderest feelings to know her sensitiveness to such attacks; and when she sheds tears over the *Times* critique—of all things in the world to weep over—our heart bleeds indeed.

(pp. 441-43)

I am not aware that Charlotte Brontë on any other occasion wrote to an editor about any review of her books. (p. 443)

> *W. Robertson Nicoll, "Charlotte Brontë and One of Her Critics," in* The Bookman, *New York, Vol. X, January, 1900, pp. 441-43.*

Andrew D. Hook (essay date 1970)

[*Hook is a Scottish educator and critic. In the following excerpt, he views the struggle between feeling and reason as the primary theme of* Villette.]

Villette is Charlotte Brontë's last and most searching exploration and analysis of the [conflict between imagination and responsibility] that had troubled her so long. Only now the implications and consequences of that conflict are seen as extending into further areas of human experience. The world of romantic daydream, of visionary delight and hope, is as appealingly portrayed as ever, but the rocks on which that world is wrecked are presented less in terms of moral and religious negatives and more in terms of the nature of reality itself. Such an extension of meaning is characteristic of the book. In one sense, however, *Villette* represents a narrowing of focus compared with *Jane Eyre.* Whereas in *Jane Eyre* the world of romantic excitement is given partial externalization in character and event, in *Villette* its existence is almost wholly internalized within the mind of the novel's protagonist, Lucy Snowe. Such a development is perhaps the only one through which the world of romance can be properly assimilated into a novel committed to an essential realism.

With its action so largely internalized, *Villette* is above all a psychological novel: its drama is the drama of a consciousness. Whose consciousness is indicated by the novel's narrative method? That it is told in the first person by Lucy Snowe is a clear suggestion of its subject; a failure to recognize this is the source of most of the common objections to the book. If Lucy Snowe is to be seen for much of the story as no more than a rather colorless onlooker who serves as narrator, then it is true that large sections of the novel are scarcely relevant; and it is equally true that about half way through interest is switched from one set of characters to a new set. But Charlotte Brontë makes Lucy Snowe narrator precisely to draw attention formally and dramatically to her centrality. This is true no matter what personal qualities, dull or interesting, prim or passionate, her telling of the story reveals. Character and event are important in *Villette* only in relation to Lucy Snowe's response, as first-person narrator, to them. Just as much as in a novel by James it is the story of the story that really matters. It is through the central recording consciousness of Lucy that the coherence of *Villette* is achieved.

If character and event in *Villette* are subordinate to the consciousness that renders these, then the nature of that consciousness comes very much into question. We have Charlotte Brontë's own word for it that Lucy's name is of symbolic value. The comment is a familiar one. "A cold name she must have . . . for she has about her an external coldness." Notice that the coldness is carefully defined as "external" only. Of course some characters in the novel never see beyond externals. Dr. John, for example, never learns to see Lucy as anything other than quiet, retiring, self-effacing; for him she is "quiet Lucy Snowe," his "inoffensive shadow"; she suffers from "overgravity in tastes and manner—want of colour in character and costume." M. de Bassohmpierre, Lucy feels, sees her as "the essence of the sedate and discreet," "the pink and pattern of governess-correctness." For Ginevra Fanshawe she is unfeeling throughout. Of course the impression suggested by these descriptions is one which Lucy in a sense consciously creates; her colorless exterior is a symbol of an internal stance that she struggles to maintain. She describes herself as "tame and still by habit." When the Bretton household is disturbed by Polly's grief at the departure of her father, "I, Lucy Snowe, was calm." In fact Lucy seems to be fully conscious of the implications of her name. After a night of turmoil, occasioned by her recognition that Mme. Beck is suspicious of her relationship with Dr. John, she reports that "next day I was again Lucy Snowe."

But that Lucy should be so disturbed as a result of her awareness of Mme. Beck's suspicions points to the side of her nature that is opposed to the colorless calm of her exterior. Lucy's inner life is as active, variable, passionate and feeling as her external is passive. The "repose of her nature," disturbed by Mme. Beck, if it exists at all, is the consequence of strict inner discipline. It is a condition that has to be struggled towards, and once attained is irresolutely defended. That she does feel, and sometimes with passionate intensity, Lucy occasionally admits: "I had feelings: passive as I lived, little as I spoke, cold as I looked, when I thought of past days I *could* feel. . . ." This acknowledgement by Lucy of her capacity to feel comes quite soon after her arrival at the Pensionnat of Mme. Beck and clearly hints at a discontent with the superficial calm of her existence there. The reappearance of Dr. John has no doubt contributed to her disturbed state. That she is disturbed is made very clear:

> At that time, I well remember whatever could excite—certain accidents of the weather, for instance, were almost dreaded by me, because they woke the being I was always lulling, and stirred up a craving cry I could not satisfy.

The ensuing thunderstorm lifts Lucy to a pitch of intense emotional excitement. For a moment the wildness of the storm releases all her pent-up desires to escape from the nugatory present. But the romantic intensity of this is quickly "knocked on the head" in the following paragraph, and a kind of calm restored. The price of that calm is suggested by the Jael and Sisera reference which Charlotte Brontë uses to define it. "Unlike Sisera," the feelings in question "did not die: they were but transiently stunned, and at intervals would turn on the nail with a rebellious wrench; then did the temples bleed, and the brain thrill to its core." The almost masochistic physical immediacy of this is disturbing. But it leaves no room for doubting the vivid, emotional, passionate quality of Lucy Snowe's inner nature.

The division within Lucy Snowe suggested by her external coldness and her inner anguish implies two quite different stances towards life. What these are an examination of the opening episodes of *Villette* will help to clarify. The story opens in a house in Bretton's "calm old streets." The house is an asylum of peace and tranquillity. "The large peaceful rooms, the well-arranged furniture, the clear wide windows, the balcony outside, looking down on a fine antique street, where Sundays and holidays seemed always to abide—so quiet was its atmosphere, so clean its pavement—these things pleased me well." Despite its lack of incident, Lucy Snowe is very much at home in this world: "The charm of variety there was not, nor the excitement of incident; but I liked peace so well, and sought stimulus so little, that when the latter came I almost felt

it a disturbance, and wished rather it had still held aloof." The Brettons, in whose house Lucy is living, match the equitableness of their environment. Graham Bretton's inheritance from his mother includes "her spirits of that tone and equality which are better than a fortune to the possessor." Such spirits are the guarantee of a life of comparative peace, even if they deprive their possessor of both the heights and depths of feeling. Into this Sunday world of the Brettons, all calm and peace and quiet, comes the fantastic, elfin figure of Polly. In strong contrast to the Brettons, Polly is quintessentially feeling and imagination. Her devotion to her father in the first place, and subsequently to Graham Bretton, is powerful and tenacious. But the very strength and intensity of her feelings make her exquisitely vulnerable. So much so that Lucy Snowe fears for her amid "the shocks and repulses, the humiliations and desolations" which she believes to be part of the "battle with this life." Polly then is a small example for Lucy, a sketch of the dangers which are bound up with the life of feeling.

Lucy's own stay in the calm world of Bretton proves to be only temporary. (Soon even the Brettons are to learn that such tranquillity and ease are short-lived.) After leaving Bretton Lucy passes over the next eight years of her life, though indicating that they were years in which there

Title page of Villette.

was no return to the safe harbour of a Bretton. "I will permit the reader," she says, "to picture me . . . as a bark slumbering through halcyon weather, in a harbour still as glass—the steersman stretched on the little deck, his face up to heaven, his eyes closed: buried, if you will, in a long prayer." Notice that the romantic dream the reader is allowed is imaged very much as Bretton had been; the suggestion is of a calm, still, comfortably uneventful existence, perhaps even once again of a perennial Sunday. The "real" sea on which Lucy sails in these years is, on the contrary, tempest-tossed.

The action of these opening chapters of the book, like so much of the action that is to come, is a kind of extended metaphor. Through it Charlotte Brontë establishes the two main poles of the novel's movement. At once on the external level of Lucy's life, and, more important, on the internal level of her mind and consciousness, the major rhythm of *Villette* is that between calm and excitement, between quiet passivity and action, between engagement with life, despite all its shocks and desolations, and retreat from life. The text of the novel often offers and contrasts categories of experience of a more definite and more limited kind: Reason and Feeling preeminently, Reason and Imagination, Necessity and Hope, but all of these are subsumed within the larger rhythms I have described. As is the case in *Jane Eyre,* Charlotte's interpretive glosses often seem narrower than the experience of the novel warrants.

On the level of external action *Villette*'s major movements involve Lucy's search for some haven of calm where she will be sheltered from the suffering produced by the storms of experience. Driven by unexplained necessities, she comes to London on her way to the continent. At first she is fearful and confused. But the old inn in which she stays provides her with temporary security sufficient to give her a momentary sense of the pleasures of involvement in the busy life of the city streets. After the stresses and strains of the channel crossing, and the difficulties with which she has to contend on arrival, the Pensionnat of Mme. Beck again appears as a kind of retreat, a place of safety and security. (Later we are frequently reminded of the way in which the school is insulated from the busy life of the great city around it: "Quite near were wide streets brightly lit, teeming at this moment with life. . . . " Finally, the security of the Pensionnat will become that of a prison.) After Lucy's mental and physical breakdown, the house of the Bretton family into which she wakes is another temporary asylum where peace is briefly rediscovered. And finally there is the house provided by M. Paul, overlooking the Eden-like garden, where Lucy's school is to be set up, and where for one day M. Paul and she are together. Each of these resting places is achieved after a period of intense inner strain and torment.

This large rhythm, however, of periods of difficulty and danger followed by intervals of comparative calm and tranquillity, is only a mirror of the novel's more essential internal movement, similarly a question of rising and falling rhythms of inner passivity and acceptance on the one hand, emotional excitement and turmoil on the other. Even when Lucy's external life is at its most uneventful,

her inner life is never entirely quiescent. In her early days at the Pensionnat her impulse towards a quiet obscurity is for the moment satisfied, but even then she talks of her "two lives—the life of thought, and that of reality," and opposes "the strange necromantic joys of fancy" to "daily bread, hourly work, and a roof of shelter." The possibility of conflict between Lucy's two lives, with their hint of the old opposition between Angria and the more immediate calls of duty, is clear enough. Such a conflict does of course occur and reoccur, though a clash between "thought" and "reality" is only one of several possible definitions of the conflict's nature and source. Rarely indeed does Lucy's internal life attain to the calm tranquillity she encourages herself to seek.

After the introductory account of the Bretton world, *Villette* pauses again before undertaking its central narrative of Lucy's experience. The Miss Marchmont episode both reinforces the implications of the initial Bretton experience, and suggests a stance to be adopted in light of these. Polly, a mere child, suffers because of the intensity of her feelings. Miss Marchmont's experience of the life of passionate feeling and hope is more mature, but the outcome is the same: suffering. For Lucy there is again the note of warning. But Miss Marchmont offers Lucy a further lesson: the lesson of suffering accepted and endured. As Jane Eyre believes she should emulate Helen Burns, so Lucy Snowe tries always to learn Miss Marchmont's lesson. Miss Marchmont's is the stance towards experience that Lucy admires and which she sometimes believes herself to have achieved.

In both these opening episodes, then, Lucy finds a temporary retreat, a shelter from the challenges and risks of life, where she can indulge the "cold" side of her nature, the impulse to remain only the uninvolved observer of life. Both episodes contain suggestions about the nature of the world outside and the dangers that follow from engagement with it. The larger rhythm of the novel involves movements from and towards the calm tranquillity of the Bretton world and the passive stoicism of Miss Marchmont. What the reader recognises, as Lucy does not, is that in the first episode calmness, peace and tranquillity are polarized against sensibility, feeling, and imagination; and that stoical endurance in the second is sustained only by the memory of a happiness achieved, however fleetingly. The cost of that calm tranquillity which Lucy seeks is apparently the complete rejection of the feelings and imagination which are part of her being; hence the inner anguish that belies the external coldness of her nature.

In the opening episodes of *Villette* Lucy Snowe's role is only that of observer. What she observes hints at the nature of the conflict she is soon to experience in her own person. But to understand that conflict more fully it is necessary to move on to her personal experience which is the novel's primary subject. The major rhythm I have identified develops through Lucy's relationships first with Dr. John, then with M. Paul. In other words it is the passion of love which challenges most seriously the calm repose of Lucy's nature. Harriet Martineau objected to what she felt to be *Villette*'s preoccupation with the force of love in women's lives. But in the novel love is important, not as it were for its romantic self, but because it is the sharpest focus of feeling, excitement, and imagination. Such a definition gives love its significance, suggests its danger, and explains why it is inevitably Charlotte Brontë's prime subject.

Feeling, excitement, and imagination are all resisted by Lucy Snowe because, perhaps from her early experiences at Bretton and with Miss Marchmont, she believes she knows their dangers. Jane Eyre, we recall, struggled to check and subdue her feelings, usually in accordance with some moral or religious ideal. Lucy may not listen to the voices of feeling and hope, not so much because to do so is morally wrong, but because she believes that such voices direct her towards a painfully unrealizable world. With their promise of a life of excitement and fulfilment they are supremely appealing, but what they effect is only renewed awareness of a world permanently beyond reach: beyond reach, that is, of all except the favored few, such as Paulina, for whom life really is a romance. To combat these voices, Lucy calls on the power of reason. Reason tells her to abjure the world of the passional imagination; only thus may ultimate despair be avoided. Better surely to be a mere onlooker on life, colorless and obscure perhaps, but nonetheless preserving a calm, tranquil repose otherwise unattainable.

But Lucy's inner nature rebels against the conclusions of reason. And that rebellion is supported by Charlotte Brontë. In the first place, both Lucy and the reader are offered an example of the consequences for a human being of the denial of feeling. In the portrait of Madame Beck the dehumanizing effect of such a denial is clearly revealed. Lucy admires Madame Beck for her efficiency and her professional competence, but in the end she sees that Madame Beck is heartless. Her physiognomy is a reliable indicator of her personal qualities:

> . . . her forehead was high but narrow; it expressed capacity and some benevolence, but no expanse; nor did her peaceful but watchful eye ever know the fire which is kindled in the heart or the softness which flows thence.

Madame Beck's benevolence is of a purely rational kind. She is entirely devoid of feelings of sympathy: " . . . to attempt to touch her heart was the surest way to rouse her antipathy, and to make of her a secret foe. It proved to her that she had no heart to be touched. . . . " Madame Beck's behavior in the rest of the novel will amount to no more than an active confirmation of the characteristics ascribed to her here. Again, it is in the area of feeling that the inadequacy of Dr. John too is finally recognized. The cool equanimity that he normally possesses, the Bretton calm that he embodies, exists at the expense of at least the deepest experiences of human feeling. Recognizing this frees Lucy from his spell. On the occasion of their watching the performance of the actress Vashti Lucy comes to full understanding of the basic contrast between Dr. John and herself. Vashti's acting disturbs the deep foundations of Lucy's nature. Dr. John remains unmoved:

> Her agony did not pain him, her wild moan— worse than a shriek—did not much move him; her fury revolted him somewhat, but not to the

point of horror. Cool young Briton! The pale cliffs of his own England do not look down on the tides of the channel more calmly than he watched the Pythian inspiration of that night.

There is much that is right about Dr. John's infatuation with the empty-headed, unfeeling Ginevra Fanshawe.

In their coolness towards the world of feeling, Madame Beck and Dr. John are merely expressing what is fundamental to their natures. Lucy Snowe's nature is alien to theirs; hence the disastrous consequences of her attempts to equal their cool dispassionateness in her own life. Lucy's attempt to discipline and restrain the emotional side of her nature brings her at least once to total nervous and spiritual breakdown. Alone in the Pensionnat in the late part of summer, physically exhausted by the demands made on her by the cretin, a child incapable of normal human feelings, whom she is looking after, Lucy's external environment mirrors her internal condition. The impulse to hope, to imagine a life beyond that of drab duty, has been repressed and denied to the extent that Lucy is destroying her truest self. Hence the collapse that brings her in the end to the confessional. The account of this breakdown contains some of the most brilliant passages in the novel. They suggest most powerfully how the denied and thwarted imagination takes control in dream and trance sequences as soon as rational checks begin to give way:

> The solitude and the stillness of the long dormitory could not be borne any longer; the ghastly white beds were turning into spectres—the coronal of each became a death's head, huge and sunbleached—dead dreams of an elder world and mightier race lay frozen in their wide gaping eyeholes.

The nightmare quality of such a passage is powerful evidence of the degree of dislocation in Lucy's nervous state that unflinching self-dedication to the calls of duty and responsibility produces. The hot, arid Indian-summer days in which this episode in Lucy's experience occurs are interrupted by fierce equinoctial storms: a fitting image of the manner in which Lucy's attempt to accept an existence devoid of any kind of visionary hope or excitement is overwhelmed by an eruption of uncontrollable feelings from the repressed and thwarted side of her nature.

If these powerful sequences suggest Charlotte Brontë's unqualified recognition of the dangers that result from total rejection of the world of feeling and imagination, contrasting scenes suggest the dangers on the other side of the unchecked indulgence of feeling. Juxtaposing these scenes will serve once again to clarify the fundamental conflicts that are explored in the subject-matter and form of *Villette.* What Lucy Snowe understands as the dangers implicit in the unchecked indulgence of feeling and the imagination emerges after her performance in the play directed by M. Paul. M. Paul's reading of her skull is proved correct. When Lucy allows herself to get inside the role assigned to her she discovers that play she can, even as M. Paul had insisted. But in the cool light of day she rejects her triumph in terms that are highly significant:

> Yet the next day when I thought it over, I quite disapproved of these amateur perform-

ances. . . . A keen relish for dramatic expression had revealed itself as part of my nature; to cherish and exercise this newfound faculty might gift me with a world of delight, but it would not do for a mere looker-on at life; the strength and longing must be put by. . . .

Through Lucy's acting "a world of delight" is brought within her grasp. But that world is rejected as inappropriate to "a mere looker-on at life." There is a suggestion here of how closely related Charlotte Brontë saw the world of imaginative reality, as she understood it, and the actual world of social and moral responsibility. The imaginative world of acting is not to be easily set aside from the concerns of the actual. The imaginative world is a feeling world above all; it draws on and acts upon the passionate side of experience; and the feelings it indulges and releases—feelings of hope, expectancy, fulfilment—are as dangerously real as those produced by any other stimulus. Rejecting her acting, Lucy is struggling to master her own passionate nature, to choke off a mode of *self-expression* which if encouraged would be self-indulgent.

This reading of Lucy's rejection of her own acting is reinforced subsequently by her account of her response to the great actress Vashti. Lucy's account of Vashti's performance is so impassioned as to be almost incoherent. But the telling confusion is that between the role Vashti is playing and the actress herself. Is it to her performance or to the actress that Lucy responds with such burning intensity? The point is that Charlotte Brontë blurs any such distinction. It is the passion that Vashti both supremely embodies and superbly projects that concerns her. The passion that Lucy witnesses is so overwhelmingly real that it challenges the orthodoxies of conventional morality. Lucy is possessed by Vashti's passion, but not swept away. Her response is deep and full; but self-control survives. "Hate and Murder and Madness incarnate, (Vashti) stood," she tells us.

> It was a marvellous sight; a mighty revelation.
> It was a spectacle low, horrible, immoral (II:7).

The ambivalence in Charlotte Brontë's response to the world of the romantic imagination could not be more surely pointed. In Vashti's performance, as experienced by Lucy Snowe, art and morality are openly pitted against each other. For Lucy and for Charlotte Brontë it is a crucial moment of truth.

But the episode is not complete at this point. One uncomfortable truth is followed by another. The evening ends with powerful confirmation of the dangers that are the consequence of the unchecked indulgence of passionate feeling. The fiery passion of the stage is translated into the rumor of actual fire in the theatre. Immediately the audience becomes a struggling, jostling, mindless mob. It is only Dr. John's cool self-control that saves the day. The moral is clear and it is taken to heart by Lucy Snowe. Where Jane Eyre runs away from her feelings, Lucy tries to preserve self-control by stifling hers. The burying of Dr. John's letters is both literal and symbolic.

What these various episodes in Lucy's experience after her arrival in the Pensionnat of Madame Beck suggest is an enlargement and development of hints contained in the opening chapters of the novel. If the price of the calm repose of nature is the total denial of the experience of feeling, then the paying of the price produces a kind of death, a self-denial that in a normally sensible person leads to physical and spiritual collapse. Uninhibited indulgence of feeling, on the other hand, produces an equally destructive moral anarchy: the self becomes the prisoner of forces which both encourage the distortion of reality and threaten to deprive it of its proper freedom. Lucy Snowe's fate is to become aware in her own experience of both these dangers; to feel the threat of both within herself. For most of the novel she is struggling with one or the other of them. What she has to learn is that there is no salvation to be found either in repression and self-denial or in visionary, romantic yearnings. There is no answer to be found either in the ultimately self-destructive role of the mere onlooker on life or in Dr. John. Above all Lucy needs to come to terms with both sides of her nature. Hence the importance of M. Paul. With M. Paul she is finally able to be wholly herself, because his nature is like her own. "You are patient, and I am choleric," M. Paul says, "you are quiet and pale, and I am tanned and fiery; you are a strict Protestant, and I am a sort of lay Jesuit: but we are alike—there is affinity." M. Paul goes on to develop his sense of the likeness between them, and he is right to do so. The affinity is there, and it is the source of the mutual self-understanding which distinguishes their relationship from that between Lucy and Dr. John, M. de Bassohmpierre, Madame Beck and the rest, and which finally brings them together.

Lucy's love for M. Paul provides such resolution as *Villette* offers for the broadly moral and psychological conflicts it explores. But the fact that these conflicts are clarified by (for example) acting scenes reminds us again of the complex relationship that Charlotte Brontë recognized between the worlds of moral choice and the aesthetic imagination. The sense in which the imagination has become a moral issue in *Villette* is hinted at by Lucy's behavior over her role in M. Paul's play. She agrees to play the part, but she refuses to "dress up" for it. She will not disguise what she really is. This is in small Charlotte Brontë's mode of writing in *Villette.* The disguise of romance is abandoned in favor of a basic realism. Hence the retreat in *Villette* from the more Gothic elements of plot and character in *Jane Eyre.* The trappings of the world of romance persist in the later novel in the legend of the nun, and the use made of it by Ginevra and de Hamal. But the point is the sham/deceitful quality of such romantic stuff; it deceives but does not seriously challenge the rational world. (One may nonetheless isolate one of the novel's weaknesses here. Undeniably too much attention is paid to the nun, the mysterious *billet-doux,* the shadowy figures in the garden walk. The explanation is to be found in the use of the first person narrative. As James argued, the danger of such a narrative mode is its "fluency" in the longer piece. What we are interested in is not the mysteriously romantic events themselves, but Lucy's reaction to them. How will she cope with these extraordinary manifestations? But as narrator she has to tell us what the events are, their circumstances, and the rest. At such points Lucy's roles as narrator and protagonist conflict.)

The world of romance, then, as it appears in the external

action of *Villette* is a factitious one, appropriate to certain characters whose grasp of reality is limited, but something nonetheless to be seen through and rejected. The episodes involving the nun interestingly also involve aspects of Lucy's self-delusion. The nun appears in the attic where Lucy is reading one of Dr. John's letters; she appears again in the attic, where Lucy had been locked by M. Paul to learn her part in the play, when Lucy is about to leave with Dr. John to see Vashti at the theatre; the episode of the burial of the letters at the base of the tree where the nun is supposed to have been entombed is also associated with the appearance of the mysterious figure. And last of all, there is the confusion of the legendary nun with the dead Justine Marie—against whom, for no obvious reason, M. Paul warns Lucy—along with Lucy's mistake about the relationship between M. Paul and the living Justine Marie. All of these episodes involve either errors of judgement or unrealizable visionary hopes and dreams; and all are associated with moments of high romantic mystery and sensation. The linking of romance with delusion in some form is insisted on.

The same argument may be used in relation to the concluding section of the novel, which has often been attacked as inferior to the rest. In the account of the efforts made to keep M. Paul and Lucy apart there is clearly a large admixture of the Gothic in both character and event. But again one may recognize an association between a more Gothic vision of the nature of reality, and the falsity and deviousness of those who manipulate that reality. It is as if here, for Charlotte Brontë, the worlds of Roman Catholicism and Gothic romance become organically related as subject-matter and style. The aesthetic sleight-of-hand of the one becomes perhaps the moral jesuiticalness of the other.

Whatever the nature of their external action, the final chapters of *Villette* do nothing to undermine the realism of the portrait of Lucy Snowe. "Cloud" is the climax of the novel and in this chapter Lucy's inner conflicts are partially resolved. Driven by an overwhelming need to act rather than merely to be acted upon; a need to fight back against an imposed passivity; a need to assert her individuality and her freedom, Lucy finds herself escaping out of the prison of the sleeping school into the fast-flowing current of life in Villette on festival night. Responding to the promptings of her deepest nature, Lucy denies the rational self that is constantly advising that security and calm and the avoidance of active suffering are to be discovered in the passive role of the mere onlooker at life. The strictest self-control is yielding in the face of pressures whose source is passionate feeling and an awakened imagination. However far the reader may respect such a development, Charlotte Brontë's own feelings clearly remain ambivalent. Lucy's behavior is explained away as the consequence of a drug administered to her by her enemies. This it is that is responsible for her irrational, impulsive behavior. More important, however, is the fact that the drug is explicitly identified as a surrogate for the imagination. The drug, we learn, had produced the opposite of its intended effect:

> Instead of stupor, came excitement. I became alive to new thought—to reverie peculiar in colouring. A gathering call ran among the faculties,

> their bugles sang, their trumpets rang an untimely summons. Imagination was roused from her rest, and she came forth impetuous and venturous.

It was Imagination that lured Lucy to leave "the glimmering gloom, the narrow limits, the oppressive heat of the dormitory," and "follow her forth into dew, coolness, and glory." Imagination speaks here in such rhetorically suspect terms that one is tempted to believe that Charlotte intended an aesthetic reflexion of Lucy's drugged state. Certainly much of Lucy's account of her experiences that night beautifully suggests the twilight world between dream or nightmare and vision. Nevertheless, it is more probable that Lucy's excited condition is an accurate reflexion, as Charlotte Brontë sees it, of that produced by imagination's power. In other words the "drug" has a moral, rather than aesthetic, significance. It allows Charlotte to continue to suggest the moral uncertainty she felt about the status of the imagination. And the grounds of that uncertainty are further suggested by the errors of judgment, the overheated fancies that Lucy falls victim to in her "distempered state" (as Southey would have called it). Yet the release from the prison of the self that Lucy experiences remains for her fundamentally necessary and right. Only thus, through the imagination, whatever its perils, may she enter the world of feeling where the truth about herself is to be discovered.

In *Villette,* just as in *Jane Eyre,* Charlotte Brontë sets high value on individual independence and freedom. Both Jane Eyre and Lucy Snowe have a healthy sense of their own worth, and many of their trials arise from their need to assert and preserve their individuality. Even the necessity of rational self-control may be understood in these terms. Subjection to passionate feeling involves the temporary loss of individual identity. But what Lucy discovers in this closing section of the book is that freedom is not to be defined only as a negative preservation of individual independence, and is not to be achieved at the expense of feeling and the imagination.

Obedient to the forces that have sent her out into the festive life of Villette, Lucy is made to recognize her commitment to a love "furnace—tried by pain." The mistake over M. Paul's relationship with Justine Marie may strike the reader as a meretricious device to hold his interest. But it is Lucy who is deceived rather than the reader; and the self-deception is central to her understanding of her own position. The notion that M. Paul is to marry someone else is almost welcome to her. Such an outcome, she imagines, will put an end to the feelings that have meant "hourly torment," disturbing the calm repose of her nature. Once again, as it were, she will be Lucy Snowe. The truth, she believes, has set her free: "Truth stripped away Falsehood, and Flattery, and Expectancy, and here I stand—free." But the degree of self-delusion in this is immediately made obvious: "Nothing remained now but to take my freedom to my chamber, to carry it with me to my bed and see what I could make of it." For Lucy there is in fact to be no return to the kind of freedom that is obtained at the expense of feeling. The "drug" that has directed Lucy's behavior on the night of the fête may have distorted reality, but an awakened imagination has also made her recognize the truth. Lucy is now at last allowed the freedom to feel, intensely, urgently, and in the closing pages of the novel that freedom, with M. Paul, is fleetingly enjoyed. Fleetingly, that is, in the real world of duties accepted and of suffering endured; in the world of romance, perhaps, the end is a different one. In either case the value of that freedom remains. (pp. 143-56)

Andrew D. Hook, "Charlotte Brontë, the Imagination, and 'Villette'," in The Brontës: A Collection of Critical Essays, *edited by Ian Gregor, Prentice-Hall, Inc., 1970, pp. 137-56.*

Kate Millett   (essay date 1970)

[*In her* Sexual Politics (1970), *a highly controversial work of literary and cultural criticism, Millett argued for the inclusion of sexuality in political discourse, studied the background of women's struggle for cultural empowerment, and denounced the patriarchal ideology—rooted in the psychoanalytic writings of Sigmund Freud—that she found in the works of D. H. Lawrence, Henry Miller, and Norman Mailer. In the preface to* Sexual Politics, *Millett wrote: "Literary criticism is not restricted to a dutiful round of adulation, but is capable of seizing upon the larger insights which literature affords into the life it describes, or interprets, or even distorts." In the following excerpt from that work, Millett offers a reading of* Villette *as a subversive chronicle of a woman unwilling to accept her role in male-dominated society.*]

[Charlotte Brontë's **Villette** is a book too subversive to be popular.] In Lucy one may perceive what effects her life in a male-supremacist society has upon the psyche of a woman. She is bitter and she is honest; a neurotic revolutionary full of conflict, backsliding, anger, terrible self-doubt, and an unconquerable determination to win through. She is a pair of eyes watching society; weighing, ridiculing, judging. A piece of furniture whom no one notices, Lucy sees everything and reports, cynically, compassionately, truthfully, analytically. She is no one, because she lacks any trait that might render her visible: beauty, money, conformity. Only a superb mind imperfectly developed and a soul so omnivorously large it casts every other character into the shadows, she is the great exception, the rest only the great mediocre rule.

Lucy is a woman who has watched men and can tell you what they are as seen by the woman they fail to notice. Some are like John Graham Bretton, charming egoists. Their beauty, for Brontë is perhaps the first woman who ever admitted in print that women find men beautiful, amazes and hurts her. Bretton is two people: one is Graham the treasured and privileged man-child seen through the eyes of a slighted sister, whether the distant idolator be Lucy or Missy Home. Brontë keeps breaking people into two parts so we can see their divided and conflicting emotions; Missy is the worshipful sister, Lucy the envious one. Together they represent the situation of the girl in the family. Bretton is both the spoiled son Graham, and the successful doctor John, and in both roles Lucy envies, loves and hates him. Never does the situation permit her to love him in peace, nor him to take notice of her in any

but the most tepid and patronizing good humor: sterile, indifferent. His beauty and goodness make him lovable; his privilege and egotism make him hateful. The enormous deprivation of her existence causes Lucy to resemble a ghetto child peering up at a Harvard man—envy, admiration, resentment and dislike; yet with a tremendous urge to love—if it were possible to love one so removed, so diffident, so oppressive, so rich, disdainful and unjustly superior in place.

If the male is not the delightful and infuriating egoist whom maturity means learning to relinquish one's "crush" on, he is the male one encounters a bit later in life when one tries to make one's way. He is Paul Emanuel, the voice of piety, conventionality, male supremacy, callow chauvinism terrified of female "competition." John is unconquerable; he will never acknowledge any woman who is not beautiful or rich, his only qualifications; he loved Fanshawe's stupidity just as readily as Paulina Mary's virtue. Women are decorative objects to him. Paul is easier to cope with; in his sexual antagonism there is something more tractable. John Graham never saw Lucy; Paul sees her and hates her. Here it is possible to establish contact and, as the story is all a fantasy of success (a type of success utterly impossible to achieve in Brontë's period, and so necessarily fantastic) Paul is met and persuaded. To his sneer that she is ignorant and women are dolts, Lucy replies with phenomenal intellectual effort. Despite the impossible atmosphere he gives off as a pedagogue, the bullying, the captivity in overheated rooms, the endless spying, the bowdlerizing of her texts—she learns. It is his ridicule that forces her to achieve, pokes her into development, deprives her of the somnolence of ladyhood, its small ambitions, timidity, and self-doubt.

Lucy watches women—again from a double and even more complicated point of vantage. She studies Ginevra Fanshawe the flirt, an idiot beauty callously using men to acquire what she has been carefully taught to want: admiration, money, the petty power of dominating a puppy. Fanshawe is beautiful too, and Lucy, in every respect the product of her society as well as its enemy and rebel, has been schooled to love this beauty. It stirs her. The book is full of references to the desire such beauty arouses in her. To express it, Brontë invents the device of an afternoon of amateur theatrics. Lucy is dragged into them at the last moment to play Fanshawe's lover. It is another of Paul's bullying schemes (he locks her in an attic in the July heat to be sure she learns her lines) to coerce her into courage and achievement. Lucy succeeds miraculously, and she makes love to Fanshawe on stage in one of the most indecorous scenes one may come upon in the entire Victorian novel. (Brontë is too much an insurrectionary to acknowledge any convention beyond the literary and the most astonishing things occur continuously in her fiction.) Just as maturity and success lie in outgrowing an infatuation with Graham's masculine egotism, or Paul's bullying but productive chauvinism, they are also a matter of renouncing a masculine lust for Fanshawe. She is too dumb to love, too silly to want or to permit oneself to be wounded by. The dialogue between the two young women is brutal; Fanshawe parades her beauty with the double purpose of making Lucy capitulate before it, acknowledge herself an ugly woman and therefore inferior; or propose herself a suitor to it and therefore a captive through desire. For Ginevra knows critical Lucy would be the best catch of all, the biggest conquest. Lucy holds her own in these cruel sessions and won't be had either way. Ultimately, she transcends them and Fanshawe altogether, who fades into the mere butterfly she is and disappears from the book.

The other women Lucy watches are Madame Beck and Mrs. Bretton. Both are older women, one a mother, one a businesswoman and head of a school. They are two of the most efficient women one can meet anywhere in fiction. Lucy, who, like Charlotte Brontë, lacked a mother, regards older women as the embodiment of competence, and what she loves in them is their brilliant ability to manage. While Victorian masculine fantasy saw only tender, quivering incapacity in such women, Lucy perceives them as big, capable ships and herself only a little boat. But the big ships are afloat because they knew how to compromise; Lucy does not plan to. The big ships are convention. For all the playful banter of her relationship with her son, Mrs. Bretton stands for a stale and selfless maternity, bent on living vicariously through her adored boy's success. Pleasant matron that she is, she would sacrifice any daughter in the world for the comfort of his lordly breakfast, and Lucy knows it. Mrs. Bretton's conventional motherhood is only the warm perfection of chauvinist sentiment. Then there is Madame Beck, a tower of convention, the tireless functionary of European sexual inhibition, watching every move of the young women under her Jehovah-like and unsleeping surveillance; getting up at night to examine Lucy's underwear, reading her letters to sniff out traces of sex in them, watching for missives thrown from windows to her pupils. Both these women are still young and ripe for sexuality. Mrs. Bretton fulfills her own in flirtation with her son:

"Mamma, I'm in a dangerous way."

"As if that interested me," said Mrs. Bretton.

"Alas! the cruelty of my lot!" responded her son. "Never man had a more unsentimental mother than mine; she never seems to think that such a calamity can befall her as a daughter-in-law."

"If I don't, it is not for want of having that same calamity held over my head; you have threatened me with it for the last ten years. 'Mamma, I am going to be married soon!' was the cry before you were well out of jackets."

"But mother, one of these days it will be realized. All of a sudden, when you think you are most secure, I shall go forth like Jacob or Esau, or any other patriarch, and take me a wife, perhaps of these which are of the daughters of the land."

"At your peril, John Graham! that is all."

Beck is more sensually alive and would be delighted to take on John Graham, but of course she is not sufficiently young, beautiful, or socially prominent for his tastes. Real as her own sexuality is, she will gracefully acknowledge his rejection, and serenely carry on the business, while cheerfully stamping out the intrusion of the least hint of sex in any corner of her establishment. As the educator of young females, Madame Beck is a perpetual policewoman, a virtual forewoman of patriarchal society. No system of subjection could operate for two seconds without its collaborators, and Beck is a splendid example of the breed.

Finally, there is Paulina Mary, the golden one, the perfect woman, John Graham's pretty Polly, the apple of her daddy's eye. Lucy had no father to dote upon her, nor any John to court her, and she is painfully aware that Paulina is lucky. Yet there is one flaw in this female paragon—she is a child of eight—delightful when she appears as Missy Home at the beginning of the book; clever, affectionate, precocious—but nauseating when she reappears as a woman of nineteen and still a mental infant. Paulina is well-meaning and well loved. Even Lucy is fond of her from time to time, but she is also appalled that society's perfect woman must be a cute preadolescent. Having surveyed the lot, Lucy prefers to be like none of them. Looking over all the "role models" her world presents, the adoring mother, the efficient prison matron, the merciless flirt, the baby-goddess, Lucy, whose most genuine trial is that she has been born into a world where there are no adequate figures to imitate so that she is forced to grope her way alone, a pioneer without precedents, turns her back on the bunch of them. Better to go back to something solidly her own—deal with mathematics, Paul Emanuel, and the job.

Lucy has watched men look at women, has studied the image of woman in her culture. There is probably nothing so subversive in the book as that afternoon in the Brussels museum when she scrutinizes the two faces of woman whom the male has fashioned, one for his entertainment, one for her instruction: Rubens' Cleopatra and the Academician's four pictures of the virtuous female. Lucy's deliberately philistine account of Cleopatra is very entertaining:

> It represented a woman, considerably larger, I thought, than the life. I calculated that this lady, put into a scale of magnitude suitable for the reception of a commodity of bulk, would infallibly turn from fourteen to sixteen stones. She was indeed extremely well fed. Very much butchers' meat, to say nothing of bread, vegetables, and liquids, must she have consumed to attain that breadth and height, that wealth of muscle, that affluence of flesh. She lay half-reclined on a couch, why, it would be difficult to say; broad daylight blazed round her; she appeared in hearty health, strong enough to do the work of two plain cooks; she could not plead a weak spine; she ought to have been standing, or at least sitting bolt upright. She had no business to lounge away the noon on a sofa . . . Then, for the wretched untidiness surrounding her, there could be no excuse. Pots and pans, perhaps I ought to say vases and goblets, were rolled here and there on the foreground; a perfect rubbish of flowers was mixed amongst them, and an absurd and disorderly mass of certain upholstery smothered the couch, and cumbered the floor.

This "coarse and preposterous canvas," this "enormous

piece of claptrap," as Lucy nominates the masturbatory fantasy she perceives in it, is the male dream of an open and panting odalisque, the sheer carnality floating always in the back of his mind, and can be matched only by its obverse—the image of woman he would foist on the woman herself. Cleopatra is for masculine delectation only, and when Paul catches Lucy contemplating the painting he is deeply shocked: "How dare you, a young person, sit cooly down, with the self-possession of a garçon, and look at *that* picture?" A despot, as Lucy describes him so often, he is deeply offended, even affronted, that a young woman should see what he immediately settles down to gaze at. Paul forbids Lucy to look upon Cleopatra, and forces her to sit in a dull corner and study several mawkish daubs the conventional mind has designed for her:

> . . . a set of four, denominated in the catalogue, "La vie d'une femme." They were painted in a remarkable style, flat, dead, pale and formal. The first represented a "Jeune Fille," coming out of a church door, a missal in her hand, her dress very prim, her eyes cast down, her mouth pursed up—the image of a most villainous, little, precocious she-hypocrite. The second, a "Mariée" with a long white veil, kneeling at a pire-dieu in her chamber, holding her hands plastered together, finger to finger, and showing the whites of her eyes in the most exasperating manner. The third, a "Jeune Mère" hanging disconsolate over a clayey and puffy baby with a face like an unwholesome full moon. The fourth, a "Veuve," being a black woman, holding by the hand a black little girl [black because in mourning] and the twain studiously surveying an elegant French monument . . . All these four "Anges" were grim and grey as burglars, and cold and vapid as ghosts. What women to live with! insecure, ill-humored, bloodless, brainless nonentities! As bad in their way as the indolent gipsy giantess, the Cleopatra, in hers.

In this comic instance of sight taboo, the social schizophrenia within masculine culture, not only the hypocrisy of the double standard, but its purpose and intentions are exposed. It has converted one woman into sex symbol, flesh devoid of mentality or personality, "cunt"—this for itself to gaze upon. And unto woman herself is reserved the wearisome piety of academic icons with their frank propaganda of serviceable humility.

The disparity in the contradiction of images represented by the two pictures explains the techniques of *Villette* better than any other moment in the novel. It is a division in the culture which Brontë is retorting to by splitting her people in half and dividing Lucy's own responses into a fluctuating negative and positive. The other dichotomy is between her newness, her revolutionary spirit, and the residue of the old ways which infects her soul. This inner conflict is complemented by an exterior one between her ambitions and desires and the near impossibility of their fulfillment. There are obstacles everywhere, social and financial. The hard realities of the sexual caste system frustrate her as well as its mentality. Curiously enough, the obstacles drive her on. Lucy represents not only Brontë's, but what must have been, and probably still remains, the am-

bition of every conscious young woman in the world. She wants to be free; she is mad to escape, to learn, to work, to go places. She envies every man his occupation, John his medicine, Paul his scholarship, just as she envied them their education. Both had the finest obtainable and it was given to them as a preparation for life. Lucy was given nothing so substantial:

> . . . picture me for the next eight years, as a bark slumbering through halcyon weather, in a harbour as still as glass—the steersman stretched on the little deck, his face up to heaven, his eyes closed . . . A great many women and girls are supposed to pass their lives something in that fashion; why not I with the rest? . . . However, it cannot be concealed that in that case, I must somehow have fallen overboard, or there must have been a wreck at last.

She is traumatically cast out of the middle class quite unprepared to live, for all the world had expected her to exist parasitically. She now lacks the prerequisites: a face, respectable social connections, and parents to place her. She is a serf without a proprietor who must become a wage slave, namely a governess or teacher. The only way out, and it's a desperate track, is to learn the world and books. *Villette* chronicles her formal and informal education in the acquisition of her own competence through both.

But what work can Lucy do; what occupations are open to her? Paid companion, infant nurse, governess, schoolteacher. As they are arranged, each is but another name for servant. Each involves starvation wages which only a lifetime of saving could ever convert to ransom. There is another humiliation in the fact of servant status which rested with particular severity on middle-class women who in taking employment are falling a step below the class of their birth. (While a paid companion, Lucy encounters a schoolmate now the mistress of a household—Lucy had been visiting another servant in the kitchen.) Furthermore, these occupations involve "living-in" and a twenty-four-hour surveillance tantamount to imprisonment. The only circumstances under which Lucy is permitted an occupation are such that they make financial independence and personal fulfillment impossible. It is not very hard to understand her envy at the gratification and status which Paul and John are given automatically in their professions. One might well ask, as Lucy does unceasingly, is it worth it then, under these conditions, to work? Is it not easier to keep falling into daydreams about prince charmings who will elevate one to royalty, or so they claim? At any rate, they could provide easy security and a social position cheaply attained. They will provide, if nothing else, the sexual gratification which women occupied like Lucy are utterly forbidden to enjoy.

Villette reads, at times, like another debate between the opposed mentalities of Ruskin and Mill. Lucy is forever alternating between hankering after the sugared hopes of chivalric rescue, and the strenuous realism of Mill's analysis. Brontë demonstrates thereby that she knows what she is about. In her circumstances, Lucy would not be creditable if she were not continuously about to surrender to convention; if she were not by turns silly as well as sensible. So there are many moments when she wishes she were as pretty as Fanshawe, as rich as Polly, occasions when she would happily forgo life itself at a sign that Graham recognizes she was alive. Born to a situation where she is subject to life-and-death judgments based on artificial standards of beauty, Lucy is subject to a compulsive mirror obsession, whereby each time she looks in the glass she denies her existence—she does not appear in the mirror. One of the most interesting cases of inferiority feelings in literature, Lucy despises her exterior self, and can build an inner being only through self-hatred. Yet living in a culture which takes masochism to be a normal phenomenon in females, and even conditions them to enjoy it, Lucy faces and conquers the attractions Paul's sadism might have held.

Charlotte Brontë has her public censor as well as her private one to deal with. This accounts for the deviousness of her fictional devices, her continual flirtation with the bogs of sentimentality which period feeling mandates she sink in though she be damned if she will. Every Victorian novel is expected to end in a happy marriage; those written by women are required to. Brontë pretends to compromise; convention is appeased by the pasteboard wedding of Paulina Mary and Prince John; cheated in Lucy's escape.

Escape is all over the book; *Villette* reads like one long meditation on a prison break. Lucy will not marry Paul even after the tyrant has softened. He has been her jailer all through the novel, but the sly and crafty captive in Lucy is bent on evading him anyway. She plays tame, learns all he has to teach her of the secrets of the establishment—its mathematics and Latin and self-confidence. She plays pupil to a man who hates and fears intelligent women and boasts of having caused the only woman teacher whose learning ever challenged his own to lose her job. Lucy endures the baiting about the "natural inferiority of females" with which Paul tortures her all through the lesson, and understands that only the outer surface of his bigotry melts when she proves a good student and thereby flatters his pedagogic vanity. Yet in his simplicity he has been hoodwinked into giving her the keys. The moment they are in her hand, and she has beguiled him into lending her money, renting her a school of her own, and facilitated her daring in slipping from the claws of Madame Beck—she's gone. The keeper turned kind must be eluded anyway; Paul turned lover is drowned.

Lucy is free. Free is alone; given a choice between "love" in its most agreeable contemporary manifestation, and freedom, Lucy chose to retain the individualist humanity she had shored up, even at the expense of sexuality. The sentimental reader is also free to call Lucy "warped," but Charlotte Brontë is hard-minded enough to know that there was no man in Lucy's society with whom she could have lived and still been free. On those occasions when Brontë did marry off her heroines, the happy end is so fraudulent, the marriages so hollow, they read like satire, or cynical tracts against love itself. There was, in Lucy's position, just as in the Brontës' own, no other solution available.

As there is no remedy to sexual politics in marriage, Lucy very logically doesn't marry. But it is also impossible for

Brontë's father, Reverend Patrick Brontë, insisted that Villette *end happily.*

a Victorian novel to recommend a woman not marry. So Paul suffers a quiet sea burial. Had Brontë's heroine "adjusted" herself to society, compromised, and gone under, we should never have heard from her. Had Brontë herself not grown up in a house of half-mad sisters with a domestic tyrant for father, no "prospects," as marital security was referred to, and with only the confines of governessing and celibacy staring at her from the future, her chief release the group fantasy of "Angria," that collective dream these strange siblings played all their lives, composing stories about a never-never land where women could rule, exercise power, govern the state, declare night and day, death and life—then we would never have heard from Charlotte either. Had that been the case, we might never have known what a resurrected soul wished to tell upon emerging from several millennia of subordination. Literary criticism of the Brontës has been a long game of masculine prejudice wherein the player either proves they can't write and are hopeless primitives, whereupon the critic sets himself up like a schoolmaster to edit their stuff and point out where they went wrong, or converts them into case histories from the wilds, occasionally prefacing his moves with a few pseudo-sympathetic remarks about the windy house on the moors, or old maidhood, following with an attack on every truth the novels contain, waged by anxious pedants who fear Charlotte might "castrate" them or Emily "unman" them with her passion. There is bitterness and anger in *Villette*—and rightly so. One finds a good deal of it in Richard Wright's *Black Boy,* too. To label it neurotic is to mistake symptom for cause in the hope of protecting oneself from what could be upsetting.

What should surprise us is not Lucy's wry annoyance, but her affection and compassion—even her wit. *Villette* is one of the wittier novels in English and one of the rare witty books in an age which specialized in sentimental comedy. What is most satisfying of all is the astonishing degree of consciousness one finds in the work, the justice of its analysis, the fairness of its observations, the generous degree of self-criticism. Although occasionally flawed with mawkish nonsense (there is a creditable amount of Victorian syrup in *Villette*), it is nevertheless one of the most interesting books of the period and, as an expression of revolutionary sensibility, a work of some importance. (pp. 140-47)

> *Kate Millett, "The Sexual Revolution, First Phase: 1830-1930," in her* Sexual Politics, *Doubleday & Company, Inc., 1970, pp. 61-156.*

Q. D. Leavis   (essay date 1972)

[*Leavis was an English critic, essayist, and editor. Her professional alliance with her husband, F. R. Leavis, resulted in several literary collaborations, including the successful quarterly periodical* Scrutiny, *in which she published many critical essays. Leavis stressed that "literary criticism is not a mystic rapture but a process of the intelligence," suggesting that a responsible critic should remain objective and eschew impressionistic responses to a work. Most importantly, she asserted, a work should not be judged on the basis of its moral value. In the following excerpt, Leavis speculates about the autobiographical sources of various elements of* Villette *and discusses the novel's structure as a function of Brontë's need for self-expression.*]

Charlotte had further developed the interests, peculiar to herself, that [appeared] . . . in *The Professor,* in the course of writing *Jane Eyre* and *Shirley,* the former being a great advance in technical achievement, finding a form absolutely fitted to embody the themes. And though *Shirley* seems to us less of an achievement, she herself wrote: 'I took great pains with *Shirley*.' Thus the steady sequence of novelwriting (*The Professor* written presumably in 1845, *Jane Eyre* started in 1846, *Shirley* written in 1848-9, showing an almost continuous practice of the medium) meant that she knew her medium and her own capacities thoroughly by the time she started *Villette* (probably in 1851). She was however delayed constantly in the writing by ill health, and her vitality was sapped by her private troubles as well, but these were resolved happily by her father's at last consenting to her marrying his curate Arthur Nicholls in 1854, the year following the publication of the novel which had taken a couple of years to write. It is interesting to note what were the impelling elements that amalgamated at this date. In 1850 she had visited Scotland (of which Mr Home in *Villette* is a native) and wrote afterwards that it is 'the Scottish national character, that grand character which gives the land its true charm, its true greatness'—though no doubt she had been assisted in this insight by her enthusiastic frequentation of

the novels of Scott from childhood onwards. In 1851, while spending a month in London she saw Rachel 'the great French actress' perform; the impression made on Charlotte who was as fascinated in spite of herself by the theatre as by the Roman Catholic religious rites, is introduced into *Villette* in the chapter 'Vashti': 'It was a spectacle low, horrible, immoral.' The next day she went to see another performance that affected her in the same way: Cardinal Wiseman holding a confirmation—'impiously theatrical', she reported. This would recall her painful experiences of the Catholic world of Brussels, where she had written home to Emily of 'their idolatrous "messe"' and had become estranged from her employer Mme Héger. That lady (who in due course was indignantly recognized as a caricature by her family in Mme Beck) was, as Mrs Gaskell tells us, 'not merely a Roman Catholic, she was *dévote* . . . and her conscience was in the hands of her religious guides' and she was incensed therefore by Charlotte's uncompromising witnessing to the Protestant truths. The consciousness that M. Héger, the inspiration for M. Paul Emanuel, was, though not himself a bigot, also inalienably Catholic and under the dominion of his wife, had left her in social and moral isolation that produced the psychological condition she calls 'Hypochondria' (first described in *The Professor*). This condition leads Lucy Snowe to trying the resources of the confessional as well as to the painful dependence on the letters of Dr Bretton. Charlotte herself had depended for friendship and affection on a correspondence with M. Héger after her return home from Brussels but broke off the correspondence on finding that it was a cause of jealousy or resentment to his wife. The painfulness sustained throughout *Villette* must derive from such bitter memories. In the same visit to London Charlotte had attended Thackeray's lecture where incidents attributed in *Villette* to the lecture in Brussels had taken place. She had then made the acquaintance of her publisher and of his mother, Mrs Smith, and letters at this time to that lady show that she was in many respects the original of Mrs Bretton, Lucy's godmother, who stands in such a wholesome and protective relation to Lucy without any real understanding of what Lucy is at bottom. It must be borne in mind also that *Villette* was written slowly and at intervals broken by bouts of ill health, some of them mental anguish due to isolation and despair, in which, quite evidently, the most painful experiences of her past life thrust themselves on her (though she herself wrote characteristically of her use of real life in her fictions: 'We only suffer reality to *suggest,* never to *dictate*', and 'I hold that a work of fiction ought to be a work of creation'). Mrs Gaskell saw her recourse to writing novels now, in her loneliness, as self-therapy: 'The interests of the persons in her novels supplied the lack of interest in her life; and Memory and Imagination found their appropriate work, and ceased to prey upon her vitals.' She missed while writing *Villette* the discussions about their work that the sisters had always held at nights—fault-finding as well as sympathizing—until only the one was left and the faithful servant told Mrs Gaskell on her first visit to the parsonage: 'now my heart aches to hear Miss Brontë walking, walking, on alone', every night. Charlotte's most intelligent friend, the 'Rose Yorke' of *Shirley,* told Mrs Gaskell that Charlotte, the ambitious and energizing member of the family, had organized the publication first of the sisters' volume of verse and then of a novel each, because she thought of literary fame as 'a passport to the society of clever people' but that 'When at last she got it, she lamented that it was of no use. Her solitary life had disqualified her for society. Her fame, when it came, seemed to make no difference to her. She was just as solitary, and her life as deficient in interest as before.' Yet it was at this dreariest of all times in Charlotte's life, left alone with her father and thinking her preferred suitor would never be allowed to marry her, that a visitor gained the impression which she subsequently described thus in a letter to Mrs Gaskell:

> Miss Brontë put me so in mind of her own Jane Eyre. She looked smaller than ever and moved about the house so quietly and noiselessly just like a little bird, barring that all birds are joyous, and that joy can never have entered that house since it was first built. Now there is something touching in the sight of that little creature entombed in such a place, and moving about herself like a spirit, especially when you think that the slight still frame encloses a force of strong fiery life, which nothing has been able to freeze or extinguish.

The Professor had ended in success for both tutor and governess—a happy and financially prosperous marriage based on mutual respect and the united purpose of a working professional partnership culminating in a leisured retirement together with an interesting son to rear (Charlotte did not then look forward to a life passed in teaching schoolgirls or tending a demanding father). *Villette* replaces this pleasant daydream by a tragic withdrawal of all happiness, for not only is the death by shipwreck of Lucy's betrothed envisaged (veiled, to please her father, but uncompromisingly forecast) but there is also, it seems to me, the recognition that no marriage could take place and work between the Protestant English Lucy Snowe and the Jesuit-trained and -dominated foreigner.

The radical difference between *The Professor* and *Villette* is a technical one—not merely technical of course—the change of narrator from a man to a woman. This everyone sees as a gain. It may be asked why Charlotte originally used a male persona at all. There are two reasons: the obvious one, which led Mary Ann Evans to write under the name 'George Eliot' and the Brontë girls to choose to add to their pen name of Bell three Christian names (Acton, Ellis, and Currer) which suggested masculine authors. The other reason is more likely to have been secondary to this, as giving extra protection against being slighted or accused of impropriety as a woman: writing from the point of view of a William Crimsworth gave the authoress more freedom to treat the relations between the sexes with the frankness and fire of unconventional arguments, it also gave more imaginative scope, a proof of genius demanded by Coleridge in his statement of the principle that a creative artist should initially be seen to choose a situation as far as possible from his own to write about. In *Villette,* as in *Jane Eyre,* Charlotte succumbed to the temptations of the more directly personal autobiography, though she claimed that Jane Eyre was not herself 'any further than being plain and small', and she took pains to make Lucy

Snowe even less attractive than Jane, concentrating on those aspects of herself which she evidently wished to examine. In this matter we have the evidence of a remarkable letter to her publisher [dated 6 November 1852; see excerpt above] in which she answers his criticism that Lucy will 'be thought morbid and weak' by replying:

> I consider she *is* both morbid and weak at times . . . and anybody living her life would necessarily become morbid. It was no impetus of healthy feeling which urged her to the confessional, for instance; it was the semi-delirium of solitary grief and sickness. If, however, the book does not express all this, there must be a great fault somewhere.

All the episodes on which the charge of morbidity and what is here classed as 'weakness' could be made were in the identical or similar forms experienced by the author herself, which she recognizes in the last sentence I have quoted as the reason for writing the novel. But Charlotte was not weak except physically since she never gave in to her misfortunes save on the occasion of once succumbing to the use of the confessional, no sooner done than repented.

And yet the novel is not a document for the psychiatrist but a deliberate work of art. There is self-criticism and a holding aloof of her grief and sickness, and this has produced the schematic form that *Villette,* like *Jane Eyre* and *Wuthering Heights,* has taken. All these novels are equally the products of thought and planning, and *Villette* bears an interesting technical relation to both *The Professor* and *Jane Eyre,* for each novel shows successively a development of idea and a greater richness and profundity of treating it.

Here we must make an exception of the episodes devoted to the Nun, which may be seen as an unfortunate inheritance from Mrs Radcliffe and the Gothic novels of horror that the Brontë children had read with evident *empressement.* But why, we naturally ask, should it have survived in Charlotte's last novel, having been suppressed after the early manuscript fictions of her youthful scribblings? There is nothing of the sort in *The Professor* or *Shirley* and, except for the concealed mad woman in *Jane Eyre* and her inexplicable appearances at night, there is no source of terror. It seems to me due to her unhappy experience in failing to get *The Professor* published. Though she had tried six publishers before giving it up and starting *Jane Eyre,* it was rejected by all, and she was never able to get it published in her lifetime in spite of her attempts to persuade Smith, Elder & Co., who had done so well out of her, to add it to their list of her successful novels. The reasons they had all given for rejecting this first novel, evidently peculiarly dear to its author, were, she told the critic G. H. Lewes, that though 'original and faithful to nature such a work would not sell' because 'it was deficient in "startling interest" and "thrilling excitement"', so that it would never suit the circulating libraries'. Hence, we may conclude, the importation, to satisfy publisher and circulating libraries, of 'startling interest' and 'thrilling excitement' into her later novels—the mystery of the mad wife secreted in the heart of Thornfield with her 'goblin laugh, distinct, formal, mirthless', the more legitimate excitement provided by the Luddite riots in *Shirley,* and the detective-story element in *Villette* in both the deception about Dr John's identity (which readers rightly resent as unfair) and the bogus supernatural theme of the Nun: *Villette,* a rewriting and rethinking of *The Professor,* was *not* to be refused publication if Charlotte could help it. (Correspondence with her publisher about the manuscript as she sent it to him in instalments shows her insecurity and her doubts as to its success.) Her use of the pseudo-supernatural to play on the reader's nerves follows Mrs Radcliffe and her school of Gothic fiction in the determination to have it both ways: there is the thrill of the terror of the supernatural; but, eventually, a rational explanation of what had apparently been miraculous satisfies the eighteenth century's rationalism and the Protestant's common sense. Charlotte Brontë was no true Romantic, for Romantic writers really believed in the supernatural (or tried to pretend that they did) and did not explain it away when they had made use of it. Byron in the last episode of *Don Juan* ends with the very similar anti-Romantic revelation that the supernatural friar haunting Juan is actually an amorous lady using the friar's garb as cover, and it seems probable to me that Charlotte, who at eighteen recommended Byron's poetry to a friend as 'first-rate' (along with Shakespeare, Milton, and Wordsworth) had borrowed the idea and merely reversed the sexes to produce de Hamal disguised as a nun to further his pursuit of Ginevra.

A genuine source of excitement in *Villette,* not present in *The Professor,* is the battle of wits and wills and temperaments between Lucy and Paul Emanuel. Complementary in his irritability and egotism to Lucy's self-restraint and humble desire to learn, and an intellectual she can respect, he also has the necessary warmth to thaw her coldness and give her the love she craves as well as psychic support. The relation of Lucy to her 'master', if curious, is psychologically convincing and founded in a truth of experience recognized by Charlotte in these passages from a letter home from Brussels, during her first spell there when she had Emily as companion, where I see the very germ of *Villette.*

> I was 26 years old a week or two since; and at this ripe time of life I am a schoolgirl, and, on the whole, very happy in that capacity. It felt very strange at first to submit to authority instead of exercising it—to obey orders instead of giving them; but I like that state of things . . . It is natural to me to submit, and very unnatural to command.

> The difference in country and religion makes a broad line of demarcation between us and all the rest. We are completely isolated in the midst of numbers. Yet I think I am never unhappy; my present life is so delightful, so congenial to my own nature, compared to that of a governess.

In *Villette* the opposed cultures sketched in *The Professor* are located in two symbolic centres which, with their inhabitants, are played off against each other as moral-sociological concepts. There is Bretton in England, and there is Villette across the sea, and then Bretton establishes itself in Villette-land but is not assimilated, any more than Lucy can be united with M. Paul Emanuel. *Bretton*

is of course Britain, and our heroine Lucy Snowe is godchild of the Brettons of Bretton, a thorough Englishwoman. The other people there are called *Home*—Mr Home is half Lowland Scotch, Charlotte admiring the Lowland Scotch character and having a theory that the combination of English and Scotch produces one of the best types; and his kinsman, red-haired Graham Bretton, is described as a Celtic type. The symbolic intention is rather too obvious perhaps—the whole constituting Great Britain. Britain is exquisitely typified by the minster town, peaceful, clean (the cleanliness is associated with the quiet and the order and the sense of a perpetual Sunday atmosphere in the place to suggest a spiritual quality), and Lucy's visits to Bretton remind her of a beatific episode in *Pilgrim's Progress.* Britain and Home—the British Protestant culture: the intention is plain. (Practically all the names in *Villette* are symbolic, and Bunyan must have been closer to her here than to any other novelist, often as he stands in the background of English novelists.)

A real and remarkable subtlety, however, is to be found in the use of little Polly in the early chapters. She is, we see, only a variation on the child Jane Eyre and the child Victor Crimsworth and the first three chapters are given up to an exposition of her equally exquisite sensibility for suffering and her need of affection, but in a totally different relation. Lucy Snowe is in the limited scenes at Bretton as a mere spectator, presented as a neutral and even adversely critical one, for example when the child's father leaves her at Mrs Bretton's:

> During an ensuing space of some minutes, I perceived she endured agony. She went through, in that brief interval of her infant life, emotions such as some never feel; it was in her constitution; she would have more of such instants if she lived. Nobody spoke. Mrs Bretton, being a mother, shed a tear or two. Graham, who was writing, lifted up his eyes and gazed at her. I, Lucy Snowe, was calm.

That is, Lucy characteristically conceals her real feelings, which are much more sympathetic than those of the others, in an affectation, almost—to avoid revealing that she is one of the same nature as Polly. It is not until the child's little history is finished and she is about to disappear in this character from the book, when Lucy, taking the 'elfish' creature in her arms, gives her true reaction, reflecting:

> How will she get through this world, or battle with this life? How will she bear the shocks and repulses, the humiliations and desolations, which books, and my own reason, tell me are prepared for all flesh?

that we realize that this *is* Lucy Snowe and that the questions relate to herself. Polly, she says, 'departed the next day; trembling like a leaf when she took leave, but exercising self-command'. The child represents Lucy's sensibility externalized, suffering for its delicacy and proud refinement as ordinary souls do not. Her history is to be Lucy's history, not least in the relation to Graham Bretton we have witnessed. Lucy Snowe is what the world sees, to all appearance calm, cold as her name implies, self-disciplined; little Polly is an externalization of her inner self (always characterized as 'elfin' or 'faery-like' throughout the book, suggesting something supernatural and spiritual in essence).

The forecast in the first three chapters of Lucy's relation to Graham Bretton, the forecast enacted by Polly, is followed immediately by the history of Miss Marchmont, the intention being to prepare the reader emotionally for a tragic outcome. This prefigures Lucy's later history which ends with her lover drowned at sea on his way home to marry her. Miss Marchmont when young was robbed by violent death of *her* bridegroom and lives on 'stern and morose', treasuring in her memory the year when there was 'a living spring—a warm glad summer—strength of hope under the ice-bound waters'. The formal, stilted language of this episode is intended to mark it, like the play within *Hamlet,* by its stylization as an epitome framed off from the text. Lucy, whose fate has thus been sketched for us (she lets drop that *she,* Lucy, is now an old white-haired woman telling *her* story) crosses the sea on a ship called the *Vivid*—other ships called the *Consort,* the *Phoenix,* and so on, are not hers, she notes—reminding us of Jane Eyre's desire for 'other and more vivid kinds of goodness' than a woman's conventional allowance (a child's or a good woman's—Adèle's and Mrs Fairfax's). Painfully Lucy arrives at Villette. Here instead of an English home is a foreign girls' school, instead of forthright Mrs Bretton is Mme Beck ('her name was Modeste; it ought to have been Ignacia'). English probity is contrasted with Catholic intrigue, the English system of trust with the French system of *'surveillance',* English delicacy of feeling with Latin coarseness and 'realism', Lucy's external coldness but inner intense sensibility with Mme Beck's appearance of *'bonté'* that covers only callous self-interest; and the moral obliquity or absence of any sense of conscience among the pupils is registered by the contrast with the self-respect of the English girls (only partially undermined in the case of the frivolous Ginevra Fanshawe, who marries a foreign count). This is all rendered with the most convincing concreteness. The unfeeling and unprincipled upbringing by Mme Beck of her daughters contrasts significantly with Polly's by her loving Scotch father. Only in M. Paul does Lucy find that fineness of nature, warmth of feelings, and disinterestedness can exist in the atmosphere of Villette. But neither Lucy nor M. Paul can conceivably be converted by the other, and the closing shipwreck is, as Charlotte rightly felt, inevitable. The comparison with Julien Sorel's sojourn in the seminary (in *Le rouge et le noir*) is interesting because whereas Stendhal's morally superior hero conquers his environment by strategy and cunning, by assimilating himself to it in externals, the Englishwoman manifests her moral superiority by inflexibility and undisguised aversion. In consequence, she suffers such an extremity of isolation that, like Jane Eyre, she is driven beyond her own control and has a break in consciousness. This happens on her leaving the church where she has gone to obey an irresistible impulse to make use of the confessional: this is the point where she touches bottom, when she is driven to behave *as if she were a Catholic* and belonged to the community of Villette. At this, the tension of the Protestant–Catholic conflict breaks and the dark waters close over her, she drops lifeless in the street. No doubt it was from *Villette* that Hawthorne took the idea of making

Hilda, the New England girl in *The Marble Faun* (1859), enter the confessional at a crisis, he having been struck by the dramatic situation it presents. But in Hawthorne the incident is not related to the rest of the novel and is preposterous; indeed it is morally offensive. We can see how, in contrast, the incident is led up to in *Villette* and is an integral part of the structure, the turning point in both the plot and the moral scheme.

Lucy recovers herself in a new place which turns out, as in *Jane Eyre,* to be the home of her kindred; she is thus provided with affection, social status, and a congenial environment (Bretton transported abroad). The pattern is similar in *Jane Eyre,* where Jane in extremity of isolation is rescued by her kindred the Rivers household, but this is not a mere repetition of that, and the treatment of it all is even more astonishingly original than in the earlier book. The night-wandering ending in a psycho-physical collapse is in both books a symbolic account of the experience of acute isolation followed by the opposite experience, of being taken into a family, of *belonging.* Lucy says: 'I seemed to pitch headlong down an abyss', and thereupon begins the next chapter ('Auld Lang Syne') with an account of the sensations she had when recovering. There is a terrifying momentary time lag before the memory functions again. 'The divorced mates, Spirit and Substance, were hard to reunite: they greeted each other, not in an embrace, but a racking sort of struggle.' This experience Charlotte Brontë daringly extends to give it symbolic dimensions. 'The life-machine presently resumed its wonted and regular working', Lucy says, but she cannot recall her surroundings; though familiar she cannot place them except as belonging to another time and country, a different phase of existence from her recent life in Villette. Even when she recollects that the contents of the blue room were those of her godmother's drawing-room at Bretton, she knows the room itself is not that but one unknown to her. Dropping off again she finds on regaining consciousness that she has left lamp-lit night and blueness for 'leaden gloom' and sea-green surroundings, where she thrillingly recognized 'Bretton! Bretton! and ten years shone reflected in that mirror.'

The author means to show Lucy recognizing a past phase of her life without being able to connect it with the present, owing to the split in her life between Bretton and Villette. 'Where my soul went during that swoon I cannot tell', the chapter begins, and what we are shown is the soul rising from the 'abyss' out of the blue and up from the depths of the sea (the blue chamber and the sea-green). Is this fanciful? No, for in the next chapter we find they had this significance for the writer:

> My calm little room seemed somehow like a cave in the sea. There was no colour about it, except that white and pale green, suggestive of foam and deep water: the blanched cornice was adorned with shell-shaped ornaments, and there were white mouldings like dolphins in the ceiling angles. Even that one touch of colour visible in the red satin pincushion bore affinity to coral; even that dark, shining glass might have mirrored a mermaid. When I closed my eyes, I heard a gale, subsiding at last, bearing upon the house-front like a settling swell upon a rock-

base. I heard it drawn and withdrawn far, far off, like a tide retiring from a shore of the upper world—a world so high above that the rush of its largest waves, the dash of its fiercest breakers, could sound down in this submarine home, only like murmurs and a lullaby.

The movement of the prose endorses the meaning. There is plainly no danger in attributing to the details of these novels the maximum meaning, the greatest significance, the widest-ranging interpretation that we may be able to find for them, for we can be sure the author strove to put it there herself. We must not overlook either the simile just before this passage which likens her godmother to a 'stately ship crossing safe on smooth seas' and herself to a lifeboat manned by 'the half-drowned lifeboat man', 'only putting to sea when cloud encounters water, when danger and death divide between them the rule of the great deep'. Half-drowned, she has risen through the sea that separates Villette from Bretton, to safety and a fresh start in a regained Bretton which sustains her against Villette. The recognition scene is completed by the reappearance of Paulina, now a woman. She also has suddenly acquired status, riches, a title, and a new name in the foreign land. She and Lucy rediscover each other in a magical scene of recognition in the sea-green chamber, where she says to Lucy who fails to recognize her as little Polly, though knowing her as Countess de Bassompierre: 'No, not Miss de Bassompierre for *you.* Go back to Bretton. Remember Mr Home.' Again she shares Lucy's life with the peculiar sympathy of another self, for she is a parallel self—what Lucy might have been in favourable circumstances—and she acts out the destiny that Lucy had formerly desired for *her*self, becoming Graham Bretton's wife. It is when Lucy has seen that Paulina and Graham are drawn to each other by their complementary natures, as in the opening of the novel, that she makes the decision to stand alone, burying his letters that had sustained her in her isolation. This is yet another break in her life, but it represents a healthy movement towards independence, as she recognizes when sealing up the letters:

> The impulse under which I acted, the mood controlling me, were similar to the impulse and mood which had induced me to visit the confessional . . . I was not only going to hide a treasure—I meant also to bury a grief . . . This done, I rested . . . I felt, not happy, far otherwise, but strong with reinforced strength.

Therefore when, in the second remarkable night scene, she wanders through Villette *en fête* under the influence of Mme Beck's narcotic, she remains equally aloof from both the Home-Bretton party and the Beck-Emanuel clan as she encounters each in turn. When recognized by Graham, who wishes her to join them, she insists on being 'let alone'.

The passages I have quoted above substantiate my . . . contention that the structure we find here is different from that of a rigidly controlled novel like *The Magic Mountain, Jude the Obscure,* or *The Custom of the Country* (which I specify because they are recognized as novels which *have* structure). It is not, like theirs, a structure just sufficiently covered by its materials, like a kite, and like a

kite tethered by a line; it is like a living bird winging away free but on a flight with an object. One explanation of this live quality, I think, is that Charlotte needed to write these novels: they are a form of self-expression, not confessions (like Constant's *Adolphe* or Tolstoy's *The Kreutzer Sonata*), but communications. The frequent reference to the reader is oppressive to us, but it was the sense of a reader there to impart them to that made her write down and evaluate those highly-charged experiences, for it was only by arranging them so that they convey a meaning for someone else that she could be eased. Yet, it would be quite unjust to suggest that she was (as Lord David Cecil for instance, alleges in his standard work *Early Victorian Novelists*) 'extremely simple' and 'naïve'. What she did for the novel she did consciously, as is proved by her criticism of Jane Austen. She wished to write, unlike Miss Austen, as 'a complete woman', and part of that undertaking was to draw on the submerged levels of being to convey her sense of the nature and quality of living. No novelist before would have described a character in the terms she uses for Diana Rivers in ***Jane Eyre:*** 'In her there was an affluence of life and certainty of flow, such as excited my wonder, while it baffled my comprehension'; or for Lucy Snowe: 'I still felt life at life's sources.' (pp. 205-17)

> *Q. D. Leavis, " 'Villette'," in her* Collected Essays: The Englishness of the English Novel, *Vol. I, edited by G. Singh, Cambridge University Press, 1983, pp. 195-227.*

Janice Carlisle   (essay date 1979)

[*In the following excerpt, Carlisle analyzes the complexity of the first-person narrative in* Villette, *discussing Lucy's evasive treatment of the past as a reflection of her suppressed emotional life.*]

Recounting one of the more famous anecdotes of the fabled life at Haworth parsonage, Patrick Brontë once described the result of his desire to know what his very young children were thinking: "happening to have a mask in the house, I told them all to stand and speak boldly from under the cover of that mask." The father suspected that the everyday behavior of his children was itself a mask, an assumed pose of innocence that veiled "more than [he] had yet discovered." By means of his ruse he hoped to counter that deception; the mask would conceal the face and identity of the speaker in order to reveal the child's heart. The episode is one of those telling revelations of both character and the forces that mold character. Even at the age of eight, Charlotte Brontë was being encouraged to adopt subversive modes of self-expression. The form of this little drama would become the form of her art. Like Thackeray, who fled the responsibilities of speaking *in propria persona* by creating narrators such as Barry Lyndon or Arthur Pendennis, Brontë was most comfortable when presenting narratives mediated through a consciousness other than her own; from the earliest extant juvenilia to the fragment of the novel begun just before her death, she spoke with most freedom when she spoke through the voices of characters like Captain Tree or Charles Wellesley Townshend, Jane Eyre or Mrs. Chalfont. This mode was never more central to Brontë's art than in the case of

Villette. Lucy Snowe is the mask under cover of which Brontë conceals her identity in order to reveal the unappealing reality of her emotional life and its central figures, M. Heger and George Smith. The mask, however, performs this function in the service of art. The novel is a mirror in which reality is transformed to grant the emotional and aesthetic satisfactions that life invariably withholds.

Villette, the result of this process, is indeed a private document, but its privacy is a function of Lucy Snowe's life and character, not its author's. Brontë was able to distance herself from her own experience and even from facets of her own personality so that we do not need the facts of her life to explain or justify the novel. Yet *Villette* is genuinely puzzling, and it presents mysteries that we might be tempted to unlock with the key of biography. Its first reader, George Smith, responded to the manuscript with a pained silence so prolonged that it almost induced Brontë to journey to London to discover what had gone amiss. Even she seemed at least partially unaware of the implications of her novel. Like Lucy naïvely suggesting that her cold exterior represents her true identity, Brontë commented soon after finishing *Villette,* "Unless I am mistaken the emotion of the book will be found to be kept throughout in tolerable subjection." She was, of course, mistaken, and one might say of Charlotte and *Villette* what Charlotte said of Emily and *Wuthering Heights,* "Having formed these beings, she did not know what she had done." Charlotte Brontë firmly believed that writers are mastered by a force that they themselves do not comprehend—"something that at times strangely wills and works for itself"—but even the powers of unconscious creative agency do not explain the questions the novel raises. What are we to make of its disjointed chronology,

Anne, Emily, and Charlotte Brontë as painted by their brother Branwell, about 1835.

its shifts of tone and subject, its patent evasions, and the inconclusiveness of its ending? Does the novel reveal the view of a woman who accepts suffering as the dispensation of a just Providence? Or does it, in Matthew Arnold's words [in a letter dated 14 April 1853], display the author's "hunger, rebellion, and rage"? On a first reading, the novel almost always seems as "preternatural in its power" as George Eliot found it [in a letter dated 11 February 1853], but most readers—and here I speak for myself and my students—wonder if its power is not the result of emotions profoundly confused and confusing. Yet if we begin to look more closely at Lucy Snowe, at the shape and form of Brontë's mask, what has seemed perplexing or contradictory about her story reveals a clarity and persuasive emotional logic that shine through even the most apparently trivial or irrelevant detail.

The qualities that Lucy displays as the narrator of her own life and the qualities of *Villette* as the mirror of her experience are most easily defined if we set the novel in the context of its contemporary tradition, the art of autobiography at the Victorian midcentury. As Leigh Hunt noted in 1850, autobiography had "abounded of late years in literary quarters," and the trend only continued to increase in the early years of the 1850's. The popularity of *Jane Eyre* (1847) had been an important impetus to the widespread adoption of the form. Because of the generous gifts of books from her publishers and a growing circle of literary friends, Charlotte Brontë was well aware of this development. During the fall of 1849, when *Shirley* was being published, she began reading Dickens' *David Copperfield,* the first in a number of autobiographical works that she read before starting *Villette.* If "autobiographical" is defined formally in terms of first-person narration, then this group of works includes memoirs and poetry as well as fiction: the "Recollections" that preface Southey's *Life and Correspondence,* Hunt's *Autobiography,* and Tennyson's *In Memoriam.* The most significant work, however, was the posthumous 1850 edition of Wordsworth's *Prelude.* In all the autobiographical works that Charlotte Brontë read in 1849 and 1850, the central issues of memory and the past are treated in a highly self-conscious manner. To each of these writers, memory is the source and proof of personal identity: as Southey comments, "at two years old . . . my recollection begins; prior identity I have none" ("Recollections"). The effect of this widespread emphasis on memory seems clear. Though Jane Eyre had been called upon to recount her past experience, only in *Villette* and one of the sketches that preceded it does Brontë treat memory as a problematic function. *Henry Esmond,* a novel that Brontë read in manuscript as she was writing *Villette,* testifies to the predominance of the same concerns: for the first time in Thackeray's career, memory itself becomes the subject of analysis and description.

Autobiography is, almost by definition, a form that strives to accommodate fact and desire, circumstances as they actually occurred and the longing that they—or oneself—had been somehow different. The complexity of memory is beautifully imaged in Wordsworth's well-known comparison of the man who looks through the "surface of the past" to a man looking over the side of a boat on a still lake: he

... often is perplexed and cannot part
The shadow from the substance, rocks and sky,
Mountains and clouds, reflected in the depth
Of that clear flood, from things which there
    abide
In their true dwelling; now is crossed by gleam
Of his own image, by a sun-beam now,
And wavering motions sent he knows not
    whence. . . .

The past self is the product of a number of refracted images: the uneven mirror of the lake reflects the sky, the sun, and the face of the watcher as it communicates the ever-moving objects on its bottom: shadow and substance merge indistinguishably. Most potent are the shadows cast by the longing to perceive an image of self that is acceptable if not flattering. Biographical research has shown us the extent to which such feelings can shape the "facts" recorded in autobiographical documents. Wordsworth omits the story of Annette Vallon from *The Prelude,* perhaps because she had little relevance to the account of his poetic discipline, more probably because his own part in the affair involved unattractive qualities that he did not care to reveal. In his *Confessions* Rousseau similarly distorts the chronology of his sojourn at Les Charmettes so that he does not have to acknowledge the quality of Mme. de Warens' less than exclusive affection for him. Not constrained even as much as Wordsworth or Rousseau by the need to be faithful to actual events, Brontë uses the freedom of her fictional autobiography to increase the complexity of interpenetrating and refracted images of self. Why she would need to do so seems clear. For neither Brontë nor Lucy Snowe can the facts or circumstances of experience offer any satisfaction. Family is gone; suitors have disappeared. M. Paul is dead; Graham Bretton, married to another woman, is dead to Lucy. Memory can only reveal a past of promise and hope turned to present deprivation; it is primarily a record of losses and humiliations. David Copperfield or Jane Eyre can see every untoward event in their lives as a step in the direction of the happy resolution of past difficulties—Agnes and Rochester wait at the end of their narrative journeys. No such consolation is available to Lucy. Her dilemma is like that of *In Memoriam:* events can yield fulfillment only through a change in the perspective of the individual who has suffered through them. Lucy must find the little satisfaction that her life affords through the pattern which she imposes on it, through the way in which she chooses to relate events: memory must mold experience into a form that is acceptable, a form that will "suffice," if not actually console. Lucy must depend on essentially subversive ways of appeasing memory.

Commenting on other people and their petty vanities, Lucy notes "wherever an accumulation of small defences is found . . . there, be sure, it is needed." *Villette* is a carapace of defenses against the almost intolerable pain of memory, and the first of the ways in which Lucy tries to assuage that pain is the simplest: she ignores one of the most prominent themes of midcentury autobiography by flatly refusing to acknowledge the cost of retrospection. Even in a treatment of the past as unremittingly cheerful as Leigh Hunt's, the writer still looks back on his narrative and notes, "I can never forget the pain of mind which

some of the passages cost me." Likewise, Southey claims with calm satisfaction, "I have lived in the sunshine, and am still looking forward with hope," while he speaks of the "courage" he has had to find "to live again in remembrance with the dead, so much as I must needs do in retracing the course of my life." The pain of loss is the predominant tone in much of David Copperfield's narrative, and the valiant, but futile efforts of Mr. Dick illustrate the frustrations faced by any man who tries to write "a Memorial about his own history." But Lucy does not deal with the problem so directly. Indeed she never lets us know that for her recollection is something less than an occasion for tranquillity. In the context of her character, such evasions make sense. She has been trained by untoward circumstances to hide her feelings, to pretend that she is the "unobtrusive article of furniture." that the other characters take her to be. Throughout her earlier experience in Bretton and at Mme. Beck's, she has learned the benefit of "telling tales," of presenting elliptical accounts of events that do not involve any embarrassing revelations of her feelings. In one rather comically self-conscious instance, she tells Ginevra that her callous mockery of Graham and his mother has caused him acute suffering—she has told a tale, a lie, to satisfy Ginevra's expectations. Lucy often treats the reader and his conventional demands for a gratifying story as cavalierly as she has treated Ginevra. She buries her feelings in her "heretic narrative." as surely as she has buried her affections in the jar she entombs beneath the pear-tree in Mme. Beck's garden. She tells us that one must struggle "with the natural character, the strong native bent of the heart," that one must follow the dictates of Reason rather than Feeling and present to the world a surface that is "regulated," quiet, and "equable." To see beyond the supposedly imperturbable, opaque surface of Lucy's story is the reader's most challenging responsibility. Only by examining a crucial event from the narrator's earlier experience can we begin to understand the pain she inevitably feels whenever she thinks of her past.

At the opening of Volume II, Brontë presents one of the most complete of Victorian speculations on the dangers and terrors of memory, but her analysis is as remarkable for its indirection as for its power. Instead of letting the older Lucy tell us what it means to revive thoughts of the past, Brontë subjects the younger Lucy to a literal return of the "scenes and days" of her "girlhood." The effect is something like watching Alice fall down the rabbithole of imagination: mental phenomena are rendered as physical objects and sequences of narrative. Brontë sets this scene in "Auld Lang Syne" at a moment of crisis. Lucy has been left to spend the long vacation alone at Mme. Beck's *pensionnat.* After fainting in a street beyond the church where she has attended confession, she wakes to experience an involuntary and unexpected rebirth into a strangely familiar world. "With pain, with reluctance, with a moan and a long shiver," Lucy finds herself in an environment that seems ghostlike. At one of those oddly resonant moments so frequent in *Villette,* Lucy faces a mirror and sees the skull-like image of a dead self: "In this mirror . . . I looked spectral; my eyes larger and more hollow, my hair darker than was natural, by contrast with my thin and ashen face." As she begins to recognize the objects in the drawing room as the furniture from her godmother's house in Bretton, Lucy becomes increasingly skeptical about her own identity or sanity. She then falls asleep—only to wake in another room that intensifies her earlier sense of uncanny recognition. Again, Lucy looks into a mirror; instead of seeing a ghostly image of herself, she sees the past: "Bretton! Bretton! and ten years ago shone reflected in that mirror. And why did Bretton and my fourteenth year haunt me thus? Why, if they came at all, did they not return complete?" To return to the past, as Lucy literally does here, is to journey into a world that is spectral because it is dead, a world that calls into question the stability and substantiality of one's identity.

There is, of course, a logical explanation for Lucy's hallucinatory vision of "auld lang syne." After recognizing a portrait of Graham Bretton, Lucy soon discovers his mother sitting by her bedside. Although Lucy chooses not to reveal her identity, she learns that the past has been revived in the present simply because the Brettons have moved themselves and their belongings from England to Labassecour. As she becomes accustomed to her reinstatement in the world of her childhood, she describes even its comforts in a way that again suggests the emotional cost of memory. She rests in her bedroom and thinks of her "calm little room" as a "cave in the sea":

> There was no colour about it, except that white and pale green, suggestive of foam and deep water; the blanched cornice was adorned with shell-shaped ornaments, and there were white mouldings like dolphins in the ceiling-angles. Even that one touch of colour visible in the red satin pincushion bore affinity to coral; even that dark, shining glass might have mirrored a mermaid. When I closed my eyes, I heard a gale, subsiding at last, bearing upon the house-front like a setting swell upon a rock-base. I heard it drawn and withdrawn far, far off, like a tide retiring from a shore of the upper world—a world so high above that the rush of its largest waves, the dash of its fiercest breakers could sound down in this submarine home, only like murmurs and a lullaby.

La Terrasse literally offers Lucy a refuge in the past. The scene evokes some of the most eloquent language in *Villette,* yet its lyrical qualities are themselves warnings against the seductive and potentially dangerous powers of memory. Like other Victorian descriptions of the past, this passage is an image of a withdrawal that is also a regression. In the womblike "submarine home" of memory, one is protected from the storms of adult experience; there the sound of conflict is magically transformed into a lullaby. The context of the passage offers further warning that the peace of this withdrawal is deceptive and its comfort merely temporary. Like every other retreat Lucy finds, it must be abandoned; like every moment of calm, it will be disturbed. Only four chapters later, Lucy suffers a "Reaction" when she returns to Mme. Beck's school: the responsibilities of maturity must inevitably replace the joys and security of childhood. Lucy now must live by "imperious rules, prohibiting under deadly penalties all weak retrospect of happiness past; commanding a patient journeying through the wilderness of the present."

From these events the twenty-three-year-old character learns an impressive lesson that the older narrator is not likely to overlook. To relive the sorrows of the past is to revive their pain; to relive its joys is to relinquish them once more. Though Lucy's retreat to La Terrasse, to the cave in the sea, is a time of peace and fulfillment, it renders more unbearable the present solitude and struggle which she must endure. Like Vashti, Lucy remembers the heaven she has left, and "Heaven's light" can only serve to disclose the "forlorn remoteness" of her "exile." By making a narrative return to the scenes of her past, the older Lucy is forcing herself to do what Graham unwittingly does to her when he brings to La Terrasse the sick English schoolteacher he does not recognize. In the face of such difficulties, simple reticence is no adequate defense. Without giving the reader any direct indication of the principles that underlie her treatment of the past, the narrator responds to the events or characters she recalls in ways that vary according to the emotional challenges they entail. Like the young woman responding to the unfolding revelations of her stay at La Terrasse, the older woman allows her attitudes toward the past to develop according to a coherent "plot" roughly equivalent to the volume divisions of the novel: her visit to Bretton when she was fourteen and her first term at Mme. Beck's *pensionnat* in Volume I; her renewed acquaintance with the Brettons and the Homes in the second volume; and the relationship with M. Paul that dominates the action of the third volume. But the narrator never acknowledges that such a development is taking place. The reader must discover for himself how and why these psychological processes are at work. Again the practice of Brontë's contemporaries helps define Lucy's more unconventional modes of dealing with the past.

Dickens, Hunt, Southey, Wordsworth and Tennyson all agree on the central problem that memory presents: the difficulty of defining one's temporal perspective on the past. Wordsworth is, of course, the subtlest commentator on this question. As he explains, the man who tells his own story may feel that the difference between his past and present selves creates in him "two consciousnesses," separate identities with no relation to each other. Conversely, these two selves may interpenetrate. Speaking of his undergraduate days, Wordsworth admits: "Of these and other kindred notices / I cannot say what portion is in truth / The naked recollection of that time, / And what may rather have been called to life / By after-meditation." The narrator may present his "naked recollection"—his initial impressions of an event—or the product of his "after-meditation": his first impressions may be altered or effaced by his knowledge of later events or his more mature understanding of himself. Although they may not be as dismayed by their autobiographical tasks as Mr. Dick, all these writers openly admit that they are often baffled by the relation between their past and present selves. Like Wordsworth, they conscientiously warn us when, in Hunt's words, they "bring [their] night-thoughts into the morning of life." Southey, for instance, speaks of an acquaintance: "I look back upon his inoffensive and monotonous course of life with a compassion which I was then not capable of feeling." The Prologue to *In Memoriam* notifies the reader that the present-tense lyrics that follow are actually records of the first impressions of a past experience of grief. Dickens' careful handling of tenses is an even more remarkable indication of the care with which an author may balance the presentation of the narrator's first impressions against his later understanding of them. The use of the historical present is, of course, frequent in *David Copperfield,* especially in the first half of the novel as David tries to recapture the feelings of childhood. David's evolving identity is defined by present-tense chapters such as "I Observe" and his various "Retrospects." Yet the use of the tense can also express the strength of the older narrator's feelings about his past experience: the warehouse where David works as a child contains "things, not of many years ago, in my mind, but of the present instant." Dickens is exceedingly careful to distinguish between the historical present of the revivified past and the present tense appropriate to his narrative activity. David adds qualifications such as "according to my present way of thinking" whenever his "later understanding comes . . . to [his] aid." At one point, he even employs the two uses of the tense in one sentence so that he can distinguish between them: "I am a sensible fellow [at seventeen years], I believe—I believe, on looking back, I mean—." Here irony emphasizes the demarcation between past and present; the narrator's "I believe" becomes a telling comment on the sense with which the seventeen-year-old credits himself.

Such self-conscious treatments of memory and its perplexing effects are characteristic of the autobiographical works Charlotte Brontë read as she approached the writing of *Villette.* By comparison Lucy Snowe's attitude toward her retrospective activity seems almost naïve. Again she simply avoids the issue. Her reticence about her narrative role suggests that, for her, memory involves neither pain nor complicated temporal perspectives. Indeed her most straightforward comment on the question—the one too often accepted as definitive—implies that *Villette* is entirely the product of mature "after-meditation": "(for I speak of a time gone by: my hair which till a late period withstood the frosts of time, lies now, at last white, under a white cap, like snow beneath snow)." Lucy, now an old woman, tells the story of her younger self. The passage is reminiscent of Southey's comments on his old age or David's reference to the twenty years that separate his present self from the events he recounts. We are asked to believe that Lucy brings to the story of her youth all the serenity and calm resignation implicit in the image of her whitened hair. As we have learned from "Auld Lang Syne," however, memory has not always been a capacity that Lucy has been able to exercise with such painless ease. In another passage describing the attitudes of her younger self, Lucy has noted, "Oh, my childhood! I had feelings: passive as I lived, little as I spoke, cold as I looked, when I thought of past days, I *could* feel." The older narrator differs in no essential way from the young woman who makes this statement. A look at the first three chapters of *Villette* reveals the complex distortions of temporal perspective that her feelings create.

As conventional autobiography, these chapters are woefully inadequate. As an indication of the essential qualities of Lucy's relation to her past, they display an admirable degree of emotional logic. Reticence, of course, predomi-

nates. Neither the narrator's past nor present self is the ostensible subject here. Lucy refuses to tell us about her own childhood; rather she depicts her adolescent acquaintance with the child Paulina Home. We are asked to assume that Lucy offers us her first impressions of this relationship. Her apparently detached, yet ultimately hostile attitude toward this child creates the main difficulty. In Lucy's view of her, Paulina is scarcely human. She arrives in Bretton a "shawled bundle"; even when she emerges, Lucy repeatedly calls her "it" or the "creature" or a "mere doll." She continually views Paulina's love for her father or Graham as "absurd" or grotesquely dehumanizing. At one point Lucy even suggests that Paulina, the "little Odalisque," is faintly immoral. We might be tempted to attribute these shrewish comments to Lucy's adolescent jealousy. There is reason enough for that response. Before Paulina arrives, Lucy reigns supreme in Mrs. Bretton's affections. Paulina causes a "change" in this situation that is all the more disturbing because it is so "unexpected." This quaint child takes Lucy's place, and Lucy is forced to watch as Mrs. Bretton lavishes her attention on Paulina. Lucy finds the reunion between Paulina and her father "oppressing" simply because she is excluded from that or any other scene of parental fondness. Yet there are at work here forces—covert emotions, confused perceptions—that simply cannot be explained as the first impressions of even the most jealous of fourteen-year-old girls.

Though the narrator betrays no emotional involvement in the Bretton scenes she recalls, we need to know why she would begin her own story at that point in her experience. One answer is obvious: like the vignettes of the child and nature in *The Prelude,* like David Copperfield's precocious fascination with the subject of marriage, Paulina's stay in Bretton has a central thematic role in *Villette.* It illustrates what Lucy knows to be the basic structure of human relationships: emotional bonds are forged by the pressure of a woman's great need, and they are inevitably disrupted by "fate" or a man's fickle indifference. More importantly, Lucy's depiction of Paulina defines a central quality of her own memory: the emotional resonance of a particular scene often has little relation to Lucy's "naked recollection," and the narrator's temporal perspective on an event usually becomes apparent only after she has moved on to recount later incidents in her life. Without giving the reader any warning, Lucy allows her "later understanding" to efface her first impressions of Paulina. Only after we have read well into the second volume of *Villette* do we realize that Lucy's memory of the Bretton scenes elicits an extremely defensive response because they prophesy the most disturbing crisis in her later experience.

The events of Volume II recapitulate those in the first three chapters and explain why Lucy should find those earlier events significant. The incidents that occur when Lucy is fourteen are exactly reenacted when she is twenty-three. After the distressing isolation of the long vacation—comparable to the "unsettled sadness" of her kinfolk's home when she is fourteen—Lucy again finds herself with her godmother, "happier, easier, more at home" than she has been for years. Bretton and the past have been revived for her. She is again pampered by Mrs. Bretton and treated to sight-seeing and entertainments by John. Again Paulina usurps Lucy's place. When Graham first meets the Homes at the theatre, he tells them that the lady with him, Lucy, is "neither hindrance nor incumbrance." She is certainly no incumbrance on his affections. She is completely forgotten for seven weeks after the renewal of the relationship between the Brettons and the Homes. Even the seemingly insignificant details of the second volume have their precursors in the first three chapters. When Lucy finally returns to her "own little sea-green room" at La Terrasse, she finds that Paulina has installed herself there and that she is herself the "intruder," just as she has earlier gone up to her bedroom at Bretton and found, without warning, that a crib and a chest have been added for another child's use. Paulina's sewing, her lisping speech, her servile and tender doting on the men, all repeat her earlier behavior. Lucy even uses the same allusion to describe the two episodes in her life. Her visits in Bretton "resembled the sojourn of Christian and Hopeful beside a certain pleasant stream." Later, Graham's attention is "a goodly river on whose banks I had sojourned, of whose waves a few reviving drops had trickled to my lips." In both cases the comfort is taken away: the river "bend[s] to another course," Paulina. Lucy's treatment of the earlier Bretton scenes must bear all the weight of a mature woman's jealousy, yet she cannot admit to herself—much less to her reader—that she has ever experienced such feelings.

To reticence, then, Lucy adds a second defense against her memories of the past: even the indirect revelation of both the narrator and the character's emotional involvement may be transferred from the scene which elicited it to another, less painful scene. Because the events recorded in the second volume of *Villette* are ultimately more significant than the events of Lucy's adolescence, she displaces her feelings about Paulina's second entry into her life onto the story of her first intrusion into the Bretton world of security and affection. The scene at Bretton, for all its pretence of calm objectivity, is a scene recollected so much in the light of later events that the initial emotions are ignored while the narrator tries to avoid depicting her own present response to her memory of the scene. The result of this process is a curious sort of freedom. By attributing to her adolescent experience all her harsh attitudes toward Paulina, Lucy can recount her rival's later role in the second volume as if it had no relation to her own hopes and desires. She can ignore the cruelty of Graham's indifference. The emotional energy appropriate to the later event has already been expended. The reader's response to this complex interweaving of temporal perspectives must be less immediately productive. The reader can begin to understand the considerations that have shaped Lucy's account of an event only long after she has finished relating that part of her story. *Villette* would seem to be a novel that must be read backwards or, at very least, reread if one is to judge the narrator's perspective accurately.

Lucy's unacknowledged love for Graham Bretton is, of course, the reason for her evasive treatment of the past in Volume II. Like Paulina, Lucy is naturally reticent about affection that is not reciprocated. In a characteristically deceptive parenthetical statement, she denies entertaining any "warmer feelings" for Graham. Even years later when her hair has turned to gray, Lucy abides by the convention that a woman should not speak of love until she has been spoken to. Beyond such social prohibitions there is a more important reason for Lucy's silence. The memory of this unrequited love, the mere thought of which carries with it the certain knowledge of unfulfilled desires and wasted emotions, is so painful that it cannot be confronted openly. Like Paulina's letters to Graham, however, Lucy's narrative does "glow" with the "unconfessed confession" of her love. Indeed, Thackeray, confusing Lucy with Charlotte Brontë, felt moved to make a condescendingly amused comment on the author's "naïve confession of being in love with 2 men at the same time." Only as the novel reaches its conclusion, do we discover the full extent of the narrator's involvement with these concealed past emotions and, therefore, the justice of Thackeray's comment.

Four chapters before the end of *Villette,* when Lucy is describing her hallucinatory responses to the characters gathered at the fête in the park, she refers in an uncharacteristic fashion to events that occur after the close of her story. Here, for the first and only time in the novel, she confesses to the reader her past love for Graham Bretton and, more importantly, her present undiminished capacity to love him:

> I believe in that goodly mansion, his heart, he kept one little place under the skylights where Lucy might have entertainment, if she chose to call. It was not so handsome as the chambers where he lodged his male friends . . . still less did it resemble the pavilion where his marriage feast was splendidly spread; yet, gradually, by long and equal kindness, he proved to me that he kept one little closet, over the door of which was written "Lucy's Room." I kept a room for him, too—a place of which I never took the measure, either by rule or compass: I think it was like the tent of Peri-Banou. All my life I carried it folded in the hollow of my hand—yet, released from that hold and constriction, I know not but its innate capacity for expanse might have magnified it into a tabernacle for a host.

As Lucy has said of her younger self, "I *could* feel." This confession completely invalidates her earlier claim to the resigned objectivity of old age. At any time, presumably even as she tells her story, Graham could find in her heart a place splendid enough for a god. Coming as late as it does, offset by its placement among opium-induced visions, this avowal merely highlights the disconcerting complexity of the temporal perspectives in *Villette.*

This confession gives us the clue we need if we are to understand the narrator's earlier attitudes toward Graham and his place in her past. Because her feelings are so often at stake, she can never present her "naked recollections" of these events. The excessive emotions that typify her responses to Graham can be explained only by the later feelings she never mentions. Although her first meeting with Dr. John is too brief to allow her to realize that he is Graham Bretton, she reacts to this stranger who leads her through Villette with all the exaggerated trust that a Victorian wife might place in the husband who will lead her through life: "as to distrusting him, or his advice, or his address, I should almost as soon have thought of distrusting the Bible. There was goodness in his countenance, and honour in his bright eyes. . . . I believe I would have followed [his] frank tread, through continual night, to the world's end." The tone here is clearly inappropriate. Lucy's response seems proof of almost hysterical desperation or a naïve adoration of "bright eyes." Many chapters later we learn that her extravagant claims of faith in this stranger can be attributed to her later recognition of him as the man she would marry if she could. Memory has clearly responded to the pressures exerted on it by the knowledge of later events. The reader, however, is asked to accept this passage as the rendering of a first impression; there are no clues to the perspective from which the event is actually viewed. Such evasions continue. The most obvious was noticed by E. M. Forster [in his *Aspects of the Novel*, 1927]. Lucy violates the one essential convention of autobiographical form—if the reader does not demand to share the narrator's sense of later events, he does have the right to know what the character realizes at the time of any given event. For six chapters before she finds herself at La Terrasse, Lucy refuses to tell us that she knows that Dr. John and Graham Bretton are one and the same character. (pp. 262-75)

[Finding] fugitive modes of self-expression is a central convention of nineteenth-century autobiography. The writer whose work is a mirror of his experience naturally emphasizes those events or characters within it which serve as miniature reflections of self. The pretence of distance between the writer and his reflection is, however, absolutely essential to the success of this kind of self-analysis. Wordsworth, for instance, inserted in *The Prelude* a description of himself that he had written earlier, but he found he had to conceal it as a meditation on the dead Winander boy if he were to acknowledge that a facet of himself had likewise perished. On another occasion he refers to the story of Vaudracour and Julia because Vaudracour is a repressed version of the self who fell in love with Annette Vallon. *In Memoriam* is the record of similar processes. Tennyson continuously seeks out analogues for his feelings—he is variously defined as the widow, the linnet, the expectant or disappointed lover—and he explains this proliferation of analogues by noting that the love he feels "sees himself in all he sees." In one passage he recalls a dream in which he has seen Hallam's troubled face. He wakes and realizes, "It is the trouble of my youth / That foolish sleep transfers to thee [Hallam]." The art of autobiography, like Tennyson's dream, rests on such projections of self. Patrick Brontë's mask, seemingly the bright idea of a concerned parent, is a device that has a natural role in autobiography. By exploring self as if it were another identity, the autobiographer can confront its hidden facets with honesty and often profoundly acute scrutiny. Lucy's use of this device is unusual only because it invariably achieves for her an otherwise unattainable emotional gratification.

Brontë defines even more clearly the tradition behind *Villette* when Lucy says of Paulina, "I wondered to find my thoughts hers: there are certain things in which we so rarely meet with our double that it seems a miracle when that chance befals." Lucy uses precisely the right word here. Paulina is her double, but that fact is a function of her own

perception, not the result of the workings of Providence or fortune. Unlike Lucy, Brontë would not be blind to the psychological implications of that term. In *The Spell*, one of the more coherent works of the juvenilia, she had followed the model of Hogg's *Confessions of a Justified Sinner* (1824) when she created for the Duke of Zamorna a twin brother, an "alter-ego" and "repetition" to explain his "unfathomable, incomprehensible nature." Lucy, a character considerably more advanced in complexity than even Zamorna, deserves and indeed requires a *doppelgänger*. Paulina, Ginevra, and even Vashti are extensions of a technique that Brontë would have remembered from her early reading of Romantic fiction and from her own adolescent Angrian works. Yet the psychological process involved in the creation of doubles is as much akin to the conventions of autobiography as it is characteristic of the Gothic or Romantic imagination expressed in *The Devil's Elixir* or Hogg's *Confessions*. Otto Rank defined the link between doubles and narcissism as the desire to perceive a version of self that triumphs over mortality; autobiography, by definition a narcissistic endeavor, would seem the genre particularly suited to such modes of perception. In fact, both *David Copperfield* and *Villette* attest to the vitality and significance of the double in midcentury autobiography.

Like Tennyson and Wordsworth, both David and Lucy share the propensity to project versions of themselves onto other characters such as Steerforth, Traddles, Ginevra, or Miss Marchmont, but they also refuse to recognize the doubles who figure forth their own sexual identities— Uriah Heep and the Nun. This situation is not at all surprising. Both David and Lucy suffer from a similar inability to recognize themselves when they literally look into a mirror. David's hatred for Uriah is the only expression he can give the "secret current" of his emotions, his love for Agnes. Uriah's role in his story is consistently tied to David's attitude toward his adopted "sister." Uriah takes over David's bedroom in the Wickfield household; he aspires to Agnes' hand in marriage—all when David himself is involved in his courtship of Dora and their subsequent marriage. David acts out his self-disgust and punishes his own hidden desires when he slaps Uriah. If there were any question about the nature of David's feelings, it would be swept away by his response when Uriah announces his plan to marry Agnes:

> I believe I had a delirious idea of seizing the red-hot poker out of the fire, and running him through with it. It went from me with a shock, like a ball fired from a rifle: but the image of Agnes, outraged by so much as a thought of this red-headed animal's, remained in my mind. . . . He seemed to swell and grow before my eyes . . . and the strange feeling . . . that all this had occurred before, at some indefinite time, and that I knew what he was going to say next, took possession of me.

David, of course, knows what Uriah will say next because Uriah expresses what he feels; the concatenation of libidinal energies in this passage is attributed to both characters, not just to Uriah. Interestingly, Brontë inverts this use of the double—and indeed the larger tradition of which it is an example—in her treatment of the nun. While Dickens uses Uriah to objectify the sexual impulses that David must deny, Lucy Snowe's nun projects the refusal to express such energies: the sin in *Villette* is not desire, but the repression of desire. The nun first appears when Lucy receives a letter from Graham, when she is trying to summon reason to restrain emotion. As Graham quite accurately comments, the nun is specifically his enemy. Only after she has buried Graham's letter and her hope that he might reciprocate her feelings does Lucy welcome and even reach out to touch the spectral figure she has earlier fled. David leaves the side of Dora's deathbed so that he can travel to Dover and aid in the defeat of Uriah's ambitions; when it seems most likely that Dora's death will render his feelings for Agnes acceptable, David literally puts them in prison. Lucy, however, destroys her double when she recognizes the strength of her love for M. Paul; after seeing Justine Marie in the park with Paul, she can express her jealous desire to possess him and, later that evening, tear to pieces the clothes worn by the nun.

Yet memory must further complicate these earlier psychological processes. Brontë gives the tradition of the double a final and unconventional twist by turning Lucy's lover into yet another of her second selves. Paul is, first and foremost, Graham's replacement. If Graham is the romantic hero of *Villette,* Paul is its "Christian hero." Patterned after the initial tie between Lucy and Graham, Paul's love first finds expression in the idea of a sibling affection. Just as the Frenchman represents a more satisfying version of the young English doctor, he is also another Lucy. At one point he even forces her to look in a mirror so that she can see the "affinity" between them. His irritable actions, like Lucy's reserve, conceal the "inner flame" he shares with both Lucy and Paulina. This identification, in turn, affects Lucy's position. Paul's love, his frequently demonstrated jealousy, his fiery nature allow Lucy to assume the role that Graham has played in Volumes I and II. Like the earlier Graham, she becomes the unresponsive object of love: she is "placid" in the face of Paul's tempestuous emotions; she experiences "a certain smugness of composure, indeed, scarcely in my habits, and pleasantly novel to my feelings." That Paul, playing Lucy's earlier role, wins her affection and respect, is, by analogy, a final triumph over Graham's indifference. By describing Paul as if he were going through a course of emotions that she herself has previously experienced, Lucy manages to have it both ways. Because Paul is a man, he can reveal his feelings and therefore act out the responses that Lucy has previously denied. Even the quality of Paul's speech depends on Lucy's actions and characterization. When he explains that his capacity for love "died in the past—in the present it lies buried—its grave is deep-dug, well-heaped, and many winters old," he is recapitulating the scene in which Lucy buries the symbol of her love for Graham under the pear-tree in the garden. Paul's exaggerated jealousy also reveals Lucy's carefully concealed responses to Graham. As Lucy allows herself to play the roles of both Paulina and Graham, Paul's character becomes identified with those of Graham and Lucy.

Late in *Villette* Lucy makes what seems to be a wholly gratuitous and nearly absurd statement that again empha-

Arthur Bell Nicholls proposed to Brontë the month before Villette *was published.*

sizes the transformations that her imagination perpetually effects. After asking Lucy for her friendship, Paul fails to meet her at their usual hour for lessons. Instead he works in the garden outside the schoolroom and "fondles" the spaniel Sylvie, "calling her tender names in a tender voice." Lucy describes the dog and then comments, "I never saw her, but I thought of Paulina de Bassompierre: forgive the association, reader, it *would* occur." This strange "association" is explained in the next sentence: "M. Paul petted and patted her; the endearments she received were not to be wondered at; she invited affection by her beauty and her vivacious life." Paulina must appear one more time as a threat to Lucy's hold on a man's affections. Here, however, her rival for Paul's love is no more likely to succeed than she herself could have succeeded against Paulina's claims on Graham. Her apology for this "association" is either disingenuous or naïve. Such associations, doublings and identifications are the distinguishing characteristic of a narrative which constantly mirrors back the images of Lucy's suppressed emotional life. At one point she says of Graham, "He was a born victor, as some are born vanquished." Lucy consistently sees herself as one of the vanquished. But if some victors are born, Lucy's narrative proves that others can be made. During the course of the third volume, the fact of Paul's love allows Lucy to triumph. More importantly, the way in which she describes that love, the form that memory imposes on events through "associations," allows her to triumph one last time over that "born victor," Graham Bretton.

During their first meeting at La Terrasse, Paulina explains

herself to Lucy by paraphrasing a line from Wordsworth: "The child of seven years lives yet in the girl of seventeen." The rest of the epigraph to the "Intimations of Immortality" ode is equally applicable to Paulina: "And I would wish my days to be / Bound each to each by natural piety." Paulina's quite Wordsworthian sense of the past—as opposed to Graham's propensity to live in and for the present moment—elicits Lucy's unqualified approval and admiration: "Her eyes were the eyes of one who can remember; one whose childhood does not fade like a dream, nor whose youth vanish like a sunbeam. She would not take life, loosely and incoherently, in parts, and let one season slip as she entered on another: she would retain and add; often review from the commencement, and so grow in harmony and consistency as she grew in years." This passage recalls Wordsworth's desire to use the narration of his past experience to "understand [him]self": "my hope has been, that I might fetch / Invigorating thoughts from former years; / Might fix the wavering balance of my mind." Memory, for both Paulina and Wordsworth, is literally a source of integrity, that sense of a self that is "consistent," "harmonious," and unwavering. The connections between past and present selves that are wrought by memory are proof of the organic growth of a distinct identity. Addressing Venus, the morning and the evening star, Tennyson makes the same point: "Thou, like my present and my past, / Thy place is changed; thou art the same." By the end of *David Copperfield,* the narrator can claim a similar faith in the coherent patterns that memory imposes on his life. Earlier he has seen an absolute division between the young boy he was and the man he has become: "That little fellow seems to be no part of me; I remember him as something left behind upon the road of life—as something I have passed, rather than have actually been—and almost think of him as of some one else." By the time he proposes to Agnes, however, his narrative "journey" has linked the two selves: "Long miles of road then opened out before my mind; and, toiling on, I saw a ragged way-worn boy forsaken and neglected, who should come to call even [Agnes'] heart now beating against mine, his own." Paulina's sense of the past, then, embodies a common nineteenth-century ideal, one that would appear again as the central piety of *The Mill on the Floss.*

Paulina's ability to give "a full greeting to the Past" is yet another way in which she is a refined version of Lucy's less than ideal self. Lucy has said of her younger self that she has lived "two lives"; that sense of division is appropriate to her narrative activity as well. The moments of clarity she achieves in Volume III fade in the "Finis" with which *Villette* ends. Here again memory too painful for expression must be evasively cloaked in vague generalizations and patently ironic statements of resolution. Earlier Lucy's childhood, unlike Paulina's, has "fade[d] like a dream." At the end of the novel, Lucy lets another "season slip" because its revival would be unbearable. Though the evasions at the end of *Villette* were a response to Patrick Brontë's demand for a happy ending, Charlotte Brontë's attempt to "veil the fate in oracular words," as Elizabeth Gaskell called the process, is an appropriate final demonstration of the nature of Lucy's memory. The workings of memory implicit in her narrative correspond to the stages depicted in "Auld Lang Syne." During the child-

hood sections of *Villette,* Lucy is a ghost-like presence on the periphery of the action. Later she finds herself "happier, easier, more at home" in the past as she has felt during her stay at La Terrasse. But the comfort offered by memory is a promise of inevitable dispossession. The fact of Paul's death makes the past as uninhabitable as Lucy's earlier need to earn a living has made La Terrasse. Yet in the interval before she must acknowledge the fact of her ultimate and continuing deprivation, Lucy makes at least partial peace with her past. In her hands the already highly developed conventions of autobiography reach a new level of complexity and subtlety. Both character and creator construct a narrative mirror in which self appears vindicated against the slights experience has dealt them and consoled for the indifference with which others have treated them. (pp. 282-87)

Janice Carlisle, "The Face in the Mirror: 'Villette' and the Conventions of Autobiography," in ELH, *Vol. 46, No. 2, Summer, 1979, pp. 262-89.*

Mary Jacobus   (essay date 1986)

[*Jacobus is an English educator and critic whose views are informed by feminist and psychoanalytic interpretive strategies. In the following essay, she draws upon Freud's concept of the uncanny to explain Lucy Snowe's character.*]

> "Is this enough? Is it to live? . . . Does virtue lie in abnegation of self? I do not believe it. . . . Each human being has his share of rights. I suspect it would conduce to the happiness and welfare of all, if each knew his allotment, and held to it as tenaciously as the martyr to his creed. Queer thoughts these, that surge in my mind: are they right thoughts? I am not certain."

Caroline Helstone's assertion of the inalienable rights of self, in Brontë's *Shirley* (1849), I take to be the seed of her *Villette* (1853)—in which repression returns vengefully on the heroine in the form of a ghostly nun. But *Villette* is not simply about the perils of repression. It is a text formally fissured by its own repressions, concealing a buried letter. Lucy Snowe writes two letters to Graham Bretton, one "under the dry, stinting check of Reason," the other "according to the full, liberal impulse of Feeling"—one for his benefit, censored and punishingly rational, the other for hers, an outpouring of her innermost self. The same doubleness informs the novel as a whole, making it secretive, unstable and subversive. The narrative and representational conventions of Victorian realism are constantly threatened by an incompletely repressed Romanticism. Supernatural haunting and satanic revolt, delusion and dream, disrupt a text which can give no formal recognition to either Romantic or Gothic modes. The buried letter of Romanticism becomes the discourse of the Other, as the novel's unconscious—not just Lucy's—struggles for articulation within the confines of mid-nineteenth-century realism. The resulting distortions and mutilations in themselves constitute an aspect of the novel's meaning, like the distortions of a dream text. But there is more to be found in *Villette* than the incompatibility of realist and Romantic modes. It is haunted by the unacknowledged phantom of feminism, and by the strangeness of fiction itself. Its displacements and substitutions, like its silences and dislocations, are a reminder that fiction is the peculiar reserve both of repression and of the *Unheimliche*—the uncanny which, in Freud's words, "is in reality nothing new or alien, but something which is familiar and old-established in the mind and which has become alienated from it only through the process of repression." Lucy's haunted self-estrangement encodes the novel's alienation from its ghostly subtext.

"Why is *Villette* disagreeable?" asked Matthew Arnold [in a letter dated 14 April 1853]—"Because the writer's mind contains nothing but hunger, rebellion and rage, and therefore that is all she can, in fact put into her book." The same qualities inspired Kate Millett's polemicizing of *Villette* as a radical feminist text ("one long meditation on a prison break") [see excerpt dated 1970]. Arnold and Millett are alike in proposing an unmediated relationship between author and work. It is easy to dismiss this collapsing of Charlotte Brontë and her fictional creation, Lucy Snowe; in her letters the novelist writes punitively of her heroine [in a letter dated 6 November 1852; see excerpt above], "I can hardly express what subtlety of thought made me decide upon giving her a cold name" and [in a letter dated 3 November 1852], "I am not leniently disposed towards Miss *Frost.* . . . I never meant to appoint her lines in pleasant places." Yet the assumption that autobiographical release fuels the novel is natural enough, and not only because the letters evince the same straining after dissociation as the novel itself. For *Villette,* belonging as it appears to do to the tradition of the *roman personnel* (the lived fiction), invites its readers to make just such a covert identification between Charlotte Brontë and her creation—and then frustrates it. The novel's real oddity lies in perversely withholding its true subject, Lucy Snowe, by an act of repression which mimics hers. Her invisibility is more than evasive; it is devious, duplicitous. Lucy lies to us. Her deliberate ruses, omissions and falsifications break the unwritten contract of first-person narrative (the confidence between reader and "I") and unsettle our faith in the reliability of the text. "I, Lucy Snowe, plead guiltless of that curse, an overheated and discursive imagination," she tells us; but the same sentence goes on to speak of the infant Paulina's incommensurately powerful grief "haunting" the room—as Lucy herself will later be haunted by the "discursive" imagination she denies. "I, Lucy Snowe, was calm," she insists again, after a heart-rending account of Paulina's parting from her father (disclosing the lie): "she dropped on her knees at a chair with a cry—'Papa!' It was low and long; a sort of 'Why has thou forsaken me?' " Riven with such contradictions, Lucy's narrative calls itself into question by forcing us to misread it. "I seemed to hold two lives—the life of thought, and that of reality," she tells us later; the hidden life of thought strives ceaselessly to evade her censorship in the very language she uses: that of supernatural haunting and the Christian Passion—the product of an inverted martyrdom in which Lucy renounces her share of rights instead of cleaving to them.

At the start of the novel, Lucy observes and narrates an-

other's drama, the diminutive Paulina's. Of her own painful circumstances we learn only that she has been shipwrecked in the metaphoric tempest which recurs at moments of crisis through the novel: "To this hour, when I have the nightmare, it repeats the rush and saltiness of briny waves in my throat, and their icy pressure on my lungs." Paulina's grief—that of the abandoned child cast among strangers—has in any case already acted out Lucy's. Asking no pity for herself, Lucy earlier had invoked it for her surrogate: "How will she get through this world, or battle with this life? How will she bear the shocks and repulses, the humiliations and desolations . . . ?" So, too, Paulina's premature love for the adolescent Graham Bretton is at once a displacement and a prefiguration of Lucy's future relationship with him; just as later, Miss Marchmont's state of erotic arrest and confinement are annexed to Lucy herself: "Two hot, close rooms thus became my world. . . . All within me became narrowed to my lot." As the novel quarries deeper into Lucy's subconscious, the displacement becomes more bizarre. Confined alone at the Rue Fossette during the long vacation, she finds herself looking after a cretin—a creature conjured from nowhere to be her "strange, deformed companion," an image of deranged self who "would sit for hours together moping and mowing and distorting her features with indescribable grimaces." That the heartsick Miss Marchmont and the untamed cretin, warped in mind and body, are aspects of Lucy's repression (as Paulina had been an aspect of her loss) hardly needs emphasizing. Her regression from child to invalid to cretin parodies and reverses the Romantic quest for self which is the real "plot" (the conspiracy of silence) of *Villette.* "Who *are* you, Miss Snowe?" asks Ginevra Fanshawe inquisitively—"But *are* you anybody? . . . Do—*do* tell me who you are!" And, "If you really are the nobody I once thought you, you must be a cool hand." A cool hand indeed; for Lucy's invisibility is a calculated deception—a blank screen on which others project their view of her. To Graham Bretton she is "a being inoffensive as a shadow"; to M. Paul, denouncing her in a melodramatic hiss, she is dangerously, sexually, insurgent—"vous avez l'air bien triste, soumise, rêveuse, mais vous ne l'êtes pas. . . . Sauvage! la flamme à l'âme, l'éclair aux yeux!"

Lucy withholds her true identity from us as well as from the characters whose presence as actors in the novel defines her absence. The most disconcerting of her reticences, and the least functional, concerns her recognition of the medical attendant at the Rue Fossette (Dr. John) as Graham Bretton. The "idea, new, sudden, and startling" which strikes Lucy as she observes him one day at the Pensionnat Beck is not disclosed to the reader until her return to the scene of her and Paulina's childhood love, the reconstituted Bretton household: "I first recognized him on that occasion, noted several chapters back. . . . To *say* anything on the subject, to *hint* at my discovery, had not suited my habit of thought." Instead of declaring herself, Lucy prefers to retain her social invisibility—at this stage she is still employed as a nursery-governess. Her strategic silence conceals the private life which Mme. Beck's system of surveillance is at pains to detect, while she herself sets about detecting the clandestine flirtation between Dr. John ("Isadore," in this role) and Ginevra, much as she had earlier observed the love game between Graham and the infant Paulina. The novel is full of such voyeurisms (Mme. Beck herself is scarcely more on the watch than Lucy)—exhibitions in which Lucy casts herself as an onlooker, passive yet all powerful. Even when she takes the stage herself, during the school play of Chapter 14, she contrives to combine the two roles—at once spectator and participant in the sexual drama which she enacts between "Isadore," Ginevra, and her gallant, de Hamal (between the "Ours" or sincere lover, the coquette, and the fop whose part Lucy plays). Here the divide between stage and audience, watcher and watched, is piquantly removed in the interests of a more complex and ambiguous drama; Lucy also crosses the sexual divide—impersonating a man while clad as a woman from the waist down. In the same way, the frisson lies in Lucy's nonsubservience to her spectator role, as the game of master/slave in *Jane Eyre* is spiced by Jane's insubordination to her master. Jane discovers a taste for sexual mastery in preference to the more conventional role of mistress: Lucy discovers in herself "a keen relish for dramatic expression" and, carried away by she knows not what, transforms her part into an unorthodox piece of intersexual rivalry—"I acted to please myself."

"But it would not do for a mere looker-on at life" (p. 211). Lucy's invisibility is an aspect of her oppression: the actress, Vashti, is an aspect of her hidden revolt. As a middle-class woman, Lucy can only be employed within the home or its educational colony, the school; but that "home," since she is employee and not "mistress," must remain alien. Though increasingly professionalized, the role of teacher retains many of the anomalies of the governess figure in her differing guises (mother substitute, educator, companion). The governess is peculiarly the victim of middle-class sexual ideology, for the only role open to her is that of bringing up children while marriage and motherhood themselves are paradoxically taboo for her within the family that employs her. Economically nonnegotiable (nonexchangeable), she is denied both social and sexual recognition: "No one knows exactly how to treat her." Significantly, Lucy prefers the relative independence of remaining a teacher in Mme. Beck's pensionnat to Mr. Home's offer of employment as Paulina's companion; while Mme. Beck sees in Lucy's bid to marry M. Paul a threat to the economic and family interests on which her establishment is founded (Lucy will ultimately set up a rival school). Charlotte Brontë's letters have much to say both about the "condition of woman" question and about being a governess; but this, finally, of the woman whose destiny it is to be unmarried:

> when patience had done its utmost and industry its best, whether in the case of women or operatives, and when both are baffled, and pain and want triumph, the sufferer is free, and is entitled, at last to send up to Heaven any piercing cry for relief, if by that he can hope to obtain succour.

In *Villette,* that piercing cry is uttered by an actress whose release of "hunger, rebellion and rage" sets the theater literally alight with its revolutionary force.

Vashti is a female version of the central Romantic protagonist, the satanic rebel and fallen angel whose damnation is a function of divine tyranny (Blake's Urizen, Byron's Jehovah of sacrifices, Shelley's Jupiter):

> Pain, for her, has no result in good; tears water no harvest of wisdom: on sickness, on death itself, she looks with the eye of a rebel. Wicked, perhaps, she is, but also she is strong; and her strength has conquered Beauty, has overcome Grace, and bound both at her side, captives peerlessly fair, and docile as fair. Even in the uttermost frenzy of energy is each maenad movement royally, imperially, incedingly upborne. Her hair, flying loose in revel or war, is still an angel's hair, and glorious under a halo. Fallen, insurgent, banished, she remembers the heaven where she rebelled. Heaven's light, following her exile, pierces its confines, and discloses their forlorn remoteness.

Villette can only be silent about the true nature and origin of Lucy's oppression; like Charlotte Brontë's letters, it neither questions the enshrining of marriage within Victorian sexual ideology, nor pursues its economic and social consequences for women. But what the novel cannot say is eloquently inscribed in its subtext—in the "discursive" activity of Lucy's (over-) heated imagination, and in the agitated notation and heightened language which signal it. Here her mingled identification, revulsion and admiration are tellingly juxtaposed with Graham Bretton's indifference to the spectacle. We witness not only his lack of affinity "for what belonged to storm, what was wild and intense, dangerous, sudden, and flaming"—for the Romantic mode which defines Lucy's own insurgent inner life; we witness also his sexual judgment on "a woman, not an artist: it was a branding judgement." "Branded" as a fallen woman, a rebel against conventional morality, Vashti is at once déclassé and thereby permitted to retain her potency—a demonic symbol of sexual energy created by a woman (actress/author) in contrast to the static, male-fabricated images of woman exhibited for Lucy's inspection in an earlier chapter: Cleopatra on one hand, the *Jeune Fille/Mariée/Jeune Mère/Veuve* on the other (woman as sexual object or as bearer of ideology). "Where was the artist of the Cleopatra? Let *him* come and sit down and study this different vision" (my italics), demands Lucy—in whose scandalous pink dress M. Paul detects a latent scarlet woman.

"*Heimlich* is a word the meaning of which develops in the direction of ambivalence, until it finally coincides with its opposite, *unheimlich.*" Thus Freud, for whom the uncanny in fiction provided "a much more fertile province than the uncanny in real life, for it contains the whole of the latter and something more besides." Lucy's dreamlike propulsion from one world to another—from her childhood at Bretton, to Miss Marchmont's sickroom, to the Pensionnat Beck, and back again to Bretton—makes resourceful use of this fertile province, suspending the laws of probability for those of the mind. Narrative dislocation in *Villette* insists on the irreducible otherness, the strangeness and arbitrariness, of inner experience. Lucy's return to the past (or the return of her past?) is ushered in by a nightmare of estrangement—"Methought the well-loved dead . . . met me elsewhere, alienated"—and she recovers consciousness after her desperate visit to the confessional amidst the decor of the *Unheimliche:* "all my eye rested on struck it as spectral," "These articles of furniture could not be real, solid arm-chairs, looking-glasses, and wash-stands—they must be the ghosts of such articles." The real becomes spectral, the past alien, the familiar strange; the lost home (*heimlich*) and the uncanny (*unheimlich*) coincide. Like Vashti, Lucy is an exile from the paradisal world of Bretton; even when restored miraculously to it, she cannot remain there. Its true inmate is not the satanic rebel and fallen angel, but the angelic, spiritualized Paulina—whose surname, appropriately, is Home. By marrying her (it is she whom he rescues from the threatened conflagration in the theater) Graham Bretton ensures the continuation of the status quo. But their conventional love story—child bride taken in charge by medical father substitute—is upstaged by Lucy's more innovatory and disturbing inner drama. In this internalized theater, the part that doubles Lucy's is taken by a (supposed) ghost. Freud's essay on the uncanny offers a classic formulation of Gothic strategy: "the writer creates a kind of uncertainty in us . . . by not letting us know, no doubt purposely, whether he is taking us into the real world or into a purely fantastic one of his own creation." The effect of this uncertainty in Charlotte Brontë's novel is to challenge the monopolistic claims of realism on "reality"—to render its representations no less fictive and arbitrary than the Gothic and Romantic modes usually viewed as parasitic. Moreover, as Freud suggests, a peculiarly powerful effect is achieved when the writer pretends to move in the world of common reality and then oversteps it, "betraying us to the superstitiousness which we have ostensibly surmounted." The grudge which we feel against the attempted deceit is just that retained by readers and critics of *Villette* toward the nun of the Rue Fossette—in whom repression, the uncanny, and the unacknowledged phantom of feminism combine to subvert the novel's facade of realism.

A realist reading of *Villette* must relegate the nun to the level of Gothic machinery; indicatively both Kate Millett (for whom the novel is a manifesto of sexual politics) and Terry Eagleton (for whom it is a Marxist myth of power) ignore her ambiguous presence. But just because the device is so cumbrous and unnecessary in realist terms—Ginevra's gallant dressed up for their clandestine assignations—it must have another function. In effect, it symbolizes not only Lucy's repression, but the novelist's freedom to evoke or inhibit the *Unheimliche;* to lift or impose censorship. The nun thus becomes the phantom or psychic reality which representation represses, evading the censorship of realism as de Hamal himself evades the forbidden ground of the Pensionnat Beck under Mme. Beck's censoring eyes. In his medical capacity, Graham Bretton diagnoses "a case of spectral illusion . . . resulting from long-continued mental conflict." But as it turns out, the rationalist explanation is debunked by the fictive reality of the novel itself: "doctors are so self-opinionated, so immovable in their dry, materialist views," Lucy comments with apparent perversity; yet the text vindicates her. The legend of the nun, buried alive in a vault under the Methuselah pear tree "for some sin against her vow," is introduced early on but lies dormant until passion threatens to reassert itself. The first apparition—summoned up, it

seems, by Lucy's love for Graham Bretton—occurs when she plunges into the vaultlike depths of "the deep, black, cold garret" to enjoy his precious letter:

> Are there wicked things, not human, which envy human bliss? Are there evil influences haunting the air, and poisoning it for man? What was near me? . . .
>
> Something in that vast solitary garret sounded strangely. Most surely and certainly I heard, as it seemed, a stealthy foot on that floor: a sort of gliding out from the direction of the black recess haunted by the malefactor cloaks. I turned: my light was dim; the room was long—but, as I live! I saw in the middle of that ghostly chamber a figure all black or white; the skirts straight, narrow, black; the head bandaged, veiled, white.
>
> Say what you will, reader—tell me I was nervous, or mad; affirm that I was unsettled by the excitement of that letter; declare that I dreamed: this I vow—I saw there—in that room—on that night—an image like—a NUN.

The sheerest melodrama? or a bold refutation of "common reality"? Lucy's challenge—"Say what you will, reader"—defies us to find the narrative incredible or the author unreliable.

For the reader, there is no knowing how to take the nun; is Lucy deceiving us again? A brief admonitory sighting marks her visit to the theater (an unexplained light in the *grenier*); but the next full apparition occurs at a similar moment of high emotional significance—on the still, dim, electric evening when she buries her letters from Graham, and her love for him, in a hole under the Methuselah pear tree:

> the moon, so dim hitherto, seemed to shine out somewhat brighter: a ray gleamed even white before me, and a shadow became distinct and marked. I looked more narrowly, to make out the cause of this well-defined contrast appearing a little suddenly in the obscure alley: whiter and blacker it grew on my eye: it took shape with instantaneous transformation. I stood about three yards from a tall, sable-robed, snowy-veiled woman.
>
> Five minutes passed. I neither fled nor shrieked. She was there still. I spoke.
>
> "Who are you? and why do you come to me?"

Lucy here both hides a treasure and entombs a grief; does the nun confront her to assert their kinship? The third apparition—aroused to vengeful anger—is provoked by M. Paul's declaration of affinity between himself and Lucy ("we are alike—there is affinity. Do you see it, mademoiselle, when you look in the glass?"). The birth of love and the turbulent reactivation of repression occur simultaneously:

> Yes; there scarce stirred a breeze, and that heavy tree was convulsed, whilst the feathery shrubs stood still. For some minutes amongst the wood and leafage a rending and heaving went on. Dark as it was, it seemed to me that something more solid than either night-shadow, or branch-

shadow, blackened out of the boles. At last the struggle ceased. What birth succeeded this travail? What Dryad was born of these throes? We watched fixedly. A sudden bell rang in the house—the prayer-bell. Instantly into our alley there came . . . an apparition, all black and white. With a sort of angry rush—close, close past our faces—swept swiftly the very NUN herself! Never had I seen her so clearly. She looked tall of stature, and fierce of gesture. As she went, the wind rose sobbing; the rain poured wild and cold; the whole night seemed to feel her.

Natural and supernatural are brought ambiguously into play; the nun is at once "solid," material, and capable of bringing about changes in the weather—"betraying us to the superstitiousness we have ostensibly surmounted."

Lucy's question ("Who are you?") remains unanswered, but the nun's ambiguous status—at once real and spectral, both a deceit practiced on Lucy and her psychic double—has important implications for the system of representation employed in the novel. The configuration of characters around Lucy is equally expressive of her quest for identity and of her self-estrangement. Mrs. Bretton, Mme. Beck, Ginevra, the detestable Zélie de St. Pierre and the adorable Paulina are the images of women (the good and bad mothers, the rivals and sisters) through whom Lucy both defines and fails to recognize herself, placed as she is at the center of a distorting hall of mirrors in which each projection is obedient to her feelings of gratitude, rivalry, attraction, hatred or envy. No other woman in the novel has any identity except as Lucy herself bestows it. The absent center exerts a centripetal force on the other characters, making them all facets of the consciousness whose passions animate them. And yet such is the level which a realist reading of *Villette* would claim as stable, objective, autonomous, in contrast to the phantasmal subjective world represented by the nun and the Gothic hinterland to which she belongs. At this point one must acknowledge the powerful presence of fantasy in Charlotte Brontë's fiction. M. Paul, no less than Lucy's rivals (the images to whom she must submit or over whom she may triumph), is animated by a wish fulfillment which it is surely justifiable to see as Charlotte Brontë's own. But far from detracting from the fiction, the release of fantasy both energizes *Villette* and satisfies that part of the reader which also desires constantly to reject reality for the sake of an obedient, controllable, narcissistically pleasurable image of self and its relation to the world. From the scene in which Ginevra triumphantly contrasts herself and Lucy in the mirror, to Lucy's unexpected glimpse of herself in public with Graham Bretton and his mother ("a third person in a pink dress and black lace mantle . . . it might have been worse"), to M. Paul's declaration of affinity ("Do you see it . . . when you look in the glass? Do you observe that your forehead is shaped like mine—that your eyes are cut like mine?"), we trace, not so much the rehabilitation of the plain heroine, as the persistence of the Lacanian mirror phase. Or, to put it in terms of text rather than plot, we too are confronted by an image in which signifier and signified have imaginary correspondence—by a seductive representational illusion which denies the lack or absence central to all signification. The nun stands opposed to this imaginary plentitude of sign or image. Too easily identified as the specter of repression, or as the double of Lucy's repressed self, she is nonetheless recalcitrantly other; "Who are you?" asks Lucy, not recognizing her. She is the joker in the pack, the alien, ex-centric self which no image can mirror—only the structure of language. Like the purloined letter in [Jacques] Lacan's reading of the Poe story, where the meaning of the letter (the autonomous signifier) lies in its function in the plot rather than its actual contents, the nun derives her significance from her place in the signifying chain. She has one function in relation to Lucy, another in relation to M. Paul, and another again in relation to Ginevra. The different meanings intersect but do not merge; the threads cross and intertwine without becoming one. Her uncanniness lies in unsettling the "mirroring" conventions of representation present elsewhere in *Villette,* and in validating Gothic and Romantic modes, not as "discursive" and parasitic, but—because shifting, unstable, arbitrary and dominated by desire—as the system of signification which can more properly articulate the self.

What are we to make of Lucy's extraordinary narrative? Which level of the text finally claims priority? Pursuit of the nun to the novel's climax—the phantasmagoric scenes of Lucy's drugged nocturnal expedition to the illuminated park—provides an answer of sorts. The nun has by this time manifested herself in another guise, as the external obstacle to marriage between Lucy and M. Paul; that is, his supposed devotion to the dead, sainted Justine Marie (and, with her, to Roman Catholicism) whose nun-like portrait is pointedly exhibited to Lucy by Père Silas, as well as his guardianship of a bouncing, all too alive ward of the same name. Her presence at the climax of the novel perfectly illustrates Charlotte Brontë's deviousness, the strategy by which her heroine's consciousness at once distorts, and, in doing so, creates a truth that is essentially a fiction. In this coda-like sequence, all the characters of the novel are paraded before the apparently invisible Lucy in their happy family parties—the Brettons and Homes; the Becks, Père Silas and Mme. Walravens; and lastly, after an elaborate buildup of expectation and delay, M. Paul and his ward. Thus Lucy is ostensibly returned to her original role of excluded spectator. But there is a difference. This time it is she who is *metteur en scène* in a drama of her own making. First comes "the crisis and the revelation," the long-awaited arrival of the nun or her double, Justine Marie—heightened by Lucy's anticipatory memories of her earlier hauntings:

> It is over. The moment and the nun are come. The crisis and the revelation are passed by.
>
> The flambeau glares still within a yard, held up in a park-keeper's hand; its long eager tongue of flame almost licks the figure of the Expected—there—where she stands full in my sight! What is she like? What does she wear? How does she look? Who is she?
>
> There are many masks in the Park to-night, and as the hour wears late, so strange a feeling of revelry and mystery begins to spread abroad that scarce would you discredit me, reader, were I to say that she is like the nun of the attic, that she

wears black skirts and white head-clothes, that she looks the resurrection of the flesh, and that she is a risen ghost.

All falsities—all figments! We will not deal in this gear. Let us be honest, and cut, as heretofore, from the homely web of truth.

Homely, though, is an ill-chosen word. What I see is not precisely homely. A girl of Villette stands there. . . .

"*Heimlich* is a word the meaning of which develops in the direction of ambivalence." Once again it is the living and not the dead, the familiar and not the strange, that becomes uncanny; not least because the bathos fails to proceed as expected.

The transformation of spectral nun into bourgeois belle is followed by yet another audacious reversal—a denial of reality whereby Lucy invents an engagement between M. Paul and his ward, a fiction whose basis ("his nun was indeed buried") is the truth of her own autonomous imagination:

Thus it must be. The revelation was indeed come. Presentiment had not been mistaken in her impulse; there is a kind of presentiment which never *is* mistaken; it was I who had for a moment miscalculated; not seeing the true bearing of the oracle, I had thought she muttered of vision when, in truth, her prediction touched reality.

I might have paused longer upon what I saw; I might have deliberated ere I drew inferences. Some perhaps would have held the premises doubtful, the proofs insufficient; some slow sceptics would have incredulously examined, ere they conclusively accepted the project of a marriage between a poor and unselfish man of forty, and his wealthy ward of eighteen; but far from me such shifts and palliatives, far from me such temporary evasion of the actual, such coward fleeing from the dread, the swift-footed, the all-overtaking Fact, such feeble suspense of submission to her the sole sovereign, such paltering and faltering resistance to the Power whose errand is to march conquering and to conquer, such traitor defection from the TRUTH.

Is this Lucy's final and most outrageous lie? or, as the text insists in the face of its heavily alliterative irony, the novel's central "truth"?—that the imagination usurps on the real to create its own fictions; that Lucy is essentially and inevitably single.

The self-torturing narrative and masochistic imagery ("I invoked Conviction to nail upon me the certainty, abhorred while embraced") speed Lucy back to her solitary dormitory in the Rue Fossette, to the effigy of the nun on her bed, and the empty garments which signal "the resurrection of the flesh":

Tempered by late incidents, my nerves disdained hysteria. Warm from illuminations, and music, and thronging thousands, thoroughly lashed up by a new scourge, I defied spectra. In a moment, without exclamation, I had rushed on the haunted couch; nothing leaped out, or sprung, or

stirred; all the movement was mine, so was all the life, the reality, the substance, the force; as my instinct felt. I tore her up—the incubus! I held her on high—the goblin! I shook her loose—the mystery! And down she fell—down all round me—down in shreds and fragments— and I trode upon her.

The phrasing is odd and significant: "all the movement was mine, so was all the life, the reality, the substance, the force." The wardrobe mockingly bequeathed to Lucy by the eloped Ginevra and de Hamal labels her as the nun of the Rue Fossette—at once accusing her of animating the specter from within herself, and forcing her to recognize its true identity.

But of course the narrative doesn't leave things here, although the ambiguous ending cunningly attempts to do so—at once uniting Lucy and M. Paul in their educational idyll, and severing them for ever. The final evasion ("Trouble no quiet, kind heart; leave sunny imaginations hope") was clearly designed to satisfy the conventional novel reader as well as Charlotte Brontë's father. But there is more to it. Of the two letters she writes to Graham Bretton, Lucy tells us: "To speak truth, I compromised matters; I served two masters: I bowed down in the house of Rimmon, and lifted the heart at another shrine." The entire novel, not just its ending, bears the marks of this compromise—between Victorian romance and the Romantic imagination, between the realist novel and Gothicism. The relationship between the two texts is as arbitrary as that between the two letters; as the signified slides under the signifier, so the buried letter bears an ex-centric relation to the public version. This is not to say that the real meaning of *Villette,* "the TRUTH," lies in its ghostly subtext. Rather, it lies in the relationship between the two, which points to what the novel cannot say about itself—to the real conditions of its literary possibility. Instead of correcting the novel into a false coherence, we should see in its ruptured and ambiguous discourse the source of its uncanny power. The double ending, in reversing the truth/fiction hierarchy, not only reinstates fantasy as a dominant rather than parasitic version of reality, but at the same time suggests that there can be no firm ground; only a perpetual de-centering.

Fittingly, the sleight of hand is carried out with the aid of metaphors drawn from the Romantic paradox of creation-in-destruction. The tempest by which Lucy's earliest loss is signified becomes an apocalyptic upheaval prophesying rebirth as well as death when the time comes for her to leave Miss Marchmont ("disturbed volcanic action . . . rivers suddenly rushing above their banks . . . strange high tides flowing furiously in on low sea-coasts"). In the same way, Lucy's loss of consciousness before her rebirth into the Bretton household, later in the novel, is heralded by renewed images of Shelleyan storm—"I only wished that I had wings and could ascend the gale, spread and repose my pinions on its strength, career in its course, sweep where it swept." There is thus a profound ambiguity in the Romantic cataclysm which shipwrecks Lucy's happiness at the end of the novel:

The skies hang full and dark—a rack sails from the west; the clouds cast themselves into strange forms—arches and broad radiations; there rise resplendent mornings—glorious, royal, purple as monarch in his state; the heavens are one flame; so wild are they, they rival battle at its thickest—so bloody, they shame Victory in her pride. I know some signs of the sky; I have noted them ever since childhood. God, watch that sail! Oh! guard it!

. . . . .

That storm roared frenzied for seven days. It did not cease till the Atlantic was strewn with wrecks: it did not lull till the deeps had gorged their full of sustenance. Not till the destroying angel of tempest had achieved his perfect work, would he fold the wings whose waft was thunder—the tremor of whose plumes was storm.

John Martin and the Angel of Death transform Lucy's premonition of loss into an apocalyptic victory of the imagination. By admitting to the incompatibility of the world of thought and the world of reality, Lucy becomes a truly reliable narrator—single and double at the same time. And by tacitly affirming the centrality of shipwreck, loss and deprivation to the workings of her imagination, Charlotte Brontë also reveals the deepest sources of her own creativity.

A Bloomian reading would presumably see the nun as an emblem of repression in a belated text whose sexual anguish, like that of Tennyson's "Mariana," masks influence anxiety (note the analogous presence of the Methuselah pear tree and "Mariana"'s poplar). A plausible case could be made for misreading *Villette* in the same way. Charlotte Brontë's imagination was nurtured on Romanticism ("that burning clime where we have sojourned too long—its skies flame—the glow of sunset is always upon it"), but the world of Angria had to be repressed in the interests of Victorian realism: "When I first began to write . . . I restrained imagination, eschewed romance, repressed excitement." It was no more possible to write a Romantic novel in the mid-nineteenth century than to read one, as the bewildered and imperceptive reviews of *Wuthering Heights* (1847) reveal. Unlike her sister, Emily Brontë refused to bow down in the house of Rimmon, and in an important sense, hers is the repressed presence in *Villette.* Lucy's unwilling return to consciousness in the Bretton household ("Where my soul went during that swoon I cannot tell. . . . She may have gone upward, and come in sight of her eternal home. . . . I know she reentered her prison with pain, with reluctance") resembles nothing so much as Emily Brontë's "Prisoner" after visionary flight: "Oh, dreadful is the check—intense the agony / When the ear begins to hear and the eye begins to see." Her invocation "To Imagination" underlies *Villette*'s paean to the Imagination in the face of Reason's tyranny (" 'But if I feel, may I *never* express?' '*Never!*' declared Reason.") Emily Brontë had written, "So hopeless is the world without, / The world within I doubly prize," and welcomed a "benignant power, / Sure solacer of human cares"—

> Reason indeed may oft complain
> For Nature's sad reality,
> And tell the suffering heart how vain

> Its cherished dreams must always be;
> And truth may rudely trample down
> The flowers of Fancy newly blown.

> But thou art ever there to bring
> The hovering visions back and breathe
> New glories o'er the blighted spring
> And call a lovelier life from death,
> And whisper with a voice divine
> Of real worlds as bright as thine.

Charlotte Brontë, in turn, creates one of the most remarkable invocations to Imagination in Victorian literature—a passage that criticism of *Villette* has proved consistently unable to assimilate, or even acknowledge:

> Often has Reason turned me out by night, in mid-winter, on cold snow. . . . Then, looking up, have I seen in the sky a head amidst circling stars, of which the midmost and the brightest lent a ray sympathetic and attent. A spirit, softer and better than Human Reason, has descended with quiet flight to the waste—bringing all round her a sphere of air borrowed of eternal summer; bringing perfume of flowers which cannot fade—fragrance of trees whose fruit is life; bringing breezes pure from a world whose day needs no sun to lighten it. My hunger has this good angel appeased with food, sweet and strange, gathered amongst gleaming angels. . . . Divine, compassionate, succourable influence! When I bend the knee to other than God, it shall be at thy white and winged feet, beautiful on mountain or on plain. Temples have been reared to the Sun—altars dedicated to the Moon. Oh, greater glory! To thee neither hands build, nor lips consecrate; but hearts, through ages, are faithful to thy worship. A dwelling thou hast, too wide for walls, too high for dome—a temple whose floors are space—rites whose mysteries transpire in presence, to the kindling, the harmony of worlds!

The dizzying and visionary prose strains, like Shelley's poetry, away from the actual toward enkindled abstractions that image the human mind. But the deity that the temple of the heart enshrines is female; like the embodiment of rebellion and rage (Vashti), the spirit that succours the mind's hunger has been triumphantly feminized.

"Nothing but hunger, rebellion and rage. . . . No fine writing can hide this thoroughly, and it will be fatal to her in the long run"—Arnold's prognosis was wrong (Charlotte Brontë died of pregnancy), but revealingly poses a split between rebellion and "fine writing." The divorce of the Romantic imagination from its revolutionary impulse poses special problems for Victorian Romantics. Where vision had once meant a prophetic denunciation of the status quo and the imagining of radical alternatives, it comes to threaten madness or mob violence. Losing its socially transforming role, it can only turn inward to self-destructive solipsism. Charlotte Brontë's own mistrust erupts in *Villette* with the fire that flames out during Vashti's performance or in the vacation nightmare which drives Lucy to the confessional; while the spectral nun (the Alastor of the Rue Fossette?) has to be laid in order to free Lucy from the burden of the autonomous imagination and allow her to become an economically independent headmistress. There are added complications for a woman writer. The drive to female emancipation, while fueled by revolutionary energy, had an ultimately conservative aim—successful integration into existing social structures; "I am a rising character: once an old lady's companion, then a nursery-governess, now a schoolteacher," Lucy boasts ironically to Ginevra. Moreover, while the novel's pervasive feminization of the Romantic Imagination is a triumph, it runs the attendant risk of creating a female ghetto. The annexing of special powers of feeling and intuition to women and its consequences (their relegation to incompetent dependency) has an equally strong Romantic tradition; women, idiots and children, like the debased version of the Romantic poet, become at once privileged and (legally) irresponsible. The problem is illuminated by situating Charlotte Brontë's novels within a specifically feminist tradition. *Villette*'s crushing opposition between Reason and Imagination is also present in Mary Wollstonecraft's writing. *The Rights of Woman*—directed against the infantilizing Rousseauistic ideal of feminine "sensibility"—not only advocates the advantages for women of a rational (rather than sentimental) education, but attempts to insert the author herself into the predominantly male discourse of Enlightenment Reason, or "sense." Yet, paradoxically, it is within this shaping Rousseauistic sensibility that Mary Wollstonecraft operates as both woman and writer—creating in her two highly autobiographical novels, *Mary* (1788) and, ten years later, *The Wrongs of Woman,* fictions which, even as they anatomize the constitution of femininity within the confines of "sensibility," cannot escape its informing preoccupations and literary influence. Though their concepts of Reason differ, the same split is felt by Charlotte Brontë. In *Villette,* Reason is the wicked and "envenomed" stepmother as opposed to the succoring, nourishing, consoling "daughter of heaven," Imagination. It is within this primal yet divisive relationship that the novelist herself is constituted as woman and writer—nurtured on Romanticism, fostered by uncongenial Reason. The duality haunts her novel, dividing it as Lucy is divided against herself.

It is surely no longer the case, as Kate Millett asserted in 1970, that literary criticism of the Brontës is "a long game of masculine prejudice wherein the player either proves they can't write and are hopeless primitives . . . or converts them into case histories from the wilds." But feminist criticism still has a special task in relation to Charlotte Brontë's novels. That task is not to explain away, but to explain—to theorize—the incoherencies and compromises, inconsistencies and dislocations, which provoked the "can't write" jibe in the first place; to suggest, in other words, the source of Matthew Arnold's disquiet. It is enough to point to the part played by realism and Reason respectively in Charlotte Brontë's double quest for literary form and for female emancipation. To do so relocates her writing, not in a neurotic northern hinterland ("case histories from the wilds"), but in the mainstream of Victorian literary production—its legacy of Romanticism complicated in her case by the conflict between a revolutionary impulse toward feminism and its tendency to confine women within irrationality. And what of the feminist critic? Isn't she in the same position as Charlotte Brontë, the writer, and her character, Lucy Snowe?—bound, if she's

to gain both a living and a hearing, to install herself within the prevailing conventions of academic literary criticism. To this extent, hers must also be an ex-centric text, a displacement into criticism of the hunger, rebellion, and rage which make Lucy an estranged image of self. Constituted within conditions essentially unchanged since those of Mary Wollstonecraft and Charlotte Brontë (i.e. patriarchy) and experiencing similar contradictions within herself and society, the feminist critic faces the same disjunction—removed, however, to the disjunction between literary response and critical discourse. The novel itself becomes the discourse of the Other, making its presence felt in the distortions and mutilations of critical selectivity. What strategy remains, beyond unsettling the illusory objectivity of criticism? Surely also to unfold a novel whose very repressions become an eloquent testimony to imaginative freedom, whose ruptures provide access to a double text, and whose doubles animate, as well as haunt, the fiction they trouble. In the last resort, the buried letter of Romanticism and the phantom of feminism both owe their uncanny power to their subterranean and unacknowledged presence—to repression itself, the subject of Charlotte Brontë's most haunting novel, and fiction's special reserve. (pp. 41-61)

> *Mary Jacobus, "The Buried Letter: 'Villette',"* in her Reading Woman: Essays in Feminist Criticism, *Columbia University Press, 1986, pp. 41-61.*

Steven Millhauser   (essay date 1987)

[*Millhauser is a novelist and short story writer whose works often explore the imaginative worlds of children and the role of the artist in society. In the following essay, he describes* Villette *as a novel of inner conflict, focusing on the haunting quality of the novel's imagery.*]

Villette, Charlotte Brontë's fourth and final novel, begun when she was thirty-five and lonely, and completed some sixteen months later at a time when she routinely described her life as a "pale blank" and "weary burden," is the darkest and most disturbing novel of the exuberant Victorian era. The story it tells is oddly uneventful. Lucy Snowe, a lonely woman of twenty-two who has been orphaned in adolescence, leaves England to seek her livelihood abroad. She goes to Villette, the capital of the kingdom of Labassecour, where she finds work as a nursery maid at a boarding school for girls and is soon advanced to the position of English teacher. She falls in love with an English doctor, who does not return her love; she then falls in love with a professor of literature at the boarding school, who declares his love for her in the penultimate chapter, one day before he sets sail on a three-year journey. The novel ends rather abruptly with Lucy Snowe awaiting the return of her beloved, who, it is strongly hinted, dies in a storm.

Such is the plot of *Villette,* that story of two unconsummated loves. But beneath this plot runs a darker story, which finds expression in the events of the external action but which also runs its own dangerous and fitful course, and it is this dark underplot that seizes the imagination

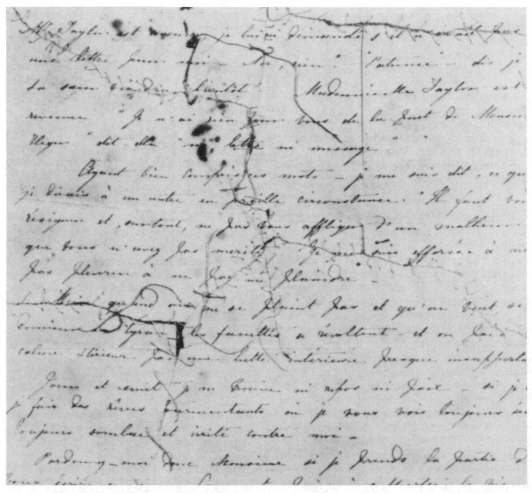

An 1845 letter from Brontë to M. Heger, torn up by him and sewn back together by his wife. Heger appears in The Professor *as William Crimsworth and in* Villette *as Paul Emanuel.*

and compels it powerfully through the novel's forty-two chapters. It is the story of a soul in anguish, tormented by a deep desolation of loneliness, and bitterly divided against itself as it struggles to crush down its always rising cry. That cry is a cry for nourishment, for the quenching of heart-thirst, for more life, and it is at odds with a harsh puritanical conviction that one must be content with one's wretched lot. *Villette* is a minute history of unsuccessful repression. This darker story moves in alternating rhythms of constriction and eruption, and culminates in two widely spaced and extraordinarily powerful scenes: Lucy Snowe's suffering and breakdown during a long vacation, and her drugged half-mad midnight wandering through the streets of Villette into a festive park. At its blackest moments the novel puts one in mind of the "terrible sonnets" of Gerard Manley Hopkins, and of his anguished and solemn cry: "Send my roots rain."

A look at the constricted, eruptive inner world of the novel in its first third, culminating in the breakdown in chapter fifteen, will suggest the book's inward emphasis and dark progress. The story is narrated by Lucy Snowe and opens with three prologuelike chapters from her fifteenth year, after which there is an abrupt eight-year break. In the pro-

logue Lucy Snowe seems curiously absent, barely speaking of herself while directing our attention to a group of three characters who later reappear in the city of Villette. Even so, we have a sharp, troubling sense of her. As early as the fifth paragraph we hear of a mysterious "unsettled sadness" in her life—a theme that will swell into breakdown. We hear of her "cool" nature, which at once invites attention to her name. She likes peace and quiet; she fears "stimulus." She compares herself to another girl and says: "These sudden, dangerous natures—*sensitive* as they are called—offer many a curious spectacle to those whom a cooler temperament has secured from participation in their angular vagaries." It is not a remark calculated to draw a reader's sympathy, and it should be said at once that the success of Lucy Snowe as a character depends in large part on her stringency, her gravity, her secretive and boxed-in nature, her pinched puritanical primness, her extreme lack of all that is meant by feminine charm. The coldness is intentional; Charlotte Brontë wrote to her editor that "A cold name she must have . . . for she has about her an external coldness" [see letter dated 6 November 1852]. When we meet her eight years later, in the first of three transitional chapters leading to Villette, she has lost her vague "kindred": her aloneness is now complete. She becomes companion to the invalid Miss Marchmont. "Two hot, close rooms thus became my world; and a crippled old woman my mistress, my friend, my all . . . I forgot that there were fields, woods, rivers, seas, an everchanging sky outside the steam-dimmed lattice of this sick-chamber; I was almost content to forget it. All within me became narrowed to my lot." This narrowing of her nature in response to a narrowing of circumstance is characteristic, but the words set up a counterpressure: the very act of enumerating all that her steam-dimmed life excludes serves to thrust them into the reader's awareness, while to be "almost content" is to be, however mildly, discontent.

Miss Marchmont dies, and Lucy finds the resolution to go to London. For the first time, we hear directly of a nature beneath her nature: "Indeed, I had a staid manner of my own which ere now had been as good to me as a cloak and hood of hodden grey; since under its favour I had been enabled to achieve with impunity, and even approbation, deeds that, if attempted with an excited and unsettled air, would in some minds have stamped me as a dreamer and zealot." It is an extraordinary confession, though one that somehow doesn't surprise us: the continual insistence on coolness, on calmness, on "steady self-possession," on lack of imagination, on passivity, on the absence of "artistic temperament" arouses in the reader an alertness to opposites. Images of secret, dangerous inner forces begin to appear. As she travels to Villette in chapter seven, she experiences feelings of joy—despite the "deadening influences" in the surrounding landscape. But a powerful counterimage arises: "These feelings, however, were well kept in check by the secret but ceaseless consciousness of anxiety lying in wait on enjoyment, like a tiger crouched in a jungle. The breathing of that beast of prey was in my ear always; his fierce heart panted close against mine; he never stirred in his lair but I felt him; I knew he waited only for sun-down to bound ravenous from his ambush."

In the next seven chapters, as Lucy Snowe establishes herself in the boarding school and begins to feel attracted to a handsome English doctor who barely notices her, we begin to hear of deeper discontents. Images of repression multiply. "In catalepsy and a dead trance, I studiously held the quick of my nature." Stormy weather excites her strangely; it "woke the being I was always lulling, and stirred up a craving cry I could not satisfy." One night there is a thunderstorm. "The tempest took hold of me with tyranny: I was roughly roused and obliged to live." The wild storm that erupts is an emblem of her desperate need, and seems to burst from within her. "I could not go in: too resistless was the delight of staying with the wild hour, black and full of thunder, pealing out such an ode as language never delivered to man—too terribly glorious, the spectacle of clouds, split and pierced by white and blinding bolts." The image here is inescapably sexual, but it is more than that: it figures forth the longed-for breaking of her spiritual trance, the cleaving of her frozen nature by some life-releasing ax. Such images are the secret life of the book, the dark tiger-blood that flows through the narrative veins and stirs the book to dangerous life. Images of curbing-in, of reining, abound, as well as hints of

a more "impulsive" strain; and slowly we approach chapter fifteen, "The Long Vacation."

It is a harrowing chapter, the most powerful evocation of anguished loneliness in English fiction. For eight weeks of late summer and early fall Lucy Snowe is left alone in the "huge empty house," with no companion except a servant and an imbecile pupil. The long isolation brings her inner crisis to a head; images of death, of paralysis, of aridity, of famine pour from her. In the fourth week a raging storm fails to release her: "the beating rain crushed me with a deadlier paralysis than I had experienced while the air had remained serene." She takes to wandering; the language grows more intense. "A goad thrust me on, a fever forbade me to rest; a want of companionship maintained in my soul the cravings of a most deadly famine. I often walked all day, through the burning noon and arid afternoon, and the dusk evening, and came back with moonrise." In her long agony of loneliness nothing helps. "I really believe," she says to herself in the very accents of madness, "my nerves are getting overstretched: my mind has suffered somewhat too much; a malady is growing upon it—what shall I do?" She can no longer sleep, but lies in "a strange fever of the nerves and blood." Nightmare racks her. One evening—"and I was not delirious: I was in my sane mind"—she dresses and goes out into the rain, leaving the house that was "crushing as the slab of a tomb." Church bells draw her; despite her fierce Protestant aversion to Romanism she enters the Catholic church, and in desperate loneliness is drawn to the confessional, where she pours out her grief into the ear of an unknown priest.

This desperate outpouring represents the climax of the long series of eruptions chronicled in the earlier chapters, as well as in "The Long Vacation" itself. It is the final spiritual eruption before her collapse, and directly follows her physical eruption from the tomblike boarding school. In fact the fifteenth chapter affects us as a succession of physical and mental eruptions: a wild wandering of the streets, a nightmare, a bursting forth from the tomb, an outpouring of words into a priestly ear. Such rendings and tearings, however necessary, can result only in ruin, and after leaving the church Lucy collapses in the street.

If the first third of *Villette* is primarily dark—and there is a great deal of literal darkness, such as night scenes and dark storms and a dark attic and a dark alley in a garden—the next third begins in the brightness of Lucy's recovery and dawning happiness, only to take a turn into darkness as she recounts the long slow misery of her unrequited love for Graham Bretton. At one point an attempted tone of unprotesting acceptance is shattered by a cry: "Oh!—to speak truth, and drop that tone of a false calm which, long to sustain, outwears nature's endurance." Here eruption makes itself felt in the text itself. Only in the last third of the novel does the darkness begin to clear and the oppression to lift as slowly, doubtfully, painfully Lucy Snowe spins out threads of attachment to the swarthy little irritable ugly professor who at first had seemed to her "a harsh apparition." At the end she achieves the shadowed happiness of requited but unfulfilled love—as well as a school of her own. The entire novel gives the impression of a long dark night of storm, easing gradually to an overcast morning through whose pale gray clouds there bursts, for a moment, a single sunshaft, perhaps more beautiful than sun itself. But the storm returns. We are spared Jane Eyre's immortally embarrassing words: "Reader, I married him."

Despite the general movement from oppression to ease, from "heart-poverty" (chapter 13) to "a relieved heart" (chapter 41), from hell to Eden ("such moonlight as fell on Eden"), the scenes of lonely suffering have such intensity that they burn more vividly than all others into the reader's mind, inflaming the imagination and filling it with a kind of hunger for darkness. Readers are cruel. Though we may think we care about a character as we might about a person, what we crave is always the deepest, most dangerous point to which a writer's craft can lead us. Charlotte Brontë had an extreme talent for the depiction of a certain kind of suffering; she is learnèd in pain, a scholar in sorrow. *Villette* is a wound—a black book of pain. It impresses the imagination not as a love story but as a hymn of suffering, a journey through vast tracts of inward dark. Indeed Lucy Snowe is aware that her knowledge of pain separates her from others, and at times there is a touch of pride in her sorrow-scholarship, a faint scorn for those who cannot understand her. "On these points mine was a state of mind out of their experience."

The continual turn inward, the close attention to spiritual events, the meticulous narration of minute changes in emotion, connect *Villette* to that branch of English fiction which derives from *Clarissa* rather than *Tom Jones*. But if Charlotte Brontë in her last book looks backward to Richardson, she also looks forward to the modern novel, and especially to those quintessentially modern novels in which a hampered nature seeks release. To my mind there is a curious affinity between *Villette* and the more densely organized *Portrait of the Artist as a Young Man:* each insists on the extreme isolation of its protagonist, each emphasizes a tumultuous inner life, each moves in a rhythm of constriction and release, and each surges toward climaxes rich in significant imagery. Lucy Snowe's restless wandering through the streets of Villette, culminating in a flood of desperate speech, is echoed sixty years later by Stephen Dedalus's restless wandering through the streets of Dublin, culminating in the releasing touch of his tongue to the tongue of a prostitute.

Despite the emphasis on inward struggle, *Villette* is set in a carefully observed and minutely particularized world: the world of Madame Beck's boarding school. But Charlotte Brontë's skill in describing the objects of that world is rarely more than adequate, and often deserts her for the vague or hand-me-down phrase. Sometimes, almost as if by accident, something is seen with sudden swift sharpness, as when Lucy crosses a square "on whose pavement drops almost as large as a five-franc piece were now slowly darkening." More often flowers are fragrant, and sunshine glorious; breezes have an alarming tendency to kiss people; faces often and architecture always elude her. She is good at furniture, and at rooms in general. Her sense of color is most exact in the description of dresses (pale lilac, deep crimson, purple-grey). She watches how people move

(of Madame Beck: " . . . some people's movements provoke the soul by their loose awkwardness, hers satisfied by their trim compactness"). But she is without the vivid gift of fanatical particularization, achieved through a brilliant use of simile or metaphor, that marks a Dickens, for example, and compels us to remember Peggotty's forefinger "roughened by needlework, like a pocket nutmeg-grater." But Charlotte Brontë's descriptive powers improve noticeably whenever Lucy Snowe ceases merely to record the look of things out of narrative necessity, and through inward necessity mixes herself into the description. We then have less a photograph than a record of feelings expressed through images in the outer world. She is good at storms, and at night scenes where darkness creates confusion and objects loom half-seen. She is best whenever the line between external and internal becomes uncertain, when the world approaches hallucination—as in her drugged walk through the "wanderer-wooing summer night" and her arrival in the dreamlike park.

But her descriptive powers achieve their finest precision when she turns to the shadowy inner world itself. Here she frequently resorts to the Bible, and less often to *The Arabian Nights,* for images to convey inward states. She is particularly strong at rendering states of failed repression:

> I did long, achingly then and for four-and-twenty hours afterwards, for something to fetch me out of my present existence, and lead me upwards and onwards. This longing, and all of a similar kind, it was necessary to knock on the head; which I did, figuratively, after the manner of Jael to Sisera, driving a nail through their temples. Unlike Sisera, they did not die: they were but transiently stunned, and at intervals would turn on the nail with a rebellious wrench: then did the temples bleed, and the brain thrill to the core.

In the novel's most startling and disturbing image, worthy of a Jacobean playwright, Lucy Snowe describes her former love for Graham Bretton:

> Was this feeling dead? I do not know, but it was buried. Sometimes I thought the tomb unquiet, and dreamed strangely of disturbed earth, and of hair, still golden and living, obtruded through coffin-chinks.

She is capable of describing brighter feelings, though often they emerge from darkness. Thus does Lucy Snowe begin to fall in love with Graham Bretton:

> Conceive a dell, deep-hollowed in forest secrecy; it lies in dimness and mist: its turf is dank, its herbage pale and humid. A storm or an axe makes a wide gap amongst the oak-trees; the breeze sweeps in; the sun looks down; the sad, cold dell becomes a deep cup of lustre; high summer pours her blue glory and her golden light out of that beauteous sky, which till now the starved hollow never saw.

Here the "golden light" and "beauteous sky" should not be charged with vagueness—they function perfectly as emblems, and all that matters is the contrast between blue-and-gold on the one hand and dim-and-dank on the other. A reader attuned to the novel's pattern of eruptions will notice that familiar storm, that liberating ax. The image, and the book itself, betrays a secret craving for violence, for the destruction of inner impediment. It is the same ax that the youthful Kafka longed for, when he wrote that a book should be an ax to break the frozen sea within us.

All three of these descriptive passages are highly active, and become little stories within the larger story. These secondary stories do not merely reveal and illuminate the feelings they describe, but temporarily replace or annihilate the larger story. To a certain extent this is true of all comparisons, all metaphors. But whereas Dickens's nutmeg-grinder is a homely image that places Peggotty's thumb squarely in a world containing both thumbs and nutmeg-grinders, the Brontë images tend to draw us out of the world of the novel into a dark realm where a warrior bleeds in a tent, a living man is buried in a coffin, a tireless ax cuts its way into the heart of a forest. By pulling us temporarily out of the novel, by exercising over us for a moment the power of story, the images tend to dissolve the world of the novel. This act of dissolution, operating within the very style of the book, directs us away from the external world into the inner world, and subtly reinforces the inward emphasis of the entire novel.

A book, then, of "inward conflict": the phrase is Lucy Snowe's. The story moves toward an hallucinatory climax, followed by a resolution in returned love, but the overwhelming impression remains one of restless suffering. An old Yorkshire servant of the Brontës once told Mrs. Gaskell that when the Brontë girls were children, "Miss Brontë and Miss Emily & Miss Anne used to put away their sewing after prayers & walk all three one after the other round the table in the parlour till near eleven o'clock. Miss Emily walked as long as she could, & when she died Miss Anne & Miss Brontë took it up,—and now my heart aches to hear Miss Brontë walking, walking, on alone." The image of Charlotte Brontë walking round and round the table in the spectral footsteps of her dead sisters is as haunting as any in *Villette.* It may serve as emblem for that dark and restless book. (pp. 176-84)

> *Steven Millhauser, in a review of 'Villette,' in Grand Street, Vol. 6, No. 2, Winter, 1987, pp. 176-84.*

Sally Shuttleworth   (essay date 1987)

[*Shuttleworth is an English educator and critic with an interest in the relationship between literature and science. In the following essay, she notes Brontë's familiarity with nineteenth-century psychological theory and discusses the ways in which her use of that knowledge in* Villette *challenged the patriarchal views of the medical establishment and contemporary society.*]

The fame of the "mad wife" in *Jane Eyre* has ensured that the writings of Charlotte Brontë are firmly associated in the public mind with a preoccupation with madness. Brontë's interest in the demarcation of insanity is not restricted to this one text but is pursued in her final novel, *Villette,* where the narrator is subject, seemingly, to hallucinations, undergoes a nervous collapse, and discusses her symptoms at great length with a doctor. Despite this fore-grounding of medical expertise, no one has, as yet, placed *Villette* in the context of the intense psychological debates conducted in the scientific writings and popular press of the mid-Victorian era.

Insanity and nervous disease were the subject of acute public concern at this time. The mid-century witnessed the founding of public asylums and the professionalization of the medical treatment of insanity, developments which were accompanied by detailed discussions in the periodical press concerning the functions and processes of the mind. The aim of this essay is to place *Villette* within this social and scientific discourse on psychology, and to analyze the ways in which the novel both absorbs and resists the definitions and codifications of female experience offered by the male medical establishment.

Charlotte Brontë takes as her subject in *Villette* the inner processes of mind of a subject who defines herself, at one stage in her narrative, as "constitutionally nervous." When writing *Jane Eyre,* Brontë had deliberately created a split between Jane and her "dark double"—the concealed and imprisoned "mad" wife of Rochester—offering, through a process of analogy and contrast, an analysis of the social construction of insanity. In *Villette* she confronts the issue of psychological instability more directly through the figure of her narrator, Lucy Snowe, focusing now, not on the flamboyant extreme of "mania," but on the more subtle area of the constitution of neurosis. Through the autobiographical account of "calm," "shadow-like" Lucy, the archetypal unreliable narrator, Brontë both explores and interrogates contemporary theories of mental alienation.

The text of *Villette* is dominated by the practice of surveillance. The constant self-surveillance and concealment which marks Lucy's own narrative account is figured socially in the institutional practices of those who surround her. All characters spy on others, attempting, covertly, to read and interpret the external signs of faces, minds, and actions. Madame Beck runs her school according to the watchwords " 'surveillance,' 'espionage' "; M. Paul reads Lucy's countenance on her arrival in Villette, and later studies her through his "magic lattice"; and Père Silas focuses on her "the surveillance of a sleepless eye"—the Roman Catholic confessional. Lucy is subjected to educational, professional, and religious surveillance. Each observer tries to read her inner self through the interpretation of outer signs. This practice takes its most authoritative form in the narrative in the medical judgments of Dr. John.

After Lucy's first encounter with the nun, as she is attempting to read Dr. John's letter, he in turn tries to "read" her: "I look on you now from a professional point of view, and I read, perhaps, all you would conceal—in your eye, which is curiously vivid and restless: in your cheek, which the blood has forsaken; in your hand, which you cannot steady." Dr. John directs onto Lucy the gaze of medical authority, calmly confident of his ability to define inner experience from outer signs. His verdict is distinguished by his insistence on his professional status, and by his unshakable belief that, no matter how hard Lucy might try to hide from his gaze, he would penetrate through to her innermost secrets. The rhetoric of unveiling and penetrating the truth, so prevalent in nineteenth-century science, is here located as a discourse of power: male science unveils female nature.

All those who subject Lucy to surveillance present her with interpretations of her mind and character, but only Dr. John claims the authority of science for his interpretation (though M. Paul, to a lesser extent, also assumes this power when he offers a phrenological reading of her skull). Against the descriptive labels offered by Madame Beck and Père Silas, Dr. John presents a whole language of analysis and a theory of psychological functioning. His diagnosis on this occasion is that it is "a matter of the nerves," a "case of spectral illusion . . . following on and resulting from long-continued mental conflict." The terms of his analysis are drawn directly from contemporary medical science where the subject of "spectral illusion" proved a constant source of debate. Against more visionary explanations of the nun, who functions as a site of crucial interpretative conflict in the text, he offers a materialist explanation based on the functioning of the nervous system. On one level, the text falsifies Dr. John's materialist explanation by presenting an even more material cause—the physical presence of the Count de Hamal masquerading as a nun. The authority of science is not, however, thereby erased from the text. The very inadequacy of the "literal" explanation, indeed, feeds further speculation into the question of the relationship between body and mind which functions as a subtext in the novel. As readers interpreting the signs of Lucy's discourse, we are constantly tempted by the text into reenacting the role of Dr. John, as we attempt to pierce through the external linguistic signs of the narrative to a concealed unity lying below. The text, however, frustrates all such quests for a hidden unitary meaning, deliberately undermining the social and psychological presuppositions which underlie such a quest.

In focusing interpretative attention in the novel on Lucy's "sightings" of the nun, Brontë is deliberately raising the issue of Lucy's psychological stability. Hallucinations, as Brontë was clearly aware, were classically regarded as signs of madness. Lucy herself invokes this mode of explanation on her first glimpse of the nun, challenging the reader to say, "I was nervous, or mad." Despite Lucy's stated resistance to Dr. John's system of analysis, she constantly employs contemporary scientific language to describe her own psychological functioning. The term "nervous system," which she finds alien and technical when used by Dr. John, has already figured largely in her narrative. Other terms from contemporary scientific discourse, such as "monomania," "hypochondria," and "hysteria" are also employed with precision in her analysis. Scientific language in the novel is not confined to Dr. John's specific diagnoses—the imposition of "male reason" on a largely Gothic text—it frames Lucy's narrative construction of her self.

In order to understand Brontë's explorations of the psyche in *Villette* it is essential to place the novel in the context of mid-nineteenth-century medical and social debate. Unlike her contemporaries George Eliot and Wilkie Collins,

for instance, who explicitly recorded their indebtedness to psychological theory, Brontë has not generally been noted for her interest in this area. Evidence from her novels and letters, however, which are permeated with contemporary psychological vocabulary, suggests a rather different picture. The following analysis will draw on the diverse sources through which psychological debate penetrated into the Haworth household: local newspapers, periodicals, texts in the Keighley Mechanics' Institute Library, and, perhaps most significantly, the Reverend Brontë's secular bible: Thomas John Graham's *Domestic Medicine*. This text, which clearly stands behind the authority of Dr. John Graham Bretton, has been annotated throughout by Patrick Brontë, revealing a wealth of reading in psychological medicine and a personal interest in nervous diseases (Patrick records his fears concerning his own psychological health, and the symptoms of Branwell).

The preoccupation with nervous disorder in *Villette* reflects contemporary social concern. The mid-Victorian press was full of alarmist reports concerning supposed dramatic increases in the numbers of the insane, while the borders between sanity and insanity also seemed to be called into question. As a writer observed in the *Times,* July 1853, "Nothing can be more slightly defined than the line of demarcation between sanity and insanity. . . . Make the definition too narrow, it becomes meaningless; make it too wide, the whole human race are involved in the drag-net." The observation reflects the radical shift in social attitudes toward insanity in the nineteenth century which culminated in the passing of the two Lunatic Acts in 1845 and the setting up of public asylums. For the first time the insane were sharply distinguished from the criminal or pauper. This development was directly related, however, to the rise of theories of "moral management" for the treatment of the insane, which stressed the recuperability of the mentally ill, thus breaking down any absolute barrier between sanity and insanity. While earlier theorists had tended to stress the animal nature of the insane, the moral managers stressed their membership in a common humanity. Thus at the same time that insanity was being constructed as a distinct social category, the borders separating it from sanity were also being eroded.

The social and institutional change signaled by the founding of the public asylums was underpinned by the growing professionalization of medical practice, and by the growth of a new specialty—alienism, or psychological medicine. Doctors henceforth claimed the exclusive right to define and treat insanity. Their claims to authority were supported by developments in physiological research which designated the brain and nervous system as the site of mental life. The social and philosophical debate concerning the constitution of the self is crystallized in each era in the discussion of insanity, as Roy Porter clearly demonstrates in his analysis of the eighteenth century in this volume. The crucial term in pre-1860s debate was control. At the same time that the popular and scientific press offered increasing numbers of articles on dreams, apparitions, and the operations of the unconscious mind, the dominant ideology remained that of self-control, as exemplified in John Barlow's work entitled *Man's Power over Himself to Prevent or Control Insanity* (1843). Popular response to mesmerism underlined this duality. Thus one critic could account for the attraction of mesmerism in terms only of an "imbecility of the nervous system, a ready abandonment of the will, a facility in relinquishing every endowment which makes man *human*" ["What is Mesmerism?" *Blackwood's* 70 (1851)]. Fear of the loss of control, of public exposure, underlies this attack. Emphasis on an individual's necessary responsibility for action is coupled with an overwhelming sense that control is at every moment liable to be overthrown.

The nineteenth-century preoccupation with control has been linked, by Andrew Scull, to the economic nexus. The shift in the treatment of the insane, as the external mechanisms of restraint of whips and chains were replaced by an emphasis on internal control and the inner discipline of the mind, was directly related, he argues, to the rise of laissez-faire economics: lunatics, like the industrial work force, had to be taught the principles of " 'rational' self-interest" which governed the marketplace. The individualist philosophy encapsulated in Samuel Smiles's notion of "self-help" governed the treatment of the insane. The asylum formed a microcosm of Victorian society: social and psychological ordering was achieved through constant surveillance, or "careful watching," and its psychological reflex, the internalization of social controls.

Women held a different relationship to this system than men: the medical construction of categories of insanity reinforced the sexual stereotypes of social discourse. The debates concerning self-control were underpinned by the traditional nature-culture polarity; women were assimilated to the side of nature. The metaphorical construction of nature as female . . . is given practical force here. As the preeminent theorist of insanity, [J. E. D. Esquirol, in his *Mental Maladies, A Treatise on Insanity,* 1845], observed: "Physical causes act more frequently upon women than men." Menstruation, childbirth, lactation, all contributed to the myth of "feminine vulnerability": women were seen to possess a biological predisposition to insanity. The social construction of women, which endowed them with feeling, but little reason, also thereby reduced their capacity to resist the onslaughts of the body. Thus at the same time that the Victorian social code ruthlessly enforced ideas of "modesty" and "decorum" in female behavior, it also presented women with an image of their own powerlessness actively to achieve these qualities. In the mid-century criminal trial, where insanity had come to be a recognized plea, women, like children and idiots, were held to be not "responsible" for their actions.

The success of this medicosocial constitution of the feminine can be judged, as Showalter has observed [in her "Victorian Women and Insanity," *Victorian Studies* 23 (1980)], by the evident collusion of middle-class women in this process: "how eagerly they embraced insanity as an explanation of their unfeminine impulses, and welcomed the cures that would extinguish the forbidden throb of sexuality or ambition." In analysis of *Villette,* I will be concerned to examine how far Lucy Snowe, in constructing her narrative, resists such collusion, and how far she recapitulates the definitions and codifications of female experience offered by the male medical establishment.

Brontë's depiction of Lucy's life shows clearly how institutional practices of surveillance are inscribed within the self. Medical surveillance is matched by Madame Beck's professional control, which Lucy relates directly to the practices of industry, referring to her "system of managing and regulating this mass of machinery." Madame Beck's machine seems to function independently of any personal intervention, operating rather on the participants' internalization of the mechanisms of control. As Foucault observes of the principles of Bentham's Panopticon (which he takes as paradigmatic of nineteenth-century modes of social control), "He who is subjected to a field of visibility, and who knows it, assumes responsibility for the constraints of power; he makes them play spontaneously upon himself; he inscribes in himself the power relation in which he simultaneously plays both roles; he becomes the principle of his own subjection" [*Discipline and Punish: The Birth of a Prison,* 1979]. Lucy clearly demonstrates this psychological pattern, allowing all her actions to be dictated by the sense that she might be overlooked. Thus at one stage she even invests inanimate nature with the qualities of spy: "the eyes of the flowers had gained vision, and the knots in the tree-boles listened like secret ears."

The third form of surveillance to which Lucy is subject is that of the Roman Catholic church. Her impulse to confession—the voluntary revelation of the secrets of the inner self—represents for Lucy the nadir of her mental state. Worn out by suffering consequent on her internalization of the social contradictions of the female role, she sacrifices the last vestiges of her autonomy, thus opening herself up to the continued intervention of both medical and religious authorities in her life (and precipitating her entry into the "very safe asylum" offered by the Brettons). Père Silas proves even more assiduous in his "treatment" than Dr. John. From that moment on, as he later informs her, he had not "for a day lost sight of you, nor for an hour failed to take in you a rooted interest." He envisages her "passed under the discipline of Rome, moulded by her high training, inoculated with her salutary doctrines" (the manuscript originally read "sane" doctrines). With its aim of total dominion over the mind through the discipline of its sane/salutary doctrines, Lucy's Roman Catholic church replicates precisely the alientists' system of moral management of the insane.

The perceived threat of the church to Lucy does not end with her confession. As her relationship with Dr. John is subject always to the scrutiny of Madame Beck "glid[ing] ghost-like through the house, watching and spying everywhere," so her relationship with M. Paul is attended by that "ghostly troubler," Père Silas, and the threat of the confessional: "We were under the surveillance of a sleepless eye: Rome watched jealously her son through that mystic lattice at which I had knelt once, and to which M. Emmanuel drew nigh month by month—the sliding panel of the confessional." Lucy's use of the term "magic lattice" echoes, significantly, M. Paul's description of his "post of observation," his window overlooking the garden, where he sits and "reads" "female human nature": "Ah, magic lattice! what miracles of discovery hast thou wrought." The "magic lattice" forms another medium for the male gaze to penetrate through to the recesses of the female psyche, furnishing information which is then appropriated to judge and censor, in accordance with male definitions of female decorum (M. Paul rejects Zelie St. Pierre on the basis of his observations). Lucy herself, M. Paul observes, wants "checking, regulating, and keeping down." She needs "watching, and watching over." Lucy vehemently repudiates M. Paul's methods: "To study the human heart thus, is to banquet secretly and sacrilegiously on Eve's apples. I wish you were a Protestant." The phrase "Eve's apples," used in connection with the voyeuristic practice of spying on women, takes on a decisive sexual charge. The implicit connection, made throughout the book, between Roman Catholicism and the threatened exposure, and suppression, of female sexuality is here brought to the surface.

The school legend of the nun "buried alive, for some sin against her vow" establishes a chain of association between nuns, ghosts, and sexuality which reverberates throughout the novel. Lucy, burying her precious letters from Dr. John above the nun's grave, is associating the unspecified "sin" with sexual transgression. Her "sightings" of the nun occur, significantly, at moments of heightened sexual tension, while the ghostly pursuit to which she is subject seems to embody externally her own activities of self-suppression. Lucy's violent antagonism to Roman Catholicism, treated so often by critics as an intrusion of Brontë's personal prejudice, stems from this sexual nexus. The intensity of her response is signaled initially by her seemingly excessive reactions to the nightly "lecture pieuse": "it made me so burning hot, and my temples and my heart and my wrist throbbed so fast, and my sleep afterwards was so broken with excitement, that I could sit no longer." The description of the content of the tales helps explain Lucy's extreme response: they contain "the dread boasts of confessors, who had wickedly abused their office, trampling to deep degradation high-born ladies, making of countesses and princesses the most tormented slaves under the sun." It is this "abuse of office" which Lucy most fears: the subjection of the self to a male authority consequent on the revelation of the inner self. The explicit sexual nature of this subjection is suggested by the only named tale, that of Elizabeth of Hungary, whose source for Brontë was Charles Kingsley's virulently anti-Catholic poem *The Saint's Tragedy*. The poem chronicles the effects, in Kingsley's view, of the "Manichean contempt" for sexuality of the Roman Catholic church: Elizabeth's guilt concerning sexual desire leads to her total subjection to her priest, whose motives are seen to be an unsavory mixture of sexual lust, worldly ambition, and crude love of power.

In constructing Lucy's self-contradictory narrative, with its displacements, evasions, and ghostly sightings, which clearly signal to the modern reader the presence of sexual repression, Brontë was not unconsciously articulating patterns in the human psyche which were to remain unrecognized, or even untheorized, until the advent of Freud. Sexuality, and specifically female sexuality, was frequently cited as a primary cause of nervous disorder and insanity in nineteenth-century discussions of mental illness. Ideas of women's sexual neurasthenia, as exemplified in Acton's writings, were directly counterpointed by theories of female psychology which stressed women's "vulnerability": the mysterious processes of menstruation (whose causes remained, for the mid-Victorians, threateningly inexplicable), childbirth, and lactation, which linked them to the natural world, also predisposed them, physiologically, to passion. In the seventeenth century, William Harvey had drawn a comparision between women and animals in heat, observing that "in like manner women occasionally become insane through ungratified desire." They are saved only through "good nurture," and innate modesty. Virtually the same sentiments were repeated in the nineteenth century by the progressive alienist John Bucknill: "Religious and moral principles alone give strength to the female mind," he observed. "When these are weakened or removed by disease, the subterranean fires become active, and the crater gives forth smoke and flame" (a process which is literally embodied by Brontë in the burning of Thornfield by the demonic Mrs. Rochester, and in the outbreak of fire in the theater as the "fallen angel" Vashti is acting).

The idea of a specific sexual cause of mental disorder reappeared with renewed force in the nineteenth century following the work of Pinel (acknowledged founder of the new "humanitarian" treatment of the insane), who suggested that mental alienation might proceed, not from an organic disease of the brain, but rather from a "moral" (or functional) disorder. His influential study of mental alienation stressed sexuality as a major factor in hysteria (a disorder which, although no longer attributed to the wanderings of the womb, was still recognized as a primarily female province). Medical texts of the nineteenth century emphasized repeatedly that hysteria occurred mainly in young, unmarried women.

By the mid-century, commentators, eschewing earlier coyness, directly addressed the possible destructive consequences of continence. Thus Feuchtersleben argued, for example, in *The Principles of Medical Psychology* (1845, Eng. trans. 1847), that hysteria arose most frequently in women from "the want of exercise in those sexual functions intended by nature for use and disappointed desire or hope." The equation of women's "natural" state and sexual activity figures even more decisively in Robert Carter's study *On the Pathology and Treatment of Hysteria* (1853), which outlines the first systematic theory of repression. Carter argues that the suppression of sexual passion is one of the primary causes of hysteria, and women, both by nature and social convention, are rendered more susceptible than men. Although woman is "much under [the] dominion" of sexual desire, "if unmarried and chaste, [she] is compelled to restrain every manifestation of its sway." While Harvey extolled the "good nurture" and "innate modesty" of women which enabled them to "tranquilize the inordinate passions of the mind," Carter turns this formulation on its head, to show how social conventions of female passivity actually produce insanity.

Brontë's endorsement of Carter's position is clearly revealed in **Shirley,** where the disappointed Caroline, denied the social right to address her lover, reflects on the life of the old maid, comparing it directly to the life-denying existence of nuns, "with their close cell, their iron lamp, their robe strait as a shroud, their bed narrow as a coffin. . . . these having violated nature, their natural likings and antipathies are reversed: they grow altogether morbid." Denial of sexuality is explicitly associated with the violation of nature. As in Carter's theory of repression, natural energies, if thwarted, turn back on themselves to create perverted forms. The attractive Caroline is not permitted to become "morbid." She is subjected instead to the physical ailment of brain fever which allows her mental faculties and personality to remain fundamentally intact. In *Villette,* by contrast, Brontë actively explores the mental effects of repression, exposing, through the twists and turns of her narrative, the morbid processes of mind of her designedly uncongenial "Miss Frost."

The question of Lucy's actual instability must remain unanswered if we, as readers, are to avoid falling into the error of Dr. John in assuming unproblematic access to a realm of hidden "truth." It is possible, however, to trace the degree to which Lucy, in analysis of her own history, draws on the constructions of appropriate and "insane" feminine behavior to be found in mid-nineteenth-century psychological science. In her explicit use of contemporary scientific terms, Lucy draws attention to the explanatory complexes which underpin the often unconscious associations that direct her interpretation of behavior. Her first noticeable use of scientific terminology occurs in her judgment on what she perceives to be the emotional excesses of the child Polly's behavior with regard to her father: "This, I perceived, was a one-idead nature; betraying that monomaniac tendency I have ever thought the most unfortunate with which man or woman can be cursed." The idea of monomania, displaced here onto Polly, is later appropriated by Lucy for herself to describe her distress at losing Dr. John's letter: " 'Oh! they have taken my letter!' cried the grovelling, groping, monomaniac." The "curse" of monomania to which Lucy here refers was first defined by Esquirol as an "anormal condition of the physical or moral sensibility, with a circumscribed and fixed delirium." In the more developed definition of James Prichard, the chief popularizer of Esquirol's theories in England, monomania was seen as a form of "partial insanity, in which the understanding is partially disordered or under the influence of some particular illusion, referring to one subject, and involving one train of ideas, while the intellectual powers appear, when exercised on other subjects, to be in a great measure unimpaired." Monomania was thus a form of insanity, unmarked by mania, which could exist within the compass of normal life. Esquirol's categories of insanity were founded on assumptions of "feminine vulnerability." Women, he believed, were more susceptible, both physiologically and psychologically, to religious and erotic melancholy, and hence to the "hallucinations the most strange and frequent " of religious and erotic monomania (a conjunction of religion and sexuality which clearly lies behind the figure of the nun).

Lucy's monomania follows the course of Esquirol's erotic monomania, which he defines as a literal disease, a "chronic cerebral affection . . . characterized by an excessive passion." Reflecting the cultural attitudes of his era, Esquirol divides sexual afflictions into chaste erotomania, whose origins lie in the imagination, and "obscene,"

"shameful and humiliating" nymphomania and satyriasis, which originate in the organs of reproduction. Erotomaniacs' affections are "chaste and honourable"; they "never pass the limits of propriety." Instead, they tend to "forget themselves; vow a pure, and often secret devotion to the object of their love; make themselves slaves to it; execute its orders with a fidelity often puerile; and obey also the caprices that are connected with it." The description offers an outline of Lucy's "chaste," obsessional behavior; her devotion to Dr. John, like that of the erotomaniac, is secret.

Esquirol's formulation of erotomania, like his other categories of insanity, dresses recognized social stereotypes in the authority of science. In his hands, the disease becomes socially respectable. Erotomaniacs, he insists, do not, even in fantasy, seek fulfillment of their desires: "The erotomaniac neither desires, nor dreams even, of the favors to which he might aspire from the object of his insane tenderness." The social repression, so evident in Lucy's narrative, which forbade women the articulation, or even conscious acknowledgment, of their desires, is encoded in his very definition of the disease. Esquirol's theory of erotomania, however, does not merely reinforce accepted social wisdom: chaste, hopeless passion is transformed into a cerebral disease, and must henceforth be treated as a possible symptom of insanity. The fear of mental illness signaled by Lucy's references to monomania underpins all her narrative: insanity is no longer limited to the recognizably disruptive forces of sexual desire, which may be locked away in the attic, but lurks as an incipient threat even in the "chaste" repressed imaginings of the "respectable" woman.

The structure of *Jane Eyre* had seemed to vindicate the mid-Victorian ideological position that successful regulation of the mental economy would lead to material social success. Bertha is sent to her death so that Jane can achieve the bourgeois dream. *Villette,* a more radical work than *Jane Eyre,* refuses this compromise. The novel calls into question the doctrine of control, thus implicitly challenging the economic model of healthy regulation which underpinned mid-Victorian theories of social, psychological, and physiological functioning. The mind, like the body, or the social economy, was to be treated as a system to be guided, regulated, and controlled. As John Elliotson observed [in *Human Physiology,* 1840], "the laws of the mind are precisely those of the functions of all other organs,—a certain degree of excitement strengthens it; too much exhausts it." In the mental as in the social economy, the aim must be to obtain maximum efficiency, neither overstretching nor underdeploying the natural resources. Theories of insanity drew on this model. Whether the cause were seen to be physical or moral, menstrual irregularities or the exclusive direction of the efforts of the mind into one channel, the net effect was that of unbalancing the body's natural economy which was founded on the free flow of "secretions" and a hierarchical regulation of the mental forces. Such theories of the bodily economy were based, however, on normative, gender-specific, codes of social behavior. The social construction of insanity went hand in hand with that of femininity.

Lucy, in her vocabulary, seems initially to endorse enthusiastically the world view propounded by contemporary alienists and phrenologists, that cultivation of the correct faculties and suppression of the troublesome lower propensities would lead directly to social advancement. Launched in her teaching career she feels satisfied "I was getting on; not lying the stagnant prey of mould and rust, but polishing my faculties and and whetting them to a keen edge with constant use." Such confidence soon dissolves, however, to be replaced by a rather different theory of social and psychological life. Brontë still uses the vocabulary of regulation and control, but to rather different effect. Lucy's efforts at regulation are no longer seen to be healthful. She strives for a literal form of live burial, recapitulating the experience of the nun: "in catalepsy and a dead trance, I studiously held the quick of my nature." In a world where inner energies, when duly regulated, can find no external outlet, it is better, Lucy argues, that they be suppressed, if they are not to become self-consuming. Alternatively, they should be allowed to range in the world of fantasy. Thus she deliberately rejects Hag Reason, for the saving spirit of the imagination, while the "Real"—that realm to which the moral managers sought so assiduously to return their patients—is figured for her in the iconography of the fallen women: "Presently the rude Real burst coarsely in—all evil, grovelling, and repellent as she too often is." The description, which prefigures the emergence of that "grovelling, groping, monomaniac" Lucy herself, suggests the consequences for women of living according to male-defined reality (the "Real" here is the casket containing the love letter which simultaneously dismisses Lucy as a sexual possibility and condemns her as a monster). Lucy's narrative, which dissolves the real into the imaginary, challenges male constructions of the social and psychological world.

This is not to suggest, however, that Lucy thereby steps entirely outside the formulations of psychological experience to be found in contemporary science. Her descriptions of her sufferings during the long vacation follow medical wisdom in assigning both physical and moral causes for this "strange fever of the nerves and blood." Her sexual fantasies and nightmares of rejection are underpinned by the responsiveness of her physical frame to the storms and tempests outside, held by contemporary alienists to occasion and exacerbate insanity. In thus projecting herself as a physical system, at the mercy of external physical changes, Lucy is able to deny her responsibility for her mental disorder: it is her "nervous system" which cannot stand the strain; the controlling rational ego is dissolved into the body. The figure of the cretin, however, with its "propensity . . . to evil," stands as a warning projection of a model of mind where the physical is dominant, and the passions and propensities are not subject to any mental restraint.

Lucy seems to shift in and out of physiological explanation of the self at her convenience. In opposition to Dr. John, she denies understanding his diagnosis: "I am not quite sure what my nervous system is, but I was dreadfully low-spirited." Her attempt to define why she went to confession is marked by a similar resistance: "I suppose you will think me mad for taking such a step, but I could not help

it: I suppose it was all the fault of what you call my 'nervous system'." Lucy's resistance to Dr. John seems to stem less from the actual content of his medical verdicts than from his reduction of her to a bundle of symptoms, open to his professional definition and control.

Her battle for control over self-definition and interpretation of the processes of her own mind is not conducted solely with Dr. John; the fiery M. Paul also enters the lists. On encountering Lucy in the art gallery after her illness, M. Paul berates her for her unfeminine behavior in not being able to look after the cretin: "Women who are worthy the name," he proclaims, "ought infinitely to surpass our coarse, fallible, self-indulgent sex, in the power to perform such duties." The covert subject of this conversation is clearly the model of the female mind which suggested that women are more "naturally" able than men to suppress their "evil propensities." Lucy, in self-defense, resorts to another male model of the female mind, asserting a physical illness: "I had a nervous fever: my mind was ill." Diminished responsibility, which figured so largely in mid-Victorian trials of female criminals, becomes the basis of her excuse for "unwomanly" conduct. Unlike Dr. John, M. Paul refuses to accept this model of the mind and so draws attention back again to his own image of the constitution of the feminine. Dismissing the idea of nervous fever, he points instead to Lucy's "temerity" in gazing at the picture of Cleopatra. The portrait of the fleshy Cleopatra, and the four pictures of "La vie d'une femme," "cold and vapid as ghosts," which M. Paul prefers for Lucy's instruction in the arts of femininity, take on iconographic significance in the narrative, representing the two alternative models for womanhood created by men. Lucy's challenge to these models, implicit throughout her narrative, takes decisive form in the Vashti section.

The narrative sequence which culminates in the performance of Vashti actually starts, not in the theater, but with Lucy's apparent sighting, that evening, of the nun. Dr. John, refusing to respect her reticence, invokes once more his professional authority to diagnose the symptoms of her "raised look," thus provoking Lucy's angry dismissal of his explanation: "Of course with him, it was held to be another effect of the same cause: it was all optical illusion—nervous malady, and so on. Not one bit did I believe him; but I dared not contradict: doctors are so self-opinionated, so immovable in their dry, materialist views." Lucy rejects the "doctor's" opinion on principle, although his physiological explanation appears perhaps surprisingly close to views she herself has expressed elsewhere. The grounds of her objection to Dr. John's "dry" materialism are made explicit, however, in her analysis of their mutual responses to the performance of Vashti.

For Lucy, Vashti on stage transcends socially imposed sex roles; she is neither woman nor man, but a devil, a literal embodiment of inner passion: "Hate and Murder and Madness incarnate, she stood." Lucy's response is to invoke the male author of a rather different image of womanhood: "Where was the artist of the Cleopatra? Let him come and sit down and study this different version. Let him seek here the mighty brawn, the muscle, the abounding blood, the full-fed flesh he worshipped: let all materialists draw nigh and look on." In a significant elision, Lucy has drawn together the materialism of doctors who seek to explain the processes of the mind with reference only to the physiological behavior of the nerves, and the materialism of men who construct their images of women with reference only to the physical attributes of the flesh. The creation of the feminine in male-executed art is directly allied to the medical construction of women.

Lucy perceives, in Vashti, a force which could reenact the miracle of the Red Sea, drowning Paul Peter Rubens (*sic*) and "all the army of his fat women," but Dr. John remains unresponsive to her challenge. He replicates, in the "intense curiosity" with which he watches her performance, the professional gaze he has recently imposed on Lucy. His verdict underscores, for Lucy, his indifference to the inner movements of female experience: "he judged her as a woman, not an artist: it was a branding judgment." Dr. John's response is determined entirely by predefined categories of suitable female behavior. As in his medical practice, he is insulated from any attempt to understand the causes or experiential detail of the cases he is examining through his possession of a socially validated system of classification which allows him to speak with unreflecting authority. Like his counterparts in the Book of Esther (from where the name Vashti is drawn), he trusts to the codification of male power to protect him from the "demonic" challenge of female energy. (Queen Vashti's refusal to show her beauty to the people at the king's command had provoked, from a worried male oligarchy, a proclamation "into every province according to the writing thereof, and to every people after their language, that every man should bear rule in his own house" [Esther, 1:22]).

In choosing to equate medical and artistic constructions of the female identity through the notion of "materialism," Brontë was drawing on the terms of contemporary debate. As an artistic term, implying the "tendency to lay stress on the material aspects of the objects represented," the word materialism seems to date only from the 1850s (*O.E.D.*). Although the philosophical usage of materialism dates back to the eighteenth century, it had, at the time of Brontë's writing, become the focus of a virulent social and theological debate concerning the development of psychological theories which stressed that the brain was the organ of mind. Phrenology and mesmerism were located, in the popular press, at the center of this controversy, as evidenced by the 1851 *Blackwood's* article which inveighed against the phreno-mesmerism of authors who believed that "upon the materialism of life rest the great phenomena of what we were wont to call mind." Lucy's objections to materialism are not based on the religious grounds of contemporary debate; nor, as her own use of physiological vocabulary demonstrates, are they founded on an opposition to physiological explanation of the mind per se. Her rejection of medical and artistic materialism stems rather from the rigid and incomplete nature of their conception; she objects less to the idea of an interrelationship between body and mind than to their rather partial vision of this union. Under the medical and artistic gaze, woman is *reduced* to flesh and the material functioning of nerves.

In describing the impact of Vashti, Lucy herself employs the vocabulary of contemporary physiological psychology; Vashti's acting, "instead of merely irritating imagination with the thought of what *might* be done, at the same time fevering the nerves because it was *not* done, disclosed power like a deep, swollen, winter river, thundering in cataract, and bearing the soul, like a leaf, on the steep and steely sweep of its descent." The term "irritating" here is a technical one as used, for example, in Graham's observation that "the nervous headache generally occurs in persons with a peculiar irritability of the nervous system." Coupled with the idea of "fevering the nerves," it suggests two different levels of response within the nervous system, while the concluding imagery of the thundering river draws on physiological ideas of channeled energy within the brain. The power disclosed is both internal and external: it describes the force of Vashti's own inner energy, and the impact on the observer, Lucy. In this metaphorical usage of contemporary physiological theory, Brontë dramatizes an even closer integration of body and mind than physiology envisaged, while simultaneously breaking down traditional boundaries of the self. Mind is not reduced to body, it becomes literally "embodied," as Lucy earlier observed: "To her, what hurts becomes immediately embodied: she looks on it as a thing that can be attacked, worried down, torn in shreds. Scarcely a substance herself, she grapples to conflict with abstractions. Before calamity she is a tigress; she rends her woes, shivers them in convulsed abhorrence." While the artist reduces woman to a material expanse of flesh, and the doctor to a mere encasement of nerves, Vashti reveals a true union between the worlds of mind and body: abstractions, the experiential details of mental life which physiology cannot describe, are given material form. In her treatment of Vashti, as throughout the novel, Brontë actually employs contemporary physiological theory to break through the narrow definition of the self it proposes.

The description of Vashti tearing hurt into shreds anticipates Lucy's later destruction of the figure of the nun:

> All the movement was mine, so was all the life, the reality, the substance, the force; as my instinct felt. I tore her up—the incubus! I held her on high—the goblin! I shook her loose—the mystery! And down she fell—down all round me—down in shreds and fragments—and I trode upon her.

Like Vashti, Lucy undertakes a material destruction of an inner hurt: the force and *substance* are Lucy's own. The term "incubus," with its associations of sexuality and mental disturbance, draws together the arenas of physical and mental life. In nineteenth-century psychological usage, incubus had become synonymous with nightmare. In a passage noted by Patrick Brontë in his *Domestic Medicine,* Robert Macnish observed, in *The Philosophy of Sleep,* that it was possible to suffer nightmare while awake and in "perfect possession of [the] faculties." Macnish records that he had "undergone the greatest tortures, being haunted by spectres, hags, and every sort of phantom—having, at the same time, a full consciousness that I was labouring under incubus, and that all the terrifying objects around me were the creations of my own brain." Brontë takes this idea of waking nightmare, or incubus, one stage further, giving it a literal embodiment in her fiction which defies attempts to demarcate the boundaries between "creations of the brain" and external forms.

Brontë offers, in **Villette,** a thorough materialization of the self. The construct "Lucy" is not a unified mental entity, located within a physiological frame, but rather a continuous process which extends beyond the confines of the flesh. Lucy's entire mode of self-articulation breaks down the hierarchy of outer and inner life upon which definitions of the "Real" (and sanity) depend. Her description of the death of Hope, for instance, parallels that of the literal burial of the letters: "In the end I closed the eyes of my dead, covered its face, and composed its limbs with great calm." The burial itself is figured as the wrapping of grief in a "winding-sheet." Later, as Lucy pauses beside the grave, she recalls "the passage of feeling therein buried." Metaphor has become inoperable: it functions, as Lucy's text makes clear, only if the speaker endorses normative social demarcations between different states. Thus the classrooms which initially only "seem" to Lucy to be like jails quickly become "filled with spectral and intolerable memories, laid miserable amongst their straw and their manacles." The controlling distance of "seems" is collapsed, as "memories," normally restricted to the realm of the mind, take on vivid physical form.

Lucy's intricate dramatizations of her feelings undermine traditional divisions between external social process and inner mental life, revealing their fictional status. Her tale of Jael, Sisera, and Heber, for example, simultaneously portrays physiological pain, psychological conflict, and the social drama of repression. Speaking of her desire to be drawn out of her present existence, Lucy observes:

> This longing, and all of a similar kind, it was necessary to knock on the head; which I did, figuratively, after the manner of Jael to Sisera, driving a nail through their temples. Unlike Sisera, they did not die: they were but transiently stunned, and at intervals would turn on the nail with a rebellious wrench; then did the temples bleed, and the brain thrill to its core.

The distinction between figural and literal quickly fades, as the inner psychic drama develops, the the rebellious desires themselves perpetuate their torture, in a description which captures the physiological and psychological experience of socially inflicted repression (the term "thrill" carried the medically precise meaning, in the mid-nineteenth century, of "vibratory movement, resonance, or murmur").

The famous account of Lucy's opiate-induced wanderings into the night landscape of Villette also dissolves the divisions between inner and outer realms, as social experience now takes on the qualities of mental life, defying the normal boundaries of time and space. Amidst the physical forms of Cleopatra's Egypt, Lucy witnesses the figures of her inner thoughts parade before her eyes. Even here, however, where she seems most free from external social controls, she is still subject to fears of surveillance: she feels Dr. John's gaze "oppressing" her, seeming ready to grasp "my identity . . . between his never tyrannous, but always powerful hands." As dominant male, and doctor,

empowered by society to diagnose the inner movements of mind, and legislate on mental disease, Dr. John threatens Lucy's carefully nurtured sense of self. Identity, as Brontë has shown throughout **Villette,** is not a given, but rather a tenuous process of negotiation between the subject and surrounding social forces.

The opposition to male materialism, voiced by Lucy in her confrontation with medical authority, gives dramatic expression to the interrogation of male constructions of the female psyche which underpins the narrative form of **Villette.** In seeking to avoid the surveillance of religious, educational and medical figures, trying to render herself illegible, Lucy attempts to assume control over the processes of her own self-definition. Yet her narrative, as I have argued, reveals a clear internalization of the categories and terms of contemporary medical psychology. Lucy employs physiological explanations of mental life and appropriates to herself theories of a female predisposition to neurosis and monomania. In creating the autobiography of her troubled heroine, whose commitment to evasion and displacement is articulated in the very title of her book, Brontë explores both the social implications of contemporary psychological theory and its inner consequences. The form of her account, with its dissolution of divisions between inner psychological life and the material social world, suggests an alternative vision—one that challenges the normative psychological vision implicit in male definitions of the "Real." (pp. 313-32)

> *Sally Shuttleworth, " 'The Surveillance of a Sleepless Eye': The Constitution of Neurosis in 'Villette',"* in One Culture: Essays in Science and Literature, *edited by George Levine, The University of Wisconsin Press, 1987, pp. 313-35.*

Robert M. Polhemus   (essay date 1990)

[*Polhemus is an American educator and critic who has described his work as an investigation into the "relationship between the rise and flourishing of the novel and the search and need for areas of secular faith to replace orthodox faith." In the following excerpt, he discusses Brontë's treatment of love and erotic longing in* Villette.]

In **Villette,** Polly Home de Bassompierre quotes from Schiller: "Oh, Holy One, call back your child, I have known earthly happiness, I have lived and loved!" To Lucy Snowe, the first-person narrator, she then muses: "Lived and loved!. . . is that the summit of earthly happiness, the end of life—to love? I don't think it is. It may be the extreme of mortal misery, it may be sheer waste of time, and fruitless torture of feeling. If Schiller had said to *be* loved—he might have come nearer the truth. Is not that another thing, Lucy, to be loved?" "I suppose it may be," says Lucy, in her characteristically repressive mode, "but why consider the subject? . . . we will not talk about love." But she will write about it—in fact, about little else.

This dialogue gets to the crux of the novel and expresses the need that made love a nineteenth-century faith despite its ravages. The problematic relationship between love and the power of expression, between desire and repression, between love and identity, love and the sacred, love and the novel, all figure throughout the book. The repressive, enchanting "holy one" is the erotic god as well as the Christian God, and *Villette* shows as well as any text the continuing, oscillating displacement between the one and the other in nineteenth-century sensibility. Charlotte Brontë knew all the arguments against romantic love—they lived in her nerves—but she imagines it as a necessity. The holy trinity of her being, like Lucy Snowe's, consists of love, Christian faith, and writing; and though the parts are finally inseparable, the greatest of these is love. Without erotic emotion, there is no faith and no lasting word of God.

The controversial logic of *Villette* says that the self, until it is loved, lacks definition, reality, and voice; only by feeling love from another or being in love can the personality take form in the world. Only love can repress the power of death and bring the word that gives sanctity to being. "You're nobody," goes the song, "until somebody loves you." You're also nobody if you do not find a means to express love.

Charlotte Brontë's sorrowful, wonderfully original, but demanding novel is as suffused with desire as *Wuthering Heights* and just as important a testament of love and erotic history. *Villette,* however, is the most inward and Protestant of fictions. Unlike the flamboyant *Wuthering Heights,* it avoids violent outbursts of passion or ecstatic dialogue. It has inspired no songs, operas, or movies; it has no witty, lively heroine like Elizabeth Bennet, no self-dramatizing fireball like Catherine Earnshaw, no image of beauty and sacrifice like Lucy Ashton. Instead it features neurotic Lucy Snowe who lacks beauty, charm, health, wealth, and family. Shabbily genteel, she is one of those nineteenth-century "relative creatures," women fated to flutter on the periphery of middle-class life and notice. Lucy must work as a paid lady's companion, a governess, a school teacher and school keeper. What have such marginal, apparently self-effacing people to do with love? Brontë, who once *was* such a creature, tries to render a story that will make readers know and care. Her unconventional heroine's repressed mien and emotional displacement hide a monomaniacal lovesickness. Love is to Lucy as money is to a pauper: something whose absence and need define her. The condition of her life is erotic hysteria and what she calls "heart-poverty."

Villette is as somber and uncompromising as a Samuel Beckett novel—*love* "how it is," not "as you like it." Brontë, like Beckett, insists on the terrible, drab compromises and the compulsive fictionalizing that the hunger for love foists on people. She questions erotic faith, even while she subscribes to it. Charlotte Brontë is a Calvinist of the heart. Some are saved and some are damned on earth by love, and erotic providence and its signs show everywhere. On the one hand, the novel deflates romantic illusions about some one-and-only, Mr.-or-Miss-Right kind of love coming beautifully along; but on the other, no novel more insistently slashes away at the opposite sentimentality, the naive who-needs-*them,* I-can-make-it-on-my-own school of sublimation and pseudopragmatism. In its bitterness and honesty, *Villette* pushes readers to focus on just what

they seldom want to face, especially in times when the ideologies of quantification, individualism, and equality flourish: namely, the inevitably demeaning conditions of dependency—the radical imperfections and insufficiencies both in themselves and in those they love that make love so imperative, fragile, and death-haunted.

As love becomes faith, Scripture feeds the Novel. "Many waters cannot quench love," says the Bible, "neither can the floods drown it" (Song of Solomon, 8:7). Charlotte Brontë's imagination takes those canonical words and forms from them her controlling imagery and her narrative of being in love. The intention of the text is to reconcile human love and Christian faith; but in *Villette,* as in *Jane Eyre,* faith in love both conflicts and fuses with Christian calling. This novel of religious yearning reads like a *Pilgrim's Progress* of Victorian love. Charlotte, proudly Protestant and much more orthodox than Emily, steeps her book and her protagonist-narrator Lucy Snowe in the language, typology, and cadence of the Bible, religious tracts, sermons, confessional narratives, and moral testimony, but she uses the tone and forms of religious writing to explore erotic faith. She also uses personal erotic experience to breathe life into these old forms of Christian testament.

Doubt and strain permeate the text: if faith, hope, and charity are to have a chance in hearts and in the world, then Christian idealism must blend with erotic love; but Jehovah and the god of love may not be reconcilable. The dilemma Charlotte Brontë faced was awful: How do you keep erotic longing and faith from being a curse to some poor hapless souls and bodies, as Christian belief is to those who believe themselves damnable? *Villette* struggles with that predicament.

Everything in it exists in a double context: Christian and erotic. It is no accident, for example, that the first man Lucy loves has the same name as the herald of faith, John the Baptist, or that her true lover and savior, whose epistles from afar inspire her, is called Paul Emanuel. Moving through Lucy's text is like traveling through some land whose people and ethos are shaped by the accretion of two powerful religions. Her narrative needs to be read like a passage from Revelations, an evangelical autobiography, and a Freudian case history all in one.

The novel's meaning and structure may be complex, but the basic story is simple. Lucy Snowe, pathetic ugly duckling, suffers many trials, including an unrequited love for the handsome Dr. John. By the end, however, at a boarding school in the mythical foreign city of Villette, she wins the love of a fellow teacher, a good, if flawed, man, Paul Emanuel. Through their faith in one another, she achieves both vocational success—a career as head of her own school—and the power of imaginative expression. Though it seems clear that Paul dies at sea before they can be married, Lucy finds the strength to articulate her vision of the world out of her experience of being in love and being loved. The shadow of death and loss, however, chills even requited love. She tells the chronological story of her life only up to the time she comes to possess love, and then stops. Even though the "first person" who sets down this account refers to herself as a white-haired older woman, she tells nothing of the thirty years or more between the ocean storm that presumably drowned Paul and the time of writing. *Villette* is not the story of a life, but the story of love and its inscription.

The novel, in its images of love life, raises bitter questions. If love makes life worth living and a person cannot bloom without it, what then is an unattractive, unloved, and apparently unlovable woman to do? *Villette* offers no solution except to pursue and imagine love in a way that makes it possible to go on living, and there is no guarantee that the pursuit will bring anything except a renewal of suffering. Lucy Snowe must follow both her erotic and her professional vocation. Working hard, aspiring morally, fighting for good in the immediate circumstances of life are for Charlotte Brontë ways of bettering the world and the self, gaining esteem and self-respect, and thus possibly making oneself lovable. Another tactic is to repress and discipline hopeless erotic desire, so that the deflected energy can find new possibilities for love and make one's inner life glow with enchantment—the kind of enchantment that can turn disparate material into art and, as happens in *Villette,* a frog into a prince. Lucy has to undergo the kind of humiliating ritual that eros usually requires: she has to switch her love from a man who loves someone else to one who can love her. And then she has to try to preserve that love when physically it no longer exists. If you can't be with the one you love—to paraphrase the modern lyric—then find a way to love the one you're with (even if you can only be with that one through the power of imagination and art).

Equivocal Thackeray, sincere admirer and cruel patronizer of Charlotte Brontë, wrote [in a letter dated 4 April 1853], "That's a plaguy book, that *Villette.* How clever it is! and how I don't like the heroine. . . . " That is just the point. The heroine is not a type who can gain easily the liking of men on which women's life and fate so much depend. In a letter to a young woman, Thackeray set out, with nasty, sexist shrewdness, a great problem of the author and Lucy—and the whole age:

> The poor little woman of genius! the fiery eager brave tremulous homely-faced creature! I can read a great deal of her life as I fancy her in her book, and see that rather than have fame, rather than any other earthly good or mayhap heavenly one she wants some Tomkins or another to love her and be in love with. But you see she is a little bit of a creature without a penny worth of good looks, . . . and no Tomkins will come. You girls with pretty faces . . . will get dozens of young fellows fluttering about you—whereas here is one genius, a noble heart longing to mate itself and destined to wither away into old maidenhood with no chance to fulfil the burning desire.

Though a Tomkins (Arthur Nicholls, her father's curate) afterwards *did* dismally come, Thackeray rightly sensed that the book grew out of Charlotte Brontë's thwarted desire for love.

She suffered from her hopeless love for Monsieur Héger and made the novel out of her life. Héger was her teacher and the proprietor, with his wife, of the school she and Emily attended in Brussels to prepare themselves to teach, to which she returned alone, and from which she had to leave in sorrow and mental confusion, forced out by Madame Héger and an impossible situation. This love and the agony of both knowing and trying to deny that it was obsessive, humiliating, unrequited, and morally wrong—and that she was condemned to go on fantasizing about it in her loneliness—shaped her mind and art for the rest of her life.

Other men and experiences fed into the eroticism of the novel. Charlotte seems to have fallen in unrequited, if not all-consuming, love with her publisher, George Smith, a "prototype" of Dr. John. (She displaced the rejection of love from the Héger figure to the Smith figure, and that transferral indicates, among many other things, just how excruciatingly difficult and shameful it can be to imagine that the person you love most passionately—the love of your life—really does not love or want you. Brontë can render John's rejection, and she can drown Paul, but she cannot write that Paul would not find her lovable.) Also she turned down a proposal of marriage—à la Paul's—from ugly little James Taylor, Smith's partner, on his way out to India for five years. And behind these unconsummated relationships lay the kingdom of death which the world, taking her family one by one, showed itself to be.

Lucy Snowe writes about providence—erotic providence. For her, erotic providence is world, life, and destiny ordered and given meaning by the desire for human love; and the force of love and desire is what allows her to regard Divine Providence with stoic faith. Lucy is one of the great case studies in the fiction of repression, and what she represses is whatever threatens to close off or delimit the working of a mystical providence. She undertakes to do through her text what religion and religious institutions try to do: to repress death, control desire, and show that individual life matters. Her first-person narration—the first-person world—is the creation of providential erotic desire, and she represses what would separate her perception from the creative energy of that desire.

This repression works both negatively and positively. When, loveless, she equates the idea of self with hopeless desire, then she suppresses her personality and memory. Her repression, however, though it makes her an unreliable narrator, leads her to project her frustrated desire and patterns of imagination everywhere. She fears the pain of exposure, but she also fears being cut off and alienated from the outside world. The tension disorients her being. In her prose and psychology, she displaces, transfers, and fuses her self into other characters, objects, places, sights, nature, and even providence itself. The overriding pattern—a pattern, I need hardly say, we find in the life of her author—is to sublimate desire into language.

Disorientation: Villette, the little city of competing faiths, the capital of a small Low Country, lies to the east of England and within the fluid boundaries of Lucy's mind, an erotic New Jerusalem where the walls between self and not-self quietly come tumbling down. Inner and outer life have no fixed demarcation in *Villette.* Lucy's repression helps create the erotic enchantment of her vision and works to idealize love or preserve the possibility of forming and holding onto such an idealization. It also helps to blend her libidinous desire into her labor (including her narrative) and her vocational ambitions. The book therefore presents a small-scale version of the way Victorian sexual repression was ideally supposed to work in large: faith in love would be preserved and great quantities of energy would flow into good and constructive works.

Repression, displacement, and enchantment characterize *Villette,* where nothing can be taken at face value because all appears through Lucy's words and eye. The novel reads like the testimony of a voyeur: deflected, displaced desire, skewed self-regard, and passion eroticize everything. A concert, a painting, a play, an actress performing, clothing, a king—all are tinged, framed, and inscribed with personal meaning by a love-hungry mind. Erotic desire expropriates anything—art, architecture, public ceremony—to tell its tale. And almost everything magically connects, as in a land of pure enchantment, which Villette is. The characters who live in England are sure to show up years later in Villette; the Dr. John who saves her and who tends the sick at the girls' school is sure to be the Graham Bretton of the opening, and so on. This is a world of romance ordered and composed by Eros, for that is how Brontë imagines Lucy's ordering and composition of her text. (pp. 108-13)

To be enchanted is to be caught in a spell, and Lucy Snowe's story lies in the spell of writing that seeks to express love and repress death. That spell transfixes time, so that Lucy's narrative, though at first it may seem to move chronologically, is actually synchronous, like the hundred dormant years for Sleeping Beauty after the prince's kiss awakens her, or like our past when we recollect it. The

idea of enchantment, as in fairy tales, Vermeer's painting [*A Woman Standing at a Virginal*], or *Villette,* often features the absent figure of an awaited lover and stresses the power of love to overcome the threat of death. Charlotte Brontë, the last survivor of her siblings, kept learning all her short life the lesson that anything she loved or attached herself to would die or be denied her. In *Villette* she is trying to imagine—as Emily so differently does in *Wuthering Heights*—how and whether love could be stronger than death.

The novel is both progressive and circular. Time as well as emotion and experience is repressed and displaced. For example, we find the most probable allusion to Lucy's state of mind, life, and faith as an older woman not at the end, but near the beginning in her account of Miss Marchmont; and this report comes immediately after Lucy has displaced the repressed emotion of her own traumatic childhood and apparent motherlessness by projecting it onto Polly Home, the only child we see in the novel. Thus in this "heretic narrative," we seem to have the essential beginning and end of Lucy's autobiography, but they take place in other characters' lives and almost before the story gets started. Not only does the action on the last page precede the setting down of the words on the first page—the usual convention of first-person narratives—but also the events, the images, the very language of the last chapter are necessary to understand and appreciate the novel from the beginning. Anyone trying to grasp the full significance and power of *Villette* comes eventually to see that it must, in effect, be read backwards as well as forwards.

Nothing does more to cast a singular spell over the novel than Lucy's fusion of past and present at the end and her

Haworth Parsonage, Brontë's residence from 1820 until her death in 1855.

refusal to tell Paul's fate directly or mention her own after his final voyage. In the last chapter, Paul, having engaged to marry her, must leave Villette to spend three years working in the Caribbean. Anxious for his return, Lucy, when his time is up, moves her prose from past tense to present, her eager memory making all contemporaneous. Brontë imagines her writing these pregnant words: "I thought I loved him when he went away; I love him now in another degree; he is more my own." On the last two pages she describes, in vivid present tense, the killer storm that strews wrecks and corpses, but she does not say explicitly that Emanuel drowned.

We need to look carefully at the book's penultimate paragraph: "Here pause: pause at once. There is enough said. Trouble no quiet, kind heart; leave sunny imaginations hope. Let it be theirs to conceive the delight of joy born again fresh out of great terror, the rapture of rescue from peril, the wondrous reprieve from dread, the fruition of return. Let them picture union and a happy succeeding life."

This is complex, ambivalent prose. Brontë plays with "the happy ending," that sentimental heaven of popular novels. Sardonically, she edges near parody of the conventional courtship novel which, after all, narrates the match of lovers, but then stops the story before they have to live together. With a bitter twist, she makes explicit the void that is implicit, for example, in Austen. But the paragraph also fuses the language and imagery of love with that of Christian faith. It can be read as an orthodox vision of immortality and resurrection as well as a rosy romantic ending. Lucy's wish for those "sunny imaginations" accords nicely with Christian hope and doctrine. Her narrative and experience cast doubt on the efficacy of institutional faith, but the irony and weight of the passage are demeaned only if we think of those "sunny imaginations" belonging to mere sentimentalists who cannot face a mortal fact. These sunny ones can also be seen as the conventionally faithful. Charlotte Brontë struggles against despair by trying to imagine a blend of traditional and erotic faith that would avoid the deceptions of each, but she also sees the cant of mush-minded optimism.

Lucy Snowe is not "sunny." She has the imagination of moonlight—romantic, melancholy, slightly distorting, misty, and "loony"—a light in shadows and darkness, a light depending upon a nineteenth-century womanly process of visionary experience and reflection. ("Imagination," she reports, showed her "a moon supreme, in an element deep and splendid.") We know that Brontë had planned to kill Paul, but her father wanted a happy ending, and we know that she simply could not imagine a happy marriage for Lucy without distorting her sense of truth. The main point, however, about the climax is surely the repression itself. Everything that has come before is connected to her radical strategy of avoiding closure.

Muting the fate of the man and the relationship shows both the extraordinary reticence and the willpower of Brontë and her narrator. For all we know from the text, Lucy Snowe lives her life—a life that, from the only evidence she gives, has been devoted to love—as a virgin, never knowing the intimacy of the flesh. The final pages confirm as her lasting reality her idealization of love: "I

love him now in another degree; he is more my own." Karen Chase [in her *Eros and Psyche*] calls this process "the lover denied, the love affirmed," and it shows the reason for the prevalence and force of erotic faith. In *Villette*'s metamorphosis of a male lover into a woman's spiritual love, the novelist and the novel show how idealizing love is not some abstract, precious phenomenon but action that grows out of desperate need and deprivation. "I love him . . . in another degree; he is more my own": I find, in the oddly brave repression of what might be called *carnal knowledge*—in order that an erotic present can be possessed lastingly in words and memory—the full religious aspiration and power of the erotic imagination. By idealizing romantic love and suspending questions about its physical, time-doomed nature, many Victorians and others have sought to transcend the finitude of particular flesh and affections and make of love an open-ended creed and comfort.

The prose of Lucy's key paragraph both does and does not cede authority: it gives direct responsibilities to the readers to define themselves, but it wraps itself proudly—even arrogantly—in mystery, and glorifies the writer and writing. It suppresses material fact and, what is more, death. Paul's letters, she tells us in this last chapter, were the "living water" that sustained her life, the spring of her energy: "He sat down, he took pen and paper, because he loved Lucy and had much to say to her." As she moves to the end, she is reciprocating, trying to inscribe herself with him in an epitaphic text, and to make their love live in narrative.

Lucy offers words that carry many meanings and connotations, some of them contradictory. That paragraph says that some lucky people do not know the deadly unfairness and sorrow of life, and that telling them would do no good. It says that true believers can imagine that no matter what the tragedy of earthly life, they will rejoin their loved ones and God in eternal life. It implies both that love might create an enchanted world where there is no death and that such belief is Pollyannish. It says that by refusing, in narrative, to make death the end of things, the writer might throw emphasis on life and preserve it through memory. It says also that as the world seems to promise intimacy, but then withholds it, so I, Lucy Snowe, shall withhold the intimacy I have implicitly promised you readers. And what it unmistakably says to careful readers is that what is here denied or omitted through repression here breaks through elsewhere, that is, *what I don't say now, you will find coloring what I have written before.* (pp. 114-17)

The book begins, as it ends, with passive-aggressive reserve. The pre-*Villette* chapters stand as an overture to all that follows, but we cannot realize their art and meaning until the end. Lucy, already in her fourteenth year, says nothing about her family and antecedents. Childhood, a kind of perverse Eden in *Wuthering Heights* and a nightmare in *Jane Eyre,* does not exist in Lucy's history, except by indirection as an ominously silent chasm. In the first chapter, at her godmother's, Lucy tells about the arrival of little Polly Home, the unhappy marriage of Polly's parents, and the disgraceful history of Polly's mother, but gives not a line about her own parentage or early life. Polly, at the start and throughout the text, usurps Lucy's place in the affections of the Brettons—mother and, especially, son—but Lucy also projects onto Polly, as she does with other characters to come, her own repressed desires and concerns. Let me repeat, because the text's implicit claim for the power of love and libido to determine perception (and, in novels, the first-person point of view) lies in this fact: *There is no absolute sense of a discrete, objective other who can be known and spoken of outside of the observer's conscious or unconscious erotic desire. When we talk of others, we talk of ourselves and what we want and love; we can't help it.*

Lucy's vision oscillates; other figures—Polly for example—reflect both projections of her self and detached images of the not-self. Right from the start, Polly's grief over separation from her father and her role as the one who alienates affection from Lucy look like reenactments by Lucy from her own "unspeakable" childhood. The whole episode of Polly in the first three chapters smacks of a screen memory for a sensitive girl traumatized by the arrival of a younger sibling. Lucy swings wildly between expressing strong hostility to others, especially females, and vicariously identifying with them—two basic, common strategies in sibling relationships. René Girard's general theory of mimetic desire as the heart of erotic love—the idea that love is mediated and we love what another loves—finds good grounds of support both in the relationship of Lucy and Polly and in the existence of sibling rivalry and incestuous impulses that comprise for us original, if not eternal, triangles.

For much of the novel, Polly-Paulina is what Lucy would like to be, but is not. To understand Lucy, her narrative, and love in **Villette,** we need to watch her watching Polly: "I, Lucy Snowe, plead guiltless of that curse, an overheated and discursive imagination [just what *does* characterize her]; but whenever . . . I found her seated in a corner alone . . . that room seemed to me not inhabited, but haunted." Lucy is herself possessed by the spirits of others, and through Polly she imagines *herself.* "Papa!" cries the small girl when her father goes off: "It was low and long; a sort of 'Why hast thou forsaken me?' . . . I perceived she endured agony. She went through, in that brief interval of her infant life, emotions such as some never feel; it was in her constitution. . . . I, Lucy Snowe, was calm. The little creature . . . contended with an intolerable feeling; and, ere long, in some degree, repressed it." We cannot tell the watcher from the sufferer here. Lucy's daring, almost blasphemous words tie religion and God to a specific need—and lack—of human love; they show her fascination with martyrdom and sacrifice; they feature repression, and they repeat her formulaic denial of emotion, the defense mechanism that casts its dislocating spell over the text.

Lucy then gives a moving account of Polly's transferred love for sixteen-year-old Graham Bretton, one of the few places in literature where we find expressed with delicacy the common, but rarely discussed, passion of a young child's falling in love with an older person. But what Lucy does not report until many years later is that she too at that time was in love with Graham—that the whole story, in fact, starts with her being in love and that she provoked and mediated Polly's love. Ten years after, in Villette, Lucy recognizes in Dr. John's house "a portrait."

> It seemed a youth of sixteen. . . . Any romantic little school-girl might almost have loved it in its frame. . . . Ah! that portrait used to hang in the breakfast-room . . . : somewhat too high, as I thought. I well remember how I used to mount a music-stool for the purpose of unhooking it, holding it in my hand, and searching into those bonny wells of eyes, whose glance under their hazel lashes seemed like a pencilled laugh. . . . I hardly believed fancy could improve on the curve of that mouth, or of the chin; even *my* ignorance knew that both were beautiful. . . . Once, by way of test, I took little Missy Home, and, lifting her in my arms, told her to look at the picture.
>
> "Do you like it, Polly?" I asked. She never answered, but gazed long, and at last a darkness went trembling through her sensitive eyes, as she said, "Put me down." So I put her down, saying to myself: "The child feels it too."

Lucy, the writer of narrative, like Brontë, begins by showing another her love, and she keeps on, even if she tells her story by reflections. Being in love frames her life. This would-be disdainer of emotionalism, in fact, was mooning over Graham's picture like any other "romantic schoolgirl." She offers readers the vision of her life and desire almost in the same way as she offers the vision of her love to Polly. The image of the older girl holding the younger up, watching her reaction, teaching her—by fanning mimetic desire—to love the same person she does, suggests the unpredictable wonder in love and the forms it takes. Such a scene deflates that cynical *mot* of La Rochefoucauld, "People would never fall in love, if they had not been told about it," because it says that to be human *is* to tell people of love, by word, deed, gesture, and art. It makes a good symbol not only for what Brontë does in **Villette,** but for what distinguished Victorian fiction did so well: namely, to hold unawakened erotic nature up to a mirroring art of desire.

If Polly is Lucy's surrogate as a child, Miss Marchmont, the "maiden lady" Lucy tends for two claustrophobic years before going to Villette, previews her later life. The chapter "Miss Marchmont" rereads like an abstract of the plot, the tone, the matter and manner of the book. Marchmont dies, but on the night of her death, she tells Lucy of her tragic love. By the end of the book, we see that her experience is completely fused with Lucy's text and fate. Nearly all the radiating symbols and images by which Brontë organizes the novel show up first in Marchmont's tale: "I . . . feel," says she, telling of the night her lover died, "the . . . firelight warming me, playing on my silk dress, and . . . showing me my own young figure in a glass. I see the moon of a calm winter night, float full, clear and cold, over . . . the silvered turf of my grounds. . . . The flames had died in the fire, but it was a bright mass yet; the moon was mounting high, but she was still visible from the lattice." We have in these lines the moon, that shining satellite—symbol of fertility, flow, imagination, feminine being, and bonding, and more particularly, symbol of Lucy, light bringer in the night. We have also frozen water, clothes, images of fashion, fire—representing passion and love—and the reflecting mirror and the lattice, devices for looking and spying. The prose gives us in imagistic form the very name of Lucy Snowe and it tells us that her identity may be projected through the entire text.

Of her long-dead lover, Marchmont tells Lucy, "[I]f few women have suffered as I did in his loss, few have enjoyed what I did in his love." Nearing death, she says, in words that Lucy will later echo, "I can say with sincerity, what I never tried to say before—Inscrutable God, Thy will be done! And at this moment I can believe that death will restore me to Frank. I never believed it till now."

Erotic faith is here regenerating Christian faith. That is Charlotte Brontë's project in the novel. Like her sister Emily, she makes the idea of a desirable heaven depend on the strength and endurance of individual human love. But Marchmont ends on a typical nineteenth-century note of doubt: "You see I still think of Frank more than of God; and unless it be counted that in thus loving the creature so much, so long, and so exclusively, I have not at least blasphemed the Creator, small is my chance of salvation. What do you think, Lucy, of these things? Be my chaplain and tell me." In other words, can God and Eros be reconciled? The tension that exists between them, the feeling that "salvation" is impossible without both, the hope and doubt that both can bring light within the single soul— that is what Marchmont is articulating, what Lucy is projecting into her, and what Charlotte Brontë is rendering. To comprehend the function and enterprise of the nineteenth-century novel we must take these words of this overture to *Villette* seriously: the writer of the text—the new scripture—is to be the chaplain of erotic faith, and significantly here the chaplain, that is, "one appointed to conduct religious services for a society," is a woman.

Lucy says she "had no words" then; but later, near the end, when her own life parallels Marchmont's, she does. Speaking of God's blessing on the lucky, Lucy turns to her own misfortune and takes up both her old mentor's questioning of God's motives and her resigned faith ("Thy will be done!"). Rhetorically Lucy asserts the orthodox creed:

> His will be done, as done it surely will be, whether we humble ourselves to resignation or not. The impulse of creation forwards it. . . . Proof of a life to come must be given. In fire and in blood, if needful, must that proof be written. . . . In fire and in blood does it cross our own experience. . . . Pilgrims and brother mourners, join in friendly company. Dark through the wilderness of this world stretches the way for most of us: . . . be our cross our banner. . . . Let us . . . keep the faith, reliant in the issue to come off more than conquerors: "Art thou not form everlasting mine Holy One? WE SHALL NOT DIE!"

Faith means a way of preserving life. Though this Christian exhortation verges on pietistic rant (Charlotte Chaplain?), few who consider the agony out of which Lucy writes or the reality of Brontë's own experience will fail to find it moving. With all of her siblings dead and her love

life at nil, the author must have felt proud to write such words and hopeful that they could touch her readers. As for Lucy, she has just told the life story of Polly and her old love Dr. John, who—she quickly summarizes—live a full and happy life with many children, much love, and all the good things that the world can offer. And she is about to inform us that her new love, Paul, is leaving Villette without declaring his love for her.

I want to stress two points:

1. God, in Lucy's sermon, is an author much like her; they both follow the same pattern. He brings to his creation fierce discipline which tests faith, generates mystery, and issues in a form of afterlife. The pattern of this Christian faith, like the pattern of erotic faith in her text, features repression and displacement, and offers a somber hope of undying enchantment.

2. Brontë immediately undercuts, even blasphemes, her onward-Christian-soldiers piece with an astounding juxtaposition. These words directly follow it: "On a Thursday morning we were all assembled in classe, waiting for the lesson of literature. The hour was come; we expected the master [Monsieur Paul]." "The lesson of literature" and "the master," the term of the faithful for Jesus, used just at this point and shortly after followed by other references to "M. Emanuel," casting him typologically as the awaited savior, intimate Lucy's true faith in love and show that she just cannot separate religion, writing, and love.

One of the primary images of the novel, the mysterious "ghost" nun who appears from time to time to Lucy and others, provides an apt symbol for love's impersonation of Christianity in the novel: "she" turns out to be de Hamal, the lover of the coquette Ginevra Fanshawe, in masquerade. . . . The nun's costume sums up a meaning that Brontë reiterates in passage after passage: love walks in the guise of religion; it takes over religious habits and vocabulary; it is life even if it takes the form of death; it moves with sacral aspect through the enchanted atmosphere of the novel. (pp. 119-23)

In *Villette,* writing and love feed into each other, even become interchangeable. Faith must be legible. Love becomes the occasion for writing, and letters have an important part in the story. To write with creative freedom and power you need love, but writing itself inspires love, and love generates imagination that makes faith possible.

The goal of a human being, as set forth in this novel and in much nineteenth-century thought, is to imagine, create, and live a love narrative. That is why the heroine must leave the church, lose all consciousness, and then awake in the house of her love, a place that, figuratively speaking, she never again leaves, though its owner changes. One project of Lucy Snowe's text is to transcribe a demystifying and then a remystifying of romantic love. We see that she can love more than one man, that she can switch her passion from a girl's notion of a romantic paragon to a man she knows has obvious faults, and that such a man's love can animate her creative spirit. But before she can be refreshed by love, she first must come to acknowledge that she feels it and can value it. John prepares the way for Emanuel.

Letters, for Lucy, are fetishes of love. Ink is the blood of her erotic life and faith. The free and open correspondence between Paul and herself in the final chapter is what enables her to survive, and the letter she gets from Dr. John first gives her identity and hope because it tells her that someone she loves could actually care about her. She treats John's letters as if they were living beings, and when he stops writing her, she prepares a funeral and actually *buries* them. No act could better symbolize the powerful erotic charge that letters carried for the Victorians or what they meant historically to women.

When Lucy meditates on how she might reply to a letter she thinks, "[W]here the bodily presence is weak and the speech contemptible, surely there cannot be error in making written language the medium of better utterance than faltering lips can achieve?" Look at the implications of that sentence: Writing might allow a despised, plain woman to equal or better a privileged man's force of expression. It might compensate for all kinds of physical and social inferiority through genius, and it might be a way of making one's vision last.

Lucy's repression must have an end, in the sense of both a finish and an aim. Her self-censor leads her to one of her most perverse acts. Thrilled by Dr. John's letter, she writes him back, pouring out her "sincere heart." If anything is to come of her love, this is her opportunity. But she tells us then that "Reason" makes her "snatch the full sheets, read, sneer, erase, tear up, re-write, fold, seal, direct, and send a terse, curt missive of a page. She did right." The monosyllabic diction and blunt syntax hammer out these self-mutilating blows to the heart and show the terrible split in Lucy. Being in love for her means, as it often did for nineteenth-century women, both a striving for intimacy and a withholding of intimacy for fear that the dignity and fragile selfhood that signs of affection nurture would be swamped in a sea of rejection. Lucy's repressive reason, in Brontë's prose, bludgeons any hope of a serious romance with Dr. John. The absence of the letter of love kills the spirit.

Repression's end comes in the outpouring of her heart to Paul in their last meetings, in the freedom of their letters, and in the narrative she writes. What Lucy calls "Reason" is, she says, "envenomed as a step-mother [the simile offers a clue to her early sorrow and the repression of her childhood]. If I have obeyed her it has chiefly been with the obedience of fear, not of love." Her imagination, however, eventually flourishes, making even Belgium fascinating and the experience of a drab teacher in an undistinguished school wondrous. But this imagination depends on some requited love if it is to become what Lucy calls "intercommunion," the mysterious rite of inspired communication with others by the "kindling" word.

Strangely, the horrible repression by "Reason" works, and the eerily disciplined will that makes her tear up and bury precious letters brings her to conquer romantic myth and win the rational love of Paul Emanuel. But how flat that sounds. The full human and historical relevance of this novel will only come through if we try to understand the genuine hunger signified in the term *love-starved*. "Heart-poverty" means what it says: an absence of sustenance

that can destroy well-being as surely as the penury to which it so often is related. To the pitiful little epistolary tomb, Lucy speaks final words that bring home again the awful power of erotic providence. "Good night, Dr. John; you are good, you are beautiful; but you are not mine." To subsist, this woman Lucy Snowe needs, as the imagery specifically tells us, the coin of reciprocal love: "The love born of beauty was not mine; I had nothing in common with it: . . . but another love, venturing diffidently into life after long acquaintance, furnace-tried by pain, stamped by constancy, consolidated by affection's pure and durable alloy, submitted by intellect to intellect's own tests, . . . this Love that laughed at Passion, . . . in *this* Love I had a vested interest." That is the language of erotic economics. She is describing the indispensable *exchange* of love—love that the imagination must once more somehow enrich. Lucy fits Paul typologically into her religious framework as a miraculous Christian agent of salvation (e.g., "Emanuel," "He was come"; "Be ready for me"; "He was my king"; her "Pauline" epistle), but as a *human* savior.

Villette presents a revealing analogy between the structure of erotic faith and Christianity. Brontë shows us the force of love in Lucy's world, that love made manifest in the flesh of Paul, and the power of erotic imagination to inscribe itself and make love live in her narrative. That trinity parallels the popularly understood Christian trinity of nineteenth-century Protestant sensibility: God the immanent ruler of all things; Christ, divinity in the form of human flesh; and Scripture, the Holy Word of God and manifestation of the Holy Ghost. In the phantasmagoric, psychedelic night journey through Villette's illuminated park (chs. 38, 39), Lucy finds her Holy Ghost, "Imagination": "With scorn she looked on Matter, her mate—. . . . 'this night I will have *my* will. . . . Look forth and view the night!' was her cry." The personification of imagination not only tells us that there is no disjunction here between Lucy's inner and outer life, no clear divisions between what exists and what she perceives; it also shows her becoming conscious of the power that can translate matter to spirit through language—that can, in other words, achieve through the mode of writing her desire to transform an absent lover into present love. This power is religious, erotic, and narrative.

The narrative subordinates the forms of Christian belief and the religious conflict between Lucy and Paul to their relationship. Both Lucy and Paul come to choose love for one another over their respective Protestant and Roman Catholic convictions. Brontë sets out clearly their religious differences (see chap. 36, "The Apple of Discord") and then makes the subject of their last communication a belief in love so strong that it acquiesces in tolerance for the other's brand of Christianity and dismisses their conflict. Her scripture, therefore, imagines nothing less than a shift—a displacement—in the priority of faith from God and the interpretation of his will, to love. (pp. 129-31)

From the beginning, Brontë's rendering of love in *Villette* has been controversial, and Harriet Martineau's 1853 review [in the *Daily News;* 3 February] set out the issues for critical debate:

An atmosphere of pain hangs about the whole. . . . All the female characters, in all their thoughts and lives, are full of one thing, or are regarded by the reader in the light of that one thought—love. . . . And so dominant is this idea—so incessant is the writer's tendency to describe the need of being loved, that the heroine . . . leaves the reader at last under the uncomfortable impression of her having either entertained a double love, or allowed one to supersede another without notification of the transition. It is not thus in real life. There are substantial, heartfelt interests for women of all ages, and under ordinary circumstance, quite apart from love.

A split between these two friends was inevitable, given their different allegiances. A dedicated novelist for whom writing is a sacred vocation must sometimes represent erotics otherwise than would a person whose ruling passion is to lead a broad political movement and advocate directly the betterment of women's lives. From the Brontë sisters' perspective, like that of so many modern writers, righteous priority to even the best of causes risks promoting art that can become the equivalent of that deceiving *La vie d'une femme:* simplistic, constricting work inspired by, and serving doctrinaire views of, political and moral correctness—views that, of course, may be perfectly valid.

Exactly what Martineau objects to—that awful telling of the raw need for love and the compulsive nature of erotic desire as it shapes perception—is what burns *Villette* into memory. People who have known sufficient requited love may plausibly claim that it is overrated, as prosperous people may claim that money can't buy happiness. Lucy Snowe, writing her narrative, was not such a figure.

In a preface to *Villette* the novelist Mary Ward, at the end of the nineteenth century, explained how and why, for women, the subject matter of love, which later would seem to many a dependency drug, could mean the chance for literary achievement and the opportunity to combine, in the novel, feminine religious insight and feeling with feminist aspirations:

> What may be said to be the main secret, the central cause not only of her [Charlotte Brontë's] success, but, generally, of the success of women in fiction, during the present century? . . . As a rule, so far, women have been poets in and through the novel. . . . they are here among the recognised 'masters of those who know.' . . . For the one subject which they have eternally at command, which is interesting to all the world, and whereof large tracts are naturally and wholly their own, is the subject of love—love of many kinds indeed, but preeminently the love between man and woman. . . . The modern novel reflects the craving . . . for that feeling which expresses the heart's defiance of the facts which crush it, . . . and brings up, or seems to bring up, the secrets of the infinite.

Ward is describing the inner city of Villette, scene of expanding consciousness.

Harriet Martineau wrote to Charlotte, "I do not like the love, either the kind or degree of it; and its prevalence in the book." Brontë replied, "I know what love is as I understand it; and if man or woman should be ashamed of feeling such love, then is there nothing right, noble, faithful, truthful, unselfish in this earth, as I comprehend rectitude, nobleness, fidelity, truth, and disinterestedness—Yours sincerely—To differ from you gives me keen pain." That is religious sentiment—pure and not so simple. She was trying to establish a faith that would be true to her experience. Erotic faith might not bring happiness, but it could offer a reason for being and an incarnation—an inscription—of meaning. It could make the flesh into word.

Brontë is imagining how, for a woman of religious feeling, a lover's vocation can merge with an artist's vocation—erotic faith with aesthetic faith. In *To the Lighthouse,* Virginia Woolf, deeply influenced by Charlotte Brontë, delves into the mind of the unmarried artist Lily Briscoe and, for me, nicely sums up the feeling and nature of love in *Villette:*

> [F]rom the dawn of time odes have been sung to love; wreaths heaped and roses; and if you asked nine people out of ten they would say they wanted nothing but this—love; while the women, judging from her own experience, would all the time be feeling, This is not what we want; there is nothing more tedious, puerile, and inhumane than this; yet it is also beautiful and necessary.

Charlotte Brontë, with her death-cursed family history, knew that erotic faith, like most religions, finally rests on the principle of sacrifice; and faith in the sacrificial effect of displaced love was her link to immortality. How else can we account for these heartfelt words in Lucy Snowe's narrative? "Proof of a life to come must be given. In fire and in blood, if needful, must that proof be *written*" (italics mine). (pp. 135-36)

> *Robert M. Polhemus, "Faithful Repression and Erotic Enchantment: Charlotte Brontë's 'Villette' (1853)," in his* Erotic Faith: Being in Love from Jane Austen to D. H. Lawrence, *The University of Chicago Press, 1990, pp. 108-36.*

FURTHER READING

Blake, Kathleen. *"Villette:* 'How Shall I Keep Well?' " In her *Love and the Woman Question in Victorian Literature,* pp. 56-75. Totowa, N.J.: Barnes & Noble, 1983.
  Discusses Lucy Snowe's self-definition as "loverless and inexpectant of love" in the context of the novel's themes of sexual repression.

Bledsoe, Robert. "Snow beneath Snow: A Reconsideration of the Virgin of *Villette.*" In *Gender and Literary Voice,* edited by Janet Todd, pp. 214-22. New York: Holmes & Meier, 1980.
  Warns readers of *Villette* against sympathizing with or admiring the independence of Lucy Snowe, claiming

that the character is "infinitely pitiable, but not lovable, not mature, and not triumphant."

Briganti, Chiara. "Charlotte Brontë's *Villette:* The History of Desire." *West Virginia University Philological Papers* 35 (1989): 8-20.
Suggests that the town Villette, and not the character Lucy Snowe, is the chief focus of the novel.

Burkhart, Charles. "The Nuns of *Villette.*" *The Victorian Newsletter* 44 (Fall 1973): 8-13.
Examines the stories about nuns in *Villette* for their relevance to an understanding of Lucy Snowe's sexual impulses.

Clark-Beattie, Rosemary. "Fables of Rebellion: Anti-Catholicism and the Structure of *Villette.*" *ELH* 53, No. 4 (Winter 1986): 821-47.
Exploration of Brontë's treatment of Catholicism as a form of "institutional tyranny" in *Villette.*

Colby, Robert A. "*Villette* and the Life of the Mind." *PMLA* LXXV, No. 4 (September 1960): 410-19.
Influential defense of *Villette* as Brontë's "most profound accomplishment." Colby highlights the depth and complexity of Lucy Snowe's character and champions the novel as a forerunner of literary depictions of the subconscious.

———. "*Villette:* Lucy Snowe and the Good Governess." In his *Fiction with a Purpose: Major and Minor Nineteenth-Century Novels,* pp. 178-211. Bloomington: Indiana University Press, 1967.
Views *Villette* as Brontë's "*Bildungsroman* of a writer."

Coursen, Herbert R., Jr. "Storm and Calm in *Villette.*" *Discourse* V, No. 3 (Summer 1962): 318-333.
Inquiry into actual and metaphorical storms in *Villette.*

Craik, W. A. "*Villette.*" In her *The Brontë Novels,* pp. 158-201. London: Methuen, 1968.
Favors the interpretation of the novel "as an interior study of an extraordinary personality."

Crosby, Christina. "Charlotte Brontë's Haunted Text." *Studies in English Literature, 1500-1900* 24, No. 4 (Autumn 1984): 701-15.
Interprets *Villette* as "both the compelling narrative of a woman's accession to her proper place and a text which continually displaces identities and definitions."

DeLamotte, Eugenia C. "*Villette:* Demystifying Women's Gothic." In her *Perils of the Night: A Feminist Study of Nineteenth-Century Gothic,* pp. 229-289. New York: Oxford University Press, 1990.
Argues that *Villette* contains an intensification of the Gothic conventions found in *Jane Eyre.*

Review of *Villette,* by Charlotte Brontë. *Dublin University Magazine* 42, No. 251 (November 1853): 612-15.
Favorable early notice.

Eagleton, Terry. "*Villette.*" In his *Myths of Power: A Marxist Study of the Brontës,* pp. 61-73. London: Macmillan Press, 1975.
Perceives *Villette* as a novel "jumpily unpredictable in its variations of hostility and approbation" in its treatment of bourgeois values.

Review of *Villette,* by Charlotte Brontë. *The Examiner,* No. 2,349 (5 February 1853): 84-5.
Favorable early notice.

Falconer, J. A. "*The Professor* and *Villette:* A Study of Development." *English Studies* 9, Nos. 1-6 (1927): 33-7.
Compares *Villette* to Brontë's first novel, and argues that *Villette* contains the maturer and more successful treatment of a teacher-pupil relationship.

Fleishman, Avrom. "*Villette:* Pilgrim of the Imagination." In his *Figures of Autobiography: The Language of Self-Writing in Victorian and Modern England,* pp. 219-34. Berkeley and Los Angeles: University of California Press, 1983.
Supports the position that Brontë created Lucy Snowe as a reflection of her own nature and character.

Freeman, Janet. "Looking on at Life: Objectivity and Intimacy in *Villette.*" *Philological Quarterly* 67, No. 4 (Fall 1988): 481-511.
Discusses *Villette* as a meditation on the opposition between observing and acting.

Gérin, Winifred. "Writing *Villette.*" In her *Charlotte Brontë: The Evolution of Genius,* pp. 486-512. London: Oxford University Press, 1967.
Biographical analysis arguing that "the true subject of *Villette* is . . . loneliness, the theme that most obsessed the writer's mind during the period—probably sixteen months in all—she was writing the book."

Gilbert, Sandra M. and Gubar, Susan. "The Buried Life of Lucy Snowe." In *The Madwoman in the Attic: The Woman Writer and the Nineteenth-Century Literary Imagination,* pp. 399-440. New Haven, Conn.: Yale University Press, 1979.
Influential feminist reading of *Villette.* Gilbert and Gubar provide a chapter-by-chapter examination of the novel, commenting on its treatment of love, its anti-Catholic sentiment, and its apparently misleading narrative style.

Goldfarb, Russell M. "Charlotte Brontë's *Villette.*" In his *Sexual Repression and Victorian Literature,* pp. 139-57. Lewisburg, Pa.: Bucknell University Press, 1970.
Contends that "Lucy Snowe is a sexually frigid young woman who learns to come to terms with her abnormal sexuality during the course of the novel."

Review of *Villette,* by Charlotte Brontë. *Graham's Magazine,* Philadelphia XLII, No. 5 (May 1853): 633-34.
Early review of *Villette* describing its principal theme as "the illustration of the idea that character is destiny, and what is called fate is really disposition."

Hawthorn, Jeremy. "No Room of One's Own: Charlotte Brontë's *Villette.*" In his *Multiple Personality and the Disintegration of Literary Character: From Oliver Goldsmith to Sylvia Plath,* pp. 73-83. New York: St. Martin's Press, 1983.
Attributes the novel's "obsessive concern for secrecy" to "the need for the powerless, educated woman to create an inner space in which to indulge repressed aspects of her personality, an inner space that performs the same function for a woman that the outer space of the work, and town, performs for a man."

Heilman, Robert B. "Tulip-Hood, Streaks, and Other Strange Bedfellows: Style in *Villette.*" *Studies in the Novel* 14, No. 3 (Fall 1982): 223-47.

Notes the influence of eighteenth-century prose styles on *Villette*.

Johnson, E. D. H. " 'Daring the Dread Glance': Charlotte Brontë's Treatment of the Supernatural in *Villette*." *Nineteenth-Century Fiction* 20, No. 4 (March 1966): 325-36.
  Views the gothic elements in *Villette* as stylistically incongruous, but thematically essential.

Johnson, Patricia E.. " 'This Heretic Narrative': The Strategy of the Split Narrative in Charlotte Brontë's *Villette*." *Studies in English Literature, 1500-1900* 30, No. 4 (Autumn 1990): 617-31.
  Traces the dichotomous narrative in *Villette*, noting that it enables Lucy Snowe to disclose both the private and public aspects of her character.

Keefe, Robert. "Exile: *Villette*." In his *Charlotte Brontë's World of Death*, pp. 149-84. Austin: University of Texas Press, 1979.
  Interprets *Villette* as an expression of Brontë's suicidal urges.

Knies, Earl A. "The Dual Vision: *Villette*." In his *The Art of Charlotte Brontë*, pp. 171-203. Athens: Ohio University Press, 1969.
  Discusses Lucy Snowe as a narrator.

Lawrence, Karen. "The Cypher: Disclosure and Reticence in *Villette*." *Nineteenth-Century Literature* 42, No. 4 (March 1988): 448-66.
  Considers Lucy Snowe a remarkable protagonist because, unlike women portrayed in conventional art and literature, "she is primarily a viewer rather than a viewed object."

Lenta, Margaret. "The Tone of Protest: An Interpretation of Charlotte Brontë's *Villette*." *English Studies* 64, No. 5 (October 1983): 422-32.
  Objects to most feminist readings of *Villette*, specifically to that of Kate Millett (see essay above dated 1970). "The feminist critic," writes Lenta, "looking at *Villette*, must try to decide whether the vision offered of women's lives is distorted by morbidity which arises, not from [Brontë's] sufferings as a woman, which were related to society's expectations of all women, but from the tragic losses which she had experienced."

Lewes, George Henry. "*Ruth* and *Villette*." *The Westminster and Foreign Quarterly Review* 58 (1 April 1853): 474-91.
  An originally unsigned review referring to *Villette* as "a work of astonishing power and passion."

Litvak, Joseph. "Charlotte Brontë and the Scene of Instruction: Authority and Subversion in *Villette*." *Nineteenth-Century Literature* 42, No. 4 (March 1988): 467-89.
  Studies the novel's "thematics of acting and spectatorship."

Martin, Robert Bernard. "*Villette*." In his *The Accents of Persuasion: Charlotte Brontë's Novels*, pp. 143-86. London: Faber & Faber, 1966.
  Asserts that "*Villette* is unobtrusively full of hints that Miss Brontë had accepted the traditional view of human redemption as not only transcending earthly life but also throwing over it the comforting awareness that human sorrow is at worst transient."

Moglen, Helene. "*Villette*: The Romantic Experience as Psychoanalysis." In her *Charlotte Brontë: The Self Conceived*, pp. 190-229. New York: W. W. Norton, 1976.
  Describes *Villette* as Brontë's most introspective novel.

Myer, Valerie Grosvenor. "*Villette*." In her *Charlotte Brontë: Truculent Spirit*, pp. 188-206. Totowa, N.J.: Barnes & Noble, 1987.
  Cites numerous contemporary interpretations of *Villette* in a general discussion of the book's themes and structure.

O'Dea, Gregory S. "Narrator and Reader in Charlotte Brontë's *Villette*." *South Atlantic Review* 53, No. 1 (January 1988): 41-57.
  Assesses Lucy Snowe as an untrustworthy narrator.

Passel, Anne. *Charlotte and Emily Brontë: An Annotated Bibliography*. New York: Garland Publishing, 1979, 359 p.
  Contains a section listing criticism of *Villette*.

Peters, Margot. "*Villette*." In her *Unquiet Soul: A Biography of Charlotte Brontë*, pp. 336-57. Garden City, N.Y.: Doubleday & Company, 1975.
  Chronicles Brontë's life during the writing of *Villette*.

Rabinowitz, Nancy Sorkin. " 'Faithful Narrator' or 'Partial Eulogist': First-Person Narration in Brontë's *Villette*." *The Journal of Narrative Technique* 15, No. 3 (Fall 1985): 244-55.
  Depicts Lucy Snowe as a skillful narrator fully conscious of how to use language to her advantage.

Silver, Brenda R. "The Reflecting Reader in *Villette*." In *The Voyage In: Fictions of Female Development*, edited by Elizabeth Abel, Marianne Hirsch, and Elizabeth Langland, pp. 90-111. Hanover, N.H.: University Press of New England, 1983.
  Observes that *Villette* "employs characteristics of both the artificially plausible narrative and the seemingly arbitrary narrative that in fact inscribes an alternative ideology, and both these narrative modes are encoded in [Lucy Snowe's] dialogue with the reader."

Review of *Villette*, by Charlotte Brontë. *The Spectator*, No. 1,285 (12 February 1853): 155-56.
  Judges the character of Lucy Snowe: "One might almost say that she took a savage delight in refusing to be comforted, in a position indeed of isolation and hardship, but one still that a large experience of mankind and the miseries incident to the lot of humanity would hardly pronounce to be by comparison either a miserable or a degraded lot."

Vrettos, Athena. "From Neurosis to Narrative: The Private Life of the Nerves in *Villette* and *Daniel Deronda*." *Victorian Studies* 33, No. 4 (Summer 1990): 551-79.
  Compares the depiction of neurosis in *Villette* with that in George Eliot's *Daniel Deronda*. Vrettos observes that both portrayals draw upon "established literary stereotypes," and share "figurative vocabulary . . . to portray the experience of nervous illness."

Waring, S. M. "Charlotte Brontë's Lucy Snowe." *Harper's New Monthly* CLXXXIX, No. 32 (February 1866): 368-71.
  Character analysis of Lucy Snowe, praising her insight and sense of humor.

Fyodor Dostoevsky

1821-1881

(Full name Fyodor Mikhailovich Dostoevsky; also transliterated as Dostoevski, Dostoyevsky, and Dostoevskij) Russian novelist, short story writer, and essayist.

The following entry presents criticism of Dostoevsky's novella *Zapiski iz podpol'ya* (1864; *Notes from the Underground;* also translated as *Letters from the Underworld*). For a discussion of Dostoevsky's complete career, see *NCLC,* Vol. 2; for criticism devoted to his novels *Prestuplenye i nakazanye* (*Crime and Punishment*) and *Besy* (*The Possessed*), see *NCLC,* Vols. 7 and 21, respectively.

Acclaimed as one of the classics of modern literature for its experimental form and style, thematic complexity, and innovative depiction of character psychology, *Notes from the Underground* is perhaps the most influential of Dostoevsky's works. The novella consists of "notes" on the philosophy and experiences of a retired, embittered recluse living in squalor in St. Petersburg. In creating the fictional author of the notes, who is commonly designated the "underground man" by critics, Dostoevsky introduced the antihero into Russian literature and firmly established the archetype of the outsider in world literature. The underground man has been cited as the figurative progenitor of various fictional characters of Franz Kafka, André Gide, Hermann Hesse, Jean-Paul Sartre, and Albert Camus, among others, and has prompted Colin Wilson to praise *Notes* as "a uniquely great monument of Existentialist thought." The philosophical dimension of the novella, however, is only one aspect of a work that also fuses sociology, psychology, and politics. Although critics disagree on the central theme of the novella, Avrahm Yarmolinsky has expressed the critical consensus on the work's position within Dostoevsky's canon: "The importance of *Notes from the Underground* is out of all proportion to the size of the piece. The ideas of which it is the vehicle are essential to his later, more massive works. It is the prologue to his novels."

In 1849 Dostoevsky was exiled to Siberia for his participation in the Petrashevsky Circle, a liberal political discussion group. Originally sentenced to be shot, Dostoevsky and twenty other members of the group received last-minute reprieves from the czar, and their sentences were commuted to hard labor. Dostoevsky spent four years in a penal settlement at Omsk under extremely harsh conditions. While a prisoner, he experienced his first epileptic seizure and suffered from various other maladies. The impression made by coarse and brutal yet strong-willed fellow convicts, most of whom were from the lower classes, and his reading of the New Testament, the only book permitted, led to a marked change in Dostoevsky's views. His earlier moderate socialism, infused with a high regard for Western intellectualism, gave way to a religiously based faith in community and Russian peasant values. Upon his release from the labor camp, he was made to serve an addi-

tional four years in the military in Siberia. In 1857, Dostoevsky married Maria Dmitrievna Isaev, who suffered from tuberculosis, and became stepfather to her profligate son Paul. He returned to St. Petersburg in 1859 to find the political atmosphere much more radical than it had been ten years earlier, as evinced by the depiction in Ivan Turgenev's novel *Ottsy i deti* (1862; *Fathers and Sons*) of an extreme political type then coming into existence in Russia: the nihilist. This individual rejects every aspect of political, social, and cultural life, believing in nothing save empirical science. Dostoevsky, with his brother Mikhail, started the magazine *Vremya* (*Time*), in which he published his novel *Ynizhenye i oskorblenye* (1861; *The Insulted and Injured*) and his Siberian reminiscences *Zapiski iz myortvogo doma* (1862; *Notes from the House of the Dead*). *Vremya* was a successful venture but government censors, who inspected and edited the political content of all publications, suppressed the magazine for a May 24, 1863 article considered supportive of the Polish rebellion. (Poland was at that time occupied by the Russian Empire.) In the summer of 1862, Dostoevsky traveled through Europe seeking treatment for his epilepsy; a year later, after the closing of *Vremya,* he returned there to meet his young mistress, Apollinaria Suslova. Financially strapped as a result of his gambling while abroad and the suppression of his magazine, Dostoevsky returned home to his dying wife. His travels in Europe left him with an enduring antipathy for Western culture, which he had come to view as decadent and hollow. Shortly after his return to St. Petersburg, Dostoevsky and his brother established a second journal, *Epokha* (*Epoch*). Part I of *Notes from the Underground* was published in the magazine in March of 1864. Dostoevsky's wife died April 19, 1864, one month before the publication of Part II.

The notes of the underground man consist of two sections, "The Underground," a theoretical screed setting forth the fictional author's personal philosophy, and "Apropos of the Wet Snow," in which he recollects experiences that he had in his twenty-fourth year that anticipate his present condition and philosophy. In the course of his diatribe, the fictional author reveals many traits: he is ineffectual, resentful, alienated, ambivalent, introspective, and self-contradictory. Although he claims that his first-person, monologic notes are not written for anyone else, he nevertheless addresses an imaginary audience and anticipates its responses, thus giving the notes the tenor of dialogue. In "The Underground," the author attacks contemporary theories on the nature of humanity and maintains a refusal to submit to a life defined by laws of reason and science, an existence that he metaphorically equates with the incogitant passivity of a "piano-key." This denial has led him to acts of perversity and debauchery in the attempt to demonstrate free will and the intangible human qualities that he claims to cherish: "What a man needs is simply and solely *independent* volition, whatever that independence may cost and wherever it may lead." The first incident described in "Apropos of the Wet Snow" is an ambiguous encounter with an army officer that the underground man interprets as an affront to himself. For two years the underground man plots a revenge that produces equally ambiguous results. The author then relates another story in which he intrudes upon a dinner party held by former schoolmates and proceeds to embarrass himself by insulting the others and flaunting his averred superior intelligence. When the party subsides, the underground man follows his former schoolmates to a brothel, where he asserts his superiority over a prostitute, Liza (also transliterated as Lisa), whom he manipulates with noble speech and a lofty offer of assistance. Three days later, Liza appears at the underground man's abode, only to realize his meanness and unhappiness. The underground man is humiliated at having been exposed and is unable to accept her consoling love. Shortly after the close of this story the notes abruptly end, with the underground man purporting that he will write no more. The heretofore silent "editor" of the notes adds the following postscript: "This is not the end, however, of the 'Notes' of this paradoxical writer. He could not help going on. But to us too it seems that this will be a good place to stop."

The thematic complexity of *Notes from the Underground* has generated a wide variety of interpretations. Many critics have contended that *Notes from the Underground* is a parody of Nikolai Chernyshevsky's *What Is to Be Done?*, an 1863 utopian novel that propounds a radical socialist philosophy of enlightened self-interest, referred to as "rational egoism". This philosophy asserts the absolute hegemony of reason, insisting that all human behavior is dictated by rational laws of nature. In *What Is to Be Done?*, Chernyshevsky evoked the image of the Crystal Palace, a structure originally constructed for London's 1851 World's Fair, as the ideal of human rationality. The underground man, however, attacks this triumph of science and engineering as a symbol of the absence of spontaneity and freedom. In *Notes,* critics have maintained, Dostoevsky showed the moral and psychological incompatibility of an autonomous personality and the purely deterministic world heralded by Chernyshevsky and other socialist radicals. Based on the underground man's argument that "after all, twice two is four is not life, gentlemen, but the beginning of death," *Notes* has been considered an argument for existential choice and, similarly, a protest against utilitarianism, materialism, and positivism. In the same vein, critics have viewed the underground man as either an exponent of unrestricted freedom and a continual striving for power or an advocate of nihilism, both of which reject all civic and moral law. In this respect, many scholars have noted that the novella presages the philosophy of Friedrich Nietzsche. Others have perceived the underground man simply as the embodiment of evil, an explanation that rests largely on his apparent morbidity, maliciousness, immorality, and sado-masochistic desire to humiliate and suffer humiliation. Alternative readings have construed *Notes* as a condemnation of the spiritual malaise of Dostoevsky's age, a theological cry of despair over moral disintegration, or a parody of a literary "confession." Some critics have insisted that the novella advances religious orthodoxy and, more specifically, the primacy of Christian faith. Advocates of this view have relied largely on the section excised by the government censor from Part I of the original manuscript, in which Dostoevsky expressed the possibility of redemption for the underground man through suffering, love, and Christ. Dostoevsky decried the cutting of his work but did not reinstate the deleted passage, which is now lost, in subsequent editions. Most commentators have approved the result of the censor's action, maintaining that the work would otherwise have been didactic and therefore less powerful. Furthermore, this passage would tend to provide a specific conclusion to the conflicts presented in *Notes,* which otherwise resist such resolution. Commentators have often observed that the underground man's spiralling logic and pervasive relativism preclude his ever solving the dilemmas he confronts.

The psychological aspects of the work have also received close attention. Scholars have termed *Notes* the self-revelation of a pathological personality diversely diagnosed as narcissistic, borderline psychotic, paranoid, compulsive, or repressed. Yarmolinsky has contended that "the story is a perfect anatomy of the neurotic temperament, with its compulsions, its inhibitions, its emotional ambivalence and consequent discords, every expression of a disruptive maladjustment." Some critics have found in Dostoevsky's own troubles a basis for the autobiographical, agitated tone of his *Notes*. These commentators have suggested, variously, that Dostoevsky himself felt burdened by an overly sensitive consciousness, derived pleasure from depraved acts, or was rejecting the social Romanticism of his youth. Many have held that the novella disparages the narrow intellectualism and overrefined consciousness that Dostoevsky ascribed to Russians who were, in his estimation, contaminated by the corrupt rationalist trends of western European thought. Still others have focused on the underground man as a social type representative of individuals unable to establish a bond with humanity: an anonymous and isolated figure within a metropolis who experiences hostility toward the mechanized and bureaucratic aspects of society. Apologists of this view have stressed the significance of Dostoevsky's prefatory assertion, which offers insight into the antecedents of the underground man: "The author of these Notes and the Notes themselves, are both, of course, imaginary. All the same, if we take into consideration the conditions that have shaped our society, people like the writer not only may, but must, exist in that society."

Notes from the Underground has been cited as the first work to extensively employ "fantastic realism," the depiction of an extreme, possible instance of reality as opposed to the portrayal of a prosaic actuality. Described by Gary Rosenshield as having "perhaps the most complex narrational structure of all Dostoevskij's work," *Notes* incorporates many innovations, including an incomplete and untrustworthy narrative, a narrator who verbally attacks the reader, and a structure that is both temporally nonlinear and circular—the events in the second section chronologically precede and, in a sense, lead to the philosophy propounded in the first section. Critics have also praised the novella for fusing ideas and plot, thereby dramatizing the abstract and, according to George Steiner, achieving "a rare instance of creative equilibrium between poetic and philosophic powers."

Notes from the Underground was a pivotal work for Dostoevsky for its inauguration of themes prominent in his later novels and its introduction of the acutely self-analytical, spiritually torn hero, who is a prototype for many other of his characters. However, the importance of *Notes* extends far beyond its significance in Dostoevsky's career, as evinced in Steiner's estimation of the novella: " . . . when the traditional literary elements in [*Notes from the Underground*] have been set aside, and when close affinities to Dostoevsky's other works have been noted, the profound originality of the thing continues to assert itself. Chords previously unheard had been struck with admirable precision. No other text by Dostoevsky has exerted more influence on twentieth-century thought or technique."

(See also *Short Story Criticism,* Vol. 2)

Vasily Rozanov   (essay date 1906)

[*A Russian journalist and philosopher, Rozanov was a prominent critic known for his innovative, interpretative approaches to literature and original and personal style of writing. He married Apollinaria Suslova, the former mistress of Dostoevsky, when Rozanov was twenty-four*

and Suslova was forty. His first book, On Understanding *(1886), is an anti-rational philosophical study and a bitter polemic against the University of Moscow. His* Legenda o velikom inkvizitore *(1891;* The Legend of the Grand Inquisitor*), a study of Dostoevsky's The Brothers Karamazov, introduced a new critical approach to the author and aided revival of interest in Dostoevsky. In the following excerpt from a 1906 translation of the third edition of that work, Rozanov stresses the high value placed upon free will in* Notes from the Underground.]

In reading [***Notes from the Underground***], one is unexpectedly struck by our need for annotated editions—annotated not from the standpoint of the form and origin of literary works, as is already done, but from the standpoint of their contents and meaning—in order finally to decide the question of whether the idea contained in them is true, or whether it is false, and why, and to decide this by joint efforts, to decide it thoroughly and rigorously, in a way accessible only to science. For example, every line of ***Notes from the Underground*** is important; it is impossible to reduce the book to general formulas. Moreover, no thinking person can pass over the assertions made in it without considering them carefully.

There never was a writer in our literature whose ideals were so completely divorced from present-day reality. The thought never for a moment occurred to Dostoevsky to try to preserve this way of life and merely improve a thing or two in it. Because of the generalizing cast of his mind, he directed all his attention toward the evil concealed in the general system of a historically developed life; hence his hatred of and disdain for all hope of improving anything by means of individual changes; hence his animosity towards our parties of progressives and Westerners. Perceiving only the "general," he passed directly from reality to the extreme in the ideal, and the first thing he encountered there was the hope of raising, with the help of reason, an edifice of human life so perfect that it would give peace to man, crown history, and put an end to suffering. His criticism of this idea runs through all his works; it was expressed for the first time, and moreover in the greatest detail, in ***Notes from the Underground.***

The man from the underground is a person who has withdrawn deep within himself. He hates life and spitefully criticizes the ideal of the rational utopians on the basis of a precise knowledge of human nature, which he acquired through a long and lonely observation of himself and of history.

The outline of his criticism is as follows: man carries within himself, in an undeveloped state, a complex world of inclinations that have not yet been discovered—and their discovery will determine his future history just as inevitably as the existence of these inclinations in him now is certain. Therefore, the predetermination of history and its crown by our reason alone will always be empty talk without any real importance.

Among those inclinations, in so far as they have already revealed themselves during the course of history, there is so much that is incomprehensibly strange and irrational that it is impossible to find any intelligent formula that would satisfy human nature. Is not happiness the principle on which this formula can be constructed? But does not man sometimes crave suffering? Are there really any pleasures for which Hamlet would give up the torments of his consciousness? Are not order and regularity the common features of every final system of human relations? And yet, do we not sometimes love chaos, destruction, and disorder even more passionately than we do regularity and creation? Is it possible to find a person who would do only what is necessary and good his whole life long? And would he not, by limiting himself to this for so long, experience a strange weariness; would he not shift, at least briefly, to the poetry of instinctive actions? Finally, will not all happiness disappear for man if there disappears for him the feeling of novelty, of everything unexpected, everything capriciously changeable—things to which he now adapts his way of life, and in so doing experiences much distress, but an equal joy? Does not uniformity for everyone contradict the fundamental principle of human nature—individuality—and does not the constancy of the future and of the "ideal" contradict his free will, his thirst for choosing something or other in his own way, sometimes contrary to an external, even a rational, decision? And can man really be happy without freedom, without individuality? Without all this, with the eternal absence of novelty, will not instincts be irresistibly aroused in him such as will shatter the adamantine nature of every formula: and man will wish for suffering, destruction, blood, for everything except that to which his formula has doomed him for all eternity; in the same way that a person confined too long to a light, warm room will cut his hands on the glass of the windowpanes and run naked out into the cold, merely so as not to have to remain any longer in his former surroundings? Was it not this feeling of spiritual weariness that led Seneca into intrigue and crime? And was it not this that made Cleopatra stick gold pins into the breasts of her black slave girls, while eagerly looking them in the face, watching their trembling, smiling lips, and their frightened eyes? And finally, will the never-changing possession of the achieved ideal really satisfy a person for whom wishing, striving, and achieving is an irresistible need? And does rationality, on the whole, exhaust human nature? But obviously that is the only thing that its very creator—reason—can give to a final formula.

By nature, man is a completely irrational creature; therefore, reason can neither completely explain him nor completely satisfy him. No matter how persistent is the work of thought, it will never cover all of reality; it will answer the demands of the imaginary man, but not those of the real one. Hidden in man is the instinct for creation, and this was precisely what gave him life, what rewarded him with suffering and joy—things that reason can neither understand nor change.

The rational is one thing; the mystical is another thing again. And while it is inaccessible to the touch and power of science, it can be arrived at through religion. Hence the development of the mystical in Dostoevsky and the concentration of his interest on all that is religious, something we observe in the second and chief period of his work, which began with *Crime and Punishment.* (pp. 47-51)

Vasily Rozanov, in his Dostoevsky and the Legend of the Grand Inquisitor, *translated by Spencer E. Roberts, Cornell University Press, 1972, 232 p.*

J. Middleton Murry   (essay date 1916)

[*Murry is recognized as one of the most significant English critics of the twentieth century, noted for his studies of major authors and for his contributions to modern critical theory. Perceiving an integral relationship between literature and religion, Murry believed that the literary critic must be concerned with the moral as well as the aesthetic dimensions of a given work. While his critical approach led some commentators to question his ability to render objective assessments of the authors he discussed, his essays are nevertheless valued for their originality and insight. In the following excerpt, Murry asserts that the narrator of* Notes from the Underground, *who is the tortured victim of his own heightened consciousness, is Dostoevsky's rendering of himself.*]

[In *The Insulted and Injured* Dostoevsky] sets down only what he saw and felt: What he thought he hid close within his heart, while he sought the way of unburdening his deeper soul, which was his passionate mind.

And within a year or two, after *The House of the Dead* had been written, he ventured to reveal something of that which was hidden. The imaginary writer of *Letters from the Underworld* is a man of thought, and not of action. He does not live at all, but thinks, and his thought has paralysed his being, until he can only sit down and contemplate the world that is, which he abhors yet can by no means escape. Evil and pain, they tell him, are the visible working of the iron laws of Nature: the things that are must be. "What have *I* to do with the laws of Nature, or with arithmetic," he answers, "when all the time those laws and the formula that twice two make four do not meet with my acceptance? Of course I am not going to beat my head against a wall if I have not strength enough to do so; yet I am not going to accept that wall merely because I have to run up against it and have no means to knock it down." This is at last open rebellion, even though it be confined within the ferment of his own soul. He will not accept life; he cannot refuse. To live demands a grosser soul than his; for in his acute sensibility the equilibrium which Dostoevsky the youth had sought between the inward life and the outward is lost beyond recovery. So clearly does he recognise the vanity of action, that the only actions left to him are those in which he has at least a faint hope of momentarily overwhelming his consciousness with the extremity of sensation. Therefore his existence passes in the underworld, from which he makes sudden and fantastic irruptions into the upper air of decent normal life, only because he knows that he will suffer there the torments of the damned.

These torments are all he has to hope for from life. If he folds his hands in contemplation, he suffers both from what he contemplates and yet more from the longing to break the bands of his inertia and to act, for his longing to act is infinitely greater than that of the man of action, not merely because the springs of action are weakened in him and he desires that which he has not, but because he is conscious of his own personality, and knows that he must assert his will simply for the sake of asserting his will. Even the existence of that will he has to prove to himself; therefore the actions of that will are bound to be senseless and evil and fantastical, precisely because they are crucial. Deliberately to do a senseless or an evil or a fantastical thing is to have asserted one's will in the highest, and to have convinced one's self of its reality, because no power on earth save the individual will could have accomplished it. That is his only reply to the life which he cannot accept. But to do good and to behave sensibly, they say, is in his interests. What does he care about his interests?

> I tell you that there is one occasion and one occasion only when man can wilfully, consciously desiderate for himself that which is foolish and harmful. This is the occasion when he yearns *to have the right* to desiderate for himself what is foolish and harmful and to be bound by no obligation whatever to desiderate anything that is sensible. It is his crowning folly; it is herein we see his ineradicable wayfulness. Yet such folly may also be the best thing in the world for him, even though it work him harm and contradict our soundest conclusions on the subject of his interests. This is because it is possible for his folly to preserve to him under all circumstances the chiefest and most valuable of all his possessions—his personality, his individuality.

This is a searching dialectic. Doubtless it underlay the evil Prince Valkovsky's "What's not nonsense is personality—myself " [in ***The Insulted and Injured***], but Dostoevsky had not dared to lend it to him. Nevertheless, the obscure writer of the ***Letters from the Underworld*** confesses to a similar taste for ugly debauchery. Though his reasoning is ostensibly a protest against materialist and positivist philosophers, it strikes far beyond these obvious enemies. Not only the good of the positivist is impotent before it, but what other good can stand against it?

But Dostoevsky forbore to draw the last conclusion from his own logic. He left it so that it could be said that these confessions were no more than the ravings of a crazy, morbid mind. There is nothing crazy in the argument, however. Certainly it was only a skirmish before the battle, but it was fought with the skill of a master of strategy, and it was fought on a straight issue: Consciousness *contra mundum.* Of course the writer of those letters was a noxious insect which must be destroyed. But what if, given a certain datum, his noxiousness is inevitable? And further, what if that datum is nothing less than the possession of that which mankind has come to recognise as the proud differentia of man, of *homo sapiens:* the conscious reason? Is one who possesses this consciousness in the highest degree and has the courage to act upon it, to be destroyed as a noxious insect by the majority of other men who possess it in a lesser form or not at all? What if life has reached in the modern man a final form whose destruction by its own elements is inevitable? What if the good man, the normal man, the sound man, the living man, the social man are forms already superseded by something other which can find only in the underworld a possibility of continued existence, which desires to live, but cannot, because the conscious mind desires to accept life, but cannot?

The underworldling had thought these things. "True," he says,

> the normal man is gross—but then the normal man may have to be gross. How indeed do you know that his grossness is not one of his very best points? Anyway, I grow daily more confirmed in my suspicion that if one were to take the antithesis of the normal man—that is to say, the man of acute sensibility, the man who hails not from Nature's womb, but from a chemical retort—this comes rather too close to mysticism, a thing which I also suspect—the man born of the retort would sometimes feel so conscious that he was being outclassed by his antithesis, the man of action, that he would come to look upon himself despite his acute sensibility as a mouse rather than a human being. . . .

Yet wherein is he less than human? There is only one answer to this: because he feels and thinks more than his fellows. It is surely only a malignant mockery to suppose that a man who is more richly endowed with the essentially human faculties than other men, is less a man than they. Here is the beginning of an ugly and desperate paradox. It is true that he knows himself not a man, but a creature compounded in a chemical retort; but he also knows that the chemical process is that of life itself. He is one of the first of the new men who by the excess of their humanity are inhuman; and upon what power falls the responsibility of his creation? "Civilisation," he says, "develops nothing in man save an added capacity to receive impressions," and he might have added, "and to think upon the impressions he has received." In himself the last progress of the human consciousness has ended in a cul-de-sac.

So he lives in the underworld, his hands folded in contemplation, brooding upon the evil which life has wrought in himself. He has no desire, though he knows that he is a mouse in their comparison, to have the freedom of the company of the children of the day. He envies them, yet he would not accept life on their conditions, for he is, after all, more a man than they.

> That is to say, though I envy him, I find the underworld better—yet I am lying. I am lying because, even as I know that two and two make four, so do I know that it is not the underworld which is so much better, but something else, something else,—something for which I am hungry, but which I shall never find. Ah no! To the devil with the underworld! . . .

And this something else is a Way of life. The underworld is only living death. The tormented soul of this mouse-man longs to *be,* to resign nothing of his humanity and yet to live. He longs for that which he knows to be impossible, for something within him whispers that it may yet be possible in defiance of his reason and his consciousness. But since upon these alone he must depend to show him the way to the future beatitude, he knows he will never slake his thirst at the fountain of life.

In the story of "The Falling Sleet," he tells a ghastly history of one of his irruptions into the life that is, of how he desired and won the love of a simple heart, how he hated the woman who loved him and whom he loved, how he outraged her and drove her away in a final inspiration of devilish cruelty and was left alone once more. It was inevitable: and the secret of its inevitability is in the terrible words which Dostoevsky once used in *The Journal of an Author,* when, protesting against the panacea of love for humanity, he said that "love for suffering humanity in a soul which knows it can bring no alleviation to that suffering, will be changed into a hatred of humanity." That, he said, was profounder, even though they did not understand it, than all the gospels of all the preaching of universal love. And the outcast of the underworld, though he desired to love and to be loved, had within him a stronger desire, that he should not deceive himself or another by love. Love was no remedy for him who suffered from the contemplation of the whole life of which love was only a part; and truly it was better for the woman that she should have been driven away even as she was than that she should have remained with him or he with her. He was in rebellion against life, and since a man cannot live in rebellion, he did not live. There was no hope for him in life, nor any for one who should unite her life with his. He had deliberately and inevitably put himself outside life; he chose the underworld, because there was no other place for him, and if, when he yielded to the longing within him to be swallowed up in life, to act and to forget and to live, his action was cruel and revolting, that too was inevitable. His being was set in absolute negation to the life of which love is the noblest part.

But he was a sick soul, a mind diseased, a man corrupted by his own thought! Sickness is a two-edged conception. He was abnormal, it is true, and he and Dostoevsky in him was clearly conscious of the abyss that lay between his nature and that of normal men. But abnormality is not the same as sickness. What is sick cannot be sound, but the abnormal may well be true. What reason is there to suppose that the way of health and the way of truth are the same? We may argue endlessly that we dare not suppose that life should itself contain the principle of its own destruction, but why should it not? What evidence can a man derive from the contemplation of life which could make such a conception absurd? The conception is irrational; but life itself is irrational. Life seems to have evolved the human reason for the singularly irrational purpose of making known its own irrationality. The conception is terrible; life itself is not less terrible.

Mais autres temps, autres mœurs. There is another philosophy descended upon the earth in recent times. It may be thought that Dostoevsky's underworldling would find a stouter opponent in M. Bergson than in the positivists and social reformers of his day. If he had miraculously anticipated the doctrine of the bankruptcy of the reason, he had not known that the way of intuition and instinct was open to him. Perhaps he was not quite so simple. If the reason is bankrupt, man is not the less condemned to use it and to put faith in it. If he would resign its privilege, he cannot for all his desire. He is born to the purple. For better or worse it is his so long as mankind shall continue. And if by reason he has decided that reason is unprofitable, it is

not likely to be atrophied by the destructive force of its own logic. Nor can man, still possessed of and possessed by reason, fling himself into the nirvana of instinct and intuition. The underworldling was not so simple-minded though he made the same attempt. Instinct and intuition are not detachable parts of the human soul. They are permeated now by the conscious reason and are changed. The underworldling made the attempt to lose his consciousness in them, with tragedy inevitable for a conclusion. Perhaps there is more real philosophy in his proud and final challenge to the normal, living men, that he, for all his sordidness and unchanging despair, had yet *lived* more than they.

> Well, gentlemen, heaven forbid that I should justify myself by seeking to include all my fellow-men with myself; yet, so far as I am concerned, I have but carried to a finish in my life, what you have never even dared to carry half-way, although you have constantly mistaken your cowardice for prudence, and have constantly cheated yourselves with comforting reflections. The truth is that I have been more *alive* than you. That is all. But look a little closer. We do not even know where present-day reality is to be found, nor what it is called. Whenever we are left to our own devices, and deprived of our bookish rules, we at once grow confused—we do not know what to do, nor what to observe, nor what to love, nor what to hate, nor what to respect, nor what to despise. We grow weary of being human beings at all—of possessing real, individual flesh and blood. We are *ashamed* of being human—we count it beneath our dignity. . . .

He is grown weary of his humanity. He must possess his soul in patience until out of his bankruptcy and impotence a new thing is created: but in the age-long waiting for the miracle what shall he do?

Dostoevsky, who was the man, had his one cure and his one refuge in creating him after his own image. Doubtless he knew that the solace of this activity might be denied to other men. They might even be stronger men and bolder. Had not even the villain Valkovsky let fall a dangerous word, one dangerous in itself, but altogether too dangerously near the exacter reasoning of the underworld? "What a man most needs is an *independent* will—no matter what the cost of such independence of volition, nor what it lead to. Yet the devil only knows what man's will—" The rest of that broken sentence is not the next chapter in the *Letters from the Underworld,* but in the rest of Dostoevsky's work. Suppose the anodyne of literary creation denied, suppose a man too strong to remain in the underworld, even though it is not a place but a state of soul, then there might be strange things to chronicle. "The devil only knows. . . . " It is true; but there have been those—Mihailovsky was one—who were convinced that they had seen the light of the Evil One in Dostoevsky's eyes. (pp. 90-101)

J. Middleton Murry, in his Fyodor Dostoevsky: A Critical Study, *1916. Reprint by Russell & Russell, 1966, 263 p.*

D. S. Mirsky (essay date 1926)

[*Mirsky was a Russian prince who fled his country after the Bolshevik Revolution and settled in London. While in England, he wrote two important histories of Russian literature,* Contemporary Russian Literature *(1926) and* A History of Russian Literature *(1926). In 1932 Mirsky returned to the USSR, where he continued to write literary criticism. Soviet censors objected to his work and he was eventually exiled to Siberia; he disappeared in 1937. In the following excerpt from the 1949 condensed edition of* A History of Russian Literature, *Mirsky extols* Notes from the Underground *as a work that transcends classification as mere art or literature due to the philosophic depths it plumbs.*]

Memoirs from Underground, the work that introduces us, chronologically, to the "mature" Dostoyévsky, contains at once the essence of his essential self. It cannot be regarded as imaginative literature pure and simple. There is in it quite as much philosophy as literature. It would have to be connected with his journalistic writings were it not that it proceeded from a deeper and more significant spiritual level of his personality. The work occupies a central place in the creation of Dostoyévsky. Here his essential tragical intuition is expressed in the most unadulterated and ruthless form. It transcends art and literature, and its place is among the great mystical revelations of mankind. The faith in the supreme value of the human personality and its freedom, and in the irrational religious and tragic foundation of the spiritual universe, which is above reason, above the distinction of good and evil (the faith, ultimately, of all mystical religion), is expressed in a paradoxical, unexpected, and entirely spontaneous form. The central position of **Memoirs from Underground** in the work of Dostoyévsky was first discerned by Nietzsche and Rózanov. It stands in the center of the writings of Shestóv, the greatest of Dostoyévsky's commentators. Viewed as literature, it is also the most original of Dostoyévsky's works, although also the most unpleasant and the most "cruel." It cannot be recommended to those who are not either sufficiently strong to overcome it or sufficiently innocent to remain unpoisoned. It is a strong poison, which is most safely left untouched. (p. 273)

> D. S. Mirsky, *"The Age of Realism: The Novelists (II)," in his* A History of Russian Literature Comprising "A History of Russian Literature" and "Contemporary Russian Literature," *edited by Francis J. Whitfield, Alfred A. Knopf, 1949, pp. 245-90.*

Julius Meier-Graefe (essay date 1928)

[*A German art critic and the author of nearly fifty books on art and travel, Meier-Graefe was known internationally as the author of the definitive biography of Vincent van Gogh, as an early champion of van Gogh's work, and as the founder of four art magazines—*Pan *in 1894,* Dekorative Kunst *in 1896,* L'Art décorative *in 1898, and* Germinal *in 1899. He generally employed an historical perspective in his study of aesthetics and focused on the artistic extremes of ancient art and Impressionism and Post-Impressionism. His writing was generally nontech-* nical and readable and expressed such iconoclastic theories as the averred superiority of Egyptian art to that of ancient Greece. In the following excerpt from his sympathetic biography* Dostoevsky: The Man and His Work *(1928), Meier-Graefe refutes the claims of such critics as Leo Shestov that Dostoevsky introduced a Nietzschean transvaluation of morals in* Notes from the Underground, *arguing instead that this work evinces a probable, though dramatic, development of ideas introduced in* The Double *and expatiated in later works.*]

[**Letters from the Underworld**] remains fragmentary. A finished work would not have intensified the atmosphere. It is already perfect in itself. For that reason we have to accept the fragments in the spirit of toleration with which we admire the mutilated Gothic-like modellings of Michelangelo or the half-destroyed second Anatomy of Rembrandt. The rhythm is not alone not restrained by the limitation of incompleteness but is actually enhanced. Only in the first moments are the monologue and the loose linking-up of the episodes disturbing, just as in the first moment we are disconcerted by the missing limb of a *torso*. It is a mere superficiality. We ourselves can see to the rounding off of the work without Dostoevsky and we do it, as far as necessary, instantaneously. Without our efforts to this end no new synthesis can take place. But with these memoirs Dostoevsky has done more than set us on the new path. He accompanies us almost to the end, running, it is true, rather than walking. We must be careful not to jump to premature conclusions on the strength of passages which have been skipped. All commentaries on the Russian which are concerned with his idea and attempt to formulate it by means of false inferences are exposed to this danger. Over-haste may lead to inferences such as those of Leo Shestov, the restless Russian philosopher, who, from fragments only half understood, deduced Dostoevsky's kinship to Nietzsche. The consequences of this typical blunder, largely responsible for the antagonism against the poet both in Russia and, recently, in Germany, may be so considerable that further consideration of Shestov's work is imperative.

Shestov has educed from the **Letters from the Underworld** a type of "underworldling" with whom he believes he can identify Dostoevsky. The memoirs are unquestionably a more or less free autobiography of the period in which they were written; it is quite unnecessary to refute the harmless note at the beginning of the work in which Dostoevsky explains that the writer of the memoirs is a fictitious person. It is important to consider over what period of time the work was spread, that is, whether it took one year, two years, or only a few days. Shestov ignores this factor. Of course Dostoevsky must have had the thoughts of the underworldling, otherwise he could not have expressed them. Of course Shakespeare must have imagined himself into every possible kind of rascal. His thoughts about humanity must therefore be educed from his entire work.

Shestov fails to notice Dostoevsky's development, particularly this most important part, the inevitable struggle against sentimentality. He mistakes the process of inurement for the final renunciation of feeling. Because Dostoevsky absolves himself from the Schilleresque—not from Schiller, . . . he is to disclaim all his ideals. Does that really happen even in these necessarily transient fragments which immediately succeed the most nauseous and disastrous work? They are neither written at the same time as nor do they precede *The Insulted and Injured,* as Shestov seems to suggest. The sequence is important. It must not be forgotten that Dostoevsky wanted to rid himself of the nauseous taste and to say something more important. It is perfectly clear from these fragments, brimful of mockery and scepticism, that he felt the need to purge himself of conventional notions. If the underworldling is feelingless, then so were Daumier, Rembrandt, and Grünewald. Shestov compares Tolstoy's method of adjustment. We can dispense with that. It is just people like Tolstoy who prove how deep the acid must eat in before it reaches healthy flesh. That leads Michailovsky to the "cruel talent." Can a necessary operation be cruel? The underworldling was hard to himself and needed to be. Overwrought sentimentality leads him to despair. Who despairs? The "Schilleresque" underworldling, the Schilleresque Dostoevsky for that matter, thus a part of Dostoevsky! Even the people whom the underworldling addresses and who are very surely and speedily drawn, needed cruelty. Does Dostoevsky on that account murder hope? Shestov believes that the underworldling jeers at all construction because he sticks his tongue out at the indestructible palace of crystal. But in the tenth chapter of the first part there is a detailed discussion of the joys of sticking out the tongue, and it is not very far-fetched to assume that the crystal-castle stands for an indestructible notion of utter futility.

It is not necessary to have been in the *katorga* to share this aversion. But, for the rest, this sceptic is quite prepared to prefer a decent house to a hencoop in which, in case of need, it is possible to keep dry; indeed in certain circumstances to prefer a palace of crystal. "I would willingly," he says,

> have my tongue cut right out in sheer gratitude if only I could be relieved of the desire to stick it out. How can I help that it is impossible to make such an arrangement and that one has to be satisfied with lodgings? Why am I so constituted that I am compelled to cherish such desires? Does then my whole spiritual constitution only pursue the aim of bringing me to perceive its own deception? Is that the whole intention? I cannot believe it.

He comes to the eulogy of seclusion. Since he loathes normal beings, he finds isolation better, but, it is doubtless understood, only because he does not find what he seeks. "The best," he says, "is positively and certainly not seclusion. To the devil with seclusion!"

All sorts of things can, of course, be deduced from such spasms. To make the moods a basis of philosophy seems to me a serious matter. In order to prove that the underworldling's egoism leads to Nietzschean master-morality, Shestov quotes the cold repulse of Lisa, the poor harlot, who comes for "moral support." "Do you know what I really want?" he asks her. "That you all of you go to the devil! That's all! I need peace. For a song I'd instantly hand over the whole world. Is the world to go to the dogs, or am I not to have tea? I say, let the world go to the dogs, so long as I always have my tea!" To which Shestov adds: "Who has ever thought of putting words of such unexampled cynicism into his hero's mouth? Just to the very Dostoevsky who not so long ago spoke with such warmth and upright feeling concerning the destiny of man."

And therewith Shestov seeks to prove an important stage in the transformation of Dostoevsky's "humanity" and couples with it far-reaching inferences.

It is difficult to grasp that Dostoevsky's tone in itself did not perplex his interpreter. This lack of fine perception is at the root of many errors. Moreover, if Shestov had examined more closely an exactly parallel situation, Raskolnikov's first conversation with Sonia, the street-girl, in a riper work [*Crime and Punishment*], to which these memoirs served as an immediate preface, he would have been convinced of the narrow-mindedness and hastiness of his conclusions. He does, in fact, touch once on this parallel and imputes to the conversation with Sonia a special significance which Dostoevsky did not intend. Sonia is to give Raskolnikov what the knowledge of the "scholar" Razumihin cannot give him. (How does Shestov arrive at making Razumihin, the primitive man of feeling, the "blockhead" as he is called in the novel, the representative of knowledge?) He also quotes the climax of the conversation, Sonia's reading of the Bible, and refers to Raskolnikov's hope in the miracle of Lazarus, but merely in order to substantiate Dostoevsky's egoism in choosing, not a passage which was acceptable to recognized morality, but Lazarus, who fitted into Raskolnikov's situation, because, so at least Shestov believes, the immortality promised by the parable appears consistent with the belief in immortal egoism. He asserts that Dostoevsky was convinced "that a single passage torn from the context of the holy writing was perhaps not truth at all but became a lie." If only Shestov and his numerous followers could have been convinced that this procedure could not lead to creative literature, he would not have rejected, because it did not serve his purpose, such a masterpiece as *The Idiot,* would not have ignored *The Possessed,* a pamphlet, *A Raw Youth,* the impassioned protest against the superman, and would not have flung on to the rubbish-heap Alyosha [in *The Brothers Karamazov*], the purest of all affirmers. This philosophy destroys creative literature, and it is open to question whether the "idea" which Shestov evolves can offer sufficient compensation.

Let us keep to the underworld den and consider more carefully Shestov's important example, the above-mentioned words to Lisa "let the world go to the dogs—," because this passage is characteristic not only of the narrator's dialecticism but also of the author's method. The cynical words occur at a psychological moment which Dostoevsky has carefully prepared. The underworldling has awaited Lisa for days, has secretly indulged in hopes of saving and marrying Lisa and of thus saving himself. It must be remembered what has happened in the brothel. Lisa is perhaps his last refuge. She does not arrive. Therefore, after he has been scorned by his old school-fellows, in whose company his hopeless longing has brought him into an impossible situation, he is now rejected even by the

Woodcut depicting a tormented underground man.

whore. In the meantime he is, as usual, persistently wrangling with Apollo, his servant. This Apollo was expressly installed by the devil to torment him. The scene with his "tormentor" degenerates almost into a brawl and drives the underworldling into a violent rage. In the middle of this scene Lisa suddenly appears. Naturally he feels "crushed, ridiculous, in ignominious confusion." Then all his irritation is poured upon his visitor. Dostoevsky says explicitly in the scene with Apollo, "If it were not for Lisa none of all that would have occurred," so that the tormentor owes his existence to the yearning for Lisa. Moreover, this remark would certainly not have been necessary. The beginning of the scene with Lisa aggravates his exasperation. In order to entertain Lisa he is forced to make his peace with Apollo, to implore Apollo to buy tea and rusks as quickly as possible, and for three horrible minutes he does not know whether the brute will go or not. When the servant is at last out of the way and the underworldling returns to Lisa, he begins to wonder whether he should not simply go off, just as he is, in his tattered dressing-gown. In the presence of Lisa his fury with Apollo overpowers him.

> "I shall kill him!" I yelled, striking the table. I was raving and at the same time had quite a clear notion of how stupid it was to rave like that.
>
> "You don't know, Lisa, what this tormentor means to me. He is my torturer—"
>
> And all at once I burst into tears. That was a fit. I was horribly ashamed while I sobbed, but I could not control myself.

The cynical words to Lisa, to which Shestov objected, could long since have been introduced without incriminating the unfortunate man, but Dostoevsky is still preparing. His psychology works faultlessly. After the "fit" Apollo brings the tea. This ordinary prosaic tea seems "wretched and unseemly" to the abnormally excited man after all that has happened. Who could not understand him? "Lisa, I suppose you despise me?" Only now comes the first attack on Lisa, not by any means a bolt from the blue. "I was angry with myself but, of course, she had to pay for it. A sudden wrath against her surged in my heart. She is responsible for everything, I thought."

But it still goes on. He struggles with himself, feels "the nauseous blackguardism of his spiteful stupidity," tries to conquer himself. If Lisa had not been so tactless at this moment, he would perhaps have been able to restrain himself. But it is just at this very moment that she informs him of her laudable resolve to quit the brothel. Nothing was more natural than to say it at this moment since she hoped thereby to free him of his suffering, and it is just as obvious that being informed at this moment was bound to be an intolerable profanity to him. And thereupon he razes the whole building and abandons himself to raving, in the course of which occur the words quoted by Shestov. These words are only few in a whole web which take the sting out of cynicism and yet sharpen it again and again. It suffices carefully to read such passages once, to follow the origin, the outburst and the dying down of the explosion, in order once and for all to be proof against the errors of Shestov and his colleagues. Dostoevsky's psychology always overwhelms us with a mass of detail, and only by means of his art does he succeed in retaining his spontaneity and in concealing the moral. It seems that he is too successful.

He is still saddled with the reproach of having portrayed, not the trill of the nightingale and blossoming roses and the beloved's amber-look, as it goes in the story of the Lisbon earthquake, but this underworld den. But since he had chosen the subject his task could not have been better fulfilled.

False interpretation, inadmissible isolation of the hero's phrases, which must not be removed either from their atmosphere or, still less, from their psychological context if they are to retain their original and quite definite significance, misled Shestov into regarding the poet as a transvaluer of all values. In effect, Dostoevsky, in his progress through human nature, did come into contact with the region in which supermen dwell. Unquestionably the topography of this fever-region particularly attracted him all his life. He recognized its immense significance for travellers weary of Europe, and jealously inhaled its poisonous vapours. Nietzsche may have believed that he leant on Dostoevsky for support, and it can serve to enhance Nietzsche's psychology. It is of no importance to criticism of Dostoevsky.

This typical example proves how questionable is the application of the epithet "cruel" to Dostoevsky's methods. Actually his incentive was nothing more or less than the unswerving devotion of a poet emancipated not from morals but from the roof-garden. Instead of recognizing this path to universality, a path across which thousands of candles cast the light of day, Shestov considers Dostoevsky the forerunner and relative of the philosopher "who was the first to decorate his banner with the terrible words: Apotheosis of cruelty." In so far as it is possible to pervert facts it has here been done to perfection.

This procedure is a matter of course to-day and is practised by every possible Shestov on every possible occasion. This mental indolence proves how deeply we are all sunk in an underworld den. We, on the other hand, fail to benefit by the poison which stimulated the underworldling. Old shibboleths are only flung aside to make room for *cli-*

chés which are more easily workable. A poet whose very nature demanded bold leaps in the dark and whose profile cannot be caught with a carpenter's pencil, is not to be set on a Procrustes' bed. He needs to become black just because he lights up the darkness. Instead of letting him illuminate them, people paint him over and perhaps even imagine that this adds to his greatness by rendering him more intelligible.

Attempts have been made to trace the experience which provoked the fanatical exasperation of these memoirs. Shestov and others unjustifiably blame Siberia. It was not the *katorga* which gave birth to the underworld refuge. It dates back . . . to Dostoevsky's earliest emotions, first expressed in **The Double.** The rudiments of the underworld are found in Golyadkin's habitation, but Golyadkin is simple and stupid. His brain was not capable of generalizing his personal experience and lapsed into delusion. Not a little has been added to the hero's knowledge in twenty years. His power of resistance and his capacity for suffering have grown, but so has his tension. The anthropomorphic sentiment of the conservative Golyadkin is moderate beside the intellectual fantasy of the underworld man. The latter is certainly not disposed to soothe his twofold or manifold existence with the false product of a harmless madness, and to compound his claim on the world around with touching self-expropriation.

Naturally Siberia contributed to the preparation of this tension, and perhaps more than his experiences in the *katorga,* what followed the *katorga.* Still, it will not do to take isolated incidents in order to explain this turning-point in the poet's career. The tension is the natural consequence of every experience as well as of every quality of the man himself. Over the underworld den broods a sky of brimstone. The underworldling still squats in inactivity, meditates and chatters. How should I induce them not to laugh at my wretchedness? How should I show them that I am not a "little worm"? That is the sense of the monologue. The question swells and festers in the underworld den and presses towards an outlet. The monologue is not an outlet but merely a bridge to something else. Every line heralds the birth of tragedy. (pp. 102-10)

> *Julius Meier-Graefe, in his* Dostoevsky: The Man and His Work, *translated by Herbert H. Marks, George Routledge and Sons Ltd., 1928, 406 p.*

Edward Hallett Carr   (essay date 1931)

[*Carr was an English educator, political historian, and biographer whose greatest achievement was his fourteen-volume history of the Soviet Union from 1917-29. In the following excerpt from his biography of Dostoevsky, he discusses the author's mental and physical distress at the time he wrote* Notes from the Underground *but denies that the work is an autobiographical depiction of spiritual or philosophical crisis.*]

Before the end of the Russian October [in 1863], Dostoevsky was back in Petersburg. He joined his wife in Vladimir, and together they moved about the middle of November to Moscow. There all the winter Maria Dmitriev-na lay slowly dying, passing through the familiar phases of advanced consumption—depression, irritation and wild pathetic optimism. Except for one or two brief visits to Petersburg, Dostoevsky remained at her side, at first alone, later supported by the dying woman's sister. It was not in his nature to become altogether indifferent to a woman who had once infatuated him. A better man might have been less patient; a more blameless husband might have been less tender to one who had never loved him and whom he had long ceased to love. But the capacity for sinning, and for sinning without remorse, carried with it a capacity for unstinting forgiveness of sins against himself. The wrongs she had done him, the wrongs he had done her, the defects of her character and of his, were forgotten; and there remained on his side nothing but the tenderness of pure pity, pity unspoiled by even the most fleeting sense of condescension or superior virtue.

While his mother lay on her sick-bed in Moscow, young Paul Isaev [Dostoevsky's stepson] was pursuing his studies and his pleasures in Petersburg. There was nothing in his parentage to promise stability of character; and an indulgent upbringing had confirmed him in the pleasant habits of an idler and a licensed scapegrace. When at Semipalatinsk the curly-haired boy often had "played the fool and refused to learn," the doting stepfather accepted it as being "in the order of things." It was difficult to look with equal complacency on the same behaviour at the age of sixteen. When Maria Dmitrievna was moved to Vladimir and Dostoevsky went abroad, Paul had been left in the Petersburg flat in the charge of a tutor named Rodevich; but this arrangement did not prevent the boy from devoting his time and energies to the acquisition of precocious worldly experience rather than to more orthodox forms of learning. His favourite resort was the Yusupov Garden, the Vauxhall of Petersburg, and it was not long before he had installed a prostitute in the flat. Dostoevsky's letters to his stepson from abroad during the summer and autumn, and from Moscow in the winter, alternate pathetically between expressions of affection, obviously sincere, and confidence, no less obviously misplaced, and bitter heartfelt reproaches—reproaches that he does not take the trouble to write, reproaches, when he does write, that his letters are misspelt and illiterate, reproaches for dissipation and extravagance.

It was even worse when Paul came to Moscow on a New Year visit. His behaviour to his sick mother was so intolerable that he had to be sent back post-haste to Petersburg—probably the very result which he wished to produce.

> He is extraordinarily irresponsible [wrote Dostoevsky to his sister-in-law] and the whole trouble is that he does not know how to behave with a very sick woman. Of course, Maria Dmitrievna's illness has made her irritable to the last degree. . . . I am terribly grieved for her, and life for me here is no bed of roses. But I feel I am necessary to her and therefore remain.

There are few moments of Dostoevsky's life which inspire us with more unmixed sympathy than these of his faithful watch by the dying consumptive's bedside.

The spectacle of his wife's agony, the irregular courses of

his stepson and, perhaps, the unquiet emotions of the past summer had reacted on Dostoevsky's diseased nervous system. During the first week in Moscow he had two epileptic fits, "one very severe." In a letter to his brother in February he records two more fits; he has been ill for a fortnight; his old trouble, piles, has recurred and been followed by inflammation of the bladder; he does not keep his bed, but can "neither stand nor sit." Towards the end of the month he risked a journey to Petersburg, but suffered agonies both there and after his return. By the end of March, the main symptoms had passed away leaving an aftermath of weariness, weakness and jagged nerves.

Financial anxieties, except when he was actually on the verge of starvation, never weighed heavily on Dostoevsky; and they probably counted for little among the other troubles of the moment. His position and outlook were indeed rather better than usual. It is true that he had no immediate source of income. But he had returned to Russia with the balance of Boborykin's 300 roubles in his pocket; and at the end of November he received 3,000 roubles as his share of the legacy of rich uncle Kumanin (the husband of his mother's sister) who, having been bedridden with paralysis for eight years, had just opportunely expired. This windfall enabled him to pay back his debt to the Fund for Needy Men of Letters, and to meet the needs of existence for a few months; and as usual when he had money, his pen remained idle. By the spring the money was gone and he was once more reduced to begging small sums from his scarcely less poverty-stricken brother Michael in Petersburg. Finally, in April, Boborykin, who must long since have despaired of getting the promised story, curtly demanded his money back. Dostoevsky tried to digest his humiliation by being rude to his creditor; but he took the only possible course of appealing to Michael, who once more advanced the necessary sum to save his brother's name from disgrace.

The winter for Michael had been one long struggle to repair the family fortunes. The *Vremya* was dead; but the authorities agreed, after a decent interval, to permit its resurrection under a new name. The first name proposed for the revived journal was *Pravda* ("Truth"); but this designation was rejected by the censorship as being dangerous and unduly tendencious. The next title suggested was colourless enough to win official approbation; the new journal was to be called the *Epocha*. But delay followed delay; and instead of the *Epocha* making its bow at the beginning of the year, nothing was published till the last week in March, when a double number for January-February was at last delivered to an attenuated number of patient subscribers.

Fyodor followed the struggles and disasters from Moscow with an agonised interest. After the closure of the *Vremya* in the preceding May, he had not written a line for seven or eight months; and when he at last sat down to write his *Memoirs from Underground* for the second number of the *Epocha,* the words did not flow easily from his pen.

> I am a sick man. I am a malicious man. I am an unprepossessing man. I think I have a pain in my spleen. Of course, I really don't understand my pains, and cannot tell exactly what is aching. I

am taking no remedies and never have taken remedies, though I respect medicine and doctors. . . . No, I refuse remedies out of malice. You probably fail to understand that. Well, I understand. Naturally, I shall not be able to explain to you whom I am getting at with this malice of mine. . . . I know better than anyone that I shall harm only myself and nobody else. But all the same, if I refuse remedies, it is out of malice. I have a pain in my spleen; well, let it ache all the worse.

These opening sentences of the *Memoirs* seem pregnant with all the concentrated bitterness of this winter of unalloyed misery: the wife coughing out her life in the next room, the mistress who had played him false in France, the spoilt and heartless stepson wasting his substance in Petersburg, the recurrent attacks of epilepsy, and the painful malady which would let him "neither sit nor stand." Even the season of the year played its part in the mood of the *Memoirs.* Every Russian, and every foreigner who has lived in Russia, is familiar with the enervating effects of those last weeks of the seemingly interminable Russian winter, when frost alternates with thaw and still delays the long-awaited spring.

> To-day snow is falling, [concludes the first part of the *Memoirs*] half-wet, yellow, dirty snow. Yesterday it was snowing too, and the day before it was snowing. I think it must be the wet snow which brought this story to my mind. So let it be called "A Story of the Wet Snow."

The *Memoirs* have in recent years received an almost exaggerated amount of attention from critics and students of Dostoevsky. They fall into two parts: the first is an exposition of the philosophy of malice, the second relates an incident, or rather a series of incidents, from the life of the supposed narrator, the malicious man. The first part may seem inadequate as philosophy, the second as fiction; but in their queer way the *Memoirs* are as original as anything Dostoevsky ever wrote. Many years later the critic Rozanov, Polina Suslova's [Dostoevsky's mistress'] husband, drew from them the inspiration for some of the most capricious of his writings; and Rozanov declared that, if a statue of him were ever erected, he should be depicted putting out his tongue at the reader. This exactly defines the attitude of the man from "underground"; his constant delight is to put out his tongue not merely at the reader but at the world at large and even at himself. The *Memoirs from Underground* lack the broad humanity and tolerance which inspire Dostoevsky's greater works; they reflect too much of the pain and distraction in the midst of which they were composed.

The book has, nevertheless, an important place in Dostoevsky's development; it was his first incursion into philosophy, and forms in a certain sense an introduction to the series of his great novels. In the previous year there had appeared a work whose historical significance far exceeds its small literary merit, a novel by the radical publicist Chernyshevsky entitled *What Is to be Done?* It is the picture of a Utopian state of society in which perfect happiness is attained by everyone pursuing untrammelled the satisfaction of his own rational desires. In the eyes of

Chernyshevsky, a pupil of J. S. Mill, reason and self-interest are the sole sanctions of morality; man commits evil actions only through misapprehension of the true nature of his interests; and intellectual enlightenment is the infallible road to right conduct. The *Memoirs from Underground* are an answer to the philosophy of Chernyshevsky. It had by this time become one of Dostoevsky's strongest convictions that human nature is not, as optimistic utilitarians of Chernyshevsky's kidney believed, fundamentally and essentially good; and that man, in virtue of one side of his nature, may desire and choose evil, knowing it to be evil. This conviction finds its first expression in these *Memoirs:*

> Who was it, pray, who first declared and proclaimed that man behaves like a blackguard only because he does not know his true interests; and that if he were enlightened and had his eyes opened to his true, normal interests, he would straightway cease to behave like a blackguard and become good and honourable, inasmuch as, being enlightened and understanding his true advantages, he would see his advantage in goodness? . . . O excellent young man! O pure, innocent babe!

The whole history of mankind, argues Dostoevsky, "from the flood to the Schleswig-Holstein period" (it was the moment of the forcible occupation of the duchies by joint Austrian and Prussian forces), is a record of human irrationality. Man may love to build, like the ant in his ant-hill; but he also loves to destroy. He loves to indulge his caprice, to sin deliberately against his own interests merely in order to free himself from the tyranny of reason, of "twice two are four." Such were the bold paradoxes maintained by Dostoevsky in the year 1864. The age of optimism, of faith in a morality established by science and reason, has now long passed away. The irrational chaos of human nature has become a platitude, and we no longer require a subterranean philosopher to put out his tongue at us in order to compel belief in it. It is one of the most important points on which Dostoevsky anticipated modern psychology.

The *Memoirs from Underground* mark then a stage in the growth of Dostoevsky's thought. Many critics, including most German writers on Dostoevsky and Middleton Murry in English, attach to them a profounder significance. It is suggested that Dostoevsky did in fact pass in this winter of 1863-4 through a spiritual crisis in which he rebelled against accepted morality and vindicated to his own satisfaction the right to sin; and that the *Memoirs* are the record of his own soul-shattering experience. The theory is an illustration of the danger of seeking autobiographical material in professed works of fiction. It will not hold water; and it is hard to believe that the critics who maintain it have read Dostoevsky's private letters of the period, not all of which were available when the theory was first propounded. During his sojourn in Moscow which lasted from November 1863 to the end of April 1864, Dostoevsky wrote twenty-one letters which are extant; of these, twelve are letters to his brother Michael, from whom he concealed none of his affairs or his thoughts. They are letters of a man wrestling with every

form of material difficulty and disaster, and overwhelmed with every kind of mental and physical distress; but they contain no single hint of any spiritual crisis or of any tormenting preoccupation with questions of faith and philosophy. Nor is the evidence exclusively negative. In a letter to Michael of March 26th he refers to the excisions made by the censorship in the first part of the *Memoirs:*

> What swine the censors are! The passages where I railed at everything and *made show* of blaspheming [Dostoevsky's own underlining] are allowed; but the passage where I deduced from all this the necessity of belief in Christ is cut out.

These are not the words of a man who has passed through a furnace of doubt and revolt; and they prove that the demonstration of the love of evil as a fundamental element in human nature was followed in the original text (which is lost to us) by an argument of "the necessity of belief in Christ." In other words, far from being a cry of revolt, the book was a vindication of religious orthodoxy against the materialistic ethics of Chernyshevsky. (pp. 115-22)

> *Edward Hallett Carr, in his* Dostoevsky: A New Biography, 1821-1881, *George Allen & Unwin Ltd., 1931, 331 p.*

Ralph E. Matlaw   (essay date 1958)

[*A German-born American educator and critic, Matlaw was an authority on nineteenth-century Russian literature, a professor of Slavic languages, and the translator and editor of works by Anton Chekhov, Ivan Turgenev, Leo Tolstoy, Fyodor Dostoevsky, and Appolon Grigor'ev. In the following excerpt, he studies aspects of structure, symbolism, and narration that contribute to the artistic and thematic unity of* Notes from the Underground.]

In the literature on *Notes from the Underground* the protagonist is always called "the underground man" (*podpol'nyj chelovek*), as if he were an archetypal entity, rather than "the narrator," an accepted literary convention of the *Icherzählung*. The nomenclature is significant, for critics have treated the work as the turning point in Dostoevsky's development, ransacked it for philosophical, political, and sociological formulas, noted the profound psychology, but have never analyzed the *Notes* in detail as an artifact. By so doing critics distort the *Notes* structurally and substantively, because they concentrate on and over-emphasize the first part of the work almost to the exclusion of the second, and because they accept and discuss the narrator's formulations in this part without analyzing them as the expression of a literary creation. The purpose of this study is to examine the unity of the *Notes:* to ascertain the relationships of its two parts; to indicate the thematic function of ordering episodes in a particular sequence; to note the recurrence of certain objects, the symbolism involved therein, and its effect on the unity of the *Notes;* finally, to assess the effect of artful integration on the apparent "meaning" of the work.

To treat the *Notes* as an artistic whole—to find the real, rather than the mechanical principle of organization—involves first the problem of time sequence. Events in Part II antedate those of Part I by fourteen to sixteen years.

What is the purpose of such displacement? The simplest answer might be that such sequence obviates accounting for the time gap. The second part can have no apt conclusion. Since it reconstructs the narrator's experience, it might well continue his story to the time he commits his "notes" to paper. Indeed, at the end of the work, to the last sentence, "I don't want to write more from 'underground', " Dostoevsky appends the comment "the notes of this paradoxalist do not end here, however. He could not refrain from continuing them, but it seems to us that we may stop here." Were the two sections placed chronologically, there would be a hiatus between the end of his experiences and his philosophical formulations; the emergence of one from the other might seem insufficiently motivated as a change from narrative to "logical" exposition. Another possibility is that the second part, particularly in 1864, must have seemed particularly repellent to the reader. Why read, or even write, so tortured and in some respects disgusting a work? In the first section, though the psychological mechanism is no less evident, the narrator propounds a series of brilliant paradoxes, through which he attempts to establish his intellectual superiority, so that his vagaries in the second part now seem to him to be presented against a backdrop which slightly attenuates them. Finally, this narrator is a new phenomenon in literature and must be so marked. Hence Dostoevsky's footnote:

> The author of these notes and the "Notes" themselves are, of course, imaginary. Nevertheless, such persons as the writer of these notes not only may, but positively must exist in our society, considering those circumstances under which our society in general was formed. I wanted to expose to the public more clearly than is usually done one of the characters of the recent past. He is one of the representatives of the current generation. In this excerpt, entitled "Underground," this person introduces himself, his views, and, as it were, tries to explain the reasons why he appeared and had to appear in our midst. In the following excerpt will appear the real "notes" of this person about several events in his life.

Although these answers begin to explain the structure, they do not satisfactorily account for the higher organization so characteristic in Dostoevsky. For even a cursory reading reveals that the work is of a piece—stylistically, intellectually, psychologically the *Notes* are a single sustained effort. They take the form of an extended monologue, but are full of suggestions of dialogue: "you say," "you laugh," "this is all that you say," "yes, gentlemen," and so on. Such locutions also appear, to a lesser degree, in the *Writer's Diary,* but with a different function. The narrator, by his own admission, is writing a confession, and maintains that the oratorical flourishes simply exist so that he may express himself most easily and clearly. But this device in turn gives the work the illusion of dialogue and makes it seem like a sustained polemic with an opponent, as if the narrator were anticipating objections. Like all confessions, the narrator's postulates the existence of an auditor, but psychologically the auditor here is never passive and cannot be so for this is a confession to one's self—the auditor and confessor are one. The *Notes* may

even be considered as a parody of confession which, in religious terms, is ostensibly preceded by contrition, but here is replaced by proud (though ambivalent) self-defense. The confession is not Augustinian but Rousseauistic, with the added temporal notation of Musset's title, *Confessions d'un enfant du siècle.* The literary roots of the narrator's confession are unmistakable. Rousseau appears not only as the propounder of the *homme de la nature et de la vérité* in the first part, but also in an explicit comment at its end. The narrator approves Heine's criticism of Rousseau and autobiography—that a man will lie about himself out of sheer vanity—but he also adduces it as proof that his confession is true, unexaggerated, since it is not meant for publication.

The narrator is correct in his contention, though not in the manner he thinks. Dostoevsky's psychological insight permits him to trace a portrait which is, or can be, clear to the reader despite the narrator's evasions, repetitions, contradictions, self-lacerations. At their deepest level the narrator's analyses are honestly meant. That they appear not to be so, or to be incorrect, must be attributed to the fact that these analyses and judgments are distorted by the narrator's personality. The reader must constantly discount the distorting prism, and assess the narrator's incorrect judgments about others and himself in terms of what they tell about the narrator. To put it more clearly, the narrator is portrayed twice. His own statements account for his actions at one level, yet his statements are not trustworthy. Dostoevsky indicates the profounder psychological level, which is manifest in the contradiction between the narrator's analyses and his behavior. Parenthetically, it might be pointed out that the narrator's knowledge is not emotional but rational; although he claims that the *Notes* are "hardly literature so much as corrective punishment," the *Notes,* unlike those of the *Adolescent* [*A Raw Youth*], have no ameliorative or therapeutic value to their ostensible author.

If the *Notes* are to be considered as a psychological document, then the structure, and even its confessional aspect, gains another dimension. The relationship of the two parts might be described as follows: most of the interest of the *Notes* for the narrator consists in his recreation of the experiences in Part II. But the narrator is not at first capable of committing himself to such an exposition. He evades the subject, attempts to build up his ego by rationalization, by philosophical speculation, and avoids the recapitulation of his past until the time that the need for disclosure and security in such disclosure coincide. From this point of view practically all the first part is a false start, leading the reader away from the real subject of the work. Dostoevsky had originally indicated the true center of the book himself. The only significant change from the first printed text to the second is the elimination of the last sentence in Dostoevsky's footnote: "Thus this first excerpt should be considered as an introduction to the whole book, almost as a foreword."

A psychological principle of organization seems to account most satisfactorily for the sequence of the *Notes,* but it does not solve all the problems of organization. Against his will the narrator exposes himself almost as much in the first as in the second part. And if one ignores other dimensions of the work and their relation to the psychological, the *Notes* then do not properly weight Part I as the synthesis, the result of the narrator's life in Part II. Moreover, even psychological confession does not account for the highly selective nature and progression of episodes in what at first appears to be merely a chronological recapitulation. So that if psychologically the narrative properly progresses from the first to the second part, chronologically and rationally Part II leads back into the formulations of Part I. Neither the narrator nor Dostoevsky stresses this (except in the concluding footnote), but as we shall see, the narrator's psychological pattern does not in itself account for all of his social behavior: society and the particular historical moment affect his personality. And the interaction of the psychological, social, and intellectual create the dramatic tension and structure of the *Notes.*

Dostoevsky's style and his narrative method consist of an interpenetration of "naturalistic" and metaphysical elements. He introduces real events and philosophical speculations as two facets of the same subject, frequently (as in the "odor of sanctity" in the *Brothers Karamazov*) presenting a naturalistic explanation concomitantly with a mystic one. The opposition of real to ideal implies an ethical core which, in a social context, postulates in part the quest of the individual for his place in the world. It is so stated in Gogol's "Cloak" which, with his "Nevsky Prospect," is a forerunner of important concepts in the *Notes.* The quest is psychological as well as ethical, and Dostoevsky's contribution to the problem lies in the development of its psychological aspect and can be illustrated by means of his earlier story, the *Double.* Misinterpretation of the *Double* has tended to obliterate the organic unity of Dostoevsky's psychological and social thought. Realizing that the *Double* failed, Dostoevsky continually wished to rewrite the work, but finally realized that it would have to be completely recast. However, only the form was bad—the idea remained artistically unrealized. Dostoevsky even betrays his dualistic procedure in his defense of the *Double* in the *Writer's Diary:* "Why should I lose a wonderful idea, and an extraordinary type in his social importance, which I first discovered, and whose herald I was?" Further he states "the idea was quite clear, and I have never expressed anything more important in my work." This idea is obviously not clinical schizophrenia but an ethical idea which contrasts man's aspiration (in the "double") with his actual position. The fact that the double exists is indubitably psychological; the reason for its existence, in Dostoevsky's work, is primarily social. In the *Notes* we may clearly see Dostoevsky's ethical-psychological duality in operation, and may also note in passing the change of attitude by the author from the detachment and disdain of the *Double* to sympathetic treatment of the narrator and his problems in the *Notes.*

In the second part of the *Notes* each of the episodes is carefully selected to point out socio-ethical considerations simultaneously with psychological ones. These appear in different balances: sometimes one element predominates, sometimes another; both are always present. I shall here touch only on four episodes—that with the officer, the farewell party for Zverkov, the affair with Liza, and the

attitude of the narrator to his servant Apollon—in an attempt to see how Dostoevsky's method gradually forces the narrator into his final position.

The narrator attempts to avenge himself against an officer who, during a quarrel with another man "moved me from where I was standing to another spot and passed by as though he had not noticed me." The narrator does not demand an immediate apology but later, in various ways, for several years (!) he attempts to revenge this slight. Occasionally he spots the officer on the Nevsky Prospect, where the narrator

> used to wriggle like an eel among the passers-by, in the most unseemly fashion, continually moving aside to make way for generals, for officers of the Guards and the Hussars, or for ladies. In those minutes I used to feel a convulsive twinge at my heart, and hot all down my back at the mere thought of the wretchedness of my dress, of the wretchedness and vulgarity of my little scurrying figure.

The future underground man, usually immersed in books and daydreaming, is drawn to the Nevsky at every possible opportunity, drawn to partake in the rush and movement of life. The Nevsky in this sense is almost a commonplace of Russian literature. Dostoevsky's distinctive use emphasizes the narrator's "continually moving aside," his being forced outside the stream of life while the social parade passes him in both directions. Of the officer the narrator observes that "he too went out of his way for generals and persons of high rank, and he too shifted among them like an eel. But people like me, or even neater than I, he simply walked over." Social stratification, then, forces the officer to step aside, but the narrator, as a lower creature in the scale, must *continually* step aside. He has no stature either in his own estimation (a psychological fact), or in that of the Nevsky strollers (a social comment).

His "audacious" plan for revenge consists in attempting to force the officer to yield the right of way. To achieve his end, the narrator makes elaborate preparations: "To begin with, when I carried out my plan I should have to look very decent, and I had to think of my clothes. In any case, if, for instance, there were any sort of public scandal . . . I must be well dressed; that inspires respect and of itself puts us in some way on equal footing in the eyes of high society." By dint of financial hardship the narrator improves his appearance. Similarly, Akaky Akakevich in the *Cloak* saves in order to purchase his garment. The sacrifice for each is crucial, since the goal for both represents the emotional awakening of the character. The officer's crime was lack of notice, lack of consideration for a fellow being. By improving his appearance, the narrator defeats the primary social purpose of his plan, since the respect he may obtain will be merely a tribute to his external appearance. Thus his rationalization leads him to duplicate the officer's crime: he is unable to consider himself a social being. His behavior is socially conditioned—the material emphasis has been inculcated too strongly—but his inability to exact revenge is also motivated psychologically. His diffidence, his vanity, insist that he present an external appearance corresponding to what he considers his intellectual superiority. Similarly, he cannot carry out his plan for psychological reasons. At the last minute he always steps aside, once even falling ignominiously at the officer's feet. Finally the narrator closes his eyes and collides with the officer, who

> did not even look around and pretended not to notice it. But he was only pretending, I am convinced of it, I am convinced of it to this day! Of course, I got the worst of it—he was stronger—but that was not the point. The point was that I had attained my goal, I had kept up my dignity, I had not yielded a step, and had put myself publicly on an equal social footing with him.

The narrator's vanity had precluded any possibility of social atonement by the officer. Psychologically, the narrator *must* feel that he has triumphed, though his insistence suggests he does not. Admission that the officer did not notice him would be unbearable: it would annihilate him, destroy the very foundation of his personality. Even failure is preferable to nonrecognition, since failure at least implies the possibility of success, and thereby provides the narrator a point of contact with humanity. He ends the episode by remarking: "The officer was later transferred. I have not seen him now for fourteen years. What is the dear fellow (*golubchik*) doing now? Whom is he walking over?" Although used sarcastically, the term of endearment (*golubchik*) is in part seriously meant, and presents an inverted protest, for to the narrator the officer represents a form—perhaps the worst form—of social intercourse. And the protest becomes the more poignant as the narrator anticipates similar experiences by other men, members of the same social and historical community. The personal psychology, however, still dominates. There is apparently a genuine interest in maintaining the fleeting contact, the brief moment of social and psychological achievement.

The second major event is again precipitated by a combination of social and psychological forces. The narrator experiences one of those rare moments when he feels a need for human companionship. But since the day is a Thursday and the only person whose house he frequents (his superior, Setochin, who also figures in the *Double*) receives only on Tuesday, the narrator must hold his desire in abeyance. He finally decides to visit a former classmate and there insinuates himself into the farewell party for Zverkov. This episode is one of the clearest examples of the narrator's psychological mechanism. He constantly realizes that he should not act as he does, but nevertheless each action is calculated to antagonize the other participants and elicit their disdain. Also, the difference between the narrator's quotations of dialogue and his interpretation of their meanings indicates that after the episode with the officer he has reached a point at which social intercourse is no longer feasible for him. He misinterprets Zverkov's motives when the latter first greets him, and Zverkov's final remark, "Insulted? *You* insulted *me?* Understand, sir, that you could never, under any circumstances, possibly insult *me*," is interpreted only psychologically, whereas the remark also has overtones of social inequality or might be construed as a combination of exasperation and social differentiation. But the point here is precisely to indicate, in comparison with the narrator's youth and school days, and with the Nevsky episode, that

the question of social inequality has now become for the narrator almost entirely a psychological problem of individual value.

During the trip to the brothel and the events there (about which more in the next section), and simultaneously with the romantic phantasy about revenge, the narrator has an inkling that he will disgrace rather than vindicate himself. Nevertheless, despite his hesitation and vacillation, he feels compelled to bring the event to its inevitable conclusion, to discover his essential self. This scene is clearly the keystone of the *Notes* but it is projected by means of an irony that operates at a second remove. Dostoevsky brilliantly exploits a symbolic touch to forewarn the reader of the added intricacy. Material standards were previously shown to be inadequate because they were limited by rationality. They may also be inadequate because they are misrepresented by psychological irrationality. Thus the narrator's dissatisfaction with his personality finds one mode of expression in his undue concern for sartorial elegance, a product of the same distortion that leads him to intense dissatisfaction with his face. In describing his attitude he also states his desideratum: "Let my face even be ugly, so long as it seems lofty, expressive, and above all *extremely* intelligent." It therefore follows that he also expects his face to reflect his tortured feelings when he arrives at the brothel. As he approaches Liza he looks at a mirror: "My harassed face struck me as particularly revolting, pale, angry, abject, with dishevelled hair." Everything that follows seems to the narrator to be motivated by and to exemplify his vilest, most repulsive traits. Like the narrator's assumption about his face, this is only *his* view, and his view of the image in the mirror is a distortion of a false view. But Dostoevsky forces the reader to acknowledge that ultimately the narrator interprets the picture in the mirror correctly: the mirror reflects an agonized face. The appearance and the reality have fused. Similarly, the reader must now discount the narrator's view of his motivation in talking to Liza and accept his sermon as the direct expression of the narrator's profoundest convictions and deepest needs. The scene presents the narrator's views directly, and the reader only tends to question them because the narrator describes them as artificial and because some of his views of "love" are highly personal, though so noted by him. The sermon contradicts most of the rational strictures and self-characterizations of the narrator but leads to the same conclusions that the paradoxes of Part I imply. The verbal pattern is atypical: this time the narrator consciously uses an emotional, even sentimental, harangue, and minimizes intellectual, rational exposition. He later denies that his speech represents his real vision because it is atypical of his style, though he justifies its use for Liza. The stylized eloquence in the external form of the sermon corresponds to a reversal in the narrator's subject matter: not material advancement but the soul and love are its contents. It rejects his previous criteria by being directed at a person of no intellectual ability (but even she comments on the "bookish" nature of his speech), a person who according to Part I would be unworthy of his attention. The scene emphasizes that the narrator has dramatically tried, and spectacularly succeeded, in arousing an ignorant soul and has led it out of an acquiescence to and involvement in humanity's shoddier side to an appreciation of its individuality, value, and even grandeur. The narrator has salvaged one life, and in his concern for an "insignificant" person has demonstrated the mainspring of his view of man. The success of his effort, both on Liza and on himself (for he becomes involved in his own eloquence and is moved by it) indicates that he has found and developed the basic issues to which man responds.

The narrator cannot operate long at this emotional level, and realizes his incapacity almost immediately. He proceeds to describe his relationship with Apollon, which is very rich in meanings. If the narrator's report can be trusted, the portrait of Apollon indicates, beneath the mask of human dignity, the same malicious, sadistic traits characteristic of the narrator. He is thus an extension of the narrator's personality, a proof, as it were, of his ubiquity in the modern world, and once more refers the reader to Dostoevsky's footnote. The relationship is complex, for the narrator enjoys the so-called "tortures" Apollon inflicts on him, which he anticipates and provokes. There is no motivation for Apollon's remaining with the narrator unless one accepts the narrator's estimate of his servant or else vouchsafes him enormous compassion and stature. Yet Apollon has additional meanings: he is another of those who consider the external side of man supreme, but, paradoxically, is a servant who achieves true (or as the narrator sees it, false) human dignity. And as one who delights in reading psalms aloud, and who ultimately turns into a professional funeral psalm reader, he intones a symbolic *requiescat* over the narrator while still in his service. Thus Apollon is introduced at this point to balance the narrator's humanistic achievement with Liza and to reintroduce his psychological estrangement.

In anticipating Liza's visit, the narrator reflects on the circumstance that he will appear to her in all his miserable poverty and slovenliness. Again human beings are to be judged by their appearance rather than their intrinsic value. Yet the narrator, having once broken through his assumed intellectualism to experience a relationship founded on a fundamental human need, would repeat such experiences if he were capable of so doing. He realizes the difference between the need and the action, the social and the personal, when he objects to poverty: "Oh, the beastliness! And it isn't the beastliness of it that matters most! There is something more important, more loathsome, viler! Yes, viler! And to put on that dishonest lying mask again!" The lying mask, that is, his speech to Liza, is rejected, and the narrator's second protest is directed against the psychological barrier erected between himself and man; it reaffirms his alienation from society.

To accept unquestioningly the narrator's abstractions in Part I, the results of his cerebrations and psychological rationalizations, would necessitate, if only for reasons of consistency, accepting the accuracy and validity of the depictions as well as the judgments of events in Part II. That Dostoevsky does not intend the reader to do so, that, in fact, he expects the narrative to communicate, by artistic deployment, more and perhaps different generalizations about the narrator than the narrator can make by generalization and description, may be illustrated by tracing the symbolism of objects in the *Notes.* Here one must distinguish between the symbolic value objects assume for the narrator, and the symbolism arising from the narrator's story, but apparent only to the reader.

Because so much of Dostoevsky consists of dramatic dialogue there is little descriptive prose; in the *Notes* there is almost none. Here as elsewhere Dostoevsky makes symbolic use of objects and of attitudes expressed through objects, though these must necessarily appear as speech. Among objects the following bear significant relation to the story: clothes (noted earlier in the Nevsky episode), eyes, snow, tables, walls, doors, and glass. A closer look at these will show yet another artistic connection between the two parts and simultaneously offer a further insight into Dostoevsky's method.

We have previously seen that to the narrator clothes are an index of personal success. They appear with other connotations as well. Thus in Part I the first object the narrator finds antipathetic is the clanking sword of an officer. The problem of dress recurs before the party, first when the narrator brushes his own shoes because he fears that Apollon would never consent to clean twice in a single day, and again when he thinks about the state of his clothes and the yellow spot on his trousers. (One must note here the onus of the "Yellow Passport" carried by prostitutes, as well as the Russian designation, "yellow spot," for that part of the retina most sensitive to light.) Similarly, his old dressing gown, in which he feels sure Liza will see him, and which even in his own eyes is the symbol of poverty, is exactly the object he tries to wrap around himself when she does appear. Apparently it offers no protection except the psychological one of displaying his poverty. More telling is the fact that real contact between him and Liza is necessarily made while he is without clothes, and at a time when he is rawest psychologically. When he dresses at the brothel he immediately loses the possibility for personal contact and resumes his facade, with which clothes may be equated. When Liza visits him, he recognizes that the psychological situation of the brothel is reversed, and notes its symbolic counterpart in Liza's festive appearance and his own dressing gown. But the clearest proof of the symbolic use of clothes occurs in the brief spell when the narrator acts from the heart—a distinction he insists upon when he says about the money he pressed into Liza's hand, "though I did that cruel thing purposely, it was not an impulse from the heart, but came from my evil brain." In that brief span, between the time she leaves and that moment on the street when he realizes the futility of pursuit, he is concerned only with his need, not with his intellect. When he rushes after her, clothes lose the value the narrator usually attaches to them, become neutral and, paradoxically, assume their most striking symbolic function by indicating the profundity of the moment: "A minute later I flew like a madman to dress, flinging on what I could at random, and ran headlong after her."

Connected with the psychological and the social behavior expressed by the emphasis on clothes is a continual emphasis on eyes, the verb *to see,* and the chiaroscuro of Petersburg. The narrator, like others in the *Double* and *Pos-*

sessed, finds it impossible to look anyone directly in the eyes, turns away, and at the same time has a constant paranoiac feeling of being observed. (The objection to the crystal palace is therefore apposite even in this context.) At least as early as *Oedipus Rex* eyes and seeing are used as symbols for understanding or knowledge and reason. In the *Notes,* both in the introspections of Part I and the episodes of Part II, they repeatedly indicate that the narrator cannot see clearly, cannot evaluate properly, refuses to understand or is incapable of it.

This configuration also appears in conjunction with snow, which is usually treated as a white, pristine covering, either pleasant or inimical, but in either case endowed with an elemental beauty. In the *Notes,* in Petersburg, it is yellow, dingy, wet, unpleasant, troublesome; Dostoevsky uses it for maximum symbolic effect. The narrator almost at the outset admits that the Petersburg climate is bad for him, but only returns to the subject at the end of Part I, when he makes the important statement, "I fancy it is the wet snow which has reminded me of that incident, which I cannot shake off now. And so let it be a story apropos of the wet snow." In the same manner, after the dinner party, when the narrator jumps into a sleigh to follow his friends, he particularly remembers the driver and horse, covered with "wet and, as it were, warm snow. It was hot and steaming." This time the narrator becomes depressed by snow in a different way. He realizes during the ride that his behavior is foolish, but decides to carry on. He unbuttons his coat, and the snow, in big wet flakes, drifts under his coat, his jacket, and his tie. It melts there and he remarks "I did not wrap myself up—all was lost anyway." Clearly he betrays the same romantic attitude as that of the scene of revenge he conjures up en route. But just as clearly, although this is a crucial episode in his experience, it cannot be the scene he recalls at the end of Part I. Nevertheless it forms one part of it. The narrator mentions "deserted street lights gleaming sullenly in the snowy darkness like torches at a funeral" (an echo of Apollon's calling). He uses the topic of snow (again in conjunction with funerals and darkness) to start his conversation with Liza. The most effective use of snow occurs at the end, when Liza runs into the street and the narrator follows her. This time it falls in masses, perpendicularly, ready to cover everything, "the pavement and the empty street as though with a pillow. There was no one in the street, no sound was to be heard. The streetlights gave a disconsolate and useless glimmer." The narrator ends his search, and indeed the image has been exploited fully. The snow, which originally hung over him, dingy, and could not be shaken off, and which reminded him of the experiences of Part II, now serves to cover Liza's steps. But it can never obliterate the narrator's experience. It can only settle on him, a mantle which will never be worn lightly, lit by lights which do not sufficiently illuminate.

The most important symbol in the *Notes,* however, is obviously the wall. The narrator describes himself at first as having a corner, then later uses the image of a cornered mouse coming up against a wall. The narrator occupies a whole room, not a corner, but like the mouse he is cornered and shut in by the wall. The wall successively represents to the narrator single-minded purpose, finality, all

that is in keeping with the normal, stupid, average man; then, in turn, it stands for natural science, for the laws of nature, for mathematics, for Darwin and heredity, for theories of virtue and enlightened self-interest, in short, for anything that can be connected with rational theories of the nineteenth century. With the wall may be associated the crystal palace, the highest stage of human utopia, which is wall-like because it is deterministic and rational, and because it eliminates all possibility for man to show his individuality and free will. The wall, then, embodies a paradox, for it represents those things designed to improve the lot of man, but in practice tending to destroy that which is most valuable in him. It symbolizes the positive, final views against which the narrator rails, and also stands as a barrier between man and his fullest expression of the self. Through the wall, however, one may assert one's individuality, even if only by making one's neighbors aware of one's toothache. Recognition of the wall leads the narrator to a consciousness of the wall as a symbol for isolation in Part I. In Part II it operates for the reader as the culminating symbol of the narrative. The narrator has, in his rooms high in a Petersburg tenement, achieved the ultimate in isolation when he forces Liza to leave. He listens to her steps as she runs down the stairs, shouts her name and then notes: "I heard the stiff outer glass door open heavily with a creak and slam violently. The sound echoed up the stairs." This is what the narrator had dreaded when hesitating whether or not to follow to the brothel. Through his romantic posturing he communicates his very real despair, since he realizes that his behavior will precipitate him into ultimate isolation. Dostoevsky, to paraphrase Poe, is writing not of Petersburg, but of the soul. And when the door—a glass door—slams shut, the symbol of the wall is dramatically complete.

The narrator, then, through a complex series of psychological and social motivations is actually driven to the philosophical position enunciated in the first part. Like his sermon to Liza, his protest has another and a deeper validity than that which he assigns to it. But it becomes artistically meaningful only if seen in terms of the whole work, if his ideas are studied not exclusively for their meaning, but contextually, as the expression of a personality whose generalizations are masked by a highly developed and personalized irony because this is the only form in which he is willing to admit his profound concern for his fellow beings.

Moreover, Dostoevsky specifically calls the narrator a "paradoxalist" so it behooves the reader to examine the narrator's ideas with some care. The first paradox is implied in the title. The English rendering of *podpol'e* as 'underground' is perfect, for in both languages there is a connotative difference between cellar and underground. The adjective *underground* as well as the noun indicate a secret organization, in modern times invariably a revolutionary one. The title clearly implies this, since the narrator's residence (which has other important symbolic overtones) is always above ground. But underground movements in Russia of the 1860's are precisely those against which the narrator inveighs, so that logically he should be considered reactionary rather than revolutionary. On the other hand, both in terms of respect for individual human value

Maria Dmitrievna Isaev, Dostoevsky's first wife.

and in terms of present day antiutopian attitudes, the narrator is the true revolutionary and his contemporaries are not. The title also carries the modern overtones of 'subconscious' which Dostoevsky had found in C. G. Carus and German romanticism, and which is in any case a central theme of the work (the will as irrational). A whole galaxy of paradoxes may be traced in the *Notes.* On the psychological level, the paradox consists of the difference between the narrator's self-analysis, self-comprehension, and his behavior, which contradicts such analysis; of suffering as a palliative; in social theory, the paradoxes of individual supremacy and social stratification, of a utopia for all men and the insignificance and expendability of any particular individual, of utopian idealism destroying humanism, of progress and regression; at the same time, the narrator's view of the soul as "filth." On the philosophical level, where the ramifications are broadest, the paradox presents the problems of free will and determined behavior (as opposed to the psychological statement of the same problem), of conscience and consciousness (*soznanie* means both 'realization' and 'conscience'—cognitive and ethical) which makes man a superior being to the *animaux domestiques* and yet in his superiority destroys him; the paradox of consciousness leading to inertia; the paradox of reason being denied and minimized by the only tool which will adequately do so—reason itself. Stemming from this is the paradox of integration in society and isolation from it and, in literary terms, the creation of an anti-

hero who is a hero, and writing directed against the process of writing.

The narrator protests against positivism; he contends that belief in chemically created man and consciousness smacks of its own kind of mysticism, but he has no acceptable escape from such a world. He finds a release in books and dreams, particularly the latter. Indeed, both in the first part and at the very end of the second, he echoes Piskarev's remark in the *Nevsky Prospect* about the superiority of dreams and books to reality:

> "Real life" (*zhivaja zhizn'*) oppressed me with its novelty so much that I could hardly breathe . . . for we are all cripples, every one of us more or less. We are so divorced from it that we feel at once a sort of loathing for "real life," and so cannot bear to be reminded of it. We have almost come to look upon "real life" as an effort, almost as hard work, and we are all privately agreed that it is better in books.

Much of the narrator's view of himself is, of course, a dream, a projection, in literary terms, of the romantic outcast and of the lone avenger (he mentions Pushkin's Silvio [*The Shot*] and Lermontov's *Masquerade*). He dreams of himself as a hero, for his notion is that a hero cannot defile himself—even the evil he does is accepted and forgiven. Still, he recognizes that dreams are caused by "real life" behavior, that his most hideous dreams follow days in which he considers his behavior as particularly despicable. Ultimately he recognizes the futility of this method of escape. He particularly emphasizes at the end that he has not created anything interesting in the *Notes,* for a novel needs a hero, while all the traits of the antihero are *expressly* gathered together in this work. There is no middle ground for the narrator: "be a hero or an insect." The middle is crass, stupid, uninteresting. But Dostoevsky's creation has shown himself to be if not the average man, at least typical of nineteenth- (and twentieth-) century man. The narrator claims at one point that it is not so much the end or goal of life but its very process which is interesting and important. This, his most positive affirmation, aptly characterizes the *Notes* themselves.

No social or personal redemption is possible for the narrator. The view he takes of man, which, like Ivan Karamazov's, is founded on a denial of love, might almost be stated in terms of a generalization from the *Writer's Diary:* "The consciousness of complete impotence to help suffering humanity or to do it any good or alleviate its lot can even, despite our belief in humanity's suffering, change that feeling for humanity from love into hatred." The possibility of a solution, however, did at one time exist in the *Notes.* In a letter to his brother Michael, Dostoevsky wrote on 26 March 1864:

> I am also bewailing my *Notes.* Terrible misprints, and it would have been better not to print the penultimate chapter [of Pt. I] at all (that chapter where the very idea is stated), than to print it in that form, that is, with sentences left out and contradicting itself. But what can be done? Those swine of censors left in the passages where I railed at everything and *pretended* to blaspheme; but they deleted the passage where

> I deduced from all this the *necessity of belief in Christ.*

Dostoevsky did not try to reintroduce the passage in subsequent editions, and his omission makes the work more effective, since a comparable view is implied in the scene with Liza and its rejection there is dramatically justified. Nothing can exist for the narrator; even religion is merely a fiction.

The tragedy of the narrator, and that inherent in the *Notes,* is particularly gloomy and hopeless because in the dramatic and structural terms of the story there is no escape. All roads are blocked; the wall blocks action, thought, sentiment. But a wall shuts out as well as in. The narrator has values which cannot be shared by his doctrinaire contemporaries. Gide's self-conscious characterization of the main idea of the *Notes* as " 'celui qui pense n'agit point . . . ,' et de là à prétendre que l'action présuppose certaine médiocrité intellectuelle, il n'y a qu'un pas" completely inverts the story's meaning. For the narrator admits that the underground is not really what he wants, that he seeks something totally different. But since psychology and philosophy are inseparable in the *Notes* he cannot find a positive conclusion for either one. The real point, the import of the *Notes,* is that action consists in apprehending the conflict, in gauging what Malraux calls the only two characters of tragedy, the hero and his sense of life. If there is no escape, there is realization and sympathy. There is the paradoxical recognition in the total terms of the *Notes* that humanism as well as neurosis underlies the narrator's protest, and that even refusal to accept the wall is in itself an assertion of man's stature. (pp. 101-09)

> *Ralph E. Matlaw, "Structure and Integration in 'Notes from the Underground'," in* PMLA, *Vol. LXXIII, No. 1, March, 1958, pp. 101-09.*

Robert Louis Jackson   (essay date 1958)

[*An American educator and critic, Jackson's work as editor and author has focused on the study of Dostoevsky. In the following excerpt, he provides an exposition of* Notes from the Underground *as Dostoevsky's pivotal work, noting that the underground man prefigures the rationalistic "antiheroes" of numerous subsequent works, including Raskolnikov in* Crime and Punishment *and Ivan in* The Brothers Karamazov.]

> The underground, the underground, the poet of the underground! The feuilleton writers repeat this as though there were something degrading in it for me. Fools, this is *my glory, because truth is here.*
>
> From the notebooks of Dostoevsky

The role of *Notes from the Underground* in Dostoevsky's works is complex; its ramifications extend throughout his writings. *Notes from the Underground* is a key work in which Dostoevsky develops the main themes of his great novels. These themes may be broadly stated as criticism of the idea that society can be reorganized on a permanently happy basis by means of reason, and criticism of the educated Russian man, morally and intellectually di-

vorced from the people and poisoned by a rationalistic ethic. The theme of freedom—the search for a way out of the "underground", the exploration of these paths and the dangers confronting man in this quest—is really begun in *Notes from the Underground.*

The Underground Man occupies a transitional position in Dostoevsky's works: he represents in part the culmination of Dostoevsky's study and defense of the "little man", and he represents as well the beginning of Dostoevsky's critical examination of the anti-hero and social apostate. It is in the Underground Man that the timid rebellion of Devushkin [in *Poor Folk*] takes on the destructive character that Dostoevsky will condemn in Raskolnikov [in *Crime and Punishment*].

When Chernyshevsky in his novel *What Is to be Done?* contrasted the enlightened rational egotism of the "new man" (Lopukhov, Kirsanov, Rakhmetov) with the unenlightened egotism of the petty, stupid egotist, he invited the malicious and hysterical rage of Dostoevsky's "little man". The latter in his misery and suffering was very far indeed from the lofty idealism and self-confident philosophy of the rationalists. But this "little man", as he rebels in *Notes from the Underground* is more than a rebellious Devushkin: he is conceived as one of Russian society's negative types, a former adherent of the rationalists, crippled by rationalism and by the deleterious influence of the "beautiful and lofty".

Thus, the theme of defense of the "little man" is interwoven with Dostoevsky's attack on rationalism. It is the synthesis of these themes which explains the complex ideological dialectic of *Notes from the Underground.*

In *Crime and Punishment* (*Prestuplenie i nakazanie,* 1866) and subsequent works the theme of anti-hero and social apostate is separated from the theme of the "little man". Dostoevsky turns from his earlier concentration on the "little man" to embrace a wider circle of imagery, including types which more realistically belong to the stratum of the educated Russian man of the nineteenth century.

In *Crime and Punishment* Dostoevsky, as though recoiling from his complicity with "underground" rebellion, does not use the Underground Man's philosophy of negation and rebellion as a means of attacking rationalist and utilitarian doctrines. The basic polarity in this work—as in later works—is love, self-sacrifice, religious reconciliation with reality as opposed to rationalist rebellion. This polarity is present in *Notes from the Underground,* but it is subordinated to the struggle of the Underground Man against rationalism—the most dynamic ideological tension in the work. Dostoevsky's essentially supports his rebellious Underground Man in this struggle. In *Crime and Punishment,* however, he joins rebel and rationalist in the figure of Raskolnikov and, continuing his attack on the rationalists, in effect withdraws his support from the rebel.

The central fact of rationalism, as it is presented in *Notes from the Underground,* is its inevitable violation of the individual. This idea, expressed by Razumikhin in *Crime and Punishment* is illustrated by the whole tragic drama of Raskolnikov. Raskolnikov's crime is, in part, a rationalistic distortion, arrived at through utilitarian humanism, ratiocination and self-isolation. The Underground Man's "game" with Liza, his testing of ego, is paralleled in *Crime and Punishment* by Raskolnikov's experiment. It is the voice of the Underground Man that is heard in Raskolnikov's cry: "Freedom and power, but chiefly power! Over every trembling creature and over the whole ant hill! That is the goal! Remember that!"

Raskolnikov's apocalyptic vision of the destruction of society on earth (in the Epilogue of *Crime and Punishment*) symbolizes his own tragedy. "Spirits endowed with reason and will" introduce moral chaos and destruction into society, just as "reason" helped lead Raskolnikov to moral chaos and disaster. Reason alone provides no foundation for moral behavior. This idea is first developed in *Notes from the Underground.*

The theme of evil "spirits endowed with intellect and will" introducing destruction and chaos into the life of society is developed in Dostoevsky's novel *The Devils* (*Besy,* 1871). Shatov gives direct voice to the anti-rationalist theme. The "beautiful dreams" of the "lovers of humanity" in *Notes from the Underground* have degenerated in *The Devils* into the nightmare of Shigalevism. The division of humanity into superior "underground" men and the stupid "herd" (*Notes from the Underground*), into those with the right to transgress and those who "like to be obedient" (*Crime and Punishment*) is now reincarnated in Shigalev's system of earthly paradise—a paradise "based on the facts of nature and very logical". Shigalev is a "fanatical lover of humanity". Stepan Verkhovensky in *The Devils* is disclosed as the spiritual link between the idealism of the 1840's and Shigalevism.

The monstrous program of Shigalev and Petr Verkhovensky is no more than a codification of the despotic strivings of the Underground Man. "Starting from unlimited freedom I arrive at unlimited despotism," Shigalev remarks. This idea, in its psychological content, is born in the "underground" where freedom for the individual is freedom to tyrannize, to subjugate, to debauch, to expand.

There can be no other social paradise on earth except a Shigalevian one—Shigalev emphasizes. "He is perhaps much nearer to realism than anyone," observes the lame teacher, "and his earthly paradise is almost the real one, the very one for the loss of which mankind is sighing, indeed if it ever existed." The theme of man's inability to bear freedom is expressed by Murin in "The Landlady" ("Khozyaika", 1847). "Give a weak man freedom and he will bind it himself and return it to you," The Underground Man, at the conclusion of his "notes", expresses a similar pessimistic thought. "Well, just try, just give us, for example, a little more independence, untie the hands of any of us, broaden the sphere of our activity, relax the control and we—yes, I assure you—immediately should beg to be under control again." This thought, too, lies at the basis of the conception of "The Legend of the Grand Inquisitor". Man is "weak and vile", the Grand Inquisitor declares. Man cannot support the burden of freedom of choice. Happiness and rest for his tormented, suffering soul will only come when man renounces freedom and hands over his burden to those who will voluntarily as-sume his sufferings. This is a central idea of "The Legend of the Grand Inquisitor". It is antithetical to the rebellious spirit of the Underground Man, but it is rooted in the deep despair of *Notes from the Underground.*

"The Legend of the Grand Inquisitor" is the intellectual fruit of Dostoevsky's greatest rationalist and sceptic, Ivan Karamazov; in the last of Dostoevsky's great anti-heroes, the "disease of consciousness" attains its highest development. Ivan is dominated by the pride of intellect, the pride of reason. ". . . Ivan doesn't love anybody," Fedor Karamazov keenly observed. Yet the egotism of Ivan, like the egotism of the Underground Man, has not crushed a passionate idealism.

The Underground Man's rejection of the rationalists' "crystal palace" world harmony is related to Ivan's rejection of God's world, of the possibility of world harmony. The Underground Man rejects the world harmony of the rationalists because it is based on an ignoring and negation of suffering, of contradiction, of the irrational element in life. Ivan with his "Euclidian reason" cannot accept a world harmony that is based upon the tears and suffering of children, upon tears and suffering that are unatoned for. He cannot accept a world that is not justified by reason. Here the "reason" of Ivan is not restrictive and negative, but positive. "I do not want harmony, out of love for humanity I do not want it."

Thus, both the anti-rationalist Underground Man and the rationalist Ivan arrive at the same conclusion—the conclusion of uncompromising idealists—namely, that a harmony which does not cope with the problem of suffering, the problem of the irrational, is unacceptable. The Underground Man does not reject the ideal of the crystal palace: it is, after all, an ideal for him, too; he rejects only the chicken coop which is, he feels, what the crystal palace of the rationalists amounts to. "Destroy my desires, eradicate my ideals, show me something better and I will follow you." Ivan essentially could say the same thing. Ivan does not reject God (the highest incarnation of the ideal), he rejects an imperfect "God's world".

While the Underground Man's insistence on the absolute fulfillment of the ideal is supported by Dostoevsky, Ivan's uncompromising idealism is viewed by Dostoevsky as ultimately destructive and negative (although Dostoevsky shares Ivan's pain and despair over suffering). Dostoevsky seems ready in *The Brothers Karamazov* to accept less than the whole ideal; he reveals in "The Legend of the Grand Inquisitor" what Rozanov [in his study *The Legend of the Grand Inquisitor*] has described as a certain "weariness". Pessimism and despair about the fate of man unite the Underground Man and Ivan; but the despair that leads the Underground Man to the idea of the never-ending rebellion of the individual against any and all encroachment on his freedom evokes in Ivan "The Legend of the Grand Inquisitor".

Dostoevsky's negative attitude towards Ivan's rationalistic insistence on the absolute ideal reflects a more realistic approach to suffering and evil: in *The Brothers Karamazov* Dostoevsky clearly and powerfully challenges the dreamer and idealist who—like the Underground Man—

demands everything "ready made". The "dreaming kind of love", Zosima observes, "thirsts for quick heroism rapidly performed and in the sight of all. . . . Active love, on the other hand, is work and endurance. . . ."

The elder Zosima has a keen understanding of "underground" psychology. He observes:

> The man who lies to himself and who listens to his own lies comes to such a pass that he is no longer able to distinguish any truth either in himself or in his surroundings and, therefore, loses all respect for himself and for others. And having no respect for anyone, he ceases to love, and lacking love, in order to occupy and distract himself he gives way to passions and coarse pleasures and sinks to bestiality in his vices, and all from continual lying both to people and to himself. The man who lies to himself can be offended more easily than anyone. You know it is sometimes very pleasant to take offense, isn't it? And a man may know that nobody has insulted him, and that he himself has invented the insult and lied for show, exaggerated in order to make it picturesque, in a word, has made a mountain out of a mole hill—he knows that himself, but still he will be the first to take offense, and will revel in his resentment until he feels great pleasure in it, and so pass to genuine vindictiveness.

Zosima's words seem directed at the Underground Man himself. And, significantly, they are directed at Fedor Karamazov—spiritual brother of the Underground Man. In Fedor Karamazov may be found the same self-deception, the same tortured posturing, the same cynical and shameless behavior that is characteristic of the Underground Man. He delights in his shamelessness and in his moral fall. In Fedor Karamazov, as in the Underground man, shamelessness, deliberate malice, is the distorted expression of humiliation.

Self-humiliation is a source of pleasure to many of Dostoevsky's heroes. These "underground" feelings are experienced, for example, by Stavrogin in *The Devils.* Stavrogin writes in his "confession":

> Every exceedingly disgraceful, immeasurably humiliating, vile and, above all, ridiculous situation in which I have happened to be in my life, always aroused in me, alongside of an immeasurable anger, an incredible delight. It was just the same in moments of crime and in moments when my life was in danger. If I were stealing something, I would feel, while committing the theft, an ecstasy from the consciousness of the depths of my vileness. It was not the vileness that I loved (here my reason was usually quite intact), but I enjoyed the ecstasy that came from the tormenting consciousness of my debased action.

The Underground Man has identical feelings. He relates that he would return to his den after a night of debauchery and experience "a secret, abnormal, vile pleasure" in the consciousness that "today I committed another disgusting deed. . . ." ". . . The pleasure here came precisely from a too vivid consciousness of one's degradation." Stavrogin's pleasure in being slapped recalls the tormenting pleasure of the Underground Man at this form of hu-

miliation. "When I have been slapped," Stavrogin observes, "(and I have been slapped twice in my life) that [feeling] was even here, in spite of a terrible anger. But if one can restrain one's anger in such circumstances, the pleasure will exceed all expectations."

Stavrogin is perhaps Dostoevsky's most sinister embodiment of the anti-hero. Divorce from the people and the "living life", idleness and boredom, love of oneself and of one's own psychologizing, cold, formalized intellect, the confusion of moral criteria, delight in self-humiliation—these features unite the Underground Man and Stavrogin: but the dialectic of internal struggle, so intense and everpresent in the Underground Man, is felt feebly in Stavrogin. The features of his personality have become frozen like the features of his face.

The theme of the coexistence of lofty feeling and sentimentality with "underground" filth and vileness is one which preoccupies Dostoevsky in his works. Dostoevsky's *Eternal Husband (Vechny muzh,* 1870) is a remarkable study of this phenomenon. Pavel Trusotsky (a betrayed romantic like the Underground Man) is a living "Schiller in the image of a Quasimodo". The eternal husband, Trusotsky, loved the former lover of his wife, Velchaninov, with malice. He came "in order to knife me, but thought that he was coming to 'embrace and weep'," Velchaninov observed, adding: "The most monstrous monster is the monster with noble feelings. . . ." Velchaninov recognizes in Trusotsky "underground filth", as he later recognizes in himself an "underground man". In Trusotsky Dostoevsky created a psychological type extremely close to the Underground Man.

Eternal Husband, Dostoevsky wrote N. N. Strakhov March 18, 1869, was written in response to a request that he write in the manner of *Notes from the Underground.* "But this is not *Notes from the Underground,* it is something quite different in form, although the essence is the same, my eternal essence. . . ."

A study in ambivalent consciousness, many of Dostoevsky's heroes, like Trusotsky, love—in their hatred and malice—and hate—in their loving. "Yes, he loved me *out of malice,*" Velchaninov remarks of Trusotsky; "this is the strongest kind of love." The same ambivalence seems to have lent a special intensity to Dostoevsky's feelings towards the romanticism of the 1840's. The furious malice of *Notes from the Underground* is not explained alone by the simplicities of the rationalists; it suggests also a man who is trampling something that is hateful because it was extremely dear.

Many pages from *Raw Youth (Podrostok,* 1876) recall *Notes from the Underground.* As in *Notes from the Underground,* the writer of these "notes" is the hero of his own story. The hero, Arkady Dolgoruki, cannot "restrain" himself from writing; yet, he insists, he will never write his autobiography. "One has to be too disgustingly in love with oneself in order to write without shame about oneself." He considers it "indecent and vile" to display one's inner soul on the literary market place, yet with vexation he foresees that it will be impossible to "get along completely without a description of feelings, without reflections (perhaps even vulgar ones): such is the corrupting influence any literary enterprise has on a man, even though it is undertaken only for himself." He is writing for himself, but he is continually addressing the "reader".

> . . . The reader, perhaps, will be horrified by the frankness of my confession [a reference to his "idea" of becoming a Rothschild], and will in all simplicity ask himself: how is it that the author does not blush? I answer: I am not writing for publication . . . And therefore, if in these notes I sometimes address the reader, that is only a device. My reader is an imaginary person.

Raw Youth is broader in scope than *Notes from the Underground.* There is a complex drama and a complex web of themes. But in the person of Arkady Dolgoruki, Dostoevsky presents a variation of the Underground Man. Arkady reveals the same "underground" pattern of behavior:

> Was there malice in me? I don't know, perhaps there was. Strange to say, I always had, perhaps from my earliest childhood, the following characteristic: if I was maltreated, oppressed, insulted to the last degree, I always manifested an insatiable desire passively to submit to insult and even to increase my humiliations beyond the desires of my offender. "All right, you have humiliated me, well, I will humiliate myself even more; go ahead, look and enjoy it!" Touchard beat me and wanted to show that I was a lackey and not a Senator's son, and so I at once entered into the role of a lackey at that time . . . I could have kept up a passive hatred and underground malice in this way for years.

In Arkady, Dostoevsky explores the formative years of the "underground" individual—a theme briefly but intensely developed in *Notes from the Underground.* The retreat of the humiliated youth into brooding isolation, the striving for power (as a purely subjective need), the preoccupation in this connection with the psychological experiment, the "underground" faculty of "cherishing in one's soul the loftiest ideal side by side with the most extreme vileness, and all this absolutely sincerely", the ambivalence of rebellious lackeyism, the growing "spider's soul"—characterize Arkady Dolgoruki.

Arkady challenges his socialist-minded companions, and his words seem to come right out of *Notes from the Underground:*

> Nothing is clear in our society, gentlemen. Indeed, you deny God, you deny heroic feats; but just what deaf, blind, dull inertia could compel me to act in one way, if it is more advantageous to me to act in another way? You say: "a rational attitude towards humanity is all to my advantage." But what if I find all these rational notions, all these barracks and phalansteries irrational? What the devil do I care for them, for the future when I only live once in the world! Permit me to decide myself what is to my own advantage: it is more enjoyable. How is it my affair what happens in a thousand years with all your humanity if for all this, according to your code, I am to get neither love, nor future life, nor recognition for my efforts? No, indeed, if that's how

it is then I'd rather live for myself in the most ignorant way, and it would be a good thing if they all went to perdition!

If Pavel Trusotsky and Arkady Dolgoruki are close to the Underground Man, the same may be said of Liputin in *The Devils*—a vain, malicious minor official, a punctilious little man and petty despot—and of the dying consumptive Ippolit Terentiev in *The Idiot* (*Idiot,* 1868). "Après moi le déluge" is the title Terentiev affixes to his "confession", a profoundly "underground" document. He regards himself as sentenced to death by dark, deaf and insolent forces of nature—and he rebels. His last decision is to commit suicide, the only thing he still has time to begin and end of his own free will. He writes:

> Let me tell you that there is a limit to disgrace in the consciousness of one's own insignificance and powerlessness beyond which a man cannot go, and after which he begins to feel a tremendous pleasure in his own disgrace.

Pleasure in one's own disgrace, a pleasure that is intensified by rebellion against that very disgrace, is the essence of "underground" being.

Two heroes of Dostoevsky who seem almost to re-embody the Underground Man are the hero of the brief sketch **"The Verdict"** (**"Prigovor"**, October, 1876, *Diary of a Writer*) and the hero of **"A Meek One"** (**"Krotkaya"**, November, 1876, *Diary of a Writer*).

Dostoevsky is discussing the problem of suicide. In **"The Verdict"** he offers to the reader the "deliberation of a suicide *out of boredom*—of course, a materialist". Dostoevsky discloses, in the words of his "materialist", a sequence of logical thought leading the hero to self-destruction. The monologue of the "materialist" is an example of the complete formalization of the thinking processes:

> To be conscious means to suffer: but I do not wish to suffer—because why should I consent to suffer? Nature through my consciousness tells me about some kind of harmony of the whole. . . . It tells me that I—although I know quite well that I cannot and never will participate in the "harmony of the whole," and that, indeed, I will never even know what it means—it tells me that nevertheless I must submit to this message, humble myself, accept suffering in the form of the harmony of the whole and agree to live. . . . But my consciousness is not harmony, but on the contrary disharmony: because I am unhappy with it. Look, who is happy in this world and what kind of people *consent* to live? Precisely those who are like animals and come nearest to their type by virtue of the low development of their consciousness.

One immediately recognizes the Underground Man in this "materialist"—the lonely, suffering, egotistical, rationalizing man divorced from the "living life". Like the Underground Man, he is tormented by the "harmony of the whole", by an oppressive Euclidian reality, by a feeling of the senselessness of suffering in which "there is no guilty one".

Like Arkady Dolgoruki, this materialist cannot be happy "even in the face of the most lofty and *immediate* happiness of love for neighbor and for mankind", since he knows that "tomorrow all this will perish: and I, and all this happiness, and all this love, and all humanity will be transformed into nothing, into former chaos". He "will not and cannot be happy on condition of being threatened by tomorrow's zero".

The hero of **"The Verdict"** contains elements of both the Underground Man and Ivan Karamazov. Even accepting the possibility of a rational and scientific organization of life on earth, of man's future happiness, Dostoevsky's "materialist" believes, the mere thought that "because of some inert laws nature found it necessary to torture man for thousands of years before bringing him to this happiness is unbearably outrageous". This same thought, of course, underlies Ivan's rejection of a future harmony. Further, contemplating the sad thought that man may have been placed on earth for an "insolent experiment", Dostoevsky's "materialist" observes:

> The sadness of this thought consists chiefly in the fact that once again there is no guilty one; nobody conducted the experiment; there is nobody to curse, since everything simply happened according to the dead laws of nature which I simply do not understand, with which my consciousness can in no way reconcile itself.

Indignation against senseless suffering in which "there is no guilty one", rebellion against the "laws of nature" which symbolize this suffering is, of course, the heart of *Notes from the Underground.* The Underground Man, rebelling, rebels in the name of his own personal suffering; Ivan, rebelling against God's world, rebels in the name of suffering mankind.

Dostoevsky's "materialist", unable to reconcile himself with the "dead laws of nature", sentences nature—which has brought him into existence for suffering—to annihilation, together with himself. "And since I cannot destroy nature, I am destroying only myself, solely from the boredom of enduring a tyranny in which there is no guilty one."

Suicide, in **"The Verdict"**, is presented as the logical end result of "underground" malice and negation. In **"The Verdict"** Dostoevsky discloses his clear understanding that the *perpetuum mobile* of such a type as the Underground Man inevitably must come to a halt. In **"The Verdict"** the "underground" type, like so many other Dostoevsky heroes, is viewed at the moment of crisis and catastrophe. **"The Verdict"** could be an epilogue to *Notes from the Underground.*

The hero of Dostoevsky's story **"A Meek One"** is one of the most terrible of Dostoevsky's heroes. One recognizes in this pawnbroker who quotes Goethe the face of the Underground Man. The hero of *Notes from the Underground* and the hero of **"A Meek One"** are one man.

Dostoevsky's pawnbroker describes himself as a coward and egotist, a man of difficult and ridiculous character, a dreamer, never liked in school. In this tragedy—related by the pawnbroker himself—Dostoevsky exposes the mechanism of a corrupt, rationalistic consciousness. The story is in essence a development of the Underground Man's "game" with Liza. This is the attempt of a degraded man, a spiritual despot, to play the hero, the deliverer, to make another soul pay for his spiritual injuries. The pawnbroker subjects his bride to his "system", his "idea"—the idea of meeting her enthusiasm with silence. He is proud and he wants her to discover his pride for herself. "I wanted her to be standing before me in homage for the sake of my sufferings. . . . " In essence, the pawnbroker wishes to fortify his ego by "conquering" his bride; and he enjoys the idea of her humiliation.

When his experiment ends in tragedy, in the suicide of his bride, he cannot help feeling that he "made some mistake here! Something went wrong here. Everything was clear, my plan was as clear as the sky." Dostoevsky's pawnbroker is a man in whom moral consciousness is dead.

In **"A Meek One"**, as in **"The Verdict"**, Dostoevsky further analyzes the hero of *Notes from the Underground.* The heroes of these two stories closely resemble the Underground Man: it is Dostoevsky's orientation towards this "underground" type that has changed. There is no poetry or pathos in the heroes of **"The Verdict"** and **"A Meek One"**—here all is *Wahrheit;* there are no extenuating circumstances from the life of the "little man" to arouse the reader's sympathy; there are no conflicting ideological themes such as the theme of the defense of free will. A comparison of **"The Verdict"** and **"A Meek One"** with *Notes from the Underground* suggests the meaning of Dostoevsky's remark to Pochinkovskaya about *Notes from the Underground*—"Es is schon ein überwundener Standpunkt." What Dostoevsky had transcended was his support of the rebellious individual.

" 'People, love one another!' Who said that? Whose commandment is that?" the hero of **"A Meek One"** asks at the end of his reminiscences. Man is alone; he is trapped in his singleness, in his egoistic self-consciousness. Only through merging of the self in the totality, in brotherhood, will man break out of the circle of his loneliness. This idea—Dostoevsky's great antithesis to the "underground"—is most vividly expressed in the last of Dostoevsky's works—*The Brothers Karamazov.*

Brotherhood, Zosima's "secret visitor" observes, will come only after man has passed through a period of human isolation.

> The kind that is now prevalent everywhere, and especially in our century, but it has not yet reached its limit, and its end is not yet in sight. Because everyone is now striving to isolate his person as much as possible, wants to experience in himself the fullness of life, whereas from all his efforts there comes instead of the fullness of life only complete self-destruction, because instead of the complete self-determination of his being he falls into absolute isolation. Because everyone in our century has divided into units, each one is withdrawing into his hole, each one is holding himself aloof from the next person, is hiding, and hiding what he possesses, and ends by being repelled by other people, and repelling people from himself. He accumulates wealth in

isolation and thinks: how strong I am now and how secure, but the madman does not know that the more he accumulates, the more he sinks into self-destructive impotence. Because he is accustomed to rely on himself alone and to separate himself as a unit from the whole, he has taught his soul not to believe in human help, in people and in humanity, and only trembles lest he lose his money and the privileges he has acquired through it. Everywhere these days the human mind is sneeringly refusing to understand that the true security of the individual lies not in his personal, isolated efforts, but in general social solidarity. But it will inevitably happen that an end will come to this terrible isolation. . . .

These observations disclose Dostoevsky's deepest insight into his epoch—"and the end is not yet in sight". The atomization of the individual in society, the atrophy of his social instincts, the separation from humane values, is a phenomenon of the 19th and 20th centuries.

Notes from the Underground is a germinal work in Dostoevsky's major period of creative work after exile. It is not surprising, therefore, that it plays a central role in the Russian literature that fell under the shadow of Dostoevsky. (pp. 49-63)

> *Robert Louis Jackson, in his* Dostoevsky's Underground Man in Russian Literature, *Mouton & Co., 1958, 223 p.*

George Steiner   (essay date 1959)

[*Steiner is a French-born American critic, poet, and fiction writer. He has described his approach to literary criticism as "a kind of continuous inquiry into and conjecture about the relations between literature and society, between poetic value and humane conduct." A central concern of his critical thought is whether or not literature can survive the barbarism of the modern world, particularly in view of the Holocaust. Though some commentators have found fault with his sometimes exuberant prose style, Steiner is generally regarded as a perceptive and extremely erudite critic. In the following excerpt, he praises Dostoevsky's innovative application of standard literary techniques to effect a profoundly original union of philosophic content and literary form in* Notes from the Underground.]

There is . . . a substantial literature concerning the psychological and psychoanalytic material in the *Letters from the Underworld.* Of all of Dostoevsky's "surfaces," none yields less resistance to this style of approach. It is lent cogency, moreover, by the fact that the work was composed at a time when its author was suffering grievous emotional upheavals.

But while allowing the eminent fascination of the *Letters* from the points of view of metaphysics and psychology, one should not overlook the way in which Dostoevsky converted prevailing literary devices and conventions to his particular ends. Live burial, descents into caverns, maelstroms or sewers, and the figure of the redeeming prostitute were commonplace of romantic melodrama. The underworld which the narrator "carries within him"

has specific literary and historical intonations; it was not necessarily that of Dostoevsky himself. Indeed, in the brief prefatory note, the novelist says that he is depicting a character "peculiar to the present age," and that his personality is "due to the *milieu* which all of us share in Russia." In that respect, the whole work belongs with other Dostoevskyan polemics against spiritual nihilism.

At the end of Part I, Dostoevsky considers the problem of literary form. The narrator proposes to set down a manual of total candour: "I wish, in particular, to try whether one can *ever* be really open with oneself—*ever* be really fearless of any item of truth." The sentence echoes the celebrated opening paragraph of Rousseau's *Confessions,* and the Dostoevskyan narrator promptly observes that Heine thought Rousseau a liar "partly out of set purpose, and partly out of vanity." He adds: "I believe that Heine is right." Heine's presence in this context is illustrative of how the symbolic imagination works: by virtue of his long and cruel entombment in the *Matratzengruft*—literally in a burial vault of illness—Heine had become an archetype of the underground man. Contrary to Montaigne or Cellini or Rousseau,

> though I may seem to be writing for the eye of a reader, I do so out of mere show, and because I find that that kind of writing comes easier. It is all mere form—all a mere empty form, for which I shall never have a reader.

This fiction is conveyed through a traditional device which Poe used to similar effects; we are asked to believe that a manuscript never intended for publication has been anonymously "transcribed."

Such claims to privacy are, of course, rhetorical. But a real problem is at issue. With the irruption of the unconscious into poetics, with the endeavour to portray characters in their divided entirety, classical methods of narrative and discourse became inadequate. Dostoevsky believed that the dilemma of inadequate form—Rousseau's *Confessions*—entailed the more significant dilemma of inadequate truth. Modern literature has sought to resolve this problem in various ways, but neither the alternate use of "public" and "private" speech in O'Neill's *Strange Interlude* nor the stream of consciousness perfected by Joyce and Hermann Broch has proved wholly satisfactory. What we can hear of the language of the unconscious falls too readily into our own syntax. Perhaps we do not yet know how to listen.

The *Letters from the Underworld* are experimental in range of content rather than in dislocation or deepening of narrative form. Once again, the primary mode is dramatic: by compressing the course of outward happenings into a series of crises, Dostoevsky caused the narrator to speak with a frenzied candour which human beings, under less final circumstances, reserve for their unavowed thoughts. In the *Letters,* soul and unreason confront each other in extremity, and the reader overhears truths as awesome as the truths Dante overheard in hell.

The setting is arch-Dostoevskyan: "a mean, shabby room" on the fringes of St. Petersburg—"the most abstract, the most deviously-minded city on this terrestrial sphere of ours." The weather is in the appropriate key:

> Today half-melted, yellow, dirty snow is falling. It was falling yesterday, and it does so nearly every day. I believe that it is the wet snow which has reminded me of the episode of which I cannot rid my thoughts; so here goes for my confession *àpropos* of the fall of sleet.

The next sentence, which opens Part II, reads:

> At that time I was only twenty-four and, so far, had lived a dull ill-regulated existence that was well-nigh as solitary as that of a savage.

One is reminded of Villon—the first great voice from the underground of the European metropolis. In him, also, meditation followed on *les neiges d'antan* and the attainment of *l'an de mon trentiesme aage* (and is it not a fine coincidence that the old saint's legend of Mary the Egyptian, to which Villon refers in several poems, should reappear in *Raw Youth*?).

The "I" of the *Letters* says repeatedly that his philosophy "is the fruit of forty years in the underworld," of forty years spent in the isolation of self-scrutiny. It is difficult to dismiss the echo of the forty years passed by Israel in the desert or of Christ's forty days in the wilderness. For the *Letters from the Underworld* cannot be considered in isolation. They are closely related to the symbolic values and thematic material of Dostoevsky's major fictions. Thus, the prostitute is called Liza. In the final tableau she sits on the floor, sobbing:

> By this time she knew all. She knew that I had outraged her to the core, and that (how am I to express it?) my short-lived passion had sprung only from a desire for vengeance, from a yearning to subject her to a new indignity. . . .

The lines are a gloss on the scene between Liza and Stavrogin in *The Possessed* and prefigure Dostoevsky's treatment of the relations between Raskolnikov and Sonia in *Crime and Punishment.* Nor is the Dostoevskyan emblem of primordial evil lacking in the narrator's tale. When he asks Liza why she left her father's house to come to a brothel, she hints at some mysterious infamy: "But what if things were *worse* there than here?" Unconsciously—the dramatization being as subtle and open to every shift of value as it is in Shakespeare—the underground man seizes on her hint. He confesses that if he had a daughter, "I should love her even more than I did my sons." He tells of a father who kisses his girl's hands and feet "and folds her in his arms as she lies asleep." The immediate reference would seem to be to Balzac's *Père Goriot.* Beyond it lies the motif of father-daughter incest which, in the guise of the Cenci affair, had fascinated Shelley, Stendhal, Landor, Swinburne, Hawthorne, and even Melville. The narrator makes a revealing admission; he would not have his daughter marry:

> Because, by heavens, I should have been jealous. What? She to kiss another man—to love a stranger more than she did her father? It hurts me even to think of it!

And he concludes with the classical Freudian insight that "the man whom the daughter loves is generally the man who cuts the worst figure in her father's eyes."

In the *Letters* we even find traces of the myth of the "double" which Dostoevsky's conception of the human soul had, in fact, rendered archaic. The surly Apollon is both the underground man's servant and his inseparable shadow:

> My present tenement was an isolated one, and therefore my sheath, my box into which I could withdraw from all humanity; and for some infernal reason or another Apollon always seemed to form part of it. Consequently for seven whole years I found myself unable to make up my mind to dismiss him.

And yet, when the traditional literary elements in the *Letters* have been set aside, and when close affinities to Dostoevsky's other works have been noted, the profound originality of the thing continues to assert itself. Chords previously unheard had been struck with admirable precision. No other text by Dostoevsky has exerted more influence on twentieth-century thought or technique.

The portrayal of the narrator is an achievement for which one does not find a genuine precedent:

> I wish to tell you, gentlemen (no matter whether you care to hear it or not), why I have never been able to become an insect. I solemnly declare to you that I have often *wished* to become an insect, but could never attain my desire.

This notion, which obviously contains the germ for Kafka's *Metamorphosis,* is pursued throughout the narrative. Other personages look upon the speaker "as some kind of ordinary fly." He describes himself as "the foulest . . . the most ill-gained worm upon earth." In themselves, these images are not new. The source of Dostoevsky's insect symbolism has, indeed, been traced to Balzac. What is new and terrifying is the sustained methodic use of such imagery to "inhumanize" and dehumanize man. The narrator "crouches" in his lair and waits "in his cranny." The sense of animality infects his consciousness. The ancient metaphors linking man to worms and vermin, the representation of man's death, in *King Lear,* as a wanton massacre of flies, are transformed by Dostoevsky into psychological realities, into actual conditions of the mind. The tragedy of the underground man is, literally, his retreat from manhood. This retreat is made explicit through the cruel impotence of his assault on Liza. In the end, he sees matters plainly:

> We grow weary of being human beings at all—of possessing real, individual flesh and blood. We are ashamed of being human—we account it beneath our dignity.

If there is one main element contributed by modern literature to our world view, it is precisely this sense of dehumanization.

What has brought it on? Perhaps it is a result of the industrialization of life, of the downgrading of the human person through the blank, nameless monotony of industrial processes. In the *Letters,* Dostoevsky describes "the throng of hurrying workmen and artisans (their faces worn almost to brutality).'' With Engels and Zola, he was one of the first to realize what factory labour can do to eradicate individual traits or the play of intelligence in a man's face. But, whatever its origins, the "shame of being human" has, in our century, assumed proportions grimmer than those foreseen by Dostoevsky. In his parable *Les Bêtes,* Pierre Gascar tells how the kingdom of the beasts supplants that of men in the world of concentration camps and gas chambers. And in a minor, yet grave key, James Thurber has shown the waking of the animals behind the imperfect, rent covering of the human skin. For since the *Letters from the Underworld* we know that the insect is gaining on the part of man. Ancient mythology dealt with men who were half-gods; post-Dostoevskyan mythology depicts roaches who are half-man.

The *Letters* carried to a new finality the conception of the non-heroic. Mario Praz has shown that the abandonment of the heroic type was one of the major currents in Victorian fiction. Gogol and Goncharov had made of the non-heroic protagonist a figure symbolic of contemporaneous Russia. But Dostoevsky went further. His narrator not only affects a sense of degradation and self-loathing; he is genuinely odious. He recounts his abject experiences "as a well-merited punishment" and does so with hysterical malevolence. Consider Gogol's terrifying *Diary of a Madman* and Turgeniev's *Journal of a Superfluous Man;* both are essays in the non-heroic, but both move us to compassion through grace and irony of presentment. Tolstoy's Ivan Ilych [in "The Death of Ivan Ilych"], a truly mediocre and selfish creature, is, at the last, ennobled by the tenacity of his despair. In the *Letters,* however, Dostoevsky treats his material with a withering touch. The "transcriber" indicates in the postscript that this "dealer in paradoxes" wrote further notes but that these were not worth preserving. We are left with an intended nothingness.

In his portrayal of the "anti-hero" Dostoevsky has had a legion of disciples. Add to his method the more ancient tradition of the picaresque and you find the sinful confessor of Gide's novels. Camus's *The Fall* is a palpable imitation of the tone and structure of the *Letters;* in Genet the logic of avowal and degradation is carried to the excremental.

Finally, the *Letters from the Underworld* are of tremendous importance in that they formulated, with utmost clarity, a critique of pure reason which had been gathering impetus in much of romantic art. Some of the passages in which the narrator mutinies against natural law have become touchstones of twentieth-century metaphysics:

> Good Lord! What have *I* to do with the laws of Nature, or with arithmetic, when all the time those laws and the formula that twice two make four do not meet with my acceptance! Of course, I am not going to beat my head against a wall if I have not the requisite strength to do so; yet I am not going to *accept* that wall merely because I have run up against it, and have no means to knock it down.

How can man's will attain total freedom "except by thrusting through the wall," asked Ahab [in Herman Melville's *Moby Dick*]. Non-Euclidean geometry and the more

Fyodor Dostoevsky, three years before publication of Notes from the Underground.

abstruse reveries of modern algebra were to breach some of these walls of axiom. But the rebellion of the Dostoevskyan narrator is all-encompassing. With his derisive rejection of the *savants,* the Hegelian idealists and the believers in rational progress, he offered a declaration of independence from reason. Long before his existentialist followers, the man from the underground proclaimed the majesty of the absurd. This is why Dostoevsky is so often cited in the pantheon of modern metaphysics with other mutineers against liberal empiricism—Pascal, Blake, Kierkegaard, and Nietzsche.

It would be fascinating to inquire into the sources of the Dostoevskyan dialectic. Condorcet asserted that if men said *calculemus*—if they grasped the tools of reason in a Newtonian world—nature would yield her answers. Dostoevsky said "No." He said "No" to Spencerian faith in progress and to the rational physiology of Claude Bernard (a man of genius whom Dimitri Karamazov [in *The Brothers Karamazov*] refers to with particular rage). One might examine the elements of Rousseauism in the underground man's contempt for formal authority and in his obsession with the primacy of will. For between Rousseau's pronouncement that the private conscience is an "infallible judge of good and evil, making man similar to God," and the narrator's conviction that he can dismiss natural law and the categories of conventional logic, there is a complex but authentic link. These matters pertain, however, to a more technical study.

What needs emphasizing is the fact that the *Letters from the Underworld* were a brilliant solution to the problem of philosophic content within the literary form. Unlike the *contes philosophiques* of the enlightenment or the novels of Goethe, in which the part of speculation is so deliberately exterior to the fiction, the *Letters* coalesce the abstract with the dramatized—or in Aristotelian terminology, they fuse "thought" with "plot." In point of genre, neither Nietzsche's *Zarathustra* nor the theological allegories of Kierkegaard impress one as equally successful. Together with Schiller, to whom he looked as a constant model, Dostoevsky achieved a rare instance of creative equilibrium between poetic and philosophic powers.

The *Letters from the Underworld* are, indeed, a Dostoevskyan *summa*—even if we grant that the narrator's views cannot be identified with the novelist's political program and official Orthodoxy. It is appropriate that the contrast with Tolstoy should nowhere be more final. Even in abjection, a Tolstoyan personage remains man; if anything, his humanity deepens and grows lustrous with disgrace. As Isaiah Berlin puts it, Tolstoy saw men "in natural, unaltering daylight." The hallucinatory collapse of the human into the bestial was alien to his view. Even at its most brutal, Tolstoyan pessimism was amended by a central belief that human beings would not merely "endure," to use Faulkner's distinction, but also "prevail."

Tolstoy's "non-heroes"—as, for example, the narrator of the *Kreutzer Sonata*—have a humaneness in suffering and a moral assertiveness which set them worlds apart from the bilious masochism of the underground man. The difference flashes through beautifully in a dialogue between Shakespeare's Apemantus and the fallen Timon [both from *Timon of Athens*]. Even when the latter is reduced to hatred and self-mockery, it appears as if the "bleak air" were still his "boisterous chamberlain."

Tolstoy's philosophy, for all its rejection of the schoolmen and the idealists, is profoundly rationalistic. During his whole life he sought for a unifying principle through which the multitudinous individuality of observed experience could be reconciled to an apprehension of order. Dostoevsky's homage to the absurd, his assault on the ordinary mechanics of tautology and definition, would have seemed to Tolstoy a peevish madness. Tolstoy was, in Vyazemsky's phrase, a "negativist." But his negations were axe-strokes to carve a clearing for the light. His portrayal of life culminates in humanism, in that final "Yes" of Molly Bloom's soliloquy [in James Joyce's *Ulysses*]. In his journal for July 19, 1896, Tolstoy recorded seeing a clump of burdock in the midst of a ploughed field; one shoot was alive.

> black from dust, but still alive and red in the centre. . . . It makes me want to write. It asserts life to the end, and alone in the midst of the whole field, somehow or other has asserted it.

The narrator of the *Letters from the Underworld* expresses through his acts and language a final "No." When Tolstoy remarked to Gorky that Dostoevsky "ought to have made himself acquainted with the teachings of Confucius or the Buddhists; that would have calmed him down," the underground man must have howled derisively from his lair. Our times have given substance to his derision. The *univers concentrationnaire*—the world of the death camps—confirms beyond denial Dostoevsky's insights into the savagery of men, into their inclination, both as individuals and as hordes, to stamp out within themselves the embers of humanity. The subterranean narrator defines his species as "A creature which walks on two legs and is devoid of gratitude." Tolstoy also realized that there was no abundance of gratitude, but instead of "creature" he would always have written "man."

That we should, at times, think him old-fashioned marks the desecration of our estate. (pp. 221-30)

George Steiner, *"Dostoevsky," in his* Tolstoy or Dostoevsky: An Essay in the Old Criticism, *Alfred A. Knopf, Inc., 1959, pp. 132-254.*

Joseph Frank   (essay date 1961)

[*An American educator and critic, Frank is the author of three parts of a projected five-volume biography entitled* Dostoevsky *(1976-). Each volume in this highly lauded, authoritative work addresses a seminal period in the novelist's life. Frank devotes a chapter in the third volume,* Dostoevsky: The Stir of Liberation, 1860-1865 *(1986) [see Further Reading] to a discussion of* Notes from the Underground, *the work that he states "shaped my whole approach to Dostoevsky's work." In the following essay, Frank maintains that Dostoevsky intended* Notes from the Underground *as a parody of the social Romanticism of the 1840s and Russian Nihilism of the 1860s.*]

Few works in modern literature are more widely read or more often cited than Dostoevsky's *Notes from Underground.* The designation "underground man" has entered into the vocabulary of the modern educated consciousness, and this character has now begun—like Hamlet, Don Quixote, Don Juan and Faust—to take on the symbolic stature of one of the great archetypal literary creations. No book or essay on the situation of modern culture would be complete without some allusion to Dostoevsky's figure. Every important cultural development of the past half-century—Nietzscheanism, Freudianism, Expressionism, Surrealism, Crisis Theology, Existentialism—has claimed the underground man as its own; and when he has not been adopted as a prophetic anticipation, he has been held up to exhibition as a luridly repulsive warning.

Indeed, *Notes from Underground* by now would seem to have been discussed from every conceivable point of view—with one single but important exception. For this exception is the point of view of Dostoevsky himself. Critics are ready to expatiate at the drop of a hat—amid an increasingly suffocating smokescreen of erudite irrelevancies and melodramatic pseudo-profundities—on the vast "cultural significance" of *Notes from Underground.* Meanwhile, the real point of Dostoevsky's fascinating little work has gotten completely lost in the shuffle.

What was Dostoevsky himself trying to do? Everyone knows that *Notes from Underground* was originally begun as a polemic inspired by Dostoevsky's opposition to the Socialist radicals of his time (popularly called Nihilists as a result of the label affixed to them in Turgenev's *Fathers and Sons*). The outstanding spokesman for the Russian radicals at this moment was Nicolai G. Chernyshevsky, whose Utopian novel *What Is To Be Done?* had appeared in the spring of 1863 and had caused a sensation. *Notes from Underground* was intended as an answer to *What Is To Be Done?*; and the accepted account of the relation between them runs as follows.

Chernyshevsky and the radicals believed that man was innately good and amenable to reason, and that, once enlightened as to his true interests, reason and science would ultimately enable him to construct a perfect society. Dostoevsky, on the other hand, believed that man was innately evil, irrational, capricious and destructive; not reason but only faith in Christ could ever succeed in helping him to master the chaos of his impulses. This view of *Notes from Underground* was first advanced by the Russian religious philosopher V. V. Rozanov in his brilliant study, *The Legend of the Grand Inquisitor* (1890). And regardless of the differing explanations offered for the genesis of Dostoevsky's *Weltanschauung,* this interpretation of *Notes from Underground* has continued to reign unchallenged ever since.

Despite the hegemony it has enjoyed, however, Rozanov's theory is at best only a beguiling and misleading half-truth. Rozanov was not primarily concerned with interpreting Dostoevsky's art but with enlisting the awe-inspiring name of the novelist on the side of his religious philosophy; and he unduly emphasizes one pole of the actual dialectic of the work, bringing it to the foreground as the entire meaning of the whole with a total disregard for context. Worst of all, he sees the underground man only as the simple negative of what Dostoevsky was attacking—the irrational against reason, evil and moral chaos against purposive social activity.

If this interpretation were true, then we could only conclude that Dostoevsky was just about the worst polemicist in all of literary history. Could Dostoevsky really have imagined that any reader in his right mind would *prefer* the world of the underground man as an alternative to Chernyshevsky's idyllic Socialist Utopia? Hardly! Dostoevsky was by no means as simple-minded or as maladroit as admirers like Rozanov—though certainly without fully realizing it themselves—would make him out to be. In reality his attack on Chernyshevsky and the Nihilists is a good deal more insidious, subtle and effective than Dostoevsky ever has been given credit for.

Beginning with V. L. Komarovich in 1924, a number of Russian critics have explored in detail the relation between *Notes from Underground* and *What Is To Be Done?* It is now clear that whole sections of Dostoevsky's novella—for example, the attempt of the underground man to

bump into an officer on the Nevsky Prospect, or the famous encounter with the prostitute Lisa—were conceived entirely as *parodies* of specific episodes in Chernyshevsky's book. The uncovering of these parodies provided the first real glimpse into the inner logic of Dostoevsky's artistry; but the Russian critics themselves have never pressed their own insights home with sufficient rigor. What they have failed to realize is that *Notes from Underground* as a whole—not only certain details and episodes—was conceived and executed as one magnificent satirical parody.

This parody, however, does not consist merely in rejecting Nihilism and setting up a competing version of "human nature" in its place. Rather, since parody is ridicule by *imitation,* Dostoevsky assimilates the major doctrines of Russian Nihilism into the life of his underground man; and by revealing the hopeless dilemmas in which he lands as a result, Dostoevsky intends to undermine these doctrines from within. The tragedy of the underground man does not arise, as is popularly supposed, because of his rejection of reason. It derives from his acceptance of *all* the implications of "reason" in its then-current Russian incarnation—and particularly those implications which the advocates of reason like Chernyshevsky blithely preferred to overlook or deny.

Dostoevsky himself clearly pointed to his use of parody in the footnote appended to the title of his novella. "Both the author of the *Notes* and the *Notes* themselves," he writes, "are, of course, fictitious. Nevertheless, such persons as the author of such memoirs not only may, but must, exist in our society, if we take into consideration the circumstances which led to the formation of our society. It was my intention to bring before our reading public, more conspicuously than is usually done, one of the characters of our recent past. He is one of the representatives of a generation that is still with us." Dostoevsky here is obviously talking about the formation of Russian ("our") society, not—as has often been claimed—about the society of nineteenth-century Western Europe or of "modern culture." And Russian society, as Dostoevsky could expect all his readers to know, had been formed by the successive accretions of Western influence that had streamed into Russia since the time of Peter the Great. The underground man embodies and reflects the latest phases of this evolution in himself; he is a parodistic *persona* whose life exemplifies the serio-comic impasse of this historical process.

Only if we approach *Notes from Underground* in this way can we understand Dostoevsky's choice of subject-matter and method of organization. The work consists of two tableaux selected from the life of the underground man—but each episode also, and more importantly, corresponds to a different and very crucial moment in the spiritual history of the Russian intelligentsia. The first section shows the underground man in the ideological grip of the Nihilism of the Sixties; the second, as a perfect product of the social Romanticism of the Forties. Each section of the work thus reveals the differing manner in which the personality of the educated Russian—depending on the dominant ideology of the moment—had been disorganized and disrupted by the attempt to live according to alien doctrines and ideals. This also explains the peculiar construction of the work, which reverses chronological sequence and proceeds backward in time. The Nihilism of the Sixties was uppermost in the consciousness of Dostoevsky's readers, and had provided the immediate inspiration for the story. Since the underground man was not primarily a private individual but a social type, Dostoevsky sacrifices the natural biographical order of inner growth and development to obtain as much polemical timeliness as possible from the very first page.

Notes from Underground, then, is not the self-revelation of a pathological personality, not a theological cry of despair over the evils of "human nature," least of all a work expressing Dostoevsky's involuntary adoption of Nietzsche's philosophy of "immoralism" and the will to power. On the contrary, it is a brilliantly ironic Swiftian parody remarkable for its self-conscious mastery, satirical control and Machiavellian finesse. But to prove this contention we must set the work back in the context from which it came, and endeavor to supply the framework of coordinates on which Dostoevsky depended to obtain his effects.

The famous opening tirade of *Notes from Underground* gives us an unforgettable picture of the underground man stewing in his Petersburg "funk-hole" and mulling over the peculiarities of his character—or rather, his total inability to become a character. Nothing could be more abject, petty and ridiculous than the image he gives of his life. He refuses to be treated for a liver ailment out of "spite"; he remembers an attempt made in his youth, when he was still in the civil service, to browbeat an officer for no reason other than the assertion of petty vanity; he boasts of his honesty, and then, when he realizes how "contemptible" such boasting is, he deliberately lets it stand to degrade himself even more in the eyes of the reader.

The underground man, indeed, seems to be nothing more than a chaos of conflicting emotional impulses; and his conflict may be defined as that of a search for his own character—his quest for himself. "I did not even know how to become anything," he says, "either spiteful or good, either a blackguard or an honest man, either a hero or an insect." At the very moment when he feels most conscious of "the sublime and the beautiful," he tells us, he was also "guilty of the most contemptible actions which—well, which, in fact, everybody is guilty of, but which, as though on purpose, I only happened to commit when I was most conscious that they ought not to be committed." Why, he asks plaintively, should this be so?

The answer to this question has invariably been sought in some "abnormal" or "psychopathic" trait of the underground man, which is then usually traced to the hidden recesses of Dostoevsky's own psychology. But the underground man's monologue provides a perfectly plausible answer to his question. "Whatever happened," he assures us, "happened in accordance with the normal and fundamental laws of intensified consciousness and by a sort of inertia which is a direct consequence of those laws, and . . . therefore you could not only not change yourself, but you simply couldn't make any attempt to." Dostoevsky, in other words, attributes to his underground man a belief in *scientific determinism.* The underground man, who remarks that he is "well-educated enough not to be superstitious," is quite well up on the most enlightened opinion of his time; he knows all about science and the laws of intensified consciousness; and he accepts the fact that whatever he does is inevitable and unalterable because it is totally determined by the laws of nature.

The moral impotence of the underground man thus springs directly from his acceptance of one of the cornerstones of Chernyshevsky's thought—absolute determinism. This aspect of Chernyshevsky's philosophy is mentioned only incidentally in *What Is To Be Done?*; and the behavior of some of the characters—as Chernyshevsky himself is embarrassedly forced to concede—can hardly be reconciled with this doctrine. Nonetheless, in his resounding article on *The Anthropological Principle in Philosophy* (1860), which was equally if not more famous than his novel, Chernyshevsky had flatly denied the existence of anything remotely resembling free will—or, for that matter, any kind of will. An act of will, according to Chernyshevsky, is "only the subjective impression which accompanies in our minds the rise of thoughts or actions from preceding thoughts, actions or external facts." Dostoevsky thus begins his parody of Nihilism by having the underground man use Chernyshevsky's philosophy as an excuse for his moral flaccidity. Under the magic wand of Chernyshevsky's determinism, *if taken seriously and consequentially,* all moral action has become impossible.

With skillful dialectical ingenuity, Dostoevsky displays the bewildered demoralization of his character before this unprecedented situation. The underground man, for instance, imagines that he wishes to forgive someone magnanimously for having slapped him in the face; but the more he thinks about it, the more impossible such an action becomes. "For I should most certainly not have known what to do with my magnanimity—neither to forgive, since the man who would have slapped my face would most probably have done it in obedience to the laws of nature; nor to forget, since though even if it is the law of nature, it hurts all the same."

Or suppose he wishes to act the other way round—not to forgive magnanimously but to take revenge. How can one take revenge when nobody is to blame for anything? "One look and the object disappears into thin air, your reasons evaporate, there is no guilty man, the injury is no longer an injury but just fate, something in the nature of toothache for which no one can be blamed." That is why, as the underground man says, "the direct, the inevitable and the legitimate result of consciousness is to make all action impossible." Or, if any action is taken—say on the matter of revenge—then "it would merely be out of spite." Spite is not a valid cause for any kind of action, but it is the only one left when the "laws of nature" make any other response illegitimate.

In such passages, the moral vacuum created by the underground man's acceptance of scientific determinism is expressed with unrivalled psychological acumen. But while, as a well-trained member of the intelligentsia, reason forces him to accept determinism, it is impossible for him humanly to live with its conclusions. As a result of the laws of intensified consciousness, he writes sardonically, "you are quite right in being a blackguard, as though it were any consolation to the blackguard that he actually is a blackguard." Or, as regards the slap in the face, it is impossible to forget because "though even if it is the law of nature, it hurts all the same." Both these comments pose a total human reaction—a moral revulsion at being a blackguard, an upsurge of anger at the insult of being slapped—against a scientific rationale that dissolves all human responsibility and thus all possibility of a human response. "Reason" tells the underground man that feelings of guilt or even of indignation are totally irrational and unjustified; but conscience and a sense of dignity are not "reasonable"—happily for mankind—and they manage to assert themselves all the same.

It is this assertion of the moral-emotive level of the personality, striving to keep alive its significance in the face of the laws of nature, that is expressed by the underground man's so-called "masochism." He confesses, in a much-commented passage:

> I felt a sort of secret, abnormal, contemptible delight when, on coming home on one of the foulest nights in Petersburg, I used to realize intensely that again I had been guilty of some dastardly action that day . . . and inwardly, secretly, I used to go on nagging myself, worrying myself, accusing myself, till at last the bitterness I felt turned into a sort of shameful, damnable sweetness, and finally, into real positive delight! Yes, into delight! . . . The feeling of delight was there just because *I was so intensely aware of my own degradation.*

Whatever a passage of this kind may reveal about Dostoevsky's psyche to the trained clinical eye, in the context of *Notes from Underground* it does not refer to Dostoevsky but to the underground man; and it has a specific dramatic function. The ambiguous "delight" of the underground man arises from the moral-emotive response of his *human nature* to the blank nullity of the *laws of nature.* It signifies his refusal to abdicate his conscience and submit silently to determinism, even though his reason assures him that there is nothing he can really do to change for the better. The "masochism" of the underground man thus has a *reverse* significance from that usually attributed to it. Instead of being a sign of pathological abnormality, it is in reality an indication of the underground man's paradoxical spiritual health—his preservation of his moral sense.

It is only from this perspective, with its deceptive transvaluation of the normal moral horizon, that we can grasp the underground man's relation to the imaginary interlocutor with whom he argues all through the first part of *Notes from Underground.* This interlocutor is obviously a follower of Chernyshevsky, a man of action, *l'homme de la nature et de la vérité;* and the underground man, as we see, *accepts* his theory that all human life is simply a mechanical product of the laws of nature. But the underground man knows what the man of action does not—that this theory makes all moral action impossible, or at least meaningless. "I envy such a man with all the forces of my embittered heart," says the underground man. "He is stupid—I am not disputing that. But perhaps the normal man

should be stupid." The normal man, for example, the man of action, inspired by a feeling of revenge, "goes straight to his goal, like a mad bull, with lowered horns." He does not realize that what he thinks of as the basis for his action, i.e., justice, is a ludicrously old-fashioned and unscientific prejudice eliminated by the laws of nature. It is only his stupidity that allows him to maintain his complacency, and to look on the underground man's squirmings with unfeigned contempt. Or conversely, the men of action "capitulate in all sincerity" before the "stone wall" of scientific determinism and the laws of nature, which exert "a sort of calming influence upon them, a sort of final and morally decisive influence and perhaps even a mystic one." The plain men of action simply do not understand that scientific determinism does not allow them to be "morally decisive" about anything; and they accept its conclusions with a smug awareness of being up-to-date, while they go on behaving exactly as in the past.

Very different is the response of the ignominious underground man, who knows only too well what the "stone wall" really means and, as a consequence, can only nurse a despicable resentment that he cannot justly discharge against anybody. But the underground man, with his well-known "masochism," cannot help behaving *as if* some sort of free human response were still possible and meaningful—"consequently there is only one solution left, namely, knocking your head against the wall as hard as you can." "Is it not much better to understand everything," cries the underground man, "to be aware of everything, to be conscious of all the impossibilities and stone walls? Not to be reconciled to any of those impossibilities or stone walls if you hate being reconciled to them? To reach by way of the most irrefutable logical combinations the most hideous conclusions on the eternal theme that it is somehow your own fault if there is a stone wall, though again it is abundantly clear that it is not your fault at all, and therefore to abandon yourself sensuously to doing nothing, and silently and impotently gnashing your teeth?"

Here, at first sight, the paradoxes of the underground man appear to reach a paroxysm of psychopathic self-accusation; but once we understand the logic of Dostoevsky's creation, it is quite clear that nobody in the world can be guilty of anything except the underground man. He knows that the idea of guilt, along with all other moral notions, has been abolished by the laws of nature; yet he persists in having moral responses just the same. And since there is nowhere else for him to assign moral responsibility, by the most irrefutable logic he and he alone is to blame for everything.

The portrait of the underground man we have been tracing is developed up through Chapter VI of the first part of *Notes from Underground.* And, as we have tried to show, it is based on an imaginative dramatization of a double movement: the acceptance of Chernyshevsky's determinism by the underground man's reason, but its rejection by his moral-emotive instincts. It is only from this point of view, indeed, that we can grasp the complex raillery of Dostoevsky's creation. The self-mockery of the underground man, the disgusted pejoratives he uses about himself, have usually been taken literally; but as we have seen in the case of "masochism," such a literal reading entirely misses Dostoevsky's meaning. In the same way, the continual self-derision of the underground man is intended to convey a consummate tragi-comic irony.

The underground man becomes what he is because his life is the *reductio ad absurdum* of the metaphysics of the man of action; and the more repulsive and hideous he portrays this life (and himself) as being, the more he underlines the incredible obtuseness of his self-confident judge. Far from wishing to portray the underground man as the embodiment of *evil*, the whole purpose of **Notes from Underground** is quite the opposite. Only in a world where human choice can make a difference, only where there is no absolute determinism, is any morality possible at all; and Dostoevsky adroitly defends the underground man's "capriciousness" as the necessary precondition for any morality whatsoever.

Beginning with Chapter VII of **Notes from Underground,** Dostoevsky shifts his target of attack. Up to this point he has been aiming at Chernyshevsky's metaphysics in its most general formulation; but now he turns to his ethics of "rational egoism" on the one hand, and, on the other, to the ideal of the Crystal Palace. Both these doctrines are exploded by the use of the same strategy that Dostoevsky has already employed—his technique, as it were, of projection into the absolute. Dostoevsky, that is, places himself imaginatively at the position where the doctrine he wishes to attack has already achieved its goal; and then he demonstrates the moral-psychological incompatibility of this achievement with some aspect of the nature of man—in this case, man's need to feel spiritually free and morally responsible. This is what Dostoevsky meant when he spoke of the "fantastic realism" of his work—a realism of the possible and the extreme rather than of the median and the actual; and his first large-scale use of this "fantastic realism" occurs in **Notes from Underground.**

In the first part of this section, the underground man waxes merry over the "theory of the regeneration of the whole human race by means of the system of its own advantages." But what *is* man's true advantage? Can it only be found by "taking the average of statistical figures and relying on scientific and economic formulas"? "That's the trouble, gentlemen," says the underground man commiseratingly,

> that there exists something which is dearer to almost every man than his greatest good, or (not to upset the logic of my argument) that there exists one most valuable good (the one, too, that is being constantly overlooked, namely, the one we are talking about) which is greater and more desirable than all other goods, and for the sake of which a man, if need be, is ready to challenge all law, that is to say, reason, honor, peace, prosperity—in short, all those excellent and useful things, provided he can obtain that primary and most desirable good which is dearer to him than anything in the world.

The tone and language of this passage, with its pretense of philosophical precision, is clearly a parody of some of the more laborious passages in *The Anthropological Principle.* Even more important, however, is to understand why

Dostoevsky's "one most valuable good" is placed in such immitigable opposition to "reason, honor, peace, prosperity," etc. The ultimate goal of Chernyshevsky's ethics of "rational egoism" was the creation of a sanctified humanity which, out of sheer rational calculations of self-interest, had lost the very possibility of doing evil. A true "rational egoist," according to Chernyshevsky, "may say to himself: I will be wicked, I will do people harm; but he will not be able to do that any more than a clever man can be a fool even if he wanted to be one." Not Dostoevsky but Chernyshevsky had posed the alternative: either moral freedom, i.e., the freedom to *choose* between good and evil, or "reason" with all its material advantages. And the answer of the underground man is that man's need to feel himself free and morally autonomous is precisely the "one most valuable good" for which he is ready to sacrifice all the others. To obtain this "good" he will "deliberately and consciously desire something that is injurious, stupid, even outrageously stupid, just because he wants *to have the right* to desire for himself even what is very stupid and not to be bound by an obligation to desire only what is sensible." For at all events, however stupid and unreasonable this "good" may be, "it preserves what is most precious and most important to us, namely, our personality and our individuality."

The underground man's rejection of "rational egoism" paves the way for his reaction against its ultimate ideal in the future—the world of the Crystal Palace. In this future Utopia, described in *What Is To Be Done?,* all the laws of nature governing society will have been discovered. Here Dostoevsky is no longer dramatizing the moral-psychological impossibility of a purely deterministic world; the laws of nature are now seen in the light of their future triumphs, which will guide man's way to overwhelming material prosperity. The Crystal Palace was modelled, as all Chernyshevsky's readers knew, on the Fourierist phalanstery; and Fourier had calculated and combined all the details of life in the phalanstery with a precision that was not only mathematical but maniacal. The phalanstery, as Emile Faguet once pithily remarked, "c'est l'Arcadie d'un chef de bureau."

The triumph of the Crystal Palace presupposes that science will have taught man that his free-will, in addition to being a regrettable speculative error, was also a positive hindrance to his welfare. For science proves that man "possesses neither will nor caprices, and never has done, and . . . he himself is nothing more than a sort of piano-key or organ-stop." (Fourier, it might be mentioned, spoke of the phalanstery as embodying the laws and principles of "harmony." His chief disciple, Victor Considerant, in a famous Socialist treatise mentioned anagrammatically in *What Is To Be Done?* compared human passions to a "clavier" whose notes could be blended into such harmony: hence Dostoevsky's musical imagery.) The trouble is, however, that man is "phenomenally ungrateful. I'm even inclined," says the underground man, "to believe that the best definition of man is—a creature who walks on two legs and is ungrateful." For even if you

> shower all the earthly blessings upon him, drown him in happiness, head over ears, so that only bubbles should be visible on the surface, or

bestow such economic prosperity upon him as would leave him with nothing to do but sleep, eat cakes, and only worry about keeping world history going . . . even then he will, man will, out of sheer ingratitude . . . play a dirty trick on you.

This "dirty trick" is precisely that he will throw everything overboard, will set his heart on the most uneconomic and positively harmful nonsense, "for the sole purpose of proving to himself (as though that were so necessary) that men are still men and not keys on a piano."

At this point, the underground man rises to a climactic vision of universal chaos which duplicates, on the socio-historical level, the chaos of the underground man's life in the earlier chapters. And in both cases, the cause of this chaos is the same—the revolt of the personality against the vision of a world in which personality and free-will have no further reason for being. For even if such a world could really be created,

> even if he [man] really were nothing but a piano-key, even if this were proved to him by natural science and mathematically, even then he would refuse to come to his senses. . . . And if he has no other remedy, he will plan destruction and chaos, he will devise all sorts of sufferings. . . . If you say that this, too, can be calculated by the mathematical table—chaos, and darkness, and curses—so that the mere possibility of calculating it all before hand would stop it all and reason would triumph in the end—well, if that were to happen man would go purposely mad in order to rid himself of reason and carry his point.

Nothing in **Notes from Underground,** at first sight, seems more daring and shocking than this invocation to the gods of darkness—to destruction, chaos, and madness. And, not surprisingly, all interpreters of Dostoevsky have invariably taken it with the same literalness with which they took the underground man's "masochism" and "immorality." None have paid the slightest attention to the hypothetical and conditional form in which Dostoevsky cast these assertions, nor have they seen them in the light of his projection of the future ideal of the Crystal Palace. In fact, however, the senseless and self-destructive revolt of freedom is envisaged by Dostoevsky *only* as a last-ditch defense, in circumstances where man has no other way of preserving the autonomy of his personality. Indeed, the underground man himself makes abundantly clear that his frenetic harangue does not refer to man as he actually *exists* in ordinary "irrational" life; it applies to man as he might be forced to *become* if Chernyshevsky's Fourierist Utopia were ever realized. For after lividly declaiming in the name of curses, darkness and chaos, the underground man returns to reality for a moment and adds: "And how is one after that to resist the temptation to rejoice that all this has not happened yet and that so far desire depends on the devil alone knows what."

Once having envisaged the completion of the Crystal Palace, however, the underground man continues, in Chapter IX, to question the confidence of Chernyshevsky and the Socialist radicals that such an ideal was what man really wanted. "Man likes to create and clear paths—that is un-

Main Hall of the Crystal Palace, a structure at London's Universal Exhibition of 1851 and a symbol invoked by both Nikolai Chernyshevsky in his What Is to Be Done? *and the underground man in* Notes from the Underground.

deniable," the underground man agrees; man wishes to accomplish useful and socially productive labor. But the underground man denies that man wishes to achieve the static secular Apocalypse of the Crystal Palace, to reach the literal end of history when all further striving, moral struggle, and inner conflict will have ceased. Perhaps man

> is instinctively afraid of reaching the goal and completing the building he is erecting? . . . Perhaps he only loves building it and not living in it, preferring to leave it later *aux animaux domestiques* such as ants, sheep, etc., etc., . . . They [ants] have one marvelous building of this kind, a building that is forever indestructible—the ant-hill.

The ideal of the "ant-hill" is suitable *aux animaux domestiques* exactly because they have no inkling of man's need to feel creative and free—because all they desire is to complete their appointed tasks in conformity with reason and the laws of nature through all eternity.

This comparison of the Socialist ideal to an "ant-hill" was a commonplace in the Russian journalism of the period, but the use of such an image here as a symbol for the secular end of history very probably derives from Alexander Herzen. "If humanity went straight to some goal," Herzen wrote in *From the Other Shore* (1855), "there would be no history, only logic; humanity would stop in some finished form, in a spontaneous *status quo* like the animals . . . Besides, if the libretto existed, history would lose all interest, it would become futile, boring, ridiculous." Of all Herzen's works, Dostoevsky publicly expressed special admiration for *From the Other Shore;* and the similarity is too great to be accidental. Now Herzen, more than any other single individual, was responsible for the propagation of Socialist ideas in Russia; but he never accepted the Nihilist scientism and determinism of the Sixties. Like Dostoevsky himself, Herzen was a member of the generation of the Forties which had been nurtured on Schelling and Hegel; and no member of this generation, regardless of politics, ever succumbed completely to the lure of mechanical materialism. Dostoevsky here is thus using the Forties to argue against the Sixties, as he was to do later again in *The Devils* (1871-1872). And this interplay between the generations, as we shall see, is of first importance for understanding the meaning of *Notes from Underground* as a whole.

The ultimate argument of the underground man against the Crystal Palace is that it outlaws suffering. "In the Crystal Palace it is unthinkable; suffering is doubt, it is negation, and what sort of Crystal Palace would it be if one were to have any doubts about it? And yet I am convinced that man will never renounce real suffering, that is to say, destruction and chaos. Suffering! Why it's the sole cause of consciousness!" Within the ideological context of *Notes from Underground,* "suffering" clearly has the same function as "masochism" or as the underground man's inverted irony. It is the only way left of keeping alive his "consciousness" as a human being, of asserting his personality, individuality and moral responsibility. And in returning to the problem of "consciousness" at this point—the end of Chapter IX—Dostoevsky brings his demolition of the Crystal Palace into relation with his earlier chapters, establishing the unity of what appears to be the underground man's spasmodic and disorderly tirade.

In Chapter X, the penultimate section of *Notes from Underground,* the reader becomes aware of a new note being struck, or rather, of a note which had hitherto remained in the background suddenly ringing out above all the others. Up to this point, the self-torture and suffering of the underground man had been made amply evident. Still, the underground man's sacrilegious assertion that he had found "delight" in his suffering, and the sarcastic satisfaction with which he flaunts this "delight" before the horrified eyes of his interlocutor, somewhat mitigates our sense of his anguish. But in Chapter X, we become aware of how literally unbearable the situation of the underground man really is.

Torn between the convictions of his reason and the revolt of his conscience and feelings, the underground man cries out: "Surely I have not been made for the sole purpose of drawing the conclusion that the way I am made is a piece of rank deceit? Can this be the sole purpose? I don't believe it." The underground man is desperately searching for some solution to his racking dilemma; and he makes very clear that the underground revolt of the personality, valuable though it may be, is by no means a positive answer. "I rejected the Crystal Palace myself for the sole reason that one would not be allowed to stick out one's tongue at it" (again a self-mocking and derisive image for the revolt of moral freedom). "But I did not say that be-

cause I am so fond of sticking out my tongue. . . . On the contrary, I'd gladly have let my tongue be cut off out of gratitude if things could be so arranged that I should have no wish to stick it out at all."

Dostoevsky leaves us in no doubt that the underground man, far from rejecting all ideals, is desperately searching for one that would truly satisfy the needs of his spirit. Such an ideal would not spur his personality to revolt in rabid frenzy; on the contrary, it would lead to the willing surrender of himself in its favor. This alternative ideal obviously could only be one which, recognizing the autonomy of the will and the freedom of the personality, appealed to the moral nature of man instead of to "reason" and self-interest in the service of determinism. From a letter of Dostoevsky's we know that Chapter X originally contained some clear indication that this alternative ideal was that of Christ; but this part of the text was mangled both by the censors and by the carelessness of the proof readers.

"I am not at all happy about my article," Dostoevsky wrote after the publication of the first part of *Notes from Underground;* "there are terrible proofreading errors, and it would have been better not to publish the penultimate chapter (the most important, where the very idea of the whole article is expressed) rather than to publish it this way, that is, with twisted sentences and contradictions. But what can one do? What swine the censors are! Where I derided everything, and sometimes blasphemed *for appearance,* they let it get by, but when from all this I deduced the necessity of belief in Christ, they cut it out. Why, are the censors perhaps conspiring against the government?"

Dostoevsky, we may assume, corrected some of these errors when he revised the magazine text for publication in book form; but while the alternative ideal to the Crystal Palace is clearly enough indicated, some confusion still remains in the final text. This confusion arises when, in Chapter X, the underground man begins to compare the Crystal Palace to another structure that would be a "real" palace instead of a hencoop.

"You see" he says, "if it [the Crystal Palace] were not a palace but a hencoop, and if it should rain, I might crawl into it to avoid getting wet, but I would never pretend that the hencoop was a palace out of gratitude to it for sheltering me from the rain. You laugh and you tell me that in such circumstances even a hencoop is as good as a palace. Yes, I reply, it certainly is if the only purpose in life is not to get wet." It is not the usefulness of the hencoop that is impugned by the underground man, but the fact that it is mistaken for a palace, i.e., that in return for its practical advantages it has been elevated into mankind's ideal. But the underground man refuses to accept the hencoop-*qua*-palace as *his* ideal. "But what is to be done if I've got it into my head that that [i.e., not to get wet] is not the only purpose of life, and that if one has to live, one had better live in a palace?"

Here, as we can see, the underground man poses a "true" against the "false" palace; and this is the point at which the confusion occurs. For the underground man develops this comparison as follows: "For the time being," he says,

. . . I refuse to accept a hencoop for a palace.
The Crystal Palace may be just an idle dream, it
may be against all the laws of nature, I may have
invented it because of my own stupidity, because
of certain old and irrational habits of my generation. But what do I care whether it is against the
laws of nature? What does it matter so long as
it exists in my desires, or rather exists while my
desires exist?

Now it is obvious that something is wrong here: the "Crystal Palace" mentioned in this passage is the *opposite* of everything it has stood for throughout the rest of the text.

This latter "Crystal Palace" is a structure that exists
against the laws of nature instead of being their embodiment; it is an answer to man's desires and not their suppression. Moreover, the underground man's allusion to
"certain old and irrational habits of my generation" reminds us that he is a member of the generation of the Forties. This paves the way for part two of the work, and also
indicates Dostoevsky's recognition that the Forties—
whatever else this era may have been guilty of from his
point of view—still believed in the existence of the will and
in the importance of feeling and desire. In any case, it is
clear that the "Crystal Palace" of this citation refers to the
"true" palace which is *not* a hencoop; but the fact that
Dostoevsky allows the same designation to stand for both
"palaces" cannot help but baffle the reader.

Despite Dostoevsky's indication of this alternative ideal,
however, the essence of his conception of the underground
man requires the latter to remain trapped in the negative
phase of the revolt for freedom. He longs for another ideal,
he knows that it must exist, but—accepting determinism
and the laws of nature—he does not yet know how to attain it. All he can do is affirm despairingly: "I know that
I shall never be content with a compromise, with an everlasting and recurring zero because it exists according to
the laws of nature and *actually* exists. I will not accept as
the crown of all my desires a big house with model flats
for the poor on a lease of ninety-nine hundred and ninety-
nine years."

And our last glimpse of the underground man, in the final
Chapter XI, masterfully depicts this state of mind, in
which he both denies and affirms his underground revolt
and his "dark cellar" in the space of a few lines.

Though I have said that I envy the normal man
to the point of exasperation, I wouldn't care to
be in his place in the circumstances in which I
find him (though I shall never cease envying
him. No, no, the dark cellar is, at any rate, of
much greater advantage to me!). In the dark cellar one can at least. . . . Sorry, I'm afraid I am
exaggerating. I am exaggerating because I know,
as well as twice-two, that it is not the dark cellar
that is better, but something else, something else
altogether, something I long for but cannot find.
To hell with the dark cellar!

What that "something else" is, and why the underground
man cannot attain it, forms the substance of the second
part of *Notes from Underground.*

The second part of *Notes from Underground* is subtitled:

"Apropos of the Wet Snow." Since the snow plays no role
whatever in the story, one may wonder why Dostoevsky
chose to highlight it in this manner. The answer is: to
heighten the symbolic atmosphere. This subtitle, along
with the quotation from Nekrasov used as epigraph, serves
to set this second part firmly in the ideological ambiance
that Dostoevsky wishes to evoke. It had already been
noted in the Forties (by P. V. Annenkov) that writers of
the "natural school" were fond of employing "wet snow"
as a typical feature of the Petersburg landscape; and Dostoevsky uses it to summon up instantly an image of Petersburg in the Forties—an image of the most "abstract and
premeditated city in the whole world," whose very existence had become symbolic in Russian literature for the
violence and unnaturalness of the Russian adaption to
Western culture. In addition, the poem by Nekrasov also
conjures up the moral and spiritual climate of the period.

Nekrasov's famous poem, to which Dostoevsky had also
alluded ironically in an earlier work—*The Friend of the
Family* (1859)—reproduces the pathetic confession of a
repentant prostitute redeemed from her degraded life by
the author:

When with a word of fervent conviction,
From the lowest dregs of dark affliction,
A soul from eternal doom I saved;

Citing some further lines, Dostoevsky suddenly cuts it
short with etc., etc.,—thereby indirectly indicating his
feeling that the poem was completely conventional chatter. The redemption-of-a-prostitute theme, which runs
from social Romantics like Eugène Sue, George Sand and
Hugo right through to Tolstoy's *Resurrection* (1899), had
become a commonplace in the Russian literature of the
Forties and also figures as a minor incident in *What Is To
Be Done?*. The climactic episode in the second part of
Notes from Underground—the encounter between the underground man and the prostitute Lisa—is clearly an ironic parody and reversal of this social Romantic cliché.

The second part of *Notes from Underground,* then, is intended to satirize the sentimental social Romanticism of
the Forties just as the first part had satirized the Nihilism
of the Sixties. And a good deal of light is thrown on this
second part by articles that Dostoevsky published in his
magazine *Time* in the years immediately preceding the
composition of his novella. The Forties, Dostoevsky wrote
in 1860, had been the moment when "the spirit of analysis
penetrated into our intellectual classes. . . . Then everything was done according to principle, we lived according
to principles, and we had a horrible fear of doing anything
not according to the latest ideas." All spontaneity and un-
self-consciousness was lost; not to live by the light of "the
latest ideas" was literally unthinkable. And under the influence of "the latest ideas" a new social type appeared
among the Russian intelligentsia—the "Byronic natures,"
the liberal idealists of the Forties.

As Dostoevsky describes them, these idealists were burning to help "humanity"; but they could find no occupation
worthy of their powers. "They said it was not really worth
the trouble to become angry and curse—that everything
was so dirty that one hardly had the desire to wiggle a single finger, and that a good dinner was worth more than

anything." All this was taken as the fine irony of despair, even when these idealists became fat and rosy-cheeked— or even when, as sometimes happened, they began to cheat at cards and were caught with their hands in someone else's pockets. But since these idealists were always longing to "sacrifice" themselves for "the good of humanity," Dostoevsky tauntingly pretends to take them at their word. Why, he asks, should they not really accomplish a sacrifice—and perhaps go so far as to teach a serf child to read? "Sacrifice yourselves, O giants," he bitingly enjoins them, "for the good of all. . . . Sacrifice yourselves completely, with your sublime temperament and your sublime ideas—lower yourselves, shrink yourselves, to this one particular child."

The social Romanticism of the Forties, in Dostoevsky's opinion, had fostered an inflated "egoism of principle," which allowed the Russian intelligentsia to live in a dream-world of "universal" beneficence while actually nursing their own vanity with perfect moral complacency. And the moral task confronting these liberal idealists was to live up to their own pretensions, i.e., to turn their abstract love of "humanity," which chiefly served to heighten their own self-esteem, into a concrete act of self-sacrifice directed toward a particular, concrete individual. This is of course precisely the theme of the second part of *Notes from Underground;* and we find a corresponding shift of style and treatment to accord with the new atmosphere of the period. Earlier the irony had been harsh, grating, jarring; the final argument of the underground man against the world of the Crystal Palace could only be the rage of madness and self-destruction. But what now comes to the foreground is a lighter comic tone of burlesque and caricature.

The youthful underground man, as Dostoevsky conceives him, is stuffed full of bookish ideas culled from the European and Russian Romantics and social Romantics—"I could not speak" he says of himself, "except 'as though I was reading from a book.'" Describing his own life he writes: "At home I mostly spent my time reading . . . it [the reading] excited, delighted and tormented me." All through the second part there are constant allusions to the artificiality of his responses ("how paltry, *unliterary,* and commonplace the whole affair would be," he thinks at one point). Entire sections are nothing but an extended burlesque of the underground man's stilted and pedantic reactions to the simplest human situations; and it is a testimony to the power of received ideas that Dostoevsky's sharply derisive comedy should so long have gone unnoticed. This comedy predominates in all the episodes preceding the meeting with the prostitute Lisa; for in these the underground man is caught in what we may call a "dialectic of vanity," which parallels the "dialectic of determinism" in part one. The underground man's vanity convinces him of his own intellectual superiority and he despises everybody; but when he realizes that he cannot rest without *their* recognition of his superiority, he hates others for their indifference and falls into self-loathing at his own humiliating dependence. This is the inevitable dialectic of an egoism which cannot forget about itself for a moment, and, in seeking to wrest recognition from the world, only receives dislike and hostility in return. Psychologically,

this dialectic duplicates the conflict of all against all that arises socially from the Western European principle of egoistic individualism. And Dostoevsky's implication is that the underground man—an "educated man, a modern intellectual," as he gleefully calls himself—has, as a result of imbibing the European culture popular in Russia in the Forties, lost almost all capacity for undistorted and selfless moral feeling.

The comedy changes into tragedy, however, when the underground man finally encounters another human being who fails to respond in the accustomed fashion. Dostoevsky was well aware of this alteration in texture, and, while working on the second part of his novella, wrote to his brother Mikhail: "You understand what is called a *transition* in music. Exactly the same thing happens here. In the first chapter, seemingly, there is just chatter; but suddenly this chatter, in the last two chapters, is resolved by a catastrophe." (In the final version the catastrophe is actually developed through Chapters V to X). This catastrophe is the incident with the prostitute Lisa, which resolves the conflict between imaginary sentimental idealism and ethical reality in dexterous fashion. And, by the ironic paradox of the conclusion, it reveals all the shabbiness of the intelligentsia's "ideals" when confronted with spontaneous and unselfish love.

The incident with Lisa begins on the underground man's arrival in the brothel. The proprietress treats him like any other patron and a girl enters. As he goes out with her, he catches sight of himself in a mirror: "My flustered face looked utterly revolting to me: pale, evil, mean, with dishevelled hair. 'It's all right, I'm glad of it,' I thought, I'm glad that I'll seem repulsive to her. I like that. . . ." Not having been able either to subdue his companions earlier or to insult them with sufficient weight to be taken seriously, the underground man characteristically anticipates revenging himself on the helpless girl. The more repulsive he is to her, the more his egoism and need for domination will be satisfied by forcing her to submit to his desires. It is not by physical submission alone, however, that the underground man attains his triumph over Lisa. For when he becomes aware of her hostile and resentful attitude, "a peevish thought stirred in my mind and seemed to pass all over my body like some vile sensation." This thought takes the form of an effort to play on Lisa's feelings, and to triumph over her not only physically but morally as well.

The underground man thus proceeds to break down the armor of indifference and assumed cynicism by which Lisa protects herself against the debasing circumstances of her life. Mingling horrible details of degradation with images of felicity whose banality makes them all the more poignant—and drawing on Balzac's *Le Père Goriot* in the process—the underground man succeeds in bringing to the surface Lisa's true feelings about herself and causing the total humiliation of her emotional breakdown. None of this was of course meant seriously; the underground man simply had been carried away by the power of his own eloquence. But this time his words hit home—Lisa is too young, naive and helpless to see through their falsity. "I worked myself up into so pathetic a state" he says, "that

I felt a lump rising in my throat and—all of a sudden I stopped . . . and, bending over apprehensively, began to listen with a violently beating heart." Lisa's bosom was heaving spasmodically, and she was making harrowing efforts to contain her sobs. "She bit the pillow, she bit her arm till it bled (I saw it afterwards), or clutching at her dishevelled hair with her fingers, went rigid with that superhuman effort, holding her breath and clenching her teeth."

The underground man, carried away by his victory, cannot resist living up to the exalted role of hero and benefactor that he had so often given himself in fantasy. When he leaves Lisa he gives her his address with a lordly gesture, inviting her to come and see him; and it is on this gesture that Dostoevsky turns the *dénouement* of the second part. For the moment the underground man emerges from the self-adulatory haze of his charlatanism, he is stricken with terror. He cannot bear the thought that Lisa might see him as he really is—wrapped in his shabby dressing-gown, living in his squalid "funk-hole," completely under the thumb of his manservant Apollon, immersed in all the exterior poverty and ignominy of his daily life. Never for a moment does it occur to him that he might help her nonetheless; he is so absorbed in himself that the only thought of her as a reality is an obscure sense of guilt. "Inside me, deep down in my heart and conscience, something kept stirring, would not die, and manifested itself in a feeling of poignant anguish."

After a few days pass and Lisa does not appear, the underground man becomes more cheerful; at times, he says, "I even began indulging in rather sweet day-dreams." These all concerned the process of Lisa's re-education, her confession of love for him, and his own confession that

> I did not dare lay claim to your heart first because I knew you were under my influence and was afraid that, out of gratitude, you would deliberately force yourself to respond to my love, that you would rouse a feeling in your heart which perhaps did not really exist, and I did not want this because it—it would be sheer despotism on my part—it would have been indelicate. . . . (Well, in short, here I got myself entangled in a sort of European, George-Sandian inexpressibly noble subtleties).

Interspersed with these reveries—which are a slap both at Sand's importance in the Forties, and the strong Sandian influence in *What Is To Be Done?*—is the low comedy of the underground man's efforts to bend the stubborn Apollon to his will. Dostoevsky, as it were, here uses the classical theatrical technique of two identical plots, one serious and the other farcical; and he interweaves them adroitly by having Lisa enter when the underground man is revealing all of his hysterical impotence in face of the imperturbably Apollon.

By this time, the underground man has reached a dangerous pitch of frustration and nervous exasperation. He breaks down completely before the bewildered Lisa, sobbing and complaining that he is "tortured" by Apollon. But all this is so humiliating that he cannot help turning on her in spiteful fury when, by stammering that she wishes to get out of the brothel, she reminds him of all that has taken place. And here he breaks into a famous tirade, in which he tells her the bitter truth about their relation: "To avenge my wounded pride on someone, to get my own back, I vented my spite on you and I laughed at you. I had been humiliated, so I too wanted to humiliate someone." With the typical inversion of his egoist's logic, he shouts: "I shall never forgive you for the tears which I was shedding before you a minute ago . . . Nor shall I ever forgive *you* for what I am confessing to you!"

But at this point, a strange thing occurs—strange at least to the underground man. Instead of flaring up herself and hitting back—the only response the underground man is accustomed to—Lisa realizes that he too is unhappy and suffering. She throws herself into his arms to console *him,* and they both break into tears; but given the character of the underground man, who cannot respond selflessly to any feelings, such a moment cannot last very long. "It . . . occurred to me just then, overwrought as I was, that our parts were now completely changed, that she was the heroine now, while I was exactly the same crushed and humiliated creature as she had appeared to me that night four days before." And not out of love but out of hate, the underground man makes love to her on the spot to revenge himself on *her* for having dared to try to console him. Even more, to make his revenge complete and humiliate her further, he slips a five-rouble note into her hand; but though completely broken by this encounter, Lisa manages to fling the money on the table unnoticed before leaving.

All the moral depravity of the underground man is starkly revealed in this climactic scene—or perhaps not so much depravity as moral impotence. For he retains his moral awareness all through the novella, although his egoism prevents him from ever putting this awareness into practice. Even here, when he finds the five-rouble note, he distractedly rushes out after Lisa in the silent, snow-filled street to ask her forgiveness. But then, pulling himself up short, he realizes the futility of all his agitation. For he understands very well that "I could not possibly have loved anyone because, I repeat, to me love meant to tyrannize and be morally superior."

And as he turns slowly home, he conceives the most diabolic rationalization of all for his conduct.

> Will it not be better, [he thinks] suppressing the living pain in [his] heart . . . that she should now carry that insult away with her for ever? What is an insult but a sort of purification? It is the most corrosive and painful form of consciousness! . . . The memory of that humiliation will raise her and purify her by hatred, and, well, perhaps also by forgiveness . . . And, really . . . which is better: cheap happiness or exalted suffering? Well, which is better?

With this final stabbing irony, Dostoevsky allows his underground man to use the very idea of purification through suffering as a rationalization for his viciousness. In so doing, he returns to the main theme of the first part and places it in a new light. "Consciousness" and "suffering" were seen to be values when the underground man, out of a need to preserve his human identity, wished to suffer *himself* rather than to rationalize his conduct as an effect of the laws of nature. But so long as these values remain a function only of egoism, there is always the possibility that they will be devilishly interpreted primarily to cause *others* to suffer as a way of purifying *their* souls. And here, we might add, Dostoevsky has provided an inadvertent but prophetic parody on all those critics who have so often accused him of advocating an indiscriminate "salvation through suffering."

As the second part of *Notes from Underground* comes to an end, the underground man again returns to his frustrated isolation. For one moment he had caught a glimpse of the way out of his racking dialectic. Lisa's complete disregard of her own humiliation, her whole-souled identification with the underground man's torments—in short, her capacity for selfless love and self-sacrifice—is the only way to break the sorcerer's spell of egocentricity. When she rushes into the arms of the underground man, not thinking of herself but only of *his* suffering, she is at the same time illustrating that "something else" which his egoism will never allow him to attain. This "something else" is the ideal of the voluntary self-sacrifice of the personality out of love. In his encounter with Lisa, the underground man has met this ideal in the flesh; and his failure to respond to its appeal dooms him irrevocably for the future.

Nonetheless, if we look at *Notes from Underground* as a whole, we see that the idealistic egoism of the Forties, with its cultivation of a sense of spiritual *noblesse* and its emphasis on individual moral consciousness, does not merely have a negative value. It was precisely because of such "old and irrational habits" of his generation that, as we noted, the underground man held out against the Nihilism of the Sixties; and this is the relation between the Forties and Sixties that continues to prevail in Dostoevsky's work. Egocentric though it may have been, the sentimental idealism of the Forties still stressed the importance of free-will and preserved a sense of the inner autonomy of the personality. Such a sense is the presupposition for any human world whatever; and this is the basis on which Dostoevsky defends "egoism." But so long as such egoism remains self-centered, it is not by itself a moral act; more is required, as we see in part two, for the underground man to achieve moral self-definition. Exactly the same relation between the two generations was later portrayed in *The Devils,* where the sentimental idealism of the old liberal Stepan Trofimovitch Verkhovensky is far superior morally to the utilitarian ruthlessness of Peter Verkhovensky; but Stepan Trofimovitch is himself morally impotent, and, like the underground man in part two, rhetorically longs for some contact with "reality."

As a coda to the entire work, Dostoevsky offers some remarks in which *both* ideologies of the radical intelligentsia are rejected; and in which we hear the same plea to return to the Russian "soil" that echoes in Dostoevsky's articles. For these ideologies have disoriented the natural, instinctive, spontaneous, spiritual reactions of the Russian intelligentsia to the point where, without such foreign ideas, they are totally helpless; but so long as they cling to such crutches, they can never learn to walk by themselves.

"Leave us alone without any books," writes the underground man caustically, "and we shall at once get confused, lose ourselves in a maze, we shall not know what to cling to, what to hold on to, what to love and what to hate, what to respect and what to despise. We even find it hard to be men, men of *real* flesh and blood, *our own* flesh and blood." And to reply that the underground man is only speaking for himself, Dostoevsky reaffirms the "typicality" he had stressed in the opening footnote, while at the same time defining the technique of satirical exaggeration and parodistic caricature that he had used. "For my part," remarks the underground man, "I have merely carried to extremes in my life what you have not dared to carry even half-way, and, in addition, you have mistaken your cowardice for common sense and have found comfort in that, deceiving yourselves." Nothing, it seems to me, could more amply confirm the interpretation of *Notes from Underground* offered in these pages. (pp. 1-33)

Joseph Frank, "Nihilism and 'Notes from Underground'," in The Sewanee Review, *Vol. LXIX, No. 1, Winter, 1961, pp. 1-33.*

Ronald Hingley   (essay date 1962)

[*Hingley has written extensively on Russian literature and history and has translated the plays and stories of Anton Chekhov. In the following excerpt, he maintains that* Notes from the Underground *is an autobiographical display of Dostoevsky's perverse penchant for suffering and debauchery.*]

[*Notes from Underground*], a short novel, [is] the only short work which has exercised on Dostoyevsky's critics a fascination comparable with that of his later long novels. It has been spoken of as the 'prelude' to the five-act tragedy of the great novels from *Crime and Punishment* to *The Brothers Karamazov.* There are arguments in favour of this view, for the links with Dostoyevsky's future to be found in *Notes from Underground* are indeed numerous and important. In particular it is his first attempt at a philosophical novel, an enterprise into which he plunged with enthusiasm. This short work contains a greater proportion of theorizing than any of the fiction which followed it, not excluding *The Brothers Karamazov.*

The theoretical sections of the novel, like the narrative which follows, are put into the mouth of Dostoyevsky's unnamed Narrator, who will be referred to as the 'Underground Man'. As his title suggests, this is a figure from the past. The Underground Man is another in the series of 'St. Petersburg dreamers', being the most developed and interesting member of the group, but possessing the familiar stigmata. He is an isolated, lonely figure who lurks in poverty and introspective misery in his 'corner', and like other members of the group is a distorted portrait of Dostoyevsky himself during the eighteen-forties. There is reference to his 'touchiness', 'irritability' and 'pride,' all words which Dostoyevsky applied to himself on many occasions in his letters.

Dostoyevsky also attributes to his Underground Man his own passion for reading, together with the romantic dreams in which he had indulged in the eighteen-forties, those dreams termed 'Schilleresque' about everything 'noble and beautiful' which had incurred the sneers of Prince Valkovsky in *Insulted and Injured.* These romantic imaginings of the Underground Man are described as alternating with bouts of *razvrat* (debauchery), a word which occurs repeatedly in Dostoyevsky's writings. Dostoyevskian debauches usually take place off-stage, as it were, being hinted at in oracular language, and form part of the regular build-up of his Bogeymen. Here they are attributed to one of the self-portrait characters.

> Sometimes I used to get terribly bored. . . . I used to feel the need of movement, and would suddenly plunge into dark subterranean, loathsome . . . petty debauchery. Because of my perpetual pathological irritability my passions were sharp and burning. . . . I used to feel a hysterical thirst for contradictions and contrasts—hence my plunges into debauchery.

Is the 'debauch' also autobiographical, and if so what kind of debauchery does Dostoyevsky have in mind?

Alcoholic debauchery can be ruled out. Though drunkenness figures in his fiction (Marmeladov in *Crime and Punishment* being his most notable alcoholic) this was not among Dostoyevsky's many human weaknesses. But it does seem almost certain that in the dark days of the eighteen-forties he was at least an occasional visitor to the brothels of St. Petersburg. The point is almost clinched in a letter of November, 1845, in which he remarks to his brother Mikhail: 'The Minnas, Klaras and Mariannas [these were intended to be understood as the names of prostitutes] have become excessively pretty, but are damned expensive.' Unless Dostoyevsky was romancing here—always a possibility—this was his own brand of *razvrat.* If so this is another autobiographical trait in his Underground Man, whose visit to a brothel brings on the climax of the novel.

To the alternation between high thinking and low living must be added another more familiar contradiction which the Underground Man shares with his creator. This is his ambivalent attitude to humiliation. The Underground Man is yet another oscillator up and down the 'humiliation slot'. He is a predator and victim by turns, alternating between situations in which he courts humiliation and situations in which he himself humiliates and tyrannizes others. 'I'd been humiliated,' he remarks at one point, 'and so I wanted to humiliate. I'd been treated like a dishcloth, and so I too wanted to show my power.'

The Underground Man resembles previous self-portrait characters, such as the Narrator from *Insulted and Injured,* in being the product of introspective inspiration. But he differs from these characters, and even more strikingly from previous humiliation-oscillators (of whom Foma Fomich in *The Village of Stepanchikovo* was the most important forerunner) in the amount of introspective theorizing put into his mouth. This is his special characteristic. He outdoes all other characters in Dostoyevsky in the profundity of his self-analysis.

He is also one of the most sensitive, 'as if [he remarks of himself at one stage] I'd had my skin flayed off me and the mere touch of air hurt me'. This sensitivity, which he

terms *soznaniye* (consciousness) is one of his main introspective preoccupations. He wishes, for example, that he had been equipped with only the ordinary human allocation of consciousness, 'that is a half or a quarter of the portion allotted to a highly developed man in our unhappy nineteenth century, especially to one who has the added misfortune of living in St. Petersburg, the most abstract and contrived city on the face of the globe'. All consciousness, he claims, is a disease.

Notes from Underground is curiously constructed, the first part of the book (about one-third of its total length) being devoted entirely to theory, while the second part contains the narrative. Part One is again subdivided into two sections, of which the first is devoted to this theme of 'consciousness' (Dostoyevsky's term will be kept here, although it may be helpful in attempting to understand his somewhat involved arguments to remember that 'hypersensitivity' perhaps conveys better what he had in mind).

The Underground Man's reflections on 'consciousness' are particularly revealing, the most significant pointers here being his pleasures. One of these is to commit some vile and irretrievable deed.

> I used to experience a sort of secret, abnormal, base little pleasure in returning on some excessively foul St. Petersburg night to my corner and in being *violently conscious* of the fact that here I was today having again committed a vile deed and that what I had done was again irretrievable. Secretly and internally I would gnaw, rasp and suck myself on account of it to the point when my grief at last turned into a kind of base and accursed sweetness, and finally into a positive and serious pleasure.

One comic feature is the imaginary dialogue which the Underground Man conducts with his reader, as when he goes on to discuss another and even more strange source of enjoyment—having toothache.

> 'Ha! ha! ha!' you will shout with a laugh. 'After this you'll even be finding pleasure in toothache!'
>
> 'So what? There *is* pleasure even in toothache,' I shall answer. 'I've had toothache for a whole month. I know what it is. This is of course something that people don't put up with in an angry silence. They groan. But these are not frank groans, they are groans with a dose of malevolence. And the malevolence is the whole point. It is precisely in these groans that the sufferer expresses his pleasure. . . . I ask you, gentlemen, to have a good listen some time to the groans of an educated man of the nineteenth century who is suffering from toothache, say on the second or third day, when he is already beginning to groan differently from the first day, that is, not simply because he has toothache. He doesn't groan like some crude *muzhik,* but as a man touched by progress and European civilization. . . . He knows that even the audience for whom he's putting on the performance, and all his family have already begun to listen to him with loathing, don't believe him for an instant, and realize perfectly well that he could groan differently, more simply and without all these trills and twists.'

To this exotic pleasure may be added the satisfaction which the Underground Man claims that he would receive if someone were to slap his face, and the pleasure which he derives in the narrative section of the book from the many occasions on which he takes and gives offence.

These perversities of the Underground Man provide a key to an important quality in Dostoyevsky's own make-up—an addiction to violent sensation, with the important qualification that it was violent mental sensation which attracted him. To physical sensation he remained relatively indifferent, in spite of the attractions of toothache described in *Notes from Underground.* And it was precisely the violence of the sensation and not its quality which interested him. One might phrase it differently by saying that he would rather be violently unhappy than mildly happy, though his attitude to this changed in the last few years of his life. The same point is put in different words by the Underground Man, when he asks the rhetorical question: 'Which is better? Cheap happiness or lofty sufferings?'

Dostoyevsky himself was the same kind of emotional self-flagellant as his Underground Man, although it is necessary not to lose a sense of proportion here, for it was Dostoyevsky's habit in his fiction to take a human trait, whether observed in himself or others, and to carry it to the most extreme possible degree. It is doubtful whether Dostoyevsky was quite such an extreme example of 'consciousness', even in the difficult period of the eighteen-forties, as his Underground Man. But he was fairly far along the road. Reference has been made above to his courtship of Isayeva, in which he seems to have sought, not satisfaction in love, but extreme mental vibration. A love affair of the mid-sixties, in which this tendency was carried even further, must shortly be considered. To this will be added a new addiction exactly suited to maintain the shuddering vibrations in which he delighted—gambling.

More trivial matters also were exploited as a source of emotional vibration. An illustration of this is found in a letter written to his brother Mikhail when Dostoyevsky was eighteen.

> You will not believe what a sweet trembling of the heart I experience when I am brought one of your letters. And I have discovered a new form of pleasure, a strange one—tormenting myself. I take your letter, turn it over for several minutes in my hands, feel it to see if it is of adequate weight, and, having looked my fill and taken my fill of delight over the sealed envelope, put it in my pocket. . . . You will not believe what a sensual [*sladostrastnoye*] condition of soul, feelings and heart this brings! And in this way I sometimes wait for about a quarter of an hour. In the end I fall greedily on the packet, tear the seal, and devour your lines.

Dostoyevsky's craving for strong mental sensations perhaps explains his indifference to alcohol, a drug for those who wish to dull that 'consciousness' in which he found so much perverse pleasure. This craving for sensation is part of the secret of his art, since it is his ability to squeeze the last drop of emotional stimulation out of a scene which often contributes to his strongest effects.

The characterization of the 'conscious' man is completed by an analysis of his diametrical opposite, the 'man of action'. This term illustrates one of the points made about the conscious man, who is inhibited from action by his excess of consciousness. The man of action, also termed the 'normal', 'straightforward' and 'real' man, is saved by his stupidity. He can do things like taking revenge on someone who has insulted him, an activity denied to the 'violently conscious mouse', as the Underground Man describes himself.

So much for the beginning of the philosophical First Part of *Notes from Underground.* The passage continues with an apparent change of subject as Dostoyevsky settles in the saddle of what was to become his favourite hobby-horse and mounts his first full-scale fictional attack on the fashionable theory which he would from now on regard as the major heresy of his time: the idea that human society should or could be reorganized on the basis of enlightened self-interest. From now on Dostoyevsky's hatred of this idea remained the ruling passion of his life, but he rarely exceeded the eloquence with which he denounced it in *Notes from Underground.* (pp. 69-73)

Ronald Hingley, in his The Undiscovered Dostoyevsky, *Hamish Hamilton, 1962, 241 p.*

Mikhail Bakhtin   (essay date 1963)

[*A respected twentieth-century Russian essayist, literary theorist, and philosopher of language, Bakhtin is best known for his influence on the Structuralist and Semiotic literary movements. His works include* Formal'nyi metod v literaturovedenii *(1928;* The Formal Method in Literary Scholarship, *1978),* Problemy poetiki Dostoevskogo *(1963;* Problems of Dostoevsky's Poetics, *1984), and* Voprosy literatury i esteiki *(1975;* The Dialogic Imagination, *1981). Bakhtin's early writings were sometimes published under the names of various friends because, as a Christian, his views came into ideological conflict with Russian Marxist thought. In his critical writings, Bahktin particularly emphasized the concept of discourse* (slovo) *and advocated the idea that literature must be studied along with its sociological and cultural context. In the following excerpt from* Problems of Dostoevsky's Poetics, *he maintains that the underground man's discourse with an imagined audience is a continually evolving dialectic and, as such, has no constant, external point of reference.*]

Notes from Underground is a confessional *Ich-Erzählung* ["first person narration"]. Originally the work was entitled *A Confession.* And it is in fact an authentic confession. Of course, "confession" is understood here not in the personal sense. The author's intention is refracted here, as in any *Ich-Erzählung;* this is not a personal document but a work of art.

In the confession of the Underground Man what strikes us first of all is its extreme and acute dialogization: there is literally not a single monologically firm, undissociated word. From the very first sentence the hero's speech has already begun to cringe and break under the influence of the anticipated words of another, with whom the hero, from the very first step, enters into the most intense internal polemic.

"I am a sick man . . . I am a spiteful man. I am an unpleasant man." Thus begins the confession. The ellipsis and the abrupt change of tone after it are significant. The hero began in a somewhat plaintive tone "I am a sick man," but was immediately enraged by that tone: it looked as if he were complaining and needed sympathy, as if he were seeking that sympathy in another person, as if he needed another person! And then there occurs an abrupt dialogic turnaround, one of those typical breaks in accent so characteristic of the whole style of the *Notes,* as if the hero wants to say: You, perhaps, were led to believe from my first word that I am seeking your sympathy, so take this: I am a spiteful man. I am an unpleasant man!

Characteristic here is a gradual increase in negative tone (to spite the other) under the influence of the other's anticipated reaction. Such breaks in accent always lead to an accumulation of ever-intensifying abusive words or words that are, in any case, unflattering to the other person, as in this example:

> To live longer than forty years is bad manners; it is vulgar, immoral. Who does live beyond forty? Answer that, sincerely and honestly. I will tell you who: fools and worthless people do. I tell all old men that to their face, all those respectable old men, all those silver-haired and reverend old men! I tell the whole world that to its face. I have a right to say so, for I'll go on living to sixty myself. I'll live till seventy! Till eighty! Wait, let me catch my breath.

In the opening words of the confession, this internal polemic with the other is concealed. But the other's words are present invisibly, determining the style of speech from within. Midway into the first paragraph, however, the polemic has already broken out into the open: the anticipated response of the other takes root in the narration, although, to be sure, still in a weakened form. "No, I refuse to treat it out of spite. You probably will not understand that. Well, but *I* understand it."

At the end of the third paragraph there is already a very characteristic anticipation of the other's reaction:

> Well, are you not imagining, gentlemen, that I am repenting for something now, that I am asking your forgiveness for something? I am sure you are imagining that. However, I assure you it does not matter to me if you are.

At the end of the next paragraph comes the above-quoted polemical attack against the "reverend old men." The following paragraph begins directly with the anticipation of a response to the preceding paragraph:

> No doubt you think, gentlemen, that I want to amuse you. You are mistaken in that, too. I am not at all such a merry person as you imagine, or as you may imagine; however, if irritated by all this babble (and I can feel that you are irritated) you decide to ask me just who I am—then

my answer is, I am a certain low-ranked civil servant.

The next paragraph again ends with an anticipated response:

> . . . I'll bet you think I am writing all this to show off, to be witty at the expense of men of action; and what is more, that out of ill-bred showing-off, I am clanking a sword, like my officer.

Later on such endings to paragraphs become more rare, but it remains true that all basic semantic sections of the work become sharper and more shrill near the end, in open anticipation of someone else's response.

Thus the entire style of the *Notes* is subject to the most powerful and all-determining influence of other people's words, which either act on speech covertly from within as in the beginning of the work, or which, as the anticipated response of another person, take root in the very fabric of speech, as in those above-quoted ending passages. The work does not contain a single word gravitating exclusively toward itself and its referential object; that is, there is not a single monologic word. We shall see that this intense relationship to another's consciousness in the Underground Man is complicated by an equally intense relationship to his own self. But first we shall make a brief structural analysis of this act of anticipating another's response.

Such anticipation is marked by one peculiar structural trait: it tends toward a vicious circle. The tendency of these anticipations can be reduced to a necessity to retain for oneself the final word. This final word must express the hero's full independence from the views and words of the other person, his complete indifference to the other's opinion and the other's evaluation. What he fears most of all is that people might think he is repenting before someone, that he is asking someone's forgiveness, that he is reconciling himself to someone else's judgment or evaluation, that his self-affirmation is somehow in need of affirmation and recognition by another. And it is in this direction that he anticipates the other's response. But precisely in this act of anticipating the other's response and in responding to it he again demonstrates to the other (and to himself) his own dependence on this other. He *fears* that the other might think he *fears* that other's opinion. But through this fear he immediately demonstrates his own dependence on the other's consciousness, his own inability to be at peace with his own definition of self. With his refutation, he confirms precisely what he wishes to refute, and he knows it. Hence the inescapable circle in which the hero's self-consciousness and discourse are trapped: "Well, are you not imagining, gentlemen, that I am repenting for something now? . . . I am sure you are imagining that. However, I assure you it does not matter to me if you are. . . . "

During that night out on the town, the Underground Man, insulted by his companions, wants to show them that he pays them no attention:

> I smiled contemptuously and walked up and down the other side of the room, opposite the sofa, along the wall, from the table to the stove and back again. I tried my very utmost to show

them that I could do without them, and yet I purposely stomped with my boots, thumping with my heels. But it was all in vain. They paid no attention at all.

Meanwhile our underground hero recognizes all this perfectly well himself, and understands perfectly well the impossibility of escaping from that circle in which his attitude toward the other moves. Thanks to this attitude toward the other's consciousness, a peculiar *perpetuum mobile* is achieved, made up of his internal polemic with another and with himself, an endless dialogue where one reply begets another, which begets a third, and so on to infinity, and all of this without any forward motion.

Here is an example of that inescapable *perpetuum mobile* of the dialogized self-consciousness:

> You will say that it is vulgar and base to drag all this [the hero's dreaming—M. B.] into public after all the tears and raptures I have myself admitted. But why is it base? Can you imagine that I am ashamed of it all, and that it was stupider than anything in your life, gentlemen? And I can assure you that some of these fancies were by no means badly composed. Not everything took place on the shores of Lake Como. And yet you are right—it really is vulgar and base. And what is most base of all is that I have now started to justify myself to you. And even more base than that is my making this remark now. But that's enough, or, after all, there will be no end to it; each step will be more base than the last.

Before us is an example of a vicious circle of dialogue which can neither be finished nor finalized. The formal significance of such inescapable dialogic oppositions in Dostoevsky's work is very great. But nowhere in his subsequent works does this opposition appear in such naked, abstractly precise, one could even say directly mathematical, form.

As a result of the Underground Man's attitude toward the other's consciousness and its discourse—extraordinary dependence upon it and at the same time extreme hostility toward it and nonacceptance of its judgments—his narration takes on one highly essential artistic characteristic. This is a deliberate clumsiness of style, albeit subject to a certain artistic logic. His discourse does not flaunt itself and cannot flaunt itself, for there is no one before whom it can flaunt. It does not, after all, gravitate naively toward itself and its referential object. It is addressed to another person and to the speaker himself (in his internal dialogue with himself). And in both of these directions it wants least of all to flaunt itself and be "artistic" in the usual sense of the word. In its attitude toward the other person it strives to be deliberately inelegant, to "spite" him and his tastes in all respects. But this discourse takes the same position even in regard to the speaker himself, for one's attitude toward oneself is inseparably interwoven with one's attitude toward another. Thus discourse is pointedly cynical, calculatedly cynical, yet also anguished. It strives to play the holy fool, for holy-foolishness is indeed a sort of form, a sort of aestheticism—but, as it were, in reverse.

As a result, the prosaic triteness of the portrayal of his inner life is carried to extreme limits. In its material, in its theme, the first part of *Notes from Underground* is lyrical. From a formal point of view, this is the same prose lyric of spiritual and emotional quest, of spiritual unfulfillment that we find, for example, in Turgenev's "Phantoms" or "Enough," or in any lyrical page from a confessional *Ich-Erzählung* or a page from [Goethe's] *Werther*. But this is a peculiar sort of lyric, analogous to the lyrical expression of a toothache.

This expression of a toothache, oriented in an internally polemical way toward the listener and toward the sufferer, is spoken by the Underground Hero himself, and he speaks of it, of course, not by chance. He suggests eavesdropping on the groans of an "educated man of the nineteenth century" who suffers from a toothache, on the second or third day of his illness. He tries to expose the peculiar sensuality behind this whole cynical expression of pain, an expression intended for the "public":

> His moans become nasty, disgustingly spiteful, and go on for whole days and nights. And, after all, he himself knows that he does not benefit at all from his moans; he knows better than anyone that he is only lacerating and irritating himself and others in vain; he knows that even the audience for whom he is exerting himself and his whole family now listen to him with loathing, do not believe him for a second, and that deep down they understand that he could moan differently, more simply, without trills and flourishes, and that he is only indulging himself like that out of spite, out of malice. Well, sensuality exists precisely in all these consciousnesses and infamies. "It seems I am troubling you, I am lacerating your hearts, I am keeping everyone in the house awake. Well, stay awake then, you, too, feel every minute that I have a toothache. I am no longer the hero to you now that I tried to appear before, but simply a nasty person, a scoundrel. Well, let it be that way, then! I am very glad that you see through me. Is it nasty for you to hear my foul moans? Well, let it be nasty. Here I will let you have an even nastier flourish in a minute. . . ."

Of course any implied comparison here between the structure of the Underground Man's confession and the expression of a toothache is on the level of parodic exaggeration, and in this sense is cynical. But the orientation of this expression of a toothache, with all its "trills and flourishes," nevertheless does, in its relation to the listener and to the speaker himself, reflect very accurately the orientation of discourse in a confession—although, we repeat, it reflects not objectively but in a taunting, parodically exaggerating style. . . . (pp. 227-32)

The destruction of one's own image in another's eyes, the sullying of that image in another's eyes as an ultimate desperate effort to free oneself from the power of the other's consciousness and to break through to one's self for the self alone—this, in fact, is the orientation of the Underground Man's entire confession. For this reason he makes his discourse about himself deliberately ugly. He wants to kill in himself any desire to appear the hero in others' eyes (and in his own): "I am no longer the hero to you now that

I tried to appear before, but simply a nasty person, a scoundrel. . . ."

To accomplish this he must banish from his discourse all epic and lyrical tones, all "heroizing" tones; he must make his discourse *cynically* objective. A soberly objective definition of himself, without exaggeration or mockery, is impossible for a hero from the underground, because such a soberly prosaic definition would presuppose a word without a sideward glance, a word without a loophole; neither the one nor the other exist on his verbal palette. True, he is continually trying to break through to such a word, to break through to spiritual sobriety, but for him the path lies through cynicism and holy-foolishness. He has neither freed himself from the power of the other's consciousness nor admitted its power over him, he is for now merely struggling with it, polemicizing with it maliciously, not able to accept it but also not able to reject it. In this striving to trample down his own image and his own discourse as they exist in and for the other person, one can hear not only the desire for sober self-definition, but also a desire to annoy the other person; and this forces him to overdo his sobriety, mockingly exaggerating it to the point of cynicism and holy-foolishness: "Is it nasty for you to hear my foul moans? Well, let it be nasty. Here I will let you have an even nastier flourish in a minute. . . . "

But the underground hero's word about himself is not only a word with a sideward glance; it is also, as we have said, a word with a loophole. The influence of the loophole on the style of his confession is so great that his style cannot be understood without a consideration of its formal activity. The word with a loophole has enormous significance in Dostoevsky's works in general, especially in the later works. And here we pass on to another aspect of the structure of *Notes from Underground*: the hero's attitude toward his own self, which throughout the course of the entire work is interwoven and combined with his dialogue with another.

What, then, is this loophole of consciousness and of the word?

A loophole is the retention for oneself of the possibility for altering the ultimate, final meaning of one's own words. If a word retains such a loophole this must inevitably be reflected in its structure. This potential other meaning, that is, the loophole left open, accompanies the word like a shadow. Judged by its meaning alone, the word with a loophole should be an ultimate word and does present itself as such, but in fact it is only the penultimate word and places after itself only a conditional, not a final, period.

For example, the confessional self-definition with a loophole (the most widespread form in Dostoevsky) is, judging by its meaning, an ultimate word about oneself, a final definition of oneself, but in fact it is forever taking into account internally the responsive, contrary evaluation of oneself made by another. The hero who repents and condemns himself actually wants only to provoke praise and acceptance by another. Condemning himself, he wants and demands that the other person dispute this self-definition, and he leaves himself a loophole in case the other person should suddenly in fact agree with him, with

his self-condemnation, and not make use of his privilege as the other.

Here is how the hero from the underground tells of his "literary" dreams:

> I, for instance, was triumphant over everyone; everyone, of course, lay in the dust and was *forced* to recognize my superiority *spontaneously*, and I forgave them all. I, a famous poet, and a courtier, fell in love; I inherited countless millions and immediately devoted them to humanity, and *at the same time I confessed before all the people my shameful deeds, which, of course, were not merely shameful, but contained an enormous amount of "the sublime and the beautiful," something in the Manfred style. Everyone would weep and kiss me (what idiots they would be if they did not),* while I would go barefoot and hungry preaching new ideas and fighting a victorious Austerlitz against the reactionaries.

Here he ironically relates dreams of heroic deeds with a loophole, dreams of confession with a loophole. He casts a parodic light on these dreams. But his very next words betray the fact that his repentant confession of his dreams has its own loophole, too, and that he himself is prepared to find in these dreams and in his very confessing of them something, if not in the Manfred style, then at least in the realm of "the sublime and the beautiful," if anyone should happen to agree with him that the dreams are indeed base and vulgar: "You will say that it is vulgar and base to drag all this into public after all the tears and raptures I have myself admitted. But why is it base? Can you imagine that I am ashamed of it all, and that it was stupider than anything in your life, gentlemen? And I can assure you that some of these fancies were by no means badly composed. . . . "

And this passage, already cited by us above, is caught up in the vicious circle of self-consciousness with a sideward glance.

The loophole creates a special type of fictive ultimate word about oneself with an unclosed tone to it, obtrusively peering into the other's eyes and demanding from the other a sincere refutation. . . . [The] word with a loophole achieves especially sharp expression in Ippolit's confession [in *The Idiot*], but it is to one degree or another inherent in all the confessional self-utterances of Dostoevsky's heroes. The loophole makes all the heroes' self-definitions unstable, the word in them has no hard and fast meaning, and at any moment, like a chameleon, it is ready to change its tone and its ultimate meaning.

The loophole makes the hero ambiguous and elusive even for himself. In order to break through to his self the hero must travel a very long road. The loophole profoundly distorts his attitude toward himself. The hero does not know whose opinion, whose statement is ultimately the final judgment on him: is it his own repentant and censuring judgment, or on the contrary is it another person's opinion that he desires and has compelled into being, an opinion that accepts and vindicates him? The image of Nastasya Filippovna [in *The Idiot*], for example, is built almost entirely on this motif alone. Considering herself guilty, a fallen woman, she simultaneously assumes that the other person, precisely as the other, is obliged to vindicate her and cannot consider her guilty. She genuinely quarrels with Myshkin, who vindicates her in everything, but she equally genuinely despises and rejects all those who agree with her self-condemnation and consider her a fallen woman. Ultimately Nastasya Filippovna does not know even her own final word on herself: does she really consider herself a fallen woman, or does she vindicate herself? Self-condemnation and self-vindication, divided between two voices—I condemn myself, another vindicates me—but anticipated by a single voice, create in that voice interruptions and an internal duality. An anticipated and obligatory vindication by the other merges with self-condemnation, and both tones begin to sound simultaneously in that voice, resulting in abrupt interruptions and sudden transitions. Such is the voice of Nastasya Filippovna, such is the style of her discourse. Her entire inner life (and, as we shall see, her outward life as well) is reduced to a search for herself and for her own undivided voice beneath the two voices that have made their home in her.

The Underground Man conducts the same sort of inescapable dialogue with himself that he conducts with the other person. He cannot merge completely with himself in a unified monologic voice simply by leaving the other's voice entirely outside himself (whatever that voice might be, without a loophole), for, as is the case with Golyadkin [in **The Double**] his voice must also perform the function of surrogate for the other person. He cannot reach an agreement with himself, but neither can he stop talking with himself. The style of his discourse about himself is organically alien to the period, alien to finalization, both in its separate aspects and as a whole. This is the style of internally endless speech which can be mechanically cut off but cannot be organically completed.

But precisely for that reason is Dostoevsky able to conclude his work in a way so organic and appropriate for the hero; he concludes it on precisely that which would foreground the tendency toward eternal endlessness embedded in his hero's notes.

> But enough; I don't want to write more from "underground" . . .
>
> The "notes" of this paradoxalist do not end here, however. He could not resist and continued them. But it also seems to me that we may stop here.

In conclusion we will comment upon two additional characteristics of the Underground Man. Not only his discourse but his face too has its sideward glance, its loophole, and all the phenomena resulting from these. It is as if interference, voices interrupting one another, penetrate his entire body, depriving him of self-sufficiency and unambiguousness. The Underground Man hates his own face, because in it he senses the power of another person over him, the power of that other's evaluations and opinions. He himself looks on his own face with another's eyes, with the eyes of the other. And this alien glance interruptedly merges with his own glance and creates in him a peculiar hatred toward his own face:

> For instance, I hated my face; I thought it disgusting, and even suspected that there was something base in its expression and therefore every time I turned up at the office I painfully tried to behave as independently as possible so that I might not be suspected of being base, and to give my face as noble an expression as possible. "Let my face even be ugly," I thought, "but let it be noble, expressive, and above all, extremely intelligent." But I was absolutely and painfully certain that my face could never express those perfections; but what was worst of all, I thought it positively stupid-looking. And I would have been quite satisfied if I could have looked intelligent. In fact, I would even have put up with looking base if, at the same time, my face could have been thought terribly intelligent.

Just as he deliberately makes his discourse about himself unattractive, so is he made happy by the unattractiveness of his face:

> I happened to look at myself in the mirror. My harassed face struck me as extremely revolting, pale, spiteful, nasty, with disheveled hair. "No matter, I am glad of it," I thought; "I am glad that I shall seem revolting to her; I like that."

This polemic with the other on the subject of himself is complicated in **Notes from Underground** by his polemic with the other on the subject of the world and society. The underground hero, in contrast to Devushkin [in **Poor Folk**] and Golyadkin, is an ideologist.

In his ideological discourse we can easily uncover the same phenomena that are present in his discourse about himself. His discourse about the world is both overtly and covertly polemical; it polemicizes not only with other people, with other ideologies, but also with the very subject of its thinking—with the world and its order. And in this discourse on the world there are two voices, as it were, sounding for him, among which he cannot find himself and his own world, because even the world he defines with a loophole. Just as his body has become an "interrupted" thing in his own eyes, so is the world, nature, society perceived by him as "interrupted." In each of his thoughts about them there is a battle of voices, evaluations, points of view. In everything he senses above all *someone else's will* predetermining him. It is within the framework of this alien will that he perceives the world order, nature with its mechanical necessity, the social order. His own thought is developed and structured as *the thought of someone personally insulted by the world order,* personally humiliated by its blind necessity. This imparts a profoundly intimate and passionate character to his ideological discourse, and permits it to become tightly interwoven with his discourse about himself. It seems (and such indeed was Dostoevsky's intent) that we are dealing here with a single discourse, and only by arriving at himself will the hero arrive at his world. Discourse about the world, just like discourse about oneself, is profoundly dialogic: the hero casts an energetic reproach at the world order, even at the mechanical necessity of nature, as if he were talking not about the world but with the world. (pp. 232-36)

The discourse of the Underground Man is entirely a discourse-address. To speak, for him, means to address some-one; to speak about himself means to address his own self with his own discourse; to speak about another person means to address that other person; to speak about the world means to address the world. But while speaking with himself, with another, with the world, he simultaneously addresses a third party as well: he squints his eyes to the side, toward the listener, the witness, the judge. This simultaneous triple-directedness of his discourse and the fact that he does not acknowledge any object without addressing it is also responsible for the extraordinarily vivid, restless, agitated, and one might say, obtrusive nature of this discourse. It cannot be seen as a lyrical or epic discourse, calmly gravitating toward itself and its referential object; no, first and foremost one reacts to it, responds to it, is drawn into its game; it is capable of agitating and irritating, almost like the personal address of a living person. It destroys footlights, but not because of its concern for topical issues or for reasons that have any direct philosophical significance, but precisely because of that formal structure analyzed by us above.

The element of *address* is essential to every discourse in Dostoevsky, narrative discourse as well as the discourse of the hero. In Dostoevsky's world generally there is nothing merely thing-like, no mere matter, no object—there are only subjects. Therefore there is no word-judgment, no word about an object, no secondhand referential word—there is only the word as address, the word dialogically contacting another word, a word about a word addressed to a word. (pp. 236-37)

> *Mikhail Bakhtin, in his* Problems of Dostoevsky's Poetics: Theory and History of Literature, Vol. 8, *edited and translated by Caryl Emerson, University of Minnesota Press, 1984, 333 p.*

Donald Fanger   (essay date 1965)

[*An American educator and critic, Fanger has edited and written several works about Russian writers. In the following excerpt, he contends that* Notes from the Underground *signifies Dostoevsky's shift of emphasis from social and psychological to metaphysical concerns in his treatment of inhabitants of St. Petersburg.*]

Notes from Underground is generally considered to inaugurate Dostoevsky's second and major period; but it does so by bringing to an end his first period. If the antihero (as he calls himself) marks by his incandescent self-consciousness "an abrupt change in Dostoevsky's approach to characterization" [Ernest J. Simmons; see Further Reading], he also represents a projection into the grotesque of some of his literary predecessors' main traits. He is, as the author notes carefully on his first page, "one of the characters of the recent past" whom "I wanted to expose to public view more clearly than is usually done." The means to this exposure are magnification and concentration (one would like to say hyperbole, but the character is too uncomfortably plausible for that): "I have, after all, only carried to an extreme in my life what you have not dared to carry even halfway," the narrator declares to his imaginary interlocutors. What, exactly, does he represent of the recent past, and what has he carried to an extreme?

He represents the evolution of the dreamer of the forties, condemned (as the hero of **"White Nights"** foresaw at the end of his adventure with Nastenka) by the fervor of his dreams to an ever deepening solitude, and discovering that solitude may be at the same time an unavoidable and an untenable way of life, that the appetites it encloses do not wither but only turn inward, consuming the ego and issuing in masochism and "dark, subterranean, loathsome—not vice, but petty vice." He is tormented by dreams he can neither disavow nor realize and drawn intermittently to a reality he cannot embrace: "I was never able to take more than three months of dreaming at a time without beginning to feel an irresistible need to plunge into society." So when reality intrudes to show up the dreams, he must ridicule them, for he is too intelligent to ignore reality. Yet the dreams—which are of what life should be—are too far superior to that reality to be relinquished. He is condemned to a perpetual vacillation, a perpetual, impotent imbalance:

> But how much love, oh Lord, how much love I would feel in those dreams of mine, in those "escapes into the sublime and the beautiful." Though it was fantastic love, though it was never in fact applied to anything human, still there was so much of it, of this love, that afterward one did not even feel the need to apply it in practice: that would have been a superfluous luxury. Everything, however, always ended happily by a lazy and rapturous transition into the realm of art; that is, into beautiful forms of existence which were stolen, ready made, from poets and novelists and adapted to all sorts of functions and needs. I, for instance, am triumphant over everyone; everyone, of course, lies in the dust and is forced to recognize all my perfections voluntarily, while I forgive them all. I, a famous poet and courtier, fall in love; I receive countless millions and immediately donate them to humanity, and at the same time I confess before all the people my shameful deeds—which, of course, are not simply shameful, but contain an extraordinary amount of "the sublime and the beautiful," something in the Manfred style. Everyone weeps and kisses me . . . while I go off barefoot and hungry to preach new ideas and smash the reactionaries at Austerlitz. Then a march is played, an amnesty is declared, the Pope agrees to leave Rome for Brazil; then there is a ball for the whole of Italy at the Villa Borghese on the shores of Lake Como—Lake Como having been moved to Rome for the occasion; then comes a scene in the bushes, and so on and so forth—know what I mean?

The dream is progressively caricatured and finally ridiculed, but its context leaves the main emphasis on the opening cry from the heart. The same emphasis appears in the final scene with the prostitute Liza when, after he has tried intentionally to humiliate her by confessing the duplicity of his "fine words" in the brothel, she responds by opening her arms in a gesture of profound sympathy, to which he can only sob out: "They won't let me—I can't be—good!"

This is his main ethical impulse—to be good, but impossibly, loftily, romantically good. The "they" who will not let him are a complex lot: his own dreamer's conditions, bound to be disappointed; his neurotic craving to bring on a humiliation he regards as inevitable; and, concretely, those few vulgar acquaintances whom, as a young man, he could neither live with nor without. The end of the scene at the Hotel de Paris is thus painfully typical. He has provoked a scandal, and now his dreamer's impulse tears from him a sudden apology:

> "I ask for your friendship, Zverkov; I insulted you, but—"
>
> "Insulted? You-u insulted me-e-e! Allow me to inform you, sir, that under no circumstances could you ever insult *me*."

The impulse no sooner appears than it is frustrated.

The underground man is clearly not to be explained by the circumstances of his childhood alone; yet these circumstances, as much as we know of them, are significant. He was an orphan, sent by distant and indifferent relations to a school where, "lonely, already crushed by their reproaches, already brooding and silent, looking savagely at everything around him," hating and envying the vulgarity of his schoolfellows, he endured their jibes in almost total isolation. In Petersburg he is a clerk and a dreamer, like so many early Dostoevsky heroes. His situations sounds, in fact, like a composite summary of all their situations: "My life was even then gloomy, disorderly, and solitary to the point of savagery. I associated with no one, even avoided talking, and hid in my corner more and more. On the job, in the office I even tried not to look at anyone, and I was very well aware that my co-workers considered me . . . an eccentric." The incident of his borrowing money to buy a beaver collar so that he might assert his dignity in public against the anonymous officer on the Nevsky is a grotesque variation on the situation of Makar Devushkin [in *Poor Folk*], as well as on that of his predecessor, Akaky Akakievich [in Gogol's "The Overcoat"]. A Soviet critic's characterization of the typical Dostoevsky hero of the 1840s fits him perfectly:

> Dostoevsky's hero is thrown into the world lonely and orphaned. Alone he stands against a threatening, elusive, and implacable order of things [*zakonomernost*]. He is unable to get close to people; the wicked trample him; the benevolence of others provides neither salvation nor relief. He is an isolated monad, everything is against him; he perishes or is saved by flight into seclusion; he shrinks into himself, but even there the implacable hand of "fate" reaches him. [V. Ya. Kirpotin in *F. M. Dostoevsky: Tvorchesky put (1821-1859)*]

But the underground man is writing in the 1860s, and this description can comprehend neither the psychological complexity that twenty years of aloneness have refined nor the new perspective that a different epoch in the life of the nation (as in the life of the author himself) was to lend. He is the first of Dostoevsky's obsessed talkers, and his "notes" are the first of many confessions. The men of the forties, Dostoevsky included, assumed that they knew what human nature was. But the underground man, speaking for the later Dostoevsky, challenges all these assumptions, in part I by argument and in part II simply by being. While Chernyshevsky with his doctrines of rational self-interest was simplifying the nature of man, Dostoevsky, through this extreme spokesman, was complicating it; while Chernyshevsky was reducing psychology to a scheme, Dostoevsky was proclaiming it an irreducible chaos. In each case, the contention served a further end. Chernyshevsky's novel, *What Is To Be Done?* (which Dostoevsky plainly had in mind when he wrote the *Notes*), pointed a political lesson, showed a way to social change through its pictures of the "new men." Dostoevsky's had rather an antipolitical point: it sought to show the hopelessness of social or political change without a prior regeneration of each individual. The man who had written Russia's first social novel in the forties now renounced the social as an independent category, and he did the same thing for the psychological: both were to be understood, both were to be completed and transcended by religion. The censor, with his legendary stupidity, deleted the passage in which the underground man said as much—and so made absolutely vicious a circle that Dostoevsky had made only relatively so. It would take us too far afield to speculate why Dostoevsky made no attempts in later editions to restore this cut. What is important here is to note that, while others were seeking to adapt the political utopianism of the forties and make it more practical, the former utopian socialist Dostoevsky was trying to show the impossibility of any such adaptation.

The tragedy of the underground man, then, does grow out of the pathos of the earlier works, from whose world he has survived, improbably, "like a mouse in its hole." His is not a Petersburg story only because his notes are not a story—as he himself insists:

> Wouldn't it be better to end my "Notes" here? It seems to me that it was a mistake to start writing them. . . . After all, to tell long stories, for example, about how I have ruined my life through moral disintegration in my corner, through lack of human contact, through loss of touch with everything vital, and vain spite in my underground world, is really not interesting; a novel needs a hero, and all the traits of an antihero have been *deliberately* brought together here, and what is most important, all this will produce an extremely unpleasant impression, because we have lost touch with life, we are all cripples, every one of us, more or less.

But his existence is a Petersburg existence, as he himself is aware. In the period of his affair with Liza, he lived in an apartment that was "my privacy, my shell, my case, in which I hid from all mankind," wrapped up in that anonymity and isolation from "living life" which is one of the main marks of the metropolis and one of the main themes in Dostoevsky's evocation of it. When he would venture out on the Nevsky Prospect, it was "a martyrdom, a constant, intolerable humiliation at the thought, which turned into a constant and direct sensation, that I was a fly in the eyes of this whole world, a vile, obscene fly—more intelligent than all of them, more cultured, more noble, of course, but a fly that was constantly yielding to everyone,

Nikolai Chernyshevsky, whose utopian What Is to Be Done? *(1863) and the radical socialist philosophy propounded therein are considered by many critics to be the parodied subjects of* Notes from the Underground *(1864).*

insulted and injured by everyone." The later, final stage of such an existence is his living, at the time of writing, in a wretched room on the outskirts of the city.

> I am told that the Petersburg climate is getting to be bad for me, and that with my poor means it is very expensive to live in Petersburg. I know all that, I know it better than all these experienced and sage counselors. But I am staying in Petersburg; I won't leave Petersburg! I won't leave because . . . Bah, after all it makes absolutely no difference whether I leave or don't leave.

The reason, though unexpresssed, is clearly implied when he speaks a few lines later of "the particular misfortune of inhabiting Petersburg, the most abstract and intentional city in the whole world." It is, simply, that he belongs there, in this city formed unnaturally ("There are," he notes, "intentional and unintentional cities") by the will of a man, on inhospitable ground, *in the service of an idea.* There is an ontological consonance between the "anti-city" built in violation of the natural laws of growth and this anti-hero divorced from life—perhaps even a case of cause and effect. The narrator of *The Insulted and Injured* had referred pointedly to the abnormal life of the capital; here Dostoevsky, in a signed note, states on the first page

that "such persons as the [imaginary] writer of these notes not only may, but must exist in our society, when you consider the circumstances under which our society was in general formed." The qualification ("in general") signals a major change of emphasis, a philosophical bias that will henceforth be dominant. Once a theater for social-psychological dramas, Dostoevsky's Petersburg now takes on a broader metaphysical dimension, which envelops the psychological, much as the underground man's speculations envelop his psychological nature while not ceasing to depend on it. As for the social, it remains, but ambiguously: vividly illustrative, it can "explain" only so much. It is almost a decoy, a bait for shallow understandings.

We shall see the implications of this change in Dostoevsky's next novel. What we have in the *Notes* is a brilliant experimental sketch. Its narrator is an extreme representative of the newly seen city, but one who loses none of his representativeness for all that. "As for me," the narrator concludes, "I have, after all, only carried to an extreme in my life what you have not dared to carry even halfway, and what's more, you have taken your cowardice for prudence, and found comfort in that self-deception." So we get the image of the underground—an image, incidentally, that problems of translation and usage have tended to obscure. The Russian word, *podpolie,* suggests the space under the floorboards of a house, a sense the narrator plays upon when he compares himself to a mouse and when he tells his imaginary audience, "For forty years I have been there listening to these words of yours through a crack."

The man of the 1840s still exists in the 1860s, but he has long since reached an impasse, which his reason is able to comprehend but not to resolve. Two years later, Dostoevsky was to place a new hero—a young man of the sixties—in a similar isolation, there to mature theories quite different but comparable in their extremity, and then to test them in action by transgressing against "living life." Psychologically and ideologically, *Notes from Underground* prepares *Crime and Punishment*—the most finished embodiment of Dostoevsky's myth of Petersburg. (pp. 177-83)

> *Donald Fanger, "Evolution of the Myth: From 'Poor Folk' to 'Notes from Underground'," in his* Dostoevsky and Romantic Realism: A Study of Dostoevsky in Relation to Balzac, Dickens, and Gogol, *Cambridge, Mass.: Harvard University Press, 1965, pp. 152-83.*

Ralph Harper (essay date 1965)

[*In the following excerpt, Harper asserts that the narrator of* Notes from the Underground *is representative of individuals repressed by society.*]

The Double is interesting now mainly because it was Dostoevsky's first attempt to describe repression. He wrote it three years before he was sent to Siberia. It is long-winded, and Dostoevsky soon knew enough about repression not to be satisfied with its unrealistic simplification. It is a story of pathological schizophrenia, and seems to have little or no moral significance. The main character, Mr.

Golyadkin, is a so-called titular councilor in some Petersburg section of the civil service, an unimportant official doing some undefined paper-pushing. He would like to be envied by colleagues, and loved by the daughter of the boss. He is neither envied nor loved, and makes a fool of himself one day when he masquerades on borrowed money as a wealthy playboy. Humiliated by the disrespect of everyone he tries to impress, he begins to see his double, another Mr. Golyadkin, working in the same office, prospering as the real Mr. Golyadkin declines. In the end "our hero," as Dostoevsky tiresomely calls him, is removed to the madhouse.

Although Mr. Golyadkin is obviously suffering from the many frustrations of a small man in a big city, neither he nor his maker makes this explicit. His schizophrenia is certainly involuntary. When he consults a doctor, he is told to change his habits but not his habitat. "Entertainment, for instance, and friends—you should visit your acquaintances and not be hostile to the bottle . . . likewise keep cheerful company." The prescription is useless because the diagnosis has missed the mark. Dostoevsky's "double" is an early figure of anonymous urban man, no roots, no home, no job worth doing. Looked at from the outside he is both comic and pathetic by turns, and neither the author nor the reader is tempted to identify himself with his bewilderment. Never again did Dostoevsky write of an hallucinatory double.

When he next took up the problem of repressed personality, after returning from his prison experiences in Siberia, he described (in *Notes from Underground*) the life of another anonymous man who not only does have some idea of the meaning of his predicament but who uses affective and moral ambivalence as a way out. *The Double* is told in the third person; *Notes from Underground* is told in the first. The Underground Man does not have a proper name; he could be anyone living in the same circumstances. In fact, the author insists in a note, the Underground Man "not only may but positively must exist in our society, when we consider the circumstances in the midst of which our society is formed. . . . He is one of the representatives of a generation still living." These "notes" are autobiographical in tone, and the reader gets involved in the emotions of the narrator without intending to, they are so embarrassingly uninhibited.

The Underground Man is also a civil servant, a bachelor without friends. He was practically an orphan, and treated badly at school. He too is tiresomely garrulous, and yet timid in public, a dreamer rather than a doer. But he has a habit of humiliating himself before others in order to be noticed. He is the first of Dostoevsky's many buffoons. He is not necessarily psychotic, however much his behavior imitates the symptoms of schizophrenia. From beginning to end he knows what he is doing. He speaks of himself as sick from the inertia and over-consciousness of his time, and yet we wonder why spite should be particularly symptomatic of that sickness and that time. Why not the opposite, depression?

The Underground Man does not, unlike Mr. Golyadkin, bother with doctors; he already knows what is ailing him and knows there is no cure. Spite keeps him going. Because no one thing or person is repressing him, he cannot vent his spite in a concentrated way; he is generally spiteful. We would call his brooding consciousness the repressed inwardness of one who should be able to see his situation in terms of the infinite judgment of God or of human love. The Underground Man himself certainly does not see it this way. He does not even know why his age is the age of over-consciousness. Nor does he connect inertia with the social conditions of his life and of Russia in the mid-nineteenth century. Even Dostoevsky at this time did no more than remind readers that this anonymous man could be anyone. The solution that the Underground Man reaches for in his spite is very different from the solution of Mr. Golyadkin.

While Mr. Golyadkin dreams of marrying a rich official's daughter, the Underground Man has dreams too, "dreams of faith, hope, love, the good and the beautiful." He says, "It is worth noting that these attacks of the good and the beautiful visited me even during the period of dissipation and just at the times when I was touching the bottom." This is the first symptom of doubleness, a simultaneity of good and evil. Mr. Golyadkin does not show this symptom. The basic difference is that the Underground Man not only has some idea of his predicament, he tries to meet it by acting spitefully. It is one thing to hurt someone deliberately, it is another to hurt someone deliberately and both enjoy and loathe doing so. The Underground Man's spite is not pretense; he really is spiteful. And in this he may appear like *l'homme de ressentiment* that both Kierkegaard and Nietzsche wrote about. But he is not bourgeois. He does not resent other people being more distinguished than himself; he resents their indifference to him. He resents living in a world where there is no place for him. He does not resent other persons; he resents the fact that he cannot be taken for a person too, and not just as a minor official in an office force. No wonder he does not want to do what is expected of him, to be a good citizen and virtuous. He does not care for somebody else's notions of what is to his advantage. As far as he can understand his own wants, all he needs is to act freely. But we can see that he is already not dependent on anyone. Why then does he worry about independence? Because he confuses independence with his real need, recognition, love. All he owns is his pride, and the refusal to succumb to what is expected of him. The conflict in him between his pride and his need for recognition is accordingly expressed in the form most flattering to pride as a need for independence.

The Underground Man would like to demonstrate his independence and at the same time be recognized, without giving anything of himself, by crushing someone else who would, if he cared, crush him. But the young blood he tested this on pushed him aside without noticing him. What such a lonely pride needs is a love that will both comfort him with recognition and attract his energies away from self-isolation. The prostitute Liza, who comes to him with gratitude and love, only draws on herself the malice of a weak man who has become so wounded by the anonymity of his life and spitefulness that his only possible relationship to someone else is treating her as he has been treated, as a thing. Love comes to him, and he realizes his need for it, too late. Too late he runs after her into the street, "to ask her forgiveness." Too late he suffers from remorse. And yet in his misery he never doubts that even had he found her, he would have treated her spitefully again. Spite is his way of life. The Underground Man never speaks of God, and he does not say he wants to be loved. If inwardness can be repressed, if decisiveness can be withheld or frustrated, why should not the very consciousness of inwardness be suppressed too? The Underground Man cannot reach out for the right solution to his predicament, and he knows this. But he does not know his predicament completely either. Did Dostoevsky himself at this time? Or was Dostoevsky only sure that sadism and masochism are responses to a repressive climate that many were already conditioned by?

The Underground Man, conscious of his own emptiness and isolation, resents himself as well as his society. Having no experience of a society which is a community rather than a bureaucracy, how could he be expected to surrender to anyone when the opportunity comes? He can respond only with the character that his society expects of him, anonymously, without regard for personal feelings. When he says that he cannot think of love except as tyrannizing over someone else (foreshadowing Sartre), we understand that he is not likely to learn from a prostitute. The Underground Man is Dostoevsky's first serious diabolic character, the first to make a self-conscious attempt to define his own fate. But he does not yet know all the terms of reference of this fate. He has not been able to see his situation more clearly because no one else can either. Without a shared experience, or shared inquiry, without a more developed philosophical preparation, man is left with the only measure he does possess, his pride. The next best course then is the one the Underground Man takes, the destructive and self-destructive career of resentment, revenge, sadism-masochism. In the society in which Dostoevsky was living, it was not unusual to say that nihilism is the only way of preserving one's self-respect. "Everyone loves evil," "sin is sweet"—these are phrases from a later novel, but they express a leaning towards the abyss of nihilism which appears for the first time in literature, after the Renaissance is well over and modern times under way. It is a course that romantic isolation as a whole took. In Dostoevsky's novels, however, it was a carefully designed response to the anonymity of life in a disintegrating society. Nihilism had become a game for the overfed and the under-recognized alike.

The double's simultaneity shatters the Aristotelian law of contradiction, for he loves and hates at the same time. Of course, this is not the first time the law had been broken; it had been shattered also in the Pauline conception of original sin. "For that which I do, I allow not. For what I would, that do I not; but what I hate, that I do." Kierkegaard also had maintained that Aristotle's law was binding only on reason, not on the personality as a whole. The Incarnation, two natures in one person, is the sharpest affront of all to reason. Nothing made Kierkegaard more exasperated than his contemporaries' inability to see the impossibility of a rational acceptance of the Incarnation. But the double not only predicates contraries of the same thing at the same time, he breaks the classical ethical principle that no man does evil knowingly. So logic and ethics topple together. The double does evil knowingly and exultingly. He wants to hurt, even destroy, what he loves most. He has no doubt as to what he loves and how much. And one cannot excuse his immorality by suggesting that he loves himself more. Dostoevsky began to write of doubleness of this kind only after he himself had lived with criminals in Siberia. The simultaneity of the double, and the double's attraction to evil, are themes that haunted him the rest of his life. All he adds is the metaphysical structure of inwardness as he later came to see it.

The Underground Man, in the name of over-consciousness, objects to being bound, in an age of reflection, to what is rational, what is expected of him. He does not want to be "some sort of impossible, generalized man." He says that men in his day are oppressed at being men—men with a real individual body and blood. He objects not only to the nineteenth century; he objects to civilization itself. Perhaps reason loses its appeal when it is left in man without a supporting order of reality independent of the mind, an order which can justify both man and reason. Without such an order the sensitive individual does not know even how to express his loneliness except as over-consciousness. In this manner the Underground Man's brooding is the closest he can get to real inwardness. But it is inwardness all the same, because he knows that he is on trial, even though he does not want to, and will not, accept external judgment of himself. He knows life as a series of situations in which recognition and meaning are for unexplained reasons missing; he keeps his head clear by supplying his own justification, acting the stranger at the same time he feels remorseful for being so. But his characteristic resentment indicates that he has an instinct for a different kind of life in which spite would be neither possible nor necessary. He does not bring such a life to the front of his mind where he could have it to choose or reject. He rejects, e.g., in Liza, an opportunity, not a way of life. As the bourgeois is caught in a mesh of his own conventions, so the Underground Man, rising deliberately above the insane fate of the bourgeois Golyadkin, is repelled by the routines and anonymity of modern life which allow the good and the lovely to come to man only accidentally. (pp. 40-6)

> *Ralph Harper, "Excursion into Chaos," in his* The Seventh Solitude: Man's Isolation in Kierkegaard, Dostoevsky, and Nietzsche, *The Johns Hopkins Press, 1965, pp. 36-60.*

Thomas M. Kavanagh (essay date 1972)

[*In the following excerpt, Kavanagh provides a structuralist examination of* Notes from the Underground, *arguing that the fragmented form and structure of the work mirrors its content: the "fractured" and "polymorphous" consciousness of the narrator.*]

As a short, deceptively accessible, and above all engaging text, **Notes from Underground** nonetheless manifests an independence and self-sufficiency that reassert themselves each time this work is subjected to an attempted critical domination. Hardly longer than many of the studies devoted to it, **Notes from Underground** manages, with each rereading, to escape those categories which various critical discourses have imposed upon it.

No doubt it is this independence, the work's refusal to be caught up in any language other than its own, which has made it an almost inevitable test-case for every cultural development appearing on the recent intellectual horizon. Nietzscheanism, Freudianism, Existentialism—these are but a few of the contemporary perspectives which have attempted to establish an intellectual legitimacy by finding in the narrator of *Notes from Underground* their own putative parentage. Few could rival this narrator for the number and startling diversity of those who have found in his anguish their own.

The major difficulties involved in the analysis of this text stem from what might be called its "chinese box" structure: the reader must penetrate through two distinct levels of authorial discourse before arriving at anything resembling the straightforward narration with which we usually identify the novel. The entire text is enclosed, as it were, in those parentheses opened by the authorial voice as it first states that both the notes and their author are fictitious, but then goes on to explain that in the first excerpt "this man" (i.e., the narrational voice) will introduce himself and present his views while in the second excerpt we will be dealing with his actual "notes" on certain events of his life. The closing of this authorial parenthesis, coming at the end of the text, does little to clarify the situation with its simple statement that the notes do not actually end here, but that he is of the opinion that one might just as well stop here.

In a parallel movement the first-person narrational voice, once introduced, takes up well over half the text in a surprisingly long prolegomenon to the actual relation of any "story." (pp. 491-92)

This convoluted structure brings into focus the central problem of any critical analysis of *Notes from Underground*: how, in spite of the obvious break between the first and second parts, is one to account for the immediately felt unity and integration of these two "fragments"? In our estimation all previous attempts to explain this unity have proven insufficient because of their exclusive consideration of the work's symbolic status: they have concerned themselves only with *what* the text says while neglecting its existence as a free and self-defining act of language concomitant with a formal unity that the text itself creates. We shall later refer to these formal aspects (the corresponding *how* of the message) as the work's iconic status.

The hypotheses set forth to explain this work have been as numerous as they are contradictory. The pathological egotism of an insane author, the theological despair of a man placed face to face with the evil of human nature, immoralism and the will to power, the existential bleeding of the self confronted by the other: dissimilar as they might be, each has followed the classical critical journey going from the work as product to arrive at the author as origin. To understand the work is to understand this author: in describing the creator's state of mind the critic can come closest to an adequate delineation of his creation. (p. 492)

Our claim is that the inadequacy of such critical approaches derives from a refusal to accept the literary sign as being iconic *as well as* symbolic. Symbolic refers here to any sign related to its meaning by virtue of an exterior and arbitrary code. As a thing of language, the literary text obviously makes use of an initially symbolic semiotics; it is through a purely conventional, communally shared code, a language, that any given graphic image comes to represent a series of definable concepts.

Both historical (the parody of Chernyshevsky thesis) and psychological (the Nietzschean-Existentialist-Irony theses) criticism share the common premise of what might be called the *doubly symbolic status of the literary sign:* as the text's individual words take on meaning by virtue of a particular linguistic code, so also does the work as a whole take on meaning by reason of its being caught up in a second code which is to be found outside the text itself. The critic's task is to explicate and defend the relevancy of the particular code he has chosen as his domain. Historian, psychologist, sociologist, psychoanalyst—each sings the siren's song of the vanishing text.

The icon, on the other hand, is a sign related to its meaning by virtue of an immediate resemblance of the signifying object to the thing signified. The union of sign and meaning is thus independent of any prior code or convention. A portrait would be the icon of a man's face; a blueprint, the icon of a building. This call for an acceptance of the literary sign as iconic should not be misunderstood. The most obvious example of the linguistic icon, the direct resemblance of the acoustic image to its natural referent (onomatopoeia) is certainly a phenomenon of limited interest. Much more important to the study of literature is what might be called the *indirect* iconic status achieved by the literary use of language. The real problem here is that implied by the seemingly contradictory reference to an "indirect" iconic status which is in some way "achieved" rather than given. The icon is founded on a natural resemblance of the signifier to the thing signified. This alone would seem to imply its foundation in some pre-existing, objective reality. It is obvious, however, that any language is initially dependent upon an arbitrary, symbolic use of signs. The apparent contradiction is resolved when we cease to see language as a system which is *only* symbolic. The literary text, originating as must all language from a symbolic use of the sign, manages, through a mutual and self-defining system of relationships on the level of the words themselves, to create a second nature, a nature proper only to the text itself and perceptible in the *form* of the verbal chain rather than in its symbolic content. The mimesis proper to the literary text is not that which would make of it an imitation of that radically *other* order of some supposedly objective historical or psychological reality, but rather that which makes of the work's thematics the icon of its unfolding form. The text's constantly redefined relation of word to word becomes both the elaboration of its second nature and the locus of its iconic status. To read a literary work is to open oneself to the creation of this new nature, a nature fabricated by words and existing only within words. The form does not mirror a preexisting content, but instead creates that content which is the icon of its form.

Part I of *Notes from Underground* is . . . characterized by a particular thematic content: that of the anti-utopia. In approaching this text the reader, however, is immediately struck by something quite different from any given thematics:

> I'm a sick man . . . a mean man. There's nothing attractive about me. I think there's something wrong with my liver. But, actually, I don't understand a damn thing about my sickness; I'm not even too sure what it is that's ailing me. I'm not under the treatment and never have been, although I have great respect for medicine and doctors. Moreover, I'm morbidly superstitious—enough, at least, to respect medicine. With my education I shouldn't be superstitious, but I am just the same. No, I'd say I refuse medical help simply out of contrariness. I don't expect you to understand that, but it's so. Of course, I can't explain whom I'm trying to fool this way. I'm fully aware that I can't spite the doctors by refusing their help. I know very well that I'm harming myself and no one else. But still, it's out of spite that I refuse to ask for the doctors' help. So my liver hurts? Good, let it hurt even more!

The halting tone, the constant change in direction, the inability to initiate any unilinear development—all these elements impress themselves upon the reader as the perception of a *form*. The grammatical variants of the first person (*I, me, myself*) appear no less than twenty-six times in the space of one paragraph. There is, however, no unity within this "I." Its only constant is its absolute instability. The act of writing becomes centered on the endless spectacle of the self. To write of the "I" is to forever retreat from one perspective to a second, often contradictory perspective on this infinitely "explicable" self: why do I write as I write of what I write?

What is said can be just as easily unsaid. The text abounds in sentences such as "I was lying just now" and "Don't believe what I was just saying." This constant perspectivism, this spontaneous multiplication of the "I," alienates the reader from all preconceptions as to the text's supposedly mimetic nature. The chain of words is nothing more than the always inadequate attempt to stabilize within a fixed form the mercurial self. This self is fissured by its own lucidity—the inevitable separation of the "I" as analyzed from the "I" as analyst. Acute awareness implies an inability to accept as final or even durative any one posture. Lucidity is a disease: "But I still say that not only too much lucidity, but any amount at all is a disease. That's where I stand. But let's leave that for the moment too." The symptom of this disease is the act of writing—the frantic attempt to capture, to determine, to deaden within one signified meaning that which is pure dynamism: "Obviously in order to act, one must be fully satisfied and free of all misgivings beforehand. But take me: how can I ever be sure? Where am I to look for it? I exercise my power of reasoning, and in my case, every time I think I have found a primary cause I see another cause that seems to be truly primary, and so on and so forth, indefinitely." Language is sundered from the representation of a definable reality: it opens itself instead to the transformations of a narrative consciousness whose discursive movement exactly parallels that of language itself.

The thematic content of Part I, that of the anti-utopia, now becomes visible as an icon of its form. This form, that of the polymorphous "I" engaged in an unending quest of self-awareness, has, in manifesting itself within a symbolic linguistic code, created a second nature (a nature proper to and concomitant with the text) in terms of which the failure of utopia becomes an iconization of the fractured "I." The "I" exists as its incompletion, as its self-perpetuating transformations. The writing continues, the text "goes on," only so long as these transformations can continue. To accept the realm of utopia is to accept the rule of objective laws swallowing up and standardizing all those whom they govern. To enter utopia is to build roads away from the self. To enter utopia is to die as an individual and to cease to write. The choice is absolute: one must live either in the crystal palace of utopia's objective constructions or in that hole in the floor where dwells the narrator of *Notes from Underground.* This hole, this absence hollowed out of the material world, becomes the locus of both the liberty of the self and the power to write.

As readers we are forced to leave behind the classical dichotomy of form and content. No content—as the prior presence of an idea, meaning, or theme—is here drawn up, restructured, and set out according to some form which has been arbitrarily imposed upon it. Through the arraying of words and the shaping of a language, an initially symbolic code achieves, through its form, the iconic motivation of a second and properly literary order of nature.

Closing the circle one might reconsider that point marked as the most appropriate entry into this text: the thematics of the narration, the thematics of Part II. In reading this one senses something quite different from the simple recounting of an anecdote. Everything said is, as it were, absorbed in the very particular manner of its saying. Much as in *Crime and Punishment,* all reference to an anecdote is phantasmagorized by the reader's confinement within the perspective of an agonized central consciousness. We see only the world of shadows flickering upon an unbroken and painful awareness of self. The plenum of things and persons is abandoned for the protective absence of the mousehole: "But I changed my mind and decided to merge, full of rage, into the background." Almost nothing "happens" and the text becomes a series of fractured, multiple perspectives on the myriad possibilities offered by the self as placed in various hypothetical situations. The characters, or rather the disincarnated names occurring in the verbal chain, are nothing more than a projection of the many-faceted narrational "I."

The other exists as an expression of the self. The importance and function of this other is created by and subordinated to the purely subjective dialectic of self-awareness. The standard pattern of this self-awareness is that of a movement from the *hypothetically acting* "I" to the *self-condemning* "I" and finally, by a process of reversal, to the *self-congratulating* "I": "I constantly tortured myself with the humiliating thought, which turned into a physical feeling, that, to the world, I was nothing but a dirty, pestiferous fly—more intelligent, sensitive and noble than the lot of them, of course." The place and value of the other is everywhere a function of these changing and purely subjective moods. . . . At the moment of hypothetical action (the narrator, in fact, almost never really acts) the other is posited as equal, as he who must be confronted as an as yet unspecified resistance. Passing to the second stage of self-judgment and self-condemnation this other comes to be seen as infinitely superior to the self. It is this projected other who provides the perspective from which the self is condemned. At the final stage, that of self-congratulation, the other is relegated to an inferior position; he above whom the narrator, by reason of greater lucidity, is able to place himself. Action itself is sapped of any effective relation to reality. The only drama taking place is that of the self reacting and relating to the self. Nothing could be more unconvincing than any proof eked out of this realm of the other: "But the worst, the most depressing realization was that I already knew that I didn't really need any of it—I had no wish to tame, crush, or charm them, and the result wouldn't be worth a kopek to me once I'd achieved it." No matter what is done or happens, its meaning never depends on the event alone, but on the ever changing attitude of the "I" toward that event. An action's meaning is abolished or reversed simply because what is done must always be enclosed within the ever redefining parentheses of the self: "You came because of all the 'touching' things I said the other night. But, for your information, I was laughing at you then, just as I'm laughing at you now. Why are you trembling? Yes, I say I was laughing."

The centrality of the act of writing, as the attempted yet never successful capture of the self by the self, to the integration of Parts I and II is most apparent in its relationship to the two previously mentioned cycles of this second section: the Zverkov and the Liza cycles. The exclusively thematic analysis underlined its ultimate inadequacy to the text as a whole. Returning to this problem, one might show how these cycles do, in fact, function as an icon of the textual "I" engaged in the above described act of self-analysis. . . . In moving from the first to the second episode the position of the narrator is reversed. He who is condemned in one context becomes, in a different context, he who condemns.

But what are these contexts? Examining the reasons why the narrator is able to condemn Liza, one realizes that each of them is based on an aspect of her condition that is exactly similar to that of the narrator. He is able to draw a vivid picture of her fate precisely because this same fate is his own. Both will end in a cheap coffin followed by a nonexistent cortege to a swampy winter's grave. The dying words of the Haymarket whore can be used as an exemplum in the narrator's homily only because they represent what is his own ultimate fear: "You'll moan in vain: 'Let me out; let me back into the world, kind people. My life was no life. It was spent between being used as a doormat and drinking in taverns. Give me one more chance, kind people, to live'." In terms of the reasons why she is condemned, Liza is the narrator's double. It is not surprising that they do, in fact, change roles: "The thought also flashed through the turmoil in my head that we had definitely changed places, Liza and I, that now she had the

heroic role, and I was the beaten-down, crushed creature she had been that night over there." (pp. 500-06)

[Zverkov and his three friends condemn the narrator.] In so condemning, however, they posit a relationship to him which is the mirror image of the narrator's later condemnation of Liza. Zverkov depicts the narrator as the antithesis of the conventional manly virtues of amorous and material conquest just as the narrator condemns Liza as the antithesis of the conventional womanly virtues of a successful marriage and happy family. The narrator drunkenly protests his own value to Zverkov in the same pathetic and ineffectual way that Liza attempts to retrieve a sense of self-worth in producing the medical student's marriage proposal.

Both Zverkov and Liza are, as it were, projections, signs, icons of the more fundamental relationship of the writing "I," of the self-examining narrational consciousness to itself. The textual form of the polymorphous "I" expresses itself through a series of icons radically separated from all reality. There remains but one relationship—that of the writer writing of the self. [The Condemning "I" writes of the Condemned "I" and vice versa.]

"Ah! What a lot of words!" screams the narrator, and it is as a self-defining, self-perpetuating chain of words that this text exists. The word is not a symbolic reference to some objective reality existing outside the text, but rather the inaugural absence of all reality. To write the story of the self is to exclude the writing of any other story lying outside that self. Action, as a significant contact with "reality," is impossible. Such a relationship would presume the union of the beholding "I" with the "I" beheld. Without this union the "I" is unable to turn away from its own hypnotic spectacle.

The real world is the utopic myth created by a self calcified in bad faith. Only a self so alienated and so deadened is capable of diverting from itself its own disintegrating gaze. The living self, the writhing self, the writing self, the self caught up and existing in an on-going act of language finds refuge in none of the substantive nominalizations offered him by a language radically alienated from its own movement and force:

> If only my doing nothing were due to laziness! How I'd respect myself then! Yes, respect, because I would know that I could be lazy at least, that I had at least one definite feature in me, something positive, something I could be sure of. To the question "Who is he?" people would answer, "A lazy man." It would be wonderful to hear that. It would imply that I could be clearly characterized, that there was something to be said about me. "A lazy man." Why, it's a calling, a vocation, a career, ladies and gentlemen! Don't laugh, it's the truth. I'd be a member of the foremost club in the land, and my full-time occupation would be constant respect for myself.

Were this self but capable of being one thing, of assuming one name, of appropriating to itself one adjective, it could then escape its unending existence as the movement, the transformation, the sliding of one word into another.

But were such a calcification to occur the fundamental

movement of language would be denied. The text would cease—deadened, caught within that utopian objectivity from which it represents the unique escape. *Notes from Underground* derives its force, its resolute "literarity," not from a subtle parody of certain now forgotten social movements, but rather from its status as the self-contained story of its story, as the story of its creation as an on-going act of language: "And each question brings up so many more unanswered questions that a fatal pool of sticky muck is formed, consisting of the mouse's doubts and torments."

One ceases his scrutiny of this icon not because he has exhausted its meaning but by reason of a free choice to no longer look upon it: "Actually the notes of this lover of paradoxes do not end here. He couldn't resist and went on writing. But we are of the opinion that one might just as well stop here." (pp. 506-07)

> *Thomas M. Kavanagh, "Dostoyevsky's 'Notes from Underground': The Form of Fiction," in* Texas Studies in Literature and Language, *Vol. XIV, No. 3, Fall, 1972, pp. 491-507.*

Reed Merrill (essay date 1973)

[*In the following excerpt, Merrill observes that as the underground man's persistent statements and acts of negation deny resolution and finality to the story he relates, so does* Notes from the Underground *refute the claim that literature is a source of immutable truths.*]

The narrator of Fyodor Dostoevsky's *Notes from Underground (Zapiski iz podpol'ya)* is representative of the base zero of human existence; as he points out in his tirade against every positive principle, all multiples of zero contain the same depressing result. Like Lermontov's Pechorin in *A Hero of Our Time (Geroi Nashego Vremeni),* the Underground Man is in the border state of the aesthetic-ethical, but unlike Pechorin he has placed almost total emphasis on the ethical sphere. His "adventures" into society have invariably resulted in the discovery that the worldly, external life of immediacy and personal gratification is totally empty of meaning, but he nevertheless persists in his craving by turning the idea of the immediate into his own consciousness and by attempting to use the immediate and all its inherent ambiguities of decision-making to bring him final peace. Unfortunately, his reflections upon past events only serve to bolster his negativism and to verify his belief that somehow his life of paradox can be finally resolved with dialectical proofs in self-willed isolation. Karl Jaspers ["The Will to Communicate," in *The Modern Tradition: Backgrounds of Modern Literature,* ed. Richard Ellman and Charles Feidelson, Jr., 1965] has referred to such mistaken ideals as "great seductions."

> The great seductions are: through belief in God to withdraw from men; through supposed knowledge of the absolute truth to justify one's isolation; through supposed possession of being itself to fall into a state of complacency that is in truth lovelessness. And to these may be added the assertion that every man is a self-contained monad, that no one can emerge from himself, that communication is a delusion.

The difference between Pechorin and the Underground Man is the difference between what Søren Kierkegaard refers to as immature and mature thought. Pechorin has fatalistic doubts and accepts the world as evil and impossible to fathom; the Underground Man is a developed thinker, a dialectician who has transformed his understanding of the emptiness of the aesthetic life into complete inwardness. His suspicion of mankind's sacred ideals has led him to negate everything, especially himself, and his alternative to the stalemate of multiple zero is to withdraw from life, a moral cripple. The Underground Man is all too aware of the weakness of his position of total subjectivity. His response to ethical imperatives is constant doubt, and fear that he will never find peace.

Lermontov's Pechorin fits Kierkegaard's category of "aesthetic indifference"; he is the individual whose life is consumed by immediacy and whose thought is unreflective and undifferentiated. Dostoevsky's Underground Man falls in the ethical category of "either/or"; he makes decisions and choices between good and evil. According to Nicholas Berdyaev [in his *Dostoevsky*], the Underground Man has found freedom through his dialectic but has discovered that freedom to be a hellish burden.

> The first manifestations of newly-freed man are exaggerated individualism, self-isolation, and rebellion against the exterior harmony of the world; he develops an unhealthy self-love which moves him to explore the lower regions of his being. He begins to burrow from the surface of the earth, an "underworld man," a shapeless, ugly creature, makes his appearance and exhibits his dialectic.

The purpose of the Underground Man's confession is to bring to light his subjective concepts—"essential secrets"—in a direct form of expression though he knows that expression is as variable and inconsistent as life itself and that language is the unreliable witness to an impossibility of communication. The fact that he is unable to find any "permanent" values through his dialectic of reason forces him to resort to the immediately sensed as the truth of his experience. The fact that he argues in the undifferentiated immediate is his remaining and restrictive tie with the aesthetic sphere. Philosophically, the immediately sensed involves undifferentiated cognition; hence the constant shifting in his narration from negative to positive and back again, never with final resolution. This is reflected both in the content of the Underground Man's argument and in the textual form of the argument itself. It is not surprising that Lev Shestov has referred to *Notes from Underground* as a more powerful and consistent presentation of the problems of rationalism than Kant's *Critique of Pure Reason.*

Kierkegaard has called the middle ground between the ethical and the aesthetic the difference between existing and not existing. The narrator of *Notes* is somewhere between "an imaginative inwardness which evokes the possibilities with intensified passion, with sufficient dialectical power to transform all into nothing in despair" and "an ethical pathos, which with a quiet, incorruptible, and yet infinite passion of resolve embraces the modest ethical task, and edified thereby stands self-revealed before God and man" [Kierkegaard, *Either/Or*].

The Underground Man has tragic capability. Like the classical hero, he is willing to stand or fall by his own acts; he is also willing to accept universal guilt, though he finds it difficult to rise from his state of passivity and suffering. As a consequence, he gathers all his analytical powers together to battle his suffering with the logic of his mind. The Underground Man (Kierkegaard's counterpart is "modern man") finds that analysis leads to greater and greater subjectivity and a conscious shirking of acts for ruminations and conservative proddings into possibility. He finds that he cannot accept any ethical concept except his own suffering and doubt, and he insists that somehow his freedom from the bondage of doubt can be achieved only through his subjectivity. He hopes that he will eventually discover the royal way to individual freedom through pure subjectivity but finds that he cannot move toward the sphere of the religious (faith in metaphysical ideals) because such a move would demand a complete denial of his rationality. Instead he remains stubbornly in ethical isolation, hoping that he will eventually break the code and evolve a logical system for his life which will allow him subjective freedom in a frame of ethical behavior. By not accepting a principle of limitation, the modern tragic hero becomes embedded in an eternal struggle between his personal guilt and suffering and the problem of evil. He becomes a monad attempting to recreate his world through ethical ideas which he vainly hopes will maintain his freedom and perpetuate his theories while obtaining a new good. He believes that creative thinking can replace the weakness of faith or the wasted life of the aesthetic immediate.

This elevation of self is based upon evil as the source of tragedy, but according to Kierkegaard, it is comic in result, for the good intentions of the solipsist will always fall short. Kierkegaard derives the modern theory of tragicomedy from this kind of situation.

> Our age strives to let the whole tragic destiny become transubstantiated in individuality and subjectivity. One would know nothing to say about the hero's past life, one would throw his whole life upon his shoulders, as being the result of his own acts, would make him accountable for everything, but in so doing, one would also transform his aesthetic guilt into an ethical one. The tragic hero thus becomes bad; evil becomes precisely the tragic subject; but evil has no aesthetic interest, and sin is not an element. This mistaken endeavor certainly has its cause in the whole tendency of our age toward the comic.

It is the sense of the tragicomic which now pervades contemporary literature in such concepts as the absurd, the problem of alienation, the so-called "language of silence," and in the emphasis upon apocalyptic theories. Kierkegaard insists, and it seems that a great many contemporary writers largely concur, that willful isolation and self-emulation at the expense of faith in metaphysical absolutes or transcendent ideals leads to tragi-comic consequences. According to Kierkegaard,

> The comic lies exactly in isolation; when one

would maintain the tragic within this isolation, then one gets evil in all its baseness, not the truly tragic guilt in its ambiguous innocence. It is not difficult, when one looks about in modern literature, to find examples.

This often comical "mistaken endeavor" of the modern hero suggests that the solipsist has placed himself in the grotesque position of being alienated both from the world of metaphysics and from the ethical values of his fellow man. Dostoevsky recognized this situation, and in *Notes from Underground* presented the dilemma of the free ethical man in a formal and philosophical setting suited to expressing this dilemma.

Wolfgang Kayser has suggested [in *The Grotesque in Art and Literature*] that the consequence of man's alienation and his effort to purge the universe of the demonic is illustrated in the grotesque motif. Dostoevsky uses the situation of alienation and the desire for purgation as both setting and persuasive device. His methodical destruction of his reader's pattern of expectation is accomplished by the negation of every stock response through constant shifts of emphasis and by ironic reversals in the narrative.

There are ways a reader can avoid a serious confrontation with the Underground Man, the principal one being to consider him an example of total immorality and decadence (the current Russian Marxist critical opinion) or to consider him an example of Dostoevsky's parody of nihilism and socialist idealism (a minority opinion at best). In fact *Notes from Underground* is a basic text for problems of today and must be understood on the terms of the Underground Man's own argument.

To ask oneself about the problem of reality involves a whole series of paradoxes with which the Underground Man is all too familiar. If, for instance, one strives to find reality on the aesthetic plane, one can discover it only in theories of possibility, since possibility is a higher form to the aesthetic man than ethics. On the ethical plane, reality is a consequence of individual determination. A higher reality is found in faith and in the belief that there is truth in those transcendent values lying outside the individual personality—belief in the existence of others, including the belief that [according to Kierkegaard in his *Concluding Unscientific Postscript*] "God has existed in time."

It is Kierkegaard's prophetic contention that without faith ethical man must struggle from paradox to paradox, through self-examination after self-examination, in a fruitless, often self-destructive attempt to find ontological fixity and that his efforts are doomed to failure without transcendent faith. *Notes from Underground* is a fictional analogue of Kierkegaard's hypothesis, and its narrator is an ethical dialectician whose investigations cover every alternative to transcendent faith in his attempts to find, in his own consciousness, reasonable answers to important questions.

The structure of the novella itself enhances the philosophical argument of the narrator. The first section of his apology involves a thorough examination of the internal world of his self-consciousness and complicated analyses of epistemological, metaphysical, and ontological problems; the second section encompasses retrospective examinations of the causes of the effects shown in section one and an explanation of the events in the external world which have brought about his self-willed exile and his philosophy of bitter isolation. The two sections of the narrative fit the intrinsic-extrinsic pattern and the causal structure of the novel in a mechanical sense as do the arguments of the narrator himself in a rhetorical sense. It is no accident that the final result of form and persuasion is wholly negative and ambiguous, because both form and content express the Underground Man in the same state of militant confusion at the end as at the beginning of his tirade. Dostoevsky, like Lermontov before him, and Tolstoy, James, and Joyce after him, realized that it was necessary to create a structure to fit the character of his protagonist, and for this he utilized (and in large part helped establish) what Leon Edel calls the "subjective novel," a more precise extension of the concept of the psychological novel.

The principal problem in the subjective novel is authorial distance—not in the sense of establishing final judgments of "how the author felt" in regard to his characters (especially to his hero) but in allowing the characters to work out their own destinies without cumbersome and distracting intrusions by the author. In the subjective novel, the author remains only a disinterested or ironic commentator and, as Joyce stated [in *A Portrait of the Artist As a Young Man*], is finally "refined out of existence." In his subjective, or confessional, novel, Dostoevsky has taken full advantage of the intrinsic weakness of the confessional genre—its episodic nature and lack of boundaries and its tendency to autobiography—to suggest in the fragmented arguments of the narrator that disorder and inconsistency are facts of life. Dostoevsky has turned the weakness of the confessional form to good purpose in every instance, for the structural "deficiencies" of the intrinsic form (seemingly random speech in part one, a spastic series of events in part two, with no ending—only an editorial intrusion and arbitrary cutting-off) parallel the "deficiencies" of the apologist himself. The notes of the Underground Man are abruptly terminated by a disgusted "editor" in recognition of the open-ended nature of an argument which will never be resolved. The Underground Man will go on insisting upon his position of defiance, contempt, and eternal analytics even though at the point of the editor's cutting-off he has said, "But enough; I don't want to write more from 'Underground.'" Hypothetically, there is no end to the Underground Man's analytics. Because there seem to be no answers to the serious challenges presented by the exponent of freedom and suffering, the novella itself is left open and unresolved.

In a footnote to the first section of *Notes from Underground,* the editor immediately makes clear that he wants to be carefully separated from the writer of the notes. The diarist is made out to be a very special case—an example for his generation—hence the justification for the editor's publishing his statements regardless of their deviations from the normal, as much for cautionary as for literary value. Even though the editor makes clear his objectivity, he has not prepared the reader for the shock of the Underground Man's first statement. It would be difficult to find

in all of literature a more disconcerting beginning than that of *Notes from Underground:*

> I am a sick man. . . . I am a spiteful man. I am an unattractive man. I believe my liver is diseased. However, I know nothing at all about my disease, and do not know for certain what ails me. I don't consult a doctor for it, and never have, though I have a respect for medicine and doctors. Besides, I am extremely superstitious, sufficiently so to respect medicine, anyway (I am well-educated enough not to be superstitious, but I am superstitious). No, I refuse to consult a doctor from spite. That you probably will not understand. Well, I understand it, though.

The first paragraph is an introduction to the argumentative devices to which the Underground Man will resort throughout his confession. His statements will be always spontaneous, unreflective, and constantly equivocated by counterstatements, and when a positive conclusion is suggested (the fact that he is well enough educated not to be superstitious, but is nevertheless superstitious), it is almost immediately negated. This consistent negation is the kind of verbal gymnastic found throughout the text. His constant use of qualifiers ("however," "though," "besides," "perhaps," "of course") shows his willful refusal to formulate a concrete statement. His equivocal languages reflects his relativism, his systematic and analytic attempts to cancel out each idea that presents itself to his consciousness, and his dialectical ability to turn the canceled statement into a nagging, negative remainder.

The narrator's confrontation with the reader is constantly couched in reference to the Other, the "gentlemen" readers. He finds "opposite elements" encompassing his existence, driving him to despair. He is quick to point out that he is not denying the value of his despair and confusion, only regretting the fact that he seems unable to discover any valid alternatives to them.

> It was not only that I could not become spiteful. I did not know how to become anything: neither spiteful nor kind, neither a rascal nor an honest man, neither a hero nor an insect. Now, I am living out my life in my corner, taunting myself with the spiteful and useless consolation that an intelligent man cannot become anything seriously, and it is only the fool who becomes anything.

The Underground Man's retirement is self-enforced; since he has found himself to be totally different from other people and unable to cope with their collective eccentricities, isolation seems to be the only alternative. His misery and withdrawal are certainly not a pose; yet he finds solace in his misery and in the fact that he is a master of inversion. He is capable of turning bile into honey, of converting his self-loathing into "positive real enjoyment!" He is capable of relishing his hopeless condition, of finding humor in vice and evil in goodness. He exhibits all the characteristics of the pathological personality when he states that he has assumed a position of "the enjoyment, of course, of despair; . . . in despair there are the most intense enjoyments, especially when one is very acutely conscious of the hopelessness of one's position."

For the balance of his impassioned monologue, the Underground Man illustrates his points with symbols which are easily converted so that their values as correspondences will be specific. There is no ambiguity in their meanings; they represent positive ideals of the crowd, which disgust him for their innocence. The symbols are in themselves parodies, literally clichés, of the mentality he is criticizing. The "Crystal Palace" is a symbol with historical basis as well as an image of an ideal existence; it is the consolation of utopian socialism or of any collective idea which denies man his will to freedom. The blank wall is the symbol of man's consolation, the image of fate and acceptance. Nothing can be done to circumvent a wall except to believe in its predetermined existence as a kind of final cause. He suggests that "men of action," whose mentalities are most often direct and unthinking, will dash themselves like enraged bulls against walls and, finding that the walls have stopped them with brutal finality, will immediately turn the effect to good cause by saying that walls are surely a necessity. The wall is turned into an ideal by default.

In his careful analysis of Dostoevsky's novels Konstantin Mochulsky has obviated criticism of Dostoevsky's works for a lack of structure and a crudity of style by demonstrating that Dostoevsky was virtuoso in his efforts to establish new stylistic and structural ideas in the dramatic context of his novels. *Notes from Underground* is the most notable of Dostoevsky's works for its combination of style and form, and the fact that Dostoevsky created a rhetorical position, to quote Wayne Booth [in his *The Rhetoric of Fiction*, 1961], of *"deliberate confusion of the reader about fundamental truth,"* does not prove Dostoevsky's clumsiness, ambiguity, or immortality as a writer but rather his masterful ability to make the form fit the subject matter of his novel. Nowhere in literature can there be found a more conclusive rejoinder to an insistence that a novel contain "fundamental truths" than in *Notes from Underground;* how could Dostoevsky's novel be understood on any level of intelligent cognition by a reader insisting on fundamental truths as he began to read the tirade of a man who has been totally sickened by a world filled with "fundamental truths"? The Underground Man *knows* that there are no truths except those temporarily created by his own caprice and that whoever maintains faith in abstract absolutes and innocent hopes is not only deceived but dangerous. The idea that literature contains fundamental truths suggests the belief that the world contains blank walls—satisfying determinisms—against which a wanderer may fall with satisfaction after suffering frustrations and setbacks. This suggests the "moral duplicity" which underlines most nineteenth-century (and some twentieth-century) fiction where certain authors insist that there is some sort of "legalized" dogma of values which lies somewhere at the end of each work. *Notes from Underground* suggests the danger of such oversimplifications of ethical and moral value, which should be as unacceptable today as Calvin's concept of the "elect." Both deny reason and the truth of human experience. Unfortunate as it may seem to those who insist upon "proper endings," there is a dominant belief today in the concepts presented by the Underground Man because of his belief in freedom regardless of the consequences and his contempt for moral encyclicals or group theories and for such hopeless dreams as Wayne Booth's "true meaning of events." The Underground Man has reason to feel contempt for a man who seeks bondage and not freedom. Experience cannot be compartmentalized. When there is a suggestion that it can be, it is time to move on and to reject the commonality of an experience as an illusion. When it is said that there is "true" meaning to an event, the statement can be relegated to the already jammed files of the Crystal Palace.

Alan Friedman has suggested [in his *The Turn of the Novel,* 1966] that the rejection of "clarity," "proper aesthetic distance," and "true meaning of events" is the rejection of the old moral laws of the nineteenth century; they are turned literally inside out to find values in their opposites. There is as much value in negative rhetoric as in positive argument, and the narrator of *Notes from Underground* illustrates the value of negation as one of the necessary paths to understanding. Even "the problem of distance" is purposely made ambiguous in *Notes from Underground.* Booth refers to the problem of distance as the establishment of a firm separation of author and characters so that the reader will know which thoughts and actions are the character's and which are the author's, to determine conclusively in what relation the author stands to his fictional characters. There is no doubt that in some earlier fiction this problem caused authors confusion and necessarily resulted in confusion of the reader. This sort of critical approach is negative at best, for it assumes that modern writers lead the unsuspecting reader and critic into a labyrinth of problems which have been purposely created by authors who find little value in differentiating between fictional and real characters. Again, *Notes from Underground* provides an example of the problem of distance, for critics are still arguing about "how Dostoevsky felt" about his Underground Man. If the historical Dostoevsky *were* the editor of *Notes* (which is a bold assumption at best), his attitude would still be one of condescension, boredom, or better, the recognition that the ravings of the paradoxicalist are unresolvable. If we assume that the first version of the novel, the "Christian" version, which was censored and never restored, was considered to be adequate, then one could claim that the Underground Man finally found salvation of one kind or another though this is to deny the fact of the extant novella and its intrinsic form. The question of Dostoevsky's opinion of *Notes from Underground* is as unresolvable as is the question of his belief in a quasi-Christian new revivalism or his belief that doubt was the only final value.

Some critics (Berdyaev, Mochulsky, Simmons, Wasiolek) maintain that the Underground Man is one of the dark heroes and negative characters who stand in contrast to Dostoevsky's people of God (Myshkin [in *The Idiot*], Alyosha, Father Zossima [both in *The Brothers Karamazov*], Sonya Marmeladov [in *Crime and Punishment*]) who are a step higher on the path to God; others maintain that the negative heroes are the personification of Dostoevsky's final doubts. Mihajlo Mihajlov is one of these. He states [in his *Russian Themes,* 1968]:

> That Dostoevsky's critics should have taken Sonya for his ideal is incomprehensible. His ideal might rather be the underground man, in whom Shestov was the first to see a true medi-

eval martyr and saint who refuses to bow before precisely those objective natural laws which Dostoevsky's critics glorified. And yet it is in the underground man that these critics might have found proof of their belief that man is born good and that it is circumstances which make him bad. "They won't let me be good," says the underground man.

It is ironic that the solution to the problem of Dostoevsky's real opinion of *Notes from Underground* will never be finally and conclusively determined any more than will the problem of distance in the novel be resolved.

The biographical fallacy will likely continue to dominate American criticism, along with its newly discovered appendage, the rhetorical fallacy, in which fictional persuasion can seemingly be found to contain moral truths and can be judged on those terms as good or bad fiction according to clarity or morality of its creator and its characters. Confessional novels, subjective and autobiographical novels, and novels which express such contemporary ideas as the fact that there are no final truths, no moral imperatives, and that freedom is a lonely and wholly individual problem, will always suggest that the old duplicities of morality and clarity of point of view are serious pitfalls and wrong-headed attempts to understand fiction which is pointed in other directions.

The determined objective of the Underground Man is to prove conclusively that he is free to choose and to act. He also knows that his position must always be unresolved, that it must be a condition of active revolt and creation as long as he lives. He must even repudiate the idea of concluding his struggle, for this would be a capitulation to a defined goal which is another blank wall. "He will launch a curse upon the world, as only man can curse (it is his privilege, the primary distinction between him and the other animals)" because the curse may obtain his objective—to prove that he is a man and not a piano-key. He will create chaos, pervert possibility, even purposely go mad in order to destroy reason and gain his freedom to choose. A free man destroys not necessarily from perversity but from an inherent fear of completion; he cannot be domesticated and live in an "ant-heap" but lives for the idea not for projects such as building leak-proof dikes and digging endless ditches. He is tragicomical in his obstinate insistence on taking the other side, assuming the alter opinion, maintaining the stance of the devil's advocate. He accepts suffering, doubt, and negation only because they prove his existence, his consciousness, and his individuality.

It is impossible to support the belief that the Underground Man is an example of existential bad faith and that, like Camus' Clamence [in *The Fall*], he is a judge-penitent whose bad example only serves to enforce a kind of recalcitrant and meeching subservience. The Underground Man does not exalt servitude but screams for freedom regardless of the conditions of suffering. He has done nothing wrong, and even if he had, he is a free man who can decide between right and wrong. The fact that his diatribe is cut off by his editor does not in any sense weaken the case of the Underground Man but only proves that his argument is beyond resolution. Apologies, servitude, total

loss of personal identity in the case of penitence are as foreign to the Underground Man as is faith in the final kingdom. Camus' Clamence accepts the conventional and bases his whole existence on explanations of an action which took place in the past, but the Underground Man does not have to justify; when he finds himself attempting to do so, he immediately counters with negatives, paradoxes, ironies, and self-parodies, for he knows that justification for past acts is a sign of bad faith. At worst, he is a relativist who knows that relativism is not the answer to freedom. He is not an incoherent, babbling madman, nor is he philosophically weak and indecisive. He is neurotic, even characteristically paranoid, but he can be excused for that. He knows his situation; he desires to break out of it with a newly discovered dialectic of freedom. His editor lost faith in him, but his editor was not necessarily the biographical Dostoevsky. (pp. 505-16)

Reed Merrill, "The Mistaken Endeavor: Dostoevsky's 'Notes from Underground'," in Modern Fiction Studies, *Vol. 18, No. 4, Winter, 1972-73, pp. 505-16.*

Bernard J. Paris   (essay date 1973)

[*An American educator and critic, Paris describes his method as the employment of psychoanalytic theory in "the analysis of literary character, authorial fantasies, and in the personality which can be inferred from all of an author's works." In the following essay, he uses the theories of Karen Horney, the noted German-born American psychoanalyst and critic of Freudian practices, in a detailed psychological study of the narrator of* Notes from the Underground *that seeks to explain the narrator's divided nature.*]

The most difficult task confronting the reader of *Notes from Underground* is to make sense of the vacillating, inconsistent, and often bizarre behavior of the underground man. How are we to account for the disparity between his ideals and his deeds, for his spite and self-destructiveness? What is the relationship between the ideas he expresses in Part I and the events he portrays in Part II? What is the connection, if any, between his philosophy and his way of living?

In their efforts to answer such questions, critics have employed two distinct modes of analysis, thematic and psychological. Thematic analysis tries to account for the underground man by showing what he meant to Dostoevsky, what Dostoevsky was trying to say, through him, about his time and about the nature and condition of man. Ingenious as much of it has been, thematic analysis has not been entirely satisfactory, partly because the mimetic portrait of the underground man continually escapes its categories, but mainly because *Notes from Underground* does not interpret the experience it portrays. It is possible to infer from our whole knowledge of Dostoevsky's life and writings what significance his character may have had if he had chosen to give his story a thematic structure; but the fact is that there are few reliable guides in the work itself to the implied author's attitudes and beliefs. The underground man functions, of course, as an interpreter of his own experience, but we have no reason to believe that his interpretations are trustworthy or that they are affirmed by the work.

The psychological approach seems more appropriate. The novel is essentially a portrait of a character. Its every aspect, including the philosophical speculations of Part I and the way in which the material is ordered, is an expression of the underground man's psyche. When we have understood the peculiar inner logic of that psyche, we will have understood the work as a whole and the function of each of its parts. There have been several psychological analyses of the underground man, but none provides as full an explanation of his character, his ideas, and his behavior as I shall attempt here, with the aid of Karen Horney's theories of neurosis. Horney's is a psychology of inner conflict that explains from without the same kinds of experience that Dostoevsky, and many other great novelists, have grasped from within. Since Horneyan psychology is not widely known among students of literature, I shall preface my analysis of *Notes from Underground* with a brief account of her system.

In an atmosphere of warmth, security, and esteem, says Horney [in her *Neurosis and Human Growth: The Struggle toward Self-Realization*, 1950], a child "will develop . . . the unique alive forces of his real self: the clarity and depth of his own feelings, thoughts, wishes, interests . . . the special capacities or gifts he may have; the faculty to express himself, and to relate himself to others with his spontaneous feelings. All this will in time enable him to find his set of values and his aims in life." Under unfavorable conditions, when the people around him are prevented by their own neurotic needs from relating to him with love and respect, the child develops a "feeling of being isolated and helpless in a world conceived as potentially hostile." This feeling of "basic anxiety" makes the child fearful of spontaneity, and, forsaking his real self, he develops neurotic strategies for coping with his environment.

These strategies are of three kinds: the individual can adopt the self-effacing or compliant solution and move toward people; he can develop the aggressive or expansive solution and move against people; or he can become detached or resigned and move away from people. Each of these solutions produces its own set of character traits and beliefs.

The person in whom self-effacing trends are dominant becomes weak, humble, and dependent; he values goodness and love above all else and tends to glorify suffering. He tries to overcome his basic anxiety by gaining approval and by controlling others through his need of them. He is appeasing and conciliatory and tends to blame himself and to feel guilty whenever he quarrels with another, feels disappointed, or is criticized. He has powerful taboos against "all that is presumptuous, selfish, and aggressive," believes in turning the other cheek, and tends to see the world as displaying a providential order in which virtue is rewarded. He needs to lose his identity in something larger and more powerful than himself.

The predominantly aggressive person tries to be strong, efficient, and exploitative. What appeals to him most is not love, but mastery. He is ambitious, craves recognition, ab-

hors helplessness, and is ashamed of defeat or suffering. He believes that might makes right and that the world is a jungle in which each man is out for himself. He is ruthless and cynical, trusts no one, and is out to get others before they get him. He wants to be hard and tough and regards all manifestation of feeling as sloppy sentimentality. Considerateness, compassion, loyalty, and self-sacrifice he scorns as signs of weakness; those who value such qualities are his natural victims.

The basically detached person worships freedom and strives to be independent of both outer and inner demands. He pursues neither love nor mastery; he wants, rather, to be left alone, to have nothing expected of him and to be subject to no restrictions. He values intelligence, imagination, and individuality, believes in the power of will, and often has great psychological insight. The detached person handles a threatening world by removing himself from its power and by shutting others out of his inner life. He disdains the pursuit of worldly success and has a profound aversion to effort. He has a very strong need for superiority and usually looks down upon his fellows with condescension; but he realizes his ambition in imagination rather than through actual accomplishments. In order to avoid being dependent on the environment, he tries to subdue his inner cravings and to be content with little. He cultivates a "don't care" attitude and protects himself against frustration by believing that "nothing matters." He seeks privacy, finds it a great strain to associate with others, and may go to pieces if his magic circle is entered and he is thrown into intimate contact with another person.

In the course of neurotic development, the individual will come to make all three of the defensive moves compulsively; and, since they involve incompatible character structures and value systems, he will be torn by inner conflicts. In order to gain some sense of wholeness, he will emphasize one move more than the others and will become predominantly self-effacing, expansive, or resigned. The other trends will continue to exist quite powerfully, but they will be condemned and suppressed. The "basic conflict" will not have been resolved, but will simply have gone underground. When the submerged trends are for some reason brought closer to the surface, the individual will experience severe inner turmoil, and he may be paralyzed, unable to move in any direction at all.

While interpersonal difficulties are creating the basic conflict and the movements toward, against, and away from people, the concomitant intra-psychic problems are producing their own self-defeating strategies. The destructive attitudes of others, his alienation from his real self, and his self-hatred make the individual feel terribly weak and worthless. To compensate for this he creates, with the aid of his imagination, an "idealized image" of himself and embarks upon a search for glory: "In this process he endows himself with unlimited powers and with exalted faculties; he becomes a hero, a genius, a supreme lover, a saint, a god."

The creation of the idealized image produces not only the search for glory but a whole structure of neurotic strategies that Horney calls "the pride system." The idealized image leads the individual to make both exaggerated *claims for* himself and excessive *demands upon* himself. He takes an intense pride ("neurotic pride") in the attributes of his idealized self, and on the basis of these attributes he makes "neurotic claims" upon others. He feels outraged unless he is treated in a way appropriate to his status as a very special being. His neurotic claims make him extremely vulnerable, of course, for their frustration threatens to confront him with his "despised self," with the sense of worthlessness from which he is fleeing. Either he is all, or he is nothing. Indeed, it is because he feels himself to be nothing that he must claim to be all: he who can be a man does not need to be God.

The individual's pride in his idealized self also leads him to impose stringent demands and taboos upon himself ("the tyranny of the should"). The function of the "shoulds" is "to make oneself over into one's idealized self: *the premise on which they operate is that nothing should be, or is, impossible for oneself.*" Since the idealized image is for the most part a glorification of the self-effacing, expansive, and resigned solutions, the individual's "shoulds" are determined largely by the character traits and values associated with his predominant trend. The "shoulds" are a defense against self-loathing, but, like other neurotic defenses, they tend to aggravate the condition they are employed to cure. Not only do they increase self-alienation, but they also intensify self-hate, for they are impossible to live up to. The penalty for failure is the most severe feeling of worthlessness and self-contempt. This, indeed, is why the "shoulds" have such a tyrannical power.

It is not difficult to see that, in Horneyan terms, the underground man's predominant solution is detachment. His values, character structure, and life-style all display the characteristics of this solution. He prizes freedom, will, caprice, individuality, peace, and intellectual superiority above all else, and has a profound aversion toward anything suggesting coercion, conformity to law, ordinariness, or stupidity. When his privacy is invaded or emotional demands are made of him (as in the episode with Liza), he becomes hysterical. He defends himself against his feelings of shame and failure by protestations of indifference—"I don't care"; "it doesn't matter"—and by escaping into dreams of glory: "I was a terrible dreamer, I would dream for three months on end, tucked away in my corner. . . . I suddenly became a hero." He has the same "onlooker" attitude toward himself that he has toward life and is, as a result, an excellent observer of his own inner processes. [This phenomenon is described in Horney's *Our Inner Conflicts: A Constructive Theory of Neurosis,* 1945.] His *explanations* of these processes are often rationalizations, however, and are not to be trusted.

At almost every stage of his life the underground man leads an extremely solitary existence. By the age of twenty-four, he tells us, his life was already "gloomy, ill-regulated, and as solitary as that of a savage. I made friends with no one and positively avoided talking, and buried myself more and more in my hole." As soon as he receives a small inheritance, he retires from service and withdraws almost entirely into his underground world: "my lodging was my private solitude, my shell, my cave, in which I concealed myself from all mankind." Some of the intrapsychic forces behind this behavior are suggested by Horney's description of withdrawal as a way of protecting pride:

> He [the person employing this defense] does not embark on any serious pursuits commensurate with his gifts lest he fail to be a brilliant success. . . . So, according to his economic status, he either does nothing worth while or sticks to a mediocre job and restricts his expenses rigidly. In more than one way he lives beneath his means. In the long run this makes it necessary for him to withdraw farther from others, because he cannot face the fact of lagging behind his age group and therefore shuns comparisons or questions from anybody about his work. In order to endure life he must now entrench himself more firmly in his fantasy world. But, since all these measures are more a camouflage than a remedy for his pride, he may start to cultivate his neuroses because the neurosis with a capital N then becomes a precious alibi for the lack of accomplishment.

It seems evident that the underground man was driven to an extreme form of the detached solution by a singularly bleak and loveless childhood. He was completely deprived of the warmth, reinforcement, and protection of family life; and his resulting oddness (defensiveness) made him an object of scorn and derision to his peers. He was sent to school, he tells us, "by distant relatives upon whom I was dependent and of whom I have heard nothing since—they sent me there a forlorn, silent boy, already crushed by their reproaches, already troubled by doubt, and looking with savage distrust at every one." His schoolfellows met him "with spiteful and merciless jibes" because he "was not like any of them"; and he "hated them from the first" and shut himself "away from every one in timid, wounded and disproportionate pride." Feeling alone and helpless in a hostile world, he tried to cope with his anxiety by withdrawing from others and nourishing a belief in his own superiority.

By the time of his encounter with Liza, the underground man is himself aware of the connection between his homelessness and his detachment. "If I had had a home from childhood," he tells Liza, "I shouldn't be what I am now. I often think that. However bad it may be at home, anyway they are your father and mother, and not enemies, strangers. Once a year at least, they'll show their love of you. Anyway, you are at home. I grew up without a home; and perhaps that's why I've turned so . . . unfeeling." These remarks, which introduce a glowing description of the joys (even in suffering) of family life, show a profound yearning in the underground man for the human warmth and intimacy of which he has been deprived. But since he has never been loved, he cannot help sensing the world as composed of enemies and strangers; and it is understandable that, despite a strong desire to do so, he cannot open himself to others and entrust himself to them.

In his school years, the underground man moved not only away from, but also against and toward his fellows. He tried to insulate himself from his schoolfellows' contempt and from his own feelings of inadequacy by keeping aloof and by scorning their stupidity and their respect for success. But he could not detach himself sufficiently to become indifferent to their mockery, and he was consumed by hatred and a desire for vindictive triumph: " . . . by then I did not desire their affection: on the contrary I continually longed for their humiliation. To escape from their derision I purposely began to make all the progress I could with my studies and forced my way to the very top. This impressed them. . . . The mockery ceased, but the hostility remained, and cold and strained relations became permanent between us." "In the end," however, he could not bear this estrangement, and he began to move toward his fellows, but with little success. When his relationships were not "strained" because of his aloofness and distrust, they were marred by his desire to "exercise unbounded sway over" the partner and his contempt for the weakness of anyone who would allow himself to be dominated.

We begin to see here the way in which the underground man's contradictory trends result in inconsistencies. His detachment leads him to scorn success, but his aggressive needs make him force his way to the top. When he leaves school, he gives up "the special job" for which he "had been destined so as to break all ties, to curse [his] past and shake the dust from off [his] feet"; but he is deeply humiliated by his poverty and the insignificance of his position, and he feels terribly inferior to his more prosperous schoolmates. He craves intimacy so much that he frightens his friend with his "passionate affection"; but his fear of closeness makes him aloof and distrustful. When he succeeds in establishing a relationship, he is driven by his need for mastery into becoming a tyrant and his aggressive values lead him to despise devoted souls.

By the time of the Zverkov-Liza episode, the underground man's basic character structure has been formed; it changes little from then on. He is a detached person whose aggressive and compliant trends are very close to awareness and rather evenly balanced. They exist mainly as attitudes (his life-style is determined by detachment), but they sometimes drive him into behavior from which he almost immediately recoils. He oscillates between identifying with his proud and with his despised selves, between feeling like a god and like a piece of dung. As an analysis of several key passages and episodes will show, a great many of the underground man's vacillations and contradictions become intelligible when we see him as beset by inner conflicts in which tendencies toward detachment, compliance, and aggression, with their interpersonal and intrapsychic ramifications, are all powerfully at work.

In the opening pages of his "notes," when he is describing his life in the government service, the underground man tells us that he was "a spiteful official. I was rude and took pleasure in being so. . . . When petitioners used to come for information to the table at which I sat, I used to grind my teeth at them, and felt intense enjoyment when I succeeded in making anybody unhappy. I almost always did succeed. For the most part they were all timid people—of course, they were petitioners." This sadistic behavior releases some of the underground man's pent-up hostility and gives him a feeling of power that is deeply satisfying. But his compliant trends, which are quite close to the surface, prevent him from wholeheartedly enjoying his triumphs and lead him, indeed, to a denial of his spitefulness.

> But do you know, gentlemen, what was the chief point about my spite? Why, the whole point, the real sting of it lay in the fact that continually, even in the moment of the acutest spleen, I was inwardly conscious with shame that I was not only not a spiteful but not even an embittered man, that I was simply scaring sparrows at random and amusing myself by it. I might foam at the mouth, but bring me a doll to play with, give me a cup of tea with sugar in it, and maybe I should be appeased. I might even be genuinely touched, though probably I should grind my teeth at myself afterwards and lie awake at night with shame for months after. That was my way.

> I was lying when I said just now that I was a spiteful official. I was lying from spite. I was simply amusing myself with the petitioners and with the officer, and in reality I never could become spiteful. I was conscious every moment in myself of many, very many elements absolutely opposite to that. I felt them positively swarming in me, these opposite elements. I knew that they had been swarming in me all my life and craving some outlet from me, but I would not let them, would not let them, purposely, would not let them come out. They tormented me till I was ashamed: they drove me to convulsions and—sickened me, at last, how they sickened me! Now, are not you fancying, gentlemen, that I am expressing remorse for something now, that I am asking your forgiveness for something? I am sure you are fancying that. . . . However, I assure you I do not care if you are.

In the first paragraph of this passage the underground man denies that he was a spiteful or an embittered man for two reasons. His awareness of his compliant tendencies makes him feel that his aggressive behavior does not reflect what he really is, and the "shoulds" created by his compliant trends make it impossible for him to admit his anger and his cruelty to himself. At the same time, however, the "shoulds" dictated by his aggressive trends are in operation, and he is ashamed of his softness, of the ease with which he can be touched and appeased. The aggressive part of him wants to be unabashedly sadistic and is full of contempt for his sentimentality; hence, when he is touched or appeased he grinds his teeth at himself and lies awake "with shame for months after." His compliant side is by no means the weaker in this conflict, however, for it forces him to deny the reality of his anger and cruelty. His conclusion that he was "simply scaring sparrows at random and amusing" himself by it testifies to his sense of his aggressive self as an empty facade, but it is hardly an adequate explanation of his behavior. It does accord, however, with the dictates of his detachment, which demands that his behavior be undetermined ("random") and that he have no strong feelings (he was "simply . . . amusing" himself).

The violence of his inner conflict is evident in the second paragraph, when he speaks of the absolutely "opposite elements" (impulses toward compliance) which have been "swarming" in him all his life and which he "purposely"

Apollinaria Suslova, formerly Dostoevsky's mistress and later the wife of noted Dostoevsky scholar Vasily Rozanov.

will not let come out. They "torment" him because they force him to hate himself for both his aggressiveness and his detachment; they must be suppressed because they threaten the other two moves in the most profound way. His aggressive self must repel trends that would judge it to be evil, and his detached self is deeply frightened of impulses that would drive him into unbearable intimacy and dependency. His aggressive values make him "ashamed" of being tormented by the thrust of his softer nature. Part of the underground man's difficulty, of course, is that his conflicting trends are not only all very powerful, but they are also all very close to the surface, so that he is driven to "convulsions" and "sickened" by the warfare between them. His detachment, which becomes more and more profound as he grows older, is in part an effort at resolving his conflicts by moving away from them. He attempts to substitute an intellectual awareness of his conflicting trends for the direct and painful experiencing of them; and, in a manner typical of the detached person, he takes great pride in his self-knowledge and intelligence.

His denial, at the end of the second paragraph, that he has been expressing remorse and asking for forgiveness and his expression of indifference as to what his readers may

think both seem motivated by a combination of aggressive and detached values. His aggressive side cannot admit to feelings of remorse and defensiveness, especially when such feelings are generated by compliant drives; and it urges him to get back at the readers, who have been feeling superior, by denying the importance of their thoughts and judgments. The denial that he is experiencing uncomfortable feelings and that he cares about the readers' opinions is also generated by his need not to care, not to be vulnerable, either to himself or to others. It is no more to be taken at face value than is his declaration that he is not a spiteful man.

The underground man really is spiteful; he really is remorseful; and he really is indifferent. Like the romantic he describes, he has "great breadth." His problem is that since he contains everything, he feels that he is nothing; none of his attributes really defines his nature. "It was not only that I could not become spiteful," he tells us, "I did not know how to become anything: neither spiteful nor kind, neither a rascal nor an honest man, neither a hero nor an insect." He cannot become anything because he is almost totally self-alienated, and the neurotic character structure that has replaced his real self has not achieved even a spurious integration. None of his acts, impulses, or values is an authentic expression of his real self; every one is subject to almost immediate repudiation by the conflicting components of his defense system. It is no wonder that he feels self-less, without definition or substantial reality. He is, in fact, a hollow man, a puppet pulled about by his contradictory compulsions, who, ironically, takes his slavery as an evidence of freedom.

In his relations with Liza the underground man displays again the manysidedness of his character. His initial impulse is, of course, aggressive; he restores his pride, after the humiliations of the dinner, through sexual mastery and by successfully playing upon Liza's feelings. He is motivated not only by a need for vindictive triumph, however, but also by a feeling of rapport with Liza, a desire for human contact, and a long frustrated craving for self-expression.

His impassioned speeches to Liza are to a certain extent made up for the occasion and carefully calculated to produce their effect, but much of their content is drawn from his own long-harbored fantasies and fears. When we examine his speeches we find that they are largely an expression of his self-effacing and detached attitudes: they celebrate love and family life and depict with horror the slavery of the harlot's life. His glorification of married love and of parenthood and his assertion that love is "everything," that "with love one can live even without happiness," reveal more vividly than anything else in the novel his yearning for human warmth and intimacy. If his praise of love is an expression of his own dreams, his picture of the horrors of enslavement is an expression of his own fears. "But when are you free?" he asks Liza. "Only think what you are giving up here!" "It is an accursed bondage. I know it."

The underground man hammers at Liza until she responds; but when she does respond, with despair and "an impulsive movement towards" him, he becomes "panic-stricken," is filled with "terror," and makes haste "to get away—to disappear." He gives her his address partly as a response to her need and partly to facilitate a quick escape. He is overwhelmed by the sight of her feelings and dreads the intimacy they imply.

When he gets home he is beset by feelings of fear, rage, remorse, and desire. His predominant feeling is anxiety at the thought of Liza's invading his "private solitude" and finding him out. Yesterday he "seemed such a hero to her," but if she discovers his poverty and abjectness his triumph will be lost; he will once again be humiliated. Liza's arrival will bring reality into his retreat, his "cave," his "shell," the realm of his dreams, and confront him with his actual self, which he despises. She will bring with her, moreover, emotional demands which threaten his basic defense and to which he cannot possibly respond. He knows, therefore, that he will "be panic-stricken as usual."

When Liza does arrive the underground man is paralyzed, wishes to run away, is angry with himself, is angry with her, blames her for everything, wishes to kill her, does not care what happens, assaults her verbally, reveals his baseness, calls himself a scoundrel, wishes for peace, tells her he does not care about her, and urges her to go. When Liza understands his unhappiness and reacts with compassion, their roles are completely changed: she is "now the heroine," while he is "just such a crushed and humiliated creature as she had been before me that night." A "feeling of mastery and possession" flames up in his heart, and he makes love to her as "an act of vengeance." His pride restored, he becomes terribly impatient for her to leave. As she leaves he degrades her yet further by thrusting a five-ruble note into her hand; but as soon as she is gone he rushes after her "in shame and despair."

The affair with Liza leaves the underground man overwhelmed by remorse and tortured by self-hate. He hates himself for his treatment of her. He hates himself because he longs desperately for love, and he realizes that he will always be cut off from it by his own nature. He has withdrawn from reality in order to protect his pride, to preserve his idealized image; the experience with Liza confronts him with his own warped and destructive nature, and he is flooded with self-contempt: "Had I not recognized that day, for the hundredth time, what I was worth?"

His need to tell the story of his relations with Liza indicates that the underground man has never been able to resolve the feelings of remorse and despair that they engendered in him. As he narrates the events of long ago, he is once again overcome by self-loathing; and he not only reports his earlier self-accusations, but adds new ones: he is incredibly "spiteful and stupid," "incapable of love," corrupted by being "so out of touch with 'real life'." It is no wonder that he has no wish to go on with his "Notes." He had begun Part II with the hope of obtaining "actual relief from writing"; but he has only succeeded in administering to himself "a corrective punishment." The only thing that he can do with such experiences is to run away from them; and so, for the time at least, he gives up writing from "underground."

The underground man is sick, and knows that he is sick, and hates his sickness; but he is trapped by it and must live with it; hence he glorifies it. "People do pride themselves on their diseases," he tells us, "and I do, may be, more than any one." His withdrawal, his inertia and indecision, his vacillations and contradictions all become marks of superiority, sources of pride. He is diseased, to be sure; but his disease is that of being "too conscious," too intelligent; and it places him far above the stupid normal men of action whom he so envies and so despises.

As the underground man sees it, one of the primary differences between the stupid normal man and the man of acute consciousness is the inability of the conscious man to make up his "mind to do anything," and particularly his inability to take revenge. He cannot believe in his right to vengeance because he can discover no basic principles upon which to act and judge. All that science can tell him is that everything is determined and no one is responsible. If he ignores questions of justice and virtue, however, and acts simply out of spite, he finds that he has "not even spite. . . . In consequence again of those accursed laws of consciousness, anger in me is subject to chemical disintegration."

The underground man has given us an accurate picture of his conscious mental processes; but he has not correctly identified the source of his difficulties. He is incapable of wholehearted feelings of anger not because he is so acutely conscious or philosophically at sea, but because, though he is full of rage, he has powerful taboos against both feeling and acting out his anger. His "doubts and questions" derive not so much from his intelligence as from the conflicting impulses of his own nature, which find a sophisticated conscious expression in his relativistic and deterministic attitudes. It is the laws of neurosis, not the "laws of consciousness," that make his anger subject to "chemical disintegration." His vengeful feelings violate the taboos of his self-effacing trends and imperil his detachment by threatening to embroil him in conflict; he handles them on the conscious level by rationalizing them away and unconsciously by converting them into self-hate and self-destructiveness.

Intellect alone can never provide the foundation for which the underground man is looking; that can be found only in the authentic values and strivings of the real self. Since the underground man is almost totally alienated from his real self, his intellect is an instrument not of self-actualization, but almost wholly of rationalization. It is driven by three almost equally powerful neurotic trends, and it oscillates endlessly, settling nowhere. In one of his tirades of self-accusation, the underground man reveals that he knows this: "You boast of consciousness, but you are not sure of your ground, for though your mind works, yet your heart is darkened and corrupt, and you cannot have a full, genuine consciousness without a pure heart."

The underground man's inaction is a product not only of his self-alienation and inner division, but also of his pride system. By doing nothing he can preserve the possibility of being everything, a god, a hero. For the underground man nothing "but the foremost place" will do; and "for that very reason," he explains, he "quite contentedly" occupies "the lowest in reality. Either to be a hero or to grovel in the mud—there was nothing between." Any real activity is bound to fall short of his goals, to threaten his pride, to confront him with self-hate; this is why his experiences with Zverkov and Liza are so devastating to him. Hence, in the manner typical of the detached person, he gives up active strivings and seeks to actualize his idealized image almost wholly in imagination.

The underground man is not completely divorced from himself. He concludes that "it is better to do nothing! Better conscious inertia! And so hurrah for underground!" But he immediately confesses that "it is not underground that is better, but something different, quite different, for which I am thirsting, but which I cannot find! Damn underground!" I suggest that the something better for which he is thirsting but which he can neither find nor define is authentic, self-realizing existence. He expresses this longing only once, though we may assume that it contributes to his despair and to his efforts at honesty. Most of the time he cannot afford to recognize how truly lost he is.

Perhaps the most striking indication of the severity of the underground man's neurosis is the intensity of his self-hate. From beginning to end his notes are filled with incidences of extreme self-contempt, self-accusation, self-frustration, self-torture, and self-destructiveness. The underground man feels hated, despised, spat upon. Alternating with his claim of superiority is a sense of utter insignificance; he describes himself as a fly, a mouse, an insect, a worm, an eel. He accuses himself of being corrupted, out of touch with life, incapable of love. His liver is diseased, but he won't consult a doctor; Petersburg is too expensive and the climate is bad for him, but he won't leave. At a certain period he repeatedly takes strolls along the Nevsky which are not strolls "so much as a series of innumerable miseries, humiliations and resentments." "Why I inflicted this torture upon myself, why I went to the Nevsky, I don't know. I felt simply drawn there at every possible opportunity."

The underground man's self-hate originated, of course, in his early experiences of rejection and of self-betrayal. He develops his pride system in order to compensate for his feelings of worthlessness and inadequacy; but the pride system itself and the devices that he employs to protect his pride weaken him further and intensify his self-hate. He himself recognizes that his self-idealization and the demands that he makes upon himself cause him both to loathe himself and to feel despised by others: "It is clear to me now that, owing to my unbounded vanity and to the higher standard I set for myself, I often looked at myself with furious discontent, which verged on loathing, and so I inwardly attributed the same feeling to every one." Characteristically, he manages to take pride in his self-hate by seeing it as a sign of his intellectual and moral superiority: "A cultivated and decent man cannot be vain without setting a fearfully high standard for himself, and without despising and almost hating himself at certain moments."

Though the underground man has some understanding of his self-hate, there are aspects of it which puzzle him. He is puzzled, for example, by the disparity between his ideals and his actions. He not only fails to live up to his ideals,

but he seems compelled to violate them. His spells of dissipation often begin "at the very moments" when he is "most capable of feeling every refinement of all that is 'good and beautiful'." He feels that this is "not accidental" in him, "but as though it were bound to be so." At first he struggles in agony against his depravity, then he comes to feel that it is his normal condition, and finally he takes pleasure in it.

There are several reasons why an intense consciousness of the good and the beautiful compels the underground man to degrade himself. We have already seen that he grovels in the mud because of his need to be a hero; he occupies the lowest place in reality because nothing but the foremost place will do. The more conscious he is of the good and the beautiful, the more anxious he becomes; for he cannot fulfill the demands of his "shoulds" and his pride system threatens to collapse. He protects his idealized image by not trying to live up to it; his dissipation is a defense against failure. It is, at the same time, a punishment for failure. He cannot be aware of his ideals without also being aware of his failure to live up to them, and this is bound to generate intense self-hate and a need for relief through self-flagellation. Yet another motive for the underground man's dissipation is his need to rebel against his "shoulds." Being predominantly a detached person, he cannot stand any form of coercion. Such people, says Horney, "may go through alternating phases of self-castigating 'goodness' and a wild protest against any standards. . . . there may be a constant shuttling between an 'I should' and 'no, I won't.' . . . Often these people give the impression of spontaneity and mistake their contradictory attitudes toward their shoulds for 'freedom.'"

The underground man finds an "enjoyment in the very feeling of his own degradation," which "sometimes reaches the highest degree of voluptuousness." He has "taken up [his] pen" in order to understand this "strange enjoyment"; but he finds it "so subtle, so difficult of analysis," that it is impossible to fathom "all the intricacies of this pleasure." The underground man's pleasure in his self-degradation is, indeed, intricate. For one thing, he is seeking to escape pain through pain. "The specific masochistic way of lulling psychic pains," says Horney [in her *New Ways in Psychoanalysis*, 1939], "is to intensify them and wholly surrender to them. By the person's wallowing in humiliation his pain of self-contempt is narcotized and may then be turned into a gratifying experience." As we have seen, the underground man's consciousness of his ideals fills him with a sense of failure and activates his self-hate. His reaction is to plunge into dissipation, to sink more deeply into his mire, and to be more and more inclined "to sink into it altogether." By intensifying his misery "and wallowing in self-accusations and feelings of unworthiness," Horney observes, "the masochistic person may derive satisfaction from an orgy of self-degradation." The pain of self-reproach gives way to the pleasure of self-pity.

It is not only feelings of degradation that the underground man enjoys wallowing in, but also feelings of hopelessness, feelings that he has "reached the last barrier," that it is horrible, but that he can never change. He is one of those [described by Horney] "who, despairing of ever being able to measure up to [their] standards, have consciously or unconsciously resolved to be as 'bad' as possible." Such a person wallows in his badness "with a kind of desperate delight." By losing everything, he protects himself against future blows to his pride and the pain of future defeat.

The underground man feels hopeless about resolving his problems and hopeless about living up to his "shoulds." To escape the pain of his futile struggles and endless self-reproaches, he longs to have his pride crushed, to feel that he is foredoomed, that he might as well sink "in silent impotence . . . into luxurious inertia." His debauchery is a way of crushing his own pride, of proving to himself that he is irremediably lost. With at least part of his being, the underground man longs to be crushed, to be swallowed up, to have his identity obliterated and his impotence confirmed. This is why he wants to be thrown out of the tavern window and can imagine being glad of a slap in the face: "why then the consciousness of being rubbed into a pulp would positively overwhelm one." He wishes to escape from his inner torments by losing his selfhood, by being overwhelmed, by having his struggles and agonies subsumed into some larger, implacable phenomenon. This is why he likes to see himself as a helpless victim of the laws of nature.

Just as the underground man derives an enjoyment from being in "complete slavery" to his teeth, so he also takes a certain satisfaction in recognizing his slavery to his compulsions and to his inner paralysis, which he sees as a product of "the normal fundamental laws of over-acute consciousness, and . . . the inertia that [is] the direct result of those laws." By seeing himself as a victim of the laws of nature he tries to disclaim responsibility for his weaknesses and to defend himself against his self-hate and guilt: "a decent man is bound to be a coward and a slave. It is the law of nature for all decent people all over the earth." This defense does not work, however; and he turns the fact that he continues to feel guilt into one more reason for feeling trapped, abused, full of self-pity.

The underground man feels that there is no rational solution to the problem of responsibility, and he sees himself as a victim of existential uncertainty: "it is simply a mess, no knowing what and no knowing who, but in spite of all these uncertainties and jugglings, still there is an ache in you, and the more you do not know, the worse the ache." It is quite natural for the underground man to see his problem as a product of the human condition, but it should be clear to us by now that it is part of his sickness. His ache can never be stilled because his personality can never be integrated. His feelings of enslavement and his feelings of responsibility are both products of his defense system; they can never be reconciled because they serve contradictory needs.

The underground man is so famous for his defense of free will and his defiance of necessity that it is somewhat surprising to realize that he also sees himself as a helpless victim of nature's laws and that he has a number of motives for doing so. His motives for denying necessity are, of course, equally strong, if not stronger, and issue in the philosophic passages that have attracted so much attention.

Replying to the rationalistic and utilitarian thinkers of his day, the underground man attacks the philosophy of enlightened self-interest. He cannot accept the idea that man "only does nasty things because he does not know his own interest." Man's destructiveness is not simply the product of his ignorance; it derives in part from nonrational forces in his nature that can never be eradicated by "common sense and science." Since man's will is governed only in small part by reason, a rational demonstration of his true normal interests will never compel him to will only the good. The rationalists have left out of their calculations, moreover, man's "most advantageous advantage," which is not "honour, peace, prosperity," or any of the goals that reason dictates, but the exercise of his caprice, the expression of his "own sweet foolish will." What man wants "is simply *independent* choice, whatever that independence may cost and wherever it may lead."

The rationalists dream of a scientific utopia in which all human behavior will have been subsumed under the laws of nature and in which our rational self-interest will have been thoroughly calculated. As the underground man sees it, men would never consent to this state of affairs, even if it were attainable; for the price of happiness would be freedom, the most advantageous advantage. They would "kick over the whole show and scatter rationalism to the winds" simply so they could "live once more at [their] own sweet foolish will."

The strongest part of the underground man's argument is his insistence upon the influence of nonrational forces on human behavior. His own experience is living proof that knowing the good by no means compels one to do the good. Indeed, as we have seen, consciousness of "the good and the beautiful" produces in him dissipation and depravity. It is no wonder that he sees "theories for explaining to mankind their real normal interests, in order that . . . they may at once become good and noble" as "mere logical exercises." His inner conflicts, the disparity between his ideals and his behavior, and his experience of powerful self-destructive forces gives the underground man a penetrating insight into the inadequacy of rationalist psychology, which simply leaves out of account the existence of unconscious motivations and neurotic compulsions.

The fact that the underground man makes some valid objections to the rationalist psychology does not necessarily mean that his own version of human nature is a balanced or accurate one. As we might expect, he sees his own traits as characteristic of the species and his own highest value as "the most precious thing for mankind." He does this not only because he is given to generalizing from his own experience, but also because he needs the reassurance of believing that in reality everyone is like him. It is important for him to affirm that it is not simply he, but all men who love suffering, chaos, and destruction. Human history provides powerful evidence for his contention; but this means that neurosis is widespread and not necessarily that man is essentially a self-destructive being.

The underground man is threatened not only by the utilitarian philosophers' belief in man's rationality, but also by their contention that human behavior is lawful and that it can therefore be explained, predicted, and controlled. His arguments on this subject have far less cogency than his attack on the overestimation of reason. Their vehemence and near-hysteria indicate a high level of anxiety against which he must defend himself by a process of compulsive rationalization. His attack on the utilitarians is but a single episode in his lifelong battle against necessity. "The laws of nature," he tells us, "have continually all my life offended me more than anything." He has "always been afraid of . . . mathematical certainty," and he is "afraid of it now." "Mathematical certainty" is, to him, "something insufferable": "Twice two makes four seems to me simply a piece of insolence. Twice two makes four is a pert coxcomb who stands with arms akimbo barring your path and spitting."

The underground man dislikes the laws of nature and the fact that twice two makes four for a number of reasons. "The more a person is alienated from himself," observes Horney, "the more his mind becomes supreme reality. . . . This is why the pride in . . . the supremacy of the mind . . . is a regular occurrence in all neurosis." The laws of nature and of arithmetic limit the power of mind, of will, to determine reality. They insufferably frustrate our neurotic claims, insolently deny our personal grandeur, and bar the path to the actualization of our idealized image, which they force us to recognize as an imaginary construction. Many neurotics, says Horney, "have an intense . . . aversion to the realization that they [are] subject to *any* necessity. The mere words 'rules,' 'necessities,' or 'restrictions' may make them shudder. . . . In their private world everything is possible—to them. The recognition of any necessity applying to themselves, therefore, would actually pull them down from their lofty world into actuality, where they would be subject to the same natural laws as anybody else." In order to sustain his pride system, it is necessary for the underground man to deny reality, to ignore or defy the actual conditions of life.

The underground man's intense aversion to the laws of nature and of arithmetic is a product not only of his self-alienation and self-glorification, but also of his particular neurotic solution, which is detachment. As we have seen, the detached person loathes all forms of restraint or coercion and has a compulsive need for freedom and independence. The underground man's hatred of the laws of nature and fear of mathematical certainty is, in effect, a phobic reaction. He is unusually disturbed by twice two makes four.

He is unusually disturbed, also, by the possibility that human behavior may someday be explicable, that "a formula" will be discovered "for all our desires and caprices." If this happens, he contends, "then, most likely, man will at once cease to feel desire, indeed, he will be certain to. For who would want to choose by rule? Besides, he will at once be transformed into an organ stop or something of the sort." Here, as elsewhere, the underground man confuses descriptive with prescriptive law. But his confusion could never be cleared up by a logical explanation; because of his hypersensitivity to constraint he *feels* descriptive laws to be prescriptive. If he must feel and choose by rule, then the only way he can maintain his freedom is to feel nothing and to choose nothing. One of the reasons why the doctrine of enlightened self-interest is so abhorrent to him is that, as he perceives it, it contains an element of compulsion; man will be "compelled" by reason "not to want to set his will against his normal interests." If reason compels him to do good, he will, if need be, "purposely go mad in order to be rid of reason and gain his point!"

The underground man's affirmation of freedom as the most advantageous advantage is, like his hypersensitivity to constraint, symptomatic of his detachment. The compliant person finds the meaning of life in love; the aggressive person finds it in mastery. For the detached person the highest value of all is freedom, independence. This can be a healthy value, and any appeal to it tends to be stirring; but, as Horney points out, "the fallacy here is that he looks upon independence as an end in itself and ignores the fact that its value depends ultimately upon what he does with it. His independence, like the whole phenomenon of detachment of which it is a part, has a negative orientation; it is aimed at *not* being influenced, coerced, tied, obligated." The underground man does not wish to be free so that he can fulfill his human potentialities. For him freedom is the goal of life, the highest fulfillment, and he is ready to embrace suffering, chaos, and destruction in order to have it.

One reason why the underground man wants freedom so much is that he possesses so little of it. His behavior is extremely compulsive; and, as we have seen, he is aware of the inevitability of his reactions and feels them to be expressions of natural law. His hatred of the laws of nature is in part a hatred of his own compulsiveness, which he longs to escape. There are times when he mistakes his contradictory attitudes toward his "shoulds" for freedom; but his vacillations and his rebellions are themselves compulsive. He glorifies his self-destructiveness as an evidence of free will and the futility of reason; but he is nowhere more driven than in this behavior, which, far from being capricious or incomprehensible, is thoroughly explicable in terms of his neurosis. He prizes caprice because "it preserves for us what is most precious . . . our individuality"; but he is incapable of spontaneity and feels like an automaton that is manipulated by forces beyond its control. That is why, to him, "the whole work of man seems to consist in nothing but proving to himself every minute that he is a man and not a piano-key!" There is a germ of health in his craving for autonomy, but a man who is truly in possession of himself does not feel a need to fight every minute against the threat of obliteration. It is the underground man's self-alienation and not the laws of nature, the certitude of mathematics, or the philosophy of the rationalists that threatens to transform him "from a human being into an organ-stop."

It is my contention that, whatever Dostoevsky's thematic intentions may have been, the philosophic arguments that take up Sections vii-ix of Part I are quite consonant with the underground man's character structure and are both better understood and more permanently interesting as expressions of his neurosis than as thematic affirmations of the implied author. It is possible to see them as Dostoevsky's reply to utilitarian ethics and rationalist psychology, as a clue to Dostoevsky's conception of human nature and human values, or as an early expression of some of the central motifs of existentialism. Whatever their historical, biographical, or philosophical import, however, they are first and foremost an integral part of Dostoevsky's incredibly complex and subtle portrait of his character. As such they have an enduring mimetic truth that will make them fascinating even when their ideological content seems antiquated. (pp. 511-22)

> Bernard J. Paris, " 'Notes from Underground':
> A Horneyan Analysis," in PMLA, Vol. 88, No.
> 3, May, 1973, pp. 511-22.

Terrence Doody   (essay date 1975)

[*In the following excerpt, Doody claims that the confessional form of* Notes from the Underground *demonstrates that a sense of community is essential to the process of determining individual identity. However, the critic states, the underground man's refusal to share in community by subverting his audience denies him selfhood.*]

The narrator of Dostoevsky's **Notes from Underground** has two different audiences for his confession: the "gentlemen" he addresses throughout the polemic of Part One, and the reader given to him by his "editor." The Underground Man knows nothing of the reader; and at the end of the polemic, he tries to dismiss the "gentlemen" as a device created for his own convenience.

> I, however, am writing for myself, and wish to declare once and for all that if I write as though I were addressing readers, that is simply because it is easier for me to write in that way. It is merely a question of form, only an empty form—I shall never have readers. I have made this plain already.
>
> I don't wish to be hampered by any restrictions in compiling my notes. I shall not attempt any system or method. I will jot things down as I remember them.
>
> But here, perhaps, someone will take me at my word and ask me: if you really don't count on readers, why do you make such compacts with yourself—and on paper too—that is, that you won't attempt any system or method, that you will jot things down as you remember them, etc., etc.? Why do you keep explaining? Why do you keep apologizing?
>
> Well, there it is, I answer.

The reader is not dismissed so easily, however, for he is still there to read the ensuing notes, which demonstrate that the Underground Man's need for an audience's recognition and confirmation is constant, desperate, and essential. He needs an audience in order to define himself, to realize his identity. Yet he cannot admit to that need, so he cannot entrust himself to anything but a fictionalized audience that he conceives to exploit and then repudiate. It is never "merely a question of form" with the Underground Man; it is, rather, always a question of form. And the forms he uses are ultimately dishonest and self-destructive because he uses them to evade or forestall his own realization.

Dostoevsky's intentions for **Notes from Underground** are different from his narrator's and quite complex; and by placing the polemic first, he sets the reader up to be manipulated into two very different reactions to the Underground Man. If the polemic were to come in its proper chronological place, after the notes of reminiscence, it would lose much of its cogency and meaning. But faced with it immediately, the reader cannot be sure of the narrator's real motive for confessing, of Dostoevsky's distance from his character, or of his own status as audience. This uncertainty and confusion of distance contribute to the polemic's great credibility and suasive force, and they allow Dostoevsky to make his own argument through the narrator before the narrator is allowed to reveal himself and inadvertently raise questions about his own authority. For if the Underground Man is eventually undermined by his compulsive self-delusion and mistrust, he is initially a faithful and convincing spokesman against the rationalism that Dostoevsky himself finds so dangerous and naive.

The confession is an almost inevitable instrument for the case that both the narrator and author want to make against the social planners whose systems and progressive ideals deny a place to anyone like the Underground Man. A confession is a personal history that seeks to express the essential nature of the self, its ontological truth, to an audience that represents the kind of community the speaker needs to confirm his identity. This need for community is nicely epitomized in the line from Novalis that Conrad took as the epigraph to *Lord Jim:* "It is certain my conviction gains infinitely, the moment another soul will believe in it." Not just any other soul will do as a confessor, however. For the speaker's choice of an audience, his attitude toward it, can be as definitive of himself as anything he then goes on to say. And his motive for seeking an audience in the first place is essential to the reason he presents himself in a confession rather than in some other mode of autobiography.

The Confessions of St. Augustine, for instance, proceed from the conversion that enfolds him in the Christian community and provides him with a comprehensive myth—a theology, a theory of history, and a system of values—that he shares with all orthodox Christians. Augustine addresses his confessions in penitence and gratitude to an omniscient God, who already knows what he is going to say; Augustine publishes them, however, for the sake of the community and the alleviation of his own distress. As an "insider," Augustine can treat his personal history as representative. The events of his life may be interesting and instructive in their own right (especially since Augustine is a famous convert and writes as bishop of Hippo), but their greatest value for the orthodox audience is that Augustine can interpret them to demonstrate the necessity of grace and benefits of conversion. In this respect, his confessions are an act of solidarity with the community that shares his belief, a rite of mutual confirmation. For a more intimate audience of friends, however, Augustine writes in an unanticipated literary form in an attempt to define himself. For the conversion that interrupts his life and re-defines him rather intensifies than assuages Augustine's famous restlessness, and he writes out of the realization that his conversion alone has not provided any "final security." So in examining the pressure the past still exerts and the temptations that continue to bother him, he opens himself to the solace of his friends' companionship and prayers. Augustine's need to know himself in the eyes of his immediate company and his interest in his ineluctably private experience are exactly what make his confessions more than simply a Christian apology and what make Augustine himself accessible to the nonbelievers who can share his sense of introspective loneliness, his dislocation in time, and all the difficulties, as Stevens says, of "what it is to be."

Rousseau writes his confessions [*The Confessions of Jean-Jacques Rousseau*] out of the need for a similar confirmation and solace. But his need is, perhaps, more extreme than Augustine's because Rousseau's confessions follow upon a crisis, his decision (around 1750) to repudiate the conventions of his society and to live according to the principle of his own nature. He confesses, therefore, to justify that decision by justifying himself, ontologically; and he does not have the orthodox audience or circle of friends to rely on that Augustine has. For Rousseau defines himself as an "outsider" and writes *against* what has been his natural community, all those people who no longer understand him. The audience he addresses, after a perfunctory invocation of the Deity, is the community of readers that will be created by virtue of its sympathy for him.

> It was not so much my literary celebrity as the change in my character, which dates from this time, that evoked their jealousy; they would perhaps have forgiven me for brilliance in the act of writing; but they could not forgive me for setting up an example by my conduct; this appeared to put them out. I was born for friendship; my easy and gentle disposition had no difficulty in fostering it. So long as I lived unknown to the public, I was loved by all who knew me, and had not a single enemy. But as soon as I made a name I ceased to have friends. That was a very great misfortune. A still greater one was that I was surrounded by people who took the name of friend, and used the rights it gave them only to drag me to my undoing.

This statement probably has its share of the disingenuous, but it does reveal Rousseau's need for the sympathy and understanding, indeed for the friendship, that will ratify his decision and prove his essential self still lovable.

Though Rousseau is a formidable rhetorician (and a famous polemicist as Augustine was), in his confessions he says he need only be honest, be himself, for his just readers to render a favorable verdict.

> I should like in some way to make my soul transparent to the reader's eye, and for that purpose I am trying to present it from all points of view, to show it in all lights, and to contrive that none

> of its movements shall escape his notice, so that he may judge for himself of the principle which has produced them.

> My duty is to tell the truth; my readers' to be just, and that is all that I shall ever ask of them.

Yet, clearly Rousseau asks for more than justice and courts the reader constantly by showing him how treacherous most other people are, even his wife and his friend Diderot. Rousseau's strategy in this is designed to foster the sympathy he needs because it encourages the reader to think of himself as also "born for friendship," more sensitive and understanding than others, less mean-spirited and conventional.

Like Rousseau, the Underground Man is motivated by the crisis of his isolation. But in the polemic he never treats it as a crisis; he treats it as an advantage for the superior insight it affords. So he too writes against his audience: explicitly trying to dominate the gentlemen as though to win a debate; implicitly defining himself by his opposition. The outsider may have some doubts about who he is exactly, but he usually knows what he is not; if he cannot be sure of who will comprise his sympathetic audience, he can define quite clearly who it will not be. In arguing against the "gentlemen," the Underground Man seems also to be arguing *through* them to an audience he cannot yet identify, for it is an audience he will create in the process of defining himself.

To do this, the Underground Man makes no pretense about his honesty or humility; he never overtly courts the audience or seeks its sympathy. On the contrary, he argues his case with great, aggressive self-confidence in order to defeat the "gentlemen" and destroy their rationalist position, and he begins his attack in the first sentence—"I am a sick man . . . I am a spiteful man"—when he puts off the sympathetic response his illness could evoke by immediately changing his plea to a much less sympathetic cause. Then he admits to a lie he could never have been suspected of; and by doing so, he indicates how enthusiastically he will manipulate the conventions and expectations of his discourse. He makes himself a difficult man to answer because he pursues his argument with such speed, through so many shifts of tone and attitude, that there is no logical principle on which to build a response. For instance, after arguing quite seriously about the problems of acting on the basis of a primary cause, he immediately begins the ironic celebration of the "loafer"—"why, after all, it is a calling and an appointment, it is a career, gentlemen." And these remarks slide through a parody of the esthete's devotion to "the sublime and the beautiful" into the serious argument that freedom of choice is in itself a more "advantageous advantage" than the pursuit of enlightened self-interest.

Although he cannot readily be anticipated at any turn in his argument, the narrator nonetheless keeps silencing the "gentlemen" by anticipating their objections and turning them into the evidence of his own insight, authority, and control.

> It is so subtle, sometimes so difficult to analyze consciously, that somewhat limited people, or

simply people with strong nerves, will not understand anything at all in it. "Possibly," you will add on your own account with a grin, "people who have never received a slap in the face will not understand it either," and in that way you will politely hint to me that I, too, perhaps, have been slapped in the face in my life, and so I speak as an expert. I'll bet that you are thinking that. But set your minds at rest, gentlemen. I have not received a slap in the face, though it doesn't matter to me at all what you may think about it. Possibly, I even myself regret that I have given so few slaps in the face during my life. But enough, not another word on the subject of such extreme interest to you.

Moreover, he neutralizes even *ad hominem* objections by defiantly admitting to every fault he knows himself to have. For instance: "You laugh? I am delighted. My jokes, gentlemen, are of course in bad taste, uneven, involved, lacking self-confidence. But of course that is because I do not respect myself. Can a man with consciousness respect himself at all?" In arguing like this, the Underground Man is at once defiant, condescending, deliberately outrageous; sometimes he is even funny, as when he says: " . . . for I'll go on living to sixty myself. I'll live till seventy! Till eighty! Wait, let me catch my breath." But he never seems desperate, for he is always in command of his own position, his argument, his audience, and his style.

In the course of the polemic, the narrator becomes the most convincing evidence of the case he is making. This "self-authorization" is obviously necessary for any outsider who, in explaining his own experience, cannot invoke the full support of shared conventions (as Augustine can use the language of Scripture to formulate even his most private experience); and the need for the confessional speaker to authorize himself is the source of both his *style* and of the intense rhetoric that confessions support so well. Because it deals with essential self, the confession is a natural mode of expression for the alienated; but more than that, it is also a natural opportunity for the discovery and articulation of a new mode of being. Confessions like Augustine's and Rousseau's have been the issue not only of their personal situations, but also of critical, transitional periods in history when an exact definition of the self has become important for an entire culture. Augustine's audience lived through the fall of Rome and in an era of great theological controversy. And Rousseau's audience, of course, has come to see him as a great spokesman, if not the innovator, of a major phase in modern Western culture. In both cases, a prophetic authority has accrued to each of them from the immediate audiences that have seen in each confession a truer image of themselves.

The presence of the "gentlemen" in the polemic indicates that it is Dostoevsky's plan to give his narrator some prophetic authority, at least temporarily, by bringing the reader as close as possible to the narrator's position throughout Part One. For these "gentlemen" are so easily mastered that they are, like Rousseau's ex-friends, rhetorical whipping boys from whom the reader is strongly encouraged to distance himself. As the reader moves away from them and their beliefs, he moves necessarily closer to the Underground Man; and in doing so, he moves toward something like the Underground Man's "hyperconsciousness," which is an excessive but valuable quality in these circumstances and the virtue the Underground Man has to offer.

As an opponent of rationalism and all its systems, the narrator cannot propose another system as an alternative. The "will" he argues for is, as the method of his own argument demonstrates, anti-systematic. He can only hope to expose the fallacy of rationalist assumptions, counter their abstractions with the example of his own experience, and liberate whatever audience he has into self-conscious individuality. So, in one sense, he is perfectly right in denying the existence of an audience he keeps addressing, for this too thwarts a rational expectation and becomes a paradox that, like all the other paradoxes he explores, keeps his argument open-ended and leaves his audience self-consciously suspended in the argument's general irresolution. As Robert M. Adams says [in his *Strains of Discord: Studies in Literary Openness*]:

> A characteristic, then, of one sort of open-formed work is the direct and unmediated quality of its relation to the audience. By imputing to its reader no character at all, or condition purely negative, the work in closed form disguises or minimizes its essentially relativist relation to the reader. Works in the open form make this relativism explicit. They often imply an image of man as an essentially divided and self-antagonistic creature. Although he may be ignorant of this fact at first, the work brings him to a realization of it; and to do so it must stand at once closer to the reader and further from its own actions or characters. Its proper effect always precludes simple identification between reader and character; an element of self-consciousness enters into the proper reaction to the work in open form.

Adam's description of the effect of open form is a fairly accurate, if moderate, description of what the Underground Man himself seems to stand for and wish his audience to recognize: not "simple identification," but the self-consciousness that admits to "the image of man as an essentially divided and self-antagonistic creature."

So, before the unfolding of Part Two, the narrator sounds pretty much like what he wants to be: a superior intelligence in radical opposition to modern society. And he has convinced the reader, given to him by Dostoevsky, of the validity of his argument against the rationalist "gentlemen." This effect is not the end of *Notes from Underground,* however. Dostoevsky has more to reveal about his narrator and a serious qualification to apply. And Dostoevsky's reader comes to understand this qualification as he is allowed to acquire some distance from the narrator by seeing him in circumstances where other audiences have met him and have been allowed to respond. These encounters reveal the Underground Man's motive for confessing as he does and prove that the strategy he adopts for the polemic is not simply a brilliant technique, but the result of a compulsion that has determined his whole life. For this man with no name, who says he "slavishly worshipped the conventional in everything external," and whose fantasy life is often an act of plagiarism, cannot open or entrust himself to anyone else. Instead he plays roles and he hopes, by the strength of his performance, to cast everyone he meets into the role of an audience that will validate his new persona. He has been driven underground because his earlier roles have all failed: he could neither sustain his own part, nor compel his audiences to maintain theirs. In retrospect, therefore, the polemic comes to be seen as a superior version of the performances he has been giving with less success throughout his whole life because, for the polemic, he has invented an audience that cannot respond to deny him.

One of Dostoevsky's fundamental points is that the narrator, who argues so well for the freedom of the individual at almost any cost, cannot be free alone. He must be free before someone who will validate his freedom, so he must rely on a form like the confession which is designed to give him the audience he needs. This use of confession is perfectly appropriate, but the Underground Man ultimately abuses the confession's formal intention by excluding from his audience any real reader. He is confessing to himself, and undermining even this are the revelations in the narrative that he does not know he is making.

The first major episode of Part Two is the narrator's least successful attempt to create an audience out of the officer in the tavern who refuses to recognize his presence and moves him like a piece of furniture. The narrator has no immediate response because he fears the "literary" strategies he first considers will be jeered at and the *point d'honneur* misunderstood. Some years later, he writes a satire against the officer, which goes unpublished because the particular convention is by then outmoded. Later still, he writes a similarly anachronistic letter, demanding an apology and proposing a duel, which he hopes will reveal the fineness of his sensibility and move the officer "to fling himself on my neck and offer me his friendship." He never sends the letter, of course, and finally decides he must settle for a humbler form of recognition by bumping into the man on the Nevsky. Yet even this physical response, which is years late, involves a role and reliance on convention because the Underground Man has to dress up to play the part of a boulevardier.

Despite all of this deliberateness, he finally acts out of impulse.

> The night before I had made up my mind not to carry out my fatal plan, and to abandon it all, and with that goal in mind I went to the Nevsky for the last time, just to see how I would abandon it all. Suddenly, three paces from my enemy, I unexpectedly made up my mind—I closed my eyes, and we ran full tilt, shoulder to shoulder, into each other! I did not budge an inch and passed him on a perfectly equal footing! He did not even look around and pretended not to notice it; but he was only pretending. I am convinced of that. I am convinced of that to this day! Of course, I got the worst of it—he was stronger, but that was not the point. The point was that I had attained my goal, I had kept up my dignity. I had not yielded a step, and had put myself publicly on an equal social footing with him.

The narrator's claim that the officer only pretended not to notice is itself a pretense that is now the narrator's only means of "controlling" the officer's response. What the reader notices, however, is the narrator's self-deception. For it is clear, from the narrator's own account, that the officer did not notice. And what the reader hears in place of the flip self-deprecation of the polemic is a strident insistence that discloses the narrator's need for both personal acceptance and a sustaining belief in his own intelligence. At this point, it is difficult to hold that the Underground Man understands himself in a way that would have allowed him to achieve the performance of Part One.

The Underground Man is a bit more successful in subsequent episodes as he creates situations that allow him to talk. Again out of impulse, he talks himself into Simonov's party for Zverkov. He knows these men from his school days, and they even make some attempt to include him graciously. If they are not an eager audience to the narrator's role of old school chum and fellow gallant, they are at least more accessible than the officer from the tavern and more willing to play along. However, the narrator's loathing for himself and the entire situation eventually breaks down all semblances of accord. After insults, recriminations, and too much to drink, he begins stomping up and down the room while the others continue the party. He demonstrates his integrity by his "silence," but he cannot simply go because departure would mean relinquishing the audience before whom he must display his superiority and contempt. The scene ends when his audience walks out on him.

At the end of Part One, the Underground Man says that one reason for writing these episodes from his past is "to be able to criticize myself and improve my style." Throughout the polemic, though, he has argued that improvement or progress of any kind is impossible. In principle he has implied that style is the man; in practice he does not accept the fatalistic limitations of Buffon's formula. For the Underground Man's solution to the failure of one role or style is the adoption of another, with the unstated hope that a new persona will constitute a new personality. So, as he follows his retreating audience to the brothel, he fantasizes a role in which he wins a spectacular revenge against Zverkov. Then he admits that the fantasy is taken from Pushkin and Lermontov. This admission is not the kind of self-criticism he has promised; the fantasy is a stylistic improvement only in so far as the *imaginary* Zverkov cannot now ignore the narrator's act. As the Underground Man pursues his audience in quest of an identity, it becomes clear that he can never change himself. He can only hope to win a more pliable, submissive witness—like the "gentlemen" of the polemic who are held to silence, or Liza the prostitute.

Initially, Liza is the narrator's most suitable audience. Young, inexperienced, submissive by profession, she provides him with the opportunity for his most voluble performance: "I began to feel myself what I was saying and warmed to the subject. I was already longing to expound the cherished *little ideas* I had brooded over in my corner. Something suddenly flared up in me. An object had 'appeared' before me." The Underground Man goes on to celebrate the standard pieties of love, marriage, and life at home. Toward the end of his speech, he admits to being "really excited" by his own performance. Liza herself recognizes that he is merely rehearsing conventions: "Why you—you speak exactly like a book," she says. But the intensity of the Underground Man's act eventually crushes her. In accepting all of the loathing and defeat he projects onto her, she accepts in effect his definition of her as the kind of audience she should play to his role of enlightened, compassionate freedom.

The Underground Man is aware of Liza's suffering; he is even troubled by it and eager to release her, to escape her. Nevertheless, his first act the following day is indicative of the self-concern that blinds him to a real understanding of the forms he uses for his public roles. Apparently inspired by his success with Liza, he returns home to write an apology to Simonov for his behavior at the party.

> To this hour I am lost in admiration when I recall the truly gentlemanly, good-natured, candid tone of my letter. With tact and good taste, and, above all, entirely without superfluous words, I blamed myself for all that had happened. . . . I was especially pleased with that "certain lightness," almost carelessness (strictly within the bounds of politeness, however), which was suddenly reflected in my style, and better than any possible arguments, gave them at once to understand that I took rather an independent view of "all that unpleasantness last night"; that I was by no means so utterly crushed as you, gentlemen, probably imagine; but on the contrary that I looked at it as a gentleman serenely respecting himself should. "On a young hero's past no censure it cast!"
>
> "There is, after all, even an aristocratic playfulness about it!" I thought admiringly, as I read over the letter.

The Underground Man is no more aware of his self-deception here than he is about the success of his encounter with the officer on the Nevsky. It does not occur to him that Simonov would be able to see through the postures of "tact," "good taste," and "the young hero's past," for the narrator's insight into his audience is only as sharp as his insight into himself. So, it comes as no real surprise that he cannot accept Liza when she comes, later that day, to profess her love. For in complying with the Underground Man's wishes, she is also breaking character by asking him to respond to her authentically. His authentic response is terror and brutal cynicism. Yet he chases after her down the street because it is as difficult for him to relinquish an audience as it is to fire his servant Apollon, who is his most constant audience and the easy winner of all the power games the Underground Man tries to play.

Throughout these episodes, the Underground Man seems to feel, not that he is misunderstood, but understood only too well, especially by Liza and Apollon. At the end, he also seems to fear that the non-existent "gentlemen" understand him too. As he tries to bring his notes to a close, he once again anticipates their objections and seems momentarily to side with them against the "anti-hero" he has created in his "story." But he can sustain this alliance, which suggests both a critical distance from himself and a trust in others, no longer than he can sustain the earlier claim that his address is only an empty form. For immediately he turns on the "gentlemen" and justifies his own courageous sense of "real life."

> "Speak for yourself," you will say, "and for your miseries in your underground holes, but don't dare say 'all of us.'" Excuse me, gentlemen, after all I do not mean to justify myself with "all of us." As for what concerns me in particular I have only, after all, in my life carried to an extreme what you have not dared to carry halfway, and what's more, you have taken your cowardice for good sense, and have found comfort in deceiving yourselves. So that perhaps, after all, there is more "life" in me than in you. Look into it more carefully! After all, we don't even know where living exists now, what it is, and what it is called. . . . We are even oppressed by being men with real individual body and blood. . . . Soon we shall somehow contrive to be born from an idea.

The irony of these last lines is almost pat: no one is more oppressed by his real individuality than the Underground Man; no one labors more anxiously to realize a self-conception.

The narrator's final tone sets in high relief the calm, uninsistent authority of the "editor's" final note. At a sudden and obvious distance from the Underground Man, the editor speaks directly to the reader with the assurance that they understand the narrator so well, almost nothing need be said. His understatement is convincing and even eloquent: "The 'notes' of this paradoxalist do not end here, however. He could not resist and continued them. But it also seems to me that we may stop here."

It has been argued recently [by Reed Merrill; see excerpt dated 1973] that "The fact that his diatribe is cut off by his editor does not in any sense weaken the case of the Underground Man but only proves that his argument is beyond resolution." Yes, but his argument is not the only thing at stake. Dostoevsky locates the polemic first so that it may have its full effect, but he does not locate the identity of his narrator in the polemic alone. Moreover, by making *Notes from Underground* a confession rather than a journal, a diary, or a lyric narrative (like Camus's *The Stranger*), Dostoevsky emphasizes the formal importance of all the audiences the Underground Man addresses—including the reader, who is immediately engaged by the Underground Man but never acknowledged as necessary. All modes of autobiography are incomplete, open-ended, unresolved. But by making its formal commitment to an audience, the confession finds an end for its own activity in the community it can sponsor. And it is precisely because the narrator cannot entrust himself to anyone else that he violates his confession and loses control of it. His argument against the rationalists stands, but he falls into the empty freedom of the rhetoric he addresses to no one.

The Underground Man has said that Rousseau told lies to his audience out of vanity, but that he will tell the truth because he has no real audience to entertain. However, the Underground Man does not know the full truth about himself; and though the confessional form he adopts and everything he says attest to his need for an audience's confirmation, he does not understand (as Rousseau does) what that audience can do for him: which is to ratify the value and inescapability of his suffering and save him from his isolation. No community—whether it is institutionalized like Augustine's or continually self-generating like Rousseau's—can resolve every human problem. And the reader who subscribes to the values of suffering, experience, and self-knowledge which the Underground Man stands for—and which Dostoevsky wants to rescue from rationalism—cannot resolve the Underground Man's argument either, unless he wants to do so under the auspices of an extrinsic authority like Kierkegaard or Nietzsche. But it is impossible for the reader, who understands more about the Underground Man than he does himself, to attribute to him the superiority he wants so desperately. For through the form of the confession and without any intrusion, Dostoevsky has demonstrated that rationalism is not sufficiently answered by the narrator's romantic existentialism, which defines personal identity in the self alone. So the Underground Man is exactly right, with a terrible double irony, about having no readers. For by the end the readers are all Dostoevsky's, whose own argument is that identity is constituted in the individual's experience of community. As we read the final editorial note and share its understanding, we leave the narrator as abruptly as Simonov left him at the party—all by himself. (pp. 27-37)

> *Terrence Doody, "The Underground Man's Confession and His Audience," in* Rice University Studies, *Vol. 61, No. 1, Winter, 1975, pp. 27-38.*

Gary Rosenshield (essay date 1984)

[*In the following excerpt, Rosenshield argues that the possibility of spiritual redemption exists upon the open-ended completion of* Notes from the Underground.]

The fate of Dostoevskij's Underground Man is generally considered to be a dismal one. Yet we know from a letter to his brother Mixail, dated 26 March 1864, in which he berates the censors for having made significant cuts in the next-to-last chapter of Part One of *Notes from the Underground,* that Dostoevskij once entertained considerable hopes for his hero. "The misprints are horrendous; it would have been better not to print the next-to-last chapter at all (the most important one, where the idea of the work is itself expressed) than print it as it is, that is, with its many deleted phrases and self-contradictions. But what can one do? Where I mocked everything and sometimes blasphemed *for show*—that the beastly censors let by, but where I showed from all this the necessity of faith and Christ, that they forbade. What's wrong with the censors, are they engaged in a plot against the government?" Unfortunately, the manuscript copies of *Notes from the Underground* have not survived and Dostoevskij never restored the original text. As we have it, *Notes from the Underground* makes no mention of Christ; and it seems to end in the same vein as it begins: that is with the hero still busy writing away, with no unmistakable sign of progress toward a solution to his numerous serious problems.

A close examination of the text, however, reveals that even in the final version, with all the mangled phrases and deleted passages in the tenth chapter of Part One, Dostoevskij does not leave the Underground Man without hope of resolving his philosophical, moral, and psychological difficulties—and of eventually experiencing spiritual regeneration. The possibility of this regeneration, to be sure, is not explicitly presented, but, as I hope to show, it is strongly implied, and it is as well motivated psychologically as the implied regenerations of several of the heroes of Dostoevskij's later novels.

In fact, though the censor must have deleted from Chapter Ten of Part One several passages having to do with faith and Christ, there is a good deal of evidence from the letters that the deletion did not substantially upset Dostoevskij's basic plan. It would seem that Dostoevskij never had the intention of saving the Underground Man in the novel itself, as, for example, he would save Raskol'nikov in the epilogue of *Crime and Punishment.* Rather he employed the memoir (Part Two)—and the Underground Man's present confrontation in it of his "crime"—to motivate only the possibility of his hero's salvation. His salvation would come—if it did at all—through the acceptance and appreciation of the ideal of compassion and self-sacrifice embodied in the prostitute Liza: the theme of Chapter Ten, Part Two.

One of the signs pointing to the possibility of the Underground Man's regeneration is his remarkable similarity in situation—despite some obvious differences in character and circumstance—to the "saved" heroes of Dostoevskij's later fiction, in particular, Raskol'nikov [in *Crime and Punishment*], the Ridiculous Man [in **"The Dream of a Ridiculous Man"**], and Dmitrij and Ivan Karamazov [in *The Brothers Karamazov*]. It is true that the Underground Man is not saved at the end of the novel, but neither are the others: they have taken, at most, only the first important step toward regeneration. Furthermore, it is implied that for all of them a long period of suffering and additional testing lies ahead. As the narrator of *Crime and Punishment* says of Raskol'nikov, the only major character of Dostoevskij's whose salvation is explicitly prophesied: "He did not even know that the new life would not be his for nothing, that it must be dearly bought, and paid for with great and heroic struggles yet to come."

More important, in the Underground Man we find, as in all of these heroes, the same elements presented as necessary for resurrection into a new life and the experience of a hitherto undreamed-of reality: the acknowledgment and acceptance of responsibility; compassion; guilt (both conscious and unconscious); the compulsion to confess; and the need to expiate the crimes contemplated or committed. Critics have overlooked the presence of these qualities, indeed powers, in the Underground Man, it seems to me, because they have failed sufficiently to distinguish between the younger and older Underground Man and consequently to appreciate the progress the narrator has made in the sixteen years since he experienced the events of Part Two.

Notes from the Underground has perhaps the most complex narrational structure of all Dostoevskij's work. Part

One, told from the point of view of the older Underground Man, is straightforward. Part Two, however, works on several narrational planes at the same time, relating the ideas and feelings of the Underground Man sixteen years ago, as they are remembered by a now much older narrator, as well as the present ideas and feelings of this older narrator about his present and past selves. As a result of this narrative situation a significant ironic distance is established between the Underground Man's younger and older selves, a distance, moreover, which is underlined by the narrator's numerous statements explicitly explaining the differences between his present and past perceptions of the same events. This ironic distance is especially important because it is the author's most effective means of bringing out the differences between the experiencing and narrating personae on which the Underground Man's possibility for moral and spiritual renewal is based.

One of the most unmistakable signs of this possibility for renewal is the older Underground Man's full acknowledgment of his responsibility for both his past and present situations. He, of course, does not argue that his life was in no way shaped by the circumstances in which he found himself, but rather that these circumstances played much less of a role than his freely made decisions. The Underground Man, in other words, accepts the "logical" consequences of his own argument in Part One and takes responsibility for the exercise of his freedom.

In the first episode of Part Two, for example, the Underground Man consciously plans a confrontation with an army officer who he maintains treated him disrespectfully. Looking back, he is rather amused by the incident, presenting it all as an excuse for a self-indulgent adventure in which the officer was totally unaware of the role in which his younger self had cast him. Similarly, the Underground Man presents himself as directly responsible for his humiliation at the going-away party for Zverkov. Though to be sure, he in part depicts himself as a victim, he shows as well that at all times he knew exactly what he was doing, but willfully refused to do otherwise.

The Liza episode differs significantly from the other two episodes in that the Underground Man is much less the victim—in fact, he is clearly the aggressor—and consequently he feels greater responsibility. The harm that the Underground Man does himself by rejecting Liza's love and compassion, losing perhaps a chance of escaping his deadly isolation, is indeed great; but the harm he does Liza is far greater still, for by violating her soul and destroying her hope he possibly condemns her to that terrible fate which several days before he had so graphically described to her and from which he had "nobly" offered her rescue. As in the other episodes, the narrator confesses that he knew even then what he was doing to Liza; but he goes much further, adding that in fact he wanted to humiliate her, that her humiliation was even pleasurable to him. "I had already sensed for quite some time that I had turned her whole soul upside down and I had wrung her heart and the more I became convinced of this, the more I wanted to attain my end as quickly and as forcefully as possible." Although the younger Underground Man knew what he was doing while he was doing it, he did not, nor

Mikhail Dostoevsky, brother of Fyodor and co-founder of the magazines Vremya *and* Epokha, *the journal in which the 1864* Notes from the Underground *was first published.*

could he, appreciate the moral and psychological consequences of his actions. This the narrator begins to do only sixteen years later. Time has not effaced for him the "criminal" deed of the past; on the contrary his crime haunts him now more than ever, and he feels far more responsible now than he did then. In fact, it is clear that the confession itself is to a large degree motivated by the narrator's increasing recognition of his responsibility for his past actions. But this is also a case of reciprocal cause and effect, for at the same time it is only the narrator's confrontation of his own past actions in the confession that makes him recognize the enormity of his "crime" against Liza and his responsibility for it.

How much the narrator's sense of responsibility differs from that of his younger self is evident in his description of his treatment of Liza before their "love-making" in his apartment. The younger Underground Man at first thinks that he has dealt Liza a final humiliating blow by giving her money; and then is taken aback when he finds out that she has secretly left the money behind in the room. The narrator cannot, as it were, refrain from commenting on his former ignorance. "Well! I might have expected that she would do that. Might I have? No, I was such an egoist, I was, in fact, so lacking in respect for my fellow-creatures that I could not even imagine she would do so. . . ." The narrator's statement that because of his egoism he was incapable of even imagining what Liza would do also suggests that he no longer is afflicted, in his own view, by the same egoism, or at least, not to the degree that it blinds him to such unpleasant truths. But more important it shows that the narrator now is clearly holding himself responsible for something that he was unable or refused to hold himself responsible for some sixteen years before.

Another indication of the narrator's willingness, even passionate desire, to take responsibility for his actions is the devastating irony with which he treats all his earlier attempts to rationalize his cruelty to Liza.

> 'And won't it be better, won't it be better,' I fantasized afterwards at home, stifling the living pang of my heart with fantastic dreams. 'Won't it be better for her to take the insult away with her forever? An insult—why it is purification; it is a most stinging and painful consciousness! Tomorrow I should have defiled her soul and have exhausted her heart, while now the insult will never die in her, and however loathesome the filth awaiting her—the insult will elevate and purify her . . . by hatred . . . h'm . . . perhaps too, by forgiveness. . . . But will all that really make things easier for her?'

The narrator presents his past justifications for his cruel treatment of Liza as obvious rationalizations. Whereas the younger Underground Man's imagination prevents him from seeing the truth and acknowledging responsibility, the narrator's imagination—as embodied in the story he writes about himself—is continually used to reveal the truth to himself and to compel him to assert that responsibility. By calling these rationalizations fantasies (*fantazii*) the narrator suggests the superiority of his present understanding of reality to his past understanding; for the narrator implies that these rationalizations are fantastic because they can have been arrived at only by someone who has lost contact with reality. They represent the ignorance peculiar to the isolated consciousness. Since the ignorance is more moral than intellectual, this passage, like the one treated above, has important implications regarding changes that have been occurring in the Underground Man since the events of Part Two. If the Underground Man is still an isolated intellectual, his isolation is of a qualitatively different sort than it was sixteen years earlier. Of course, the narrator, as is evident from Part One, has by no means solved any of his major problems; but his narrative shows that he has not spent these last sixteen years of suffering in vain. However lost and confused he appears to himself, he is presented by the implied author as being closer to seeing the light now than he was before, and closer even than those who have continued to live lives based on abstractions and have remained completely unaware that they have done so.

The narrator's acceptance of responsibility in Part Two also has a direct bearing on the interpretation of Part One; for it shows that Part One, far from being the Underground Man's rationalization of his early behavior, provides, in its passionate and rebellious defense of free will, a philosophical justification of his desire to take responsibility for his actions. The Underground Man knows that without free will responsibility is meaningless; however since there is still so much of the rationalist in the Underground Man, he must "prove" that free will exists in order

to feel comfortable with his "irrational" acceptance of responsibility for his past behavior. Conversely, Part Two gives the older Underground Man's existential proof—based on his present feelings of guilt for past behavior—of the validity of the human category of responsibility.

Another attribute of the Underground Man which is as important as acceptance of responsibility in establishing his potential for renewal, and even redemption, is compassion—in particular, the compassion of the *older* Underground Man for Liza. In its presentation of compassion, the *Notes* is most similar to **"The Dream of a Ridiculous Man,"** in which the hero's compassion for a little girl, whose desperate pleas he initially disregards, first prevents him from shooting himself and then inspires the dreams that lead to his implied recovery. (The dreams and visions of Raskol'nikov, Dmitrij and Ivan Karamazov, *mutatis mutandis,* have a similar effect.) But as with responsibility, determining the exact nature of the Underground Man's compassion is complicated by the form of the narration. Here again it is necessary carefully to distinguish the point of view of the younger and older Underground Man.

The narrator reveals that at the time of the events he felt compassion for Liza, particularly when she visited him in his apartment to tell him that she wanted to leave the brothel, "My heart simply ached from pity for her awkwardness and unnecessary candor, but immediately something ugly suppressed all pity in me, it egged me on even more." Pity, to be sure, is a relatively weak feeling in the younger Underground Man, easily suppressed by spite, vanity, and vindictiveness. But just as important, much of the pity that the younger Underground Man feels for Liza is self-induced, elicited more by the sentimental stories he has told her than by her actual situation. Further, he exploits this pity to exert his will over her: when he sees that she responds to what seems to her to be genuine compassion, he immediately takes advantage, and turns her soul upside down by means of it.

> And I was so carried away by my own words that I began to get a lump in my throat myself, and . . . and all at once I stopped, sat up in dismay, and bending over apprehensively began to listen with a beating heart. I had reason to be troubled.

> I had already sensed for some time that I had turned her soul upside down and I had wrung her heart, and the more I became convinced of this, the more I wanted to attain my end as quickly and as forcefully as possible. It was the exercise of my skill that carried me away.

Whereas compassion for the younger Underground Man is a means of self-aggrandizement, for the older Underground Man it is one of his prime means of overcoming the self. It is true that the Underground Man's compassion is clearly too late for Liza (a fact that the Underground Man must live with for the rest of his life), but it is not, in all respects, too late for the Underground Man, since his capacity now to suffer for another human being constitutes an important sign of his potential for spiritual renewal. It is ironic that sixteen years after the original romance, Liza, by means of the older Underground Man's recollection of the events, once again offers the Underground Man a chance for renewal, but this time not so much through her compassion for him, but through the compassion elicited in him by her fate, that is, not so much through her compassion for his suffering, but his compassion for hers.

If the confession is largely motivated by compassion, compassion, in its turn, is elicited and heightened by the confession, that is, by the very act of telling the story, by the dramatic reenactment of the events, by their particular artistic representation. In contrast to the destructive use to which the Underground Man put the story sixteen years earlier, he uses the present story—the confession—and the compassion it evokes in him, to increase his own suffering and by doing so to expiate his crime. And, in fact, at a number of especially painful memories, the narrator interjects in mid-sentence an anguished *bednaja* in reference to Liza (significantly, with no irony intended) as though he were so overcome with compassion that he cannot complete his thought without giving immediate expression to his emotion.

Another unmistakable sign of the narrator's compassion for Liza is his consistent presentation of her as meek, naive, and defenseless, especially in her unequal battle with his younger self. (Dostoevskij uses the same technique, though in a more exaggerated form, in portraying Lužin's "crime" against Sonja in *Crime and Punishment*.) The narrator presents himself as the predator and Liza as the victim in order to elicit compassion for her in his hypothetical reader (the artistic function of the device) as well as in himself, as the real audience of his own work (the edificatory function of the device).

But of all the feelings necessary for regeneration in Dostoevskij's later fiction the most important is unquestionably guilt. And in the *Notes* we see Dostoevskij for the first time using it as the foundation for the possibility of his hero's spiritual renewal. But here again understanding the specific role of guilt in the novel, like that of responsibility and compassion, is complicated by point of view. Both the younger and older Underground Man clearly distinguish between good and evil and both experience guilt; yet their knowledge and feelings of guilt differ significantly. We have already seen the younger Underground Man's ambivalent feelings toward Liza, the simultaneous existence in him of both pity and hatred for her: similarly, the younger Underground Man feels guilt over Liza even when tormenting her. But though he suffers from the pangs of remorse throughout his brief romance with Liza, he often is unaware of the nature of his own feelings. The guilt manifests itself mainly in an acute but indefinite anxiety, the reasons for which the younger Underground Man cannot understand. The narrator writes of the younger Underground Man's feelings after returning from the brothel: "I could not make out what was wrong with me, I could not find the clue, something seemed to be rising up continually in my soul, painfully, and refusing to be appeased. I returned home completely upset; it was just as though some crime was lying on my conscience." The younger Underground Man thinks he is most upset by the insult he received at the going-away party for Zverkov; he does not at all realize that he is suffering for his gratuitous cruelty to Liza. We are presented with still another example of the Underground Man's ego-engendered blindness. In the above passage, it is, perhaps, at first difficult to distinguish between the experiencing and narrative selves of the Underground Man, for the narrator expresses what seems to be his present knowledge in the past tense. But we can tell that the description of the Underground Man's condition here is clearly from the point of view of the narrator because the narrator recounts not what the Underground Man was thinking but what he felt—what he had not or could not have put into words.

The younger Underground Man does not understand the reason for his suffering because his guilt is to a considerable extent subconscious. The older narrator, on the other hand, is painfully conscious of his feelings of guilt, and they have not abated with time. "But I did not know then that fifteen years later I should still in imagination see Liza, with the same pitiful, distorted, inappropriate smile which was on her face at that minute." The depth of the narrator's recognized guilt is revealed by his inability to assuage it other than through the written word. He cannot keep it bottled inside him; he must express it in writing, and not only to himself but to an audience as well—however hypothetical that audience might be. In *Crime and Punishment,* Raskol'nikov's confession is not a completely satisfactory one until it is, among other things, a public one; Ivan Karamazov's confession is not a complete one—**"The Grand Inquisitor,"** for example—until he goes before the court. The confession, that is, the story the Underground Man tells about himself, becomes the quintessential expression of his guilt; but it is more than an expression of guilt still felt, it is also an act of expiation of that guilt. The Underground Man suffers as much in retelling the story as he did in experiencing the events. "Even now, after so many years, it is almost too painful to recall all this. In fact, there is a great deal now which is painful for me to recall, but . . . isn't it about time that I put an end to these *Notes?* It seems to me that I made a mistake in beginning them. At least, I have been ashamed all the time I have been writing this *tale (povest')*: it must be then that this is not really literature, but corrective punishment (*ispravitel'noe nakazanie*)." Raskol'nikov's dreams after the murder—in effect, his relivings of the crime—can be looked at in much the same way. Although it may or may not be that the Underground Man's crime against Liza is a form of self-punishment, the confession engendered by this crime certainly is. *Notes from the Underground,* like most of Dostoevskij's works, is in essence a novel about crime and corrective (*ispravitel'noe*) punishment, and it is from the crime itself that the forces arise which lead the criminal to atonement—and the chance for regeneration that perhaps could not have been possible before it had occurred.

The Underground Man of course is not "saved" in the end—that is, given new hope—in the same way Raskol'nikov is in the epilogue of *Crime and Punishment.* But if we compare Raskol'nikov's situation at the end of the novel proper with that of the Underground Man at the end of the *Notes,* we see that the Underground Man has made at least as much "progress" toward renewal as Raskol'nikov has made in *Crime and Punishment.* Well into the second chapter of the epilogue, Raskol'nikov not only feels no conscious guilt or remorse for the murder, which he does not consider a crime, he even refuses to take responsibility for it, often rationalizing it away as a cruel joke of fate. Dostoevskij presents the Underground Man still writing at the end of the *Notes,* but he is struggling to find a way out of his dilemma. Moreover, in contrast to Raskol'nikov, he has fully acknowledged and accepted his responsibility and guilt. Though the confession he writes reveals that he still has a long way to go—and this is true for all of Dostoevskij's heroes whose regeneration is implied—he has reached that point of almost total despair which directly precedes the revelation of a new way for those of Dostoevskij's lost souls who have retained their lust for life and have continued to be moved by compassion for the suffering of others.

In the *Notes* the revelation of the way is implied, not explicitly stated; and it must be so because the Underground Man, like Raskol'nikov, does not believe that he will experience spiritual renewal. He feels that he is as badly off as he was sixteen years before. The older Underground Man has as little knowledge of his future and his possibilities of a way out of his impasse as Raskol'nikov or Ivan Karamazov at comparable stages in their lives. This only the implied author—and therefore the reader—can know. There is as great a distance in the *Notes* between the points of view of the older Underground Man and the implied author as there is between the points of view of the older and younger Underground Man. The older Underground Man writes a confession, as it were, out of physical necessity and he goes on writing because he cannot stop; but he does not know—he cannot know—that this writing is in itself an essential first step out of the underground.

The Underground Man's limited understanding of his own situation is particularly evident in the following passage relating to sacrificial love, in which the older narrator explains why he had been unable fifteen years earlier to understand Liza's desire to love him.

> Even in my underground dreams I did not imagine love except as a struggle. I began it always with hatred and ended it with moral subjugation and afterwards I never knew what to do with the subjugated object. And why is that so incredible, when I had succeeded in so corrupting myself morally, when I had become so out of touch with "real life," as to have actually thought a little earlier of reproaching her, and putting her to shame for having come to me to hear pathetic words; and I did not even guess that she had come not to hear pathetic words, but to love me, because to a woman all resurrection (*voskresenie*)—all salvation (*spasenie*) from any sort of ruin, and all renewal (*vozroždenie*)—is included in love and manifests itself only in that form.

The younger Underground Man is, of course, well aware of the idea of the nobility of sacrificial love, but his knowledge of it is only from books, a type of knowledge which the older Underground Man both directly and indirectly condemns throughout Part Two. Moreover, as is obvious from his dreams, the young Underground Man sees self-sacrifice as another means of self-aggrandizement; he fails

to see the necessity, or even possibility, of such an ideal existing if only as a guiding force in life. The older Underground Man's views certainly differ dramatically from those of his younger self. Yet although he presents his former egoistic love in the most negative terms, in effect, calling it a perversion of true love and the primary cause of his failure to live a "real" life, and although he now clearly appreciates the nobility of Liza's sacrifice, of self-sacrifice in general—the willingness to subordinate the demands of the ego for the sake of another—the older narrator nevertheless does not himself have a complete understanding of the role that sacrificial love can, and should, play in his own life. He does not realize that, according to the novel, this type of love is the highest manifestation of not only the female personality, but the male personality as well. In fact, it almost sounds as though the older Underground Man were envious of Liza in particular and women in general; for it seems to him that only they can achieve what he himself is desperately trying to achieve: resurrection, salvation, and regeneration. The three almost synonymous nouns in close proximity underline in the tenth and last chapter of Part Two the possibilities—not probabilities—for the Underground Man which were originally sounded in Chapter Ten of Part One.

In most of the criticism on the *Notes,* especially the most recent, the Underground Man's confession—which, as I have shown, figures as the basis on which the turn in the Underground Man's fate may be achieved—is held to be not only ineffectual but even positively harmful. His statements at the end of Part One on the nature of confessions are invariably interpreted as proof that the Underground Man's confession, like Rousseau's, is bound to be shot through with distortion, rationalization, and vanity, and constitutes, in the end, essentially an exercise in self-glorification. It cannot be denied that we can find all of the above in the Underground Man's confession, and even expect to (we find, by the way, exactly the same characteristics in Raskol'nikov's confession right into the second chapter of the epilogue), but the fact that confessions may have many self-serving motives does not mean that they cannot at the same time be primarily, or at least on balance, salutary, to the self as well as to others. Every case in Dostoevskij's novels must be examined on an individual basis. Furthermore, it is not necessary that a confession tell the absolute truth—if there is such a thing as autobiographical truth—or even be reliable on the major points to serve its prime function: to reveal the most significant facts about its author, in the Underground Man's case, both his great suffering (which the reader cannot but feel) and his attempt to arrive at the truth. The confessor may not know the truth, but, as we have repeatedly seen, Dostoevskij has him reveal the truth about himself, for the reader, through his partial truths and even outright misconceptions about himself. The "confessions" of Montesquieu, Rousseau, and Heine are beside the point here; for the *Notes* is not Dostoevskij's confession, but the Underground Man's, a confession from which Dostoevskij maintains an ironic distance throughout. One also wonders whether Dostoevskij would have worked out a sophisticated narrative system in which the narrator is separated from his "story" by sixteen years and great differences of perception and judgment intermingle only to undercut it in the end by showing that the Underground Man's attempt to come to terms with his past is really no more meaningful than his earlier sentimental and self-aggrandizing fantasies. In the Underground Man's case at least, the confession records not the stasis of the soul but the slow and harrowing struggle and progress of a soul toward spiritual regeneration. The Underground Man's confession, as an indication of this progress, is not invalidated by virtue of its being a confession; nor is it invalidated by its incompleteness; nor even by its lies. That the Underground Man is still writing at the end is not a sign of motion without forward movement, but the novel's way of showing that the search is continuing—as it must—for the search itself is the most certain indication of the presence of that living life (*živaja žizn'*) which keeps open the possibility of rebirth.

The potential efficacy of the Underground Man's confession can perhaps nowhere be better appreciated than when the Liza episode of Part Two is viewed in its polemical relationship with the Marion episode of Rousseau's *Confessions.* In one of the earliest sections of his autobiography, Rousseau confesses that when he was sixteen he committed a crime against an innocent young girl from the country, named Marion, by falsely accusing her of having stolen a ribbon that he himself had taken. As a result of his action Marion was dismissed from her position as a cook in the household, and since her reputation was irreparably tarnished, her chances of further employment were severely damaged. Although he never really knew what became of her, Rousseau always looked upon himself as the cause of Marion's ruin. In a passage very similar to one in the *Notes,* Rousseau states that for forty years he has been tormented by remorse for his nefarious deed and that he has taken up writing the confession to rid himself of the great burden it has for so long placed on his conscience. But as is typical in the *Confessions,* Rousseau presents the other side of his "crime." He did not accuse Marion out of deliberate wickedness; in fact, he liked Marion and his heart was torn because of what he had done. But so great was his childish fear of public shame that he could not confess that it was he who had stolen the article. Further, Rousseau argues that his age should be taken into account. Since he was only a child, his crime amounted in reality to nothing more than weakness (*faiblesse*). What torments him then is not so much the intention of his actions, but their consequences. But even with regard to consequences, Rousseau sees the other side, pointing out the beneficial effects of his misdeed. The impression alone of that sole offense, he writes, secured him for the rest of his life "against any act that might prove criminal in its results." It also made him an unceasing enemy of untruth, a stance which led, he says, to forty years of misfortune. Rousseau concludes the chapter expressing the hope that his confession here will terminate his life-long expiation of his crime. And it seems, at least in the *Confessions,* this hope is realized, for he makes no further mention of Marion in the following 500 or so pages of text.

If Dostoevskij had wanted to undermine the Underground Man's confession, to reveal its self-serving and self-defeating nature, one, of course, could hardly imagine a literary situation that Dostoevskij could more easily ex-

ploit than Rousseau's justification of his crime-but-not-a-crime. But on closer inspection, we see that Dostoevskij is not merely reproducing the *effects* of Rousseau's confession (something, after all, which should not surprise us), but rather using similar methods and effects for quite different purposes. What is perhaps most striking at first is the relative weight of the Liza and Marion episodes in their respective works. Whereas Rousseau devotes only four pages to Marion, Dostoevskij devotes almost half of the novel to Liza. In the *Confessions,* the Marion episode occurs near the beginning and it is never mentioned again, partly because the *Confessions* is a chronological account of a life; however, in the *Notes* the Liza episode, although it occurs sixteen years before the actual time of writing, is the most important action of the work, the action which the rest of the work leads up to. One cannot help getting the impression that Liza has had a much stronger effect on the Underground Man's life (and of course it should have) than Marion had on Rousseau's. The Underground Man cannot stop thinking and now writing about it. What is more, in contrast to Rousseau, the Underground Man uses every method at his disposal to emphasize his responsibility for his actions toward Liza. He is not writing an autobiography justifying his actions, as is Rousseau, but a philosophical treatise (Part One) and a personal history (Part Two) equally supporting his need and moral duty to take responsibility for his actions. That his treatment of Liza was a moral crime and not a misdeed is made explicit throughout by the Underground Man, a fact which becomes clearer the more Rousseau's work is used as a basis of comparison. Rousseau is able to reduce his crime to childish naughtiness that may have had unfortunate consequences. This the Underground Man cannot and *will* not do.

Furthermore, it is also important to note that at sixteen (the age of Rousseau in the Marion episode), the Underground Man had a relationship with a boy at school that may also have had unfortunate consequences, a relationship that is similar to and foreshadows the one that he has eight years later with Liza. But Dostoevskij, as it were answering Rousseau, repeats the situation when the Underground Man is an adult, twenty-four years old—about the same age as Raskol'nikov—when his actions can no longer be explained away as a childish weakness. The Underground Man does not argue, as Rousseau does, that his heart was in the right place, and that all that tormented him was the possible harmful consequences of his actions. In fact, he explicitly states, as we have seen, that his motivations from the start were far from exemplary, that he wanted to humiliate Liza and satisfy his wounded ego. In addition, not only was he aware of what the terrible consequences of a life like Liza's might be, he used the lurid description of those consequences in order to get Liza more firmly in his power. All this the older Underground Man admits. Surely to understand this admission as a form of self-glorification, a sort of one-upmanship on Rousseau, is not properly to appreciate the suffering that Dostoevskij is able to convey throughout the Underground Man's tortured monologue; it is also to argue in effect that Dostoevskij is employing a good deal of ammunition to destroy a ridiculously easy target (Rousseau's justification of his crime), a justification which seems almost to "self-deconstruct."

Rousseau argues that his misdeed had, at least for himself, the beneficial effect of making him a better man, the proof of which was the Jobian misfortunes he suffered as a defender of the truth. Now however true such an analysis of the Marion incident may have been in Rousseau's real or even his fictionalized life (the *Confessions*), most readers cannot but take the author's justification—Rousseau uses the verb *s'excuser*—as a sign of immodesty and self-deception and therefore a serious obstacle to belief. If the Underground Man's crime—like Raskol'nikov's in *Crime and Punishment*—was to play an important role in his spiritual regeneration, Dostoevskij could not risk having the Underground Man explicitly speak of the possible "good" consequences of his "evil" actions, for to do so would naturally call into question the sincerity of the Underground Man's statement of responsibility and thus the possible beneficial effects of the crime. Perhaps this is why the Underground Man rarely attempts to justify his crime in contrast, for instance, to Raskol'nikov in *Crime and Punishment.* In a third-person narrative, characters can get away with a great deal of self-justification and still appear sympathetic—Marmeladov [in *Crime and Punishment*] and Raskol'nikov—because of counterbalancing descriptions of their sufferings by an objective third-person narrator. But since a first-person narrator is telling his own story and cannot provide an objective or at least an outside view of his own feelings and thoughts, he must, if he is at all to be believed, at all costs avoid those justifications that we find in Rousseau. In contrast to the crime of Rousseau, the crime of the Underground Man (and here of course we are dealing only with Rousseau's own analysis of his behavior) did not lead to a life of honest and upright behavior causing him untold misfortune. On the contrary, the Underground Man, we are to believe, indulged in a great deal of behavior which repels him, about which he feels guilt, and for which we see him suffering in the present. If there is to be any saving grace to his disgraceful behavior he must not be conscious of it, as Raskol'nikov is not and cannot be conscious of the paradoxical benefits of his murder of the pawnbroker. Rousseau saves himself in his confession and ascribes the cause; the Underground Man can do no such thing for he cannot see—and must not see—that there is hope for him in these terms, that is, as a consequence of his crime against Liza. Can one, for example, seriously imagine Raskol'nikov *consciously* hoping that the murder of Alena Ivanovna—or Ivan Karamazov *consciously* hoping that the murder of his father—may lead to his spiritual regeneration. Obviously to have them hope so in the novel proper would have seriously impeded the reader's acceptance of any possible renewal for them.

In the end we do not and cannot know what will happen to the Underground Man: the ending is an open one. But if guilt, acknowledgment of responsibility, and compassion for the suffering of others can provide the basis of spiritual renewal, one cannot say that there is no hope for the Underground Man. To maintain that there is no hope for the Underground Man, especially if we take the Underground Man as an everyman, is to argue that the novel

shows that guilt, compassion, and suffering are of no redemptive value. To so argue is to fail to appreciate the moral dialectic of the novel, to appreciate that all-important ambiguity and resonance with which Dostoevskij invests the fate of his hero. (pp. 324-37)

> Gary Rosenshield, "The Fate of Dostoevskij's Underground Man: The Case for an Open Ending," in Slavic and East-European Journal, *n.s. Vol. 28, No. 3, Fall, 1984, pp. 324-39.*

Dominick LaCapra   (essay date 1987)

[*An American critic and historian, LaCapra promotes the use of interpretive techniques from disciplines such as literary criticism and philosophy as an alternative to the traditional methods in the fields of intellectual and social history. He defines his purpose as an attempt "to revive a Renaissance ideal of historiography." In the following excerpt, LaCapra documents the paradoxical element of* Notes from the Underground, *which lends the work resonance and continuing relevance.*]

> If anyone proved to me that Christ was outside the truth, and it *really* was so that the truth was outside Christ, then I should prefer to remain with Christ than with the truth.
>
> Fyodor Dostoevsky

If one were to inquire into the question of the relationship between Dostoevsky's context and his texts, one could do worse than to begin with the commonplace idea of the breakdown of tradition. The crucial form this breakdown took for Dostoevsky was, of course, religious crisis. The Westernized intellectual had a privileged relation to the crisis as one who both aggravated it and came to an acute critical consciousness of it. For Dostoevsky, the West itself embodied an ideology of free, critical inquiry and secular rationalism that endangered traditional religious faith.

The Underground Man is in one sense the limiting case or extreme representative of the Westernized intellectual. And there was a sense in which Dostoevsky could never fully eliminate from himself what he saw as the Western influence—the nexus between freedom and critical questioning that contested or even endangered faith. His inner division might itself be taken as indicative of the dubiousness of the very binary opposition between West and East, for it bears witness to the problematic insertion of the West in the East (and vice versa).

In his life, Dostoevsky at first subscribed to what he later saw as a Westernized position and placed secular faith in radical politics, and his later reaction against radical politics coincided with his movement toward Russian Orthodox religion. As a young man he sympathized with radical groups that opposed the role in Russia of a despotic political regime, a reactionary church, and a secret police and spy system. Their criticism was fed by a familiarity with Western thinkers such as Saint-Simon and Fourier. In the late 1840s, Dostoevsky was a member of the Durov circle within the larger Petrashevsky circle, a group of reformers who met to read and discuss socialist and liberal literature.

Perhaps unrealistically, Dostoevsky believed that had this circle not been liquidated, it would have gone on to take revolutionary action and would have had large-scale popular support. The Durov circle was the most activist group within the Petrashevsky circle. Its members believed that violence might be necessary and took a terroristic oath of revolutionary solidarity to kill any member who betrayed the group. (There is similar group in *The Possessed,* and one of the more probing aspects of this novel is its disclosure of the way privileged groups might themselves be permeated with revolutionary ideas.)

The 1848 Revolution in France led to a crackdown in Russia, and in 1849 Dostoevsky was slated for execution. In melodramatic fashion, a courier from the Czar arrived at the eleventh hour with a commuted sentence. This gesture, confirming the divine-right status of the ruler in his command over life and death, had a telling effect upon the prisoners. One of the condemned went mad. Dostoevsky himself apparently was filled with mystical awe.

Dostoevsky subsequently spent four years in Siberia under extremely harsh conditions and dated his epileptic seizures from this period in his life. He explicitly looked upon his imprisonment as a merited punishment that enabled him to atone for the errors of his corrupt youth. And he sought solace and salvation in religion. The only book he had in prison was the New Testament. It was shortly after his release from prison that he wrote to his brother the words that serve as my epigraph. Yet whether or not these words are accurate with respect to Dostoevsky's lived relation to religion, they do not serve to characterize the treatment of religion in his novels. For in them there is no simple alternative between belief and disbelief, revealed religion and secular "truth." Rather, religious belief is powerfully contested even when it is powerfully affirmed, and the most extreme atheist exists on the margin of possible belief. It is the abiding value of Mikhail Bakhtin's analysis [*Problems of Dostoevsky's Poetics,* 1963] to have brought out the internally "dialogized" nature of all ideologies in Dostoevsky's literary texts.

Still, upon leaving prison, Dostoevsky saw political radicalism as both wrongheaded and sinful. In the 1860s he condemned the new generation of radicals whose most prominent exponent was Chernyshevsky. One explicit object of caricature, parody, and polemical attack in *Notes from Underground* is of course Chernyshevsky's *What Is to Be Done?* with its faith in rationalism and progress. Dostoevsky himself seemed increasingly to tend toward a conservative but populistically based Slavism. He openly affirmed the value of Russian Orthodox religion, mother Russia, and the simple, pious Russian people.

In 1862 a trip to western Europe (discussed in *Winter Notes on Summer Impressions*) confirmed Dostoevsky in his convictions. He saw capitals such as Paris and London as the scene of egotism, materialism, and hypocrisy. The West was decadent. By contrast, Dostoevsky affirmed the need for self-sacrifice, compassion, and brotherly love.

Certain things, however, remained relatively constant or changed only in degree in Dostoevsky's outlook over time. He was always opposed to what he saw as the total West-ernization of Russia. He rejected extreme liberalism and believed that it could only encourage a flight from freedom. He also attacked capitalism from the beginning to the end of his life. He opposed the introduction of capitalism in Russia because he thought it would upset the old order and give rise to divisive class conflict. He also always believed in the special mission of Russia and her people. From his perspective, the most Russia should do with the Western tradition was to overcome it in a higher synthesis. Indeed, he saw Russia in an idealized light as a synthesizing force with a capacity for universal reconcilability, universal humanity. And he always believed that intellectuals in Russia should avoid the twin dangers of extreme Westernization and uprooted detachment from the people. The uprooted Westernized intellectual was the stereotypical "superfluous man"—and *Notes from Underground* contains this prevalent theme of Russian literature. Dostoevsky thought Russian intellectuals should not emulate Westerners but see in the people the salvation of Russia. In his idealized view of Russia, her faith, and her people, Dostoevsky seemed to find the saving grace of suffering and compassion.

What Dostoevsky came to see more forcefully in time—and to oppose vehemently—was the possibility that Russia faced its greatest threat of disruption from its Westernized intellectuals. Here, from the opposite end of the ideological spectrum, one seems to have a remarkable convergence with the thought of Lenin. But Russia in Dostoevsky's time, in contrast to Lenin's, had as yet no significant capitalistic bourgeoisie or proletariat. And Dostoevsky opposed the large-scale introduction of capitalism precisely because it would create conditions incompatible with his values. Yet even without these conditions, a Westernized intelligentsia was an active force that might upset the status quo. The apparent and apparently decisive difference between the young and the later Dostoevsky was the difference between support of, and opposition to, this possibility. But in his novels and perhaps in his life—certainly in the relation between the two—the will to believe does not simply and complacently culminate in belief, and the "Westernized" other is within as well as without. One name for this "Westernized" other is the Underground Man.

In *Notes from Underground,* one finds at least two modes of "dialogue" (in the Bakhtinian sense) that are not simple opposites. First and most obvious is the broken but often terribly funny dialogue of an evasive voice internally divided against itself. "Dialogue" here takes the form of split monologue. This internally dialogized, sidesplitting monologist is always on the lookout for loopholes. He can level existing structures, and he generates paradoxes that are explosive, often hilariously so. But these paradoxes seem to lead nowhere. In a sense, one has here the voice of the self-conscious and explicitly self-parodic superfluous man or Westernized intellectual.

The second dialogue or aspect of dialogue is the hint or hope of a transformative relationship where an interanimation of voices may have a regenerative function. The Underground Man both evades and seeks this transformation. This second and more submerged possibility of dialogue is indicated at two important places in the text (which are discussed below). On another level, it may be implied in the relation between the writer and the reader of the text.

These two dialogues and the voices related to them are mutually implicated in a kind of life and death struggle. And the relations among author, narrator, and reader are also complex and multivoiced.

Dostoevsky as author seems to take his distance from the Underground Man at one very strategic place—at the very beginning of the text. But he does so in an imperious and perhaps suspect way. In an introductory note to the title, which is actually signed by Dostoevsky, he seems to reduce the text to a mere document, a detached case history of a representative character of modern times.

> The author of these notes and the "Notes" themselves are, of course, imaginary. Nevertheless, such persons as the writer of these notes, not only may, but positively must, exist in our society, considering those circumstances under which our society was in general formed. I wanted to expose to the public more clearly than it is done usually, one of the characters of the recent past. He is one of the representatives of the current generation. In this excerpt, entitled "Underground," this person introduces himself, his views, and, as it were, tries to explain the reasons why he appeared and was bound to appear in our midst. In the following excerpt, the actual notes of this person about several events in his life will appear. *Fyodor Dostoevsky.*

In his own name and with the authority of his signature, Dostoevsky thus seems to position himself securely above the mouse-man of the text, the Westernized intellectual caught in traps of his social conditioning and his own morbid making. But the obvious question is whether this note totally masters the work and play of the text by providing an exclusive or privileged way of reading it. For one thing, the note itself may not entirely escape the self-contestatory movements generated by the text, for it may be read as a parodic echo of the beginning of Mikhail Lermontov's *Hero of Our Time* and thus not be taken entirely "straight." One danger of simply taking the note at face value is that this interpretive gesture would deprive the text of much of its force, disimplicate both writer and reader from its challenge, and render nugatory many of its most gripping movements.

At the end of the text, in another complex gesture to which I shall return, distance is again put between the author and the Underground Man in a manner not quite identical to that of the initial note. For the rest of the text, the Underground Man is himself the narrator, speaking in the first person. Yet he does not have a proper name that would clearly attach his "I" to someone whose identity could be underwritten with a signature. This fact adds to the indeterminate status of the narrator-protagonist and furthers his complicity with both the author and the reader. The interactions among Dostoevsky as author, the Underground Man as narrator, and the reader form an intricate network of relations of proximity and distance—even of love and hate.

The narrative is divided into two parts: "The Underground" and "Apropos of Wet Snow." Part One is chiefly a conceptual or theoretical form of discourse in which the Underground Man in the present tense reflects or theorizes about consciousness and its (sometimes hilarious) paradoxes. It is like a self-parodic preface to a phenomenology of alienation and resentment. The Underground Man is introduced as a retired civil servant who has, at the age of forty, settled into a rut in life. He has decided, at the threshold of middle age, to reflect on existence, and he gives us his parodic credo. Part Two is largely a narrative of previous events, a story that involves a remembrance of things past, occurrences at the age of twenty-four. It can also be funny, but it is at times serious and searing, especially at the end. Twenty-four is of course another liminal age—the threshold of adult maturity.

The relation between the two parts is an offset superimposition of threshold on threshold. In significant ways the parts seem paradoxically to undercut each other and to exist in a bewildering form of counterpoint, for each part is a suspicious alibi or pretext for the existence of the other. And neither part has a fully cogent *raison d'être*. "Alibi" literally means "in another place," and each part of the *Notes* displaces (or disorients and de-Westernizes) the other and is partially inside its counterpart: there are events in Part One and theorizing in Part Two.

The Underground Man writes Part One to introduce Part Two and Part Two to illustrate Part One. This is the simplest and most commonsensical relation between the parts. Yet the relations between the parts are complex, involving displacement, repression, and even distortion. The text enacts dreamwork, and scenes are often dreamlike. One sign of displacement and distortion is the fact that the servant who appears as an unnamed woman in Part One becomes a man—Apollon—in Part Two. The sex of the servant is reversed as one moves from part to part, and as a male he acquires a name—a name that recalls Apollo.

The problem of displacement and distortion cuts across many levels—that of the relation of consciousness to life, of theory to events, of Part One to Part Two. Hyperconsciousness distorts and displaces life, excessive theory distorts and displaces events, Part One distorts and displaces Part Two, and vice versa. In addition, the excessive theorizing of Part One can be seen as a way of repressing or delaying as well as illuminating—at times artificially or even falsely—the narration of events in Part Two. It is a way of beating about the bush and not getting to the point. But one cannot take the first part as a simple theoretical statement or even as diversionary intellectual free (or fore) play. It is not entirely serious in tenor; it carnivalizes theory, (proleptically) including psychoanalytic theory, which one might be tempted to use uncritically in interpreting the text. And in Part One there is explicit criticism of a fully coherent and comprehensive theory of human behavior.

As for the chronology of the text, Part One is something that occurs after the fact of the events of Part Two. Yet it is placed first in the text; the relation between the time of narration and the time of the narrated phenomena is reversed. And once in each part the broken dialogue that evades issues intimates the possibility of a transformation, though the possibility is quickly sidestepped by the Underground Man: the "Damn Underground" passage and its sequel in the first part; in the second part the suggestion of love with Liza, which is followed by a departure from the narrative past tense and a return to the present tense and the accusatory tone of Part One.

Let us look at these two parts and their relationship more closely. Part One leads to Part Two through the image of wet snow. The condensed and largely theoretical first part thus culminates in an image which, by an apparent process of free association in the remembrance of things past, triggers in the second part a process of recollection of seemingly repressed or avoided events. The image of wet snow is paradoxical, for it joins the two parts with a bond that is as elusive and insubstantial as wet snow itself. Yet the snow fills a gap between the parts and invites us to interpret it. I offer three more or less plausible interpretations suggested by the text—but they do not entirely account for this seemingly aleatory yet necessary image that has the important function of enabling the transition from Part One to Part Two.

First, the wet, yellow, dingy snow is an obvious symbol of lost purity. Wet snow exists in contrast to a utopia or at least a livable life (what Dostoevsky sometimes refers to as "living life"), a life not distorted by hyperconsciousness, perhaps a life of faith, perhaps something else (a life of both heart and mind?). In the text as we have it, the alternative to wet snow remains as elusive and insubstantial as wet snow itself.

Second, the image of wet snow is related to the writing process. Writing tries to do something with wet snow, to give an account of it:

> Today, for instance, I am particularly oppressed by a certain memory from the distant past. It came back to my mind vividly a few days ago, and since then, has remained with me like an annoying tune that one cannot get rid of. And yet I must get rid of it. I have hundreds of such memories, but at times some single one stands out from the hundreds and oppresses me. For some reason I believe that if I write it down I will get rid of it. Why not try?

Writing is thus to exorcise an obsessive image. Yet Part Two begins with a poem by Nicolai Nekrasov that is blatantly an object of parody. Writing thus does not seem to serve the purpose of working through and exorcizing compulsive or obsessive memories related to the events of the second part.

A third thing recalled or brought to mind by wet snow is the polluting potential of the city where falling snow quickly turns to dirt and mud. The urban environment of the Underground Man is the city of Petersburg, and there is an obvious elective affinity between the man and his city.

> To be hyperconscious is a disease, a real positive disease. Ordinary human consciousness would be too much for man's everyday needs, that is, half or a quarter of the amount which falls to the lot of a cultivated man of our unfortunate nineteenth century, especially one who has the par-

ticular misfortune to inhabit Petersburg, the most abstract and intentional city in the whole world.

Petersburg was literally an abstract and premeditated or intentional city. It was a masterpiece of rationalized urban planning that had no natural foundation: it was built on a bog. And it was illuminated by the northern lights, white lights that Dostoevsky saw as unnatural, demonic. With the white lights, there was no natural rhythm between darkness and light but only continual, eerie illumination. Like his city, the Underground Man is an artificial construct, built on a bog and illuminated by the white lights of a hyperconscious, dissociated lucidity.

The increasing obviousness of these interpretations should serve as a signal that they are not altogether acceptable. The Underground Man seems clearly to be the product of a distorted form of civilization. But in this text the alternative to him is neither a naive utopia of natural simplicity nor a life of unquestioned faith. Nor is the Underground Man a purely negative figure. He is a bewilderingly paradoxical combination of the lowest and the highest in humanity. He is both below and above the statistical norm. The reader is tempted to follow the lead of the introductory authorial note and to see him simply as a case history if not as a convenient scapegoat, but the text brings out his ambivalence in ways that contest giving in to this temptation.

Especially in his weak and evasive side, the Underground Man seems below the common level of humanity. In a more literal translation of the title, he is the man from under the floorboards—a mouse-man. He would, it seems, love to have a fixed identity, even to be known definitively as a lazy person. But he has no clear-cut identity, no "I", and hence his use of the "I" in narration must be paradoxical. His seeming confession avoids the full revelation of himself, which is the ostensible object of the confessional mode. He cannot bare all because he has no "all" to bare. His self or character is split, a fractured nonentity of many contradictory levels and voices. The narrative he employs explores his double or multiple binds. In his ordinary reality, he is abject and desperate, a hole-and-corner man with a perpetual yellow stain on his pants. In his dreams, he is titanic—an overman. Yet his imagination, which fabricates these dreams, is oppressive. It tyrannizes over him. He is perpetually looking at himself as he does something and is petrified by his own look, which internalizes the oppressive look of others. Embittered, frustrated, and resentful in his alienation from society, he tries to make his presence felt and to act by forcing himself on or bumping into others in boorish, ridiculous, or brutal ways. He is forever rattling a non-existent sword. In his inverted existence, suffering and degradation become both masochistic sources of pleasure and sadistic bases for attacks upon others. He is like a stand-up comic of the morbid psyche. At times he is close to being an antiintellectual intellectual who uses logic to destroy logic and who delights in sophistic, self-indulgent, evasive rhetoric.

Yet at least two further points may be made about him. First, his use of irony, parody, and self-parody is in part effective. He does demolish the grounds for narrow, one-sided rationality, closed systems, and simplistic solutions to life's problems. He defends from underground the partially creative force of radical criticism and even of chaos and destruction. He is the bearer of negative capability in a postromantic age, and he insists upon the power of ambivalence and mystery in life's economy. Here his forceful and near hysterical sense of humor plays a crucial role: he laughs and ridicules things into a state that reveals their questionableness. In performing this feat, he is not invidious. He also dismembers, anatomizes, and carnivalizes his own hyperconscious self in a grotesque and convulsive way. He is a lucid juggler, a fool who is diabolical and perhaps a bit holy. At the very least he is unsettling, and he may unsettle the reader. The text can be effective only if the reader *is* unsettled and does not simply look down upon the narrator and his antics.

A second related point is that he may be superior to the unselfconscious reader who relies on simplistic solutions and safe, invidious irony to feel superior to the Underground Man. Baited and berated by his wily adversary, this reader is inclined to carry superficiality to new heights and to rely on ideological complacency to put the Underground Man securely in his place. Yet the Underground Man is already inside this reader in a way that the reader may repress or deny in order to retain a sense of normality and superiority. But the text insistently challenges strategies of avoidance and denial. Not only is the reader actually someone who is reading this book to acquire insight into himself or herself; the reader is made part of the text by the narrative technique itself. The Underground Man addresses the reader as if the reader were a part of himself and of the text. The reader is thus internalized by the Underground Man and may at times be internally persuaded by him. Indeed, the Underground Man and the reader are reciprocally inside one another in an agonistic relation that both courts and evades reciprocity. The force of the text depends upon this mutual internalization and uncanny (non)recognition. If what seems terribly unfamiliar and disconcerting does not register as strangely familiar or at least as inhospitably within the threatened self, the text remains powerless: it makes no claim upon the reader and becomes an inert case history.

In Part One the reader is offered a number of other personae or roles to try on for size—roles even less tenable than that of the Underground Man. These roles or personae are often related to the views of other writers; they are ways the text internalizes other texts or existential options as masks or stylized caricatures. These seeming alternatives to the underground are objects of devastating criticism and uproarious parody: for example, there is the stupid and limited man of action with his relation to the wall; the advocate of the sublime and the beautiful—a parodic version of the romantic beautiful soul; *l'homme de la nature et de la vérité*—a caricature of Rousseau. The obvious question not directly addressed but at least intimated is whether there are other options not so easily reduced to comic-book versions and able to pose more potent challenges to the hyperbolic onslaughts of the Underground Man.

One especially important persona or role model for the

reader in Part One is the ideologist who affirms pure, one-sided rationality that eliminates everything questionable in life and reduces all problems to puzzles. As I indicated earlier, a literary and political source for this model is Chernyshevsky in *What Is to Be Done?*—perhaps too easy an adversary for the Underground Man's polemical verve. The images related to this model are those of the organ stop, the piano key, the chicken coop, the crystal palace, the "two plus two" approach to life. The less caricatural and quite "realistic" object of attack here is the tendency toward an exclusive technological rationality that in its very occlusion of any broader and more internally contested version of reason invites seemingly irrational outbursts and self-indulgent yet self-lacerating refusals.

In one sense, the Underground Man lies by saying that he writes only for himself. All his words are uttered with an almost paranoid sideward glance at the reader. Yet in another sense, his statement is true, for he has already taken the reader into his own split self as an alter ego. His very narrative technique is to anticipate what the reader will say; to undercut, frustrate, or provocatively play with the reader's expectation; to put words into the reader's mouth, refuse to let the reader put words into his mouth, and try to end up thumbing his nose, sticking out his tongue, or perhaps even baring his narrative behind at the reader. Often the Underground Man makes the reader play the role of straight man in burlesque and comic scenes—intellectual analogues of a Punch-and-Judy show. But the Underground Man not only intimidates but also fears the reader, for he both dreads and desperately desires the type of understanding or insight into himself that would enable something approximating communication. This very strong form of ambivalence in him prevents his relation to the reader from being reduced to a classical master-slave dialectic. One cannot sketch out stages of inferiority and superiority or clear-cut procedures of domination and subordination in the life-and-death struggle between the Underground Man and his internalized other. Nor is their labile and mutually implicated agon resolvable in some future totality. Whatever is beyond underground that the Underground Man hopes for yet cannot reach would seem to be different both from his way and from a speculatively "dialectical" *Aufhebung* of it.

In the story itself, the highly complex figure of Apollon is like the reader in certain ways. In a sense he is another persona or mask—an alter ego—internalized by the Underground Man as a fluid projection of himself. Apollon is a servant who is his master's master, yet he has at best a paradoxical, inconclusive master-slave relation to the Underground Man. He is a retainer who should serve the master but who judges him and is tyrannical instead. He is like the Apollonian in relation to the Dionysian, or the superego in relation to the id. He is, however, also part of the Underground Man's fragmented self. At times he even seems like a hallucination or at least a very shadowy figure in a dreamlike world. He is related to the question of distortion, but he is also a belated carnivalesque figure and a mask—a servant who at times behaves like a master in a topsy-turvy world that is devoid of any regulated collective rhythm of social life wherein institutionalized carnival might alternate with work and ordinary life. The Underground Man and Apollon must play it by ear, and their almost Beckettian vis-à-vis, in its shifting, surly, and pathetic interdependence, threatens to be emblematic of relations in general.

The critique of a total system, particularly one of utility or advantage, receives an intriguing (and shockingly contemporary) textual development in section 7 of Part One.

> Oh, tell me, who first declared, who first proclaimed, that man only does nasty things because he does not know his own real interests; and that if he were enlightened, if his eyes were opened to his real normal interests, man would at once cease to do nasty things, would at once become good and noble because, being enlightened and understanding his real advantage, he would see his own advantage in the good and nothing else, and we all know that not a single man can knowingly act to his own disadvantage.

Whoever the first proclaimer of these enlightened tidings may have been, they bring the name of Socrates immediately to mind. "Oh, the babe! Oh, the pure, innocent child!" exclaims the Underground Man, and he is off on his histrionic yet impassioned dismemberment of the "advantage" theory of systematic closure:

> Why, in the first place, when in all these thousands of years has there ever been a time when man has acted only for his own advantage? What is to be done with the millions of facts that bear witness that men, *knowingly,* that is, fully understanding their real advantages, have left them in the background and have rushed headlong on another path, to risk, to chance, compelled to this course by nobody and by nothing, but, as it were, precisely because they did not want the beaten track, and stubbornly, wilfully, went off on another difficult, absurd way seeking it almost in the darkness.

After this pathos-charged invocation of the empirical resistance to closure (which is not fixated as a uniquely modern or modernist phenomenon), the Underground Man raises more conceptual and definitional questions:

> Advantage! What is advantage? And will you take it upon yourself to define with perfect accuracy in exactly what the advantage of man consists of? And what if it so happens that a man's advantage *sometimes* not only may, but even must, consist exactly in his desiring under certain conditions what is harmful to himself and not what is advantageous.

This quasi-philosophical outburst recalls the earlier invocation of masochistic pleasure in pain, "enjoyment [. . .] in the hyperconsciousness of one's own degradation," with no possibility of escape or change for the better. In the face of anticipated laughter as the ridiculing response of his interlocutor, the narrator plays his trump card:

> Why does it happen that all these statisticians, sages and lovers of humanity, when they calculate human advantages invariably leave one out? They don't even take it into their calculation in the form in which it should be taken, and the whole reckoning depends upon that. There would be no great harm to take it, this advantage, and to add it to the list. But the trouble is, that this strange advantage does not fall under any classification and does not figure in any list.

The supplementary advantage that gives the slip to any system of classification paradoxically leads the narrator to the question of the "one most advantageous advantage (the very one omitted of which we spoke just now) which is more important and more advantageous than all other advantages." The paradox here is that to name this advantage would bring it under the very system that it presumably eludes—a quasi-theological situation. Faced with this double bind, the narrator defers mentioning the "most advantageous advantage" and teases the reader with its delayed disclosure. Then, at the end of section 7, he apparently does name it:

> One's own free unfettered choice, one's own fancy, however wild it may be, one's own fancy worked up at times to frenzy—why that is the "most advantageous advantage" which we have overlooked, which comes under no classification and through which all systems and theories are continually thrown to the devil. And how do these sages know that man must necessarily need a rationally advantageous choice? What man needs is simply *independent* choice, whatever that independence may cost and wherever it may lead. Well, choice after all, the devil only knows. . . .

Reducing radical desire to need and naming the "most advantageous advantage" would seem to encompass the supplementary play of excess and lack within the system it deconstructs and displaces. Yet the manner in which the "advantage" is named keeps both its contestatory force and its dubiousness in play. Choice itself is taken to the extreme point of wildness and frenzy, thus transgressing the boundaries implied by choice and naming. Independence itself is stressed with a simplicity that would seem indistinguishable from intransigently obdurate irresponsibility. The section ends with a seemingly aimless ellipsis and a deferment of knowledge to the proverbial devil. Yet in this movement, "choice" has been returned to "chance," which is where the section began before the invocation of the "most advantageous advantage." Thus the revelation is itself *trompe-l'oeil,* and what narrative expectation led one to believe would be an ultimate disclosure or a fully convincing argument becomes caught up in repetition. What is notoriously absent between "chance" and "choice," as both mediation and supplement, is precisely a flexible yet binding structure of relationships or an institutional network of norms and roles that might enable social life to achieve a "livable" rhythm countering both abstract, totalizing systems and the appeal of absolute risk or chance/choice. Given this significant absence, a restless critical animus agitates thought and destroys false "utopian" solutions, but nothing constructive may arise as an alternative to the given, however limited in effect, self-critical in nature, and open to contestatory forces such an alternative must remain. To offer the "filling in" of this absence as a "total solution" to the problems explored in the text would be to encase it in precisely the kind of utilitarian or sociologistic armature that it effectively dismantles. To avoid posing the institutional and social problem as related to a significant modification of the terms explored in the text would be to remain unquestioningly within its limits, turns, and aporetic impasses.

Yet I have already intimated that, especially at two points, the broken but at times critical and funny dialogue activated in the text seems on the verge of exploding, and the momentary hope of a more regenerative dialogue is hinted at, only to be avoided by the Underground Man. Toward the end of Part One, before the appearance of the image of wet snow, the Underground Man seems close to self-insight but immediately resorts to defensiveness, shying away from reciprocity with the reader. "I know myself as surely as two times two makes four, that it is not at all underground that is better, but something different, quite different, for which I long but which I cannot find! Damn underground!" The intrusion of a self-parodic reference to the "two times two" philosophy of life introduces a dissonant note, but the exclamatory force of this statement is still insistent.

In Part Two, in a somewhat analogous place in the text, one has Liza, who also seems to damn the underground and to represent a genuine possibility of communication and self-insight through love. Her potential as a saving grace is enhanced by the fact that it comes after the hysterically ridiculous failure of human contact in the *pas de deux* with the boorish officer on the Nevsky prospect and the abortive scene of renewed friendship with Zverkov and company. Liza, genuinely taken in by the bookish words and fictitious poses of the Underground Man, suffers in a self-sacrificing way that promises hope. She is of course the pure prostitute, and the unavoidable question is whether she is too stereotyped to be altogether credible as the carrier of redemption. Indeed, she too may be read as a parody of a character in Chernyshevsky's *What Is to Be Done?* And the Nekrasov poem that introduces Part Two announces the love scene in an extremely deflationary fashion. Yet, in her love, Liza does seem to have gone beyond the man of resentment, and the Underground Man resents this very fact. Liza makes him feel like a fool because she seems willing to accept him with all his foolishness.

In a gratuitous act that is premeditated but unmotivated, the Underground Man refuses her offer of a seemingly saving love: he places money in her hand and reduces her act to the gesture of a prostitute. As the Underground Man himself puts it, "I can say this for certain: though I did that cruel thing purposely, it was not an impulse from the heart, but came from my evil brain. This cruelty was so affected, so purposely made up, so completely a product of the brain, of *books,* that I could not keep it up for a minute—first I rushed to the corner to avoid seeing her, and then in shame and despair rushed after Liza." Of course, it is too late for the Underground Man. But it is noteworthy that his most vile act is not a product of pure unreason or excess. Rather it has a false model and amounts to a resentful literary gesture—an act of cruelty committed without cruelty.

In a letter to his brother, Dostoevsky intimates that the censors deleted a passage in which he gave his own religious idea of an alternative to the underground. In Part One, section 10 there had been a passage stating that the Underground Man could have been saved by faith and Christ. The obvious question is whether this solution would have seemed highly out of place in the context of the *Notes,* especially if it were not developed in a compelling way, as it is to some extent in *The Brothers Karamazov.* The censors may unknowingly have acted like good literary critics here, although they were probably concerned with eliminating what might have seemed contaminated by blasphemy in such a text. In any case, it is significant that Dostoevsky did not reinsert the deleted passages in subsequent editions of the *Notes.* In the text we have, the path not taken comes in the form of human love and compassion without religious sanction—the offer of love by Liza, an offer warped by its stereotypical frame and outrageously implausible in nature but moving nonetheless.

With Liza gone, the style of the Underground Man toward the end of Part Two reverts to the style of Part One. He writes in the present tense and becomes direct, didactic, and accusatory in addressing or even indicting the reader. He seems to be forcing on the reader the realization that he or she too carries around an encrypted Underground Man.

> Even now, many years later, I somehow remember all this as very bad. I have many bad memories now, but—hadn't I better end my "Notes" here? I believe I made a mistake in beginning to write this *story;* so it's hardly literature so much as corrective punishment. After all, to tell long stories, for example, showing how I have ruined my life by morally rotting in my corner, through lack of fitting environment, through divorce from reality, and vainglorious spite in my underground, would certainly not be interesting; a novel needs a hero, and all the traits of an antihero are *expressly* gathered together here, and what matters most, it all produces an unpleasant impression, for we are all divorced from life, we are all cripples, every one of us, more or less. We are all so far divorced from it that we immediately feel a sort of loathing for actual "real life," and so cannot even stand to be reminded of it. After all, we have reached the point of almost looking at actual "real life" as an effort, almost as hard work, and we are all privately agreed that it is better in books. And why do we sometimes fret, why are we perverse and ask for something else? We don't know why ourselves. It would be worse for us if our capricious requests were granted.

The wary reader might well ask what "actual 'real life'" (or "living life") means, especially in the mouth of the Underground Man, and whether it transcends all the problems explored by him in this far-from-bookish text. It would be easy to agree that "it would be worse for us if our capricious requests were granted." But the statement that we are all crippled, more or less, has a strong impact even if the reader might object to being called a cripple by a cripple who may still be projecting and trying to engender complicity with the reader. Still, these penultimate statements seem forceful because they are the only instances where the dark prince of obliqueness and indirection drops his ironic pose and makes direct and rather pathetic statements. Indeed, these are statements that might open him up to ironic counterattack by a reader whom he, in accordance with his own skewed pedagogical imperative, has helped to educate. For here he seems to expose his face and not simply his behind. To the last, however, the Underground Man anticipates the response of the reader and, unable to shut up, continues:

> "Speak for yourself," you will say, "and for your miseries in your underground holes, but don't dare to say 'all of us.' " Excuse me, gentlemen, after all I do not mean to justify myself with that "all of us." As for what concerns me in particular I have only, after all, in my life carried to an extreme what you have not dared to carry halfway, and what's more, you have taken your cowardice for good sense, and have found comfort in deceiving yourselves. So that perhaps, after all, there is more "life" in me than in you.

In this rather didactic rejoinder, the Underground Man invokes Dostoevsky's highest value—living life. And in rather biblical tones, he seems to appeal to the story of the Good Samaritan, the story of an alien who is closer to virtue than the upright religious officials who pass by a person in need. In any event, toward the end of the text, Dostoevsky seems close to the Underground Man, seems to side with him in the accusations he hurls at the complacent reader enjoying feelings of superiority. But "life" in the passage I just quoted is itself in quotes, as is "real life" (or "living life") in the earlier passage—indicating that Dostoevsky is not willing to place his values in the Underground Man's mouth in an unqualified way. And after this passage, distance is taken from the Underground Man in a manner different from but reminiscent of the author's gesture in the note to the title of the text. The question is whether in these gestures Dostoevsky opens the possibility for a "dialogue" or exchange with the reader who does not feel securely superior to the Underground Man but who does agree that something different is desirable.

The last words of the text follow a break (indicated by a line in the Matlaw translation): "The 'notes' of this paradoxicalist do not end here, however. He could not resist and continued them. But it also seems to me that we may stop here." There is no ending to the notes of the Underground Man. After evading the possibility (however problematic) of a certain kind of "ending" in love, there is no ending to the infinite series of paradoxes and vicious circles he can generate. The Underground Man may go on cutting capers until he kicks off. The text has no satisfying ending, and so it is arbitrarily terminated. Yet an arbitrary termination may paradoxically be the only plausible ending to this kind of text—one that, like the image of wet snow, is both aleatory and necessary.

This terminal passage has a clear shift in voice, but the direction of the shift is not clear. Unlike the introductory note, the final passage bears no signature. Who terminates the text as the great liquidator? Who are the "me" and the "we" referred to in the seeming *hors-texte?* Who contractually agrees to stop here? One can give no self-certain and

definite answer to these questions. In a sense, language has come to its limits, at least in this discursive context. One might, however, suggest that this "ending" that is not an ending terminates the complicity between the author and the Underground Man and opens up the possibility of a relationship between the (reversible roles of) writer and reader in the context of a more general "textuality." (Indeed, it is dubious to continue, as I have done, to follow the established convention of employing the name, "the Underground Man," to designate the narrator, for it gives him a nominal consistency and a semblance of a unified self that the text itself questions and that the concluding passage obliterates.)

The text of the ***Notes*** provides no answers to the questions it raises; it restricts itself to intimations of the need for another way. Marking its own limits, it thus refuses any purely symbolic or cathartic solution to the problems it has explored with hyperbolic insistence and intensity. But in shifting grounds and opening the text to a problematic writer-reader relation that is emblematic of relations "outside" this text (in its delimited and conventional specificity), this parodic, paradoxical, and extremely "modern" text may come close to older forms of parable from which it differs markedly—notably in its self-conscious difficulty in coming to an end. (pp. 35-55)

> *Dominick LaCapra, "Notes on Dostoevsky's 'Notes from Underground',"* in his *History, Politics, and the Novel,* Cornell University Press, 1987, pp. 35-55.

FURTHER READING

Abood, Edward F. "Fyodor Dostoevsky: *Notes from Underground."* In his *Underground Man,* pp. 13-29. San Francisco: Chandler & Sharp Publishers, 1973.

> Addresses *Notes from the Underground* as a satire of Chernyshevsky's *What Is to Be Done?* and determines that "by a curious twist, Underground Man and his imaginary opponents of Part I end up in the same camp. Like them, he is first and foremost an intellectual, who attempts to confine experience within a theoretical framework devoid of passion and impulse."

Beatty, Joseph. "From Rebellion and Alienation to Salutary Freedom: A Study in *Notes from Underground." Soundings* LXI, No. 2 (Summer 1978): 182-205.

> Examines *Notes* in an effort to "exhibit a deeper, more satisfying account of freedom than that of rebellious, irrational caprice."

Beebe, Maurice, and Newton, Christopher. "Dostoevsky in English: A Selected Checklist of Criticism and Translations." *Modern Fiction Studies* 4, No. 3 (Autumn 1958): 271-91.

> Selected bibliography of studies about Dostoevsky organized according to individual works, including *Notes from the Underground.*

Bercovitch, Sacvan. "Dramatic Irony in *Notes from the Un-*

derground." The Slavic and East European Journal VIII, No. 3 (Spring 1964): 284-91.

> Espies the self-deception of the narrator of *Notes from the Underground,* contending that he attempts to justify his life by presenting it as the result of choice, though dramatic irony, evident "in the unspoken but implicit truth," reveals that "his 'free choice' rests in every case upon a false alternative."

Bouson, J. Brooks. "Narcissistic Vulnerability and Rage in Dostoevsky's *Notes from Underground.*" In his *The Empathic Reader: A Study of the Narcissistic Character and the Drama of the Self,* pp. 33-50. Amherst: The University of Massachusetts Press, 1989.

> Analyzes the ways in which the readers of *Notes from the Underground* "become implicated in the pathological drama enacted in the text, caught up in the same narcissistic script the anti-hero stages with the imaginary gentlemen."

Cardaci, Paul F. "Dostoevsky's Underground as Allusion and Symbol." *Symposium* XXVIII, No. 3 (Fall 1974): 248-58.

> Examines the idea of the underground in *Notes from the Underground* as a symbol that "not only defines the conflict, the narrator, but also brings together structure, character, and theme to give the work its essential unity."

Carrier, Warren. "Artistic Form and Unity in *Notes from Underground.*" *Renascence* XVI, No. 3 (Spring 1964): 142-45.

> Study of the structure of *Notes from the Underground,* which is called "a compelling artistic whole": "The final movement of the story is circular; we begin with the situation of Part One, move to Part Two to discover its active origin, return to Part One, in effect, since chronologically it precedes."

Consigny, Scott. "The Paradox of Textuality: Writing as Entrapment and Deliverance in *Notes from Underground.*" *Canadian-American Slavic Studies* 12, No. 3 (Fall 1978): 341-52.

> Contends that the underground man is trapped by "textuality" and his own "literariness" and, therefore, cannot directly perceive "reality." Consigny further argues that the underground man's use of paradox and other rhetorical devices leads readers to the "paradoxical recognition . . . that when we understand the underground man's text, we may be able to abandon it" and escape the entrapment of textuality.

Darring, Gerald, and Darring, Walter. "Dostoevsky's Prophetic *Notes.*" *Genre* VI, No. 4 (December 1973): 388-403.

> Interprets *Notes from the Underground* as part of a trilogy, together with Dostoevsky's *Notes from the House of the Dead* and *Winter Notes on Summer Impressions,* that contains "an allegory of life." The Darrings determine that "the testimony of our social experience, as Dostoevsky has forseen it, is that the bases of morality . . . have failed."

Fagin, N. Bryllion. "Dostoevsky's Underground Man Takes Over." *The Antioch Review* XIII, No. 1 (March 1953): 23-32.

> Acknowledges the warning offered by *Notes from the Underground* of the capriciousness of the "secret self" and exposes the incompatibility of Soviet socialist doctrine and Dostoevsky's emphasis on the individual.

Frank, Joseph. "*Notes from Underground.*" In his *Dostoevsky: The Stir of Liberation, 1860-1865,* pp. 310-47. Princeton, N.J.: Princeton University Press, 1986.

> Claims that *Notes from the Underground* is a literary milestone in Dostoevsky's artistic development. While Frank's analysis of the work is extensive, his position remains essentially the same as expressed in an essay published earlier in his career [see excerpt dated 1961].

Fremantle, Anne; Simmons, Ernest J.; and Bryson, Lyman. "Feodor Dostoevsky: *Notes from Underground.*" *The Invitation to Learning Reader* 6, Nos. 2/3 (April-June 1956): 137-44.

> Transcript of a general discussion of *Notes from the Underground* that was first broadcast May 20, 1956.

Gregg, Richard. "Apollo Underground: His Master's Still, Small Voice." *The Russian Review* 32, No. 1 (January 1973): 64-71.

> Freudian analysis of Apollon's function in *Notes from the Underground* in which Gregg finds a "singular congruency" between the manservant's function and the role of the superego.

Hall, J. R. "Abstraction in Dostoyevsky's *Notes from the Underground.*" *The Modern Language Review* 76, No. 1 (January 1981): 129-37.

> Perceives in the narrator of *Notes from the Underground* an abstract intellectualism that degenerates progressively into solipsism and allows his position to be undermined in the eyes of the reader.

Holquist, Michael. "The Search for a Story: *White Nights, Winter Notes on Summer Impressions,* and *Notes from the Underground.*" In his *Dostoevsky and the Novel,* pp. 35-74. Princeton, N.J.: Princeton University Press, 1977.

> Maintains that the narrator of *Notes from the Underground* must shape his experiences into stories to imbue his life with meaning and order. "Perhaps it is the case that *in order* to live, men are condemned to tell [stories]," Holquist concludes.

Jones, Malcolm V. "*Notes from Underground:* The Cult of Perversity." In his *Dostoyevsky: The Novel of Discord,* pp. 55-66. London: Elek Books Ltd., 1976.

> Contends that the narrator of *Notes from the Underground* views perversity as a rebuke to rationalism and scientific determinism.

————. "Dostoevsky: *Notes from Underground.*" In *The Voice of a Giant: Essays on Seven Russian Prose Classics,* pp. 55-65, edited by Roger Cockrell and David Richards. Exeter, England: University of Exeter, 1985.

> Maintains that "the Underground Man's philosophical attitudes are rooted not only in contemporary cultural and philosophical views, but also in his own personality disorder. In trying to resolve the philosophical question he is also trying to resolve his spiritual problems, and in both he fails."

Leatherbarrow, William J. "Enlightened Malevolence III: *Notes from Underground.*" In his *Fedor Dostoevsky,* pp. 63-8. Twayne's World Authors Series, A Survey of the World's Literature: Russia, edited by Charles A. Moser. Boston: Twayne Publishers, 1981.

> Observes that *Notes from the Underground* is "perhaps the greatest critique of narrow intellectualism and over-

refined consciousness ever written, as well as a disturbing rejection of the ideals of the Enlightenment."

Lednicki, Waclaw. "Dostoevsky—The Man from Underground." In his *Russia, Poland and the West: Essays in Literary and Cultural History,* pp. 180-248. New York: Roy Publishers, 1954.

    Enumerates the literary influences on Dostoevsky's *Notes from the Underground,* focusing on the importance of Pushkin and Turgenev.

Lethcoe, James. "Self-Deception in Dostoevskij's *Notes from the Underground.*" *The Slavic and East European Journal* X, No. 1 (Spring 1966): 9-21.

    Concludes that self-deception is a major theme in *Notes from the Underground* and that "recognition of this theme provides a satisfactory explanation for the claims of . . . critics that the underground man's testimony is unreliable." Lethcoe makes extensive use of quotations from the Russian text of *Notes from the Underground.*

Nabokov, Vladimir. *"Memoirs from a Mousehole."* In *Vladimir Nabokov: Lectures on Russian Literature,* edited by Fredson Bowers, pp. 115-25. New York: Harcourt Brace Jovanovich, 1981.

    Commentary on the style of *Notes from the Underground,* which Nabokov calls "the best picture we have of Dostoevski's themes and formulas and intonations."

Peace, Richard. "Early Writing and *Notes from Underground.*" In his *Dostoyevsky: An Examination of the Major Novels,* pp. 1-18. London: Cambridge University Press, 1971.

    Views Dostoevsky's *Notes from the Underground* as "an introduction to his major novels." According to Peace, the work evinces "a strong polemical element" and rejects the romantic idealism of the 1840s as well as Chernyshevsky's philosophy of enlightened self-interest ("rational egoism") of the 1860s.

Pfleger, Karl. "Dostoievsky, the Man from the Underworld." In his *Wrestlers with Christ,* translated by E. I. Watkin, pp. 185-220. New York: Sheed & Ward, 1937.

    Includes commentary on the despairing and demonic quality of *Notes from the Underground* in a discussion of the interplay between Dostoevsky's Christian faith and his writing.

Powys, John Cowper. "Memoirs from the Underground." In his *Dostoievsky,* pp. 82-7. London: John Lane The Bodley Head, 1946.

    Discusses the psychology of the narrator of *Notes from the Underground,* declaring that Dostoevsky's work "is a revelation of the power of the lonely, self-existent, unpropitiated human mind."

Rice, Martin P. "Dostoevskii's *Notes from Underground* and Hegel's 'Master and Slave.'" *Canadian-American Slavic Studies* 8, No. 3 (Fall 1974): 359-69.

    Compares sections of Hegel's *Phenomenology* with Dostoevsky's *Notes from the Underground,* observing that *Notes* "appears to be the complete artistic exposition of the psychological and philosophical insights contained in Hegel's understanding of the development of consciousness."

Sanborn, Pat. "Nasty Pleasures in *Notes from Underground.*" *North Dakota Quarterly* 54, No. 2 (Spring 1986): 200-11.

    Detects an analysis of pleasure in *Notes from the Under-

ground* that involves frank scrutiny of traditional conceptions of pleasure. Sanborn suggests that the underground man's identification of pain and despair as sources of satisfaction necessitates a revaluation of pleasure.

Scott, Nathan A., Jr. "Dostoevski—Tragedian of the Modern Excursion into Unbelief." In *The Tragic Vision and the Christian Faith,* edited by Nathan A. Scott, Jr., pp. 189-210. New York: Association Press, 1957.

    Includes the narrator of *Notes from the Underground* among Dostoevsky's central characters who struggle in a modern existential void caused by secularism. Scott asserts that the narrator "is a captive to the awful solitude that overtakes the human spirit when it finds itself inhabiting a world from which the gracious reality of 'Presence' has been banished."

Simmons, Ernest J. *"Notes from the Underground."* In his *Dostoevsky: The Making of a Novelist,* pp. 98-111. London: John Lehmann, 1950.

    Study of *Notes from the Underground* with a strong biographical influence, focusing especially on Dostoevsky's affair with Polina Suslova.

Smalley, Barbara. "The Compulsive Patterns of Dostoyevsky's Underground Man." *Studies in Short Fiction* 10, No. 4 (Fall 1973): 389-96.

    Argues that the narrator's compulsive personality bars attainment of the freedom that he seeks: "The underground man's brilliant exposition of his right to caprice and choice is at one and the same time his brilliant demonstration that for him no such power of choice is possible."

Spilka, Mark. "Playing Crazy in the Underground." *The Minnesota Review* VI, No. 3 (1966): 233-43.

    Likens the conscious perversity of the narrator of *Notes from the Underground* to behavioral traits observed in the borderline psychotic personality.

Traschen, I. "Dostoyevsky's *Notes from Underground.*" *Accent* XVI, No. 4 (Autumn 1956): 255-64.

    Describes Dostoevsky's attitude toward the narrator of *Notes from the Underground* as "ambiguous" and declares the narrator's romanticism and godless intellectualism sterile.

Troyat, Henry. *"Notes from the Underground."* In his *Firebrand: The Life of Dostoevsky,* translated by Norbert Guterman, pp. 248-90. New York: Roy Publishers, 1946.

    Discusses the underground man as a representative type in Dostoevsky's fiction and identifies the figure in several of the author's works in addition to *Notes from the Underground.*

Wasiolek, Edward. *"Notes from the Underground* and Dostoevsky's Moral Dialectic." In his *Dostoevsky: The Major Fiction,* pp. 39-59. Cambridge, Mass.: The M.I.T. Press, 1964.

    Perceives a moral dialectic in *Notes from the Underground* in which the universal happiness represented by the Crystal Palace is achieved at the expense of individuality and aberration. Ironically, Wasiolek observes, as a result of this opposition "the very aberrational traits for which the Crystal Palace is a solution become elevated into traits of universal value."

Weisberg, Richard. "An Example Not to Follow: *Ressenti-*

ment and the Underground Man." *Modern Fiction Studies* 21, No. 4 (Winter 1975-76): 553-63.

> Declares that the "fundamental truth" of *Notes from the Underground* is: "Not all overly developed intellects are admirable, and . . . a life defined by literary formulations and a total absence of social spontaneity cannot produce a 'free' or useful philosophy."

Wilson, Colin. "The Question of Identity." In his *The Outsider*, pp. 147-77. Boston: Houghton Mifflin Co., 1956.

> Discussion of the identity of the outsider as depicted in literature. Wilson cites *Notes from the Underground* as "the first major treatment of the Outsider theme in modern literature," adding that it conveys "the tortured, self-divided nature" of this figure.

Yarmolinsky, Avrahm. "Ends and Beginnings." In his *Dostoevsky: His Life and Art,* pp. 177-92. New Jersey: S. G. Phillips, 1957.

> Describes the events of Dostoevsky's life surrounding the writing of *Notes from the Underground* and the influence of Chernyshevsky's philosophy of enlightened self-interest. Yarmolinsky closes his consideration of the novella with the following claim: "The importance of *Notes from the Underground* is out of proportion to the size of the piece. The ideas of which it is the vehicle are essential to [Dostoevsky's] later, more massive works."

Mihail Eminescu

1850-1889

(Also Mihai Eminescu; born Mihail Imin or Emin; surname changed to Iminovici or Eminovici) Romanian poet, dramatist, and journalist.

Eminescu is considered the foremost Romanian poet of the nineteenth century and the leading exemplar of Romanticism in Romanian literature. His use of Romanian folklore in his works and his frequent portrayal of Romanian peasants have led to his reputation as his country's national poet. Aurel Martin has described Eminescu as "a superlative expression of ethnical sensibility, a voice authorized and competent to represent the Romanian nation in mankind's concert."

Eminescu was born in a region of northern Moldavia rich in cultural and historical traditions. He spent his childhood exploring the Romanian countryside, learning the folktales and legends that would later play a prominent role in his poetry. In 1866, at the age of sixteen, he left home to travel with a theatrical company as prompter and copyist; his first poems were published in *Familia,* a Budapest periodical, at this time. In 1869 Eminescu entered the University of Vienna to study philosophy. The following year several of Eminescu's poems were published in the influential periodical *Convorbiri literare,* issued by the literary society Junimea, marking the beginning of critical recognition of his works. In 1872 Junimea contributed financially to Eminescu's further education in Berlin, where he was exposed to German Romantic literature and was influenced by Arthur Schopenhauer's philosophy of pessimism. After two years of study in Berlin, Eminescu moved to the Romanian city of Iaşi, where he worked as director of the University Central Library. This position enabled him to extensively research the medieval literature and folklore of Romania. In 1877, Eminescu moved to Bucharest, accepting a position as editor of *Timpul,* an important daily newspaper. During the next six years, Eminescu wrote prolifically, producing most of his poetry in addition to abundant journalistic work. Eminescu's creative output ceased in 1883 when he first displayed symptoms of a debilitating mental illness attributable to inherited syphilis. He died in a Bucharest asylum in 1889.

Eminescu believed that a significant national literature was essential to the formation of a national identity: "Each national literature is the focus of the national spirit, upon which rays converge from every direction of spiritual life." As a young poet, Eminescu was enthralled with the revolutionary heroes of Romania's recent past, and he extolled the virtues of the common people, speaking for those he felt to be victims of oppressive authority. These sentiments are expressed most vividly in such early poems as "Împărat şi proletar" ("Emperor and Proletarian") and "Inger şi Demon" ("Angel and Demon"). Zoe Dumitrescu-Buşulenga notes that, although Eminescu remained a champion of the oppressed throughout his life,

after seeing many revolutionary struggles fail throughout Europe, he became convinced that "evil and selfishness were omnipotent." Biographers conclude that this disillusionment with contemporary society increased Eminescu's tendency to delve into an idealized past. "Călin," considered one of his most important poems, fuses the epic and lyric genres, combining medieval legend with idyllic descriptions of the Romanian countryside and the virtues of peasant life. In his later works Eminescu explored, as Dumitrescu-Buşulenga has explained, "the philosophic problem of human existence . . . and more especially that of the condition of the genius." Eminescu's masterpiece "Luceafărul" ("Hyperion") reflects this theme in its depiction of what Eminescu perceived as the immeasurable distance between the genius and the rest of humanity.

Although his popular and critical success during his lifetime was limited, Eminescu is now considered by many critics to be the greatest poet in Romanian literature. Expressing his theory of Eminescu's influence, Nicolae Iorga has stated: "No other writer of his time possessed his wonderful gift of creating a perfect synthesis, in which all the influences of the period, wedded to his own powerful and pure voice, resolve themselves into a single harmony."

PRINCIPAL WORKS

Poesii (poetry) 1884
[*Poems,* 1980]

Zoe Dumitrescu-Buşulenga   (essay date 1976)

[*In the following essay, Dumitrescu-Buşulenga discusses Eminescu as a representative author of the Romantic movement in nineteenth-century European literature.*]

Mihai Eminescu is the last romantic poet in European literature and he preserved in his life and work the romantic artists' characteristics. Continually aspiring after a higher ethic and artistic life, searching the truth with pathos and consistently refusing compromises, Eminescu was permanently in conflict with the people of his time, because of his non-conforming attitude, of the sincerity in the facts of his life and the loftiness of his thinking.

His youth, nourished by the memories of 1848 of his dearest teacher Aron Pumnul, is that of a former ardent man of forty-eight. He experienced intensely certain moments of remarkable social dynamics, on the European plane—the Italian *Resorgimento* around the sixties, then the Paris Commune—during the time when he was a student in Vienna. This rebellious passion, this "Sturm und Drang" passion pervades all the poet's *juvenilia* (we are referring to the poems **"Horia"** and **"Andrei Mureşan," "Corrupt Youth," "Angel and Daemon," "Emperor and Proletarian"** and reaches a climax in the novel of the revolution of 1848 in Transylvania **Barren Genius.** For Eminescu this is the time when he worshipped the men of forty-eight, as the poem **"Epigones"** reveals and so many other testimonies too. In this first stage of the Eminescian thinking and creative work, the poet took a great interest in the ideas and culture of the European peoples who were continuing the struggle for freedom. The young man—as Ibrăileanu too shows in *The Critical Spirit in Romanian Culture*—was carefully following what was happening in France and Italy and he saw in Victor Hugo the "bard of liberty"; he became acquainted with the Romantic sources through the French romanticists taken over by Romanian writers such as Vasile Alecsandri, Ion Heliade Rădulescu, Dimitrie Bolintineanu. But the successive defeats of the revolutions gradually made him think it was impossible to interfere in the social and moral life in which he believed ever more firmly that evil and selfishness were omnipotent. Naturally, besides this, there was the heavy burden of personal disappointments which began very early, the humiliations expressed so distressingly in his future **"Epistles."** It was under these circumstances, decisive for Eminescu, that he became acquainted with Schopenhauer, with his philosophy—the expression of a moment of fatigue and disappointment (and which, by no means casually, had be-

come popular in Germany only after 1851). The bitter disappointment Eminescu felt became more pronounced under the combined influences of these circumstances, which created in the poet the orientation towards the "archaic myth", towards "Dacism" and mediaevalism which he now considered "Golden ages." This transition from Titanic rebellion to conservatism or to metaphysics was peculiar to European romanticism more especially to the early generation of English romantic poets. It is less pronounced in Wordsworth's poetry, but very manifest in Coleridge's and Southey's poems. The difference, however, between Eminescu and the English romantics consists in the permanence of what we might call the "demophile" passion. His attachment to the people, his love for the "people of destitution," for the peasant and for the "positive" classes—which he saw were becoming more and more oppressed by the growing capitalism—lasted throughout his life, constituting, as a matter of fact, the substance of the political articles he published from 1877 on in the daily *Timpul* (The Time).

Broadly speaking, the stage that followed is divided between romanticism and neo-classicism. Under the potent influence of Romanian folklore and of German romanticism, which he had a thorough knowledge of, Eminescu clarified his poetical retina and lent great transparence to the substance of his sensitiveness, while his expression acquired more and more musical modulations. A delightful paradisiacal nature, the nature of Romania transfigured according to the models of folklore, entered his universe, enriching it with the exceptional freshness of places after which he keeps aspiring. Likewise folklore itself appears under a great many aspects and will be, until the end, the model of perfection and the guarantee of a contact with the perennial sources of the folk spirit.

From **"Hapless Dionis"** to **"The Morning Star,"** the philosophic problem of human existence is raised and more especially that of the condition of the genius, implied in the romantic interpretation of certain myths (Lucifer, Hyperion) in which the solution is given by consolation through absolute cognition which, when he was a youth, accompanied love and towards the end he dispensed with (but with how much suffering!). As he was nearing maturity, Eminescu was more and more haunted by the idea of classical perfection. "The eye of the ancient world" meant for him perfection; as a matter of fact Homer (as well as Kalidasa and Shakespeare) was for the Romanian poet an ideal to attain. Indeed, his last works express his aspiration after classicism by trying to objectify the sufferings of his personal condition and by tempering his romantic violences, an aspiration which manifested itself both under the influence of the classical models and under that of folklore, considered by Eminescu a classical source *par excellence.*

The whole of Eminescu's work belongs, however, to the most typical works of European romanticism. It sprang from a characteristic attitude towards romanticism, from a dimension of this spirit, the absolute aspiration after a demiurgic domination of the world. Hence, in his youth, the impulse to overthrow the world and rebuild it, then, in full maturity, his aspiration after the domination of the world by means of philosophic cognition, by absolute cognition.

Helped by a most fecund genius and by a vast culture, Eminescu created a highly original vision of the world, which makes him both similar to romantic creators and, at the same time, singles him out among them. Overthrowing the objective laws of the world, on a cosmic scale, he resorted to folklore and to ancient myths and built a universe of his own which lives in every fragment of his work, published during his life or after his death.

The poet followed up numerous aspects of life in most of its elements, from cosmogony to apocalypse, from the beginnings of the world to its end. The heavens and the sea, as fundamental sources of life, were permanently made use of. The heavenly bodies helped him in the daring cosmic flights which his fantasy undertook deep down into the depths of creation, for he explored with "gigantic imagination" the inter-sidereal spaces, he measured the Einstein distances in light-years (**"To the Star"**); with Hyperion he dived into the galaxies and reached near the active centre of the universe, thirsting, as he was, after the absolute (**"Hapless Dionis," "1st Epistle," "The Morning Star"**). Eminescu was not fascinated, as all romantics were, only by the strange nocturnal light of the moon, he only wished to send the demiurgic forces of the genius to this still unexplored heavenly body. **"Hapless Dionis,"** a fantastic short story, proves what is in European romanticism a new way of dealing with the Luciferic myth, with specific quests and solutions; the poet builds new worlds on the moon, attempting to make up for the imperfection of the only one known so far, the one he lived in, by increasing the number of suns and morning stars in the universe, by remaking a luxuriant paradisiacal nature in which the magus-genius can take refuge only with his beloved.

Actuated by the same thirst for perfection, Eminescu divided the world into two parts: one was the zone of the eternal creatures, which he had become acquainted with through a neo-Platonic gnostic philosophy or the traditions of popular books he knew so well, and a second one, that of the mortals, those who "lived under a lucky star or were persecuted by fate." He aspired intensely after the former at the time of his daring youth, investigating the initial causes, trying to wring from them their secrets, achieving syntheses based on Romanian history and spirituality (starting from the Dacian philosophy, alleged to have been related to the Hindu one, to neo-Platonism and gnosis, as we have already mentioned above). He admitted he was defeated in his riper age, but found consolation in philosophic cognition.

Like all great poets, Eminescu often dealt with the problem of time in his work. For each of the two worlds he let two kinds of time flow: a cosmic time correlated to continuous creation, and another time commensurate with the mortals. The passing of the macrotime had no effect on the great life of the immortals who live in spheres where vicissitudes are absent. As for the mortals, time means the first source of the drama. And as he grew older, Eminescu granted ever more importance to meditations on time, which acquired a specific timbre in European romanticism. The enormous distance between childhood and the moment of the loss of childhood, measured in time, overwhelmed the lyrical hero who feels it everywhere in the poetry of his riper age as a dark ghost. Time makes the thrill of the great cosmic mystery disappear in him, the thrill usually felt at sunset (**"Like Clouds Have Passed the Years . . ."**). The isolation, the solitude which time and the loss of love contribute to, ring dolefully in **"From the Waves of Time,"** where lovers get lost like monads in the huge, merciless billows of the same time whose effects are felt everywhere with excruciating keenness. But at times, an attempt at emerging from time (such as for instance in (**"Passing by the Odd Number of Poplars"**) through the feeling of perenniality of the genius, suggests the existence of another dimension which is eternal; when confronted with this new dimension, the existence in time appears still more distressing.

As a matter of fact, speaking philosophically, Eminescu's attitude to time differs as we follow it up from his youth to his disappointed riper age. Bitterly hostile to time as all romantics were, who employed the most varied practices and perspectives in order to vanquish it, he wanted, like the German romantics, like Hoffmann or Novalis, to abolish its baneful effects on man. Thus he too imagined magic practices (the magus very frequent in Eminescu's work is one more proof of his demiurgic aspirations) as in **"Hapless Dionis," "The Tale of the Magus Travelling in the Stars," "The Ghosts"** as well as the ancient idea of metempsychosis which allows him to walk unhindered along the dimensions of time, thus defeated (**"The Avatars of Pharaoh Tla," "Hapless Dionis"**).

On the other hand, later, when his youthful demiurgic daring feats ceased, he tried to deny time, showing in his poetry that the dimensions of the past and of the future were nothing but illusions and that the whole existence happens in a continuous present (**"You Add Tomorrow to Your Days"**). The Buddhist philosophy, the neo-Platonic one, then Kant, the German romantic philosophy, from Fichte and Schelling to Schopenhauer, gave him in turns the satisfaction of following up certain difficult and learned constructions which he expressed in verse, in a synthesis of personal thinking, replete with senses and ideas. Eminescu was to such an extent a thinking poet first of all, a poet of ideas, that both his lyrical poetry of folklore inspiration and his love poetry (nevertheless so preponderant in the whole of his work) bear the stamp of his thinking, of philosophic significances.

Folklore was the area where the poet always met his own people, an area in which Eminescu kept moving uninterruptedly, from his young age to the end. Both the English and the German romantic poets made full use of folklore in their poetry and in their prose; their aim was to revive the Middle Ages long gone by, to achieve picturesqueness and to refresh the national lyrical sources. Eminescu discovered folklore by instinct, at a very early age, in his adolescence he even grew up in it, considering that he spent his childhood like any other peasant's son. He made use of it in his work only later, starting from the Viennese period and, most likely, under the theoretical influence of Herder and the German romantic school.

For Eminescu folklore became a school he attended uninterruptedly and from which he learned a specific kind of wisdom, the philosophy of his own people and the consummate clarity of the form. Unlike other European romanticists, Eminescu tried to fully identify himself with popular creation, with its aesthetic and philosophic features, by penetrating with care and toil into folklore. Thus, from 1869-1870, his work was permeated with all the species and constituent elements of folklore. When he published the tale **"Prince Charming the Tear-Born,"** he was imbued with the reminiscences of the fantastic in the German romantic literature, the same when he finished **"Călin—Leaves from a Fairy Tale,"** in which I seem to detect sure traces of his recent reading of the novel Heinrich von Ofterdingen by Novalis. But everything was filtered through his genuine Romanian mind and through a solid, autochthonous, undeniable vision. And the love poetry of his brighter period was expressed, like his fairy tales, in autochthonous landscapes and personages (**"The Fairy Tale Queen," "Prince Charming of the Lime Tree," "The Tale of the Lime Tree,"** and others).

In the poems of folklore inspiration, the poet's meditation on time and on human life continues in a very unusual form for the world romantic literature. For example, in a piece of poetry such as **"Forest, Oh My Forest"** the "wanderer's" admiring questions, when he comes back to his native forests (Forest dear, with quiet streams / All in this world flowing seem / Time goes past but only thou / still art young and younger now), the forest answers with indifferent superiority: "What is time, when every night / Shines for me the stars' peaceful light" . . . For the forest, an eternal element for the Romanian romantic, time does not flow, it has no power over the forest. But against this background of the eternity of nature (present in Rousseau, Herder, Schiller) "Man alone is changeable / A Wanderer on earth . . . " This creates again a dramatic contrast for the human condition, from the angle of time.

Eminescu's contribution to European romantic love poetry is also original, more especially in point of the ideas connected with love, in point of the philosophic aspect he lends to love. The poet tried to fully achieve his own personality in love too, as a corollary of his aspirations after the absolute. This supreme, superior function of love appears in the diversity of the aspects in which love accompanies Eminescu's hero: as a rebel (**"Angel and Daemon," Barren Genius**), as a wanderer among the stars and a demiurge (**"Hapless Dionis"**), but more especially as an artist and a creator (**"Epistles IV"** and **"V"**). Love plays a great part in the Eminescian personality, associated with the loftiest intellectual and spiritual activities. And in this sense we can find philosophic equivalences in the love poetry of the "dolce stil nuovo", where the woman "donna angelicata" transforms the artist's intellectual, moral, spiritual potentialities into fact, or in Goethe where "Das ewig Weibliche" becomes the same as the neo-classical idea of the "beautiful soul" embodied in a few of the women in *Wilhelm Meister* or *Iphigenia auf Tauris,* so beneficent for the man near them.

With Eminescu the angel-woman appeared at the beginning of his poetical career, a sign of his great trust in woman and more especially in the sense of her love for the creator. He conferred on woman a noble role and a unique dignity and associated her, by the perfection of purity and the depth of affection he thought she feels, to his demiurgic work. It was only when he was unhappy in love—his individual drama with no chances of return—that he renounced, subjectively and grieved, the philosophic idea that woman was fated to grasp or to arouse in the creator specific powers.

As regards the technique of his verses, the Eminescian poetics in his riper age holds again an interesting and original place in Romantic poetics. I mentioned his creative road oriented from its very beginnings (which were a sort of *Sturm und Drang* for him) towards a musicality and an imagery free especially from any contact with German romanticism and later towards a neo-classicism in which the romantic grandiloquence was ever more moderate, the same as the expression of his own sufferings expressed in fine, softer tones. But with Eminescu there existed, as the Magyar professor Láslo Gáldi pointed out, unlike with other Romantics, an evolution towards new values of poetical expression, opening up the way to a technique of highest musical suggestions, like that of the symbolists, but without renouncing accessibility. Pieces of poetry such as **"And If the Branches . . .",** some of the sonnets (especially **"When Even the Voice of Thoughts Is Silent"**), the great poem **"The Morning Star"** attain a very lofty degree in poetical expression, all the more so as the most profound thoughts are perfectly well conveyed, intensified by the perfect essential word.

Thus all the motifs of European romanticism are present in Eminescu's poetry too, which is an entire universe of ideas and images, a unitary personal universe, although all the ideas and the motifs had been present in almost one century of pre-romanticism and romanticism. But they belong to him due to the final melting in the crucible of his personal vision of the world expressed in what we generally call "Eminescian style". The modality in which every motif is renewed, its integration in a conception and a new original vision lending it new values, equally open to the data of national culture and to those of universal culture, is the modality with which any great poet of the world compels recognition. And Eminescu is one of them. (pp. 68-71)

> *Zoe Dumitrescu-Buşulenga, "A Great Romantic: Mihai Eminescu," in* Romanian Review, *Vol. 30, No. 1, 1976, pp. 68-71.*

Aurel Martin   (essay date 1978)

[*In the following essay, Martin focuses on Eminescu as the national poet of Romania.*]

Who is Mihai Eminescu? Any Romanian will answer, without a moment's thinking: Our national poet. In other words, a superlative expression of ethnical sensibility, a voice authorized and competent to represent the Romanian nation in mankind's concert, the axiological synthesis of the historical moment, one of the greatest lyrical poets of world literature, comparable—in his uniqueness—with Byron, Hugo, Hölderlin, Leopardi, Lermontov, Petöfi,

Mickiewic, therefore with the luminaries of European Romanticism. A revolutionary poet in terms of attitude, of modality, of metaphorical approach and manner, of background and outlook, of trailblazing, a man of his own times, actively present in the immediacy of the "there and then", divining the valences of the primordial, envisaging perspectives and acquiring an unmistakable timbre for his voice. The voice of a poet whose life-span only lasted 39 years (1850-1889), whose creative manifestation ended at 33 years—the moment when his only volume printed during his life-time appeared—yet bequeathing to posterity an inestimable treasure of verse, of rough versions and variants—illustrative in themselves, on the scale of the idea of a model. A model in which Romanian neo-romantics as well as neo-classicists, symbolists as well as avant-garde poets, found their parent. In fact this holds good for the entire Romanian poetry of the 20th century. Lucian Blaga and George Bacovia, Tudor Arghezi and Ion Pillat, Alexandru Philippide and Mihai Beniuc, Emil Botta as well as Geo Bogza and Nichita Stănescu no less than Ioan Alexandru, very much as countless other poets. Each of them particularizing a certain colour of Eminescu's spectrum, one of his options in point of themes, one or another of his existential queries, one area of the universe which he investigated gnoseologically. Each of them claiming descendence from Eminescu in point of problems tackled. From Him seen as a Demiurge. Crisscrossing the continent of the human soul, distilling so many faces of virtuality, revealing the antitheses of dialectics from the angles of ethics and beauty, of the real and the ideal, of the extremes ("angel and demon", "Venus and Madonna", "emperor and proletarian"), but also of emotional reconciliations. An Eminescu springing from the landscapes of Bukovina in northern Romania, a traveller through the landscapes of Transylvania in western Romania, a student who attended courses at the universities of Vienna and Berlin, who eventually settled in Bucharest, summating life's essential experiences. Experiences also conjugating employments such as that of a prompter for theatrical companies, a librarian at Jassy University, a school-inspector, a journalist. In this last capacity he ranked among the most representative Romanian journalists—a term of reference to this very day. Through the passion with which he lived his ideas, through the polemic verve of expression and the deep political involvement of each gesture. An evolutionist in his outlook, he also shared a strong feeling of tradition and of the national model; a great patriot, he militated for the achievement of the unitary and sovereign Romanian state, conceived by analogy with the life of bees, as a state of the working people—of the "positive classes"—without stratification and without any servitude on a foreign plane; a moralist, he shared the worship of values, within a context in which literature and the arts were meant, in his acceptation, to educate people, to become levers of progress, to lend lofty significations to their humanistic message.

A poet, a prose-writer and a playwright, Mihai Eminescu marked in Romanian literature the exceptional moment of the meeting (identification) between the genius (as an individual value) and genius (as a value of collective, ethnical thinking and sensibility). Between the particular and the general. The general which, in his case, in fact embraces humanity as a whole. It is not at all fortuitous that he always took for his model Shakespeare, whom he styled "the great Briton," to whom he dedicated a genuine ode and whom he more than once conjured up in superlative terms. His second model was Romanian folklore—one of the richest and most generous in the world, in point of problems and themes, in point of philosophical as well as emotional vibration, open to whatever is truly human. Models—that is universes. "Eminescianized," though. In a unique orchestral transcription. Time, space, life, death, love, hatred, landscapes, the real and the fantastic, myths, existential adventures, the search for one's own self, gnoseological interrogation, the joy of living, the chimera of happiness, ethical antinomies, the possible and the impossible, the tragic and the comic, setting deeds on a cosmic orbit, etc., etc.—are all integrated within a system of obsessions and relations which confers a timbre with polyphonic nuances upon his literary approach, attitude and manner. Specialists in literary sources discern in this system universal as well as national points of reference, ancient as well as modern, Oriental (particularly Indian) as well as European (particularly German). Undoubtedly bookish as a stimulus, it nevertheless changed into an authoritative personal vision on the scale of synthesis. Summing up—at the level of the 19th century, the century of the nations' awakening—attitudes which are at the same time Homeric, Ovidian, Horatian, Dantesque, Goliardic, Illuministic, pre-romantic, romantic, pre-Raphaelite—variants of heroic poetry of various types, of melancholy, of *carpe diem,* of the cathartic elegy, the impact between the celestial and the telluric, the euphoria of the Dionysian liberating man from servitudes, the consciousness of demophilism, the tear and the voice of revolt, serenity as well as the urge to action, political wisdom, the return to immemorial beginnings, to the genesis of the world, when the non-being became being, when reality was metaphorized in mythology and when man imagined himself as deity, the species disseminating itself into typologies, surviving through mutations, interferences and adstrata, through synchronies, through associations, but more especially through dissociations and assimilations, through absorptions. A process of ineffable complexity, apt to be outlined at the height of Eminescu's horizon only in the perspective of the epic. The constellation of history asserting the latter in the premonitory penumbra of *fortuna labilis,* of *memento mori,* of triumphant Evil. On the other hand, the same history validating the fact that a wise (and proud) Romanian hospodar (like Mircea the Old in **"The Third Epistle"** may give a scathing rebuff to the mightiest figure of his day—the Sultan who had no intuition of the elementary truth that he would come up against ("What stirs here in this country, be it river, breeze, or oak"). That confrontations were battles. That they revealed ideals and heroes. That ideals nominalized freedom, equity, ethics, democracy. That the heroes—as exemplary, repressive or generous entities, legendary in a traditional way or merely supervening to the scale of hypothetical values—threw out into bold relief definitions of the national spirit. That the situations of conflict conjured up also evolved under the sun of significations. Of implication in the dialectics of history, of making the latter stand out in the perspective of the desirable future ("for your past, a future worthy of our nation"), of reiterating ancestral virtues, of outgrowing blasé attitudes, easy-going conventionality, frivolousness and wantonness, hypocrisy, the cohort of undermining venial sins, whatever capitalist "civilization" brought in its wake, estranging man from his own essence.

Eminescu's poetry is nothing but a plea for dis-alienation. For liberating the individual as well as the community from any servitudes. The premise being the identification of existential contradictions, reducible to the schema Good-Evil, to the variant possible-impossible, to that of "will" and "can", of being aware of limits as well as of discerning beyond them the fascinating continent of revelations geometrized by eyes capable to discern the fantastic. Of being a magus travelling among the stars, in an attempt at deciphering the beauties as well as the laws of the cosmos, of imagining (as in **"Hyperion"**) the dramatic idyll between an earthly woman and an astral spirit, of observing that antitheses characterize both the visible and the invisible elements of the macrocosm and microcosm. But also of being a Dionysus (or a Hyperion) for whom happiness (*id est* fulfillment) does not necessarily involve the flight towards demiurgical heights, but rather the realistic satisfaction offered by elementary human dreams. In the first place, through escape in the midst of Nature. Or, to put it more accurately: reintegration within Nature. In the forest, on the borders of a lake, under the cascade of linden-tree blossoms, on the shore of the sea. Where everything throbs with vitality, where biological rhythms appear to be sempiternal, the Uranian is reflected in the Neptunian, the ocean claims descendence from the celestial, beautifully penning in time and space a status of the human condition, both real and desiderative. A status which Eminescu expresses in his oxymoron: "painfully sweet". A syntagm so difficult to convey, owing to its polysemous inflexions, however much we referred to some proposition of Schopenhauer's, related in its gamut of problems. While offering a deeper grounding for the relation between these terms, in fact Eminescu invites one to a transcendentalization of living. Which—on an erotic plane—is translated into the fairy-like vision in **"Călin"** (**"Fragments from a Tale"**), into that of the revolt in **"Mortua est,"** into the suavely diaphanous one in **"So Fresh and Frail,"** into a call like "Oh, come to the wood!", in the symbol of the "sky-blue flower", in that of **"Prince Charming of the Linden Tree"**, in a synthesis-poem like **"If Branches . . .",**—to put it tersely, in *survival*. In *love*. A feeling which is quite defining on the scale of safeguarding moral values. Through its human essence. Through its perenniality. Through its enigmatic nature. Essentially heroic. Heroic even when love could be styled anti-love. When it is sublimated into hatred, scorn, curses. When the dialogue turns into a diatribe-monologue, and the image isolated *pro toto* is Delilah, as in **"The Fifth Epistle."** Because, in this case, by denying, the dream asserts something. The dream, that is the ideal. The ideal, that is the detachment from alienation. As the moon is within Eminescu's landscapes, which for the most part are benighted. The all-conquering moon. Empress of all waves, of the silver forests, "the queen of night", of Life and Death.

With Eminescu, death is a *leitmotiv*. Itinerant. Loaded

with traditional atomic charges. Placed under the shield of the most diverse heraldic valences. Man, objects, vegetation, the fauna, rocks—all acknowledge its mastery. And yet, an aphorism of immortality—all "die only to be born again". To be born, to live and to perish, making up the trichotomy of time itself. As duration, through resumption. The same in all seasons of mankind. It is not fortuitous, I think, that in Eminescu's vocabulary there is an obsessive recurrence of the idea expressed by the word *the same*. *The same* equalling the Eleatic utterance of changelessness, of fatality, of laws and rules, but also of death's impotence. Existential dynamics outclassing—century after century—the prospect of the Apocalypse. Validating—again century after century—the idea that *the same* spells *Life, Progress*. That life and progress, like love and patriotism, enter the polysemy of the concept of dis-alienation.

A concept which renders Eminescu topical to an extent which nobody can deny. The topicality of his para-temporal presence. Of the hunger for the ideal. Of the thirst for non-evil. Of the yearning to discover "the word which expresses the truth". Of the belief that the latter is also expressed by "life's prose", as well as by its opposite, that the sense of life is self-perfection, that the future of the community is again to find the very Self. Where the ethos converges upon the ethnos. Catching a glimpse of the portrait of human personality painted in infinitesimal spots of a myriad colours. Sharing the consciousness of the Self. Contemporary to absolute Time. Discontented. Restless. Walling itself up as if with myths. Freeing itself through lucidity. Through romantic irony. Through the paradoxical identity between "to be" and "not to be".

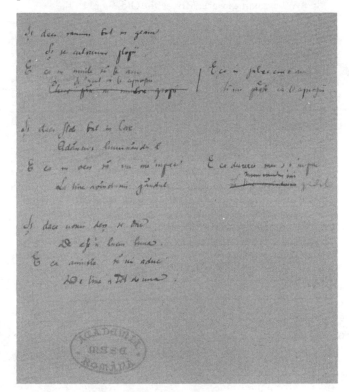

The manuscript of "Şi dacă" ("And if ").

Imagining the aggressor forest in *Macbeth* no less than the idea of Puck's and Ariel's beauty. And (why not?) that of the Dark Lady in the *Sonnets.* Making one's mark as the Shakespeare of Romanian poetry. A Shakespeare to whom—while being aware of the tribulations in his biography—negligible ones, after all—we acknowledge the kinship of genius. In whatever exists as such. Anticipating the judgment of value. Stating that Eminescu is a Shakespeare. And yet that Eminescu is not a Shakespeare. Very much as he is neither a Byron nor a Shelley nor a Lermontov . . . Nor . . . Because he is Eminescu. Unique. Appreciated by Romanians as such. As a summit and a creed.

Half a century after Eminescu's death, one of the youngest poets of that time, Mihai Beniuc, exclaimed in an anthological poem: "We, young poets all, / can never vie with Eminescu". The exclamation certified not the iconolatry of one generation but of several generations. Not the worship of a few people, but that of an entire nation. Transsubstantiated rather recently by an even younger successor, Marin Sorescu, in a thrilling hymn ("They Had to Have a Name") dedicated to the man who equalled the nominalized with the anonymous:

> There was no Eminescu.
>
> There was only a fine country
> On the shore of a sea,
> Where the waves tie white knots
> In the uncombed beard of a king—
> Like waters, like flowing trees
> In which the moon had its round nest.
> And more particularly there were some simple
>   people
> Whose names were: Mircea the Old, Stephen the
>   Great,
> Or plainer still: shepherds and ploughmen,
> Who—of an evening, around the fire—
> Enjoyed reciting poems;
> "The Ewe-Lamb" and "Hyperion" and "The
>   Third Epistle".
>
> But as now and then they heard
> Their mastiffs barking at their sheepfold,
> They left to fight the invading Tartars
> And the Avars and the Huns and the Poles
> And the Turks too.
>   . . . .
>
> There were moreover deep forests
> And a youth who would talk with them,
> Asking them why they swayed without a breath
>   of wind?
>   . . . . .
>
> Also there were some linden-trees,
> And the young couple who knew
> How to make their blossoms snow
> Into a kiss.
> And some birds or some clouds
> Which kept floating over them
> Like long, soft-moving plains.
>
> And since all of these
> Had to have a name,
> One name alone,
> They were named

Eminescu.

(pp. 21-9)

Aurel Martin, in a foreword to Poems *by Mihai Eminescu, translated by Leon Leviţchi and Andrei Bantaş, Minerva Publishing House, 1978, pp. 21-9.*

Ion Dodu Bălan   (essay date 1981)

[*In the following essay, Bălan presents an overview of Eminescu's works.*]

Mihai Eminescu, the Romanian national bard, one of the great romanticists in world literature, was first and foremost a poet of nature and of love, upon which he conferred the proportions of a cosmic mystery. In his verse—touching upon deep and serious metaphysical meanings—the ecstasy of pure love is brought to the frontiers of suffering and death. He also cultivated meditative lyricism, with echoes from Schopenhauer, opposing the lonely and immortal genius to human transience. His **"Lucea-fărul"** (**"Hyperion"** or **"The Evening Star"**) is a cosmologic love poem with profound gnoseological senses; **"Memento mori"** is a vast sociogonic panorama of human civilizations since Afro-Asian antiquity down to the modern world of the French Revolution and the Napoleonic wars; **"Scrisorile"** (**"The Epistles"**) are long narratives or meditations, the first of them including a splendid cosmogonic scene often compared with the hymn of creation in *Rig-Veda;* **"Împărat si proletar"** (**"Emperor and Proletarian"**) is an acute meditation in the spirit of social philosophy, while **"Odă în metru antic"** (**"Ode in Ancient Metre"**) and **"Glossa"** (**"The Gloss"**), one more poem in classical form, exude an existential intensity that is equally thrilling to a modern reader:

GLOSSA
(The Gloss)

> Time will come and time will fly,
> All is old, but new in kind;
> What is right and what is wry
> You should ponder in your mind;
> Don't be Hope's or Terror's thrall;
> Wave-like things like waves shall pass;
> Should they urge or should they call,
> Keep as cool as ice or glass.
>
> Many sounds our ears will touch,
> Much—before our eyes—will glisten;
> Who can bear in mind so much
> And to all is fain to listen;
> Finding your own self anew
> You should loftily stand by,
> Even though with vain ado
> Time will come and time will fly.
>
> Nor should reason's icy scales
> Bend their needle, out of measure,
> To'ards the moment with swift sails
> Fleetingly disguised as pleasure,
> Which is born out of its knell,
> Just for moments, you may find;
> To whoever knows it well,
> All is old, but new in kind.

In the world's dramatic show,
Deem yourself a looker-on:
Should some men feign joy or woe,
Their true face you'll read anon;
Should they weep or insults dart—
Inwardly rejoicing, lie.
Sifting out from all their art
What is right and what is wry!

Both the future and the past
Are but sides of that same page:
In beginnings, ends are cast
For whoever can be sage;
All that was or e'er will be
In the present we can find;
But as to its vanity,
You should ponder in your mind.

Eminescu's world outlook incorporated the kind of scientific knowledge about the universe, nature and society that was prevalent in his time. Illustrative in this respect is the poem **"La steaua" ("Up to the Star")** in which he integrated love into his vision of the world:

Up to the star that's just appeared
The journey's long, and so
For thousand years its light's careered
To reach us here, below.

It may have faded on its way
Of old, in blue spheres bright,
Though only now its shining ray
Unfolds to this our sight.

The image of the star that died
Comes slowly to the fore;
It used to be when it would hide—
We see what is no more.

And likewise, while our yearning dove
Died in the deepest night,
The light of the extinguished love
Still follows us in flight.

Eminescu's love poems proper offer a wealth of feelings: within a complex philosophical and generalizing conception of love, the poet blends down-to-earth sensuousness with sad meditations on transience. Here are excerpts from **"Atît de fragedă" ("So Fresh and Frail")**:

So fresh and frail you are, my love,
You seem a snow-white cherry-flower,
And like an angel from above
You cross my life's course at this hour.

Your steps on carpets fall like beams
—Silk rustles softly under them—
You float as airily as dreams
From lovely head to graceful hem.

. . . . .

To see you was my fault alone;
I can't forgive myself again;
My dream of light I will atone
By stretching out my arms in vain.

Before me you will rise one morning—
The deathless Virgin to portray—
A coronet your brow adorning.
Whereto? Will you return some day?

Pictures of nature and village scenes may be beautifully absorbed into the poet's wordly eroticism, but despair and tragedy underlie even ecstasy as in this quotation from **"Floare albastră" ("Sky-Blue Flower")**:

If you grant me then a kiss
Not a soul will ever know
'Twill be secret; even so:
It is no one's business!

When through boughs we see the moon—
Empress of the summer night—
By the waist you'll hold me tight
And together we shall spoon.

While descending under bowers
To our village in the glen
I'll give you a kiss again
Sweet as shyly hiding flowers.

And if reaching mother's gate
We shall whisper in the dark
Nobody will mind our lark:
Just who cares my love's so great?

One more kiss—she vanishes.
I stay in the moonlight dazed:
Oh, how beautiful, how crazed,
And how sweet my flower is!

. . . . .

Wonder sweet, you left your thrall:
Our love lived but an hour.
Sky-blue flower, sky blue flower! . . .
Sad is this world after all!

It is moreover worth noting that Eminescu's erotic poems included also the poet's other passions or affections; for instance, his love of literature—with Shakespeare taking a foremost place—was clearly stated in his early poem **"Cărțile" ("The Books")**:

Oh, Shakespeare, whom I sadly ponder oft
Thou art the gentle brother of my soul;
The wealthy springs of verse thou bringst aloft
Leap to my mind—and I repeat them whole.
Thus cruel art thou and yet so very soft;
Thy words—a tempest, yet they gently roll;
In God and thee man many faces sees;
Thou tell'st us more than hosts of centuries.

If I had been coeval to thy rise
Wouldst thou indeed have been so dear
to me?
What'er I feel, be it or wrong or wise
—Suffice it that I feel—I owe to thee.
'Tis thou alone that opened'st wide my eyes
I read the world's great riddle with thy key
E'en if with thee I err, I love my fault:
To be like thee's the glory I exalt.

Alongside Eminescu's verse, his prose pieces—e.g. **"Sărmanul Dionis" ("The Wretched Dionysos")**, **"Avatarii faraonului Tlá" ("Pharaoh Tla's Avatars")**, the novel *Geniu pustiu* **(*Barren Genius*)**—and his highly poetical dramatic sketches built a brilliant work, an exceptional synthesis of the entire Romanian spirituality and an artistic expression apt to arouse high aesthetic emotions. Wherever and whenever Romanians mention Eminescu's name, they feel they are expressing their own selves, including whatever is linked to their spiritual existence, to their universe of thoughts and feelings, to their glorious history, to the charming language in **"Miorita"** and to the incurable longing in the *doinas.* Eminescu is the poet of all generations of Romanians, a true national poet whose verses are remembered by everybody, deeply engraved in their souls like aphorisms pithily embodying a nation's specific features. In a brilliant self-confession he stated his fundamental allegiance: "The God of Geniuses has sipped me from my people, very much as the sun drinks in a cloud out of the sea of bitterness".

Most people agree that Eminescu's masterpiece is the legend which he called **"Luceafărul"** (in Romanian it stands for both the evening and the morning star, at the same time being the symbol of handsomeness and brilliancy). In a nutshell, it is the story of the fair princess who falls in love with the bright star that she watches night after night. The star—Hyperion (**"Luceafărul"**)—is charmed by her beauty and feelings, responds to them and asks his celestial father to turn him into a mortal so that he may join his bride. Confronted with her fickleness, however, he stays away from lowly earthlings and resumes the burden of his cool immortality. In many interpretations, the poem is an allegory of the impossibility for a genius to adapt or lower himself to the condition of ordinary philistines. Below we quote from the young princess's confession of her love for Hyperion:

> You are as handsome as in sleep
> Can but a daemon be;
> Yet never shall I take and keep
> That path you show to me.
>
> My heartstrings ache when every eve
> You vent your cruel desire,
> Your eyes, so gloomy, make me grieve,
> And scorching is their fire

Hyperion's travel through space to the throne of his Godly Father acquires the dimensions of a cosmogonic description:

> Off went the star. And as he went,
> His wings grew more and more
> And myriads of years were spent
> For every hour that wore.
>
> There was a sky of stars beneath,
> A sky of sky o'erhead—
> Like to a bolt with ne'er a death
> Among the worlds he sped.
>
> And from the valleys of the pit
> He upwards spun his way;
> He saw how lights sprang up and lit
> As on the earliest day,
>
> How like a sea they girdled him,
> And swam and heaved about . . .
> And flew and flew, an ache-borne whim,
> Till everything died out;
>
> For where he reached there was no bourne,
> To see there was no eye.
> And from the chaos to be born
> Time vainly made a try.

> And there was nothing. There was, though,
> A thirst that did oppress,
> A gaping gulf above, below,
> Like blind forgetfulness.

In **"Luceafărul"** (Hyperion) and in many other poems, Eminescu gave voice to the whole universe of the existence of the Romanian people. His own attitude towards life and death, the grave judgement passed upon history and upon mankind's successive civilizations, his views on the fate of a man of genius, his humaneness, worship of work, love of beauty and truth, his propensity to meditation and reflection, his keen feeling for nature (which in his vision feels and thinks like a man), his longing, yearning and grief, his sense of humour, his patriotism and his striving for social equity—features that are typical of the Romanian people—all burn with unique intensity in Hyperion's soul:

> From heavy, dark eternity
> Deliver me, o Lord,
> For ever hallowed may'st Thou be
> And praised throughout the world.
>
> O, ask me, Father, anything
> But change my fortune now;
> O'er Fount of Life Thou art the king,
> The death-dispenser Thou;
>
> My aura of eternity,
> My fiery looks, retrieve,
> And, in exchange, for love grant me
> A single hour's leave.
>
> From chaos come, I would return
> To chaos, oh, most Blessed,
> For out of rest eternal born,
> I yearn again for rest.

The awareness of death as well as of eternity, the experience of the irreversible flow of time, the delight with the Romanian geographical space, the boundless confidence in Romania's historical destiny are further fundamental elements of Eminescu's universe. Better than anybody else, in thrilling verse of ardent patriotism like those in **"Scrisoares a treia"** (**"The Third Epistle"**) Eminescu managed to conjure up the glorious past of his people who, against all hardships, knew how to preserve their national entity in perfect dignity.

He also succeeded in raising the language of Romanian poetry to summits undreamt of before, while imprinting his fantastic personality upon each one of its articulations. Even nowadays Romanians use certain words being conscious of the additional expressiveness that Eminescu lent them. In the grave and enchanted harmony of his poetic language, he expressed the whole range of feelings of the human soul, from the pure charm of childhood and the thirst for life, bright aspirations and sad falls, to the disturbing mystery of death. In harmonies of faultless musical quality, he re-created the beauty of Romania's Nature, projecting the image of Moldavian hills at dusk in a cosmic perspective, or allowing the sea with its sailing-ships to suggest the irreversible flow of time:

> Citadels traced
> Afloat in loneliness
> Moving on limitless

Stretches of waste

For Romanians, Nature carries in it part of Eminescu's soul:

> On a hill the moon is rising like a hearth of
> dying fire
> Reddening the ancient forests, the lone castle
> with
> its spire.
> [Translated by Leon Leviţchi]

With the first hoar frost, migratory birds always fly away as if accompanied by one of Eminescu's touching elegies:

> Behold, the swallows take to flight
> And nut-trees follow autumn's rite,
> The frost has ruined grape and plum.
> Why don't you come, why don't you come?

The rustling of the copper-coloured forests, the murmur of springs and of the vast expanses of water where "the lowly-bending branches / Hide a plot of terraced ground"; the lake "where clouds have woven / A fine, gossamery shade / Bent asunder by wave-motions / And with gems of light in-laid" [Translated by Leon Leviţchi]; the acacias that "shed their leafage, with wind and autumn's brume"; "the poplars odd in number", "the soft and woolly clouds spreading on a royal bed", the miraculous landscape "with rivers of fire, with a silver-bronze string / With shores of incense, with flowers that sing", "hosts of flowers on the beds", "the gardens in bloom and the flower groves", the year-laden mountains—"Carpathians with lofty crests of rock" and whatever embodies in memorable expressions the very essence of the Romanian land reverberates in amplified echoes in Romanians' consciousness, lending new dimensions to their thoughts and feelings. His very popular poem **"Ce te legeni codrule" ("Forest, Why D'You Swing So Low?")** is a fine sample to that effect.

> "Forest, why d'you swing so low?
> With your branches bending so,
> There's no rain and no winds blow!"
> "You should not be wond'ring why
> For my time so swift does fly.
> Nights grow longer, days grow shorter
> Leaving of my leaves a quarter;
> Sideways does the wind strike leaves,
> Me of songsters it bereaves—
> Cutting like a scimitar;
> Winter's here and summer's far!
> What else could I do but sway
> While birds go in flight away?
> Over tops of trees upright
> Flocks of swallows pass in flight
> Taking all my thoughts along
> And my luck as well, erelong;
> And they follow one another
> Darkening this world and t'other;
> Fluttering their wings they drift
> And they fly like moments swift;
> So they leave me, in great haste,
> Withered, bare, benumbed and waste
> All alone, just with my yearning—
> Echoing each other's burning".

Turning to folklore, Eminescu insisted particularly on the grave lyrical species like the *doina*, the song of grief or

longing; his poetry became the people's own singing. Longing and restlessness in Eminescu's poetry are the same as in Romanian folklore.

It is thanks to Eminescu's glory that Romanian culture got access to universality by adding to its credit the last of the great romantics, acknowledged as a poet of world value. (pp. 35-44)

> *Ion Dodu Bălan, "Mihai Eminescu," in his* A Concise History of Romanian Literature, *translated by Andrei Bantaş, Academy of Social and Political Sciences, 1981, pp. 35-45.*

Mihai Drăgan (essay date 1987)

[*In the following essay, Drăgan relates Eminescu's view on the importance of a national literature as a means of establishing a national identity.*]

If a writer's disloyalty and creative insubordination to what has been characterized the force of a great artist as Paul Valéry said, then Mihai Eminescu is disloyal to his predecessors, though not directly and openly, in poetical manifestos and insurgent articles, but only indirectly, in the hidden part of his work, in the region of great ebullition represented by the arcana of his working laboratory, where the dissatisfaction and revolt of the genius turns at first against himself, his chiefest concern being that of achieving a new poetry and literature which is, at the same time, a new language.

But Eminescu no longer wrote (with the partial exception of a few texts published in his youth, in the magazine *Familia*) to satisfy the social conventions of the day, the taste of a certain public, too much habituated to the poetry of a Vasile Alecsandri and Dimitrie Bolintineanu. Already in those young years (the prestudent period, as the critic G. Călinescu styled it), Eminescu began to write in virtue of powers conformable to himself, the momentary spontaneity, facile like any spontaneity risen from juvenile enthusiasm, being replaced by a kind of demonic unrest, by lucidity and a critical attitude, by the self-imposed task of relentlessly watching his own poetical work in a subterranean opposition to "the conceited, naive productions of our forerunners", significant but not sufficient for him, and especially to those of his contemporaries, "state and cold" (letter to Iacob Negruzzi, June 1870), in a word, spontaneity and fervour have been replaced by an immense creative force.

What did the young Eminescu think about the literature and culture of the past and of his own time? The question is of capital significance, as it involves an intellectual process with two perfectly complementary sides: the way in which the romantic visionary took a deep interest in our national culture (including folklore) and, at the same time his ability to get beyond this space—strictly delimited by the vicissitudes of history—and create, from the height of his demonic genius, spiritual values that take us into the realm of universality.

Eminescu is, according to Constantin Noica's profound observation, "a cultural conscience behind us," "a cultural conscience open to everything," an extraordinary proof of this being his notebooks, similar to Leonardo da Vinci's. It should be noted that to Eminescu nothing makes sense without conscience, an absolute conscience. Culture and literature, as seen by the still very young poet and thinker, signify the creation and orderliness of his mind, deeply integrated with the national consciousness, which he understood to be not only a historical reality circumscribing the Romanian geographic and spiritual area, but also an immanent one, whose original datum constantly points to, and justifies, eternity.

It is almost amazing that already in his agitated youth of romantic peregrination, when he excitedly participated in the life activities around him (the most significant experience being that of the theatre), displaying a keen consciousness of historicity, Eminescu would also turn against history (even so far as to put up what Noica once called "a resistance to history"), which enabled him to inhabit the realm of metaphysical contemplation, propitious to the creation of spiritual values in the grand perspective of eternity.

It can be said that the essence of Eminescu's spirit resided throughout his meteoric career, in this profound symbiosis between his *historical consciousness* (early manifest in multiple and complex forms) and his *consciousness of creation on the metaphorical plane,* as opposed to historicity, regionalism, short-lived presentness. The problem is of capital importance to understanding the destiny of our culture, as Eminescu conceived of it at the time.

In the process of formation of Eminescu's creative personality we can already discover the firmness of his critical consciousness, as one of the prime elements of this personality's richness and inner unity. The idea of publishing a book of poetry and, probably one of prose at the age of 19 or 20, was not born of some juvenile impatience, or of a vainglory that Eminescu never entertained. No doubt, this idea rose from a new comprehension of the writer's function and of the role of literature as against all that was being written and commented upon in an age of transition like that after the revolution of 1848.

A text with an important idea, although rather unfinished in terms of linguistic expression, is **"The Opposite Page,"** written by Eminescu in 1868 with the stated intention of being a preface to an "original story", possibly one to his novel *Lone Genius,* as believed by Perpessicius and, more recently, by Aurelia Rusu.

Beyond the self-ironical tone, there are in this text a few valuable hints revealing Eminescu's thoughts and concerns in that period of uncommon creative feverishness. One actually finds, on the two planes of plot development, represented by "Mrs. World" and "Mr. Destiny", a number of reflections on the nature of the literary text and the writer's status, beyond the atmosphere of the day, rather unfavourable to productions far ahead of the timeserving spirit of the *milieu,* in which humbugs and nonentities were in the front ranks.

In the **"Opposite Page"** Eminescu rises not so much against himself—now, in 1868, he already knows exactly what he wants—as against the ossified usages of the time, against the spirit of the out-of-date traditionalism, which

denied any understanding and recognition of genuine value. Essential to the position taken by the author—who defines himself as a sceptic—is the observation that "in Romania, almost all that is written is badly written, that is, as good as not written, and what is not written cannot be read either," this being a reference to the literary productions of the day, profuse and mediocre, then already under strong and systematic attack from the *Junimea* literary society and its review, *Convorbiri literare,* through the incisive pen of Titu Maiorescu.

This text can be related to other remarks made by Eminescu about the same time, and expressed even more emphatically, to the effect that the "lone genius", discontented with the entire reality of his time, begins to judge it from an "absolute" point of view. This would soon lead him to great dissatisfaction with this reality, with its miseries, falseness and injustice, with the noxious effects of the so-called democracy that had emerged, on waves of rhetoric, after the defeat of the 1848 revolution. One of these remarks, illustrative of Eminescu's critical thinking, is found in the marginal notes on his plans for a play, **Mira** (about 1867–68): "but look at the statistics of Romanian literature, pierce them with your eyes to better see the progress we are making—*progress* being an ironical metaphor for *regress,* since anyone viewing things in their absolute essence will easily realize that the step taken backwards, negatively, is longer, far longer than the positive one."

The starting point of Eminescu's criticism was established—even before the poet's contact with Kantian philosophy—in a perspective "looking at things in their absolute essence," whence the irreducible contradiction (antithesis) between an ideal of culture and culture that can be achieved, he thinks, by the true *creative mind* of the nation, and the historical reality of his time, deeply contradictory and, in many regards, irrelevant by its many forms of minor culture, obsequious and degrading imitations of foreign models. To stand in the shadow of great cultures (French culture, at the time) is to be condemned to sterility, to numbness of the national creative instinct and, ultimately, to shutting this instinct in the basement of a history which rhythmically, peaceably pursues its biological course but which remains anonymous by its lack of creation and participation in the great European spirituality and culture.

One fundamental theme of the future journalist's meditations was the approach from a new angle—almost a dialectical one—to what the young Eminescu, who in 1868 began translating H. Th. Rötscher's *The Art of Dramatic Performance,* calls in a marginal note, "the characteristic and internal individuality of the people itself." In this connexion, the poet wrote that an approach from the idea of *historical necessity* in the perspective of *historical duration,* of the relentless will to make history in its natural, specific evolution instead of accepting it as it should not be, "is the absolute condition of a natural history, that it should take account of a nation's spiritual movements, of the sum total of the impressions created in its soul by various incidents and circumstances. The red thread, the antithesis to the outside circumstances, is the characteristic and internal individuality of the people itself—this must be our guide through the maze of history, only that this individuality must be understood, and it must also be understood that all its combination with the occurrences of the time are organic and conformable to this individuality itself. An approach without the national individuality as the characterizing part of the facts is simply unthinkable."

History, and implicitly culture, is understood by Eminescu *problematically,* as a constant will to progress and aspiration for an organic creation of its own, inside its specificity, of the "national individuality," without however remaining captive to regionalism and the trivial immediate, in a word, to the ephemeral. The true way of reaching history is that of highly original, individualized spiritual creation, beyond the limitations of unpropitious historical time and in full agreement with the requirements of eternity.

Also in his youth, probably at the start of his Viennese studies, Eminescu noted these thoughts of extraordinary significance in terms of profundity and practical perspective:

> Moment one, the peoples learn to think; moment two, they think about themselves; three, they think about the whole world and for the whole world. One is receptive, two emancipates the national individuality from the burden of reception, enabling it to think of its own cause, three, lastly, is the golden flower in which the whole world rejoices.

> Why? A strange question. Nothing is easier than creating thousands upon thousands of plans and means to one and the same end, plans and means of the most flowery and beautiful. But why? An idea must come to life [in] a manner precluding any possibility of its becoming a different one—thus and only thus.

Viewing all problems and realities (nation, one's homeland, poetry, society, the state, culture, art, love, truth, justice, work, value, etc.) "in their absolute essence" grew with Eminescu into an unswerving line of thought, though not from an absolutist romantic impulse but from the genius's irrepressible need to think and create differently than had done his forerunners, enthusiastic but lacking the depth of originality, and his contemporaries of the "transition stage," confused by ambitions, the shine and fanfare of hollow rhetoric, but incapable of having a "historical sense." (The phrase is Eminescu's.)

To be a nation really culturally-conscious, a people must follow a *possibility* that is exclusively its own, born of its own organic individuality. The three stages in a people's evolution towards self-consciousness, which is always a consciousness of spiritual culture, mentioned by Eminescu, are conceived dialectically, from the angle of a small culture that can become great through the nation's will to progress. The creator's aspiration is now to be able, through his total involvement in the Romanian nation's spirituality, to "think about the whole world and for the whole world," and thus to pass on, by profoundly assimilating the national spirit, the people's "pre-existent genius," from the ethnic localism of the 1848 period to uni-

versality. (At the end of his essay *The New Direction,* 1872, Titu Maiorescu spoke of the need "to discover, none the less, and to formulate ideas for the whole world," "without missing the national element.") This must be achieved not through craftsmanship—easy to learn by imitation—but through a wide range of newly created spiritual values, which is nothing but an emanation of genius. To Goethe, as is known, the essence of creation was genius, "The demonic spirit of genius," rather than craftsmanship, which holds perfectly true for Eminescu's manner of thinking and acting.

The culture and literature of the forerunners, from a period preceding the year 1848, are to Eminescu (and this can also be seen from a letter to Iacob Negruzzi in June 1870) an example of simple, true faith in nationality and the spirit of the times, in the *public* they were writing for: "when I am in the presence of these elders, of the past decades' literature, I seem to be in a warm room . . . " One feels that those people were in direct contact with a certain public, large or small, yet none the less a public (*Fragmentarium*). The forerunners were men of vision, enthusiastic proponents of the great ideas of their time; their literature, not particularly valuable in itself, was full of genuine, not artificial feelings, and was destined for sensitive readers, who, while lacking an aesthetic education that could meet the requirements of the day, romantically saw a precursor in the poet and took heed of his prophetic words.

The notes mentioned above, written in Eminescu's student years (most probably early in that period) express, like the letter to Iacob Negruzzi, an antithesis between the spirit of the "elders" ("the blessed visionary natures" of **"The Epigones"**) and the "moderns," that is, the poet's contemporaries. The concept of "modern," applied by Eminescu to most of the contemporary writers (certainly, in contrast to the idea of durability, hence classicality) obviously includes a hint of exhaustion, devitalization and decadence ("the sickly air"). Eminescu speaks about all this with much candour, as if in a diary not confined to trivial details and private matters, but committing the writer's conscience to a lucid confrontation with itself and with the reality of the time, which often met him with contempt and violence, for "merit and qualities are to the world a challenge to duel" (*Fragmentarium*). The confrontation with the "moderns" (his contemporaries) is done through a flexible approach, whose essential notes are, however, unassailingly logical:

> With the moderns I feel as if in a cold room, and in a cold room, anyone knows this, something seems to be *lacking,* not warmth itself but something touchable, as if on the blank wall something had been that is no more, or the family's feeling when someone has died in the house. It's a kind of vacancy everyone feels so keenly, as if things were missing from the house, not just a man's body. Another man may come in, but your feeling won't change. As if you were accustomed to seeing the frame with another portrait, and the portrait in another frame. With most of our modern authors one promptly feels that they are not for the public, nor the public for them, well, that they are not rings in the chain of our culture's historical continuity, being as it were,

extra muros. And this is the fate of all cultures unnaturally imported as ours. They are not covered by the long road of condensing the ideas in the people's skulls, and thus are something that can be neither grasped (nor) conceived, they are rings from the evolution of an alien head, (a) walnut branch out of which, when already half-grown, you wished to raise an oak, while only through the dissolution of that branch in the soil could atoms be produced that go into the structure of the oak as well.

This text, which gives off the grand breathing of Eminescu's enthusiastic, romantic spirit, contains in a nutshell a basic theme of his thought: the right to independent existence of a people endowed with national consciousness can be achieved only by participation in history with original spiritual values, as plenary expressions of its freedom and its own creative mind, not as imitations of foreign cultural forms or, simply, as cultural aspects that only fill some momentary requirements, transient like anything serving the trivially ephemeral and, hence, excluded from eternity.

Romanian culture and civilization, as they were seen by Eminescu about the year 1870 were for the most part alien to the national spirit, instead of being cogent arguments in favour of developing it and enhancing its contribution to mankind's progress. The many reasons for this were placed by the thinker in close inter-relations, illustrative of a picture amplifying to the absolute the revolt of genius against the contradictory present. They also supply him with many arguments supporting a disillusionment that began, from his youth, to be a part of the gigantic prospect of universal nothingness.

It is certain that doubt and scepticism were essential and primordial elements of Eminescu's structure, along with the extraordinary vigour of his mind and with a disposition, obvious in his late adolescence and early youth, to be an extrovert and to passionately communicate with people around him. The ancestral sadness continually amplified by the shadow of death that hovered, like a huge bird of prey, over most of his family ("the pitiless hereditary fatality", in Maiorescu's words), the personal drama (erotical most often, and with uncommon implications for his life), the spectre of the ruthless disease and, perhaps, occasionally, some indefinite melancholy, as in the case of so many other romantics, were paralleled in Eminescu by unbound confidence in the nation's abilities and by a demonic lucidity of thought that reached truly colossal dimensions in his *œuvre.* These contrary elements lent Eminescu's consciousness, in its striving to harmonize them, a tragic sense by the total assumption of the existence and realities of his time.

The root which eventually caught all the fibres of Eminescu's spirit, turning it into a cosmic pessimism, was the cruelly contradicting and oppressive reality of his day (with its multiple aspects), which dramatically faced the poet from his early youth, as his universal genius caused him to consider everything in an absolute perspective. This profound implication in the history of his time signified an utmost sharpening of the critical spirit, its orientation towards highly polemic forms (pamphleteering in-

Statue of Eminescu.

cluded) and, at the same time, a withdrawal from the arena of worldly struggle, where the genius felt alone, isolated, into the realm of poetic contemplation, where spiritual values are created and where Eminescu is happily at home, since art, as a compensatory element, turns into everlasting duration.

Most of the truths thought and visionarily stated by Eminescu are of an absolute character, and the distance between them and the realities of his time was so great that it caused in his personality a split unimaginable in a man's real (normal) existence, but reduced by the writer himself by a harmonizing of the contraries, often at a cosmic level, in his work.

In fact the young Eminescu, even before he went to Vienna—one capital of nineteenth-century European spirituality—posed, with amazing clear-sightedness, the problem of truth in a philosophical perspective related to the personality of a genius linked to a given historical period and, primarily, to the spirituality of the people that produced him. Man, the poet thinks, "is the product of his attending circumstances" and "truth, as man's creation, is likewise an effect of the attending circumstances," (***Fragmentarium***), whence its relativity ("What one century tells us, the others will deny"—**"Mortua est!"**) and consequently, the impossibility to define it. Since "to a great mind everything's a problem," Eminescu is convinced that the truth, as sought by this romantic thirsting for the absolute, can be found only within his own soul: "Just as the fish can only live in water, my soul can live only in me"; "this is my fate: for truth / To seek only within my heart" (**"If You Speak, I'll Pretend Deafness . . . "**).

What "painfully touches" him, hence his drama perpetually verging on the tragic, arose from "the disagreement between the icon borne by it" (by the soul) and the reality of his time, in which dominant positions were held by demagogical rhetoric ("the tyranny of rhetoric", as his contemporary I. L. Caragiale would say), by the confusion of petty politics, by falsehood, injustice, aggressive upstart nullity, in a world by all that is essentially opposed to the freedom, spiritual values and organic progress for which Eminescu struggled with the utmost conviction and fervour.

His self-consistency was absolute, and so was the striving of his conscience in seeking for, and unimpededly proclaiming, the truth. A manuscript note from Iaşi period symbolically concentrates a correlation between thought, fervour and truth: "fervour is the juice that gives life to thought. Only that it should have a lofty object, and the loftiest is, no doubt, truth." (*Fragmentarium*). Thus conceived and projected into the space of a genius' manifestations, fervour is not a mere emotional attitude that can vary with the mood and circumstances, but a deep belief in the powers of the mind, in idea and its penetrations, if it truly comes from a total assumption of the national reality and from understanding the mechanism of its growth beyond everything that is transient and doomed to vanish into the dust of time.

To better delimit the defining elements of the "lone genius's" revolt in the plane of theoretical thought about culture and literature, it is necessary to comment on a few significant ideas found in another of his notes from the same Viennese period when, in our opinion, we should place Eminescu's most representative meditations upon our present field of interest. With the inflexible determination of the future journalist, Eminescu wrote that

> an immature, false maturity, incapable of grasping the principle of life, is sweeping the country from end to end, an artificial culture, imported from the four corners of the world, is being imposed on the Romanian spirit, which it has already corrupted [to] a certain degree. We Romanians in the Principalities are in the unfavourable position of being governed by a cultured generation that is in no wise connected with the nation, for we have never made use of such preventative means as can protect a nation from foreign influence.
>
>   (*Fragmentarium*).

Imitation and form *without a content* are, in Eminescu's view, totally exterior to the organic process of real evolution and modernization of Romanian civilization, nay a serious danger to the national being itself. Under the historical conditions for the period, which the thinker very aptly describes, the essential thing was precisely to strengthen the Romanian people's cultural consciousness, pointing out its belonging to an old durable spiritual community, in which the language plays a capital unifying role.

Concerned from his youth about the historical "continuity law," though not in the superficial aspects of its problems, generally unessential to determining the nation's spiritual identity, Eminescu considers that progress in language in no way signifies abandoning or depreciating—as it happened with "our innovators" (the fanciful philologists of the day)—the old structure of the Romanian tongue. The language is the very mark and genius of nationality and it justifies its importance as social and psychological organism, as well as its unifying role in the people's spiritual life, to the extent that it transcends the value of a mere means of communication between people, growing into "an essential element of, nay, a criterion for culture," to the effect that a man's speech and writing "will reveal his degree of culture," and "the maturity of the public culture of the people's spirit is seen mainly in its language." Moreover, Eminescu holds, in the perspective of the sublime text of expressiveness to which he was going to put the Romanian language, that, in fact, "the linguistic value and power, the kind of style and expression found with a people, are reflected and manifested in its national literature. This is the source from which all will take."

One leitmotif of Eminescu's critical thought is markedly and clearly noticeable in this period of demonic unrest and of fundamental final options as to the origin of spiritual values. All his efforts are turned—theoretically also—to an in-depth change in understanding the essential part that the national literature can play in asserting the people's spiritual identity in the consciousness of the world. Eminescu no longer views literature as an indifferent expression of the present reality, fatally subject to transcience, but ascribes to it, in the perspective of the "absolute foundation" of things, an aesthetic and human significance aimed at eternity. In other words, literature as a unique expression of our spirituality and of our national language's creative capacity, plays a decisive role in strengthening the national consciousness, in promoting and protecting our very nationality. The note (from his student years) titled **"The Role of the National Literature in the Public Spirit,"** from which we have quoted, ends with a thought perfectly illustrative of Eminescu's profound, never out-of-date theoretical position: "each national literature is the focus of the national spirit, upon which rays converge from every direction of spiritual life; it shows the level of spiritual public life."

Appealing to the sovereign authority of the national language to which he submitted in order to recreate it, Eminescu, still young, was the first Romanian to think, in a universal perspective, that a strong national literature presupposes the creation of a language of its own, the transformation of the expressive capabilities of the people's language into a language that could confine the feeling and thinking originality of the "national genius." With Eminescu, we can speak of the myth of the national writer whose genius, as a sublimated expression of the nation's genius, is equally in history and against it, and, oppressed by the tragicalness of life, creates for eternity. (pp. 54-62)

Mihai Drăgan, "Eminescu—National Consciousness and Culture," in Romanian Review, *Vol. 41, No. 1, 1987, pp. 54-62.*

Edgar Papu (essay date 1989)

[*In the following essay, Papu demonstrates the reasons for the universality of Eminescu's poetry.*]

Far from being an isolated phenomenon, a great personality in the history of artistic creation or thinking is a term of a relation with far-reaching consequences. This is why, no matter how acute the exclusive intrinsic understanding of a poet might be, it still does not have all the necessary elements to reveal his value in its entirety. It is only by connecting it with certain implications from the outside that a work of art can show its real axiologic importance. In other words, it results from the whole set of relations where its author is a mere term. In such a more comprehensive configuration its value is evinced gradually at two different stages: the first aims at establishing his place within national culture and the second goes further, namely tries to find his rank in world culture. With Mihai Eminescu, the Romanian people's greatest poet, the distinct contribution of these two stages is quite obvious. Establishing the poet's position in his national culture offers, indeed, a more accurate picture of his value, but only from a partial and, therefore, relative viewpoint. It is only the next stage, that is, finding his place in universality, that can really have its decisive say in this respect. It is the only way to offer an unquestionable appreciation of his absolute value.

Who is Eminescu in Romanian culture? Roughly speaking, this is well known. Even if new contributions are and will still be discovered, they are to be added to something already familiar. But who is Eminescu in world culture? This is a question pushing us into a rather vague field of his identity. And it is this very aspect that really matters in the attempt at describing Eminescu's greatness and value.

This is what accounts for the interest taken today in the idea of Eminescu's universality. But this idea is in a stage when it is not clearly outlined, it is often mixed up with the question of the distribution and success of his work abroad. It goes without saying that the two interests condition each other, but they are distinct in their essence. One of them is a question of useful cultural policy focusing on a national value, the other one is a purely scientific question aimed at spotting the new, important contributions of this value at world level. We are interested in the latter only (some aspects of the other question will be dealt with in certain respects).

Once these explanations have been given, we have also to add that we start from the assumption that the fact is admitted in principle. That is we do no longer think it necessary to demonstrate the idea in itself, which we have mentioned in the title of our article. The general intuition of this work clearly convinces us that it is of a more than lim-ited local interest. However, we can confine ourselves to what was already known. Consequently, the general idea of Eminescu's universality has to be clarified more strictly. What makes Eminescu universal? To what extent is he universal (there are various stages here too)? What means do we use to prove the universality we have attributed to him? These are questions to which definite answers have to be given, not mere assertions in principle.

A poet manages to join the world flow of assets by three distinct ways. First he reaches this stage by enriching and bringing to utmost perfection—not achieved up to that time—some already existing expressions rendered imperfectly. Second, the poet becomes universal when, by the new, valid elements of his literary creation, he substantially contributes to the completion of the most representative features of the moment he lives at. Finally, he can also attain universality if his work includes some rich anticipating elements heralding the future. And Eminescu brilliantly used all these three ways. But he did no longer live to make a synthesis of his numerous contributions as Dante, Shakespeare or Goethe used to do owing to their longer period of literary creation. Though incompletely linked to one another, there are in Eminescu's work the elements of a whole which are as grandiose as those due to the most important poets of the world. But we shall stand aside from the temptation of hypotheses, which can often mix up what we wish and what exists; we shall only aim at those elements capable to give a complete clarification of the question we are concerned with. Therefore, what we have to do is to take separately the three ways by which the Romanian poet reached universality.

Now we shall deal with the first one. Under this aspect Eminescu enriches Romanticism and elevates it to the last stage of perfection. This general hint can be followed more accurately on various planes. First of all, the prospect of the great remoteness, where the poet is to be traced back ontologically, finds one of its starting points in Romanticism too, as it was illustrated, among others, by Novalis. But here Eminescu surpasses not only the Romantic character, but also all the other already known antecedents. Indeed, he appears to be the greatest poet of remoteness in all literature of the world. When saying this, we are not referring to the less important quantitative character of this aspect, but to the qualitative one, that is to the fulfillment continuously projected by his substantial outlook against the infinite space and time of creation. Other poets, such as Hugo, for instance, may have left him behind as regards the extensiveness and volume of remoteness. But it was Eminescu alone who could grasp the intrinsic value of this aspect, its depth rich in meaning. "Without creating Hugo's hallucinating vision", said critic Aurel Sasu, "Eminescu is more complex as he associates to the vast aspect of horizontality the depth of phenomena, the real of mystery and the nearness of myth . . . The descriptiveness of the former is replaced by the latter with a more subtle process of revelation, hence the illumination when reading Eminescu's poetry." With slight changes adequate to the various similar cases, this confrontation can also be valid in a possible relation to Keats, Byron and many other poets, be they Romantic or non-Romantic ones.

Passing to a related field of concerns, we can say that Eminescu's remoteness is imbued with a number of representations, in which the poet turns out to be highly skilful in giving shape to the most daring ineffable imaginings. Some of them are the motive representations. The great dynamic expressions, the far-reaching gestures, cosmically projected, are spread in the modern world by Romantic titanism too, from Keats to Hugo; the latter one is actually one of the poets suggesting to Eminescu the motif of the fall of the worlds. However, Hugo's outwardly descriptive manner was far from the endless suggestive power of Eminescu's evocations, which are superior to all Romantic antecedents in this respect. In their depth quite impossible to define, the great cosmic gestures—one of them is throwing Orpheus' harp in chaos as described in the poem **"Memento mori"**—point to Eminescu as one of the greatest titanic poets of the world.

As for the full experience of remoteness, conceived of in its substance, Eminescu inverts the man-cosmos relationship as compared to Romanticism. I have already said that he conveyed his own experience in the whole range of ontologic changes of the endless universe. Therefore, the Romantic anthropomorphism of nature—with its entire theoretical descent from the *Einfühlung* aesthetics—becomes a cosmorphism of man. The human being as personified by the man of genius is an infinite nature itself. This will entail two new contributions not only as regards Romantic visionary motifs, but also as regards the fabulous of all times. First, in the field of mythical metamorphoses, it is no longer man who changes into a natural element, but the natural element into man, as is the case with Eminescu's famous poem, **"Hyperion."** Second, and we are referring to **"Hyperion"** too, the Romantic idea of the exceptional superiority, represented by the solitary genius, does no longer materialize in an anthropomorphous spirit, but in a representation of the untamed force of nature. In both cases that Romantic élan of becoming one with the rest of the world, of the relationship between "man and the Whole" does no longer show an impulse of the human subjective initiative, but of a cosmic consciousness which the poet has beyond his own self. Here Eminescu begins one of the first démarches to objectify Romanticism, to pass to a kind of Neo-Romanticism and to the new cosmic dimension of modern lyrical poetry.

Descending from the realm of the great remoteness to the realm of inner life, the experience of the sweetness characteristic of Eminescu derives from the Romantic voluptuous melancholy and dreaming too. This feature of Romanticism spread into European lyrical poetry especially through Lamartine, "the poet of the inner harmony and silence." But such a sweet repose, which, with that poet, seems to be a compensation looked for by the "tired man who has lost his balance," becomes the object of a widespread groundless epigonism. This outwardly Lamartinian attitude had ravaged Romanian lyrical poetry, it had even come to contaminate the literary creation of a great poet like Vasile Alecsandri with its insipid sweetness. Under such circumstances Eminescu is the first lyrical poet to experience sweetness with such an intensity and richness in nuances that he rises high above the starting point of the first Romantic initiative. The poet goes even

deeper into the most unexpected feelings brought about by this subtle sensation, including the longing (actually he was the first great Romanian poet to talk about it). Therefore, Eminescu does not only go beyond the borders of Romanticism as regards his way of expressing sweetness lyrically, but, in this respect, he was equalled by Dante alone in the entire world literature. Of course he lays the revelation of this phenomenon on other bases and with other means, but it is also as an expression that casts light on an ineffable zone of inner experiences.

Eminescu crowned Romanticism, surpassing it in so many respects. Thus, the poet brilliantly earned his universality. But he also reached universality by following the second way mentioned above. That is, he substantially contributed to the entire poetic configuration in the late 19th century, in other words to the historical present of his time. The fact that, being not known enough, his work was not popular at that time is, as I have already said, a mere question regarding the flow of assets, not one referring to his effective universality. Similar circumstances were connected with other illustrious artistic personalities too. For instance, all along the 17th century, Shakespeare was completely ignored outside the national culture he belonged to. At other times the same happened to Dante, Caldéron de la Barca and many other poets ranking highest in the hierarchy of world values. Therefore, irrespective of their work being well known or ignored, we shall consider Eminescu's contribution to the poetic output of his time.

This is why we have to correct the way in which the poet is identified in the context of the time he represented. Eminescu's being labelled as a "late Romantic" seems not appropriate to us for two reasons. First, any late appearance in a literary or artistic trend or movement is not necessarily a belated appearance. Such a name is to be applied to epigonic expressions. Here is one example only: Eminescu's contemporary, the German poet Geibel, is indeed a "belated Romantic." But, on the contrary, a late appearance can be the acme of the literary trend it stands for. The specific categories of the 13th century will be illustrated by Dante no sooner than in the 14th century when he wrote *Divina Commedia*. He is not a belated, but a culminating expression of medieval allegorism for all that. Maybe not an exactly identical case, but, anyway, one of its variants is also evinced by the Eminescu phenomenon as against Romanticism, as we think one could infer from our previous illustrations. What we have not yet illustrated is the second reason why we think it wrong to label Eminescu as a "belated Romantic," which mars that great Romanian poet's prestige. The ground of our statement is that, in a certain respect, his literary creation does not point to him as a Romantic poet only, but also as one of the best representatives of post-Romantic poetry, which is actually the time when he wrote his work. The poet substantially takes part in defining the distinctive features of his time. This is the second aspect of Eminescu's universality, which we are now going to clarify in its various aspects.

The first item of our discussion will be the much commented upon Schopenhauer influence, a fact which, for the beginning, makes us remind readers of some elementary data. It is known that the philosopher published his *Die Welt als Wille und Vorstellung* no sooner than 1849. Although it had been written as early as 1849, therefore in full Romantic swing, this work could not at all mould the components proper of Romanticism as it was not known at that time. Quite evident in the latter half of the 19th century only, the philosophic famous work is rather the source of a *fin de siècle* atmosphere, especially in its German variant, which extends its action even later, up to the time of Thomas Mann as a young man. And Eminescu is among the first great European poets who prove the influence of Schopenhauer's philosophy. In this respect he is preceded only by some remarkable figures of Germany of that time, by Wagner and Nietzsche among others. Quite true, the great Hungarian poet Madách preceded him by about ten years, but this may, of course, be accounted for by Hungary's belonging at that time to a political entity placed under the sign of Germanism and of its culture implicitly. But Eminescu is the first great poet not included in this German or Germanized sphere whose work reveals the penetration of this philosopher's thinking.

As a matter of fact, the above-mentioned antecedents of the culture to which Schopenhauer belonged could not be too remote in time from the moment when the Romanian poet came to know *Die Welt als Wille und Vorstellung,* that is within a matter of twenty years after its publication. Nietzsche himself came to know it not long before. Therefore, Eminescu can be considered an original participant in the first Schopenhauer manifestations in modern poetry. In this configuration his originality results from the totally loose character of the relationship he establishes with the German thinker. With him Schopenhauer's philosophy discharges no constitutive function, as with Wagner or Nietzsche, but one meant to confirm, to stress the meaning of uselessness and, therefore, of renunciation, which the poet had appropriated from elsewhere.

Still, in Eminescu's work there are some Romantic equivocal aspects of this philosopher's influence. But there are other aspects in which Eminescu unquestionably leaves Romanticism behind and turns into one of the best representatives of poetry in the latter half of the 19th century. Regarded in his exemplary expression, the Romantic poet moves into an ideal zone he wished for. This zone, no matter whether it is myth as with Hölderlin, dream as with Novalis, utopic fantasy as with Shelley, the spiritual adventure as with Byron or, on the contrary, the harmony of inner peace as with Lamartine, this zone we were talking about, irrespective of the content of its ideality, engulfs all sensitiveness typical of Romanticism. It is Baudelaire's "modernism" that, for the first time, breaks this Romantic monotony, as we might call it, and establishes the dramatic clash between ideal and reality, a clash devoid of any illusions. This dualism, brought about by the new penetration of deep-going and unforgiving lucidity, is popular with all great Symbolists who followed the author of *Les fleurs du mal* in the 19th century. Its characteristics can equally be spotted in Rimbaud's, Verlaine's and Mallarmé's poems.

Independently, but concurrently with them, Eminescu brilliantly stands for an identical attitude to be discerned in the same lucid post-Romantic tension between ideal and reality. It goes without saying that he was also backed by the similarity of Schopenhauer's views with that attitude, but at least to the same extent the stimulus came to him from some elements existing beforehand in him too. The dramatic contrast between the two sapiential orders, between remoteness and nearness, between the world of imagination and the real one, between the fulfilled elemental erotomorphism and the imperfect worldly eroticism, eroticism he evoked with striking sincerity, all this reveals Eminescu in the modern light of his time. Far from being influenced by others, he is the first to create—together with the great poets of that time and on the same place with them—one of the fundamental poetic tenets of the time, which will extend its influence into the 20th century too.

Finally, the modern character of the artistic outlook recorded so far can be rounded off with an equally advanced character as regards the very physiognomy of Eminescu's art understood in its structure. And in this respect the poet intensifies—in the proper meaning of the word—poetry in the latter half of the 20th century. Here, in his poetry, the elementary Romantic character is enriched by a refined component, made up of subtle crystallizations specific to an entire atmosphere of post-Romantic lyricism with a "modern" tinge. But the idea of artistic refinement refers to a too complex, and consequently, too vague nation if one wants to know its general definition only, to which we have confined ourselves. It can really be understood only if the registers making it up are considered separately. From among them mention should be made of the optical angle and the way perceptions are received, the selective order of motifs, the way to treat the material. And in all these registers, besides being a remarkable Romantic, Eminescu also becomes a fine representative of the moment he lived at, which he enriches with his unequalled art.

First, as regards sense perception, Eminescu appears to be one of the most accomplished representatives in synaesthesia in lyrical poetry. For the beginning we shall give some examples we have already used in other cases, which we are now going to illustrate taking into account the new interest. We have mentioned some visual structures which are so complex that they cannot be seen, only felt and, in that case, are suggestively sensed by the poet through hypothetical hearing. That wonderful harmony of the thoughtful forest is the imponderable and only supposed auditive perception of the blossoms falling in a lime-tree forest, an image which the poet records visually when the completing close-up is near. An identical relation is conveyed by a line in **"Călin the Fool"** which we have mentioned when dealing with the Eminescu's sweetness: "For any branch is a string and any leaf is a speaking tongue." The identification by auditive attributes of some elements meant to be seen, such as the branch and the leaf, stands proof to an ample conversion of the visual forest into an equally ample sound notion.

From among the illustrations used in other contexts, mention should be made of one which, by the deep intuition underlying it, transcends the Eminescu moment and rather integrates itself into a kind of intuition specific to this century. As it is a species of synaesthesia we had better remember it now. We are referring to the verse "And you'll hear grass growing." In the previous cases, that is the lime-tree blossoms, the branch or the leaf, the visual hindrance is connected solely with the large number of these elements which, when in a whole forest, cannot be seen all at a time. But when it comes to the growing grass, this hindrance is to be attached to a more secret order, which is anyway more impressive. It is an image meant for the eye and also forbidden to it by the great secret of nature, which, to André Gide's mind, probably conceals its action under the cover of night. In his *Journals* the French writer confessed that, for years on end, he watched for the moment when flowers burst open in spring. But all was in vain. Everytime he found the flowers already open. Changing a visual phenomenon into an auditive one, which is nevertheless inaccessible to sight, Eminescu uses synaesthesia not on the common plane of sensations, but in the register of a secret of things, when his intuition senses, in other words, it listens to, and invisibly perceives a secret concoction of nature he can see only in its effects.

In the end we are going to resort to some examples which we have not used so far, to point out other nuances of the Eminescu synaesthesia too. One of them is, for instance, the description of a precise visual image which is made of olfactory material. In the poem **"Miradoniz"** he imagines "incense-filled tree-hollows . . . with rocks of myrrh that have been broken into bits." Such an association is no isolated phenomenon, it is almost an obsession with Eminescu (it appears in **"Memento mori"** and his prose too). Incense and myrrh create only olfactory representations, which, as regards eyesight, extend to some evanescent images of fumigations at the most. Eminescu changes these data of olfaction into huge, massive plastic expressions, where visuality mingles with some marked tactile influences (hollows, rocks).

Synaesthesia becomes so intense and refined here that again it supersedes by far the means of the time being comparable to some modes of comprehending things specific of our century. We are thinking of the analogy with the famous tree perceived by hearing from one of Rilke's sonnets to Orpheus. The Orpheic singing is so intense that the suggestion of its growth and arborescence creates the visual image of the tree in sound registers. A similar case is to be found in Eminescu before that. In that transfigured nature in **"Miradoniz,"** the odoriferous sensation is so strong and dense that in its own compass of smells it adequately concentrates its power in the visual-tactile of the hollow or rock scattered into fragments. These two images do not make up mere vague fantasies, they are precisely differentiated into synaesthetic suggestions of remarkable profoundness. The hollow is the symbol of closed concentration suggesting the compact durability of heavy miasmas which will not lose their intensity by scattering. On the contrary, rocks reveal also a concentration of strong fragrances which this time, unrestricted from all sides, can scatter yet without fading. Pulverization into effluvia moving away from the olfactory source turns here into big fragments in the still striking sensation they produce.

Finally, in the illustration of the last synaesthetic nuance, the poet confers visual attributes on invisible elements related at most to motive and tactile representations. Thus, in **"Demonism"** he speaks about the breathing of that "golden air." In his vision, the "molten and transparent" gold whereby he describes the air is part of a larger range, that of an ascendingly transfigured nature. This nature ennobled by the vision often discloses all its aspects in colours and substances more previous than the real ones. However, they correspond to the same sensory range. Vergil, for instance, sees the battle of Actium as taking place in a world of gold as it is disclosed to him by the images on Aeneas' shield. By that he changes not only the object of visualization but also visualization itself. In its turn, the transfiguration operated by Eminescu who frequently employs gold as a means of imparting a hieratic quality to things is mostly related to visual expressions, too, like the element itself that is going to clothe them. This can be especially seen in **"Memento mori"** from the initial line in which only the example of that golden sky points to the relation of gold to an element which we do not perceive by visual means but only by motive or tactile ones. Much like in the case of the incense hollow and of the myrrh rocks Eminescu illustrates here the rarer and extremely refined instance of synaesthetic adaptation to the register of a violently transfigured nature.

Synaesthetic intuition had developed powerfully as early as the German Romanticism but its existence in poetry has proved to be much older continuing without break from the Ancient Times as attested by that "ater odor" (heavy smell) in Vergil's Aeneid. However with few really refined exceptions in Arab poetry, the conversion of a sensory perception into another was in former times the object of a more comprehensive, simpler and more nondifferentiated look. Baudelaire was the first to programmatically adapt synaesthesia to the finest and most profound nuance particularization or dissociation. As known, Rimbaud furthered this line thus preparing one of the essential refined components of the modernist poetic climate. In his turn, Eminescu, by a variety of modes, the differentiated subtleness and unexpected originality of his synaesthetic adaptations, illustrates this phenomenon also in its modern range and he does it at the same time with the prominent French Symbolists.

Eminescu's synaesthesis is an instance of his post-Romantic refinement only in the order of artistic vision, that is of the manner of intuitively grasping things. But, the same refinement can be regarded starting from a series of motifs. Of course, these, too, cannot be separated from a certain vision in harmony with them. However, in this case, the manner of seeing is no longer comprised in an initial position as in the case of synaesthesia. Now, the standpoint is prescribed only by the previous specific of the motif. First we come across the very motif of the domestic interior, of the town, of the animal model and only then do we associate it with the standpoint of the intimate lyrical poetry, of the Impressionist sketch, of Parnassian fine arts. This is an entirely distinct section of Eminescu's refinement. We return to the phrase "post-Romantic refinement" which makes us see in Eminescu the bearer of an effective world value of the moment he represents. Such a value comes first of all from the poet's original contribution to that moment itself. With Eminescu, the refinement of motifs is not identical to artificiality, luxury, or their isolation from nature. His refined eye pierces directly into the soul of things with no previous overornate draping.

The serene voluptuousness of the domestic interior results not from the luxury of the objects but from their simple and charming animism as one can see from the line "In a dust heap, lay the grinder, ancient, knotty out of gear" in **"Călin" ("Fragments from a Tale")**. The animist virtue conferred by Eminescu on that hand mill turns it into a true being as is the unpretentious interior in the much later vision of Maeterlinck or of some decadents. The life of the objects is associated with their quiet, with a calm which far from being identical to that suggested by Baudelaire conveys on a small scale the very great lifefulness of nature's rest. Equally original is Eminescu as regards the new motif of the town in poetry. The stylized symbolist park, the sentimental sight of urban melancholy is replaced by him by the vegetative atmosphere of our old patriarchal town. Although vegetation and the moon itself become mere details of urban periphery losing their wild function, they however reveal, much like in the case of the domestic interior that Eminescu's refinement rejects the interference of the artificial—detectable in any "modernism" of the past century—and remind, even indirectly and weakly of the great cradle of nature. Finally, as a last series of motifs the rare image, selected by Parnassus especially from the register of animal exoticism, is attached by Eminescu to some specimens of the familiar, surrounding nature. In this case, too, that cold, slightly strained bookishness transparent in exotic ostentation gives way with our poet to a direct attraction to the surrounding natural world. Everywhere, the refined expression of things is dissociate from the decadent injunction which the notion of refinement often implies. By so doing the poet sometimes goes further than his contemporaries revealing that fine keenness of insight related to the simplicity, and understatement of motifs, a feature to be found only in the early 20th century.

But it is not only the standpoint and motifs that reveal Eminescu's modern refinement. This is equally obvious in the so important sphere of artistic treatment. Here, our objective goes especially to the register of Eminescu's sounds. That in this respect, too, Eminescu leaves behind the old range of the Romanticism is more than evident. The fluid romantic melody results from spontaneous feelings freely reproducing the profuse volutes of fantasy. For this reason, the musicality of the Romantics—with the exception of Hölderlin, almost ignored by them—appears to be merely melodic. Only with the appearance of the great Symbolists—anticipated by Poe and Nerval—and we are referring to Baudelaire first, then to Verlaine and especially Mallarmé—did it change into a harmonic musicality, wholly and deliberately elaborate. At the same time with them but without any trace of influence Eminescu contributed to one of the fundamental fabrics of the most advanced poetry of his time.

Eminescu's musicality is not only reproducing, like that of nature, but also searching, like that of the great composer. It explores, on the one hand, the depths of its being in all the resources convertible into sounds and, on the other hand, the infinite world of language from the angle of the creative associations of sounds and of refined psychophonic effects. Thus, the ensemble of sounds results from a twofold handling, brought in the last analysis to convergence in that unique phenomenon termed by Tudor Vianu "Eminescu's harmony." For instance in the lines "From chaos come I would return / To chaos, oh, most Blessed" he produces such an exquisite construction of vocalic echoes suggesting the moving closer and moving away, the infinite regret and infinite desire. In "Water springs weep murmuring clear" we are also faced with an instance of laborious association of sounds to assimilate the quiver of the springing water to that crying in order to strike a unique chord of the two, major and minor, registers. Such a crystallization of sounds to the end of obtaining an objective value of poetry on the basis of its phonic structure highlights again Eminescu's creative synchronism with the moment where he carried out his activity.

There are therefore many instances in which to the poet universality as a climactic figure of the Romanticism we could add his quality of an essential contributor to the setting of the poetic feature of his post-Romantic epoch.

But, we have stated that a poet can become universal in a third manner as well, that of precursor, of harbinger of future ideas. This last mode of universality is also specific of Eminescu. As one could see, some anticipative indices took shape also by the two previous paths: but such-like indices could not be dissociated from the broader contexts where they appeared only as particular aspects. Here, we shall narrow the range to other anticipatic meanings and forms which enable us to regard them independently.

Thus in **"Ode (In Sapphic Metre)"** which seems to us to reach the summit of distillation towards the essence of being in Eminescu's poetry, the poet develops to the degree of utmost concentration a whole existential dialectic: the poet pursues with stringency the process of entering the state of being in parallel with that of moving out of the state of alienation. From the first line "That I'm doomed to die I believed it never" when the poet still lives enwrapped in the robe of illusion, he moves on to the tragical risk, to the experience of desperation which will propel him into the threshold zone ("Burning alive . . . in flames I'm melting") the only place where he will be able to look for himself in a state of non alienation ("O give me back my own selfhood"), in the equal disalienating imminence of his own death ("That I may in quietness die"). Here Eminescu starts from a repudiation of Romanticism to reach that existentialism cultivated only in our century and which tends to the rediscovery of the being in limit-experiences. Of course, concerns or even full existentialists existed in the past century prior to our poet. But they produced in other fields or genres like drawing or prose. Eminescu knew neither Kierkegaard's *Treatise on Desperation* nor Georg Büchner's drama *Wojzek,* a work discovered and published after Eminescu had ceased his activity. Quite independent of them, the **"Ode (In Sapphic Metre)"** remains perhaps the first valuable piece of existentialist poetry in the world.

Another forerunning feature stands out from the minus zone of Eminescu's grotesque. We have referred somewhere else to the only relative grotesque of the Romantics and the radical grotesque of Eminescu who, affectively destroying a structure touches on the modern asburd. As regards the Romanticism, we have pointed to this fundamental alteration in the special instance of the nightmare; with Eminescu, its grotesque features no longer are particularized, momentary, substitutable, they become durable and attain cosmic proportions. Finally, the closeness to the absurd is also revealed by certain categories of the language. Among them the deliberately striking mixture with the grossest prose, a means of expression copiously used by modern poetry to ruin the preexistent poetic structures. Therefore, in this case, Eminescu fully performs the function of a forerunner, in point of both the internal relations of the grotesque and its linguistic specificity.

In the same order of anticipative resources, we should mention another fundamental feature which could be identified with accuracy only in the light of the last decades. What we want to say is that the poet outdistanced his epoch also by a certain type of active visualization enabling him to see into the depth of things with the eye of our century. This is obvious especially from various expressions of the near register where we could see several instances of optic virtues similar to those acquired by both the art of film and the mode of seeing springing from it.

Such an instance is the expressive detail brought into the foreground and deliberately employed to suggest the whole atmosphere. Let's take, for instance, the following image from **"Călin" ("Fragments from a Tale")**. " . . . At a bench-end, in a pot / Burnt the black wick of rushlight, filling with red mist the cot." This detail, subserved to the ensemble in the case of a passive perception, is here alive and sovereign, as if seen by a magnifying eye, by an original dilation of its size, coming to fill a whole scene. The active virtue of Eminescu's visual perception inverts the order of things and organizes it differently as happens in the motion picture close-ups. Now it is not the ensemble that contains the detail, not the small and partial element that naturally enters the large and complete one, but it is the detail that contains the ensemble; it suggestively incorporates it in itself through the mediacy of a modern eye which not only records but also thinks and operates associations. In this respect, we come across in Eminescu's works with infinitely more subtle optic procedures. In suchlike cases, the poet varies with incredible refinement the distances of panoramic perspectives by bringing the landscape closer to man and not vice versa. We are thinking of the well-known lines in the Fourth Satire: "Ever larger looms the forest, it approaches fast and faster (And so does above the waters the moon disk)". We recognize here the movement of the huge eye of a camera with all the effects of changing dimensions, angles and distances applied to the same object. The power of Eminescu's eye to control space and change it according to his will, to make it mobile, to decompose and recompose it reached

quite early that acuity known only by our century, in some of its literary expressions included.

Finally, what casts light on Eminescu's contemporary virtues is the cultivation of blank verse and not in the inceptive form inaugurated by some symbolists like Gustave Kahn but in the advanced and radical one of today. Poems like **"Oh, Clear Up Cold Dark . . . ," "Demonism,"** or **"Miradoniz"** appear as having been written in a slightly rhymed prose, fragmented only typographically into verses. Sometimes, the very idea appears syncopated resembling some poems of our days. A clear illustration thereof is provided by the following two lines from **"Oh, Clear Up Cold Dark . . . "**: " . . . Sweet ones, with eyes / soft, large, blue, . . . as white as lilies." In traditional poetry, and in Eminescu's too, the immediate attributes rounding off a notion fuse into a single body with that notion as the indissoluble part of the same line. To give an example also with the eye motif, let us take the following images from **"Călin:** "O thou, mortal, transient shadow, with eyes full of sad unrest." In this case, the determinants *sad* and *unrest* are placed quite close to the eyes in the respective line. On the contrary, in the above example from **"Oh, Clear Up Cold Dark . . . "** we come across the mentioned modern-type syncope. The immediate determinants are no longer placed in the same line with *eyes,* now a dismembered notion, broken by an interval, with its attributes *soft, large, blue* appearing now only in the following line. Therefore, not only as general makeup but also as the character of some of the most intimate relations, the blank verse of contemporary poetry was anticipated by Eminescu. All these are fundamental indications of the poet's universality also in what means anticipation.

Eminescu not only employed all the three means deciding the universal character of an artist but he also illustrated them by the most essential expressions. The stamp of universality in such a complete form is to be found only with the greatest world poets. Time and not the exceptional quality of his artistic call was the only element missing for his substantial contributions to make a genuine synthesis of the past present and future as Dante, Shakespeare or Goethe had achieved in their time. At the age of 33, for this is the age at which the flame of Eminescu's spirit waned away, Dante had not produced *Divina Commedia,* nor had Shakespeare written *Hamlet* and Goethe *Faustus.* For this reason, we take the liberty to describe our poet as a more unfortunate equal of the three. More unfortunate but the more touching for us, as the highest symbol of the aspirations of greatness, so many times stifled, of the Romanians' history and past. Seeking to demonstrate the degree of Eminescu's universality, we actually want to share with others this right to be proud, right which we had reserved only for us until now. The highest pride of the Romanians appears thus to be one of the highest prides of the world, another example where human limits have been overcome. (pp. 89-101)

Edgar Papu, "Universal in Scope," in Romanian Review, *Vol. 43, No. 1, 1989, pp. 89-101.*

Al. Piru (essay date 1989)

[In the following essay, Piru offers a survey of Eminescu's dramatic works.]

The recent publication of the eighth volume of Eminescu's **Works,** ten years after the fourth volume of drama released by Minerva Publishing House, opens a discussion on Eminescu's theatre, a part of his creation finally completely published. First we shall deal with the original drama. There are only a few completed but not thoroughly finalized works, published during the author's lifetime (only **Lost Love—Lost Life,** inspired from Alecsandri's *Emmi,* like his **"Mortua Est"** and **"Andrei Muresanu"**—a dramatic poem in three variants—were posthumously published), the rest being smaller or bigger writings, fragments, disparate notes or mere projects. G. Călinescu was the first critic who put the texts together and commented them on a topic most often suggested by the author himself. The new editors put together the variants and, following the coherence and logics of the facts, the adjacent texts, thus getting the most plausible sequence Eminescu might have imagined for his planned dramatic work.

His first dramatic work, dating back to 1868–1869, could be **Mira,** after the name of a character that had obsessed Eminescu and that was resembling Miradoniz, of a poem dated 1872, where she is considered a Weltgeist, a spirit of the world. The initial project contains Toma Nour as well, the character of his unfinished novel, **Lone Genius,** bearing either this very name, or being called Popa and Hilariu, Michael the Brave's envoy to replace Prince Ieremia Movilă with his son Miron-Ştefan or with Marcu, Michael's son. In that play, Mira is Ieremia Movilă's daughter and Miron-Ştefan considers her "the world's princess." Toma Nour has to kill her to prevent Movilă's projected alliance with the Pole king, as she had been promised to be the king's bride. Eminescu followed as a model Schiller's plays *Kabale und Liebe* and *Don Carlos* (Posa's scene with Phylipp). Posa is seen there as "a golden cloud rising from the sea of love," echoing in Toma Nour's words: "The God of genius drew me out of the people, like the sun which is drawing a golden cloud from the sea of bitterness." There are also suggestions from *Romeo and Juliet.* Magdalina (the Prince's mistress), who loved Miron-Ştefan and was aware that had she poisoned Mira, she would have lost his love, gave Mira only a narcotic. Thinking that Mira had died, Toma Nour's son meditates on the theme of death just like in **"Mortua est."** Miron told Magdalina that they were both his father's victims. Mira came back as a ghost (the poet being influenced by Goethe's *Torquato Tasso*) and Toma Nour assured Miron that the ghost is really existing and that he could give life to it. Miron recited some lines from the poem "Lyre Broken against the Rocky World," subsequently turned into "Casandra's Song," changed into the "Fiddler's Song." But finally, urged by Magdalina, Mira wanted to kill Miron, but she fell at his feet; as he rejected her, she killed herself. Miron finally got mad. He was replaced for a while by Prince Marcu, Michael the Brave's son. Michael was defeated and Marcu killed, so Toma Nour's plans failed.

Mira appeared again in a draft of Act V, of the unfinished play **Petru Rareş** (1869-1870), being this time the daughter of Arbore, the Minister of War. She was considered "the killer angel" and poisoned Ştefan cel Tînăr, the son of Bogdan cel Orb, in order to free the throne for Petru Rareş. When the latter came to the crowning ceremony, acclaimed by the people, she poisoned herself, shouting: "I want to remain a sacred virgin."

Mira was the demoniac somnambulant, loved by the angel—poet laureate—Maio and by Petru Majă (Rareş) in the almost completed drama **Stephen the Younger.** She was also Arbore's daughter, a man of the old world, preserver of the glorious traditions handed down to him by Stephen the Great himself: "When, like a wondrous fire-hearted sun / That takes golden clouds out of the sea of bitterness, / He took me out of the sea, out of the people / To royal ranks, to brilliant throne." One can notice fragments of verses from **Mira,** some of which were attributed to Toma Nour. Ştefăniţă—a Faustian spirit, suffering from melancholy (he even recited the lines of Eminescu's poem titled **"Melancholy"**)—who wanted nevertheless to enjoy worldly pleasures, confident in his alliances, doubted by the old man, killed him and wanted to marry Mira, who had been promised to Maio. After her father's death, just like in Faust, she was offered other, unearthly, opportunities and the play ended there. Though Maio, a noble spirit, gave in, Petru Rareş could not aspire to Mira's love. He did not appear in the play anywhere else but on the cast, with the explanation that he was inspired by an "Italian passion" while Ştefăniţă was haunted by an "Arab love." Petru Rareş' portrait was not detailed any further than the coronation moment in a previous project, **The Last of the Muşat Kin** (1869-1870).

Special importance is attached to the drama **Decebalus** written during the poet's Berlin epoch (1873-1874), because of the philosophy of history it contains, an influence from Dio Cassius, mingled with echoes from Montesquieu, and Dochia's words about Genesis ("Oh, why are we not living at the time / When there was no being or non-being . . . ") make Călinescu think of the pessimistic words of Dushanta (Sakuntala); it sounds in fact very much like the cosmogony of **"The First Epistle."** Of great interest is the independent text published as such by Aurelia Creţu in *Manuscriptum* review (1983, No, 3) titled **"In Search of the Earth's Peace."** The messenger is Pater Celsus (coming from high above), his name recalling that of Hyperion (the one hovering above the ground)—i.e., a titan. An adjacent text, unpublished so far, contains the cue of the king who made the following description: "Oh, you titans, poor titans / Who are said to have been chased away from Heavens / Why have they fallen? . . . Can it be / Because of their boundless aspiration? / Because of their boundless heart?"

Whether the fragment **The King and the Knight,** formerly called **Elfrida** (but the name was changed either to Mira or to Sara) could be a translation (Eminescu was at the time thinking of plays with antithetic heroes, like Grachus Baboeuf-Catilina, Morny-Grachus Baboeuf), the **Monk and the Face** is the last part of the poem **"The Starless King's Son"** or the **"Tale of the Magus Roaming among the Stars,"** turned into a play. It is possible to take the magus as a Prospero, if we think of the King's son as a Caliban. Another similitude with Shakespeare's *The Tempest* could be the motif "life is a dream" present with Eminescu as well.

Eminescu made a plan sometime in 1876 to write a *Dramatic Dodecameron,* that is a sequel of plays to be acted during a fortnight (one daily) inspired with slight alterations from the history of Moldavia, since the foundation to Alexandru Lăpuşneanu. Out of his list he had completed to various degrees only *Petru rareş* and *Stephen the Younger.* Starting 1876, he wrote *Gruie sînger* and *Bogdan-Dragoş.* The first is inspired from Vasile Alecsandri's legend. Mihnea Sînger, together with his wife, Irina, killed Prince Iuga Ologul, who was known in history as the son of Giurgiu, the brother of Roman, Alexander the Kind's father. Princess Maria cursed Mihnea to have a parricide son. And indeed, Gruie Sînger killed his father while hunting, taking him for a bear, and lived with his mother Irina, like Oedipus. The second play, written until 1878, took information from *Fragmente zur Geschichte der Rumänen I,* by Eudoxiu Hurmuzachi; Bogdan-Dragoş was the son of Prince Dragul, who had promised, upon his death, to leave the throne to his cousin Sas. (In fact Sas was Dragoş' son, Bogdan being the real founder of Moldavia). Bogdana, Sas' wife, gradually poisoned Dragul and planned Bogdan-Dragoş's death. Suspecting those machinations, Dragul sent Bogdan to go hunting, and, as Ştefan, Sas' son, was sleeping in Bogdan's bed, Sas stabbed his own son to death. The poet changed Dragul with Iuga, Mihnea Singer with Sas and Irina with Bogdana. The following love story between Bogdan and Anna, the daughter, of Toader Lupăşteanu, a landlord from the Bistriţa Valley, is the substance matter of another play, *Dragoş's Wedding,* with a new character, Roman Bodei, Dragoş' confidential servant. Anna is the second name of Veronica Micle, the poet's lover; the play intended therefore to be an image of an archaic wedding, a metaphor for the poet's much dreamt of union with Veronica Ana Micle. *Gruie sînger* contained the texts of some poems, i.e. the posthumous **"When I Saw You"**, **"Venere"** and **"Jealousy"**, while *Bogdan-Dragoş—Dragoş's Wedding* included the variant of **"So Fresh and Frail"** (published by Eminescu in 1879), **"O'er the Tree Tops,"** (published in Maiorescu's edition), **"Lost for Me, Smiling You Walk By"**, **"I Could not Be up to You"**, **"Under the Cloudy Sky"**, **"Renunciation."** Other fragments resembled **"Fourth Epistle"** and **"The Twin Brothers"** Despite some historic inaccuracies, *Bogdan-Dragoş* was the best accomplished and maybe the most exquisite historic drama written by Eminescu.

In the prose fragment *Alexander the Kind* (1879-1880), the prince declared in his first cue: "We have been reigning for thirty years," so Ringala, whom he had divorced ten years earlier, could not appear in scene two. The drama was abandoned, as the poet had not sufficient sources of information (he did not know, for instance, that Iliaş and Ştephen were stepbrothers and that it was Stanca, Stephen's mother, who had been drowned by Iliaş).

Alexandru Lăpuşneanu (1879-1881), the play that was to end the the *Dodecameron,* was also unfinished. But the few

Title page of Eminescu's Poesii.

fragments that were written are exquisite, with flawless verses. The main topic is the murder of Gruie, who had objected to Lăpuşneanu's order (given by the Turks) to destroy the Moldavian citadels. The murderer was treasurer Ioan. Bringing a letter from Lăpuşneanu, declaring Gruie's liberation, Ioan used it to convince Bogdana to give in, which she had accepted. But hearing that her husband had been murdered, she asked the Prince to make justice. Lăpuşneanu, who had pretended in the beginning to forbid a proper funeral for Gruie—in fact one of the adepts of the Prince's policy of restoration of the old patriotic traditions—conceded to put an end to that case, if the treasurer married Bogdana, making her the heiress of all his belonging, to which the Prince himself added a number of estates. Missing his point, the two thanked the Prince, who made a funeral address, praising Gruie and inviting everybody to Bogdana's wedding, making a slight hint that there would be an imminent death, that of Ioan. So, that judgement favoured Bogdana, only because she was mother of Gruie's children, who had been thus avenged. Though cruel, the judge is right, as the crowds considered him: "He's too cruel and heartless . . . but his judgement is divine." There are no details common with the famous short story *Alexandru Lăpuşneanu,* by Negruzzi.

Eminescu had been thinking first of a Romanian *Macbeth,* but then he took *Timon of Athens* as a model.

A few more or less dramatic plays, like *The Tale,* (with a ceremonial character), *Reason and Heart* (focusing on the wedding of a widow, who could have been Veronica), various poems written purposely for the plays or reviewed by the poet himself were published by some editors among the posthumous texts (such like **"Andrei Mureşanu."** Separately were published: *Cassiodor,* a reflexive, juvenile monologue, a draft for a character comedy, fragments of the comedies *The Infamy, Cruelty and Despair or the Black Cave and the Wretched Incense Burners,* or *Elvira and Her Desperate Love for a Ludicrous King, The King's Judgement, The Prince's Justice, Daddy's Gogu, By the Fireside, Cenuşotcă* (only a list of characters). The draft comedy *Bedlam*(*Bedlam-Comodie*) must be associated to the British lunatic asylum, founded in 1247, bearing the name of Bedlam (coming from Bethlehem) with wandering lunatics (Tom o'Bedlam) and beggar lunatics (Bess o'Bedlam). Edgar, the son of the Earl of Gloucester, in Shakespeare's *King Lear,* disguised himself as Tom o'Bedlam.

Eminescu placed the hospital in a mountain resort, where groups of Bedlamites "are strolling one by one / in thinner or bigger ranks / coming together or going apart / sweetly, gently gurgling." The verses were first published by Perpessicius in *Works V,* 653, the section *Exercises and Debris, Romancero español* being a criticism addressed to Iacob Negruzzi, who had adapted, without admitting it, Augustin Moreto's comedy *El desdén con el desdén* that had also influenced Molière's *La Princesse d'Elide,* Carlo Gozzi's *Principessa Filosofa,* Camil Petrescu's *Dona Diana* (influenced by Gozzi). Eminescu must have read Moreto's comedy in a German version. The joke dated back to 1870 and was published first by Perpessicius in *Works IV, Posthumous Poems.*

We shall further deal with the plays completely or partially translated or only copied by Eminescu. The one-act drama *Histrion* by Guillom Jerwitz is the oldest. It is one of the *Dramatische Kleinigheiten* published in Dresden in 1865 by the obscure Wilhelm Jerwitz. The Romanian version with strong Transylvanian dialectical influences could have been made by somebody else who had used a French version, as he had called the author Guilom giving the play the title *Histrion* (*Histrio* in German). It must have been dated 1868, when Eminescu had already copied the one-act comedy *The Night Dragon* by Hyppolite Lucas (starting 1866), translated by P. I. Georgescu, the vaudeville *Margo contessa,* translated from French and the comedy *A Slap or the Coward Brave,* translated by the same person from a French play staged at Palais Royal. The ancient Greeks and Romans called Histrion any comedy actor, in modern times the word refers to the jester, while at present it refers to the talentless if not hypocritical or quack comedian. Jerwitz' drama presented an old, forgotten, derelict actor who hoped at least for Felice's, his step son, success. That happened indeed, the boy acting under a foreign name (Dallma) Histrio was very happy and before the audience realized that the new actor was his son, he died with happiness, which pointed to the importance

and nobility of the great actors that dedicate their lives to art. We do not know whether the play has ever been staged in Romania. It was first published by Ilarie Chendi in 1906 in *Convorbiri literare,* and we think it is one of the translations copied by Eminescu.

In the "draft for Mira" where the character bearing this name had to be Ieremia Movilă's daughter, Eminescu referred to the scene between Tasso and Eleonora in Goethe's play *Torquato Tasso* act V, last scene, in writing the scene in which Miron-Ştefan, the son of Toma Nour, Michael the Brave's messenger met Mira. A fragment of 19 verses was left of this play translated by Eminescu, containing a dialogue between Princess Leonora d'Este and Leonora Sanvitale. The fragment was not used in Mira and it is too short to illustrate the text translated by Eminescu at the time from *The Art of Dramatic Representation Scientifically Approached in its Organic Connections,* by Enric Theodor Rötscher: "Less contradictory antithesis require more subtle nuances. Thus the princess in *Tasso,* a more introvert, suffering and melancholic person has to have a fundamentally slower tempo than Leonora Sanvitale, who is more lively and worldly."

The poet copied only the characters' list of the play *The Diplomat* by Eugène Scribe and Germain Delavigne, for unknown reasons. There was no need to resort to the German version of the play where Count Moreno is the envoy of Belgium and not of Spain. Noteworthy is the fact that Eminescu had selected for a translation or adaption *Bedlam Comedy,* which hints to Scribe's *Une visite á Bedlam.* In 1876 Eminescu might have been looking for fragments for his column in *Curierul de Iaşi,* where he had published a dialogue between Alexander the Great and Diogenes, as an excerpt from *Alexander and Diogenes,* a drama by Fr. Bodenstedt. When Alexander menaced that he could kill him, Diogenes answered that he could as much kill himself. And as he did not accept any gift and had no wish, except of not been deprived of what he could not been given, such as for instance, of the sunlight, he received the following answer from Alexander: "Had I not been Alexander, I'd have liked to be Diogenes."

Another comedy was drafted at about the same period, but the date is not sure. It was the *Ephesus Widow,* inspired from Lessing's *Die Matrone von Ephesus. Ein Lustspiel in einen Aufzuge* from *Dramatische Entwürfe und Fragmente,* making great divagations in case he had not made use also of Ernst Raupach's homonymous play. Eminescu's characters were a proconsul, three conspirators, their sympathiser, Suphis, who wanted to steal Meander's corpse, Talamon, the young dead man, Cinara, his widow, Mysis, a slave (present also with Lessing), Areion, a Roman soldier. The widow is supposed to have facilitated the replacement of the hanged Meander's corpse with that of her dead husband's. G. Călinescu's suggestion that the text was hinting at Veronica Micle's frivolity is ungrounded. But when the so-called draft was made in 1876, Veronica was not a widow yet. The relationship between the two is better reflected in the second half of the play *Bogdan-Dragoş* almost completed in 1878. Eminescu translated beyond any doubt *Vîrful cu dor, A Romanian Ballad in Three Parts* by F. de Laroc (Carmen Sylva) and

Laïs, an ancient one-act comedy, after Karl Saar's version in *Le joueur de flûte* by Emile Augier.

Vîrful cu dor is an example of an etiological text, explaining the name of the peak in the Bucegi Mountains: "In olden times / A youth had yonder died / A whole winter had he spent / In the bleak forest by himself / Until a deadly longing / Melting his heart away." Here is in fact the motif of the young shepherd from folk Ballad *Miorița,* whose last wish is expressed also by Eminescu in his poem **"The Boon which I Last Crave",** begun in Iaşi, in 1876. The originality of Eminescu's lines resounds also in the translation of the German ballad. The text was adapted for music by Zdislaw Lubicz and it had to be re-translated into Italian by L. F. Paganini. Thus, the "opera" was staged in January 1879 with G. Perugini playing Ionel, Miss A. Veratti Dorul, Miss Lavassey Maria. The ballad was published in all its three variants at the same time. Eminescu signed as M. E-scu.

Laïs is one of the early eight versified plays written by Emile Augier (*The Flute Player*), published in 1850. Eminescu's title, *Laïs,* is taken from the German version *Laïs oder Der Flotenspieler* by Karl Saar, a Frenchman by origin, born in Vienna on July 3, 1850. As that translation was published in 1888, in *Reclams Universal Bibliotek,* it was assumed that Eminescu might have written it using both texts, the French and the German one, being at the time in a short relapse of good health. Saar's translation might have been published at least ten years even before the *R.U.B.,* as he had already translated other plays written by Augier, Augier and Sandeau, and several others. Augier was known to have opposed the style of Dumas-fils to the tough style of *Mariage d'Olympe* (1855) and *Les Lionnes pauvres* (1858), after the model of Théodore Barrière the one who had sentenced the cruel courtesan in *Les filles de Marbre* (see also Eminescu's poem dated 1866, **"The Love of a Marble"**). Laïs is the name of a courtesan, probably coined after the famous Thaïs, who was courted by two rich merchants, Psamis of Corinth and Bomilkar of Carthage (the action takes place in Corinth) and the flute-player shepherd Chalkidias, under the name of Ariobarsanes. Chalkidias loved Laïs and to make her notice him, he became a slave and was sold, but he would not marry her unless he were sure she loved him and parted with her courtesan's life. Laïs was seduced by Chalkidias' lines in which he reminded her of old love promises, since they had been kids and she had been called Timandra.

Eminescu could not have written such exquisite verses in 1888, when N. Petraşcu asked Maiorescu to read Eminescu's supposedly original translation. The poet had written two copies, offering one to the National Theatre, but it had not been staged. Maiorescu added the name of Augier and of his play, not that of the German translator and made slight interventions in the text, no more than four.

Augier had been indirectly known by the Romanian public at an earlier date by means of Alecsandri's adaptation of *Le gendre de M. Poirier* (1855), under the title *Hagi Petcu's Son-in-Law.* Other two plays by Augier, *Les Effrontés* and *Le Fils de Giboyer* (1861–1862) (written in prose) influenced Alecsandri in his comedy *Boieri şi Cio-*

coi, in 1873. There followed Eminescu's version, then that of Al. Macedonski (in verses as well), titled *Iadeş!* (1880) after *Gabrielle* (1849) by Augier.

Eminescu's last translation was connected to his drama **Alexandru Lăpuşneanu** and consists of the first 134 lines of W. Shakespeare's *The Life of Timon of Athens.* That version is dated 1880-1881, like the play itself, as much as he managed to write of it. After that, the poet wrote neither original drama nor translations. We suppose that *Timon of Athens* was translated from German making also use of the English original, as this was Eminescu's habit in translations. (pp. 79-86)

> *Al. Piru, "The Dramatic Dodecameron," in* Romanian Review, *Vol. 43, No. 3, 1989, pp. 79-86.*

George Munteanu   (essay date 1989)

[*In the following essay, Munteanu examines Eminescu's creative process.*]

Preceded by Bălcescu and the whole series of martyrs to whom he used to give so much thought, Eminescu was doomed to an existence as impressive as his own work, which may be given endless interpretations just like his life. It is commonly known that the poet possessed a quality indispensable to any individual with great inborn features that may turn him into a spokesman or a reformer. We are talking here about consistency, unfaltering agreement between thoughts and deeds, life and work, rendered in time ever more visible by the hardships Eminescu had to face, adding other new meanings to the original ones. The sense of personal dignity possessed him to the same great extent as his sense of responsibility towards his own people. It was not ostentatiously that the poet lived his short life in complete self oblivion, absorbed to his final breath by the works of his spirit. The honours and comforts of life had obstinately avoided him, but he never thought of pursuing them for himself. He contented himself with endless, industrious work carried out in his temporary jobs, but especially in his personal training for the act of creation and for his creation itself, a realm where he has never been matched in point of proficiency and functionality.

Being so exigent with himself, he was right in asking as much from his contemporaries, from life as a whole, from the whole structure of the world. His thorough and powerful genius, of a Romantic essence in the best sense of the word, determined him to ask for consummate perfection in all fields. We, the offspring of the great poet and of his Romantic age, consider ourselves as more "realistic" and think that we cannot come closer to the absolute than in the timeless succession of the generations. But in the innermost Romantic part of our soul we cannot but understand Eminescu and his whole way of being as a pure symbol of the eternally human aspiration after something different than we had been given. Thrown at the bottom of aerial ocean, impossible to be discriminated from the water, land or aery beings except the awareness of the humiliations we are subjected to by gravitation, we are always thinking to Eminescu, as he is the one to sublimely avenge such humiliations. The hieroglyph of his existence reiterates the hieroglyph of mankind's existence as a whole, whose latency we think surpasses by far the biologic rectitude and its present consequences. In a sequal of utmost counsels, where good, truth and beauty have the same meaning, the rectitude of Eminescu's existence exhausts the wisdom of this land's existence, of the existence of the species on other meridians. Brancusi's *Endless Column* is his counterpart . . .

We could also ask ourselves how can Eminescu's intelligence be studied in a different way? Understanding it, naturally, as the structural fundament of the poet's personality. And we have to take it as such, not only as it is suggested by the whole orientation of contemporary thinking, but also as anybody is aware—except *ad-hoc* descriptions—of the fact that Eminescu used to be one of the most cultivated and intelligent 19th-century poets, but the "idea" (in the Platonic sense) is the very germinative cell of his work.

But Eminescu could not be a spontaneous mind, in the usual sense of the word, as his remarkable dissociative qualities happened to be of more subordinated kind than it happens to be with associative minds, synthetic integrative prospects. Eminescu was aware of that, careful as he was with all his problems, and even noted it in a seemingly impersonal meditation:

> I can imagine learned people, but deprived of a personal talent, that is carriers of an inert being, like a dark hall with an entrance and exit door. Exterior ideas come in through one door, crossing the darkness and going out through the exit door, indifferent, lonely and cold. The mind of a talented man is like a well lit up room with walls made of mirrors. Ideas are coming cold and different indeed from outside but what a whirlwind is awaiting for them inside! The strongest light points out other ideas either similar, or contradictory, debates, concessions, and the great ideas, i.e. the core of his inner life are watching them, trying to match them without contradicting each other. And how do they come out of that well-lit room? Most of them, formerly contradictory, come out united, knowing well each other being fully aware of their relationships, being thus let known to the audience who feel confronted by a harmonious and attractive universe.

Though nobody has paid it any attention, that meditation contains a very suggestive and "modern" description of the features of synthetic thinking, as taken by Eminescu himself. But synthetic intelligence is obviously producing something only after complex accumulations, obscurely gathered at all levels and bound together by the so less disciplinable imagination. The mechanism that starts it is intuition (that doubtful outcome of organically fulfilled syntheses), not the analysis. It is a rather sudden "illumination" than a methodical progress towards a previously circumscribed goal. That is why, even though they cannot be completely separated, the synthetic natures are keeping aloof from the uninterrupted objectiveness of the analytical ones, pointing out a slower rhythm, not so striking as the other's mobility. But there is always a reverse, which has to be also understood, beyond any absolutizations and omissions of intermediary meanings. As unpredictable as nature itself, the synthetic frames of mind are as solid as nature in its results, as impossible to be subjected to an ultimate analysis. Exclusively creative as compared to their opposites, which are rather reproductive, the synthetic minds undertake everything to the end, as their development laws require them to pass through the whole inferno of experience and the limbo of reflection in order to get the right to become manifest, which is the same with a redemption, with an ecstasy. That is why they get the necessary matter by seemingly crooked strange sometimes, but always difficult ways, but they are much more comprehensive (gathering huge amounts of information sometimes from unthought-of areas), completely assimilating, offering the world organically structured productions. The more diverging the synthetic mind's knowledgeable antennae, directed as they are towards the poles of seen and unseen realms, the more acute the tension between the consciousness and unconsciousness, the bigger the unity of the demiurgic centre: an imaginative maelström, attracting everything as in a gravitational breakdown, before passing on to a sovereign creative expansion.

Eminescu seems to have represented the most remarkable Romanian pattern of the demonic nature of such a human being, with all its implications. Its prodigious and uninterrupted inner creation sets forth its own standards from very early stages, hardly agreeing to what could not get naturally integrated, but especially hardly intelligible for those that considered themselves called upon to guide his progress in real life. Psychologically speaking, the poet had no other outlook on things than that of a character in *Cezara:*

> I have a strange mind and heart. Nothing goes in directly. An idea takes days on end to float on the surface of the mind, without impressing or interesting me. Several days afterwards, it goes deep down my mind, joining others already existing there and gets deep roots. . . . My feelings are the same. I may see a man dropping dead in the street and I have no reaction for the time being . . . but several hours later I remember him and start crying . . . I do cry a lot and cannot forget him at all.

Could the poet's attitude have any other consequence than procrastination, when the events were forcing his inner rhythm? The poet clearly showed that to Maiorescu in 1874, when the latter pressed Eminescu to go in for his doctor's degree. The letters we are talking about are valuable sentimental documents, offering an involuntary phenomenologic analysis of the "hardships" of synthesizing intelligence. After indirectly postponing, explaining how many things he would have to study in order to deliver a philosophy course and how long it would take him to assimilate what he had studied and to put them into words for the students "bearing the specific and fresh touch of my spirit," he put it bluntly: "When I have to give a straight answer (yes or no), I generally do not say anything and my genuine primeval character comes out without any further hesitation: I'm dawdling." This assertion is capable of casting light on Eminescu's failures in his practical life and on certain attitudes possible to be checked at any time. The same constant feature pertains in the great solitudes he used to plunge in as a teenager, without any attempt at saving face when he was taken unawares, or in his putting off his doctor's thesis, the persuasive Maiorescu not being more convincing, in this respect, than the strict Gheorghe Eminovici, the poet's father, or in his perpetually intended marriage with Veronica Micle. In fact, the poet had no special initiative, not even in his own field, the endeavours of the spirit, that is, but he knew to discern the virtual proportions and to make a decisive contribution to carry out other people's initiatives. What would have been the "România junǎ", the Putna festivities, the very *Junimea* literary circle, or the Romanian Romanticism without Eminescu's dedicated and farsighted work? One may thus draw the conclusion that, putting an end to all necessary anticipations, his "primeval nature" placed him in the rearguard, befitting any synthesizing nature. But his genial individuality made these who came after him take him as a trailblazer, a Hyperion. This is the "satisfaction" of synthesizing natures—posthumous, in most cases, and directly related to the test of time—of Shakespeare, the poet's main mentor, of Poe or Baudelaire, his peers in many respects. . . .

But besides the outstanding gift of his expression, all Eminescu's prodigalities stem up from his unusual capacity of comprehension and assimilation, which is a secondary demiurgic synthesis, of pushing back elements into their former unity, but from a perpetually new coign of vantage. Genius with Eminescu is mainly that, which has been realized by all trustworthy critics from Maiorescu onwards. Ibrǎileanu, for instance, had found a brilliant formula:

> Eminescu used to be an accomplished entity. He had been endowed plentifully, all sensations, a comprehensive imagination, an outstanding intelligence. He had summed up all ages of mankind and individuals alike. Sensitive and imaginative, like a primitive, candid and curious like a child—newly born against the grandeur of the universe, he was both a knowledgeable scholar and a metaphysical abstractor of ideas.

But to have been able to train as a scholar of history and of political economy, to have been capable of understanding and experiencing the metaphysical problems like a career philosopher, of foreseeing the movements of the universe like an astrologer but of being aware of them only as an Orpheus stands proof, among others, that he is the most gifted synthesizing nature of the whole Romanian people. More than that, one could say that this is one of those extremely rare occasions, cropping up only at millenary intervals, when nature is summoning all necessary means to get to know itself directly, to make all efforts afterwards to scatter them away, frightened by what it had been revealed. "Of a whole day I glean so much, as if a thousand had I lived," runs a line by Eminescu seemingly symbolic for the primeval gifts bestowed upon him by nature. Other lines, most of which intimating the obsession that he would be thunder stricken by Apollo, are auspicious for his other propensity: "Everything is marked for me, I myself a mask may be / Demiurge is urging me, and enticing / Rendering me happy of being your peer / To

fascinate me and not call him on his name." Eminescu's existence, personality and work is taking shape between these two tendencies, bearing the mark of an antique magnificence and tragism, with an impending but permanently postponed feeling deeply rooted in our soul, of a decisive redeeming answer to the question of our existence. Who has labelled this with the worn-out term of pessimism? Summing up eternal human condition, Eminescu's intelligence is grieving for anything, except itself, even though it claims it does so. To put it otherwise, the whole meaning of Eminescu's existence focussed on the struggle of being as free as possible to ponder over the fettered part of human condition. Seen from an absolute vantage, nobody can ask more of mankind or even of its best representatives, for the simple reason that given this share, it was bestowed with everything it needed for its ascent towards an infinite freedom or a freedom necessarily measured with the gauge of the infinite.

Specially privileged as already shown, the structure of Eminescu's genius showed its qualities, its initial "project" not only through the dynamic of its innermost functions. The astonishing thing is that it happened to come up in equally privileged circumstances, that is at the crossroad of some forces that suited him and others. That was the great opportunity offered to one of the most "unlucky" persons of the whole Romanian people.

Studying the components of that "opportunity," the consonant forces, we have to make the objective observation that, contrary to Maiorescu's later opinions, Eminescu might have become something else. As all his closest friends would have liked him to cultivate these virtues they thought they had discovered with him, being aware of his multiple qualities, but not of the single one that submitted all the others. We know about the efforts made in this respect by the critic himself, the last of a series of more or less important "tutors" (his father, Pascaly, Slavici, and so many others). The very events of his life, the more memorable happenings seem to have illustrated this restrictive rule, their nefarious symbol being his ill health. But, contrary to the common idea that he lacked determination, he had always put up—despite Nietzsche's opinion—an attitude suggested by the latter's saying that "the most powerful man is the one with a sole idea," which is perfectly understandable. The genuine synthesizing natures are not a mixtum composition of disparate qualities, open to any kind of activity. They are strictly structured acting like a necessity, structuring inexorably its components, subordinating them to a single one determining the type of initiatives, which happened to be, in Eminescu's case, "A deeply rooted and stubborn longing / For a peerless beauty" (**"Muşat and the Weirds"**) turning into a boundless fancy. But dedicated to art as he used to be, through his very structure of his ideas and living his inexorable destiny which makes his biography and work equally impressive Eminescu was faced with the first consonant possibility out of the more numerous ones we are going to deal with. It is indeed the first, as art is the most synthetic form of spiritual activity and it is experienced as such, when it comes to evaluating the possibilities of human condition to exert itself under the most specific forms, to expressing itself freely, to finding one's own identity. Sciences and philosophy are beyond comparison, and in such a case it is clear why Cantemir and Iorga—giants of synthesizing natures in themselves—did not acquire Eminescu's status among his conationals.

From among all arts, Eminescu dedicated himself to literature, especially to lyricism. We have to dwell a little on this idea, even if it might look rather inferred, but it is similar to those consonances that paved the way for the poet's vocation substantiating his message. Otherwise we would not be able to discriminate him from Heliade or Haşdeu, huge comprehensive spirits, as well, but deprived of constant preoccupations, coherence and depth characteristic to the genuinely synthesizing natures. Had he been endowed with a frailer structure of the creative capacities, had he been born at another stage of the literary evolution, in a country with different traditions, Eminescu might have taken up prosewriting in the tradition of *Gold, Grandeur and Love* or *At Master Vasile Creangă's Manor,* which could have given birth to a great social novel in the spirit of early realism. And why not the ambitious dramatic *Dodecameron* or the other play drafts obsessively present in his manuscripts? But at that time the assertion that the "Romanian is an inborn poet" had not become a *mot d'esprit* as it is now, but it used to be a feeling not fulfilled yet and a longing. How could he have not believed that saying, he who was the very embodiment of the idea of poetry and had foretold a day before joining the Junimea that the "king of contemporary poetry" must also be succeeded by a "poets' emperor"? And he was naturally favoured by the best option with all its consequences to match his gifts in one more way. Grounded in so many ways on the imagination, which among others ways at the bottom of Eminescu's soul, lyrics enhanced once more his position as its representative, because it really is the most synthetical literary form. (That is why the "ineffable" is a mere word, a convenient excuse for the incapacity of selecting without losses the elements of lyrical synthesis, in the same way as the discovery of "poetry" in the works of prosewriters or playwrights is a compliment and a way of inferring that they had acquired an equivalent comprehension.)

Eminescu's openly declared thoroughly romantic spirit used to give a lot of trouble at the time when Romanticism ran counter the opinions of a certain sociological criticism. He had been placed among the critical realists for a while. But afterwards, when the proofs could no longer be denied the critics tried to preserve at least a few "elements" of critical realism. And so on. It would seem illogical to remind such things, unless their logics would not introduce us in various types of positivism, in separating those elements that have to be taken together, in order to understand them. Eminescu would have asserted himself as a Romantic poet anyway, owing to his synthesizing nature, made up of permanently strained polarities. But the poet had to feel it that way and get integrated into Romanticism, summing up its successes at a time when it was the most daring aspiration ever known after total, final syntheses. Sterile discussions have been going on about the "contradictions" of the Romantic poet, of the respective trend, of certain works written under its influence. But this refers to two distinct things. First, that their minds would be more analytical and dissociable and would not encompass the scope of the Romanticists' syntheses. Second, that the idea of "synthesis" is devised, in such cases, as a mechanical association of some identical, inert elements, deprived of any specific identity and tension, of the functions of dialectical complementariness. But a worthy organically structured synthesis involves a necessary and indestructible *complexia oppositorum.* That is, in the case of Romanticism, a combination of "optimism" and "pessimism," of the joy of living with weariness of life, of the real and the imaginative, the local and the exotic, of the most violent verism and ethereal sceneries, comic and tragic, culture and nature, terrestrial and cosmic—and over and over again, with wide, unthought-of overlappings. To put it briefly, it is the espousal of existential antinomies under the sign of a very many-sided *Weltanschauung* (together with their incumbing aesthetization), turning thus into a rediscovery of the *Being* in its original, Heraclitean sense. Could Eminescu have not felt at ease, could he have not identified himself in the Romantic tempest? The truth is that such superb encompassings of things were another lucky consonance for him, one of the numerous other consonances that had roused his synthesizing propinquities, increasing their complexity, refining them, turning the most important Romanian poet into one of the few genuine "classics" of Romanticism in world literature.

It should not be forgotten that Eminescu's age was characterized by imminences, by necessary perennial syntheses, in the realm of culture. Three previous generations had been searching for a *via magna,* to be able to utter memorable ideas on the Romanian soul, assimilating in a very short time the patterns and techniques of modern literary criticism, testing ways of enhancing the expressiveness of their ancestors' language. Being often successful in smaller areas and topics, failing in most cases in their attempts at making a comprehensive whole, those heroic forerunners had the common sense to consider themselves the "labourers"—as Alecu Russo put it—meant to gather the materials and the unflinching belief that the architects of their much-dreamt-of edifice were still to come. And those great masters, the classics, headed by the one who would overpass them, Eminescu, were born at a given time, out of a simultaneous process, similar to that of the bonfires built on top of the hills to herald some important events. What an astonishing example this is in point of the characteristic logic of the development of various realms, and how many interpretations the "scientific" slanderers of criticism had given! The founders of our literary classicism could not have been prevented to ascend to the highest status of representatives, though they had been hurt in so many ways by the world in which they were doomed to be born, as individuals with a certain precarious, almost anonymous status. They were forced to that by certain laws running independently from the inimic rules of the time, the rules of transition from the stop-gap searchings to full crystalizations. This statute was equally and impetuously established by the norms of their own synthesizing nature, obvious in each and every case, irrespective of the realms approached and the specific styles. Hence, in the order of literary immanences, Eminescu's encounter with his epoch was consonant, essentially favourable, against any certain broadly enough circulated preconceived ideas.

A rather significant role in this sense was played by Junimea Society and Maiorescu even if their effort to understand and assist the oeuvre of such an absolute spirit was by the very nature of things insufficient and eroded by intermittences. Given the specific literary circumstances of his epoch and of those who had prepared it, it is even more clear why Eminescu celebrated so passionately in his **"Epigones,"** his lesser and greater predecessors, as all of them had in one way or another smoothed his path to gain a name as a classic.

The last question, from the vantage of Eminescu's permanence, concerns the nature of the poet's in-depth relations with the Romanian nation. The way Eminescu considered his own people, its permanent, defining virtues is standing out clearly from the answer Prince Mircea gives to Bajazet (**"The Third Epistle"**): "Emperors who thought too narrow for their needs the globe's four quarters / Also visited this country to demand our land and waters . . . / I am loath to boast or fright you, but, note well, on coming round, / They all got into great trouble and were levelled with the ground." What does this allegation mean? Of course, the fact that the we, others, Romanian belong to the world, that they are not alienated from it and hence, the Romanian people's force of assimilation. It is a feature put to the test and confirmed so many times after Eminescu, and historians show that it governed even the making of the Romanian people, as both Romans and Dacians used to be great assimilators, both in matters material and cultural. Later in keeping with an ethnogenetic structure, synthetical *par excellence,* originating from forefathers who in their turn were *ex toto orbe romano et dacico,* the settlement of the Romanians "on the road of all evils" turned from curse into benefic circumstance. Compelled by their location and their tormented history to stay not isolated, they were thus helped not to become as indurated as by sclerosis. We, Romanians, have used the opportunity to settle lastingly in the bedrock of our own inner evolution and be at the same time careful about the whims of fate and about the kins projecting their gaze outside their confines. Our so-called "ahistory" was, therefore, organic in thought, curious contemplation and word. This was the amount of history turned into epos that we needed by then, and we got it from transhumance—afar from minor ways, in this context, for it helped us to be anytime substantially present all through the places of our origins. Worth noting is also the fact that by its functions transhumance was for our age, then, the bulky and natural precedent of what is now understood by the Goethean concept of *Wanderjahre.* As a matter of fact this may also be taken otherwise: had we lived in *a history stricto sensu,* we would not have been able to assimilate in such spectacular terms the forms of modern life and would have been assimilated by them.

For, the question we are posed—to better understand Eminescu's exponential force—what have we contributed, we, others, Romanians, to widen the horizons of the world? First, a language without dialects and at the same time, of an unimaginable complexity in its unity, amazing by topic briskness, words of infinite reverberations (born as if directly from the realities they are defining), verbal moods able to cover all the zones of the palpable and the impalpable, inclusive of the prodigious power to absorb, to turn Romanian all the words needed from other languages. It's not characteristic of the Romanians and therefore we are not interested to know—as Elvin Kuhn, the German linguist believes—if "at the turn of the year 2000 the Romanian language will be able to settle international relations" (the assertion starts from its assimilating capacity). But what we know for sure is that the language we have got is endowed with all the guarantees of perpetuity for and the blossoming of the spirit of our nation. We have come before the world with a literature and a large spectrum of folk arts, with our metaphysics and a very rich system of empiric sciences, which we have to deepen even more for a long time to come, in order to know clearly, without constraint how we are. During the more ungrateful, documentarily speaking, days of his time, Eminescu has thoroughly done it but his undertaking was pallidly espoused and followed. Proof of his undertaking is not so much his poems in folk style, but the presence and functions of longing in his work, that overwhelm the meanings deriving from various other newer or older philosophical systems, and assimilate them in a way that is still open to study. For us Romanians, longing is the equivalent, in an absolutely Romanian way, of the *Weltanschauung,* it is the most truthful mirror of the Romanian way of being. It is in longing that persists synthetically not synchretically (that is in a harmony seen as integrating tension, not as a mechanical built-up), the whole gamut of moods from the "Dionysian to the Apollonian one," all the antinomies of human existence and spirit. Who said that the *hybris,* excessive feelings and experience are alien to the Romanian, that he is all poise, balance buttressed by an always watchful reasoning? But reason, even if only in principle, would be the safest way to spiritual dryness if devoid of the substance to be set into order by the great vitalist élans. Curing itself of any preconceived ideas about the "specific," Romanian longing appears at one end with the suffering for what it is and would better not be or by what is not imperiously necessary to the human being, or of what it was and is irretrievably lost, and to the other end with the pleasure of wishing, of hope, of the representation of plenitude (be it even in the sphere of the possible). By longing, the Romanian spirit confesses the fact that it has chosen the hardest existential solution, but also the most human one plenarily: the solution to assume the experience of the real from the vantage of a nostalgia of the absolute.

Replete with the inflexions of longing, close to the core of this Romanian-type of *Weltanschauung,* one can better grasp why it is so specific for the Romanians to accept everything human. But it is also deeply specific for them to leave nothing human develop unilaterally, to leave nothing human go along blind alleys. We are "realistic", of course, as so many have remarked, but we also know that life without longing would be nothing else than savagery, which becomes not to our soul. Or, is this not a proof that we are "romantical enough? We must admit, when we are told, that we have inherited from our Roman ancestors their wisdom (*cum mente*), that every thing is done *bona mens,* with the precision—as a folk adage goes—that we also wish to have the "Moldavian's second thought." It is more complete, more truthful, in this way, implying something from our *sui generis* becoming as a people, which happily turned us dialectical. Intelligence with the Romanians, when one is surely endowed with, is necessarily warm-hearted, and affectivity—so strong with them—appears although under the garb of discretion, owing to a strong sense of the ridicule. Romanian skepticism, real to be sure, is nor total nor dissolving, but only a form of fecund expectation, implying side by side with the things one may have doubts about also a possibility of the contrary proof. Generally, expressions of the ego are also present, but they never hurt common sense, never come into clash with the specifically Romanian humaneness. There is also a complementarity, therefore an antidote to the baits of unilaterality. Which cannot but mean that we are a pre-eminently synthesizing nation and—among the nations having the same profile—we are offering the world an original equation: this synthesis is one of the whole Being, placed under the sign of an "unboundless longing" (as Eminescu would have put it) which commits us in everything to the very end. And, thus, the Eminescian "miracle" appears now clearer against another horizon: the most open understanding of his outlook on the Romanian people, his terrible fury against those tempted to scoff at the "language, at the forefathers, at customs," of his material and artistic life lived against the horizons of longing. His synthesizing genius appeared within a nation synthesizing *par excellence*.

But when it so happened that so many fields of force overlapped one another, that so many "waves" have met in a point of ideal convergence, it was only natural that they all grew into a huge almost unexplainable slope whose peak has been fixed for ever by perennial artistic expression far up in the heavenly sky. Maybe Eminescu himself was amazed when he first realized and put it down on paper that "The God of genius sucked me from my people like the Sun that sucks a golden cloud from a sea of sorrow." (pp. 99-108)

> *George Munteanu, "A Synthetic Genius," in* Romanian Review, *Vol. 43, No. 4, 1989, pp. 99-108.*

Dumitru Vatamaniuc   (essay date 1989)

[*In the following essay, Vatamaniuc surveys Eminescu's journalistic writings.*]

Eminescu's journalistic activity is made of several clearcut stages corresponding to his own status within the sociopolitical context. The poet made his journalistic début in 1870, as a student in Vienna. From the very beginning he pivots his newsman's work on three main topics, which he unfailingly advocates all along his journalistic career. In his first article **"Our Theatrical Repertory,"** published in *Familia* (edited by Iosif Vulcan) in January 1870, he focusses on the theatrical movement examining it in close connection with the struggle of the Romanians in the Austro-Hungarian Empire for the assertion of their cultural rights. This second article, **"Critical Words,"** was printed by *Albina,* Vincenţiu Babeş's gazette, in January 1870, too. Eminescu was advocating again for the Romanians' cultural establishments under the Austro-Hungarian Empire, committed in the support of the strug-

gle for national emancipation. His next coverage is formed of a series of articles on political life (**"Let Us Gather in Congress," "Union Means Power,"** and **"Equilibrium"**) published by *Federaţiunea* (chief-editor Alexandru Roman) in April 1870. Eminescu censures in them the Dual pact concluded between the Court of Vienna and the Budapest governments, characterising that political act as "a diplomatic fiction." Eminescu criticizes the very constitutional bases of the Austro-Hungarian Dual Monarchy against which he enters a literary action still open in literary history. Eminescu is thus involved in the struggle carried on by the Romanians under the Austro-Hungarian Empire and addresses also a call to national solidarity and fraternisation with the other peoples in the Empire, an act by which he outruns many of his contemporaries in the political struggle.

Eminescu's Viennese studies are coeval with another distinct moment in his journalistic activity—the preparation of and the celebration of the Putna Festivities in August 1871. He is the Secretary of the Central Committee for the festivities organized at Stephen the Great's tomb and in this capacity he draws up the *Appeals* to the public and the students of colleges and universities: with his open letter to Dumitru Brătianu, signed by him and Pamfil Dan, and his article **"Note on the Projected Gathering at Stephen the Great's Tomb at Putna"** published in *Convorbiri literare,* in September 1870, he produces a philosophical interpretation of this expression of national solidarity.

Eminescu is director of the Central Library of Iaşi between 1874 and 1875 and school inspector between 1875 and 1876. His journalistic writings of those years have a bookish touch. He presents Constantin Bălăcescu's literary activity and Al. Odobescu's essay *Pseudo-kynegeticos,* in which he defines the art of the archaeologist. He delivers a lecture on "Austrian Influence on the Romanians in the Principalities," subsequently published, in *Convorbiri literare,* in 1876. This is the first work of a synthetical character in his journalistic career, prefiguring Eminescu's main socio-political theses subsequently sustained and expanded in numerous of his articles. The study is buttressed by a rich historic information, partly unused or unpublished yet by other researchers. The life experience gathered as a school inspector fuels his journalistic articles. Eminescu comes into direct contact with the countryside and gets acquainted with the peasants' life, with everything that it meant, with all the sufferings endured, the abuse committed by the officialdom, landowners and tenants.

A switch in Eminescu's personal status occurs in May 1876, when he gets a job as editor on the staff of *Curierul de Iaşi,* a job he fills until October 1877. This is the moment the poet becomes a professional newsman, a career which best meets his fighter's personality. *Curierul de Iaşi* was an administrative gazette that had only one page reserved for "unofficial matters." Eminescu's activity at this gazette follows in the trails of Gheorghe Asachi, Vasile Alecsandri, Mihail Kogălniceanu, who had turned their reviews and newspapers into publications of an encyclopaedic character. *Curierul de Iaşi* appeared thrice a week and Eminescu published the sole "informal" page of cultural, economic and political information. He offers the readers a genuine diary of the war waged by the Serbians and the Montenegrins against the Ottoman Empire, hails the proclamation of Romania's state independence and eulogizes the valiance of the Romanian Army on Balkan theatres of war.

Eminescu gets a job on the editorial staff of the newspaper *Timpul* (late October 1877—June 1883). Apparently nothing is changed in the poet's personal status. But only apparently. For as an editor at *Timpul,* he has not any more the responsibility of everything published by him as it happened when he edited the "informal" page of the Iaşi gazette. The poet chooses to write home and foreign affairs commentaries and only incidentally makes cultural coverage.

Eminescu becomes editor-in-chief of *Timpul* in February 1880, and holds this office until December 1881. This is the climax of his journalistic career. Everything published by *Timpul* is first seen by him and he is accused that he has transformed the Bucharest daily—the press organ of the Conservative Party—into his own newspaper. To this time date the series of articles **"Studies on the Situation"** and **"Movables Credit,"** the most thorough study of the matter ever made. The poet planned to have it published in volume form, as his manuscripts prove it.

The political switch of the Conservative Party to the "young liberals" prompts Eminescu to hand over the leadership of *Timpul* to Gr. G. Păucescu and he remains on the staff as chief-editor for political affairs. His articles preserve the same high standing but he writes much less. As a matter of fact he is obliged to write three articles a week. In June 1882 he goes on holidays to Constanţa and sees the sea for the first time. His poem **"The Boon Which I Last Crave,"** and its variants, was written before the poet would be "not far from the seaside."

The first fit of his illness determines him to interrupt his journalistic activity in June 1883. He resumes this career in 1888 as a contributor to *România liberă,* then to *Fintina Blanduziei* that published his last articles in January 1889. The contributions to these two publications form the epilogue of his journalistic career.

His journalistic productions between 1870 and 1889 show the poet's perfectly coherent system of thinking. When his coverage does not fit his system of thinking he does not drop the subject but draws the necessary demarcation. G. Călinescu rightfully noted that even the Schopenhauerian theses that had played an obvious influence on the poet were vested with significances absent in the work of the German philosopher.

Eminescu is governed in his journalistic activity by the fundamental principle of the primacy of work and he never makes the least concession from it. He judges the development of Romanian society according to this principle which he advocates with all his intellectual power and stylistic brilliance. According to this principle each individual—maintains the poet—has to produce at least as much as he consumes and he extends the principle to the whole society. The state is presented as a natural product not as a social contract between individuals. The mission of the

state is to protect the productive forces and limit, through its bodies, the non-productive factors. The head of the state, irrespective of his status—president, king, emperor—justifies his presence only if he watches the implementation of the laws protecting the productive forces and limiting the unproductive ones. The political parties are justified also only if they gear their activity onto that matter. When examining the situation in Romania, he notes that this very principle is not observed: non-productive factors have considerably multiplied, and grabbed the state. Eminescu defines the non-productive factors as a "superposed stratum," that lived on the exploitation of "positive" classes, represented, first and foremost this time, by the peasantry. The definition devised by him for the "superposed stratum" is grounded on economic criteria and has nothing to do with races. This is best illustrated by the inclusion in the "superposed stratum" of the category of "scribblers" made up prevailingly of autochthons. The ruling prince, who became a king, did not justify his presence at the head of the state, and he accuses the political parties of having a role ambition—to govern, and of acting prompted by utter demagogy.

Eminescu reiterates often his freedom of thinking. In his opinion, the governing political parties or those who aspired to take over the power, should nominate enlightened people, whatever their political colour who wished to serve the nation's interests. Eminescu advocated this principle in a central press organ of an opposition party. This comes to explain why the politicians of the Conservative Party have removed him from the executive board of *Timpul,* an unqualifiable act, serving politically biassed interests.

Eminescu makes daily coverage and, besides discussing questions of a general interest, he involves himself in hottop issues. He writes a series of articles concerning Romania's relations with the neighbouring empires, the "Eastern Question," the War of Independence, territorial changes, amendment of the Constitution, the Danubian question, the setting up of banks, the buying back of the railways, the education reform, the cultural movement. The poet also launches at *Timpul* a press campaign concerning the "Danubian question." The Austro-Hungarian Empire claimed the leadership of the Danubian Commission and prevailing vote, though it was not a riparian country on the lower course of the Danube. Eminescu takes a stand against these claims, claims that aimed at subordinating the country to the neighbouring empire; he does not take into account the colour of political parties, interested as they were by then in a rapprochement with the Austro-Hungarian Empire and he goes on with the press campaign against those interests, in defence of national sovereignty.

Eminescu's journalistic texts, either covering questions of public interest, or touching everyday topics, is unfailingly future-oriented. The poet is deeply concerned for the future of his people and advances chiefly economic solutions. Romania should not remain an agrarian country, and one should impose its growing into an industrial one. Hence, he supports the idea of protectionism, in defense of national output. He thinks, and this is quite significant, that industrial work has an educational role. This work, shows the poet, creates new abilities, develops human intelligence and contributes, side by side with material production to the elevation of a people's cultural level.

Eminescu is criticized by the time's press for his stand against "content-void forms," a formula by which he meant the introduction of some western institutional forms, inadequate to the indigenous fund. This question is the gist of many of his articles, the poet advocating the substantiation of the new forms with a real contents, by supplanting the incapable and corrupt people with well-trained, honest ones, ready to serve their people.

Eminescu maintained thus protectionist measures, the gaining of new abilities owing to industrial work and the investment of a real content to institutions likely to help the Romanian people elevate itself at European material and cultural standards.

Future oriented and pivoted on these topics, Eminescu's journalistic activity identifies the barriers hampering the normal development of Romanian society. The main obstacle was work evasion and the worrying swelling of the number of "scribblers," who lived at the expense of "positive classes, "subjected, more and more to a pauperization process. This entailed all the other hardships, as for instance the lowering of productive capacity of the "positive classes, the peasantry in particular and the alarmingly dramatic decrease of nativity among the "positive classes," which threatened the very existence of the nation. Work used to be replaced by demagogy, which institutes itself as a promotion criterion in social hierarchy and gets ascendency over the "positive classes." The political parties' ultimate goal was to grab power and to place their acolytes in important offices. Eminescu criticizes from this vantage the Liberal Party within which he distinguishes a grouping called by him the "red party," represented by C. A. Rosetti and the newspaper *Romănul,* and another, more moderate one, represented by I. C. Brătianu. The poet blames the "reds" of not taking account in their undertakings of Romania's realities. The comparison drawn by Eminescu between the Liberal and the Conservative party tipped, at that particular historic moment, the scales in favour of the latter. The Conservative Party was represented by notable political personalities, who also had a solid cultural standing, such as Titu Maiorescu (which was not the case with C. A. Rosetti and I. C. Brătianu) not to speak of E. Costinescu, E. Carada and others whose name is frequently quoted in Eminescu's articles. The towering personality of the Liberal Party was, in Eminescu's opinion, M. Kogălniceanu, separated by Eminescu from the "reds" and other liberals. The Liberal Party enjoyed nevertheless a much larger social basis than the Conservative one, made up of the ascending bourgeoisie. This comes to explain why the authority of the Conservative Party members was fading away in step with the disappearance of the political personalities, who would soon leave the scene of political life. Eminescu counterposes to the "new icons" (the liberal government) the "old icons", illustrative of the economic situation of the "positive classes" and the Romanian society's progress in those times. The poet is reproached to plead for a return to the past

which is not justified by his journalistic activity. The poet himself shows repeatedly that a return to the past is impossible given the irreversibility of historical development. The poet does not invoke any "old icons." He only thinks of the epochs of Mircea the Great, Alexander the Kind, Stephen the Great, Matei Basarab, and, of a more recent one, that of Alexandru Ioan Cuza. Those epochs, and the ruling princes are evoked for their stability, for their military strength, for wise government, which taken together, ensured the independence and progress of Romanian society.

Eminescu is animated in his journalism by his confidence that all the evils sickening society at his time could be eradicated. The poet serves his credo with a dedication which goes to self-sacrifice. His criticism is addressed to the monarchy, to the political parties, the state administration, from minister and prefect, to mayor, and eventually to the "scribbler." His words of praise are addressed to a sole institution, the Army. This is explained by the fact that he considered it as formed of the peasantry, the "positive class," that had to make the greatest sacrifices both at time of peace and of war. On the other hand, the Army was not so much at the beck and call of the political parties and was, in Eminescu's opinion, the sole guarantee of defence of the Romanian national state's independence.

Eminescu's contemporaries were taught by his "old icons" and "new icons" lessons for the future development of Romanian society. If they could not be applied then, their future orientation proved consonant with the historical development half a century later. (pp. 216-21)

Dumitru Vatamaniuc, "Ardency of the Journalistic Word," in Romanian Review, *Vol. 43, Nos. 5-6, 1989, pp. 216-21.*

FURTHER READING

Al-George, Sergiu. "Eminescu—The Archetype." *Romanian Review* 42, No. 7 (1988): 39-50.

   Explores the influence of East Indian culture on Eminescu.

Bădescu, Ilie. "Sociological Horizon." *Romanian Review* 40, No. 1 (1986): 23-31.

   Focuses on sociological insights in Eminescu's journalism.

Bhose, Amita. "Eminescu, Tagore, Kalidasa." *Romanian Review* 42, No. 7 (1988): 70-7.

   Demonstrates that "in order to study the evolution of Eminescu's thinking and to seek the grounds for his proclivity for India, it is necessary to look back to his early writings."

————. "Cosmology of Mihai Eminescu." *Cahiers Roumains d'Etudes Littéraires* 2 (1989): 76-85.

   Defines "Eminescu's vision of the evolution of the world" as outlined in his poetry.

Carduner, Jean; Roşu, Lucian; Natanson, Karl, eds. *Mihai Eminescu: Symposium Dedicated to the 135th Anniversary of the Greatest Romanian Poet.* Ann Arbor: The Department of Romance Languages, 1985, 122 p.
  Contains studies and translations of Eminescu's poetry.

Drăgan, Mihai. "National Consciousness and Prescience." *Romanian Review* 43, Nos. 5-6 (1989): 198-207.
  Explores the development of Eminescu's concept of national identity.

Dumitrescu-Buşulenga, Zoe. "A Poet in the Destiny of His People." *Romanian Review* 43, Nos. 5-6 (1989): 4-6.
  Discusses the response of critics, historians, and the reading public to Eminescu's poetry in the years since his death.

Gáldi, László. "Petőfi and Eminescu." *The American Slavic and East European Review* VII (1948): 171-79.
  Addresses "the parallel characteristics" of Hungarian poet Sándor Petőfi and Eminescu.

Iorga, Nicolae. Introduction to *Poems of Mihail Eminescu,* translated by E. Sylvia Pankhurst and I. O. Stefanovici, pp. xiii-xix. London: Kegan Paul, Trench, Trubner & Co., 1930.
  Describes Eminescu as "one of those rare spirits in whom one seems to hear, not the individual, but the people itself, united and embodied in him."

MacGregor-Hastie, Roy. Introduction to *Mihai Eminescu: Poems,* translated by Roy MacGregor-Hastie, pp. 4-23. Cluj-Napoca, Romania: Dacia Publishing House, 1980.
  Discusses the Romanian language and explains difficulties encountered in the translation of Eminescu's poems into English.

Mihăescu, Valentin F. "The Sap of Ideas." *Romanian Review* 40, No. 1 (1986): 36-41.
  Discusses the relationship between Eminescu's poetry and his journalism, describing them "as two complementary undertakings, two illustrations of one and the same set of ideas."

Oprea, Alexandru. "The Journalist's Physiognomy." *Romanian Review* 40, No. 1 (1986): 10-23.
  Contends that Eminescu's journalism "justified the concept of the committed writer as a sensitive seismograph and spokesman of his nation's sorrows and aspirations."

Popa, George. "Is 'Hyperion' a Drama of Time?" *Cahiers Roumains d'Etudes Littéraires* 2 (1989): 46-58.
  Explores "various philosophical interpretations given to Eminescu's masterpiece, 'Luceafarul.' "

Popescu, Corina. "Eminescu and Leopardi: the Revelation of the Infinite." *Romanian Review* 42, No. 11 (1988): 85-94.
  Describes a "spiritual kinship" between Eminescu and the Italian poet Giacomo Leopardi.

"Eminescu as Seen by His Contemporaries." *Romanian Review* 40, No. 1 (1986): 42-80.
  Recollections of Eminescu by six of his contemporaries, including I. L. Caragiale and Iacob Negruzzi.

Scarlat, Mircea. "Aesthetic Interest." *Romanian Review* 40, No. 1 (1986): 31-6.
  Focuses on the literary value of Eminescu's journalism, with "its many-sided artistic qualities, in full consonance with the poet's genius."

Sorescu, Roxana. "Eminescu and Poe." *Romanian Review* 41, No. 11 (1987): 62-8.
  Compares Eminescu's poem "Melancholy" to Edgar Allan Poe's tale "The Fall of the House of Usher."

Tappe, E. D. "The Centenary of Mihai Eminescu." *The American Slavic and East European Review* X (1951): 50-5.
  Praises Eminescu's lyric poetry, describing him as a "treasure of Rumanian literature."

Todoran, Eugen. "The Sacred Mountain and the Abysmal Phenomenon." *Cahiers Roumains d'Etudes Littéraires* 2 (1989): 12-25.
  Compares opposing critical approaches to Eminescu's works expressed by Tudor Arghezi and Lucian Blaga.

Zub, Al. "Assuming National History." *Romanian Review* 43, Nos. 5-6 (1989): 221-26.
  Discusses Eminescu's poetry as "a meditation on history as human destiny and adventure."

Samuel Ferguson

1810-1886

Irish poet, short story writer, essayist, and dramatist.

Ferguson was one of the first poets to draw on Irish history and folklore as sources of literary inspiration. Lauded for their vivid evocation of Irish mythical characters, many of Ferguson's poems adapt ancient Celtic battle sagas to address themes of Irish strength and nobility. His work was seminal in the development of an Irish national literature and played a significant role in the Irish Literary Renaissance during the late nineteenth and early twentieth centuries, influencing such writers as William Butler Yeats, James Joyce, and John Millington Synge.

Born in Belfast in 1810, Ferguson was raised in a Protestant family. He received his primary and secondary education at the Belfast Academical Institution, which was dedicated to the promotion of unity between Irish Protestants, who favored continued union with Great Britain, and Irish Catholics, who had long agitated for an independent republic. The question of religious sectarianism in Ireland became a compelling concern for Ferguson, who several times modified his views on the subject. In 1832, while he was studying law in Dublin, Ferguson published his first poem, "The Forging of the Anchor," in *Blackwood's Edinburgh Magazine,* and for the next six years he continued to publish poems, essays and short stories in Irish literary journals. One of his most significant works during this period, "Dialogue between the Head and Heart of an Irish Protestant," was published in the *Dublin University Review* in November, 1833. In this essay, Ferguson gave what many consider to be a cogent and passionate voice to the sentiments of members of the Protestant ruling class, describing the dilemma of an individual who feels compassion for his Catholic countrymen because of the limited educational and economic opportunities afforded them, yet is convinced that their problems stem from intellectual and cultural inferiority. In the same year, Ferguson published a short story depicting fourteenth-century life in Ireland entitled "Return of the Claneboy." He later remarked that this work was "the first indication of my ambition to raise the native element of Irish History to a dignified level," adding that this ambition "may be taken as the key to almost all the literary work of my subsequent life." After 1833, Ferguson's conception of the Irish people as two distinct groups separated by religion began to fade as his study of Irish history inspired him to concentrate on the common heritage of the two groups rather than the seemingly irreconcilable differences.

Ferguson stopped writing poetry for some time after he was appointed to the Irish bar in 1838, but he continued to read extensively in Irish history. The famine in Ireland in 1847, during which the English government failed to offer relief to the largely Catholic peasantry, and the work of Thomas Davis, the founder of the pro-republic Young

Ireland political movement and the *Nation* magazine, increased Ferguson's sympathy for Catholics and he began to act on his nonsectarian views. In 1848, he defended Dalton Williams, a Catholic who was falsely accused of treason. Although the others who were accused along with Williams were convicted, Ferguson's expert defense of his client resulted in an acquittal. Later that same year, Ferguson met and married Mary Catherine Guinness, the daughter of one of the wealthiest Protestant businessmen in Ireland. Biographers maintain that because of the prominence of his wife's family in the Anglo-Irish community, Ferguson's expression of nonsectarian views effectively ceased. In 1867 he gave up the practice of law to accept the position of Deputy Keeper of Public Records, and for the next two decades he concentrated increasingly on literary and historical pursuits, writing poetry as well as studying and translating ancient Celtic works. Ferguson died in 1886.

Critics praise Ferguson's poetry for its vivid depiction of the life of the ancient Celts, noting that his careful study of the culture added veracity to his writings and set him apart from other writers, such as James Mangan, who used Celtic legends as the basis for poetry but failed to create a realistic portrait of the Celtic period. Robert Welch has observed that Ferguson's is "an objective poetry, delighting in the externals of the old Irish world, its swift, energetic, often brutal physicality." Critics find this attention to detail most effective in Ferguson's shorter poems, including "The Vengeance of the Welshmen of Tirawley" (1845), a poem recounting the conflict between two Welsh clans who had settled in the west of Ireland that is widely considered Ferguson's best work. His most ambitious project, *Congal,* is an epic poem based on the legend of the seventh-century Battle of Moira between Domnal, High King of Ulster, and the Congal clan. While critics praise Ferguson's treatment of high adventure and epic themes in the poem, they find the narrative weakened by frequent moralizing. Ferguson has also been faulted for ineffective use of prosodic conventions and poetic imagery, although some critics have asserted that these technical flaws were the result of his attempt to imitate the poetic style and linguistic cadences of his Celtic-language sources.

Commentators who were also participants in the Irish Literary Renaissance highly praised Ferguson's work, particularly celebrating his efforts to reinvigorate Irish literature with Celtic subjects. Yeats pronounced Ferguson "the greatest poet Ireland has produced, because the most central and most Celtic." However, subsequent critics have suggested that Yeats overestimated Ferguson's poetic abilities and note that his primary contributions to modern literature were his painstaking illumination of the roots of Irish culture and his use of such materials to establish a uniquely Irish literary tradition. Alfred Deering concluded that whoever writes "the Literary History of Ireland, will take his point of departure from the work of Sir Samuel Ferguson."

(See also *Dictionary of Literary Biography,* Vol. 32.)

PRINCIPAL WORKS

The Cromlech on Howth   (poetry) 1861
Lays of the Western Gael, and Other Poems (poetry) 1865
Father Tom and the Pope; or, A Night at the Vatican (prose) 1867
Congal: A Poem in Five Books (poetry) 1872
Deirdre: A One-Act Drama of Old Irish Story   (drama) 1880
Poems (poetry) 1880
The Forging of the Anchor (poetry) 1883
The Hibernian Nights' Entertainments   (short stories) 1887
Lays of the Red Branch (poetry) 1897
Poems of Sir Samuel Ferguson (poetry) 1916
Poems (poetry) 1963

The Dublin Review   (essay date 1865)

[*In the following excerpt, the critic reviews Ferguson's*

Lays of the Western Gael, and Other Poems, praising the Irish spirit in the poet's expression.]

Mr. Ferguson has accomplished the problem of conveying the absolute spirit of Irish poetry into English verse, and he has done so under the most difficult conceivable conditions—for he prefers a certain simple and unluxuriant structure in the plan of his poems, and he uses in their composition the most strictly Saxon words he can find. But all the accessories and figures, and still more a certain weird melody in the rhythm, that reminds the ear of the wild grace of the native music, indicate at every turn what Mr. Froude has half-reproachfully called "the subtle spell of the Irish mind." It is not surprising to find even careful and accomplished English critics unable to reach to the essential meaning of this poetry, which to many evidently appears as bald as the style of Burns first seemed to Southron eyes, when he became the fashion at Edinburgh eighty years ago. And yet to master the dialect of Burns is at least as difficult as to master the dialect of Chaucer, while Mr. Ferguson rarely uses a word that would not be passed by Swift or Defoe. Before one of the most beautiful, simple, and graceful of his later poems, a recent critic paused, evidently dismayed by the introduction, of which, however, not willing to dispute the beauty, he quoted a few lines. It was an old Irish legend, versified with surpassing grace and spirit, of which this is the argument. Fergus MacRoy, King of Ulster in the old Pagan times, was a very good king of his kind. He loved his people and they loved him. He was handsome, and strong, and tall. He bore himself well in war and in the chase. He drank with discretion. Nevertheless his life had two troubles. He did not love the law; and he did love a widow. To listen as Chief Justiciary to the causes, of which a constant crop sprang up at Emania, tares and corn thickly set together, troubled him sorely. To make verses to the widow on the other hand, came as easy as sipping usquebaugh or metheglin. He proposed, and though a king was refused; but not discouraged, pressed his suit again and again. And at last Nessa the fair yielded, but she made a condition that her son Conor should sit on the judgment-seat daily by his stepfather's side. This easily agreed, Nessa became Queen, while, as Fergus tells the tale:

> While in council and debate
> Conor daily by me sate;
> Modest was his mien in sooth,
> Beautiful the studious youth,
>
> Questioning with eager gaze,
> All the reasons and the ways
> In the which, and why because
> Kings administer the laws.

In this wise a year passed, the youth diligently observant, with faculties ripening and brightening as his Majesty's grew more consciously rusty and slow; and then a crisis came, which Mr. Ferguson describes in verses of which it is hard to say whether they best deserve the coif or the laurel, for in every line there is the sharp wit of the lawyer as well as the vivid fancy of the poet:—

> Till upon a day in Court
> Rose a plea of weightier sort,
> Tangled as a briary thicket

Were the rights and wrongs intricate

Which the litigants disputed,
Challenged, mooted, and confuted,
Till when all the plea was ended
Nought at all I comprehended.

Scorning an affected show
Of the thing I did not know,
Yet my own defect to hide,
I said, "Boy judge, thou decide."

Conor with unalter'd mien,
In a clear sweet voice serene,
Took in hand the tangled skein,
And began to make it plain.

As a sheep-dog sorts his cattle,
As a king arrays his battle,
So the facts on either side
He did marshal and divide.

Every branching side-dispute
Traced he downward to the root
Of the strife's main stem, and there
Laid the ground of difference bare.

Then to scope of either cause,
Set the compass of the laws,
This adopting, that rejecting,—
Reasons to a head collecting,—

As a charging cohort goes
Through and over scatter'd foes,
So, from point to point, he brought
Onward still the weight of thought

Through all error and confusion,
Till he set the clear conclusion
Standing like a king alone,
All things adverse overthrown,

And gave judgment clear and sound:—
Praises filled the hall around;
Yes, the man that lost the cause
Hardly could withhold applause.

In these exquisite verses, the language is as strict to the point as if it were taken from Mr. Smith's "Action at Law;" but the reader will remark how every figure reminds him, and yet not in any mere mimetic fashion, of the spirit and illustrations of the Ossianic poetry. Nevertheless each word taken by itself is simple Saxon. Its Celtic character only runs like a vein through the poem, but it colours and saturates it through and through.

The greatest of Mr. Ferguson's poems, however, is undoubtedly **"The Welshmen of Tirawley,"** a ballad which we do not fear to say, is unsurpassed in the English language, or perhaps in even the Spanish. Its epic proportion and integrity, the vivid picturesqueness of its phraseology, its wild and original metre, its extraordinary realisation of the laws and customs of an Irish clan's daily life, the stern brevity of its general narrative, and the richness of its figures, though all barbaric pearl and gold, give it a pre-eminent place among ballads. Scott would have devoted three volumes to the story, were it not for the difficulty of telling some of its incidents. Mr. Ferguson exhibits no little skill in the way that he hurries his readers past what he could not altogether omit. For the facts upon which the

ballad is founded are simply horrible, and they are historically true. (pp. 307-09)

["The Welshmen of Tirawley"] is indeed unique in its order: no Irish ballad approaches its wild sublimity and the thoroughness of detail with which it is conceived and executed. The only Irish narrative ballad which can bear a general comparison with it is Mr. Florence MacCarthy's "Foray of Con O'Donnell," a poem as perfect in its historical reality, in the aptness of all its figures, illustrations, and feats of phrase to a purely Celtic ideal, and which even surpasses **"The Welshmen"** in a certain easy and lissome grace of melody, that falls on the ear like the delicately drawn notes of Carolan's music. But this grace is disdained by the grim and compressed character which animates every line of Mr. Ferguson's ballad. His other works, fine of fancy and ripe of phrase as they are, fall far below it. **"The Tain Quest"** does not on the whole enthral the reader, or magnetize the memory. **"The Healing of Conall Carnach,"** and **"The Burial of King Cormac"** are poems that will hold their place in many future Books of Irish Ballads; they are unusually spirited versifications of passages from the more heroic period of early Irish history; but excepting occasional lines, they only appear to be the versifications of already written legends. The ballad of Grace O'Malley, commonly called **"Grana Uaile,"** may be advantageously contrasted with these, and it contains some verses of singular power—as, for example, where the poet denies the imputation of piracy against this lady who loved to roam the high seas under her own commission—

But no: 'twas not for sordid spoil
Of barque or sea-board borough,
She plough'd with unfatiguing toil
The fluent-rolling furrow;
Delighting on the broad-back'd deep
To feel the quivering galley
Strain up the opposing hill, and sweep
Down the withdrawing valley.

"Aideen's Grave" is a poem of a different kind, full of an exquisite melancholy grace; and where Ossian is supposed to apostrophize his future imitator, it is as if he thought after the manner of the Fenians, but was withal master of every symphony of the English tongue,—

Imperfect in an alien speech
When wandering here some child of chance,
Through pangs of keen delight shall reach
The gift of utterance,—
To speak the air, the sky to speak,
The freshness of the hill to tell,
Who roaming bare Ben Edar's peak,
And Aideen's briary dell,
And gazing on the Cromlech vast,
And on the mountain and the sea,
Shall catch communion with the past,
And mix himself with me.

There are lines in this poem that a little remind us of Gray, as—

At Gavra, when by Oscar's side
She rode *the ridge of war;*

and again in the **"Farewell to Deirdre"** there is something in the cast and rhythm of the poem, rather than in any individual word or line, that recalls Scott's "Farewell to North Maven." But to say so is not to hit blots. Mr. Ferguson's is beyond question the most thoroughly original vein of poetry that any Irish Bard of late days has wrought out. . . . (pp. 314-15)

> *A review of "Lays of the Western Gael and Other Poems," in* The Dublin Review, *n.s., Vol. IV, No. VIII, second quarter, 1865, pp. 307-15.*

W. B. Yeats   (essay date 1886)

[*The leading figure of the Irish Renaissance and a major poet in twentieth-century literature, Yeats was also an active critic of his contemporaries' works. As a critic he judged the works of others according to his own poetic values of sincerity, passion, and vital imagination. In the following excerpt from an essay that originally appeared in the* Dublin Review *in 1886, he applauds Ferguson's use of material from Irish legends, extolling him as Ireland's greatest poet.*]

In the literature of every country there are two classes, the creative and the critical. In Scotland all the poets have been Scotch in feeling, or, as we would call it, national, and the cultured and critical public read their books, and applauded, for the nation was homogeneous. Over here things have gone according to an altogether different fashion.

It has not paid to praise things Irish, or write on Irish subjects; but the poet, who is, as far as he is a poet at all, by the very nature of his calling a man of convictions and principle, has gone on remaining true to himself and his country, singing for those who cannot reward him with wealth or fame, who cannot even understand what he loves most in his work. This he has done while the Irish critic, who should be a man of convictions, but generally becomes, by the force of circumstances a man of tact, industry, and judgment; who studies the *convenances* of the literary world and praises what it is conformable to praise, has remained with his ears to the ground listening for the faintest echo of English thought. Meanwhile the poet has become silent or careless, for everywhere the supply ultimately depends on the demand. If Ireland has produced no great poet, it is not that her poetic impulse has run dry, but because her critics have failed her, for every community is a solidarity, all depending upon each, and each upon all. Heaven and earth have not seen the man who could go on producing great work without a sensitive and exacting audience. Why did a writer like Sir Samuel Ferguson publish in a long life so little poetry, and after he had given evidences of such new and vivid power, become no longer vocal, and busy himself mainly with matters of research?

The greatest of his faculties was killed long ago by indifference.

It is a question whether the most distinguished of our critics, Professor [Edward Dowden of Trinity College], would not only have more consulted the interests of his country, but more also, in the long run, his own dignity and reputation, which are dear to all Irishmen, if he had devoted some of those elaborate pages which he has spent on the much bewritten George Eliot, to a man like the subject of this article. A few pages from him would have made it impossible for a journal like the *Academy* to write in 1880, that Sir Samuel Ferguson should have published his poetry only for his intimate friends, and that it did not even 'rise to the low water-mark of poetry.' Remember this was not said of a young man, but one old, who had finished his life's labour. If Sir Samuel Ferguson had written to the glory of that, from a moral point of view, more than dubious achievement, British civilization, the critics, probably including Professor Dowden, would have taken care of his reputation.

Lately another professor of Trinity appears to have taken most pleasure in writing [in the *Athenaeum* (14 August 1886), see Further Reading], not that the author of **Congal** was a fine poet, nor that he was a profound antiquarian, but in assuring us that he was an 'orderly citizen'; which, if it means anything, means, I suppose, that unlike Socrates, he never felt the weight of the law for his opinions.

'I would,' said one of the most famous of living English poets [William Morris] to the author of this article, 'gladly lecture in Dublin on Irish literature, but the people know too little about it.'

The most cultivated of Irish readers are only anxious to be academic, and to be servile to English notions. If Sir Samuel Ferguson had written of Arthur and of Guinevere, they would have received him gladly; that he chose rather to tell of Congal and of desolate and queenly Deirdre, we give him full-hearted thanks; he has restored to our hills and rivers their epic interest. The nation has found in Davis a battle call, as in Mangan its cry of despair; but he only, the one Homeric poet of our time, could give us immortal companions still wet with the dew of their primal world.

To know the meaning and mission of any poet we must study his works as a whole. Sir Samuel Ferguson has himself pointed out how this may best be done in his own case. He tells us that the main poems in his first volume and his last should be read in the following order:—**"Twins of Macha"** (*Poems,*) **"The Naming of Cuchullin"** (*Poems,*) **"Abdication of Fergus"** (*Lays of the Western Gael,*) **"Mesgedra"** (*Poems,*) **"Deirdre"** (*Poems,*) **"Conary"** (*Poems,*) **"Healing of Conall Carnach"** (*Lays,*) **"The Tain Quest"** (*Lays.*)

"The Twins of Macha" and **"The Naming of Cuchullin"** give us the keynote of his work—that simplicity, which is force. He is never florid, never for a moment rhetorical. We see at once that he has the supreme gifts of the storyteller—imagination enough to make history read like romance, and simplicity enough to make romance read like history.

The boy Setanta approaching at night the house of the great smith, Cullan, is attacked by the smith's gigantic watch dog and kills it. The old man laments the loss of his faithful hound:—

> Boy, for his sake who bid thee to my board
> I give thee welcome: for thine own sake, no.
> For thou hast slain my servant and my friend,
> The hound I loved, that, fierce, intractable

To all men else, was ever mild to me.
He knew me; and he knew my uttered words,
All my commandments, as a man might know;
More than a man he knew my looks and tones
And turns of gesture, and discerned my mind
Unspoken, if in grief or if in joy.
He was my pride, my strength, my company,
For I am childless; and that hand of thine
Has left an old man lonely in the world.

The boy declares that till he has trained the watchdog's whelp to take the place of the dead hound, he himself will guard the house, remaining at his post by day and by night. Those who are standing by cry out that henceforth his name shall be Cuchullin, the 'Hound of Cullan.' All this is told with such simplicity and sincerity that we seem to be no longer in this modern decade, but listening to some simple and savage old chief telling his companions round a forest fire, of something his own eyes have seen. There is not much fancy, little of the subtler forms of music. Many a minor English poet whom the world will make haste to forget, has more of these; but here are the very things which he has not, the germinal thoughts of poetry.

The **"Abdication of Fergus"** follows next in the cycle. The poet-king, who loves hunting and the freedom of the great wood, far better than the councils is delighted by the wisdom with which his stepson who sits beside him on the judgment seat, arrays in some most tangled case argument against argument—

> As a sheep-dog sorts his cattle,
> As a king arrays his battle.

He takes from his head the crown and lays it beside him on the bench. Let Fergus tell his own tale.

> And I rose, and on my feet
> Standing by the judgment-seat,
> Took the circlet from my head,
> Laid it on the bench and said:—
>
> 'Men of Uladh, I resign
> That which is not rightly mine,
> That a worthier than I
> May your judge's place supply.
>
> Lo, it is no easy thing
> For a man to be a king,
> Judging well, as should behove
> One who claims a people's love.
>
> Uladh's judgment-seat to fill
> I have neither wit nor will.
> One is here may justly claim
> Both the function and the name.
>
> Conor is of royal blood:
> Fair he is; I trust him good;
> Wise he is we all may say
> Who have heard his words to-day.
>
> Take him therefore in my room,
> Letting me the place assume—
> Office but with life to end—
> Of his counseller and friend.'
>
> So young Conor gained the crown;
> So I laid the kingship down;

Laying with it as I went
All I knew of discontent.

In **"Mesgedra,"** Conall Carnach, after Cuchullin the greatest of the Red-Branch chieftains, finds his enemy, Mesgedra, with one arm disabled, taking sanctuary under a sacred tree, and, in order that they may fight on equal terms, binds one of his own arms to his side, and when a chance blow releases it, binds it again.

We now come to **"Deirdre,"** which I hold to be the greatest of Sir Samuel Ferguson's poems. It is in no manner possible to do it justice by quotation. There is an admirable, but altogether trivial, English poet called Edmund Gosse. If fate compelled me to review his work, and to review also some princely ancient Homer or Aeschylus, and to do this by the method of short quotations, the admirable Londoner, in the minds of many readers, would rule the roost. For in his works grow luxuriantly those forms of fancy and of verbal felicity that are above all things *portable;* while the mighty heathen sought rather after breadth and golden severity, knowing well that the merely pretty is contraband of art. With him beauty lies in great masses—thought woven with thought—each line, the sustainer of his fellow. Take a beauty from that which surrounds it—its colour is faded, its plumage is ruffled—it is dead.

In this Sir Samuel Ferguson was like the ancients; not that he was an imitator, as Matthew Arnold in "Sobrah and Rustum," but for a much better reason; he was *like* them—like them in nature, for his spirit had sat with the old heroes of his country. In **"Deirdre"** he has restored to us a fragment of the buried Odyssey of Ireland.

In Scotch Glen Etive, Naisi, Son of Usnach, lives in exile with his two brothers and his bride—his Deirdre, for he has carried her off from a little lonely island in a lake where the king, Conor, had hidden her away in charge of her nurse and an old Druid, that he might make her his mistress when her beauty had grown to full flower. Deirdre is entirely happy, for love is all-sufficient for her; not so her lover—he longs for war, and to sit once more in council with his peers. Suddenly is heard through Glen Etive the hunting-call of ex-king Fergus. He brings a pardon.

Of all those who return with him Deirdre alone is sad, she knows the peace is treacherous, that Conor is only seeking to bring her once more into his power. None believes her. Are they not safe under the protection of Fergus? But no; she will not place trust in one who gave up his kingdom so lightly. They reach land. Fergus is enticed away by a ruse of King Conor. Their protectors now are the two young sons of Fergus. How beautiful, as they ride across the country, is that talk between Deirdre and the youngest of the two, who afterwards dies for her. He does not love the company of warriors:—

> I would rather, if I might,
> Frequent the open country, and converse
> With shepherds, hunters, and such innocents.

Then they talk of love, these two, so young, and yet so different; the one on the threshold of life, the other, who has known wandering and weariness. He loves all the world, for in her whom he loves are all the world's perfections. There is something maternal in her reply:

> Long be thou happy in believing so.

Then turning to the other son, who afterwards betrays her, she seeks to sound his nature also. He is one of those who apply to all the moral obligations of life the corrosive power of the intellect, and she, who knows only how to feel and believe, murmurs sadly, half to herself:

> Oh yonder see the lake in prospect fair,
> It lies beneath us, like a polished shield.
> Ah, me! methinks I could imagine it
> Cast down by some despairing deity
> Flying before the unbelief of men.

Close by this lake is the 'Red-Branch' house, where their journey ends.

I have not space to tell how, point by point, she sees fate drawing near them—how to the very end Naisi, the simple soldier, sits calmly playing chess even when they are surrounded—how Conor comes with his magic shield that was hammered in the sea by fairy smiths, and how there was between it and the seas of Ireland a strange sympathy, so that when it is smitten they all surge. I have not space to tell how the sons of Usnach are slain, but I cannot resist quoting in full the beautiful lament of Deirdre:

> The lions of the hill are gone
> And I am left alone—alone—
> Dig the grave both wide and deep,
> For I am sick, and fain would sleep!
>
> The falcons of the wood are flown,
> And I am left alone—alone—
> Dig the grave both deep and wide,
> And let us slumber side by side.
>
> The dragons of the rock are sleeping,
> Sleep that wakes not for our weeping;
> Dig the grave and make it ready;
> Lay me on my true[-]love's body.
>
> Lay their spears and bucklers bright
> By the warriors' sides aright;
> Many a day the three before me
> On their linkèd bucklers bore me.
>
> Lay upon the low grave floor,
> 'Neath each head, the blue claymore;
> Many a time the noble three
> Redden'd these blue blades for me.
>
> Lay the collars, as is meet,
> Of their greyhounds at their feet;
> Many a time for me have they
> Brought the tall red deer to bay.
>
> Sweet companions ye were ever—
> Harsh to me, your sister, never;
> Woods and wilds and misty valleys
> Were, with you, as good's a palace.
>
> Oh! to hear my true-love singing,
> Sweet as sound of trumpet ringing;
> Like the sway of ocean swelling
> Roll'd his deep voice round our dwelling.
>
> Oh! to hear the echoes pealing

> Round our green and fairy sheeling,
> When the three, with soaring chorus
> Pass'd the silent skylark o'er us.
>
> Echo, now sleep, morn and even—
> Lark alone enchant the heaven!—
> Ardan's lips are scant of breath,
> Nessa's tongue is cold in death.
>
> Stag exult on glen and mountain—
> Salmon, leap from loch to fountain—
> Herons in the free air warm ye—
> Usnach's sons no more will harm ye!
>
> Erin's stay no more you are,
> Rulers of the ridge of war;
> Never more 'twill be your fate
> To keep the beam of battle straight.
>
> Woe is me! By fraud and wrong,
> Traitors false and tyrants strong,
> Fell Clan Usnach, bought and sold,
> For Barach's feast and Conor's gold!
>
> Woe to Emain, roof and wall!—
> Woe to Red Branch, hearth and hall!—
> Tenfold woe and black dishonour
> To the foul and false Clan Conor!
>
> Dig the grave both wide and deep,
> Sick I am, and fain would sleep!
> Dig the grave and make it ready,
> Lay me on my true-love's body!

This is not the version in the text but an earlier and more beautiful one—a version from the Irish, which I have followed Judge O'Hagan's lead in quoting from the *Lays of the Western Gael.* I know not any lament so piercing.

No one will deny excellence to the Idylls of the King; no one will say that Lord Tennyson's Girton girls do not look well in those old costumes of dead chivalry. No one will deny that he has thrown over everything a glamour of radiant words—that the candelabras shine brightly on the fancy ball. Yet here is that which the Idylls do not at any time contain, beauty at once feminine and heroic. But as Lord Tennyson's ideal women will never find a flawless sympathy outside the upper English middle class, so this Deirdre will never, maybe, win entire credence outside the limits—wide enough they are—of the Irish race.

There is a great gap that Sir Samuel Ferguson never filled up between this poem and the next. Here should have come the record of the foiled vengeance of Fergus.

In **"Conary"**, a pirate fleet is shown us, lying off Howth, commanded by the banished foster brothers of King Conary and the British pirate Ingcel. Spies have been sent on shore. They return. 'What say ye?' They have seen a line of seventeen chariots—in the first, reverend men, judges or poets; in the second heralds; in the third an aged man, 'full-grey, majestical, of face serene;' in the others a numerous household. 'What heard ye?' They have heard one within a guest-house lighting a fire for the reception of a king. The pirates land; a spy is sent before them—he approaches the guest-house and hears within—

> A hum as of a crowd of feasting men.
> Princely the murmur, as when voices strong

Of far-heard captains on the front of war,
Sink low and sweet in company of queens.

On his return he describes one by one the great chiefs of Ireland that he saw within, and Ferragon, foster brother of Conary, declares their names. There is Cormac Condlongas, son of Conor, who in rage for the betrayal of the sons of Usnach, made war on his father and his kin.

The nine he sat among,
Were men of steadfast looks, that at his word,
So seemed it me, would stay not to inquire
Whose kindred were they be might bid them
slay.

'I knew them also,' answered Ferragon.
'Of them 'tis said they never slew a man
For evil deed, and never spared a man
For good deed; but as ordered, duteous slew
Or slew not. Shun that nine, unless your heads
Be cased in caskets made of adamant.'

There too is Conall Carnach:

Fair-haired he is,
And yellow-bearded, with an eye of blue.
He sits apart and wears a wistful look,
As if he missed some friend's companionship.
Then Ferragon, not waiting question, cried:
Gods! all the foremost, all the valiantest
Of Erin's champions, gathered in one place
For our destruction, are assembled here!
That man is Conall Carnach; and the friend
He looks for vainly with a wistful eye
Is great Cuchullin: he no more shall share
The upper bench with Conall; since the tomb
Holds him, by hand of Conall well avenged.

One by one the great chieftains are re-created for us in words like the clang of hammer on anvil in fashioning a sword. The arch-king Conary is there.

One I saw
Seated apart: before his couch there hung
A silver broidered curtain; grey he was,
Of aspect mild, benevolent, composed.
A cloak he wore of colour like the haze
Of a May morning when the sun shines warm
On dewy meads and fresh ploughed tillage land
Variously beautiful, with border broad
Of golden woof that glittered to his knee
A stream of light. Before him on the floor
A juggler played his feats; nine balls he had
And flung them upward, eight in air at once,
And one in hand! Like swarm of summer bees
They danced and circled, till his eye met mine;
Then he could catch no more; but down they fell
And rolled upon the floor. 'An evil eye
Has seen me,' said the juggler.

The spy has observed others who were not warriors:

I saw three slender, three face-shaven men
Robed in red mantles and with caps of red.
No swords had they, nor bore they spear or
shield,
But each man on his knee a bag-pipe held
With jewelled chanter flashing as he moved,
And mouthpiece ready to supply the wind.

'What pipers these?'

These pipers of a truth
If so it be that I mistake them not,
Appear not often in men's halls of glee:
Men of the *Sidhe* they are.

. . . . .

To-night their pipes will play us to our ships
With strains of triumph; or their fingers' ends
Shall never close the stops of music more.

The attack is sounded. Conary sends one troop of his warriors against them, bidding one of the strange pipers sound a pibroch for the onset:

'Yea, mighty king,' said one,
'The strain I play ye shall remember long,'
And put the mouthpiece to his lips. At once
It seemed as earth and sky were sound alone,
And every sound a maddening battle-call,
So spread desire of fight through breast and
brain.

They drive all before them and force a way through the enemy, but fainter and fainter to the ears of Conary comes the sound of the music and the swords. For the treacherous piping has led them far away into the darkness by an irresistible spell; and now the king bids another troop go out against the pirates:

And let another piper play you on.

Again the sound of the music and the swords comes fainter and fainter. Conall Carnach must seek them with a third troop, and to these is appointed the third piper:

'Trust not these pipers, I am but a child,'
Said Ferflath; 'but I know they are not men
Of mankind, and will pipe you all to harm,'
'Peace, little prince,' said Conall, 'trust in me.
I shall but make one circuit of the house.'

They sally out, and those within first hear the sound of 'legions overthrown,' but soon 'clamour and scream' grow fainter in the distance. Now that it is too late they see the truth:

The gods
Have given us over to the spirits who dwell
Beneath the earth.

The great arch-king himself prepares for 'battle long disused,' and with his household, 'steward and butler, cupbearer and groom,' goes out against his besiegers.

In the moment of victory he is attacked by a terrible thirst, and cries out for water. Cecht, the only great warrior who remains with him, sets out with the child Ferflath to find it in a distant well. Twice it is spilt, and when at last in the gray of the morning they return, the arch-king is slain, and the three strayed troops stand round him:

As men who doubted did they dream or wake,
Or were they honest, to be judged, or base.

These things are supposed to have happened near the spot where Donnybrook bridge now stands, and there, a few years ago, some workmen found a sword and spear-head of immense antiquity, and a mass of headless skeletons.

I have not space to do much more than mention the next

two poems. Though lucid and beautiful, they are of much less importance than Deirdre or Conary. In these latter the wave of song reaches its greatest volume of sound and strength. In the **"Healing of Conall Carnach"** it ebbs with soft notes that are almost idyllic, and with a half regretful prophecy of change.

"The Tain Quest" tells how in the course of ages the poem in which Fergus had recorded the previous stories is lost, and the bards have sought it everywhere in vain. At last Murgen, the chief bard's son, resting in a lonely valley find[s] written on the stone on which he leaned, that there Fergus was buried. He calls upon the ghost of the dead warrior to rise and give the Tain once more to the world. Vainly he conjures him by the name of Love, by his Nessa's eyes, by the heroic deeds of his son. At last he conjures him by the sacred name of Song:

> In dark days near at hand
> Song shall be the only treasure left them in their
>   native land.

Fergus rises:

> . . . . A mist and a flush
> Of brazen sandals blended with a mantle's waf-
>   ture green.

So the song is recovered, but Murgen has to give his life in exchange.

There is a wonderful incident full of Celtic irony in the epic of *Congal.* The great chief, from whom the poem takes its name, having driven all his enemies before him, finds himself suddenly face to face with an idiot boy with a bill-hook for sword and the head of a cauldron for a shield. Congal turns away half in scorn and half in pity, but as he turns the idiot wounds him mortally with the bill-hook, and seeking out his king, reports what he has done. The king, in gratitude, promises him great gifts:

> "Tis good,' said Cuanna, and sat down, and
>   from the gravelly soil
> Picking the pebbles smooth, began to toss with
>   patient toil
> The little stones from hand to hand, alternate
>   back and palm,
> Regardless of the presence round, and lapsed in
>   childish calm.

Meanwhile a notorious coward seeing Congal faint from loss of blood, resolves to win the glory of having killed him. He severs Congal's wrist with a sword-cut, and the hand is driven far over the ground grasping, but he who gave the sword-cut has fled without waiting to see the effect of his blow. So the most famous warrior of his time bleeds to death, slain by the hands of an idiot boy and a coward.

In thus describing these poems I have not sought to convey to my readers, for it were hopeless, their fine momentum, the sign manual of the great writers. I am in every way satisfied if I have made plain the personality of the work.

I must now speak of the slighter poems. To these it is more possible to do justice by quotation.

It is a long cry from the days of Congal to those of Davis:—

> I walked through Ballinderry in the springtime,
> When the bud was on the tree;
> And I said, in every fresh-ploughed field behold-
>   ing
> The sowers striding free,
> Scattering broadcast forth the corn in golden
>   plenty
> On the quick seed-clasping soil,
> Even such, this day, among the fresh-stirred
>   hearts of Erin,
> Thomas Davis is thy toil.

> . . . . .

> O brave young men, my love, my pride, my
>   promise,
> 'Tis on you my hopes are set
> In manliness, in kindliness, in justice,
> To make Erin a nation yet;
> Self-respecting, self-relying, self-advancing,
> In union or in severance, free and strong—
> And if God grant this, then, under God, to
>   Thomas Davis
> Let the greater praise belong.

Thus wrote Sir Samuel Ferguson at the time of his friend's death. Of the sincerity of the national feeling running through this and all his other poems he gave earnest by being at one time an ardent politician. Towards the last, however, when he had exchanged poetry for antiquarian studies, his Nationalism (in the political sense), though not his patriotism, became less ardent, 'Years robbed him of courage,' as Wordsworth said of himself in a moment of melancholy insight.

Beautiful with their desire for some stronger life, one with the rapture of the sea and the stars, are those opening lines from **"Grace O'Malley"**—

> She left the close-air'd land of trees
> And Proud MacWilliam's palace,
> For clear, bare Clare's health-salted breeze,
> Her oarsmen and her galleys:
> And where, beside the bending strand
> The rock and billow wrestle,
> Between the deep sea and the land
> She built her Island Castle.

> The Spanish captains, sailing by
> For Newport, with amazement
> Behold the cannon'd longship lic
> Moored to the lady's casement;
> And, covering coin and cup of gold
> In haste their hatches under,
> They whispered, "Tis a pirate's bold;
> She sails the seas for plunder!'

> But no; 'twas not for sordid spoil
> Of barque or sea-board borough
> She plough'd, with unfatiguing toil,
> The fluent-rolling furrow;
> Delighting, on the broad-back'd deep,
> To feel the quivering galley
> Strain up the opposing hill, and sweep
> Down the withdrawing valley

> Or, sped before a driving blast,

> By following seas uplifted,
> Catch, from the huge heaps heaving past,
> And from the spray they drifted,
> And from the winds that toss'd the crest
> Of each wide-shouldering giant,
> The smack of freedom and the zest
> Of rapturous life defiant.

Almost all the poetry of this age is written by students, for students. But Ferguson's is truly bardic, appealing to all natures alike, to the great concourse of the people, for it has gone deeper than knowledge or fancy, deeper than the intelligence which knows of difference—of the good and the evil, of the foolish and the wise, of this one and of that—to the universal emotions that have not heard of aristocracies, down to where Brahman and Sudra are not even names.

The following lines from the poem to Brittany, are very different, with their love of peace and their regret for the past. Those who remember that last year's address of Renan's on the same subject will notice how like it they are in temper and substance:

> Leave to him—to the vehement man
> Of the Loire, of the Seine, of the Rhone,—
> In the Idea's high pathways to march in the van,
> To o'erthrow, and set up the o'erthrown:
>
> Be it thine in the broad beaten ways
> That the world's simple seniors have trod,
> To walk with soft steps, living peaceable days,
> And on earth not forgetful of God.
>
> Nor repine that thy lot has been cast
> With the things of the old time before,
> For to thee are committed the keys of the past,
> Oh grey monumental Arvôr!

Of all the lesser poems of Sir Samuel Ferguson there is none more beautiful than that on the burial of Aideen, who died of grief for the death of Oscar, and whose grave is the cromlech at Howth:—

> They heaved the stone; they heap'd the cairn,
> Said Ossian. 'In a queenly grave
> We leave her, 'mong the fields of fern,
> Between the cliff and wave.
>
> 'The cliff behind stands clear and bare,
> And bare, above, the heathery steep
> Scales the clear heaven's expanse, to where
> The Danaan Druids sleep.
>
> 'And all the sands that, left and right,
> The grassy isthmus-ridge confine,
> In yellow bars lie bare and bright
> Among the sparkling brine.
>
> 'A clear pure air pervades the scene,
> In loneliness and awe secure;
> Meet spot to sepulchre a queen
> Who in her life was pure.
>
> 'Here, far from camp and chase removed,
> Apart in Nature's quiet room,
> The music that alive she loved
> Shall cheer her in the tomb.
>
> 'The humming of the noontide bees,
> The larks loud carol all day long,

> And borne on evening's salted breeze,
> The clanking sea-bird's song
>
> 'Shall round her airy chamber float,
> And with the whispering winds and streams,
> Attune to Nature's tenderest note
> The tenor of her dreams.
>
> 'And oft, at tranquil eve's decline,
> When full tides lip the old Green Plain,
> The lowing of Moynalty's kine
> Shall round her breathe again.
>
> 'In sweet remembrance of the days
> When, duteous, in the lowly vale,
> Unconscious of my Oscar's gaze,
> She filled the fragrant pail.

. . . . . .

> 'Farewell! the strength of men is worn;
> The night approaches dark and chill;
> Sleep, till perchance an endless morn
> Descend the glittering hill.'
>
> Of Oscar and Aideen bereft,
> So Ossian sang. The Fenians sped
> Three mighty shouts to heaven; and left
> Ben-Edar to the dead.

At once the fault and the beauty of the nature-description of most modern poets is that for them the stars, and streams, the leaves, and the animals, are only masks behind which go on the sad soliloquies of a nineteenth century egoism. When the world was fresh they gave us a clear glass to see the world through, but slowly, as nature lost her newness, or they began more and more to live in cities or for some other cause, the glass was dyed with ever deepening colours, and now we scarcely see what lies beyond because of the pictures that are painted all over it. But here is one who brings us a clear glass once more.

The author of these poems is the greatest poet Ireland has produced, because the most central and most Celtic. Whatever the future may bring forth in the way of a truly great and national literature—and now that the race is so large, so widely spread, and so conscious of its unity, the years are ripe—will find its morning in these three volumes of one who was made by the purifying flame of National sentiment the one man of his time who wrote heroic poetry—one who, among the somewhat sybaritic singers of his day, was like some aged sea-king sitting among the inland wheat and poppies—the savour of the sea about him, and its strength.

In these poems and the legends they contain lies the refutation of the calumnies of England and those amongst us who are false to their country. We are often told that we are men of infirm will and lavish lips, planning one thing and doing another, seeking this to-day and that tomorrow. But a widely different story do these legends tell. The mind of the Celt loves to linger on images of persistance [*sic*]; implacable hate, implacable love, on Conor and Deirdre, and Setanta watching by the door of Cullan, and the long waiting of the blind Lynott.

Of all the many things the past bequeaths to the future, the greatest are great legends; they are the mothers of nations. I hold it the duty of every Irish reader to study those of his own country till they are familiar as his own hands, for in them is the Celtic heart.

If you will do this you will perhaps be saved in their high companionship from that leprosy of the modern—tepid emotions and many aims. Many aims, when the greatest of the earth often owned but two—two linked and arduous thoughts—fatherland and song. For them the personal perplexities of life grew dim and there alone remained its noble sorrows and its noble joys.

I do not appeal to the professorial classes, who, in Ireland, at least, appear at no time to have thought of the affairs of their country till they first feared for their emoluments—nor do I appeal to the shoddy society of 'West Britonism,'—but to those young men clustered here and there throughout our land, whom the emotion of Patriotism has lifted into that world of selfless passion in which heroic deeds are possible and heroic poetry credible. (pp. 88-104)

> W. B. Yeats, "The Poetry of Sir Samuel Ferguson—II," in his Uncollected Prose, edited by John P. Frayne, Columbia University Press, 1970, pp. 87-104.

Aubrey De Vere   (essay date 1889)

[De Vere was an Irish poet. In the following excerpt, he offers a favorable assessment of Congal and "Aideen's Grave".]

Sir Samuel Ferguson's poetry has a very special character of its own. It does not profess, like a host of recent poems, to be a revealer of mysteries, metaphysical or psychological; and it has as little affinity with those works which reproduce the old tales of the Greek mythology,—a vintage rich indeed, but the grape-skins of which have perhaps been sucked too often since they were cast aside, their best wine duly stored by the gatherers of an earlier day. The mediæval legends have contributed nothing to the materials of [Ferguson's *Poems*]; and it seldom aims at the illustration of modern life, the hardest crux of modern poetry. It is drawn from sources less known among us, more than two-thirds of it being founded on the earliest remains of Irish romance. Sir Samuel Ferguson has already given us two remarkable volumes, in which analogous themes are treated, viz. *Congal*, a tale of Ireland's "Heroic Age," and *Lays of the Western Gael,* in which last events taken from historical as well as legendary periods are recorded. Nearly all the Irish poems in this volume belong to Ireland's Pagan time.

Unfortunately, but few of the Irish manuscripts illustrating that time have as yet been translated, whether in the form of verse or in that of prose,—the latter the better, because the truer, form, except when, as in this instance, the verse is at once thoroughly free and thoroughly faithful to the *spirit* of the original. These poems are, however, not translations; but, in passing through the imagination of a modern Irish poet, the ancient song seems to have lost nothing of that native note which combines the barbaric with the sweet. The legendary poems are entitled, "Mes-

gedra," "Fergus Wry-Mouth," "The Naming of Cuchullin," "Conary," "Deirdre," and "The Twins of Macha." Among the most representative are "Conary" and "The Naming of Cuchullin," the former being essentially epic in character, while the latter resembles a fragment from a lyrical drama. (pp. 98-9)

[The qualities of Ferguson's poetry] are those characteristic of the noble, not the ignoble, poetry, viz. passion, imagination, vigour, an epic largeness of conception, wide human sympathies, vivid and truthful description; while with these it unites none of the vulgar stimulants for exhausted or morbid poetic appetites, whether the epicurean seasoning, the sceptical, or the revolutionary. Its diction is pure, its metre full of variety; and with these merits, common to all true poetry, it unites an insight which only a man of genius can possess into the special characteristics of those ancient times and manners which are so frequently its subject. His Irish poetry is Irish, not, like a good deal which bears that name, *i.e.* by dint of being bad English, while stuffed with but the vulgarer accidents, not the essential characteristics of Gaelic Ireland—not thus, but by having the genuine Gaelic spirit in it. That spirit, like the Irish airs, its most authentic expression, has much of the minor key about it, and many "shrill notes of anger" besides; but alike with its sadness, its fierceness, and its wild fits of mirth, a witching tenderness is mingled; and all those qualities are largely found in Sir Samuel Ferguson's poetry. Whoever follows his footsteps up the purple glens of old Erin will not fail to hear the wild slogan of the clan, and farther off "the horns of Elfland faintly blowing." Such poetry can hardly fail sooner or later to conquer that difficulty which the most accomplished Englishmen often find in understanding poetry which worthily illustrates the highest Irish themes, even when the critic is patient with modern Irish comedy in its vulgarest forms. Poetry on its lower levels will gratify low appetites, notwithstanding serious diversities in national tastes: it is when poetry deals worthily with what is at once high and characteristic that the diversities and latent antagonisms of national tastes are tested, such diversities as Mr. Matthew Arnold has admirably illustrated in his essay on "Celtic Literature." Whether Sir Samuel Ferguson's poetry is destined to become ever well known either in the land of his forefathers or in that land whose ancient annals he has illustrated so well, few can guess; but it is at least as likely to interest Englishmen as those Irishmen who prefer the aspirations of modern continental Socialists to the glories of their country in the ages of Loyalty and of Faith. In both countries "Conary" and "Congal" will find readers, however; and their award will be, "The author of these poems added another string to the great English harp—the Gaelic string." (pp. 123-25)

> Aubrey De Vere, "Poems by Sir Samuel Ferguson," in his Essays: Chiefly Literary & Ethical, Macmillan and Co., 1889, pp. 98-125.

Alfred Perceval Graves   (essay date 1913)

[Graves was an Irish poet, scholar, and contemporary of Ferguson. In the following excerpt, he offers an overview *of Ferguson's poetry and examines his significance in Irish literature.*]

Sir Samuel Ferguson was unquestionably the Irish poet of the past century who has most powerfully influenced the literary history of his country. It was in his writings that was decisively begun the great work of restoring to Ireland the spiritual treasure it had sacrificed in losing the Gaelic tongue. He was, however, no mere antiquarian. He was also a scholar, and a patriot in the highest sense of the word. He had friends in all parties, for he was in no sense a political partisan. Indeed, though with strong Irish National feeling—of which he gave evidence in some of his earlier ballads, and which came to the front in his successful defence of Richard Dalton Williams, the Young Ireland poet, when tried for treason-felony—he felt that the highest duty he owed his country was that of a poet and prose writer above party. But in his poetic capacity, as pointed out by Mr. W. B. Yeats, "he was wiser than Young Ireland in the choice of his models; for while drawing not less than they from purely Irish sources, he turned to the great poets of the world for his style," and notably to Homer: and the result is that, as Roden Noel puts it, "**Congal** and his shorter Irish heroic poems combine in a striking manner the vague, undefined shadowy grandeur, the supernatural glamour of northern romance, with the self-restraint, distinct symmetrical outline, ordered proportion and organic construction of the Greek classic." More than this, as his brother poet and friend, Aubrey de Vere, urges [see excerpt dated 1889], "its qualities are those characteristic of the noble, not the ignoble poetry—viz., passion, imagination, vigour, an epic largeness of conception, wide human sympathies, vivid and truthful description—while with them it unites none of the vulgar stimulants for exhausted or morbid poetic appetite, whether the epicurean seasoning, the sceptical, or the revolutionary."

Ferguson differs from those who regard the realm of poetry as another world detachable from this—a life mystical, non-human, non-moral—the life, if you will, of fairy, demon, or demi-god. Indeed, he was in no danger of falling into this illusion. He was absolutely human and practical; broad and sympathetic-minded both. Yet for entire success as a poet in his particular day he had to struggle against difficulties constitutional, accidental, and of his own seeking. His very versatility rendered difficult that entire devotion of his energies to his art, of which Tennyson is the great modern example. He could not spare the time, even had he possessed the taste, for that fastidious word-for-word finish in verse to which the late Laureate accustomed the critics, and through them the educated public, which undoubtedly, for the time being, militated against the success of Ferguson's poetry.

Then he was deliberately facing the fact that the Irish themes he had set his heart upon had no public behind them. A generation before, they would have had the support of a cultured and unprovincialised Irish upper class; a generation later they would have claimed attention, in Ferguson's hands, as the noblest outcome of the Irish literary revival. He was therefore both before and after his time, and realised his position to the full. Indeed, when I once spoke to him with regret of the neglect of all but Irish

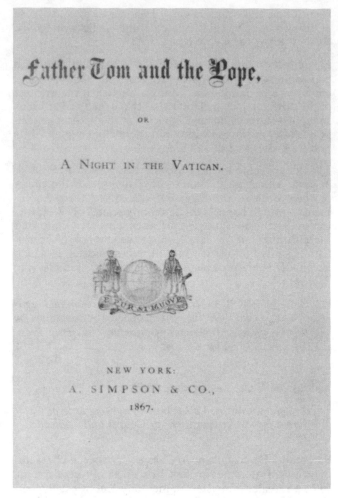

Title page for Father Tom and the Pope, *Ferguson's anti-Catholic satire first published in* Blackwood's Edinburgh Magazine *in 1838.*

political literature, he acknowledged it, but with the quiet expression of his confidence that "his time would come." Edward Dowden explains the fact that **Congal** had not hit the popular taste in the following passage of a letter to Sir Samuel:

> A poem with epic breadth and thews is not likely to be popular now. A diseased and over-sensitive nerve is a qualification for the writing of poetry at present, much more than a thoughtful brain or strength of muscle. Some little bit of novel sensibility, a delight in such colours as French milliners send over for ladies' bonnets, or the nosing of certain curious odours, is enough to make the fortune of a small poet. What seems to me most noteworthy in your poems is the union of culture with simplicity and strength. Their refinement is large and strong, not curious and diseased; and they have spaces and movements which give one a feeling like the sea or the air on a headland. I had not meant to say anything of **Congal**, but somehow this came and said itself.

Nothing could be more truly appreciative of Ferguson's work than this. That fine saying, "Your poems have spaces and movements which give one a feeling like the sea or the air on a headland," may be here illustrated by one of the greatest passages in *Congal;* indeed, it in all probability suggested the criticism to Dr. Dowden. It may be quoted, moreover, as a telling example of how Ferguson's careless or rough treatment of detail is carried off by the largeness of his conception and movement:

> He looking landward from the brow of some
> great sea-cape's head,
> Bray or Ben Edar—sees beneath, in silent pag-
> eant grand,
> Slow fields of sunshine spread o'er fields of rich,
> corn-bearing land,
> Red glebe and meadow margin green commin-
> gling to the view
> With yellow stubble, browning woods, and up-
> land tracts of blue;
> Then, sated with the pomp of fields, turns sea-
> ward to the verge
> Where, mingling with the murmuring wash
> made by the far-down surge,
> Comes up the clangorous song of birds unseen,
> that, low beneath,
> Poised off the rock, ply underfoot; and, 'mid the
> blossoming heath,
> And mint-sweet herb that loves the ledge rare-
> air'd, at ease reclined,
> Surveys the wide pale-heaving floor crisped by
> a curling wind;
> With all its shifting, shadowy belts, and chasing
> scopes of green,
> Sun-strown, foam-freckled, sail-embossed, and
> blackening squalls between,
> And slant, cerulean-skirted showers that with a
> drowsy sound,
> Heard inward, of ebullient waves, stalk all the
> horizon round;
> And, haply, being a citizen just 'scaped from
> some disease
> That long has held him sick indoors, now, in the
> brine-fresh breeze,
> Health-salted, bathes; and says, the while he
> breathes reviving bliss,
> "I am not good enough, O God, nor pure
> enough for this!"

The ear educated to Tennyson's or Swinburne's verse would be jarred by the heavy aggregation of consonants here and there in the passage. But as a presentment of country, cliff, and ocean, it is alike so broad and delicate in colour and movement that it rises visibly before us, till the echo of the sea is in our ears, and we breathe and smell its keen savours. Then the human note with which it closes is inexpressibly touching.

It is not, however, implied that Ferguson is wanting in the musical ear or the appreciation of fine poetical craftsmanship, but rather suggested that, unlike Tennyson and other writers, he is not *sectus ad unguem* in everything he attempts, because he is not careful to be so. Moreover, like Wordsworth, he did not always write when his best mood was upon him. And hence like Wordsworth and, I may add, Browning, he will live in selections, though large selections, from his works, rather than in their entirety. Yet, **"The Forging of the Anchor"** is a remarkably finished achievement for a young man of one-and-twenty, and

"The Fairy Thorn," another early poem, is exquisite wizardry itself. True, it appears to have been conceived and executed with a rapidity which was inspiration, and is indeed one of Ferguson's gems without flaw.

Next come Ferguson's Translations from the Irish which arose from his study of his country's language along with O'Hagan, afterwards Lord Chancellor, and above all George Fox, a young Belfast man, of whom he writes in after life:

> His discourse possessed a fascination equal to all that I have heard ascribed to that of Coleridge, and under his influence my poetic faculty, which had already shown itself in the ballad of Willy Gilliland, acquired strength for the production of **"The Forging of the Anchor,"** published in *Blackwood* in May 1832. We had formed a private class for the study of Irish. The early history of Ulster had already seized on my imagination, and the **"Return of Claneboy,"** a prose romance which I contributed about that time to *Blackwood,* may be regarded as the first indication of my ambition to raise the native elements of Irish History to a dignified level; and this ambition, I think, may be taken as the key to almost all the literary work of my subsequent life.

George Fox probably died young. "He left Belfast to push his fortunes in British Guiana," writes Lady Ferguson in her memoirs of her husband [see Further Reading], and no doubt succumbed to its unhealthy climate. His youthful friends heard no more of him. They spared no efforts, through a long period of years, to learn his fate.

When Ferguson, in 1864, published in his *Lays of the Western Gael* his **"Versions from the Irish,"** which had appeared first in the *Dublin University Magazine* of 1834 in the form of translations with a Commentary from Hardiman's Irish Minstrelsy, he would not include one of the best among them, as he considered George Fox entitled to share in the authorship of **"The County Mayo,"** and when almost fifty years had passed since his early friend had been heard of, and he, in 1880, published his *Poems,* the volume bore this brief and touching dedication—*Georgio, Amico, Condiscipulo, Instauratori.*

Ferguson's translations from the Irish differ from Miss Brooke's and Miss Balfour's versions and those of other translators preceding him, by their assimilation of Irish idioms and the Irish spirit into English verse without violence—indeed, with a happy judgment which lends a delightful effect to these lyrics. Edward Walsh has scarcely excelled Ferguson in this field; and Dr. Sigerson and Dr. Hyde, though they come much closer to the original metres, rarely go past him in poetical feeling and passion.

For the very character of the originals calls for simple treatment, and high polish would have spoilt Ferguson's verse translations from the Irish.

Ferguson was now casting round for nobler themes to work upon, whilst keeping his hand in at these translations from the Irish. Patriotic to the core, he was above all things eager to achieve something lofty in literature for Ireland's sake—something that might help to lift her from the intellectual flats upon which she had fallen.

Moreover, another Belfast friend and mentor, Dr. Robert Gordon, was keeping him up to his highest poetical self by a series of memorable letters, extracts from which Lady Ferguson gives in her Biography of Sir Samuel, as thus:

> "You rejoice me, I speak seriously, by saying you are 'doing.' To be and to do. O Ferguson, those little words contain the sum of all man's destiny. You are strong, and I would have you strike some note that will reverberate down the vista of time. Will you, Ferguson?"

In the course of his delightful New Year's Epistle to Robert Gordon, M.D., dated 1st of January, 1845, Ferguson thus responds to his friends' appeal:

> For ilka day I'm growin' stranger
> To speak my mind in love or anger;
> And, hech! ere it be muckle langer,
> You'll see appearin'
> Some offerin's o' nae cauld haranguer,
> Put out for Erin.
>
> Lord, for ane day o' service done her!
> Lord, for ane hour's sunlight upon her!
> Here, Fortune, tak' warld's wealth and honour,
> You're no' my debtor,
> Let me but rive ae link asunder
> O' Erin's fetter!
>
> Let me but help to shape the sentence
> Will put the pith o' independence,
> O' self-respect in self-acquaintance,
> And manly pride
> Intil and Eber-Scot's descendants—
> Take a' beside!
>
> Let me but help to get the truth
> Set fast in ilka brother's mouth,
> Whatever accents, north or south,
> His tongue may use,
> And there's ambition, riches, youth;
> Tak' which you choose!

But before he had ripened for the full outcome of his genius Ferguson anticipated it by one of the noblest laments in our language, **"Thomas Davis: an Elegy,"** 1845, a poignant expression of his grief at the death of his friend, the famous young National leader.

Sir Charles Gavan Duffy tells us that

> Ferguson, who lay on a bed of sickness when Davis died, impatient that for the moment he could not declare it in public, asked me to come to him, that he might ease his heart by expressing in private his sense of what he had lost. He read me fragments of a poem written under these circumstances, the most Celtic in structure and spirit of all the elegies laid on the tomb of Davis. The last verse sounded like a prophecy; it was, at any rate, a powerful incentive to take up our task anew.
>
> (pp. 36-42)

The Irish potato famine now intervened, and drove Ferguson into the *sæva indignatio* of Juvenal at the Government mismanagement, which had multiplied its horrors a hundredfold.

No one knew this better than himself, for he was secretary to the Irish Council, whose wise advice, tendered to the English Parliament, was rejected in favour of futile experimental legislation in the way of relief-road making and so forth. Convinced that a Parliament after Grattan's model would have saved the country, he became a Repealer and one of the poets of Repeal.

> Deem not, O generous English hearts, who gave
> Your noble aid our sinking Isle to save,
> This breast, though heated in its Country's feud,
> Owns aught towards *you* but perfect gratitude.
>
> . . . . .
>
> But, frankly, while we thank you all who sent
> Your alms, so thank we not your Parliament,
> Who, what they gave, from treasures of our own
> Gave, if you call it giving, this half loan,
> Half gift from the recipients to themselves
> Of their own millions, be they tens or twelves;
> Our own as well as yours: our Irish brows
> Had sweated for them; though your Commons'
>   House,
> Forgetting your four hundred millions debt,
> When first in partnership our nations met,
> Against our twenty-four (you then two-fold
> The poorer people), call them British Gold.
> No; for these drafts on our United Banks
> We owe no gratitude, and give no thanks!
> More than you'd give to us, if Dorsetshire
> Or York a like assistance should require;
> Or than you gave us when, to compensate
> Your slave-owners, you charged our common
>   state
> Twice the amount: no, but we rather give
> Our curses, and will give them while we live,
> To that pernicious blind conceit and pride,
> Wherewith the aids we asked you misapplied.
>
> . . . . .
>
> Sure, for our wretched Country's various ills
> We've got, a man would think, enough of bills—
> Bills to make paupers, bills to feed them made;
> Bills to make sure that paupers' bills are paid;
> Bills in each phrase of economic slang;
> Bills to transport the men they dare not hang.
> (I mean no want of courage physical,
> 'Tis Conscience doth make cowards of us all!)

Allowance must be made for the passionate bitterness or this invective from the circumstances that Ferguson had seen the Irish peasantry he loved dying of starvation before his very eyes and because of the neglect of the British Government of ordinary precautions for "more than a third of the potato crop throughout the island was gone, in some districts more than half, and at the same time the bulk of the remaining supplies, cattle and corn, butter, beef and pork, which would have fed all the inhabitants, continued to be exported to England to pay the rent of farms which would no longer yield the cultivators their ordinary food."

Ferguson, however, lived to turn this fine power of literary invective against the successors of the Young Ireland poets and patriots with whom he had sympathised when he found them descending from the high aspirations and manly action of Davis and Duffy to what he characterised as "a sordid social war of classes carried on by the vilest methods."

In his satiric poems **"The Curse of the Joyces"** and **"At the Polo Ground"**—an analysis in Browning's manner of Carey's frame of mind before giving the fatal signal to the assassins of Mr. Burke and Lord Frederick Cavendish—and in his Dublin eclogue **"In Carey's Footsteps,"** he exposes the cruelties of the boycotting system of political agitation with unsparing severity.

In 1864 appeared Ferguson's *Lays of the Western Gael,* a gratifying surprise even to many of his friends, owing to the inclusion in it of fresh and finer work than he had yet achieved. Their point of departure is thus well described by Mr. A. M. Williams, the American critic [see Further Reading]:

> The *Lays of the Western Gael* are a series of ballads founded on events in Celtic history, and derived from the Early Chronicles and poems. They are original in form and substance, the ballad form and measure being unknown to the early Celtic poets of Ireland; but they preserve in a wonderful degree the ancient spirit, and give a picture of the ancient times with all the art of verity. They have a solemnity of measure like the voice of one of the ancient bards chanting of
>
> > Old forgotten far-off things
> > And battles long ago,
>
> and they are clothed with the mists of a melancholy age. They include such subjects as **"The Tain Quest,"** the search of the bard for the lost lay of the great cattle-raid of Queen Maeve of Connaught, and its recovery, by invocation, from the voice of its dead author, who rises in misty form above his grave; **"The Healing of Conall Carnach,"** a story of violated sanctuary and its punishment; **"The Welshmen of Tirawley,"** one of the most spirited and original, and which has been pronounced by Mr. Swinburne as amongst the finest of modern ballads, telling of a cruel mulct inflicted upon the members of a Welsh Colony and its vengeance; and other incidents in early Irish history. In his poems, rather than in Macpherson's *Ossian* or in the literal translations, will the modern reader find the voice of the ancient Celtic bards speaking to the intelligence of to-day in their own tones, without false change and dilution, or the confusion and dimness of an ancient language.

Of the longer lays thus far published, **"The Tain Quest"** found the greatest acceptance with his poetic compeers, and the most notable criticism of it was that of Thomas Aird, the fine Scottish poet, author of *The Devil's Dream on Mount Aksbeck:*

> In all respects **"The Tain Quest"** is one of the most striking poems of our day. Specially do I admire the artistic skill with which you have doubted the interest of the Quest itself by introducing in the most natural and unencumbering way so many of the best points of the *Great Cattle Foray,* the subject-matter of the *Tain.* The shield has long been grand in poetry; you have made it grander. The refusal of Fergus to stir to the force of private sympathy, but his instantaneous recognition of the patriotic necessity of song, is a just and noble conception.
>
> The power of the Bard over the rude men of Gort; the filial piety of the sons of Sanchan, and their brotherly love; that mysterious Vapour, and that terrible blast of entrance, and the closing malediction by the Maiden, are all very notable towards the consummation of effect. As for the kissing of the champions in the pauses of the fight, I know of nothing in the reaches of our human blood so marvellously striking and sweet; you have now made it immortal in song. However admirably expressed, the last stanza is an error in art. Surely you spoil the grand close, and the whole piece, by appending your own personality of interference as a commentator on the malediction. Might I not further say (with a peculiar smile) you make the preordained fulfilment of Malison a sublime apology for Irish Grub Street?

The sting in the tail of Aird's fine judgment is deserved, and it is curious to observe that Ferguson has been similarly unlucky in **"The Welshmen of Tirawley"** in this attempt to tag a comment on to the end of a tale which he has so nobly adorned. That magnificently savage lay should end with the ante-penultimate stanza.

This tendency to act at times as a commentator on his own work and to present it at others in a too ponderously Latinised form, as well as the careless, not to say bluff, disregard for verbal delicacies into which he now and again lapses, are the only proclivities to which exception can be taken in Ferguson's technique. For his method is uniformly manly, and his occasional periods of majestic inspiration sweep our minor critical objections before them, as the blast from his Mananan's mantle swept the chieftain and his hound into the valley like leaves before the wind.

We have taken Ferguson to our hearts as we take our best brother, loving his very ponderosities and carelessnesses as part and parcel of his greatness, as we love the kindred qualities in Samuel Johnson—for the sake of the man and the gentleman.

In 1872 appeared *Congal,* which Ferguson describes in a letter to Father Russell as an epic poem of greater length and higher literary pretension than his *Lays of the Western Gael.*

An epic requires a great subject, and he who writes it must have vision and manliness closely allied to his nature, else how can he realise the heroic ideal? These are Ferguson's pre-eminent qualities. He is manly. His heroes proclaim it in their every action, their every utterance; and his tender portrait of Lafinda could only have been drawn by a gallant gentleman. He has vision. The terrible shapes and Celtic superstitions—the Giant Walker, the Washer of the Ford—loom monstrously before us as he sings; and he marshals the contending hosts at Moyra with a magnificent realism to which we know no modern parallel.

His subject is a great old-world tale of love and hate, and ambition and jealousy, and craft and courage—a splendid story of the last heroic stand made by Celtic Paganism against the Irish Champions of the Cross.

But great though much of *Congal* undoubtedly is, Ferguson's genius was to break into finest flower at the last.

The volume of 1880 contains some striking verse of a religious, philosophical and personal kind, including the searching **"Two Voices,"** the trenchant and yet more touching **"Three Thoughts,"** the noble lines entitled **"The Morning's Hinges,"** and the lofty **"Hymn of the Fishermen"**—a poem written after a surmounted danger of shipwreck. But in **"Deirdre"** and **"Conary"** he reaches his fullest height as a poet, and the best that has been said or could well be said about them comes from William Allingham and Aubrey de Vere—the two Irishmen of his time whose opinion should interest, if not influence, us most.

Allingham wrote on receipt of the volume: "Many thoughts of my own swarmed about the pages as I turned them, like bees in a lime-tree. In your style high culture is reconciled with simplicity, directness, and originality; and nothing can be happier than your enrichment of English speech with Irish forms without the least violence. All the Irish poems are very remarkable, but **"Deirdre"** I count the chief triumph. Its peculiar form of unity is perfectly managed, while in general effect it recalls nothing so much as a Greek play."

Mr. Aubrey de Vere and Mr. Yeats, and perhaps the larger proportion of the other leading Irish critics, prefer **"Conary"** to **"Deirdre."**

"It would be difficult," writes De Vere,

> to find, amid our recent literature, a poem which at once aims as high as **"Conary"** and as adequately fulfils its aim . . . Novel to English readers as is such a poetic theme, and embarrassing as are a few of the Gaelic names, the work belongs to the "great" style of poetry—that style which is characterised by simplicity, breadth of effect, a careless strength full of movement, but with nothing of the merely sensational about it, and an entire absence of those unclassic tricks that belong to meaner verse. It has caught thoroughly that epic character so remarkable in those Bardic Legends which were transmitted orally through ages when Homer must have been a name unknown in Ireland.

To sum up: though at times over-scholarly and nodding now and again—as all the great unconscious poets, from Homer down, will occasionally nod, as opposed to the little self-conscious ones who are never caught napping—Ferguson is always human, always simple, always strong. Sense ever goes before sound with him. He is no mere reed for blowing music through. He takes you into no gorgeous jungle of colour and scent, and stealing serpent and ravening beast, where perspective is lost and will paralysed, and passion riots unrestrained. No! What Mr. W. B. Yeats finely wrote of him [see excerpt dated 1886] is still true today:

> The author of these poems is the greatest poet Ireland has produced, because the most central

and most Celtic. Whatever the future may bring forth in the way of a truly great and national literature—and now that the race is so large, so widely spread, and so conscious of its unity, the years are ripe—will find its morning in these three volumes of one who was made by the purifying flame of national sentiment the one man of his time who wrote heroic poetry—one who, among the somewhat sybaritic singers of his day, was like some aged sea-king sitting among the inland wheat and poppies—the savour of the sea about him and its strength.

(pp. 44-50)

Alfred Perceval Graves, "Sir Samuel Ferguson," in his Irish Literary and Musical Studies, *Elkin Mathews, 1913, pp. 36-50.*

Ernest Boyd   (essay date 1922)

[*An Irish-American writer and translator, Boyd was a prominent literary critic known for his erudite, honest, and often satirical critiques. In the candidly wrought essays which form his important studies of Irish literature,* Ireland's Literary Renaissance *and* The Contemporary Dramas of Ireland *(1917), Boyd evaluated Irish literary works apart from English literature. In the following excerpt from the former work, Boyd examines Ferguson's crucial role in the development of an Irish national literature.*]

Ferguson was a distinguished Gaelic scholar. His studies in archæological research gave him direct access to the treasures of Ireland's ancient history and literature, which were only imperfectly revealed to [his predecessor, James] Mangan in the literal translations from the Gaelic, furnished by his learned friends O'Daly and O'Curry. With the intuition of genius, Mangan was able to sense the spirit that lay behind these transcriptions. Ferguson infused his verse with that spirit as the reward of years of antiquarian labours. His work was not confined to literature, but covered the whole field of Irish culture, history, architecture, law, music and antiquities. The public recognition of his services to Irish scholarship was his appointment as Deputy Keeper of the Records, and subsequently his election as President of the Royal Irish Academy. He set himself to lay the foundations of a national literature worthy of Ireland, realising that something more substantial than the aggressive patriotism of *The Nation* must provide the subject matter of Irish art.

While a young man Ferguson attracted attention as a poet in the pages of *Blackwood's* magazine, and between the ages of twenty and thirty he contributed to the *Dublin University Review* the series of historic tales afterwards published as **The Hibernian Nights' Entertainments.** These were his first attempts to put the old legends and stories into circulation. In 1867 he published his first volume of verse, **Lays of the Western Gael,** which was followed in 1872 by the more ambitious epic, **Congal.** A volume of collected **Poems** appeared in 1880, and attached directly to the first book of **Lays,** by its treatment of further incidents in the Red Branch legendary cycle. These two works gave a strong impulse to the return to Irish legend which is so distinctive a feature of the Revival. This rendering in English verse of the Conorian cycle of the Red Branch history is the foundation of a new literature. Here, for the first time in Anglo-Irish poetry, is outlined the tragic history of the House of Usnach, of the loves of Naisi and Deirdre, the Helen and Paris of Ireland's antiquity, and the mighty deeds of Cuchulain, who dominates Irish bardic history, as Achilles dominated the Greek epic.

The older,—Conorian,—legend has always found more favour than the later Ossianic. The love story of Deirdre, for example, has never ceased, since Ferguson, to engage the attention of the poets. As early as 1876 the *Deirdre* of R. D. Joyce awakened popular response, and since 1880, the date of Ferguson's version, the subject has been treated by Douglas Hyde, John Todhunter, T. W. Rolleston, A.E., J. M. Synge, W. B. Yeats, and others of lesser importance. On the other hand, the corresponding tale of Diarmuid and Grania from the later legend has attracted comparatively few, none of whom has been quite successful. Ferguson, in his *Lays,* has treated the pathetic incident of the death of Diarmuid and his last meeting with Finn. Katharine Tynan, in her second volume of verse, *Shamrocks,* gave a sympathetic rendering of the story, but it still awaits a worthy interpretation. The dramatists have similarly failed in their treatment. Neither the *Diarmuid and Grania* due to the strange collaboration of George Moore and W. B. Yeats, nor the recent *Grania* of Lady Gregory, can be compared with the dramas which have had Deirdre for their subject. The latter, it is true, offers material of a naturally more dramatic quality. The story falls of its own accord into the five acts of classical tragedy, and, involving as it does the destiny of the entire House of Usnach, it is not surprising that it should transcend the more circumscribed interest of the Diarmuid and Grania episode. The Fate of the Sons of Usnach seems from the earliest times to have been sung by the bards, for whom the tragedy had the same fascination it has exercised upon the modern poets. Indeed, as Dr. Sigerson has pointed out, there is reason to suppose that Deirdre was the first tragedy, outside of the classic languages, in the literature of Europe.

It was natural that Ferguson, with his ambition to found a national literature, should think of writing an Irish epic. In *Lays of the Western Gael* he had already adapted to English verse portions of the great Gaelic epic, the *Tain-Bo-Cuaigne,* but these episodes were never welded together, and made no pretence of fulfilling the need of Anglo-Irish literature for a work of epical dimensions. For this purpose something more was demanded of the poet than that he should be a translator or adapter. It was necessary to take the material supplied by the transcripts of the ancient tales of the bards, to divest it of many of the extravagancies which conceal the true grandeur and poetry of the bardic songs, and to remould it into one of those beautiful, homogeneous narratives with which we associate the great epic poems of literature. In the bardic romance known as *The Battle of Moyra,* Ferguson believed he had found a subject susceptible of such treatment, and for some years he strove to embody it in a poem of epic quality. The result of his labours was the publication in 1872 of *Congal.* This, however, was but the partial fulfilment of his original purpose. As he confessed in his preface, the "inherent repugnancies" of the subject proved "too obstinate for recon-

cilement." Instead of following the plan of the original story, he was obliged to recast the material, and to concentrate his attention upon Congal, the principal personage in the Gaelic text, while retaining the Battle of Moyra as the culminating incident.

The theme seems, indeed, peculiarly adapted to epic treatment, possessing, as it does, breadth of significance and unity and continuity of action. The struggle between the forces of Congal and Domnal transcend the interest of simple warfare, and the battle at Moyra marks the last stand of bardic and pagan Ireland against the forces of Christianity and clericalism. In spite of having abandoned his first project, Ferguson succeeded in imparting to *Congal* some of the qualities which his original conception would naturally have possessed. He peoples his narrative of the expedition of Prince Congal against Domnal, king of Erin, with the terrible, gigantic figures of Celtic mythology. Mananan mac Lir, the great sea-god of Irish antiquity, strides through these pages with giant steps, while the ghastly Washer of the Ford, most horrible of banshees, is evoked with the vividness of reality.

Ferguson's work is valuable as representing a definite stage in the development of Anglo-Irish literature. It must be judged by its relative rather than by its absolute merits. As we have seen, he was more than a poet, he was an antiquarian whose manifold activities, though all directed towards the reconstruction of the Gaelic past, could not but interfere with his efforts in the field of pure literature. He did not bring to poetry that concentration of purpose and jealous care for perfection of finish, which are necessary to the creation of great verse. The most effective passages in *Congal* are marred by metrical weaknesses, the clashing of consonants and awkward cæsuræ, all indicating a certain roughness of composition also visible in the shorter poems. Frequently, on the other hand, there is a vigour and freshness which enable Ferguson to achieve his effects, in spite of poor craftmanship. It is necessary to remember the difficulties with which he had to contend.

We are now so familiar with the material that we forget how strange it was in Ferguson's time. To the natural difficulties of all pioneer work must be added the problem of finding euphonious equivalents for the old Gaelic names and of grappling in English with the redundant fluency of the old language. In his notes to *Congal* Ferguson refers to these "word-cataracts," where such orgies of descriptive epithet abound as the following:

> The deep-clear-watered, foamy crested, terribly-
>   resounding,
> Lofty leaping, prone-descending, ocean-calf-
>   abounding,
> Fishy fruitful, salmon-teeming, many-coloured,
>   sunny beaming,
> Heady-eddied, horrid thund'ring, ocean-
>   prodigy-engend'ring,
> Billow-raging, battle waging, merman-haunted,
>   poet-vaunted,
> Royal, patrimonial, old torrent of Eas-Roe.

That he should have risen so successfully to the exigencies of his task must weigh with us in estimating the defects and qualities of Ferguson's verse. If we miss the more delicate verbal effects to which many of his successors have attained, we find in him a grasp of subject, a simple grandeur, with frequent passages of genuine inspiration, which compensate the absence of a more perfect technique. At times, especially in his longer works, we are more sensible of the hand of the scholar than of the poet. It was fortunate that, sometimes, at least, scholarship and poetry were combined. The disappearance of Gaelic from the mainstream of Irish life was so complete that it seemed condemned to exist obscurely in the libraries of the learned societies. Once having lapsed into the domain of scholarship, the annals and achievement of Gaelic Ireland could only be restored through the intervention of a scholar, but a scholar who would reach the ear of the unlearned.

The work of restoration demanded the co-operation of learning and imagination, and in Ferguson a man was found who combined the necessary qualifications. He was able to see the past with the eyes of a scholar and to interpret it with the mind of a poet. It was thus his privilege to possess the key that unlocked the gates through which the stream of modern Irish literature was to pass. He set free the Celtic spirit, imprisoned in the shell of an almost extinct language, and obscured by the dust of political turmoil. It is significant that Ferguson obtained immediate recognition from Aubrey de Vere, William Allingham, and such of his contemporaries as were to prepare the way of the new poetic revival. The year of his death, 1886, saw the publication of *Mosada,* the first book of W. B. Yeats, who has since been so completely identified with the Celtic spirit in Irish literature. As indicating the relation of Ferguson to the young generation, and, consequently, his influence upon the Literary Revival, Yeats's criticism of that date may be quoted [see excerpt dated 1886]: "The author of these poems is the greatest poet Ireland has produced, because the most central and the most Celtic. Whatever the future may bring forth in the way of a truly great and national literature . . . will find its morning in these three volumes of one who was made by the purifying flame of national sentiment, the one man of his time who wrote heroic poetry." (pp. 20-5)

> *Ernest Boyd, "Precursors," in his* Ireland's Literary Renaissance, *revised edition, Alfred A. Knopf, 1922, pp. 15-25.*

Arthur Deering   (essay date 1931)

[*Deering was an American scholar and critic. In the following excerpt, he assesses Ferguson's technical skills as a poet, and, finding them flawed, concludes that his abiding legacy is his influence on later writers.*]

Ferguson, the poet, would receive but scant consideration at the hands of the sharp critic. I think he has violated every rule listed in the canon of good prosody. There is no doubt in the world but that he knew poetry when he saw it. But, whether he was indifferent, or lazy, or cock-sure of his own intuitive touch, is hard to say. This is certain; he never revised a poem after it once got into print. He probably regarded poetry as a natural outpouring, and he forgot that the poet must have a certain amount of cunning and skill to direct that outpouring.

That he has no fine sense of rhythmic consciousness is evidenced in the way he has cast his various themes in inappropriate measures. He seems to know nothing of that free and irregular English swing which sings itself into English ears.

Closely associated with rhythm is the element of stress. This element presupposes the fact that important words are to be put in stressed positions, providing always that those accents which are certain and definite are not liable to change. When Ferguson safely locates an important word in a stressed position he often violates the principle of accent. This results in some unacceptable pronunciations.

Perhaps in no other point does Ferguson so outrage one's sensibilities as in the use of rime. The extremes to which he goes in forcing rime words into a kind of relationship is enough to convince even the casual reader that the man must have been tone deaf. It is evident that he was not aware of this weakness, for he chose a rime scheme for all his extended work that would put an unbearable strain on any man's resources. If I were to enumerate these violations the references would cover all but four of his poems. He seldom ever wrote over fifty lines of aa, bb, verse, but that he violated this important canon of poetic art. May I add, that by no stretch of the imagination could his violations be considered as resolved rimes or near rimes.

In his choice of diction, Ferguson falls far short of the true poet. He has given us no words that blend with eeriness or witchery. There is nothing in his diction to emphasize the gulf between suggestion and mere statement. He gives us no connotative words that fling up great vivid images.

Ferguson's use of stanzaic structure is the most artificial of all his poetic technique. It appears that he chose his stanza form arbitrarily, or it may be that he simply wrote down what came into his mind. The result is that very few stanzas show a single complete thought. Enjambment comes in so frequently that we wonder why he took the trouble to set off the lines into stanzas. Most surely he knew nothing of the pattern of the poem when he set out to write.

It would be manifestly unfair for me to judge a man entirely by his technique. Even though his songs did not burst from his heart, still, he worked in materials that had lain dormant for years, and it will be for his materials that he will be remembered. Ferguson wrote at first, as many of the English poets of his day were writing, with nothing at all important to say. The drift, then, was away from the essential and the perennial. Grace, simplicity, and originality were little thought of. But Ferguson turned from conventional English themes to Irish myth. His pioneering here led others to the same rich field. It was not as if he had written the last word on the subject. It was not as if he had cast it all into an unforgettable mold, as if he had given it the final touch. No! On the contrary, he was too much of a Victorian. Although he had an attraction for the Celtic nature, as is witnessed in his *Adieu to Brittany,* he was continually unable to understand the Celtic soul. The frank sensuousness of the Celtic tales, their cruelty, their patent immorality, their pagan philosophy, quite nauseated him. He felt that he simply had to reduce them to the terms of Victorian morality and customs. Other men, coming later, with more universal sympathy, with more cosmic souls, and evidently with more Celtic blood, took up the lode that Ferguson had uncovered, and have worked the raw ores into something precious and refined.

Ferguson did not have the skill to recapture moments of glory. He made draftsmen's plates of the old monuments of Celtic lore. He had no ability to work into the legends that suggestive power which carries the reader beyond the imaginable. This power of suggestion is commensurate with the poet's ability to use figures of speech. Ferguson depicts rather than suggests. The only places wherein his figures flash out brilliantly were already figures in the originals from which he worked. Ferguson, essentially a man of the cold, scholastic type, could never aspire to anything beyond the hope of an appeal to the intellect. Of creative genius, that is the making of beauty for the sheer joy of it, he had none. (pp. 108-10)

[Ferguson was popular with anthologists in his day.] Of late years, however, he has been passed over by all collectors save those working in the Anglo-Irish field. The work these latter men have selected from him has been, for the most part, his translations.

The mention of translations brings a clearer light on Ferguson's skill as a poet. Two of his most famous translations: *Cean Dubh Deelish,* and *The Fair Hills of Ireland,* have been done by others. In all cases the work of the other poets deserves the preference. Dora Sigerson's, *Cean duv deelish,* is passionately human, while Sir Samuel's is politely formal. Edward Walker's, *The Fair Hills of Eire Ogh;* Mangan's, *The Fair Hills of Eiré O;* and George Sigerson's, *The Fair Hills of Eire,* are all superior in quality, spirit, and Celtic atmosphere, to Ferguson's translation of Donagh Mac Con Mara's original.

What can be said of Ferguson as a poet? In the face of all the laudatory criticism . . . , I have to come to the conclusion that Sir Samuel was but a hard conscientious worker. A scholar who longed to paint in imperishable verse pictures and incidents which he first had to reduce to cold logic; then to remold in the conventions of his time and of his social circle. Conservative, cautious, plush-curtainy, smug, Tory, as he was, he could not step outside of his character, even under the light of his flare.

This much, however, he did do. He checked the flood of maudlin sentiment that welled up out of *The Nation.* He threw a cloak of dignity around the hitherto despised Celtic legend. While Tennyson was purging adultery from the Arthurian Romance, Ferguson was weaving a few halos for the neglected figures of the Red Branch Cycle, for the lonely figures of the Western Gaels. In doing these things he gave inspiration to the coming generation, to the host of reborn Celtic writers. Though the younger men were to employ means which Ferguson deplored, still, his ends were their ends. In this respect he deserves a high position among the workers in Anglo-Irish Literature. (pp. 110-11)

Arthur Deering, in his Sir Samuel Ferguson, Poet and Antiquarian, *n.p., 1931, 150 p.*

Padraic Colum   (essay date 1963)

[*An Irish poet, dramatist, editor, and critic, Colum was one of the major writers of the Irish Literary Renaissance. He was most noted for his efforts to make better-known the varied heritage of Irish literature through his writings and public lectures, but he is perhaps most important as a historical dramatist who established many precedents for the Irish national theater. Colum's poetry incorporated his knowledge of dramatic technique. In addition, his poems are admired because they do not display the nationalistic didacticism so prevalent in the poetry of his contemporaries. Because of his close and genuine links with the people and culture of Ireland, he is considered one of the few authentic national poets of Ireland. In the following excerpt, Colum discusses Ferguson's poetry, suggesting that the poet's work possesses power despite flaws in technique.*]

Reading [Ferguson's **Lays of the Western Gael** and **The Lays of the Red Branch**] now one sees that the bulk of them have small imaginative energy. And if we compare any of them with a "lay" by a modern poet, Yeats's "Death of Cuchullain"—the poem, not the drama—we notice that something very necessary in poetry that evokes the ancient world is absent in these collections. There is nothing in them that characterises a personage. Yeats has given his Cuchullain and Emer lines that convey character. Ferguson fails to do this. There is some characterisation in **"The Tain Quest"** and **"The Death of Dermid."** **"The Abdication of Fergus"** and **"Aideen's Grave"** are certainly memorable, but, curiously, they are separated from the age of the heroes: they read as elegiac poems.

The poet who pioneered an Irish poetry based on epical themes—the scholars Hennessy and O'Donovan had revealed them to him—would very likely have been surprised if a critic placed before **The Lays of the Red Branch** and **The Lays of the Western Gael, Congal,** the Ulster ballad, **"Anna Grace"** and, more particularly, pieces that must have seemed incidental to him, his translations of traditional love-songs. Such a placing would be right, I believe. In the music of the harpers, the music that Bunting saved, the music that he and Petrie delighted in, and in the language he had learned with enthusiastic companions, Ferguson had a surer guide into the world of the Gael than in the translations furnished him by the scholars. Jeremiah Joseph Callanan had already brought into English the rhythm of the Gaelic folk-song—

'Tis down by the lake where the wild tree fringes
   its sides,
That the maid of my heart, my fair one of Heaven, abides.
I think as at eve she wanders its mazes along,
The birds go to sleep by the sweet wild twist of
   her song.

But Ferguson used this distinctive rhythm to more purpose—

Oh, fair maid, remember the green hillside,
Remember how I hunted about the valleys wide;
Time now has worn me; my locks have turned
   to grey,
The year is scarce and I am poor, but send me
   not, love, away.

And more truly than the translator of "The Outlaw of Loch Lene," he has got the sense that we expect to find in the popular songs of the penal days, the sense of oppression and defiance. Callanan's poem must be highly rated among translations from Irish into English, but **"Cashel of Munster," "The Coolun,"** have a sense of abandonment that, in those days of misfortune, must have been in the lives of the people. (pp. 6-7)

In an essay which he wrote Ferguson stated the condition on which a writer could deal with traditional material: he should be able to look the past in the face. This he does not do in **Lays of the Western Gael** and **Lays of the Red Branch.** He seems to be under the impression that his personages, because they belong to the national record, should be presented with dignity—the sort of dignity with which Tennyson invested his Arthur, Lancelot, Guinevere, and other worthies of Camelot. However, as a student of literature he noted that Aeschylus, Sophocles and Euripides wrote out of a traditional material that included rapes, robberies, murders. Once, when he did not have to impose standards that he thought were becoming to national heroes, when his personages were Burkes, Barretts, Lynotts, he looked the past in the face, and made himself the impressive poet of rapes, robberies and murders. His **"Vengeance of the Welshmen of Tirawley"** is the one ballad by an Irish poet that can be put beside the Border Ballads.

It is an outstanding achievement. The very rudeness of its stanza form has appropriateness. And the last stanza which might be rejected as a mere comment has validity: it gives us the sense that what we have heard or read were actual occurrences, and that the record presented is factual, historical. It is a loss that the judgment given by the Brehons is so far outside our time that we have to have an explanation of it: in a swiftly moving ballad immediate comprehension in needful; a climax depending on our sympathy with the institutions of fosterage and the eric makes for a loss of interest in the story. **"The Vengeance of the Welshmen of Tirawley"** because of its local and temporal circumstances, not for any failure in the poet's power, cannot have the wide appeal that its stark drama entitles it to.

Samuel Ferguson knew what up to his time Irish writers did not know, something of early Irish literature and what was great and exceptional in it. Taking the saga of "The Destruction of Da Derga's Hostel" in Hennessy's translation and "The Feast of Dun na Nee" in O'Donovan's translation, he made narrative poems out of them, **"Conaire"** and **Congal. . . . Congal** is monumental as a narrative poem: indeed it was intended to be, and Ferguson spoke of it as, an epic. But to write a narrative of three thousand five hundred lines or thereabouts, and keep it readable through metrical invention with shifts of interest, is something that no poet writing in English in the past two hundred years has been able to accomplish. Yeats saved "The Wanderings of Oisin" from monotony by changing the metrical pattern from episode to episode, but in doing this he broke the unity of the story. There is no variation of pattern in **Congal;** the successive rhyme through incident after incident becomes tiring. However,

there are certain passages in the poem that have completeness as narrative and these are given in this selection. In his early and unsurpassed **"Anna Grace,"** Ferguson brought eeriness into the situation, an eeriness that makes the action memorable. He does the like in a part of **Congal:**—the episodes of the Giant Walker and the Washer at the Ford have an eeriness that makes them outstanding in the narrative. And the scene that follows them, the confrontation of Congal by his betrothed Lafinda and her guardian, rounds off this part of Congal's history.

Towards the end of his writing life Ferguson wrote to the editor of *The Irish Monthly Magazine,* Father Russell, noting the fact that little attention had been paid to his poetry in "the great centres of criticism in England," going on to say, "My business is, regardless of such discouragement, to do what I can in the formation of a characteristic school of letters for my own country." We must honor him for that declaration. (pp. 8-10)

Padraic Colum, in an introduction to The Poems of Samuel Ferguson *edited by Padraic Colum, Allen Figgis, 1963, 1-12.*

Robert O'Driscoll   (essay date 1971)

[*O'Driscoll is a Canadian scholar and educator specializing in Irish studies. In the following excerpt, he describes Ferguson's use of Irish history and folklore for inspiration.*]

Two events, one literary and one historical, lie behind the conscious movement for an Irish national literature. The literary event was the publication in the early 1760's of James Macpherson's translations of what he claimed were authentic poems of Ossian. These, as every undergraduate knows, were forgeries in that they purported to be translations of a third-century poet. Nevertheless the work did have a profound influence on European literature and attracted attention to a body of tradition which to this point had only been locally known. Interest was revived in Irish music, legend, literature, and history; and the work of Sylvester O'Halloran, Ferdinando Warner, J. H. Wynne, Charlotte Brooke, Joseph Cooper Walker, James Hely, Charles Vallancey and a host of others can be attributed directly or indirectly to Macpherson's influence, and to the desire of these scholars to vindicate their country's claim to an ancient and honorable literature and history. In addition, societies were organized to examine and publish the manuscripts in which the Irish tradition was preserved. In 1786 the Royal Irish Academy was founded and, some time later, the Scottish Highland Society, the Hiberno-Celtic Society, the Gaelic Society. It was under the patronage of the Gaelic Society that the first complete edition and translation of an Irish legend was made: Theophilus O'Flangan's edition of the Deirdre legend in 1808.

The other event that lies behind the movement for an Irish national literature, the historical event, was the founding in 1791 of the United Irish Society, which proposed as its chief objects the abolition of "all unnatural religious distinctions," the union of Irishmen "against the unjust influence of Great Britain," and the establishment of "true representation in a national Parliament." It was broken as a political force in 1798, but in 1810 its principles were altered from a political to an educational ideal, as the writer of the original prospectus of the Society, William Drennan, founded the Royal Belfast Academical Institution, setting down as one of its chief aims the encouragement of communication between "pupils of all religious denominations . . . by frequent and friendly intercourse, in the common business of education, by which means a new turn might be given to the national character and habits, and all the children of Ireland should know and love each other." From an educational to a literary ideal was as natural although not as clear a transition. It was attempted, however, by one of the pupils of the Institution, by Samuel Ferguson, who advocated that the most effective way of dissipating the prejudices of his countrymen was by turning their thoughts from narrow political interests to the study of their country's history, antiquities, and literature.

But despite the influence of the Belfast Academical Institution Ferguson expresses in his early writings intolerance for his Roman Catholic countrymen and a deep distrust of the motives of the Roman Catholic Church in Ireland. The Roman Church, he believed at this time, was simply a mixture of error and superstition:

> between the outworks of trick and legerdemain, and the citadel of church supremacy what a wilderness of error inexplicable—what pitfalls, traps, and labyrinths—what sloughs and stenches of superstition! But, above all and beyond all, what a rampart in the deluded people's love? For the Irish priesthood hold the hearts of their seduced victims in even firmer bondage than their minds ["**A Dialogue between the Head and Heart of an Irish Protestant**," *Dublin University Magazine,* II (November, 1833), 586].

Yet though Ferguson's dislike of Catholicism was great, his love of Ireland was greater: "I am an Irishman and a Protestant," he writes in an unpublished letter, but "I was an Irishman before I was a Protestant." Consequently in 1833 his interest in the welfare of his country was such as to lead him to investigate the literary legacy of his Catholic countrymen. The result was four essays on Irish poetry that he published in the newly-founded *Dublin University Magazine* in 1834 and to which he appended translations of original Irish poems, translations in which he broke boldly with the established tradition of Anglo-Irish translation and in which he consciously furnished later poets with a model where simplicity had not been sacrificed to sophistication nor truth to convention.

Translations from the Irish had been made before, the most important being Charlotte Brooke's *Reliques of Irish Poetry* in 1789 and those included in James Hardiman's *Irish Minstrelsy* in 1831. These works are important because despite their many drawbacks they focused considerable attention on Irish poetry and dissipated some of the suspicion and contempt with which it was then regarded. Unfortunately, however, all of the translators imposed on their Irish originals the metrical patterns and conventional language of contemporary English poetry. For despite their realization of the need to preserve the spirit of the

bards, and the repeated assertions of their genuine attempts to do so, they were unwilling to follow the irregular metrical patterns of the originals and unwilling to translate the vigorous, simple, and sometimes homely idiom as directly and as simply as possible. Instead they all felt compelled to sophisticate the sentiments of the originals by using a highly ornate and artificial language, and by fitting the loose and unemphatic measures to alien and inflexible English metrical patterns.

In 1834 Ferguson censured the work of these translators and made his own in an attempt to give as close a representation in English verse of the thought, measure, and idiom of the original poems as the exigencies of translation permitted. In doing this he successfully transferred the distinctive features of Irish poetry to English poetry. Indeed, it was not until Ferguson's translations were made, nor those of his independent forerunner, Jeremiah Callanan, that, in Yeats's words, "anything of an honest style came into use" [*A Book of Irish Verse,* (1895)]. Callahan pioneered the pattern that Ferguson established, attempting in a few of his translations "a union of Gaelic thought, rhythm, and vowel patterns" [B. G. MacCarthy in "Jeremiah J. Callanan: His Poetry," in *Studies,* XXXV (September, 1946), p. 394]. It is in Callanan's wake that Ferguson follows, Callanan's style that he emulates, Callanan's music that he makes subtler and more diversified. Ferguson is consequently the first influential Anglo-Irish poet to preserve in his English translations the shape, sound, and sentiment of his Irish originals. Always he preserves, ungarnished and unsophisticated, the sentiments of the originals. And the disciplined form, the strict and athletic movement he gave his translations of early bardic remains he replaced in his versions of seventeenth- and eighteenth-century love poems by a more fluidic line of varying tempo, the long swinging line with its wavering unemphatic rhythm, the distinctive measure later used with such variation and effect by Mangan, Walsh, Sigerson, Hyde, Yeats, AE, and others.

It is well to remember Ferguson's achievement as a translator of Irish poetry, but equally important to realize that if his literary exertions had been confined solely to this field of Anglo-Irish literature he would be a far less significant figure in 19th-century Ireland than he is. Ferguson was not interested in translation as a pastime, nor even as an art. He was filled with the broader desire of creating for his country a distinctive national literature. He believed that this literature would not only be the means of realizing the destiny which he considered rightfully Ireland's but would also provide a link between people of diverse convictions: it would, he argued, minimize and ultimately remove the antipathies between Orange and Green, Protestant and Catholic, aristocrat and peasant. To this end he dedicated a long life of versatile literary activity. He turned from the conventional poetic themes of his day to ancient Irish history and legend. He dignified and popularized this material and made it the subject matter of a new and distinctive literature.

When he began to write Ferguson could see two fairly distinct schools of Anglo-Irish literature. One, the Donnybrook Fair school, of which he claimed Mrs. S. C. Hall,

Thomas Crofton Croker, Samuel Lover, and Charles Lever were examples, produced works that were Irish more by accidentals than by substance and attempted to focus the contrast between the "sober, industrious, law-abiding" English citizen and the "drunken, wrangling, lawless" Irish peasant. The other school, of which Ferguson claimed Charlotte Brooke, James Hardiman and his translators were examples, painted a contrasted picture of Irish life and literature, attempting to dignify and sophisticate the Irishman to the point of proving that not only was he very human but also very British. Both schools were equally untrue to Irish life and character: "The one school exaggerated peculiarities until the picture of Irish life was a mere caricature; while the other suppressed whatever did not conform to the British standard of behaviour and expression."

Ferguson saw the need for Ireland's developing literature to be in close contact with contemporary life, but separated as he was from the Irish people by background, taste, and temperament, and feeling that the church to which they adhered was a secret mixture of medieval superstition and Renaissance intrigue, he realized that he could never give a genuine literary presentation of Irish peasant life. He left this, therefore, for his friend William Carleton and turned, instead, to ancient Ireland.

Slowly his idea for an Irish national literature developed. By 1837 it had advanced to the point which he could see on the strictly utilitarian level the social function such a literature could serve. By this time also he had realized that much material was inaccessible to the historian and creative writer, that the only way in which it could be made available to both was through the slow and painstaking labors of the antiquary. Three years later he had fully formulated the means for achieving his literary ideal. As he prophetically put it later: "A new root of society has been planted, and a new flower of civilization has yet to bloom, in this western world. It has been bathed with tears, and nourished under sighs; but, by God's favour, it will yet send its perfume down all the avenues of time" ["The Annals of the Four Masters," *Dublin University Magazine* (May 1848)].

By 1840 the challenge had been issued, and during the next decade it was answered. In 1842 the *Nation* was founded and the principle of action which Ferguson had been advocating for almost ten years in the not-too-influential *Dublin University Magazine,* the principle of unity through self-reliance, self-education, and self-help was disseminated to an attentive country. Ferguson, however, did not approve of the political basis that was now given this idea. Consequently, he did not contribute to the *Nation,* but during its turbulent six-year history quietly applied himself "to the prosecution of my original design to keep the Irish subject up to a higher standard, and to discountenance that helotism which has so often vulgarized the efforts of Irish writers, seeking to gain the ephemeral applause of the magazines and newspapers of the metropolis" [quoted in *Sir Samuel Ferguson in the Ireland of His Day,* by Lady Ferguson; see Further Reading]. The abortive armed uprising of 1848 convinced him that some-

thing more permanent than political exertion was necessary before Ireland could realize her rightful destiny:

> We have, indeed, been involved in a sea of troubles; but in the midst of that confusion and repulsion, the reconciling power of mind has been at work, settling and establishing itself on sure foundations, by unseen, but great and preserving labour; for these noble works of learning which day by day begin to show their heads above the waves of misfortune around us, rest upon deep and solid substructions, such as assure us that they will yet become centres of gathering intelligence—will spread, and unite, and grow green with culture, and be covered with harvests, while storms shall blow, and waves fret at their feet in vain [*Dublin University Magazine* (May, 1848)].

During the whole period, however, his hopes for a national literature were high. Davis had quickened the prospects for its achievement by disseminating national spirit and literature among millions of Irish people. Whether consciously or unconsciously, one part of Ferguson's challenge of 1840 had been answered, and what must have been even more gratifying for him was that the other part was receiving just as interested attention. For it is important to remember that Ferguson in 1840 not only wanted a literature binding Irishmen of different backgrounds, but that he had advocated that this developing literature must have its foundation in the fact of ancient Irish history and legend. This foundation in fact, he felt, could only be provided by the careful investigations of the antiquary. Again the challenge was answered. The 1840's in Ireland were a decade of antiquarian achievement. It saw the beginnings of the work of the great scholar, Eugene O'Curry, the publication of George Petrie's *Ecclesiastical Architecture of Ireland,* and of John O'Donovan's thesaurus of native Irish history, *The Annals of the Four Masters.* It witnessed the activity of an energetic Ordnance Survey Committee, the formation of the Irish Archaeological Society, the Celtic Society, and what eventually became the Royal Society of Antiquaries. And, more importantly, it established the necessity and value of antiquarian and poetic collaboration: in 1842 John O'Donovan published his edition of *The Banquet of Dun Na N-Gedh and the Battle of Magh Rath,* and in 1844, with this material before him, Ferguson began **Congal,** the first substantial English poem based on Irish legend.

In December, 1849, Ferguson wrote to William Allingham: "I have now full confidence in the creation of a pure home literature, and invite all the geniuses of the country to rally in Dublin." By 1849 his decision had been made. The ideal had become practical while the material was becoming available. Now all that was needed was to forge the heroic material into heroic poetry, to take its confused splendors, its fragmentary, scattered, and unrelated parts and make it into something it was not before, to infuse it, as Lascelles Abercrombie would say, with a "single presiding unity of artistic purpose," to make it symbolize significant patterns in the nation's destiny. But in 1849 Ferguson could not see many poets with either the ability or the will to undertake this demanding work. By the end of the 1840's most of Ireland's literary figures had died or had been ostracized. Davis had died in 1845, Mangan in 1849, and Moore—not that his genius suited him to the task—was to die in 1852. Most of the Young Irelanders had been ostracized for their participation in the 1848 rising. As for the other prospects, William Allingham and Aubrey De Vere were too busy acquainting themselves with conventional English form, matter, and personages to devote the time and energy necessary for the creation of a national literature. Ferguson could see only one candidate for the job, and that was himself. So he began his task with a courage and single-mindedness that was able to sustain him through years of literary neglect, cut off as he was from the main stream of English literature and laboring as he was alone and without encouragement in the unaccepted field of Celtic legend.

About 1849 he was working on the first draft of his epic **Congal,** a poem which presents the final clash of paganism and Christianity in 7th-century Ireland. But although complete and ready for publication in 1861, **Congal** was not published until 1872. The chief reason for this delay seems to have been Ferguson's fear of the reception the poem would be given by a public antipathetic to Ireland and to Irish publications, and for the most part ignorant, or at least sceptical, of the value of Irish legend as subject matter for poetry. Consequently, to prepare its way, he decided to publish in 1865 the **Lays of the Western Gael,** a volume of shorter, less ambitious poems illustrating some of the main epochs of Irish legend.

The **Lays of the Western Gael** is significant for a number of reasons: first, it contained the translations from the Irish that Ferguson had published in the *Dublin University Magazine* in 1834, translations in which, as we have seen, he broke boldly with the established tradition of Anglo-Irish translation; second, it contained poems which possess the seeds of the "Celtic Twilight," poems in which the fairy is not a diminutive creature of fancy introduced to give local coloring or a supernatural atmosphere, but which has become for almost the first time in Anglo-Irish literature an imaginative reality. Third, the volume provided the first serious poetic presentation in English of the legendary material which ultimately became the chief source of inspiration for Irish poets and dramatists. It is thus Ferguson, and not any of his contemporaries, who is the true precursor, we may even say the originator, of the literary revival at the end of the 19th-century, Ferguson who approached the past with the eyes of a scholar, and interpreted it with the mind of a poet: "The work of restoration demanded the co-operation of learning and imagination, and in Ferguson a man was found who combined the necessary qualifications. . . . It was thus his privilege to possess the key that unlocked the gates through which the stream of modern Irish literature was to pass. He set free the Celtic spirit, imprisoned in the shell of an almost extinct language, and obscured by the dust of political turmoil" [Ernest Boyd; see exerpt dated 1922].

Several of his contemporaries certainly had the will to use Irish legendary material, but all lacked one or other of the essential qualifications for turning it into the basis for a national literature. James Clarence Mangan's translations generally capture the fire and lament of the originals: in-

deed so deeply does Mangan enter into the spirit of the poems he is translating that one of his original poems, "A Vision of Connaught in the Thirteenth Century," could easily be an authentic *aisling.* But, as noted earlier, some of Mangan's best translations were directly inspired by Ferguson's, and he wrote no poems based on the earlier cycles of Irish legend. Several of Ferguson's other contemporaries had to be content with historical ballads. Thomas Davis, for example, on whom Ferguson's influence has yet to be explored, realized the value of Irish legend for poetry, but could only write ballads illustrating some of the later epochs of Irish history. He lacked the knowledge and, it may even be said, the dedication to make sustained poetic renderings of Irish legend. The same is true of Thomas D'Arcy McGee who, although a finer poet than Davis and although capable of catching some of the splendor of early Celtic life and legend in a few of his poems, was also denied this source of poetic inspiration. Denis Florence MacCarthy and Aubrey de Vere, also, had to content themselves for a considerable time with Irish history and the available legends of the saints before they had the example and the knowledge to create poems from the early material. As for the other noteworthy 19th-century Irish poet, William Allingham, although presenting an interesting picture of contemporary Ireland in *Laurence Bloomfield* (1864), and although later writing lyrics of low

Drawing of Ferguson at the time of his marriage to Mary Catherine Guinness.

life and poems based on fairy traditions, he never found poetic inspiration in Irish legend.

The importance of the *Lays of the Western Gael* in the history of Anglo-Irish literature is, therefore, difficult to over-estimate. But when published, slightly over a hundred years ago, it was practically ignored. Of the English periodicals of the time, only the *Athenaeum* reviewed it favorably. A writer in the *Saturday Review* [January 1865] made the following assessment:

> There is perhaps no class of matters, historical or legendary, in which it is so hard to get up an interest as in matters purely Celtic. . . . We imagine this from seeing how utterly impossible it is to get up any interest about the Celt pure and simple as we see him in Wales and Ireland. No one cares for any Welsh hero except Arthur, and people care for Arthur only because they do not realize he was Welsh. . . . The Irishman, the "Western Gael" of Mr. Ferguson, is, if possible, more hopeless still. It would require a great genius indeed to make us care in the least for tales which we know are not history and which have acquired no fame or interest as legends. . . . But we cannot think Mr. Ferguson has succeeded in the attempt. . . . There are pretty bits enough here and there, but the thing, as a whole, is decidedly wearisome. . . . If Mr. Ferguson's lines arouse any desire to know more about Crunn and Macha, it is not because of their grandeur, but because of their grotesqueness.

The reviewer's ignorance of Irish legend, his uncompromising denial of its use as legitimate subject matter for poetry, and his errors of fact and interpretation considerably lessen the force and sting his conclusions might otherwise have had.

Congal followed in 1872 and attracted even less attention than *Lays of the Western Gael.* Ferguson's third volume of poetry was published in 1880; it contained his finest narrative poem, **"Conary"**, and the first dramatic presentation of the Deirdre legend.

It is striking how closely the themes of Ferguson's poetry paralleled the events of his life. *Congal* was composed at a time when his hopes for a national literature were high, when he felt that it was merely a matter of time before Celtic legend became a central source of inspiration for writers; thus the tumultuous defiance, the youthful exuberance and enthusiasm for his subject which characterized his life during this period characterized also his epic poem. The exuberance passed, leaving a more mature and a more thoughtful man. During his second period of poetic development he went on to depict a pagan world on the verge of Christianity, a primordial society poised on the threshold of a new era. So it was, he thought, with Ireland at the time. He felt that she, too, was poised on the threshold of a great new era of social unification, economic prosperity, and intellectual achievement, that all of these things were to be the indirect results of a national literature; thus it was with mixed feelings of impatience and nostalgia that he anticipated the change. By the late 1870's, however, it had become increasingly clear to Ferguson that this change would not take place in Ireland

during his lifetime. But this realization, disheartening as it must have been, did not lead him to abandon his efforts to create a national literature; it simply resulted in a strange fascination for the theme of fatalism. There is in his poetry of this date, in **"Deirdre"** and **"Conary"**, a passive acceptance of the harsh decrees of a repressive Fate. He shows how pitiable and powerless man is at the hands of Fate, how his most carefully laid plans are ruthlessly frustrated, how he is duped by guile and pushed unlovingly into a cold untimely grave.

Ferguson was caught between two currents. His refusal to pander to the popular taste for political literature cut him off from the Irish public, and his choice to write poetry based on Irish legend from contemporary English criticism. His death in 1886 seemed to shock some critics into an appreciation of his dedicated labors to provide Ireland with a distinctive literature. For a brief period, while Irish lore and legend were in the ascendant, Ferguson enjoyed some recognition, but as the Irish subject grew in popularity, as the blue-bleak embers of the Irish tradition were finally made to fall and gall and gash the gold-vermilion of the Literary Revival, as the scope of the revival expanded and as its interest was pushed deeper and deeper into original material, as its imaginative exponents gripped with greater and greater intensity the mind of the age, so also did Ferguson sink more and more out of sight, overshadowed by the brilliance and appeal of these later-day writers. But now that the impact of the Revival is over, the literary historian can study objectively its course and see the parts in their true perspective.

It is interesting to read some of Ferguson's last references to his plans for a national literature, considering that during those years, with his work completed and his ideal unachieved, he was only repeating his words of fifty years earlier, but repeating them with the same faith, determination, and courage. Witness:

> I see only friends falling and failing around me, and must be content to go my ways leaving undone a great deal that I ought to have done; but I have lived, and loved, and done something if not all I might . . . [to make] the voice of this despised people of ours heard high up Olympus.

and

> I think we have amongst us enough of ability to lay the foundations of such a school of letters here as will be honourable also to the country. That has been the great aim I have had in view of all my efforts. . . . A Dublin School would, I think, restore good taste and good English in our current poetry, now over-run with gaspings, affectation, pet words, and bad prosody. . . . The history of this country furnishes plenty of material; its native literature more. But the people—idle, *feckless* as they are—are a game breed, and won't disappear before the face of any other competitors for existence here; and they must have their history and their humanities *to-lites qualites.* I trust in God they will yet recognise as friends the men who revolt against the present teachings given them by those who would make them knaves and cowards.

and

> I don't despair at all for my country. Knaves, cowards, assassins, at present represent her; but this scum floats on a substratum of noble qualities. I am old, but, if I do not see it, I shall close my eyes in the faith of her resurrection.

and

> We will have to make a literature for this country whatever be the fate of this or that policy. . . . It must be lofty, moral, and distinctly Irish. . . . The Poets will save the people whom the rogues and cowards have corrupted. I shall not live, I daresay, to see the salvation, but I shall die believing in it. I have, indeed, had a warning not to expect long-deferred events.

Ferguson did not live to see the "salvation" of the Irish nation, but his fear that the event would be "long-deferred" proved groundless. For only two months after his death, W. B. Yeats, then on the threshold of his literary career, boldly took up Ferguson's prophecy to make one of his own, a prophecy for an Irish national literature which, he claimed, would find its morning in Ferguson and his heroic poetry:

> The author of these poems is the greatest poet Ireland has produced, because the most central and most Celtic. Whatever the future may bring forth in the way of a truly great and national literature—and now that the race is so large, so widely spread, and so conscious of its unity, the years are ripe—will find its morning in these three volumes [Ferguson's *Lays of the Western Gael, Congal,* and *Poems*] of one who was made by the purifying flame of National sentiment the one man of his time who wrote heroic poetry— one who, among the somewhat sybaritic singers of his day, was like some aged sea-king sitting among the inland wheat and poppies—the savour of the sea around him, and its strength [see excerpt dated 1886].

(pp. 82-95)

Robert O'Driscoll, "Ferguson and the Idea of an Irish National Literature," in Éire-Ireland, *Vol. VI, No. 1, Spring, 1971, pp. 82-95.*

Terence Brown   (essay date 1975)

[*Brown is an Irish educator and scholar who has extensively studied Irish culture and literature. In the following excerpt, he examines Ferguson's works in light of the poet's social and political views.*]

Samuel Ferguson was born of a Scots planter family in Belfast in 1810. His people had settled in Antrim in the seventeenth century and had been substantial landholders since that time. Ferguson's father was, however, extremely improvident and it was his mother who had to maintain family standards as their fortunes waned. Ferguson was educated, nevertheless, at the Belfast Royal Academy, then at the Academical Institution and Trinity College, Dublin. Belfast, in Ferguson's youth was without doubt an Irish town—'as British as Birmingham' is a formulation that would have cut little ice with a generation that

remembered the United Irishmen, and before that the Dungannon convention, nor with those who may have attended the great harp festival in 1792. At school Ferguson fell under the influence of nationally inclined young men, and in particular of one, George Fox. Ferguson wrote of his early associates:

> Amongst my schoolfellows and youthful associates in Belfast were the late Mr John Maclean, afterwards the London millionaire, and Lord O'Hagan. We three used greatly to affect the society of another young Belfast man, Mr George Fox, son of a widow lady resident in North Street in that our common native town. Mr Fox, to judge of him by the influence he exercised on the minds of two at least of our coterie, will be recognised as a man of singular ability and attractiveness of conversation. His discourse, indeed, possessed a fascination equal to all that I have heard of Coleridge. Under these influences my poetic faculty, which had already shown itself in the ballad of **'Willy Gilliland'** acquired strength . . . We had formed a private class for the study of Irish. The early history of Ulster had seized my imagination, and the **'Return of Claneboy'**, a prose romance which I had contributed about that time to *Blackwood,* may be regarded as the first indication of my ambition to raise the native elements of Irish poetry to a dignified level; and that ambition I think may be taken as the key to almost all the literary work of my subsequent life [quoted in *Sir Samuel Ferguson in the Ireland of His Day* by Lady Ferguson; see Further Reading].

This ambition was indeed lifelong. Throughout his career as barrister at law, Deputy Keeper of the Records Office in Dublin, scholar, antiquary, President of the Royal Irish Academy, and Victorian knight and public man, Ferguson wrote poetry which took as its basis the 'matter of Ireland'. How Ferguson treated that material and what his treatment implies is worth study.

Samuel Ferguson, for all the stodginess of his public persona (his letters and speeches often echo standard Victorian pieties), was a man in a very remarkable position: he was by marriage a member of the Protestant Ascendancy, a descendant of Scots settlers, who fell under the spell of native Irish traditions, legends and literature. A Unionist in politics almost all his life, he nevertheless had a role to play, small though it was, and against his own best intentions, in the development of modern Irish nationalism.

It was Ferguson's often-expressed contention that a firm respect for the Union of Great Britain and Ireland did not preclude one from asserting a proper pride in one's own native land and its best traditions and products. Thus he apparently felt no conflict between his Tory political loyalties and his national feelings. Only once, in the years of the Famine, was he ever tempted by the Repeal movement, and that in a rather dilatory manner considering the urgency of the situation. Nationalism for Ferguson did not necessarily imply separatism. Yet one should not question the fervour of his nationalist feelings, perhaps derived from his friend Fox and nurtured in the revolutionary romantic nationalism fashionable in his youth (Ferguson's brother died fighting for Bolivia and his friend James Emerson Tennent enlisted in the Greek cause). He had no doubt at all that he was an Irishman, indeed one of the best kind of Irishman, and he resented profoundly any suggestion to the contrary. In 1834 he published an extensive review of Hardiman's *Irish Minstrelsy* [in *Dublin University Magazine*]. This review takes Hardiman sternly to task for, as Ferguson saw it, dividing Catholic Ireland from Protestant Ireland by making the Gaelic past the sole preserve of the Catholic Irish: 'O ye fair hills of holy Ireland, who is he who ventures to stand between us and your Catholic sons' goodwill?'

Throughout the review and other essays he published in his twenties, Ferguson preached nationalism, but a nationalism that was to include all types of Irishmen. In 1834 we find him writing a passage that might well come from the pen of a nationalist fanatic in the midst of the political struggle that came in the early twentieth century:

> We believe that great proportion of the characteristics of a people are inherent, not fictitious; and that there are as essential differences between the genius's as between the physical appearances of nations. We believe that . . . no stultifying operation of mere security, plenty, or laborious regularity could ever, without actual physical transubstantiation, reduce the native Irishman to the stolid standard of the sober Saxon.

This is the ideology of a militant nationalism, if one cared to take it seriously. Two years later he was writing (perhaps in more measured tones, but with no diminution of nationalist zeal): 'We must be Irish in mental achievements or we are nothing' and 'The development of a new national genius is an era in the history of human life,' and he eulogises a

> young nation entering the lists of intellectual competition, striking out paths of enquiry hitherto untrodden, creating styles and schools hitherto unimagined . . . perhaps in the collision of intellects throwing light upon questions till then involved in undissipated darkness.

It should be pointed out that when Ferguson writes in this fashion he does so in the service of a nationalism that will allow a flowering of the Irish intellect rather than a violent assertion of her spiritual identity. Yet the violence of his rhetoric is of the kind that might be employed in the service of a much less gentlemanly nationalism than Ferguson would have hoped to see.

Why did Ferguson then write in this way, in a rhetoric that could serve causes far from those he had in mind? Conor Cruise O'Brien in his book *States of Ireland* has applied and developed Frantz Fanon's categories of colonists and colonised to the Irish situation, and particularly to the Protestant nationalists of the Irish literary revival. He writes:

> The natives they idealized were those who had remained most thoroughly native: and unfortunately they idealized these in ways that did not appear to the Catholic *colonisés* to be ideal.

Such an analysis creates in O'Brien's book an explanatory context for Yeats's frequent attacks upon the Catholic *bourgeoisie* who fumbled in their greasy till when they should have obeyed Yeats's calls to nationhood, and for the fact that J. M. Synge, although a Dublin Protestant, chose the vital life of the Irish peasantry to present his vision of Ireland. Their nationalism was of a peculiarly insulting kind. They venerated an idealised image of the peasantry in scorn of the middle class's vulgar material aspirations. O'Brien seems convinced that this emotional response to their situation is entirely due to their status as colonists. I doubt this, since it is a common feature of nationalist ideologues to scorn the majority of their fellowcitizens who do not share their urge for racial purity, for the primitive sources of the tribe and the spiritual possibilities inherent for the people in a liberation struggle. European nationalists have idealised many unsuspecting peasantries. Such romantic rejection of sophistication and vulgar modernity has by no means been a prerogative of colonial classes. Rather it has been a recurrent gratification for romantics or for the disaffected, whether their alienation was from the sterilities of garrison culture or from a dismissive and unappreciative bourgeois society.

Samuel Ferguson at moments in his writing displayed an almost Yeatsian contempt for the vulgarity of Catholic political aspirations and established his own version of the ideal Celt. He was probably reacting to his coloniser's position, but was also reflecting standard romantic nationalist tendencies. In his review of Hardiman's *Irish Minstrelsy* we encounter the following extraordinary passage:

> Let us contribute our aid to the auspicious undertaking, and introduce the Saxon and the Scottish Protestant to an acquaintance with poetical genius of a people hitherto unknown to them, as being known only in a character incompatible with sincerity or plain dealing. The present century will not answer the conditions of our enquiry. We will look nearer to times when they who had high treason in their hearts had arms in their hands, and honest defiance on their faces—when the game of nations was played boldly and won fairly—when victors and vanquished could afford to seem what they really were, and genuine feeling found utterance undisguised, in the passionate sincerity of exultation or despair. We will leave the idiotic brawler, the bankrupt and fraudulent demagogue, the crawling incendiary, the scheming, jesuitical, ambitious priest—that perverse rabble, on whom the mire in which they have wallowed for the last quarter of a century has caked into a crust like the armour of the Egyptian beast, till they are case hardened invulnerably in the filth of habitual impudence, ingratitude, hypocrisy, envy and malice; so that it were but a vain defilement of aught manly or honourable to advance it against such panoply of every foul component—we will leave them to their employment of reproach and agitation, and sing the songs of men who might well rise from honourable graves, and affright the midnight echoes of Aughrim or Benburb with their lamentations, if they could know that their descendants were fools enough to be led by such a directory of knaves and cowards.

We recognise the 'fraudulent demagogue'—O'Connell, having won Emancipation was turning his energies to the Repeal movement—but who, we might ask, is 'the bankrupt' or 'the scheming jesuitical, ambitious priest'?

In his poetry Ferguson introduces us to the Celts who 'could afford to seem what they really were', to the Celts of bold yet simple virtues, to what he described in another part of the essay as 'bold men and chaste women' who are 'the elements of a nation, though its metropolis be a kraal and its *via regis* a sheeptrack'. We can therefore see Ferguson's ambition 'to raise the native elements of Irish story to a dignified level' in the nationalist context in which it was originally meaningful.

Ferguson's poems present us with idealised peasant girls who would have gladdened the hearts of those who hated *The Playboy of the Western World*. Of course, his poems **'Molly Astore'**, **'Nora of the Amber Hair'**, and **'Kitty Tyrrell'** are translations from the Gaelic, but Ferguson obviously delighted in their subjects' uncorrupted, peasant simplicity. Kitty would accept the addresses of her rustic swain but reject the advances of a fast-talking criminal from Co. Wicklow.

> Ah would that I never had seen your bright
>   head,
> Your little pen's writing or step light and free;
> But if once my Lord Bishop the blessing had said
> I'd soon have my Kitty across the salt sea:
> She's fair as the swan of the silver white down,
> Than music she's sweeter, than sunshine more
>   bright;
> There's never an ale-house, from this to the
>   town,
> In which I won't drink her good health before
>   night.

Ferguson is even happier with martial subjects. It is strange that the cultural nationalist who desired the emergence of an Irish mind was so little moved in his poetry by the traditions of medieval Christian scholarship, but chose instead to tell tales of pagan revenge and brutal vitality. This remained true throughout his career. In his public life he allowed himself only a brief flirtation with Young Ireland (probably because Thomas Davis was a cultivated Protestant) and with the Repeal movement before settling into a staid Unionism and horror of physical force. It seems deeply ironical that when the Celt did stand up openly with arms in his hands, Ferguson, who in his poetry idealised the martial prowess of the Gaelic past, was horrified. He was appalled by political violence of any kind, and was particularly distressed by the Phoenix Park murders towards the end of his life, producing in response a long dramatic monologue in the manner of Browning in an attempt to understand the event. He seems to me to have been an unselfconscious man of considerable talents who was almost unaware in the midst of a busy life of the implications of his own imaginative preoccupations. He did once attempt to suppress some of his patriotic poems 'lest by any means, the Nationalists should claim him for their own'. But, as W. B. Yeats remarked [in *Dublin University Review* (November, 1886)], 'The suppression was not carried far enough. We claim him through every line. Irish singers, who are genuinely Irish in thought, subject and style, must, whether they will or no, nourish the forces that make for the political liberties of Ireland.' To write, in the midst of a century of political turmoil, poems which celebrate Gaelic military exploit was, to say the least, ill-advised for one who supported the Union. And Ferguson's work was indeed to bear strange fruit when planted in the fertile ground of W. B. Yeats's youthful imagination, when that poet claimed him for his own.

Ferguson portrayed Celtic militarism in many poems. Often an excessive regard for manliness and strength in his heroes make them merely the stolid, unbelievable, imaginings of a Victorian gentleman as they stomp about clothed in stock diction. At other times, however, Ferguson let the violence and energy of his inspiring sources imprint itself on his own work. His verse then achieves a real power. **'The Burial of King Cormac'**, for example, is directly and energetically brutal:

> They loosed their curse against the king;
> They cursed him in his flesh and bones;
> And daily in their mystic ring
> They turn'd the maledictive stones,
>
> Till, where at meat the monarch sate,
> Amid the revel and the wine,
> He choked upon the food he ate,
> At Sletty, southward of the Boyne.

Occasionally, Ferguson manages a primitive bluntness evoking an heroic period when issues did not admit of much discussion. So in **'Fergus Wry-Mouth'**

> Fergus theron slew the maid;
> And, to Loch Rury's brink in haste conveyed
> Went in at Fertais.

'The Welshmen of Tirawley' is one of Ferguson's best known poems. Swinburne thought it the finest Irish ballad ever written. It is a tale of conquest and uncompromising vengeance: as an Anglo-Norman crime is avenged by a group of Welsh settlers in medieval Ireland. Patrick Power has remarked of the poem [in *The Story of Anglo-Irish Poetry*, 1967]: 'There is a note of ferocity in this ballad . . . which looks very like the uncompromising material that turns up so often in Gaelic folksong.' The poem's primitive force is partly an effect of its vigorous rough-hewn rhythms, the battle cry of its refrain, and partly of its treatment of a material that must have seemed to the Victorian ear very barbaric indeed. The Welshmen of the tale are offered a grim choice by their victors—blinding or castration. They naturally choose blinding, hoping to sire offspring who will wreak vengeance for their sufferings. All but one of them are drowned as they stumble unseeingly into a swift-flowing river. The sole survivor swears revenge.

> For 'tis neither in eye or eyesight that a man
> Bears the fortunes of himself and his clan,
> But in the manly mind.
> These darken'd orbs behind,
> That your needles could never find
> Though they ran
> Through my heart-strings!
> Sing the vengeance of the Welshmen of Tirawley.

Ferguson's major work was his poem *Congal* which he published in 1872. In this he attempts to elevate Irish materials to a dignified level by treating them in the epic manner. The poet took as his source a Middle Irish text known as 'The Banquet of Dún na nGedh' and recast it into a clumsy fourteen-syllable line, liberally illustrating the poem's heroic action with epic similes in the Miltonic manner. Dr Johnson's remark on *Paradise Lost,* that no man has ever wished it longer, may also be applied to *Congal.* Yet it has virtues. Although the similes break up the action with tedious regularity, some of them evoke a fresh exhilarating impression of primitive nature. The work thus gave Edward Dowden, the distinguished Professor of English Literature at Trinity College, Dublin, 'a feeling like the sea, or the air on a headland'. The poem also achieves moments of sonorous grandeur and rhetorical strength, particularly when Ferguson adapts the Miltonic device of tolling proper names to an Irish context. Thus:

> Three hundred years and three and one, it is
>   since at the date
> Three hundred-thirty-three from Christ, these
>   three laid desolate
> Emania, Ulster's royal seat till then, and over-
>   ran
> All that Clan Rury theretofore to westward of
>   the Bann
> And southward of the Yewry held; from which
>   time hitherto
> Ultonia's bounds embrace no more than at this
>   day they do,
> From Mourne to Rathlin; small the tract: yet in
>   that little space
> Ambition how exorbitant, how huge a pride has
>   place!

Other felicitous touches are the poem's multiple word-coinages. The sea is imagined, for instance, as 'swift-keel clasping gulfs of ocean', while such coinages, closely observed details of the natural world, consolidate the impression of an open-air society, a vision of Ireland as a free, fresh island of seascape, spaciousness, winds and scudding clouds.

The narrative element of the work recounts the events surrounding the Battle of Moyra, fought in the seventh century between Congal Claen, hereditary sub-king of Ulster, and Domnal, high-king of Ireland, in which the invading forces of the pagan Congal are completely routed by the Christian Domnal's army, and the hero is himself slain. In telling his tale, Ferguson reveals himself to have an almost Yeatsian admiration for heroic failure. That reverence for the solitary hero facing insurmountable odds that Yeats expressed in his Cuchulain poems, and which (partly through the Irish literary revival's popularising a view of Parnell's downfall as analogous to Cuchulain's fight with the sea, and its recognition of the virtue of lost causes) entered the traditions of modern Irish nationalism, is the dominant mood of Ferguson's *Congal.* Ferguson knows that the forces of progress represented by Domnal must triumph, but his sympathies are all with Congal. Lady Wilde (Oscar's mother, who as 'Speranza' had contributed nationalist verses to the Young Irelanders' newspaper, *The Nation*) wrote to Ferguson, noting and responding favourably to this aspect of the poem and mak-

ing the political analogy. It is a very interesting letter which is worth quoting at length. She treats the poem as a piece of nationalist propaganda:

> I have read and re-read and thought much over this poem. Congal seems to me to typify Ireland. He has the noble, pure, loving nature of his race—still clinging to the old, from instinctive faith and reverence, through all the shadowy forebodings that he is fighting for a lost cause; and the supernatural here has a weird reality and deep significance. It is the expression of our own presentiments. The pathetic beauty and interest of Congal's career is heightened by the consciousness that he is fated, doomed . . . Yet he fights on, with the self-immolating zeal of a martyr, for the old prejudices of his nation, his fathers, his childhood, against the new ideas that overthrew all he reverenced. Still, all our sympathies are with Congal—with the suffering, the fated the wronged—for a beautiful nature underlies all. So it is with Ireland . . .
>
> The death of Congal, too, has a pathetic significance . . .
>
> Here again I find a symbolism to our poor Irish cause: always led by a hero, always slain by a fool.

So Ferguson in *Congal* presents a vision of Irish military virtue that would have satisfied the Fenians, an image of aristocratic, solitary heroism that would have pleased the literary revivalists in their veneration of Parnell, and a grasp of the emotional possibilities of self-sacrifice in a lost cause, 'the self-immolating zeal of a martyr' that would have stimulated Pádraic Pearse. And all this was from the pen of a Belfast-born member of the Ascendancy of Conservative politics. That Ferguson unwittingly wrote work that could bear such an interpretation as Lady Wilde provides, explains why the young Yeats, under the spell of the old Fenian military leader John O'Leary, found Ferguson 'the greatest poet Ireland has produced, because the most central and most Celtic' and could assert with evangelistic zeal:

> Whatever the future may bring forth in the way of a truly great and national literature . . . will find its morning in these . . . volumes of one who was made by the purifying flame of National sentiment the one of his time who wrote heroic poetry—one who, among the somewhat sybaritic singers of his day, was like some aged sea-king sitting among the inland wheat and poppies—the savour of the sea about him, and its strength [see excerpt dated 1886].

Ferguson was 'Celtic' in a further important way that must have not only appealed directly to Yeats, but also anticipated a strand in modern Irish nationalism that Yeats helped sustain. He had a considerable, if perhaps unconscious, sympathy for a pre-Christian Irish paganism of the kind that Synge felt he found in Aran, and a respect for the 'Ulster peasant's tenacious piety toward his pre-Christian superstitions' similar to that felt by Yeats for the peasantry of Sligo. As Malcolm Brown has written in his study *The Politics of Irish Literature,*

Yeats's youthful discovery of . . . Ferguson provided the base for his unique contribution to Irish thought, the proposition that Ireland's purest essence was located in the peasants' primitive belief in holy wells and fairy thorns and in those supernatural 'pale windy people' who dwelt with 'white lillies among dim shadows, [in] windy twilights over grey sands'.

This apprehension, expressed most powerfully in Synge and Yeats, which implies that a true nationalism must reject Catholic Christianity, that

the unappeasable host
Is comelier than candles at Mother Mary's feet

becomes an often-expressed theme in twentieth-century cultural nationalist literature, in the literary theme of conflict between priest and poet. It is present in embryonic form in Ferguson's **'The Burial of King Cormac'**, in *Congal,* and in **'The Fairy Thorn'**.

In **'The Burial of King Cormac'** the newly converted king refuses pagan burial at Brugh and expresses a desire to be buried at Rossnaree, for

'twas at Ross that first I knew
One, Unseen, who is God alone.

His captains, however, determine to disobey his dying orders, and they try to bear his corpse to the tomb of his ancestors. The elements this time are Christianised, and the Boyne river, on the side of the angels, foils their plan by casting up the coffin at Rossnaree where pious shepherds bury it. But one cannot help feeling that the captains were ill-used—that it is proper that an Irish king should be interred with his fathers. In *Congal,* although we know, as in Yeats's 'The Wanderings of Oisin', that St Patrick has triumphed, we regret the passing of the pagan order. The central lines of Book I concern a great feast at which three bards sing of the civilisation that is under threat. They urge Congal to action; the poets are the true patriots. One of them exults in an identification with past heroes, calls for battle in the name of the dead.

But come; resound the noble deeds and swell the
chant of praise
In memory of the men who did the deeds of
other days;
The old bard-honoring, fearless days, exulting
Ulster saw.
. . . .
Burst, blackening clouds that hang aloof o'er
perjured Domnal's halls!
Dash down, with all your flaming bolts, the
fraud-cemented walls,
Till through your thunder-riven palls heaven's
light anew be poured
In Law and Justice, Wealth and Song, on Congal's throne restored!

'The Fairy Thorn' is by contrast lyrical and magical, but it evokes an Irish countryside of pagan mysteriousness that knows nothing of Christian morality. The poem is strangely sexual, druidic in a way that makes Yeats's early exercises in the same mode seem literary and artificial. The soul of Ireland, the spirit of her secret and essential places is 'unchristened', utterly herself. The poem tells of a group of young girls going to a dance at twilight around a fairy thorn. They are seduced by the atmosphere, beauty and magic of the experience, and by the extraordinarily sensual fairy-folk. One of their number is drawn away by the fairies.

Thus clasp'd and prostrate all, with their heads
together bow'd,
Soft o'er their bosoms' beating—the only human
sound—
They hear the silky footsteps of the silent fairy
crowd,
Like a river in the air, gliding round.

. . . . .

They feel their tresses twine with her parting
locks of gold,
And the curls elastic falling, as her head withdraws;
They feel her sliding arms from their tranced
arms unfold,
But they may not look to see the cause.

Late in life Ferguson, depressed by the political unrest of the 1880s, felt that his artistic and cultural mission had met with little success. He might well have been more depressed had he known the kind of future his work would have as the young W. B. Yeats built upon its implications for his own propagandist purposes. But he would surely have been cheered to know that he is remembered today primarily as the poet of **'The Fairy Thorn'** and, in his long poem *Conary* and in a few lyrics, of some of the best verse written in nineteenth-century Ireland. (pp. 29-41)

Terence Brown, "Samuel Ferguson: Cultural Nationalism," in his Northern Voices: Poets from Ulster, *Rowman and Littlefield, 1975, 29-41.*

Robert Welch   (essay date 1980)

[*Welch is an Irish scholar and critic. In the following excerpt, he discusses Ferguson's use of traditional Celtic material, arguing that Ferguson's motivation for using Irish myths in his work was to legitimize the development of modern Irish literature by establishing its connection with the past.*]

Considering the quiet life [Ferguson] led, the content of much of his poetry is quite surprising, in that [he] had an astonishing sympathy with the more brutal and violent aspects of Irish literary tradition. As Terence Brown has pointed out, we might have expected him to be drawn to the medieval Irish devotional tradition, especially as he was inclined to regard modern Irish Protestantism as the true inheritor of the spirit of resistance to Papal authority, which was a feature of the Celtic church [see excerpt dated 1975]. Scholarship in this area had not gone very far in Ferguson's lifetime, but there can be no doubt that he was more at home temperamentally in the wider—and wilder—spaces of pagan Ireland. In his essays on Hardiman . . . it was his object to determine what it was that constituted national sentiment, or identity. In his poetry this too was his object; he wanted the verse to respond to the intense, often savage sincerity of the Celtic nature, as he saw it. He wanted it to show forth the Irish capacity for devoted loyalty, (even when that loyalty was given to a wrong or brutal cause), its innate, if simple, heroism and nobility.

This romanticized view of the essential Celt is, as Terence Brown has shown, remarkably similar to the version of the Irish peasant Yeats and Synge were later to fashion, much to the anger of the newly-risen Catholic middle classes, many of whom had been peasants themselves only a generation or two before, and who resented Yeats's scorn at them for betraying what they considered themselves well out of. Although Ferguson's Gaelic Ireland is a romanticization, it is not one done in soft lights and delicate hues and vague allusive word tones. On the contrary, it is a vividly rendered masculine world done in bold broad strokes, with little attention to the niceties of characterization. It is an energetic world, violent, bloody and unpredictable, with most of the action taking place outdoors. Nature is a constant backdrop to the events, and more often than not those events are given precise locations, imitating the topographical character of a good deal of Gaelic story.

All the time we are conscious of Ferguson's continuing preoccupation with the 'facts' of that Gaelic world he wished to re-present imaginatively in as faithful a manner as he could. Often the effect is harsh, where he makes an attempt to present in English an impression of what the original Irish was like, stylistically. In **'Fergus Wry-Mouth',** for example, he makes a reasonably successful attempt at capturing the often terse, almost sardonic quality of the dialogues in Irish saga as they survive in manuscript. King Fergus has been given the power to walk under water by the fairies, with the warning that he must never attempt to explore Loch Rury. He does, and meets a monster, called the Muirdris, who is so hideous that the sight of it

> Hung all his visage sideways with affright.
> He fled. He gained the bank. 'How seems my
>   cheer,
> Oh Mwena?' 'Ill!' replied the Charioteer.
> 'But rest thee. Sleep thy wildness will compose'.
> He slept.

This is awkward, but it is an awkwardness that has for its object immediacy. Indeed, one of the qualities of Ferguson's original poems is their freshness, their air of somewhat rough but alert attention to detail. It is an objective poetry, delighting in the externals of the old Irish world, its swift, energetic, often brutal physicality. Congal, in the hall of Dunangay, where he has been insulted by the Christian high king Domnal, describes how he, in support of Domnal, killed Sweeney Menn, Domnal's predecessor and lawful king:

> 'on the sunny sward
> Before the fort, sat Sweeney Menn, amid his
>   royal guard,
> He and his nobles chess-playing. Right through
>   the middle band
> I went, and no man's licence asked, Garr-
>   Congail in my hand,
> And out through Sweeney's body, where he sat
>   against the wall,
> 'Twas I that sent Garr-Congail in presence of
>   them all.

> And out through Sweeney's body till the stone
>   gave back the blow,
> 'Twas I that day at Aileach made keen Garr-
>   Congail go'.

He revels in the martial, savage imagery. These are a major feature of his sources anyway, and as he points out in a note to **'Mesgedra',** they should no more repel the reader than Medea's cauldron or the supper of Thyestes. The reader should not allow the atrocities to blind him to what is behind them. Behind them are the 'characteristic forms of grandeur' of the ancient Celt, his savage nobility and strength, and his capacity for direct energetic action. This energy, expressed in the martial imagery seems to be what Ferguson most associated with the essential temperament of the race. His verse is at its best when it strains in its excitement to catch that energy, and make it live again in a modern unsatisfactory language. In **'Conary'** there is a passage which does this very successfully, a passage describing the effect of the war-pipe on fighting men. The piper is one of the three red pipers Conary, the high king, saw before him on his way to the hostel of Da Derga, and they are an evil omen for him. The pipers are of the sidhe, and have power over him because he has disregarded various taboos. Later, surrounded in Da Derga by invaders, he sends out a force of men on a circuit of the hostel in an attempt to repel the enemy, fatally asking one of the red pipers to lead them into combat. The piper excites their feelings so intensely that he can draw them away from the hostel:

> 'Yea, mighty king', said one,
> 'The strain I play ye shall remember long',
> And put the mouthpiece to his lips. At once—
> It seemed as earth and sky were sound alone,
> And every sound a maddening battle-call,
> So spread desire of fight through every breast
>   and brain,
> And every arm to feat of combat strung.
> Forth went the sallying hosts: the hosts within
> Heard the enlarging tumult from their doors
> Roll outward; and the clash and clamour heard
> Of falling foes before; and, over it,
> The yelling pibroch; but, anon, the din
> Grew distant and more distant.

Ferguson had a horror of violence, of civil war, of anything that would disrupt the ordered pattern of things. He was drawn to the Protestant Repeal Association, because he thought that some measure of self-determination was the only way to avoid the complete collapse of Irish society, which would follow the extermination of the Irish gentry. English policy with regard to Ireland seemed intent on that extermination of the privileged. **'Conary'** is a poem about a society breaking down, and there is nothing anyone can do about it, because Conary, the high king, is fated to break all his taboos. There is a malignancy around him, which his kindly, peace-loving nature cannot control. Among the invaders there are some Irish, foster-brothers of Conary, in fact, whom he failed to punish severely, sending them into exile instead of killing them. With them also are two of Conary's own brothers, who joined the others for the excitement of it. One of these, Lomna Druth, pleads with the British pirate Ingcel, not to attack the hostel where Conary is staying the night. In killing the inhabitants, he will be killing 'the life, the soul itself / Of our whole nation', because the people gathered in the hostel are all those who 'minister our loftier life':

> For, slay our reverend sages of the law,
> Slay him who puts the law they teach in act;
> Slay our sweet poets, and our sacred bards,
> Who keep the continuity of time
> By fame perpetual of renowned deeds;
> Slay our experienced captains who prepare
> The youth for martial manhood, and the charge
> Of public freedom, as befits a state
> Self-governed, self-sufficing, self-contained;
> Slay all that minister our loftier life,
> Now by this evil chance assembled here,
> You leave us but the carcass of a state,
> A rabble ripe to rot, and yield the land
> To foreign masters and perpetual shame.

The plea of Lomna Druth is a conservative plea in that he wishes to dissuade Ingcel from disrupting the established mode of life in Ireland, its hereditary, hierarchical nature. If he does invade, there will be but rabble left. All independence will be sacrificed forever; the state will no longer be able to govern itself. The conservatism of Lomna Druth has within it a desire to safeguard Ireland's self-determination. Lomna Druth is overruled, the British pirate Ingcel is interested only in plunder. He has no interest in Ireland's well-being.

Lomna Druth's futile plea expresses Ferguson's conservative nationalism, whereas the ruthlessness of Ingcel could stand for the exploitative and unsympathetic attitude of the British government towards Ireland, about which Ferguson frequently complained.

It is clear that Ferguson's re-tellings of Irish saga are no mere satisfying of a taste on his part for the archaic and barbaric. They show a desire to re-present, as faithfully as possible, those 'facts' of Gaelic history and legend which would enlarge the imaginative scope of the contemporary Irishman, and make his intellectual life more authentic, because more in contact with his own past.

There is a sense that this project can only hope to succeed partially, if succeed at all. In **'Aideen's Grave'** the poet Ossian sings a burial dirge over the dead Aideen, who has died of grief on hearing of the death of Oscar, Ossian's son, at the battle of Gavra. They inter her at Howth under the great cromlech. Ossian's lament takes a strange turn halfway through and he imagines how the life he knows will pass away, how the language he is controlling now at this dramatic moment will fail. Even the marks on Aideen's stone will in time wear away. Then he imagines someone in some far distant time attempting to sympathize with the lay he is singing now, with his time and with his grief. The someone is, of course, Ferguson, but Ferguson's reviving of that grief can only be 'imperfect':

> The long forgotten lay I sing
> May only ages hence revive,
> (As eagle with a wounded wing
> To soar again might strive,)
>
> Imperfect, in an alien speech,
> When, wandering here, some child of chance
> Through pangs of keen delight shall reach

The gift of utterance,—

> To speak the air, the sky to speak,
> The freshness of the hill to tell,
> Who, roaming bare Ben Edar's peak
> And Aideen's briary dell,
>
> And gazing on the Cromlech vast
> And on the mountain and the sea,
> Shall catch communion with the past
> And mix himself with me.

There is something of Eliot's desire for impersonality here; Ferguson wishes 'to speak the air', not to speak of himself, to mix himself with the dead hero, rather than assert his own uniqueness in the here and now. Self-assertion, energy, belonged to those men in the past. Now speech itself is imperfect. It is not the total speech of Ossian. Life has waned:

> Of Oscar and Aideen bereft,
> So Ossian sang. The Fenians sped
> Three mighty shouts to heaven; and left
> Ben Edar to the dead.

There is a strong feeling here that 'the dead' are all those who have followed the Fenians, those Dubliners of Joyce who go to Howth for day trips from time to time, those Dubliners of Ferguson's own day, and Ferguson himself, who used to go there to recover from his periodic breakdowns in health.

Ferguson, in his re-tellings of Gaelic saga, or episodes from Irish history (like for example, his well-known savage ballad, **'The Welshmen of Tirawley'**), tried to reinvigorate the 'dead' imagination of his own time by recreating the energetic vitality of the old Irish world, as he saw it. Whenever he speaks of the poets of his own day he is inclined to regard them as somewhat unhealthy and unmanly in their search for 'recondite thought and curious felicities of expression which of late in our literature, have become too much the fashion'. His ideal was Burns, not because Burns made much of the ancient traditions of Scotland in the way that Ferguson was trying to do for Ireland, but because Burns, to Ferguson's mind, seemed in contact with the simple actualities of his own time, Burns 'spoke the air' of his own locality with an authenticity denied to most poets from the time of Ossian. His speech was less 'imperfect' than that of Ferguson, stronger, 'manlier' (one of Ferguson's favourite words) than the 'nosers of curious odours' (Edward Dowden's phrase) of his own time. An Irish poet could not hope for the kind of authenticity that Burns had, seeing that rural Irish society had not as yet progressed to the stage of civilisation needed for a poet like Burns to emerge.

Urban poetry was by definition a diseased imposture, so it was necessary to retain as much contact as possible with the countryside, especially the countryside of one's upbringing. That for Ferguson was the countryside of county Antrim, especially those vales east of Lough Neagh, a territory that had, strangely enough, been colonized by Lowlands Scots, who still spoke the dialect of Burns up to Ferguson's time. It is not surprising then to find that his great epic hero comes from that area, Rathmore Moy-Linny. Like Yeats after him, Ferguson

thought
All that we did, all that we said or sang
Must come from contact with the soil, from that
Contact everything Antaeus—like grew strong.

But it seemed to Ferguson that in his time the soil had gone sour and dead, and so was incapable of such a flourishing growth as Burns. That soil had to be re-invigorated with memories of former growth, former energy, former richness. Thus Ferguson's Irish sagas attempted to 'raise the native elements of Irish story to a dignified level; and that ambition I think may be taken as the key to almost all the literary work of my . . . life'. They were to fertilize the soil for the coming of the truly representative national poet, the Irish Burns. Thomas Moore was not he, not only because he was not a Protestant, and so lacking (as Ferguson saw it) the fearlessness and manliness such a poet would need, but because Ferguson recognized in him a lack of attack, a lack of the directness such a poet should have. In January 1845, in one of two essays on Burns, he accurately foretold that the representative Irish poet, when he would come, would come from the middle classes, not the farming class, as in Burns's case, as it would be only among the middle classes that sufficient independence of spirit would be bred into the man's bone.

What happened followed fairly exactly Ferguson's prediction: Yeats was of the Protestant middle classes, fiercely proud of his family's independence of spirit, and indeed using Ferguson's poetry as a seed bed for his own vigorous imagination, building Ferguson, especially in his early writing, into a kind of Homeric figure among the 'sybaritic' poets of his day, praising him for a kind of rough-hewn massiveness.

One thing that Ferguson would probably have disapproved of in Yeats's re-handling of him soon after his death was the way in which Yeats made him out to be a kind of revolutionary nationalist. This was a natural enough thing for Yeats to do, as Ferguson had laid so much stress on the essential nature of the Celt, different in character and imagination from the 'stolid Saxon'. Such radical theorizing is dear to the hearts of all revolutionary nationalists, but we cannot make Ferguson out to be an unconscious Fenian (in the modern, political, not the Ossianic sense) in spite of all his superficial conservatism. His fascination with racial theorizing, while undoubtedly a contributory factor to the political outlook of Yeats and, later again, Pearse, was something he shared with many Victorians, among them Matthew Arnold, and no one could accuse the English public school inspector of being either an unconscious Fenian, or a proto-Fascist.

Terence Brown has argued that in his revelling in fierce martial imagery, Ferguson was unconsciously responding to the contemporary political forces of his time. War was what the Fenians were after, and here, in Ferguson's versions of saga, were images of war associated with racial purity. Brown points out that civil disruption terrified Ferguson's conservative attitude (an attitude expressed in **'Conary'**). It may be that Ferguson's attraction to the violent, the savage, the unpredictable in nature and humanity, was, as well as being a re-call of Celtic energy, also an exorcism of the violence of a turbulent present, with all its tensions and complexities.

This is not self-expression in the usual sense of the word; it has more in common with the 'objective correlative' of Eliot, where images and narrative, entirely separate from personality, carry the emotional charge which refuses to be stated directly. The narrative and its accompanying images (often images of violence in Ferguson's sagas) help to dissolve the tension of living in a turbulent present more completely than any attempt at direct statement of that tension. It is in the long poem *Congal,* in the complexities of its narrative structure, that we find the most complete and probably unconscious exegesis of the tensions in the mind of a conservative Irish Protestant in the latter half of the nineteenth century.

Ferguson based *Congal* (1872) on the two historical tales, *Cath Muighe Rath,* and its introductory pre-tale *Fled Dúin na nGéd,* the *Battle of Moyra* and *The Banquet of Dunangay.* These historical tales were edited in 1842, by John O'Donovan and William Hennessy, and published by the Irish Archaeological Society. From then on the two tales occupied Ferguson's imagination. He was attracted to them for their broad theme, which had to do with the dis-establishment of the old, native order in Irish society by the forces of Christianity and progress. Congal, a sub-king of Ulster, ruling from Rathmore Moy-Linny near Antrim (Ferguson's own area) is drawn into conflict with Domnal, high king of Ireland ruling from Dunangay on the Boyne, because of an actual or imagined insult (it is left unclear in the poem) at the feast to which the high king has invited him. Congal cannot be simply equated with the old order, although all the poets in the first book of the poem are very eager to do so. Most of the poets, as preservers of the Gaelic order, have retired to Ulster, where they receive protection from Kellach the Halt, Chief of Mourne, and uncle to Congal. 'Erin's churls' (the followers of Domnal and the priests), have banished the poets, and they now have sanctuary in the 'sheltering, song-preserving hills' of Ulster, where they still teach 'the better Bardic utterance', awaiting the day of liberation.

Congal, on his way to the feast at Dunangay, is asked to stay the night at the court of Kellach the Halt, where the poets sing to him, in disdain of the high king's messenger who has accompanied him, songs that can only be called seditious. One of the poets, Cical, identifies Congal with Slanga, son of Partholan, one of the first invaders of Ireland. When he 'saw the sunshine flame / On Congal's crest' he knew him to be Slanga reborn. Ardan too, the chief-poet, claims Congal as the champion of Ulster's suppressed rights. He reminds him of the richness and extent of Ulster, of the magnificence of the tributes to which he is traditionally entitled, of his responsibility, as it were, to the landscape itself, the sense that 'abrupt Easroe / In many a tawny leap and whirl' belongs to him and he to it in ways that the new order represented by Domnal cannot comprehend. Ardan then looses a traditional curse on the high king, a curse wherein Ardan imagines the natural forces also leagued against Domnal. He makes himself out to be their spokesman:

From livid lips of desperate men who bear enormous wrong,
Heaven cannot hold it; but the curse outbursting
from on high
In blight and plague, on plant and man, blasts
all beneath the sky.
Burst, blackening clouds that hang aloof o'er
perjured Domnal's halls!
Dash down, with all your flaming bolts, the
fraud-cemented walls,
Till through your thunder-riven palls heaven's
light anew be poured
In Law and Justice, Wealth and Song, on Congal's throne restored!

The heaven here is not the heaven of Domnal, but that
other pagan heaven of Ardan. Congal has mixed feelings
about these bardic tributes. To Ardan he says 'for thy lay
/ I thank thee and I thank thee not'. He and Domnal have
sworn peace, even though his lands have been reduced.
Furthermore, although Ferguson does not go to any great
trouble to give Congal any depth of character, he is conspicuous for his independence from bardic belief, and
from Christian belief also. He simply wishes to get on with
the practical business of living, of settling down with Lafinda, his betrothed. He would let the past be with the
dead, but those around him are intent on keeping the dead
alive and on invoking the unseen forces on all possible occasions. For this reason, the dead will not stay dead, the
unseen trouble the living. When war is decided upon, Congal himself hears a tumult in the mountains, 'as of immeasurable herds a-droving all around'. Then there is a sound
as of shale dislodged from the summit and Ardan cries out
with excitement that it is the herdsman-god Borcha,
climbing to his herd-seat as of old, where he sat and counted the numbers of his flock. This, for Ardan, means that
the 'Powers / Unseen that round us live and move' are on
their side, the side of the poets, of Kellach and of Congal.
However, Congal wants nothing to do with these unseen
forces. If he is to fight, he wants to fight with manly arms
alone.

The unseen forces, however, will not stay out of the action.
They haunt it and their intentions are inscrutable. It is almost as if they themselves do not know what they are
doing. To some extent they are in the grip of the way
events have gone in the tangible Ireland of Congal and
Domnal, to some extent they are subject to incomprehensible laws of their own. Manannan Mac Lir, ancient pro-
tector of Ireland, appears to Congal while he and his army
are encamped on the way to the battlefield of Moyra. The
huge shape tramps around the camp, and Congal goes out
to speak with it. He sees, vaguely, the great bulk striding
through the white mist, 'like a man much grieved, who
walks alone / Considering of a cruel wrong'. Congal addresses it, asking it why it comes now to trouble his sleep
before a battle, but there is no reply. Ardan later tells him
that Manannan's power has now gone, but that he revisits
Ireland when evil destinies threaten it, uselessly to haunt
the outcome.

Crossing the river Ollarva the army are confronted with
the horrifying spectre of the Washer of the Ford, leaving
bloodstained tunics and the limbs and heads of men in the
water. The stream approaching her is 'tranquil, clear and

bright' but downwards from her 'the blood-polluted flood
rode turbid'. From the mess of tangled limbs she lifts up
a head, saying, 'thine own head, oh Congal'. This episode,
of the Washer of the Ford, Ferguson took from an account
of the wars between two septs of the O'Briens entitled *The
Wars of Turlogh* written in 1549 by one Mac Craith. It is
discussed in the third of Ferguson's Hardiman articles and
the hag's speech quoted there matches very closely the one
she makes to Congal in the later poem. All that this shows
is that the barbaric imagery fascinated Ferguson, and he
was glad to incorporate it in a poem which revels in it. It
also increases the reader's sense of the chaos of the unseen
forces that surround the human actors in *Congal.* Congal
who, despite the fact that he has his doubts about the ancestral argument for war of Ardan and Kellach the Halt,
is nevertheless fighting for the old ways, finds himself confronted with manifestations out of native legend that
threaten and terrify. Eventually he takes what is, under
the circumstances, a fairly rationalist view, and maintains
that all these 'phantasms' are in fact created by the curses
of the priests that surround Domnal, to dishearten the just
army of Congal. But, according to Congal, his men are independent, free, unsuperstitious; the 'weak ghosts' sent
out by the priest-ridden Domnal can have no power over
them. Their cause is just, they must win, and with that he
and his men move on to 'Moyra's fated field'.

They do not win, Congal is given his death wound from
behind with a bill-hook by Cuanna, an idiot, son of Ultan-
Long-Hand. He eventually swoons from loss of blood, and
through a combination of the powers of Manannan and
Borcha is spirited away in a great storm back to his native
Antrim. He finds that Ardan also has been brought from
the battle in the same way. They find themselves in 'grassy
Collin' outside a convent founded by Brigid, where Lafinda has become a novice. She tends the dying hero in his
last moments, during which he is granted an extraordinary vision from which Lafinda piously averts her eyes. It
is a vision of Manannan Mac Lir in benign aspect, a vision
of blessed plenty, of sweetness and release. The god reveals
himself as the countryside is when it is beautiful, when
there seems no distance between perceiver and perceived:

No longer soiled with stain of earth, what
seemed his mantle shone
Rich with innumerable hues refulgent, such as
one
Beholds, and thankful-hearted he, who casts
abroad his gaze
O'er some rich tillage-country-side, when mellow Autumn days
Gild all the sheafy foodful stooks; and broad before him spread,—
Bray or Ben-Edar—sees beneath, in silent pag-
eant grand,
Slow fields of sunshine spread o'er fields of rich
corn-bearing land;
Red glebe and meadow-margin green commin-
gling to the view
With yellow stubble, browning woods, and up-
land tracts of blue.

The simile goes on for another fourteen lines, during
which it is revealed that the 'he' who looks out over this
richness is a citizen just recovered from an illness which

has kept him 'long indoors'. The simile is not simply a distraction, but helps to make the vision granted to Congal at the end all the more vivid. He, Congal, at the point of death, is like the modern citizen recovered from a disease. All the beauty of the Irish countryside breaks fresh upon the sight, and this freshness, this sweetness, is the true Manannan Mac Lir, free from the toil, the blood, the fury and complexity of human strife. It is an amazingly good close to a very confused poem. Congal says:

> my deeds of strife and bloodshed seem
> No longer mine, but as the shapes and shadows
>   of a dream:
> And I myself, as one oppressed with sleep's deceptive shows,
> Awaking only now to life, when life is at its
>   close.

Congal, when he dies, is brought into the sacred enclosure; those who bring him in offer sanctuary to Ardan as well from the hosts of the approaching Domnal. He, however, his king having attained illumination outside the convent, decides to remain outside as well, 'while up the hill the hosts of Domnal came'.

A great deal has been said in the past about the faults of *Congal.* Many critics begin their demolition with the unsuitability of the metre for a sustained narrative which is self-consciously attempting to be dignified. It is a resurrection of the Chapmanesque fourteener, which has an irresistible tendency to degenerate into the sing-song of the ballad measure. Many of the criticisms levelled at the metre are just, but it does at times attain what Ferguson desired, a long loose flowing measure, with floating stresses, a nineteenth century version of what Ferguson imagined a bardic chant to be like.

To find fault with the poem's metre, however, is only to scratch the surface. More complicated is the fact that our sympathies are confused, and this confusion is hardly deliberate on Ferguson's part. It is, however, a very rich and suggestive confusion. Congal is the hero; that at least is clear. Lady Wilde recognised this immediately; writing in the year *Congal* was published she says:

> Congal seems to me to typify Ireland. He has the noble, pure, loving nature of his race—still clinging to the old, from instinctive faith and reverence, through all the shadowy forebodings that he is fighting for a lost cause; and the supernatural here has a weird reality and deep significance. It is the expression of our own presentiments . . . Yet he fights on, with the self-immolating zeal of a martyr, for the old prejudices of his nation, his fathers, his childhood, against the new ideas that overthrew all he reverenced . . . The death of Congal, too, has a pathetic significance . . . Here again I find a symbolism to our poor Irish cause; always led by a hero, always slain by a fool. I must talk over this, and a great deal more in the epic, when I see you.

Terence Brown has recently argued that here Ferguson was (probably unconsciously) contributing to the growth of one of the favourite icons of later nationalists, the failed yet noble hero, whose failure testifies to his authenticity.

There is truth in this, and certainly Ferguson wished his hero to stand for a central feature of the Irish identity. Congal is a martyr for a failed cause. Yet when we look more closely the picture loses some of this clarity, valuable though it is from the point of view of nineteenth century political history, and the growth of its dangerous iconographies.

Congal has something essentially Irish about him. But he is no credulous heathen. He is not drawn into the fight by the appeals to legendary rights of the bards, though he is touched by their eloquence. He is a pagan, but a very independent one. He will have no truck with their superstitions, though the narrative of the poem makes clear that there are unseen forces operating on human life. The bards think that these forces are on the side of the man who is trying to oppose the new order, an order that will surely be inimical to them, but the forces seem to have little sympathy either way. If anything they lean towards the new order of Domnal, making Congal's journey to Moyra so fraught with fatal omens. They seem to enjoy making appearances, and a march to a forthcoming battle presents a good opportunity for powerful manifestations. Congal remains suspicious of them, and attributes them to the priests that he sees as running King Domnal's life for him. Congal is a strange mixture of Celtic nobility (as Ferguson saw it) and Protestant independence of mind.

In the poem, however, that independence is doomed. The day is to be with the new order. The Ulstermen see Domnal as priest-ridden; according to the poets he is something of a proto-materialist, exiling the poets, so that their influence is confined. In their view he disregards 'life's needful charge of knowledge'. From the Ulster point of view in the poem he looks like an image of the Victorian, middle class, Irish Catholicism against which Yeats was later to rage, that fearful Catholicism which 'dried the marrow from the bone'. But that is the Ulster point of view *in the poem.*

The total picture of Domnal that *Ferguson* gives us is not at all an unsympathetic one. Throughout the poem he behaves nobly, and indeed the insult that first occasioned the strife may not have been intended. Especially notable is his behaviour towards Cuanna, the idiot boy who killed Congal. Cuanna's stepmother would appear to be responsible for the boy's idiocy; she, when he was a boy, scared him out of his wits by showing him a doll dressed as a goblin, so that her own son could assume his place. Domnal takes the boy seriously and assures him of justice. In all Ferguson makes Domnal a noble opponent to Congal, but at the close it is Congal who has the true vision of Ireland, when Manannan Mac Lir puts off his shapeless indeterminateness (though not his silence) and shows him the blessedness of natural things, a blessedness he only comes to see on the point of death. And he sees it outside the convent where Lafinda, his loved one, has, to put it crudely, gone over to the enemy.

What are we to make of all this? Congal is the essential Celt (according to Ferguson), manly, noble, fearless, undaunted by the unseen and indeterminate forces of Ireland's legendary past. These forces are massive and violent, and no one has a satisfactory way of dealing with them. It might be argued that they are in the poem only because Ferguson delighted in the vague, the massive, that their chaos is merely a failure on Ferguson's part to organise his heathen machinery properly. Even so, such a failure would be a significant one, indicating Ferguson's powerlessness in the face of the massive and often brutal energy he saw as being characteristic of Irish identity, and of Irish art. It was an energy he at once tried to tame, and yet convey to the modern Irishman.

In the poem Congal regards these manifestations of power and violence as the 'weak' demons of priestcraft, but he is shown to be wrong; they are more than that. (As Lady Wilde said, they have 'a weird reality and deep significance!') They are an energy underlying whatever it means to be Irish, and to be Irish is to be involved with them to some extent at least. To be a poet is to be especially susceptible to their power, as the poets in the poem are, except that they misinterpret them also. These great indeterminate shapes are powerful blurred images of the turbulence that underlies Irish history. They also seethe beneath the present, threatening to fracture whatever frail structures good-willed men try to erect on the basis of sanity and understanding. So their blurred outline in the poem is the terrified sketch of the violence that is constantly under the surface of Irish life, portrayed by a man who, more than anything, longed for stability.

Ferguson is fair to Domnal, although the Ulstermen are not; he and they are, after all, enemies. Although Domnal is just and noble according to his lights, it is to Congal that Manannan reveals himself at the end in benign aspect. This is the true vision of Ireland. So, out of the great blur that surrounds the poem in the persons of the native deities, out of the confusion of sympathies deriving from Ferguson's fair-mindedness in dealing with Domnal, a proposition begins to emerge, a proposition that Ferguson held all his life: that the only true Irishman is a Protestant, because only he has the independence of spirit that can keep him clear of the turmoil of Irish life. He can give, because he is free to refuse. He can serve Ireland because only he can make that severance between head and heart necessary to sane life and progress. Her Catholic sons, though their desire to serve is also intense, always tend to lose themselves in the blur of energy that Congal manages to hold at a distance. That energy is violent, unpredictable, destructive. Only by holding it at a distance can normal life (and that is all that any sane man wants) be possible. It is a curiously Augustan stance, but Ferguson was not the only Victorian who by temperament belonged to the age of Grattan's parliament.

Before 1850 or thereabouts, it had been Ferguson's ambition to establish a living equation between past and present in Ireland. He saw it as his Protestant responsibility to make that past live in a spirit of sane, free enquiry. That done, national self-respect would be enhanced, and with it national independence. In *Congal,* Ferguson's most ambitious poem, that independence is defeated, although it is given a vision of the true Ireland at the close. The future belongs to Domnal and his priests, his centralization and his favourites. Even Lafinda herself has become a nun. Finally, irony of ironies, Congal himself is to be interred in the convent enclosure. The poem is, at root, a lament for the passing of Ireland as Ferguson knew it, and that, for him, meant the best of Ireland. The country is to pass over to the modern mixed society, that will not be without justice, but the day of the rabblement will have begun. The 'plebeianizing' tendency he spoke of in 1848 is irreversible; Ireland is handed over to the dead, the violent, and the democratic. (pp. 139-54)

> *Robert Welch, "Sir Samuel Ferguson: The Two Races of Ireland," in his* Irish Poetry from Moore to Yeats, *Barnes & Noble, 1980, pp. 116-55.*

FURTHER READING

"Current Literature." *The Academy* 18, No. 429 (24 July 1880): 60.
    Brief negative review of Ferguson's *Poems* in which the critic states: "We would suggest that it would be more reverent if persons who have not the gifts necessary for composing poetry would confine themselves entirely to secular subjects."

"Obituary: Sir Samuel Ferguson." *The Academy* 30, No. 746 (21 August 1886): 120-22.
    Retrospective summary of Ferguson's career.

"Sir Samuel Ferguson." *The Athenaeum* No. 3068 (14 August 1886): 205.
    Obituary tribute in which the critic suggests that in "his anxiety to revive a distinctively Irish literature [Ferguson] perhaps sacrificed some of the popularity of his books."

Becket, John J. à. "An Irish Poet." *The Catholic World* XLVII, No. 278 (May 1888): 164-72.
    Positive assessment of Ferguson's works focusing on his use of Irish materials.

"Sir Samuel Ferguson." *Blackwood's Edinburgh Magazine* CXL, No. DCCCLIII (November 1886): 621-41.
    Overview of Ferguson's poetry providing numerous examples and excerpts from the poet's works.

"Sir Samuel Ferguson's Life." *Blackwood's Edinburgh Magazine* CLIX, No. DCCCCLXVI (April 1896): 613-24.
    Review of Mary Catherine Ferguson's biography of her husband (cited below). The critic also provides commentary on Ferguson's career and significance.

Brown, Malcolm. *Sir Samuel Ferguson.* Lewisburg, N.J.: Bucknell University Press, 1973, 101 p.
    Concise biography of Ferguson.

Clark, David R. "Yeats's Fishermen and Samuel Ferguson's 'Willy Gilliland'." In *Irish Studies 1,* edited by P. J. Drudy, pp. 73-83. Cambridge: Cambridge University Press, 1980.
    Comparative analysis in which Clark contends that Ferguson's "Willy Gilliland" was the inspiration for Yeats's fishermen figures in "The Fisherman" and "The Tower."

Fackler, Herbert. "Sir Samuel Ferguson: 'The Death of the

Children of Usnach' (1834) and *Deirdre* (1880)." *Éire-Ireland* VII, No. I (1972): 84-95.

> Compares Ferguson's two versions of the tale of Deirdre, the prose version published in the *The Hibernian Nights' Entertainments* and the verse drama *Deirdre*.

Ferguson, Lady. *Sir Samuel Ferguson in the Ireland of His Day.* 2 vols. Edinburgh: William Blackwood and Sons, 1896.

> Authoritative biography of Ferguson written by his wife.

"Aubrey De Vere on Samuel Ferguson." *The Irish Monthly* 15, No. 166 (1887): 224-26.

> Brief article containing a letter written by De Vere in which he praises Ferguson, remarking that the poet's work "is Irish not . . . by dint of being bad English, stuffed with the mannerisms not of Ireland but of the Irish peasant class;—not thus, but by having the true Gaelic *spirit* in it."

Kinsella, Thomas. "From a Lecture on 'Irish Poetry and the Nineteenth Century' at the Merriman Festival, Ennis, Co. Clare, September, 1968." In *Davis, Mangan, Ferguson? Tradition and the Irish Writer: Writings by W. B. Yeats and by Thomas Kinsella,* pp. 67-70. Dublin: Dolmen Press, 1970.

Lecture in which Kinsella discusses the poetry of Ferguson and James Mangan, specifically arguing that Yeats's claims of Ferguson's poetic greatness are exaggerated.

O'Driscoll, Robert. *An Ascendancy of the Heart.* Toronto: Macmillan Company, 1976, 84 p.

> Traces Ferguson's ideological development through his prose and poetic works.

[O'Hagan, John]. "The Poetry of Sir Samuel Ferguson." *The Irish Monthly* 12, Nos. 131, 134 (May, August 1884).

> Review of *Congal* and the poems that were inspired by the *Tain Bo Cuailgne,* containing detailed plot summaries of the legends from which Ferguson's poems were drawn.

Williams, Alfred M. "Sir Samuel Ferguson and Celtic Poetry." In his *Studies in Folk-song and Popular Poetry,* pp. 131-65. 1895. Reprint. Darby, Pa.: Folcroft Library Editions, 1975.

> Overview of Ferguson's major poems including *Congal* and "Aideen's Grave." Williams includes a concise summary of the plot of *Congal*.

Francis Jeffrey

1773-1850

Scottish critic and editor.

Among the nineteenth century's most influential literary critics, Jeffrey was one of the founders of the *Edinburgh Review,* a popular monthly magazine featuring book reviews as well as social and political commentary. In addition to serving for twenty-seven years as editor of the *Review,* he wrote much of its literary criticism, a selection of which he published as *Contributions to the Edinburgh Review* (1844). Jeffrey is perhaps best remembered for the outspoken and unsparing nature of his criticism, particularly his censure of some Romantic poets, exemplified in his notorious comment on William Wordsworth's *Excursion* (1814): "This will never do."

Jeffrey was born in Edinburgh, the eldest son of a deputy clerk in the Scottish Court of Sessions. In 1781 he was sent to the prestigious Edinburgh High School, and in 1787 he continued his studies at Glasgow College where he focused on literature, philosophy, and law. During this time his political views were influenced by the Whig party, which advocated limiting the power of the monarchy and increasing the role of Parliament in determining policy. Leaving Glasgow in 1789, Jeffrey entered Oxford University but returned to Edinburgh one year later to continue his law studies; he was summoned to the Scottish bar in 1794. As an attorney in Edinburgh, Jeffrey became acquainted with that city's literary society, developing friendships with Sydney Smith and Henry Brougham. Perceiving a need for a literary publication that incorporated the Whig party's liberal views, Jeffrey, Smith, and Brougham formed the *Edinburgh Review* in 1802, and Jeffrey became its editor-in-chief the following year.

The *Edinburgh Review* was an immediate success, providing social and literary commentary that was, in the words of George Saintsbury, "violently partisan, unhesitatingly personal, and more inclined to find fault, the more distinguished the subject was." As a chief contributor of reviews, Jeffrey evaluated the popular literature of the time, including works by Sir Walter Scott, Madame de Staël, Samuel Taylor Coleridge, William Wordsworth, and Johann Wolfgang von Goethe. While his confrontational style made him popular among the general public, it incited anger among those authors with whom he found fault. In 1806 his unfavorable commentary on Thomas Moore's *Epistles, Odes, and Other Poems* prompted the poet to challenge Jeffrey to a duel, but the altercation was stopped by police and the two men eventually became friends. Considered by many of his contemporaries to be an authority on aesthetics, Jeffrey was invited to contribute an entry to the *Encyclopedia Britannica,* which published his "Essay on Beauty" in 1811. In addition to earning recognition as an editor and essayist, Jeffrey enjoyed considerable success in his law practice, and in 1829 he left the *Review* to accept a position as Dean of Faculty in the law

school of Edinburgh University. Over the next twenty years, as the Whig party's reformist principles gained acceptance, Jeffrey sought a career in the Scottish parliament; he became Lord Advocate in 1830 and Lord of Session in 1834, an office in which he served until his death in 1850.

Despite his reputation as a dictatorial arbiter of literary merit, Jeffrey's aesthetic doctrine, set forth in "An Essay on Beauty," purports liberal and highly subjective criteria for beauty, suggesting that it is defined by each person, based on his or her values and past experiences. However, Jeffrey argued that in order to be of literary or artistic merit, a work must appeal to the diverse personal experiences and values of a wide audience. Jeffrey's aim in criticism, characterized by John A. Taylor as the "Whiggish hope for the general improvement of taste," was to direct public attention to instances in which a writer's work failed or succeeded at such universal appeal. His essays praise realistic depictions of the commonplace in poetry by George Crabbe while dismissing as pretentious nonsense the espousal of mysticism in Romantic poetry by Wordsworth and Coleridge. At the same time, Jeffrey commended John Keats as a poet in the Elizabethan tradition, particularly in his employment of classical themes. Jeffrey's political and social principles assumed a restrictive role in his attempt to gauge universal appeal, and has prompted critics to question the fairness of his literary estimations.

Attempts to account for Jeffrey's taste predominate among critical analyses of his work. Often citing a passage in which Jeffrey predicted that Romanticism, represented by such poets as Lord Byron, Percy Bysshe Shelley, and Wordsworth, would be soon forgotten, while the poetry of Samuel Rogers and Thomas Campbell would be long remembered, critics during the second half of the nineteenth century tended to ridicule Jeffrey, citing him as a critic dedicated only to maintaining the status quo. Leslie Stephen considered Jeffrey undeserving of serious critical attention, characterizing him as grossly incompetent, a "Mr. Much-Afraid or a Mr. Despondency." Other late-nineteenth-century commentators emphasized Jeffrey's relatively conservative approach to literature as destructive to his credibility. George Saintsbury cited "Whig recognition of the rights of man, joined to a kind of bureaucratical distrust and terror of the common people" as a chief inconsistency in Jeffrey's work.

A reevaluation of Jeffrey's critical capacity was prompted in 1899 by Lewis Gates, who suggested that Romanticism's decline in popularity among turn-of-the-century readers would allow for a more judicious examination of Jeffrey's contributions to literary criticism. In defending Jeffrey's hostile reviews of works by Wordsworth, Coleridge, and Robert Southey, Gates observed that Jeffrey's tastes did not reflect a lack of literary acumen, but rather his inability to accept Romanticism as a viable philosophical doctrine. Jeffrey took issue in particular with the intense mysticism of some Romantic writers. According to Gates, "As long as Romanticism seemed chiefly decorative, as in Scott or Keats, Jeffrey could tolerate it or even delight in it." Similarly, Joseph M. Beatty, Jr., noted that "Jeffrey was a man with a matter-of-fact point of view: he did not believe that it was necessary to spiritualize nature that was in itself sublimely beautiful." Subsequent commentators have sought to shift critical focus away from the validity of Jeffrey's judgments in order to explore his theories on the writer's social and political responsibilities. Peter F. Morgan argues that Jeffrey was strongly influenced by eighteenth-century essayists who emphasized literature's moral responsibility toward its audience. The popularity Jeffrey enjoyed during his lifetime has also precipitated critical discussion. John A. Taylor has explored ways in which Jeffrey's essays masterfully combine "didacticism and entertainment" to promote the mass circulation of the literary periodical, a historically significant event in publishing. Acknowledging that his opinions often diverge markedly from those of modern commentators, critics have nevertheless defended Jeffrey's pragmatic approach as, in the words of Beatty, "essentially sane," and have acknowledged his contributions to the development of literary theory as an autonomous and popular study.

PRINCIPAL WORKS

Contributions to the Edinburgh Review. 4 vols. (criticism) 1844
Jeffrey's Literary Criticism (criticism) 1910
Jeffrey's Criticism: A Selection (criticism) 1983

William Hazlitt   (essay date 1825)

[*Hazlitt was one of the most important critics of the Romantic age. He was a deft stylist, a master of the familiar essay, and a leader in what was later termed "impressionist criticism": a form of personal analysis directly opposed to the universal standards of critical judgment accepted by many eighteenth-century critics. Hazlitt popularized the critical techniques of evocation, metaphor, aphorism, and personal reference, and, acutely aware of the abstract nature of literature as well as the limitations of his audience in understanding questions of aesthetics and style, he strove to produce palatable literary criticism. In the following excerpt, he characterizes Jeffrey as an eloquent and judicious critic.*]

Mr. Jeffrey is the Editor of the *Edinburgh Review,* and is understood to have contributed nearly a fourth part of the articles from its commencement. No man is better qualified for this situation; nor indeed so much so. He is certainly a person in advance of the age, and yet perfectly fitted both by knowledge and habits of mind to put a curb upon its rash and headlong spirit. He is thoroughly acquainted with the progress and pretensions of modern literature and philosophy; and to this he adds the natural acuteness and discrimination of the logician with the habitual caution and coolness of his profession. If the *Edinburgh Review* may be considered as the organ of or at all pledged to a party, that party is at least a respectable one, and is placed in the middle between two extremes. The Editor is bound to lend a patient hearing to the most paradoxical opinions and extravagant theories which have resulted in our times from the "infinite agitation of wit," but he is disposed to qualify them by a number of practical objections, of speculative doubts, of checks and drawbacks, arising out of actual circumstances and prevailing opinions, or the frailties of human nature. He has a great range of knowledge, an incessant activity of mind; but the suspension of his judgment, the well-balanced moderation of his sentiments, is the consequence of the very discursiveness of his reason. What may be considered as a *commonplace* conclusion is often the result of a comprehensive view of all the circumstances of a case. Paradox, violence, nay even originality of conception is not seldom owing to our dwelling long and pertinaciously on some one part of a subject, instead of attending to the whole. Mr. Jeffrey is neither a bigot nor an enthusiast. He is not the dupe of the prejudices of others, nor of his own. He is not wedded to any dogma, he is not long the sport of any whim; before he can settle in any fond or fantastic opinion, another starts up to match it, like beads on sparkling wine. A too restless display of talent, a too undisguised statement of all that can be said for and against a question, is perhaps the great fault that is to be attributed to him. Where there is so much power and prejudice to contend with in the opposite scale, it may be thought that the balance of truth can hardly be held with a slack or an even hand; and that the infusion of a little more visionary speculation, of a little more popular indignation into the great Whig Review would be an advantage both to itself and to the cause of freedom. Much of this effect is chargeable less on an Epicurean levity of feeling or on party-trammels, than on real sanguineness of disposition, and a certain fineness of professional tact. Our sprightly Scotchman is not of a desponding and gloomy turn of mind. He argues well for the future hopes of mankind from the smallest beginnings, watches the slow, gradual reluctant growth of liberal views, and smiling sees the aloe of Reform blossom at the end of a hundred years; while the habitual subtlety of his mind makes him perceive decided advantages where vulgar ignorance or passion sees only doubts and difficulty; and a flaw in an adversary's argument stands him instead of the shout of a mob, the votes of a majority, or the fate of a pitched battle. The Editor is satisfied with his own conclusions, and does not make himself uneasy about the fate of mankind. The issue, he thinks, will verify his moderate and well-founded expectations.—We believe also that late events have given a more decided turn to Mr. Jeffrey's mind, and that he feels that as in the struggle between liberty and slavery, the views of the one party have been laid bare with their success, so the exertions on the other side should become more strenuous, and a more positive stand be made against the avowed and appalling encroachments of priestcraft and arbitrary power.

The characteristics of Mr. Jeffrey's general style as a writer correspond, we think, with what we have here stated as the characteristics of his mind. He is a master of the foils; he makes an exulting display of the dazzling fence of wit and argument. His strength consists in great range of knowledge, an equal familiarity with the principles and the details of a subject, and in a glancing brilliancy and rapidity of style. Indeed, we doubt whether the brilliancy of his manner does not resolve itself into the rapidity, the variety and aptness of his illustrations. His pen is never at a loss, never stands still; and would dazzle for this reason alone, like an eye that is ever in motion. Mr. Jeffrey is far from a flowery or affected writer; he has few tropes or figures, still less any odd startling thoughts or quaint innovations in expression:—but he has a constant supply of ingenious solutions and pertinent examples; he never proses, never grows dull, never wears an argument to tatters; and by the number, the liveliness and facility of his transitions, keeps up that appearance of vivacity, of novel and sparkling effect, for which others are too often indebted to singularity of combination or tinsel ornaments.

It may be discovered, by a nice observer, that Mr. Jeffrey's style of composition is that of a person accustomed to public speaking. There is no pause, no meagreness, no inanimateness, but a flow, a redundance and volubility like that of a stream or of a rolling-stone. The language is more copious than select, and sometimes two or three words perform the office of one. This copiousness and facility is perhaps an advantage in *extempore* speaking, where no stop or break is allowed in the discourse, and where any word

or any number of words almost is better than coming to a dead stand; but in written compositions it gives an air of either too much carelessness or too much labour. Mr. Jeffrey's excellence, as a public speaker, has betrayed him into this peculiarity. He makes fewer *blots* in addressing an audience than any one we remember to have heard. There is not a hair's-breadth space between any two of his words, nor is there a single expression either ill-chosen or out of its place. He speaks without stopping to take breath, with ease, with point, with elegance, and without "spinning the thread of his verbosity finer than the staple of his argument." He may be said to weave words into any shapes he pleases for use or ornament, as the glass-blower moulds the vitreous fluid with his breath; and his sentences shine like glass from their polished smoothness, and are equally transparent. His style of eloquence, indeed, is remarkable for neatness, for correctness, and epigrammatic point; and he has applied this as a standard to his written compositions, where the very same degree of correctness and precision produces from the contrast between writing and speaking, an agreeable diffuseness, freedom and animation. Whenever the Scotch advocate has appeared at the bar of the English House of Lords, he has been admired by those who were in the habit of attending to speeches there, as having the greatest fluency of language and the greatest subtlety of distinction of any one of the profession. The law-reporters were as little able to follow him from the extreme rapidity of his utterance as from the tenuity and evanescent nature of his reasoning.

Mr. Jeffrey's conversation is equally lively, various, and instructive. There is no subject on which he is not *au fait:* no company in which he is not ready to scatter his pearls for sport. Whether it be politics, or poetry, or science, or anecdote, or wit, or raillery, he takes up his cue without effort, without preparation, and appears equally incapable of tiring himself or his hearers. His only difficulty seems to be, not to speak, but to be silent. There is a constitutional buoyancy and elasticity of mind about him that cannot subside into repose, much less sink into dulness. There may be more original talkers, persons who occasionally surprise or interest you more; few, if any, with a more uninterrupted flow of cheerfulness and animal spirits, with a greater fund of information, and with fewer specimens of the *bathos* in their conversation. He is never absurd, nor has he any favourite points which he is always bringing forward. It cannot be denied that there is something bordering on petulance of manner, but it is of that least offensive kind which may be accounted for from merit and from success, and implies no exclusive pretensions nor the least particle of ill-will to others. On the contrary, Mr. Jeffrey is profuse of his encomiums and admiration of others, but still with a certain reservation of a right to differ or to blame. He cannot rest on one side of a question: he is obliged by a mercurial habit and disposition to vary his point of view. If he is ever tedious, it is from an excess of liveliness: he oppresses from a sense of airy lightness. He is always setting out on a fresh scent: there are always *relays* of topics; the harness is put to, and he rattles away as delightfully and as briskly as ever. New causes are called; he holds a brief in his hand for every possible question. This is a fault. Mr. Jeffrey is not obtrusive, is not impatient of opposition, is not unwilling to be interrupted;

but what is said by another, seems to make no impression on him; he is bound to dispute, to answer it, as if he was in Court, or as if it were in a paltry Debating Society, where young beginners were trying their hands. This is not to maintain a character, or for want of good-nature—it is a thoughtless habit. He cannot help cross-examining a witness, or stating the adverse view of the question. He listens not to judge, but to reply. In consequence of this, you can as little tell the impression your observations make on him as what weight to assign to his. Mr. Jeffrey shines in mixed company; he is not good in a *tête-à-tête*. You can only show your wisdom or your wit in general society: but in private your follies or your weaknesses are not the least interesting topics; and our critic has neither any of his own to confess, nor does he take delight in hearing those of others. (Indeed in Scotland generally, the display of personal character, the indulging your whims and humours in the presence of a friend, is not much encouraged—every one there is looked upon in the light of a machine or a collection of topics. They turn you round like a cylinder to see what use they can make of you, and drag you into a dispute with as little ceremony as they would drag out an article from an Encyclopedia. They criticise every thing, analyse everything, argue upon every thing, dogmatise upon every thing; and the bundle of your habits, feelings, humours, follies and pursuits is regarded by them no more than a bundle of old clothes. They stop you in a sentiment by a question or a stare, and cut you short in a narrative by the time of night.) The accomplished and ingenious person of whom we speak, has been a little infected by the tone of his countrymen—he is too didactic, too pugnacious, too full of electrical shocks . . . , and reposes too little on his own excellent good sense his own love of ease, his cordial frankness of temper and unaffected candour. He ought to have belonged to us! (pp. 185-89)

> *William Hazlitt, "Mr. Jeffrey," in his* The Spirit of the Age; or, Contemporary Portraits, *J. B. Lippincott Company, 1825, pp. 179-90.*

James Moncreiff   (essay date 1844)

[*In the following excerpt, Moncreiff offers a favorable estimation of* Contributions to the Edinburgh Review.]

While the [*Edinburgh Review*] was received with singular favour by the public generally, the feelings it excited were by no means those of unmingled admiration in all quarters. On the contrary, it hit so hard the prejudices of many influential classes, that its vigour and ability only rendered it the more obnoxious. Authors were also not unwilling to impugn the partiality or fairness of a tribunal, through the ordeal of which so few could pass with credit. In looking into the *Memoirs of William Taylor,* lately published, we find, in the letters of Southey, who was a great correspondent of his, a good illustration of the feelings by which our author and his *Review* were regarded by the irritable race to which the poet belonged. He never speaks of Jeffrey but with a degree of bitterness which indicates much of the fear, as well as the smart, of injured vanity; and we have no doubt that many of his tuneful brethren at that time participated in his sentiments. It is worth remarking, however, that Taylor, so far from taking the trouble to apply

any balm to his wounds, never fails to put in a word of praise of the Scotch Reviewers. Taylor's commendation is valuable, as the expression of the opinion of a rival critic, speaking of genius which had eclipsed his own. He was the principal contributor to the *Monthly Review,* and is fairly entitled to the praise, not only of having done much to introduce the taste for German literature in this country, but also of having first adventured the broader and more scientific style of criticism which the *Edinburgh Review* afterwards carried to so much perfection. While he was well able to appreciate the kindred merits of the new Journal, the simplicity and disinterestedness of his praise adds greatly to its value. "It is not," he says in 1809, in answer to one of Southey's invectives, "with Jeffrey's politics that I am in love; but with his brilliant and definite expressions, and his subtle argumentative power. I have not seen the *Quarterly Review.* It is said to rival that of Jeffrey; *but I should be surprised if there is literary strength enough in any other combination to teach so many good opinions so well as the Edinburgh Reviewers.*"

This brings us to speak of [**Contributions to the Edinburgh Review**], and of its author, the director and head of this formidable confederacy. It is simply a reprint of selected articles from the *Review,* without any addition by the author, with the exception of the preface, and some occasional notes. Here and there he has curtailed an article, sometimes to adapt it to modern readers, and sometimes for other reasons, explained at the places where they occur. Apart from its other merits, it cannot fail to interest as a memorial of the wisdom, policy, and triumphs of the government of the autocrat of criticism, to which, unlike most abdicated monarchs, he looks calmly back with honest but well-tempered pride, undisturbed by the cravings of ambition, and undisquieted by the recollection of former strife. The dignity proper to his station may have, in some degree, moderated the vivacity and point for which the subjects of the little annotations scattered up and down these volumes afford considerable scope; but, on the other hand, there is something most attractive in the mellowed light thrown over the whole, from a flame which once burned so fiercely;—in the gentle candour and the unassuming and considerate reflection, untinctured by a single drop of gall, with which he recurs to conflicts which are now matter of history in our literary annals. Not a vestige is to be found there of the touchy vanity common to authorship; nor even of the natural dogmatism of a man engaged during an ardent life in the maintenance of strong opinions. It is with a kind of apologetic diffidence, rather than with any vaunt of consistency, that in writing of his earlier feuds, he intimates that he still thinks as he then thought, but with all kind words of the antagonists who remain, and kinder of those who are departed, and an amiable and unbidden regret for the strength of words, which grate upon his memory, while he cannot feel them to be undeserved. Such was the mind of the man whose name at one time, among a certain class, was a synonym for bitterness, revilings, and all uncharitableness, and who certainly enjoyed no small amount of fear and hatred among those who knew nothing of him except through the terrors of his lash.

It is not fair, perhaps, to contrast the ebullitions of a poet impatient of the recent smart, with the quiet reminiscences of such a work as this; but having just spoken of Southey, and we would wish to speak reverently of the memory of so powerful an intellect, we cannot but turn to the tribute paid by the once dreaded critic to the two most inveterate of his adversaries.

> I have, in my time, said petulant and provoking things of Mr. Southey:—and such as I would not say now. But I am not conscious that I was ever unfair to his poetry: and if I have noted what I thought its faults, in too arrogant and derisive a spirit, I think I have never failed to give hearty and cordial praise to its beauties—and generally dwelt much more largely on the latter than the former. Few things, at all events, would now grieve me more, than to think I might give pain to his many friends and admirers, by reprinting, so soon after his death, any thing which might appear derogatory either to his character or his genius; and therefore, though I cannot say that I have substantially changed any of the opinions I have formerly expressed as to his writings, I only insert in this publication my review of his last considerable poem; which may be taken as conveying my matured opinion of his merits—and will be felt, I trust, to have done no scanty or unwilling justice to his great and peculiar powers.
>
> [Vol. iii., p. 133.]

> I have spoken in many places rather too bitterly and confidently of the faults of Mr. Wordsworth's poetry: And forgetting, that even on my own view of them, they were but faults of taste, or venial self-partiality, have sometimes visited them, I fear, with an asperity which should be reserved for objects of moral reprobation. If I were now to deal with the whole question of his poetical merits, though my judgment might not be substantially different, I hope I should repress the greater part of these *vivacités* of expression: And indeed, so strong has been my feeling in this way, that considering how much I have always loved many of the attributes of his genius, and how entirely I respect his character, it did at first occur to me whether it was quite fitting that, in my old age and his, I should include in this publication any of those critiques which may have formerly given pain or offence to him or his admirers. But, when I reflected that the mischief, if there really ever was any, was long ago done, and that I still retain, in substance, the opinions which I should now like to have seen more gently expressed, I felt that to omit all notice of them on the present occasion, might be held to import a retractation which I am as far as possible from intending; or even be represented as a very shabby way of backing out of sentiments which should either be manfully persisted in, or openly renounced, and abandoned as untenable.

> I finally resolved, therefore, to reprint my review of 'The Excursion;' which contains a pretty, full view of my griefs and charges against Mr. Wordsworth; set forth, too, I believe, in a more temperate strain than most of my other inculpations—and of which I think I may now venture to say farther, that if the faults are unsparingly noted, the beauties are not penuriously or grudgingly allowed; but commended to the admiration of the reader with at least as much heartiness and good-will.
>
> [Vol. ii., p. 233.]

The preface is conceived in the same gentle spirit. The episode concerning Sir Walter Scott, with which it concludes, is not without interest; but we would certainly have preferred its omission. *Pace tanti nominis,* it was hardly worth Jeffrey's while to have taken such anxious notice of the observation, even though it came from Scott.

It is explained in the preface, that these volumes do not contain a third of the author's contributions to the *Review,* independently of the constant labour of revising, altering, and editing those of his coadjutors. When it is recollected that the party on whom this task was thrown, was, during the entire period, a barrister in great practice, and that he arrived ultimately at the highest honours, both officially and professionally, which a Scottish advocate can hold, some idea may be formed of the wonderful versatility of powers and rapidity of execution which he must have had at his command. Any one who has had the duty of an editor imposed on him, will understand how greatly the extensive occupations of the reviewer enhance the merits of his literary labours. For a dull, ill-tempered man, fancy could not imagine a more refined and perfect torment than the life of an editor. Tied to a stake—a mark for every disappointed friend or foe to fling at—daily devoured by the petulance of authors—the jealousies and intolerable delays of contributors, and the grumblings of publishers—and doomed to a task never ending—still beginning—more hopeless and interminable than the labours of the fabled sisters, "speeding to-day, to be put back tomorrow"—an editor might well require leisure the most uninterrupted, and patience almost patriarchal, if he hoped to enjoy his life, or to retain it long. Indeed we are satisfied, that not all the intellectual qualities which he brought to the service, could have enabled Lord Jeffrey triumphantly to accomplish both his literary and professional distinctions, but for a natural sweetness and suavity of temper, that left his mind serene and unruffled for all his tasks, and enabled him to throw off with his books, equally the harassments of the editor, and the anxieties of the law.

Written amid such avocations, the selections contained in these volumes are presented to the public in a separate shape. The articles are arranged, not chronologically, but under distinct classes of general literature, history, poetry, politics, and miscellaneous subjects.

This arrangement has certainly the advantage of presenting, in a continuous and unbroken view, the author's sentiments on the varied subjects embraced in the collection. On the other hand, it exposes the articles themselves, as the author seems to be aware, to the most trying test to which they could be subjected. As despatches sent out from time to time—orders in Council, so to speak, promulgated as occasion or delinquency required—it might frequently happen that the same doctrines might be often enforced, and the same reprimands repeated with advantage. But when, thus collected, after the emergencies have passed away, and read continuously as contemporaneous essays, it was inevitable that they should present the recurrence of analogous discussions to a much greater degree than would be either natural or agreeable in a connected work; and the classification adopted, of course increases the effect of these repetitions.

This defect is most prominent in those treatises, which are otherwise the most valuable; as the author most frequently reverts to those topics on which he had thought most deeply, and which he considered most important. In fact, it is a defect quite inseparable from the style of composition. We do not say, as Fox did of reported speeches, that if these treatises make a good book, they must have been bad reviews; but nothing can be clearer, than that in following out a bold and extensive system of criticism, intended and adapted to correct the corrupted taste of the age, much of their weight and influence depended on the frequency with which the blow was repeated. Articles which stand side by side in these volumes, were separated by the distance of years; and during the interval, the changes in public feeling, or the revolutions of literature, gave zest and propriety to reflections, which, as they are here placed, seem merely echoes or reproductions of the thoughts of a few pages before.

Perhaps there is another leading feature of these Essays, which is calculated to diminish their popularity as a connected work; we mean the didactic or metaphysical cast which distinguish the most elaborate of their number. The prevalent taste for studies of that nature which reigned in Scotland at their date, naturally led the pupils of Reid and Stewart to exercise on literature and politics, the habits of inquiry which they had learned in those celebrated schools. Fashion has, in some degree, antiquated the science; and at the present day, the mysticism of metaphysics is more in favour than its pure inductions. But while it cannot be denied, that this character of the work before us may detract a little from its qualifications as a competitor for popular favour, it is far from diminishing its intrinsic merit. It was, as we have said, one of the leading objects of the *Review,* to introduce and enforce more correct principles of reasoning and taste. As Lord Jeffrey says in his preface, the "*Review* aimed high from the first:"—

> And refusing to confine itself to the humble task of pronouncing on the mere literary merits of the works that came before it, professed to go deeply into *the Principles* on which its judgments were to be rested; as well as to take large and original views of all the important questions to which those works might relate. And, on the whole, I think it is now pretty generally admitted, that it attained the end it aimed at. Many errors there were, of course, and some considerable blunders; abundance of indiscretions, especially in the earlier Numbers; and far too many excesses, both of party zeal, overweening confidence, and intemperate blame. But with all these drawbacks, I think it must be allowed to have substantially succeeded—in familiarizing the public mind (that is, the minds of very many individuals) with higher speculations, and sounder and larger views of the great objects of human pursuit, than had ever before been brought as effectually home to their apprehensions, and also in permanently

raising the standard, and increasing the influence of all such occasional writings, not only in this country, but over the greater part of Europe, and the free States of America; while it proportionally enlarged the capacity, and improved the relish, of the growing multitudes to whom such writings were addressed, for 'the stronger meats' which were then first provided for their digestion.

Now, in the attainment of this object, it was essential that the subjects of controversy should be reduced to their elements, and that the foundation of a more solid and enduring canon of judgment should be laid on a correct basis of sound principle. Hence the great utility of that habit of analysis which was favoured by the taste of the time, and of which our author is so great a master. It is true, some of these analytical processes read now like a series of self-evident propositions; and we sometimes think it was hardly worth while to use an instrument so subtile to extract so plain a truth. But it must be borne in mind, that what we think self-evident and axiomatic, were the very propositions, the denial or disregard of which lay at the root of the misgovernment and perverted taste of the day; and the fact, that these principles, which were so utterly forgotten when his labours commenced, and so frequently derided and repudiated during his advocacy of them, are now received and acknowledged on all hands as rudimental—so that the demonstration of them appears superfluous—is perhaps the most flattering testimony which could be paid to the efficiency and moral influence of his writings.

No better illustration of these remarks occurs to us than the Review of Mr. Leckie's "Essay on the British Government." So gross and foolish a libel on constitutional liberty, would hardly, perhaps, at present find a reader, and certainly not a reviewer; nor, on the other hand, would any politician, or class of politicians, so far commit themselves with the public, as to deny, that all government flows from the people, and has the good of the people as its only end. But when this elaborate defence of very plain principles was composed, a man was not thought either a knave or a fool, but, on the contrary, a truly loyal British subject, deserving of great rewards, and very often receiving them, who stood up for the divine right of kings, and the sinfulness of questioning the absolute wisdom of any constituted authority. Nor must we rashly conclude, that although such notions are now obsolete, they are necessarily extinct. We have seen some strange resurrections in our own day. Opinions which have at any time taken a strong hold on intelligent men, never die, however pernicious or absurd; nor is a country or age ever safe against their reappearance. It was by exorcisms such as those of the *Edinburgh Review,* that the incantations which deluded the nation were broken, and the rabble rout dispersed; but even now, when so many seem disposed to forsake modern light for ancient darkness, and when we find dogmas which we thought buried with the monks that held them, reacquiring their power over even the learned and enlightened, it is impossible to say how soon we may be sent back to the very demonstrations which we think so elementary, for weapons to defend all we hold sacred in our national institutions.

But passing from these peculiarities, we regard this work as a very valuable addition to the permanent literature of the country. It is a book not to be read only—but studied. It is a vast repertory, or rather a system or institute, embracing the whole circle of letters—if we except the exact sciences—and contains within itself, not in a desultory form, but in a well digested scheme, more original conception, bold and fearless speculation, and just reasoning on all kinds and varieties of subjects than are to be found in any English writer with whom we are acquainted, within the present or the last generation.

It would be a very unwarrantable trespass on the time of our readers, to follow our author in detail through the work before us. It presents all the variety of an undulating landscape, with deep recesses and sunny glades, and smooth still lakes, and dashing torrents, and here and there less fertile plains, and anon bright broad green meadows, redolent of cheerfulness and joy. We could but faintly sketch its more prominent and striking features; for it seems very ill spent labour to attempt to describe or condense writings which have been to us as household words from our youth, and with which our readers are probably as familiar as ourselves. We cannot, however, dismiss our subject without inquiring a little more anxiously into our author's peculiar merits and qualities as a writer, and an attempt to form a somewhat more specific estimate of the school of criticism, of which he was the founder and the head.

The most natural comparison, as we have said before, to which every one is prompted to subject these volumes, is to the writings of Sydney Smith and Macaulay: and on a first or superficial impression, the comparison is not in their favour. The quaint wit of Sydney Smith, and Macaulay's stately rolling periods, and glittering images, beguile the time more quickly, and rivet the attention closer. Those who expected to find Jeffrey's essays of a similar stamp, have probably read or tried to read, the book, with a feeling of disappointment. It wants sustained interest for the more indolent class of readers, and is not a work for a lounger to skim over of a morning. The difference arises in a great measure from causes we have already adverted to: for these articles are truly *criticisms*—intended to teach and instruct. But in other respects they have merits of a higher order, and in a higher degree than either of these authors. In the first place, as pure English compositions, we think Jeffrey's writings incomparably superior, not only to his brother reviewers, but to most writers of his time. Sydney Smith's style is careless though effective. Macaulay's is an artificial costume. He is always in full dress, and marches perpetually to the same majestic but rather pompous strain. We read through his three volumes with great delight, but as we read, the everlasting reverberation of his sentences, like a great sea wave on a sandy beach, made our head reel at last. Jeffrey does not drive over the ground so smoothly, but he is infinitely better worth loitering with. His choice of words is unbounded, and his felicity of expression, to the most impalpable shade of discrimination, almost miraculous. Playful, lively, and full of illustration, no subject is so dull or so dry that he cannot invest it with interest, and none so trifling that it cannot acquire dignity or elegance from his pencil. He can

rise to the heights of the most exalted argument, or gossip with equal ease with Mary Montague or Pepys, and neither his flights nor his descents seem to cost him an effort, or to interrupt the unencumbered flow of his thoughts. Other writers have been more stately, more accurate, more witty, more florid, than he; but few have ever combined so much facility and so much excellence in all. In playful satire, he stands, in our opinion, without a rival in his time. It was his favourite and most dreaded weapon, of which his rapid fancy, quick sense of the ridiculous, and his command of happy expression, rendered him as complete a master as ever practised the art.

Independently, however, of mere style, and apart from the great variety of subject embraced by his pen, the distinguishing feature of his writings, and that in which he excels his contemporary Reviewers, is the deep vein of practical thought which runs throughout them all. He is not what would now-a-days be thought an *original* thinker. He has no mysteries. He does not startle by unexpected fancies, or by everyday thoughts arrayed in half-intelligible language. On the contrary, he plainly eschews such things as offences against good taste and nature, and handles them unmercifully when they come under his cognizance. In particular, he is altogether untainted by the bastard philosophizing strain which the passion for German literature has introduced of late years—which, in our humble judgment, has obscured and damaged a great deal of vigorous thought, which, in a sober, natural, and English dress, would have been far more distinguished and useful. But the habit of his mind is to search after principle, and to discover the germs of truths in the more complicated phases of intellect, and the artificial states of society. He is the professed votary of simplicity and nature in all their forms, and therefore the whole strain of his reflections, which are always clear, acute, and just, and very frequently profound, is to deduce from his subject some general principle in ethics or dialectics, by which a canon or rule may be derived for general guidance and instruction.

In his preface, he remarks—

> If I might be permitted farther to state, in what particular department, and generally, on account of what, I should most wish to claim a share of those merits, I should certainly say, that it was by having constantly endeavoured to combine ethical precepts with literary criticism, and earnestly sought to impress my readers with a sense, both of the close connexion between sound intellectual attainments and the higher elements of duty and enjoyment; and of the just and ultimate subordination of the former to the latter. The praise, in short, to which I aspire, and to merit which I am conscious that my efforts were most constantly directed, is, that I have, more uniformly and earnestly than any preceding critic, made the moral tendencies of the works under consideration a leading subject of discussion; and neglected no opportunity, in reviews of poems and novels, as well as of graver productions, of elucidating the true constituents of human happiness and virtue: and combating those besetting prejudices and errors of opinion which appear so often to withhold men from the path of their duty—or to array them in foolish

and fatal hostility to each other. I cannot, of course, do more, in this place, than *intimate* this proud claim: But, for the proof—or at least the explanation of it—I think I may venture to refer to the greater part of the papers that follow.

With one qualification, we think, he is well entitled to the praise which he here assumes. He has a strong and ardent love of humanity, and delights to look on the sunny side of life. Human griefs and passions—the deeper sorrows and the minute unhappinesses of existence—find constant sympathy with him; and no little joy, no flash of true-hearted merriment, fails to find an echo in his breast. He is none of those grumblers of whom Seneca speaks, who accuse the order of the world, and would wish the gods amended, not themselves. He admires and deeply venerates all that is august and glorious in this visible diurnal sphere, and labours, with earnest sincerity, to teach those lessons of high philosophy by which he thinks public and social happiness consist.

The qualification we refer to, is one which, perhaps, might have no place, if the volumes alone were before us; but in considering the school of criticism which he founded, and the decrees of that tribunal of which he was the head, it is impossible to omit the remark, that the highest and truest standard of right, if it was admitted at all, was never allowed to occupy its appropriate place. Let us not be misunderstood. There is nothing in the Essays before us which can do violence to the keenest religious sense; indeed, if we except one or two casual expressions in the review of Hayley's *Life of Cowper,* there is little we could wish altered in that respect. On the other hand, there are many passages—as, for instance, in the remarks on *Bishop Heber's Journal*—which breathe a tone of deep reverence for sacred things. With the scourging of hypocrisy, and the exposure of pretended sanctity, we should not only not quarrel, but sympathize. Nor is the least agreeable impression produced by these volumes, that softened and more solemn air which time and experience always produce on minds truly great. We do not complain, however, of what we find, but we desiderate what is absent. In so far as the critic derived his laws of judicial determination from the eternal truths of morality, and deals his censure and awards his praise in proportion as the great ends of man appear to be advanced or injured by the subject of the inquiry, he approached to the formation of a perfect standard of criticism. But why should the process stop there? If, after all, the true canon is to be found in the tendency to ameliorate and improve the race, will not that rule be purer and more perfect, if it embrace not temporal only, but the eternal interests of man, and have reference not merely to fallible conscience and a clouded moral sense, but to the clear unchanging dictates of divine truth? The spirit of evangelical religion applied as a rule of judgment, is so far from excluding or superseding the principles of taste, that it strengthens and purifies these principles, and superadds an unfailing touchstone to that ethical test which Lord Jeffrey claims as his ultimate criterion of right:—with this difference, that certainty is substituted for speculation, at best doubtful, and AUTHORITY comes in to confirm the wavering opinions of man on the great questions of moral excellence and fitness. There is no more

reason why a sound spirit of religion should quench the lamp of genius, or shed a gloom over the paths of literature, than there is for a similar effect being produced by making both subservient to a spirit of mere morality. If the moral musings of the sages of antiquity only give additional interest to their writings, and charm while they instruct;—if we love to stray with Plato in meditation through academic groves, or dwell with rapture over the darkened but delightful wanderings of Cicero after a futurity he dimly foresaw, but could not fathom;—if in these ancients, *their* religion, dim and doubtful, detracts nothing, but only adds to their classic grace—why should the charm be lost because we walk in broad noon, where they groped in twilight? Or, if moral judgments can best discern and preserve truth and unity, and nature, in all manifestations of intellect, surely those judgments must be the most accurate and the most exalting, which are founded on an unerring rule of right, and embrace the welfare of man, even in his everlasting destiny?

The true operation of the spirit of religious truth as a criterion of just criticism, is a subject which would lead us far away from our present theme; it deserves separate and full consideration for itself. We must, however, observe, that it would be impossible to speak of the *Edinburgh Review,* as a work—at least of its earlier and most celebrated numbers—without the use of terms of much stronger reprehension. Its careless, and even scoffing tone, and a certain irreligious air which it assumed, exposed it justly to great reproach, and did more to counteract the influence of the great and enlarged principles which it advocated, and to blunt the point of its brilliant sarcasm, than any other element. The age in which it started was one of much professed attachment to the Church, and clamorous fear of bringing her into danger, but of little real piety, and one in which sincere and simple religion was despised and derided equally by the sceptic and the bigot. By such articles as that on Missions in 1807, not only was just offence and scandal given to the serious part of the community, but an excuse was afforded to those to whom the cry of "Church in danger" was convenient, to raise a popular outcry against an antagonist otherwise so formidable. It may not perhaps be easy to estimate accurately the amount of injury which was done to the really free and enlightened principles which it was the professed object of the *Review* to proclaim, by thus associating them in the minds of many good and worthy people with infidelity or carelessness, and inducing the belief that those who held the first, must of necessity be tinged with the last also. It is satisfactory to find, that while the great principles of freedom, and the just rules of thought, for which the *Review* contended, have gained strength every year of their advocacy, those very evangelical opinions, which were made the subject of ridicule and assault, have, like "birds of a tempest-loving kind," beat steadily up against the storm, until they have even found a resting-place in the pages of some of their opponents.

The principal department to which our author turned his attention, and to which the most important and effective of these criticisms relate, is that of belles lettres and poetry. The dissertations which these volumes contain on the lighter literature of our language, and the inquiries into

the elements in which the merit and excellence of true poetry consist, were those on which the critic's reputation
was first founded. It does not follow, that they form the
most interesting articles to a modern reader. But it was in
that field that the power and effect of the *Review* was most
eminently successful. Prior to the establishment of the
Quarterly Review, Jeffrey remained absolute monarch of
this kingdom; and although there may be some things
which seem to us rather elementary, and others that appear to be unnecessarily repeated, when we read these Essays now, we owe to him more, perhaps, than we have the
means of calculating, for his constant, unceasing, and
powerful efforts in the erection and defence of a sound
standard of taste.

The foundation of his principles of criticism, and the cause
also of his success in permanently establishing them, is to
be found in his deep admiration, and thorough knowledge
of the early English dramatists. Indeed, it must be admitted, that he draws little either on classical literature or the
foreign writers of modern Europe; and this, perhaps, detracts from his reputation as a catholic author. It increased, however, that which is his greatest recommendation, the thoroughly *English* spirit which pervades all his
dissertations. For the first time, for nearly a century, the
public were sent back to refresh themselves at those long-
forgotten springs. Dryden was perhaps the last example
of the nervous English writers. Pope borrowed from him
"the long resounding line," and indeed improved on his
master, if not in strength, at least in the rhythm and melody of his diction. But as the founder of a school, he led
away his followers in a search after pointed antithesis and
glittering conceits from the manly, vigorous style of those
ancient models, on which Milton formed his majestic
numbers, and from which Dryden learned the secret of his
power. So much, indeed, did the fashion introduced by the
brilliant wits of Queen Anne cast into the shade their
rougher and more masculine predecessors, that during the
last century Shakespeare himself was considered as an obsolete writer of a more vulgar and a ruder age. It is Jeffrey's greatest triumph to have instilled into the minds of
his countrymen a sound appreciation and befitting reverence for these great fathers of English song, and to have
recalled the taste for the graces of natural thought and
passion, of which they are such abundant storehouses.
(pp. 258-70)

> *James Moncreiff, in a review of "Contributions
> to the Edinburgh Review," in* The North Brit-
> ish Review, *Vol. I, No. I, May, 1844, pp. 252-
> 84.*

Thomas Carlyle   (essay date 1867)

[*A noted nineteenth-century essayist, historian, critic,
and social commentator, Carlyle was a central figure of
the Victorian age in England. In his writings, Carlyle
advocated a Christian work ethic and stressed the importance of order, piety, and spiritual fulfillment. Known
to his contemporaries as the "Sage of Chelsea," Carlyle
exerted a powerful moral influence in an era of rapidly
shifting values. In the following excerpt from an essay*

*originally published in 1867, he assesses strengths and
weaknesses in Jeffrey's criticism.*]

Jeffrey was perhaps at the height of his reputation about
1816; his *Edinburgh Review* a kind of Delphic oracle and
voice of the inspired for great majorities of what is called
the 'intelligent public,' and himself regarded universally
as a man of consummate penetration and the *facile
princeps* in the department he had chosen to cultivate and
practise. In the half-century that has followed, what a
change in all this! the fine gold become dim to such a degree, and the Trismegistus hardly now regarded as a
Megas by anyone, or by the generality remembered at all.
He may be said to have begun the rash reckless style of cri-
ticising everything in heaven and earth by appeal to *Molière's maid;* 'Do *you* like it?' '*Don't* you like it?' a style
which in hands more and more inferior to that sound-
hearted old lady and him, has since grown gradually to
such immeasurable length among us; and he himself is one
of the first that suffers by it. If praise and blame are to be
perfected, not in the mouth of Molière's maid only but in
that of mischievous precocious babes and sucklings, you
will arrive at singular judgments by degrees! Jeffrey was
by no means the supreme in criticism or in anything else;
but it is certain there has no critic appeared among us
since who was worth naming beside him; and his influence
for good and for evil in literature and otherwise has been
very great. Democracy, the gradual uprise and rule in all
things of roaring million-headed unreflecting, darkly suffering darkly sinning 'Demos,' come to call its old superiors to account at its maddest of tribunals; nothing in my
time has so forwarded all this as Jeffrey and his once famous *Edinburgh Review.*

He was not deep enough, pious or reverent enough, to
have been great in literature; but he was a man intrinsically of veracity; said nothing without meaning it to some
considerable degree, had the quickest perceptions, excellent practical discernment of what lay before him; was in
earnest too, though not 'dreadfully in earnest;' in short
was well fitted to set forth that *Edinburgh Review* (at the
dull opening of our now so tumultuous century), and become coryphæus of his generation in the waste, wide-
spreading and incalculable course appointed *it* among the
centuries! I used to find in him a finer talent than any he
has evidenced in writing. This was chiefly when he got to
speak Scotch, and gave me anecdotes of old Scotch Brax-
fields and vernacular (often enough but not always cynical) curiosities of that type; which he did with a greatness
of gusto quite peculiar to the topic, with a fine and deep
sense of humour, of real comic mirth, much beyond what
was noticeable in him otherwise; not to speak of the perfection of the mimicry, which itself was something. I used
to think to myself, 'Here is a man whom they have knead-
ed into the shape of an Edinburgh reviewer, and clothed
the soul of in Whig formulas and blue and yellow; but he
might have been a beautiful Goldoni too, or some thing
better in that kind, and have given us *comedies* and aerial
pictures true and poetic of human life in a far other way!'
There was something of Voltaire in him, something even
in bodily features; those bright-beaming, swift and piercing hazel eyes, with their accompaniment of rapid keen expression in the other lineaments of face, resembled one's

notion of Voltaire; and in the voice too there was a fine half-plangent kind of metallic ringing tone which used to remind me of what I fancied Voltaire's voice might have been: 'voix sombre et majestueuse,' Duvernet calls it. The culture and respective natal scenery of the two men had been very different; nor was their *magnitude* of faculty anything like the same, had their respective kinds of it been much more identical than they were. You could not define Jeffrey to have been more than a potential Voltaire; say 'Scotch Voltaire'; with about as much reason (which was not very much) as they used in Edinburgh to call old Playfair the 'Scotch D'Alembert.' Our Voltaire too, whatever else might be said of him, was at least worth a large multiple of our D'Alembert! A beautiful little man the former of these, and a bright island to me and to mine in the sea of things, of whom it is now again mournful and painful to take farewell. (pp. 63-6)

> Thomas Carlyle, "Lord Jeffrey," in his Reminiscences, Vol. II, *edited by James Anthony Froude, 1881. Reprint by Scholarly Press, Inc., 1971, pp. 1-66.*

Leslie Stephen   (essay date 1878)

[*Stephen was one of the best-known English literary critics of the Victorian age. Contending that the role of criticism is to translate into intellectual terms that which is represented by character, symbol, and event in literature, Stephen based his critical practice on the belief that all writing is nothing more than an imaginative rendering, in concrete terms, of a writer's philosophy. While some scholars argue that Stephen produced biographical judgments of writers rather than criticism of their work, others praise his insight and intellectual vigor. In the following excerpt, he provides an overview of Jeffrey's career, defining his critical disposition as pessimistic and insincere.*]

Jeffrey's collected articles include about eighty out of two hundred reviews, nearly all contributed to the *Edinburgh* within its first period of twenty-five years. They fill four volumes, and are distributed under the seven heads— general literature, history, poetry, metaphysics, fiction, politics, and miscellaneous. Certainly there is versatility enough implied in such a list, and we may be sure that he has ample opportunity for displaying whatever may be in him. It is, however, easy to dismiss some of these divisions. Jeffrey knew history as an English gentleman of average cultivation knew it; that is to say, not enough to justify him in writing about it. He knew as much of metaphysics as a clever lad was likely to pick up at Edinburgh during the reign of Dugald Stewart; his essays in that kind, though they show some aptitude and abundant confidence, do not now deserve serious attention. His chief speculative performance was an essay upon beauty contributed to the *Encyclopædia Britannica,* of which his biographer says quaintly that it is "as sound as the subject admits of." It is crude and meagre in substance. The principal conclusion is the rather unsatisfactory one for a professional critic that there are no particular rules about beauty, and consequently that one taste is about as good as another. Nobody, however, could be less inclined to

apply this over liberal theory to questions of literary taste. There, he evidently holds, there is most decidedly a right and wrong, and everybody is very plainly in the wrong who differs from himself.

Jeffrey's chief fame—or, should we say, notoriety?—was gained, and his merit should be tested by his success, in this department. The greatest triumph that a literary critic can win is the early recognition of genius not yet appreciated by his contemporaries. The next test of his merit is his capacity for pronouncing sound judgment upon controversies which are fully before the public; and, finally, no inconsiderable merit must be allowed to any critic who has a vigorous taste of his own—not hopelessly eccentric or silly—and expresses it with true literary force. If not a judge, he may in that case be a useful advocate.

What can we say for Jeffrey upon this understanding? Did he ever encourage a rising genius? The sole approach to such a success is an appreciative notice of Keats, which would be the more satisfactory if poor Keats had not been previously assailed by the opposition journal. The other judgments are for the most part pronounced upon men already celebrated; and the single phrase which has survived is the celebrated "This will never do," directed against Wordsworth's *Excursion.* Every critic is liable to blunder; but Jeffrey's blundering is amazingly systematic and comprehensive. In the last of his poetical critiques (October 1829) he sums up his critical experience. He doubts whether Mrs. Hemans, whom he is reviewing at the time, will be immortal. "The tuneful quartos of Southey," he says, "are already little better than lumber; and the rich melodies of Keats and Shelley, and the fantastical emphasis of Wordsworth, and the plebeian pathos of Crabbe, are melting fast from the field of vision. The novels of Scott have put out his poetry. Even the splendid strains of Moore are fading into distance and dimness, except where they have been married to immortal music; and the blazing star of Byron himself is receding from its place of pride." Who survive this general decay? Not Coleridge, who is not even mentioned; nor is Mrs. Hemans secure. The two who show least marks of decay are—of all people in the world—Rogers and Campbell! It is only to be added that this summary was republished in 1843, by which time the true proportions of the great reputations of the period were becoming more obvious to an ordinary observer. It seems almost incredible now that any sane critic should pick out Rogers and Campbell as the sole enduring relics from the age of Wordsworth, Shelley, Keats, Coleridge, and Byron.

Doubtless a critic should rather draw the moral of his own fallibility than of his superiority to Jeffrey. Criticism is a still more perishing commodity than poetry. Jeffrey was a man of unusual intelligence and quickness of feeling; and a follower in his steps should think twice before he ventures to cast the first stone. If all critics who have grossly blundered are therefore to be pronounced utterly incompetent, we should, I fear, have to condemn nearly every one who has taken up the profession. Not only Dennis and Rymer, but Dryden, Pope, Addison, Johnson, Gray, Wordsworth, Byron, and even Coleridge, down to the last new critic in the latest and most fashionable journals, would have to be censured. Still there are blunders and blunders; and some of Jeffrey's sins in that kind are such as it is not very easy to forgive. If he attacked great men, it has been said in his defence, he attacked those parts of their writings which were really objectionable. And, of course, nobody will deny that (for example) Wordsworth's wilful and ostentatious inversion of accepted rules presented a very tempting mark to the critic. But—to say nothing of Jeffrey's failure to discharge adequately the correlative duty of generous praise—it must be admitted that his ridicule seems to strike pretty much at random. He picks out Southey, certainly the least eminent of the so-called school of Wordsworth, Coleridge, and Lamb, as the one writer of the set whose poetry deserves serious consideration; and, besides attacking Wordsworth's faults, his occasional flatness and childishness, selects some of his finest poems (*e.g.* the "Ode on the Intimations of Immortality") as flagrant specimens of the hopelessly absurd.

The *White Doe of Rylstone* may not be Wordsworth's best work; but a man who begins a review of it by proclaiming it to be "the very worst poem ever imprinted in a quarto volume," who follows up this remark by unmixed and indiscriminating abuse, and who publishes the review twenty-eight years later as expressing his mature convictions, is certainly proclaiming his own gross incompetence. Or, again, Jeffrey writes about [Goethe's] *Wilhelm Meister* (in 1824), knowing its high reputation in Germany, and finds in it nothing but a text for a dissertation upon the amazing eccentricity of national taste which can admire "sheer nonsense," and at length proclaims himself tired of extracting "so much trash." There is a kind of indecency, a wanton disregard of the general consensus of opinion in such treatment of a contemporary classic (then just translated by Mr. Carlyle, and so brought within Jeffrey's sphere) which one would hope to be now impossible. It is true that Jeffrey relents a little at the end, admits that Goethe has "great talent," and would like to withdraw some of his censure. Whilst, therefore, he regards it as an instance of that diversity of national taste which makes a writer idolized in one country who would not be tolerated in another, he would hold it out rather as an object of wonder than contempt. Though the greater part "would not be endured, and, indeed, could not have been written in England," there are many passages of which any country might naturally be proud. Truly this is an illustration of Jeffrey's fundamental principle that taste has no laws, and is a matter of accidental caprice.

It may be said that better critics have erred with equal recklessness. De Quincey, who could be an admirable critic where his indolent prejudices were not concerned, is even more dead to the merits of Goethe. Byron's critical remarks are generally worth reading, in spite of his wilful eccentricity; and he spoke of Wordsworth and Southey still more brutally than Jeffrey, and admired Rogers as unreasonably. In such cases we may admit the principle already suggested, that even the most reckless criticism has a kind of value when it implies a genuine (even though a mistaken) taste. So long as a man says sincerely what he thinks, he tells us something worth knowing.

Unluckily this is just where Jeffrey is apt to fail; though he affects to be a dictator, he is really a follower of the fashion. He could put up with Rogers' flattest "correctness," Moore's most intolerable tinsel, and even Southey's most ponderous epic poetry, because admiration was respectable. He could endorse, though rather coldly, the general verdict in Scott's favour, only guarding his dignity by some not too judicious criticism; preferring, for example, the sham romantic business of the *Lay* to the incomparable vigour of the rough moss-troopers

> Who sought the beeves that made their broth,
> In Scotland and in England both—

terribly undignified lines, as Jeffrey thinks. So far, though his judicial swagger strikes us now as rather absurd, and we feel that he is passing sentence on bigger men than himself, he does fairly enough. But, unluckily, the *Edinburgh* wanted a butt. All lively critical journals, it would seem, resemble the old-fashioned squires who kept a badger ready to be baited whenever a little amusement was desirable. The rising school of Lake poets, with their austere professions and real weaknesses, was just the game to show a little sport; and, accordingly, poor Jeffrey blundered into grievous misapprehensions, and has survived chiefly by his worst errors. The simple fact is, that he accepted whatever seemed to a hasty observer to be the safest opinion, that which was current in the most orthodox critical circles, and expressed it with rather more point than his neighbours. But his criticism implies no serious thought or any deeper sentiment than pleasure at having found a good laughing-stock. The most unmistakeable bit of genuine expression of his own feelings in Jeffrey's writings is, I think, to be found in his letters to Dickens. "Oh! my dear, dear Dickens!" he exclaims, "what a No. 5" (of *Dombey and Son*) "you have now given us. I have so cried and sobbed over it last night and again this morning, and felt my heart purified by those tears, and blessed and loved you for making me shed them; and I never can bless and love you enough. Since that divine Nelly was found dead on her humble couch, beneath the snow and ivy, there has been nothing like the actual dying of that sweet Paul in the summer sunshine of that lofty room." The emotion is a little senile, and most of us think it misplaced; but at least it is genuine. The earlier thunders of the *Edinburgh Review* have lost their terrors, because they are in fact mere echoes of commonplace opinion. They are often clever enough and have all the air of judicial authority, but we feel that they are empty shams, concealing no solid core of strong personal feeling even of the perverse variety. The critic has been asking himself, not "What do I feel?" but "What is the correct remark to make?"

Jeffrey's political writing suggests, I think, in some respects a higher estimate of his merits. He has not, it is true, very strong convictions, but his sentiments are liberal in the better sense of the word, and he has a more philosophical tone than is usual with English publicists. He appreciates the truths, now become commonplace, that the political constitution of the country should be developed so as to give free play for the underlying social forces without breaking abruptly with the old traditions. He combats with dignity the narrow prejudices which led to a policy of rigid repression, and which, in his opinion, could only lead to revolution. But the effect of his principles is not a little marred by a certain timidity both of character and intellect. Hopefulness should be the mark of an ardent reformer, and Jeffrey seems to be always decided by his fears. His favourite topic is the advantage of a strong middle party, for he is terribly afraid of a collision between the two extremes; he can only look forwards to despotism if the Tories triumph, and a sweeping revolution if they are beaten. Meanwhile, for many years he thinks it most probable that both parties will be swallowed up by the common enemy. Never was there such a determined croaker. In 1808 he suspects that Bonaparte will be in Dublin in about fifteen months, when he, if he survives, will try to go to America. In 1811 he expects Bonaparte to be in Ireland in eighteen months, and asks how England can then be kept, and whether it would be worth keeping? France is certain to conquer the continent, and our interference will only "exasperate and accelerate." Bonaparte's invasion of Russia in 1813 made him still more gloomy. He rejoiced at the French defeat as one delivered from a great terror, but the return of the Emperor dejects him again. All he can say of the war (just before Waterloo) is that he is "mortally afraid of it," and that he hates Bonaparte "because he makes me more afraid than anybody else." In 1819 he anticipates "tragical scenes" and a sanguinary revolution; in 1821 he thinks as ill as ever "of the state and prospects of the country," though with less alarm of speedy mischief; and in 1822 he looks forward to revolutionary wars all over the continent, from which we may possibly escape by reason of our "miserable poverty;" whilst it is probable that our old tyrannies and corruptions will last for some 4,000 or 5,000 years longer.

A stalwart politician, Whig or Tory, is rarely developed out of a Mr. Much-Afraid or a Mr. Despondency; they are too closely related to Mr. Facing-Both-Ways. Jeffrey thinks it generally a duty to conceal his fears and affect a confidence which he does not feel; but perhaps the best piece of writing in his essays is that in which he for once gives full expression to his pessimist sentiment. It occurs in a review of a book in which Madame de Staël maintains the doctrine of human perfectibility. Jeffrey explains his more despondent view in a really eloquent passage. He thinks that the increase of educated intelligence will not diminish the permanent causes of human misery. War will be as common as ever, wealth will be used with at least equal selfishness, luxury and dissipation will increase, enthusiasm diminish, intellectual originality will become rarer, the division of labour will make men's lives pettier and more mechanical, and pauperism grow with the development of manufactures. When republishing his essays Jeffrey expresses his continued adherence to these views, and they are more interesting than most of his work, because they have at least the merits of originality and sincerity. Still, one cannot help observing that if the *Edinburgh Review* was an efficient organ of progress, it was not from any ardent faith in progress entertained by its chief conductor. (pp. 225-29)

Leslie Stephen, "Hours in a Library: The First Edinburgh Reviewers," in The Cornhill Magazine, *Vol. XXXVIII, August, 1878, pp. 218-34.*

George Saintsbury   (essay date 1887)

[*Saintsbury has been called the most influential English literary historian and critic of the late nineteenth and early twentieth centuries. His studies of French literature, particularly* A History of the French Novel *(1917-1919), established him as a leading authority on such writers as Guy de Maupassant and Honoré de Balzac. Saintsbury adhered to two distinct sets of critical standards: one for the novel and the other for poetry and drama. As a critic of the novel, he maintained that its "substance must always be life not thought, conduct not belief, the passions of the intellect, manners and morals not creeds and theories. . . . The novel is . . . mainly and firstly a criticism of life." As a critic of poetry and drama, Saintsbury was a radical formalist who frequently asserted that subject is of little importance, and that "the so-called 'formal' part is of the essence." René Wellek has praised Saintsbury's critical faculties: his "enormous reading, the almost universal scope of his subject matter, the zest and zeal of his exposition," and "the audacity with which he handles the most ambitious and unattempted arguments." In the following excerpt, Saintsbury assesses the strengths and weaknesses of Jeffrey's critical arguments in* Contributions to the Edinburgh Review.]

In reading Jeffrey's [*Contributions to the Edinburgh Review,* I vol. London, 1853] nowadays, the critical reader finds it considerably more difficult to gain and keep the author's own point of view than in the case of any other great English critic. With Hazlitt, with Coleridge, with Wilson, with Carlyle, with Macaulay, we very soon fall into step, so to speak, with our author. If we cannot exactly prophesy what he will say on any given subject, we can make a pretty shrewd guess at it; and when, as it seems to us, he stumbles and shies, we have a sort of feeling beforehand that he is going to do it, and a decided inkling of the reason. But my own experience is, that a modern reader of Jeffrey, who takes him systematically, and endeavours to trace cause and effect in him, is liable to be constantly thrown out before he finds the secret. For Jeffrey, in the most puzzling way, lies between the ancients and the moderns in matter of criticism, and we never quite know where to have him. It is ten to one, for instance, that the novice approaches him with the idea that he is a "classic" of the old rock. Imagine the said novice's confusion, when he finds Jeffrey not merely exalting Shakespeare to the skies, but warmly praising Elizabethan poetry in general, anticipating Mr Matthew Arnold almost literally, in the estimate of Dryden and Pope as classics of our prose, and hailing with tears of joy the herald of the emancipation in Cowper. Surely our novice may be excused if, despite certain misgiving memories of such reviews as that of *The Lay of the Last Minstrel,* he concludes that Jeffrey has been maligned, and that he was really a Romantic before Romanticism. Unhappy novice! he will find his new conclusion not less rapidly and more completely staggered than his old. Indeed, until the clue is once gained, Jeffrey must appear to be one of the most incomprehensibly inconsistent of writers and of critics. On one page he declares that Campbell's extracts from Chamberlayne's *Pharonnida* have made him "quite impatient for an opportunity of perusing the whole poem,"—Romantic surely, quite Romantic. "The tameness and poorness of the serious style of Addison and Swift,"—Romantic again, quite Romantic. Yet when we come to Jeffrey's own contemporaries, he constantly appears as much bewigged and befogged with pseudo-classicism as M. de Jouy himself. He commits himself, in the year of grace 1829, to the statement that "the rich melodies of Keats and Shelley, and the fantastical emphasis of Wordsworth are melting fast from the field of our vision," while he contrasts with this "rapid withering of the laurel" the "comparative absence of marks of decay" on Rogers and Campbell. The poets of his own time whom he praises most heartily, and with least reserve, are Campbell and Crabbe; and he is quite as enthusiastic over *Theodric* and *Gertrude* as over the two great war-pieces of the same author, which are worth a hundred *Gertrudes* and about ten thousand *Theodrics*. Reviewing Scott, not merely when they were personal friends (they were always that), but when Scott was a contributor to the *Edinburgh,* and giving general praise to *The Lay,* he glances with an unmistakable meaning at the "dignity of the subject," regrets the "imitation and antiquarian researches," and criticises the versification in a way which shows that he had not in the least grasped its scheme. It is hardly necessary to quote his well-known attacks on Wordsworth; but, though I am myself anything but a Wordsworthian, and would willingly give up to chaos and old night nineteen-twentieths of the "extremely valooable chains of thought" which the good man used to forge, it is in the first place quite clear that the twentieth ought to have saved him from Jeffrey's claws; in the second, that the critic constantly selects the wrong things as well as the right for condemnation and ridicule; and in the third, that he would have praised, or at any rate not blamed, in another, the very things which he blames in Wordsworth. Even his praise of Crabbe, excessive as it may now appear, is diversified by curious patches of blame which seem to me at any rate, singularly uncritical. There are, for instance, a very great many worse jests in poetry than,

> Oh, had he learnt to make the wig he wears!

—which Jeffrey pronounces a misplaced piece of buffoonery. I cannot help thinking that if Campbell instead of Southey had written the lines,

> To see brute nature scorn him and renounce
> Its homage to the human form divine,

Jeffrey would, to say the least, not have hinted that they were "little better than drivelling." But I do not think that when Jeffrey wrote these things, or when he actually perpetrated such almost unforgivable phrases as "stuff about dancing daffodils," he was speaking away from his sincere conviction. On the contrary, though partisanship may frequently have determined the suppression or the utterance, the emphasising or the softening, of his opinions, I do not think that he ever said anything but what he sincerely thought. The problem, therefore, is to discover and define, if possible, the critical standpoint of a man whose judgment was at once so acute and so purblind; who could write the admirable surveys of English poetry contained in the essays on Mme de Staël and Campbell, and yet be guilty of the stuff (we thank him for the word) about the dancing daffodils; who could talk of "the splendid strains

of Moore" (though I have myself a relatively high opinion of Moore) and pronounce *The White Doe of Rylstone* (though I am not very fond of that animal as a whole) "the very worst poem he ever saw printed in a quarto volume"; who could really appreciate parts even of Wordsworth himself, and yet sneer at the very finest passages of the poems he partly admired. It is unnecessary to multiply inconsistencies, because the reader who does not want the trouble of reading Jeffrey must be content to take them for granted, and the reader who does read Jeffrey will discover them in plenty for himself. But they are not limited, it should be said, to purely literary criticism; and they appear, if not quite so strongly, in his estimates of personal character, and even in his purely political arguments.

The explanation, as far as there is any (and perhaps such explanations, as Hume says of another matter, only push ignorance a stage farther back), seems to me to lie in what I can only call the Gallicanism of Jeffrey's mind and character. As Horace Walpole has been pronounced the most French of Englishmen, so may Francis Jeffrey be pronounced the most French of Scotchmen. The reader of his letters, no less than the reader of his essays, constantly comes across the most curious and multiform instances of this Frenchness. The early priggishness is French; the effusive domestic affection is French; the antipathy to dogmatic theology, combined with general recognition of the Supreme Being, is French; the talk (I had almost said the chatter) about virtue and sympathy, and so forth, is French; the Whig recognition of the rights of man, joined to a kind of bureaucratical distrust and terror of the common people (a combination almost unknown in England), is French. Everybody remembers the ingenious argument in *Peter Simple* that the French were quite as brave as the English, indeed more so, but that they were extraordinarily ticklish. Jeffrey, we have seen, was very far from being a coward, but he was very ticklish indeed. His private letters throw the most curious light possible on the secret, as far as he was concerned, of the earlier Whig opposition to the war, and of the later Whig advocacy of reform. Jeffrey by no means thought the cause of the Revolution divine, like the Friends of Liberty, or admired Napoleon like Hazlitt, or believed in the inherent right of Manchester and Birmingham to representation like the zealots of 1830. But he was always dreadfully afraid of invasion in the first place, and of popular insurrection in the second; and he wanted peace and reform to calm his fears. As a young man he was, with a lack of confidence in his countrymen probably unparalleled in a Scotchman, sure that a French corporal's guard might march from end to end of Scotland, and a French privateer's boat's crew carry off "the fattest cattle and the fairest women" (these are his very words) "of any Scotch seaboard county." The famous, or infamous, Cevallos article—an ungenerous and pusillanimous attack on the Spanish patriots, which practically founded the *Quarterly Review,* by finally disgusting all Tories and many Whigs with the *Edinburgh*—was, it seems, prompted merely by the conviction that the Spanish cause was hopeless, and that maintaining it, or assisting it, must lead to mere useless bloodshed. He felt profoundly the crime of Napoleon's rule; but he thought Napoleon unconquerable, and so did his best to prevent him from being conquered. He was sure that the multitude would revolt if reform was not granted; and he was, therefore, eager for reform. Later, he got into his head the oddest crotchet of all his life, which was that a Conservative government, with a sort of approval from the people generally, and especially from the English peasantry, would scheme for a *coup d'état,* and (his own words again) "make mincemeat of their opponents in a single year." He may be said almost to have left the world in a state of despair over the probable results of the Revolutions of 1848-49; and it is impossible to guess what would have happened to him if he had survived to witness the Second of December. Never was there such a case, at least among Englishmen, of timorous pugnacity and plucky pessimism. But it would be by no means difficult to parallel the temperament in France; and, indeed, the comparative frequency of it there, may be thought to be no small cause of the political and military disasters of the country.

In literature, and especially in criticism, Jeffrey's characteristics were still more decidedly and unquestionably French. He came into the world almost too soon to feel the German impulse, even if he had been disposed to feel it. But, as a matter of fact, he was not at all disposed. The faults of taste of the German Romantic School, its alternate homeliness and extravagance, its abuse of the supernatural, its undoubted offences against order and proportion, scandalised him only a little less than they would have scandalised Voltaire and did scandalise the later Voltairians. Jeffrey was perfectly prepared to be Romantic up to a certain point,—the point which he had himself reached in his early course of independent reading and criticism. He was even a little inclined to sympathise with the Reverend Mr Bowles on the great question whether Pope was a poet; and, as I have said, he uses, about the older English literature, phrases which might almost satisfy a fanatic of the school of Hazlitt or of Lamb. He is, if anything, rather too severe on French as compared with English drama. Yet, when he comes to his own contemporaries, and sometimes even in reference to earlier writers, we find him slipping into those purely arbitrary severities of condemnation, those capricious stigmatisings of this as improper, and that as vulgar, and the other as unbecoming, which are the characteristics of the pseudo-correct and pseudo-classical school of criticism. He was a great admirer of Cowper, and yet he is shocked by Cowper's use, in his translation of Homer, of the phrases, "to entreat Achilles to a calm" (evidently he had forgotten Shakespeare's "pursue him and entreat him to a peace"), "this wrangler here," "like a fellow of no worth." He was certainly not likely to be unjust to Charles James Fox. So he is unhappy, rather than contemptuous, over such excellent phrases as "swearing away the lives," "crying injustice," "fond of ill-treating." These appear to Mr Aristarchus Jeffrey too "homely and familiar," too "low and vapid"; while a harmless and rather agreeable Shakespearian parallel of Fox's seems to him downright impropriety. The fun of the thing is that the passage turns on the well-known misuse of "flat burglary"; and if Jeffrey had had a little more sense of humour (his deficiency in which, for all his keen wit, is another Gallic note in him), he must have seen that the words were ludicrously applicable to his own condemnation and his own frame of mind. These settings-up of a wholly arbitrary canon of mere taste, these

excommunicatings of such and such a thing as "low" and "improper," without assigned or assignable reason, are eminently Gallic. They may be found not merely in the older school before 1830, but in almost all French critics up to the present day: there is perhaps not one, with the single exception of Sainte-Beuve, who is habitually free from them. The critic may be quite unable to say why *tarte à la crème* is such a shocking expression, or even to produce any important authority for the shockingness of it. But he is quite certain that it is shocking. Jeffrey is but too much given to protesting against *tarte à la crème;* and the reasons for his error are almost exactly the same as in the case of the usual Frenchman; that is to say, a very just and wholesome preference for order, proportion, literary orthodoxy, freedom from will-worship and eccentric divagations, unfortunately distorted by a certain absence of catholicity, by a tendency to regard novelty as bad, merely because it is novelty, and by a curious reluctance, as Lamb has it of another great man of the same generation, to go shares with any newcomer in literary commerce.

But when these reservations have been made, when his standpoint has been clearly discovered and marked out, and when some little tricks, such as the affectation of delivering judgments without appeal, which is still kept up by a few, though very few, reviewers, have been further allowed for, Jeffrey is a most admirable essayist and critic. As an essayist, a writer of *causeries,* I do not think he has been surpassed among Englishmen in the art of interweaving quotation, abstract, and comment. The best proof of his felicity in this respect is that in almost all the books which he has reviewed (and he has reviewed many of the most interesting books in literature) the passages and traits, the anecdotes and phrases, which have made most mark in the general memory, and which are often remembered with very indistinct consciousness of their origin, are to be found in his reviews. Sometimes the very perfection of his skill in this respect makes it rather difficult to know where he is abstracting or paraphrasing, and where he is speaking outright and for himself; but that is a very small fault. Yet his merits as an essayist, though considerable, are not to be compared, even to the extent to which Hazlitt's are to be compared, with his merits as a critic, and especially as a literary critic. It would be interesting to criticise his political criticism; but it is always best to keep politics out where it can be managed. Besides, Jeffrey as a political critic is a subject of almost exclusively historical interest, while as a literary critic he is important at this very day, and perhaps more important than he was in his own. For the spirit of merely æsthetic criticism, which was in his day only in its infancy, has long been full grown and rampant; so that, good work as it has done in its time, it decidedly needs chastening by an admixture of the dogmatic criticism, which at least tries to keep its impressions together and in order, and to connect them into some coherent doctrine and creed.

Of this dogmatic criticism Jeffrey, with all his shortcomings, is perhaps the very best example that we have in English. He had addressed himself more directly and theoretically to literary criticism than Lockhart. Prejudiced as he often was, he was not affected by the wild gusts of personal and political passion which frequently blew Hazlitt a thousand miles off the course of true criticism. He keeps his eye on the object, which De Quincey seldom does. He is not affected by that desire to preach on certain pet subjects which affects the admirable critical faculty of Carlyle. He never blusters and splashes at random like Wilson. And he never indulges in the mannered and rather superfluous graces which marred, to some tastes, the work of his successor in critical authority, if there has been any such, the author of *Essays in Criticism*.

Let us, as we just now looked through Jeffrey's work to pick out the less favourable characteristics which distinguish his position, look through it again to see those qualities which he shares, but in greater measure than most, with all good critics. The literary essay which stands first in his collected works is on Madame de Staël. Now that good lady, of whom some judges in these days do not think very much, was a kind of goddess on earth in literature, however much she might bore them in life, to the English Whig party in general; while Jeffrey's French tastes must have made her, or at least her books, specially attractive to him. Accordingly he has written a great deal about her, no less than three essays appearing in the collected works. Writing at least partly in her lifetime and under the influences just glanced at, he is of course profuse in compliments. But it is very amusing and highly instructive to observe how, in the intervals of these compliments, he contrives to take the good Corinne to pieces, to smash up her ingenious Perfectibilism, and to put in order her rather rash literary judgments. It is in connection also with her, that he gives one of the best of not a few general sketches of the history of literature which his work contains. Of course there are here, as always, isolated expressions as to which, however much we admit that Jeffrey was a clever man, we cannot agree with Jeffrey. He thinks Aristophanes "coarse" and "vulgar" while (though nobody of course can deny the coarseness) Aristophanes and vulgarity are certainly many miles asunder. We may protest against the chronological, even more than against the critical, blunder which couples Cowley and Donne, putting Donne, moreover, who wrote long before Cowley was born, and differs from him in genius almost as the author of the *Iliad* does from the author of the *Henriade*, second. But hardly anything in English criticism is better than Jeffrey's discussion of the general French imputation of "want of taste and politeness" to English and German writers, especially English. It is a very general, and a very mistaken, notion that the Romantic movement in France has done away with this imputation to a great extent. On the contrary, though it has long been a kind of fashion in France to admire Shakespeare, and though since the labours of MM. Taine and Montégut, the study of English literature generally has grown and flourished, it is, I believe, the very rarest thing to find a Frenchman who, in his heart of hearts, does not cling to the old "pearls in the dung-heap" idea, not merely in reference to Shakespeare, but to English writers, and especially English humorists, generally. Nothing can be more admirable than Jeffrey's comments on this matter. They are especially admirable because they are not made from the point of view of a *Romantique à tous crins;* because, as has been already pointed out, he himself is largely penetrated by the very preference for order and proportion which is at the bottom of the

French mistake; and because he is, therefore, arguing in a tongue understood of those whom he censures. Another essay which may be read with especial advantage is that on Scott's edition of Swift. Here, again, there was a kind of test subject, and perhaps Jeffrey does not come quite scatheless out of the trial: to me, at any rate, his account of Swift's political and moral conduct and character seems both uncritical and unfair. But here, too, the value of his literary criticism shows itself. He might very easily have been tempted to extend his injustice from the writer to the writings, especially since, as has been elsewhere shown, he was by no means a fanatical admirer of the Augustan age, and thought the serious style of Addison and Swift tame and poor. It is possible of course, here also, to find things that seem to be errors, both in the general sketch which Jeffrey, according to his custom, prefixes, and in the particular remarks on Swift himself. For instance, to deny fancy to the author of the *Tale of a Tub,* of *Gulliver,* and of the *Polite Conversation,* is very odd indeed. But there are few instances of a greater triumph of sound literary judgment over political and personal prejudice than Jeffrey's description, not merely of the great works just mentioned (it is curious, and illustrates his defective appreciation of humour, that he likes the greatest least, and is positively unjust to the *Tale of a Tub*), but also of those wonderful pamphlets, articles, lampoons, skits (libels if any one likes), which proved too strong for the generalship of Marlborough and the administrative talents of Godolphin; and which are perhaps the only literary works that ever really changed, for a not inconsiderable period, the government of England. "Considered," he says, "with a view to the purposes for which they were intended, they have probably never been equalled in any period of the world." They certainly have not; but to find a Whig, and a Whig writing in the very moment of Tory triumph after Waterloo, ready to admit the fact, is not a trivial thing. Another excellent example of Jeffrey's strength, by no means unmixed with examples of his weakness, is to be found in his essays on Cowper. I have already given some of the weakness: the strength is to be found in his general description of Cowper's revolt, thought so daring at the time, now so apparently moderate, against poetic diction. These instances are to be found under miscellaneous sections, biographical, historical, and so forth; but the reader will naturally turn to the considerable divisions headed Poetry and Fiction. Here are the chief rocks of offence already indicated, and here also are many excellent things which deserve reading. Here is the remarkable essay, quoted above, on Campbell's *Specimens.* Here is the criticism of Weber's edition of Ford, and another of those critical surveys of the course of English literature which Jeffrey was so fond of doing, and which he did so well, together with some remarks on the magnificently spendthrift style of our Elizabethan dramatists which would deserve almost the first place in an anthology of his critical beauties. The paper on Hazlitt's *Characters of Shakespeare* (Hazlitt was an *Edinburgh* reviewer, and his biographer, not Jeffrey's, has chronicled a remarkable piece of generosity on Jeffrey's part towards his wayward contributor) is a little defaced by a patronising spirit, not, indeed, of that memorably mistaken kind which induced the famous and unlucky sentence to Macvey Napier about Carlyle, but something in the spirit of the schoolmaster who observes, "See this clever boy of mine, and only think how much better I could do it myself." Yet it contains some admirable passages on Shakespeare, if not on Hazlitt; and it would be impossible to deny that its hinted condemnation of Hazlitt's "desultory and capricious acuteness" is just enough. On the other hand, how significant is it of Jeffrey's own limitations that he should protest against Hazlitt's sympathy with such "conceits and puerilities" as the immortal and unmatchable

> Take him and cut him out in little stars,

with the rest of the passage. But there you have the French spirit. I do not believe that there ever was a Frenchman since the seventeenth century (unless perchance it was Gérard de Nerval, and he was not quite sane), who could put his hand on his heart and deny that the little stars seemed to him puerile and conceited.

Jeffrey's dealings with Byron (I do not now speak of the article on *Hours of Idleness,* which was simply a just rebuke of really puerile and conceited rubbish) are not, to me, very satisfactory. The critic seems, in the rather numerous articles which he has devoted to the "noble Poet," as they used to call him, to have felt his genius unduly rebuked by that of his subject. He spends a great deal, and surely an unnecessarily great deal, of time in solemnly, and no doubt quite sincerely, rebuking Byron's morality; and in doing so he is sometimes almost absurd. He calls him "not more obscene perhaps than Dryden or Prior," which is simply ludicrous, because it is very rare that this particular word can be applied to Byron at all, while even the staunchest champion must admit that it applies to glorious John and to dear Mat Prior. He helps, unconsciously no doubt, to spread the very contagion which he denounces, by talking about Byron's demoniacal power, going so far as actually to contrast *Manfred* with Marlowe to the advantage of the former. And he is so completely overcome by what he calls the "dreadful tone of sincerity" of this "puissant spirit," that he never seems to have had leisure or courage to apply the critical tests and solvents of which few men have had a greater command. Had he done so, it is impossible not to believe that, whether he did or did not pronounce Byron's sentiment to be as theatrical, as vulgar, and as false as it seems to some later critics, he would at any rate have substituted for his edifying but rather irrelevant moral denunciations some exposure of those gross faults in style and metre, in phrase and form, which now disgust us.

There are many essays remaining on which I should like to comment if there were room enough. But I have only space for a few more general remarks on his general characteristics, and especially those which, as Sainte-Beuve said to the altered Jeffrey of our altered days, are "important to us." Let me repeat then that the peculiar value of Jeffrey is not, as is that of Coleridge, of Hazlitt, or of Lamb, in very subtle, very profound, or very original views of his subjects. He is neither a critical Columbus nor a critical Socrates; he neither opens up undiscovered countries, nor provokes and stimulates to the discovery of them. His strength lies in the combination of a fairly wide range of sympathy with an extraordinary shrewdness and

good sense in applying that sympathy. Tested for range alone, or for subtlety alone, he will frequently be found wanting; but he almost invariably catches up those who have thus outstripped him, when the subject of the trial is shifted to soundness of estimate, intelligent connection of view, and absence of eccentricity. And it must be again and again repeated that Jeffrey is by no means justly chargeable with the Dryasdust failings so often attributed to academic criticism. They said that on the actual Bench he worried counsel a little too much, but that his decisions were almost invariably sound. Not quite so much perhaps can be said for his other exercise of the judicial function. But however much he may sometimes seem to carp and complain, however much we may sometimes wish for a little more equity and a little less law, it is astonishing how weighty Jeffrey's critical judgments are after three-quarters of a century which has seen so many seeming heavy things grow light. There may be much that he does not see; there may be some things which he is physically unable to see; but what he does see, he sees with a clearness, and co-ordinates in its bearings on other things seen with a precision, which are hardly to be matched among the fluctuating and diverse race of critics. (pp. 90-105)

> *George Saintsbury, "Jeffrey," in his* The Collected Essays and Papers of George Saintsbury, 1875-1920, Vol. I, *1923. Reprint by Johnson Reprint Corporation, 1969, pp. 79-105.*

Lewis E. Gates   (essay date 1899)

[*In the following excerpt, Gates examines Jeffrey's objections to the Romantic movement in English literature, proposing that this negative reaction was chiefly responsible for the decline in his popularity as a critic.*]

How has it happened that Jeffrey's lustre, once so brilliant, has paled in our day into that of a fifth-rate luminary? Was his earlier reputation wholly undeserved? Or is the "dumb forgetfulness" that has overtaken him a real case of literary injustice? Probably Jeffrey is now oftenest remembered for his unluckily haughty reprimand to Wordsworth, "This will never do!"—a sentence which is popularly taken to be an incontestable proof of critical incapacity. Yet as regards the artistic worth of the *Excursion,* the poem against which Jeffrey was protesting, judges are at present nearer in agreement with Jeffrey than with Wordsworth. Ought not Jeffrey, the critic, then, to benefit somewhat from the latter-day reaction against overweening Romanticism?

Doubtless, Jeffrey's fate is in part merely an illustration of the transiency of critical fame. Jeffrey, like Rymer and John Dennis, has gone the deciduous way of all writers of literature about literature, save the few who have been actually themselves, in their prose, creators of beauty. Yet probably there is also something exceptional in Jeffrey's case,—in his earlier complete ascendency and in the later sorry disinheriting that has overtaken him. Jeffrey's reputation was really a composite affair, due fully as much to the timely-happy establishment of the *Edinburgh Review* as to his own personal cleverness, great as that was. On

Jeffrey, the editor, was reflected all the shining success of the first brilliant English *Review.* To understand, then, the waxing and the waning of Jeffrey's literary reputation, a somewhat careful analysis will be needed not simply of his critical genius, but also of the methods for making that genius effective which fortune offered him and his own keen practical instincts worked out successfully. As for his individual worth as a critic, the truth will be found to lie, as so often happens, about midway between the eulogists and the cavillers. Judged even by present standards, Jeffrey was a notably effective critic; he made blunders not a few, but he was acute, entertaining, and suggestive, even when he went astray; he excelled in rapid analysis, apt illustration, and audacious satire. (pp. 4-5)

A rapid and pungent style and great adroitness and attractiveness in exposition were doubtless largely responsible for Jeffrey's constant success with his public. But, in addition to these formal excellences, Jeffrey was remarkably well equipped and well trained for the part of a universal genius. Instinct had been beforehand with him and led him to prepare himself during a good many years of faithful study for just the part he was to play. When he had to choose a profession he decided for the bar, and he was called as a barrister in 1796. But both before this decision and during his actual legal studies, he read widely and systematically by himself in general literature, political theory, history, and philosophy; and during all this patient, private reading, at Glasgow University, at Edinburgh, and afterwards at Oxford, he was busy, with canny Scotch diligence, at note-books, in which facts and ideas and theorizings were recorded and worked out. His mind was conspicuously vivacious and alert,—swift to catch up and make its own new knowledge, whether about books or life. This keenness of intellectual scent was always characteristic of him. Even Matthew Arnold has conceded to him one trait of the ideal critic—*curiosity.* A very different commentator, Mrs. Carlyle, makes special mention, after a call from him, of his "dark, penetrating" eyes, that "had been taking note of most things in God's universe."

Besides the results of this patient self-discipline, and of this wide ranging and swiftly appropriating intellectual interest, Jeffrey had, in a very high degree, the barrister's power of seizing, comprehending, and controlling, quickly and surely, a vast mass of new facts. He could "get up" an unfamiliar subject with unsurpassable readiness and completeness. His mastery of his subject in a review-article seems often like the successful barrister's knowledge of his brief: he knows whatever he needs to know to carry the matter in hand triumphantly through.

His way of unfolding a subject is always deft and delightful to follow. He had a sure expository instinct. Point by point, the most complex problem takes on, under his treatment, at least a specious simplicity, and the most abstract theorem, alluring familiarity, and definiteness. He is generous with illustrations and examples and mischievous in giving them a satirical turn. Despite his Scotch bias towards theorizing, he knows and "hugs" his facts, and his discussions always keep close to experience.

His breadth of view is remarkable, if his work be compared with that of eighteenth-century critics. Whatever the book or question under discussion, Jeffrey lifts it into the region of general principles, and is not content with formal judgments of literary worth or with random comments on special points. He is really bent on setting up "a free play of ideas" over the literature and the modes of life that he criticises, and on orienting his readers as regards not simply the special work under discussion, but the whole field of art or of study to which it belongs. That his theories, at least in literary matters, were not always searching or profound, that they will not, in sweep and thoroughness, bear comparison with those, for example, of Coleridge, the great system-weaver of the Romanticists, is undoubtedly true. Yet even in literary theory Jeffrey, as will be presently shown, hit on some notable truths; he partially comprehended and applied the historical method for the study of literature; he worked out with Alison an interpretation of beauty, which, though false in its emphasis and distorted, recognized and illustrated with great acuteness one highly important and comparatively neglected source of æsthetic emotion; and, despite much mistaken ridicule of Romantic poetry and much insensibility to its quintessential power and charm, he showed his critical insight in his protests against certain radical defects alike in the ethical and in the æsthetic theory of the Romanticists,—defects which, as Jeffrey contended and as modern criticism admits, do much to invalidate Romantic poetry, both as a criticism of life and as a permanently invigorating imaginative stimulus. But even apart from the absolute correctness or finality of Jeffrey's theorizing, his practice of raising criticism into the region of general principles and of examining the material worth of books even more searchingly than their barely formal qualities, was a renovating change in criticism, and at once gave new consideration and dignity to the work of the critic. Mind was at any rate fermenting in whatever Jeffrey wrote, and for the most part the writing of earlier reviewers had been a barren waste of words.

Finally, Jeffrey's style startled and challenged and terrified and amused, and through its briskness and audacity, its swift sparkle and gay bravado, its satire and banter, its impetuous fulness and unfailing wealth of fact and illustration fairly captivated a public that was used to the humdrum, conventional speech of penny-a-lining critics. There is a fine vein of mischief in Jeffrey that leads continually to very grateful ridicule of pedantry, dulness, and all kinds of absurdity. Even the devoutest Wordsworthian will, if he be not an ingrained prig, relish Jeffrey's raillery at the expense of Wordsworth's occasional pompous ineptitude. And if Jeffrey's vivacity still seems amusing, how much more irresistible must his style have seemed before the days of Hazlitt and Lamb and Macaulay and Carlyle. His dash and wit and audacity were new in literary criticism, and for the time being seemed to the public almost more than mortal.

Whether or no all these qualities of Jeffrey's genius and style are those of the ideal literary critic, they were fitted to gain him success and renown as a brilliant, argumentative writer on literary topics. And, in point of fact, this is what Jeffrey really was; he was a typically well equipped and skilful middleman of ideas. He found an increasingly large Liberal or Whig public anxious to have its beliefs expressed plausibly, its feelings justified, and its taste made clear to itself and gently improved. The Whig "sheep looked up," and Jeffrey fed them. He did much the same work in general literary, social, and political theory that Macaulay did later in history. Macaulay's historical essays, also published in the *Edinburgh Review,* were, as Cotter Morison has pointed out, "great historical cartoons," specially adapted for the popularization of history, and specially suited to the knowledge and aspirations of an intelligent middle-class public. Jeffrey's essays in literature had much this same character and value. They interpreted the freshest, most vital thought of the time, so far as possible in harmony with Whig formulas, and judged it by Whig standards; they made happily articulate Whig prejudices on all subjects, from the French Revolution to Wordsworth's peasant poetry. By their masterly exposition, their incisive argument, and their wit, they entertained even those whom they exasperated. Their success was prompt and unexampled.

It has already been hinted that the qualities of Jeffrey's genius and style, great as may have been their value for the work he accomplished, are not, when judged from the modern point of view, altogether those of the ideal literary critic. This is particularly true if appreciation be included as a vital part of the critic's task. Jeffrey rarely *appreciates* a piece of literature, interprets it imaginatively, lends himself to its peculiar charm, and expresses this charm through sympathetic symbolism. His readiness and his plausibility are not the only points in which Jeffrey the critic suggests Jeffrey the advocate. He has the defects as well as the merits of the lawyer in literature. He is always for or against his author; he is always making points. The intellectual interest preponderates in his critical work, and his discussions often seem, particularly to a reader of modern impressionistic criticism, hard, unsympathetic, searchingly analytical, repellingly abstract and systematic. He is always on the watch; he never lends himself confidingly to his author and takes passively and gratefully the mood and the images his author suggests. He never loiters or dreams. He is full of business and bustle, and perpetually distracts his readers with his sense of the need of making definite progress. He is one of those responsible folk who believe that

> Nothing of itself will come
> But we must still be seeking.

For delicate and subtle appreciation, then, of the best modern type it is useless to look in Jeffrey's essays.

Of course, historically, such criticism could hardly have been expected in 1803. The critical tradition that Jeffrey fell heir to was that of the dogmatists,—the tradition that came down from Ascham, the pedagogue, through the hands of the would-be autocrats, Rymer and Dennis, to Dr. Johnson. The theories of the dogmatists suffered many changes, but remained nevertheless true to one fundamental principle: the critic was to be accepted as an infallible judge in literature because of his familiarity with certain models or certain abstract rules, the imitation or the observance of which was essential to good art. The dogmatic critic deemed himself lord of literature by a kind of divine right. Ascham believed in the plenary artistic inspiration

of the Greek and Latin classics, and posed as the authentic interpreter of the sacred literary word. The pseudo-classical critics, Rymer and Dennis, based themselves also partly on authority, but even more upon reason; they pretended to rule by the divine right of pure logic. Their implicit postulate might be likened to Hobbes's theory in politics; they substantially held that the strongest must keep order in the commonwealth, and that in the literary commonwealth this duty fell to the intellectually strongest. Accordingly, these critics administered justice magisterially in accordance with a strict code of laws; they had laws for the epic poet, laws for the writer of comedy, laws for the satirist, laws for the writer of tragedy; the author of every new piece of literature was called up to the bar and reprimanded for the least illegality. In short, the dogmatic critic regarded himself and was generally regarded as able to apply absolute tests of merit to all literary work, and as the final authority on all doubtful matters of taste.

Now, Jeffrey was the inheritor of this tradition in criticism, and naturally adopted at times its tyrannical tone and manner towards public and authors. Yet, following his temperamental fondness for compromises, for middle parties and mediating measures, Jeffrey never tried formally to defend this old doctrine or represented himself as an absolute lawgiver in literature. Nowhere does he lay down a complete set of principles, like the rules of Bossu for epic poetry, or those of Rapin for the drama, by which excellence in any form of literature may be absolutely tested. Such a high-and-dry Tory theory of criticism does not suggest itself to Jeffrey as tenable. He is a Whig in taste as in politics, and desires in both spheres the supremacy of a chosen aristocracy. In his essay on Scott's *Lady of the Lake* he declares the standard of literary excellence to reside in "the taste of a few . . . persons, eminently qualified, by natural sensibility and long experience and reflection, to perceive all beauties that really exist, as well as to settle the relative value and importance of all the different sorts of beauty." Jeffrey regards himself as one of the choicest spirits of this chosen aristocracy, and it is as the exponent of the best current opinion that he speaks on all questions of taste.

It follows that, when Jeffrey is dealing with purely literary questions, he is less argumentative than at other times, and that what has been said of his viewing every subject in the light of general principles is least applicable to his dogmatic essays on literature. When, for example, he attacks *Wilhelm Meister* or the *Excursion,* he does so simply and frankly in terms of his temperament. Wordsworth's mysticism baffles him, and he condemns it; Goethe's sordid realism and sentiment offend his man-of-the-world taste and he anathematizes them. His custom in such hostile criticisms is to let his own taste masquerade as that of "the judicious observer" or "the modern public." His faith in his own personal equation is unquestioning and devout. Whatever fails to fall in with his bias is a fair mark for his bitterest invective. Goethe's *Wilhelm Meister,* for example, is "sheer nonsense," "ludicrously unnatural," full of "pure childishness or mere folly," "vulgar and obscure," full of "absurdities and affectations." These terms are, for the most part, mere circumlocutions for Jeffrey's dislike, mere roundabout ways of saying that the book is not to his taste. As for coming to an understanding with author or reader about the ends of prose fiction or the best methods of reaching those ends, Jeffrey never thinks of such an attempt. He simply takes up various passages and declares he does not comprehend them, or does not fancy the subjects they treat of, or does not like the author's ideas or methods. He gives no reasons for his likes or dislikes, but is content to express them emphatically and picturesquely. This is, of course, dogmatism pure and simple, and a dogmatism, too, more irritating than the dogmatism that argues, for it seems more arbitrary and more challenging. Of this tone and method, Coleridge complains in the twenty-first chapter of his *Biographia Literaria,* when, in commenting on current critical literature, he protests against "the substitution of assertion for argument" and against "the frequency of arbitrary and sometimes petulant verdicts."

But, irritating as is this pragmatic, unreasoning dogmatism, it is nevertheless plainly a step forward from the view that makes the critic absolute lawgiver in art. As the Whig position in politics is midway between absolute monarchy and democracy, so what we may term the Whig compromise in criticism stands midway between the tyranny of earlier critics and our modern freedom. The mere recognition of the fact that the critic speaks with authority only as representing a *coterie,* only as interpreting public opinion, is plainly a change for the better. The critic no longer regards himself as by divine right lord alike of public and authors; he no longer measures literary success solely by changeless, abstract formulas of excellence; he admits more or less explicitly that the taste of living readers, not rules drawn from the works of dead writers, must decide what in literature is good or bad. He still, to be sure, limits arbitrarily the circle whose taste he regards as a valid test; but it is plain that a new principle has implicitly been accepted, and that the way is opened for the development and recognition of all kinds of beauty and power the public may require.

Jeffrey himself, however, seems never to have suspected the conclusions that might legitimately be drawn from the ideas that he was helping to make current. He seems to have had no qualm of doubt touching his right to dogmatize on the merits and defects of art as violently as a critic of the older school. In theory, he held that all artistic excellence is relative; but in practice, he never let this doctrine mitigate the severity of his judgments. He asserts in his review of *Alison on Taste* that "what a man feels distinctly to be beautiful, *is beautiful* to him"; and that so far as the individual is concerned all pleasure in art is equally real and justifiable. Yet this doctrine seems never to have paralyzed in the least his faith in the superior worth of his own kind of pleasure; and he upbraids Wordsworth and Coleridge just as indignantly for not ministering to that pleasure, as if he had some abstract standard of poetic excellence, of which he could prove they fell short.

When we try to define Jeffrey's taste and to determine just what he liked and disliked in literature, we find an odd combination of sympathies and antipathies. Mr. Leslie Stephen has spoken of him as in politics an eighteenth-century survival [see excerpt dated 1878]; but this formula, apt as it is for his politics, scarcely applies to his taste in literature. The typical eighteenth-century man of letters was a pseudo-classicist; and beyond the pseudo-classical point of view Jeffrey had passed, just as certainly as he had never reached the Romantic point of view. Of Pope, for example, he says: he is "much the best we think of the classical Continental school; but he is not to be compared with the masters—nor with the pupils—of that Old English one from which there had been so lamentable an apostasy." Addison he condemns for his "extreme caution, timidity, and flatness," and he declares that "the narrowness of his range in poetical sentiment and diction, and the utter want either of passion or of brilliancy, render it difficult to believe that he was born under the same sun with Shakespeare." These opinions are proof patent of Jeffrey's contempt for pseudo-classicism. Then, too, Jeffrey is, as he himself boasts, almost superstitious in his reverence for Shakespeare. More significant still is his admiration for other Elizabethan dramatists, like Beaumont, Fletcher, Ford, and Webster. "Of the old English dramatists," he assures us in his essay on Ford, "it may be said, in general, that they are more poetical, and more original in their diction, than the dramatists of any other age or country. Their scenes abound more in varied images, and gratuitous excursions of fancy. Their illustrations and figures of speech are more borrowed from rural life, and from the simple occupations or universal feelings of mankind. They are not confined to a certain range of dignified expressions, nor restricted to a particular assortment of imagery, beyond which it is not lawful to look for embellishments." Finally, he even commends Coleridge's great favourite, Jeremy Taylor, as enthusiastically as Coleridge himself could do: "There is in any one of the prose folios of Jeremy Taylor," he asserts, "more fine fancy and original imagery—more brilliant conceptions and glowing expressions—more new figures, and new applications of old figures—more, in short, of the body and the soul of poetry, than in all the odes and the epics that have since been produced in Europe."

Such judgments as these mark Jeffrey as, at any rate, not an eighteenth-century survival; they must be duly borne in mind when a formula is being sought for his literary taste. Fully as significant, though in a different way, is the series of essays on the poet Crabbe. If the praise of the Elizabethans seems to argue an almost Romantic bias in Jeffrey and to suggest that after all his tastes are very like those of Wordsworth and Coleridge, the Crabbe essays at once reveal his antipathy to the men of the new age and show how far he is from even being willing to allow its prophets to prophesy in peace and obscurity.

Throughout his praise of Crabbe, Jeffrey is by implication condemning Wordsworth; nor does he confine himself to this roundabout method of attacking Romanticism. In the very first essay on Crabbe (1807), he turns aside from his subject to ridicule by name, "the Wordsworths, and the Southeys, and Coleridges, and all that ambitious fraternity," and contrasts at great length Crabbe's sanity with Wordsworth's mysticism. "Mr. Crabbe exhibits the common people of England pretty much as they are"; whereas "Mr. Wordsworth and his associates . . . introduce us to beings whose existence was not previously suspected by the acutest observers of nature; and excite an interest for them—where they do excite any interest—more by an eloquent and refined analysis of their own capricious feelings, than by any obvious or intelligible ground of sympathy in their situation." With Crabbe, Jeffrey feels he is on solid ground, dealing with a man who sees life clearly and sensibly, as he himself sees it; and in his enthusiastic praise of the minute fidelity of Crabbe, of his uncompromising truth and realism, and of his freedom from all meretricious effects, from affectation, and from absurd mysticism, we have at once the measure of Jeffrey's poetic sensibility and the sure evidence of his inability to sympathize genuinely with "the Lakers."

Of course, for the classic passages expressing his impatience of the new movement, we must go to the essays on Wordsworth's *Excursion* and *White Doe.* Jeffrey's objections to the Lakers fall under four heads: First, the new poets are nonsensically mystical; secondly, they falsify life by showing it through a distorting medium of personal emotion, *i.e.* they are misleadingly subjective; thirdly, they are guilty of grotesque bad taste in their democratic realism; fourthly, they are pedantically earnest and serious in their treatment of art, and inexcusably pretentious in their proclamation of a new gospel of life. Mysticism, intense individuality of feeling, naturalism, and "high seriousness,"—these were the qualities that in the new art particularly exasperated Jeffrey; and inasmuch as these were the very qualities to which, in the eyes of its devotees, the new art owed its special potency, the division between Jeffrey and the Romanticists was sufficiently deep and irreconcilable.

Wordsworth's transcendentalism, his intense spiritual consciousness, his inveterate fashion of apprehending all nature as instinct with spiritual force and of converting "this whole Of suns and worlds and men" and "all that it inherits" into a series of splendid imaginative symbols of moral and spiritual truth,—these qualities of Wordsworth's genius were for his admirers among his most characteristic sources of power, and tended to place him as an imaginative interpreter of life far above those Elizabethan writers whom Jeffrey, too, in opposition to the eighteenth century, pretended to reverence. But these were just the qualities in Wordsworth's genius that seemed to Jeffrey most reprehensible. After quoting a typical passage where Wordsworth's transcendentalism finds free utterance, Jeffrey exclaims: "This is a fair sample of that rapturous mysticism which eludes all comprehension, and fills the despairing reader with painful giddiness and terror." Jeffrey's woe is by no means feigned. We cannot doubt that his whole mental life was perturbed by such of Wordsworth's poems as the great *Ode,* and that it was an act of self-preservation on his part to burst into indignant ridicule and violent protest. To find a man of Wordsworth's age and literary experience deliberately penning such bewildering stanzas and expressing such unintelligible emotions, shook for the moment Jeffrey's faith in his own little, well-ordered universe, and then, as he recovered from his earthquake, escaped from its vapours, and felt secure once more in the clear, every-day light of common sense, led him into fierce invective against the cause of his momentary panic.

Hardly less impatient is Jeffrey of Wordsworth's subjectivity than of his mysticism. Why cannot Wordsworth feel about life as other people feel about it, as any well-bred, cultivated man of the world feels about it? When such a man sees a poor old peasant gathering leeches in a pool, he pulls out his purse, gives him a shilling, and walks on, speculating about the state of the poor law; Wordsworth, on the contrary, bursts into a strange fit of raving about Chatterton and Burns, and "mighty poets in their misery dead," and then in some mysterious fashion converts the peasant's stolidity into a defence against these gloomy thoughts. This way of treating the peasant seems to Jeffrey utterly unjustifiable, both because of its grotesque mysticism, and because it thrusts a personal *motif* discourteously into the face of the public and falsifies ludicrously the peasant's character and life. Wordsworth has no right, Jeffrey insists, to treat the peasant merely as the symbol of his own peculiar mood. Here, as in his protest against Wordsworth's mysticism, Jeffrey pleads for common sense and the commonplace; he is the type of what Lamb calls "the Caledonian intellect," which rejects scornfully ideas that cannot be adequately expressed in good plain terms, and grasped "by twelve men on a jury."

Crabbe's superiority to the Lakers lies for Jeffrey chiefly in the fact that he has no idiosyncrasies, though he has many mannerisms; he expresses no new theories and no peculiar emotions in his portrayal of common life. Hence his choice of vulgar subjects is endurable—even highly commendable. His peasants are the well-known peasants of every-day England, with whose hard lot it behoves an enlightened Whig to sympathize—from a distance. But a realism that, like Wordsworth's, professes to find in these poor peasants the deepest spiritual insight and the purest springs of moral life, is simply for Jeffrey grotesque in its maladroitness and confusion of values. Sydney Smith used to say, "If I am doomed to be a slave at all, I would rather be the slave of a king than a cobbler." And this same prejudice against any topsy-turvy reassignment of values was largely responsible for Jeffrey's dislike of Wordsworth's peasants and of his treatment of common life. If peasants keep their places, as Crabbe's peasants do, they may perfectly well be brought into the precincts of poetry; but to exalt them into types of moral virtue and into heavenly messengers of divine truth, is to "make tyrants of cobblers." Jacobinism in art, as in politics, is to Jeffrey detestable.

In fact, all the pretensions of the new school to illustrate by its art a new gospel of life were intensely disagreeable to Jeffrey. As long as Romanticism seemed chiefly decorative, as in Scott or Keats, Jeffrey could tolerate it or even delight in it. But the moment it began, whether in Byron or Wordsworth, to take itself seriously, and to struggle to express new moral and spiritual ideals, Jeffrey protested. Just here lies the key to what some critics have found a rather perplexing problem,—the reasons for the varying degrees of Jeffrey's sympathy with the poets of his day. Let the poet remain a mere master of the revels, or a mere magician calling up by his incantations in verse a gorgeous phantasmagoria of sights and sounds for the delectation of idle readers, and Jeffrey will consent to admire him and will commend his fertility of invention, his wealth of imagination, his "rich lights of fancy," and "his flowers of poetry." Keats's luxuriant pictures of Greek life in *Endymion,* Jeffrey finds irresistible in the "intoxication of their sweetness" and in "the enchantments which they so lavishly present." Moore and Campbell, he regards as the most admirable of the Romanticists, and their works as the very best of the somewhat extravagant modern school. Writing in 1829, he arranges recent poets in the following order, according to the probable duration of their fame:

> The tuneful quartos of Southey are already little better than lumber:—and the rich melodies of Keats and Shelley,—and the fantastical emphasis of Wordsworth,—and the plebeian pathos of Crabbe, are melting fast from the field of our view. The novels of Scott have put out his poetry. Even the splendid strains of Moore are fading into distance and dimness . . . and the blazing star of Byron himself is receding from its place of pride. . . . The two who have the longest withstood this rapid withering of the laurel . . . are Rogers and Campbell; neither of them, it may be remarked, voluminous writers, and both distinguished rather for the fine taste and consummate elegance of their writings, than for that fiery passion, and disdainful vehemence, which seemed for a time to be so much more in favour with the public.

Now a glance at Jeffrey's list of poets makes it clear that those for whom he prophesies lasting fame are either pseudo-classicists or decorative Romanticists, and that those whose day he declares to be over are for the most part poets whose Romanticism was a vital principle. Rogers is, of course, a genuine representative of the pseudo-classical tradition, with all its devotion to form, its self-restraint, its poverty of imagination, and its distrust of passion. Moore, whom Jeffrey places late in his list of fading luminaries, and Campbell, whom he finds most nearly unchanging in lustre, are both in a way Romanticists; but they are alike in seeking chiefly for decorative effects and in not taking their art too seriously. So long, then, as the fire and the heat of Romanticism spent themselves merely in giving imaginative splendour to style, Jeffrey could tolerate the movement, and could even regard it with favour, as a return to that power and fervour and wild beauty that he had taught himself to admire in Elizabethan poetry. But the moment the new energy was suffered to penetrate life itself and to convert the conventional world of dead fact, through the vitalizing power of passion, into a genuinely new poetic material, then Jeffrey stood aghast at what seemed to him a return to chaos. Byron with his fiery bursts of selfish passion, Wordsworth with his steadily glowing consciousness of the infinite, and Shelley with his "white heat of transcendentalism," were all alike for Jeffrey portentously dangerous forces and unhealthy phenomena.

For the most part, in his attacks upon Romantic poetry, Jeffrey indulges in little philosophizing; he is content with wit, satire, epigram, and clever self-assertion. And yet, in the last analysis, there is a vital connection between his rejection of Romanticism and his abstract theorizings on beauty,—small pains as he has taken to bring out this obscure relationship. A complete account of his temperament and taste ought to show how the same instincts that led to his hostility to Wordsworth and Coleridge expressed themselves formally, and tried to justify themselves, through the theory of Beauty which he worked out with Alison's help.

According to Jeffrey's account of the matter, a beautiful object owes its beauty to its power to call up in the observer latent past experiences of pleasure and pain. These little fragments of past joy and sorrow gather closely round the object and blend in a kind of blurred halo of delight which we call beauty. Suppose that an observer looks out upon a luxuriant country landscape; the winding road calls back to him (though without his conscious recognition of the fact) leisurely afternoon drives; the green meadows suggest (again obscurely) past sympathy with shepherds and grazing flocks and rustic prosperity; the cottages surreptitiously wake memories of home joys and content about the hearthstone. And so the imagination garners out of the summer landscape a myriad evanescent associations with past life, which, too slight and swift to be detected separately by thought, nevertheless unite like the harmonics of a musical note to produce the peculiar character that we call beauty. This being the nature of beauty, it follows that every individual's past will limit and create for him his beauty in the present; his foregone pleasures and pains will alone make possible those echoes of intense feeling which in the present combine into the single chord of beauty. According to every man's past, then, is his present sense of beauty; and as no two men have the same past, no two men can have the same perceptions of beauty in the present.

Jeffrey accepts unhesitatingly the conclusions involved in this doctrine, and asserts that beauty is wholly relative; that whatever seems to a man beautiful is for him beautiful; and that no sensible debate is possible over the legitimacy of the beauty that a man's special temperament manufactures. So long as a man confines himself to *enjoying* beauty, he remains beyond criticism in the magic region of his own private experience. But the moment he offers himself as a creator or interpreter of beauty for others, he must take into account the scope and nature of common experience and try to appeal imaginatively to associations which are likely to be in the hearts of all. This is precisely, Jeffrey once or twice implies, what Romanticists like Wordsworth and Coleridge failed to do. They tried to impose on the public their own curiously whimsical associations of pleasure and pain; they were incredibly presumptuous in their belief that their own quaint, countryside blisses and sorrows and their own droll exaltations and despairs over peddlers and beggars and leech-gatherers must have universal value for mankind. Here for Jeffrey lay the wilful and colossal egotism of Romantic art; and once more we find him posing as the foe of idiosyncrasy and arbitrary whim, and as the representative of a cultivated aristocracy of intelligence and social experience and taste, who, after all, have something like a common fund of feelings and associations on which art can draw.

As for the actual worth of Jeffrey's theory of beauty, its fault lies in trying to stretch into a universal formula what is really only a partial explanation of the facts. The beauty that Jeffrey lays stress on—the kind of beauty that comes from the suggestiveness of objects—is duly recognized nowadays under the name of beauty of *expression.* The possible origin of beauty through association of ideas had not been thoroughly considered before the days of Jeffrey and Alison, and their work was therefore new and historically important. But beside beauty that comes from this source,—beside beauty of expression,—there are beauty of form and beauty of material; neither of these is recognized by Jeffrey as an independent variety, and examples of each he tries, with really heroic ingenuity, to reduce to beauty of expression. The beauty of a Greek temple is explained as depending solely on a swift, unconscious recognition of the stability, costliness, splendour, and antiquity of the structure. The beauty of special colours or of chords of music is derived, not at all from the intrinsic quality of the sensations,—the hue or the musical sound,—but wholly from subtle associations with past pleasure and pain. Thus Jeffrey's theory becomes distorted and misleading in spite of the truthfulness of much of his observation and the real subtlety and acuteness of many of his interpretations. The quintessential in art, the pleasure that art gives through pure form and the inexplicable ministry of sensation, Jeffrey is least sensitive to, and is continually looking askance at and trying to forget or to account for as merely disguised human sympathy.

CONTRIBUTIONS

TO THE

EDINBURGH REVIEW.

BY

FRANCIS JEFFREY,

NOW ONE OF THE JUDGES OF THE COURT OF SESSION IN SCOTLAND

FOUR VOLUMES.

COMPLETE IN ONE.

NEW YORK:
D. APPLETON AND COMPANY,
346 & 348 BROADWAY.
M.DCCC.LX.

Title page of the third edition of Contributions.

Besides the light it throws on Jeffrey's quarrel with Romanticism, his theory of beauty is of special significance because it emphasizes the genuineness and intensity of his ethical interest. All artistic pleasure is for Jeffrey merely human sympathy in masquerade—past love for one's fellows, delicately revived in the music of art. The only man, then, who can have a wide range of artistic pleasure is he who in the past has shared generously in the lives of his comrades. Holding this theory of art, Jeffrey in his literary criticism naturally laid great stress on the ethical qualities of books and authors. Accordingly, in the preface to his *Contributions to the Edinburgh Review,* Jeffrey claims special credit for his frequent use of the ethical point of view.

> If I might be permitted farther, to state, in what particular department, and generally, on account of what, I should most wish to claim a share of those merits, I should certainly say, that it was by having constantly endeavoured to combine Ethical precepts with Literary Criticism, and earnestly sought to impress my readers with a sense, both of the close connection between sound intellectual attainments and the higher elements of duty and enjoyment; and of the just and ultimate subordination of the former to the latter. The praise, in short, to which I aspire, and to merit which I am conscious that my efforts were most constantly directed, is, that I have, more uniformly and earnestly than any preceding critic, made the Moral tendencies of the works under consideration a leading subject of discussion.

This "proud claim," as Jeffrey calls it, seems amply justified when we compare Jeffrey's essays either with the critical essays in the earlier Reviews, or with the more formal and elaborate critical essays of the eighteenth century. Even Dr. Johnson with all his didacticism had little notion of extracting from a piece of literature the subtle spirit of good or of evil by which it draws men this way or that way in conduct. An obvious infringement of good morals in speech or in plot he was sure to condemn, and a formal inculcation of moral truth he was sure to recognize and approve. But neither in Johnson, nor anywhere else before Jeffrey, do we find a critic constantly attempting to detect and define the moral atmosphere that pervades the whole work of an author, and to determine the relation between this moral atmosphere and the author's personality as man and as artist. To have perceived the value of this ethical criticism, to have practised it skilfully, and to have fostered a taste for it, these are true claims to distinction; and Jeffrey's services in these directions have been too often forgotten. The greater breadth of view of later critics and their surer appreciation of ethical values should not be allowed to deprive Jeffrey of his honour as a pioneer in ethical criticism. (pp. 7-33)

Regarded, then, from a modern point of view, Jeffrey, as a literary critic, takes shape somewhat as follows: As an appreciator he is sadly to seek, owing largely to over-intellectualism and disputatiousness. As a dogmatic critic he is even yet thoroughly readable because of his dashing style, his deft and ready handling, his shrewd common sense, and his sincerity; he expressed brilliantly the tastes and antipathies of a large circle of cultivated people of considerable social distinction, who, while not peculiarly artistic or literary, read widely and intelligently, and felt keenly and delicately, though within a somewhat limited range. Even in his dogmatic criticism, however, his faults are obvious; his dogmatism is peremptory; his tone, often bitter; and his prejudices are as scarlet. On the other hand, for giving a strong ethical trend to literary criticism, he deserves all honour. His social sympathies were intense and alert; they fixed the character of his whole theory of beauty, and continually expressed themselves in his comments upon books and authors. Through his persistently ethical interpretations of literature, he really enlarged the borders of literary criticism. As for his historical criticism, it cannot be said to have much permanent value. Into the general theory on which the use of the historical method rests, Jeffrey shows considerable insight; but he was by nature and by training a dogmatist, not a scientific student of fact. Though his theorizings led him to believe speculatively in the relativity of beauty, and though he recognized abstractly that literature must vary from age to age as the time-spirit varies, yet he rarely let these convictions affect his tone or method in the treatment of literature; he is as round and intolerant in his blame of Addison or Pope as if he had never been within seeing distance of the historical point of view. In short, the disinterestedness of science was foreign to Jeffrey's nature; he was primarily and distinctively, not an investigator or interpreter, but a censor bent on praise or blame.

These very characteristics of his criticism, however, were of a kind to bring Jeffrey, in 1803, great glory. With some disguise until 1809, when the Tory *Quarterly Review* was founded, undisguisedly thereafter, Jeffrey was the great Whig champion in all that pertained to letters. From a partisan critic, audacious and brilliant dogmatism was just what was sure to win the widest hearing. Moreover, in accounting for Jeffrey's enormous popularity, the trashiness and insipidity of earlier review-writing must be kept in mind. Reviewing had been the pet occupation of Grub street; penny-a-liners had impressed upon criticism all their own unloveliness and feebleness; review articles seemed to issue from under-fed, torpid brains and anæmic bodies. Jeffrey's reviewing was the very incarnation of health, vigour, and prosperity.

Finally, Jeffrey profited in name and fame more than it is easy now to compute from the happy opportuneness of a new literary form, a literary form that was made possible through the establishment of the *Edinburgh Review.* This Review differed in many of its business arrangements and in its mode of publication from preceding Reviews; it was established in accordance with a new conception of the scope of review-writing, and of the relation of reviewers to the public. As the result of this new conception and these new relations, literary criticism, which had hitherto been merely more or less ingenious talk about technical matters, was transformed into the earnest and vigorous discussion of literature as the expression of all that was significant and absorbing in the life of the time. And as still further results of the new policy, reviewing and reviewers came into hitherto unknown honour; the *Edinburgh Review* was adored or was hated and feared throughout the length and breadth of the land, and Jeffrey was universally regarded as demonic in his versatility, brilliancy, penetration, and vigour. Much of Jeffrey's great prestige as a critic must be set down as due to his having long stood as the visible symbol of the success of the new style of reviewing. (pp. 39-41)

Jeffrey profited from the conspiracy of a great many fortunate circumstances, and for a series of years enjoyed, as dictator of the policy of the *Edinburgh Review,* a reputation as critic that was really far beyond what his intrinsic merit justified. Leigh Hunt and Lamb were much more delicate and imaginative appreciators of literature than Jeffrey; Hazlitt, despite his waywardness and arrogance, was a subtler and more stimulating literary interpreter. Coleridge was incomparably Jeffrey's superior in penetrating insight, in learning and scholarship, in philosophic scope, and in refinement and sureness of taste. Yet Jeffrey, by dint of his cleverness, versatility, brilliancy, readiness of resource, and, above all, because of his commanding position as the director of the new Whig *Review,* outstripped all these competitors and imposed himself on public opinion as the typically infallible critic of his day and generation. His personal charm, too, worked in his favour; his Whig following was enthusiastically loyal. Everything tended to increase, for the time being, his fame as a literary autocrat.

The later reaction, which has so nearly consigned Jeffrey to the region of unread authors, was in its turn extreme, and yet followed naturally. Wordsworth and Coleridge, whom Jeffrey had assailed persistently till he had become in the public mind the representative foe of Romanticism, had won their cause, and been received by wider and wider circles of the most cultivated and discerning readers as among the foremost poets of their age. Jeffrey, their archenemy, suffered correspondingly in public esteem. Time seemed to have proved him wrong in one of his most strenuously asserted prejudices. Moreover, this particular defeat was merely one special instance of the evil effect that far-reaching influences were having upon Jeffrey's reputation. His modes of conceiving life were being outgrown. His genial, man-of-the-world wisdom and somewhat narrow range of feeling seemed more and more unsatisfactory, as the public gradually made their own the deeper spiritual experience of idealistic poets, like Shelley, and of transcendental prose-writers, like Carlyle. Jeffrey's dry intellectuality and his shallow associational psychology seemed unequal to the vital problems in art and in ethics that the new age was canvassing. Moreover, his autocratic style and omniscient air had been caught up by all the quarterly Reviews, and no longer served to distinguish him; the methods and the tone of the *Edinburgh* were copied far and wide, and the critics of the new generation were quite a match for Jeffrey in gay, domineering assurance and in easy, swift omniscience. Jeffrey had trained many followers into his own likeness; or, at any rate, the methods and the tone that he had hit upon "survived" and had been universally received as fit.

Finally, Jeffrey's essays, even at their best, had many of the qualities of "occasional" writing, and too often seemed merely meant for the moment; the trail of the periodical was over them all. Their very rapidity, sparkle, and plausibility gave them an air of perishableness; they seemed clever and entertaining improvisations. Work of this sort could hardly hope to maintain itself permanently in public favour. Nor was the collection of his essays, that Jeffrey saw fit to publish in 1843, of a sort to make a stand against the general indifference that was clouding his fame. Two thousand pages of improvised comments on all manner of topics, from the *Memoirs of Baber* to Dugald Stewart's *Philosophical Essays,* could scarcely be expected to secure a fixed place for themselves in the affections of large masses of readers. A far smaller volume, that should have included only the essays, or portions of essays, that were best wrought in style, most vigorously thought out, and contained the most characteristic and final of Jeffrey's opinions, would have been more likely—except in so far as Jeffrey based his claims on his versatility—to have insured him permanent remembrance as critic and prose-writer.

The reaction, then, against Jeffrey was necessary and, in some degree, just. Yet, now that the air is cleared of Romantic prejudices, Jeffrey's real services to the causes both of criticism and of sound literature may be more accurately perceived and defined. Not for a moment can the student who aims at genuine insight into the history of literature and of literary opinion during the first quarter of our century afford to disregard Jeffrey and his *Edinburgh Review* Essays, or to pass him by with a phrase as a mere unsuccessful opponent of Wordsworth and Coleridge. Jeffrey influenced public opinion decisively and beneficially on a vast range of subjects. He broadened the methods of literary criticism and won for it new points of view and new fields. He put the relations between critic and public on a sounder basis, and raised the profession of literary criticism into an honourable calling. Finally, he developed English style, added to its swiftness of play and brilliant serviceableness, and prepared the way for the dazzlingly effective, if somewhat mechanical, technique of Macaulay. All these good works are nowadays too often forgotten; and on the injustice of such neglect one cannot comment more aptly than through the quotation of Jeffrey's own famous phrase—"This will never do." (pp. 59-63)

Lewis E. Gates, "Francis Jeffrey," in his Three Studies in Literature, *The Macmillan Company, 1899, pp. 1-63.*

C. T. Winchester   (essay date 1910)

[*In the following excerpt, Winchester discusses ways in which Jeffrey's work was instrumental in achieving literary recognition for the critical essay.*]

Very different literary forms have been designated by the common name Essay. In strictness, it is to Montaigne that we owe the name and the thing. His *Essais,* excellently translated by John Florio in 1583, were at once popular in England, and Bacon, fourteen years later, borrowed their title for his famous little bundles of apothegm. The influence of the *Essais,* continuing into the next century, increased with the liking for all things French after the Restoration, and is attested by Cotton's new translation in 1680. They evidently furnished the model for those

charming discursive papers by Cowley, Halifax, and Temple, which closely resemble some of the best work of Hazlitt or Lamb.

But the sudden and immense popularity of the *Tatler* and *Spectator* in the Queen Anne time brought into prominence another type of the essay. It is the peculiar praise of Addison that he knew how to give permanent charm to the familiar, even to the trivial, by nicety of literary skill. His manner is simple, yet always easy and urbane. He had nothing of importance to say; but he could say it with a suavity, humor, and grace that make the veriest nothings admirable. He was no philosopher, no statesman, and a very mediocre critic, but his little papers on a fan or a petticoat, on the foibles of Sir Roger or the vanity of Ned Softly, may last as long as the *Paradise Lost,* and very probably find more readers.

For more than half a century, the acknowledged mastery of Addison tended to popularize this literary form in which he had won such success. Before the close of the century there had appeared more than a hundred periodicals,—most of them as short-lived as the flies of a summer,—which attempted to do what had been done so brilliantly in the *Tatler* and the *Spectator.* But they all failed. The essay of the Addisonian type demands the skill of an Addison. It lost its distinctive charm even in the treatment of Goldsmith; and it becomes a solid, clumsy thing under the ponderous handling of Johnson in the *Rambler* and *Idler.* Before the close of the century its form was outgrown; the modern essay has a quite different origin.

For two hundred years, indeed, many excellent prose papers of moderate length, written upon weighty themes, political, philosophical, and critical, had appeared as prefaces, letters, pamphlets, and short treatises; but it was the new Reviews and Magazines, founded at the beginning of the nineteenth century, that produced the modern essay. Now, for the first time, we have that extended discussion of some one theme, popular in manner yet accurate in statement, and admitting high literary finish to which we now confine the name of essay. The founding of the *Edinburgh Review* in 1802, not only introduced to the public a new group of young liberal writers, it introduced a new type of writing, a type adapted to a wide range of subjects, giving expression to the author's personality, and affording scope for almost any kind of rhetorical excellence. (pp. 1-3)

It is true that the reader of to-day who turns over the early volumes of the *Edinburgh* runs the risk of finding the luminary not quite so brilliant as the accounts of its reception have led him to expect. There is certainly not so much dash and audacity in the opening numbers as one would suppose from the surprise and indignation they excited. The writers seem rather to assume a dignified assurance of manner. But any one who prepares himself by a short course of reading in what called itself criticism before 1800 will find the most homiletical passages of the [*Edinburgh Review*] "stick fiery off indeed." And it must be remembered that there is not much duller reading to be found on earth than that between the covers of *any* Review a century old, with its pother over questions settled three generations ago, and over books and men alike gathered now to a forgotten past.

It is a more serious charge against these early volumes of the *Edinburgh* and of the *Quarterly Review,* established in 1807, that they contain little or nothing of permanent value as literature. Yet this, too, was inevitable. Perhaps the most important service of the two Reviews was the intelligent guidance of opinion on public affairs. By far the larger number of the articles were on such subjects. But any periodical devoting its attention so largely to current political questions of the hour must be content to see most of its writing pass into that wallet wherein Time puts alms for oblivion. The article that is timely is seldom immortal. Only some unusual intensity, like Swift's, or some unusual philosophic vision like Burke's, can give to writing on such themes lasting value. And none of the early reviewers had either of these qualifications in any high degree.

For the literary criticism, which occupied considerable space in both Reviews, there is, perhaps, a little more to be said. The new Reviews doubtless did something to raise the quality of literary criticism. With their pretensions they could not afford to utter partial, hasty, ill-considered verdicts. Criticism was forced to justify its decisions, and to look about for some general principles. Doubtless nothing like a science of criticism was elaborated—it may be questioned whether there is any such a science; but the Reviews at least demanded from the critic careful reading, instructed judgment, and some definite views as to the grounds of literary excellence. They were, as has been said, a kind of college of criticism. Yet much of the resulting work was either very commonplace or very perverse. The Reviews certainly made some notorious mistakes. But critics, like the rest of us, are very fallible, and their worst mistakes might be pardoned them if it could be shown that they had often introduced to public notice genius not yet recognized, or removed unworthy prejudice, or anticipated in any way the verdict of the next generation. But that the Reviews rendered any such service, between 1800 and 1825, is very doubtful. A careful reading of all the critical notices in the *Edinburgh* and *Quarterly* during these years will prove that they usually followed the public taste, occasionally opposed it, but never led it. They echoed the popular admiration for Scott and Byron; but the other three great poets, Wordsworth, Shelley, and Keats, won recognition in spite of their neglect and abuse. Jeffrey's persistent attacks upon Wordsworth are matter of familiar knowledge, and unquestionably did something to retard the poet's fame; they set a fashion not yet quite outgrown. From 1815 to 1837 neither Review has anything to say of Wordsworth: having made up their verdict of condemnation, they refuse to alter or even to repeat it. Everybody remembers that the *Quarterly,* "so savage and tartarly," had the blame of killing John Keats; while the *Edinburgh* had no word of recognition for him, and only broke silence in 1820 when his brief career was closed. Shelley was abused by the *Quarterly* through three violent articles, and the cautious *Edinburgh* did not venture a word of him until 1824—two years after he was dead.

Yet, after all, the most perverse literary criticism is not without value. It at least calls attention to the book. Prob-

ably the poet himself would rather be damned than ignored. And by the discussion of faults and merits, even by the opposition he provokes, the critic does something to educate public taste; the collision of opposite opinions generates a kind of literary atmosphere and not infrequently evolves something like critical principles. Had it not been for the blind dogmatism of the *Edinburgh,* we might never have had Coleridge's *Biographia Literaria.* The criticism of the last hundred years, begun by these Reviews, has certainly done much to render public interest in literature more general and more intelligent, and thus to raise the standard of production.

It must be admitted that in all this early critical writing there are but very few papers that will find a place among English classics. Southey furnished to the *Quarterly* a body of solid and sensible prose writing, mostly on political subjects, and all of it now dusty and dead. Gifford, the editor of the *Quarterly,* was a dull-sighted, thick-skinned, heavy-handed critic, with little acumen and no delicacy, who richly deserved the flogging he got from Hazlitt. He liked to pose as a literary judge and executioner, but he wrote comparatively little himself, and that little was never of much value. Of the *Edinburgh* men, Brougham, though a vigorous and careless writer, was never ambitious of literary repute. Sydney Smith was unsurpassed as a wit, raconteur, letter-writer; but his papers in the *Edinburgh* are mostly on ecclesiastical and political topics, and only two or three of them show him at his best. The critic among the reviewers was Francis Jeffrey. From 1802 to about 1830 he was accounted beyond question the first of literary critics. As the century advanced, his fame declined. His obstinate and contemptuous depreciation of Wordsworth was remembered against him when the poet had come to his own. There were a good many irreverent people of the later generation who thought his criticism, when not commonplace, merely smart. Yet as late as 1867 Carlyle [see excerpt above] pronounced him "by no means supreme in criticism or in anything else; but it is certain that no critic has appeared among us since worth naming beside him." And only the other day, in an able and discriminating study [see excerpt dated 1899], Professor Gates was protesting against the neglect of Jeffrey's good work in Jeffrey's own famous words "This will never do!"

It is easy to understand Jeffrey's contemporary popularity. In the first place, he wrote a clear, rapid, fluent English. Doubtless he is sometimes *too* fluent and makes a little philosophy go a long way; but his style has a metallic brilliancy, not unlike that of his admirer, Macaulay. He knows how to say telling things, and he has infinite store of illustration. Then, too, like Macaulay, he is always cock-sure—which is pleasing in a critic. His sweeping assertions, his lavish use of the superlative and the unusual, give to his writing a magisterial air that most readers find very satisfying. Provided he agrees with us,—and Jeffrey never differed boldly with current opinion,—we like the critic to tell us authoritatively how we ought to feel about a book, and why we ought to feel so. We compliment ourselves on having reached substantially a sound judgment without his aid; and the loftier the critic, the greater the compliment of his agreement with us.

Then Jeffrey's criticism has always a certain hard common sense. It is clear and sane, level to the comprehension of everybody. There is nothing subtle in it. He never goes much below the surface, and cannot give you those penetrating glimpses that sometimes illuminate the whole of an author's work. He likes his meaning plain and his emotions familiar. Anything profound, mystical, or even strikingly original is likely to put him out. He emerges from the farther end of one of Wordsworth's long passages of transcendentalism blinking and angry. But the large, obvious excellences of thought and feeling, which all men perceive, he can state and appraise with intelligence and justice. He is best, therefore, on such objective writers as Scott; best of all, I think, on books like Mrs. Hutchinson's *Memoirs* or Pepys' *Diary,* that present no problems, and invite narrative treatment with copious illustrative quotations. But even in his most unsympathetic reviews, like those on the Lake School, his opinions, however blind, have a plausibility that recommends them to average prosaic common sense. He is never perverse or paradoxical of set purpose.

Jeffrey's method, unlike that of most recent critics, is dogmatic, never exactly what we have come to call impressionist. The modern critic strives to suggest the total effect upon himself of the work under review; to make you feel as the work has made him feel. He is the medium through which you are to be put *en rapport* with the author. Jeffrey's method is altogether different. He does not aim to give you an appreciation of the book, but an *estimate* of it. This is an intellectual process, a judicial process, the application of principles to reach a verdict. All Jeffrey's criticism is in this manner; he is always proving, expounding, defending. This method not only tends to conventional decisions, but it is unlikely to produce writing of the highest literary quality. For it does not appeal to our sympathy, but to our judgment; and it gives to the critic little room for the play of imagination or the expression of his own personality.

It is this method that determines the favorite form of Jeffrey's critical articles; for they are nearly all built on the same plan. They begin with an elaborate introduction, which often takes up about a third of the paper. This introduction is devoted either to a résumé of some period of literary history or to a statement of general principles on which his specific critical judgments are to be based; then follows, for the rest of the paper, a detailed estimate of the book, usually with copious excerpts to illustrate and enforce the verdict. These introductions, when of the historical sort, are usually correct in their facts, but they are superficial and show little sense of the deeper relations of literature to history. For instance, the sketch of the course of English poetry that precedes the review of Ford's *Dramatic Works* is an interesting sketch of the elementary external facts of English literary history for two centuries; but it is almost entirely without those illuminating glimpses that prove keen critical insight, and it gives you no clear notion of the ways in which the changing national life embodies itself in literature. In the instance mentioned, as in some others, the first part of the essay seems to have little connection with the rest—the introduction does not introduce. Similar comment might be made on

the opening sections of the reviews of Campbell's *English Poets* and of Goethe's *Wilhelm Meister.* Such passages are of interest as showing that Jeffrey had some dawning conception of an historical method in criticism; but he hardly had more. And he seemed quite unable to apply any such method to the literature of his own day. One would have thought, for example, that in the poetry of Byron and its wonderful vogue all over Europe, Jeffrey might have seen and pointed out some significant expression of the spirit of the age; but it cannot be said that he ever did.

The other kind of introduction, that is taken up with general critical principles, is often still more disappointing. For this formidable array of truths, which would seem to make the conclusion drawn from them quite irresistible, turns out on examination to be only the generalized expression of Francis Jeffrey's personal likes and dislikes, a set of high *priori* statements all out of his own head. He always assumes himself to be the representative of those instructed few who have authority on matters of taste, and he mistakes the limitations of his own appreciation for general laws. A good many critics, I am afraid, do that; but Jeffrey shakes still more our confidence in the stability of his judgment, not merely by the jaunty facility with which he lays down general principles, but by his unlucky denial, now and then, of some statement assumed as an eternal truth only a little while before. Thus, writing in April, 1810, an elaborate review on the poetry of Crabbe, he declares that we are all "touched more deeply as well as more frequently in real life with the sufferings of peasants than of princes . . . and an effort to interest in the feelings of the humble and obscure will call forth more deep, more numerous, and more permanent emotions than can be excited by the fortunes of princesses and heroes"; but four months later, having to explain the wonderful popularity of Scott, he decides that it is mostly due to his subject, and that "kings, warriors, knights, outlaws, minstrels, secluded damsels and true lovers" are the sort of persons to appeal to the general poetic sense. And his whole *a priori* explanation of the conditions of poetic popularity was, two years later, overset by the meteoric fame of Byron on quite different grounds. In the essay on Goethe's *Wilhelm Meister,* Jeffrey declares that "human nature is everywhere fundamentally the same"; in the review of Baber's *Memoirs,* two years later, he decides that there is "a natural and inherent difference in the character and temperament of the European and Asiatic races." One who goes straight through his essays will come upon a considerable number of such contradictions. Jeffrey's general principles we suspect are mostly made to order. He first makes up his decision upon the work under review, quite empirically, and then frames a set of universal truths to justify his decision. Mr. Leslie Stephen, indeed, goes so far as to say that Jeffrey had no real taste of his own at all, and is always asking himself, not "What do I feel?" but "What is the correct remark to make?" [see excerpt dated 1878]. But this seems to me unfair. Jeffrey, I should rather say, is always asking himself "Why ought I to feel as I do?" He has a very genuine, though limited, appreciation, and is bent on justifying it.

His various likes and dislikes are curious, and often apparently irreconcilable. Yet a little reflection will show how they all spring from a common ground of temperament. Jeffrey, if I understand him, was a singular combination—I can hardly say compound—of sense and sensibility. His emotions were easy to get at; but they were checked by anything improbable, by any shock to his prosaic sense of fact. He sincerely professed enthusiastic admiration for the romantic literature of the sixteenth century, especially the Elizabethan drama, which, he says, "I have long worshipped with a kind of idolatrous veneration"; but for the romantic literature of his own day, he had a very qualified liking. Coleridge's *Ancient Mariner* seems always to have been to him nothing better than an old sailor's foolish yarn; of *Christabel* he says—or, at all events, allowed the *Edinburgh* to say, in a review always attributed to him— that "the thing is utterly destitute of value, a mixture of raving and drivelling . . . beneath criticism." His estimate of Scott was forced up by the pressure of public opinion; but of *Marmion* he could say, in 1808: "We must remind our readers that we never entertained much partiality for this sort of composition, and ventured on a former occasion to regret that an author endowed with such talents should consume them in imitation of obsolete extravagances. . . . To write a modern romance of chivalry seems to be much such a phantasy as to build a modern abbey or an English pagoda." On the other hand, for the work of Crabbe, the most merciless of realists, he always had a great admiration. Here, he said, are the facts of life. These farmers and shopkeepers and workhouse folk are the real thing; they "represent the common people of England pretty much as they are"—not as Mr. Wordsworth's philosophical peddlers, and sententious leech-gatherers, and hysterical school masters. In a word, Jeffrey liked romanticism,—as he understood it,—and he liked realism; but he did not like them mixed. The romantic writers, he would say, may fairly abandon the present and the actual; but to throw the hues of imagination on the facts of common life, as Wordsworth attempted to do, this was merely to falsify the facts without illuminating them.

So, too, he objects to the conventional poetic diction of the eighteenth century on precisely the same grounds as Wordsworth in his famous preface, and sometimes in almost the same words. He praises Cowper without stint as the first to abandon that diction and to break away from all rigid poetic convention. Yet not the most finical classicist of the eighteenth century could have had greater dread of anything rude or undignified. Wordsworth's simplicity he accounts vulgar and puling; and he shudders politely over such very mild improprieties as the guard-room talk of the soldiers in the *Lady of the Lake*. One wonders how he would have survived a reading of—let us say— some of Rudyard Kipling's ballads. The one poet most entirely to his liking was Campbell, always proper and always sentimental. "We rejoice," he says, in opening his review of the *Gertrude of Wyoming*, "to see once more a polished and pathetic poem;" though he fears it may not appeal to the taste of an age "vitiated by babyishness" (*i.e.* of Wordsworth) "or antiquarism" (*i.e.* of Scott). In a famous passage in one of the very latest of his papers— quoted by everybody who has written anything on Jeffrey since Christopher North quoted it first in *Blackwood*— looking backward over a generation, he concludes that

Keats, Shelley, Wordsworth, Crabbe, are already passing into oblivion; Scott's novels have put out his poetry; even the splendid strains of Moore are fading into distance and dimness, and the blazing star of Byron receding from its place of pride; while the two poets who still keep the laurels fresh with no signs of fading are—Rogers and Campbell!

All of which proves, not that Jeffrey had no taste of his own, but that it was narrowed in its range, on the one hand by a hard common sense, and on the other by a rather prim sentimentality. It was his misfortune that, with his limited critical equipment, he had to deal with two or three very original poets, innovators who broke new paths for themselves. Of Shelley he never ventured any estimate at all. The great *Edinburgh* criticism of Shelley was written by Hazlitt. Byron for a time quite dazed him, as he dazed everybody. Before that overmastering genius, even Jeffrey's insistent common sense was blinded. He holds his breath over the magniloquence of *Manfred,* and avers that the dialogue which to so many of us now seems the veriest bathos is "so exquisitely managed that all sense of its impossibility is swallowed up in beauty." The worst fault of *Manfred* he declares to be, not that it is hollow and theatric, but that it "fatigues and overawes us with terror and sublimity." He has doubtless suffered most from his judgment of Wordsworth. Yet to-day the most enthusiastic Wordsworthian must admit that there is a good deal of solemn rubbish in Wordsworth, and not a little puerility. Nobody is obliged to read the whole of the *Excursion;* while as for *Goody Blake* and *Harry Gill, Alice Fell, Peter Bell,* and some dozen or more of that family, no one need much care to save them from the jaws of devouring Time. Our quarrel with Jeffrey is that he is not content to say of the *Excursion,* as Bottom says of the play, "There are things in this that will never please," but he must go on to pick out for special reprobation some of the very best passages in the poem. So in his flings at Wordsworth's simplicity, scattered through various essays,—as those on Crabbe and on Burns,—he points his ridicule by mentioning just the verses dearest to the lovers of Wordsworth, as the *Leech-Gatherer,* the *Matthew* poems, *Michael,* and what he calls "the stuff about dancing daffodils." The truth is that to the practical, mundane intelligence of Jeffrey all the most characteristic excellences of Wordsworth's poetry were quite invisible. Wordsworth's feeling of an all-pervading spiritual power in nature, his resulting conviction of the direct influence of nature upon character, his notion of the effect of the imagination on moral culture,—all this to Jeffrey was mere mystical nonsense. Wordsworth's subjective treatment of humble life, that, he thought, was a whimsical falsification of fact. There were no such plain people. He could not see it was not the peasant that made the poem, but Wordsworth's thought about the peasant. Wordsworth's poetical theories may have been right or may have been wrong; but before he condemned them Jeffrey should have understood them.

In briefest summary, then, we may admit that to Jeffrey, rather than to any other man, may be given the credit of raising the critical essay to the rank of a recognized literary form; that his writing is always brilliant and plausible; that his critical verdicts are always clear, and if upon matters within the range of his appreciation, sensible and just. On the other hand, it must also be admitted that his range of appreciation is limited; that his impressions are often worth more than the dogmas he invents to justify them; and that a considerable part of his fame was due to the immense and novel popularity of the Review which raised him for a time to literary dictatorship almost like that of Dryden or Johnson. (pp. 7-22)

> C. T. Winchester, "The New Essay—Jeffrey as Critic," in his A Group of English Essayists of the Early Nineteenth Century, 1910. Reprint by Books for Libraries Press, 1967, pp. 1-25.

Joseph M. Beatty, Jr. (essay date 1923)

[In the following excerpt, Beatty defends Jeffrey's negative assessment of Wordsworth's poetry.]

Jeffrey was a great reviewer. He was not a creative critic in the sense of being one who could tell all the author meant and all the reviewer would have meant had he written the book. He did not melt into the book and rhapsodize upon his emotions. But in an age of sentimental Germanized emotionalism, he believed in the reasonableness of intellectual activity. He considered literature, in the light of what he knew about human nature, and when he thought it deviated from the facts of life, he said, "This will never do."

Commonsense is ordinarily more likely to be right in its prohibitions than its affirmations. Based as it is upon experience, it is more likely to censure extravagant deviations from the norm of human activities than it is to judge the works that, although agreeing in the main with accepted standards, are lacking in imagination or verisimilitude. Its besetting danger is overpraise of the commonplace. Hence it is not strange that we should find Jeffrey an admirer of the genius of Rogers and Campbell. They belonged in spirit to the eighteenth century: they were polished, sentimental, interested in humanity, and reasonable. According to Jeffrey's standards, shaped also by the eighteenth century, but mellowed and rounded by a generous admixture of the sixteenth, there was little to criticize in these authors: they were typical sons of their time.

Yet after a period of one hundred years, it is evident to a student of Jeffrey and his time that his praise of Campbell and Rogers should not be permitted to obscure the excellence of his criticism of certain of his contemporaries, especially of Wordsworth. In the twentieth century, age of science and disillusion—not essentially unlike the eighteenth in its intellectual questionings—we no longer condemn Jeffrey without a hearing as a profaner of the temples of the gods. We read his reviews to find out what he really said. Usually, because we are not sentimentalists, because our love of realism has torn the veil of divinity from the Lakers, we tend to agree with him in much of his matter if not in his manner.

Most of Jeffrey's critics have censured him severely for his failure to comprehend Wordsworth's mysticism. To do so is as illogical as to censure the leopard for his spots. Only a mystic can comprehend a mystic. Jeffrey was a man with a matter-of-fact point of view: he did not believe that it was necessary to spiritualize nature that was in itself sublimely beautiful. It was sufficient to be awed by its grandeur and to feel the exhilaration of beholding sheer beauty. The element of worship may have been in his heart, but actual spiritualization of nature was beyond his comprehension. It is idle to censure Jeffrey for not accepting a point of view that even after a hundred years still has its exponents and opponents. A modern mystic will rail at the reviewer for his stupidity; a modern realist will praise him for his commonsense. Agreement is impossible.

Aside from various incidental references to Wordsworth's poems, the chief contributions of Jeffrey to the criticism of Wordsworth and his school occur in the review of Southey's Thalaba, that of Wordsworth's Poems, that of Burns's Reliques, and the still more famous reviews of The Excursion and The White Doe of Rylstone. It is upon these that we must base our opinion of Jeffrey's criticism of the greatest of the Lakers.

The review of Thalaba is Jeffrey's first detailed criticism of the new school of poetry, "dissenters from the established systems in poetry and criticism." He says that the productions of the group form a composite of the following elements: "1. The antisocial principles, and distempered sensibility of Rousseau—his discontent with the present constitution of society—his paradoxical morality, and his perpetual hankerings after some unattainable state of voluptuous virtue and perfection. 2. The simplicity and energy (horresco referens) of Kotzebue and Schiller. 3. The homeliness and harshness of some of Cowper's language and versification, interchanged occasionally with the innocence of Ambrose Philips, or the quaintness of Quarles and Dr. Donne." He notes particularly the debasing of the language and subject-matter, and complains bitterly of the social activities of the lake poets.

The discussion of the social tendencies of the new poetry is interesting as giving Jeffrey's attitude toward society and the individual.

> A splenetic and idle discontent with the institutions of society," he says, "seems to be at the bottom of all their serious and peculiar sentiments. . . . For all sorts of vice and profligacy in the lower orders of society, they have the same virtuous horror, and the same tender compassion. . . . The present vicious constitution of society alone is responsible for all these enormities: the poor sinners are but the helpless victims or instruments of its disorders, and could not possibly have avoided the errors into which they have been betrayed. . . . While the plea of moral necessity is thus artfully brought forward to convert all the excesses of the poor into innocent misfortunes, no sort of indulgence is shown to the offences of the powerful and rich. . . . If it be natural for a poor man to murder and rob, in order to make himself comfortable, it is no less natural for a rich man to gormandize and domineer, in order to have the full use of his riches. Wealth is just as valid an excuse for the one class of vices, as indigence is for the other.

Professor Harper [in *William Wordsworth. His Life, Works, and Influence.*] says of Jeffrey that "His heart had not been touched by a true sense of human brotherhood. His prejudice was political. It might, indeed, better be termed religious; for it originated in a fundamental unwillingness to acknowledge the divinity in man." Perhaps so; Jeffrey should not, however, be judged in the light of a hundred years of progress in prison reform. Even today there are many serious people who are willing to make society a universal scape-goat for individual offenses.

But a careful reading of this review makes it clear that despite his aristocratic point of view, Jeffrey was not concerned primarily with the poverty of Wordsworth's peasants or with their lowly rank. He objected to them because they were not real: "The low-bred heroes, and interesting rustics of poetry, have no sort of affinity to the real vulgar of this world; they are imaginary beings, whose characters and language are in contrast with their situation; and please those who can be pleased with them, by the marvellous and not by the nature of such a combination." This is not aristocratic indifference but a commonsense feeling for reality.

Both in the review of Burns's *Reliques* and that of *The Excursion,* Jeffrey stresses the lack of *decorum* in Wordsworth's characters. He praises Burns's *Cotter's Saturday Night* and recommends to the Lakers "the simplicity of Burns." "He has copied the spoken language of passion and affection, with infinitely more fidelity than they have ever done," he says, "on all occasions which properly admitted of such adaptation: But he has not rejected the helps of elevated language and habitual associations; nor debased his composition by an affectation of babyish interjections, and all the puling expletives of an old nurserymaid's vocabulary." In concluding the review of *The Excursion,* Jeffrey asks whether it is not plain that Wordsworth's practice of giving lofty speeches to humble persons will not expose "his work throughout to the charge of revolting incongruity, and utter disregard of probability or nature? For, after he has thus wilfully debased his moral teacher by a low occupation, is there one word that he puts into his mouth, or one sentiment of which he makes him the organ, that has the most remote reference to that occupation?"

The review of Wordsworth's *Poems* was not re-printed by Jeffrey in his volume of collected essays from *The Edinburgh Review.* It is the least discriminating of his criticisms of Wordsworth. In spite of this fact, however, it contains some of his most interesting statements about his motives in attacking the Lake Poets. "It was," he said, "precisely because the perverseness and bad taste of this new school was combined with a great deal of genius and of laudable feeling, that we were afraid of their spreading and gaining ground among us, and that we entered into the discussion with a degree of zeal and animosity which some might think unreasonable towards authors, to whom so much merit had been conceded."

Jeffrey's attitude toward Wordsworth in this review is by no means entirely hostile. To be sure, he fails to recognize the difference in quality between "The Ode to Duty" and "Alice Fell"—a serious error in judgment—but he praises the sonnets. After quoting "On the Extinction of the Venetian Republic," "London," and "I Griev'd for Buonaparte," Jeffrey exclaims, "When we look at these, and many still finer passages, in the writings of this author, it is impossible not to feel a mixture of indignation and compassion, at that strange infatuation which has bound him up from the fair exercise of his talents, and withheld from the public the many excellent productions that would otherwise have taken the place of the trash now before us. Even in the worst of these productions there are, no doubt, occasional little traits of delicate feeling and original fancy; but these are quite lost and obscured in the mass of childishness and insipidity with which they are incorporated; nor can any thing give us a more melancholy view of the debasing effects of the miserable theory, than that it has given ordinary men a right to wonder at the folly and presumption of a man gifted like Mr. Wordsworth, and make him appear, in his second avowed publication, like a bad imitator of the worst of his former productions."

In the same essay, the reviewer, in discussing *The Lyrical Ballads,* reminds his readers that "The *Lyrical Ballads* were unquestionably popular; and, we have no hesitation in saying, deservedly popular; for in spite of their occasional vulgarity, affectation, and silliness, they were undoubtedly characterised by a strong spirit of originality, or pathos, and natural feeling; and recommended to all good minds by the clear impression which they bore of the amiable dispositions and virtuous principles of the author."

Of all Jeffrey's reviews, however, the most frequently quoted are those of *The Excursion* and *The White Doe of Rylstone.* He reprinted both reviews in his collected essays. If we analyze these works we shall be able to weigh with considerable accuracy the criticism leveled at Jeffrey for his censure of the Lake Poets.

In the first place, Jeffrey's criticism of *The Excursion* is, in the main, upheld by the judgment of other critics. Aside from the questionable validity of his comment upon the poet's mysticism, his opinions are sane and rational. He is reviewing a poem that, aside from its occasional philosophical or mystical passages, is one of the Saharas of verse. At the present time it is almost unread except by special students of Wordsworth—and then too frequently in agony of spirit. We should remember that Jeffrey is here considering a specific poem, and that his criticism of it should not be considered his criticism of all Wordsworth's work.

Jeffrey's criticism is directed chiefly against the length of the poem, its weakness, and its tameness. "We have imitations of Cowper, and even of Milton, here; engrafted on the natural drawl of the Lakers—and all diluted into harmony by that profuse and irrepressible wordiness which deluges all the blank verse of this school of poetry, and lubricates and weakens the whole structure of their style."

In the second place, Jeffrey charges Wordsworth with undue obscurity and with unnecessary elaboration of self-evident ideas. He says that the work is "a tissue of moral and devotional ravings, in which innumerable changes are rung upon a few very simple and familiar ideas: But with such an accompaniment of long words, long sentences, and unwieldy phrases—and such a hubbub of strained raptures and fantastical sublimities, that it is often difficult for the most skillful and attentive student to obtain a glimpse of the author's meaning—and altogether impossible for an ordinary reader to conjecture what he is about. . . . All sorts of commonplace notions and expressions are sanctified in his eyes, by the sublime ends for which they are employed; and the mystical verbiage of the Methodist pulpit is repeated, till the speaker entertains no doubt that he is the chosen organ of divine truth and persuasion."

In the third place, Jeffrey attacks the poem for its didacticism: "more than nine tenths of it are occupied with a species of dialogue, or rather a series of long sermons or harangues which pass between the pedlar, the author, the old chaplain, and a worthy vicar, who entertains the whole party at dinner on the last day of their excursion." The reviewer has some difficulty in discovering the doctrine that the poet is trying to inculcate, but decides that, "in so far as we can collect, however, it seems to be neither more nor less than the old familiar one, that a firm belief in the providence of a wise and beneficent being must be our great stay and support under all afflictions and perplexities upon earth—and that there are indications of his power and goodness in all the aspects of the visible universe, whether living or inanimate—every part of which should therefore be regarded with love and reverence, as exponents of those great attributes. We can testify, at least, that these salutary and important truths are inculcated at far greater length, and with more repetitions, than in any ten volumes of sermons that we ever perused."

In the fourth place, Jeffrey accuses Wordsworth of silliness and triviality. In support of this charge he quotes various passages such as the one containing the ill-chosen "solemn bleat."

Although the reviewer considers the various parts of the poem in some detail, his comments are merely illustrative of his main bases of criticism—the poet's prolixity, his involved mysticism, his repetition, his didacticism, and his triviality. A modern unprejudiced reader tends to agree with Jeffrey except in his contempt for the mystical. In *The Excursion* Wordsworth was prolix, didactic, and too frequently trivial. Had the poem appeared in 1923, it is improbable that the reviewers would have treated its faults more kindly than did Jeffrey.

As might well be expected, the virtues that Jeffrey finds in Wordsworth's poem are those of the poems of the preceding age. After admitting that the author of *The Excursion* is a person "of great powers," he remarks that the poet "has frequently a force in his moral declamations, and a tenderness in his pathetic narratives, which neither his prolixity nor his affectation can altogether deprive of their effect." He emphasizes the sentimental in his author: "Mr. Wordsworth delineates only feelings—and all his adventures are of the heart"—surely no inadequate criticism of a follower of Rousseau. He says of the poet's account of the old chaplain's marriage that it is "written with great sweetness—a sweetness like that of Massinger, in his softer and more mellifluous passages."

Jeffrey's summary of the work contains his estimate of the poet himself. One of his most telling criticisms is that the characters are not true to real life. An earlier writer might have complained of the lack of *Decorum* in their portrayal. He objects to the incongruity between the lowly character and lofty sentiments, and asks pointedly whether a pedlar could engage in such "learned, abstract, and logical harangues."

In the review of *The White Doe of Rylstone,* although Jeffrey is even more brutally outspoken, his fundamental criticism is the same. "The story of the poem," he tells us, "though not capable of furnishing out matter for a quarto volume, might yet have made an interesting ballad." He notes that Wordsworth has apparently been reading Scottish ballads, but that "it unfortunately happens, that while the hobbling versification, the mean diction, and flat stupidity of these models are very exactly copied, and even improved upon, in this imitation, their rude energy, manly simplicity, and occasional felicity of expression, have totally disappeared; and instead of them, a large allowance of the author's own metaphysical sensibility, and mystical wordiness, is forced into an unnatural combination with the borrowed beauties which have just been mentioned."

Jeffrey's comment upon *The White Doe* is exasperating, yet consistent: "In the Lyrical Ballads," he says, "he was exhibited, on the whole, in a vein of very pretty deliration; but in the poem before us, he appears in a state of low and maudlin imbecility, which would not have misbecome Master Silence himself, in the close of a social day." Outrageous as is Jeffrey's manner, it is evident that his matter is based upon the dictates of commonsense. He says quite wisely that the subject is more suited for a ballad than for a quarto; that the versification is rude; and that the poem is mystically wordy.

So much for Jeffrey's comment upon Wordsworth in *The Edinburgh Review.* In re-publishing in collected form his contributions to that periodical, however, the reviewer expressed in a note, his mature judgment in regard to the poems: "I have spoken," he says, "in many places rather too bitterly and confidently of the faults of Mr. Wordsworth's poetry: And forgetting that, even on my own view of them they were but faults of taste, or venial self-partiality, have sometimes visited them, I fear, with an asperity which should be reserved for objects of Moral reprobation. If I were now to deal with the whole question of his poetical merits, though my judgment might not be substantially different, I hope I should repress the greater part of these *vivacités* of expression." He says that he has always loved "the attributes of his Genius," and respected his character. He excuses himself for re-printing his criticism of *The White Doe of Rylstone* by asserting his desire to clarify the issue between himself and the admirers of Peter Bell the Waggoner, or the Lamentations of Martha Rae, or the Sonnets on the Punishment of Death. "Now I have been assured," he remarks, "not only that there are such persons, but that almost all those who seek to exalt Mr. Wordsworth as the founder of a new school of poetry, consider these as by far his best and most characteristic productions; and would at once reject from their communion any one who did not acknowledge in them the traces of a high inspiration. Now I wish it to be understood, that when I speak with general intolerance or impatience of the school of Mr. Wordsworth, it is to the school holding these tenets, and applying these tests, that I refer."

Jeffrey's statements are borne out by those of his contemporaries. He did not actually meet Wordsworth until 1831. "Lockhart beheld the ceremony," says Henry Taylor, "and told me that Wordsworth played the part of a man of the world to perfection, much better than the smaller man." Jeffrey's early animosity was not personal. Crabbe Robinson remarks that in 1810 Coleridge said "that Jeffrey, the editor of the *Edinburgh Review,* had lately called on him, and assured him that he was a great admirer of Wordsworth's poetry, that the *Lyrical Ballads* were always on his table, and that Wordsworth had been attacked in the *Review* simply because the errors of men of genius ought to be exposed." Describing a breakfast with Rogers, Empson, and Wordsworth, the same author says:

> Empson related that Jeffrey had lately told him that so many people had thought highly of Wordsworth, that he was resolved to re-peruse his poems, and see if he had anything to retract. Empson, I believe, did not end his anecdote; he had before said to me that Jeffrey, having done so, found nothing to retract, except, perhaps, a contemptuous and flippant phrase or two. Empson says, he believed Jeffrey's distaste for Wordsworth to be honest—mere uncongeniality of mind. Talfourd, who is now going to pay Jeffrey a visit, says the same.

Granting, then, that Jeffrey's manner of criticism was honestly brutal—and Jeffrey lived in an age of brutal critics—and granting that Jeffrey's mind found the mystical uncongenial and even incomprehensible, there remains the matter of his criticism, already touched upon in part.

Among the critics of Wordsworth in his own time, Coleridge is generally admitted to be the kindliest and fairest. In the familiar passages in the *Biographia Literaria,* he notes among the defects of Wordsworth's poetry a certain *matter-of-factness,* and also "the seeming uselessness both of the project and of the anecdotes from which it is to derive support. Is there one word, for instance, attributed to the pedlar in the *Excursion,* characteristic of a Pedlar?" These are almost the words that Jeffrey used in concluding his review of the same poem. Coleridge notes also as defects, "prolixity, repetition, and an eddying, instead of progression of thought" and "thoughts and images too great for the subject."

No one knew better than Coleridge the fundamental conceptions of his fellow-poet, and no one was better qualified to judge him. Coleridge was able to comprehend the Germanized Rousseauistic mysticism in which both he and Wordsworth had steeped themselves. He was able to interpret Wordsworth as no one else could do. But in his destructive criticism, he and Jeffrey are practically in agreement.

Hazlitt, in *The Spirit of the Age,* remarks:

> We think . . . that if Mr. Wordsworth had been a more liberal and candid critic, he would have

been a more sterling writer. If a greater number of sources of pleasure had been open to him, he would have communicated pleasure to the world more frequently . . . The current of his feelings is deep, but narrow; the range of his understanding is lofty and aspiring rather than discursive. The force, the originality, the absolute truth and identity with which he feels some things, makes him indifferent to so many others.

Carlyle, writing of Jeffrey [see excerpt dated 1867], although recognizing his limitations, is not blind to his worth: "Jeffrey," he says,

> was by no means the supreme in criticism or in anything else; but it is certain there has no critic appeared among us since who was worth naming beside him; and his influence for good and for evil in literature and otherwise has been very great . . . He was not deep enough, pious or reverent enough, to have been great in literature; but he was a man intrinsically of veracity; said nothing without meaning it to some considerable degree, had the quickest perceptions, excellent practical discernment of what lay before him; was in earnest, too, though not "dreadfully in earnest."

Statements such as these from critics of Wordsworth and critics of Jeffrey, when taken with the reviews themselves, tend to clarify our conception of Jeffrey's point of view. Carlyle is a witness to his sincerity; Coleridge and Hazlitt are one with him in recognizing Wordsworth's outstanding limitations. The essential distinction between Jeffrey on the one hand and Coleridge and Hazlitt on the other is that Jeffrey judged by the standard of decorum, by his feeling for propriety and decency, by his understanding of normal human nature, whereas his two contemporaries were able sympathetically to interpret the poems as well as to censure them.

It is impossible to agree with Mr. Gates's sweeping statement that Jeffrey's attitude toward Wordsworth was determined by his political and social ideals [see excerpt dated 1899]. "In fact," Mr. Gates tells us, "all the pretensions of the new school to illustrate by its art a new gospel of life were intensely disagreeable to Jeffrey. As long as Romanticism seemed chiefly decorative, as in Scott or Keats, Jeffrey could tolerate it or even delight in it. But the moment it began, whether in Byron or Wordsworth, to take itself seriously, and to struggle to express new moral and spiritual ideals, Jeffrey protested."

Such a statement ignores the fundamental attitude of mind that expressed itself not only in Jeffrey's political point of view but also in his critical point of view. He had a judicial mind and a vast deal of Scotch commonsense. He tended to weigh all things in the scales of reason. He did not attack Wordsworth because of his radical ideas, but because it seemed to him an outrage against all decency that a man should write carelessly, at great length, and with little sense of propriety about peasants who spake with the tongues of Cambridge and Geneva.

Jeffrey could not comprehend Wordsworth's mysticism. But then, even after a hundred years, neither can Mr. Irving Babbitt. Jeffrey cannot understand how duty can "preserve the stars from wrong." Mr. Babbitt remarks that "It is not quite clear that the law of duty in the breast of man is the same law that preserves 'the stars from wrong.' " Mr. Babbitt thinks also, that "A child who at the age of six is a 'mighty prophet, seer blest,' is a highly improbable not to say impossible child." Jeffrey thought that "if Mr. Wordsworth, instead of confining himself almost entirely to the society of the dalesmen and cottagers, and little children, who form the subjects of his book, had condescended to mingle a little more with the people that were to read and judge of it, we cannot help thinking that its texture might have been considerably improved." Mr. Babbitt notes that "Wordsworth is not sparing of homely detail in his account of his leech-gatherer; but at a given moment in this poem the leech-gatherer undergoes a strange transformation; he loses all verisimilitude as a leech-gatherer and becomes a romantic symbol, a mere projection, that is, of the poet's own broodings. To push this symbolizing of mood beyond a certain point is incipient hallucination."

This paper is not a brief for rationalistic commonsense. It is simply a statement of Jeffrey's case. Stripped of its virulence, his criticism of Wordsworth was, in spite of certain limitations, essentially sane. When *The Excursion* appeared, all his critical commonsense rose in protest at its arid reaches—it was unreasonably long; it was involved; it outraged every principle of poetic decorum—and Jeffrey said, "This will never do."

The schools of commonsense and of insight can never be reconciled: the Jeffreys and the Babbitts of criticism, schooled in the fine restraint of antiquity and seeking the norm in human life, will always raise their voices in protest against the abnormal, the expressionist. They will always sound a note of warning, they will speak from the experience of the race. In general, their voices will not be heeded, but they tend to remind the dweller in the ivory tower of a world of action outside—the world of Chaucer and Shakespeare and Burns—human, puzzled, groping toward the light. (pp. 222-35)

> *Joseph M. Beatty, Jr., "Lord Jeffrey and Wordsworth," in* PMLA, *Vol. XXXVIII, No. 2, June, 1923, pp. 221-35.*

James A. Greig   (essay date 1948)

[*In the following excerpt, Greig discusses Jeffrey's critical assessments of George Crabbe, Barry Cornwall, and John Keats, poets whose works Jeffrey admired.*]

In a footnote to the **Contributions** Jeffrey said that in his reprint he had given more space to Crabbe than to any other contemporary poet—not only because he thought more highly of Crabbe than he did of most of the others, but also because he fancied that Crabbe had had less justice done to him. This obviously makes his dealings with Crabbe important to us here. A first impression might be that we have now caught sight of the Augustan in him. The remainder of the footnote does not, however, bear out this idea. The nature of Crabbe's subjects, Jeffrey remarked, was not such as to set him at the head of a school. Crabbe's claims to distinction depended "fully as much on

his great powers of observation, his skill in touching the deeper sympathies of our nature, and his power of inculcating, by their means, the most impressive lessons of humanity, as on any fine play of fancy, or grace and beauty in his delineations." Those qualities are not peculiarly Augustan. Towards the formal characteristics in Crabbe, in respect of which the poet is most obviously eighteenth-century, Jeffrey's attitude was distinctly critical. He found "some degree of unsteadiness and inconsistency" in Crabbe's "expression and versification"; he noted, without commendation, Crabbe's habit of copying "antithetical and half-punning lines" from Pope; Crabbe, he said, was "frequently misled by Darwin into a sort of mock-heroic magnificence, upon ordinary occasions"; Crabbe's "many imitations of . . . Goldsmith and Campbell" did not "always make a very harmonious combination"; some of Crabbe's verses were marked by a "tame heaviness and vulgarity." He complained too of a "want of habitual fire, and of a tone of enthusiasm in the general tenor" of Crabbe's writings. Crabbe, he said, was so unequal a writer, and sometimes so unattractive, that he required "more than any other of his degree, some explanation of his system, and some specimens of his powers, from those experienced and intrepid readers whose business it is to pioneer for the lazier sort." . . . "Considering Mr Crabbe," Jeffrey stated in another place, "as, upon the whole, the most original writer who has ever come before us . . . we have directed our remarks rather to the moral than the literary qualities of his works;—to his genius at least, rather than his taste—and to his thoughts rather than his figures of speech." "In such an author," he said, "the attributes of style and versification may fairly be considered as secondary."

The description . . . of a passage in *The Parish Register* as being "in the good old taste of Pope and Dryden" makes it clear, at the same time, that there were qualities common to Crabbe and to the Augustans that Jeffrey found it possible to admire. Among these qualities was "compression . . . a sort of sententious brevity, once thought essential to poetical composition" of which Crabbe's work afforded "now the only living example." From the "childish and absurd affectations" of certain of the authors of his day, Jeffrey declared also, he turned "with pleasure to the manly sense and correct picturing of Mr Crabbe." After being "dazzled and made giddy with the elaborate raptures and obscure originalities of these new artists" he found it "refreshing," he said, "to meet again with the spirit and nature of our old masters"—not necessarily, however, only the Augustans—in Crabbe's "nervous pages." "We trust," Jeffrey wrote in the concluding sentence of his first review of Crabbe, " . . . that he will soon appear again among the worthy supporters of the old poetical establishment, and come in time to surpass the revolutionists in fast firing, as well as in weight of metal."

The reference to "correct picturing" indicates one reason why Jeffrey felt thus drawn to Crabbe. A brief consideration of Crabbe himself reveals further affinities in taste between the two men. In his *Library* Crabbe spoke of youthful days in which he was thrilled by works teeming with "moats . . . castles . . . ghosts . . . demons . . .

black suits of armour . . . foaming steeds," and similar paraphernalia. The younger Crabbe told how, as a child, he used to delight in the fairy tales related to him by his father, "all sparkling with gold and diamonds, magic fountains and enchanted princesses." Opening, in *The Borough,* his tale of Ellen Orford, Crabbe recalled his boyhood reading: in his *Tales of the Hall* he made his Squire George one who, in his early days, mused "on tragic tales of lovers dead," and who dreamed of rescuing some lady "none on earth Of higher rank or nobler in her birth," falling in love with her, and extolling her "in glorious rhyme." Proceeding, however, with his tale of Ellen, Crabbe remarked that he soon learned there was no need to suffer any real apprehension for the heroines of romance: however dire their perils or heartrending their difficulties, they were all destined to be delivered, before the tale was fully told, unimpaired in wind, limb, virtue, and beauty, into the arms of their adorers. "These," Crabbe continued, "let us leave, and at her sorrows look. Too often seen, but seldom in a book." Few who have read Squire George's story are likely to forget the way in which that character was wrenched out of his intellectual playroom and made to see the world as it could be in reality—"a way," Jeffrey commented, "that no one but Mr Crabbe would either have thought of—or thought of describing in verse." In *The Library* Crabbe spoke of the pleasures of romance as "joys, Which Reason scatters, and which Time destroys." He thought of indulgence in romanticism, in other words, in much the same way as that in which Jeffrey thought of indulgence in certain forms of scholarship—as natural to a schoolboy but no credit to a man. Jeffrey's reference to the "childish . . . affectations" of some contemporary writers indicates that this was his attitude also to certain aspects of the romantic movement of his day.

A discussion of Crabbe's "talent for observation" throws further light on Jeffrey's conception of authenticity. The first fruit of this talent, he remarked, was generally satire—"the unmasking the vain pretenders to wisdom, and worth, and happiness, with whom society is infested." But he did not think this its "just or natural termination." The satirist's "uncharitable application" of his powers of observation he was "inclined . . . to ascribe" to love of popularity—which was well known to be best secured by successful invective—and also to "the narrowness and insufficiency of the observations themselves." The satirist made use, Jeffrey said, of only half, and the worse half, of the lessons that might be deduced from his occupation. The "true and proper effect" of a habit of observation was not to extinguish sympathy but to extend it, "to turn, no doubt, many a throb of admiration . . . into a smile . . . but at the same time to reveal much that commands our homage and excites our affection, in those humble and unexplored regions of the heart and understanding, which never engage the attention of the incurious,—and to bring the whole family of mankind nearer to a level"—we note the phrase—"by finding out latent merits as well as latent defects in all its members, and compensating the flaws that are detected in the boasted ornaments of life, by bringing to light the richness and the lustre that sleep in the mines beneath its surface." The attitude both to satire and to the obscure among mankind surely indicates that we have

travelled some distance away from the typical Augustan viewpoint.

"Mr Crabbe," Jeffrey wrote, "exhibits the common people of England pretty much as they are, and as they must appear to every one who will take the trouble of examining into their condition." Crabbe, he said, never sentimentalised his humbler characters. On the contrary, he represented certain of these "as altogether as dissipated, and more dishonest and discontented, than the profligates of higher life"; and, instead of conducting us through groves and meadows, had "led us along filthy lanes and crowded wharfs, to hospitals, alms-houses, and gin-shops." "Many ingenious writers," Jeffrey commented, "who make a very good figure with battles, nymphs, and moonlight landscapes," would find themselves helpless if set down among surroundings of that description.

Crabbe, Jeffrey felt at the same time, tended often to indulge too much in this kind of detail. His "chief fault" was to excite frequently "disgust, instead of pity or indignation, in the breasts of his readers." It was needless, Jeffrey supposed, to explain what were "the objects of disgust in physical or external existences." "These," he said, "are sufficiently plain and unequivocal; and it is universally admitted, that all mention of them must be carefully excluded from every poetical description." So far as human character was concerned, he regarded that as disgusting which represented misery without making any appeal to the reader's love, respect, or admiration. If a sufferer were amiable, the pain aroused by his suffering was enhanced into pity. Respect was awakened when to guilt there was added power. Even mean and atrocious guilt could, if efficient, arouse in the spectator sympathy for the victim and a desire for vengeance on the oppressor—which made a compound that was pleasurable on the whole. The case was different, however, when one encountered characters that were too vicious to arouse affection, and too insignificant to be a cause of misery to others. Such were "the depraved, abject, diseased, and neglected poor—creatures in whom every thing amiable or respectable has been extinguished by sordid passions or brutal debauchery;—who have no means of doing the mischief of which they are capable—whom every one despises, and no one can either love or fear." It might perhaps serve some moral purpose to set such spectacles occasionally before us, but they could never awaken either pity or horror. He knew no writer, Jeffrey said, who had sinned so deeply as Crabbe had done in portraying such pictures. It was strange that a writer of his quick observation should have failed to notice that even Shakespeare, who had "ventured every thing," had never shocked our feelings "with the crimes or the sufferings of beings absolutely without power or principle."

It would have been uncharacteristic of the Jeffrey we have come to know had this argument sprung from any desire to shut his eyes to the world's ugliness. If, he declared of *The Parish Register,* several of the groups were composed of disagreeable subjects, allowance had to be made for the author's purpose of giving an exact view of village life. "He aims," Jeffrey wrote, "at an important moral effect by this exhibition; and must not be defrauded either of that, or of the praise which is due to the coarser efforts of his pen, out of deference to the sickly delicacy of his more fastidious readers." "By the mere force of his art," he wrote of Crabbe in the review of *The Borough,* "and the novelty of his style, he forces us to attend to objects that are usually neglected, and to enter into feelings from which we are in general but too eager to escape." But Jeffrey was equally appreciative of Crabbe's more sympathetic pictures of the poor. Nothing, he said, could be more touching than the quiet suffering of Phoebe Dawson in *The Parish Register;* and he pointed out to his readers that the passage containing her story was the last piece of poetry that had been read to Fox. (It may be remembered that this tale was read also, in his last days, to Scott, who, Lockhart said, when his mind was in its full strength, could have repeated every line of it.) The felon's dream in *The Borough* appeared to Jeffrey "to derive an unspeakable charm from the lowly simplicity and humble content of the characters—at least," he added, "we cannot conceive any walk of *ladies and gentlemen* that should furnish out so sweet a picture as terminates the following extract." The *Tales,* he declared, contained a greater number of instances than did Crabbe's previous work in which the poet had "combined the natural language and manners of humble life with the energy of true passion, and the beauty of generous affection"—we notice the now very familiar last phrase—and had "unfolded, in the middling orders of the people, the workings of those finer feelings, and the stirrings of those loftier emotions which the partiality of other poets had attributed, almost exclusively, to actors on a higher scene." "If," he wrote in the article on *The Borough,* "the most admirable painting of external objects—the most minute and thorough knowledge of human character—and that warm glow of active and rational benevolence which lends a guiding light to observation, and an enchanting colour to eloquence, can entitle a poet to praise, as they do entitle him to more substantial rewards, we are persuaded that the following passage will not be speedily forgotten." A few lines from the extract he quoted show how Crabbe could, like an artist highly skilled with pen or brush, with a few easy strokes make his picture leap to the mind.

> There, in one house, throughout their lives to be,
> The pauper-palace which they hate to see:
> That giant-building, that high-bounding wall,
> Those bare-worn walks, that lofty thund'ring
>   hall,
> That large loud clock, which tolls each dreaded
>   hour,
> Those gates and locks, and all those signs of
>   power;
> It is a prison, with a milder name,
> Which few inhabit without dread or shame.

"The Lover's Journey" in Crabbe's *Tales* awakened in Jeffrey the wish, already noticed, that Crabbe had lived among Scottish scenery so that he might have had that excellent material on which to exercise his "unrivalled powers." Of the felon's dream in *The Borough* Jeffrey declared that the "exquisite accuracy and beauty of the landscape painting are such as must have recommended it to notice in poetry of any order." "We should have liked," Jeffrey wrote in the opening paragraph of his article on the *Tales,*

"a little more of the deep and tragical passions; of those passions which exalt and overwhelm the soul—to whose stormy seat the modern muses can so rarely raise their flight—and which he has wielded with such terrific force in his Sir Eustace Grey, and the Gipsy Woman." "Last, though not least," he enumerated among Crabbe's qualities in the review of *The Tales of the Hall,* "that sweet and seldom sounded chord of Lyrical inspiration, the lightest touch of which instantly charms away all harshness from his numbers, and all lowness from his themes—and at once exalts him to a level with the most energetic and inventive poets of his age." Of these criticisms also, whether or not we agree with Saintsbury that Jeffrey's praise of Crabbe is extravagant—some of us may think that this may be said of the praise in the last quotation—it cannot be held that they are appreciations of peculiarly Augustan qualities. Nor is Jeffrey's mention of Crabbe's "minute and thorough knowledge of human character" appreciation of a peculiarly Augustan quality. Such an "admirable sketch," as Jeffrey called it, as that of the completely ineffective and yet highly successful Vicar in *The Borough* appears to me, style and versification apart, as fresh to-day as when it was written. The Curate in the same poem, who "weigh'd the Greek page, and added note on note. . . . And dream'd what his Euripides would be," is, I think, still alive. The subtle psychological effects to be found in such a story as *The Patron,* the fifth of Crabbe's *Tales* are, it seems to me, as modern as those of the novel published yesterday.

It might be argued by some that in part of his criticism of Crabbe, Jeffrey was according high praise to what was not, in the highest sense of the word, poetry at all—that he was showing himself insensitive to the difference there is between writing of the Crabbe type and poetry with enchantment in it, that kind of poetry of which Shakespeare was thinking when he wrote of "the poet's eye, in a fine frenzy rolling," glancing "from heaven to earth, from earth to heaven." This is, of course, a relic of an ancient controversy. Crabbe discussed it himself in the preface to his *Tales,* quoting the passage in the *Midsummer Night's Dream* just referred to, and making the obvious comment that the question is one simply of definition. While Crabbe was prepared to concede that the work of the writer who was "of imagination all compact" was a "more dignified kind of composition" than was that of the versifier who addressed his productions to his readers' "plain sense and sober judgment," he was unwilling to grant that the former should monopolise the title of poet—remarking that this idea of poetry would exclude much of Chaucer, Dryden, and Pope, and recalling Johnson's observation that it would be difficult to frame a definition of a poet in which Pope should not be admitted. Jeffrey, we recollect, spoke of Pope as more of a satirist, moralist, wit, and critic than a poet. I do not think, however, that with his unwillingness to waste time on useless distinctions Jeffrey would have cared to pursue this discussion very far. I imagine he might have pointed out that it does not require much intelligence to perceive that Keats's famous "magic casements" passage, for instance, belongs to a different order of writing from, say, the passage in *The Newspaper* in which Crabbe, describing the conversation of comfortable people in taverns who indict

> roads, and rates that still increase;
> The murmuring poor, who will not fast in peace

mirrored a whole social attitude in a single brilliant and biting line. If we desire to mark that difference by refusing to accept the ordinary usage of language that includes both as poetry, then we have to find a new name for the second type. To call it simply verse is surely unsatisfactory. That is to confuse it with writing which has aimed at being poetry and missed its mark. Crabbe's line has hit the dead centre of its target. It seems even more unsatisfactory to describe it as prose measured out in even syllables. We have only to try expressing the idea contained in it in another way to realise how much of its effectiveness is inseparable from its rhythm.

"In poetry," [Leslie] Stephen wrote of the first *Edinburgh* reviewers, "they clung, as long as they could, to the safe old principles represented by Crabbe" [*Hours in a Library*, 1878]. This figure—of a man clinging desperately until swept from his hold by the tide of the next generation's wisdom—is inaccurate so far as Jeffrey is concerned: Jeffrey, we have seen, never abandoned his admiration of Crabbe. The remainder of Stephen's statement seems to me, however, to be completely correct: Jeffrey always clung to principles which appeared to him to be, ultimately at least, safe. He conceived it to be criticism's high office, it is becoming more and more evident, to act as a guardian of civilisation.

"Even his praise of Crabbe," Saintsbury wrote of Jeffrey [see excerpt dated 1887], "excessive as it may now appear, is diversified by curious patches of blame which seem to me at any rate, singularly uncritical. There are, for instance, a very great many worse jests in poetry than—'Oh, had he learnt to make the wig he wears!'—which Jeffrey pronounces a misplaced piece of buffoonery." We have here, it seems to me, another example of the possibly unintended process by which ordinary readers may be dazzled out of judgment. Neither the jest nor the criticism can, it is clear, be appreciated without a knowledge of the context. To the whereabouts of this Saintsbury gave no clue. The effect upon the ordinary reader of this airy allusion is, I imagine, to induce him to believe that there exists a body of experts by whom the line quoted is as immediately recognisable as is "Friends, Romans, countrymen"; and that it would be well for him, accordingly, in such formidable company, to hold his peace, even about so elementary a matter as a joke. Whether or not that assumption would be justified in every instance must be left to the conscience of any expert who may chance to read this paragraph. Perhaps our ordinary reader might be a little surprised to learn that that line is not to be found within the body of a poem in any modern edition of Crabbe's collected works—as Crabbe, being apparently less confident of the success of his jest than Saintsbury was, struck the line out of the poem in which it originally appeared.

Contact with the poetry of Barry Cornwall,—of whom it has been written that he "will be remembered as the man whom everyone loved—that company including a hundred of the greatest of the century"—moved Jeffrey to criticism which gives us some additional glimpses of his conception of the "end" of poetry, and of his dual standard of judgment. Jeffrey asserted of Cornwall that he seemed to be "altogether free from any tincture of bitterness, rancour or jealousy." It was "delightful," he said "to turn . . . to the unalloyed sweets of such poetry as Mr Cornwall's; and to refresh our fancies, and strengthen and compose our good affection, among the images of love and beauty, and gentle sympathy and sorrow, with which it everywhere presents us." The outlook in these passages is not very different from that of the man of an earlier period who declared that "he who would not be frustrate of his hope to write well hereafter in laudable things, ought himself to be a true poem," and who said that the abilities of poets "are of power . . . to imbreed and cherish in a great people the seeds of virtue and public civility, to allay the perturbations of the mind, and set the affections in right tune." "Why this," Jeffrey wrote in the second of his articles on Cornwall, "should not be thought the highest kind of poetry, we profess ourselves rather at a loss to explain;—and certainly are ourselves often in a mood to think that it is so." "In spite of his neglect of the terrible passions," he wrote also of Cornwall, "he *does* rank very high in our estimation." He enumerated, as Cornwall's models, Shakespeare in his tender, sweet, and fanciful passages, some of the other sixteenth and seventeenth century dramatists, the earlier Milton, Byron, Coleridge, Wordsworth, and Leigh Hunt. The materials, Jeffrey said, "really harmonize very tolerably." Some of this may appear extravagant praise of a poet who is now remembered, so far as he is remembered at all, mainly in connection with one not entirely fortunate lyric. One may not wish to question over-strongly the verdict of later criticism. Nevertheless it might be wise for one unacquainted with Cornwall's poetry, before springing to the conclusion that Jeffrey had in this instance jettisoned his critical taste, to glance at the two narrative poems, *A Sicilian Story* and *Marcian Colonna,* with which he chiefly dealt, or even merely at the passages he quoted from them. There will be found there in particular a passage, extracted from the latter poem, describing an ocean-voyage, that has a rhythm in its lines that is very different from the jingle of "The Sea! the Sea! the open Sea!"—though that poem too is not, to my ears, in its penultimate stanza, entirely devoid of music.

Jeffrey's criticism of Cornwall has occasioned another of those incidental tributes to him that we have noticed. "It is not often," Coventry Patmore wrote, "that the first public criticism of a poet's work is the best; and such an early judgment is especially liable to error when it includes a comparison with other and contemporary poetry. But Lord Jeffrey's estimate of 'Mr Cornwall's' writing is probably fuller and juster than anything which has been printed on the subject during the fifty-six years that have since gone by. The following extract from the *Edinburgh* notice of a *Sicilian Story* could scarcely be improved upon."

Jeffrey said of Cornwall that he had "less affectation, and far less conceit" than had Leigh Hunt, but expressed doubt whether Cornwall "could have written any thing so good, on the whole, as the beautiful story of *Rimini.*" "It is very sweet," he wrote to Moore, speaking of *Rimini,* "and very lively in many places, and is altogether piquant, as being by far the best imitation of Chaucer and some of his Italian contemporaries that modern times have produced." In the *Review,* while he noted the negligence of Hunt's style, he declared that there was "a great deal of genuine poetry in this little volume; and poetry, too, of a very peculiar and original character."

Jeffrey's appreciation of the Elizabethans, of Hogg, of Cornwall, and of Hunt, prepares us for appreciation of Keats. "Jeffrey's natural taste in poetry," Sir Sidney Colvin wrote in his *John Keats* "was conservative, and favoured the correct, the classical and traditional: but in this case, whether from genuine and personal opinion, or to please influential wellwishers of Keats on his own side in politics and criticism like Sir James Mackintosh, he on the appearance of the new volume took occasion to print, now when Keats was far past caring about it, an article on his work which was mainly in eulogy of *Endymion:* eulogy not unmixed with reasonable criticism, but in a strain, on the whole, gushing almost to excess." Colvin, it is evident, was inclined to believe that Jeffrey's personal taste alone was insufficient to account for his eulogy of Keats. *Endymion* was published in 1818. Jeffrey's review of the poem did not appear until 1820. "We had never happened," Jeffrey stated in the opening sentence of his article, "to see either of these volumes till very lately." It is possible, therefore, that in the interim someone drew his attention to the work of the new young poet. But to say this is different from suggesting that Jeffrey was prepared to tamper with his critical conscience in order to please some "influential" person or persons unknown. It is not easy to see why the editor of the most powerful literary organ of the day, a critic of British, European, and American renown—whose intractability was commented upon by his publisher Constable and by his personal friend Scott—should be supposed to have felt himself under any necessity of pleasing such persons. It is interesting, in the light of Colvin's statement, to notice how closely Jeffrey's taste and ideas, as revealed by this review, anticipated Colvin's own. "That imitation of our old writers," Jeffrey wrote, "and especially of our older dramatists, to which we cannot help flattering ourselves that we have somewhat contributed, has brought on, as it were, a second spring in our poetry;—and few of its blossoms are either more profuse of sweetness, or richer in promise, than this which is now before us." We observe that he linked Keats immediately with the Elizabethans. "Not merely," Colvin asserted, "by delight in particular poets and familiarity with favourite passages, but by rooted instinct and by his entire self-training, Keats was beyond all his contemporaries,—and it is the cardinal fact to be borne in mind about him,—the lineal descendant and direct heir of the Elizabethans." Jeffrey remarked that Keats's models for *Endymion* were "obviously" Fletcher's *Faithful Shepherdess* and Jonson's *Sad Shepherd,* and he found traces of imitation also of Milton's *Comus* and *Arcades:* Colvin mentioned the first three of these among the works that influenced Keats when he was writing the poem. Of the choral hymn to Pan in the first book of *Endymion* Jeffrey wrote that it appeared to him "to be full of beauty" and that it reminded him "in many places, of the finest strains of Sicilian—or of English poetry": Colvin numbered this hymn, along with the song of the Indian Maiden in Book IV, "among Keats's very finest achievements." Jeffrey quoted the elev-

en lines in the second book that give a picture of Cybele in her chariot, and spoke of them as "another, and more classical sketch . . . with a picture of lions that might excite the envy of Rubens, or Edwin Landseer!" Colvin quoted the same eleven lines and described the passage as "a vision of intense imaginative life expressed in verse of a noble solemnity and sonority." Jeffrey quoted the eighteen lines in the third book that describe the debris on the seafloor and remarked that the passage "comes of no ignoble lineage—nor shames its high descent": Colvin quoted the same eighteen lines and placed beside them Shakespeare's description of the dream of Clarence in Richard III. He quoted also Jeffrey's comment, describing it as "a fine phrase."

Keats, Jeffrey remarked, was, he understood, "still a very young man." His whole works, indeed, bore evidence of that. They were "full of extravagance and irregularity, rash attempts at originality, interminable wanderings, and excessive obscurity." They required therefore indulgence. Jeffrey considered, however, that they deserved it. He knew no book, he declared indeed, that he would "sooner employ as a test to ascertain whether any one had in him a native relish for poetry, and a genuine sensibility to its intrinsic charm." The "greater and more distinguished poets" had, he said, so much in them to gratify other tastes—the interest of their stories, their delineations of character, the weight and force of their maxims and sentiments, their pathos, wit, and humour—that they could captivate readers to whom their poetry was only a hindrance, as well as those to whom it constituted their chief attraction. It was only when those other recommendations were wanting, or existed in a weaker degree, that the true force of the attraction exercised by "pure poetry" could be fairly appreciated.

It is plain, nevertheless, that Jeffrey did not regard this narrow if bright stream as constituting the highest kind of poetry: we observed him describe "pure poetry," in the article on Hogg, as a "very dangerous species" of the art. Keats, Jeffrey said, dealt "too much with shadowy and incomprehensible beings": he was "too constantly rapt into an extramundane Elysium, to command a lasting interest with ordinary mortals"; and he would require to "employ the agency of more varied and coarser emotions" if he desired to take rank with "the enduring poets." He found in Keats the same pseudo-re-creation of the past that he had found elsewhere in contemporary poetry. Keats had not, in his opinion, really dealt with classical mythology; instead, "sheltering the violence of the fiction under the ancient traditionary fable," the poet had fashioned an entirely new set of characters to whom he had attached the ancient names. Jeffrey had "more than doubts of the fitness of such personages to maintain a permanent interest with the modern public"; though he remarked that this method certainly gave them the best chance that remained for them. We perceive here the reasoning that led Jeffrey to say that he could not "advise the completion" of *Hyperion.* While, he said, there were passages in the poem "of some force and grandeur," the subject was "too far removed from all the sources of human interest, to be successfully treated by any modern author." Quoting from the *Ode to a Nightingale,* he italicised in the **Contributions,** for special notice, the snatch, with human feeling in it,

> sick for home,
> She stood in tears amid the alien corn,

but not the later so celebrated "magic casements." Keats, he remarked in concluding his article, had "unquestionably a very beautiful imagination, a perfect ear for harmony, and a great familiarity with the finest diction of English poetry," but the poet would have to learn "neither to waste the good gifts of nature and study on intractable themes, nor to luxuriate too recklessly on such as are more suitable."

In *Sleep and Poetry,* after asking for "ten years" in which to "overwhelm" himself in poesy—"First," Keats wrote, "the realm I'll pass Of Flora, and old Pan," and added,

> And can I ever bid these joys farewell?
> Yes, I must pass them for a nobler life,
> Where I may find the agonies, the strife
> Of human hearts.

That, we observe, was precisely the road along which Jeffrey wanted him to travel. "Strength alone," Keats wrote,

> though of the Muses born
> Is like a fallen angel: trees uptorn,
> Darkness, and worms, and shrouds, and sepulchres
> Delight it; for it feeds upon the burrs
> And thorns of life; forgetting the great end
> Of poesy, that it should be a friend
> To soothe the cares, and lift the thoughts of man.

There we have precisely Jeffrey's conception of poetry's "great end"—and the justification of ethical criticism. "So I believe," Keats wrote in one of his letters, " . . . that works of genius are the first things in this world. No! for that sort of probity . . . which such men as Bailey possess does hold . . . the tip-top of any spiritual honours that can be paid to anything in this world." There we have precisely the Jeffreyan scale of values. "I find," Keats wrote, "there is no worthy pursuit but the idea of doing some good to the world. . . . There is but one way for me. The road lies through application, study, and thought." There we have the Jeffreyan conception of man's chief end. He had "honestly endeavoured," Jeffrey said in the preface to his **Contributions,** to select from the large mass of his articles not those which he thought most likely still to attract notice by boldness of view or vivacity of expression, but those which by enforcing what appeared to him "just principles and useful opinions" he "really thought had a tendency to make men happier and better." Once more the familiar combination! He was quite aware, Jeffrey added, of the ridicule that might be attached to this statement; but it was "the only apology" he wished to make for his re-publication. Crossing the Bay of Biscay in 1820, Keats ran into rough weather. "After the tempest had subsided," Milnes wrote, "Keats was reading the description of the storm in *Don Juan,* and cast the book on the floor in a transport of indignation. 'How horrible an example of human nature,' he cried, 'is this man, who has no pleasure left him but to gloat over and jeer at the most awful incidents of life. Oh! this is a paltry originality, which consists in making solemn things gay, and gay things solemn, and yet it will fascinate thousands, by the very diabolical outrage of their sympathies. Byron's perverted education makes him assume to feel, and try to impart to others, those depraved sensations which the want of any education excites in many.' " That, we have seen, was precisely Jeffrey's criticism. It may be that part of the attractiveness he found in Keats sprang from a subconscious perception of the fundamental harmony there was between much of his thinking and that of the younger man.

"So late as 1844," Colvin wrote on a later page than that on which appeared the first passage we extracted from him in this chapter, "Jeffrey, who in spite of the justice he had been induced to do to Keats in his lifetime, had no real belief in the new poetry and was an instinctive partisan of the conventional eighteenth-century style, could write that the 'rich melodies' of Keats and Shelley were passing out of public memory, and that the poets of their age destined to enduring fame were Campbell and Rogers." Colvin's use of the word "induced" suggests, we observe, that the purely hypothetical influence spoken of some fifty pages earlier had now become an established fact. Consideration of what has been alluded to as one of Jeffrey's "unlucky blunders" in prediction may be postponed yet awhile. So far as Keats is concerned, however, we may look, at this point, at a few other dates besides 1844. In 1818 *Blackwood's* advised "Mr John" to go "back to the shop" and the *Quarterly* reviewer of *Endymion* declared that he had been able to struggle through only the first book of the poem. Jeffrey's assertion, in opposition to these statements, that he knew no book he would sooner employ than *Endymion* as a test to ascertain whether anyone had in him a native relish for poetry seems hardly, on the face of it, evidence of unbelief in at anyrate Keats's poetry. The warmth of Jeffrey's eulogy, to which Colvin drew attention, may have been due in part to a feeling that Keats had been treated with undue harshness in the other periodicals. It must be evident by now, at the same time, that Jeffrey tended, when he was pleased with what he had been reading, to express himself hyperbolically. It was a tendency he perceived in himself. "We . . . believe we have, upon the whole," he wrote in one of his reviews of Wilson, "incurred the displeasure of the judicious much oftener by an excessive lenity, than by any undue measure of severity—for our rash and unqualified praises, than for our intemperate or embittered censures." "My natural foible," he said in a letter to Moore, "is to admire and be pleased too easily, and I am never severe except from effort and reflection." "I think it nearly impossible," Keats's first biographer wrote, nevertheless, of an extract he quoted from Jeffrey's criticism of *Endymion,* "to express, in fewer or better words, the impression usually left by this poem on those minds which, from their constitution, can claim to possess an opinion on the question." Jeffrey was not the only reviewer who criticised Keats's poetry favourably in 1820. But neither the verdicts of the other journals nor that of Jeffrey appears to have exercised much influence on the public mind on this occasion. What Keats thought of his literary position in 1821 is evident from the inscription which, "in the bitterness of his heart," he caused to be inscribed on his tombstone. In 1824 Hazlitt, writing in the *Edinburgh,* referred to "the shaft . . . venal, vulgar, venomous" that followed Keats to his grave. In the same year, however, a writer in *Blackwood's*, referring both to Hazlitt's article and to Shelley's having been drowned with a volume of Keats in his possession, delivered himself as follows: "But what a rash man Shelley was, to put to sea in a frail boat with Jack's poetry on board! Why, man, it would sink a trireme." *Blackwood's* in 1828 made "North" speak of Keats's "genius" being seen "to the best advantage" in *Lamia* and *Isabella*, but did so, Colvin remarked, "we feel, less for the sake of praising Keats than of getting in a dig at Jeffrey for having praised him tardily and indiscriminately"—surely an odd charge coming from *Blackwood's*. ("North," Colvin, and Monckton Milnes—who also spoke of Jeffrey's appreciation of Keats's genius as "somewhat tardy"—had all of course one advantage over Jeffrey. All three knew that Keats had died in 1821. It is evident from Jeffrey's review that he supposed that the "very young man" with whom he was dealing would have many years of writing life still in front of him. To gain, at barely twenty-five, from the "chieftain of the critic clan" the kind of commendation Jeffrey gave Keats might not appear, to a modern writer, to be receiving recognition too "tardily.") "Our readers," the *Quarterly* said in 1828, "have probably forgotten all about '*Endymion*, a poem,' and the other works of this young man, the all but universal roar of laughter with which they were received some ten or twelve years ago, and the ridiculous story . . . of the author's death being caused by the reviewers." "I fear," Fanny Brawne wrote of Keats in December 1829, "the kindest act would be to let him rest for ever in the obscurity to which unhappy circumstances have condemned him." Two months before that, Jeffrey had declared in the *Edinburgh*, as Colvin noted, that the "rich melodies" of Keats were fading from public memory. Does not this seem to have been simply a statement of fact? There had been up to this time no reprint of Keats's poems in Britain. There was a reprint in 1829, but only for a Paris firm, which printed for the continental market, in a collective edition of the poems of Shelley, Coleridge, and Keats. Not until 1840 did there appear the first separate British republication of Keats's collected poems. This sold badly, and before long was "remaindered." In 1843 Jeffrey returned to the charge. "I still think," he wrote in a footnote in his ***Contributions***, "that a poet of great power and promise was lost to us by the premature death of Keats . . . and regret that I did not go more largely into the exposition of his merits, in the slight notice of them, which I now venture to reprint. But though I cannot . . . without departing from the principle which must govern this republication, now supply this omission, I hope to be forgiven for having added a page or two to *the citations*,—by which my opinion of those merits was then illustrated, and is again left to the judgment of the reader." We note once more the customary attitude. This passage, read in its "honest meaning," seems hardly evidence of a lack of faith in the poetry of Keats. Not until five years after that did the first biography of the poet appear—written by Milnes, who had been one of a "Cambridge group of Shelley-Keats enthusiasts of 1830." It was, we have noted, to the reviewer who had, twenty-eight years before the publication of that first biography, expressed his appreciation of Keats's poetry that Milnes

considered it most appropriate to dedicate his memoir—with the remark that the appreciation was, when written, hazardous to even such a reputation in criticism as then was Jeffrey's. Doubtless it was not until after the publication of Milnes's work that the encyclopedical writers began to include Keats confidently among the poets. It may appear to some of the jury that it is, in these circumstances, a trifle hasty for us who live in later days to describe Jeffrey's review of 1820 as imperfect, and to speak of his recognition of Keats as slow. (pp. 153-72)

> *James A. Greig, in his* Francis Jeffrey of the Edinburgh Review, *Oliver and Boyd, 1948, 326 p.*

John A. Taylor (essay date 1975)

[*Taylor is an American educator and critic. In the following excerpt, he argues that the tone and content of much of Jeffrey's work for the* Edinburgh Review *was inspired by his aptitude for gauging popular appeal and relates this aptitude to his Whig politics.*]

Francis Jeffrey was editor of the *Edinburgh Review* from 1803 until 1829, and his magazine had a circulation of about ten thousand copies per issue. His readership was what he sometimes called "middling" and what younger radicals such as Edward Bulwer-Lytton called middle class. But Jeffrey's influence as an editor was wider than these facts indicate, and it lasted far longer into the nineteenth century than it might have been expected to do. This happened because . . . Jeffrey edited the *Edinburgh* upon the basis of an original literary formula which was given color by political dye but whose substance and composition was controlled by a calculation of the tastes and aptitudes of a popular audience. To use a twentieth century phrase, Jeffrey "slanted" the articles in his magazine towards what he conceived of as a popular reading taste. "Popular" is Jeffrey's own word. I shall also adduce evidence that Sir Walter Scott was influenced by Jeffrey's ideas concerning popular taste.

Sydney Smith edited the first three numbers of the *Edinburgh*, but it was Jeffrey who was made permanent editor when the review was put upon a business footing. Jeffrey felt some hesitation about accepting the position because he was reluctant to have it known that he was paid a salary for such work. He preferred to be a lawyer and a gentleman rather than an editor, but his legal fees were too meagre an income for the support of his family, and the promise of additional money was, he said, "a monstrous bribe for a man in my position." This original nicety with regard to money is specially interesting because Jeffrey was eventually able to make the success of the *Edinburgh Review* an important vindication not only of the independent periodical but also of the integrity of professional writers who lived by their pens. While previous journals had not been able to make attractive payment to authors whose work appeared in them, the *Edinburgh* paid its writers so handsomely that regular contributors could live upon the proceeds. It is almost as though Jeffrey conceived of the *Edinburgh* as a response to those who had learned to complain of what Oliver Goldsmith had called "a fatal revolution whereby writing is converted to a mechanic trade."

Jeffrey gave many expositions of the principles upon which he conducted the *Edinburgh Review,* for he often advised prospective contributors of the precise standards to which their writing was expected to conform. In these letters to his contributors Jeffrey defined his formula for editing the *Edinburgh* as a "popular" publication. To one such correspondent Jeffrey wrote in 1806:

> It is rather the object and the ambition of our re-
> view to step occasionally beyond the limits of
> technical details and to mingle as much general
> speculation with our critiques as the subject will
> easily admit of. To be learned and right is no
> doubt the first requisite—but to be ingenious and
> original and discursive is perhaps something
> more than the second in a publication which can
> only do good by remaining popular—and cannot
> be popular without other attractions than mere
> truth and correctness.

Jeffrey repeated these sentiments again and again. In 1804 he had defended an article he had himself written, by telling Horner:

> I am very nearly in earnest in all I have said, and
> admit only of a certain degree of inaccuracy,
> which could not well have been avoided, without
> making the doctrine less popular and compre-
> hensible.

In an 1810 letter to Horner, Jeffrey thanked him for his "kind promise to continue to illuminate the public through our pages." Asking Horner to submit his next essay as soon as possible, Jeffrey wrote:

> Make this as full, and long, and popular, as you
> can; and give us an outline of your whole doc-
> trine, rather than a full exposition of its ques-
> tionable and disputed points, which may come
> after.

I think it is clear from these passages that as an editor Jeffrey used the word "popular" with reference to literature in a vigorous but loose fashion. First, Jeffrey used "popular" to denote that blend of learning and comprehensibility which he made his goal in editing the *Edinburgh*. There can be no doubt that Jeffrey's ideas amounted in practice to an editorial formula, and there is frequent testimony that Jeffrey altered other people's writing freely, "perhaps too freely," in order to make it conform to his standards. Sir Walter Scott, who considered Jeffrey "a man of the most uncommon versatility of talent," has left us a picture of Jeffrey at work as an editor:

> One great resource to which the Edinburgh edi-
> tor turns himself, and by which he gives popu-
> larity even to the duller articles of his Review,
> is accepting contributions from persons of inferi-
> or powers of writing, provided they understand
> the books to which the criticisms relate; and as
> such are often of stupefying mediocrity, he ren-
> ders them palatable by throwing in a handful of
> spice—namely, any lively paragraph or enter-
> taining illustration that occurs to him in reading
> them over. By this sort of veneering, he converts,
> without loss of time to hindrance of business, ar-
> ticles which, in their original state, might hang
> upon the market, into such goods as are not like-
> ly to disgrace those among which they are
> placed.

Secondly, however, and without distinguishing between the two meanings, Jeffrey used the word "popular" to denote the actual success of his magazine with its readers. It will be noted in the above quotation that Scott also thought of popularity in terms which comprised both editorial "veneering" and success in "the market." The connection between presumed cause and effect was so intimate that these two practical men did not feel called upon to distinguish between them.

Important as Jeffrey's thinking on popular taste was to his work as an editor, his ideas on the subject remained inchoate. It is for this reason that I have spoken so far not of a developed theory of popular literature but rather on an editorial formula. Since Jeffrey's ideas on popular taste also shaped his literary criticism, that circumstance will be discussed later in this article. For the moment it is Jeffrey's work as an editor which concerns us.

While I do not know to what extent Jeffrey's literary use of the word "popular" was original with him, I think it is clear that, as he employed the term, it acquired particularly Whiggish connotations. Dr. Johnson's Dictionary gives what may be taken as the corresponding Tory definitions of "popular" and "popularity." The first is defined as, "1. Vulgar, plebian; 2. Suitable to the common people; 3. Beloved by the people, pleasing to the people; 4. Studious of the favour of the people;" and the second as "1. Gracious-

Drawing of Jeffrey.

ness among the people, state of being favoured by the people; 2. Representation suited to vulgar conception, what affects the vulgar." Jeffrey's usage of the term was closer to its ancient legal meaning, as *in action popular:* "affecting, concerning or open to all or any of the people; public."

It is not surprising that while Jeffrey spoke of "popular" literature in a purely literary context, he also used the word "popular" in quite another context, that of Whig politics. To John Allen, who often wrote political articles for the *Edinburgh,* Jeffrey sent many letters of advice and instruction. In these letters one sees Jeffrey's use of "popular" in relation to politics. In 1809 Jeffrey wrote to Allen:

> There are but two parties in the nation—the Tories, who are almost for tyranny, and the Democrats, who are almost for rebellion. The Whigs stand powerless and unpopular between them, and must side with, and infuse their spirit into, one or the other of them before they can do the least good. Now, the Tories will not coalesce with them, and the Democrats will. . . .

In 1810 Jeffrey wrote to Allen:

> I am very glad that the Whigs are going to do something for popularity as well as for consistency. My own opinion is, that nothing can save them or the country, but their becoming very popular in their principles, to the full extent of Whitbread's speeches in Parliament.

In an 1817 letter to Allen, Jeffrey had occasion to use both the political and the literary sense of "popular" in the same paragraph:

> Pray be as popular as you can, consistent with being rational; and be most angry at the knaves, and compassionate of the fools. One argument you will naturally consider at large. I mean the favourite one of Southey and the rest, that the power of the people has increased, is increasing, and ought to be diminished, and that the little addition made to the influence of the crown by the war and taxes is but a slight counter-balance to that increase. Now the great fallacy here is, that the increase of weight on the side of the people consists chiefly in an increase of intelligence, spirit, and activity, and that mere wealth and influence of a selfish kind can never be either safely or properly set against this sort of power and authority. In fact, it does not require to be counter-balanced at all; for it leads not to the elevation of the commons merely, but to the general improvement. . . . The natural result of such an increase of popular power is to give more direct efficiency to their agency of government, and the only way to prevent this change in the state of society from producing disorder, is to make more room for the people in the constitution.

Jeffrey's use of the word "popular" in both a political and a literary context is the bane of his work as a theorist, but it is also the key to his work as an editor. Jeffrey did not distinguish between (1) popularity as measured by the widespread readership and commercial success of the *Edinburgh Review;* (2) popularity as an editorial formula which "popularized" (in the modern sense of the word)—that is to say, which rendered simple, lucid, and interesting—the articles for his journal; (3) popularity which was synonymous with "the public" and denoted interests of the whole community excluding neither rich nor poor; (4) a popularity which denoted the interests not of the whole public but of the common people as a distinct social—and what is more important a distinct political—class. Jeffrey habitually scrambled all of these meanings of "popular" and "popularity" together; he was capable of shifting from one meaning to another in the same sentence and evidently without thinking anything of the matter.

It is only when one keeps in mind the fact that Jeffrey was a splendid editor that one is in a position to judge his achievement. His lively concern for making his opinions compatible with public acceptance of his journal was attended with such great success that Jeffrey's conception of "popular" literature and of popularity in general became one of the most influential in early nineteenth century Britain. Nevertheless, Jeffrey's very success and influence make one all the sadder that Jeffrey never bothered to make a rigorous examination of his ideas nor to give them systematic treatment in an essay or book. When Jeffrey did get free time, he devoted it not to theory but to active and practical politics.

Clearly, therefore, writers who did not share Jeffrey's Whiggish hope for the general improvement of taste, might wish to insist upon a clearer distinction than Jeffrey made between "popular" meaning all classes as distinct from any single class, and "popular" used with reference to common people and the tastes of that social class. But it is Jeffrey's accomplishment that when literary men of other political views established new reviews after 1802, they often felt obliged to make their work "popular" in the first sense—public, open to all. No longer could literary men easily regard forty thousand British readers as a vulgar mob. And Jeffrey's editorial formula was soon borrowed by persons who separated its practical application from Jeffrey's politics.

The effects of Jeffrey's work were amplified by the imitation of his literary formula in other periodicals and by the rapid rise of the circulation of the *Edinburgh* and other similar magazines. The circulation of the *Edinburgh* was soon very large in comparison to that of previous journals. It is probably not far wrong to think of the *Edinburgh Review* as selling about ten thousand copies per issue at the end of its first decade of life. Exact figures are hard to calculate for no official count was published, and one does not know what weight to give unofficial assertions that sales had reached fourteen thousand copies per issue. Whatever the precise figures were, it is certain that the circulation of the new review grew very rapidly and that it was soon selling more widely than comparable periodicals published in Britain even a few years before 1802. Back issues of the *Edinburgh* were constantly reprinted, and there was even an American edition of the review printed in New York and pirated, one assumes, from the English numbers.

The success of the *Edinburgh Review* with the reading public soon spurred rivalry, and new journals were founded in profusion. The most prominent of these were magazines which literary men of other political parties founded to combat the influence of the *Edinburgh's* Whiggery. Tories were of course particularly distressed by the avidity with which people read Jeffrey's political articles. Sir Walter Scott and the London publisher John Murray, acting at the urging of George Canning, decided to take decisive action against the *Edinburgh,* and they founded *Quarterly Review* in 1809. Canning supplied the editor of the new Tory review, William Gifford, a journalist who had previously been connected with another of Canning's protege publications, the *Anti-Jacobin Review and Magazine.*

Despite his long standing reservations about the Whiggery of the *Edinburgh,* Scott had been a frequent contributor to the magazine and a friend of Jeffrey. Scott's relationship with the *Edinburgh* was rendered particularly close by the fact that Archibald Constable, who published the *Edinburgh,* published Scott's works as well, but the principal bond which held Scott to the *Review* was his admiration for its ability to sell well and to pay its contributors handsomely. He hoped to construct upon Jeffrey's model a review which would differ from the *Edinburgh* only in its political tone. Scott explained his thoughts upon the success of the *Edinburgh* to George Ellis, whom Lockhart called Scott's "prime political confidant":

> Of this work 9000 copies are to be printed quarterly, and no genteel family can pretend to be without it, because, independent of its politics, it gives the only valuable literary criticism which can be met with. Consider, of the numbers who read this work, how many are there likely to separate the literature from the politics.

Scott strongly recommended to William Gifford, editor of the Tory *Quarterly Review,* imitation of the two principal reasons for Jeffrey's success. First was the *Edinburgh Review's* independence of booksellers and its generous payment of authors. Second was Jeffrey's ability to understand the particular points of composition which would suit an essay to public taste. In a series of letters Gifford received from Scott a first-hand account of Jeffrey's editorial methods, and thus Jeffrey's ideas on "popularity" in literature passed from one political camp to the other.

The *Quarterly Review* was carried forward with considerable success. Its circulation reached into the same general range as the *Edinburgh's,* though the earlier publication probably continued to have the advantage. Gifford remained the editor of the *Quarterly* until 1824, and the magazine proved to be, like the *Edinburgh,* a permanent feature of nineteenth century British literary life.

Literary radicals found the lessons of the *Edinburgh* school harder to learn. A succession of short-lived magazines failed to shake Jeffrey's hold upon the liberal affections of English readers. Shelley and Byron, for instance, founded a magazine called *The Liberal* in 1822, but it survived only into the following year. Finally in 1824 the great *Westminster Review* was founded and carried forward by radicals more systematic and practical than Shelley or Byron.

In the meantime, the attitude of writers, and especially those of radical writers, towards the reviews and the public they served, was quite interesting. Often enough, writers took the reviews as genuine reflections of public opinion. This was most conspicuously true of writers whose work suffered at the hands of reviewers. Byron parodied Brougham's reviews in "English Bards and Scotch Reviewers." On the other hand, it was possible to look upon the reviews as merely the playthings of the rich. The *Quarterly* was of course, the object of particular vituperation: Shelley has not permitted the world to forget how John Keats was treated in the *Quarterly,* and Hazlitt has left a description of the editor of the *Quarterly* which is a classic instance of verbal venom:

> Mr. Gifford was originally bred to some handicraft. He after wards contrived to learn Latin, and was for some time usher in a school, till he became a tutor in a nobleman's family. The low-bred, self-taught man, the pedant, and the dependent on the great, contribute to form the editor of the *Quarterly Review.* He is admirably qualified for this situation, which he has held for some years, by a happy combination of defects, natural and acquired; and in the event of his death it will be difficult to provide him a suitable successor.

Upon the whole it is probably correct to say that most contemporaries felt that the reviews defined among the reading people a sort of *pays légal.* All of the journals were rather expensive: the *Edinburgh* cost readers five shillings per issue until it was raised in price to six shillings in 1809. Six shillings was a long standard fee, and when the *Westminster Review* was founded in 1824 its price was also set at six shillings. Further, none of these magazines had a circulation comparable to that of the unstamped newspaper press.

Although the *Edinburgh* was too expensive to be bought regularly by any but relatively wealthy readers, and although its contents were not likely to make it a serious competitor for the audience of Gobbett's *Political Register,* still the audience for whom Jeffrey designed the *Edinburgh Review* was a general audience, a mixture of the whole community.

In the *Edinburgh's* famous long reviews of literary works, reviews which were anything but concise notices of current books, Jeffrey and his friends developed for readers a practical body of literary theory which, if a reader adopted it, would allow him if not to obtain an education in the classical sense, at least to master one method of approaching all types of English literature. Jeffrey himself, writing in 1844, summed up to effect and drift of his criticism:

> The *Edinburgh Review,* it is well known, aimed high from the beginning:—And, refusing to confine itself to the humble task of pronouncing on the mere literary merits of the works that name before it, professed to go deeply into the *Principles* on which its judgments were to be rested; as well as to take large and Original views of all important questions to which the works might relate. . . .
>
> I . . . endeavoured to combine Ethical precepts

with Literary Criticism, and earnestly sought to impress my readers with a sense both of the close connection between sound intellectual attainments and the higher elements of Duty and Enjoyment: and of the just and ultimate subordination of the former to the latter.

Jeffrey argued that the betterment of readers and service to the common cause of society were such serious matters that all literature could be judged with reference to them. Readers of the *Edinburgh Review* were encouraged to turn to books with practical ends in view, and to discard books, however famous or well recommended, which did not yield up their treasures to common sense and common decency. Thus, the *Edinburgh* provided readers with a surrogate education which did not require, for the understanding of English literature, that background in classical literature upon which so much previous criticism had been based.

Jeffrey was quite sanguine concerning the capacity of the public to absorb general education. He was not at all convinced that the characteristics of public—what he would have called "popular"—taste were hopelessly vulgar. He believed, on the contrary, that there was a steady improvement of taste. In reviewing Scott's edition of the works of Jonathan Swift, Jeffrey wrote in 1816:

> Now we confess we are no believers in the absolute and permanent corruption of national taste; on the contrary; we think that it is of all faculties, that which is most sure to advance and improve with time and experience; and that, with the exception of those great physical or political disasters which have given a check to civilization itself, there has always been a sensible progress in this particular; and that the general taste of each succeeding generation is better than that of its predecessors.

By the same token, Jeffrey maintained that the improvement of society and the education of public taste were the proper and almost the only proper objects of literary effort. Jeffrey rose to an unusual level of clarity on this point in his review of Madame de Stäel's *De la littérature considerée dans ses raports avec les institutions sociales* (1812):

> It is in the intelligence of the people themselves [wrote Jeffrey] that the chief bulwark of their freedom will be found to consist, and all the principles of political amelioration to originate. This is true, however, as Madame de Stäel observes, only of what she terms "la haute litterature;" or the general cultivation of Philosophy, eloquence, history, and those other departments of learning which refer chiefly to the heart and the understanding, and depend upon a knowledge of human nature, and the attentive study of all that contributes to its actual enjoyments. What is merely for delight, again, and addresses itself exclusively to the imagination, has neither so noble a genealogy, nor half so illustrious a progeny. Poetry and works of gaiety and amusement, together with music and the sister arts of painting and sculpture, have a much slighter connection either with virtue or with freedom.

This brief passage constitutes almost a manifesto in the canon of Jeffrey's critical writings in the *Edinburgh*. It explains that by "literature" he means books of all kinds, and that he placed the highest value not upon works of the imagination but upon what is now called nonfiction. Many of Jeffrey's ideas had considerable influence upon British radicals in the first half of the nineteenth century, but none was more important than this.

Jeffrey expected all books to spread improvement, and he could not understand any idea of human improvement which did not have reference to the context of human society. This placed severe limitations on Jeffrey's ability to understand imaginative literature, and it has ruined his subsequent reputation: the famous phrase "This will never do!" with which he began a review of Wordsworth's *Excursion* is perhaps Jeffrey's only living contribution to English literature. Jeffrey described Wordsworth's poem as "a tissue of moral and devotional ravings," and he condemned its "affected raptures and dull mysticism." His review of Carlyle's translation of *Wilheim Meister* is if anything more outspoken. Since that book was happily a foreign production, Jeffrey was able to blame what he considered to be its faults upon what all of his readers would naturally regard as backward social conditions. Of Goethe's novel, Jeffrey wrote:

> We must say, then, at once that we cannot enter into the spirit of this German idolatry; nor at all comprehend upon what grounds the work before us could ever be considered as admirable, or even a commendable performance. . . . it is throughout altogether unnatural . . . and, where not occupied with the professional squabbles, paltry jargon and scenical profligacy of strolling players, tumblers, and mummers (which may be said to form its staple), is conversant only with incomprehensible mystics and vulgar men of whim, with whom, if it were at all possible to understand them, it would be a baseness to be acquainted.

The point is that Jeffrey's limitations, here so graphically exposed, were deduced from the same system which controlled his shrewd and successful editorial methods. Jeffrey demanded "popularity" from a book, which is to say that he demanded of a book, first of all, that it be clear, and neither dull nor mystical. But he also thought that a writer could, at least in Britain, achieve public notice only if his work, while clear and amusing, also stimulated social improvement. Thus, Jeffrey, in reviewing works of fiction, sought to separate the merely vulgar from work whose claim upon the public mind lay in a clever combination of didacticism and entertainment. Maria Edgeworth, for instance, received Jeffrey's whole-hearted approbation.

Victorians sometimes said that it was Jeffrey's triumph to have increased the *social* importance of literature—to have made reading synonymous with education and made the two into a pastime fashionable among all classes. In this view, the *Edinburgh* is seen as the precursor of such magazines of the mid-century as Dickens' *Household Words* and *All the Year Round*. Jeffrey's ideas on popular literature, what was called earlier in this article his editorial formula, became for some Victorian critics the prototype of all mass circulation journalism of the mid century.

Walter Bagehot, for instance, put the case for this association of cause and effect in his essay "The First Edinburgh Reviewers." Bagehot pointed out that the *Edinburgh Review* reached many more readers than eighteenth century learning and eighteenth century methods of publication. Further, said Bagehot, while under eighteenth century conditions the English social order was seldom subject to important critique and thus to the power of reason and the impulse to reform, the mere existence of *Edinburgh Review,* with its relatively large audience, was enough to insure that government policies would be met continually with effective critical challenge. Education, wrote Bagehot, was the promise of the *Edinburgh Review,* and the need and passion for education among English readers of the early nineteenth century serve to raise the *Review* then to a pitch of influence which no periodical publication had ever enjoyed in England before. To Bagehot's mind, the founding of the *Edinburgh Review* marked the beginning of an era in English letters, and in fact of the modern era. "It is indeed a peculiarity of our times," he wrote:

> that we must instruct so many persons. On politics, on religion, on all less important topics still more, everyone thinks himself competent to think,—in some casual manner does think,—to the best of our means must be taught to think—rightly. . . .

Anyone who turns over pages of issues of the *Edinburgh Review* from the period of twenty-six years during which it was edited by Jeffrey, will understand the justice of Bagehot's remarks. As we have seen, the emphasis on education in the *Edinburgh* was emphatic, and the ideal of education was a very broad one—nothing less than the general improvement of society through the power of literature to spread ideas. The editor and writers of the *Edinburgh* during these years sought to educate their readers directly through long articles, often somewhat technical, upon matters as various as Irish demography, English economics, and the science of optics.

But nonetheless Bagehot believed that there was something casual in the *Edinburgh Review* and in all the literature which sprang up in imitation of its example and success. There was something, said Bagehot, not only casual but unlabored, spontaneous:

> In truth, review writing but exemplifies the casual character of modern literature. Everything about it is temporary and fragmentary. Look at a railway stall; you see books of every colour—blue, yellow, crimson, "ring-streaked, speckled, and spotted," on every subject, in every style, of every opinion, with every conceivable difference, celestial or sublunary, maleficent, beneficent—but all small. People take their literature in morsels, as they take sandwiches on a journey. . . .
>
> There is, as yet, no Act of Parliament compelling a *bona fide* traveller to read. If you wish him to read, you must make reading pleasant. You must give him short views and clear sentences. It will not answer to explain what all the things you describe are *not.* You must begin by saying what they are. There is exactly the difference between the books of this age, and those of a more laborious age, that we feel between the lecture of

a professor and the talk of the man of the world. . . .

Perhaps it was precisely Jeffrey's stance as a man of the world which put him in tune with his audience—even, as he believed with a popular audience. And perhaps this stance also has obscured his subsequent reputation with scholars. (pp. 672-80)

> *John A. Taylor, "The 'Popular' Criticism of the 'Edinburgh Review'," in* Journal of Popular Culture, *Vol. IX, No. 3, Winter, 1975, pp. 672-81.*

James Campbell (essay date 1983)

[*In the following excerpt from a review of* Jeffrey's Criticism *(1983), Campbell argues that Jeffrey's critical platform was informed by social and political conservatism.*]

Shortly after the publication of his *Odes and Epistles* in 1806, Thomas Moore picked up the latest *Edinburgh Review* and was appalled to read its criticism of his book. Rather than post off a reckless letter to the editor, Moore challenged him to a duel, and Francis Jeffrey, who was also the author of the article, accepted. The conflict was prevented by policemen, however, and the group taken down to the station. There, Jeffrey impressed Moore while lying flat on a bench and expatiating in his "oddly pronounced diction" on some literary matter, in "an ever rich and ready wardrobe of phraseology".

Other contemporaries also marvelled at Jeffrey's powers of conversation; he was famous in his lifetime as much for how he talked as for how he wrote. Of the literary celebrities of his day in Edinburgh, he was the one "whom travellers are most in a hurry to see", as J. G. Lockhart mentioned in *Peter's Letters to his Kinsfolk.* Fortunately for them, but perhaps less so for posterity, he was also the most cordial of men. "The true reviewing diet is Champagne moussu and devilled biscuit", noted sly Lockhart. In addition to being the leading contributor to his own *Edinburgh Review,* Jeffrey was also a successful Whig advocate (later Lord Advocate) and a determined socialite, who kept as keen an eye on his role in smart society as on his place in literature. Indeed, the latter came about almost by accident, since the *Edinburgh* was brought into existence as a mere diversion: "the main object of every one of us, I understand to be, our own amusement and improvement", he wrote in 1803.

Like most easy talkers, however, Jeffrey occasionally turned windbag, and the tendency inevitably spilled on to the page. For example, here he is praising Shakespeare:

> Although his sails are purple and perfumed, and his prow of beaten gold, they waft him on his voyage, not less, but more rapidly and directly than if they had been composed of baser materials. All his excellencies, like those of Nature herself, are thrown out together; and, instead of interfering with, support and recommend each other. His flowers are not tied up in garlands, nor his fruits crushed into baskets—but spring living from the soil, in all the dew and freshness of youth. . . .

And so on and so on. The generous amounts of space which nineteenth-century editors could afford to grant their contributors were often at the root of this kind of verbiage, or else behind forty pages of "The History and Development of. . . ." (what ever subject) before the first mention of the book allegedly under review. In a neat and otherwise informative introduction to *Jeffrey's Criticism* [see excerpt below], Peter Morgan tells us little of Jeffrey's writing methods, but they must have been shaped, above all, by haste. For the first issue of the *Edinburgh* he wrote six articles, which occupied seventy-five pages, and in the first few years of publication reviewed books on, among other subjects, architecture, philosophy, theology, law, geology, politics of every hue, not to mention the poetry, fiction, drama and aesthetics which form the basis of this new selection, the first since 1910. Far from being the work of a man of leisure, as is sometimes assumed, Jeffrey's essays have the stamp of productions from a fluent pen dashing to meet a deadline. A good editor would have cut most of them by half.

The mainspring of Jeffrey's criticism is his view of the relationship between literature and society. Generally, he believed that the writer's primary duty was to the public, and that what could not be said or done in full view of the public—anything which offended against his narrow idea of decency—should not be allowed to pass on to the page. It is obvious to contemporary readers who have had experience of Dostoevsky, Kafka and Camus that this view of literature and society (and therefore of the individual and society) is unimaginative, and yet Jeffrey cannot really be excused by the age he lived in. His most serious weakness as a critic resides in his unwillingness to acknowledge with full heart other powers in literature than those of social cultivation and personal refinement, and also his trepidation in the face of what he called "dangerous and turbulent emotions" in both public and private domains. The length to which Jeffrey drove this literary and emotional conservatism was itself, paradoxically, a personal eccentricity.

In his writing he is disconcertingly, even untrustworthily, self-assured, and, equally, dull. A vocabulary as well stocked as his, combined with such a lively intelligence, could hardly fail to turn up the occasional arresting phrase or original metaphor, and there are numerous dashes of insight, but in general his style is unexciting. He is less concerned with how a particular work might aid his understanding of his place among men, than among gentlemen. This was the public mask he insisted on wearing; in the preface to his four-volume **Contributions** (1844), he modestly claimed his chief merit to be the ability "to impress my readers with a sense, both of the close connection between sound intellectual attainments and the higher elements of Duty and Enjoyment; and of the just and ultimate subordination of the former to the latter."

His reviews bear this out. They are full of phrases like "the first trait of refinement in manners", "a certain tact", "the fame of the poet is popular or nothing"; and his favourite words—"noble", "decorum", "taste", "decency"— pepper the pages of this book. The contrasting terms are neatly strung together in an attack on Goethe's *Wilhelm Meister's Apprenticeship:* "absurd, puerile, incongruous, vul-

gar and affected"; it constituted "one flagrant offence against every principle of taste", which we may suppose was most revolting of all to the Prince of Reviewers.

The kind of confusion this worship of taste could lead to is revealed in his 1809 essay on Burns who, he actually writes, "had evidently a very false and crude notion of what constituted *strength* in writing". Although generally approving of Burns, Jeffrey cannot help fussing over his "contempt for prudence, decency and irregularity", the "fervour that is sometimes indelicate", and the poet's "want of polish"—all the characteristics, in short, which most appeal to us today (and, needless to say, to a large part of Burns's readership then). It is a pity that Morgan has excised from the Burns essay the section which deals with the linguistic divisions in the Scottish mind. This subject is still very much alive in Scotland today—for some, painfully so—and Jeffrey's remarks are worth reading. He suggests that the use of dialect conjures up to the older generation of his day their "schoolday innocence", that it is associated "not only with that olden time which is uniformly conceived as more pure, lofty, and simple than the present, but also with the soft and bright colours of remembered childhood". It is typical of him to distribute these emotions between old age and infancy, both of which he was entitled to regard as foreign to his own state of ever-increasing cultivation. Mention of "remembered childhood" recalls his persistent mockery of the Lake Poets, Wordsworth in particular, for their "lowliness of tone", which he equated with "silliness", "rusticity" and "childishness". What must have oppressed him in these associations was their remoteness from "polished life", their ill-fittedness to the world of affairs to which he considered he properly belonged. Whether or not he had a secret admiration for something (and it is said that he knew Wordsworth's *Lyrical Ballads* by heart) whatever was connected with the "silly" or "childish" side of life had to be publicly reviled.

Yet, not surprisingly, these "dangerous and turbulent emotions" continued to worry him. Half of the many appealing anecdotes concerning Jeffrey emphasize his personal warmth and charm, even sentimentality. When Mrs Siddons called on him unannounced and found him in floods of tears, she assumed he had suffered a dreadful bereavement—in fact, he had been reading *The Old Curiosity Shop.* Moore remembered that as the seconds fumbled with the pistols in preparation for their duel, Jeffrey talked cheerfully about the weather: the resolute refusal to display his deepest feelings in his writing has demanded a legend to balance it.

One of the effects of his personal repression was in keeping with the time. That "oddly pronounced diction" which Moore noticed as Jeffrey lay blethering on the prison bench was the result of his poor attempt to do what many Scottish gentlemen, of the eighteenth and nineteenth (and twentieth) centuries felt they had to do: cast off their native accents, which were considered to be, well, "absurd, puerile, incongruous, vulgar". Yet it is interesting to discover that Carlyle, who spent many hours in conversation with him (they fell out when Carlyle rejected his advice on a social matter) felt he was most himself when he could be "got to speak Scotch". The general remarks Jeffrey makes in the Burns essay, and elsewhere on Scott, show how great an affection, and admiration, he had for the unique robustness of Scots, even if he did not think it quite the thing for a grown-up to speak it.

So the Jeffrey we are reading in these pages (less than one tenth of **Contributions,** which was in turn less than a third of his total contribution to the *Review*) is only the critic he thought the world would wish him to be. History has proved him wrong, but perhaps he would not have minded: he was consistent with his original explanation of the founding of the *Edinburgh Review* as an amusement, and once he was made Lord Advocate in 1829 he relinquished the editorship and rarely contributed thereafter. It would not have seemed right of him to do so, and the taps which had once flowed so wonderfully were turned off, quite as easily, it seems, as they had been turned on.

> *James Campbell, "In Defence of Decency," in*
> The Times Literary Supplement, *No. 4172,*
> *March 18, 1983, p. 271.*

Peter F. Morgan   (essay date 1983)

[*Morgan is an English critic specializing in nineteenth-century English poetry and literary criticism. In the following excerpt, he discusses Jeffrey's professional associations with and editorial advice to William Wordsworth, Thomas Carlyle, and Charles Dickens.*]

[Although] Jeffrey descended to ridicule of Wordsworth there was some philosophical background and depth to his attack. The onslaught certainly affected the poet himself and produced a strong response, particularly in the 'Essay, supplementary to the Preface' of 1815, as well as in revisions of the poetry. Coleridge also leaped to his friend's defence in the *Biographia Literaria,* 1817. However, Wordsworth's poetic statement, most relevantly in *The Excursion,* 1814, remained basically unaffected either by Jeffrey's attacks or by the poet's own tinkerings and modifications of style.

In the essay of 1815 Wordsworth refutes Jeffrey's position by asserting impressively that the original poet must create the taste by which he is to be admired. He cannot rely, as Jeffrey and his school would, on 'immediate and universal' effects, since language is 'subject to endless fluctuations and arbitrary associations. The genius of the poet melts these down for his purpose.' The interaction between poet and reader, here as in the Preface to *Lyrical Ballads,* leaves small space for the mere critic. Wordsworth, like Coleridge later in *Biographia Literaria,* paints a portrait of the ideal critic, in order to show by implication how far such reviewers as Jeffrey are removed from it, but he adds that even the ideal critic is untrustworthy. He turns away towards the sensitive individual reader who, with those like him, comes to make up, not the unreliable 'public,' but the 'people' whose sanction is won only through the course of long centuries. Thus Wordsworth rejects Jeffrey, the critic—and the public—in favour of the inspired poet and the sensitive reader. The conflict, here adumbrated in the relationship between Wordsworth and Jeffrey, has remained unresolved until the present day.

Wordsworth's doughty defence of himself is supported by the judicious arguments of Coleridge in *Biographia Literaria.* In chapter XXI of that work his friend objects to the criticism of Jeffrey and the *Edinburgh Review* on five comprehensive grounds: as unphilosophical, personal, political, trivial and uncritical. Yet, in spite of Coleridge's onslaught on Jeffrey, one can still discover general points of contact between their critiques. The editor's argument lacks Coleridge's profundity, subtlety and judicial sympathy. He cannot appreciate the vital contribution of idealism towards creating the poetic whole. Nevertheless, for both journalist and theorist, poetry and criticism are general in concern. Both criticize Wordsworth's theory of poetic language and subject matter on social and aesthetic grounds. Similarly, Coleridge's view of Shakespearian imagery is parallel to that set forth by Jeffrey in his articles on Alison and Hazlitt.

Wordsworth himself was unyielding in theory to Jeffrey's attacks, but there is evidence of responsive changes in his poetic style. As he gave ground, his fame grew, until he became a central figure in the Victorian pantheon. A basic, permanent difference between Wordsworth and Jeffrey is illustrated when the poet affirms the nobility of the life of the poor peasant in Book IV of *The Excursion.* He does this as part of his attack on the spiritual shortcomings of modern society. But this onslaught was absolutely unacceptable to Jeffrey who occupied a position of literary, judicial and political authority in the society to whose values he is committed. Wordsworth's poetry has an irreducible quality of radical greatness and originality which can be diminished and obscured neither by the afterthoughts and the revisions of the poet himself, nor by the cavillings of the critic. On the other hand, the scholar must sympathize with Jeffrey, the harassed man of affairs, yearning, on behalf of himself and of the public, for spiritual refreshment. He must also appreciate the impact which Jeffrey made not only on the poet, but also on the climate of public opinion in which Wordsworth's poetry was ultimately accepted.

. . . . .

As a relatively young man Jeffrey had been harsh to his contemporary Wordsworth. He did not recant when he collected some of his contributions to the *Edinburgh Review* in 1844. On the other hand, as a man of over fifty Jeffrey lent an encouraging hand to his compatriot Carlyle, a youth of humble origin, an ungrateful graduate of Edinburgh University, without a professional career, and anxious to make his way and find a message to communicate in literature. Jeffrey soon recognized Carlyle's genius—a feeling which was to a degree reciprocated—even though his unorthodox style and opinions often enraged him.

Though Jeffrey obtusely attacked Goethe's *Wilhelm Meister's Apprenticeship,* translated by Carlyle, he later welcomed the young Germanophile as a contributor to the *Edinburgh Review,* where his articles appeared between 1827 and 1832. Carlyle seized the opportunity offered by its editor to achieve some reputation by presenting a critical appreciation of modern German literature, by re-evaluating Burns, and, later, by diagnosing the ills of contemporary English society. Carlyle's views sometimes directly opposed and contradicted those which Jeffrey himself had expressed. For example, he rejected the accusation against the Germans both of mysticism and of bad taste. His view of Burns, like that of Jeffrey, was appreciative of the poetry, but critical of the man. However, Carlyle judged not by the conventional, but by his own nascent morality of the hero. Finally, like Jeffrey, Carlyle saw his own times as turbulent, but he did not fearfully withdraw from the prospect into a defence of the gentle amelioration of the status quo by parliamentary means. On the contrary, he relished the depiction of disorder, the diagnosis of social debility, including the threadbare nature of English institutions, and the prognosis of radical remedies, both political and spiritual.

In spite of these indications of serious differences in outlook, Jeffrey's early attempts at editorial control over Carlyle were relatively mild. However, his contributor was indignant over the mutilations inflicted on the Burns article in the name of the same objections which Jeffrey had raised against Wordsworth: mysticism, exaggeration, jargon and verbosity. Jeffrey tried a milder method than that which he had employed upon Wordsworth, in order to win over Carlyle as both writer and fellow human being to what Carlyle himself called 'the joys of sociality.' This method took the form of social intercourse, including long friendly discussions and a frequent correspondence. However, though Carlyle enjoyed the debates and appreciated Jeffrey's generosity of spirit, he remained untempted. Early in the relationship, he stubbornly withdrew from Edinburgh to the isolation of Craigenputtock, where he penned the independent article on Burns and began to write *Sartor Resartus.*

It is ironical that, having scorned Jeffrey's urbane advances, Carlyle later settled in London. He himself came to judge Jeffrey as a '*Scotch* Voltaire.' Jeffrey for his part was disappointed by the younger man as he manifested himself in a later contribution to the *Edinburgh Review,* 'Characteristics':

> I fear Carlyle will not do. . . . The misfortune is, that he is very obstinate and . . . conceited, and unluckily in a place like [London], he finds people enough to abet and applaud him, to intercept the operation of the otherwise infallible remedy of general avoidance and neglect. It is a great pity, for he is a man of genius and industry, and with the capacity of being an elegant and impressive writer.

Elegance certainly was not one of Carlyle's goals. Both men continued to recognize a bond of affection between them, but when Jeffrey tried to insist upon it he went too far. His comparison of Jane Welsh to Titania and Carlyle to Bottom (himself by inference Oberon!) led to the breaking-off of the intimacy.

Carlyle himself finally summed up his view of Jeffrey, many years after his death [see excerpt dated 1867]: 'He was not deep enough, pious or reverent enough, to have been great in Literature; but he was a man intrinsically of

veracity; said nothing without meaning it in some considerable degree; had the quickest perceptions, excellent practical discernment of what lay before him; was in earnest, too, though not "dreadfully in earnest";—in short was well fitted to set forth that *Edinburgh Review . . .* and become *Coryphaeus* of his generation.'

Jeffrey, as man, editor and critic, offered Carlyle a great deal, in fact more than that individualist was willing to accept. What he did take advantage of was the platform which the *Edinburgh Review* and its editor's friendship provided for him in beginning to achieve a literary reputation. What Jeffrey offered and Carlyle did not want to accept on any terms was advice. He felt that he did not need the advice which Jeffrey proffered concerning how to manage his wife, where to live, how to get on with other people, what to write and how to think. Similarly with Jane Welsh. The advice which Jeffrey offered her, playfully and condescendingly, she rejected. The break came, never to be entirely healed. The warm friendship between the two men was never resumed.

Jeffrey's critical theorizing and political and philosophical speculations were spurned as shallow and outdated by the metaphysical Carlyle. On the other hand, Carlyle in retrospect and in a few moments of social intercourse delighted in Jeffrey's vivacity, even though he recognized all too well the limitations of its intellectual base. For Carlyle life was a struggle. In spite of this and because of the breadth of his sympathy he knew Jeffrey as a 'bright island' in the midst of the stormy ocean of experience. Memories of him rose, with others more poignant, 'benignantly luminous from the bosom of the grim dead night!' Thus Carlyle provides the reader with his characteristically emotional personal perspective from which to view Jeffrey the man and critic.

                    . . . . .

There was little trace of Jeffrey's failure in his relationships with Wordsworth and Carlyle in his friendship with Dickens. Now he was an even older man, still looking down upon the world from the eminence of the judge's bench, but no longer the public critic or the manager of men. He was instead the self-indulgent reader, though his feelings still retained the freshness of youth, influenced by the thought and sensibility of that time. Lockhart commented scornfully and unfairly: 'He who had bragged of "crushing" Skiddaw, has learned to gaze with awe upon Brixton Rise.' The element of sentimentality had always been present in Jeffrey. After all, this is another term for the cultivation of the feelings. Part of Dickens's early Victorian work appealed to the tender spot in Jeffrey's heart, and Jeffrey only lamented that he could not shed still more tears as he commented on the young writer's novels and Christmas stories as they appeared. Furthermore, he was pleased and impressed by the combination of emotional expression with material and social success in Dickens's achievement.

In his relationship with Dickens, Jeffrey was friendly and concerned. He advised him concerning financial matters. He rejoiced in the popularity of his works, and he urged him to write in such a way as to extend that popularity still further. His views of the novels are characteristic of the critic in retirement, at his ease, indulging the harmless emotions in the carefully guarded precincts of Dickens's early fiction. He expressed his immediate emotional reaction to the appearance of the characters as they struck him in the convenient form of Christmas book or monthly part. At the same time, Jeffrey's views are representative of the feelings of a large number of Dickens's contemporaries.

Jeffrey took pleasure in Dickens's portrayal of the innocent, whether comic or serious. Especially, he luxuriated in the feeling of grief over the loss of this innocence; it may be in a boy, for example, Paul Dombey. More strongly felt, the innocence is embodied in a girl who loses either by death, as Little Nell does, or by unbearable social and sexual pressures, as do Lilian in *The Chimes* and Edith Dombey. For Jeffrey such figures as Nell, Lilian and Edith were symbols of a victimization prevalent in contemporary society. He was moved by them, as he was affected by Dickens generally as a social moralist.

At the same time, Jeffrey, now the self-indulgent sentimentalist, was loath to allow the moralist his prerogative of satire. Though he accepted the comic-moral combination in Tom Pinch in *Chuzzlewit,* he criticized Dickens's caricatures at both decoratively comic and seriously thematic levels. He objected to the minor figures of the first kind in *Dombey and Son* and *David Copperfield.* He disliked the moral caricature exemplified in such variously large-scale figures as Uriah Heep, Pecksniff and Dombey. He refused the social satire, directed against the city and utilitarianism in *The Chimes,* and against American culture in *American Notes* and *Martin Chuzzlewit.*

The following paragraph on Dickens's presentation of Edith in *Dombey and Son* is typical. Jeffrey is discussing the July 1847 number of the novel:

> It is the most finished, perhaps, in diction; and in the delicacy and fineness of its touches, both of pleasantry and pathos, of any you have ever given us; while it rises to higher and deeper passions; not resting, like most of the former, in sweet thoughtfulness, and thrilling attractive tenderness, but boldly wielding all the lofty and terrible elements of tragedy, and bringing before us the appalling struggles of a proud, scornful, and repentant spirit. I am proud that you should thus shew us new views of your genius—but I shall always love its gentler magic the most; and never leave Nelly and Paul and Florence for Edith, with whatever potent spells you may invest her; though I am prepared for great things from her.

For his part, Dickens took pleasure in Jeffrey's esteem and friendship, showing his gratitude by naming his son after the critic and by dedicating *The Chimes* and *The Cricket on the Hearth* to him. What Jeffrey praised remained a strong element in Dickens's work throughout these years. Perhaps his warning concerning the anti-American element in *Martin Chuzzlewit* was heeded. More probably, his suggestion concerning a mollified fate for Edith Dombey was taken. At the same time, the caricature to which

Jeffrey objected remained an integral part of Dickens's writing.

Towards the end Jeffrey's reaction to Dickens and his fiction was marked by an exaggeration of the feeling which he displayed personally towards Carlyle and which had led him to urge his angry compatriot to come over into the camp of sociable humanity, and had even led him to make the same attempt critically with the uncongenial Wordsworth. Jeffrey's attitude towards Dickens was patronizing and comfortable. He warmed his aged heart at the fires of Dickens's youthful sentimentalism. At the same time, he applauded the novelist's success, sought to direct it to a certain extent, and gave him sensible advice concerning the management of his affairs. Here there was none of the critical animosity which marked the relationship with Wordsworth, and none of the philosophical and personal tension which characterized that with Carlyle.

This survey of personal relationships with great writers should illuminate the view of Jeffrey's critical opinions as expressed directly through his articles in the *Edinburgh Review* and indirectly through editorial policy there. For Jeffrey literature was important both personally and socially. His views are limited, but nevertheless to be respected, as often cogently argued, eloquently expressed, and to a degree representative of his time, as well as highly influential. In particular, Jeffrey enjoyed the warm humanity of Dickens, but he could not appreciate the mysticism of Wordsworth or Carlyle. Both of these reactions stemmed from his late eighteenth-century Anglo-Scottish upbringing. At the same time, and because of the same cultural heritage, Jeffrey deplored the self-imposed isolation which accompanies the mysticism of Wordsworth and Carlyle. As thinker and critic, reviewer, editor and man of affairs, as well as human being, Jeffrey resisted the notion of the isolation of the artist. He asserted a form of relationship between artist and public which won assent from Dickens and his readers, though not from Wordsworth and Carlyle, nor from posterity. Nevertheless, alternative patterns still remain to be found. (pp. 13-19)

> *Peter F. Morgan, in an introduction to* Jeffrey's Criticism, *edited by Peter F. Morgan, Scottish Academic Press, 1983, pp. 1-19.*

FURTHER READING

Bald, R. C. "Francis Jeffrey as a Literary Critic." *The Nineteenth Century and After* XCVII, No. DLXXVI (February 1925): 201-05.

> Praises Jeffrey's critical faculties, finding his principle fault to be an "excessive confidence in his own position."

"Jeffrey and Hazlitt." *Blackwood's Edinburgh Magazine* III, No. XV (June 1818): 303-06.

> Compares the principles and critical methods of Jeffrey with those of English essayist William Hazlitt.

Charvat, William. "Francis Jeffrey in America." *The New England Quarterly* XIV (June 1941): 309-34.
    Details events surrounding Jeffrey's 1812 visit to the United States, commenting on his reception by the writer Washington Irving and President James Monroe, as well as his attitude toward the American people in general.

Clive, John. *Scotch Reviewers: The* Edinburgh Review, *1802-1815.* London: Faber and Faber, 1957, 224 p.
    Attempts to "shed some light on [the *Edinburgh Review's*] origin, its editor and his editorial problems, and its chief contributors and their views on matters political, social and economic, literary, and historical. . . ."

Cockburn, Lord. *Life of Lord Jeffrey, with a Selection from His Correspondence.* 2 vols. Edinburgh: Adam and Charles Black, 1852.
    Critical biography by one of Jeffrey's law associates in Scotland.

Coleman, Deidre. "Jeffrey and Coleridge: Four Unpublished Letters." *The Wordsworth Circle* XVIII, No. 1 (Winter 1987): 39-45.
    Reprints four previously unpublished letters written in 1808 by Jeffrey to Samuel Taylor Coleridge offering the poet advice on his writing career.

Derby, J. Raymond. "The Paradox of Francis Jeffrey: Reason Versus Sensibility." *Modern Language Quarterly* 7, No. 4 (December 1946): 489-500.
    Examines ways in which "Jeffrey's identifiable reviews and surviving letters reveal inconsistencies that suggest conflict between his native sensibility and his reason."

Erdman, David V. and Zall, Paul M. "Coleridge and Jeffrey in Controversy." *Studies in Romanticism* 14, No. 1 (Winter 1975): 75-83.
    Discusses Jeffrey's role in "stimulating and, in a sense, orchestrating the mode and tone of attack" aimed at Samuel Taylor Coleridge's *Biographia Literaria* by several prominent critics.

Flynn, Philip. *Francis Jeffrey.* Newark: University of Delaware Press, 1978, 218 p.
    Studies Jeffrey's career as it was affected by the political, moral, aesthetic, and psychological perspectives prominent during his time.

Guyer, Byron. "Francis Jeffrey's 'Essay on Beauty'." *The Huntington Library Quarterly* XIII, No. 1 (1949-50): 71-85.
    Examines the philosophical influences suggested in "An Essay on Beauty", which Jeffrey composed for an entry in the 1824 *Encyclopedia Britannica.*

Hatch, Ronald B. " 'This Will Never Do'." *The Review of English Studies* n. s. XXI, No. 81 (February 1970): 56-62.
    Compares the text of the edited essays and reviews collected in *Contributions to the Edinburgh Review* to that of the originals in the *Edinburgh Review,* finding both subtle and substantial differences despite Jeffrey's claim that he revised his work very little.

Hughes, Merritt Y. "The Humanism of Francis Jeffrey." *The Modern Language Review* XVI (1921): 243-51.
    Proposes that Plato's *Republic,* and the humanistic beliefs Jeffrey derived therefrom, informed his views on poetry and may have prompted his dismissal of Wordsworth's and Coleridge's poetry.

Mellown, Muriel J. "Francis Jeffrey, Lord Byron, and *English Bards, and Scotch Reviewers.*" *Studies in Scottish Literature* XVI (1981): 80-90.
    Discusses the relationship between Jeffrey and English poet Lord Byron, proposing that "Jeffrey established a model which Byron naturally respected. In this way, Jeffrey may have contributed, albeit in a limited, indirect fashion, to the literary standards of Byron's whole career as a poet."

Moncreiff, James. "The Late Lord Jeffrey." *The North British Review* XIII, No. XXV (May 1850): 273-84.
    Obituary article highlighting Jeffrey's career and contributions to Scottish letters.

Morgan, Peter. "Carlyle, Jeffrey and the *Edinburgh Review.*" *Neophilologus* LIV (1970): 297-310.
    Discusses Jeffrey's influence on Scottish essayist Thomas Carlyle whose work Jeffrey frequently published in the *Edinburgh Review.* Morgan states that "Jeffrey's attempts at editorial control [over Carlyle], what he called 'vamping and patching,' were relatively mild. The *Edinburgh Review* needed new blood, and he was glad of Carlyle's."

————. "Francis Jeffrey as Epistolary Critic." *Studies in Scottish Literature* XVII (1982): 116-34.
    Reprints correspondence by Jeffrey to James Grahame, a Scottish cleric and poet, and Archibald Alison, a Scottish cleric and essayist, commenting on Jeffrey's "epistolary and critical tact."

Noyes, Russell. "Wordsworth and Jeffrey in Controversy." *Indiana University Publications Humanities Series,* No. 5 (1939-1941): 3-54.
    Examines Jeffrey's rejection of Wordsworth's poetry, deeming Jeffrey's criticism misinformed and slanderous.

Owen, W. J. B. "Wordsworth and Jeffrey in Collaboration." *The Review of English Studies* n. s. XV, No. 58 (May 1964): 161-67.
    Closely analyzes "parallels in wording and argument" between William Wordsworth's *Preface to the Lyrical Ballads* and Jeffrey's scathing review of Wordsworth's *Excursion,* suggesting that the *Preface* responds to the review.

Peters, John U. "Jeffrey's Keats Criticism." *Studies in Scottish Literature* X, No. 3 (January 1973): 175-85.
    Examines Jeffrey's critical methods, focusing on his reviews of Keats's poetry.

Smith, D. Nichol, ed. *Jeffrey's Literary Criticism.* London: Humphrey Milford, 1910, 216 p.
    Includes an introductory overview to Jeffrey's life and literature by Smith.

Tagart, Edward. Review of *Contributions to the Edinburgh Review,* by Francis Jeffrey. *The Westminster and Foreign Quarterly Review* LIII, No. I (April 1850): 1-38.
    Reviews the essays in Jeffrey's collection, arguing that his aesthetic principles are misinformed.

Weir, William. Review of *Life of Lord Jeffrey, with a Selection from His Correspondence,* by Lord Cockburn. *The Westminster and Foreign Quarterly Review,* LVIII, No. CXIII (1 July 1852): 95-110.
    Attacks Jeffrey's aesthetic theories, accusing him of making the poet "the victim of judicial oppression."

Wellek, René. "From Jeffrey to Shelley." In his *A History of Modern Criticism, 1750-1950: The Romantic Age*. New Haven, Conn.: Yale University Press, 1955, 459 p.

    Finds Jeffrey's critical philosophies contradictory and problematic.

Anthony Trollope

1815-1882

English novelist, autobiographer, short story writer, dramatist, and essayist.

The following entry presents criticism of Trollope's novel *Barchester Towers* (1857). For information on Trollope's complete career, see *NCLC,* Vol. 6.

Credited with establishing Trollope's reputation as one of the foremost novelists of his time, *Barchester Towers* is considered among the finest social comedies of the Victorian era. It is the second in Trollope's series of six "Barsetshire Chronicles," which collectively depict various aspects of clerical life in a small English cathedral town. *Barchester Towers* continues the story begun in *The Warden* (1855), centering largely on a political power-struggle between factions of the Anglican Church over the impending appointment of a clergyman to fill an office left vacant at the close of the earlier novel. Noted for its lively, readable style, vivid characterizations, and humorous portrayal of everyday life, *Barchester Towers* is regarded by many as the apogee of Trollope's comic achievement. Of his entire canon of fiction, which consists of more than forty novels and numerous short stories, *Barchester Towers* remains his most popular work.

A high-ranking postal official, Trollope first conceived of Barsetshire while surveying the southwestern counties of England for the Post Office; as he records in his *Autobiography* (1883): "In the course of the job I visited Salisbury, and whilst wandering there one mid-summer evening round the purlieus of the cathedral I conceived the story of *The Warden*—from whence came that series of novels of which Barchester, with its bishops, deans, and archdeacon, was the central site." While writing *Barchester Towers* Trollope kept a precise record of his daily production. Insisting that he wrote best when writing quickly, he rose early and wrote steadily for three hours before work, averaging 1,000 words per hour and eight to ten manuscript pages per day. Trollope planned *Barchester Towers* as a single-volume, two-month project; instead, the scope of the work exceeded his initial expectations, and the novel was completed in three volumes six months after he had begun writing it. As was the case with each of his novels, Trollope's wife recopied the entire manuscript of *Barchester Towers* and Trollope proofread it meticulously before submitting it to his publisher's reader, Joseph Cauvin. Cauvin praised much of the work but objected to a number of passages he considered vulgar or exaggerated. Trollope allayed his concerns in many instances by simply changing the wording of certain segments. On some matters, however, Trollope was resolute—he refused, for example, to shorten the book or to add, as his publisher wished, the subtitle "The Female Bishop." Responding to the latter suggestion, Trollope wrote: "I do not like a second title nor the one you name. I do not wish the bishop male or female to be considered the chief character in the

book." *Barchester Towers* was published, without the subtitle, in the spring of 1857. The novel was a popular and critical success, completely recouping publication costs within two months of its release and garnering a host of favorable reviews.

Resuming the story begun in *The Warden, Barchester Towers* humorously describes the political machinations that precede appointments to various offices within the Barchester diocese, including that of the wardenship of a nursing home for the elderly. The position had been vacated by Septimus Harding, who, at the close of the earlier novel, resigned when a London newspaper questioned his integrity for receiving a salary that encompassed the greatest share of charitable funds entrusted to the church for the care of residents in that institution. Using the conscientious Harding as a model of moral propriety, *Barchester Towers* further contrasts the conservative, genteel society of Barchester with the brazenly progressive world of London. The death of Barchester's bishop at the beginning of the novel is followed shortly by the appointment and arrival of Bishop Proudie, along with his domineering wife and his chaplain, the Reverend Obadiah Slope. All are of the Low Church faction in the divided Church of England, the bishop holding liberal views on doctrinal matters while his wife and chaplain denounce the "outward ceremonies" and traditions held sacred by the High Church party. Exemplified especially by the character of Slope, a fawning, unscrupulous character whom critics have compared to Uriah Heep in Charles Dickens's *David Copperfield,* these Low-Church "outsiders" from London contrast sharply with the clergy of Barchester, represented largely by Harding and his son-in-law, Archdeacon Grantly. Other characters playing a key role in the resultant "war" for control of the diocese include Dr. Vesey Stanhope, a high-ranking clergyman returning from Italy, where he had lived "in easy idleness" for twelve years; and Francis Arabin, a well-educated and eloquent young clergyman of High Church sympathy. At the novel's close, Harding rejects an offer to become Barchester's Dean; at his suggestion, the prestigious benefice is awarded to Arabin.

Barchester Towers has been described by Robin Gilmour as a "universal comic drama of change." Although the novel deals with divisions, corruption, and hypocrisy within the Anglican Church and the callous zeal of reformers, Trollope carefully avoided doctrinal or political specifics of these matters. Focusing instead on their broader social implications, he presented a conflict common to novels of the period: the struggle between an admiration of the past and a desire for permanence on one hand, and the passion for progress and social mobility on the other. To symbolize this discord, Trollope established a contrast between the world at large, represented especially by London, and the sleepy provincial town of Barchester. Evading overt political controversy, the narrator affectionately describes the comic resistance of Barchesterians to the ideas, attitudes, and actions of such outsiders as Slope, the Proudies, and the Stanhopes; at the same time, Trollope conveyed his own ideological sympathies through satirical characterizations and commentary by the narrator. For example, Slope's tasteless condescension in his dealings with the gentle Harding is typical of the improprieties of Proudie's entire Low Church faction—all of whom contrast sharply with the genteel, High Church Barchesterians. When Slope asserts to Harding that "new men are carrying out new measures, and are carting away the useless rubbish of past centuries," the narrator comments: "A man is nothing now unless he has within him a full appreciation of the new era; an era in which it would seem that neither honesty nor truth is very desirable, but in which success is the only touchstone of merit." Trollope thus objects to Low Church zeal that would sweep away all that is rich in tradition, yet recognizes, as is evident in his depiction of Vesey Stanhope, the High Church vice in tolerating what has become corrupt and useless. The common critical consensus is that Trollope neither opposed change nor viewed it as unnecessary; however, critics note that in *Barchester Towers* Trollope granted Harding the spoils, satisfying the Victorian desire for permanence in the face of unsettling social change.

Beatrice Curtis Brown called *Barchester Towers* "one of the books most entertaining to read, yet one of the less deeply interesting—it makes a shallower impact on the mind although it undoubtedly makes a lasting impact on the memory." Modern critics largely concur, asserting that the characters in *Barchester Towers* lack depth in that the author does not penetrate beyond the external manifestations of their moods and emotions, providing little more than entertainment for his readers. William Cadbury, however, has written that in *Barchester Towers* Trollope sought to achieve not a detailed, insightful rendering of the lives of Barchesterians but rather a "panoramic view of the operation of politics in social relations," necessitating distance from his characters. Cadbury explains that the reader must view each character "as an example of his type, with attributes and attitudes which we must judge. If we were to see any of these characters as we see ourselves, there would be danger of accepting their norms as ours, and thus danger of losing the panoramic view which is necessary to the comedy."

While acknowledging his skill in portraying a realistic milieu, early twentieth-century critics denigrated Trollope for the narrative intrusions prevalent in *Barchester Towers,* echoing the earlier objections of Henry James, who viewed these digressions and Trollope's use of such comic names as Dr. Fillgrave and Farmer Greenacre as "slaps at credulity." Recent critics, however, have deemed Trollope's narrator an important aspect of his artistry, providing a persona that allowed him to offer insight into human nature. Moreover, by revealing outcomes and subverting plots, Trollope's narrator effects a suspenseless story that focuses on moral contrasts between characters, fostering a sense of confidence between the reader and the narrator. In this manner, according to U. C. Knoepflmacher, Trollope achieves an "illusion of order" in which, "as sharers and participants . . . novelist and reader become tentative allies against chaos." In mid-Victorian England, "chaos" included a host of disturbing changes: dizzyingly rapid industrialization, overcrowding and urban displacement, and spiritual emptiness due to loss of faith in the tenets of orthodox Christianity. Especially distressing to Trollope was the increasingly competitive and commercial way of life that accompanied these social changes; *Barchester Towers* reasserts traditional, humanistic values, reflecting Trollope's belief that the novel should be morally instructive. Emphasizing this view, Trollope wrote in his *Autobiography* that "the novelist, if he have a conscience, must preach his sermons with the same purpose as the clergyman. . . . He can make virtue alluring and vice ugly." The success of *Barchester Towers* in so doing has been aptly stated by Knoepflmacher, who wrote: "In the invented, delightfully artificial world of Barchester, where Anthony Trollope pulls the strings, the meek actually *can* inherit the earth."

(See also *Dictionary of Literary Biography,* Vols. 21 and 57; and *Something about the Author,* Vol. 22.)

The Saturday Review, London   (essay date 1857)

[*In the following excerpt, the critic presents a favorable review of* Barchester Towers, *focusing on its successful characterizations and lively plot.*]

Barchester Towers is a very clever book. Indeed it is, if anything, too clever, and the whole story is rather too much a series of brilliant but disjointed sketches. It is a continuation of Mr. Trollope's former story, the *Warden,* and is written in the same vein, but with more power and finish. The interest chiefly turns on the fortunes of a chaplain who is in attendance on a new bishop appointed to preside over Barchester. He is of the oily school, and governs through the devotion of female admirers, and by his own consummate impudence. Naturally he stirs the wrath of the archdeacon, whom readers of the *Warden* will remember to have played so conspicuous a part in that tale. The archdeacon is furious at this interloper, and wages deadly war against him. To oppose him, he brings down from Oxford a noted adherent of the tenets most directly conflicting with those of his Exeter Hall enemy. Then comes the tug of war; for not only are the combatants at the opposite poles of English theology, but they are rivals in love, and excellently is the war described. Every chapter is full of fresh amusement; and although we know that poetical justice is sure ultimately to fall heavily on the chaplain, for a long time he has it all his own way, and treads on the necks of his foes. Such a conflict is a hard matter to describe. It is necessary to make it lively, and yet real—to give characteristic touches, and yet escape vulgarity—to handle theological disputes without bitterness, injustice, or profanity. Considering the dangers he runs, Mr. Trollope's success is wonderfully great. The theologians, unlike most theologians in novels, are thoroughly human, and retain the mixed nature of ordinary men; and, what is more, they are described impartially. The author is not a party writer, trying to run down the wrong party by painting it all black and the right party all white. He sees and paints the follies of either extreme. Then, again, he has the merit of avoiding the excess of exaggeration. He possesses an especial talent for drawing what may be called the second-class of good people—characters not noble, superior, or perfect, after the standard of human perfection, but still good and honest, with a fundamental basis of sincerity, kindliness, and religious principle, yet with a considerable proneness to temptation, and a strong consciousness that they live, and like to live, in a struggling, party-giving, comfort-seeking world. Such people are so common, and form so very large a proportion of the betterish and more respectable classes, that it requires a keen perception of the ludicrous, and some power of satire, to give distinctness to the types taken from their ranks by the novelist. Mr. Trollope manages to do this admirably; and though his pudding may have the fault of being all plums, yet we cannot deny it is excellent eating. (pp. 503-04)

> *A review of "Barchester Towers," in* The Saturday Review, *London, Vol. 3, No. 83, May 30, 1857, pp. 503-04.*

The Westminster Review (essay date 1857)

[*In the following excerpt, the critic praises Trollope's skillful storytelling in* Barchester Towers, *noting that the novel will appeal to both men and women.*]

A quarterly reviewer of novels has frequently to address his readers when the works under consideration have been perused and their contents distributed to the winds in newspaper extracts. It is seldom his part to introduce the characters and unravel the plot. A novel like *Barchester Towers,* for instance, is pretty sure to have gone the round of the circulating library before anything we may have to say touching its merits will be heard; and we can hardly expect to assist in extending its circulation in its present form, when we state our opinion of it as decidedly the cleverest novel of the season, and one of the most masculine delineations of modern life in a special class of society that we have seen for many a day. Those who have read its dashing predecessor, *The Warden,* will be quite up to the style and the story, which are both continued vigorously in *Barchester Towers,* and with renewed interest. We recommend novel readers, who have not yet made acquaintance with Mr. Trollope, to get the two books immediately. As they are likely to be few, and it is our duty to occupy ourselves with the majority, we shall speak of *Barchester Towers* as a work well known. Mr. Trollope has satisfactorily solved a problem in this production. He has, without resorting to politics, or setting out as a social reformer, given us a novel that men can enjoy, and a satire so cleverly interwoven with the story, that every incident and development renders it more pointed and telling. In general our modern prose satirists spread their canvas for a common tale, out of which they start when the occasion suits, to harangue, exhort, and scold the world in person. Mr. Trollope entrusts all this to the individuals of his story. The plot is as simple as the siege of Troy. We are sure that Mr. Slope cannot succeed, or that if he is allowed to, another three volumes will confound him. We are equally convinced that the Widow Bold will never surrender to him, or that if she should, he will have to repent it equally. Nevertheless, our appetite for the closing chapters does not languish. We are anxious for the widow, and long to get her havened out of her perilous widowhood in fast wedlock: man's great ambition to become a Bishop, and woman's wonderful art in ruling one, cannot fail to interest us exceedingly, and we hurry on without a halt to the overthrow of Slope and the rare act of self-immolation whereby the Rev. Mr. Harding refuses a deanery, value a considerable sum per annum, and bestows it on his son-in-law. The story is original in books, but common in the land: so is the villain. Mr. Slope is possessed of extraordinary powers. He cannot move without inspiring nausea even in the female bosom (for it is notorious how much the sex can bear); yet he contrives to make men jealous of him. We have all of us met somebody like Mr. Slope, and wished that, if he indeed could lay claim to the odour of sanctity, it were pleasanter to the poor human sense of smell. (pp. 594-95)

Mr. Trollope seems wanting in certain of the higher elements that make a great novelist. He does not exhibit much sway over the emotional part of our nature: though fairer readers may think that the pretty passages between Eleanor and her baby-boy show a capacity for melting woman's heart, at least. He is also a little too sketchy: the scenes are efficient in repose and richness: but let us cut short our complaints, thankful that we have a caustic and vigorous writer, who can draw men and women, and tell a story that men and women can read. (p. 596)

A review of "Barchester Towers," in The Westminster Review, *Vol. LXVIII, No. 134, October 1, 1857, pp. 594-96.*

Hugh Walpole   (essay date 1928)

[*Walpole was among England's most popular novelists
during the three decades preceding World War II. His
skill at describing settings, his gift for conceiving interesting plots, his adherence to traditional novel forms in
an age of experimentation, and his accessibility as a lecturer and public figure contributed to his wide readership in the United Kingdom and North America. In the
following excerpt, he praises the characterization in* Barchester Towers, *focusing especially on Trollope's portrayal of Mrs. Proudie.*]

What is it that gives **Barchester Towers** its unique place
amongst Trollope's novels? It is not, it may be argued, his
greatest. **The Last Chronicle, Framley Parsonage, Orley
Farm,** have all their champions. It has in it no episode as
tragically moving as Mr. Crawley's visit to Barchester in
The Last Chronicle, nothing as dramatic as the trial in
Orley Farm, as subtly true as Lady Glencora's relations
with her husband in **Can You Forgive Her?** as naturally
engaging as the situation of the sisters in **Ayala's Angel.**

Its scheme is of the slenderest, Mr. Slope, masterly though
he is, not far removed from caricature, and certain of the
scenes, like the tilting at the quintain in the Ullathorne
sports, not far removed from Lever's tomboy antics, nevertheless it remains as perhaps *the* type novel of all the
Trollope family. It is the one book of them all that you
would give to someone who said to you: "Now what is
Trollope really *like? What is* the point about Trollope?"

It has, in the first place, no *longueurs.* Its author is not yet
writing for serial publication, has not yet acquired that
fatal facility of easy, natural, but purposeless dialogue. If
the Longman reader considered that **Barchester Towers**
could be compressed into one volume, what would he have
had to say in after years to **He Knew He Was Right** and
Is He Popenjoy? and **The American Senator?**

Secondly, this book introduces and exults over one of the
greatest figures in the Barsetshire Chronicles—Mrs. Proudie.

Thirdly, the theme, slender though it is, is one eternally
attractive—the theme of the biter bit, the bully bullied, the
war between tyrants. Every reader in the world has been
in turn both Dr. Proudie and Mrs. Proudie and Mr. Slope
is the Aunt Sally of every private backyard.

But principally **Barchester Towers** is Trollope's most popular book because in it he is, from the first page to the last,
in glorious high spirits. It would be untrue to say that
there is no kindness nor gentleness in the book; that would
be as much as to imply that Mr. Harding were not present
in it—but Trollope's good spirits are constant here as they
are in no other work of his, constant but controlled, bending to the demands of creation, felt rather than heard.
There is nothing that the reader likes better than to realise
the author rejoicing in his strength, conscious of his great

powers, having them at his hand, judging their proper use,
revelling in his awareness.

This is the first time that Trollope has all his forces completely in control—the first, and we are inclined to say the
last. He was afterwards to do greater things, but nothing
again so perfectly rounded.

But of course Mrs. Proudie is sufficient of herself to ensure
a comparative immortality for any novel. Is it fanciful to
see her in the first place as a Sir Rowland Hill (afterwards
Sir Raffle Buffle) in petticoats? She is one of the three great
pillars of the Barset history, Mr. Harding and Mr. Crawley being the other two. She is not, as her creator is careful
to emphasize, a bad woman. She can be touched by the
prayers of Mrs. Quiverful, and she loves even while she
bullies her lord but not her master. She is immortal because she is real both as type and as individual. She always
rings true. Trollope has not to ask, as he too often does
about other of his creations—now is that what they would
be doing? would they be saying this or that? She is greater
than he knows.

She is great also because she expresses triumphantly Trollope's deep loathing of tyranny, oppression, unfair dealing, and it is a wonderful witness to his powers that, hating
as he does everything for which she stands, he never caricatures her personality, laughs with her as well as at her,
and feels tenderly for her at the last. In this at least he is
greater than his contemporaries Thackeray and Dickens.

His wise, balanced estimate of her allows us our own freedom of judgement. We do not hate her, because her creator does not, and so we realise her as we can never realise
anyone hated by us.

Trollope, too, shows his genius in putting up against her
a far more odious figure. Mr. Slope we are permitted to
hate; we are physically encouraged to do so. Although
even here Trollope's tenderness keeps breaking out, and
we know a moment of sympathy for the poor creature as
he bends beneath the Signora's whip.

Concerning the Stanhope family opinion will always be divided, but it is to be regretted that they do not appear
again in the succeeding books. It would have been pleasant
for Mrs. Grantley to pass, without pain, away, and that
then the Archdeacon, stirred on the Rabelaisian side of
him, should have married the Signora, the Italian husband
sufficiently deceased. One feels that Madeline has scarcely,
so far as we have been allowed to observe her, encountered
foemen worthy of her steel.

For the rest, there are some great and by now classical
scenes in this book—the scene of the Bishop's only victory, the encounter between the Signora and Mrs. Proudie
at the evening reception, the moment when Eleanor Bold
slaps Mr. Slope's face (her single praiseworthy action),
Mr. Slope at Puddingdale, Archdeacon Grantley at Plumstead, and, best of all, Mrs. Proudie and Mrs. Quiverful.

But it is here in this book that one realises for the first time
with a kind of shock of excitement all the various things
that Trollope can do, all the types of human beings that
he is able to create and understand. We are moving forward. We have advanced from the gates of Hiram's Hospi-

tal into the very heart of the town, into some of the lanes and villages of adjacent country. Trollope himself is now beginning to realise the size and variety of the landscape that he is destined to cover. (pp. 48-51)

Hugh Walpole, in his Anthony Trollope, *The Macmillan Company, 1928, 205 p.*

William Cadbury (essay date 1964)

[*In the following essay, Cadbury examines ways in which Trollope's characterizations, narrative intrusions, and parody of epic devices distance the reader from the characters and so contribute to a "panoramic" view of society in* Barchester Towers.]

Barchester Towers is one of the principal monuments of Victorian fiction, yet it has always been difficult to evaluate in terms of the Trollope canon, precisely because its excellences are of so different a kind from those of his other novels. In it Trollope's usual attempt to present characters in the round is subordinated to the attempt to present a unified world without involving us so deeply in any of his characters that they monopolize our attention. We are not to view the action only in terms of the aims and goals of the characters, as we do in such novels as *The Macdermots of Ballycloran* and *Phineas Finn,* but rather to see as a whole the social world they form. The technique of *Barchester Towers* is, in fact, a brilliant way of working out the ultimate aim of the novel of character, which is not only to elucidate character, "but to give it in such variety as to suggest a picture of society" [Edwin Muir, *The Structure of the Novel,* 1928].

If a picture of society as a unified world is to be maintained, it is necessary that we see all the characters from the outside, that they remain to us characters rather than selves, in Arthur Sewell's distinction. Sewell [in his *Character and Society in Shakespeare,* 1951] cautions us against treating the characters in drama as if they had selves: "Dramatic draughtsmanship—to create the character in the round—is not concerned . . . with that kind of actuality we have for ourselves but with that kind of actuality other people have for us." The novelist who, like Trollope, attempts to create characters in the round, can present them either way; he can emphasize the kind of reality that others have in our eyes, or he can present us with characters who have the kind of reality we have for ourselves. The kinds of conflict he presents can be entirely internal, because the novelist has a privilege which exists for the dramatist only in the clumsy device of soliloquy, that of letting us see from the inside the make-up of his characters' minds, whether or not the conflicts they feel manifest themselves in action. Hence there is no need for the novelist to present characters who are "discovered for us in the mode in which the person of the play embodies . . . a distinctive address to the world" [Sewell], or who, in Kenneth Burke's term, dance an attitude. Phineas Finn, for instance, has no attitude to dance; he merely is, without personality for himself as we are for ourselves. He has a self, the sense that he is, that he faces characters and situations, rather than a character, a conglomeration of personal attributes which may be contradictory and tangled, but

which lead to a defined attitude to life, a personality. We can learn by observation of this self, but we do it from the inside.

The figures in *Barchester Towers,* on the other hand, are designed to be seen from the outside, to exhibit typical modes of behavior by which we can know them—to be, in short, characters. Warden Harding's mind, for all its complexity, is reducible to attributes by which we know him, and while we follow his thoughts with the greatest sympathy and understand his problems as problems, we never see him from the inside as we do Phineas Finn. There is always a kind of distance between us, and when we see his thoughts and sympathize with him as he faces his problems we say "Yes, that is how someone with that character would feel," rather than "I feel it with you."

The special requirements of *Barchester Towers,* which, unlike most of Trollope's novels, is a detached, urbane, panoramic view of the operation of politics in social relations, dictate to Trollope the maintenance of distance from his characters. If he fails to keep it, the sense of character attributes is lost in a sense of personality, which at once restricts the boundaries of our attention to what the character feels and thinks, and keeps us from seeing him as an example of his type, with attributes and attitudes which we must judge. If we were to see any of these characters as we see ourselves, there would be danger of accepting their norms as ours, and thus danger of losing the panoramic view which is necessary to the comedy. All of the characters are to be ridiculous, and it is very seldom that we are ridiculous to ourselves. Trollope must keep us outside them, and the main achievement of *Barchester Towers* is the mastery of technical means for keeping us there.

But the sense of personality is of course precisely what Trollope does want in most of his novels. In the formulation of his principles of character creation in the *Autobiography* he tells us again and again that the novelist must live with his characters, must get inside and know exactly how they would respond in any situation. In a very famous passage, he tells us that the novelist

> desires to make his readers so intimately acquainted with his characters that the creations of his brain should be to them speaking, moving, living, human creatures. This he can never do unless he know those fictitious personages himself, and he can never know them well unless he can live with them in the full reality of established intimacy. . . . If the would-be novelist have aptitudes that way, all this will come to him without much struggling;—but if it do not come, I think he can only make novels of wood.

And the operation of this aspect of the creative act must be reflected in the product. As he says in the essay **"On English Prose Fiction as a Rational Amusement,"** stories "charm us . . . because we feel that men and women with flesh and blood, creatures with whom we can sympathise, are struggling amidst their woes. It all lies in that. No novel is anything, for purposes either of tragedy or of comedy, unless the reader can sympathise with the characters whose names he finds upon the page."

The kind of sympathy he here demands is clearly more involved with the characters than is the kind allowed by the outside view. And the contemporary reviewers find fault with the characterization of *Barchester Towers* on just these grounds. The reviewer for the *North British Review* [June, 1864] chides Trollope for not doing just what Trollope claims to do in the passage just quoted from the *Autobiography.* The reviewer says that "if the character of a man is to be made fully known to us, it is from within that the artist must proceed." Trollope does not do this enough for the reviewer's taste—"he has not enabled us to form a conception of what his characters are like out of the four corners of Barchester Towers." And the *Saturday Review* critic [May, 1861] of *Framley Parsonage* makes the general complaint that Trollope "paints from the outside." He is not strong at "developing or creating, but . . . depicting the behaviour of drawing-room company." But the *National Review* critic [October, 1858] of four early novels complains on the other hand (though it comes to much the same thing as the others) of too much subtlety, and says that Trollope should use "stronger shades and brighter colours in the delineation of his fictitious personages," and that because he fails to do so he "somewhat fails in awakening the sympathy of his readers." In *Barchester Towers* and *The Warden* "we are rather more inclined to be amused at than interested in the personages of the narrative."

Amusement at the personages is precisely what *Barchester Towers* is designed to supply, and the outside view of character, the lack of too deep involvement, is the way it is achieved. The novel does open, however, with an inside view, and it is partly this which sets off the old stable world of Bishop Grantly, in which selves could flourish, from the humor-dominated world of power politics of Bishop Proudie. When we see Archdeacon Grantly at the bedside of his father, we see him as a self, not a character. His ability to pray for his father's life despite his own temporal needs is a triumph of his personality.

> Thus he thought long and sadly, in deep silence, and then gazed at that still living face, and then at last dared to ask himself whether he really longed for his father's death.
>
> The effort was a salutary one, and the question was answered in a moment. The proud, wishful, worldly man, sank on his knees by the bedside, and . . . prayed eagerly that his sins might be forgiven him.

When the bishop dies, too late, there is no longer any need for the archdeacon to search his own soul. As he engages in his politics and displays all the comic richness of his character in the rest of the novel, we see him from the outside. We sympathize, for we know from this first scene what he really is, but we are sympathetically amused at his character, not deeply involved with his self. It is his character we see, for instance, when he responds to the quite unexpected news of Eleanor's engagement in a way which demonstrates Trollope's technique of the outside view. All the archdeacon says is "Good heavens!" and he says it five times, each time indicating a different state of mind, which Trollope explains. His progress from amazement to joy is thus immensely comic, because it is externalized in so characteristic a way.

The basic distinction between the outside and the inside view, then, is whether our attention is directed most strongly towards the singularizing attributes or the universalizing problems of a character. The characters in *Barchester Towers* who are most nearly presented from the inside are Harding and Arabin, because we are made to feel most deeply the complexity of the problems they face. But even here it is the eccentricity of the characters, their characteristic attitude to life, which is the main aim of the presentation. Harding is an extremely sympathetic character, yet his attitude to life is so individual that we think of him in terms of it—we could never see him as we see ourselves, as is possible with the archdeacon at his father's death-bed. After Harding has been told by Slope that he is "rubbish," his governing attribute of scrupulous self-analysis forces him to characteristic reflection: "Unfortunately for himself Mr. Harding had little . . . self-reliance. When he heard himself designated as rubbish by the Slopes of the world, he had no other resource than to make inquiry within his own bosom as to the truth of the designation." Harding is intended to appear overscrupulous, and thus we cannot identify deeply with his moral quandary, though we sympathize with it.

Because *Barchester Towers* emphasizes the outside view of character, when Trollope endows a character with a self it destroys the tone of the novel. In chapter 20, where Trollope presents what he calls an "interior view" of Arabin's character, in which he emphasizes Arabin's spiritual struggles, we lose sight of Arabin's attributes and become too much interested in the nature of the spiritual problems that he faces. Our involvement and identification with Arabin in this passage produce a disparity in tone between this and the rest of the novel, so that we never quite know how to take Arabin afterwards. But the chapter seems like a set-piece, having little to do with the rest of the book, and so when we see Arabin in action later, from the outside, we build up a separate picture of him from that of the "interior view" of his character; there remains only a slight sense of strain, as if we have two characters mixed up in our minds.

Trollope's basic practice of character creation throughout *Barchester Towers* is similar to the way he presents Arabin, though in the rest of the characters he avoids the too-close analysis of the "interior view." He describes the character in a set-piece, and then shows us the character in action, displaying the characteristics established in the description. Because Arabin and some others, particularly Madame Neroni, are such complex characters, this practice sometimes brings about the illusion of development in the characters. We tend to forget that they do not change, but rather unfold their full characters in action. Eleanor Bold, for instance, learns as her pride is beaten out of her by circumstances, but she does not grow. In a workable though improbable analogy, like King Oedipus she finds out what was in her character all along, and unlike King Lear she does not find her character changing to fit her new circumstances. We sympathize with her, but remain aloof, and do not identify with her. Her pride particularizes her, and we do not see her as we see ourselves. Thus when we are told of a character's thoughts in *Barchester Towers,* it is still, in terms of our definition, an outside view, because it reveals an attitude to life, a character rather than a self.

One of the most effective techniques of distancing a character from the reader is the creation of tension between the moral norms of the character and the moral norms of the implied author, which the reader shares. Trollope retains the outside view when exposing his characters' feelings by imposing a sense of his own values on the values which the characters hold. In the presentation of the transmutation of Eleanor's grief for John Bold into love for her baby, we sympathize entirely with Eleanor's feelings, but we perceive the gap between her feelings and the reality of the situation, and so we do not identify with her, but rather remain aloof. Trollope shows very clearly how she overreacts to the baby by emphasizing Eleanor's worship of it and the perfect ordinariness of the child—"The baby was really delightful; he took his food with a will, struck out his toes merrily whenever his legs were uncovered, and did not have fits. These are supposed to be the strongest points of baby perfection, and in all these our baby excelled." The kind of irony implicit in this contrast between the values of characters and audience is one of Trollope's favorite devices for making characters ridiculous. Mrs. Proudie, for instance, answers Lady De Courcy's expression of amazement that Madeline has captured Slope: " 'You don't know the intriguing villainy of that woman,' said Mrs. Proudie, remembering her torn flounces." She is responding to what was not actually Madeline's intriguing villainy at all, since she had nothing to do with tearing Mrs. Proudie's dress, yet Mrs. Proudie remembers with anger Madeline's laughter at her discomfiture. But it is still perfectly true that Madeline has been engaging in intrigue in captivating Slope—Mrs. Proudie responds in terms of her own values, the reader in terms of the reality which Trollope has presented.

In the same way, there is a light irony involved when Madeline says, "Parsons, I suppose, are much the same as other men, if you strip them of their black coats." The whole of **Barchester Towers** makes this very point, but the view of clerical character which the reader has is so much higher than Madeline's that for her to say it reveals more about her character than about parsons. She simply means that they can be made ridiculous by her blandishments, and she is mistaken in thinking it true of all clergymen, since Arabin remains true. To Trollope and to the reader, the remark means that parsons are as liable to be afflicted with narrowmindedness and jealousies as anyone else, but also as capable of nobility and truth.

These passages imply, since they demonstrate a difference in the responses of the characters and those of the audience, that there is a special relationship between the narrator and the audience, which itself helps to create the panoramic vision of life and to keep the reader distanced from the action. Trollope's well-known addresses and asides to the reader usually serve one of these purposes, although sometimes they can be merely petulant. Mr. Harding, for instance, is able to conceive of a marriage between Eleanor and Slope, partly because he is too easily convinced by Grantly, but partly too because "it must be remembered that such a marriage . . . did not appear so monstrous to

Slope's initial visit with Signora Neroni is brought to an abrupt conclusion by Mrs. Proudie. Illustration by Paul Hardy.

Mr. Harding, because in his charity he did not hate the chaplain as the archdeacon did, and as we do." The inclusion of the reader here is not ingenuous—Trollope is setting up a complex irony, of the type used by Thackeray, in which he blames Harding for too great charity, but blames the reader, too, for lack of charity. Slope certainly is bad, but Harding is right in seeing as little evil as possible in people. This irony, then, presents a vision of life—the sense that it is difficult to live in the world, and that the innocent is the most admirable man, though he is comic in his lack of grasp of reality.

The narrator's relationship to his novel, as well as his relationship to the reader, can be complicated, as when he discusses the character of Mrs. Proudie:

> Mrs. Proudie has not been portrayed in these pages as an agreeable or an amiable lady. There has been no intention to impress the reader much in her favour. It is ordained that all novels should have a male and a female angel, and a male and a female devil. If it be considered that this rule is obeyed in these pages, the latter character must be supposed to have fallen to the lot of Mrs. Proudie. But she was not all devil. There

was a heart inside that stiff-ribbed bodice, though not, perhaps, of large dimensions, and certainly not easily accessible.

This again is not ingenuous; by referring to a fictional character's place in the fictive world that he is creating, Trollope certainly violates the reality that critics of point of view have told us is necessary. But by contrasting Mrs. Proudie's character with our conception of her place in the novel, Trollope enforces her reality—a sense is established of life in the novel on two planes, one highly conventional and established in terms of groupings of characters, and another in which the characters live absolutely, quite apart from their places in the pattern of angel and devil and the like. This sense of a double level of life keeps the reader removed from the action, surveying it with Trollope's panoramic eye, but also makes him believe in the world of the novel as an interaction of characters who have at least partially a life of their own. The technique enables *Barchester Towers* to be both artificial and literary, as behoves a comedy, and natural and lifelike, as behoves a novel.

Henry James, in a very famous passage [from "Anthony Trollope, 1883," in *The House of Fiction,* edited by Leon Edel, 1957], objected to the distortion of the novelistic world which authorial intrusion brings about, and upbraided Trollope for inconsistency in point of view: "It is impossible to imagine what a novelist takes himself to be unless he regard himself as an historian and his narrative as a history. It is only as an historian that he has the smallest *locus standi.* As a narrator of fictitious events he is nowhere; to insert into his attempt a backbone of logic, he must relate events that are assumed to be real." Howells supported this view [William Dean Howells, *Criticism and Fiction,* 1959], and claimed that Trollope was "warped from a wholesome ideal" by devotion to the Thackerayan method. He says that Trollope wishes "to stand about in his scene, talking it over with his hands in his pockets, interrupting the action, and spoiling the illusion in which alone the truth of art resides." But the kind of illusion that James and Howells demand is precisely what Trollope does not want in *Barchester Towers.* As we have seen, the whole attempt is to keep the reader sympathetic to but uninvolved in the actions and responses of the characters. Successful creation of an illusion of reality guarantees a kind of focus on each scene and each character which would render the structure of *Barchester Towers* intolerable, as we are wrenched violently from one aspect of the plot to another. In a panoramic novel like *Barchester Towers* it is absolutely necessary to remain distant enough from the action for the mental eye to take in the panorama. As we have just seen, the illusion of reality is maintained with complete adequacy by the device of treating the characters as real people in a fictive setting—the life of the characters can occasionally break through their conventional groupings, and thus our interest in them is maintained as far as Trollope wants it.

In this way, then, Trollope's famous explanation of why he lets his readers know what is going to happen makes sense. He sets up a situation of trust between author and reader when he says of himself that he "ventures to reprobate that system which goes so far to violate all proper confidence between the author and his readers, by maintaining . . . a mystery. . . . Nay, take the last chapter if you please—learn from its pages all the results of our troubled story, and the story shall have lost none of its interest, if indeed there be any interest in it to lose." This is all simply to say that suspense of the kind necessary to the dramatic novel, the simple eagerness to learn what happens, is a supremely unimportant quality in this kind of novel. Trollope is justified in speaking directly to the reader in *Barchester Towers,* since he does not need suspense and since he does need detachment from the action. If we became too involved in the characters or in the action, the trials of good characters and the disasters of bad would become too painful. Trollope wishes to show us what life is, but he does not let us mix up his comic portrayal with reality, in the manner of romance. Jamesian critics, looking to the novel for the best kind of romance, cannot cope with the antiromantic vision, just as F. R. Leavis cannot cope with the Trollopean values of detachment and urbanity, which lack the "kind of reverent openness before life, and . . . marked moral intensity" that he feels necessary to the great tradition [*The Great Tradition,* 1954]. Different from the manner of Leavis' great tradition, "Trollope's manner," as one critic puts it, "is that of a skilled monologist speaking to an intimate, trusted and trusting individual or group" and we are asked to believe that he will "work out the situations to our satisfaction" [Edd Winfield Parks, "Trollope and the Defense of Exegesis," *NCF,* VII (1953)].

The technique described here, then, provides a perfectly respectable *locus standi* which is not that of the historian. The relationship of the author to his audience which we have just seen in *Barchester Towers* is basically that of an epic bard to his. Trollope does not employ the radical of presentation of *epos,* the direct confrontation of the audience by the bard [William Dean Howells, *Criticism and Fiction,* 1959], but the governing technical device, the mock heroic, is an imitation of it for the purposes of parody, and is still another way of keeping characters distanced from the reader. Trollope's device of giving an ironic commentary on the action, by means of mock-heroic apostrophes, substitutes for the use of a separate narrator—the tone of the apostrophes is so different from Trollope's normal narrative tone that a second narrative personality is implied. This narrator, the production of the implied author, comments on the realistic situation from the romantic point of view and thus achieves an ironic undercutting of the action.

When Trollope cries "But how shall I sing the divine wrath of Mr. Slope, or how invoke the tragic muse to describe the rage which swelled the celestial bosom of the bishop's chaplain?" he is clearly imitating the conventions of epic style, and laughing at Slope's absurdities by placing him in direct juxtaposition with Achilles. The main point of mock heroic is to give perspective, to place the tempest in the teapot, and the comparison of Trollope's clerical characters to the heroes of another tradition accomplishes this admirably.

Mrs. Proudie, of course, presents wonderful opportunities for the exercise of this device, since pomposity is so central to her character: "As Juno may have looked at Paris on Mount Ida, so did Mrs. Proudie look on Ethelbert Stanhope when he pushed the leg of the sofa into her lace train." As she ponders her revenge on Slope, she is compared to Medea, another female character in the epic tradition, but sex is not limiting: "As Achilles warmed at the sight of his armour, as Don Quixote's heart grew strong when he grasped his lance, so did Mrs. Proudie look forward to fresh laurels, as her eye fell on her husband's pillow," and she thinks of the curtain lecture she can give.

The reversal of sexes for comic effect is applied the other way around, too: "Dr. Proudie was playing Venus to [Grantly's] Juno, and he was prepared to wage an internecine war against the owner of the wished-for apple, and all his satellites, private chaplains, and others." The image of the archdeacon as warrior is used again and again: "And now, had I the pen of a mighty poet, would I sing in epic verse the noble wrath of the archdeacon." And when he has finally triumphed, he "literally made presents to everybody":

> 'Twas thus that he sang his song of triumph over Mr. Slope. This was his paean, his hymn of thanksgiving, his loud oration. He had girded himself with his sword, and gone forth to the war; now he was returning from the field laden with the spoils of the foe. The cob and the cameos, the violoncello and the pianoforte, were all as it were trophies reft from the tent of his now conquered enemy.

The epic style is here used to let us imaginatively into the archdeacon's mind, for he clearly responds to his victory over Slope as if it were an epic victory; but the epic style is used to make fun of the whole struggle as well. As is plain from many of these examples, the imagery of war governs the treatment of the power-struggle. Arabin is consistently referred to in terms of knightly tourney—Chapter 15 is entitled "The New Champion," and this epithet is used again . . . [when] Grantly again demonstrates his own lack of sense of proportion about the ecclesiastical encounters with which he is so concerned. He thinks "That paragon of a clergyman . . . that ecclesiastical knight before whose lance Mr. Slope was to fall and bite the dust, that worthy bulwark of the church as it should be . . . was—misconducting himself." Most of the characters come in for such mocking treatment. Mrs. Quiverful becomes Medea or Constance; Eleanor Bold is Lucretia to Slope's Tarquin. And the characters themselves, in an interesting variation of the device, are made to use the sense of conflict between the epic struggle and the reality of the situation to deflate each other. Madeline intends that the classical parallel deflate Slope when she tells him to avoid the example of Dido and not mix business with pleasure in his pursuit of Eleanor and herself, and the archdeacon feels an unfortunate lack of appropriateness between his vision of the real epic relationships of the antagonists and the reality of the situation:

> Dr. Gwynne was the *Deus ex machina* who was to come down upon the Barchester stage, and bring about deliverance from these terrible evils. But how can melodramatic *denouements* be properly brought about, how can vice and Mr.

Slope be punished, and virtue and the archdeacon be rewarded, while the avenging god is laid up with the gout?

Barchester Towers demonstrates, then, a variety of techniques for keeping the reader distanced from the characters and from the action, a necessary condition in presenting a panoramic view of a given social world. The most important of these are the outside view of character established through description, the simultaneous presentation of the senses of value of the author and of the characters, and the parody of epic devices by a mock-epic bard in digressions and asides to the reader. All are devices for assuring that characters, rather than selves, be presented, and all are ways of placing the action of the novel in a context in which the reality of characters and situations is kept from becoming overpowering, since the panoramic novel is fragmented by a too great illusion of reality. (pp. 509-19)

> *William Cadbury, "Character and the Mock Heroic in 'Barchester Towers',"* in Texas Studies in Literature and Language, *Vol. V, No. 4, Winter, 1964, pp. 509-19.*

James R. Kincaid   (essay date 1970)

[*Kincaid is an American educator and critic who has written extensively on nineteenth-century literature. In the following excerpt, he analyzes comic technique in* Barchester Towers.]

Trollope not only writes in the tradition of Jane Austen but shares many of her values. But if her rational and balanced comic norms might be called conservative, Trollope's are even more so. *Pride and Prejudice,* for example, is really rather blunt in its absolute rejection of those who are deluded, selfish, and mean, particularly, of course, Mrs. Bennet, and a large component of the comic satisfaction at the end is provided for by the removal from the neighborhood of their parents of both Elizabeth (whose parents' society was "so little pleasing" to her) and Jane (who runs from Netherfield Park after a year, when even "*her* affectionate heart" is unable to stand "so near a vicinity to her mother"). The struggle between parents and children basic to all comedy is seldom presented so very clearly, and, for all its emphasis on equipoise and education toward moderation, *Pride and Prejudice* takes the position traditional to all comedy in its celebration of an escape from parents. But the comedy of *Barchester Towers* avoids even this basic position; underneath all, it celebrates an escape not from parents but from children. It is one of the warmest of all the great English comic novels, but it is also one of the subtlest. Despite Henry James's oft-repeated notion that Trollope is, above all, "safe," that "he never played with a subject, never juggled with the sympathies or the credulity of his reader, was never in the least paradoxical or mystifying" ["Anthony Trollope," in *Partial Portraits,* 1888], this early novel, I believe, manages to establish itself as comic while quietly subverting many of the major tenets of traditional comedy.

Most basic, certainly, is its implicit distrust of the young— its open sneers at babies and often-cynical impatience with its principal lovers—and its corollary admiration for the aged moral center, the sixty-four-year-old Mr. Harding. But other comic principles are just as certainly overturned. Comedy, for instance, traditionally rests on an apprehension of man as a member of a social group and works to re-establish the harmony of society by eliminating or converting the individualists. *Barchester Towers,* however, directly reverses this assumption, seeing men as decent individually but dangerous, silly, or contemptible insofar as they define themselves as parts of a social organization. Similarly, comedy normally—the tradition is so firm that one almost says "naturally"—gives power to those who are approved: the good king is restored, the hero marries the girl, the money from the old will is accepted. In *Barchester Towers,* moral approval is directly proportionate to the decrease of power; Mr. Harding, the most passive and impotent character, occupies the normative position, while Mrs. Proudie and Mr. Slope, most thoroughly condemned, are in many ways the most powerful.

More generally, comedy looks to the future and envisions a society cleansed and transformed by self-knowledge and joy. Most comedies deal principally with education and the resultant transcendence of the ordinary limitations of life; they are essentially progressive, whether the progress be with Mr. Pickwick to Dulwich or with Dante to Paradise. Trollope's comedy, however, hates nothing so much as the callous notions of progress and sees forward movement as destruction. *Barchester Towers* looks to the past for its solidity and sees comic hope not in transformation but in preservation. Instead of seeking a transcendence of the ordinary, then, it revels in it. The paradise envisioned by Trollope involves what Henry James [in his *Partial Portraits*] called his "great apprehension of the real," but it is a reality made up of firm commonplaces. The most optimistic suggestion made by *Barchester Towers* is that the ordinary comforts of life are delicious, if only we perceive them fully and stop spoiling them by the continual anticipation of something better in the future. The novel sets itself squarely against the linear rhythms basic to all comedy. But these progressive and linear views are the dominant views of the nineteenth century, and the warm optimism *Barchester Towers* expresses in the commonplace is marked by a concurrent and subtle bitterness. A large part of the appeal of this intelligent and mature comedy lies in the very fact that it recognizes the impossibility of its norms. The novel opens symbolically with the advent into power of a progressive, liberal, low-church administration, one hostile to Archdeacon Grantly and fully behind the Proudies and the Slopes. It is a movement backed by *The Jupiter,* the ominous voice of the people. Time and again, the novel allows us to glimpse the futility of its old-fashioned norm and the sense that its solidity is misleading. *Barchester Towers* finally insists both on the beauty and the impossibility of its chief values and thus sacrifices the clean directness of most comedy for a vision more troubled and more complex.

Perhaps the most important thing to say about the novel's artistry is that it works to establish this complexity by a rhetoric so subtle that it seems not to be there. Rather than prodding or startling us into a special perception, Trollope urges us, paradoxically, to relax into heightened insight. It is, in fact, Trollope's much-maligned use of point of view which accounts very largely for the novel's greatness.

This point of view, particularly in the narrator's direct comments, attempts to establish a rhetoric of intimacy and relaxation. "Our doctrine," the narrator says, "is, that the author and reader should move along together in full confidence with each other" (Ch. xv). The point of this comment and, to a large extent, of the novel itself is that we are all of us men, whether bishops, archdeacons, authors, or readers. He denies explicitly the special province of the author as to knowledge and authority and also appears to deny the special province of his fiction to surprise, lecture, and edify. On the first level, the rhetoric works by a not-very-subtle flattery, giving the sense that we—the author and the reader—are undeluded, tolerant, realistic, and not bamboozled, as are the characters, by power or position. Since this rhetorical assumption is quite comfortable and appears to demand so little, the reader can easily enough accept it. The point of view thus establishes not only a sense of clear and typical realism but a relaxation of the reader's cautions and an easy identification with the novel's most important point: that the joy of life comes in renouncing power and its corollary notions of progress and in accepting the common, the kindly, and the established. Unlike most moral comedies, where the dominant rhetorical mode is attack and where the reader is asked to sharpen his critical faculties, here we are especially asked not to be so eager to judge. The tactful comedy involving Mr. Quiverful and the wardenship, for instance, makes just this point. Trollope brilliantly establishes the entirely understandable impatience of Mrs. Quiverful with her husband's apparent "sentimental pride" and over-scrupulousness. At the same time, he shows the equally understandable judgment of "the outer world" that Mr. Quiverful was rapacious and dishonorable. The narrator concludes, "It is astonishing how much difference the point of view makes in the apsect of all that we look at!" (Ch. xxiv). The rhetorical insistence is on moderation and acceptance.

At the same time, however, this basic relaxation is used to promote a clear set of values. For example, Trollope early injects some facetious and good-natured complaints about sermons: "There is, perhaps, no greater hardship at present inflicted on mankind in civilised and free countries, than the necessity of listening to sermons. No one but a preaching clergyman has, in these realms, the power of compelling an audience to sit silent, and be tormented" (Ch. vi). He goes on through a rather long paragraph on this "bore of the age," working exactly for the expansive, unbuttoned attitude in the reader that can recognize the experience as a common one and respond to this recognition with laughter. The next paragraph begins clearly in the same vein, and the reader is encouraged to lean back and companionably agree some more. But the tone and direction are quietly changed. The "preaching clergyman" becomes the "young parson," "my too self-confident juvenile friend," "my insufficient young lecturer," and the attack is shifted from the general target of boring preachers to the quite specific one of ignorant youth presuming to lecture age. Young clergymen are advised to "read to me some portion of those time-honoured discourses which our great divines have elaborated in the full maturity of their powers." Otherwise, "it all means nothing." The true harshness and severity of the last comment and of the pervasive assault on youth is masked not only by the light tone but by the introductory rhetoric, which leads us so very gently into the subject. The initial chummy platitudes do disappear, but the tone remains the same and the reader is encouraged to slide into the narrator's position here and move to the norms of this comedy. Later in the novel, then, the issue can again be brought up without the elaborate introduction. When Mr. Arabin is preparing to read himself in at St. Ewold's, the narrator reflects with deceptively genial irony on the fact that "it often surprises us that very young men can muster courage to preach for the first time to a strange congregation" (Ch. xxiii). He again goes on and on in mock wonder at how those "who have never yet passed ten thoughtful days" "are not stricken dumb by the new and awful solemnity of their position." After a few paragraphs, the irony becomes much sharper, though, as the reader is led to the very un-genial reflection that perhaps the process of ordination "banishes the natural modesty of youth." We are thus urged to relax into positions which are finally very aggressive and specialized.

Many of Trollope's famous comments on novel-writing really have much the same thematic function. The narrator reflects at one point that if Eleanor had given way to her rising tears, Arabin would have declared his love, and the whole mystery would have been cleared up. "But then," he asks with mock ingenuousness, "where would have been my novel?" (Ch. xxx). Behind the companionable and easy rhetoric established by such an invitingly artless statement is a more quiet but more important attack on these almost-young lovers. Their actions are treated as mechanical, manipulable, and therefore trivial. The narrator takes them about as seriously as he expects the reader to, and the rhetoric here contributes to the irony which attends Mrs. Bold and Arabin throughout and which helps direct our moral concern to the elderly.

Even more basically functional are his complaints about the impossibility of writing a satisfactory ending to a novel. These curious passages (see Chs. li and liii) act not to disrupt but to solidify the reader's position, first by again establishing the tone of intimacy and the rhetoric of relaxation, but more importantly by attacking the very nature of form or pattern, particularly the whole notion of finality. *Barchester Towers,* for all its conservatism, is in many ways an existential comedy and as such distrusts neat patterns which point to the future. The narrator's position is that we must apprehend life as a continuous and organic movement, not as a fixed forward-looking principle. His rhetoric brilliantly supports that very point and subtly directs our attention away from the conventional symbol of the time-bound Eleanor and Arabin, marrying, having children, and living happily ever after in power, and fixes it on the unconventional center of the novel, the weak, retiring, and old Mr. Harding.

Even more unconventional than the rhetoric, however, is the conservative comedy which is supported by the action and themes of the narrative itself. The organizing thematic principle in the novel is the notion of the fight. On all levels, clerical, academic, journalistic, and personal, the central issues involve a struggle for power. The book asks such questions as who shall be Warden?—who shall be Dean?—who will replace Mr. Bold with Eleanor? These and the equivalent questions involving value are given one answer: he who does not try. The real winners are those who do not fight. At the heart of the book is a profound protest against the competitive mode of life, and *Barchester Towers* thus establishes its comedy in direct hostility to the major progressive movements of the period: democracy and capitalism. But the issue goes deeper than this; the whole notion of power is relentlessly attacked. It is power that unites the issues of religion and love in the novel and establishes the most basic irony in the plot, when the arch-enemies Grantly and Slope end up on the same side in the war over the wardenship. All the values of the conservative comedy here arrange themselves around the central belief in passivity and its accompanying antagonism to ambition.

The novel begins, in fact, with a bleak view of power and a paradigmatic distinction between man as a human being, personally defined and decent, and man as socially defined, mad for power and dishonorable. Archdeacon Grantly's vigil at his father's death-bed brings into conflict the two sides of him, and though the question of "whether he really longed for his father's death" is finally answered negatively, the Archdeacon is not able to keep his desire for power completely under control. When his father finally dies, he itches to send his father-in-law to telegraph the ministry and is, appropriately, too late. The narrator ends the chapter by discussing the Archdeacon's disappointment and his desire for power and position. Reversing the expected terms, he removes all personal censure and attacks only the system itself. Clergymen, he says, are, like all of us, only men, and "if we look to our clergymen to be more than men, we shall probably teach ourselves to think that they are less." Thus the first chapter effectively begins to assert the need both for tolerance toward individuals and hostility toward corrupting systems of power. Though Grantly, as a worldly high-churchman, is generally completely in accord with the principles valued by the novel, Trollope has an enormous amount of fun with this sputtering organization man, so eager for power and, in the end, so impotent: all his lectures go astray, all his plots come to nothing.

The attack on the alternate camp of churchmen is, however, much sharper; for Mrs. Proudie and Mr. Slope are not only as much caught up with the lust of the fight as is the Archdeacon but, in addition, are fighting for all the wrong values. Though Trollope introduces Mr. Slope (Ch. iv) by an elaborate list of ways in which he is just like Dr. Grantly, the implied differences are more important. Where Dr. Grantly and the worldly high-church group assuage guilt, the Slopes and Proudies capitalize on it; Grantly is expansive and tolerant, while his enemies are restrictive and mean; Grantly is masculine, Slope, the most basic joke runs, is far less manly even than his cohort, Mrs. Proudie. But no comparative listing can get close to the functional use made of the Proudies and Slopes as negative illustrations to establish by contrast the novel's key position.

The Proudies, most basically, are a symbol of local warfare and perverted ambition, and Trollope uses our laughter to attack both of them. Dr. Proudie, the essence of the hen-pecked male, is still ludicrously ambitious and, sure enough, successful, all of which tells us something about the nature of success. He is known as a "useful" clergyman, a pawn of those who do indeed have power, particularly his wife. Mrs. Proudie is attacked by a very elemental sexual humor and is in the center of the line of big-bosomed, jewel-bedecked, pompous and castrating females who are eternally attacked in literature, especially in the literature of the last two centuries, from *The Pickwick Papers* to the Marx Brothers. She reflects, in part, the novel's quiet but distinct anti-feminism. By turning her into a kind of sexual amazon, who, if all else fails, can still win her battles in the bedroom, Trollope appeals to sources of humor he so often claimed to have avoided. Slope, he says, might have had some chance in his fight with Mrs. Proudie had he been able to occupy her place at night. Since he can't do this, Mrs. Proudie has, as we say, the ultimate weapon. These sorts of jokes transform both our tittering inhibitions and our sense of the grotesque into hostile laughter. Mrs. Proudie is besieged by other means too; she is not only rude but narrow, and no image is so firmly associated with her as that of the "Sabbath-day schools" and their suggestion of dreary, crushing repression. The narrator specifically identifies the ugliness of this symbol with hard work, certainly the most anti-comic work of all, bookkeeping: "These people probably did not reflect that catechisms and collects are quite as hard work to the young mind as book-keeping is to the elderly; and that quite as little feeling of worship enters into the one task as the other" (Ch. vii). Mrs. Proudie is indeed the enemy of comedy as well as the perfect comic butt. The central joke against her is that she is simply a man: she is ranked with men rather than women, the narrator says with a nudge and a wink, because of "her great strength of mind" (Ch. xxxiii). There is more than a touch of the desperate in this sort of humorous attack, but by exaggerating the threat of conflict, it can call up laughter to eliminate that conflict and thereby purify the comic society of this most basic kind of warfare. The last words on Mrs. Proudie, then—"our prayers for her are that she may live forever" (Ch. li)—reveal the true hostility behind this necessary humor of repulsion.

But compared to her chaplain, Mrs. Proudie is treated gently. It is the ambitious, progressive, and unctuous Slope who is the truly dangerous enemy and who is introduced so that the tendencies he represents may be expelled. In the process, he reveals a good deal about the norms of this comedy. The very fact that his eloquence is "not likely indeed to be persuasive with men, but [is] powerful with the softer sex" (Ch. iv), for instance, suggests that he is as feminine as Mrs. Proudie is masculine and uses a similarly elemental sexual humor to assault him. But more important, his specialized success suggests the fatal lack of discrimination—even sense—of women in general and Eleanor in particular. Women, it turns out, are unable to tell that he is "no gentleman," which, in terms of the code of **Barchester Towers,** means that they are morally blind. Slope's friends thus tell us nearly as much about him as his enemies. Eleanor is simply unable

to understand her father when he gives the central argument against Slope and, by implication, the central belief of the novel: "It can hardly be the duty of a young man rudely to assail the religious convictions of his elders in the church. Courtesy should have kept him silent, even if neither charity nor modesty could do so" (Ch. viii). When Eleanor objects that he may simply have been forced by his inner convictions to speak, Mr. Harding replies, "Believe me, my child, that Christian ministers are never called on by God's word to insult the convictions, or even the prejudices of their brethren, and that religion is at any rate not less susceptible of urbane and courteous conduct among men than any other study which men may take up." The fact that courtesy and urbanity rather than truth or righteousness are the supreme moral touchstones gets us right to the heart of this novel. Eleanor's inability to comprehend this doctrine immediately distances her from the novel's center.

But Slope's contributions are not often so indirect. He is the most vocal apostle of the new world, the oily symbol of progress and the "new man" of the country: "It is not only in Barchester," he says, "that a new man is carrying out new measures and casting away the useless rubbish of past centuries. The same thing is going on throughout the country" (Ch. xii). The "useless rubbish" in this case is Mr. Harding, a man we are forced to acknowledge as a hero. The attack on Slope, then, is an attack on *The Jupiter* and all the rude voices of discourtesy. Once the chaplain leaves Barchester, the society can function comfortably enough with the Proudies, who, at any rate, have no such horrid convictions about useless rubbish. Slope has, all along, been the chief threat to comic equilibrium, and he has been granted no virtues. It is true, of course, that Trollope makes an elaborate show of treating Slope with a consistent and fair moderation, insisting on his great courage and self-sufficiency. But Slope's courage is more aptly described by the American term, "guts," and is thus completely out of place in a world of English decency. He has, in fact, exactly the characteristics of the ruthless and cunning animals who inhabit the America of *Martin Chuzzlewit,* and in many ways Trollope echoes Dickens' great rejection of the new doctrine of "smartness" and the cult of success. Slope is a transplanted Colonel Scadder. The last reference to him makes his uncouth American newness even more explicit: "It is well known that the family of the Slopes never starve; they always fall on their feet like cats" (Ch. li). What had been matter of congratulation for Emerson in his strong celebration of the character of American youth ["Self-Reliance"], the "sturdy lad from New Hampshire or Vermont," who *"teams it, farms it, peddles"* and "always like a cat falls on his feet," becomes a matter of repulsion for Trollope in his equally strong rejection of it.

One of the major instruments of this rejection is the Stanhope family, fresh, lively, and not-very-scrupulous negative comic agents. Essentially foreigners, they not only have the clear insight of outsiders but the proper rootlessness and can act without final consequences to themselves. They do a job which the morally approved and passive cannot really handle. In their cynical and good-natured power, then, they combine the functions of Sam Weller and Alfred Jingle, adding both the necessary purgative force and the rebellious parody to the central innocence. As with most comedies (even with *Pickwick* in the case of Jingle), once their job is done, these negative agents must be gotten rid of; for their real work involves disruption, not stability. They also suggest an amusing, but also dangerous, lack of commitment. In combatting the self-deluded Proudies and Slopes, their flexibility and maneuverability are admirable, but, as Trollope insists, their very good nature hides an essential indifference, even heartlessness, and they must therefore be shipped back to Italy at the end. If we look at them too long, we might recognize their worldliness and laziness as a parody of the approved courtesy and passiveness. " 'I don't see why clergymen's sons should pay their debts more than other young men,' said Charlotte" (Ch. xix). The cynicism is welcome and sounds very much like an echo of the narrator's insistence that we are all men, but the narrator really has a secret qualification, ignored by the Stanhopes. He suggests that the best of us are all really gentlemen, pushing us upwards; the Stanhopes' cynicism levels downwards.

But Trollope handles these explosive agents with great tact. Their potential for danger is never realized, and their heartlessness is kept masked so well that they seem kindly, gentle, and, in the person of Bertie, essentially sweet. Bertie "was above, or rather below, all prejudices" (Ch. ix) and is always absolutely comfortable in his friendly indolence. He functions partly to attack work, prudence, and rigid convention and is, therefore, something of a reverse surrogate of the author and is given a kind of sneaky admiration and approval. Absolutely without self-consciousness, Bertie is the natural man and, as such, a perfect comic leveler. He enters Mrs. Proudie's reception and immediately deflates the pompous Bishop, attacking him just where he is most vulnerable—in his notion of the power given by rank:

> "I once had thoughts of being a bishop, myself."
>
> "Had thoughts of being a bishop!" said Dr. Proudie, much amazed.
>
> "That is, a parson—a parson first, you know, and a bishop afterwards. If I had once begun, I'd have stuck to it. But, on the whole, I like the Church of Rome the best."
>
> The bishop could not discuss the point, so he remained silent.
>
> "Now, there's my father," continued Bertie; "he hasn't stuck to it. I fancy he didn't like saying the same thing over so often."
>
> (Ch. xi)

Bertie continually pursues the Bishop with his conversation, and his very amiability and openness—"I was a Jew once myself"—expose the pompous churchmen. Significantly, though the majority of the clergy stare at Bertie "as though he were some unearthly apparition," "the archdeacon laughed." And that laugh carries with it the signal of moral approval for this fine comic executor. His climactic proposal (or anti-proposal) scene, then, is carefully arranged to support the most basic values. Trollope first makes it clear that Bertie is revolted by the "cold, cal-

culating, cautious cunning" (Ch. xlii) of the affair, not so much because it is iniquitous as because it is *"prudent."* He is the antithesis of the American-like Slope, instinctively repulsed by the game of power. In his gentle but firm rejection of "the new profession called matrimony" he is rejecting *all* scheming, forward-looking arrangements. He is, in this sense, a heightened but not distorted symbol of the basic tendency of the novel.

His sister Madeline plays a more complex role and brings with her a touch of a much blacker world and a more embittered spirit. However, she utilizes a kind of Freudian humor to transform her pain into clever parody and continual witty victories. She plays a role much like *Pickwick's* Jingle, who also perpetually attacks the impersonality and coldness of his environment by burlesquing it (in Chapter 7 he describes a cricket team as "flannel jackets—white trousers—anchovy sandwiches—devilled kidneys—splendid fellows—glorious"). Madeline Neroni's calling card—"La Signora Madeline / Vesey Neroni. / —Nata Stanhope"—is itself a fine parody of social forms, and she uses her daughter, "the last of the Neros," much as Becky Sharp uses little Rawdon, as an effective stage prop. Like her sister Charlotte, Madeline also sounds like the narrator: "Parsons, I suppose, are much the same as other men, if you strip them of their black coats" (Ch. x). The displacement of Madeline from the narrative center, however, is very clearly indicated by the verb "strip." Signora Neroni's function is potentially harsh, and she can, clearly, be vicious. She plays the exact negative for Mr. Harding's positive and supplies all the force and aggressiveness he lacks.

She also provides a bitter realism, which adds force and depth to the final solution: "Marriage means tyranny on one side and deceit on the other. I say that a man is a fool to sacrifice his interests for such a bargain. A woman, too generally, has no other way of living" (Ch. xv). Her cynicism is not explicitly supported, but since she does so much to ensure the solidity of the final approved society, the weight of her powerful experience and courage is assimilated into it. It is, ironically, this crippled woman who is the most powerful. She manages not only to expose the hypocrisy and unprincipled ambition of Mr. Slope and to force Arabin to recognize that the "good things of this world" are consonant with his religion (Ch. xxxviii) but actually hands him over to Eleanor, thereby arranging almost single-handedly the final disposition of the novel. For all the spider imagery associated with her, Signora Neroni has an absolutely sure moral instinct. Though she does trap the virtuous Mr. Thorne and exposes the gentle old man and his "antediluvian grimaces and compliments which he picked up from Sir Charles Grandison" (Ch. xlvi) to some ridicule, she recognizes her error. And when Mr. Slope rudely laughs at him, she springs to the old man's defense, ruthlessly exposing the chaplain's failure with Mrs. Bold and reducing him to dashing blindly from the room, while the avenged Mr. Thorne sits "laughing silently." She turns the tables in this small scene as in the novel as a whole, adjusting the proper values and correcting our own perspective. Because she is powerful, she cannot be made permanent in Barchester, but one suspects that she will be willing to come back from Italy should another Slope arrive. At any rate, she makes the cathedral town safe for the fragile values out of which the conservative comedy is built.

And all of the novel points toward the symbolic center of this comic world and the structural center of the novel in Miss Thorne's *Fête Champêtre* at Ullathorne. The party, at first seen as a monstrous dedication to illusion and the dead, ironically becomes the scene for clarity and rejuvenation, and the Thornes, viewed initially as hilariously super-annuated, move closer and closer to the normative position. Trollope's method here is extremely significant, in that he utilizes a point of view of diminishing distance to bring us closer to the Thornes and their values. Mr. Thorne is introduced in a tone of facetious detachment as a silly bore and a snob, supported by "an inward feeling of mystic superiority to those with whom he shared the common breath of outer life" (Ch. xxii). His sister, "a pure Druidess," simply exaggerates the fatuousness and obsolescence of her brother. The distance from these characters at times is so marked as to approach contempt: "Miss Thorne was very anxious to revert to the dogs. The dear good old creature was always glad to revert to anything, and had she been systematically indulged, would doubtless in time have reflected that fingers were made before forks, and have reverted accordingly." We are encouraged to laugh at these unreal and mechanistic anachronisms. The only tonal variation in this first introductory chapter involves a kind of nostalgic tolerance which is blatantly patronizing: "Who would deny her the luxury of her sighs, or the sweetness of her soft regrets!" The reader is led to view these people very much as would Mr. Slope. But Trollope, even in this chapter, slyly exposes his method: "All her follies have, we believe, been told. Her virtues were too numerous to describe, and not sufficiently interesting to deserve description." Her virtues are uninteresting only to the Slopes, and Trollope begins to reverse our position by forcing us much closer to the Thornes, quietly insisting in the next chapter on Miss Thorne's "soft heart" and essential good nature and on Mr. Thorne's honesty and generous hospitality.

By the time of the party, some ten chapters later, the Thornes' dedication to the past is taken much more seriously. They are rather like the Tudor windows at Ullathorne, not pleasing to "utilitarian" and modern, progressive minds but capable of giving immense "happiness to mankind." Instead of measurable candle-power, the Thornes give comfort and joy. Our earlier laughter is directly rebuked, as the Thornes' mechanistic unselfconsciousness is taken away and they are exposed as vulnerable and precious. In a fine scene just before the gathering, Miss Thorne tries to persuade her brother to ride at the quintain she has erected. Finally exasperated by the pressure she puts on him, he calls it a "rattletrap" (Ch. xxxv). Miss Thorne says nothing, but sips her tea and thinks of the past. As she does so, "some dim faint idea of the impracticability of her own views flitted across her brain," and it occurs to her that "perhaps after all her neighbours were wiser than herself." The sadness of this moment of self-doubt brings a single tear to her eye and Trollope uses that one tear to establish the central symbol of gentleness and kindness. "When Mr. Thorne saw the tear in her eye,

he repented himself of his contemptuous expression." Miss Thorne, "accepting the apology in her heart," goes out to the steward, Mr. Plomacy, to ask him to be lenient in checking the credentials of guests: "If they live anywhere near, let them in." In the end, they entertain nearly the whole district, and we see that the Thornes' deviation from the common standard, which had once seemed so funny, really amounts to their attempt to be truly kind and generous: "Miss Thorne, however, boldly attempted to leave the modern beaten track, and made a positive effort to entertain her guests" (Ch. xxxvi). Though she has only "moderate success," this reflects sadly on the times—not on the hostess. Later in the novel, then, after Trollope has cemented our attachment to the Thornes by this rhetoric of reversal, we can easily accept what would ordinarily appear perverse—the functional shift of love (and sexual power) from those who are young to the old Mr. Thorne: "But for real true love, love at first sight, love to devotion, love that robs a man of his sleep . . . we believe the best age is from forty-five to seventy; up to that men are generally given to mere flirting" (Ch. xxxvii).

By this point the reader is also prepared to give full authority to Mr. Harding as the moral norm. The novel does include a pair of lovers, it is true, and does give them some prominence, but it seems to me an important critical error and a distortion of the crucial themes not to recognize the ironies which attend Eleanor and Mr. Arabin and the rhetorical directions which move the reader away from them. It is particularly difficult to see how Eleanor can be accepted as a heroine. Not only is there a general distrust of women in the novel and a subtle but distinctly antifeminine tone, but there are explicit attacks on the young widow. Eleanor, very simply, is morally stupid, and the dominant image connected with her is that of the parasite, loyal, clinging, and deadly. The image is brought up immediately on her introduction: "Hers was one of those feminine hearts which cling to a husband, not with idolatry, for worship can admit of no defect in its idol, but with the perfect tenacity of ivy. As the parasite plant will follow even the defects of the trunk which it embraces, so did Eleanor cling to and love the very faults of her husband" (Ch. ii). Again, when Arabin finally proposes, the narrator insists on Eleanor's prospective happiness in the same terms: "When the ivy has found its tower, when the delicate creeper has found its strong wall, we know how the parasite plants grow and prosper" (Ch. xlix). Even more subversive is the attack on Eleanor's selfish and sloppily sentimental use of her child: "But yet she was happy in her baby. It was so sweet to press the living toy to her breast, and feel that a human being existed who did owe, and was to owe, everything to her" (Ch. ii). Her essential lack of self-knowledge is exactly like that of Thackeray's Amelia Sedley and is mirrored in the same image of child-worship as a form of self-worship. Because of this ignorance, Eleanor eagerly enters into the fighting, defending Slope often not from a sense of fairness but simply from instincts of "sheer opposition and determination not to succumb" (Ch. xxix). In the hilarious proposal scene with Mr. Slope, then, though we are expected fully to support the comic slap she gives him, we are also expected to delight in her embarrassment, the fruits of her ignorance. Both Eleanor's selfish reflections and Slope's champagne-induced "tender-pious" looks are, finally, attacked, and the scene makes fun of the triviality of young love. After this buffeting at Ullathorne, Trollope makes the criticism of Eleanor explicit. She rushes home to cuddle her boy and assert that "Mama would lie down and die if she had not her own Johnny Bold to give her comfort" (Ch. xliv). The narrator can't resist the appropriate sneer: "This kind of consolation from the world's deceit is very common. Mothers obtain it from their children, and men from their dogs. Some men even do so from their walking-sticks, which is just as rational."

While her eventual partner, Mr. Arabin, is not treated roughly, he is treated as more or less insignificant. Although not young, at "about forty" he isn't yet old enough to qualify for a favored position in this novel. As a high-churchman, most of his values can be approved of, but he has dangerous ascetic tendencies and defends conflict for its own sake in terms which run exactly counter to the belief of the novel: "But are we not here to fight? Is not ours a church militant?" (Ch. xxi). Further, his adolescent stammerings and ignorance of women are subject to a good many jokes (e.g., the ending of Ch. xxx). But he is not a bad man, only not a very important one. Trollope even laughs about having to mention the details of his engagement at all (Ch. xlviii). In the end, Arabin becomes a kind of Mr. Harding-in-training, committed to the old-fashioned and accepting from his father-in-law the deanship. Even at the last, however, Trollope throws out one final barb at this nearly-irrelevant couple. Instead of promising eternal love and proliferation of young Arabins, the narrator lets them repeat the marriage vows and cynically adds, "We have no doubt that they will keep their promises; the more especially as the Signora Neroni had left Barchester before the ceremony was performed" (Ch. liii). This Dobbin and Amelia are certainly not allowed to occupy the center of the novel.

But *Barchester Towers* is assuredly not "A Novel Without a Hero"; after virtually eliminating the standard interest in young love, the final focus rests on the true center, Mr. Harding. While Mr. Harding's values are largely defined by negation, he does display, here as in *The Warden,* an immense strength of resistance, the true power of the pacifist. He demonstrates exactly those beatitudes which the narrator blames Mr. Slope's religion for slighting: "Blessed are the meek, for they shall inherit the earth— Blessed are the merciful, for they shall obtain mercy" (Ch. iv). Mr. Harding "had nothing to seek and nothing to fear" (Ch. v), the narrator says, implying clearly that he can be unafraid *because* he has renounced the ludicrous power struggle. The definitive act of withdrawing from conflict allows Mr. Harding a unique clarity and an important capacity for self-doubt ("not . . . the usual fault of his order," Trollope sarcastically adds). His particular strength lies in his "nice appreciation of the feelings of others" (Ch. lii). He alone has the clarity and the generosity. While tolerant enough to allow "the Pope the loan of his pulpit" (Ch. vii), as Dr. Grantly says in exasperation, Mr. Harding is neither soft nor naive. He immediately dislikes Slope for all the right reasons, and he firmly resists all the pressures put on him by his friends. His final triumph, then, reverses the general terms of comedy: his satisfaction, more complete than anyone else's (Ch. lii), comes simply from escaping power. He is the strongest symbol of the most powerful impulse of the novel: the attack on the competitive instinct. In the world of fighting, Trollope argues, the man in the wrong is the one who is defensive, carefully storing up weapons, while the man in the right is confident and unarmed. "The one is never prepared for combat, the other is always ready. Therefore it is that in this world the man that is in the wrong almost invariably conquers the man that is in the right" (Ch. xxxvii). Therefore, one does not fight.

There is a good deal of melancholy behind this pacifism, and it is just this sense of self-doubt which tends to disrupt the comic simplicity and give the novel its hint of poignancy. Like Miss Thorne, Mr. Harding has moments when "he felt as though the world were sinking from his feet" (Ch. xii) and when he thinks that perhaps the Slopes are indeed right about the "useless rubbish." Though the narrator pledges to the Thornes and their kind, "May it be long before their number diminishes" (Ch. xxii), the Thornes have no descendants, and Mr. Harding's daughter hardly sustains his own values. There really is a quiet undercurrent that modifies the comic assurance with a lost-cause bitterness:

> "Everything has gone by, I believe," said Tom Staple. "The cigar has been smoked out, and we are the ashes."
>
> "Speak for yourself, Staple," said the master.
>
> "I speak for all," said the tutor, stoutly. "It is coming to that, that there will be no life left anywhere in the country."
>
> (Ch. xxxiv)

Staple's is not the only voice of the novel, of course, but it is one of the most deeply-felt. The comic confidence is also touched briefly by the vision of blunt economic necessity in the Quiverfuls and by the "look of care and pain" that sometimes plays about Madeline Neroni's eyes. This darker world, it is suggested, can make the niceties of moral conduct and warm generosity grossly irrelevant.

In any case, though the darkness of this comedy must not be overstated, an adequate appreciation of Trollope's novel demands, I think, a recognition of its complexity, its startling values, and its maturity. When Henry James praised *Barchester Towers* for its "almost Thackerayan richness," he struck exactly the right note; for Trollope's novel shares with Thackeray's masterpiece a cynicism concerning youth, a suspicion of standard novelistic formulae, a distrust of commonly-accepted heroic virtues, and even the good girl-bad girl parallel of Amelia-Becky and Eleanor-Madeline. But most important, in its values and in its particular tone, it echoes the mellow and strong sadness of *Vanity Fair.* And these are the qualities which, Geoffrey Tillotson says [in his *Thackeray the Novelist,* 1963], make Thackeray virtually unintelligible to the young: "His writings ought to be denied them, as wines should, and the latest music of Mozart and Beethoven." This is surely the voice of Mr. Harding—in a harsh mood—and reflects exactly the conservative comic spirit of Mr. Harding's world. (pp. 595-612)

James R. Kincaid, " 'Barchester Towers' and the Nature of Conservative Comedy," in ELH, *Vol. 37, No. 4, December, 1970, pp. 595-612.*

U. C. Knoepflmacher　(essay date 1971)

[*Knoepflmacher is an American educator and critic specializing in nineteenth-century fiction. In the following excerpt, he presents an overview of the themes and plot of* Barchester Towers, *discussing the importance of the narrative intrusions in the novel.*]

The word "fiction" means a lie, a deception. Yet in reading a novel we too often tend to be deceived into mistaking its invented world for fact. From its very beginning in the eighteenth century the English novel has pretended to be either history or biography. Defoe, a journalist, skillfully disguised his fiction as an account of factual occurrences; Richardson likewise obscured his own imaginative control of his epistolary novels by pretending that they merely recorded the experiences of actual people. Even Fielding, who reacted against this simulation of actuality, nonetheless helped to perpetuate the notion of the novelist-historian. Writers like Smollett, Jane Austen, and Scott added to the same confusion. For a long time, their "realism" was held to be more veracious, because presumably truer to the conditions of actual life, than the illusory fabrications of "romance."

No novelist is ever able to reproduce a precise mirror image of actual life. Although the novelist may pretend to be nothing more than a faithful chronicler or biographer, although he may claim to be absolutely scientific and accurate, we ought to remember that "no mental method of daguerreotype or photography has yet been discovered, by which the characters of men can be reduced to writing and put into grammatical language with an unerring precision of truthful description." The passage just quoted is taken from Anthony Trollope's **Barchester Towers.** It was written more than a century ago. Yet the confusion between the invented world of the novel and the actual world in which the novelist lived persists to this day. It has become a particularly troublesome obstacle in the correct appreciation of Victorian fiction, for the Victorian novel—which by and large follows the tradition of Fielding and Smollett and of Scott's historical novels—can all too easily be misread as a kind of photographic replica of nineteenth-century life. More than half of the sophomores I once asked to comment on the relevance of the "love affair" between Pip and Estella in Dickens' *Great Expectations* wrote variations of what amounted to the same contemptuous answer: Dickens, a Victorian, and hence by definition a prude in sexual matters, had shied away from presenting a "mature heterosexual relationship"; presumably, his failure to depict a "frank" affair was attributable to the timidity and repression of his age. Perhaps so. But none of the students who wrote this answer ever asked themselves what the presentation of a candid love affair, portrayed in detail, might have done to the purpose, emphasis, and very mode of *Great Expectations,* a symbolic parable and fairy tale. In arriving at their conclusion, the students had mistaken art for sociology; they had leaned on secondhand historical generalizations, instead of availing themselves directly of the standards generated by the "reality" of the novel before them.

This mistake is not only attributable to innocent undergraduates. Nor can it be ascribed exclusively to those who might confuse a fantasy tale for a "realistic" novel. It is commonly made by all of us who are seduced by the novel's feigned reality into confusing fiction with fact. And it is made particularly by those who, deluded by the verisimilitude of Victorian art, tend to misconstrue the nature of its "realism." Notwithstanding the warning of the narrator of **Barchester Towers,** three highly reputable scholars who have written on Trollope's work have occasionally lapsed into the mistake of viewing his fiction as a "daguerreotype": Michael Sadleir [in his *Trollope: A Commentary,* 1961] regarded Trollope as being above all the "voice of an epoch," a chronicler, observer, and interpreter of his age who was "concerned, consciously and literally, to portray an actuality he knew"; Bonamy Dobrée [in his *The Victorians and After: 1830-1914,* 1950] likewise felt that Trollope presented primarily "a fairly comprehensive and wholly comprehensible picture of the society in which he moved"; and Ralph H. Singleton, in his introduction to a recent edition of **Barchester Towers** [Washington Square Press, 1963], echoes these judgments and then goes on to assert that from that particular novel "we do get the clearest picture of mid-Victorian England, because Trollope was insistently preoccupied with producing just that." Inherent in all three estimates is the same confusion between fact and the artist's deliberate transmutation of fact. Although there is certainly nothing wrong in reading a novel like **Barchester Towers** as a kind of document or historical record which may tell the student of the nineteenth century something about the squabbles which took place within the Church of England at the time, this information is not what gives the novel its comprehensibility, nor, I should add, its universality. (**The Warden,** of which **Barchester Towers** is the sequel, is actually more of a historical document. Though not for that reason alone, it also happens to be a lesser work of art than **Barchester Towers.**)

The world imagined by the novelist—whether drawn according to the norms of "realism" or cast in the mold of an improbable "romance"—always contains its own ground rules. To extract these rules we must participate in its invented reality. The novelist who shapes this reality refracts, metamorphoses, and transmutes. He filters the actual world impinging on him into the fictitious world he constructs. His novel is an artifact. It is distorted by a lens which never produces an accurate "picture" of the author's own times, but rather a refraction shaped by his own idiosyncrasies, by the ideals he yearns for as well as by the fears he wants to subdue. It is a "fiction," not a chronicle, and as such offers a dimension of experience different from an objective recording of fact. We must enter this experience not as students of external history but as readers willing to share the novel's internal logic. Although separated by more than a century of changes in historical experience, the reader of today and the Trollope of 1857 can commune through their joint experience of the novel's unaltered reality.

In the remainder of this [essay], I should like to examine three devices essential to our understanding of a novel like *Barchester Towers:* setting, plot, and the elements that arise through the combination of the point of view of the characters with the novelist's use of a narrative voice. (pp. 3-6)

In *Barchester Towers*—as in most Victorian fiction—the novelist's device of setting discloses the primary characteristics of his created world. Trollope later called Barsetshire a "new shire which I added to the English counties," a "little bit of England which I myself have created." The county and its capital, the "cathedral town of Barchester," cannot be found on any map, despite their loose correspondence to Wiltshire or Hampshire, Salisbury or Winchester. Rather than a reproduction of actuality, this placid rural society contains the novelist's reaction to that actuality. Neither a Utopia nor a realm as outlandish as Swift's Lilliput or Houyhnhnmland, Trollope's Barsetshire does nonetheless reflect its creator's peculiar idiosyncrasies and concerns. Its inhabitants belong to a probable world, as probable as Hardy's Wessex or George Eliot's Loamshire, or, in our times, as Faulkner's Yoknapatawpha County. Although the Barchesterians represent a mode of life which could have existed or might exist, they embody above all that quasi-mythical, quasi-pastoral existence that Englishmen still call "Merrie England."

The opening chapters of *Barchester Towers* repeatedly call our attention to the gap which separates the imagined reality of Trollope's novel from the world to which he and his readers belong. In his first two chapters Trollope establishes a contrast he will maintain throughout the entire book: he juxtaposes quiet, sleepy Barchester to a busy outer world, an urban society similar in its composition to that formed by a good portion of his Victorian reading public. Change is the rule in this outer world: cabinets and ministries rise and fall with mechanical regularity, partisan newspapers trump up a new cause every week. Whereas provincial Barchester is self-contained, self-sufficient, and self-engrossed, London, or what the narrator calls "the world at large" (ch. 3), constantly engages in causes it does not even understand. Its Prime Ministers and Parliaments and Church Officials and Newspapers of all affiliations are always meddling and interfering. Opinions abound. If a new bishop is to be appointed for remote Barchester, why, *The British Grandmother, The Anglican Devotee,* and *The Eastern Hemisphere* must all have their say on the matter.

Trollope's novel thrives on this initial contrast between a capricious "world at large" and a sluggish provincial enclave suddenly challenged by outward changes. His "London" is semi-fictional. Rather than a mimetic copy of the world in which he and his contemporaries move, it is above all a caricature that capitalizes on his readers' own associations of London. Trollope's public would immediately understand, for instance, that the powerful *Jupiter,* that all-knowing organ which molds the opinions of an entire British nation, is the author's satirical version of the London *Times.* But if Trollope's London is only slightly distorted by the lens of his satire, Barsetshire, where time seems to run so much more slowly, is far more removed from actuality. The lingering ways of its inhabitants are endorsed by the novelist himself, though even the most Quixotic among them come to realize their dependence on "the powers" ruling the nation's changeful capital. Trollope, however, creates still another setting, even more remote than the cathedral town. At Ullathorne Court and the parish of St. Ewold, situated at the novel's innermost center, time almost stands still. It is there, in the heart of the novel, where appropriately enough the affairs of the heart are eventually settled.

Though belonging to the same uniform "reality" which prevails in the novel, these various settings are arranged according to a kind of gradation which could be represented by a series of concentric circles. On the periphery of the first circle lies the actuality to which novelist and reader belong; within the confines of that first circle lies Trollope's version of the "world at large"; the middle circle contains Barsetshire and Barchester; the innermost sphere holds Ullathorne court. Each of these areas is related. The vanities of London soon find their counterpart in Barchester, whose clergymen and merchants are after all directly connected to the capital both by the railroad and by the new "Electric Telegraph." London is a battleground for busybody parties who do as they like while pretending to pursue the general good; but this same factionalism spreads to Barchester as soon as the London interlopers disturb the town's complacency. The new bishop and his secretary bring with them the unruliness of the outer world. With their arrival, Barchester becomes a battlefield for the duration of the novel.

Ullathorne, on the other hand, seems far more impregnable. The "Court" is properly named, "for the house itself formed two sides of a quadrangle, which was completed on the other sides by a wall about twenty feet high" (ch. 22). This archaic construction, which seems to block out the world beyond it, also safeguards the slower ways of its inhabitants. The Londoners descend on Barchester by the speedy railroad; the Barchesterians in turn pride themselves on the horse-drawn carriages they ride in even for the shortest distances. But no vehicle drawn by horses can ever pass Ullathorne's "iron gate": "If you enter Ullathorne at all, you must do so, fair reader, on foot, or at least in a bathchair" (ch. 22). And yet, though farthest from the outer world, this quaint medieval bastion can never be completely cut off from the motions of change which affect all life. Its residents may lack the convenience of an electric telegraph, but "the world at large might, if it so wished, walk or drive by their iron gates. That part of the world which availed itself of the privilege was however very small." As we shall see later, those few privileged to be drawn past Ullathorne's iron gates profit from their experience.

Trollope does not introduce Ullathorne until his novel is well under way. The clash which sets the story in motion is that between London and Barchester. London's ostensible representative in the novel will be Mr. Proudie; its actual representative, Mr. Slope. While chapters one and two juxtapose Barchester to London by setting Archdeacon Grantly and Mr. Harding against those undefined forces which affect their fates, chapters three and four introduce the figures of the two intruders. Mr. Proudie represents London's self-importance; Mr. Slope, its more oblique designs. Though appointed as a rural bishop, Mr. Proudie is above all a city man. He cannot part with London, for the capital is his domain, his sphere of action: "How otherwise could he keep himself before the world? how else give to the government, in matters theological, the full benefit of his weight and talents?" (ch. 3). At the end of the novel Mr. Proudie will be able to give the government the full benefit of his weighty opinions; appointed to the House of Lords, he manages to register an occasional vote "in favour of Government views on ecclesiastical matters" (ch. 51). But while the bishop represents the empty pomp of the capital, his secretary knows how to tap its true sources of power. This power lies in his ability to exploit the changefulness of "the world at large." Like the witty servants of Roman and Elizabethan comedy who are his prototypes, the bishop's chaplain can adapt himself to change, no matter how abrupt or unforeseen. His very name, Slope, we are told by our helpful narrator, has been changed from that of the good Dr. Slop, the Catholic physician who bungled the birth of Tristram Shandy. Just as Mr. Slope has changed that eminent physician's name, so has his family changed its religion. The future lies with the Low Church party and its innovations. It is to that faction, correspondingly, that Mr. Slope theologically inclines.

The Londoners who now move towards Barchester are for Trollope the representatives of social values that deserve to be mocked. London is a fair of vanities, the breeding ground for false values, but it remains a frame of reference only. It typifies an existence as mechanical and divisive as the imaginary world of Barchester is organic and cohesive. Still, its disorder and change can easily be transplanted. Although the "world at large" represents that confusion between means and ends which Matthew Arnold was to call "machinery," Barsetshire is by no means an ideal realm made up of sweetness and light. Connected by the electric telegraph, linked by the steam locomotive, Barchester is, as Archdeacon Grantly bitterly discovers, very much affected by the decisions so casually made in the capital. It, too, cannot escape change. London oscillates between conservative and liberal governments; the cathedral town hovers uneasily between the old and the new. In London, a conservative government can fall in a matter of minutes; in the slack atmosphere of the provinces, the dying bishop holds on to life for almost a month. To the chagrin of his son, the old man is rather poor at synchronizing his timetable with that of the "world at large."

The old Bishop on his deathbed is the first figure we meet in the novel. He is as much a symbol of the inevitability of change as of Barchester's resistance to change. While the nation asks itself what party will make up the new government, Barchester simply wants to know about its own immediate future. "Who Will Be the New Bishop," is the question it asks itself, rather selfishly, though with honest concern. Even in Barchester change is unavoidable, yet the town's permutations are more deliberate than the capricious shifts of fortune that occur in London life. The old bishop, neither dead nor alive, lingers on and on. When he dies, he does so "as he had lived, peaceably,

slowly, without pain and without excitement" (ch. 1). His ways are those of Barsetshire.

The novel's contrasted settings, then, reflect degrees of antagonism between two distinct modes of life: the peaceful ways of Barchester and the offensive ways of London. Although in actual life most novelists undoubtedly prefer peace to war, a comic novel, like all comedy, relies on conflict and agitation. Trollope's aggressive Londoners are the movers of the plot. Their world at large impinges on the microcosm of Barchester and sets all characters in motion. The outsiders from that world—the Proudies, Mr. Slope, Signora Neroni, and the Stanhopes—stir up the dormant cathedral town almost as violently as the intrusion of the gigantic Gulliver stirred Lilliput. The reader, himself an outsider, is drawn into this miniscule society by venturing into Barchester, within the bishop's palace, and, eventually, past the iron gates of Ullathorne. Amused by the gyrations of the anthill that has been stirred up for him, the reader soon becomes entranced by its motions. He becomes a participant in Barchester life, sharing its petty preoccupations and insignificant squabbles.

Strife is the essence of Trollope's comedy. Chapter six of the novel is called, quite simply, "WAR!" In it Archdeacon Grantly, who had until that point never bothered to examine his doctrinal views too closely, decides that he must fight Mr. Slope in a battle to the finish. "Proudieism" and "Grantlyism" are born in a flash. The battle lines are drawn. Mock-heroic similes and metaphors begin to build up: "contest," "fight," "adversary," "champion," "combat," are the words now adopted by Barchester, the same community that, at the opening of the book, merely wanted to be left alone. In *Gulliver's Travels,* peace existed among the Lilliputian parties as well as between Lilliput and Blefuscu. The strife and contention, which start immediately upon Gulliver's arrival, end only after the Man Mountain has returned to the outer world. Pretty much the same thing occurs in ***Barchester Towers,*** partly because the novel's mode harks back to eighteenth-century comedy and satire, and partly also because Anthony Trollope, like Swift, has the conservative outlook of the Tory (there is, however, a vast difference between his Victorian Toryism and that of the Augustans).

At the end of the novel the town's slow ways reassert themselves. Peace returns to Barchester and with it the comedy is ended. The disruptive Mr. Slope is ejected, spewed out by the community: he leaves as "quickly" as he had come, and the town can return to its former immobility. Signora Neroni, that other alien, also leaves; less mobile than the nimble Mr. Slope, she departs in a far more dignified fashion and Barchester womanhood can breathe easier again. The Proudies, to be sure, do remain—some changes are inevitable. But the Bishop and his wife live mostly in London, where he can ceremoniously deliver his vote for the government in power. The only other outsider, Mr. Arabin, will become absorbed by Barchester. Its ways are his ways as well. He is an exile from London and not its deputy.

Thus, the hostilities end as abruptly as they had begun. Mr. Grantly, Barchester's self-appointed champion, finds himself vindicated. "Grantlyism" can dissolve as a political party because with Mr. Slope's departure, "Proudie-ism," too, is dead. Though the archdeacon remains disappointed in his hopes of succeeding his father, he has never really hated the new bishop or Mrs. Proudie. It is Slope, the parvenu with clammy hands, who is his archenemy. Dr. Proudie, the archdeacon decides early in the novel, has after all "been in the church *these ten years;* and they used to be a little careful ten years ago." But Slope! "How on earth such a creature got ordained!—they'll ordain anybody *now,* I know" (ch. 6, italics added). To this champion of conservatism, the old, even if only dating ten years back, must by definition be better than the new.

To Mr. Grantly the bishop's chaplain is satanic, and clearly our narrator is not overfond of the devious Mr. Slope, who speaks with "the wiles of the serpent." Yet it would be all too easy to convert Mr. Grantly into the author's spokesman, to assume that his conservatism is also that of his creator. If Trollope's point of view were truly identical with that of Grantly, then the novelist's message—rendered in the style of the "electric telegraph"—might simply read:

> "MEN FROM BAD, BAD CITY COME TO GOOD, SIMPLE COUNTRY. DISRUPT ITS ANCIENT VIRTUES WITH THEIR EVIL CITY WAYS: OFFEND GOOD COUNTRYFOLK. AROUSED BARCHESTERIANS GET RID OF BAD CITY SLICKERS, RETURN TO THEIR HABITUAL WAYS. THUS GOOD TRIUMPHS OVER EVIL. REGARDS. ANTHONY TROLLOPE."

Obviously such a message would be far too reductive, for it completely ignores Trollope's subtle injection of his values, his presentation of his own point of view. We have so far discussed setting or place and also sketched out broadly the novel's general movement or plot. Although important for our understanding of **Barchester Towers,** neither setting nor plot are sufficient in themselves.

In his candid remarks about his practice as a novelist, Trollope wrote in his **Autobiography** that he regarded plot as being "the most insignificant part of a tale." The plotting of **Barchester Towers** is hardly as complex as that of Dickens' or George Eliot's novels. Trollope's characters interact, but their interaction is produced by a series of dramatic episodes, a string of separate meetings, incidents, conversations—each vivid and memorable in itself—rather than through a tightly knit sequence of events. The situations that give rise to each of these scenes are simple in themselves: the available bishopric, almost immediately filled by Mr. Proudie; the available wardenship, alternately promised to Mr. Harding and Mr. Quiverful; the available hand (and fortune) of Eleanor Bold, desired by three separate suitors; and, halfway through the novel, the available deanery of Barchester Cathedral, aspired to by Mr. Slope, turned down by Mr. Harding, and finally awarded to Mr. Arabin.

Will Mr. Harding or Mr. Quiverful get the wardenship? Will Mr. Slope or Bertie Stanhope or Mr. Arabin get Eleanor's hand? Will a Proudieite or a Grantlyite get the Deanship? The reader knows the answers to these questions. And he knows them because he is supposed to know them. For Trollope's narrator refuses to spring unforeseen

Mrs. Proudie insists that her husband appoint Quiverful to the vacant wardenship. Illustration by Paul Hardy.

surprises on the reader (as will Dickens in *Our Mutual Friend*). Quite to the contrary, this narrator is eager to let us into his confidence: "But let the gentle-hearted reader be under no apprehension whatsoever. It is not destined that Eleanor shall marry Slope or Bertie Stanhope" (ch. 15). The remark sets us at ease—having eliminated two of Eleanor's suitors at a single stroke, we can safely guess the identity of the happy man.

The narrator gives us his doctrine that author and reader ought to move along together in perfect confidence: "Let the personages of the drama undergo ever so complete a comedy of errors among themselves, but let the spectator never mistake the Syracusan for the Ephesian; otherwise he is one of the dupes, and the part of a dupe is never dignified" (ch. 15). Why should the narrator surprise us or keep us in suspense? A peek at the novel's conclusion or the casual remark of a previous reader might easily destroy all our precious illusions. And so the narrator prefers to let us in on the follies and misconceptions of his characters and allows us to believe that only they, and not we, are the dupes. To Henry James and to Jamesian critics of the novel, these narrative intrusions seemed a crime, a "betrayal of a sacred office." In his essay on the "The Art of Fiction" James wrote:

> I was lately struck, in reading over many pages of Anthony Trollope, with his want of discretion . . . In a digression, a parenthesis or an aside, he concedes to the reader that he and this trusting friend are only "making believe." He admits that the events he narrates have not really happened, and that he can give his narrative any turn the reader may like best.

Possibly, James was thinking of passages such as that in chapter forty-three of *Barchester Towers,* where the narrator bemoans the fact that he has to dispose of "our friends" in the small remainder of "this one volume," and then goes on to wish that his publisher, Mr. Longman, would allow him a fourth volume to expatiate on further adventures (*Barchester Towers* was a so-called "three-decker," one of the three-volume novels in fashion until the end of the nineteenth century). This deliberate puncturing of our credulity occurs also in the remarks that introduce the last chapter of the book: "The end of a novel, like the end of a children's dinner-party, must be made up of sweetmeats and sugarplums." It is easy to see how such statements would have offended those who were dead serious about the art of fiction. To the outraged Henry James the mere notion that an artistic construct could be compared to the beneficent distribution of sweetmeats and sugarplums seemed a "terrible crime" indeed: "It implies that the novelist is less occupied in looking for the truth (the truth, of course I mean, that he assumes, the premises that we grant him, whatever they may be) than the historian, and in doing so it deprives him at a stroke of all his standing room." Later critics concurred. Assuming the Flaubertian notion (endorsed by Joyce) of a godlike artist who stands behind his handiwork, refined out of existence, they were as disturbed as James was by Trollope's unabashedly chatty narrator.

James' diagnosis is essentially correct. Trollope constantly calls our attention to the duping process of his art. But James' indignation is misplaced, for he failed to grant Trollope the very "premises" by which we come to place our trust in the delightful persona of the loquacious narrator. Although this narrator is indeed a spokesman for the novelist himself, he is also a character. His imperfections therefore link him both to the "dupes" in the novel and to those who, like the reader, live in an actual world of imperfection. Although he may pretend to take us into his full confidence, he can also be evasive, forcing us to make our own judgments: "My readers will guess from what I have written that I myself do not like Mr. Slope; but I am constrained to admit that he is a man of parts." The narrator's mock protestations (as in the famous incident of the slap), his calculated uncertainties, suggest that, far from destroying the "truth" of Trollope's novel, he complicates this truth for us. Like Mr. Slope, this narrator (who, as we shall later see, owes much to Thackeray's evasive Showman) can at times speak in a most "ambiguous manner."

The narrator's digressions about the course of the story do not in the least diminish our enjoyment of the novel. In fact it is precisely because his remarks allow us to anticipate the outcome of events, precisely because they establish the plot's predictability, that we cherish the individual episodes and vignettes all the more. Because we know that all will end well, that order will return to Barchester, we enjoy the disorder as long as it lasts. We take an interest in each situation and cling to the variations and complications that that situation affords. The disruptions produced by the discursive narrator only heighten our appreciation of the disruptions provided by the novel's plot.

If Trollope's narrator acts as a link between the characters and the reader, he also prevents us from becoming totally seduced by the enticing, lifelike quality of his fictive world. Although he describes and interprets the settings of the novel, although he does his very best to involve us in the events he unfolds for us, he never lets us forget that these settings and these events are feigned. The narrator thus invites us to participate in a fiction. He is a gamester who toys, for instance, with the notion that his novel is a "history." He tells us in great detail about the debates that led to the bill which regulates the administration of Hiram's Hospital, and his account sounds most authentic. But then he continues: "The bill, however, did pass, and at the time at which this history is *supposed* to commence, it had been ordained. . . . " Again and again, he maintains this pretended uncertitude. He tells us that our "present business at Barchester will not occupy us above a year *or two* at the furthest" (ch. 2, italics added). Or, in sketching Dr. Proudie's background, he informs us that the gentleman had "seven *or* eight children" (ch. 3, italics added).

The narrator also mocks our faith in the accuracy of his "history" by his repeated introduction of literary references. Squire Thorne, we are informed, is a "specimen" of the race "which a century ago was, as we are told, fairly represented by Squire Western" (ch. 22). The pretended unsureness produced by "as we are told" calls attention to the make-believe involved in a characterization that depends on literary cross-references. As mentioned above, Mr. Slope is a lineal descendant of another fictional character, Dr. Slop in *Tristram Shandy.* At least, the narrator tells us, so he has "heard it asserted." The fiction of the reporter is maintained with tongue-in-cheek: "All my researches on the subject have, however, failed in enabling me to fix the date on which the family changed its religion" (ch. 4). The effect of such statements is carefully calculated. Like the Fielding who buttonholes his readers in *Tom Jones* and *Joseph Andrews,* Trollope wants us to realize that he is in complete control of his story—that we are reading not history but fiction, devised and directed by him.

The voice of Trollope's narrator, then, complicates our initial responses to setting and plot; what is more, it also complicates our reaction to the characters themselves. Victorian fiction depends above all on the profound appeal of its characters. The Victorian novelists relied on their representation of men and women to engage their readers and establish shared sympathies and aversions. By using their characters to bring out each reader's elementary need for identification and dissociation, the novelists were able to share gratifying wishes and defenses with their public. Trollope, too, relied essentially on characterization to mold our point of view and bring it in contact with his implied beliefs. He lets his figures think, act, and speak for themselves, yet also tells us (or, more often, pretends to tell us) through the voice of his narrator what our attitudes ought to be. In the following section we will examine Trollope's handling of Archdeacon Grantly and Mr. Harding in the opening chapter and try to determine how this initial contrast helps to set up attitudes that Trollope wants us to retain for the remainder of his novel.

The opening scene of *Barchester Towers* offers an excellent illustration of Trollope's ability to manipulate our responses toward his characters. The first pages introduce us to Archdeacon Grantly, who later becomes the nominal paladin of the Barchester forces, and who should, ostensibly, become the reader's paladin as well. A competent and dedicated clergyman, he has, in effect, ruled as unofficial bishop during his father's protracted illness and therefore deserves to be appointed by the government as the old man's successor. Grantly becomes understandably offended when the newly arrived Proudies foist their opinions on him: "The archdeacon," the narrator tells us dryly, "knew his subject, and really understood the business of bishoping, which the others did not." Still, despite the legality of Grantly's claims, Trollope deliberately undercuts his characterization. Although the narrator professes that we tolerate the archdeacon's weaknesses, he denies us all possible means for such an identification.

"Proud, wishful, worldly," are the three adjectives that the narrator attaches to Grantly in the opening pages of the book. The description is repeated at the end of the first chapter:

> Our archdeacon was worldly—who among us is not so? He was ambitious—who among us is ashamed to own that "last infirmity of noble minds!" He was avaricious, my readers will say. No—it was for no love of lucre that he wished to be bishop of Barchester. He was his father's only child, and his father had left him great wealth. His preferment brought him in nearly three thousand a year. The bishopric, as cut down by the Ecclesiastical Commission, was only five. He would be a richer man as archdeacon than he could be as bishop. But he certainly did desire to play first fiddle; he did desire to sit in full lawn sleeves among the peers of the realm; and he did desire, if the truth must out, to be called "My Lord" by his reverend brethren.

The description sticks in our minds. While the narrator exculpates Mr. Grantly from being avaricious, his defense only helps to indict the archdeacon and to link him with his London adversaries. Though cast as antagonists, Slope and Grantly are more alike than not (in fact, . . . the two are the only masculine figures in a society where women fight the battles of their men). To be sure, the archdeacon is not avaricious. Slope is a fortune hunter because he wants power; Proudie is money-minded because he is vain, eager to parade his carriage before the eyes of fashionable Mayfair. But if Mr. Grantly is not avaricious, it is only because, unlike the Proudies or Slope, he happens to be rich. His ambitions, therefore, merely take a different outlet. Like Mr. Proudie, he is vain; like Mrs. Proudie or Slope,

he wants to play first fiddle. He is as power-hungry as the man he shall try to unthrone.

What convinces us most strongly that we do not want Dr. Grantly as our future paladin is the situation Trollope dramatizes in the opening chapter. More than the mere words "proud," "wishful," "worldly," "ambitious," the dominant impression is that of a son wishing to hasten his father's death. Trollope handles the situation with tact and skill. The Bishop has for all intents and purposes been dead for a month; he is in a coma, and life and death seem so much alike to this good, old, virtuous man who is so sure to find his reward in heaven. And his son's predicament is, after all, so urgent. The conservative government may fall any minute; the archdeacon is in his fifties—clearly this is his last chance. The scene is delicately rendered. It is potentially tragic (one thinks of Edmund wishing Gloucester's death). Even to non-Freudians, the situation evokes deep-rooted emotions. Trollope avoids stirring our passions too violently, and yet, at the same time, forces the archdeacon to ask himself "whether he had really longed for his father's death." The question is now out in the open. And, then, with calculated ambivalence, the novelist suppresses the direct answer we have come to expect: "The proud, wishful, worldly man, sank on his knees by the bedside, and taking the bishop's hands within his own, prayed eagerly that his *sins* might be forgiven him" (italics added). It is Dr. Grantly who has used the word "sins," not the narrator—its usage is the only admission we are allowed to glimpse. For the kneeling archdeacon's humility is short-lived. When, moments later, his father does die, his thoughts turn worldly again. He thinks of the electric telegraph at the very same time that he remembers that he must maintain a doleful appearance: "how without appearing unfeeling was he to forget his father in the bishop—to overlook what he had lost and think of what he might possibly gain?" Obviously, the possibility of gain outweighs the reality of his loss.

When at the end of the chapter the narrator steps into the story in his own voice he contributes to our uneasiness about Mr. Grantly. The question asked (but not answered) by the archdeacon before his father's death is now raised again by the narrator: "Many will think that he was wicked to grieve for the loss of episcopal power, wicked to have coveted it, nay wicked even to have thought about it, in the way and at the moments he had done so." The triple repetition of the word "wicked" is disturbing, even though the narrator now tells us that he cannot "*completely* agree" with the "censures" he attributes to his readers. What is more, the nature of his defense is deliberately inconclusive: we are asked not to expect our clergymen to be "more than men," to recognize that a lawyer does not "*sin*" in seeking to be a judge, that a young diplomat trying to rise in an embassy "entertains a fair ambition." The chapter concludes with what purports to be a simple statement of fact: "His hopes, however, were they innocent or sinful, were not fated to be realised; and Dr. Proudie was consecrated Bishop of Barchester." The wedged-in clause, "were they innocent or sinful," is unsettling. The interjected words remind us that we as readers must make the judgment that the slippery narrator refuses to provide. "Innocent"? A man who is proud, wishful, and worldly, whose desire to play first fiddle has just been emphasized, cannot be considered innocent. "Sinful"? Dr. Grantly has himself used that word. As Trollope has suggested, and as he will stress again and again, the archdeacon is as fallible as most men. Even more than the too innocuous Mr. Proudie or than the too conniving Mr. Slope, this character can act as an apt representative of the vanities which the novelist wants us to recognize in ourselves. At the same time, however, Mr. Grantly can never be the spokesman of an author who addresses us through the voice of a narrator who inevitably refuses to pass judgment. Dr. Grantly is too sure, too self-righteous for that. Although we may think him to be on the right side of the battles of Barchester, we are led to discover that all "sides," all partisanship, merely cover up the same basic human vanities: pride, ambition, the desire for influence and power.

It is significant that this first chapter should also introduce Mr. Harding, the different, timid, evasive ex-warden. It is equally noteworthy that Trollope has the old bishop die in the presence of his old friend, as well as in that of his ambitious son. Indeed, the description of the bishop who ruled with such "meek authority" resembles rather strongly that of the warden who resigned his stewardship out of meekness. Ostensibly, it is the archdeacon who is in the foreground in chapter one. It is his drama that we are interested in. But Mr. Harding, passive, undramatic, forever a bystander, is just as important to the first chapter's architecture as the manly Barchester champion. The dying old man addresses both his friend and his son; he blesses them jointly before expiring.

Mr. Harding is the archdeacon's father-in-law, yet the relationship between the two men proves to be curiously qualified, as qualified as Dr. Grantly's grief for his father. In the same sentence in which we find the two mourners yoked to each other by the death of the bishop, we learn that they have not been at all close to each other in the past: "There was more fellowship between them at that moment than there had ever been before." Moreover, this momentary "fellowship" turns out to be quite one-sided. It is Mr. Harding who, contrary to his usual ways, takes the initiative when he grasps Grantly's hands and presses them warmly. His warmness, however, is not matched by any corresponding feelings in his son-in-law. The older man's innocence is jolted when he is asked to send the telegraph message that Grantly has been composing in his mind: "Mr. Harding who had really been somewhat surprised to find Dr. Grantly, as he thought, so much affected, was rather taken aback; but he made no objection. He knew that the archdeacon had some hope of succeeding to his father's place, though he by no means knew how highly raised that hope had been."

Mr. Harding cannot fathom the extent of his son-in-law's ambitions, because Grantly's mode of thinking is too removed from his own. If the one man is ruled by the power of feeling, the other is ruled by his awareness of the power of London. The devious archdeacon tells his father-in-law that Mr. Harding must sign the message he wants to send to the prime minister; he tells him how to deliver it to the telegraph office; he even gives him a half-crown: "Mr. Harding felt very much like an errand-boy and also felt

that he was called on to perform his duties as such at rather an unseemly time." The older man is puzzled on seeing his name on the message, but is reassured by the archdeacon: "What name so proper as that of so old a friend as yourself? The Earl won't look at the name, you may be sure of that; but my dear Mr. Harding, pray don't lose any time."

The decisiveness of the younger man's tone admits no remonstration. Grantly is conscious of his dependence on "time," of the shifts of London, but it is Mr. Harding, and not the bishop's son, who is truly aware of the "unseemly time" and the unseemly gesture. We like the father-in-law, not the resolute son-in-law he only dares to address as "archdeacon," and Trollope makes us like him precisely because he is so meek and put-upon. We are therefore delighted at the sudden poetic justice that Trollope springs on us. As the old man obediently trots off to deliver the electric telegram for his scheming son-in-law—a telegram he neither composed nor wants to deliver, even though it has been signed in his own name—this aged and good-natured errand boy unwittingly gives the archdeacon the come-uppance Mr. Grantly so richly deserves. Almost by coincidence, Mr. Harding now remembers the news he had come to deliver but had forgotten in his excitement and grief over the death of his old friend: "He had found the moment so inopportune for any mundane tidings that he had repressed the words which were on his tongue." But now he recollects. " 'But archdeacon,' said he, turning back, 'I forgot to tell you—The ministry are out.' " The death of his father had raised the archdeacon's hopes; the death of the ministry kills them forever. And we rejoice.

The incident dramatized in this first chapter is a miniature of the entire novel. Mr. Harding's role in this episode is typical of his position throughout the book. Unworldly, naive, forgetful of "mundane tidings," the former warden is the exact opposite of his proud, wishful, worldly son-in-law. If Mr. Grantly wants to play first fiddle, the author of *Harding's Church Music* prefers to play his imaginary violoncello. The old man is soon dragged into the clerical warfare of Barchester by the town's self-styled champion. His extraordinary timidity is laughable, his tendency to misconstrue the feelings and motives of others, almost exasperating. Still, Trollope's novel concludes with a description of him and not of his ambitious son-in-law. What is more, in the course of the story, Mr. Harding acquires a second son-in-law, a man almost as self-effacing as himself. Mr. Arabin compensates him for the intimidating Dr. Grantly. For Mr. Harding and Mr. Arabin (whom the warden might even dare to call by his first name) are unlike the leader of their camp, who, though a High Churchman, above all resembles Mr. Slope the Low Church evangelical. Like Slope, the archdeacon forgets the precept quoted in chapter four: "Blessed are the meek, for they shall inherit the earth." And in the invented, delightfully artificial world of Barchester, where Anthony Trollope pulls the strings, the meek actually can inherit the earth.

I have used ***Barchester Towers*** to illustrate the truism that a fiction is, above all, a fiction. . . . The world created by a novelist derives its fullest identity from each reader's wishfulness, from our need to resist the encroachments of a too restrictive view of actuality. The pleasure-evoking constructs each novelist devises become continuous with the private worlds that each of us creates to ward off the threat posed by uncertainty, doubt, and change.

We should not enter a Victorian novel like *Barchester Towers* by expecting to find a faithful replica of a fixed, external reality; instead, we should regard it as a fluid fantasy that enables author and audience to react jointly against an alienating world of change and disorder. As sharers and participants in an illusion of order, novelist and reader become tentative allies against chaos. (pp. 6-24)

> *U. C. Knoepflmacher, "Introduction: Entering a Victorian Novel—'Barchester Towers'," in his* Laughter & Despair: Readings in Ten Novels of the Victorian Era, *University of California Press, 1971, pp. 3-24.*

Hugh L. Hennedy   (essay date 1971)

[*Hennedy is an American educator and critic. In the following excerpt, he praises the structural and thematic unity of Trollope's* Barchester Towers.]

[Michael Sadleir, in his *Trollope: A Commentary,* 1947] is partially right in seeing the aim of *Barchester Towers* as "the portrayal of society in a southern cathedral city". What he fails to see is that the novel is concerned with portraying a threatened, not a static, society. The exact nature of the threat and how it is met can be seen only in a detailed examination of some of the structural elements of the novel.

It is possible to look at the plotting of *Barchester Towers* in various ways. Seymour Betsky, for instance, seems to see only one plot in the novel, a plot to which some characters and incidents are connected only tangentially, if at all: "In *Barchester Towers* . . . the heart of Trollope's concern has to do with a struggle among higher clergy for political power within a cathedral town. The love story of Eleanor Bold and the Rev. Francis Arabin, the caricatured triangle of Slope, Madame Neroni, and Eleanor Bold, and the comic efforts of Bertie's proposal to Eleanor Bold—all are tangents. The sports at Ullathorne are quite extraneous, disproportionately so" ["Society in Thackeray and Trollope", in *From Dickens to Hardy,* ed. Boris Ford, 1958]. It makes at least as much sense, however, to regard the novel as having four plots, two major and two minor, the power struggle and the Eleanor Bold love affairs being the former, the fate of the Stanhopes and the position of the Thornes of Ullathorne the latter. The most sensible approach, though, lies in recognizing that *Barchester Towers,* like *The Warden,* has but two plots, but that those plots are much more complex than those of *The Warden,* for if Mr. Harding is at the center of the major plot of *The Warden,* no one person is at the center of *Barchester Towers'* power struggle: Bishop Proudie, Mrs. Proudie, Mr. Slope, and Archdeacon Grantly are all centrally engaged in the struggle; and if Eleanor has but one suitor in *The Warden,* she has three—Arabin, Slope, and Bertie Stanhope—in *Barchester Towers.* Having recognized the novel's plots, one can begin to grapple with the real critical

problems: How, if at all, do the parts of the plots relate to the wholes? How, if at all, do the two plots affect each other?

Even before the narrative proper begins, the title of the first chapter, "Who Will Be the New Bishop?" announces the first phase of the struggle for power in Barchester. If the old bishop dies before the old ministry goes out, then there will be no struggle, for the episcopal power will remain where it has been during the reign of old Dr. Grantly, a man who occupied the episcopal chair "with meek authority": it will remain in the hands of the archdeacon, the bishop's son. If the ministry should fall before the bishop's death, however, then there will be a struggle, for "No probable British prime minister but he who was now in, he who was soon to be out, would think of making a bishop of Dr. Grantly". The ministry does, of course, fall before the bishop's death, and the struggle is on. Before looking at that struggle in detail, it should first be noted that it is made possible by a shift in political power. At the very beginning of the novel, then, there is an interaction of powers: political power affects ecclesiastical power.

In case anyone should suppose that something other than power is of primary importance at the old bishop's death, Trollope takes pains at the end of Chapter 1 to clarify the archdeacon's motives: "He was avaricious, my readers will say. No—it was for no love of lucre that he wished to be bishop of Barchester. . . . He would be a richer man as archdeacon than he could be as bishop. But he certainly did desire to play first fiddle". Similarly, Trollope makes it clear that the other principal strugglers for power are motivated precisely by that desire. Mr. Slope, for instance, "wanted a wife, and he wanted money, but he wanted power more than either". And as if further to underline the importance of power in the novel, Trollope uses the word itself, or some form of it, time and time again: he uses it in at least forty of the fifty-three chapters of the novel, and in those chapters in which "power" does not appear, some substitute, such as "mastery", "authority", "jurisdiction", "rule", does. "Power", indeed, is the key word of *Barchester Towers.*

But if circumstances rather arbitrarily initiate the power struggle in Barchester, once the new bishop is named, the struggle is carried on deliberately. Bishop Proudie is to be the bishop in name, but now the question is, Who will be bishop in fact? Who will wield the episcopal power?

Though the archdeacon wielded that power while his father was alive and hoped to possess it in his own right after his father's death, he cannot really be said to be a contestant for the episcopal power once Bishop Proudie has been installed. The archdeacon moves from a position of hoping to wield the episcopal power in his own right to that of striving to limit that power. Once Mr. Slope declares war with his sermon in Barchester Cathedral, the archdeacon and his friends are put on the defensive. Theirs is a holding action; they fight to preserve as much as possible of the old order against the encroachments of the new episcopal regime.

Though the bishop is the titular head of the attacking forces [in a footnote, Hennedy adds: "The military imagery is Trollope's. It pervades the novel in a manner similar and parallel to the word 'power' "], and although insofar as he is by conviction a liberal, a whig, and a low churchman, he is the natural enemy of the archdeacon's high church forces, the real aggressors are Mr. Slope and Mrs. Proudie. The bishop is dominated by his wife, of course, but having archiepiscopal ambitions, he "by no means intended to bury himself at Barchester as his predecessor had done. No! London should still be his ground." Bishop Proudie's ambition to shine in London, then, leaves a power vacuum in Barchester.

Mr. Slope, even on his first trip to Barchester, taking note of the bishop's ambition, determines to fill the Barchester power vacuum. "He understood correctly enough to what attempts the new bishop's high spirit would soar, and he rightly guessed that public life would better suit the great man's taste, than the small details of diocesan duty. He, therefore, he, Mr. Slope, would in effect be bishop of Barchester. Such was his resolve".

And Mr. Slope's method of carrying out his resolution is just as deliberate as the resolution itself. His sermon in Barchester Cathedral is intended to be exactly what it turns out to be: an open declaration of war. Having decided that the archdeacon cannot be cajoled or flattered into accepting encroachments upon the *status quo,* Mr. Slope "saw that open battle against Dr. Grantly and all Dr. Grantly's adherents was a necessity of his position, and he deliberately planned the most expedient methods of giving offence". The sermon is one very powerful such method.

But Mr. Slope is well aware that the archdeacon and his forces are not his only enemies. "He knew that he should have a hard battle to fight, for the power and patronage of the see would be equally coveted by another great mind—Mrs. Proudie would also choose to be bishop of Barchester". It is this battle, the struggle for power between Mr. Slope and Mrs. Proudie, which is the central struggle of the novel. Had the liberal forces been united, they might very well have beaten the conservatives. As it is, the attacks on the conservatives are not so much launched for their own sakes as they are deliberately made occasions for the Slope—Mrs. Proudie struggle.

The first such occasion is the appointment of the warden for the newly reconstituted Hiram's Hospital. Though it is true that Mr. Slope and Mrs. Proudie begin in agreement that Mr. Harding shall not have the wardenship, as soon as Mr. Slope decides that because Eleanor Bold's fortune is worth having, it would be a good idea to stay on the right side of her father, then he and Mrs. Proudie are destined to come into open conflict. If Who will be the new bishop? is the first question posed by the power-struggle plot, and Who will exercise the episcopal power? the second, then the third is, Who will be the warden? If the first makes the power struggle inevitable and the second defines the essence of it, the third sets it in motion in earnest and gives Trollope another chapter title: "Who Shall Be Cock of the Walk?" By the end of this chapter, Chapter 17, Mr. Slope has not openly declared war on Mrs. Proudie, as he has already declared it on the archdeacon, but Mrs. Proudie has reacted so vigorously to his attempts to persuade the bishop to reoffer the wardenship to Mr. Har-

ding, that Mr. Slope is quite sure that there is "not room in the diocese for the energies of both himself and Mrs. Proudie".

Despite a temporary victory or two by Slope, Mrs. Proudie finally succeeds in putting her candidate, Mr. Quiverful, into the wardenship. To do so, however, she has to put down a rebellion at home, for Mr. Slope succeeds for a while in inspiring the bishop to attempt to assert his authority over his wife. But although the bishop succeeds in the daytime in driving his wife from one battlefield, his study, and even begins "to hope that he was now about to enter into a free land, a land delicious with milk which he himself might quaff, and honey which would not tantalise him by being only honey to the eye", his wife proves too powerful for him at night on another battle-field, their bed, and by the time morning arrives, the bishop has surrendered for good. If at the beginning of the novel a shift in political power makes the ecclesiastical struggle for power possible, in the middle of the work Mrs. Proudie's reassertion of domestic power assures her of her first victory over Mr. Slope, who is incapable of putting his man into the wardenship against the opposition of both the Proudies.

Mrs. Proudie's second victory over Mr. Slope does not come about through her own prowess, for although she certainly does not endorse or approve of Mr. Slope's candidacy for the deanship, it is Dr. Gwynne's influence, not Mrs. Proudie's, which secures the position for Mr. Arabin. By this time, of course, Mr. Slope has just about given up all his pretensions to episcopal power, having recognized that Mrs. Proudie possesses certain insuperable tactical advantages in the struggle to control the bishop. The deanship would make a nice consolation prize for him, though, and he still might be able to snipe away at Mrs. Proudie from the sanctuary of the cathedral. Mrs. Proudie, however, has no intention of allowing Mr. Slope any consolation. She, "the Medea of Barchester . . . had no idea of not eating Mr. Slope. Pardon him! merely get rid of him! make a dean of him! It was not so they did with their captives in her country, among people of her sort! Mr. Slope had no such mercy to expect; she would pick him to the very last bone".

Dr. Gwynne, the Master of Lazarus, has little in common with the Medea of Barchester, and soon after he encounters her in the bishop's study, he begins "to understand and to share the intense disgust which the archdeacon always expressed when Mrs. Proudie's name was mentioned". Dr. Gwynne, nevertheless, helps Mrs. Proudie complete her victory over Mr. Slope, for when, through his influence, the fourth and last question of the power-struggle plot—the question, that is, of Who is to be Dean of Barchester Cathedral?—is answered with Mr. Arabin's name, then Mr. Slope has no choice but to leave Barchester, and Mrs. Proudie's victory over him is complete.

Dr. Gwynne is not the only unintentional supporter of Mrs. Proudie's cause, however, for it is certain that Mr. Slope himself contributes to his own defeat. He does so first of all, of course, by challenging and antagonizing Mrs. Proudie in the matter of the wardenship, but some challenge was necessary in order for the fight to begin, and given the nature of the two antagonists, a fight for power between them, on some grounds or other, would seem almost inevitable. The avoidable involvement, however, the real mistake of Mr. Slope's campaign, is his entanglement with la Signora Madeline Vesey Neroni, nata Stanhope. It is one thing for him to exercise his power by summoning the Stanhopes back from Italy; it is quite another thing to pay daily visits to Signora Neroni, a woman who can give him nothing but trouble.

Mr. Slope, who is not unintelligent, is aware of the dangers of his dalliance with Madeline. He knows that scandal may reach the palace, as it does, and give Mrs. Proudie the excuse she wants to dismiss him from the bishop's service, as it does. "He knew that he was acting against the recognised principles of his life, against those laws of conduct by which he hoped to achieve much higher success. But . . . he could not help himself. Passion, for the first time in his life, passion was too strong for him". Mr. Slope, who lives to gain and exercise power, exposes himself to Mrs. Proudie's power because he is too weak to withstand the power of passion.

His passion does not grow unaided, of course, for its object deliberately seeks to strengthen it. Mrs. Proudie is not the only woman in Barchester who likes to exercise power. Indeed, Signora Neroni, physically incapacitated though she may be, is as power-hungry as anyone in the novel. Perhaps it would be more accurate to say that because she is physically incapacitated, she lusts for power over men. Trollope puts it this way: "It was necessary to her to have some man at her feet. It was the one customary excitement of her life. She delighted in the exercise of power which this gave her; it was now nearly the only food for her ambition". Once again the novel's primary plot unfolds through an interaction of powers. If the ecclesiastical power struggle begins as the result of a shift in political power, if it continues as the result of a reassertion of domestic power and moves along further through the influence of a powerful ally, Dr. Gwynne, it concludes as Signora Neroni's sexual power makes Mr. Slope especially vulnerable to Mrs. Proudie's wrath.

It is worth noting that Mr. Slope's final expulsion from Barchester, an expulsion which may remind some readers of Malvolio's final exit in *Twelfth Night* inasmuch as both he and Mr. Slope threaten revenge as they leave, is anticipated by his inglorious expulsion from the signora's presence. Signora Neroni, like Mrs. Proudie, lives to exercise power, and, again like the Medea of Barchester, she "had no pity; she knew nothing of mercy. Her present object was to put Mr. Slope down, and she was determined to do it thoroughly, now that she had him in her power". She does it thoroughly, so thoroughly that "How Mr. Slope got out of that room he never himself knew". Mr. Slope's putting-down by the signora makes a cruel scene, but it is altogether appropriate that the woman who renders Mr. Slope so helpless should play a leading role in the foreshadowing of his final exit.

As much as Trollope detests Mr. Slope, he has a certain admiration for the man's courage, and towards the end of the novel he tries to do him justice. When the appointment of Mr. Arabin to the deanship is announced, the archdea-con exults, feeling that now he has succeeded in trampling on Mr. Slope. Trollope comments at this point, however, that not the archdeacon, "but circumstances, had trampled on Mr. Slope". It is certainly true that the archdeacon has little right to claim credit for Mr. Slope's downfall. The most he has done to help his own cause is to bring Mr. Arabin to St. Ewold's and to suggest Arabin as a candidate for the deanship to Dr. Gwynne. It is also true inasmuch as Dr. Gwynne's influence in the appointment of the new dean is a matter entirely beyond Mr. Slope's control, that circumstances, not the archdeacon, thwart Mr. Slope's candidacy for the deanship. "Circumstances", however, is hardly an adequate term to cover Signora Neroni and Mrs. Proudie, and since these powerful, merciless women play a large part in the defeat of Mr. Slope, it seems more accurate to say that not the archdeacon, but circumstances and two women combine to trample on Mr. Slope.

It should be evident by this time that the various parts of the power-struggle plot cohere, that the four questions which arise during the course of the primary plot are logically tied together and that they relate to each other in a significant and causal manner. Who is to wield the episcopal power? is the central question, a question which is largely answered by means of the answers to the questions, Who is to be the new bishop? Who is to be warden? and Who is to be the new dean? It is now time to turn to the second plot, the love story, to see how its parts relate to each other and to see further how the whole of it relates to the primary plot.

If Signora Neroni's dismissal of Mr. Slope is a humiliating experience for him, his leave-taking of Eleanor Bold is also humiliating and, since she slaps him, is physically painful as well. Though she becomes very angry with her second unsuccessful suitor, Bertie Stanhope, Eleanor does not slap him, and Mr. Arabin, of course, finally succeeds in marrying Eleanor. Eleanor receives the proposals of her three suitors in various ways, but the fact that Trollope devotes a fully-developed scene to each proposal (there are probably almost as many proposals in the forty-seven Trollope novels as there are letters) is an indication that each should be seen in the light of the others. Trollope almost says as much at the beginning of his account of Mr. Arabin's proposal: "It has been told, with perhaps tedious accuracy, how Eleanor disposed of two of her lovers at Ullathorne; and it must also be told with equal accuracy, and if possible with less tedium, how she encountered Mr. Arabin". And if Eleanor reacts angrily to the money-motivated proposals of her first two suitors, Trollope underscores the difference in her reaction to Mr. Arabin's suit when he notes that Eleanor, when Arabin is temporarily at a loss for words, "looked slowly, gently, almost piteously up into his face. There was at any rate no anger there to deter him". It cannot be said that the three proposals have any direct or substantial effect upon each other, except insofar as the first two help to accustom the widow Bold to think of herself as one eligible for marriage again, but by handling the three in parallel scenes so as to emphasize their similarities and differences, Trollope manages at once to impart the proper climactic effect to the successful proposal and to bind the three together with situational unity.

The kind of unity which binds together the parts of the love plot may strike some readers as somewhat tenuous or, what may amount to the same thing, as a bit too obvious. The ways in which the love story is related to the power struggle are, perhaps, more impressive.

If, for instance, one takes Bertie as a representative of his family, then it is clear that Eleanor's three suitors not only play important parts in the struggle for power but that each is introduced into the novel in connection with the primary plot: none has his being in the novel solely to make love to Eleanor. Slope and Arabin are, of course, opposing champions of the liberal and conservative forces, and they come to Barchester as such. Similarly, the Stanhopes are summoned back from Italy not so that Bertie can make love to Eleanor Bold but so that Mr. Slope can exercise his power.

Furthermore, it is very difficult for Eleanor and her lovers to keep their love separate from their politics. Eleanor is throughout almost the whole novel suspected by her friends—somewhat tediously so, perhaps—of loving Mr. Slope. Eleanor's friends would probably not approve of Mr. Slope under any circumstances, but since he threatens their rights and privileges as members of the clerical establishment, he is just about the last man on earth they want Eleanor to fall in love with. And though Mr. Slope never has a chance with Eleanor as her lover, she does at least tolerate him socially just because her friends seem to be unduly harsh on him in clerical-political matters. He, for his part, would like to keep his love affairs and his drive for ecclesiastical power separate, but even when he takes a walk in the moonlight with Eleanor and the Stanhopes, he cannot get away from the problem of the vacant wardenship. The strollers begin by walking around the cathedral close; "then they went under the old arched gateway below St. Cuthbert's little church, and then they turned behind the grounds of the bishop's palace, and so on till they came to the bridge at the edge of town, from which passers-by can look down into the gardens of Hiram's Hospital. . . . Mr. Slope knew that the gable-ends and old brick chimneys which stood up so prettily in the moonlight, were those of Mr. Harding's late abode, and would not have stopped on such a spot, in such company, if he could have avoided it; but Miss Stanhope would not take the hint which he tried to give". By thus moving the lovers over the territory which is at stake in the power struggle Trollope effectively ties his plots together.

But though Mr. Slope tries to separate love from politics, it is he, after all, who first combines them, for it is he who decides that in order to secure Eleanor and her fortune it will be advisable for him to back her father for the wardenship. He makes this decision, by the way, while on his way home from a discussion with Mr. Quiverful about the vacant wardenship. This decision, as has been shown, leads to the first major battle between Mr. Slope and Mrs. Proudie. It should be clear, then, that the love plot is not only tied closely to the power-struggle plot, but that the one works upon the other by means of causality. Since, furthermore, Mr. Slope pursues Eleanor for her money, look-

ing upon it as he does "as a duty which he owed his religion to make himself the master of the wife and the money", it appears likely that Mr. Slope lusts for power through Eleanor, money being a form of power, just as he seeks to wield the power of the episcopal office.

Eleanor's slapping of Mr. Slope ends the first of the three proposal scenes of the novel, those scenes which Trollope arranged in ascending order. But her violent rejection of the chaplain is also the first of three rejections for Mr. Slope, for it, like Signora Neroni's expulsion of Mr. Slope from her presence, anticipates and foreshadows Mr. Slope's final dismissal from the bishop's service and from Barchester. Here too the novel's plots are beautifully woven together. One can only conclude that, from the point of view of structure, the plotting of **Barchester Towers** is admirably handled.

Power is so important in **Barchester Towers** that it is not confined to plot but assumes the status of a major theme as well, a theme so pervasive that even when the characters are engaged in apparently idle chatter about the composition of the moon, the subject of power enters the conversation. Eleanor, in replying to Bertie's question about the possibility of the moon's being composed of "pulpy gelatinous matter", says, " 'I really think it's almost wicked to talk in such a manner. How can we argue about God's power in the other stars from the laws which he has given for our rule in this one?' " But as important and pervasive as the theme of power is in the novel, it is not the primary theme, for that theme arises out of what can be done with power. Power can be used to preserve things as they are, but it can also be used in the service of change. Change is the central theme of **Barchester Towers.**

After the installation of the new bishop, Trollope wastes little time before sounding his theme. He does so at first by means of description. When the archdeacon and Mr. Harding pay their courtesy visit to their new prelate, they feel, even before Mr. Slope and Mrs. Proudie move into action, that things have changed considerably in the palace:

> His lordship was at home, and the two visitors were shown through the accustomed hall into the well-known room, where the good old bishop used to sit. The furniture had been bought at a valuation, and every chair and table, every bookshelf against the wall, and every square in the carpet, was as well known to each of them as their own bedrooms. Nevertheless they at once felt that they were strangers there. The furniture was for the most part the same, yet the place had been metamorphosed. A new sofa had been introduced, a horrid chintz affair, most unprelatical and almost irreligious, such a sofa as never yet stood in the study of any decent high church clergyman of the Church of England. The old curtains had also given way. They had, to be sure, become dingy, and that which had been originally a rich and goodly ruby had degenerated into a reddish brown. Mr. Harding, however, thought the old reddish brown much preferable to the gaudy buff-coloured trumpery moreen which Mrs. Proudie had deemed good

enough for her husband's own room in the provincial city of Barchester.

Not the least significant part of this description, perhaps, is the recognition that the room had been subject to change even while the old bishop lived. But a gradual change, a slow degeneration, is one thing; a metamorphosis, something else.

After the visit, Trollope balances his description of the metamorphosed room with a quick view of the cathedral towers. It is some time before the archdeacon is able to speak. When he and Mr. Harding reach the cathedral close, he finally manages an exclamation or two: " 'Good heavens!' exclaimed the archdeacon, as he placed his foot on the gravel walk of the close, and raising his hat with one hand, passed the other somewhat violently over his now grizzled locks. . . . 'Good heavens!'—and the archdeacon looked up to the gray pinnacles of the cathedral tower, making a mute appeal to that still living witness which had looked down on the doings of so many bishops of Barchester". The appeal may be mute but it is certainly appropriate that the archdeacon, after such a visit, should look up for consolation to a visible sign of the fact that change in Barchester is not all powerful.

Everyone seems to recognize "Barchester Towers" as a fine title for a novel. Seen simply from the point of view of grace, conciseness, and interest, it must rank among Trollope's best titles. It is also, however, an extraordinarily significant title, for in the balancing descriptions of the bishop's metamorphosed study and of the apparently unchanging pinnacles of the cathedral tower Trollope presents the central action of the novel, which has been described by one critic [William E. Cadbury, "Varieties of Form in the Novels of Anthony Trollope" (Univ. of Wisconsin Diss., 1961)] as a "movement . . . from one set of stable relationships to another, passing through a series of unstable relationships", in visible and nuclear form. The pinnacles are not absolutely unchanging, of course, but they have outlived previous bishops just as they will outlive the present one. So too Barchester is not immune from all change—bishops and deans die here as elsewhere, and wardens resign and are replaced—but it manages to retain its identity, it successfully resists metamorphosis.

Mr. Slope, though he does not finally succeed in making radical changes in Barchester, does manage once to preach a sermon in Barchester Cathedral. The setting could not be more pertinent to Trollope's theme or to Mr. Slope's purpose, and that clergyman, within the confines of the ancient structure and surrounded by the old clergy—the dean, the archdeacon, "the chancellor, the treasurer, the precentor, sundry canons and minor canons"—seizes the occasion to launch an attack upon the *status quo*. After some preliminary maneuvering, he settles to his task by criticizing the service which preceded his sermon. He does not attack the quality of the music as such; what bothers him is "the undue preponderance, which . . . music had over meaning in the beautiful service which they had just heard". He goes on to justify his criticism on the grounds of changing times: he argues "that a mode of service which was effective when outward ceremonies were of more moment than inward feelings, had become all but barbarous

at a time when inward conviction was everything, when each word of the minister's lip should fall intelligibly into the listener's heart. Formerly the religion of the multitude had been an affair of the imagination: now, in these latter days, it had become necessary that a Christian should have a reason for his faith—should not only believe but digest—not only hear, but understand".

Mr. Slope, apparently, is a believer in the doctrine of progress. It is interesting to see that Trollope, eight years after the publication of *Barchester Towers,* pointed in earnest to a movement from feeling to reason within Englishmen, which movement seems quite a bit similar to the progress from imagination to reason alluded to by Mr. Slope. Trollope noted this movement while making some preliminary remarks in an article in which he advocated reform of the English public school ["Public Schools", *Fortnightly Review,* II (1865)]. "It is the same with us Englishmen in all matters", he says. "At last, after long internal debate and painful struggle, reason within us gets the better of feeling. In almost every bosom there sits a parliament in which a conservative party is ever combating to maintain things old, while the liberal side of the house is striving to build things new. In this parliament, as in the other, the liberal side is always conquering, but its adversary is never conquered. Bit by bit, very slowly, after tedious fighting, the old wood is dragged away, and the new plantations are set in order."

Trollope was never sympathetic to violent, precipitate change, to the kind of metamorphosis that Mr. Slope tries to effect in Barchester. He probably stated his position on the subject most clearly in an essay in which he argued for the disestablishment of the Irish Church. He begins by talking about the removal of ruins and then switches to the metaphor of dead wood, the metaphor he uses in the public school essay:

> We venerate things that are old because they are old; and gently remove our ruins, fragment by fragment, with hands which love while they destroy. . . . We cannot ruthlessly cut down the half-dead tree of the grove, and tear asunder the roots, and plough and sow the soil, where the spot has been hallowed by ancient piety. The work of removal has, indeed, to be done; but it must be done tenderly, not ruthlessly. With loving hands must the old timber be dragged away, and the ground cleared for purpose of new utility ["The Irish Church", *Fortnightly Review,* II (1865)].

Mr. Slope, who does not venerate things that are old, has no intention of gently removing ruins. He talks, rather, of "casting away the useless rubbish of past centuries". Trollope probably agrees with Mr. Slope when he tells Mr. Harding that " 'Work is now required from every man who receives wages; and they who have to superintend the doing of work, and the paying of wages, are bound to see that this rule is carried out. New men . . . are now needed, and are now forthcoming in the church, as well as in other professions' ", but though he recognizes the need for new men, he cannot approve of their doing their work ruthlessly.

One critic [Roger Slakey, "Anthony Trollope: A Study in

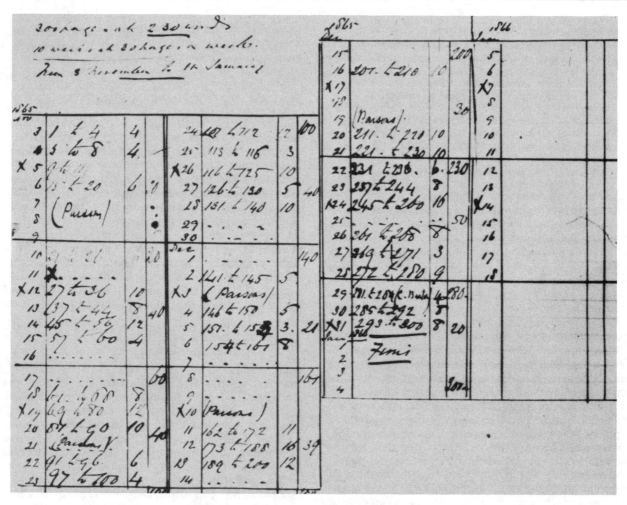

Trollope's working calendar for one of his novels.

the Foundations of Choice", Johns Hopkins Univ. Diss., 1957] has asserted that "for Trollope, change is necessary that men might be actually what in their very being they obscurely but definitely already are". Such a view of change makes sense, certainly, and it might even remind some readers of Spenser's solution to the problem of change as it is expressed in the Mutability Cantos of *The Faerie Queene,* but it is difficult to see how it applies to **Barchester Towers,** though it does seem relevant to Mr. Harding's perfecting his vocation in **The Warden** by means of his giving up the wardenship. In any event, it is certain that Trollope's attitude toward change in **Barchester Towers** is, like his position on reform in **The Warden,** not simple. It is probably best described as balanced.

Since Trollope heartily detests Mr. Slope and since at the end of the novel things appear to be very little changed in Barchester (though in fact the diocese has a new bishop, the hospital a new warden, the cathedral a new dean, and the dean a wife), a casual reader might miss Trollope's recognition of the necessity and desirability of change when it is carried out with the necessary care. Such a reader might fail to perceive the balance of Trollope's position, but he really should not, for Trollope has taken pains in the novel to satirize the unhealthy clinging to the past of

those who fail to reconcile themselves to the fact of change in human affairs. It is true that the satire directed against the Thornes of Ullathorne is gentle, affectionate, and pleasant, but it is satire nevertheless.

Trollope undoubtedly likes the Thornes better than he likes Mr. Slope, as he no doubt enjoys their foibles whereas the pretensions of the evangelical clergyman disgust him, but the point is that he does see the foibles of the Thornes as foibles, and he means it when he says that Mr. Thorne "was a man possessed of quite a sufficient number of foibles to lay him open to much ridicule". And what is true of Mr. Thorne is even more true of his sister, who, after all, regards her brother, whose favorite authors are Montaigne and Burton and who has never fully recovered from his shock at the repeal of the corn laws, as having been in his youth "a fast young man, hurried away by a too ardent temperament into democratic tendencies". Miss Thorne, for her part, "had not yet reconciled herself to the Reform Bill, and still groaned in spirit over the defalcations of the Duke as touching the Catholic Emancipation". Miss Thorne, interestingly enough, regards herself no enemy of necessary or sensible reform:

In religion, Miss Thorne was a pure Druidess.

We would not have it understood by that, that she did actually in these latter days assist at any human sacrifices, or that she was in fact hostile to the Church of Christ. She had adopted the Christian religion as a milder form of the worship of her ancestors, and always appealed to her doing so as evidence that she had no prejudices against reform, when it could be shown that reform was salutary. This reform was the most modern of any to which she had as yet acceded, it being presumed that British ladies had given up their paint and taken to some sort of petticoats before the days of St. Augustine.

It should be obvious that such characters as Mr. and Miss Thorne have every right to prominent roles in a novel primarily concerned with the subject of change. Trollope certainly seems to emphasize their thematic importance by devoting a block of eight chapters (35 through 42) to Miss Thorne's *"fête champêtre"*, that party during the course of which Eleanor Bold receives two distasteful proposals of marriage. Though one critic [Bruce McCullough, *Representative English Novelists: Defoe to Conrad,* 1946] probably had the party at Ullathorne uppermost in his mind when he characterized *Barchester Towers* as "the old loose type of novel", another [William Cadbury] has recognized it for what it is, one of the novel's two greatest scenes, the other being Mrs. Proudie's reception. Another critic [Lewis Melville (Lewis S. Benjamin), *Victorian Novelists,* 1906] has complained that "the description of the sports at Ullathorne and the desires of the Lookalofts to take precedence of the Greenacres are amusing enough, but they irritate because they needlessly stop the progress of the tale". Such an impatient reaction may be understandable, but it holds up only if one regards theme as an unimportant adjunct of tale. But even if one looks at the party strictly from the point of view of plot, it can be seen that there is a certain appropriateness in presenting the first of Mr. Slope's three rejections and the first two of Eleanor's proposals within the confines of a big scene. The further appropriateness of balancing a party given by the newly-arrived Proudies with one given by the ancient Thornes should also be obvious.

The complete party could bear much detailed analysis, but even a brief examination discloses the thematic pertinence of its parts. Miss Thorne's steward, Mr. Plomacy, for instance, is the kind of steward such a lady should have. If she still cherishes "low down in the bottom of her heart of hearts, a dear unmentioned wish for the restoration of some exiled Stuart", he had gained some distinction as a messenger for the royalist cause during the French Revolution. What Mr. Plomacy is is important, but what he does, or fails to do, at the party is equally important. One of Mr. Plomacy's duties is to keep out gate-crashers, but as experienced as he is at his business, and as well as he knows "who were welcome and who were not", and as earnestly as he tries to do his job, "Nevertheless, before the day was half over, all this was found to be useless. Almost anybody who chose to come made his way into the park". Mr. Plomacy can no more preserve the integrity of the estate by excluding the city apprentices from the party than Miss Thorne can bring back the golden age for which she sighs or revive successfully riding at the quintain. Indeed, Harry Greenacre in the dust after his attempt to ride at the quintain presents an image of the futility of extreme conservatism. There are some changes which even Miss Thorne and Mr. Plomacy are powerless to resist.

The footman who allows the Lookalofts into the Ullathorne drawing-room to mix with "the quality" had the knowledge and the power to exclude them, "But he had not the courage to tell a stout lady with a low dress, short sleeves, and satin at eight shillings a yard, that she had come to the wrong tent; he had not dared to hint to the young ladies with white dancing shoes and long gloves, that there was a place ready for them in the paddock". Mrs. Lookaloft's impudence thus gives her "the power of boasting that she had consorted on the lawn with the squire and Miss Thorne, with a countess, a bishop, and the county grandees. . . . It was a great point gained by Mrs. Lookaloft, and it might be fairly expected that from this time forward the tradesmen of Barchester would, with undoubting pens, address her husband as T. Lookaloft, Esquire". If class barriers can be thus broken down at Ullathorne, how must they be falling in the rest of the world!

So it is that while the major characters of the novel carry on their struggle for power and their love affairs at the party at Ullathorne, Mr. Plomacy, the Barchester apprentices, the Lookalofts, and the Greenacres struggle also, and if the conservatives among the major characters seem to be largely successful in retaining power and resisting drastic change, the apprentices and the Lookalofts, new men and women among the minor characters, make significant gains. Without the Thornes and their party one might have been misled by Mr. Slope's character and fate to suppose that *Barchester Towers* is simply a celebration of the successful resistance to change; with them, one must see that Trollope's attitude toward change and reform in general is as balanced as the attitude toward the malversation of charitable purposes which formed the nucleus for *The Warden.* When all is said and done, Barchester, though not metamorphosed, is not the same at the end of the novel as it is at the beginning. And that, Trollope says throughout the novel in various ways, is the way it has to be and the way it should be. (pp. 38-55)

Hugh L. Hennedy, "Trollope on Reform and Change: 'Barchester Towers'," in his Unity in Barsetshire, *Mouton, 1971, pp. 37-55.*

Joseph Wiesenfarth   (essay date 1980)

[*In the following excerpt, Wiesenfarth examines ways in which the various characters in* Barchester Towers *reflect the author's moral and ideological views.*]

Barchester Towers is a novel about ambition. It offers four prizes so representative of position and money that they are all but irresistible: the bishopric of Barchester, the wardenship of Hiram's Hospital, the cathedral deanery, and the hand of Eleanor Bold. Obidiah Slope contends vigorously for all four; Francis Arabin more moderately for two. Trollope saliently contrasts Arabin and Slope in relation to how they seek what they want. Their opposite approaches and the outcome of them conveniently organise the novel into three volumes.

Volume One (chs. 1-19) sets Slope in action. He vies with Mrs. Proudie for the bishopric while trying to retain the good will of the bishop; he uses the vacant wardenship as stick and carrot to manoeuvre Mr. Harding and Quiverful; and he plays suitor to Eleanor at the same time that he is Madeline's lover. The weakness of Slope's position is exquisitely revealed in chapter 19 when he visits the Stanhopes: he is uneasy that everyone expects Mr. Harding to be named warden and he is embarrassed that Madeline greets him as a lover while Eleanor looks on. Even when Slope gazes at the night-sky and hears Venus, Diana, and Jupiter discussed he is reminded once again of his Venus, the signora; his Diana, the widow; and his Jupiter, the London newspaper that, contrary to Mrs. Proudie's wishes, endorses Mr. Harding's return to the hospital. 'Barchester by Moonlight' is nicely arranged to remind the reader that Mr. Slope is always a man between alternatives: between Dr. and Mrs. Proudie, between Mr. Harding and Quiverful, and between Eleanor Bold and Madeline Neroni. Slope's constant dilemma is that he always wants everything and cannot decide who is most likely to satisfy him. Unlike Paris before him, he finds that no one bribe is complete enough to supersede other tempting alternative possibilities.

Volume Two (chs. 20-34) sets Arabin in action and develops his character in opposition to Slope's. Madeline puts their contrasting traits so neatly in a nutshell in chapter 38 that she reminds the reader how artfully Trollope has constructed his novel; she says to Arabin:

> He is gregarious; you are given to solitude. He is active; you are passive. He works; you think. He likes women; you despise them. He is fond of position and power; and so are you, but for directly different reasons. He loves to be praised; you very foolishly abhor it. He will gain his rewards, which will be an insipid, useful wife, a comfortable income, and a reputation for sanctimony; you will also gain yours.

These and related qualities of character are developed in comparable chapters of each volume. 'A Morning Visit' (ch. 5), for example, shows Slope abusing the archdeacon with his discontent at the physical amenities of the palace; 'St. Ewold's Parsonage' (ch. 21) shows Arabin restraining the archdeacon from repairing the parsonage, which suits him well enough as it is. 'War' (ch. 6) finds Mr. Slope preaching his 'doctrine, and not St. Paul's' for thirty minutes in the cathedral and leaving 'all Barchester . . . in a tumult.' 'Mr. Arabin Reads Himself in at St. Ewold's' (ch. 23) finds Arabin preaching 'the great Christian doctrine of faith and works combined' for twenty minutes and sending his congregation home 'to their baked mutton and pudding well pleased with their new minister.'

Volume Three (chs. 35-53) disposes of the goals of ambition sought by Arabin and Slope. In Act II of Ullathorne Sports Slope loses Eleanor and leaves Arabin to win her hand. The chaplain's defeat finds its analogue in Harry Greenacre's wild charge at the quintain—a device that when awkwardly touched unhorses a clumsy sportsman with a merciless swat. Slope's grab at Eleanor's waist earns him an immediate slap in the face that ends his untimely pursuit forever. Slope also fails to dispose of the warden-

ship as he would like to. Quiverful gets the nod from Mrs. Proudie, who has become bishop, another goal that Slope has fruitlessly pursued. Finally Mr. Harding and then Arabin are offered the deanery and the bishop's chaplain is offered nothing. Arabin, the truthful man of moderate ambition, gets the better of Slope, the deceitful man of unbridled ambition. And Madeline, who helps Arabin with Eleanor, exposes Slope to the laughter of his political and clerical rivals, Thorne and Arabin, by revealing his double-dealing in preferment and romance. Unable to choose a mistress among his Juno, Diana, and Venus, he is expelled from the palace, slapped in the face, and laughed to scorn. Slope is made to eat the apple of discord that he brazenly set rolling through the Barchester diocese.

Trollope develops this classically spare outline of his comedy in the context of age-old wisdom. Reading **Barchester Towers** is at times like dipping into the *Oxford Dictionary of Quotations*. The novel is laced with aphoristic wisdom coming from proverbs, maxims, songs, and poetry. 'There is a proverb with reference to the killing of cats,' says the narrator in chapter 1—'More ways of killing a cat than choking her with cream'—when he wants the reader to know that the outgoing prime minister has promised Archdeacon Grantly the bishopric of Barchester indirectly, not directly. Although John Bold has died an untimely death, Johnny Bold is born to Eleanor to show how 'God tempers the wind to the shorn lamb.' Trollope re-enforces this divine wisdom with hard human prudence: 'Let me ever remember my living friends, but forget them as soon as dead.' Mr. Harding hesitates to take the wardenship on Slope's terms because 'It's bad teaching an old dog tricks.' Bishop Proudie rebels against his wife just as 'Dogs have turned against their masters, and even Neopolitans against their rulers, when oppression has been too severe.' He casts his lot with Mr. Slope against Mrs. Proudie convinced that *'Ce n'est que le premier pas qui coute'*; nevertheless, he is fairly warned not to: 'Better the d— you know than the d— you don't know.' Mr. Slope is content to make slower progress with Eleanor because he knows that 'Rome was not built in a day.' When Arabin tells Eleanor that 'Charity should begin at home,' she replies, 'You should practise as well as preach.' Looking for a candidate to charge the quintain, Miss Thorne becomes philosophical: 'One man can take a horse to water, but a thousand can't make him drink.' Having drunk deeply at the *fête champêtre*, Mr. Slope resolves to go ahead with a proposal of marriage, saying to himself, 'That which has made them drunk has made me bold.' But, as Mrs. Quiverful knows, 'There's many a slip 'twixt the cup and the lip.'

This proverb appears a second time, slightly embellished, to characterize this indomitable wife's pursuit of preferment for her hapless husband. 'There might be some slip between the cup of her happiness and the lip of fruition,' but Mrs. Quiverful persists and wins the wardenship she sought. The use of the same aphoristic wisdom twice in the Quiverful story is characteristic of Trollope's using some simple sayings as leitmotifs to link segments of a strand of action. When in chapter 17, 'Who Shall be Cock of the Walk,' for instance, Mr. Slope challenges Mrs. Proudie for the bishop's apron, Trollope asks, 'Does not every cock fight best on his own dunghill?'—a question that is answered in chapter 26, 'Mrs. Proudie Wrestles and Gets a Fall'; here Slope comes to the aid of the henpecked bishop and helps him 'take a proud place upon a dunghill.' Mr. Slope has already decided that 'either he or Mrs. Proudie must go to the wall' over Hiram's Hospital—'The weakest goes to the wall'—and he feels confident of victory because he has recently overcome Mr. Harding, who has had to 'go to the wall in the manner so kindly prophesied to him by the chaplain.'

This one-line literature of worldly wisdom also shapes the matrix of Mr. Slope's most humiliating defeat. In matching wits with Madeline Neroni he more than meets his mistress: 'He was the finest fly that Barchester had hitherto afforded to her web.' Indeed, she 'sat there . . . looking at him with her great eyes, just as a great spider would look at a great fly that was quite securely caught.' And Mr. Slope is caught like Dido, who mingled 'love and business' and consequently 'fell between two stools.'

> There's an old song [says Trollope] which gives us some very good advice about courting:
>
> It's gude to be off with the auld luve
> Before ye be on wi' the new.
>
> Of the wisdom of this maxim Mr. Slope was ignorant. . . . A man should remember that between two stools he may fall to the ground.

When Madeline brings Slope to the ground, she sings to him as he tumbles:

> It's gude to be merry and wise, Mr. Slope;
> It's gude to be honest and true;
> It's gude to be off with the old love, Mr. Slope,
> Before you are on with the new.

Slope is, in the end, the cock who is kicked off his dunghill and the fly who is eaten by the spider. As one who is not off with the old love before he is on with the new, who mixes business and love, and who falls between two stools, he is presented as an offender against the accumulated wisdom of the ages. This is one reason why his foolishly pursued ambition makes him such a threat to Barchester society. Should Slope succeed in his ecclesiastical designs, the Church would suffer from his lust for power; should he succeed as a suitor, marriage would be nothing but an economic adventure. Slope is consequently a threat to the family, society's smallest unit, and to the Church, society's largest bulwark of right-conduct. Eleanor's situation is quite appropriately a personal reflection of the Church's public position; one is an image of the other. Both are misunderstood by clergymen who are called 'men of the world'; both are worth £1,200 in yearly income; both are pursued by Arabin and Slope; both are adhered to unswervingly by Mr. Harding; and both, finally, get the same dean. It is manifestly Trollope's opinion that Slope, whom he describes as a devil—and as befits the devil, a liar—is undeserving of the good things that should belong to gentlemen only: a powerful position, a handsome income, a beautiful wife, and a comfortable house. These things, the action of the novel asserts, belong by right to men like Arabin.

Such men, however, are not easily characterized. Trollope feels his powers inadequate to present a faithful picture of Arabin. He feels that 'words forsake, elude, disappoint, and play the deuce with him, till at the end of a dozen pages the man described has no more resemblance to the man conceived than the sign-board at the corner of the street has to the Duke of Cambridge.' Perhaps this is because Arabin at forty is somewhat like Trollope at forty-two and the difficulty of disengaging one personality from the other is trickier than expected. Both Arabin and Trollope were younger sons. Both attended Winchester and were meant to be fellows of New College, where neither arrived. Both had a respect for the Oxford Movement but neither became Roman Catholics. Both were inarticulate with women. Both relished the good life but neither lied or cheated to achieve it. Arabin is a blend of the same kind of 'worldliness and idealism' that characterizes Trollope's public image—but a kind of worldliness and idealism, **Barchester Towers** finally suggests, that is not sufficiently inspiring to satisfy an artist's imagination. That Trollope's difficulty in presenting Arabin adequately is not just the novelist's toying with the reader is confirmed by one critic's seeing Arabin as rescuing the novel from triviality, satire, and pessimism [Robert Polhemus, in *The Changing World of Anthony Trollope*, 1968] while another critic [see excerpt dated 1964] finds chapter 20, entitled 'Mr. Arabin,' so uncharacteristic of the rest of the novel that it becomes impossible for us to 'know how to take Arabin afterwards.'

Following on Slope's chapter, 'Barchester by Moonlight', chapter 20 links Arabin to the bishop's chaplain by way of a proverb: 'Truly he had fallen between two stools.' But Arabin fell because he underwent a series of changes connected with a growing understanding of himself and his place in life, not because he was an opportunist. He is not a trimmer who cannot decide between equally attractive alternatives; he is a late-starter who is slow to see his authentic goals in life. Arabin is shown as a man who was once a Tractarian, once an apostle, once a lonely bachelor, and once a poorly paid professor of poetry. He is now no longer content with these things because 'the daydream of his youth was over.' That daydream was founded on a stoicism that Trollope exposes as a pernicious doctrine which 'can find no believing pupils and no true teachers.' Indeed, the idea of renouncing 'wealth and worldly comfort and happiness on earth' is pronounced 'an outrage on human nature.' When Arabin belatedly comes fully to understand his own human nature, he regrets not having the good things in life: 'no wife, no bairns, no soft sward of lawn duly mown for him to lie on, no herd of attendant curates, no bowings from banker's clerks, no rich rectory.' Arabin's ambition, in short, is the natural complement of his maturity.

By way of the radical changes that Arabin undergoes Trollope maintains that to interfere with the comforts of an English gentleman—established religion, family, money, and position—is unnatural. Arabin at age forty is a convert to the doctrine that Trollope as narrator preaches at the age of forty-two. And, one should carefully note, Slope is a true believer too.

Slope wants only a little more than Arabin as far as the good life is concerned. Although Arabin never wants to be bishop, both he and Slope want to be Eleanor's husband and Barchester's dean. But Slope is an English gentleman neither by birth nor conduct, as even Mr. Harding reluctantly admits: 'He is not gentlemanlike in his manners, of that I am sure.' Slope is Trollope's more elegantly named scion of Sterne's Slop family who tries to subvert High Church practice, who makes love to a married woman, and who lies repeatedly in seeking a wife and deanery. Slope's ends tally with natural ambition—'the *nolo episcopari* . . . is . . . directly at variance with the tendency of all human wishes'—but Slope's means make him an overreacher. Trollope makes him a red man—hair of 'pale reddish hue,' face 'a little redder,' and nose like 'red-coloured cork'—a liar, and 'the d— you don't know.' The lowbred, mean-minded, callously manipulative Slope is a comic form of devil. Arabin, on the other hand, has so forthright a character that he is seen as 'a little child'. Therefore, whereas Slope is struggled against, Arabin is helped. Dr. Grantly gives him St. Ewold's, Madeline delivers Eleanor into his hands, Mr. Harding renounces the deanery in his favour, and a Whig government appoints him to clerical office. Arabin represents for every faction in the novel the best of what one reviewer [*Saturday Review*, 30 May 1857; see Smalley, ed., in Further Reading] of *Barchester Towers* called, in a happy phrase, 'the second-class of good people':

> [Trollope] has the merit of avoiding the excess of exaggeration. He possesses an especial talent for drawing what may be called the second-class of good people—characters not noble, superior or perfect, after the standard of human perfection, but still good and honest, yet with a considerable proneness to temptation, and a strong consciousness that they live, and like to live, in a struggling, party-giving, comfort-seeking world.

With Arabin the second-class of good people finds its hero and *Barchester Towers* touches ground and stands four-square. His reasonable ambitions are completely satisfied and the novel's conventional wisdom is thoroughly justified. But if *Barchester Towers* were nothing more than this would it still be a masterpiece? I hardly think so. It is every bit as much about lack of ambition and contemporary events as it is about ambition and aphoristic wisdom. This dialectic has kept the novel alive and interesting six score years and more.

Barchester Towers is larded with references contemporary to and nearly contemporary with its writing. There is even a reference to *Little Dorrit* which Dickens was writing and serialising while Trollope was writing his novel. And as an alternative to the kind of death-scenes that Mr. Popular Sentiment made famous, Trollope gives us one of another kind:

> 'God bless you, my dear,' said the bishop with feeble voice as he woke. 'God bless you—may God bless you both, my children.' And so he died.

> There was no loud rattle in the throat, no dreadful struggle, no palpable sign of death. . . . Neither Mr. Harding nor Dr. Grantly knew that life was gone, though both suspected it. . . .

> 'My lord's no more,' said Mrs. Phillips, turning round and curtseying low with solemn face; 'his lordship's gone more like a babby than any that I ever saw.'

Trollope prefers Donne to Dickens here and allows the old bishop to die as do 'virtuous men' who

> pass mildly away,
> And whisper to their souls to go,
> Whilst some of their sad friends do say,
> The breath goes now, and some say, No.

Trollope not only capitalises on Dickens and death as his novel opens but he also comments on the frequent demise of ministries in the 1850s.

There were two new governments in 1852: the Earl of Derby's in February and the Earl of Aberdeen's in December; and Palmerston formed his first cabinet in February 1855. Trollope gives his novel a contemporary, candid, and worldly-wise cachet by giving a behind-the-scenes report of what happens—so different from what we think happens—when governments change. How the 'Earl of —— in his inner library'

> stamped his foot as he thought of his heavy associates—how he all but swore as he remembered how much too clever one of them had been—my creative readers may imagine. But was he so engaged? No: history and truth compel me to deny it. He was sitting easily in a lounging chair, conning over a Newmarket list, and by his elbow on the table was lying open an uncut French novel on which he was engaged.

Trollope's outgoing Tory prime minister is suspiciously like Lord Stanley, Earl of Derby, who had a passion for books and racehorses. He preferred translating Homer to talking politics, and Disraeli complained that he could never find Derby because he was 'always at Newmarket or Doncaster.' Derby, for his part, thought Disraeli a 'scoundrel' even before his minister of the exchequer presented a free-trade budget too cleverly replete with unworkable compromises—a budget that Gladstone so mercilessly destroyed that his attack brought down Derby's government. The ministry in *Barchester Towers* is a shadow of this reality, and gives one the sense of reading a *roman à clef.* This method of grounding today's lively fiction on yesterday's lively facts is also used in part to characterize the Proudie and Grantly parties in the novel.

Both Sabbatarianism and university reform were popular topics in the 1850s. When the archdeacon and Mr. Harding pay a courtesy call to the palace, they learn that the bishop is a patron of the 'Manufacturing Towns Morning and Evening Sunday School Society'. Mrs. Proudie and Mr. Slope then demand to know their visitors' views on 'Sabbath-day schools', 'Sabbath-travelling', and 'Sabbatical amusements'. 'Mr. Harding had never been so pressed in his life,' and Archdeacon Grantly is forced to open 'the safety-valve of his anger' and emit 'visible steam' to prevent 'positive explosion and probable apoplexy.' When Slope offers Mr. Harding the wardenship, he orders him to preside over 'a Sabbath-day school' and to conduct 'morning and evening service' for the pensioners 'on the premises every Sabbath': 'for people of that class the cathedral service does not appear to me the most useful.' Slope's class-consciousness reminds one that 'when the railways began to spread, an attempt was made to stop Sunday travel, or at least to prevent third-class carriages from running' [H. D. Traill]. Indeed, at the time that Trollope was writing **Barchester Towers,** the old problem of Sunday observance—it began with the Puritans—was once again to the fore. In 1856 a bill proposing the opening of the National Gallery and the British Museum on Sundays was defeated, and Palmerston was 'obliged to accede to the Archbishop of Canterbury's request, that in deference to public opinion, the military bands in Kensington Gardens and elsewhere should be silenced.' Palmerston's friend, C. C. F. Greville, wrote in disgust that 'Cant and Puritanism are in the ascendant, and it will be well if we escape more stringent measures against Sunday occupations and amusements. It is stated that the Sabbatarians are so united and numerous that they could carry any election!' Indeed, since **Barchester Towers** begins with a change of ministries, we know that the Sabbatarians have done just that.

If the palace is identified with Sabbath-day reforms, the archdeaconry is identified with opposition to university reform at Oxford. University reform was a controversial political issue from 1850 to 1856—from Lord John Russell's letter to the Duke of Wellington announcing a Commission of Inquiry through the establishment of the Royal Commission in 1852 to the parliamentary acts of 1854 and 1856 implementing the reforms. Bishop Proudie is a member of the 'University Improvement Committee', which is about to finish its 'final report' when Grantly and Harding pay 'A Morning Visit' (ch. 5) to the palace. That report is finished by the time of 'Mrs. Proudie's Reception' (ch. 11) where it is discussed by the bishop and the archdeacon and his friends:

> 'Well, Mr. Archdeacon, after all, we have not been so hard upon you at Oxford.'
>
> 'No,' said the archdeacon, 'you've only drawn our teeth and cut out our tongues; you've allowed us still to breathe and swallow.'
>
> 'Ha, ha, ha!' laughed the bishop;. . . . 'Why, in the way we've left the matter, it's very odd if the heads of colleges don't have their own way quite as fully as when the hebdomadal board was in all its glory; what do you say, Mr. Dean?'
>
> 'An old man, my lord, never likes changes,' said the dean.

And some young men are like the old man too. Tom Staple, Arabin's and Dr. Gwynne's advisor in chapter 34, is one of them: 'Tom Staple would have willingly been impaled before a Committee of the House, could he by such self-sacrifice have infused his own spirit into the component members of the hebdomadal board.' And Arabin is another: he 'opposed tooth and nail all projects of university reform, and talked jovially over his glass of port of the ruin to be anticipated by the Church and of the sacrilege daily committed by the Whigs.' Having been seasoned at the battle of Oxford, Arabin is imported, almost as a mercenary, to fight in the battle of Barchester. But his standing with old men like Dean Trefoil on the issue of universi-

ty reform is rather a weakness than a strength of character in the 'new champion'.

Most historians agree with Woodward's assertion that 'the condition of Oxford and Cambridge invited criticism'. Like the old dean, soon to die of apoplexy, the hebdomadal board, the governing body at Oxford, 'was composed mainly of heads of houses, elderly and safe men who did not wish for change'; it was described as 'an organised torpor'. The 'sacrilege' that Arabin opposes is the decision to award degrees to those who do not subscribe to the Thirtynine Articles. Fittingly, the free-thinking Stanhope, a Cambridge drop-out, feels free to interrupt the bishop and the archdeacon's conversation to suggest further the need for university reform: 'In Germany the professors do teach; at Oxford, I believe, they only profess to do so, and sometimes not even that.' These extravagant remarks are true: the verdict of the Royal Commission was that at Oxford 'teaching was nearly extinct, and that professorial lectures had suffered something more than what the friends of the existing system called "a temporary interruption".' The Oxford partisans at Mrs. Proudie's reception nevertheless refuse to discuss the matter 'with a young man with such clothes and such a beard' as Bertie Stanhope's.

Many critics of **Barchester Towers** argue that Trollope sides with conservative clergymen against their liberal counterparts in the novel. But clearly, in chapter 11, both Bishop Proudie and Bertie have the better of the argument, as the history of university reforms that Trollope alludes to demonstrates. A univocal reading of the novel, therefore, will not do. 'It is a poor reader of Trollope,' says Ruth apRoberts [in her *Carlyle and His Contemporaries,* 1976] 'who finds only custom and the ordinary in the novels.' The contemporary events just canvassed suggest that a dialectical reading is necessary and that to achieve it we need to identify the heroes of Trollope's imagination—those [according to apRoberts] who in his 'loving detailed anatomies of custom and its interplay with the endless variations, depths, inventions and ingenuities of the human psyche' foster 'the sense of wonder in existence'.

'La Signora Madeline Vesey Neroni—Nata Stanhope' causes wonder with her gilt-edged visiting cards alone; she is presented, from the point of view of 'the second-class of good people', as decidedly dangerous and immoral. She makes only two excursions into society: at one, 'Mrs. Proudie's Reception', she defrocks an ultra-Whig female bishop; at the other, 'Miss Thorne's *Fête Champêtre*', she brings an ultra-Tory country squire to his knees. Madeline awakens all the suppressed sexual life in Barchester; men love her and women hate her:

> 'She is the most insolent creature I ever put my eyes on,' [said Mrs Proudie].
>
> 'Indeed she is,' said Lady de Courcy. 'And her conduct with men is so abominable that she is not fit to be admitted into any lady's drawing-room.'
>
> 'Dear me!' said the countess, becoming again excited, happy and merciless.

And Trollope, like Thorne, Arabin, and Slope, is half in love with his 'insolent creature' himself: 'She was a basilisk from whom an ardent lover of beauty could make no escape.'

If Arabin represents one side of Trollope's character in his gentlemanliness and decency, Madeline represents another side in her ruthless love of truth. Her function in the novel is to reveal hidden motives and expose hypocrisy; she works hand-in-glove with Trollope to get out the truth. Not only does she hold hypocrisy up to ridicule in the persons of Mrs. Proudie and Mr. Slope but she also promotes actions based on truth. Madeline's function in chapter 38 is therefore similar to Trollope's in chapter 20. Trollope reveals the unfolding character of Arabin to the reader; we know what he once wanted and what he now wants. Madeline forces Arabin to admit to himself what he wants.

> 'The greatest mistake any man ever made is to suppose that the good things of the world are not worth the winning. . . . You try to despise these good things, but you only try—you don't succeed.'
>
> 'Don't I?' said Arabin, still musing, not knowing what he said. 'I ask you the question: do you succeed?'
>
> Mr. Arabin looked at her piteously. It seemed to him as though he were being interrogated by some inner spirit of his own, to whom he could not refuse an answer and to whom he did not dare to give a false reply.
>
> 'Come, Mr. Arabin, confess; do you succeed? Is money so contemptible? Is worldly power so worthless? Is feminine beauty a trifle to be so slightly regarded by a wise man?'

Madeline draws out of Arabin that rejection of stoicism that Trollope earlier endorsed. She is an intensification of the narrative voice that refuses to live with lies. She ranges from low to high, from Mr. Slope to Mr. Thorne, revealing what should be revealed about each. But since her weapon is sex, the Victorians objected to her and called her 'desperately wicked' [*Spectator,* 16 May 1857; see Smalley, ed., in Further Reading]. Trollope even crippled her to keep her from circulating too much; nevertheless, he refused to give her up when Longman's reader called her 'a great blot on the work'. After all, she was part of himself; she was his truth within the action of the novel; she was Arabin's 'inner spirit'; she even delivered Arabin into Eleanor's hands. In Madeline's case, actions speak louder than words. And this is a principle to be kept in mind when judging Bertie Stanhope and Mr. Harding, the heroes of Trollope's imagination in ***Barchester Towers.***

Some pretty harsh things are said about Bertie Stanhope in the course of the novel, the harshest being that 'he had no principle, no regard for others, no self-respect, no desire to be other than a drone in the hive, if only he could, as a drone, get what honey was sufficient for him.' Yet he refuses to propose marriage to Eleanor in any way that could tempt her to accept him. The idea of a prudent marriage and domestic tranquillity that attracts Arabin and Slope gives Stanhope's stomach a turn: 'the most desirable lady becomes nauseous when she has to be taken as a pill.' Rather than being a man without self-respect, principle,

and a concern for others Bertie is a free spirit, a Bohemian oddity perhaps, who does not share the financial or marital goals of other more ambitious men. What has Bertie to look forward to as Eleanor's husband?

> Having satisfied his creditors with half of the widow's fortune, he would be allowed to sit down quietly at Barchester, keeping economical house with the remainder. His duty would be to rock the cradle of the late Mr. Bold's child, and his highest excitement a demure party at Plumstead Rectory. . . .

Bertie cannot bear the idea of living by the code of 'the second-class of good people'. Is he, therefore, to be condemned? If the narrator says *yes* in his harsh words, the novel says *no* in its most brilliant episodes. The artistic truth about Bertie is that he has the very best scenes in the novel.

Bertie's first great scene is a delightful social disaster. At Mrs. Proudie's reception he deflates the obsessive preoccupation of High and Low Church clergymen with their intense partisan versions of ritual and doctrine by announcing himself as having been, first, an Anglican who aspired to a bishopric; next, a Roman Catholic who was an acolyte of the Jesuits; then, a Jew who admired Sidonia; and now, obviously, a genially persistent tormenter of clergymen. Bertie also deflates the timely preoccupation of these contentious churchmen with the English university system by suggesting in no uncertain terms, as we have already seen, that the German universities are far superior. And in the justly famous unveiling scene, Bertie defrocks the pretentious, usurping lady bishop and calls forth Trollope's finest burlesque style: 'As Juno may have looked at Paris on Mount Ida, so did Mrs. Proudie look on Ethelbert Stanhope when he pushed the leg of the sofa into her lace train.' In chapters 10 and 11, Bertie deflates everything that is overblown in Barchester's clerical politics and serves the office of novelist-surrogate even more delightfully than his alluring sister.

Bertie's other great scene is a domestic triumph. He is equally adept at destroying pretension at home as he is abroad. Dr. Stanhope turns his illogical, sanctimonious parental wrath on his son when he learns that Eleanor is not to marry Bertie. As the son draws caricatures from his recollection of Miss Thorne's *fête,* his father rages against him while his sister tries to mediate between the wrath of the one and the wit of the other.

> 'Give over drawing,' said Charlotte, going up to him and taking the paper from under his hand. The caricatures, however, she preserved and showed them afterwards to the friends of the Thornes, the Proudies, and De Courcys. Bertie, deprived of his occupation, threw himself back in his chair and waited further orders.
>
> 'I think it will certainly be for the best that Bertie should leave this at once; perhaps tomorrow,' said Charlotte; 'but pray, Papa, let us arrange some scheme together.'
>
> 'If he will leave this to-morrow, I will give him £10, and he shall be paid £5 a month by the

banker at Carrara as long as he stays permanently in that place.'

'Well, sir, it won't be long,' said Bertie, 'for I shall be starved to death in about three months.'

'He must have marble to work with,' said Charlotte.

'I have plenty there in the studio to last me three months,' said Bertie. 'It will be no use attempting anything large in so limited a time—unless I do my own tombstone.'

Bertie manages this confrontation by the simple device of taking his father's pretensions of generosity to their logical conclusion, and he finds the task so easy that he can leave a record in pencil—not unlike the one Trollope has left in ink—of the social-climbing he witnessed at Ullathorne. I know of no scene in English fiction equal to this one in its use of logic to expose what is ridiculous since Elizabeth Bennet, point for point, destroyed Lady Catherine de Bourgh's ludicrous demand that she refuse to marry Darcy. Bertie Stanhope unimpeachably shares the honours of comic success with the heroine of *Pride and Prejudice*—a book that Trollope regarded as among the three best novels in the English language.

'Mr. Harding was by no means a perfect character,' says the narrator. 'In his indecision, his weakness, his proneness to be led by others, his want of self-confidence, he was very far from being perfect.' Harding is dismissed as not in the least suited to the warfare that gives the conflict its metaphorical texture in the novel. He subscribes to peace and not to Arabin's doctrine that 'Peace on earth and goodwill among men, are, like heaven, promises for the future.' He believes in 'that beautiful love which can be true to a false friend.' He is by temperament and principle unsuited to Barchester's peculiarly fractious interpretation of the church militant; he is 'a man devoid of all the combative qualifications' of a soldier in Archdeacon Grantly's army. He would rather direct the cathedral choir and play the violoncello than fight tooth and nail. Yet in spite of all these things Mr. Harding is given the last word in the novel: 'The author leaves him in the hands of his readers: not as a hero, not as a man to be admired and talked of, not as a man who should be toasted at public dinners and spoken of with conventional absurdity as a perfect divine, but as a good man, without guile, believing humbly in the religion which he has striven to teach, and guided by the precepts which he has striven to learn.' What this sentence says, in effect, is that Mr. Harding cannot be judged by the conventions of Barchester society. It affirms the very things that make him seem weak: 'Ah, thou weak man; most charitable, most Christian, but weakest of men!' No word of condemnation, one suspects, could be sweeter to a clergyman's ear.

Mr. Arabin is the novel's successful priest and Mr. Harding its failure, we are told. But it is well to remember that what Arabin gets, Harding gives away—his daughter and his deanery. Also, what Arabin represents is less satisfactory to Trollope's mind than what Harding represents. In his *Clergymen of the Church of England* Trollope praises the parson of a parish above the dean of a chapter. 'A dean,' he says, 'has little to do and a good deal to get.' In-

At his daughter's urging, Harding reads the letter written her by Slope. Illustration by Paul Hardy.

deed, if one adopts a hard line toward Arabin, one could say that he is made a dean because he is not suited to be a parson. Trollope objects to a man who 'is ordained in order that he may hold his fellowship' accepting in middle age the functions of a parish parson: 'Can anyone, we say, believe that such a one at the age of forty can be fit to go into a parish and undertake the cure of the parochial souls?'

Yet Arabin at age forty does precisely this; but the former professor of poetry is rapidly promoted to the deanery, to which he is more nearly suited: 'It is required that a clergyman shall have shown a taste for literature in some one of its branches before he can be regarded among the candidates proper for a deanery.' Mr. Harding, however, does not get to be warden and refuses to be dean; he remains vicar of St. Cuthbert's—he remains parson of a parish. His essential charity, which makes him fail as a combatant, allows him to succeed as a parson; and by the word *parson* 'the parish clergyman is designated as the palpable and visible personage of the church of his parish, making that by his presence an intelligible reality which, without him, would be an invisible idea.' Mr. Harding finds at St. Cuthbert's the truth of his calling: 'the parson in his parish must know that he has got himself into a place for which he has been expressly fitted by the orders he has taken.'

Bertie Stanhope and Septimus Harding are heroes in **Barchester Towers** because they are essentially unambitious men. It is good to be Arabin and get Eleanor and the deanery; but it is just as good, if not better, to be Bertie and Mr. Harding and refuse Eleanor and the deanery. Arabin is more typical and satisfies a conventional demand; they are unconventional and satisfy an imaginative demand. Arabin's path leads to domestic contentment; theirs to wit and wonder. Bertie scales the height of Trollope's comic genius and Mr. Harding sounds the depth of his moral sensibility. In **Barchester Towers** Trollope gives Victorian society one hero and himself and posterity two heroes, for in the working-out of his novel he is finally unable to resist his fellow artists. **Barchester Towers** itself proves that the novelist has cast his lot most imaginatively with a sculptor and a musician. (pp. 36-52)

> *Joseph Wiesenfarth, "Dialectics in 'Barchester Towers',"* in Anthony Trollope, *edited by Tony Bareham, Barnes & Noble, 1980, pp. 36-53.*

Robert M. Polhemus   (essay date 1980)

[*Polhemus is an American educator and critic who has written extensively on nineteenth-century fiction, focusing especially on "the relationship between the rise and flourishing of the novel and the search and need for areas of secular faith to replace orthodox faith." In the following excerpt, he examines the roles of the narrator, dialogue, and humor in projecting important themes and values in* Barchester Towers.]

Trollope's **Barchester Towers** is at the heart of the great comic tradition. It brings together religion and comedy and implicitly juxtaposes prayer and laughter. The most obvious thing about the novel is also the most important: the ecclesiastical establishment is made the subject of comedy, and Trollope's imagination establishes a comic church. The allegiance of Barchester's religious institution and its members has quietly passed from God to humanity, but its corporate structure remains, and Trollope respects it.

His humor, however, dissolves the aura of divinity around the church, and no matter how he might wish to deny it, the logical drift of this book implies that nothing, theoretically, is sacred—nothing, that is, is beyond comic scrutiny. Though there is no direct scoffing at the church and little that a confirmed Anglican could resent, the novel is in the broadest sense irreverent. It makes theological presumption seem ridiculous. What religious feeling there is resides not in "orthodox Christian supernaturalism" [Ruth apRoberts, *The Moral Trollope*, 1971] but in Trollope's comic vision of life. He values, and projects fictively, community, tolerance, love between men and women, the dialectical workings of social institutions and history, and humor itself.

Trollope, like Thackeray, thought of himself as a "weekday preacher" ("the novelist," he said, "if he have a conscience, must preach his sermons with the same purpose as the clergyman, and must have his own system of ethics"), and he found his humor in the "preachers" and the milieu of the church. His way of mastering the submerged spiritual tumult of his age and reconciling the clamoring religious strains in his society with the demands and realities of the changing Victorian world is to subsume and fuse ecclesiastical affairs, organized Christianity, and the energies of secularization into a wide comic perspective. In **Barchester Towers,** he imagines a comic reformation taking place.

For Trollope, change in personal and social life—the inevitable flux of circumstances and disruptions large and small—demands constant processes of reformation, i.e., perpetual readjustments of personality and behavior and continual efforts at reestablishing authority and equilibrium in the fluidity of being. These processes are the stuff of his novels. His comedy of change is especially alive to the increasing will to independence of strong-minded women and to the tensions, problems, and incongruities that new female assertiveness and ambition cause when they clash with conventional notions about feminine decorum and "a woman's place." **Barchester Towers** shows us both private and social reformations in the relationships between the sexes happening against the setting of the church, that bastion of male primacy.

Trollope's fiction is so understated and his narrative voice so unassuming that we need to keep in mind just how important his material is. In **Barchester** and its short predecessor, **The Warden,** he creates a religious, provincial society that has to adapt itself to the world's accelerating rate of change and secularizing thrust and find ways of retaining and developing its moral values, its continuity, its harmonies, and its faith. His tone is lighthearted, but it would be hard to think of a more consequential subject. It has been said that "the drama of the modern era is the decline of religion" [Peter Berger, *The Social Reality of Religion*], but, more precisely, this drama lies in the reshaping and reformation of religious drives and impulses.

Reading Trollope's comedy of clergymen makes it easier to see in retrospect how English novelists have played with the repressions of religion and with the gaping disparity between Christian profession and the practice of nominal Christians in the world. Superficially, Fielding's Parson Adams, Goldsmith's Vicar Primrose of Wakefield, and Sterne's Yorick and Dr. Slop may have influenced **Barchester Towers;** their authors, however, do not really make fun of the workings of the church or of the ecclesiastical world, nor do they have Trollope's communal focus. There is something of Peacock's spirit of communion in the parties that highlight **Barchester,** but Trollope has a much stronger feel for the particularity of life and of history. Like Dickens, he detested and wished to expose the Pecksniffian moral tyranny in his society, but he had more interest in conserving a moral tradition and a much greater faith in institutional life.

Of the comic writers, he owes most to Austen and Thackeray. From Austen he learned to develop a comic dialectic between character and community (including the importance of dialogue in representing change) and to render the intensity of personal relationships. Like her, he realized that a community without comic imagination can be stagnant, empty, and dangerous. *Barchester Towers,* like *Emma,* offers the blessings of grace upon humanity, but that grace is a gift of the author's comic understanding, not of God.

From *Vanity Fair* he learned the comic resources of shifting perspective. *Barchester Towers* treats a subject and a variety of characters of broad significance within a limited scope. As Thackeray shrinks Napoleon into Becky and the nineteenth century into his Vanity Fair, reducing and controlling them in his comedy, so Trollope shrinks the religious controversy, church factionalism, and secularization of his age into Barset. Thackeray continually brings to bear on his world the perspectives of Christian idealism in order to satirize it. Trollope's comic dialectic absorbs absolutist Christian visions and materialist points of view into a worldly perspective and makes theological views, including *contemptus mundi* and evangelicalism, part of the historical processes of the world.

From Thackeray, also, he seems to have gotten the idea of carrying over characters from one novel to another; but what was for Thackeray a minor and casual device for reminding people of his earlier books becomes in *Barchester Towers* a major innovation in British fiction and one crucial to Trollope's vision of life as a shifting but continuous communal process. By taking the characters and the setting of *The Warden* and expanding the Barchester world, Trollope turned out to be a chief English progenitor for the countless writers since who have preserved and developed their characters and fictional communities from novel to novel, e.g., Galsworthy, Ford Madox Ford, Mann, Proust, Faulkner, Powell, Lawrence, Waugh, even Joyce and Beckett—to say nothing of the lesser legion that has spawned hundreds of sagas, series, and soap operas.

Barchester Towers, with its continuing life, reflects an urge to break through the constructions of enclosed literary forms, with their traditional endings. It shows the appeal of a fantasy life that goes on and on. Trollope creates a human comedy of developing characters who interact with their evolving community and its institutions. That comedy is social but not impersonal, and it expresses both a desire and a way of seeking for permanence in the world. Extending the fictional structure beyond the covers of a single book or the limits of a single artwork is now so commonplace that we hardly give it a thought, but it says a lot about our longings for imaginative transcendence. I think it likely that the evolution of the modern fictional series has to do with secularization and a need to supplement or replace the "other world" of religion and the figures of religious myth with another kind of enduring, institutionalized fantasy life that one can somehow identify with and find some sort of psychological solace in. If there is any truth in that idea, it would seem apt that a novel and a series that chronicle the secularizing of the church should figure prominently in extending the formal domain of fiction. "We wish," says novelist John Fowles [in his *The French Lieutenant's Woman,* 1969] in words that fit Trollope neatly, "to create worlds as real as, but other than the world that is." That expresses a religious impulse, but the wish would not exist in anyone who had perfect faith in God's creation of this world and the world to come.

The opening chapter of *Barchester* is both an overture and a précis for the comic vision and mood of the whole book. "A novel," says Trollope, "should give a picture of common life enlivened by humour." What matters most, then, is the total image of the community in action, but what gives life to the whole are the personal traits and whims of its members, set off against each other. *The Warden* centers on one man, and its first words are "The Rev. Septimus Harding . . . "; but *Barchester Towers* is to be the story of a community: "In the latter days of July in the year 185—, a most important question was for ten days asked in the cathedral city of Barchester, and answered every hour in various ways—Who was to be the new Bishop?" The novel is set in moving time and poses a public question in the undifferentiated but various voices of the whole town. Before we read a proper name, we have the concern with social function and the sense of communal urgency.

> The death of old Dr. Grantly . . . took place exactly as the ministry of Lord——was going to give place to that of Lord——. . . .
>
> It was pretty well understood that the out-going premier had made his selection, and that if the question rested with him, the mitre would descend on the head of Archdeacon Grantly, the old bishop's son.

It is a wonderfully conceived situation; public and private life are inseparable. Trollope's artistry here is so delicate that it can easily be missed. Taking us into the mind of his ambitious archdeacon, he carefully balances the initial public question with a private question:

> The ministry were to be out within five days: his father was to be dead within—No, he rejected that view of the subject. . . .
>
> He tried to keep his mind away from the subject, but he could not. . . . He knew it must be now or never. . . . Thus he thought long and sadly, in deep silence, and then gazed at that still living face, and then at last dared to *ask himself* whether he really longed for his father's death.
>
> The effort was a salutary one, and *the question* was answered in a moment. The proud, wishful, worldly man, sank on his knees by the bedside, and taking the bishop's hand within his own, prayed eagerly that his sins might be forgiven him. [Italics mine.]

The exact nature of Grantly's answer may be ambiguous, but what then results shows how richly complex even a blunt personality can be. Trollope internalizes the principle of equivocation that animates Thackeray's world-view. Grantly shows himself capable of wishing for his father's death and wishing for him not to die also. The hand that he grasps is tellingly called "the bishop's" even in the moment of the son's repentance and atonement with the father. The archdeacon longs for preferment in the church and in the same instant longs to live up to Christian principles of humility too.

Harding comes in to see his officious son-in-law praying, and he is touched. Each is moved to "fellowship," and together they witness the passing of the old bishop. The "fellowship" is real, but it doesn't last. Trollope denigrates neither the dying of the gentle bishop and the passing of his pastoral way of life nor Grantly's moment of guilt and his spiritual crisis, but he revives the comic motions of worldliness and makes them follow fast upon prayer and death:

> "You cannot but rejoice that it is over," said Mr. Harding. . . .
>
> But how was he to act while his father-in-law stood there holding his hand? how, without appearing unfeeling, was he to forget his father in the bishop—to overlook what he had lost, and think only of what he might possibly gain?
>
> "No; I suppose not," said he, at last, in answer to Mr. Harding. "We have all expected it so long."

That "it," which unwittingly encompasses both the father's death and a bishopric, shows Trollope's genius for revelation in dialogue. But just as important is the internal dialogue here. The nub of experience in this book is the comedy of people having to relate to other people unlike themselves. They must define and express their desires in the context of their professional and personal relationships with others—often incongruous others—as Grantly does here in tandem with Harding.

In the presence of death, life and the hunger pangs of ambition assert themselves, and Trollope makes it funny. The comic rhythm increases, and we move back into the public world. Grantly cajoles Harding into sending the useless telegram to the newly fallen Conservative government. Trollope shifts to the world of publicity, as various newspapers speculate on who the new bishop will be. The announcement then comes that the new Liberal government is sending Bishop Proudie down from London. Death has become an aspect of the endless corporate processes of society and a cause of the comic reformation of the Barchester community.

The narrator, at the close of the chapter, returns to the private hopes of the archdeacon, now dashed, and he tentatively sympathizes with him and his worldly ambition:

> Many will think that he was wicked to grieve for the loss of episcopal power, wicked to have coveted it, nay, wicked even to have thought about it, in the way and at the moments he had done so.
>
> With such censures I cannot profess that I completely agree. . . . A lawyer does not sin in seeking to be a judge, or in compassing his wishes by all honest means. A young diplomat entertains a fair ambition when he looks forward to be the lord of a first-rate embassy; and a poor novelist when he attempts to rival Dickens . . . commits no fault, though he may be foolish. Sidney Smith truly said that in these recreant days we cannot expect to find the majesty of St. Paul beneath the cassock of a curate. If we look to our clergymen to be more than men, we shall proba-

bly teach ourselves to think that they are less. . . .

> Our archdeacon was worldly—who among us is not so?

That is the prose of a man whose heart belongs to the world and who puts faith in a career. The telling comparison of the priesthood to other professions cannot help but make the religious calling seem like any other calling. Vocation in Trollope's vision is the call of the world, and the church offers, beyond spiritual guidance, professional opportunity where one may find satisfaction, a living, and possibly distinction for oneself. Not holiness and inspiration but professional competence and humanity are the ideal qualities that emerge here for a churchman.

Notice the linkage in the passage: Grantly's emotions and wishes, which, after all, Trollope imagines, take on public significance within the world of the novel but also within the world of author and reader. The archdeacon's ambition is a subject, and so is the putative reader's response to it. Everything relates character to community, including the supposed community of readers. Grantly implicates us in Barchester, and, in a larger sense, Trollope implicates us, too, in a life made not by God but by men and women. (pp. 166-73)

. . . . .

All the main characters of *Barchester Towers* are relative creatures who together create its vision of community and comic reformation. Trollope insists on the interrelatedness of life. Hope for the future and for personal happiness lie in the flourishing of social life. Imagining how people interact, how they perceive others, how they touch and change each other, how their obsessions and individuality affect their society, how their roles and activities come to be shaped and defined, how they all work together as a collectivity—that is what fascinates him in Barchester. He would later create characters of greater depth and bring readers closer to individual men and women than he does here, but he would never imagine a more resonant community.

When I call his people "corporate characters," I mean that he sees them as parts of a functioning whole society and also that he represents individual and communal life as formed by, and inseparable from, corporate organization. Not coincidentally, this comedy was written at just that time in history when the modern corporation was being developed. The church in Trollope sometimes looks as if it were the corporation of a higher agency, since its ends, though moral, are worldly. In his Palliser series and in the chronicles of Barset, Trollope understands and makes art out of two major facts of modern life: (1) Lots of people find—or try to find—success, identity, meaning, and even a kind of transcendence in the corporate structure with which they associate themselves. (2) The dominant corporate structure in a community, though itself a constantly changing entity, sets the tone and the dramatic framework for the people of that place and tends to determine their groupings and their particular destinies. (For example, the conflict in the church in the Barset novels brings Eleanor Harding both her husbands.) Whether

Trollope is relating his characters to the church, Parliament, government, or the bureaucracy, he is busy creating the epic of organization men and women.

Barchester is dominated by the institution of organized religion. A Church of England company town, Trollope means it to be typical of an important part of the nation. Like any other institution, the church is made up of worldly and comic people of all kinds. Trollope shows how everybody, from the free-thinking Stanhopes and the old-fashioned Thornes of Ullathorne to the Barchester tradesmen and leader-writers of the London *Jupiter* (i.e., the *Times*), have a stake in Barset clerical life and the currents of ecclesiastical opinion.

He grounds the novel solidly in the religious history of its time and reflects comically the era's theological parties and strife. Slope and Mrs. Proudie represent the church's Evangelical wing; Bishop Proudie, appointed by the reforming Liberals, is a "political" bishop, willing to take orders from the government—a type very familiar in the mid-Victorian age. Grantly stands for the "high and dry" church; Dr. Arabin comes out of the Oxford Movement and champions its Anglican ideals. Even some of the particular incidents of the book had their real-life analogues; e.g., the coincidence of a falling government and a dying bishop; debates about whether cathedral services should be chanted; newspapers meddling in diocesan affairs. All of this goes to show, however, that religious affairs are part of the human comedy. For Trollope, the most important moral and religious truth—the existence of faith, hope, and charity—lies in communal life, not in theological policy or opinion.

Trollope's church is not so much a model of Anglo-Catholic faith as it is a model for displaying a secular catholic version of humanity. It loosely holds together a motley collection of mutual-interest groups and serves as the institutional body within which the maneuvering for power, influence, and security can take place. Egos shape institutions, but institutions can control and soften egoism and keep open the options and possibilities for connection between individuals. The Barchester towers express a common human idealism and give continuity to the changing scene. They are signs and physical evidence that people aspire, despite their worldly folly, to sustain and develop the moral value of their lives and of the civilization to which they belong.

Much of the moral equilibrium and integrity of Barchester depends on Harding, whose courtesy and innocent faith put the querulousness of the Proudies, Grantly, Slope, and the rest into perspective. He is the moral link between orthodox religion and the secularizing world—between past and future. A deferential man, Harding lacks the conventional strong qualities of a hero. The narrator, however, calls Harding "a good man," exactly what James Joyce would call Leopold Bloom, the great and ridiculous hero of his modern epic, and we can see Harding as a figure who connects the "foolish" Christian faith of Erasmus's *Praise of Folly* to Joyce's secular comic faith in *Ulysses.* Trollope uses Harding to relate his readers to *his* faith, which is based on kindness and sympathetic fellow-feeling. There is a touch of the holy fool about Harding and his inno-

cence. He functions as a kind of conscience to Grantly, the Oxford clerics, and the public men of London, his very being reminding people that disinterested virtue *can* exist. His special qualities—mildness, patience, tact, sensitivity to others, and a positive will *not* to dictate to them—his very *harmlessness*—are the qualities that make life tolerable in any age. He brings heart to the novel and, in fact, *is* its moral heart.

But Harding is not a symbol. He works in a practical way to preserve good relations. Breaks between people, sudden ruptures of tradition, sectarian enmity, distort the corporate nature of being. He smooths the way generously for the Proudie appointment, Quiverful, to take over as the new warden, and, feeling himself too old and passive to be dean of Barchester, he convinces others that Arabin, the only other character in the novel who shows true piety, should have the office. He moderates the contentiousness of the community and helps to join its generations.

I cannot make the significance of Mr. Harding any clearer or show how necessary he is to Trollope's communal faith than by quoting William James, in *The Varieties of Religious Experience,* when he discusses modern secularizing society's view of saintly humility:

> Here saintliness has to face the charge of preserving the unfit. . . . "Resist not evil," "Love your enemies," these are saintly maxims of which men of this world find it hard to speak without impatience. . . .
>
> And yet you are sure, as I am sure, that were the world confined to . . . hard-headed, hard-hearted, and hard-fisted methods exclusively, . . . the world would be an infinitely worse place than it is now to live in. The tender grace, not of a day that is dead, but *of a day yet to be born somehow,* with the golden rule grown natural would be cut out from the perspective of our imaginations.

Without the faintly ridiculous Harding there could be no moral imagination and no hope of virtue in the emerging society of the present and the future.

What is so impressive about the Barchester community is the way it can include so many kinds of people and points of view. Archdeacon Grantly, Dr. Slope, and Bishop Proudie are all in their own ways members of a new institutional breed, completely different from Harding. Political beings, they would be just as recognizable in pinstripes, gray flannel, or Soviet serge as in clerical garb. Grantly is an administrator jealous for the undiminished power of his profession and, like Slope, "anxious that the world should be priest-governed"; he "really understood the *business* of bishoping" (italics mine). Eager Dr. Proudie, following the main chance, "early in life adapted himself to the views held by whigs on most theological and religious subjects." A good committeeman and amenable to "those who were really in authority," he serves the reforming governmental interests that work to bring the church under the control of the modern state. In the unscrupulous and pushy Slope, Trollope gives us a fine portrait of a climbing organizational infighter, as ruthless as any beast in the modern corporate jungle. These earthy men make a mock epic of church affairs. They also show how the collective ambitions of people in the same organization can be balanced off. Trollope uses their desires to animate the community. Ironically, what results from their corporate battle is, on the whole, good. In Barchester, corporate life keeps the individual will to power in check.

The real apostle of Evangelical thought and action is Mrs. Proudie, one of the most genuinely religious people in the novel. With her sense of moral duty, her reforming obsession, her earnest inner certitude, and her utter lack of humor, she represents that oppressive, puritanical side of religion, which just asks to be ridiculed. In her unctuous language, Trollope parodies the offensive tone of certainty that marks the smug proselyte of a "higher morality." She also stars in **Barchester Towers'** comic version of the Samson theme. The traditional sexual roles often get reversed in the novel, and not only the bishop's wife but also the Stanhope girls, Mrs. Quiverful, Miss Thorne, Susan Grantly, and Eleanor seem to shear away strength from men. It is fitting that, in this novel of clerical life, women, for so long discriminated against and relegated to secondary status by the church, should romp like so many modern Delilahs through this ecclesiastical community.

Trollope often ridicules feminism, but it would never occur to the son of Frances Trollope that a woman is less important than a man. It is true that he does not imagine women leading successful independent lives or having identities that do not relate closely to men's. What we must also see, however, is that in Barchester he cannot imagine men leading lives of value that are not closely related to, and dependent upon, women's. Arabin can find fulfillment in his professional and private life only by marrying Eleanor and thereby relating himself to the community. Trollope puts a premium on the corporate relationship of the sexes, and that may be why he is without peer among English novelists in portraying marriage and in exploring the psychological connections between men and women, as the Palliser novels, for example, show.

One thing missing from Barchester before the radical and provocative Stanhope family returns is a candid sense of the ridiculous playing, from within the community, on its establishment figures; another is the alluring sport of sexuality. The reformation of Barset calls for both sex and comedy; by creating Signora Madeline Stanhope Vesey-Neroni, Trollope sets in motion both the mocking critical spirit and the farce of sexual attraction that the place needs. William James, expressing the conventional wisdom of the nineteenth century, says that "religious experience" must be "solemn": "For common men 'religion,' whatever more special meanings it may have, signifies always a *serious* state of mind." For Trollope, religion without joking will no longer do: it cannot properly put down pride, i.e., *Proudieness*.

Madeline, in her aggressive, witty talk and her sardonic laughter, exactly fulfills the definition and function of what George Meredith [in his "Essay on Comedy"] would later describe as "the Comic Spirit": "whenever they [people] wax out of proportion, overblown, affected, pretentious, bombastical, hypocritical, pedantic . . . ; whenever

it sees them self-deceived . . . drifting into vanities, congregating in absurdities . . . , plotting dementedly; whenever they are at variance with their professions; are false in humility or mined with conceit, individually, or in bulk; the Spirit . . . will look humanely malign, and cast an oblique light on them, followed by volleys of silvery laughter." This "spirit" is epitomized by a scene at Mrs. Proudie's reception, where the seductive but lame signora insists, as always, on languishing, courtesan-like, on a sofa. Mrs. Proudie, livid with raging moral prudery because her protégé, Slope, has succumbed to the siren, orders him to leave the couch.

> "Is she always like this?" said the signora. "Yes—always—madam," said Mrs. Proudie, returning; " . . . always equally adverse to impropriety of conduct of every description." . . . The signora couldn't follow her. . . . But she laughed loud, and sent the sound of it ringing through the lobby and down the stairs after Mrs. Proudie's feet. Had she been as active as Grimaldi, she could probably have taken no better revenge.

Madeline, like Becky Sharp, excels at badinage and at playing charades with the sentimental idiocies of her time. She uses role-playing and jesting to make fun of contradictions, hidden immoralities, and unconscious motives in the world. By exposing Slope, for example, and making us realize that he is the same grubby, greedy poseur in church affairs that he is in love affairs, she lets us infer the common connection between a drive for power over moral institutions and a thwarted infatuation with sexual sin. The "proper" men of Barset flock around her couch, and there she behaves with a flamboyance that kids and even makes a mockery of sex, in much the same way, and with much the same effect, as the comedienne Mae West would later do in the movies: she stimulates and then laughs at the male libido, which prudery can never quite hide.

Trollope hints that Madeline's early life included a pregnancy and the Victorian equivalent of a shotgun wedding. An internal moral censor evidently told him that the flaunting of sex, though necessary to his story, must be punished, and he made her a cripple. Though not fully realized, Madeline is one of the most interesting figures in the book. Trollope lavishes care on her speech and gives her, along with her brother Bertie, by far the best dialogue. She has a continually probing, iconoclastic wit. Like her nonconforming siblings, Bertie and the managerial Charlotte, she takes her living from the corporate church, which supports her, freethinker though she is. She is a daughter of the church, "one of the chapter," she says, and she strikes me as emblematic of the marriage that **Barchester Towers** accomplishes between the Anglican tradition and comedy. Like comedy, Madeline isn't quite respectable; but just because she is beyond the pale, "beyond the reach of Christian charity," as Mrs. Proudie puts it— *not serious*—she can send out the peals of laughter that Barset needs for renewing itself.

In the antiheroine, Madeline, whose repartee needles stuffed shirts and slaughters sacred cows, and the plot's heroine, Eleanor, we see that ingrained Victorian tendency to regard moral virtue as incompatible with critical, satirical intelligence in a woman. Again and again, Trollope, as he does here in **Barchester,** pays lip service to conventional notions of what a woman ought to be: obedient, pliable, the demure angel-in-the-house; a sweet, nurturing, familial creature who depends for her opinions and outlook on a man—someone who will "love, honor, and obey." In England, the ultimate sanction for this view of women's role lies in Christian doctrine and practice—in the church. Trollope wants to believe in the conventional Victorian ideal of womanhood; in fact, in novel after novel he says he does. He then goes right on, in the same books, to depict over and over the dilemmas and talk of those stifled, rebelliously witty women who fired his creative imagination. (Later in his fiction Trollope would bring virtue, humor, ambition, biting wit, intelligence, and vulnerability together in Glencora Palliser, Madame Max Goesler, Violet Effingham, Mabel Grex, and a host of other intelligent and whole figures in what is very likely the finest gallery of female characters ever created by a male novelist in English.)

What makes Trollope's conflict interesting, of course, is that it was—and is—cultural. What could and should women do in the world? The development and the integrity of the social community needed the full potential and participation of women of various talents. The changing status of women was and is one of the greatest social and personal problems of modern life, and Madeline's voice, her satire of conventional hypocrisy, and her immobile, crippled being bring it home to Barchester.

Madeline and her Bohemian brother Bertie don't take life seriously; they keep looking for amusement, and they work in dialectical fashion to give the Barchester world what it lacks: skepticism, flash, drama, a love of pleasure, and a touch of frivolity. Trollope stresses their good nature, but he calls them "heartless," which means, as he uses the word, that they cannot love or feel deeply. That lack distances them from us and makes them subjects as well as instruments of satire. Bertie, for example, flits idly about Europe and the Near East, dabbling in art and religion but sticking to nothing and doing no one any good. The Stanhopes look like literary ancestors of Evelyn Waugh's Bright Young People and P. G. Wodehouse's charming parasites. (That hugely famous but critically underrated antihero of twentieth-century comic fiction, Bertie Wooster, could almost be Trollope's Bertie transposed into Jeeves's company.)

Bertie shows, even as a lazy dilettante, that bohemianism can mean comic gaiety, unexpected insight, and tolerance as well as irresponsible arrogance and cultivation of the ego. Eleanor likes him because, full of candor and fun, he never professes to be moral, nor does he preach sermons at her. He acts as an agent for Trollope's subtle, but important, comic devaluing of doctrinal dispute in religion (a devaluing that implicitly means a downplaying of Christian doctrine). Clowning about comparative religion to the bishop and the Barchester clergy, he blurts such things as "I was a Jew once, myself," sapping theology of its intimidating seriousness. Creed, for him, as it has for so many others, becomes fad and entertainment. Through Bertie, Trollope expresses something that endures in the British comic tradition and, I may say, in any lively society, and that is a hedonistic longing for pleasure and jokes, for idylls of irresponsibility. Even the brains of the industrious, when they dream, enjoy fantasies of effortlessness and ambassadors from lands of milk and honey.

Trollope carefully balances the Stanhopes and their disrespectful, campy humor with another brother-and-sister pair, the anachronistic Thornes of Ullathorne. (Ullathorne, a wordplay on extreme religious conservatism, was the title of a noted reactionary Roman Catholic bishop of the day.) The Thornes—typically, Miss Thorne is much more formidable than her bachelor brother—are unashamedly reactionary and try to shut out the present by living in the past. Trollope treats them affectionately. A community, for him, is not only a gathering of people but a gathering-together of customs and mores from different times. It has temporal variety as well as human variety and stretches across years as well as land. Since it is made from the past, it must be tolerant of the past in order not to rend itself. In a rich and good culture, there must be men and women who dedicate themselves to preserving the ideals and values of other times, as do the Thornes. Trollope conceives of the Thornes, like his other characters, as typical and having communal meaning: "Such a year or two since were the Thornes," he writes, ending his slightly patronizing chapter on them. "Such, we believe, are the inhabitants of many an English country home. May it be long before their number diminishes" (22:204). He knew he was being nostalgic. Neither of the Thornes marries; they have no descendants. They do, however, aid in making the match between Arabin and Eleanor. They too are part of the comic reformation of Barset and the catholicity of Trollope's outlook.

Trollope's Barchester world goes to church and goes to parties, but going to parties predominates, and he gives over nearly a third of his text to them. Miss Thorne's party, welcoming Mr. Arabin, and Mrs. Proudie's party, when her husband becomes bishop, are central to the novel. Barchester social life revolves about institutional appointments and relations, and that is how Trollope perceives all society, as he shows later in the Palliser novels. He is the novelist laureate of parties, and social gatherings are his forte. His parties, however, are not the gluttonous feasts of Dickens or the festive comic communions of Peacock but the occasions when much important social business gets done: personal fate turns, relationships are rearranged, and characters and community, in signs, words, and gestures, reveal their real being. At parties men and women get a chance to talk to each other, courting takes place, sexual tension makes the blood jump, and the human comedy surges.

Trollope's comedy reads as if he were intending it to bring about a reunion of the diverging meanings of words by which modern society organizes itself. I mean such words as "party," "company," "corporation," "union," and "class," which have been losing their connotations of mutuality and human solidarity and now often suggest partisanship, private advantage, exclusion, and even social enmity. His parties in Barchester conserve the communal relationship and the social wholeness that potentially inhere in those words. He has a tribal sense of life, and he cares about preserving some sort of corporate integrity. Failure for him means not being able to connect with others. That is why he loves to bring people together, even very disparate people, and conjoin them in what he calls the social "sports."

Barchester's whole is greater than the sum of its parts. The life in the book has an attractiveness and a worthiness that few of the characters have if we look at them separately. Most of them—like the Proudies, Slope, the Stanhopes, Grantly, and Tom Towers—are not very nice or admirable people at all, and even Arabin, Eleanor, and Harding have their glaring shortcomings. The whole cast is not much better ethically than the figures in *Vanity Fair.* And yet the life in **Barchester Towers** seems infinitely sweeter and finer than in Thackeray's novel. The reason is that Trollope finds a value, a joyousness, and an intensity in social relationship that Thackeray does not. I am not saying that Trollope's vision is better or truer or even more conducive to great comedy; but in this novel he is much more optimistic about how people complement and compensate for each other. Henry James calls Trollope's great virtue as a writer his "complete appreciation of the usual" [James, "Anthony Trollope," in *The Future of the Novel,* edited by Leon Edel, 1956]. The meaning of that praise becomes clearer if we say that Trollope had a transfiguring faith in the usual and a talent for illuminating the wonder of it. Life, for him, is energized and made diverting by the spark of human interaction, by continuing encounter with the material world, and by the knowledge that human destiny is to be part of a community.

On almost every page he manages to convey a deep and almost obsessive interest in the minutiae of the social structure and the animation of communal relationships. His careful descriptions, for instance, of the mood and talk of different people at gatherings, of movement and positioning at parties, of the surroundings at Ullathorne and St. Ewold's parsonage, of the nagging worries that people have about what others are thinking, of the subtle nuances of behavior in social and professional hierarchies—all contribute to the *bricolage* that builds up an elaborate, thick, personal world. (pp. 173-83)

. . . . .

Trollope almost always leaves it to readers to infer the full significance of what his characters say, and the prominence he gives to dialogue is what sometimes gives his fiction the illusion of being an unmediated vision: nothing appears to stand between us and the characters. Neither the characters nor the author will *seem* to have the grasp that readers can have on the meaning and consequence of what has been said. Dialogue, then, is what makes Trollope's novels so subtle, so full of nuances, so much more intelligent than anyone would gather from the narrative commentary. It often conveys important information and profound psychological and social insight in a seemingly offhand way. In dialogue we find his characteristic and telling mode of understatement.

Understatement, a famous trait of British humor, is a comic device for slipping things past a moral censor, inter-

nal or external. It is also a *modus vivendi,* a way of making light of life's outrageousness, of not seeming to be distressingly serious and, hence, a bore; of not, in Trollope's revealing words, "seeming to have a design upon the reader." It is a mode of irony but an *indirect* mode, one that assumes a bond of communication and a superior understanding and sympathy between like-minded people attuned to recognizing and putting down crude hyperbole and self-dramatization. Understatement relies on, and encourages, a community of shared perspective.

To be good readers of Trollope's novels, we have to learn to make independent judgments about the dialogue. Look . . . at the talk between Eleanor and Arabin at the pivotal time of their courtship:

> " . . . old-fashioned things are so much the honestest."
>
> "I don't know about that," said Mr. Arabin, gently laughing. . . . "Some think that we are quickly progressing towards perfection, while others imagine that virtue is disappearing from the earth."
>
> "And you, Mr. Arabin, what do you think?" said Eleanor. . . .
>
> "What do I think, Mrs. Bold? . . . It is the bane of my life that on important subjects I acquire no fixed opinion. I think, and think, and go on thinking; and yet my thoughts are running ever in different directions. I hardly know whether or no we do lean more confidently than our fathers did on those high hopes to which we profess to aspire."
>
> "I think the world grows more worldly every day," said Eleanor.
>
> "That is because you see more of it than when you were younger. But we should hardly judge by what we see,—we see so very very little."

This conversation passes without Trollope's comment, but it is remarkable. It shows that Arabin has a wise and interesting mind: what he says about thinking and about point of view is surprisingly candid and profound; he understands that truth may be indeterminate and relative but that one needs to seek it anyway. His talk lets us know that he is honest enough to express doubt, that he senses the stagnating effect of absolutist thought, and that he has enough confidence in Eleanor to confess to her what many would regard as weakness and to tell her what truly bothers him in his intellectual life. It shows that he has changed since coming to Barchester and can now speak "with his full powers" to a woman. Her talk reveals a very conventional mind; there is great irony in her trite but idealistic sentiment, "I think the world grows more worldly." The growing worldliness of the world has brought her a large income and now, with Arabin growing more worldly, a fine new prospective husband. The statement, however, implies an innocence that charms Arabin. If we compare this dialogue with that between Arabin and Madeline, who has helped to teach him to love and enjoy the world, including rich, pretty widows, we see that, for the most part, he listens to the signora but dominates the talk with Eleanor. She allows him to express himself more comfortably and fully, and the implication is that he will have little trouble making her of one mind with him. It is easy to love those who are solicitous of our ideas and whose opinions we can help to mold.

Arabin's point about the diversity of his thinking identifies a key aspect of Trollope's fiction: for him, dialogue is an internal as well as external process. The indirect interior monologue, which becomes so important in his later novels, often takes the form of indirect inward conversation—self-dialogue. His typical characters are made up of many different, changing, sometimes conflicting social voices and parts, and he uses the method of internal debate and dialogue to help him with his characterization.

Here is a passage on Arabin's interior life that contains typical internal dialogue and understatement:

> He had, as was his wont, asked himself a great many questions, and given himself a great many answers. . . . Then he asked himself whether in truth he did love this woman; and he answered himself, not without a long struggle, but at last honestly, that he certainly did love her. He then asked himself whether he did not also love her money; and he again answered himself that he did so. But here he did not answer honestly. It was and ever had been his weakness to look for impure motives for his own conduct.

Notice that what the narrator says about Arabin's answer—that he does, indeed, love Eleanor's money—is *not* the truth that emerges. We have before us the unequivocal answer of Arabin's mind: he *does* love the idea of her money, and nothing that he says or does in the rest of the book, nothing that happens, supports the authorial comment that "he did not answer honestly." The narrator may not understand that the love for a woman and the love of her wealth can be tied to each other, but Arabin does, Trollope does, and so do we. We also learn from this internal dialogue and from several other conversations that "looking for the impure motive" in one's conduct is not a weakness but a great strength and spur to progress.

The stress on both inner and outer dialogue pulls us into a dialogue with the book. Trollope presents this seemingly casual talk among some Barchester clergymen who are visiting the old, dying dean:

> "Poor Dr. Trefoil; the best of men, but—"
>
> "It's the most comfortable dean's residence in England," said a second prebendary. "Fifteen acres in the grounds. It is better than many of the bishops' palaces."
>
> "And full two thousand a year," said the meagre doctor.
>
> "It is cut down to £ 1200," said the chancellor.
>
> "No," said the second prebendary. "It is to be fifteen. A special case was made."
>
> "No such thing," said the chancellor.
>
> "You'll find I'm right," said the prebendary.

> "I'm sure I read it in the report," said the minor canon. . . .
>
> "What do you say, Grantly?" said the meagre little doctor.
>
> "Say about what?" said the archdeacon, who had been looking as though he were thinking about his friend the dean, but who had in reality been thinking about Mr. Slope.
>
> "What is the next dean to have, twelve or fifteen?"
>
> "Twelve," said the archdeacon authoritatively, thereby putting an end at once to all doubt and dispute among his subordinates as far as that subject was concerned.

It is a typical moment in a Trollope novel.

Reading this without direct authorial guidance, I have the illusion of being not only a witness but as credible an interpreter as the narrator of what this conversation signifies. I infer that in the midst of death we are in life, that institutional identity provides continuity of life, that professional people are fascinated by the status and pay of their fellows, that the modern church is a very worldly organization, that an organization's pecking order functions even in extraordinary times, and that Grantly knows everything about the temporalities of his calling. This chatter makes fun of the religious institution, but it shows the animation of profession and the life-force even at death's door. In the fictive understatement of the dialogue I find Trollope's essential humor and comic vision. (pp. 192-96)

. . . . .

The messenger of momentous tidings of change does well to tread softly and speak ingratiatingly. The best comedians often assume a self-deprecating style and throw out audience-flattering lines in order to keep their comic license to make daring jokes and do thought-provoking routines. The narrator of ***Barchester Towers*** is self-effacing, disingenuous, shifty, playful and deferential. Trollope has to be careful of alienating his readers because he is making fun of many of the pieties of his age and is imaginatively chronicling major changes. In the communal process that shapes the world and defines life, as he renders it, there is a dialectical tension between the conventional and the unconventional, between old traditions and the uniqueness of particular new circumstances. Trollope wants to engage his readers in this process; he tries to establish community with them and mediate conflicts between what ought to be and what is. He takes his audience to be relatively conformist, poses as conventional himself, and then shows how conventions either need reforming or are shifting.

Like Thackeray's narrator, Trollope's narrator works to make us a congregation; but Trollope needs and assumes a much more diffident persona. He is preaching the possibility of a fruitful fusion of spirituality with worldly corporation and a faith in the changing earthly community, not the vanity of the world and the dismaying sameness of life. He has to be more tactful than Thackeray, who was dealing for the most part with lay sinners, that "set of people living without God in the world." He can't afford to say

Harting Grange, Trollope's country home in Sussex.

shocking things, as Thackeray can and does. Trollope, treating clergymen and their milieu—a very risky thing to do—has to handle his subject with kid gloves if he wants a broad audience to accept his comic faith.

Not wanting to make a head-on assault against sentimental conventions, he poses as independent from his characters; he lets people like the Stanhopes express unpopular ideas, while he himself makes inoffensive remarks that contradict the tenor of the text and leaves it to the readers to draw controversial conclusions. A "novelist," he says, must sometimes "submit" to his characters, by which he means that their personalities must sometimes seem strong enough to overwhelm the author's opinions and conceptual desire (e.g., Arabin *does* love Eleanor's money), and the audience must take the responsibility for judging the truth and significance of what is put before it.

Though he denies or obfuscates it, our narrator is often anticlerical and even antiecclesiastical. Notice the ambivalence and possible irony in his disclaimer of impiety:

> In endeavouring to depict the characters of the persons of whom I write, I am to a certain extent forced to speak of sacred things. I trust, however, that I shall not be thought to scoff at the pulpit, though some may imagine that I do not feel all the reverence that is due to the cloth. I may

question the infallibility of the teachers, but I hope that I shall not therefore be accused of doubt as to the thing to be taught.

Throwing out that sop to orthodoxy, Trollope almost immediately launches into a denunciation of preaching:

> There is, perhaps, no greater hardship at present inflicted on mankind in civilised and free countries, than the necessity of listening to sermons. . . . No one but a preaching clergyman can revel in platitudes, truisms, and untruisms, and yet receive, as his undisputed privilege, the same respectful demeanour as though words of impassioned eloquence, or persuasive logic, fell from his lips. . . .
>
> To me, it all means nothing; and hours are too precious to be so wasted—if one could only avoid it.

The narrator's stance is: *I ridicule human frailties but leave sacred doctrine untouched.* The disparaging of sermons and services, however, strips away sanctity from church and priest and carries at least a hint of scoffing blasphemy.

Shortly after, Trollope uses a mock-epic style to describe a meeting of the Grantly forces. He parodies *Paradise Lost* and tacitly compares Religion and Church in Miltonic England with their role in Barchester: "Then up rose Dr. Grantly; and, having thus collected the scattered wisdom of his associates, spoke forth with words of deep authority. When I say up rose the archdeacon, I speak of the inner man. . . . His hands were in his breeches pockets." The narrator's mock-heroic voice works to ridicule those who would claim their experience to be extraordinary and elevated above the social norms that govern the world of the reader. Trollope uses snatches of mock epic carefully to satirize those who presume to have an intimate relationship to "celestial minds": Grantly, Mrs. Proudie, and Slope. An archdeacon puts his hands in his pockets; a bishop's wife tears her dress; a chaplain gets his face slapped; and the narrator, using a mock-heroic style, points out ironically the common humanity of the clerical community's leading personages; their behavior is as silly and banal as other people's.

Everything about the narrator goes to prove that he too is a part of a corporate existence. Even when he intrudes in order to joke about the fictional nature of the book, he is implying that there is something so true to life and independent about the characters that certain things cannot be manipulated to satisfy his own whim. He is not always an omnipotent author. "But let the gentle-hearted reader be under no apprehension whatsoever. It is not destined that Eleanor shall marry Mr. Slope or Bertie." Trollope scoffs at fiction that stresses outcomes and upshots: "Nay, take the last chapter if you please—learn from its pages all the results of our troubled story, and the story shall have lost none of its interest." When he twits novelistic conventions, he makes fun of himself, but he is also laughing at those who prefer the conventional pap of illusion in fiction.

The narrator mocks arbitrary finalities and the disposition of private fates in novels because it is in *concluding,* in closing the book, that the analogy to reality that Trollope tries to create breaks down. The conventional, arbitrary, happy ending distorts his sense of life as a continuum. For him, the vitality of living—its meaning, its goodness and pleasure—lies not in ends but in the social dialogue and the continuing interrelationships. The last chapter of *Barchester Towers* begins, "The end of a novel, like the end of a children's dinner-party, must be made up of sweetmeats and sugar-plums." That mocking sentence says that our craving for happy finalities is childish, and it implies also that the fantasies of fiction may bring us real pleasure as long as we don't take them too seriously. Trollope usually downplays his endings, returning again and again to the same characters, writing series, imagining a second generation of fictional families; he does so because he is striving to make his fiction conform to the book of the world, and the book of the world cannot be closed. (pp. 196-200)

> *Robert M. Polhemus, "Trollope's 'Barchester Towers' (1857): Comic Reformation," in his* Comic Faith: The Great Tradition from Austen to Joyce, *The University of Chicago Press, 1980, pp. 166-203.*

Gay Sibley (essay date 1985)

[*In the following excerpt, Sibley examines the relationship between morality and "taste" in* Barchester Towers, *suggesting that Trollope used the latter as a measure of morality in the novel.*]

Several critics have remarked upon Anthony Trollope's indebtedness to Jane Austen. Bradford Booth asserts that "it is to Jane Austen, one is convinced, that Trollope owed most"; Ruth apRoberts, after stating that "Trollope beats Sterne on the grand simple decencies," goes on to affirm that "with Jane Austen we come very much closer to Trollope; early he decided *Pride and Prejudice* was the best novel in the English language"; and James Kincaid observes that Austen "provided Trollope with a method and an aesthetic" [Booth, *Anthony Trollope: Aspects of his Life and Art,* 1958; apRoberts, *The Moral Trollope,* 1971; Kincaid, *The Novels of Anthony Trollope,* 1977]. Although all of these critics point out convincing parallels, what Austen and Trollope have most in common, it seems to me, is their view of "taste" as morality, presented through narrative stances which indicate that "good taste" and "bad taste" are inextricable and irrevocably linked with classical (some would say elitist) standards; and further, that the judgments regarding such standards, even though they may at any given moment be masquerading as judgments on a character's "manners" (a factor consistently associated with "taste" in other matters as well), end finally as judgments on a character's morality.

That Austen employed such a rhetoric has been generally accepted: "If [in Austen's work]," says Jane Nardin, "a man or woman always displays good manners, it is perfectly safe for the reader to assume that his character is truly good" [Nardin, *Those Elegant Decorums: The Concept of Propriety in Jane Austen's Novels,* 1973]. At the time Trollope wrote **Barchester Towers,** however, forty-five years had passed since the publishing of *Pride and Prejudice,* and people such as Jeremy Bentham and Cardinal Newman, events such as the 1832 Reform Bill and the repeal of the Corn Laws, had intervened. Therefore, while Austen's taste-as-morality may find its echoes in Trollope, the later author's narrative approach to that concept is suitably different and notably less obvious.

Significantly, Trollope's classical hero was Cicero, and compared with Austen's ethical stance, Trollope's would appear much more "situational," as befits a time in civilization when "those elegant decorums" do not always work very well. In Cicero's *De Officiis,* says Ruth apRoberts, the author "makes ethics most specifically his business," and this work

> is the one Trollope admires beyond all others. . . . [the] relations [of *honestum* to *utile*] is a recurrent and endlessly interesting theme in Trollope, as he takes up those many cases where principle and expediency seem to be at odds, in sexual selection, in law, in problems of Church and government. Moral perception, it seems, is to be achieved only through the most meticulous examination of the case, *all* sides of it, its history, the motivation of each agent involved, the results of action or inaction, repercussions in many directions.

There are those who disagree with apRoberts's view of it. James Kincaid, for example, asserts that

> in the end, situation ethics are just not delicate or complex enough. . . . The standards are all there; they are made more difficult to apply and far more difficult to define; most of all, there is less communal agreement on what they are. But they are dependent on codes which are not to be defined by situations. The test is whether one has the proper instincts and sensitivity to behave, say, with honesty in an extremely difficult situation, but the definition of honesty is referred to the instincts and sensitivity and to the action, not to the situation. The situation tests; it is not determinant.

Kincaid's interpretation puts the onus back on the individual, and it would appear that the individual makes honest decisions based upon whether or not he or she is capable of them. And to a large extent, we are led to believe that such capability, based on "instincts and sensitivity," depends on heritage. Says Kincaid, "Trollope is forced over and over to define his villains as those who might appear to be gentlemen but who lack the first and most basic requirement: an instinctive aversion to a lie." It is this aversion that differentiates between the charms of Darcy and Wickham in *Pride and Prejudice,* and it is an aversion that seldom appears as learned behavior, or if it is learned, the knowledge has become so deeply imprinted as to operate akin to instinct. The code of the gentleman, a code based upon standards set up by the likes of Aristotle and Cicero, then, is "the most solid traditional ethical standard in Trollope."

While the classical standards of taste in behavior remain in Trollope, they are couched in an appropriate ambiguity, as befits a wider and more democratically minded audience. In contrast to Austen's confident acceptance of those standards, "Trollope's refusal to define [the] code is a recognition of its necessary flexibility." But such a recognition does not necessarily mean that Trollope is accepting a mixed bag of "situational ethics." In fact, I think it is more likely that he is retaining the same classical standards we see in Austen, but is simply adjusting his narration so that, depending on the "taste" of the reader, more than one judgment is possible regarding the "taste-as-morality" of many of the characters. In other words, instead of the clearly delineated standards of taste revealed in Austen, those standards in Trollope have been blended together in a rhetorical soup, in which several of the ingredients have lost their discernible flavor. For example, although Trollope ends *Barchester Towers* by insisting that Mr. Harding should be viewed "not as a hero," some critics doubt that he means what he says. James Kincaid insists that "the final focus rests on the true hero, Mr. Harding," while Robert Polhemus [in his *The Changing World of Anthony Trollope,* 1968] votes for Mr. Arabin: "If Barchester is to be anything more than an amusing but trivial place, [Mr. Arabin] must flourish there. The book would be satirical and pessimistic if he did not thrive." The fact is, the book may very well be "satirical and pessimistic," since a reader cannot be entirely confident of the appropriate response to many of Trollope's characters.

Such a critical ambiguity comes about in this case as a result of a move away from satire as "militant irony" in Trollope's narration. In *Barchester Towers,* only Mr. Slope and Mrs. Proudie are portrayed militantly, he a bit more than she. Nearly all of the characters but these two, of whom the narrator clearly does not approve, display a taste that could meet with approval or dismay, depending upon the taste of the individual reader and upon which side of Trollope's ambivalence that reader chooses to adopt. This is not to say that Trollope has created an unreliable narrator, but rather, that he makes it clear that all judgments about most characters within post-Reform society must be to some degree unreliable, and that no character can be portrayed as morally pristine. As apRoberts points out, in Trollope "the right and truth lie on neither side exclusively." Yet the sides exist, and as readers we are encouraged by the narrator to choose in spite of his ambivalence, whatever reservations we may have regarding the choice. Further, as I intend to show, what side we choose depends upon the narrator's convincing readers of his rightful role as arbiter of taste in behavior, and upon his also convincing us that a character's taste is a reliable indicator of morality.

In addition to the appreciation for and intimate knowledge of the works of Cicero and Jane Austen, Trollope also had been influenced by the literature of "the dandy." Bradford Booth comments that

> at the age of twenty-five [Trollope] was carefully examining the 'silverfork' novel of fashionable life. . . . As practiced by Bulwer, Disraeli, and Mrs. Gore, this was an artificial form describing an artificial society, but it was not without a kind of negative influence in promoting sounder work. . . . Largely descriptive in purpose and technique, the novel of fashionable life was written in a passive mood—a static reproduction of aristocratic life, complete in wearisome detail.

That "detail," however "wearisome," was to provide many a middle-class novelist with the information necessary to portray aristocratic life mimetically, and it would seem to have proven quite useful to Trollope in *Barchester Towers,* since what judgments the reader is encouraged to make regarding a character's morality depend, as we shall see, upon the reader's accepting the author as an arbiter of taste in other matters as well. It is not a coincidence that, in the residents of Barsetshire, "good taste" in matters of aesthetics, as well as in matters of behavior, frequently go hand in hand with a moral character.

As befits the times in which he wrote, then, Trollope's "rhetoric of taste" in *Barchester Towers* operates in a more subtle way than does Jane Austen's in *Pride and Prejudice.* In fact, one of the major differences between the two is that Trollope does not allow the concept of taste-as-morality (or its lesser brethren, taste-as-intuitive aesthetic response) to appear as a critical issue, but instead edges it in secondarily. At the root of it all, there is a very simple rhetorical device: if an author can seduce the reader with an acceptable concept and then inextricably align that concept with one not quite so acceptable, chances are the reader will be "logically" led to accept the second concept as well, however tenuous the alliance might be. In this way, *Barchester Towers* provides an excellent example of how persuasively an author may guide the minds of readers on matters of morality as it fuses with religion and politics, not by smothering with polemics which are increasingly inappropriate in a democratic age, but simply by letting readers know, through a carefully manipulated narrative tone, which side has the "good taste," i.e., which side is morally "right."

We know that Trollope had an early awareness of an interest in standards of "Taste" and that he read Edmund Burke on the sublime and the beautiful when he was eighteen. We also know how Trollope felt about religion, and we know that his stated political views ran often in opposition to his conservative opinions regarding the church. Says C. P. Snow [in his *Trollope: His Life and Art,* 1975],

> In formal terms, including ritual and social acquaintanceships, his sympathies were all with the high church. There is no doubt about that, and there is equally no doubt that this cut right across his political sympathies. In all the Barsetshire novels he is, as Victorian politicians would have called it, crossing his vote. In politics he was a Whiggish liberal, conservative about social matters, genuinely liberal about racial issues and (unlike most English intellectuals) the American Civil War. Eleven years after *Barchester Towers* he stood as a Liberal candidate for Parliament.

Given that "national politics and Church of England politics were still not separated from each other," we can expect ambivalence on this score too in the Barsetshire novels, then, and perhaps more than one example of Trollope's "crossing his vote," particularly in the area of politics, and particularly since the Reform Bill had determined a new taste-in-morality. But we will find little evidence anywhere to indicate that he abandons the "high-and-dry." Further, the careful reader cannot fail to recognize that good taste in some of the leading characters in *Barchester Towers* is one of the things that keeps the High Church high. On the other hand, in matters of social class, *Barchester Towers* provides a harbinger of an even greater ambivalence, to be reflected in Trollope's later novels. "Intellectually," says Robert Polhemus, "[Trollope] dislikes the idea of class and favors eventual equality; emotionally he is scared to death of the lower classes and has visions of crowds smashing decent order and property." As it happens, if exhibited self-consciously and used as a too-obvious marker of social class, "good taste" in *Barchester Towers* becomes almost as ridiculous as does the most inappropriate of social transgressions; but the breach of taste, because it is persistently perceived as reflective of a deficiency in moral character, remains in this novel the more serious offense.

A close reading of *Barchester Towers* reveals that Trollope has given the reader four clusters of "taste" into which the characters gather. Two clusters are represented by the main characters in the book who are essentially concerned with the power struggle between the High and Low Churches. There is embodied in Dr. Grantly, Mrs. Grantly, Eleanor Bold, the elder Stanhopes (including Charlotte), Mr. Harding, and Mr. Arabin all the elements

of decorum which, not too surprisingly, align themselves with a belief in the high-and-dry church. The laws that Dr. Grantly has set down in his clerical role, for example, are those which are "not unpalatable to the gentleman," and even when he finds his own position threatened, or finds himself dangerously angry, he still sees to it that he behaves himself. The best example of Dr. Grantly as a standard of taste (and perhaps of Trollope's ambivalence as well) appears at the beginning of the book, when the would-be bishop is torn between a genuine concern for his father's health and a guilt-ridden wish that his father will die in a hurry, enabling him to secure the bishopric. While Dr. Grantly's taste has hypocritical underpinnings here, and although the narrator makes us laugh at him, we nonetheless applaud his self-control and tend to forgive him his revealing conflict, grief and ambition being what they are. And further on, after losing the bishopric and even after the ecclesiastical horror of the first meeting with the Proudies and Mr. Slope, Dr. Grantly maintains what he perceives as his dignity when he shares his anger only with his good friend Mr. Harding and with the heavens. He realizes himself that the reason he is most angry is because the political situation is going to put him in the indecorous position of having to deal with Mr. Slope:

> Dr. Grantly did not let himself down low enough to talk about Dr. Proudie, but he saw that he would have to talk about the other members of his household, the coadjutor bishops, who had brought his lordship down, as it were, in a box, and were about to handle the wires as they willed. This in itself was a terrible vexation to the archdeacon. Could he have ignored the chaplain and have fought the bishop, there would have been, at any rate, nothing degrading in such a contest. Let the Queen make whom she would Bishop of Barchester; a man, or even an ape, when once a bishop, would be a respectable adversary, if he would but fight, himself. But what was such a person as Dr. Grantly to do when such another person as Mr. Slope was put forward as his antagonist?

If good taste provides important lines of demarcation for Dr. Grantly, as Trollope makes us believe it does, then of what use is it in an arena where the strength of it carries no weight? We see a similar frustration again in Dr. Grantly at the Ullathorne fete; when he hears that his sister-in-law has arrived with the slippy-slidy Mr. Slope, he is appalled:

> "It is perfectly shameful, or, I should rather say, shameless. She was brought here as my guest, and if she be determined to disgrace herself, she should have feeling enough not to do so before my immediate friends. I wonder how that man got himself invited. I wonder whether she had the face to bring him."

Decorum prevents Dr. Grantly from pulling Eleanor away by the hair, however, and he expresses his anger most sedately only to Mr. Arabin, who is one of his own. Even though we know Grantly's judgments about Eleanor are incorrect, because he is so powerless in the situation, and because we are led by the narrator to admire his restraint, we are correspondingly by association drawn to sympathize with the side of the High Church and to look down upon the Low, as represented by Slope *et al.* Despite Grantly's personal limitations—his stuffiness, his silent hypocrisy—his alignment with the appellation of "gentleman," given to the reader by a narrator who provides no evidence of unreliability, pulls the judgment in Grantly's favor. Further, that judgment is based upon assumptions in the culture which have their seeds in classical ethics. Edith Hamilton [in her *The Roman Way,* 1957] observed the connection: "The gentleman, the English gentleman, who has meant much to many generations, may well have had his beginnings in, certainly he was fostered by, the English schoolboy's strenuous drilling in Cicero. . . . To pass from Cicero . . . is rather like passing from Archdeacon Grantly and the pleasant people of Barset. . . . "

As it turns out, the other characters who exemplify, in their behavior and in their dress, those classical standards of restraint in their tastes are also allied with High Church beliefs. Mrs. Grantly, who "had never talked too loudly of earls and countesses, or boasted that she gave her governess sixty pounds a year, or her cook seventy," serves as the archdeacon's counterpart in propriety. Eleanor Bold, in contrast to the politically manipulative Mrs. Proudie or the sexually manipulative Signora Neroni, is a further example of tasteful womanhood in that she is, above all, largely silent, and her impact as a woman is not immediate but can even be recollected in tranquility: she is noticed in the observer's own sweet time. Her only lapse occurs when she wallops Mr. Slope for his indelicate advances, and even though the reader may feel that Slope deserves whatever he gets, the narrator still chastises Eleanor and, speaking from an omniscient loft, very nearly makes her apologize:

> She should not have raised her hand against the man. Ladies' hands, so soft, so sweet, so delicious to the touch, so graceful to the eye, so gracious in their gentle doings, were not made to belabour men's faces. The moment the deed was done Eleanor felt she had sinned against all propriety, and would have given little worlds to recall the blow. In her first agony of sorrow she all but begged the man's pardon. Her next impulse, however, and the one which she obeyed, was to run away.

Likewise, the parent Stanhopes and their elder daughter Charlotte, all products of an early English High Church upbringing, do not lack taste, for all their other drawbacks. Dr. Stanhope's "dress was always unexceptionable," and his "good taste" includes a discriminating palate. He is "an accomplished judge of wine" who "never [drinks] to excess," and is "a most inexorable critic in all affairs touching the kitchen." Mrs. Stanhope, in tandem, knows "the great architectural secret of decorating her construction and never descend[s] to construct a decoration," and Charlotte Stanhope, at the matronly age of thirty-five, "no way affect[s] the graces of youth."

Self-effacing to a fault, Mr. Harding, another representative of the "high-and-dry," allows his living to be tossed about rather than make himself unseemingly aggressive. Yet he comes closest to a display of anger when he is forced, as was Grantly before him, to lower himself to negotiate with Mr. Slope:

> [Mr. Harding] had never rated very high his own abilities or activity; but all the feelings of his heart were with the old clergy, and any antipathies of which his heart was susceptible were directed against those new, busy, uncharitable, self-lauding men, of whom Mr. Slope was so good an example.

Indeed, it is easy to see Mr. Slope as a literary descendant of Jane Austen's Mr. Collins; and since we are viewing Trollope's narrator's "new, busy, uncharitable, self-lauding men" through the eyes of a generous and gentle Mr. Harding, we are all the more likely to take sides. Therefore, when Mr. Slope signs off a letter to Mr. Harding, "Believe me to be, / My dear Mr. Harding, / Your assured friend," we understand why Mr. Harding is offended:

> Mr. Harding neither could nor would believe anything of the sort, and he thought, moreover, that Mr. Slope was rather impertinent to call himself by such a name. His assured friend, indeed! How many assured friends generally fall to the lot of a man in this world? And by what process are they made? And how much of such process had taken place as yet between Mr. Harding and Mr. Slope?

Again, the author presents for his reader an example of propriety that is hard to argue with, in that an intimacy that is thus immediate negates a true sort of intimacy dependent upon trial and time. One even hears echoes of Aristotle on "Friendship." As a result, the reader feels not only a sympathy for the impotence of Mr. Harding in such a situation, but also a sympathy for the impotence of a church position which demands decorum on the part of its adherents in circumstances wherein such standards of behavior no longer count.

And finally, Dr. Arabin is similarly careful to stay within the bound of good taste. His views of apostolic succession, though presumably based on religious right, have overtones of a near-genetic snobbery, i.e. nobody has the right to be a clergyman unless he is consecrated at the end of what can only appear as a hereditary chain. He knows not to ask for minor repairs at St. Ewold's, however, and leaves such matters to Dr. Grantly's discretion, in sharp contrast to the tasteless demands of the Proudies regarding their own clerical residence. Arabin knows, as the Proudies do not, that from Grantly's point of view it is tasteful to offer help and tasteless to ask for it. Further, for Dr. Arabin, even laughter has its crassness. "A joke that required to be laughed at was, with him, not worth uttering." Although the priggishness of both Arabin and Grantly does not encourage us as readers to feel any great affection for them, their self-restraint lures us into choosing them over the sweaty Mr. Slope or the pushy Mrs. Proudie.

I have said that these two clusters of "taste," as exhibited in **Barchester Towers,** represent the war between the High and Low Church. Were we to put those clusters along a spectrum, with "bad taste" at the left progressing linearly to "good taste" on the right, we would find the High Church folk to the right, but not so far to the right that they might present a ludicrous extreme. They are to be taken seriously, and the decorum which they exhibit is, as shown above, in many cases laudable. To the left of the spectrum, but again, not so far left as to be entirely ludicrous, are the Proudies and Mr. Slope. It would seem that Trollope wishes his reader to take these characters seriously, too, but clearly conveys to us that the taste of these characters is appalling. It is in the Proudies and Mr. Slope that bad taste operates hand in hand with Low Church political ambition and success, and we are therefore led to hold in suspicion not only the behavior and dress of these characters but also, again by association, their religious position. The "old reddish brown" curtains of the Grantly bishopric have been replaced with "gaudy buff-coloured trumpery moreen," and we are told, by the narrator, that the Proudies' new sofa is a "horrid chintz affair." Mrs. Grantly has her own horses, while "Mrs. Proudie had been hitherto jobbed about the streets of London at so much a month during the season."

And, naturally, it is not only in matters of fashion that the Proudies are errant, but in matters of behavior as well. Mrs. Proudie, particularly, is spared little mercy in the narrator's view of her womanhood: "In truth, Mrs. Proudie was all but invincible; had she married Petruchio, it may be doubted whether that arch-wife-tamer would have been able to keep her legs out of those garments which are presumed by men to be peculiarly unfitted for feminine use." While it is true that Trollope attempts occasionally to forgive Mrs. Proudie her obnoxious behavior, the narrative attempts are lame when set beside the characterization and may have come about only because Trollope might have found it extravagant so to debase any lady, even a fictional lady, however much that lady may have transgressed propriety. That she tries to run everything ends up being less a transgression on her part than on that of the husband who is so weak as to allow her to get away with it.

As for Mr. Slope, we are led to see that there is nothing less attractive or less reassuring than the manipulation of feelings to secure political patronage or money, which Mr. Slope most assuredly does in his pursuit of Eleanor Bold. And those most susceptible to having their feelings manipulated are, of course, the women. "No man—that is, no gentleman—," the narrator tells us, "could possibly be attracted by Mr. Slope, or consent to sit at the feet of so abhorrent a Gamaliel."

If we keep the spectrum of "taste" in mind, we can see that what Trollope is portraying is an inevitable blurring of the center demarcation line, not only in matters of taste, but also in matters of religion. What is threatening about Mr. Slope is that, despite his bad taste, he comes perilously close to assuming the power the narrator obviously feels belongs rightfully to the representatives of the High Church. Although the "gentlemen" are able to see through Slope, the ladies cannot, at least not right away, which enables him to thrive and spread his word almost anywhere. From the narrator's point of view, it would seem clear that someone so "tasteless" (which, as we have

seen, means "lacking in moral character"), should never be allowed to be closely allied to the center of clerical power, a belief expressed both by Dr. Grantly and by Mr. Harding. Though we are called upon by the narrator more than once to laugh at both the Proudies and Mr. Slope, and to scorn their pretentiousness, we never dismiss them as mere objects of ridicule.

At the polar ends of the spectrum of taste, Trollope moves away from the struggle for power and puts his readers into much more comfortable territory. Less is at stake in these netherlands, and through such minor characters the author is able to create some of his best scenes. To the far right of the scale, exemplifying a taste so closely allied with blood that it has become ridiculous even in the Victorian age, are Mr. and Miss Thorne of Ullathorne (Sir Leicester Dedlock of *Bleak House* falls into this same category). It is with the Ullathorne clan that Trollope begins to move more into politics (the Corn Laws, game preservation), predictably "crossing his vote," and it is with the antics of the Ullathorne fete that we see outdated standards of taste (those most closely allied with "good blood") carried to a silly extreme:

> They were, and felt themselves to be, the only true depositaries left of certain Eleusinian mysteries, of certain deep and wondrous services of worship by which alone the gods could be rightly approached. To them and them only was it now given to know these things and to perpetuate them, if that might still be done, by the careful and secret education of their children.

Mr. Thorne's favorite family battle is "written on vellum and illustrated in a most costly manner," and his position on the spectrum is so extreme as to be otherworldly and therefore foolish:

> He looked on [men whose families were of recent date] as great millionaires are apt to look on those who have small incomes; as men who have Sophocles at their fingers' end regard those who know nothing of Greek. They might doubtless be good sort of people, entitled to much praise for virtue, very admirable for talent, highly respectable in every way, but they were without the one great good gift. Such was Mr. Thorne's way of thinking on this matter; nothing could atone for the loss of good blood; nothing could neutralize its good effect.

Whatever considerations of taste are allied with the Thornes are laughable to Trollope, since their politics (of which, as we have seen, the author does not entirely approve) are growing weaker by the day and since their concern is more with blood than religion. It is noteworthy, however, that those good bloodlines demand a certain amount of respect from the novel's characters, a respect that is apart from the ridicule. Everybody, from the Grantlys to the Lookalofts, attends the Ullathorne party and at least tolerates the grotesque games which Miss Thorne forces on her guests, which games are a feeble and funny attempt to fortify a swiftly passing reverence for genealogy. Interestingly, it is through the Thornes that Trollope demonstrates the decline of the "estate," as well as the decline of the eighteenth-century view of what such an estate signifies. The description of the Thornes' home covers several pages in **Barchester Towers,** and the reader is supposed to be charmed:

> The windows opened on to the full extent of the lovely trim garden; immediately before the windows were plots of flowers in stiff, stately, stubborn little beds, each bed surrounded by a stone coping of its own; beyond, there was a low parapet wall on which stood urns and images, fawns, nymphs, satyrs, and a whole tribe of Pan's followers; and then again, beyond that, a beautiful lawn sloped away to a sunk fence which divided the garden from the park. . . . It is the colour of Ullathorne that is so remarkable. It is all of that delicious tawny hue which no stone can give, unless it has on it the vegetable richness of centuries. Strike the wall with your hand and you will think that the stone has on it no covering, but rub it carefully and you will find that the colour comes off upon your finger. No colourist that ever yet worked from a palette has been able to come up to this rich colouring of years crowding themselves on years.

Though Trollope ridicules the Thornes' reverence for genealogy, the narrative tone here reveals a wistfulness regarding the loss of such "richness of centuries." The aesthetics of Fitzwilliam Darcy's Pemberley find their echoes in Ullathorne, but the reader sees in **Barchester Towers** that the "estate," as well as the bloodlines and the accumulated aesthetics behind the creation of such an estate, has had its day. The classical standards in this case are sacrificed to the new taste-as-morality, inasmuch as the two cannot comfortably coexist.

At the other end of the scale, we see the elements of "bad taste" most actively embodied in the Lookalofts and in the younger Stanhopes. The Lookaloft women leap the "ha ha" and appear nearly bare-breasted in the drawing room, while Madeline Neroni and Bertie Stanhope, who have largely been reared in Italy, exhibit an alarming lack of English delicacy in both their behavior and dress, implying a damaged upbringing presumably brought about by an itinerant way of life. Signora Neroni's visiting card displays the worst possible taste, in that it reflects a name (Vesey) and a coronet to which, as the narrator is careful to remind us, she has no right. Her clothing further reveals a lack of judicious self-control:

> Across her brow she wore a band of red velvet, on the centre of which shone a magnificent Cupid in mosaic, the tints of whose wings were of the most lovely azure, and the colour of whose cheeks the clearest pink. On the one arm which her position required her to expose she wore three magnificent bracelets, each of different stones.

Through the use of superlatives, Trollope lets his reader know his general opinion of the Signora's taste. Further, her sexual parlaying with all available men persists in reminding everyone that sexuality is some sort of excrescence that does not necessarily have anything to do with love-leading-to-marriage. That her sexual power extends to pious clergymen and that she makes public use of this power is anathema both to "good breeding" and Christianity. That she exposes the weaknesses of the pious about her does not, in the view of the narrator, excuse her behavior.

And while Bertie Stanhope's do-nothingness is not necessarily in bad taste, his dilettantism regarding religion and education certainly is. The facility with which Bertie changes religions, for example, indicates a certain excessiveness; to talk about it is worse, and when he exposes his laudatory beliefs about German professors, we find that the reigning clergy of Barchester "could not condescend to discuss such a matter with a young man with such clothes and such a beard." Further, the narrator tells us that Bertie had none of the " 'mauvaise honte' of an Englishman" and that his clothes were "always totally opposed in every principle of colour and construction to the dress of those with whom he for the time consorted." Bertie is rather a dandy, with all that term implies, and represents how carefully Trollope studied the "silver-fork" novels of Bulwer and Disraeli.

The important thing about the Lookalofts and the younger Stanhopes is that we have been somehow led by the narrator to like them, or at least to like them better than the Proudies or Mr. Slope, in spite of their taste. We are even led to admire Madeline's spidering and Bertie's bungling, not only because they seem harmless enough in a charming sort of way, but because they set off the hypocritical superiority of those Low Church characters for whom Trollope's narrator has little sympathy—the Proudies, Mr. Slope, and their respective entourages. Madeline is even capable of illustrating that the stuffiness of Mr. Arabin and the blood-supremacy of Mr. Thorne can be "brought down" through her sexuality. The Lookalofts and the younger Stanhopes commit the ultimate sin of taste in that they are "flashy," but because they are not really threatening in any religious or political sense (the Lookaloft father will have none of this pretense, Madeline's temptation of Dr. Arabin is temporary, and Bertie Stanhope simply does not care), the reader regards them with untainted amusement, as in the case of the Ullathorne crew at the other end of the spectrum. These represent impinging fringes, and Trollope leads his readers to delight in their ability to discomfit and horrify the vying groups in the middle. The desecration of the bishop's office with the installation of the gaudy curtains was not funny; Bertie's and Madeline's desecration of the Proudie drawing room clearly is.

It is at the Proudie reception and at the Ullathorne picnic that we can see the clusters of taste in operation all at once. And if we tip the spectrum up on end, at the base of it we find Madeline tastelessly seducing, Bertie tastelessly babbling and stumbling, and the Lookalofts eliciting sneers from almost everybody. Mrs. Proudie occupies a "higher" cluster because she is able to peer down on the Lookalofts and the younger Stanhopes. Above these, Trollope gives us the Grantlys and their High Church crowd, who have the advantage of a high vantage point from which they can look down on Mrs. Proudie looking down on everyone else. And finally, at the very top are the Ullathornes, who are floating around up there in their own ether, somewhat pathetically looking down on everything. It is through such a hierarchy that the reader finds those with no political or religious power (whether they have no taste or an overabundance) to be ridiculous, those with good taste and political/religious power to be worthy of some admiration and preservation (the Grantlys and the Arabins do survive, after all), and those with bad taste and an inclination toward or a prospect of political/religious power to be unpleasant at best and, at worst, potentially dangerous.

Finally, a close look at the clusters of "taste" in Trollope's novel serves to illustrate that the use of a "rhetoric of taste" in literature can be a sneaky business. Although some may believe that there is "virtually no beating of the propagandist air in *Barchester Towers*" [Michael Sadlier, *Anthony Trollope: A Commentary,* 1927], I would have to disagree. If the narrator is good at it, as Trollope's is, we may find ourselves disapproving of a character's politics or religion without knowing quite why, until we realize that the author has been snide about the way that character decorates himself or outfits his carriage. Such "tastelessness" tends then to spill over into everything else that character does, so that, his bad taste already having been established, his ideas are now questionable, as are his politics, his religion, his friends, and so on.

Although it would be unlikely for a reader to negate Trollope's narrator's view of Mr. Slope and Mrs. Proudie, that reader cannot so comfortably condemn or praise the other characters. Given the narrative stance in *Barchester Towers,* however, we can disagree or agree more quickly with the ideas presented as a part of these characters without giving the merits or demerits of the ideas themselves much rational consideration. If we should begin a reading of *Barchester Towers* with Low Church sympathies, for example, we are likely to feel accused very soon of having "bad taste" as well. For this reason, I feel that most readers find themselves drawn to the side of the High Church in the novel, whatever their religious or political sympathies may be in their own worlds. In such a way does Trollope admit polemics with impunity, and in such a way, perhaps, is a reader polemicized unawares.

Finally, what Trollope's "rhetoric of taste" demonstrates to the reader is that people without the classical standards of taste are to be expected and accepted in the modern age, but that such people should be discouraged from occupying positions determining morality, since their questionable taste, in matters of aesthetics as well as behavior, identifies them as inevitably lacking in moral character. (pp. 38-50)

> *Gay Sibley, "The Spectrum of 'Taste' in 'Barchester Towers',"* in Studies in the Novel, *Vol. XVII, No. 1, Spring, 1985, pp. 38-52.*

Jane Nardin   (essay date 1986)

[*In the following essay, Nardin argues that* Barchester Towers *represents Trollope's least progressive and most unsympathetic portrayal of women.*]

"There is abundant evidence of antifeminism in Trollope's novels," remark the authors of a recent study [Richard Barickman, Susan MacDonald, and Myra Stark, *Corrupt*

Relations: Dickens, Thackeray, Trollope, Collins, and the Victorian Sexual System, 1982]. But, they argue, despite the unsympathetic tone often adopted by Trollope's narrators when discussing women's rights, his novels generally display a sustained and sympathetic interest in women unhappy with their restricted lives. When we look closely at the novels we see that "symbolic patterns quietly emerge and alter the very substance of the [antifeminist] surface narrative." Robert Polhemus [see excerpt dated 1980] makes a similar point about *Barchester Towers* (1857) when he argues that the narrator of this novel "poses as conventional himself, and then shows [through the story he tells] how conventions either need reform or are shifting." It seems to me, however, that the symbolic patterns concerning women's capabilities and choices that emerge from *Barchester Towers* in fact do not, as in many of Trollope's later works, undermine the conventional views that the narrator explicitly espouses. Conventions concerning a woman's proper place are indeed under attack in this novel, with its vivid portrayal of several rebellious or domineering female characters. But the patterning of events and motives in *Barchester Towers* suggests that return to an earlier mode of relations between the sexes, not reform of that mode, is desirable. Tensions between the implications of one subplot and those of another, between the narrator's pronouncements and the feelings of his characters, so important in Trollope's later work, especially where women are concerned, are far less daringly exploited in this early novel.

Perhaps Trollope never wrote a story more closely resembling classic stage comedy than the subplot of *Barchester Towers* concerning the love affair between Eleanor Bold and Mr. Arabin. Misunderstandings, strange inhibitions, failed meetings, and the interference of aging relatives and unwanted suitors prolong the romance in a stagy, almost farcical, manner that Trollope rarely employs in other novels. It is, as the narrator remarks, a "comedy of errors." But although the basic conflict in this subplot is the disagreement between Eleanor and her elders about whom she should associate with, and ultimately marry, Trollope is not here imitating the time-honored comic plot in which innocent young lovers are kept apart by the tyranny of corrupt parents or guardians, and by the values of an old order in need of reform. Instead it is Eleanor's own faulty moral values and errors of judgment that must be corrected before she and Mr. Arabin can come together. And her values are mistaken precisely because they are excessively, stupidly progressive.

Barchester Towers is a profoundly conservative novel which embodies its most positive values in the elderly Mr. Harding, who loves the past, respects the wisdom of tradition, and accepts a certain degree of human imperfection as an inevitable part of the nature of things—a man who has learned from experience that we must be tolerant, since we can never be perfect. The other members of the "high and dry" church party in Barchester share Mr. Harding's affection for tradition and his urbane tolerance, but they lack the gift for self-doubt which prevents his conservatism from becoming complacency, and his tolerance a willingness to condone injustice. The novel's villains—and it comes much closer than most Trollope novels to having actual villains—are power-loving, low-church reformers who would like to cart away the rubbish of centuries, as the worst of them, Mr. Slope, likes to call the wisdom of the past, replacing it with shallow nostrums for moral and social improvement designed by themselves.

When Slope preaches a sermon attacking cathedral services from the very pulpit of Barchester Cathedral itself, Mr. Harding, unwilling as he usually is to criticize, knows that this sort of frontal attack on ancient custom and those who love it is simply wrong. The maintenance of civility is more important than the promulgation of any private view of truth, however progressive. "It can hardly be the duty of a young man rudely to assail the religious convictions of his elders in the church," Mr. Harding tells his daughter when she suggests that Slope must have felt duty bound to express his convictions. "Courtesy should have kept him silent, even if neither charity nor modesty could do so."

Trollope does not suggest that every custom passed on from the remote past is rational or just. In *Barchester Towers,* as in other novels where this sort of issue arises, he demonstrates a keen awareness of the absurdities and inequities of many customs, and gently mocks the tendency of Englishmen, especially prosperous ones, to view radical injustices, in church patronage or parliamentary representation, for example, as charmingly picturesque. Nonetheless, there is no doubt that the emphasis in *Barchester Towers* falls on the overconfidence of those who would tamper boldly with the past, rather than on the complacency of those who love it. And Mr. Harding, who is willing to sacrifice to his sense of justice any personal advantage he might gain from the quirky traditions of the Anglican Church, shows us that a morally sensitive man can love the past without complacency. This being so, it is not surprising that Trollope cannot incorporate into this particular novel a comic plot in which the corrupt values of the past, espoused by the older generation, block the joyous conclusion.

In the main plot of *Barchester Towers,* which deals with the battle for ecclesiastical power in Barchester between the ascendant forces of the new bishop, Dr. Proudie, and the declining forces of the old-fashioned "high and dry" churchman, Archdeacon Grantly, the meddlesome arrogance of the former is, for the most part, defeated and exposed. And the comic love plot mirrors the main plot, as it tells of a woman whose head is turned when she acquires power, who tries to meddle with matters not suited to her sex, realizes that she has overreached herself, and finds happiness by finally submitting to the restrictions which tradition has placed upon women's freedom of action. In this conservative novel, the treatment of women is also conservative. *Barchester Towers'* comedy of errors begins when a woman tries to think and act for herself.

Eleanor Bold has proved a problematic character to many readers of *Barchester Towers.* The narrator's tone in speaking of her is generally indulgent to the point of sentimentality. She is "My Eleanor," or else "Poor Eleanor." She receives praise for her feminine qualities: her sweet mildness, the quiet beauty that grows slowly on those who know her well, her devotion to her first husband and her

grief at his loss. The narrator and several other characters speak of her quick, yet modest intelligence. It is hard to reconcile this chorus of adulation, however, with the impression that Eleanor's misguided or needlessly aggressive deeds and words make on the reader. Hugh Walpole thought she was "Trollope's most tiresome heroine," and many readers have agreed with his judgment. It is hard also to reconcile the narrator's tender remarks about Eleanor with the harsh or contemptuous criticism of her conduct that he occasionally voices.

James Kincaid [in his *The Novels of Anthony Trollope,* 1977] suggests that Eleanor resembles Amelia Sedley in *Vanity Fair,* and that through her character Trollope, like Thackeray, is trying to undermine the very notion of the "angel in the house"—the sweet and devoted wife and mother, whose sweetness, more closely examined, proves to be weakness, and whose devotion to her child reveals itself as a kind of twisted narcissism. Certainly this is true of Amelia, but I think there is a better way of explaining the tensions that characterize Trollope's portrayal of Eleanor. Instead of undermining the notion of the angel, Trollope implies through Eleanor's story that the angel role is indeed the appropriate one even for an intelligent young woman. She makes her mistake in assuming that she has the capacity to become something more than an angel. Eleanor's often-praised intelligence is a feminine intelligence, adequate to the demands of a homebound existence focused on "dresses, or babies, or legs of mutton," but not equal to charting an independent line of conduct in the world of ecclesiastical politics. Eleanor's misguided attempts to go beyond the angel role cause her problems and connect her morally with the arrogant overreachers of the main plot, Mr. Slope and Mrs. Proudie. The narrator may find Eleanor's eternal baby worship a bit tiresome, but his affection for her turns to real disapproval only when she tries to act independently in the world at large.

When *Barchester Towers* opens, Eleanor has just lost her husband after a short marriage. Further, she is rich, for he has left nearly a thousand a year entirely at her disposal. Up to this point, she has been a true angel, sweet and submissive. When she lived at home she "declared that whatever her father did should in her eyes be right," and after she chose to marry a highly imperfect man, she loved his very faults "as the parasite plant will follow even the defects of the trunk which it embraces." Eleanor is well-suited to this conventional Victorian role as ivy, and according to the narrator she performs it charmingly and successfully. But independence goes to her head, and she begins to think she can become an oak.

Mr. Harding, never very comfortable in the exercise of authority, is relieved to conclude that marriage and widowhood have emancipated Eleanor from his control. Even when he mistakenly concludes that she is going to marry the odious Slope, he convinces himself that he has no right to prevent the marriage. Thus, when *Barchester Towers* opens, Eleanor is for the first time in her life subject to no male authority. Intoxicated with freedom, she resents the one man who still presumes to criticize her and to offer guidance: her brother-in-law, Archdeacon Grantly. The archdeacon is an overbearing man and Eleanor "had never accustomed herself to be very abject before him." But it is only after her husband's death that Eleanor begins to find Dr. Grantly's authority more than she can bear and to rebel openly against it.

Her desire to resist the archdeacon and begin thinking for herself leaves Eleanor wide open to Mr. Slope's blandishments. Slope is an adept at manipulating bored, excitable women, the narrator tells us: "He knows how to say a soft word in the proper place; he knows how to adapt his flattery to the ears of his hearers . . . Could Mr. Slope have adapted his manners to men as well as to women . . . he might have risen to great things." Slope gets under Eleanor's guard by praising her father and her baby, and the fulsomeness of his praise fails to strike this morally tone deaf woman as odd. As the battle over ecclesiastical power and preferment between the high and low church parties in Barchester takes shape, Eleanor aligns herself with Slope and tries to convince her father to cooperate with Slope's reformist plans for Hiram's Hospital. She goes so far as to encourage Mr. Harding to add a Sabbath-day school to the establishment—ignoring both the fact that these rigidly repressive schools are absolute anathema to the high-church party, and the strangeness of appending one of them to a home for the aged. Like the novel's other reformers, Eleanor chooses the side of "progress" largely because it offers wider scope for her own energies.

Eleanor is unwilling to surrender her basically positive opinion of Slope, even though all her male friends, and her sensible elder sister, Mrs. Grantly, agree in their judgment of him, and even though his twistings and turnings as he tries to convince her of his sincerity in the matter of the hospital appointment are clearly too tortuous to be compatible with real honesty. So she convinces herself that her friends are motivated by an insane partisan zeal which prevents them from acknowledging the real virtues that underlie Slope's oily manner. "I never saw anything like you clergymen," she tells Mr. Arabin sententiously. "You wage your wars about trifles so bitterly." Only she herself, Eleanor implies, stands above party and in a spirit of charity tries to see the virtues of both sides. Eleanor's sin is spiritual pride, and in order to maintain her pride, she systematically represses her misgivings about Slope. The sense of superiority to Dr. Grantly, and the scope for independent action which her championship of Slope gives her, are too precious to relinquish. "You think Mr. Slope is a messenger direct from Satan. I think he is an industrious, well meaning clergyman. It's a pity that we differ as we do," she tells the archdeacon smugly.

Eleanor is wrong not only about Slope's character, but also about his motives for seeking her out. *Barchester Towers* has barely opened before Eleanor has acquired two suitors, Mr. Slope and Bertie Stanhope, who want her only for her money. Neither Slope, nor Bertie's sister Charlotte, who takes upon herself the task of active wooing which Bertie is too lackadaisical to pursue, is at all a subtle suitor, yet Eleanor completely fails to realize what they are after. Everyone else in the book understands Slope's and Bertie's intentions perfectly and Dr. Grantly goes so far as to warn Eleanor that Slope wants to marry her—a suggestion she repudiates indignantly. Eleanor is

an obvious target for fortune hunters, and if she herself fails to see this, it is not entirely feminine delicacy, or devotion to her late husband—as the narrator sympathetically suggests on various occasions—that cause her blindness, but in addition a startling lack of worldly wisdom. The once sheltered young girl and wife thinks she is equipped to defy advice from her elders, but she is quite mistaken.

Eleanor, indeed, is so confused about the issues she wishes to judge for herself that she flirts simultaneously with the rigid, low-church sabbatarianism of the Proudie party, and the infidelity of the Stanhope family, without any sense that she is being inconsistent. Dr. Stanhope, a well-connected clerical pluralist, has for years lived a luxuriously purposeless life on the shores of Lake Como, while curates perform the work of his various parishes. In the Stanhopes the virtues of the high-church party, tolerance and a willingness to accept imperfection, are carried so far that they become vices. Through Dr. Stanhope, Trollope explores the dangers of accepting the authority of a tradition solely because one benefits from it. All the novel's high churchmen, except Mr. Harding, incur some guilt on this point, but only Dr. Stanhope is open to the charge of using the church establishment with complete selfishness. Because they have seen their father cynically exploit the positions that time-honored customs of church patronage conferred upon him, Dr. Stanhope's three children have become skeptics who will not grant moral authority to traditional customs or beliefs. Charlotte has no religion, while Bertie moves easily from Judaism, to Catholicism, and then back to Anglicanism. Madeline Stanhope Neroni scoffs at women who fail to examine critically the customs by which they have been told to live. "She is just one of those English nonentities who would tie her head up in a bag for three months every summer, if her mother and grandmother had tied up their heads before her. It would never occur to her to think whether there was any use in submitting to such a nuisance," she remarks of Eleanor. In her flirtation with Slope, Eleanor aligns herself with those who would reform tradition; in her flirtation with the Stanhopes, she aligns herself, even more dangerously, with those who dismiss it. In both cases she rejects her own friends in order to indulge a confused inclination towards modern thought.

Like Mr. Slope, Charlotte Stanhope, listlessly seconded by Bertie, flatters Eleanor, and in this case too, Eleanor is taken in by the flattery even after she has been warned against it. The domineering manner in which the archdeacon offered his advice against Mr. Slope irritated Eleanor, but she has less excuse for disregarding the gently tactful hints of her beloved sister-in-law, Mary Bold, that the Stanhopes are unfit companions. Mary "had positively discouraged the friendship of the Stanhopes as far as her usual gentle mode of speaking had permitted. Eleanor had only laughed at her, however, when she . . . suggested that Charlotte Stanhope never went to church."

Eleanor's determination to reject the advice of her elders, in combination with her blindness concerning the motives of those who court her, ends on the day when she receives proposals from Bertie and Slope. Both proposals are fairly insulting: Bertie tells Eleanor he would rather she did not accept, and Slope, taking her acceptance for granted, embraces her. Eleanor slaps his face—an act which the narrator justifiably sees as logically concluding the course of unfeminine self-assertion in which she has indulged herself. "It were to be wished devoutly that she had not struck Mr. Slope . . . Had she been brought up by any sterner mentor than that fond father, had she lived longer under the rule of a husband, she might, perhaps, have saved herself from this great fault. . . . She was too keen in the feeling of independence, a feeling dangerous for a young woman, but one in which her position peculiarly tempted her to indulge." Eleanor's attempt to leave the safe enclosures of tradition for the high road of progress, ends in a total mess: "There was no one to whom she could turn for comfort."

This angel who tried to leave the house must beat a hasty retreat in order to achieve the happy marriage that will fittingly conclude her comic subplot. For Eleanor's arrogance and desire for power have been the main obstacles to her union with Mr. Arabin from the very start. Her championship of Slope, whose designs on her she was criminally slow to perceive, discouraged the modest Arabin from pursuing her. Her huffy dignity constantly postponed the inevitable rapprochement between them. Further, Eleanor's dislike of the condescending tone in which Mr. Arabin speaks to women—although, in her case at least, such condescension proves exaggerated rather than inappropriate—retards the development of her affection for him.

Clearly Mr. Arabin, a celibate follower of the Oxford movement, who narrowly escaped "going over" to Rome, must learn that a good wife can be as important to a clergyman as to any other man. He must stop thinking of women as if they "were little more . . . than children," stop seeing them "in the same light that one sees them regarded by many Romish priests." His doing so is a part of his return to the Anglican traditions from which he had strayed under Newman's influence. And so Arabin's new view of women is a highly conventional one. He is now prepared to grant them their "proper" place. Eleanor, he says, "would well grace any man's house" and he wants her to grace his. But ultimately the comic conclusion comes about less because Arabin realizes that he needs an angel in his house, or because he overcomes his shyness, than because Eleanor finally decides to sacrifice her pride in order to win him. He was ready to accept her long before her manner gave him any encouragement; her perversity, not his, delayed their engagement.

Trollope's desire to make this point as unambiguously as possible seems the only explanation of the scene in which Madeline Neroni decides to advise Eleanor about her relationship with Mr. Arabin. Despite Eleanor's flirtations with unconventional behavior, she is still far too repressed to appeal to the intelligent, experienced, and courageous Madeline. And Madeline also reveals a catty jealousy of Eleanor's attractions which makes the interest she takes in Eleanor's fate even more surprising. "What?" says Madeline, on learning that Charlotte proposes a match between Bertie and Eleanor, "that vapid swarthy creature in the widow's cap, who looked as though her clothes had been stuck on her back with a pitchfork!" So it is odd that Madeline should take it upon herself to advise Eleanor. But the incident is important because it contrasts with earlier scenes in which her elders advised Eleanor to pay more attention to the demands of convention. Previously, Eleanor resisted all suggestions that her rebellious behavior might get her into trouble, and resolutely asserted her own dignity and autonomy. Now Madeline tells Eleanor that unless she beats a hasty retreat, she will lose Mr. Arabin—and Eleanor listens.

Eleanor does not like Madeline any better than Madeline likes her and finds the interview between them very humiliating to her pride. Madeline tells Eleanor that though Mr. Arabin is indeed in love with her, he is "simple as a child in these matters," a man with whom "yea will stand for yea, and nay for nay," and with whom, therefore, a woman cannot coquette to prove her power or save her self-respect. Eleanor, realizing that she must "stoop to conquer," is willing for the first time in the novel to bend, because she finally understands that above all things, above her pride, dignity, and autonomy, she needs the right man to love and obey: "A glimmering of a thought came to her also,—that Mr. Arabin was too precious to be lost." Eleanor lets Madeline search her heart and finds that though there has been much in the interview "to vex her proud spirit. . . . there was, nevertheless, an understratum of joy . . . which buoyed her up wondrously." Further, "she fully resolved to follow the advice given her."

And at her next interview with Mr. Arabin, she does. In marked contrast to her earlier manner with this shy lover, Eleanor is now almost abject. Previously, to the narrator's dismay, Eleanor has been too proud to show Mr. Arabin how much she cares by breaking down in front of him, but now she cannot conceal her tears. She puts her hand confidingly on his arm, and looks "slowly, gently, almost piteously up into his face." Mr. Arabin finally takes the hint and the two become engaged. Eleanor's attempt to expand her sphere of action and thought has failed, and she is now prepared for a comic conclusion that is premised on the rightness of her return to the traditional woman's role. After the engagement, Eleanor sees that she "idolized, almost worshipped" Mr. Arabin as she once had her father, and this is the purpose for which her quick, but narrow and essentially imitative intelligence is truly suited. "When the ivy has found its tower . . . we know how the parasite plants grow and prosper. They were not created to stretch forth their branches alone, and endure without protection the summer's sun and the winter's storm. Alone they but spread themselves on the ground, and cower unseen in the dingy shade. But when they have found their firm supporters, how wonderful is their beauty."

And that's that—the pattern of Eleanor's story largely reinforces the conventional terms in which, all along, the narrator has analyzed it. Just as in the main plot of *Barchester Towers* arrogant attempts to meddle with the wisdom of the past deservedly fail, though the wisdom of the past is by no means perfect, so too, in the comic subplot,

Eleanor Bold accepts a marriage proposal from Arabin. Illustration by Paul Hardy.

traditional options for women, though restrictive, are affirmed as appropriate enough. This comedy involves a return to old-fashioned values, and not, as is so often the case with comedy, their reform.

The handling of the novel's other female characters confirms the view of women's possibilities which the comic subplot implies. For **Barchester Towers** exhibits little of the sympathy with women's extra-angelic ambitions we often find in Trollope's later work. The narrator's tone here is more consistently misogynist than is usually the case in Trollope's novels, and there is a lot of rib-digging, anti-feminist humor. Henpecked husbands like Bishop Proudie are trembling, contemptible creatures, and Mrs. Proudie should be categorized as a man "because of her great strength of mind." The narrator sees women as typically petty and hostile to each other. Charlotte Stanhope talks about Eleanor "with that sort of ill-nature which is not uncommon when one woman speaks of another." Women possess an organ by which they "instinctively, as it were, know and feel how other women are regarded by men." With this sort of humor, the narrator castigates the female characters who deviate from traditional standards of feminine propriety in their pursuit of power. He re-

serves a respectful tone only for those women who exercise power in the approved manner. And here, as with the comic subplot, the patterns that emerge from the text tend to support the narrator's views.

A knowledge of her proper place is what separates Susan Grantly, the novel's ideal wife, from Mrs. Proudie, the farcical termagant who meddles far more boldly than Eleanor Bold with ecclesiastical matters, and who tries to exercise within marriage the sort of independent power which Eleanor was unable to claim even as a widow. Because Mrs. Proudie is an immensely amusing character, readers join in the narrator's parting prayer "that she may live forever." And since her husband is quite incapable of independent thought or action, it matters little whether he is ruled by her, by Mr. Slope, or by the Government. Thus Mrs. Proudie's lust for power does little real harm, but this should not blind us to the fact that she exercises power largely for selfish reasons. Ignoring Mr. Harding's completely just claim to the Wardenship of Hiram's Hospital, Mrs. Proudie "gives" the position to Mr. Quiverful simply because she knows he will be a pliant and submissive vassal. The Quiverfuls, with their fourteen children, are deserving, but that has little to do with Mrs. Proudie's championship of them.

The Quiverfuls are reflections of the Proudies and reinforce the point made through Mrs. Proudie about the personal way in which women tend to use power. Mr. Quiverful is not a strong or consistent man, but he *can* see beyond his own interests. Even in his desperate poverty, Quiverful wants "to be right with his own conscience" and so is persuaded to recognize the validity of Mr. Harding's claim to the hospital. But Mrs. Quiverful's conscience has buckled under the pressures of want: "She recked nothing of the imaginary rights of others." Like Mrs. Proudie, with whom she shares tremendous vitality, Mrs. Quiverful cannot see beyond the personal. When she and Mrs. Proudie, between them, prevent Mr. Harding's return to the hospital, they commit an act of injustice. We sympathize with Mrs. Quiverful's dire predicament and thwarted energies, but neither she nor Mrs. Proudie is fit to exercise power outside the domestic sphere.

Susan Grantly, on the other hand, exercises power only in acceptably feminine ways. Her husband, Archdeacon Grantly, contentious and stubborn, is clearly not the easiest man in the world to live with, but Susan has made their marriage a success, giving to Plumstead Rectory an attractive "air of home." She never embarrasses her husband by challenging him openly. Her manner in private disagreement is "mild [and] seducing," and she lets her husband take the credit for her ideas whenever possible. Archdeacon Grantly often domineers, but he values his wife sincerely. When he learns that Arabin is engaged to Eleanor, he tells him tearfully that "if she does her duty by you as her sister does by me, you'll be a happy man." As a married woman, Susan is the example Eleanor must follow, while Mrs. Proudie represents a comic vision of the danger which may menace her if she continues her mistaken ways.

The single—or, in the case of Madeline Neroni, whose husband has disappeared, effectively single—women in

Barchester Towers form a similar pattern of example and warning to Eleanor. The "good" spinster is Miss Monica Thorne, who espouses the novel's conservative values in their most comically extreme form. Miss Thorne and her unmarried brother, the local squire, pride themselves on their Saxon lineage. Miss Thorne longs for the return of the era preceding the Norman conquest, speaks of Addison and Steele "as though they were still living," and in poetry is familiar with no name later than Dryden. The Christian religion, the narrator quips, "was the most modern [reform] of any to which she had as yet acceded."

Initially Miss Thorne appears no less comic than Mrs. Proudie, but as the novel progresses, her feminine kindness, modesty, and desire to make others happy begin to emerge as her most prominent traits. One scene which is crucial in humanizing Miss Thorne for the reader occurs when she is preparing for a fête-champêtre at which she fondly hopes her young guests will play some "Saxon" games, including riding at the quintain. But when she asks her brother to test the quintain for her, he cuts "her to the heart" by refusing to attack "such a rattletrap as that." She quickly recovers from her disappointment and anger, however, by reminding herself of another aspect of her conservative creed: female subservience. "It had ever been one of the rules by which Miss Thorne had regulated her conduct through life, to say nothing that could provoke her brother. . . . The head of the family should never be upbraided in his own house." Miss Thorne's principled self-suppression wins the same sort of response that Susan Grantly's does. Seeing "the tear in her eye," her brother "repented himself of his contemptuous expression" and apologized with sincere remorse.

Miss Thorne "had once declared, in one of her warmer moments, 'that now-a-days the gentlemen were all women, and the ladies all men'." The novel's other important single women, Madeline Neroni and Charlotte Stanhope, not to mention the threatening behavior of Mrs. Proudie and even of Eleanor during much of the novel, suggest that Miss Thorne's fear that traditional sex roles are breaking down ought not to be dismissed as just an irrational, reactionary terror. The structure of **Barchester Towers** implies that as he wrote it Trollope felt similar misgivings.

Like Mrs. Proudie and Mrs. Quiverful, Madeline Neroni and Charlotte Stanhope, independent, rebellious, and amusing, seem initially to undercut the novel's otherwise conservative view of the weaker sex. But I think it is possible to argue that Trollope uses Madeline and Charlotte to parody two mistaken versions of the "angel in the house" figure in order to suggest that submissive tenderness of heart is the one characteristic a true angel has to possess, the one trait that brings a woman happiness. Madeline represents the ornamental aspect of the angel figure, who should, in some versions at least, be beautiful and useless, existing solely to amuse and charm men. Certainly Madeline, witty and beautiful, but so badly crippled as to be completely unfitted for all practical purposes, is an angel in this sense. That Madeline charms by aggressively exploiting her sexuality perhaps emphasizes the discrepancy Trollope sees between the one quality that *really* makes the ornamental angel attractive, and the traits needed by a true and loving wife.

Madeline, however, might have become a better sort of angel, had she not been prevented by a combination of bad conduct and bad luck. In her youth, her unrestrained sexuality got her into trouble and she was left maimed, with an unwanted baby, deserted by her ne'er-do-well husband. Cynical about men and their professions of morality, the exceptionally clever Madeline finds amusement in exposing male hypocrisy. She truly possesses the critical insight and the ability to influence others to which Eleanor mistakenly laid claim. But Madeline is simply "the fruit of the Dead Sea, so sweet and delicious to the eye, so bitter and nauseous to the taste." Apart from occasionally exposing pretense or offering good-natured advice, there is nothing constructive she can do with her intelligence, no sphere apart from marriage to which she can apply it in a sustained way. Nurtured in the experience brought by rebellion and disaster, Madeline's intelligence is a mixed blessing at best—a woman is better off without this kind of mental power, and Madeline, for all her vitality, is very unhappy.

Home is where the heart is, and the heartlessness, which along with their good nature is the Stanhopes' leading characteristic, prevents them from becoming a real family: "It is astonishing how much each of the family was able to do . . . to prevent the well-being of the other four." Charming though Madeline is, she must be expelled from Barchester in the end. The final comment on her fitness for marriage is, appropriately, made by Miss Thorne: "She is a woman all men would like to look at; but few I imagine would be glad to take her to their hearths, even were she unmarried and not afflicted as she is." Though Madeline cleverly dismisses marriage as "tyranny on one side and deceit on the other," it is clear that the grapes are sour. In advising Eleanor not to play the coquette with Mr. Arabin, Madeline exclaims, in an "impassioned way" quite unlike her usual delivery, "what would I not give to be loved in such a way by such a man." Even Madeline would be an angel if she could, and the advice she gives Eleanor is so conventional that it might easily have come from Archdeacon Grantly. Nor is it only in arranging Eleanor and Arabin's match that Madeline aids the forces of tradition in Barchester. She protects the ultra-conservative Mr. Thorne against Slope's mockery, and inadvertently, but most effectively, humiliates Mrs. Proudie by ripping off her train. Surprisingly, Madeline fights on the side of the high church party—a tacit acknowledgement that she regrets her own rebellion against convention.

Charlotte Stanhope parodies a second aspect of the angel figure: the practical homemaker, who like many a Dickens heroine, keeps home bright and alluring by trimming the lamps, sweeping the hearths, and symmetrically arranging the tea trays. Never a beauty, Charlotte at thirty-five has left the ornamental side of angelhood to her sister and "in no way affected the graces of youth." But she runs the household. "She gave the orders, paid the bills, hired and dismissed the domestics, made the tea, carved the meat, and managed everything." Charlotte, however, is no closer to being a real angel than Madeline, for though she caters to the comforts of her family, she does so only with the selfish object of gaining power over them. The true angel makes her comfortable home a school of good moral conduct and loving self-sacrifice, which she teaches by example. Not so Charlotte. "She had aided her father in his indifference to his professional duties . . . She had encouraged her mother in idleness in order that she herself might be mistress and manager of the Stanhope household. She had encouraged and fostered the follies of her sister."

Because of her heartlessness, her mental independence, and her wish for power, and despite her unquestionable talent for the practical feminine arts, the narrator finds Charlotte sexually unclassifiable. "She was a fine young woman; and had she been a man, would have been a very fine young man." Her selfish matchmaking scheme—unlike Madeline's unselfish one—comes to naught, and she returns to Italy, where presumably she belongs. There, under her heartless management, the Stanhope family fortunes will continue to decline. The danger to the family that results when the young women become just like the young men is not as remote as it seemed when Miss Thorne first complained of this disturbing modern trend.

Madeline, Charlotte, Eleanor, and even Mrs. Proudie express dissatisfaction of one sort or another with their allotted places as "angels in the house," but *Barchester Towers* treats their desires for change far less sympathetically than Trollope's later works were often to treat the dissatisfactions of strong and intelligent women, doomed by society to pass restricted, powerless lives. It is hard to see any of them as victims of systematic male repression in the way that Alice Vavasor and Glencora Palliser in *Can You Forgive Her?*, for example, so clearly are. For all her vitality, Mrs. Proudie is little more than a comic butt; Charlotte and Madeline prove that all the abilities in the world will not help a woman to happiness if she lacks tenderness of heart; Eleanor comes to realize that her attempts to evade tradition and male authority were completely misguided. Eleanor retreats and for her the comic conclusion is therefore possible. But these other "new women," like the forces of newness represented by Mr. Slope and the low church party, remain excluded from the conservative rejoicing that marks the novel's close. (pp. 381-93)

> *Jane Nardin, "Conservative Comedy and the Women of 'Barchester Towers'," in* Studies in the Novel, *Vol. XVIII, No. 4, Winter, 1986, pp. 381-94.*

Elizabeth R. Epperly   (essay date 1989)

[*Epperly is a Canadian educator and critic. In the following excerpt, she examines Trollope's use of allusion, repetition, and patterns to define and symbolize the thoughts, attitudes, and actions of characters in* Barchester Towers.]

If we marked in red ink the allusions, clichés, tags, and general repetitions found in *Barchester Towers,* our copy would resemble the red-letter prayer-book Mrs. Proudie thought iniquitous. There are more tags and references, more extensive use of literature and repetitions in this novel than in any of Trollope's other works. Capitalizing

on the style and voice of the moderately successful *The Warden,* Trollope creates in *Barchester Towers* a comic, echoing medley made from cliché and proverb and from Shakespeare, the Bible, Scott, Thackeray, Cooper, Byron, Thomas Tusser, Milton, Sterne, Goldsmith, Henry Taylor, Goethe, Dickens, Fielding, and the classics.

Like its predecessor *The Warden* and all the good novels to follow, *Barchester Towers* is more apparently concerned with character development than social issues, even though there are distinct lessons to be learned about life in general from the important characters' reactions to the society around and to individual moral dilemmas. In fact, the clerical disputes seem excuses to follow the careers of characters Trollope had so happily created in *The Warden.* Trollope had not taken a stand on the Whiston Matter when he described Hiram's Hospital in *The Warden,* and he was certainly uninterested in reviving the religious controversies of the Oxford Movement in *Barchester Towers.* Instead, the clerical controversies are but one part of a highly complex comedy; *Barchester Towers,* as Robert Daniel says, is in the tradition of English comedy, and Trollope's narrator deflates most of the philosophical issues in an exuberant exhibition of stagecraft and mock-heroic (or merely exaggerated) embellishments.

The structure of the novel is itself playful. The characters are initially introduced as partisans in a war for clerical supremacy; the battle imagery and the mock-heroic quality of the narrator's frequent asides suggest that the entire novel will be made up of campaigns and stratagems. Then the love intrigues add another dimension to the controversy, and suggest, particularly in the Ullathorne Sports chapters, that the novel is more a protracted melodrama than a comic *Iliad.* The main characters, still identified by their Oxford labels, become more involved in Eleanor's love than in the Barchester War. And then we find that neither the war nor the romance nor the melodrama as a whole is the object of the narrator's focus.

When the love story disentangles itself and the battles over the wardenship cease, it is obvious that the core of the novel is not found in the struggle for power nor in the romance, but in the quiet ascendancy of Septimus Harding and in his response to the questions that perplex him. The whole of *Barchester Towers* operates on a kind of joyous irony. Since nothing is quite what it seems to be, we can enjoy first this and then that in the narrator's humor, as we effortlessly sort out what is of lasting and what is of passing importance in the (Barchester) world. Harding, practically alone amid so many self-absorbed or self-deluding characters, is troubled by the fundamental questions of life: What is good? What am I meant to do? What should change? What should remain the same? In the form of Slope and the arguments of the rubbish cart, Harding faces the mid-Victorian questions posed by Benthamism, by later utilitarianism, and by the Oxford Movement itself. Harding, the most apparently vulnerable and noncombative of the Barchester clergymen, finds answers—in his own humble faith—to the harrying questions that the novel's numerous comic devices expose and exploit. Thus nothing can be what it seems to be at first; we are led to suppose, along with the people of Barchester, that the real controversy will be over who will be bishop, but war fizzles out. We are led to feel that romance may be the focus of sympathetic attention, but Eleanor and Arabin are frequently foolish or irritatingly clumsy. We think, perhaps, the novel is really about the good old days and our need to preserve them, but Harding sees and knows that the Deanery—a traditional stronghold of the traditional church—should go to a younger, more energetic man, and even Monica Thorne dimly perceives the need to adapt to the times. At every turn the narrator uses comic scene and ironic allusion to share with the reader a healthy perception of the difference between enduring and apparent truths. After all the hoopla of expected battle and projected love intrigue, we welcome Septimus Harding's quietly insistent affirmation of life as the moral center of the narrator's comic whorl.

The narrator is the most vocal character in and is the director of the *Barchester Towers* comedy. To appreciate the novel's ironies, and Harding's singular position among them, one must explore the narrator's voice and control. The narrator is responsible not only for creating many of the patterns of allusions, clichés, and tags but also for repeating them—sometimes slightly altered—with different characters and in different situations. Effectively comic and exaggerated as the language may be the first time, potential for comedy is amplified by repetition (or echo) either in similar or in strikingly dissimilar circumstances. For example, the reader will recall, compare, and assess the narrator's use of Medea to characterize first the desperate but ample-hearted Mrs. Quiverful and later the enraged warrior Mrs. Proudie. The fact that the two women are leagued together makes the shared—but very different—use of Medea effective.

The narrator not only creates patterns and repeats them but also occasionally and deliberately blurs the lines between his fanciful creation of patterns and a character's own internal monologue. . . . We are not always sure whether we are reading a piece of the narrator's purely comic interpretation of the character's thought or whether the character does occasionally think the very thoughts transcribed or whether the quality of thought of the character has been represented by the allusions and clichés the narrator repeats. The blurring is intensified when certain clichés or allusions supposedly offered fancifully by the narrator are later actually spoken by the character. As Trollope's career developed there were fewer and fewer purely comic blurrings (though there are numerous somber and ironic ones), but in *Barchester Towers* they contribute substantially to the creation of an almost uniformly comic mode for the story. Many of the characters and the narrator seem to conspire to augment the boisterous comedy of thwarted power and frustrated intrigue.

So far I have argued that the whole structure of *Barchester Towers* is ironic, that Septimus Harding is a part of the ironies but is also apart from them, that the narrator directs and controls the comedy by creating and repeating certain comic patterns and formulas, and that the uniform tone of the novel is sustained by a blurring of the narrator's voice with internal monologue supposedly representative of the character's thoughts. In order to explore these aspects of the narrator's control and his treatment of Harding, we should consider the patterns created and repeated in the book by the narrator-character.

The narrator uses cliché and Latin and French tags and borrows extensively from literature—most often from drama and the Bible and the classics, but also from Scott, Fielding, Sterne, and Thackeray. The characters themselves (apart from Harding) also borrow from and use these same resources or are associated in the reader's mind with certain borrowings the narrator has used to describe them. (In Trollope's later novels it is the characters themselves who usually use the borrowings.) In *Barchester Towers* the playful narrator prepares the reader for the novel's allusive richness and for the similarities between narrator and characters.

Look at a tiny sample of the narrator's language and preoccupations. He summarizes ambition in the tag " 'last infirmity of noble minds!' " (I); says of the daily press " 'Cassandra was not believed' " (II); speaks of clergymen as " 'the bore of the age, the old man whom we Sindbads cannot shake off' " (VI); warns Slope of his danger with the old lines "It's gude to be off with the auld luve / Before ye be on wi' the new" (XXVII); or echoes Milton playfully when describing the Ullathorne difficulties of "pandemonium" and "false Cerberus" (XXXIX). Dozens of similarly playful remarks work in concert with large and small patterns to enrich the reader's appreciation of characters and their interactions.

Even the many French and Latin phrases, though they often seem more ornamental than functional, help to establish connections and patterns structurally and linguistically. In fact, within the context of the whole book, the French and Latin expressions make an ironic extension of the Ullathorne Sports satire; the French words recall the detested Normans; the Latin, the old church establishment. There are more French words in this novel than in any of Trollope's others—perhaps he was remembering his abortive *La vendée*—and a fair sprinkling of Latin (though we find the Latin tags put to better use in *The Last Chronicle of Barset, The Prime Minister,* and *The Way We Live Now*).

There are some repetitions between narrator and character, but the narrator has the greater number of distinctive language features generally. Some of the French words and phrases, apart from such anglicized borrowings as *élite* or *protégé,* are *carte du pays* (VI), *ci-devant* (XI), *de trop* (XVI), *coup de main* (XXXIV), *dénouements* (XXXIV), *déjeuner* (XXXVI), *cortège* (XXXVI), *désoeuvré* (XLII), *chef d'oeuvre* (XLV), *décolleté* (XLV), *soupçon* (twice XXVII, XLV), *fait accompli* (XLVII), *congé* (L), *couleur de rose* (LI), *mêlée* (LII). Trollope could easily have used English words, but the French reminds us of Grantly's secret copy of Rabelais, extends the satire in the observation early in the book on how politicians really spend their time (rather than "preparing his thunder for successful rivals," the former minister " . . . was sitting easily in a lounging chair, conning over a Newmarket list, and by his elbow on the table was lying open an uncut French novel on which he was engaged" [I]), and suggests the playfulness and artificiality of the novel form.

It is no accident that Miss Thorne's Sports are *fête champêtre.*

The narrator uses fewer Latin words than French, but they, too, find echoes with the characters: *rarae aves* (III), *Labor omnia vincit improbus* (XX), *particeps criminis* (XXVIII), *Deus ex machina* (XXXIV), *status quo* (XXXIV), *quid pro quo* (XXXVI), *detur digniori* (XLIII), *nil admirari* (L). The expression *nolo episcopari* (I do not wish to be made a bishop) is particularly interesting since it encapsulates much of the novel's good-humored satire of ecclesiastical struggles for power: "the *nolo episcopari,* though still in use, is so directly at variance with the tendency of all human wishes that it cannot be thought to express the true aspirations of rising priests in the Church of England" (I). In an aside, the narrator despairs of the bishop's thralldom: "Oh, my aspiring pastors, divines to whose ears *nolo episcopari* are the sweetest of words, which of you would be a bishop on such terms as these?" (XXVI).

We feel the control of the narrator-character whether he is alluding to Disraeli—"the family of Sidonia" (XIX)—or to Dickens—the bishop "read the last number of the 'Little Dorrit' of the day" (XLIII)—or to the "melodrame" within his own novel—the Stanhopes conclude "this little family comedy" (XLII). Besides the interweaving of small patterns—created from references to a variety of literary works—there are several larger repeated patterns that the narrator invites us to enjoy. The most encompassing of these comes from drama. *Barchester Towers* is full of references to drama, but also as a whole exploits techniques of stagecraft. Two large, complementary parts of the novel, the Proudie Reception and the chapters of Ullathorne Sports, are dependent on stagecraft for their full comic effect. And many of the novel's important interchanges also hinge on the narrator's creation of scenes.

In a novel about clergymen and especially about stern Evangelicals against High and High and Dry churchmen, it is ironic and therefore appropriate that Trollope should choose to use techniques of drama. He had already tried his hand at writing a play and he had read some thirty-five Beaumont and Fletcher plays while he was writing *The Warden.* Since Trollope's devotion to drama was lifelong, we would expect to find his most heavily allusive and fanciful novel filled with stagecraft. And this is the case. The most memorable parts of the novel are scenes, and the narrator and other characters make frequent satiric references to the conventions of the theatre. Doctor Proudie is called a "play Bishop," and at the close of the novel when the cheerfully ironic narrator tells us (mischievously alluding to the conclusion of *Vanity Fair*) that the end of the story must be like a children's party, we are reminded of the quality of "play" with the various puppets of the performance. Doctor Gwynne is even referred to as the wished-for "*Deus ex machina* who was to come down upon the Barchester stage, and bring about deliverance from these terrible evils" (XXXIV).

One of the most celebrated scenes of the novel takes place at Mrs. Proudie's reception; Bertie's accidental rending of Mrs. Proudie's dress is a perfect example of Trollope's use of stagecraft. The scene is pure farce. We are attached intimately to none of the characters—neither Madeline, nor Bertie, nor Mrs. Proudie—and it is time Mrs. Proudie had a set-down before the Barchester community as a whole. Who better to administer the dose to Mrs. Proudie than the children of the Italianized Dr. Stanhope, whom Mr. Slope and Mrs. Proudie together have recalled to Barchester to assist in putting down the Grantly and High and Dry faction? Mrs. Proudie demands her lace train from the kneeling Bertie (the wheel of Madeline's sofa having caught in and ripped apart the train from Mrs. Proudie's dress). With as much dignity as the tragic Druid warrior queen Bonduca in one of Trollope's collections of Beaumont and Fletcher, Mrs. Proudie booms, " 'Unhand it, Sir!' " and Trollope slyly remarks, "From what scrap of dramatic poetry she had extracted the word cannot be said; . . . " (XI). The mishap has been set up as a scene in a play, and then Mrs. Proudie uses an archaic word that the narrator, as though giving stage directions, identifies as coming from old drama. Trollope's extensive reading of old drama probably encouraged the scene painting and the pointed joke. Mrs. Proudie would style herself a tragedy queen; the narrator exposes her as an angry clown.

The techniques of drama are again openly used in another major part of the novel—Ullathorne Sports. This section, like the Jael and Sisera story in *The Last Chronicle,* has been called extraneous to the rest of the work. When we look at the Sports chapters as a microcosm of the novel, and as an end-of-novel (or third-volume) counterpart to the Proudie reception, they make perfectly good sense artistically and thematically. The division of the Sports into acts (just as the Proudie reception is divided into two parts) suggests that something of real significance is going to happen during them. Something does, but not what the reader expects from the beginning of the novel and from the emphasis on battle given in the chapters on Arabin. In the Sports we focus on Eleanor's love concerns, not the struggle for control of the bishop.

Each of the acts in the three-part melodrame apparently chronicles some misadventure in Eleanor's confused relations with Arabin. The Barchester ecclesiastical war is entirely ignored; it has disappeared and the romance is uppermost. The climax of the melodrame appears to be Eleanor's resounding slap of the tipsy Mr. Slope. But since the Sports themselves are an ironic miniature of the whole novel, we would expect, and indeed we find, that even this climax is false. The really significant event of the Sports is not Eleanor's dismissal of Slope but Harding's discovery that Eleanor despises Slope; after that discovery, the farce of Eleanor's slap and the narrator's elaborately disingenuous apology for her are but further parts of the novel's comic miscuing. And in keeping with this irony, we find that the most interesting characters are not Eleanor or Slope or Arabin or even Mr. Harding. The narrator lavishes his dramatic know-how between the actual acts of the melodrame, and on the scenes with Madeline and with the Lookalofts and the Greenacres. (Who can read the description of Madeline's triumph over Lady De Courcy and not applaud the comic staging of the piece? Madeline's remark to Mr. Slope could serve as the motto for the Sports and for the novel as a whole: " 'Ha, ha, ha. Well, that's as good as a play.' " The narrator follows up Madeline's remarks immediately by saying, "It was good as a play to any there who had eyes to observe it, and wit to comment on what they observed" [XXXVII].)

Trollope makes the Ullathorne acts richly allusive and humorous, using comic exaggerations to emphasize the themes of the novel. The Sports themselves are reminders of the Eglinton Tournament and the British obsession with Sir Walter Scott. . . . The melodrama of the Sports is also supported by the narrator's comic uses of Shakespeare. Three quotations from Shakespeare embellish the comedy of the Sports chapters. When the narrator is describing love at first sight for the older man (here Wilfred Thorne's sudden infatuation with Madeline Neroni), he uses lines from *Love's Labour's Lost*. The narrator says, "But for real true love—love at first sight, love to devotion, love that robs a man of his sleep, love that 'will gaze an eagle blind,' love that 'will hear the lowest sound when the suspicious tread of theft is stopped,' love that is 'like a Hercules, still climbing trees in the Hesperides'—we believe the best age is from forty-five to seventy; up to that men are generally given to mere flirting" (XXXVII). Though the narrator is being playful here, he is not entirely fanciful. We are invited to smile at the Thornes, but it is with the seniors in the Barchester society we find the true values that must endure. Even Arabin and Eleanor, by no means youthful, are young in Trollope's apparent scheme of things: they flounder and fumble; Arabin, because as a previously sheltered Oxford don he is experiencing what must be called emotional adolescence; Eleanor, because she is a vine fluttering in the breeze, waiting for the right wall or tree or column around which to cling and grow (the Thackerayan ivy image is used with Eleanor in both *The Warden* and *Barchester Towers*).

The second quotation, or adaptation, is from *Henry IV, II*. The clerical feasting in the tents at Ullathorne is described with " 'Twas merry in the hall when the beards wagged all' " (XXXVIII). The foolery and light-heartedness of the play are perfectly reflected in the general atmosphere of the Sports. And a comparison of Slope and Falstaff could be instructive.

The third quotation comes, ironically, from *Macbeth*. As Slope, tipsy from champagne, pursues Eleanor across the lawn so that he can propose to her, he quotes to himself, " 'That which has made them drunk has made me bold' " (XL). Slope's unconscious pun on Eleanor's last name is characteristically clumsy. And one wonders, is it Slope or Mrs. Proudie who acts as the novel's Lady Macbeth?

Shakespeare is used other times in the novel, and each light use acts as a repetition or echo of the novel's numerous comedies of error. A quotation at the end of the novel encourages us to look back at the mock melodrame as a kind of distorted *As You Like It*, with Eleanor as a rather harried Rosalind and Slope as a darkly repulsive Jaques. Ullathorne then becomes the forest of Arden, a gloriously isolated spot separate from yet deliberately exposing the foibles and concerns of the larger world outside. This play within the play technique, the melodrame within the Barchester comedy, borrowed from Elizabethan and Jacobean drama, allows the narrator to suggest, lightheartedly, parallels within the text. At the end of *Barchester Towers*

the narrator quotes from *As You Like It* to finish his own tale: "The last scene of all, as all last scenes we fear must be,

> Is second childishness, and mere oblivion,
> Sans teeth, sans eyes, sans taste, sans everything
> (LI).

Trollope's references to Shakespeare are usually richly echoic.

In Mrs. Proudie's Reception and Ullathorne Sports the narrator alludes to events and ideas in current society as well as to literature, and he fully exploits the techniques of stagecraft. The techniques used in these two prominent (melo)dramatic pieces in the novel are reinforced by the novel's many other allusions to drama (and other literature) and especially by the creation of scenes. A perfect example of the quality and extent of the narrator's deliberate repetitions and parallel uses of staging is found in the description of the three "wraths"—Grantly's, Mrs. Proudie's, and Slope's. In each of these three we experience the narrator's use of different devices (measured syntax, mock-heroic tone, literary allusion) and are at the same time reminded of the other comic characters' anger.

Since the narrator controls the major patterns of the novel—the scenes and acts, the mock-heroic flavor of battle, the comic and ironic use of literature of all varieties—we would naturally expect to find in the individual characters echoes and continuations of the narrator's preoccupations. And so it is with all except the centrally important Harding. Archdeacon Grantly's repeated tag "Good heavens!" marks him as a comically explosive character in the battles and intrigues. The French and Biblical expressions offered by him, or by the narrator interpreting him, are consistent with the individual character of the man and with the narrator's established voice. The passage declaring Grantly's "noble wrath" (echoed in Mrs. Proudie's "divine wrath" and Slope's "furious wrath") is an excellent example of Trollope's use of tag and sentence structure to create a miniature comic scene:

> "Good heavens!" exclaimed the archdeacon, as he placed his foot on the gravel walk of the close, and raising his hat with one hand, passed the other somewhat violently over his now grizzled locks; smoke issued forth from the uplifted beaver as it were a cloud of wrath, and the safety-valve of his anger opened, and emitted a visible steam, preventing positive explosion and probable apoplexy. "Good heavens!"—and the archdeacon looked up to the gray pinnacles of the cathedral tower, making a mute appeal to that still living witness which had looked down on the doings of so many bishops of Barchester (VI).

The structure of the sentence between the two "good heavens" exemplifies Trollope's deliberate control. The first exclamation is followed by exactly sixty-four words with a semicolon making a short pause between the two thirty-two-word parts. Each of the two sections in the sentence is divided by three commas which mark and emphasize the accumulation of detail. The first "good heavens" is followed by the description of the archdeacon's actions: he "exclaimed"; he "placed his foot"; while "raising his hat" he "passed the other [hand] somewhat violently over his now grizzled locks." The word *somewhat* is the only distraction from the catalogue of actions. The second part of the sentence balances the first by supplying descriptions of the actions. We see "smoke," "cloud of wrath," "safety-valve of his anger," and "visible steam." Reading the sentence aloud, as it was probably frequently read by Trollope's public, reveals a distinct pattern to the pace. The first section is read quickly and relates the actions; the second gives a vivid picture and is read slowly because it requires more effort from both the imagination and the voice. The last part of the second section, "preventing positive explosion and probable apoplexy," is neatly balanced by its deliberate parallel of "explosion" and "apoplexy" to slow down to the full stop. The next "good heavens" redirects the reader's attention from the description of the archdeacon to the archdeacon himself as he wistfully views the cathedral tower, which, in the past, has represented his stable and friendly world.

This "wrath" passage opens the chapter entitled "War," which immediately follows the sedately titled "A Morning Visit," during which Harding and Grantly are insulted deliberately by Mrs. Proudie and Mr. Slope. This courtesy visit to the new bishop is itself wonderful comedy, with Mrs. Proudie, Slope, and the bishop's creating a grating, out-of-tune calliope; as the wife and chaplain blare at their guests, the bishop squeaks, and the former harmony of Barchester is shattered in a few painful measures. Grantly suppresses his rage until he leaves the Palace, when the reader expects a full description of his explosion. The tightly controlled sentence and the significant tag "good heavens!" offer a full play in miniature.

The narrator presents Mrs. Proudie's corresponding "furious wrath" five chapters later in the dramatic piece already mentioned, "Mrs. Proudie's Reception—Concluded." A woman who quotes Scripture *at* clergymen and regains dignity with archaic expressions richly deserves the narrator's tribute of a mock-heroic departure. In the manner of Fielding, the narrator describes Mrs. Proudie's "furious wrath" as her dress is ripped apart by Bertie:

> So, when a granite battery is raised, excellent to the eyes of warfaring men, is its strength and symmetry admired. It is the work of years. Its neat embrasures, its finished parapets, its case-mated stories, show all the skill of modern science. But, anon, a small spark is applied to the treacherous fusee—a cloud of dust arises to the heavens—and then nothing is to be seen but dirt and dust and ugly fragments.
>
> We know what was the wrath of Juno when her beauty was despised. We know to what storms of passion even celestial minds can yield. As Juno may have looked at Paris on Mount Ida, so did Mrs. Proudie look on Ethelbert Stanhope when he pushed the leg of the sofa into her lace train (XI).

Whenever Mrs. Proudie or the archdeacon is incensed, there is the flavor of mock-grand style. The narrator is careful to make us feel that his "noble wrath" and her "furious wrath" have much in common. Mrs. Proudie's

anachronistic "Unhand it, Sir!", shouted at Bertie, is as characteristic and compelling as Grantly's "good heavens!"—and both people are called "Juno" in their ire. The parts of warrior and outraged deity suit equally the archdeacon and Mrs. Proudie, and the narrator's careful directing makes us appreciate the comic bond between the two.

Slope's "divine wrath" exposes his sanctimoniousness as clearly as Grantly's wrath shows his offended self-importance and Mrs. Proudie's suggests her only lightly restrained bellicosity. This third "wrath" occurs, as with Mrs. Proudie's, as a scene within a scene, this time in the third act of Ullathorne Sports when Eleanor slaps Slope. The narrator invokes the muse and dramatic precedents from Greek theatre and finally resorts to Slope's ancestor, Dr. Slop, from Sterne's *Tristram Shandy*. As with Grantly and Mrs. Proudie, the choice of mock-grand language is characteristic of the narrator but also of the comic character himself: "But how shall I sing the divine wrath of Mr. Slope, or how invoke the tragic muse to describe the rage which swelled the celestial bosom of the bishop's chaplain? Such an undertaking by no means befits the low-heeled buskin of modern fiction. The painter put a veil over Agamemnon's face when called on to depict the father's grief at the early doom of his devoted daughter" (XL). This mock-heroic aside gives way to allusions to Sterne: "He stood motionless, undecided, glaring with his eyes, thinking of the pains and penalties of Hades, and meditating how he might best devote his enemy to the infernal gods with all the passion of his accustomed eloquence. He longed in his heart to be preaching at her. 'Twas thus he was ordinarily avenged of sinning mortal men and women. Could he at once have ascended his Sunday rostrum and fulminated at her such denunciations as his spirit delighted in, his bosom would have been greatly eased" (XL). This scene with Eleanor marks the mock climax of the Ullathorne melodrama, and we know that this part of the melodrama itself was constructed to gratify the reader with a full view of Slope's failure. With him the concept of battle is carried to ridiculous extremes. Through the description of this third "wrath" we appreciate how neatly the narrator has combined, confused, blended, and repeated the novel's wars, melodramas, and romances in the different yet similar scenes.

The reader is prepared to enjoy the scenes and to relish the novel's repetitions because of the way allusions, tags, and clichés are used and repeated—with different characters throughout the novel. If we turn now from the larger patterns of *Barchester Towers* to the individual characters, we will see how thoroughly the boisterous comedy of the narrator is echoed by each of the major characters—except, of course, the purposely separate Mr. Harding.

Building on *The Warden,* the narrator in *Barchester Towers* makes Grantly's "good heavens!" his emotional index, as we have just seen with his "noble wrath." Each time Grantly uses the expression, as with Dickens's Barkis or Sarah Gamp, we feel how "dramatically" alive is the archdeacon. Grantly greets Mr. Harding's news about the deanship with " 'Good heavens!' said the archdeacon, and sank back exhausted in an easychair" (XLVII). Later,

Trollope around the year 1880.

when Harding announces Eleanor's engagement to Arabin, the archdeacon exclaims "good heavens!" five times, ending, " 'Well, well,' said he. 'Good heavens! good heavens!' and the tone of the fifth exclamation made Mr. Harding fully aware that content was reigning in the archdeacon's bosom" (L). Mrs. Grantly reflects the archdeacon's energy and responds to Eleanor's engagement to Arabin by echoing her husband: " 'Good heavens!' she exclaimed—it was the general exclamation of the rectory" (XLVIII).

Like the narrator, the archdeacon is fond of French. He says of Slope and Eleanor: " 'I see it all. . . . The sly *tartuffe!* He thinks to buy the daughter by providing for the father. He means to show how powerful he is, how good he is, and how much he is willing to do for her *beaux yeux* . . .' " (XVIII). The narrator reinforces the archdeacon's words: "The archdeacon . . . at last remained firm in his own conviction that he was destined, *malgré lui,* to be the brother-in-law of Mr. Slope" (XXXIV). Grantly contemplates Mr. Harding's proposed deanship and the narrator reflects his thoughts: "And then the great discomfiture of that arch-enemy of all that was respectable in Barchester, of that new Low Church clerical parvenu that had fallen amongst them, that alone would be worth

more, almost, than the situation itself " (XLVII). And we see, with the help of *parvenu,* that the archdeacon's traditionalism extends from his religion to the very furniture of his home. The narrator says: "In his eyes there was something democratic and *parvenu* in a round table. He imagined that dissenters and calico-printers chiefly used them, and perhaps a few literary lions more conspicuous for their wit than their gentility" (XXI).

Grantly is a convincing archdeacon, and the reader never doubts his faith, thoroughly mixed though it is with materialism. Naturally, his sermon reinforces what we know of him from his own words and from the narrator's. When Grantly introduces Arabin to his new congregation in St. Ewold's, he uses verse 10 of Philemon: "I beseech thee for my son Onesimus, whom I have begotten in my bonds" (XXIII). The narrator paraphrases Grantly's message, assuring us that though "he deprecated any comparison between himself and St. Paul," he also "took a little merit to himself for having studiously provided the best man he could without reference to patronage or favour; but he did not say that the best man according to his views was he who was best able to subdue Mr. Slope and make that gentleman's situation in Barchester too hot to be comfortable" (XXIII). Even in his choice of text Grantly exposes his militancy and pride. Though he demurs about St. Paul, he asserts his power in the diocese since the message to Philemon rests on Paul's claim for respect and obedience: "If thou count me therefore a partner, receive him as myself."

The language used to develop Mrs. Proudie is an effective combination and blurring of the narrator's fancifulness and Mrs. Proudie's own indomitable spirit. The archdeacon's archrival has the "eyes of Argus" (III) for those who offend against Sabbath observances, and she is an "episcopal Argus" (XVII) when she confronts Slope with his unclerical attentions to Madeline Neroni. We find this expression later used by some political underlings to describe the duchess of Omnium in *The Prime Minister* and understand then, as here, the implied insult to the prying female.

Mrs. Proudie is primarily a warrior, and the narrator reflects her thoughts in terms of the glories of battle. When Slope and the bishop rebel together against her, she withdraws to her own room, and there: "The air of that sacred enclosure somewhat restored her courage, and gave her more heart. As Achilles warmed at the sight of his armour, as Don Quixote's heart grew strong when he grasped his lance, so did Mrs. Proudie look forward to fresh laurels, as her eye fell on her husband's pillow" (XXVI). When the vanquished bishop stammers that he thought to mollify his wife by proposing Slope for dean, the narrator likens Mrs. Proudie to a hyena and then a cannibal as he tries to suggest the fury in her response to the bishop:

> Pleased at having her enemy converted into a dean with twelve hundred a year! Medea, when she describes the customs of her native country (I am quoting from Robson's edition), assures her astonished auditor that in her land captives, when taken, are eaten.
>
> "You pardon them?" says Medea.

"We do indeed," says the mild Grecian.

"We eat them!" says she of Colchis, with terrific energy.

Mrs. Proudie was the Medea of Barchester; she had no idea of not eating Mr. Slope. Pardon him! Merely get rid of him! Make a dean of him! It was not so they did with their captives in her country, among people of her sort! Mr. Slope had no such mercy to expect; she would pick him to the very last bone (XXXIII).

Only a few chapters before (XXV) the narrator used Medea to embellish the internal monologue of the distressed but kindly Mrs. Quiverful. The contrast between the anxious mother there and the bloodthirsty woman here is the more striking since Mrs. Proudie champions Mrs. Quiverful's cause. The narrator suggests that Mrs. Proudie's crusade for the "fourteen living children" is certainly more Medean than quixotic. The bishop wisely concludes that there is no hope in tilting "against a warrior so fully armed at all points as was Mrs. Proudie" (XXXIII).

In the final pages of the book the narrator describes Mrs. Proudie's battle tactics with a different analogy. Of her struggles with Slope he says: "They had gone through a competitive examination of considerable severity, and she had come forth the winner, *facile princeps*" (LI) (an easy first). Everything is a contest to Mrs. Proudie; she is always campaigning to prove or gain power. She uses her religion as a kind of weapon to subdue less aggressive competitors. (Mrs. Proudie uses her knowledge of the Scriptures the same way that Ferdinand Lopez in **The Prime Minister** uses his of literature: his quotations are insidious; hers are bellicose; but both realize the power of association.) When she first meets Mr. Harding she corners him and preaches: " 'Neither thou, nor thy son, nor thy daughter, nor thy manservant, nor thy maidservant,' said she impressively, and more than once, as though Mr. Harding had forgotten the words. She shook her finger at him as she quoted the favourite law, as though menacing him with punishment . . . " (V). With Dr. Gwynne she frowns and gestures while she quotes: " ' "Suffer little children, and forbid them not," ' said she. 'Are we not to remember that, Dr. Gwynne? "Take heed that ye despise not one of these little ones." Are we not to remember that, Dr. Gwynne?' And at each of these questions she raised at him her menacing forefinger" (XLIII). It is fitting that Mr. Crawley later should finally conquer Mrs. Proudie with Scripture in **The Last Chronicle of Barset.**

With Mrs. Proudie the narrator uses Scripture, myths, and mock-heroic language (itself a kind of allusion) and drama, mixing together her own angry or ill-considered words with suitably exaggerated allusion. Two allusions to Shakespeare illustrate the effective combination of the incongruous and the appropriate. The narrator quotes from *Othello* to suggest, perhaps, her warrior cunning in cajoling her repentant husband on his return to the Palace: "Nothing, however, could be more affectionately cordial than the greeting he received; the girls came out and kissed him in a manner that was quite soothing to his spirit; and Mrs. Proudie, 'albeit, unused to the melting mood,'

squeezed him in her arms, and almost in words called him her dear, darling, good, pet, little bishop" (XXXIII). The outlandish contrast between the grandeur of Othello's final speech and Mrs. Proudie's domestic flummery (spoken, too, at a time when she is again triumphant) is appropriate to the high jinks of the novel. She is best characterized, however, by an allusion to *The Taming of the Shrew:* "In truth, Mrs. Proudie was all but invincible; had she married Petruchio, it may be doubted whether that arch wife-tamer would have been able to keep her legs out of those garments which are presumed by men to be peculiarly unfitted for feminine use" (XXXIII). Mrs. Proudie is both victrix and vixen.

With Obadiah Slope the narrator and Slope together use a variety of allusions and echoes from Sterne, Dickens, Shakespeare, Bunyan, Milton, and the Bible that expose Slope's comic villainy. As mentioned earlier, Slope is introduced by the narrator as a direct descendant of Dr. Slop from Sterne's *Tristam Shandy:* "I have heard it asserted that he is lineally descended from that eminent physician who assisted at the birth of Mr. T. Shandy, and that in early years he added an 'e' to his name, for the sake of euphony . . . "(IV). The now Protestant Slope (Sterne's Dr. Slop was Catholic) "has recourse, like his great ancestor, to the fulminations of an Ernulfus: 'Thou shalt be damned in thy going in and in thy coming out—in thy eating and thy drinking.' . . . "(IV). Trollope's readers no doubt appreciated this insult to Slope, remembering Dr. Slop's embarrassment at the virulence of Ernulphus's formula for excommunication.

The description of the red-haired Slope and his clammy handshake is unmistakably reminiscent of Uriah Heep. This comic combination of Slop and Heep quotes from *Macbeth,* as we have mentioned earlier, to give him the courage to propose to Eleanor, and it is words from *Hamlet* that transfix him when Madeline later taunts him with his failure with Eleanor: " ' 'Tis conscience that makes cowards of us all.' He felt on his cheek the sharp points of Eleanor's fingers, and did not know who might have seen the blow . . . " (XLVI). It is not clear whether Slope thinks of these words himself or whether the narrator supplies them, but it matters little—they are too appropriate a condemnation of his arrogance and guilt. He recognizes, perhaps, his own position in "vanity fair" (XL) and knows that "idolaters round the altars of Baal" (XL) deserve no better. The narrator dismisses him at the end of the book with a fanciful twist of the last lines of "Lycidas": "At last he rose, and twitched his mantle blue (black), / Tomorrow to fresh woods and pastures new" (LI).

Slope fights battles in Barsetshire on two different levels, and his part in the novel provides links between the mock-heroic battles of ecclesiastical power and the melodramatic struggles of false romance. Allusions to Sterne, the Bible, and the classics connect the two different spheres of conflict. His first assault is from the pulpit. He chooses II Timothy 2:15 for his text: "Study to show thyself approved unto God, a workman that needeth not to be ashamed, rightly dividing the word of truth" (VI). He perverts the interpretation of the Scripture so that he can "ridicule, abuse and anathematize" the practises of his

High and Dry congregation. Trollope's readers will probably recall the appropriateness to Slope and his audience of the companion chapter, I Timothy 2, which gives advice to archdeacons and bishops and in advising the treatment of women foreshadows Slope's own doom: "Let the woman learn in silence with all subjection. But I suffer not a woman to teach, nor to usurp authority over the man, but to be in silence" (I Timothy 2:11-12). At any rate, Slope's attack is successful because he does, by innuendo and statement, set "all Barchester . . . by the ears" (VII).

The narrator tells us that Slope is an "abhorrent Gamaliel" (VII) who knows "the wiles of the serpent" (VIII) and has "pharisaical arrogance" (XIII). "A rich wife was a great desideratum to him" (XV); he regards Eleanor as his "embryo spouse" (XIX), tries to dupe her about the hospital with an explanation of "wheels within wheels" (XVI), and brushes aside her hesitations with "Rome was not built in a day" (XVI). He tries to make his usurpation of Mrs. Proudie a *fait accompli* (XXVI). He tries to charm Madeline by telling her that if he destroys her letters " 'they perish worthily, and are burnt on a pyre, as Dido was of old' " (XXVII). Mr. Slope's language, and that associated with him by the narrator, assures us that he is a clever, resourceful man. He is an unsuccessful soldier, and an unfortunate lover, and so is the perfect comic "male devil" for the Barchester battles and melodrama.

False romance, which is the key ingredient of the novel's melodrama, is personified in Madeline Neroni. Madeline is artificial; everything about her suggests contrivance. She herself reminds us of the novel as a novel because she thinks of herself as part of a colorful and continuing fiction. She arranges intrigues, creates scenes, dazzles her followers with wit, allusion, and repartee. Her chief object in life is to fascinate, to make scores of men fall in love with her. She personally is what Ullathorne Sports is structurally: a self-parody. She thrives on fantasy and suggests her own superficiality in the cynical extremes of her charades. She is too realistic to have genuine pride in her conquests, and too desperate not to indulge herself constantly with them. In keeping with the novel's lightness, Madeline's desperation is almost entirely effaced. Instead, the narrator and Madeline herself encourage laughter over her numerous exploits.

The narrator repeats the word *basilisk* to summarize Madeline's deadly charms: "She was a basilisk from whom an ardent lover of beauty could make no escape" (IX), a "voluptuous Rubens . . . with the power of a basilisk" (XVI); " . . . Mr. Thorne . . . yielded himself up to the basilisk . . . " (XXXVIII). She is a "painted Jezebel" (XI), as Mrs. Proudie tells us, who has eyes "bright as Lucifer's" (IX). She, like Becky Sharp, is a "noxious siren" (XXVII) who in revenge can be "as active as Grimaldi" (XI). Madeline is most fittingly characterized as a huntress in various forms: she regards Mr. Thorne as a "pheasant" "worth bagging for family uses" (XXXVIII); she fishes for Thorne first, and "The fish took the bait, was hooked, and caught, and landed" (XXXVII). At Ullathorne, too, she decides "to entrap Mr. Arabin into her net" (XXXVIII); with Slope she is merciless, because " . . . the signora was a powerful spider that made won-drous webs, and could in no way live without catching flies" (XXVII); and of Slope she "spitted him, as a boy does a cockchafer on a cork, that she might enjoy the energetic agony of his gyrations" (XXVII). The signora's charms are addictive and men are driven to her repeatedly, the narrator says, "As the Eastern idler swallows his dose of opium, as the London reprobate swallows his dose of gin . . . " (XXXVIII). Madeline's "lustrous glances" (XLI)—the pun must be intentional—captivate Slope and Arabin, the bishop and Mr. Thorne.

Signora Neroni's eyes attack and attract. She duels through eye contact with Lady De Courcy, as we have mentioned earlier, and sends her "shambling" out onto the Ullathorne lawn. Her dramatic beauty and bold techniques change most of her conversations into superb scenes. Ullathorne, itself the excuse for an elaborate "melodrame," is the perfect background for Madeline's antics.

Madeline sharpens her wit and perhaps feeds her imagination with a variety of literary pursuits. She makes more allusions in her speech than any other character in **Barchester Towers** and has a greater density of patterns associated with her than any of Trollope's characters except Josiah Crawley. Unlike Crawley, who nurtures his imagination with the classics, Madeline is an inveterate letter writer who " . . . wrote also a kind of poetry, generally in Italian, and short romances, generally in French. She read much of a desultory sort of literature, and as a modern linguist had really made great proficiency" (IX). She studies the catechism so she can remark to Slope about a proposed Sunday School, " 'I will teach them, at any rate, to submit themselves to their spiritual pastors and masters' " (XXVII). She can taunt Slope with his duplicity because she has read of St. Paul (XXVII). Her nature is most pointedly exposed in her allusions to the heroines of Shakespeare, Byron, and the classics. She mocks Dido because she fell between two stools; she mocks love in general because:

> "Who was ever successful in true love? Success in love argues that the love is false. True love is always despondent or tragical. Juliet loved, Haidee loved, Dido loved, and what came of it? Troilus loved and ceased to be a man."

> "Troilus loved and was fooled," said the more manly chaplain. "A man may love and yet not be a Troilus. All women are not Cressids."

> "No, all women are not Cressids. The falsehood is not always on the woman's side. Imogen was true, but how was she rewarded? Her lord believed her to be the paramour of the first he who came near her in his absence. Desdemona was true and was smothered. Ophelia was true and went mad. There is no happiness in love, except at the end of an English novel" (XXVII).

Madeline's cynicism adds some strength to the novel's playful criticism of sanctimony. With another allusion to Shakespeare she openly attacks Slope: " 'Why—what gulls do you men make of us,' she replied. 'How you fool us to the top of our bent; and of all men you clergymen are the most fluent of your honeyed, caressing words' " (XXVII). (pp. 14-35)

Eleanor's and Arabin's is the true romance of the novel, the one that counterbalances Madeline's heartless intrigues. It is typical of *Barchester Towers,* however, that their story is dashed with irony. Madeline is a Becky Sharp, and Eleanor is characterized by the ivy image associated with Amelia Sedley. At the beginning of the novel the narrator comments on her love for Bold: "Hers was one of those feminine hearts which cling to a husband, not with idolatry, for worship can admit of no defect in its idol, but with the perfect tenacity of ivy. As the parasite plant will follow even the defects of the trunk which it embraces, so did Eleanor cling to and love the very faults of her husband" (II). Near the end when she gives herself to Arabin the narrator again remarks, "When the ivy has found its tower, when the delicate creeper has found its strong wall, we know how the parasite plants grow and prosper" (XLIX). The end of Thackeray's novel is too similar to be ignored: "Good-by, Colonel—God bless you, honest William!—Farewell, dear Amelia—Grow green again, tender little parasite, round the rugged old oak to which you cling!" We recall that Slope thought of Ullathorne as a "vanity fair" and realize that it could be as easily Thackeray's as Bunyan's that he remembered. James Kincaid outlines the similarities between stories of Becky and Amelia, and Madeline and Eleanor. The comparison is a good one, but the analogy does not extend to Arabin. Nevertheless, Eleanor's and Madeline's similarities to the Thackeray women suggest parallels in the tone of the two novels. Their conclusions are much alike, as mentioned earlier: "Which of us is happy in this world? Which of us has his desire? or, having it, is satisfied?—Come children, let us shut up the box and the puppets, for our play is played out." Trollope's closing chapter begins: "The end of a novel, like the end of a children's dinner party, must be made up of sweetmeats and sugar-plums" (LIII). The enduring tone of *Vanity Fair,* however, is cynical; there is always a barb in the humor. In *Barchester Towers* parallels to Thackeray are but a part of a genial narrator's allusive play.

Despite the good humor, Trollope conscientiously exposes the weaknesses of all his characters with the incisiviness Thackeray shows in *Vanity Fair.* No one escapes the humor of the narrator whether described as part of the war or the melodrama or the romance. Septimus Harding belongs to none of the exuberant levels of the novel, but even he, as moral core, is not entirely exempt from the narrator's raillery. He still plays an invisible violoncello whenever he is deeply troubled, as he did in *The Warden;* he has a "want of self-confidence" (XVIII) that makes him seem a "puppet" (XXXIV) to men of Grantly's verve. The narrator laughs at some of his instances of strength—when he refuses to give up his *"pied à terre"* (XLIV) in High Street, or when he refuses to question what he thinks is Eleanor's love for Slope: "There was but little of the Roman about Mr. Harding. He could not sacrifice his Lucretia even though she should be polluted by the accepted addresses of the clerical Tarquin at the palace" (XXVIII). Ironically, it is in Harding's self-doubtings, in his persistent questions, that we see the firm faith of Bar-

chester. To men such as Grantly and Proudie and even Slope little self-examination is ever required: "The school of men to whom he [Harding] professes to belong, the Grantlys, the Gwynnes, and the old high set of Oxford divines, are afflicted with no such self-accusations as these which troubled Mr. Harding. They, as a rule, are as satisfied with the wisdom and propriety of their own conduct as can be any Mr. Slope, or any Dr. Proudie, with his own. But unfortunately for himself Mr. Harding had little of this self-reliance" (XIII). Instead, when he sees what he may have to undergo with the new appointment to the wardenship, he questions his ability to become a martyr for his beliefs. He likens his own subjection to the Proudies and Slopes to the sacrifice of St. Bartholomew, St. Sebastian, and St. Lorenzo, but without a pride in the comparison that we find in Grantly's sermon on St. Paul and Onesimus.

Harding is a completely humble man, possessed of a firmness as unobstrusive as his "velvet step" (I). He acts as a structural and moral core for the novel in characteristically quiet ways. Though it is not immediately apparent, he poses the key questions of the novel and, by example, supplies their answers. He is a catalyst for the major campaign of the clerical war—the wardenship becomes a point of contention among Grantly, Slope, and Mrs. Proudie. It is he, and not Mr. Arabin, who encounters and struggles with Slope face-to-face. It is from him that Arabin accepts the position of dean of Barchester. He opposes his powerful son-in-law, the archdeacon, concerning both the wardenship and the deanship. Structurally, he thus provides direction for the novel. Morally, he also directs the true spirit of Barchester. He rightly discerns Slope's philosophy of the times, and he shudders at the artificiality Slope advocates:

> We must talk, think, and live up to the spirit of the times, and write up to it too, if that cacoethes be upon us, or else we are nought. New men and new measures, long credit and few scruples, great success or wonderful ruin, such are now the tastes of Englishmen who know how to live. Alas, alas! Under such circumstances Mr. Harding could not but feel that he was an Englishman who did not know how to live. This new doctrine of Mr. Slope and the rubbish cart, new at least at Barchester, sadly disturbed his equanimity (XIII).

In later novels, *Phineas Redux, The Prime Minister,* and particularly *The Way We Live Now,* Trollope works out the serious implications of the frenzied "men, not measures" politics; here he uses Harding's insight into the shallowness of unthinking change as a counterpoise for the Thornes' unpractical, reactionary ways.

At the center of the mock battles and the fanciful melodramas and the boisterous allusions and patternings is Harding's faith in amelioration. Harding himself gets singular treatment from the narrator—though we smile at the mild old precentor and his violoncello, we see him as separate from the humor and the texture of the rest of the novel. It is as though the multiple linguistic devices in the whole work rest upon the simplicity of style used with Harding. In characterizing him, Trollope's narrator never uses flights of mock-heroic style or dense patterns of associative phrases or allusions. And Harding's concept of change, his antidote to the poison of men like Slope, is devoid of fanfare:

> A tear came into each eye as he reflected that all this [familiar intercourse with the old bishop] was gone. What use would the hospital be to him now? He was alone in the world, and getting old; he would soon, very soon have to go, and leave it all, as his dear old friend had gone; go, and leave the hospital, and his accustomed place in the cathedral, and his haunts and pleasures, to younger and perhaps wiser men. That chanting of his!—perhaps, in truth, the time for it had gone by. He felt as though the world were sinking from his feet; as though this, this was the time for him to turn with confidence to those hopes which he had preached with confidence to others. "What," said he to himself, "can a man's religion be worth, if it does not support him against the natural melancholy of declining years?" And, as he looked out through his dimmed eyes into the bright parterres of the bishop's garden, he felt that he had the support which he wanted (XII).

In the sad musings of an old man we find the essence of Barchester. Harding is the emblem of humane tolerance, of gentleness and kindness which transcend the petty squabbles of passing controversies. He is not a philosopher but his beliefs, like his nostalgia, are instinctive, spontaneous—fundamental to the enduring strength of Barchester. Harding's elemental goodness is like Mr. Tryan's in George Eliot's *Scenes of Clerical Life*:

> Ideas are often poor ghosts; our sun-filled eyes cannot discern them; they pass athwart us in thin vapour, and cannot make themselves felt. But sometimes they are made flesh; they breathe upon us with warm breath, they touch us with soft responsive hands, they look at us with sad sincere eyes, and speak to us in appealing tones; they are clothed in a living human soul, with all its conflicts, its faith, and its love. Then their presence is a power, then they shake us like a passion, and we are drawn after them with gentle compulsion, as flame is drawn to flame.

Barchester Towers is instinct with Septimus Harding's unassuming power. Because of him we see that change, tempered by honesty and humility, is not only good, but necessary. It is right that a worthy clergyman with fourteen children should be given a reasonable living; it is fitting that an energetic scholar and his youngish wife should come to the deanery. Unlike his belligerent son-in-law, Harding can accept parvenu clergymen and parvenu round tables, if the changes bring improvements.

Barchester Towers is a bustling novel, unique in all Trollope's writing for the density of repeated allusions, echoes, and patterns of language generally. He creates battles and melodramas and romances in an exuberant, narrator-dominated chorus of allusion, stock phrase, and proverb. The real triumph, however, is in the way we experience Harding's quiet charm through the boisterous good humor. Never again did Trollope write a novel so openly whimsical (and yet true) as *Barchester Towers.* Yet even in this height of his exuberance we feel, through Harding's ascendancy, the subtle control that characterizes all of Trollope's good novels. (pp. 40-5)

> *Elizabeth R. Epperly, in her* Patterns of Repetition in Trollope, *The Catholic University of America Press, 1989, 238 p.*

FURTHER READING

apRoberts, Ruth. *The Moral Trollope.* Athens: Ohio University Press, 1971, 203 p.
> Examines *Barchester Towers* and other works by Trollope in an analysis of Trollope's fiction and his moral concerns.

Bankert, M. S. "Newman in the Shadow of *Barchester Towers.*" *Renascence* 20, No. 3 (Spring 1968): 153-61.
> Argues that "for all its apparent levity, *Barchester Towers* is a study of the religious psychology of the nineteenth-century British churchman."

Booth, Bradford A. "Cathedral and Parish." In his *Anthony Trollope: Aspects of His Life and Art*, pp. 22-73. Bloomington: Indiana University Press, 1958.
> Discusses satiric and thematic elements in *Barchester Towers,* focusing on the characters of Mrs. Proudie and Obadiah Slope.

Edwards, P. D. "The Boundaries of Barset." In his *Anthony Trollope: His Art and Scope*, pp. 9-56. New York: St. Martin's Press, 1977.
> Contends that *Barchester Towers* "is much less artless than it pretends to be," praising "the finely sustained note of informality, mocking and self-mocking, that disguises both its sharpness of focus and its deep emotional commitment to the world it describes."

Gilmour, Robin. Introduction to *Barchester Towers,* by Anthony Trollope, pp. xv-xxxi. Middlesex, England: Penguin Books, 1983.
> Overview of the plot and prominent themes of *Barchester Towers.*

Harvey, Geoffrey. "Trollope and the Drama: Scene and Form." In his *The Art of Anthony Trollope*, pp. 38-53. New York: St. Martin's Press, 1980.
> Examines theatrical scenes in *Barchester Towers* as "microcosm[s] of the conflicting human forces in the novel," and comments on the effectiveness of Trollope's dramatic technique.

Herbert, Christopher. "Comic Imperfection." In his *Trollope and Comic Pleasure*, pp. 151-74. Chicago: University of Chicago Press, 1987.
> Examines central themes inherent in the comic aspects of *Barchester Towers.*

Jillson, Frederick F. "The 'Professional' Clergyman in Some Novels by Anthony Trollope." *Hartford Studies in Literature* I, No. 3 (1969): 185-97.
> Refutes Trollope's contention that his Barsetshire series

"paint[s] the social and not the professional lives of clergymen." Jillson examines the depictions of Hardy in *The Warden,* Slope in *Barchester Towers,* and Arabin in *The Last Chronicle of Barset,* concluding that Trollope "is faithful to the craft of the priest. His knowledge of the duties of the clergy is comprehensive and, in some areas, deep."

Kincaid, James R. *The Novels of Anthony Trollope.* Oxford: Oxford at the Clarendon Press, 1977, 302 p.

Includes a discussion of *Barchester Towers;* according to Kincaid, Trollope's Barsetshire novels comprise "a series of variations on the comic myth of renewal and preservation."

Langland, Elizabeth. "Society as Protagonist in *Nostromo* and *Barchester Towers.*" In her *Society in the Novel,* pp. 147-67. Chapel Hill: University of North Carolina Press, 1984.

Asserts that "society, a set of principles or social ideals, functions in the [*Barchester Towers*] narrative in the same way a human hero would," progressing from "a state of instability toward a qualitatively defined fate."

Lyons, Paul. "The Morality of Irony and Unreliable Narrative in Trollope's *The Warden* and *Barchester Towers.*" *South Atlantic Review* 54, No. 1 (January 1989): 41-54.

Studies the role of the narrator in conveying Trollope's moral and artistic tenets.

MacDonald, Susan Peck. "The Barchester Comedies: 1855-1860." In her *Anthony Trollope,* pp. 13-28. Boston: Twayne Publishers, 1987.

Includes a discussion of the structure of plot in *Barchester Towers.*

Pickering, Samuel F., Jr. "Trollope's Poetics and Authorial Intrusion in *The Warden* and *Barchester Towers.*" *The Journal of Narrative Technique* 3, No. 2 (May 1973): 131-40.

Examines the function of the narrator in Trollope's *The Warden* and *Barchester Towers,* concluding that "Trollope intruded . . . in order to illustrate his poetics and criticize abuses of art and literature."

Shaw, W. David. "Moral Drama in *Barchester Towers.*" *Nineteenth-Century Fiction* 19, No. 1 (June 1964): 45-54.

Explores Trollope's *Barchester Towers* as a "moral drama of self-deception and discovery."

Smalley, Donald, ed. *Trollope: The Critical Heritage.* The Critical Heritage Series, edited by B. C. Southam. London: Routledge & Kegan Paul; New York: Barnes & Noble, 1969, 572 p.

A compilation of early reviews of Trollope's works. This collection provides a reflection of his reception by his contemporaries.

Stevens, Clarence Dimick. Introduction to *Barchester Towers,* by Anthony Trollope, pp. v-xviii. New York: Charles Scribner's Sons, 1923.

Discusses Trollope's life and literary career, comparing him favorably with other prominent novelists of his day. Especially lauding Trollope's characterizations in *Barchester Towers,* Stevens concludes that his novels provide, "not only a faithful picture of Victorian manners, but also a true revelation of the universal human heart."

Super, R. H. "1853-57." In his *The Chronicler of Barsetshire: A Life of Anthony Trollope,* pp. 72-87. Ann Arbor: University of Michigan Press, 1988.

Biographical account of events surrounding the writing and publication of *Barchester Towers.*

Taylor, Robert H. "On Rereading *Barchester Towers.*" *The Princeton University Library Chronicle* 15, No. 1 (Autumn 1953): 10-15.

Overview of *Barchester Towers* that praises Trollope's "power of conviction."

Wall, Stephen. "Reappearing Characters: Barsetshire Revisited." In his *Trollope: Living with Character,* pp. 19-94. New York: Henry Holt and Company, 1988.

Analyzes characterization in *Barchester Towers,* noting that Trollope was especially "absorbed in the ways in which the twin pressures of social reality and inner nature combine to direct a man's course."

Nineteenth-Century Literature Criticism

Cumulative Indexes
Volumes 1-33

This Index Includes References to Entries in These Gale Series

Contemporary Literary Criticism presents excerpts of criticism on the works of novelists, poets, dramatists, short story writers, scriptwriters, and other creative writers who are now living or who have died since 1960.

Twentieth-Century Literary Criticism contains critical excerpts by the most significant commentators on poets, novelists, short story writers, dramatists, and philosophers who died between 1900 and 1960.

Nineteenth-Century Literature Criticism offers significant passages from criticism on authors who died between 1800 and 1899.

Literature Criticism from 1400 to 1800 compiles significant passages from the most noteworthy criticism on authors of the fifteenth through eighteenth centuries.

Classical and Medieval Literature Criticism offers excerpts of criticism on the works of world authors from classical antiquity through the fourteenth century.

Short Story Criticism compiles excerpts of criticism on short fiction by writers of all eras and nationalities.

Poetry Criticism presents excerpts of criticism on the works of poets from all eras, movements, and nationalities.

Drama Criticism presents criticism of the works of dramatists of all eras, movements, and nationalities.

Children's Literature Review includes excerpts from reviews, criticism, and commentary on works of authors and illustrators who create books for children.

Contemporary Authors Series encompasses five related series. *Contemporary Authors* provides biographical and bibliographical information on more than 97,000 writers of fiction and nonfiction. *Contemporary Authors New Revision Series* provides completely updated information on authors covered in *CA*. *Contemporary Authors Permanent Series* consists of listings for deceased and inactive authors. *Contemporary Authors Autobiography Series* presents specially commissioned autobiographies by leading contemporary writers. *Contemporary Authors Bibliographical Series* contains primary and secondary bibliographies as well as analytical bibliographical essays by authorities on major modern authors.

Dictionary of Literary Biography encompasses four related series. *Dictionary of Literary Biography* furnishes illustrated overviews of authors' lives and works. *Dictionary of Literary Biography Documentary Series* illuminates the careers of major figures through a selection of literary documents, including letters, interviews, and photographs. *Dictionary of Literary Biography Yearbook* summarizes the past year's literary activity and includes updated entries on individual authors. *Concise Dictionary of American Literary Biography* comprises six volumes of revised and updated sketches on major American authors that were originally presented in *Dictionary of Literary Biography*.

Something about the Author Series encompasses three related series. *Something about the Author* contains well-illustrated biographical sketches on juvenile and young adult authors and illustrators from all eras. *Something about the Author Autobiography Series* presents specially commissioned autobiographies by prominent authors and illustrators of books for children and young adults. *Authors & Artists for Young Adults* provides high school and junior high school students with profiles of their favorite creative artists.

Yesterday's Authors of Books for Children contains heavily illustrated entries on children's writers who died before 1961. Complete in two volumes.

Literary Criticism Series
Cumulative Author Index

This index lists all author entries in the Gale Literary Criticism Series and includes cross-references to other Gale sources. References in the index are identified as follows:

AAYA: *Authors & Artists for Young Adults,* Volumes 1-6
CAAS: *Contemporary Authors Autobiography Series,* Volumes 1-13
CA: *Contemporary Authors* (original series), Volumes 1-132
CABS: *Contemporary Authors Bibliographical Series,* Volumes 1-3
CANR: *Contemporary Authors New Revision Series,* Volumes 1-33
CAP: *Contemporary Authors Permanent Series,* Volumes 1-2
CA-R: *Contemporary Authors* (revised editions), Volumes 1-44
CDALB: *Concise Dictionary of American Literary Biography,* Volumes 1-6
CLC: *Contemporary Literary Criticism,* Volumes 1-67
CLR: *Children's Literature Review,* Volumes 1-24
CMLC: *Classical and Medieval Literature Criticism,* Volumes 1-7
DC: *Drama Criticism,* Volume 1
DLB: *Dictionary of Literary Biography,* Volumes 1-104
DLB-DS: *Dictionary of Literary Biography Documentary Series,* Volumes 1-8
DLB-Y: *Dictionary of Literary Biography Yearbook,* Volumes 1980-1988
LC: *Literature Criticism from 1400 to 1800,* Volumes 1-17
NCLC: *Nineteenth-Century Literature Criticism,* Volumes 1-33
PC: *Poetry Criticism,* Volumes 1-3
SAAS: *Something about the Author Autobiography Series,* Volumes 1-12
SATA: *Something about the Author,* Volumes 1-64
SSC: *Short Story Criticism,* Volumes 1-8
TCLC: *Twentieth-Century Literary Criticism,* Volumes 1-42
YABC: *Yesterday's Authors of Books for Children,* Volumes 1-2

Boyle, Patrick 19??-.............. CLC 19

Boyle, Thomas Coraghessan
　1948-.................... CLC 36, 55
　See also CA 120; DLB-Y 86

Brackenridge, Hugh Henry
　1748-1816 .... NCLC 7
　See also DLB 11, 37

Bradbury, Edward P. 1939-
　See Moorcock, Michael

Bradbury, Malcolm (Stanley)
　1932-.................... CLC 32, 61
　See also CANR 1; CA 1-4R; DLB 14

Bradbury, Ray(mond Douglas)
　1920-........... CLC 1, 3, 10, 15, 42
　See also CANR 2; CA 1-4R; SATA 11;
　DLB 2, 8

Bradford, Gamaliel 1863-1932..... TCLC 36
　See also DLB 17

Bradley, David (Henry), Jr. 1950- .. CLC 23
　See also CANR 26; CA 104; DLB 33

Bradley, John Ed 1959-........... CLC 55

Bradley, Marion Zimmer 1930-..... CLC 30
　See also CANR 7; CA 57-60; DLB 8

Bradstreet, Anne 1612-1672......... LC 4
　See also DLB 24; CDALB 1640-1865

Bragg, Melvyn 1939-............. CLC 10
　See also CANR 10; CA 57-60; DLB 14

Braine, John (Gerard)
　1922-1986 .... CLC 1, 3, 41
　See also CANR 1; CA 1-4R;
　obituary CA 120; DLB 15; DLB-Y 86

Brammer, Billy Lee 1930?-1978
　See Brammer, William

Brammer, William 1930?-1978 ..... CLC 31
　See also obituary CA 77-80

Brancati, Vitaliano 1907-1954..... TCLC 12
　See also CA 109

Brancato, Robin F(idler) 1936-..... CLC 35
　See also CANR 11; CA 69-72; SATA 23

Brand, Millen 1906-1980........... CLC 7
　See also CA 21-24R; obituary CA 97-100

Branden, Barbara 19??-........... CLC 44

Brandes, Georg (Morris Cohen)
　1842-1927 .... TCLC 10
　See also CA 105

Brandys, Kazimierz 1916-......... CLC 62

Branley, Franklyn M(ansfield)
　1915-...................... CLC 21
　See also CLR 13; CANR 14; CA 33-36R;
　SATA 4

Brathwaite, Edward 1930-......... CLC 11
　See also CANR 11; CA 25-28R; DLB 53

Brautigan, Richard (Gary)
　1935-1984 .... CLC 1, 3, 5, 9, 12, 34, 42
　See also CA 53-56; obituary CA 113;
　SATA 56; DLB 2, 5; DLB-Y 80, 84

Braverman, Kate 1950- .... CLC 67
　See also CA 89-92

Brecht, (Eugen) Bertolt (Friedrich)
　1898-1956 .... TCLC 1, 6, 13, 35
　See also CA 104; DLB 56

Bremer, Fredrika 1801-1865 ..... NCLC 11

Brennan, Christopher John
　1870-1932 .... TCLC 17
　See also CA 117

Brennan, Maeve 1917-............ CLC 5
　See also CA 81-84

Brentano, Clemens (Maria)
　1778-1842 .... NCLC 1
　See also DLB 90

Brenton, Howard 1942-........... CLC 31
　See also CA 69-72; DLB 13

Breslin, James 1930-
　See Breslin, Jimmy
　See also CA 73-76

Breslin, Jimmy 1930-........... CLC 4, 43
　See also Breslin, James

Bresson, Robert 1907-........... CLC 16
　See also CA 110

Breton, Andre 1896-1966... CLC 2, 9, 15, 54
　See also CAP 2; CA 19-20;
　obituary CA 25-28R; DLB 65

Breytenbach, Breyten 1939-..... CLC 23, 37
　See also CA 113, 129

Bridgers, Sue Ellen 1942- .... CLC 26
　See also CANR 11; CA 65-68; SAAS 1;
　SATA 22; DLB 52

Bridges, Robert 1844-1930........ TCLC 1
　See also CA 104; DLB 19

Bridie, James 1888-1951 .... TCLC 3
　See also Mavor, Osborne Henry
　See also DLB 10

Brin, David 1950-................ CLC 34
　See also CANR 24; CA 102

Brink, Andre (Philippus)
　1935-.................... CLC 18, 36
　See also CA 104

Brinsmead, H(esba) F(ay) 1922- .... CLC 21
　See also CANR 10; CA 21-24R; SAAS 5;
　SATA 18

Brittain, Vera (Mary) 1893?-1970... CLC 23
　See also CAP 1; CA 15-16;
　obituary CA 25-28R

Broch, Hermann 1886-1951....... TCLC 20
　See also CA 117; DLB 85

Brock, Rose 1923-
　See Hansen, Joseph

Brodkey, Harold 1930-........... CLC 56
　See also CA 111

Brodsky, Iosif Alexandrovich 1940-
　See Brodsky, Joseph (Alexandrovich)
　See also CA 41-44R

Brodsky, Joseph (Alexandrovich)
　1940-........... CLC 4, 6, 13, 36, 50
　See also Brodsky, Iosif Alexandrovich

Brodsky, Michael (Mark) 1948- .... CLC 19
　See also CANR 18; CA 102

Bromell, Henry 1947-............. CLC 5
　See also CANR 9; CA 53-56

Bromfield, Louis (Brucker)
　1896-1956 .... TCLC 11
　See also CA 107; DLB 4, 9

Broner, E(sther) M(asserman)
　1930-...................... CLC 19
　See also CANR 8, 25; CA 17-20R; DLB 28

Bronk, William 1918-............ CLC 10
　See also CANR 23; CA 89-92

Bronte, Anne 1820-1849......... NCLC 4
　See also DLB 21

Bronte, Charlotte
　1816-1855 .... NCLC 3, 8, 33
　See also DLB 21

Bronte, (Jane) Emily 1818-1848 .. NCLC 16
　See also DLB 21, 32

Brooke, Frances 1724-1789 .... LC 6
　See also DLB 39

Brooke, Henry 1703?-1783 .... LC 1
　See also DLB 39

Brooke, Rupert (Chawner)
　1887-1915.............. TCLC 2, 7
　See also CA 104; DLB 19

Brooke-Rose, Christine 1926-...... CLC 40
　See also CA 13-16R; DLB 14

Brookner, Anita 1928-...... CLC 32, 34, 51
　See also CA 114, 120; DLB-Y 87

Brooks, Cleanth 1906-............ CLC 24
　See also CA 17-20R; DLB 63

Brooks, Gwendolyn
　1917-........... CLC 1, 2, 4, 5, 15, 49
　See also CANR 1; CA 1-4R; SATA 6;
　DLB 5, 76; CDALB 1941-1968

Brooks, Mel 1926-............... CLC 12
　See also Kaminsky, Melvin
　See also CA 65-68; DLB 26

Brooks, Peter 1938-............. CLC 34
　See also CANR 1; CA 45-48

Brooks, Van Wyck 1886-1963...... CLC 29
　See also CANR 6; CA 1-4R; DLB 45, 63

Brophy, Brigid (Antonia)
　1929-.................. CLC 6, 11, 29
　See also CAAS 4; CANR 25; CA 5-8R;
　DLB 14

Brosman, Catharine Savage 1934-.... CLC 9
　See also CANR 21; CA 61-64

Broughton, T(homas) Alan 1936- ... CLC 19
　See also CANR 2, 23; CA 45-48

Broumas, Olga 1949-............. CLC 10
　See also CANR 20; CA 85-88

Brown, Charles Brockden
　1771-1810 .... NCLC 22
　See also DLB 37, 59, 73;
　CDALB 1640-1865

Brown, Christy 1932-1981......... CLC 63
　See also CA 105; obituary CA 104

Brown, Claude 1937- .... CLC 30
　See also CA 73-76

Brown, Dee (Alexander) 1908- .. CLC 18, 47
　See also CAAS 6; CANR 11; CA 13-16R;
　SATA 5; DLB-Y 80

Brown, George Douglas 1869-1902
　See Douglas, George

Brown, George Mackay 1921-.... CLC 5, 28
　See also CAAS 6; CANR 12; CA 21-24R;
　SATA 35; DLB 14, 27

Brown, Rita Mae 1944-........ CLC 18, 43
　See also CANR 2, 11; CA 45-48

Brown, Rosellen 1939-............ CLC 32
　See also CANR 14; CA 77-80

Campbell, (Ignatius) Roy (Dunnachie)
1901-1957 . . . . TCLC 5
See also CA 104; DLB 20

Campbell, Thomas 1777-1844 . . . . NCLC 19

Campbell, (William) Wilfred
1861-1918 . . . . TCLC 9
See also CA 106

Camus, Albert
1913-1960 . . . CLC 1, 2, 4, 9, 11, 14, 32, 63
See also CA 89-92; DLB 72

Canby, Vincent 1924- . . . . CLC 13
See also CA 81-84

Canetti, Elias 1905- . . . . CLC 3, 14, 25
See also CANR 23; CA 21-24R; DLB 85

Canin, Ethan 1960- . . . . CLC 55

Cape, Judith 1916-
See Page, P(atricia) K(athleen)

Capek, Karel
1890-1938 . . . . TCLC 6, 37; DC 1
See also CA 104

Capote, Truman
1924-1984 . . . . . CLC 1, 3, 8, 13, 19, 34, 38, 58; SSC 2
See also CANR 18; CA 5-8R;
obituary CA 113; DLB 2; DLB-Y 80, 84;
CDALB 1941-1968

Capra, Frank 1897- . . . . CLC 16
See also CA 61-64

Caputo, Philip 1941- . . . . CLC 32
See also CA 73-76

Card, Orson Scott 1951- . . . . CLC 44, 47, 50
See also CA 102

Cardenal, Ernesto 1925- . . . . CLC 31
See also CANR 2; CA 49-52

Carducci, Giosue 1835-1907 . . . . . . TCLC 32

Carew, Thomas 1595?-1640 . . . . LC 13

Carey, Ernestine Gilbreth 1908- . . . . CLC 17
See also CA 5-8R; SATA 2

Carey, Peter 1943- . . . . CLC 40, 55
See also CA 123, 127

Carleton, William 1794-1869 . . . . . . NCLC 3

Carlisle, Henry (Coffin) 1926- . . . . . . CLC 33
See also CANR 15; CA 13-16R

Carlson, Ron(ald F.) 1947- . . . . CLC 54
See also CA 105

Carlyle, Thomas 1795-1881 . . . . . . NCLC 22
See also DLB 55

Carman, (William) Bliss
1861-1929 . . . . TCLC 7
See also CA 104

Carpenter, Don(ald Richard)
1931- . . . . CLC 41
See also CANR 1; CA 45-48

Carpentier (y Valmont), Alejo
1904-1980 . . . . CLC 8, 11, 38
See also CANR 11; CA 65-68;
obituary CA 97-100

Carr, Emily 1871-1945 . . . . TCLC 32
See also DLB 68

Carr, John Dickson 1906-1977 . . . . . . CLC 3
See also CANR 3; CA 49-52;
obituary CA 69-72

Carr, Virginia Spencer 1929- . . . . CLC 34
See also CA 61-64

Carrier, Roch 1937- . . . . CLC 13
See also DLB 53

Carroll, James (P.) 1943- . . . . CLC 38
See also CA 81-84

Carroll, Jim 1951- . . . . CLC 35
See also CA 45-48

Carroll, Lewis 1832-1898 . . . . NCLC 2
See also Dodgson, Charles Lutwidge
See also CLR 2; DLB 18

Carroll, Paul Vincent 1900-1968 . . . . CLC 10
See also CA 9-12R; obituary CA 25-28R;
DLB 10

Carruth, Hayden 1921- . . . . CLC 4, 7, 10, 18
See also CANR 4; CA 9-12R; SATA 47;
DLB 5

Carter, Angela (Olive) 1940- . . . . . CLC 5, 41
See also CANR 12; CA 53-56; DLB 14

Carver, Raymond
1938-1988 . . . CLC 22, 36, 53, 55; SSC 8
See also CANR 17; CA 33-36R;
obituary CA 126; DLB-Y 84, 88

Cary, (Arthur) Joyce (Lunel)
1888-1957 . . . . TCLC 1, 29
See also CA 104; DLB 15

Casanova de Seingalt, Giovanni Jacopo
1725-1798 . . . . LC 13

Casares, Adolfo Bioy 1914-
See Bioy Casares, Adolfo

Casely-Hayford, J(oseph) E(phraim)
1866-1930 . . . . TCLC 24
See also CA 123

Casey, John 1880-1964
See O'Casey, Sean

Casey, John 1939- . . . . CLC 59
See also CANR 23; CA 69-72

Casey, Michael 1947- . . . . CLC 2
See also CA 65-68; DLB 5

Casey, Warren 1935- . . . . CLC 12
See also Jacobs, Jim and Casey, Warren
See also CA 101

Casona, Alejandro 1903-1965 . . . . . . CLC 49
See also Alvarez, Alejandro Rodriguez

Cassavetes, John 1929-1991 . . . . CLC 20
See also CA 85-88, 127

Cassill, R(onald) V(erlin) 1919- . . . CLC 4, 23
See also CAAS 1; CANR 7; CA 9-12R;
DLB 6

Cassity, (Allen) Turner 1929- . . . . CLC 6, 42
See also CANR 11; CA 17-20R

Castaneda, Carlos 1935?- . . . . CLC 12
See also CA 25-28R

Castedo, Elena 1937- . . . . CLC 65
See also CA 132

Castellanos, Rosario 1925-1974 . . . . . CLC 66
See also CA 131; obituary CA 53-56

Castelvetro, Lodovico 1505-1571 . . . . . LC 12

Castiglione, Baldassare 1478-1529 . . . LC 12

Castro, Rosalia de 1837-1885 . . . . . NCLC 3

Cather, Willa (Sibert)
1873-1947 . . . . . . TCLC 1, 11, 31; SSC 2
See also CA 104; SATA 30; DLB 9, 54;
DLB-DS 1; CDALB 1865-1917

Catton, (Charles) Bruce
1899-1978 . . . . CLC 35
See also CANR 7; CA 5-8R;
obituary CA 81-84; SATA 2;
obituary SATA 24; DLB 17

Cauldwell, Frank 1923-
See King, Francis (Henry)

Caunitz, William 1935- . . . . CLC 34

Causley, Charles (Stanley) 1917- . . . . . CLC 7
See also CANR 5; CA 9-12R; SATA 3;
DLB 27

Caute, (John) David 1936- . . . . CLC 29
See also CAAS 4; CANR 1; CA 1-4R;
DLB 14

Cavafy, C(onstantine) P(eter)
1863-1933 . . . . TCLC 2, 7
See also CA 104

Cavanna, Betty 1909- . . . . CLC 12
See also CANR 6; CA 9-12R; SATA 1, 30

Caxton, William 1421?-1491? . . . . LC 17

Cayrol, Jean 1911- . . . . CLC 11
See also CA 89-92; DLB 83

Cela, Camilo Jose 1916- . . . . . . CLC 4, 13, 59
See also CAAS 10; CANR 21; CA 21-24R

Celan, Paul 1920-1970 . . . . . CLC 10, 19, 53
See also Antschel, Paul
See also DLB 69

Celine, Louis-Ferdinand
1894-1961 . . . . . CLC 1, 3, 4, 7, 9, 15, 47
See also Destouches,
Louis-Ferdinand-Auguste
See also DLB 72

Cellini, Benvenuto 1500-1571 . . . . LC 7

Cendrars, Blaise 1887-1961 . . . . CLC 18
See also Sauser-Hall, Frederic

Cernuda, Luis (y Bidon)
1902-1963 . . . . CLC 54
See also CA 89-92

Cervantes (Saavedra), Miguel de
1547-1616 . . . . LC 6

Cesaire, Aime (Fernand) 1913- . . CLC 19, 32
See also CANR 24; CA 65-68

Chabon, Michael 1965?- . . . . CLC 55

Chabrol, Claude 1930- . . . . CLC 16
See also CA 110

Challans, Mary 1905-1983
See Renault, Mary
See also CA 81-84; obituary CA 111;
SATA 23; obituary SATA 36

Chambers, Aidan 1934- . . . . CLC 35
See also CANR 12; CA 25-28R; SATA 1

Chambers, James 1948-
See Cliff, Jimmy

Chambers, Robert W. 1865-1933 . . . TCLC 41

Chandler, Raymond 1888-1959 . . . TCLC 1, 7
See also CA 104

Channing, William Ellery
1780-1842 . . . . NCLC 17
See also DLB 1, 59

De la Mare, Walter (John)
1873-1956 .... TCLC **4**
See also CLR 23; CA 110; SATA 16;
DLB 19

Delaney, Shelagh 1939- .... CLC **29**
See also CA 17-20R; DLB 13

Delany, Mary (Granville Pendarves)
1700-1788 .... LC **12**

Delany, Samuel R(ay, Jr.)
1942- .... CLC **8, 14, 38**
See also CA 81-84; DLB 8, 33

De la Roche, Mazo 1885-1961 ..... CLC **14**
See also CA 85-88; DLB 68

Delbanco, Nicholas (Franklin)
1942- .... CLC **6, 13**
See also CAAS 2; CA 17-20R; DLB 6

del Castillo, Michel 1933- .... CLC **38**
See also CA 109

Deledda, Grazia 1871-1936 .... TCLC **23**
See also CA 123

Delibes (Setien), Miguel 1920- ... CLC **8, 18**
See also CANR 1; CA 45-48

DeLillo, Don
1936- .... CLC **8, 10, 13, 27, 39, 54**
See also CANR 21; CA 81-84; DLB 6

De Lisser, H(erbert) G(eorge)
1878-1944 .... TCLC **12**
See also CA 109

Deloria, Vine (Victor), Jr. 1933-.... CLC **21**
See also CANR 5, 20; CA 53-56; SATA 21

Del Vecchio, John M(ichael)
1947- .... CLC **29**
See also CA 110

de Man, Paul 1919-1983 .... CLC **55**
See also obituary CA 111; DLB 67

De Marinis, Rick 1934-........... CLC **54**
See also CANR 9, 25; CA 57-60

Demby, William 1922-........... CLC **53**
See also CA 81-84; DLB 33

Denby, Edwin (Orr) 1903-1983..... CLC **48**
See also obituary CA 110

Dennis, John 1657-1734........... LC **11**

Dennis, Nigel (Forbes) 1912-....... CLC **8**
See also CA 25-28R; obituary CA 129;
DLB 13, 15

De Palma, Brian 1940-........... CLC **20**
See also CA 109

De Quincey, Thomas 1785-1859 ... NCLC **4**

Deren, Eleanora 1908-1961
See Deren, Maya
See also obituary CA 111

Deren, Maya 1908-1961........... CLC **16**
See also Deren, Eleanora

Derleth, August (William)
1909-1971 .... CLC **31**
See also CANR 4; CA 1-4R;
obituary CA 29-32R; SATA 5; DLB 9

Derrida, Jacques 1930-........... CLC **24**
See also CA 124, 127

Desai, Anita 1937- .... CLC **19, 37**
See also CA 81-84

De Saint-Luc, Jean 1909-1981
See Glassco, John

De Sica, Vittorio 1902-1974 .... CLC **20**
See also obituary CA 117

Desnos, Robert 1900-1945........ TCLC **22**
See also CA 121

Destouches, Louis-Ferdinand-Auguste
1894-1961
See Celine, Louis-Ferdinand
See also CA 85-88

Deutsch, Babette 1895-1982 .... CLC **18**
See also CANR 4; CA 1-4R;
obituary CA 108; SATA 1;
obituary SATA 33; DLB 45

Devenant, William 1606-1649 .... LC **13**

Devkota, Laxmiprasad
1909-1959 .... TCLC **23**
See also CA 123

DeVoto, Bernard (Augustine)
1897-1955 .... TCLC **29**
See also CA 113; DLB 9

De Vries, Peter
1910- .... CLC **1, 2, 3, 7, 10, 28, 46**
See also CA 17-20R; DLB 6; DLB-Y 82

Dexter, Pete 1943-........... CLC **34, 55**
See also CA 127

Diamond, Neil (Leslie) 1941-....... CLC **30**
See also CA 108

Dick, Philip K(indred)
1928-1982 .... CLC **10, 30**
See also CANR 2, 16; CA 49-52;
obituary CA 106; DLB 8

Dickens, Charles
1812-1870 .... NCLC **3, 8, 18, 26**
See also SATA 15; DLB 21, 55, 70

Dickey, James (Lafayette)
1923- .... CLC **1, 2, 4, 7, 10, 15, 47**
See also CANR 10; CA 9-12R; CABS 2;
DLB 5; DLB-Y 82; DLB-DS 7

Dickey, William 1928-........... CLC **3, 28**
See also CANR 24; CA 9-12R; DLB 5

Dickinson, Charles 1952-.......... CLC **49**

Dickinson, Emily (Elizabeth)
1830-1886 .... NCLC **21; PC 1**
See also SATA 29; DLB 1;
CDALB 1865-1917

Dickinson, Peter (Malcolm de Brissac)
1927- .... CLC **12, 35**
See also CA 41-44R; SATA 5; DLB 87

Didion, Joan 1934-..... CLC **1, 3, 8, 14, 32**
See also CANR 14; CA 5-8R; DLB 2;
DLB-Y 81, 86; CDALB 1968-1987

Dillard, Annie 1945-........... CLC **9, 60**
See also CANR 3; CA 49-52; SATA 10;
DLB-Y 80

Dillard, R(ichard) H(enry) W(ilde)
1937- .... CLC **5**
See also CAAS 7; CANR 10; CA 21-24R;
DLB 5

Dillon, Eilis 1920-................ CLC **17**
See also CAAS 3; CANR 4; CA 9-12R;
SATA 2

Dinesen, Isak
1885-1962 .... CLC **10, 29; SSC 7**
See also Blixen, Karen (Christentze
Dinesen)
See also CANR 22

Disch, Thomas M(ichael) 1940-... CLC **7, 36**
See also CAAS 4; CANR 17; CA 21-24R;
SATA 54; DLB 8

Disraeli, Benjamin 1804-1881 ..... NCLC **2**
See also DLB 21, 55

Dixon, Paige 1911-
See Corcoran, Barbara

Dixon, Stephen 1936-............. CLC **52**
See also CANR 17; CA 89-92

Doblin, Alfred 1878-1957........ TCLC **13**
See also Doeblin, Alfred

Dobrolyubov, Nikolai Alexandrovich
1836-1861 .... NCLC **5**

Dobyns, Stephen 1941-............ CLC **37**
See also CANR 2, 18; CA 45-48

Doctorow, E(dgar) L(aurence)
1931- ..... CLC **6, 11, 15, 18, 37, 44, 65**
See also CANR 2, 33; CA 45-48; DLB 2,
28; DLB-Y 80; CDALB 1968-1987

Dodgson, Charles Lutwidge 1832-1898
See Carroll, Lewis
See also YABC 2

Doeblin, Alfred 1878-1957........ TCLC **13**
See also CA 110; DLB 66

Doerr, Harriet 1910- .... CLC **34**
See also CA 117, 122

Donaldson, Stephen R. 1947-....... CLC **46**
See also CANR 13; CA 89-92

Donleavy, J(ames) P(atrick)
1926- .... CLC **1, 4, 6, 10, 45**
See also CANR 24; CA 9-12R; DLB 6

Donnadieu, Marguerite 1914-
See Duras, Marguerite

Donne, John 1572?-1631 ...... LC **10; PC 1**

Donnell, David 1939?- .... CLC **34**

Donoso, Jose 1924-........ CLC **4, 8, 11, 32**
See also CA 81-84

Donovan, John 1928-.............. CLC **35**
See also CLR 3; CA 97-100; SATA 29

Doolittle, Hilda 1886-1961
See H(ilda) D(oolittle)
See also CA 97-100; DLB 4, 45

Dorfman, Ariel 1942-.............. CLC **48**
See also CA 124

Dorn, Ed(ward Merton) 1929-... CLC **10, 18**
See also CA 93-96; DLB 5

Dos Passos, John (Roderigo)
1896-1970 ... CLC **1, 4, 8, 11, 15, 25, 34**
See also CANR 3; CA 1-4R;
obituary CA 29-32R; DLB 4, 9;
DLB-DS 1

Dostoevsky, Fyodor
1821-1881 .... NCLC **2, 7, 21, 33; SSC 2**

Doughty, Charles (Montagu)
1843-1926 .... TCLC **27**
See also CA 115; DLB 19, 57

Douglas, George 1869-1902....... TCLC **28**

Douglas, Keith 1920-1944 .... TCLC **40**
See also DLB 27

Douglass, Frederick 1817-1895 .... NCLC **7**
See also SATA 29; DLB 1, 43, 50;
CDALB 1640-1865

Harper, Frances Ellen Watkins
    1825-1911 . . . . **TCLC 14**
    See also BLC 2; CA 125;
    brief entry CA 111; DLB 50

Harper, Michael S(teven)   1938- . . **CLC 7, 22**
    See also CANR 24; CA 33-36R; DLB 41

Harris, Christie (Lucy Irwin)
    1907- . . . . **CLC 12**
    See also CANR 6; CA 5-8R; SATA 6;
    DLB 88

Harris, Frank   1856-1931 . . . . **TCLC 24**
    See also CAAS 1; CA 109

Harris, George Washington
    1814-1869 . . . . **NCLC 23**
    See also DLB 3, 11

Harris, Joel Chandler   1848-1908 . . . **TCLC 2**
    See also YABC 1; CA 104; DLB 11, 23, 42,
    78, 91

Harris, John (Wyndham Parkes Lucas)
    Beynon   1903-1969 . . . . **CLC 19**
    See also Wyndham, John
    See also CA 102; obituary CA 89-92

Harris, MacDonald   1921- . . . . **CLC 9**
    See also Heiney, Donald (William)

Harris, Mark   1922- . . . . **CLC 19**
    See also CAAS 3; CANR 2; CA 5-8R;
    DLB 2; DLB-Y 80

Harris, (Theodore) Wilson   1921- . . . . **CLC 25**
    See also CANR 11, 27; CA 65-68

Harrison, Harry (Max)   1925- . . . . . . **CLC 42**
    See also CANR 5, 21; CA 1-4R; SATA 4;
    DLB 8

Harrison, James (Thomas)   1937- . . . **CLC 66**
    See also Harrison, Jim
    See also CANR 8; CA 13-16R

Harrison, Jim   1937- . . . . **CLC 6, 14, 33**
    See also Harrison, James (Thomas)
    See also DLB-Y 82

Harrison, Tony   1937- . . . . **CLC 43**
    See also CA 65-68; DLB 40

Harriss, Will(ard Irvin)   1922- . . . . . . **CLC 34**
    See also CA 111

Hart, Moss   1904-1961 . . . . **CLC 66**
    See also Conrad, Robert Arnold
    See also obituary CA 89-92; DLB 7

Harte, (Francis) Bret(t)
    1836?-1902 . . . . **TCLC 1, 25; SSC 8**
    See also brief entry CA 104; SATA 26;
    DLB 12, 64, 74, 79; CDALB 1865-1917

Hartley, L(eslie) P(oles)
    1895-1972 . . . . **CLC 2, 22**
    See also CA 45-48; obituary CA 37-40R;
    DLB 15

Hartman, Geoffrey H.   1929- . . . . **CLC 27**
    See also CA 117, 125; DLB 67

Haruf, Kent   19??- . . . . **CLC 34**

Harwood, Ronald   1934- . . . . **CLC 32**
    See also CANR 4; CA 1-4R; DLB 13

Hasek, Jaroslav (Matej Frantisek)
    1883-1923 . . . . **TCLC 4**
    See also CA 104, 129

Hass, Robert   1941- . . . . **CLC 18, 39**
    See also CANR 30; CA 111

Hastings, Selina   19??- . . . . **CLC 44**

Hauptmann, Gerhart (Johann Robert)
    1862-1946 . . . . **TCLC 4**
    See also CA 104; DLB 66

Havel, Vaclav   1936- . . . . **CLC 25, 58, 65**
    See also CA 104

Haviaras, Stratis   1935- . . . . **CLC 33**
    See also CA 105

Hawes, Stephen   1475?-1523? . . . . **LC 17**

Hawkes, John (Clendennin Burne, Jr.)
    1925- . . . . . . **CLC 1, 2, 3, 4, 7, 9, 14, 15,
                                            27, 49**
    See also CANR 2; CA 1-4R; DLB 2, 7;
    DLB-Y 80

Hawking, Stephen (William)
    1948- . . . . **CLC 63**
    See also CA 126, 129

Hawthorne, Julian   1846-1934 . . . . . **TCLC 25**

Hawthorne, Nathaniel
    1804-1864 . . . **NCLC 2, 10, 17, 23; SSC 3**
    See also YABC 2; DLB 1, 74;
    CDALB 1640-1865

Hayashi Fumiko   1904-1951 . . . . . . **TCLC 27**

Haycraft, Anna   19??-
    See Ellis, Alice Thomas
    See also CA 122

Hayden, Robert (Earl)
    1913-1980 . . . . **CLC 5, 9, 14, 37**
    See also BLC 2; CANR 24; CA 69-72;
    obituary CA 97-100; CABS 2; SATA 19;
    obituary SATA 26; DLB 5, 76;
    CDALB 1941-1968

Hayman, Ronald   1932- . . . . **CLC 44**
    See also CANR 18; CA 25-28R

Haywood, Eliza (Fowler)   1693?-1756 . . **LC 1**
    See also DLB 39

Hazlitt, William   1778-1830 . . . . . . **NCLC 29**

Hazzard, Shirley   1931- . . . . **CLC 18**
    See also CANR 4; CA 9-12R; DLB-Y 82

H(ilda) D(oolittle)
    1886-1961 . . . . **CLC 3, 8, 14, 31, 34**
    See also Doolittle, Hilda

Head, Bessie   1937-1986 . . . . **CLC 25, 67**
    See also BLC 2; CANR 25; CA 29-32R;
    obituary CA 119

Headon, (Nicky) Topper   1956?- . . . . **CLC 30**
    See also The Clash

Heaney, Seamus (Justin)
    1939- . . . . **CLC 5, 7, 14, 25, 37**
    See also CANR 25; CA 85-88; DLB 40

Hearn, (Patricio) Lafcadio (Tessima Carlos)
    1850-1904 . . . . **TCLC 9**
    See also CA 105; DLB 12, 78

Hearne, Vicki   1946- . . . . **CLC 56**

Hearon, Shelby   1931- . . . . **CLC 63**
    See also CANR 18; CA 25-28

Heat Moon, William Least   1939- . . . **CLC 29**

Hebert, Anne   1916- . . . . **CLC 4, 13, 29**
    See also CA 85-88; DLB 68

Hecht, Anthony (Evan)
    1923- . . . . **CLC 8, 13, 19**
    See also CANR 6; CA 9-12R; DLB 5

Hecht, Ben   1894-1964 . . . . **CLC 8**
    See also CA 85-88; DLB 7, 9, 25, 26, 28, 86

Hedayat, Sadeq   1903-1951 . . . . **TCLC 21**
    See also CA 120

Heidegger, Martin   1889-1976 . . . . . . **CLC 24**
    See also CA 81-84; obituary CA 65-68

Heidenstam, (Karl Gustaf) Verner von
    1859-1940 . . . . **TCLC 5**
    See also CA 104

Heifner, Jack   1946- . . . . **CLC 11**
    See also CA 105

Heijermans, Herman   1864-1924 . . . **TCLC 24**
    See also CA 123

Heilbrun, Carolyn G(old)   1926- . . . . . **CLC 25**
    See also CANR 1, 28; CA 45-48

Heine, Harry   1797-1856
    See Heine, Heinrich

Heine, Heinrich   1797-1856 . . . . **NCLC 4**
    See also DLB 90

Heinemann, Larry C(urtiss)   1944- . . **CLC 50**
    See also CA 110

Heiney, Donald (William)   1921- . . . . . **CLC 9**
    See also Harris, MacDonald
    See also CANR 3; CA 1-4R

Heinlein, Robert A(nson)
    1907-1988 . . . . . . **CLC 1, 3, 8, 14, 26, 55**
    See also CANR 1, 20; CA 1-4R;
    obituary CA 125; SATA 9, 56; DLB 8

Heller, Joseph
    1923- . . . . **CLC 1, 3, 5, 8, 11, 36, 63**
    See also CANR 8; CA 5-8R; CABS 1;
    DLB 2, 28; DLB-Y 80

Hellman, Lillian (Florence)
    1905?-1984 . . . . . **CLC 2, 4, 8, 14, 18, 34,
                                             44, 52; DC 1**
    See also CA 13-16R; obituary CA 112;
    DLB 7; DLB-Y 84

Helprin, Mark   1947- . . . . . **CLC 7, 10, 22, 32**
    See also CA 81-84; DLB-Y 85

Hemans, Felicia   1793-1835 . . . . . . **NCLC 29**

Hemingway, Ernest (Miller)
    1899-1961 . . . **CLC 1, 3, 6, 8, 10, 13, 19,
                            30, 34, 39, 41, 44, 50, 61; SSC 1**
    See also CA 77-80; DLB 4, 9; DLB-Y 81,
    87; DLB-DS 1; CDALB 1917-1929

Hempel, Amy   1951- . . . . **CLC 39**
    See also CA 118

Henley, Beth   1952- . . . . **CLC 23**
    See also Henley, Elizabeth Becker
    See also CABS 3; DLB-Y 86

Henley, Elizabeth Becker   1952-
    See Henley, Beth
    See also CA 107

Henley, William Ernest
    1849-1903 . . . . **TCLC 8**
    See also CA 105; DLB 19

Hennissart, Martha
    See Lathen, Emma
    See also CA 85-88

Henry, O.   1862-1910 . . . **TCLC 1, 19; SSC 5**
    See also Porter, William Sydney
    See also YABC 2; CA 104; DLB 12, 78, 79;
    CDALB 1865-1917

Henry VIII   1491-1547 . . . . **LC 10**

Hentoff, Nat(han Irving)   1925- . . . . . **CLC 26**
    See also CLR 1; CAAS 6; CANR 5, 25;
    CA 1-4R; SATA 27, 42; AAYA 4

Johnson, Uwe
1934-1984 .... CLC **5, 10, 15, 40**
See also CANR 1; CA 1-4R;
obituary CA 112; DLB 75

Johnston, George (Benson) 1913- ... CLC **51**
See also CANR 5, 20; CA 1-4R; DLB 88

Johnston, Jennifer 1930- .... CLC **7**
See also CA 85-88; DLB 14

Jolley, Elizabeth 1923-............ CLC **46**
See also CA 127

Jones, D(ouglas) G(ordon) 1929-.... CLC **10**
See also CANR 13; CA 29-32R, 113;
DLB 53

Jones, David
1895-1974 .... CLC **2, 4, 7, 13, 42**
See also CANR 28; CA 9-12R;
obituary CA 53-56; DLB 20

Jones, David Robert 1947-
See Bowie, David
See also CA 103

Jones, Diana Wynne 1934- .... CLC **26**
See also CLR 23; CANR 4, 26; CA 49-52;
SAAS 7; SATA 9

Jones, Gayl 1949-............... CLC **6, 9**
See also BLC 2; CANR 27; CA 77-80;
DLB 33

Jones, James 1921-1977.... CLC **1, 3, 10, 39**
See also CANR 6; CA 1-4R;
obituary CA 69-72; DLB 2

Jones, (Everett) LeRoi
1934- .... CLC **1, 2, 3, 5, 10, 14, 33**
See also Baraka, Amiri; Baraka, Imamu
Amiri
See also CA 21-24R

Jones, Louis B. 19??-.............. CLC **65**

Jones, Madison (Percy, Jr.) 1925- ... CLC **4**
See also CAAS 11; CANR 7; CA 13-16R

Jones, Mervyn 1922- .... CLC **10, 52**
See also CAAS 5; CANR 1; CA 45-48

Jones, Mick 1956?-................ CLC **30**
See also The Clash

Jones, Nettie 19??-................ CLC **34**

Jones, Preston 1936-1979 .... CLC **10**
See also CA 73-76; obituary CA 89-92;
DLB 7

Jones, Robert F(rancis) 1934-....... CLC **7**
See also CANR 2; CA 49-52

Jones, Rod 1953- .... CLC **50**
See also CA 128

Jones, Terry 1942?- .... CLC **21**
See also Monty Python
See also CA 112, 116; SATA 51

Jong, Erica 1942-.......... CLC **4, 6, 8, 18**
See also CANR 26; CA 73-76; DLB 2, 5, 28

Jonson, Ben(jamin) 1572(?)-1637...... LC **6**
See also DLB 62

Jordan, June 1936-.......... CLC **5, 11, 23**
See also CLR 10; CANR 25; CA 33-36R;
SATA 4; DLB 38; AAYA 2

Jordan, Pat(rick M.) 1941- .... CLC **37**
See also CANR 25; CA 33-36R

Josipovici, Gabriel (David)
1940- .... CLC **6, 43**
See also CAAS 8; CA 37-40R; DLB 14

Joubert, Joseph 1754-1824 .... NCLC **9**

Jouve, Pierre Jean 1887-1976...... CLC **47**
See also obituary CA 65-68

Joyce, James (Augustine Aloysius)
1882-1941 ...... TCLC **3, 8, 16, 26, 35;**
SSC **3**
See also CA 104, 126; DLB 10, 19, 36

Jozsef, Attila 1905-1937......... TCLC **22**
See also CA 116

Juana Ines de la Cruz 1651?-1695 .... LC **5**

Julian of Norwich 1342?-1416?....... LC **6**

Just, Ward S(wift) 1935- .... CLC **4, 27**
See also CA 25-28R

Justice, Donald (Rodney) 1925- .. CLC **6, 19**
See also CANR 26; CA 5-8R; DLB-Y 83

Kacew, Romain 1914-1980
See Gary, Romain
See also CA 108; obituary CA 102

Kacewgary, Romain 1914-1980
See Gary, Romain

Kadare, Ismail 1936- .... CLC **52**

Kadohata, Cynthia 19??- .... CLC **59**

Kafka, Franz
1883-1924 .... TCLC **2, 6, 13, 29; SSC 5**
See also CA 105, 126; DLB 81

Kahn, Roger 1927-............... CLC **30**
See also CA 25-28R; SATA 37

Kaiser, (Friedrich Karl) Georg
1878-1945 .... TCLC **9**
See also CA 106

Kaletski, Alexander 1946- .... CLC **39**
See also CA 118

Kallman, Chester (Simon)
1921-1975 .... CLC **2**
See also CANR 3; CA 45-48;
obituary CA 53-56

Kaminsky, Melvin 1926-
See Brooks, Mel
See also CANR 16; CA 65-68

Kaminsky, Stuart 1934-.......... CLC **59**
See also CANR 29; CA 73-76

Kane, Paul 1941-
See Simon, Paul

Kanin, Garson 1912-.............. CLC **22**
See also CANR 7; CA 5-8R; DLB 7

Kaniuk, Yoram 1930-............. CLC **19**

Kant, Immanuel 1724-1804 ...... NCLC **27**

Kantor, MacKinlay 1904-1977 ...... CLC **7**
See also CA 61-64; obituary CA 73-76;
DLB 9

Kaplan, David Michael 1946- ...... CLC **50**

Kaplan, James 19??-.............. CLC **59**

Karamzin, Nikolai Mikhailovich
1766-1826 .... NCLC **3**

Karapanou, Margarita 1946-....... CLC **13**
See also CA 101

Karl, Frederick R(obert) 1927- ..... CLC **34**
See also CANR 3; CA 5-8R

Kassef, Romain 1914-1980
See Gary, Romain

Katz, Steve 1935-................ CLC **47**
See also CANR 12; CA 25-28R; DLB-Y 83

Kauffman, Janet 1945-............ CLC **42**
See also CA 117; DLB-Y 86

Kaufman, Bob (Garnell)
1925-1986 .... CLC **49**
See also CANR 22; CA 41-44R;
obituary CA 118; DLB 16, 41

Kaufman, George S(imon)
1889-1961 .... CLC **38**
See also CA 108; obituary CA 93-96; DLB 7

Kaufman, Sue 1926-1977......... CLC **3, 8**
See also Barondess, Sue K(aufman)

Kavan, Anna 1904-1968........ CLC **5, 13**
See also Edmonds, Helen (Woods)
See also CANR 6; CA 5-8R

Kavanagh, Patrick (Joseph Gregory)
1905-1967 .... CLC **22**
See also CA 123; obituary CA 25-28R;
DLB 15, 20

Kawabata, Yasunari
1899-1972 .... CLC **2, 5, 9, 18**
See also CA 93-96; obituary CA 33-36R

Kaye, M(ary) M(argaret) 1909?-.... CLC **28**
See also CANR 24; CA 89-92

Kaye, Mollie 1909?-
See Kaye, M(ary) M(argaret)

Kaye-Smith, Sheila 1887-1956..... TCLC **20**
See also CA 118; DLB 36

Kazan, Elia 1909-.......... CLC **6, 16, 63**
See also CA 21-24R

Kazantzakis, Nikos
1885?-1957............. TCLC **2, 5, 33**
See also CA 105

Kazin, Alfred 1915- .... CLC **34, 38**
See also CAAS 7; CANR 1; CA 1-4R;
DLB 67

Keane, Mary Nesta (Skrine) 1904-
See Keane, Molly
See also CA 108, 114

Keane, Molly 1904- .... CLC **31**
See also Keane, Mary Nesta (Skrine)

Keates, Jonathan 19??-............ CLC **34**

Keaton, Buster 1895-1966 .... CLC **20**

Keaton, Joseph Francis 1895-1966
See Keaton, Buster

Keats, John 1795-1821...... NCLC **8; PC 1**

Keene, Donald 1922- .... CLC **34**
See also CANR 5; CA 1-4R

Keillor, Garrison 1942- .... CLC **40**
See also Keillor, Gary (Edward)
See also CA 111; SATA 58; DLB-Y 87;
AAYA 2

Keillor, Gary (Edward)
See Keillor, Garrison
See also CA 111, 117

Kell, Joseph 1917-
See Burgess (Wilson, John) Anthony

Keller, Gottfried 1819-1890....... NCLC **2**

Kellerman, Jonathan (S.) 1949-..... CLC **44**
See also CANR 29; CA 106

Kelley, William Melvin 1937-....... CLC **22**
See also CANR 27; CA 77-80; DLB 33

Kellogg, Marjorie 1922-............ CLC **2**
See also CA 81-84

Kornbluth, C(yril) M. 1923-1958.... TCLC 8
  See also CA 105; DLB 8

Korolenko, Vladimir (Galaktionovich)
  1853-1921 .... TCLC 22
  See also CA 121

Kosinski, Jerzy (Nikodem)
  1933- .... CLC 1, 2, 3, 6, 10, 15, 53
  See also CANR 9; CA 17-20R; DLB 2;
  DLB-Y 82

Kostelanetz, Richard (Cory) 1940- .. CLC 28
  See also CAAS 8; CA 13-16R

Kostrowitzki, Wilhelm Apollinaris de
  1880-1918
  See Apollinaire, Guillaume
  See also CA 104

Kotlowitz, Robert 1924-........... CLC 4
  See also CA 33-36R

Kotzebue, August (Friedrich Ferdinand) von
  1761-1819 .... NCLC 25

Kotzwinkle, William 1938- ... CLC 5, 14, 35
  See also CLR 6; CANR 3; CA 45-48;
  SATA 24

Kozol, Jonathan 1936-............ CLC 17
  See also CANR 16; CA 61-64

Kozoll, Michael 1940?-............ CLC 35

Kramer, Kathryn 19??-............ CLC 34

Kramer, Larry 1935- .... CLC 42
  See also CA 124, 126

Krasicki, Ignacy 1735-1801 .... NCLC 8

Krasinski, Zygmunt 1812-1859 .... NCLC 4

Kraus, Karl 1874-1936............ TCLC 5
  See also CA 104

Kreve, Vincas 1882-1954 .... TCLC 27

Kristofferson, Kris 1936-.......... CLC 26
  See also CA 104

Krizanc, John 1956-.............. CLC 57

Krleza, Miroslav 1893-1981........ CLC 8
  See also CA 97-100; obituary CA 105

Kroetsch, Robert (Paul)
  1927-................ CLC 5, 23, 57
  See also CANR 8; CA 17-20R; DLB 53

Kroetz, Franz Xaver 1946- .... CLC 41
  See also CA 130

Kropotkin, Peter 1842-1921....... TCLC 36
  See also CA 119

Krotkov, Yuri 1917-.............. CLC 19
  See also CA 102

Krumgold, Joseph (Quincy)
  1908-1980 .... CLC 12
  See also CANR 7; CA 9-12R;
  obituary CA 101; SATA 1, 48;
  obituary SATA 23

Krutch, Joseph Wood 1893-1970.... CLC 24
  See also CANR 4; CA 1-4R;
  obituary CA 25-28R; DLB 63

Krylov, Ivan Andreevich
  1768?-1844.................. NCLC 1

Kubin, Alfred 1877-1959 .... TCLC 23
  See also CA 112; DLB 81

Kubrick, Stanley 1928-............ CLC 16
  See also CA 81-84; DLB 26

Kumin, Maxine (Winokur)
  1925- .... CLC 5, 13, 28
  See also CAAS 8; CANR 1, 21; CA 1-4R;
  SATA 12; DLB 5

Kundera, Milan 1929- ..... CLC 4, 9, 19, 32
  See also CANR 19; CA 85-88; AAYA 2

Kunitz, Stanley J(asspon)
  1905- .... CLC 6, 11, 14
  See also CANR 26; CA 41-44R; DLB 48

Kunze, Reiner 1933-.............. CLC 10
  See also CA 93-96; DLB 75

Kuprin, Aleksandr (Ivanovich)
  1870-1938 .... TCLC 5
  See also CA 104

Kureishi, Hanif 1954-............. CLC 64

Kurosawa, Akira 1910-............ CLC 16
  See also CA 101

Kuttner, Henry 1915-1958........ TCLC 10
  See also CA 107; DLB 8

Kuzma, Greg 1944-................ CLC 7
  See also CA 33-36R

Kuzmin, Mikhail 1872?-1936..... TCLC 40

Labrunie, Gerard 1808-1855
  See Nerval, Gerard de

La Bruyere, Jean de 1645-1696..... LC 17

Laclos, Pierre Ambroise Francois Choderlos
  de 1741-1803 .... NCLC 4

La Fayette, Marie (Madelaine Pioche de la
  Vergne, Comtesse) de
  1634-1693 .... LC 2

Lafayette, Rene
  See Hubbard, L(afayette) Ron(ald)

Laforgue, Jules 1860-1887....... NCLC 5

Lagerkvist, Par (Fabian)
  1891-1974 .... CLC 7, 10, 13, 54
  See also CA 85-88; obituary CA 49-52

Lagerlof, Selma (Ottiliana Lovisa)
  1858-1940 .... TCLC 4, 36
  See also CLR 7; CA 108; SATA 15

La Guma, (Justin) Alex(ander)
  1925-1985 .... CLC 19
  See also CANR 25; CA 49-52;
  obituary CA 118

Lamartine, Alphonse (Marie Louis Prat) de
  1790-1869 .... NCLC 11

Lamb, Charles 1775-1834........ NCLC 10
  See also SATA 17

Lamming, George (William)
  1927-................... CLC 2, 4, 66
  See also BLC 2; CANR 26; CA 85-88

LaMoore, Louis Dearborn 1908?-
  See L'Amour, Louis (Dearborn)

L'Amour, Louis (Dearborn)
  1908-1988 .... CLC 25, 55
  See also CANR 3, 25; CA 1-4R;
  obituary CA 125; DLB-Y 80

Lampedusa, (Prince) Giuseppe (Maria
  Fabrizio) Tomasi di
  1896-1957 .... TCLC 13
  See also CA 111

Lampman, Archibald 1861-1899 .. NCLC 25
  See also DLB 92

Lancaster, Bruce 1896-1963........ CLC 36
  See also CAP 1; CA 9-12; SATA 9

Landis, John (David) 1950-........ CLC 26
  See also CA 112, 122

Landolfi, Tommaso 1908-1979... CLC 11, 49
  See also CA 127; obituary CA 117

Landon, Letitia Elizabeth
  1802-1838 .... NCLC 15

Landor, Walter Savage
  1775-1864 .... NCLC 14

Landwirth, Heinz 1927-
  See Lind, Jakov
  See also CANR 7; CA 11-12R

Lane, Patrick 1939-.............. CLC 25
  See also CA 97-100; DLB 53

Lang, Andrew 1844-1912......... TCLC 16
  See also CA 114; SATA 16

Lang, Fritz 1890-1976 .... CLC 20
  See also CANR 30; CA 77-80;
  obituary CA 69-72

Langer, Elinor 1939- .... CLC 34
  See also CA 121

Lanier, Sidney 1842-1881 .... NCLC 6
  See also SATA 18; DLB 64

Lanyer, Aemilia 1569-1645 .... LC 10

Lao Tzu c. 6th-3rd century B.C.... CMLC 7

Lapine, James 1949-.............. CLC 39
  See also CA 123, 130

Larbaud, Valery 1881-1957 .... TCLC 9
  See also CA 106

Lardner, Ring(gold Wilmer)
  1885-1933 .... TCLC 2, 14
  See also CA 104; DLB 11, 25, 86;
  CDALB 1917-1929

Larkin, Philip (Arthur)
  1922-1985 ... CLC 3, 5, 8, 9, 13, 18, 33,
                                 39, 64
  See also CANR 24; CA 5-8R;
  obituary CA 117; DLB 27

Larra (y Sanchez de Castro), Mariano Jose de
  1809-1837 .... NCLC 17

Larsen, Eric 1941- .... CLC 55

Larsen, Nella 1891-1964 .... CLC 37
  See also BLC 2; CA 125; DLB 51

Larson, Charles R(aymond) 1938-... CLC 31
  See also CANR 4; CA 53-56

Latham, Jean Lee 1902-........... CLC 12
  See also CANR 7; CA 5-8R; SATA 2

Lathen, Emma..................... CLC 2
  See also Hennissart, Martha; Latsis, Mary
  J(ane)

Latsis, Mary J(ane)................ CLC 2
  See also Lathen, Emma
  See also CA 85-88

Lattimore, Richmond (Alexander)
  1906-1984 .... CLC 3
  See also CANR 1; CA 1-4R;
  obituary CA 112

Laughlin, James 1914-............ CLC 49
  See also CANR 9; CA 21-24R; DLB 48

Laurence, (Jean) Margaret (Wemyss)
  1926-1987 .. CLC 3, 6, 13, 50, 62; SSC 7
  See also CA 5-8R; obituary CA 121;
  SATA 50; DLB 53

Laurent, Antoine 1952- .... CLC 50

Lewes, George Henry
  1817-1878 .... NCLC 25
  See also DLB 55

Lewis, Alun 1915-1944........... TCLC 3
  See also CA 104; DLB 20

Lewis, C(ecil) Day 1904-1972
  See Day Lewis, C(ecil)

Lewis, C(live) S(taples)
  1898-1963 .... CLC 1, 3, 6, 14, 27
  See also CLR 3; CA 81-84; SATA 13;
  DLB 15

Lewis (Winters), Janet 1899-....... CLC 41
  See also Winters, Janet Lewis
  See also CANR 29; CAP 1; CA 9-10R;
  DLB-Y 87

Lewis, Matthew Gregory
  1775-1818 .... NCLC 11
  See also DLB 39

Lewis, (Harry) Sinclair
  1885-1951 .... TCLC 4, 13, 23, 39
  See also CA 104; DLB 9; DLB-DS 1;
  CDALB 1917-1929

Lewis, (Percy) Wyndham
  1882?-1957................. TCLC 2, 9
  See also CA 104; DLB 15

Lewisohn, Ludwig 1883-1955...... TCLC 19
  See also CA 73-76, 107;
  obituary CA 29-32R; DLB 4, 9, 28

L'Heureux, John (Clarke) 1934-.... CLC 52
  See also CANR 23; CA 15-16R

Lieber, Stanley Martin 1922-
  See Lee, Stan

Lieberman, Laurence (James)
  1935-..................... CLC 4, 36
  See also CANR 8; CA 17-20R

Li Fei-kan 1904-................. CLC 18
  See also Pa Chin
  See also CA 105

Lifton, Robert Jay 1926-.......... CLC 67
  See also CANR 27; CA 17-18R

Lightfoot, Gordon (Meredith)
  1938-..................... CLC 26
  See also CA 109

Ligotti, Thomas 1953- .... CLC 44
  See also CA 123

Liliencron, Detlev von
  1844-1909 .... TCLC 18
  See also CA 117

Lima, Jose Lezama 1910-1976
  See Lezama Lima, Jose

Lima Barreto, (Alfonso Henriques de)
  1881-1922 .... TCLC 23
  See also CA 117

Limonov, Eduard 1943- .... CLC 67

Lincoln, Abraham 1809-1865..... NCLC 18

Lind, Jakov 1927-.......... CLC 1, 2, 4, 27
  See also Landwirth, Heinz
  See also CAAS 4; CA 9-12R

Lindsay, David 1876-1945........ TCLC 15
  See also CA 113

Lindsay, (Nicholas) Vachel
  1879-1931 .... TCLC 17
  See also CA 114; SATA 40; DLB 54;
  CDALB 1865-1917

Linney, Romulus 1930- .... CLC 51
  See also CA 1-4R

Li Po 701-763.................. CMLC 2

Lipsius, Justus 1547-1606 .... LC 16

Lipsyte, Robert (Michael) 1938-.... CLC 21
  See also CLR 23; CANR 8; CA 17-20R;
  SATA 5

Lish, Gordon (Jay) 1934-......... CLC 45
  See also CA 113, 117

Lispector, Clarice 1925-1977...... CLC 43
  See also obituary CA 116

Littell, Robert 1935?-............ CLC 42
  See also CA 109, 112

Little, Malcolm 1925-1965
  See also BLC 2; CA 125; obituary CA 111

Liu E 1857-1909............... TCLC 15
  See also CA 115

Lively, Penelope 1933-........ CLC 32, 50
  See also CLR 7; CANR 29; CA 41-44R;
  SATA 7; DLB 14

Livesay, Dorothy 1909- .... CLC 4, 15
  See also CAAS 8; CA 25-28R; DLB 68

Lizardi, Jose Joaquin Fernandez de
  1776-1827 .... NCLC 30

Llewellyn, Richard 1906-1983...... CLC 7
  See also Llewellyn Lloyd, Richard (Dafydd
  Vyvyan)
  See also DLB 15

Llewellyn Lloyd, Richard (Dafydd Vyvyan)
  1906-1983
  See Llewellyn, Richard
  See also CANR 7; CA 53-56;
  obituary CA 111; SATA 11, 37

Llosa, Mario Vargas 1936-
  See Vargas Llosa, Mario

Lloyd, Richard Llewellyn 1906-
  See Llewellyn, Richard

Locke, John 1632-1704 .... LC 7
  See also DLB 31

Lockhart, John Gibson
  1794-1854 .... NCLC 6

Lodge, David (John) 1935-........ CLC 36
  See also CANR 19; CA 17-20R; DLB 14

Loewinsohn, Ron(ald William)
  1937-..................... CLC 52
  See also CA 25-28R

Logan, John 1923- .... CLC 5
  See also CA 77-80; obituary CA 124; DLB 5

Lo Kuan-chung 1330?-1400? .... LC 12

Lombino, S. A. 1926-
  See Hunter, Evan

London, Jack
  1876-1916 ...... TCLC 9, 15, 39; SSC 4
  See also London, John Griffith
  See also SATA 18; DLB 8, 12, 78;
  CDALB 1865-1917

London, John Griffith 1876-1916
  See London, Jack
  See also CA 110, 119

Long, Emmett 1925-
  See Leonard, Elmore

Longbaugh, Harry 1931-
  See Goldman, William (W.)

Longfellow, Henry Wadsworth
  1807-1882 .... NCLC 2
  See also SATA 19; DLB 1, 59;
  CDALB 1640-1865

Longley, Michael 1939-.......... CLC 29
  See also CA 102; DLB 40

Longus fl. c. 2nd century- .... CMLC 7

Lopate, Phillip 1943- .... CLC 29
  See also CA 97-100; DLB-Y 80

Lopez Portillo (y Pacheco), Jose
  1920-..................... CLC 46
  See also CA 129

Lopez y Fuentes, Gregorio
  1897-1966 .... CLC 32

Lord, Bette Bao 1938-............ CLC 23
  See also CA 107; SATA 58

Lorde, Audre (Geraldine) 1934-..... CLC 18
  See also BLC 2; CANR 16, 26; CA 25-28R;
  DLB 41

Loti, Pierre 1850-1923........... TCLC 11
  See also Viaud, (Louis Marie) Julien

Lovecraft, H(oward) P(hillips)
  1890-1937 .... TCLC 4, 22; SSC 3
  See also CA 104

Lovelace, Earl 1935-.............. CLC 51
  See also CA 77-80

Lowell, Amy 1874-1925......... TCLC 1, 8
  See also CA 104; DLB 54

Lowell, James Russell 1819-1891 .. NCLC 2
  See also DLB 1, 11, 64, 79;
  CDALB 1640-1865

Lowell, Robert (Traill Spence, Jr.)
  1917-1977 ... CLC 1, 2, 3, 4, 5, 8, 9, 11,
  15, 37; PC 3
  See also CANR 26; CA 9-10R;
  obituary CA 73-76; CABS 2; DLB 5

Lowndes, Marie (Adelaide) Belloc
  1868-1947 .... TCLC 12
  See also CA 107; DLB 70

Lowry, (Clarence) Malcolm
  1909-1957 .... TCLC 6, 40
  See also CA 105, 131; DLB 15

Loy, Mina 1882-1966............. CLC 28
  See also CA 113; DLB 4, 54

Lucas, Craig....................... CLC 64

Lucas, George 1944-.............. CLC 16
  See also CANR 30; CA 77-80; SATA 56;
  AAYA 1

Lucas, Victoria 1932-1963
  See Plath, Sylvia

Ludlam, Charles 1943-1987..... CLC 46, 50
  See also CA 85-88; obituary CA 122

Ludlum, Robert 1927- .... CLC 22, 43
  See also CANR 25; CA 33-36R; DLB-Y 82

Ludwig, Ken 19??- .... CLC 60

Ludwig, Otto 1813-1865......... NCLC 4

Lugones, Leopoldo 1874-1938..... TCLC 15
  See also CA 116

Lu Hsun 1881-1936 .... TCLC 3

Lukacs, Georg 1885-1971......... CLC 24
  See also Lukacs, Gyorgy

Lukacs, Gyorgy 1885-1971
  See Lukacs, Georg
  See also CA 101; obituary CA 29-32R

Luke, Peter (Ambrose Cyprian)
  1919- .... CLC 38
  See also CA 81-84; DLB 13

Lurie (Bishop), Alison
  1926- .... CLC 4, 5, 18, 39
  See also CANR 2, 17; CA 1-4R; SATA 46;
  DLB 2

Lustig, Arnost 1926- .... CLC 56
  See also CA 69-72; SATA 56; AAYA 3

Luther, Martin 1483-1546 .... LC 9

Luzi, Mario 1914- .... CLC 13
  See also CANR 9; CA 61-64

Lynch, David 1946- .... CLC 66
  See also CA 129; brief entry CA 124

Lynn, Kenneth S(chuyler) 1923- .... CLC 50
  See also CANR 3, 27; CA 1-4R

Lytle, Andrew (Nelson) 1902- ...... CLC 22
  See also CA 9-12R; DLB 6

Lyttelton, George 1709-1773 .... LC 10

Lytton, Edward Bulwer 1803-1873
  See Bulwer-Lytton, (Lord) Edward (George
  Earle Lytton)
  See also SATA 23

Maas, Peter 1929- .... CLC 29
  See also CA 93-96

Macaulay, (Dame Emile) Rose
  1881-1958 .... TCLC 7
  See also CA 104; DLB 36

MacBeth, George (Mann)
  1932- .... CLC 2, 5, 9
  See also CA 25-28R; SATA 4; DLB 40

MacCaig, Norman (Alexander)
  1910- .... CLC 36
  See also CANR 3; CA 9-12R; DLB 27

MacCarthy, Desmond 1877-1952 .. TCLC 36

MacDermot, Thomas H. 1870-1933
  See Redcam, Tom

MacDiarmid, Hugh
  1892-1978 .... CLC 2, 4, 11, 19, 63
  See also Grieve, C(hristopher) M(urray)
  See also DLB 20

Macdonald, Cynthia 1928- ...... CLC 13, 19
  See also CANR 4; CA 49-52

MacDonald, George 1824-1905 ..... TCLC 9
  See also CA 106; SATA 33; DLB 18

MacDonald, John D(ann)
  1916-1986 .... CLC 3, 27, 44
  See also CANR 1, 19; CA 1-4R;
  obituary CA 121; DLB 8; DLB-Y 86

Macdonald, (John) Ross
  1915-1983 ...... CLC 1, 2, 3, 14, 34, 41
  See also Millar, Kenneth
  See also DLB-DS 6

MacEwen, Gwendolyn (Margaret)
  1941-1987 .... CLC 13, 55
  See also CANR 7, 22; CA 9-12R;
  obituary CA 124; SATA 50, 55; DLB 53

Machado (y Ruiz), Antonio
  1875-1939 .... TCLC 3
  See also CA 104

Machado de Assis, (Joaquim Maria)
  1839-1908 .... TCLC 10
  See also BLC 2; brief entry CA 107

Machen, Arthur (Llewelyn Jones)
  1863-1947 .... TCLC 4
  See also CA 104; DLB 36

Machiavelli, Niccolo 1469-1527 ...... LC 8

MacInnes, Colin 1914-1976 ...... CLC 4, 23
  See also CANR 21; CA 69-72;
  obituary CA 65-68; DLB 14

MacInnes, Helen (Clark)
  1907-1985 .... CLC 27, 39
  See also CANR 1, 28; CA 1-4R;
  obituary CA 65-68, 117; SATA 22, 44;
  DLB 87

Macintosh, Elizabeth 1897-1952
  See Tey, Josephine
  See also CA 110

Mackenzie, (Edward Montague) Compton
  1883-1972 .... CLC 18
  See also CAP 2; CA 21-22;
  obituary CA 37-40R; DLB 34

Mac Laverty, Bernard 1942- .... CLC 31
  See also CA 116, 118

MacLean, Alistair (Stuart)
  1922-1987 .... CLC 3, 13, 50, 63
  See also CANR 28; CA 57-60;
  obituary CA 121; SATA 23, 50

MacLeish, Archibald
  1892-1982 .... CLC 3, 8, 14
  See also CA 9-12R; obituary CA 106;
  DLB 4, 7, 45; DLB-Y 82

MacLennan, (John) Hugh
  1907- .... CLC 2, 14
  See also CA 5-8R; DLB 68

MacLeod, Alistair 1936- .... CLC 56
  See also CA 123; DLB 60

Macleod, Fiona 1855-1905
  See Sharp, William

MacNeice, (Frederick) Louis
  1907-1963 .... CLC 1, 4, 10, 53
  See also CA 85-88; DLB 10, 20

Macpherson, (Jean) Jay 1931- ...... CLC 14
  See also CA 5-8R; DLB 53

MacShane, Frank 1927- .... CLC 39
  See also CANR 3; CA 11-12R

Macumber, Mari 1896-1966
  See Sandoz, Mari (Susette)

Madach, Imre 1823-1864 .... NCLC 19

Madden, (Jerry) David 1933- .... CLC 5, 15
  See also CAAS 3; CANR 4; CA 1-4R;
  DLB 6

Madhubuti, Haki R. 1942- .... CLC 6
  See also Lee, Don L.
  See also BLC 2; CANR 24; CA 73-76;
  DLB 5, 41; DLB-DS 8

Maeterlinck, Maurice 1862-1949 ... TCLC 3
  See also CA 104

Mafouz, Naguib 1912-
  See Mahfuz, Najib

Maginn, William 1794-1842 .... NCLC 8

Mahapatra, Jayanta 1928- .... CLC 33
  See also CAAS 9; CANR 15; CA 73-76

Mahfuz Najib 1912- .... CLC 52, 55
  See also DLB-Y 88

Mahon, Derek 1941- .... CLC 27
  See also CA 113, 128; DLB 40

Mailer, Norman
  1923- ...... CLC 1, 2, 3, 4, 5, 8, 11, 14,
                        28, 39
  See also CANR 28; CA 9-12R; CABS 1;
  DLB 2, 16, 28; DLB-Y 80, 83;
  DLB-DS 3; CDALB 1968-1987

Maillet, Antonine 1929- .... CLC 54
  See also CA 115, 120; DLB 60

Mais, Roger 1905-1955 .... TCLC 8
  See also CA 105, 124

Maitland, Sara (Louise) 1950- ...... CLC 49
  See also CANR 13; CA 69-72

Major, Clarence 1936- .... CLC 3, 19, 48
  See also BLC 2; CAAS 6; CANR 13, 25;
  CA 21-24R; DLB 33

Major, Kevin 1949- .... CLC 26
  See also CLR 11; CANR 21; CA 97-100;
  SATA 32; DLB 60

Malamud, Bernard
  1914-1986 ..... CLC 1, 2, 3, 5, 8, 9, 11,
                   18, 27, 44
  See also CANR 28; CA 5-8R;
  obituary CA 118; CABS 1; DLB 2, 28;
  DLB-Y 80, 86; CDALB 1941-1968

Malcolm X 1925-1965
  See Little, Malcolm

Malherbe, Francois de 1555-1628 ..... LC 5

Mallarme, Stephane 1842-1898 .... NCLC 4

Mallet-Joris, Francoise 1930- ...... CLC 11
  See also CANR 17; CA 65-68; DLB 83

Maloff, Saul 1922- .... CLC 5
  See also CA 33-36R

Malone, Louis 1907-1963
  See MacNeice, (Frederick) Louis

Malone, Michael (Christopher)
  1942- .... CLC 43
  See also CANR 14; CA 77-80

Malory, (Sir) Thomas ?-1471 .... LC 11
  See also SATA 33, 59

Malouf, David 1934- .... CLC 28

Malraux, (Georges-) Andre
  1901-1976 ...... CLC 1, 4, 9, 13, 15, 57
  See also CAP 2; CA 21-24;
  obituary CA 69-72; DLB 72

Malzberg, Barry N. 1939- .... CLC 7
  See also CAAS 4; CANR 16; CA 61-64;
  DLB 8

Mamet, David (Alan)
  1947- .... CLC 9, 15, 34, 46
  See also CANR 15; CA 81-84, 124;
  CABS 3; DLB 7; AAYA 3

Mamoulian, Rouben 1898- .... CLC 16
  See also CA 25-28R; obituary CA 124

Mandelstam, Osip (Emilievich)
  1891?-1938? .... TCLC 2, 6
  See also CA 104

Mander, Jane 1877-1949 .... TCLC 31

Mandiargues, Andre Pieyre de
  1909- .... CLC 41
  See also CA 103; DLB 83

Mangan, James Clarence
1803-1849 .... **NCLC 27**

Manley, (Mary) Delariviere
1672?-1724. .... **LC 1**
See also DLB 39, 80

Mann, (Luiz) Heinrich 1871-1950. . . **TCLC 9**
See also CA 106; DLB 66

Mann, Thomas
1875-1955 ...... **TCLC 2, 8, 14, 21, 35;
SSC 5**
See also CA 104, 128; DLB 66

Manning, Frederic 1882-1935 ..... **TCLC 25**
See also CA 124

Manning, Olivia 1915-1980 ...... **CLC 5, 19**
See also CANR 29; CA 5-8R;
obituary CA 101

Mano, D. Keith 1942- .... **CLC 2, 10**
See also CAAS 6; CANR 26; CA 25-28R;
DLB 6

Mansfield, Katherine
1888-1923 .... **TCLC 2, 8, 39**
See also CA 104

Manso, Peter 1940- .... **CLC 39**
See also CA 29-32R

Manzoni, Alessandro 1785-1873 .. **NCLC 29**

Mapu, Abraham (ben Jekutiel)
1808-1867 .... **NCLC 18**

Marat, Jean Paul 1743-1793....... **LC 10**

Marcel, Gabriel (Honore)
1889-1973 .... **CLC 15**
See also CA 102; obituary CA 45-48

Marchbanks, Samuel 1913-
See Davies, (William) Robertson

Marie de l'Incarnation 1599-1672.... **LC 10**

Marinetti, F(ilippo) T(ommaso)
1876-1944 .... **TCLC 10**
See also CA 107

Marivaux, Pierre Carlet de Chamblain de
(1688-1763).................... **LC 4**

Markandaya, Kamala 1924-...... **CLC 8, 38**
See also Taylor, Kamala (Purnaiya)

Markfield, Wallace (Arthur) 1926-... **CLC 8**
See also CAAS 3; CA 69-72; DLB 2, 28

Markham, Robert 1922-
See Amis, Kingsley (William)

Marks, J. 1942-
See Highwater, Jamake

Markson, David 1927-............ **CLC 67**
See also CANR 1; CA 49-52

Marley, Bob 1945-1981 .... **CLC 17**
See also Marley, Robert Nesta

Marley, Robert Nesta 1945-1981
See Marley, Bob
See also CA 107; obituary CA 103

Marlowe, Christopher 1564-1593 ..... **DC 1**
See also DLB 62

Marmontel, Jean-Francois
1723-1799 .... **LC 2**

Marquand, John P(hillips)
1893-1960 .... **CLC 2, 10**
See also CA 85-88; DLB 9

Marquez, Gabriel Garcia 1928-
See Garcia Marquez, Gabriel

Marquis, Don(ald Robert Perry)
1878-1937 .... **TCLC 7**
See also CA 104; DLB 11, 25

Marryat, Frederick 1792-1848 .... **NCLC 3**
See also DLB 21

Marsh, (Dame Edith) Ngaio
1899-1982 .... **CLC 7, 53**
See also CANR 6; CA 9-12R; DLB 77

Marshall, Garry 1935?- .... **CLC 17**
See also CA 111; AAYA 3

Marshall, Paule 1929- ..... **CLC 27; SSC 3**
See also BLC 2; CANR 25; CA 77-80;
DLB 33

Marsten, Richard 1926-
See Hunter, Evan

Martin, Steve 1945?- .... **CLC 30**
See also CANR 30; CA 97-100

Martin du Gard, Roger
1881-1958 .... **TCLC 24**
See also CA 118; DLB 65

Martineau, Harriet 1802-1876.... **NCLC 26**
See also YABC 2; DLB 21, 55

Martinez Ruiz, Jose 1874-1967
See Azorin
See also CA 93-96

Martinez Sierra, Gregorio
1881-1947 .... **TCLC 6**
See also CA 104, 115

Martinez Sierra, Maria (de la O'LeJarraga)
1880?-1974.................. **TCLC 6**
See also obituary CA 115

Martinson, Harry (Edmund)
1904-1978 .... **CLC 14**
See also CA 77-80

Marvell, Andrew 1621-1678......... **LC 4**

Marx, Karl (Heinrich)
1818-1883 .... **NCLC 17**

Masaoka Shiki 1867-1902 .... **TCLC 18**

Masefield, John (Edward)
1878-1967 .... **CLC 11, 47**
See also CAP 2; CA 19-20;
obituary CA 25-28R; SATA 19; DLB 10,
19

Maso, Carole 19??-............... **CLC 44**

Mason, Bobbie Ann
1940- .... **CLC 28, 43; SSC 4**
See also CANR 11; CA 53-56; SAAS 1;
DLB-Y 87

Mason, Nick 1945-............... **CLC 35**
See also Pink Floyd

Mason, Tally 1909-1971
See Derleth, August (William)

Masters, Edgar Lee
1868?-1950......... **TCLC 2, 25; PC 1**
See also CA 104; DLB 54;
CDALB 1865-1917

Masters, Hilary 1928-............ **CLC 48**
See also CANR 13; CA 25-28R

Mastrosimone, William 19??- ...... **CLC 36**

Matheson, Richard (Burton)
1926-...................... **CLC 37**
See also CA 97-100; DLB 8, 44

Mathews, Harry 1930-......... **CLC 6, 52**
See also CAAS 6; CANR 18; CA 21-24R

Mathias, Roland (Glyn) 1915-...... **CLC 45**
See also CANR 19; CA 97-100; DLB 27

Matthews, Greg 1949- .... **CLC 45**

Matthews, William 1942-......... **CLC 40**
See also CANR 12; CA 29-32R; DLB 5

Matthias, John (Edward) 1941-...... **CLC 9**
See also CA 33-36R

Matthiessen, Peter
1927- .... **CLC 5, 7, 11, 32, 64**
See also CANR 21; CA 9-12R; SATA 27;
DLB 6

Maturin, Charles Robert
1780?-1824.................. **NCLC 6**

Matute, Ana Maria 1925- .... **CLC 11**
See also CA 89-92

Maugham, W(illiam) Somerset
1874-1965 .... **CLC 1, 11, 15, 67; SSC 8**
See also CA 5-8R; obituary CA 25-28R;
SATA 54; DLB 10, 36, 77, 100

Maupassant, (Henri Rene Albert) Guy de
1850-1893 .... **NCLC 1; SSC 1**

Mauriac, Claude 1914-............ **CLC 9**
See also CA 89-92; DLB 83

Mauriac, Francois (Charles)
1885-1970 .... **CLC 4, 9, 56**
See also CAP 2; CA 25-28; DLB 65

Mavor, Osborne Henry 1888-1951
See Bridie, James
See also CA 104

Maxwell, William (Keepers, Jr.)
1908- .... **CLC 19**
See also CA 93-96; DLB-Y 80

May, Elaine 1932- .... **CLC 16**
See also CA 124; DLB 44

Mayakovsky, Vladimir (Vladimirovich)
1893-1930 .... **TCLC 4, 18**
See also CA 104

Mayhew, Henry 1812-1887 ...... **NCLC 31**
See also DLB 18, 55

Maynard, Joyce 1953-............ **CLC 23**
See also CA 111, 129

Mayne, William (James Carter)
1928- .... **CLC 12**
See also CA 9-12R; SATA 6

Mayo, Jim 1908?-
See L'Amour, Louis (Dearborn)

Maysles, Albert 1926- and Maysles, David
1926- .... **CLC 16**
See also CA 29-32R

Maysles, Albert 1926- .... **CLC 16**
See also Maysles, Albert and Maysles,
David
See also CA 29-32R

Maysles, David 1932-............ **CLC 16**
See also Maysles, Albert and Maysles,
David

Mazer, Norma Fox 1931- .... **CLC 26**
See also CLR 23; CANR 12; CA 69-72;
SAAS 1; SATA 24

McAuley, James (Phillip)
1917-1976 .... **CLC 45**
See also CA 97-100

McBain, Ed 1926-
See Hunter, Evan

Miles, Josephine (Louise)
    1911-1985 . . . . **CLC 1, 2, 14, 34, 39**
    See also CANR 2; CA 1-4R;
    obituary CA 116; DLB 48

Mill, John Stuart 1806-1873 . . . . . **NCLC 11**
    See also DLB 55

Millar, Kenneth 1915-1983 . . . . **CLC 14**
    See also Macdonald, Ross
    See also CANR 16; CA 9-12R;
    obituary CA 110; DLB 2; DLB-Y 83;
    DLB-DS 6

Millay, Edna St. Vincent
    1892-1950 . . . . **TCLC 4**
    See also CA 103; DLB 45;
    CDALB 1917-1929

Miller, Arthur
    1915- . . . . . . **CLC 1, 2, 6, 10, 15, 26, 47;**
                          DC 1
    See also CANR 2, 30; CA 1-4R; CABS 3;
    DLB 7; CDALB 1941-1968

Miller, Henry (Valentine)
    1891-1980 . . . . **CLC 1, 2, 4, 9, 14, 43**
    See also CA 9-12R; obituary CA 97-100;
    DLB 4, 9; DLB-Y 80; CDALB 1929-1941

Miller, Jason 1939?- . . . . **CLC 2**
    See also CA 73-76; DLB 7

Miller, Sue 19??- . . . . **CLC 44**

Miller, Walter M(ichael), Jr.
    1923- . . . . **CLC 4, 30**
    See also CA 85-88; DLB 8

Millett, Kate 1934- . . . . **CLC 67**
    See also CANR 32; CA 73-76

Millhauser, Steven 1943- . . . . **CLC 21, 54**
    See also CA 108, 110, 111; DLB 2

Millin, Sarah Gertrude 1889-1968 . . **CLC 49**
    See also CA 102; obituary CA 93-96

Milne, A(lan) A(lexander)
    1882-1956 . . . . **TCLC 6**
    See also CLR 1; YABC 1; CA 104;
    DLB 10, 77

Milner, Ron(ald) 1938- . . . . **CLC 56**
    See also BLC 2; CANR 24; CA 73-76;
    DLB 38

Milosz Czeslaw
    1911- . . . . **CLC 5, 11, 22, 31, 56**
    See also CANR 23; CA 81-84

Milton, John 1608-1674 . . . . **LC 9**

Miner, Valerie (Jane) 1947- . . . . **CLC 40**
    See also CA 97-100

Minot, Susan 1956- . . . . **CLC 44**

Minus, Ed 1938- . . . . **CLC 39**

Miro (Ferrer), Gabriel (Francisco Victor)
    1879-1930 . . . . **TCLC 5**
    See also CA 104

Mishima, Yukio
    1925-1970 . . . . **CLC 2, 4, 6, 9, 27; DC 1;**
                           SSC 4
    See also Hiraoka, Kimitake

Mistral, Gabriela 1889-1957 . . . . **TCLC 2**
    See also CA 104

Mitchell, James Leslie 1901-1935
    See Gibbon, Lewis Grassic
    See also CA 104; DLB 15

Mitchell, Joni 1943- . . . . **CLC 12**
    See also CA 112

Mitchell (Marsh), Margaret (Munnerlyn)
    1900-1949 . . . . **TCLC 11**
    See also CA 109, 125; DLB 9

Mitchell, S. Weir 1829-1914 . . . . . **TCLC 36**

Mitchell, W(illiam) O(rmond)
    1914- . . . . **CLC 25**
    See also CANR 15; CA 77-80; DLB 88

Mitford, Mary Russell 1787-1855. . **NCLC 4**

Mitford, Nancy 1904-1973 . . . . **CLC 44**
    See also CA 9-12R

Miyamoto Yuriko 1899-1951 . . . . . . **TCLC 37**

Mo, Timothy 1950- . . . . **CLC 46**
    See also CA 117

Modarressi, Taghi 1931- . . . . **CLC 44**
    See also CA 121

Modiano, Patrick (Jean) 1945- . . . . . **CLC 18**
    See also CANR 17; CA 85-88; DLB 83

Mofolo, Thomas (Mokopu)
    1876-1948 . . . . **TCLC 22**
    See also BLC 2; brief entry CA 121

Mohr, Nicholasa 1935- . . . . **CLC 12**
    See also CLR 22; CANR 1; CA 49-52;
    SAAS 8; SATA 8

Mojtabai, A(nn) G(race)
    1938- . . . . **CLC 5, 9, 15, 29**
    See also CA 85-88

Moliere 1622-1673 . . . . **LC 10**

Molnar, Ferenc 1878-1952 . . . . **TCLC 20**
    See also CA 109

Momaday, N(avarre) Scott
    1934- . . . . **CLC 2, 19**
    See also CANR 14; CA 25-28R; SATA 30,
    48

Monroe, Harriet 1860-1936 . . . . . . **TCLC 12**
    See also CA 109; DLB 54, 91

Montagu, Elizabeth 1720-1800 . . . . **NCLC 7**

Montagu, Lady Mary (Pierrepont) Wortley
    1689-1762 . . . . **LC 9**

Montague, John (Patrick)
    1929- . . . . **CLC 13, 46**
    See also CANR 9; CA 9-12R; DLB 40

Montaigne, Michel (Eyquem) de
    1533-1592 . . . . **LC 8**

Montale, Eugenio 1896-1981 . . . **CLC 7, 9, 18**
    See also CANR 30; CA 17-20R;
    obituary CA 104

Montesquieu, Charles-Louis de Secondat
    1689-1755 . . . . **LC 7**

Montgomery, Marion (H., Jr.)
    1925- . . . . **CLC 7**
    See also CANR 3; CA 1-4R; DLB 6

Montgomery, Robert Bruce 1921-1978
    See Crispin, Edmund
    See also CA 104

Montherlant, Henri (Milon) de
    1896-1972 . . . . **CLC 8, 19**
    See also CA 85-88; obituary CA 37-40R;
    DLB 72

Monty Python . . . . **CLC 21**

Moodie, Susanna (Strickland)
    1803-1885 . . . . **NCLC 14**

Mooney, Ted 1951- . . . . **CLC 25**

Moorcock, Michael (John)
    1939- . . . . **CLC 5, 27, 58**
    See also CAAS 5; CANR 2, 17; CA 45-48;
    DLB 14

Moore, Brian
    1921- . . . . **CLC 1, 3, 5, 7, 8, 19, 32**
    See also CANR 1, 25; CA 1-4R

Moore, George (Augustus)
    1852-1933 . . . . **TCLC 7**
    See also CA 104; DLB 10, 18, 57

Moore, Lorrie 1957- . . . . **CLC 39, 45**
    See also Moore, Marie Lorena

Moore, Marianne (Craig)
    1887-1972 . . . **CLC 1, 2, 4, 8, 10, 13, 19,**
                                 47
    See also CANR 3; CA 1-4R;
    obituary CA 33-36R; SATA 20; DLB 45;
    CDALB 1929-1941

Moore, Marie Lorena 1957-
    See Moore, Lorrie
    See also CA 116

Moore, Thomas 1779-1852. . . . . . . **NCLC 6**

Morand, Paul 1888-1976 . . . . **CLC 41**
    See also obituary CA 69-72; DLB 65

Morante, Elsa 1918-1985 . . . . **CLC 8, 47**
    See also CA 85-88; obituary CA 117

Moravia, Alberto
    1907- . . . . **CLC 2, 7, 11, 18, 27, 46**
    See also Pincherle, Alberto

More, Hannah 1745-1833 . . . . **NCLC 27**

More, Henry 1614-1687. . . . . **LC 9**

More, (Sir) Thomas 1478-1535 . . . . . . **LC 10**

Moreas, Jean 1856-1910 . . . . **TCLC 18**

Morgan, Berry 1919- . . . . **CLC 6**
    See also CA 49-52; DLB 6

Morgan, Edwin (George) 1920- . . . . . **CLC 31**
    See also CANR 3; CA 7-8R; DLB 27

Morgan, (George) Frederick
    1922- . . . . **CLC 23**
    See also CANR 21; CA 17-20R

Morgan, Janet 1945- . . . . **CLC 39**
    See also CA 65-68

Morgan, Lady 1776?-1859 . . . . **NCLC 29**

Morgan, Robin 1941- . . . . **CLC 2**
    See also CA 69-72

Morgan, Seth 1949-1990 . . . . **CLC 65**
    See also CA 132

Morgenstern, Christian (Otto Josef Wolfgang)
    1871-1914 . . . . **TCLC 8**
    See also CA 105

Moricz, Zsigmond 1879-1942 . . . . . **TCLC 33**

Morike, Eduard (Friedrich)
    1804-1875 . . . . **NCLC 10**

Mori Ogai 1862-1922 . . . . **TCLC 14**
    See also Mori Rintaro

Mori Rintaro 1862-1922
    See Mori Ogai
    See also CA 110

Moritz, Karl Philipp 1756-1793 . . . . . . **LC 2**

Morris, Julian 1916-
    See West, Morris L.

Morris, Steveland Judkins 1950-
See Wonder, Stevie
See also CA 111

Morris, William 1834-1896 . . . . NCLC 4
See also DLB 18, 35, 57

Morris, Wright (Marion)
1910- . . . . CLC 1, 3, 7, 18, 37
See also CANR 21; CA 9-12R; DLB 2;
DLB-Y 81

Morrison, James Douglas 1943-1971
See Morrison, Jim
See also CA 73-76

Morrison, Jim 1943-1971 . . . . CLC 17
See also Morrison, James Douglas

Morrison, Toni 1931- . . . . . CLC 4, 10, 22, 55
See also BLC 2; CANR 27; CA 29-32R;
SATA 57; DLB 6, 33; DLB-Y 81;
CDALB 1968-1987; AAYA 1

Morrison, Van 1945- . . . . CLC 21
See also CA 116

Mortimer, John (Clifford)
1923- . . . . CLC 28, 43
See also CANR 21; CA 13-16R; DLB 13

Mortimer, Penelope (Ruth) 1918- . . . . CLC 5
See also CA 57-60

Mosher, Howard Frank 19??- . . . . . . CLC 62

Mosley, Nicholas 1923- . . . . CLC 43
See also CA 69-72; DLB 14

Moss, Howard
1922-1987 . . . . CLC 7, 14, 45, 50
See also CANR 1; CA 1-4R;
obituary CA 123; DLB 5

Motion, Andrew (Peter) 1952- . . . . . . CLC 47
See also DLB 40

Motley, Willard (Francis)
1912-1965 . . . . CLC 18
See also CA 117; obituary CA 106; DLB 76

Mott, Michael (Charles Alston)
1930- . . . . CLC 15, 34
See also CAAS 7; CANR 7, 29; CA 5-8R

Mowat, Farley (McGill) 1921- . . . . . CLC 26
See also CLR 20; CANR 4, 24; CA 1-4R;
SATA 3, 55; DLB 68; AAYA 1

Mphahlele, Es'kia 1919-
See Mphahlele, Ezekiel

Mphahlele, Ezekiel 1919- . . . . CLC 25
See also BLC 2; CANR 26; CA 81-84

Mqhayi, S(amuel) E(dward) K(rune Loliwe)
1875-1945 . . . . TCLC 25
See also BLC 2

Mrozek, Slawomir 1930- . . . . CLC 3, 13
See also CAAS 10; CANR 29; CA 13-16R

Mtwa, Percy 19??- . . . . CLC 47

Mueller, Lisel 1924- . . . . CLC 13, 51
See also CA 93-96

Muir, Edwin 1887-1959 . . . . TCLC 2
See also CA 104; DLB 20

Muir, John 1838-1914 . . . . TCLC 28

Mujica Lainez, Manuel
1910-1984 . . . . CLC 31
See also CA 81-84; obituary CA 112

Mukherjee, Bharati 1940- . . . . CLC 53
See also CA 107; DLB 60

Muldoon, Paul 1951- . . . . CLC 32
See also CA 113, 129; DLB 40

Mulisch, Harry (Kurt Victor)
1927- . . . . CLC 42
See also CANR 6, 26; CA 9-12R

Mull, Martin 1943- . . . . CLC 17
See also CA 105

Munford, Robert 1737?-1783 . . . . LC 5
See also DLB 31

Munro, Alice (Laidlaw)
1931- . . . . CLC 6, 10, 19, 50; SSC 3
See also CA 33-36R; SATA 29; DLB 53

Munro, H(ector) H(ugh) 1870-1916
See Saki
See also CA 104; DLB 34

Murasaki, Lady c. 11th century- . . . CMLC 1

Murdoch, (Jean) Iris
1919- . . . . . . CLC 1, 2, 3, 4, 6, 8, 11, 15,
22, 31, 51
See also CANR 8; CA 13-16R; DLB 14

Murphy, Richard 1927- . . . . CLC 41
See also CA 29-32R; DLB 40

Murphy, Sylvia 19??- . . . . CLC 34

Murphy, Thomas (Bernard) 1935- . . . CLC 51
See also CA 101

Murray, Les(lie) A(llan) 1938- . . . . . CLC 40
See also CANR 11, 27; CA 21-24R

Murry, John Middleton
1889-1957 . . . . TCLC 16
See also CA 118

Musgrave, Susan 1951- . . . . CLC 13, 54
See also CA 69-72

Musil, Robert (Edler von)
1880-1942 . . . . TCLC 12
See also CA 109; DLB 81

Musset, (Louis Charles) Alfred de
1810-1857 . . . . NCLC 7

Myers, Walter Dean 1937- . . . . CLC 35
See also BLC 2; CLR 4, 16; CANR 20;
CA 33-36R; SAAS 2; SATA 27, 41;
DLB 33; AAYA 4

Nabokov, Vladimir (Vladimirovich)
1899-1977 . . . . CLC 1, 2, 3, 6, 8, 11, 15,
23, 44, 46, 64
See also CANR 20; CA 5-8R;
obituary CA 69-72; DLB 2; DLB-Y 80;
DLB-DS 3; CDALB 1941-1968

Nagy, Laszlo 1925-1978 . . . . CLC 7
See also CA 129; obituary CA 112

Naipaul, Shiva(dhar Srinivasa)
1945-1985 . . . . CLC 32, 39
See also CA 110, 112; obituary CA 116;
DLB-Y 85

Naipaul, V(idiadhar) S(urajprasad)
1932- . . . . CLC 4, 7, 9, 13, 18, 37
See also CANR 1; CA 1-4R; DLB-Y 85

Nakos, Ioulia 1899?-
See Nakos, Lilika

Nakos, Lilika 1899?- . . . . CLC 29

Nakou, Lilika 1899?-
See Nakos, Lilika

Narayan, R(asipuram) K(rishnaswami)
1906- . . . . CLC 7, 28, 47
See also CA 81-84

Nash, (Frediric) Ogden 1902-1971 . . CLC 23
See also CAP 1; CA 13-14;
obituary CA 29-32R; SATA 2, 46;
DLB 11

Nathan, George Jean 1882-1958 . . . TCLC 18
See also CA 114

Natsume, Kinnosuke 1867-1916
See Natsume, Soseki
See also CA 104

Natsume, Soseki 1867-1916 . . . . . TCLC 2, 10
See also Natsume, Kinnosuke

Natti, (Mary) Lee 1919-
See Kingman, (Mary) Lee
See also CANR 2; CA 7-8R

Naylor, Gloria 1950- . . . . CLC 28, 52
See also BLC 3; CANR 27; CA 107;
AAYA 6

Neff, Debra 1972- . . . . CLC 59

Neihardt, John G(neisenau)
1881-1973 . . . . CLC 32
See also CAP 1; CA 13-14; DLB 9, 54

Nekrasov, Nikolai Alekseevich
1821-1878 . . . . NCLC 11

Nelligan, Emile 1879-1941 . . . . TCLC 14
See also CA 114; DLB 92

Nelson, Willie 1933- . . . . CLC 17
See also CA 107

Nemerov, Howard 1920- . . . . CLC 2, 6, 9, 36
See also CANR 1, 27; CA 1-4R; CABS 2;
DLB 5, 6; DLB-Y 83

Neruda, Pablo
1904-1973 . . . . . CLC 1, 2, 5, 7, 9, 28, 62
See also CAP 2; CA 19-20;
obituary CA 45-48

Nerval, Gerard de 1808-1855 . . . . . . NCLC 1

Nervo, (Jose) Amado (Ruiz de)
1870-1919 . . . . TCLC 11
See also CA 109

Neufeld, John (Arthur) 1938- . . . . . . CLC 17
See also CANR 11; CA 25-28R; SAAS 3;
SATA 6

Neville, Emily Cheney 1919- . . . . CLC 12
See also CANR 3; CA 5-8R; SAAS 2;
SATA 1

Newbound, Bernard Slade 1930-
See Slade, Bernard
See also CA 81-84

Newby, P(ercy) H(oward)
1918- . . . . CLC 2, 13
See also CA 5-8R; DLB 15

Newlove, Donald 1928- . . . . CLC 6
See also CANR 25; CA 29-32R

Newlove, John (Herbert) 1938- . . . . . CLC 14
See also CANR 9, 25; CA 21-24R

Newman, Charles 1938- . . . . CLC 2, 8
See also CA 21-24R

Newman, Edwin (Harold) 1919- . . . . CLC 14
See also CANR 5; CA 69-72

Newton, Suzanne 1936- . . . . CLC 35
See also CANR 14; CA 41-44R; SATA 5

Ngema, Mbongeni 1955- . . . . CLC 57

Author Index

Peacock, Molly　1947-............ **CLC 60**
See also CA 103

Peacock, Thomas Love
1785-1886 .... **NCLC 22**

Peake, Mervyn　1911-1968...... **CLC 7, 54**
See also CANR 3; CA 5-8R;
obituary CA 25-28R; SATA 23; DLB 15

Pearce, (Ann) Philippa　1920-...... **CLC 21**
See also Christie, (Ann) Philippa
See also CLR 9; CA 5-8R; SATA 1

Pearl, Eric　1934-
See Elman, Richard

Pearson, T(homas) R(eid)　1956- .... **CLC 39**
See also CA 120, 130

Peck, John　1941- .... **CLC 3**
See also CANR 3; CA 49-52

Peck, Richard　1934-............. **CLC 21**
See also CLR 15; CANR 19; CA 85-88;
SAAS 2; SATA 18; AAYA 1

Peck, Robert Newton　1928-....... **CLC 17**
See also CA 81-84; SAAS 1; SATA 21;
AAYA 3

Peckinpah, (David) Sam(uel)
1925-1984 .... **CLC 20**
See also CA 109; obituary CA 114

Pedersen, Knut　1859-1952
See Hamsun, Knut
See also CA 104, 109, 119

Peguy, Charles (Pierre)
1873-1914 .... **TCLC 10**
See also CA 107

Pepys, Samuel　1633-1703.......... **LC 11**

Percy, Walker
1916-1990 ... **CLC 2, 3, 6, 8, 14, 18, 47, 65**
See also CANR 1, 23; CA 1-4R;
obituary CA 131; DLB 2; DLB-Y 80

Perec, Georges　1936-1982 .... **CLC 56**
See also DLB 83

Pereda, Jose Maria de
1833-1906 .... **TCLC 16**

Perelman, S(idney) J(oseph)
1904-1979 ... **CLC 3, 5, 9, 15, 23, 44, 49**
See also CANR 18; CA 73-76;
obituary CA 89-92; DLB 11, 44

Peret, Benjamin　1899-1959 ...... **TCLC 20**
See also CA 117

Peretz, Isaac Leib　1852?-1915..... **TCLC 16**
See also CA 109

Perez, Galdos Benito　1853-1920 ... **TCLC 27**
See also CA 125

Perrault, Charles　1628-1703 .... **LC 2**
See also SATA 25

Perse, St.-John　1887-1975.... **CLC 4, 11, 46**
See also Leger, (Marie-Rene) Alexis
Saint-Leger

Pesetsky, Bette　1932-............. **CLC 28**

Peshkov, Alexei Maximovich　1868-1936
See Gorky, Maxim
See also CA 105

Pessoa, Fernando (Antonio Nogueira)
1888-1935 .... **TCLC 27**
See also CA 125

Peterkin, Julia (Mood)　1880-1961... **CLC 31**
See also CA 102; DLB 9

Peters, Joan K.　1945-............. **CLC 39**

Peters, Robert L(ouis)　1924-....... **CLC 7**
See also CAAS 8; CA 13-16R

Petofi, Sandor　1823-1849........ **NCLC 21**

Petrakis, Harry Mark　1923-....... **CLC 3**
See also CANR 4, 30; CA 9-12R

Petrov, Evgeny　1902-1942........ **TCLC 21**

Petry, Ann (Lane)　1908- ...... **CLC 1, 7, 18**
See also CLR 12; CAAS 6; CANR 4;
CA 5-8R; SATA 5; DLB 76

Petursson, Halligrimur　1614-1674 .... **LC 8**

Philipson, Morris (H.)　1926-....... **CLC 53**
See also CANR 4; CA 1-4R

Phillips, Jayne Anne　1952-.... **CLC 15, 33**
See also CANR 24; CA 101; DLB-Y 80

Phillips, Robert (Schaeffer)　1938-... **CLC 28**
See also CANR 8; CA 17-20R

Pica, Peter　1925-
See Aldiss, Brian W(ilson)

Piccolo, Lucio　1901-1969.......... **CLC 13**
See also CA 97-100

Pickthall, Marjorie (Lowry Christie)
1883-1922 .... **TCLC 21**
See also CA 107; DLB 92

Pico della Mirandola, Giovanni
1463-1494 .... **LC 15**

Piercy, Marge
1936-......... **CLC 3, 6, 14, 18, 27, 62**
See also CAAS 1; CANR 13; CA 21-24R

Pilnyak, Boris　1894-1937?........ **TCLC 23**

Pincherle, Alberto　1907- .... **CLC 11, 18**
See also Moravia, Alberto
See also CA 25-28R

Pineda, Cecile　1942-.............. **CLC 39**
See also CA 118

Pinero, Miguel (Gomez)
1946-1988 .... **CLC 4, 55**
See also CANR 29; CA 61-64;
obituary CA 125

Pinero, Sir Arthur Wing
1855-1934 .... **TCLC 32**
See also CA 110; DLB 10

Pinget, Robert　1919- .... **CLC 7, 13, 37**
See also CA 85-88; DLB 83

Pink Floyd........................ **CLC 35**

Pinkney, Edward　1802-1828 ..... **NCLC 31**

Pinkwater, D(aniel) M(anus)
1941- .... **CLC 35**
See also Pinkwater, Manus
See also CLR 4; CANR 12; CA 29-32R;
SAAS 3; SATA 46; AAYA 1

Pinkwater, Manus　1941-
See Pinkwater, D(aniel) M(anus)
See also SATA 8

Pinsky, Robert　1940-........ **CLC 9, 19, 38**
See also CAAS 4; CA 29-32R; DLB-Y 82

Pinter, Harold
1930- ..... **CLC 1, 3, 6, 9, 11, 15, 27, 58**
See also CA 5-8R; DLB 13

Pirandello, Luigi　1867-1936..... **TCLC 4, 29**
See also CA 104

Pirsig, Robert M(aynard)　1928- ... **CLC 4, 6**
See also CA 53-56; SATA 39

Pisarev, Dmitry Ivanovich
1840-1868 .... **NCLC 25**

Pix, Mary (Griffith)　1666-1709...... **LC 8**
See also DLB 80

Plaidy, Jean　1906-
See Hibbert, Eleanor (Burford)

Plant, Robert　1948- .... **CLC 12**

Plante, David (Robert)
1940- .... **CLC 7, 23, 38**
See also CANR 12; CA 37-40R; DLB-Y 83

Plath, Sylvia
1932-1963 .... **CLC 1, 2, 3, 5, 9, 11, 14, 17, 50, 51, 62; PC 1**
See also CAP 2; CA 19-20; DLB 5, 6;
CDALB 1941-1968

Platonov, Andrei (Platonovich)
1899-1951 .... **TCLC 14**
See also Klimentov, Andrei Platonovich
See also CA 108

Platt, Kin　1911- .... **CLC 26**
See also CANR 11; CA 17-20R; SATA 21

Plimpton, George (Ames)　1927-..... **CLC 36**
See also CA 21-24R; SATA 10

Plomer, William (Charles Franklin)
1903-1973 .... **CLC 4, 8**
See also CAP 2; CA 21-22; SATA 24;
DLB 20

Plumly, Stanley (Ross)　1939- ...... **CLC 33**
See also CA 108, 110; DLB 5

Poe, Edgar Allan
1809-1849 ... **NCLC 1, 16; PC 1; SSC 1**
See also SATA 23; DLB 3, 59, 73, 74;
CDALB 1640-1865

Pohl, Frederik　1919- .... **CLC 18**
See also CAAS 1; CANR 11; CA 61-64;
SATA 24; DLB 8

Poirier, Louis　1910-
See Gracq, Julien
See also CA 122, 126

Poitier, Sidney　1924?-............. **CLC 26**
See also CA 117

Polanski, Roman　1933- .... **CLC 16**
See also CA 77-80

Poliakoff, Stephen　1952-.......... **CLC 38**
See also CA 106; DLB 13

Police, The...................... **CLC 26**

Pollitt, Katha　1949-............. **CLC 28**
See also CA 120, 122

Pollock, Sharon　19??-............. **CLC 50**
See also DLB 60

Pomerance, Bernard　1940-........ **CLC 13**
See also CA 101

Ponge, Francis (Jean Gaston Alfred)
1899-...................... **CLC 6, 18**
See also CA 85-88; obituary CA 126

Pontoppidan, Henrik　1857-1943 ... **TCLC 29**
See also obituary CA 126

Poole, Josephine　1933-........... **CLC 17**
See also CANR 10; CA 21-24R; SAAS 2;
SATA 5

Popa, Vasko　1922-.............. **CLC 19**
See also CA 112

Ramos, Graciliano 1892-1953 ..... TCLC **32**

Rampersad, Arnold 19??-.......... CLC **44**

Ramuz, Charles-Ferdinand
1878-1947 .... TCLC **33**

Rand, Ayn 1905-1982........ CLC **3, 30, 44**
See also CANR 27; CA 13-16R;
obituary CA 105

Randall, Dudley (Felker) 1914-...... CLC **1**
See also CANR 23; CA 25-28R; DLB 41

Ransom, John Crowe
1888-1974 .... CLC **2, 4, 5, 11, 24**
See also CANR 6; CA 5-8R;
obituary CA 49-52; DLB 45, 63

Rao, Raja 1909- .... CLC **25, 56**
See also CA 73-76

Raphael, Frederic (Michael)
1931- .... CLC **2, 14**
See also CANR 1; CA 1-4R; DLB 14

Rathbone, Julian 1935- .... CLC **41**
See also CA 101

Rattigan, Terence (Mervyn)
1911-1977 .... CLC **7**
See also CA 85-88; obituary CA 73-76;
DLB 13

Ratushinskaya, Irina 1954- .... CLC **54**
See also CA 129

Raven, Simon (Arthur Noel)
1927- .... CLC **14**
See also CA 81-84

Rawley, Callman 1903-
See Rakosi, Carl
See also CANR 12; CA 21-24R

Rawlings, Marjorie Kinnan
1896-1953 .... TCLC **4**
See also YABC 1; CA 104; DLB 9, 22

Ray, Satyajit 1921-.............. CLC **16**
See also CA 114

Read, Herbert (Edward) 1893-1968 .. CLC **4**
See also CA 85-88; obituary CA 25-28R;
DLB 20

Read, Piers Paul 1941- ...... CLC **4, 10, 25**
See also CA 21-24R; SATA 21; DLB 14

Reade, Charles 1814-1884 .... NCLC **2**
See also DLB 21

Reade, Hamish 1936-
See Gray, Simon (James Holliday)

Reading, Peter 1946- .... CLC **47**
See also CA 103; DLB 40

Reaney, James 1926- .... CLC **13**
See also CA 41-44R; SATA 43; DLB 68

Rebreanu, Liviu 1885-1944 ...... TCLC **28**

Rechy, John (Francisco)
1934- .... CLC **1, 7, 14, 18**
See also CAAS 4; CANR 6; CA 5-8R;
DLB-Y 82

Redcam, Tom 1870-1933 .... TCLC **25**

Reddin, Keith 1956?- .... CLC **67**

Redgrove, Peter (William)
1932- .... CLC **6, 41**
See also CANR 3; CA 1-4R; DLB 40

Redmon (Nightingale), Anne
1943- .... CLC **22**
See also Nightingale, Anne Redmon
See also DLB-Y 86

Reed, Ishmael
1938- .... CLC **2, 3, 5, 6, 13, 32, 60**
See also CANR 25; CA 21-24R; DLB 2, 5,
33

Reed, John (Silas) 1887-1920 ...... TCLC **9**
See also CA 106

Reed, Lou 1944-................. CLC **21**

Reeve, Clara 1729-1807 .... NCLC **19**
See also DLB 39

Reid, Christopher 1949-........... CLC **33**
See also DLB 40

Reid Banks, Lynne 1929-
See Banks, Lynne Reid
See also CANR 6, 22; CA 1-4R; SATA 22

Reiner, Max 1900-
See Caldwell, (Janet Miriam) Taylor
(Holland)

Reizenstein, Elmer Leopold 1892-1967
See Rice, Elmer

Remark, Erich Paul 1898-1970
See Remarque, Erich Maria

Remarque, Erich Maria
1898-1970 .... CLC **21**
See also CA 77-80; obituary CA 29-32R;
DLB 56

Remizov, Alexey (Mikhailovich)
1877-1957 .... TCLC **27**
See also CA 125

Renan, Joseph Ernest
1823-1892 .... NCLC **26**

Renard, Jules 1864-1910 .... TCLC **17**
See also CA 117

Renault, Mary 1905-1983 .... CLC **3, 11, 17**
See also Challans, Mary
See also DLB-Y 83

Rendell, Ruth 1930- .... CLC **28, 48**
See also Vine, Barbara
See also CA 109; DLB 87

Renoir, Jean 1894-1979 .... CLC **20**
See also CA 129; obituary CA 85-88

Resnais, Alain 1922-.............. CLC **16**

Reverdy, Pierre 1899-1960 .... CLC **53**
See also CA 97-100; obituary CA 89-92

Rexroth, Kenneth
1905-1982 ...... CLC **1, 2, 6, 11, 22, 49**
See also CANR 14; CA 5-8R;
obituary CA 107; DLB 16, 48; DLB-Y 82;
CDALB 1941-1968

Reyes, Alfonso 1889-1959 .... TCLC **33**

Reyes y Basoalto, Ricardo Eliecer Neftali
1904-1973
See Neruda, Pablo

Reymont, Wladyslaw Stanislaw
1867-1925 .... TCLC **5**
See also CA 104

Reynolds, Jonathan 1942?- ...... CLC **6, 38**
See also CANR 28; CA 65-68

Reynolds, (Sir) Joshua 1723-1792.... LC **15**

Reynolds, Michael (Shane) 1937- ... CLC **44**
See also CANR 9; CA 65-68

Reznikoff, Charles 1894-1976 .... CLC **9**
See also CAP 2; CA 33-36;
obituary CA 61-64; DLB 28, 45

Rezzori, Gregor von 1914-........ CLC **25**
See also CA 122

Rhys, Jean
1890-1979 ...... CLC **2, 4, 6, 14, 19, 51**
See also CA 25-28R; obituary CA 85-88;
DLB 36

Ribeiro, Darcy 1922-.............. CLC **34**
See also CA 33-36R

Ribeiro, Joao Ubaldo (Osorio Pimentel)
1941- .... CLC **10, 67**
See also CA 81-84

Ribman, Ronald (Burt) 1932- .... CLC **7**
See also CA 21-24R

Rice, Anne 1941- .... CLC **41**
See also CANR 12; CA 65-68

Rice, Elmer 1892-1967.......... CLC **7, 49**
See also CAP 2; CA 21-22;
obituary CA 25-28R; DLB 4, 7

Rice, Tim 1944- .... CLC **21**
See also CA 103

Rich, Adrienne (Cecile)
1929- .... CLC **3, 6, 7, 11, 18, 36**
See also CANR 20; CA 9-12R; DLB 5, 67

Richard, Keith 1943- .... CLC **17**
See also CA 107

Richards, David Adam 1950-....... CLC **59**
See also CA 93-96; DLB 53

Richards, I(vor) A(rmstrong)
1893-1979 .... CLC **14, 24**
See also CA 41-44R; obituary CA 89-92;
DLB 27

Richards, Keith 1943-
See Richard, Keith
See also CA 107

Richardson, Dorothy (Miller)
1873-1957 .... TCLC **3**
See also CA 104; DLB 36

Richardson, Ethel 1870-1946
See Richardson, Henry Handel
See also CA 105

Richardson, Henry Handel
1870-1946 .... TCLC **4**
See also Richardson, Ethel

Richardson, Samuel 1689-1761 .... LC **1**
See also DLB 39

Richler, Mordecai
1931- .... CLC **3, 5, 9, 13, 18, 46**
See also CLR 17; CA 65-68; SATA 27, 44;
DLB 53

Richter, Conrad (Michael)
1890-1968 .... CLC **30**
See also CANR 23; CA 5-8R;
obituary CA 25-28R; SATA 3; DLB 9

Richter, Johann Paul Friedrich 1763-1825
See Jean Paul

Riddell, Mrs. J. H. 1832-1906..... TCLC **40**

Riding, Laura 1901-............. CLC **3, 7**
See also Jackson, Laura (Riding)

Riefenstahl, Berta Helene Amalia
1902- .... CLC **16**
See also Riefenstahl, Leni
See also CA 108

Riefenstahl, Leni 1902- .... CLC **16**
See also Riefenstahl, Berta Helene Amalia
See also CA 108

Shaara, Michael (Joseph) 1929- .... **CLC 15**
See also CA 102; obituary CA 125;
DLB-Y 83

Shackleton, C. C. 1925-
See Aldiss, Brian W(ilson)

Shacochis, Bob 1951-............. **CLC 39**
See also CA 119, 124

Shaffer, Anthony 1926- .... **CLC 19**
See also CA 110, 116; DLB 13

Shaffer, Peter (Levin)
1926- .... **CLC 5, 14, 18, 37, 60**
See also CANR 25; CA 25-28R; DLB 13

Shalamov, Varlam (Tikhonovich)
1907?-1982.................. **CLC 18**
See also obituary CA 105

Shamlu, Ahmad 1925- .... **CLC 10**

Shammas, Anton 1951-............ **CLC 55**

Shange, Ntozake 1948-....... **CLC 8, 25, 38**
See also CA 85-88; DLB 38

Shapcott, Thomas W(illiam) 1935- .. **CLC 38**
See also CA 69-72

Shapiro, Karl (Jay) 1913- ..**CLC 4, 8, 15, 53**
See also CAAS 6; CANR 1; CA 1-4R;
DLB 48

Sharp, William 1855-1905 .... **TCLC 39**

Sharpe, Tom 1928-............... **CLC 36**
See also CA 114; DLB 14

Shaw, (George) Bernard
1856-1950 .... **TCLC 3, 9, 21**
See also CA 104, 109, 119; DLB 10, 57

Shaw, Henry Wheeler
1818-1885 .... **NCLC 15**
See also DLB 11

Shaw, Irwin 1913-1984....... **CLC 7, 23, 34**
See also CANR 21; CA 13-16R;
obituary CA 112; DLB 6; DLB-Y 84;
CDALB 1941-1968

Shaw, Robert 1927-1978 .... **CLC 5**
See also CANR 4; CA 1-4R;
obituary CA 81-84; DLB 13, 14

Shawn, Wallace 1943- .... **CLC 41**
See also CA 112

Sheed, Wilfrid (John Joseph)
1930-........ **CLC 2, 4, 10, 53**
See also CA 65-68; DLB 6

Sheffey, Asa 1913-1980
See Hayden, Robert (Earl)

Sheldon, Alice (Hastings) B(radley)
1915-1987
See Tiptree, James, Jr.
See also CA 108; obituary CA 122

Shelley, Mary Wollstonecraft Godwin
1797-1851 .... **NCLC 14**
See also SATA 29

Shelley, Percy Bysshe
1792-1822 .... **NCLC 18**

Shepard, Jim 19??-................ **CLC 36**

Shepard, Lucius 19??-............. **CLC 34**
See also CA 128

Shepard, Sam
1943- .... **CLC 4, 6, 17, 34, 41, 44**
See also CANR 22; CA 69-72; DLB 7

Shepherd, Michael 1927-
See Ludlum, Robert

Sherburne, Zoa (Morin) 1912-...... **CLC 30**
See also CANR 3; CA 1-4R; SATA 3

Sheridan, Frances 1724-1766........ **LC 7**
See also DLB 39, 84

Sheridan, Richard Brinsley
1751-1816 .... **NCLC 5; DC 1**
See also DLB 89

Sherman, Jonathan Marc 1970?-.... **CLC 55**

Sherman, Martin 19??-............. **CLC 19**
See also CA 116

Sherwin, Judith Johnson 1936-... **CLC 7, 15**
See also CA 25-28R

Sherwood, Robert E(mmet)
1896-1955 .... **TCLC 3**
See also CA 104; DLB 7, 26

Shiel, M(atthew) P(hipps)
1865-1947 .... **TCLC 8**
See also CA 106

Shiga, Naoya 1883-1971.......... **CLC 33**
See also CA 101; obituary CA 33-36R

Shimazaki, Haruki 1872-1943
See Shimazaki, Toson
See also CA 105

Shimazaki, Toson 1872-1943...... **TCLC 5**
See also Shimazaki, Haruki

Sholokhov, Mikhail (Aleksandrovich)
1905-1984 .... **CLC 7, 15**
See also CA 101; obituary CA 112;
SATA 36

Sholom Aleichem 1859-1916 .... **TCLC 1, 35**
See also Rabinovitch, Sholem

Shreve, Susan Richards 1939-...... **CLC 23**
See also CAAS 5; CANR 5; CA 49-52;
SATA 41, 46

Shue, Larry 1946-1985............ **CLC 52**
See also obituary CA 117

Shulman, Alix Kates 1932- ...... **CLC 2, 10**
See also CA 29-32R; SATA 7

Shuster, Joe 1914- .... **CLC 21**

Shute (Norway), Nevil 1899-1960... **CLC 30**
See also Norway, Nevil Shute
See also CA 102; obituary CA 93-96

Shuttle, Penelope (Diane) 1947- ..... **CLC 7**
See also CA 93-96; DLB 14, 40

Siegel, Jerome 1914- .... **CLC 21**
See also CA 116

Sienkiewicz, Henryk (Adam Aleksander Pius)
1846-1916 .... **TCLC 3**
See also CA 104

Sigal, Clancy 1926-............... **CLC 7**
See also CA 1-4R

Sigourney, Lydia (Howard Huntley)
1791-1865 .... **NCLC 21**
See also DLB 1, 42, 73

Siguenza y Gongora, Carlos de
1645-1700 .... **LC 8**

Sigurjonsson, Johann 1880-1919... **TCLC 27**

Sikelianos, Angelos 1884-1951 .... **TCLC 39**

Silkin, Jon 1930- .... **CLC 2, 6, 43**
See also CAAS 5; CA 5-8R; DLB 27

Silko, Leslie Marmon 1948- .... **CLC 23**
See also CA 115, 122

Sillanpaa, Franz Eemil 1888-1964... **CLC 19**
See also CA 129; obituary CA 93-96

Sillitoe, Alan
1928- .... **CLC 1, 3, 6, 10, 19, 57**
See also CAAS 2; CANR 8, 26; CA 9-12R;
DLB 14

Silone, Ignazio 1900-1978 .... **CLC 4**
See also CAAS 2; CANR 26; CAP 2;
CA 25-28, 11-12R,; obituary CA 81-84

Silver, Joan Micklin 1935- .... **CLC 20**
See also CA 114, 121

Silverberg, Robert 1935- .... **CLC 7**
See also CAAS 3; CANR 1, 20; CA 1-4R;
SATA 13; DLB 8

Silverstein, Alvin 1933- .... **CLC 17**
See also CANR 2; CA 49-52; SATA 8

Silverstein, Virginia B(arbara Opshelor)
1937-........................ **CLC 17**
See also CANR 2; CA 49-52; SATA 8

Simak, Clifford D(onald)
1904-1988 .... **CLC 1, 55**
See also CANR 1; CA 1-4R;
obituary CA 125; DLB 8

Simenon, Georges (Jacques Christian)
1903-1989 .... **CLC 1, 2, 3, 8, 18, 47**
See also CA 85-88; obituary CA 129;
DLB 72

Simenon, Paul 1956?-
See The Clash

Simic, Charles 1938-....... **CLC 6, 9, 22, 49**
See also CAAS 4; CANR 12; CA 29-32R

Simmons, Charles (Paul) 1924-..... **CLC 57**
See also CA 89-92

Simmons, Dan 1948-.............. **CLC 44**

Simmons, James (Stewart Alexander)
1933-........................ **CLC 43**
See also CA 105; DLB 40

Simms, William Gilmore
1806-1870 .... **NCLC 3**
See also DLB 3, 30, 59, 73

Simon, Carly 1945-................ **CLC 26**
See also CA 105

Simon, Claude (Henri Eugene)
1913-................. **CLC 4, 9, 15, 39**
See also CA 89-92; DLB 83

Simon, (Marvin) Neil
1927-................ **CLC 6, 11, 31, 39**
See also CA 21-24R; DLB 7

Simon, Paul 1941- .... **CLC 17**
See also CA 116

Simonon, Paul 1956?-
See The Clash

Simpson, Louis (Aston Marantz)
1923-................. **CLC 4, 7, 9, 32**
See also CAAS 4; CANR 1; CA 1-4R;
DLB 5

Simpson, Mona (Elizabeth) 1957-... **CLC 44**
See also CA 122

Simpson, N(orman) F(rederick)
1919-........................ **CLC 29**
See also CA 11-14R; DLB 13

Sinclair, Andrew (Annandale)
1935-...................... **CLC 2, 14**
See also CAAS 5; CANR 14; CA 9-12R;
DLB 14

Tey, Josephine 1897-1952 .... TCLC **14**
See also Mackintosh, Elizabeth

Thackeray, William Makepeace
1811-1863 .... NCLC **5, 14, 22**
See also SATA 23; DLB 21, 55

Thakura, Ravindranatha 1861-1941
See Tagore, (Sir) Rabindranath
See also CA 104

Thelwell, Michael (Miles) 1939- .... CLC **22**
See also CA 101

Theroux, Alexander (Louis)
1939- .... CLC **2, 25**
See also CANR 20; CA 85-88

Theroux, Paul
1941- .... CLC **5, 8, 11, 15, 28, 46**
See also CANR 20; CA 33-36R; SATA 44;
DLB 2

Thesen, Sharon 1946- .... CLC **56**

Thibault, Jacques Anatole Francois
1844-1924
See France, Anatole
See also CA 106

Thiele, Colin (Milton) 1920- .... CLC **17**
See also CANR 12; CA 29-32R; SAAS 2;
SATA 14

Thomas, Audrey (Grace)
1935- .... CLC **7, 13, 37**
See also CA 21-24R; DLB 60

Thomas, D(onald) M(ichael)
1935- .... CLC **13, 22, 31**
See also CANR 17; CA 61-64; DLB 40

Thomas, Dylan (Marlais)
1914-1953 ..... TCLC **1, 8; PC 2; SSC 3**
See also CA 104, 120; SATA 60; DLB 13,
20

Thomas, Edward (Philip)
1878-1917 .... TCLC **10**
See also CA 106; DLB 19

Thomas, John Peter 1928-
See Thomas, Piri

Thomas, Joyce Carol 1938- .... CLC **35**
See also CLR 19; CA 113, 116; SAAS 7;
SATA 40; DLB 33

Thomas, Lewis 1913- .... CLC **35**
See also CA 85-88

Thomas, Piri 1928- .... CLC **17**
See also CA 73-76

Thomas, R(onald) S(tuart)
1913- .... CLC **6, 13, 48**
See also CAAS 4; CA 89-92; DLB 27

Thomas, Ross (Elmore) 1926- ...... CLC **39**
See also CANR 22; CA 33-36R

Thompson, Ernest 1860-1946
See Seton, Ernest (Evan) Thompson

Thompson, Francis (Joseph)
1859-1907 .... TCLC **4**
See also CA 104; DLB 19

Thompson, Hunter S(tockton)
1939- .... CLC **9, 17, 40**
See also CANR 23; CA 17-20R

Thompson, Judith 1954- .... CLC **39**

Thomson, James 1700-1748 .... LC **16**
See also DLB 95

Thomson, James 1834-1882 ...... NCLC **18**
See also DLB 35

Thoreau, Henry David
1817-1862 .... NCLC **7, 21**
See also DLB 1; CDALB 1640-1865

Thurber, James (Grover)
1894-1961 ...... CLC **5, 11, 25; SSC 1**
See also CANR 17; CA 73-76; SATA 13;
DLB 4, 11, 22

Thurman, Wallace 1902-1934 ...... TCLC **6**
See also CA 104, 124; DLB 51

Tieck, (Johann) Ludwig
1773-1853 .... NCLC **5**
See also DLB 90

Tilghman, Christopher 1948?- ...... CLC **65**

Tillinghast, Richard 1940- .... CLC **29**
See also CANR 26; CA 29-32R

Timrod, Henry 1828-1867 .... NCLC **25**

Tindall, Gillian 1938- .... CLC **7**
See also CANR 11; CA 21-24R

Tiptree, James, Jr. 1915-1987 ... CLC **48, 50**
See also Sheldon, Alice (Hastings) B(radley)
See also DLB 8

**Tocqueville, Alexis (Charles Henri Maurice
Clerel, Comte) de** 1805-1859.. NCLC **7**

Tolkien, J(ohn) R(onald) R(euel)
1892-1973 ...... CLC **1, 2, 3, 8, 12, 38**
See also CAP 2; CA 17-18;
obituary CA 45-48; SATA 2, 24, 32;
obituary SATA 24; DLB 15

Toller, Ernst 1893-1939 .... TCLC **10**
See also CA 107

Tolson, Melvin B(eaunorus)
1900?-1966................... CLC **36**
See also CA 124; obituary CA 89-92;
DLB 48, 124

Tolstoy, (Count) Alexey Nikolayevich
1883-1945 .... TCLC **18**
See also CA 107

Tolstoy, (Count) Leo (Lev Nikolaevich)
1828-1910 .... TCLC **4, 11, 17, 28**
See also CA 104, 123; SATA 26

Tomlin, Lily 1939- .... CLC **17**

Tomlin, Mary Jean 1939-
See Tomlin, Lily
See also CA 117

Tomlinson, (Alfred) Charles
1927- .... CLC **2, 4, 6, 13, 45**
See also CA 5-8R; DLB 40

Toole, John Kennedy
1937-1969 .... CLC **19, 64**
See also CA 104; DLB-Y 81

Toomer, Jean
1894-1967 ..... CLC **1, 4, 13, 22; SSC 1**
See also CA 85-88; DLB 45, 51

Torrey, E. Fuller 19??- .... CLC **34**
See also CA 119

Tosei 1644-1694
See Basho, Matsuo

Tournier, Michel 1924- ...... CLC **6, 23, 36**
See also CANR 3; CA 49-52; SATA 23;
DLB 83

Townsend, Sue 1946- .... CLC **61**
See also CA 119, 127; SATA 48, 55

Townshend, Peter (Dennis Blandford)
1945- .... CLC **17, 42**
See also CA 107

Tozzi, Federigo 1883-1920....... TCLC **31**

Traill, Catharine Parr
1802-1899 .... NCLC **31**
See also DLB 99

Trakl, Georg 1887-1914........... TCLC **5**
See also CA 104

Transtromer, Tomas (Gosta)
1931- .... CLC **52, 65**
See also CA 129; brief entry CA 117

Traven, B. 1890-1969 .... CLC **8, 11**
See also CAP 2; CA 19-20;
obituary CA 25-28R; DLB 9, 56

Tremain, Rose 1943-............. CLC **42**
See also CA 97-100; DLB 14

Tremblay, Michel 1942-........... CLC **29**
See also CA 116; DLB 60

Trevanian 1925- .... CLC **29**
See also CA 108

Trevor, William 1928- ..... CLC **7, 9, 14, 25**
See also Cox, William Trevor
See also DLB 14

Trifonov, Yuri (Valentinovich)
1925-1981 .... CLC **45**
See also obituary CA 103, 126

Trilling, Lionel 1905-1975 .... CLC **9, 11, 24**
See also CANR 10; CA 9-12R;
obituary CA 61-64; DLB 28, 63

Trogdon, William 1939-
See Heat Moon, William Least
See also CA 115, 119

Trollope, Anthony 1815-1882 .. NCLC **6, 33**
See also SATA 22; DLB 21, 57

Trollope, Frances 1780-1863 ..... NCLC **30**
See also DLB 21

Trotsky, Leon (Davidovich)
1879-1940 .... TCLC **22**
See also CA 118

Trotter (Cockburn), Catharine
1679-1749 .... LC **8**
See also DLB 84

Trow, George W. S. 1943-........ CLC **52**
See also CA 126

Troyat, Henri 1911-.............. CLC **23**
See also CANR 2; CA 45-48

Trudeau, G(arretson) B(eekman) 1948-
See Trudeau, Garry
See also CA 81-84; SATA 35

Trudeau, Garry 1948-............. CLC **12**
See also Trudeau, G(arretson) B(eekman)

Truffaut, Francois 1932-1984....... CLC **20**
See also CA 81-84; obituary CA 113

Trumbo, Dalton 1905-1976 .... CLC **19**
See also CANR 10; CA 21-24R;
obituary CA 69-72; DLB 26

Trumbull, John 1750-1831....... NCLC **30**
See also DLB 31

Tryon, Thomas 1926-........... CLC **3, 11**
See also CA 29-32R

Ts'ao Hsueh-ch'in 1715?-1763........ LC **1**

Voight, Ellen Bryant   1943- .... CLC **54**
See also CANR 11; CA 69-72

Voigt, Cynthia   1942- .... CLC **30**
See also CANR 18; CA 106; SATA 33, 48;
AAYA 3

Voinovich, Vladimir (Nikolaevich)
1932- .... CLC **10, 49**
See also CA 81-84

Voltaire 1694-1778 .... LC **14**

Von Daeniken, Erich   1935-
See Von Daniken, Erich
See also CANR 17; CA 37-40R

Von Daniken, Erich   1935- .... CLC **30**
See also Von Daeniken, Erich

Vonnegut, Kurt, Jr.
1922- ..... CLC **1, 2, 3, 4, 5, 8, 12, 22,
40, 60; SSC 8**
See also CANR 1, 25; CA 1-4R; DLB 2, 8;
DLB-Y 80; DLB-DS 3;
CDALB 1968-1988; AAYA 6

Vorster, Gordon   1924- .... CLC **34**

Voznesensky, Andrei   1933- ... CLC **1, 15, 57**
See also CA 89-92

Waddington, Miriam   1917- .... CLC **28**
See also CANR 12, 30; CA 21-24R;
DLB 68

Wagman, Fredrica   1937- .... CLC **7**
See also CA 97-100

Wagner, Richard   1813-1883 .... NCLC **9**

Wagner-Martin, Linda   1936- .... CLC **50**

Wagoner, David (Russell)
1926- .... CLC **3, 5, 15**
See also CAAS 3; CANR 2; CA 1-4R;
SATA 14; DLB 5

Wah, Fred(erick James)   1939- ..... CLC **44**
See also CA 107; DLB 60

Wahloo, Per   1926-1975 .... CLC **7**
See also CA 61-64

Wahloo, Peter   1926-1975
See Wahloo, Per

Wain, John (Barrington)
1925- .... CLC **2, 11, 15, 46**
See also CAAS 4; CANR 23; CA 5-8R;
DLB 15, 27

Wajda, Andrzej   1926- .... CLC **16**
See also CA 102

Wakefield, Dan   1932- .... CLC **7**
See also CAAS 7; CA 21-24R

Wakoski, Diane
1937- .... CLC **2, 4, 7, 9, 11, 40**
See also CAAS 1; CANR 9; CA 13-16R;
DLB 5

Walcott, Derek (Alton)
1930- .... CLC **2, 4, 9, 14, 25, 42, 67**
See also CANR 26; CA 89-92; DLB-Y 81

Waldman, Anne   1945- .... CLC **7**
See also CA 37-40R; DLB 16

Waldo, Edward Hamilton   1918-
See Sturgeon, Theodore (Hamilton)

Walker, Alice
1944- ...... CLC **5, 6, 9, 19, 27, 46, 58;
SSC 5**
See also CANR 9, 27; CA 37-40R;
SATA 31; DLB 6, 33; CDALB 1968-1988

Walker, David Harry   1911- .... CLC **14**
See also CANR 1; CA 1-4R; SATA 8

Walker, Edward Joseph   1934-
See Walker, Ted
See also CANR 12; CA 21-24R

Walker, George F.   1947- .... CLC **44, 61**
See also CANR 21; CA 103; DLB 60

Walker, Joseph A.   1935- .... CLC **19**
See also CANR 26; CA 89-92; DLB 38

Walker, Margaret (Abigail)
1915- .... CLC **1, 6**
See also CANR 26; CA 73-76; DLB 76

Walker, Ted   1934- .... CLC **13**
See also Walker, Edward Joseph
See also DLB 40

Wallace, David Foster   1962- .... CLC **50**

Wallace, Irving   1916- .... CLC **7, 13**
See also CAAS 1; CANR 1; CA 1-4R

Wallant, Edward Lewis
1926-1962 .... CLC **5, 10**
See also CANR 22; CA 1-4R; DLB 2, 28

Walpole, Horace   1717-1797 .... LC **2**
See also DLB 39

Walpole, (Sir) Hugh (Seymour)
1884-1941 .... TCLC **5**
See also CA 104; DLB 34

Walser, Martin   1927- .... CLC **27**
See also CANR 8; CA 57-60; DLB 75

Walser, Robert   1878-1956 .... TCLC **18**
See also CA 118; DLB 66

Walsh, Gillian Paton   1939-
See Walsh, Jill Paton
See also CA 37-40R; SATA 4

Walsh, Jill Paton   1939- .... CLC **35**
See also CLR 2; SAAS 3

Wambaugh, Joseph (Aloysius, Jr.)
1937- .... CLC **3, 18**
See also CA 33-36R; DLB 6; DLB-Y 83

Ward, Arthur Henry Sarsfield   1883-1959
See Rohmer, Sax
See also CA 108

Ward, Douglas Turner   1930- .... CLC **19**
See also CA 81-84; DLB 7, 38

Warhol, Andy   1928-1987 .... CLC **20**
See also CA 89-92; obituary CA 121

Warner, Francis (Robert le Plastrier)
1937- .... CLC **14**
See also CANR 11; CA 53-56

Warner, Marina   1946- .... CLC **59**
See also CANR 21; CA 65-68

Warner, Rex (Ernest)   1905-1986.... CLC **45**
See also CA 89-92; obituary CA 119;
DLB 15

Warner, Susan   1819-1885 .... NCLC **31**
See also DLB 3, 42

Warner, Sylvia Townsend
1893-1978 .... CLC **7, 19**
See also CANR 16; CA 61-64;
obituary CA 77-80; DLB 34

Warren, Mercy Otis   1728-1814... NCLC **13**
See also DLB 31

Warren, Robert Penn
1905-1989 ... CLC **1, 4, 6, 8, 10, 13, 18,
39, 53, 59; SSC 4**
See also CANR 10; CA 13-16R. 129. 130;
SATA 46; DLB 2, 48; DLB-Y 80;
CDALB 1968-1987

Warton, Thomas   1728-1790 .... LC **15**

Washington, Booker T(aliaferro)
1856-1915 .... TCLC **10**
See also CA 114, 125; SATA 28

Wassermann, Jakob   1873-1934 ..... TCLC **6**
See also CA 104; DLB 66

Wasserstein, Wendy   1950- ...... CLC **32, 59**
See also CA 121; CABS 3

Waterhouse, Keith (Spencer)
1929- .... CLC **47**
See also CA 5-8R; DLB 13, 15

Waters, Roger   1944-
See Pink Floyd

Wa Thiong'o, Ngugi
1938- .... CLC **3, 7, 13, 36**
See also Ngugi, James (Thiong'o); Ngugi wa
Thiong'o

Watkins, Paul   1964- .... CLC **55**

Watkins, Vernon (Phillips)
1906-1967 .... CLC **43**
See also CAP 1; CA 9-10;
obituary CA 25-28R; DLB 20

Waugh, Auberon (Alexander)   1939- ... CLC **7**
See also CANR 6, 22; CA 45-48; DLB 14

Waugh, Evelyn (Arthur St. John)
1903-1966 ... CLC **1, 3, 8, 13, 19, 27, 44**
See also CANR 22; CA 85-88;
obituary CA 25-28R; DLB 15

Waugh, Harriet   1944- .... CLC **6**
See also CANR 22; CA 85-88

Webb, Beatrice (Potter)
1858-1943 .... TCLC **22**
See also CA 117

Webb, Charles (Richard)   1939- ...... CLC **7**
See also CA 25-28R

Webb, James H(enry), Jr.   1946- .... CLC **22**
See also CA 81-84

Webb, Mary (Gladys Meredith)
1881-1927 .... TCLC **24**
See also CA 123; DLB 34

Webb, Phyllis   1927- .... CLC **18**
See also CANR 23; CA 104; DLB 53

Webb, Sidney (James)
1859-1947 .... TCLC **22**
See also CA 117

Webber, Andrew Lloyd   1948- ...... CLC **21**

Weber, Lenora Mattingly
1895-1971 .... CLC **12**
See also CAP 1; CA 19-20;
obituary CA 29-32R; SATA 2;
obituary SATA 26

Webster, Noah   1758-1843 .... NCLC **30**
See also DLB 1, 37, 42, 43, 73

Wedekind, (Benjamin) Frank(lin)
1864-1918 .... TCLC **7**
See also CA 104

Weidman, Jerome   1913- .... CLC **7**
See also CANR 1; CA 1-4R; DLB 28

Weil, Simone 1909-1943......... TCLC 23
See also CA 117

Weinstein, Nathan Wallenstein 1903?-1940
See West, Nathanael
See also CA 104

Weir, Peter 1944-................ CLC 20
See also CA 113, 123

Weiss, Peter (Ulrich)
1916-1982 .... CLC 3, 15, 51
See also CANR 3; CA 45-48;
obituary CA 106; DLB 69

Weiss, Theodore (Russell)
1916- .... CLC 3, 8, 14
See also CAAS 2; CA 9-12R; DLB 5

Welch, (Maurice) Denton
1915-1948 .... TCLC 22
See also CA 121

Welch, James 1940-......... CLC 6, 14, 52
See also CA 85-88

Weldon, Fay
1933- .... CLC 6, 9, 11, 19, 36, 59
See also CANR 16; CA 21-24R; DLB 14

Wellek, Rene 1903- .... CLC 28
See also CAAS 7; CANR 8; CA 5-8R;
DLB 63

Weller, Michael 1942-......... CLC 10, 53
See also CA 85-88

Weller, Paul 1958-............... CLC 26

Wellershoff, Dieter 1925-.......... CLC 46
See also CANR 16; CA 89-92

Welles, (George) Orson
1915-1985 .... CLC 20
See also CA 93-96; obituary CA 117

Wellman, Mac 1945- .... CLC 65

Wellman, Manly Wade 1903-1986 .. CLC 49
See also CANR 6, 16; CA 1-4R;
obituary CA 118; SATA 6, 47

Wells, Carolyn 1862-1942 .... TCLC 35
See also CA 113; DLB 11

Wells, H(erbert) G(eorge)
1866-1946 ...... TCLC 6, 12, 19; SSC 6
See also CA 110, 121; SATA 20; DLB 34,
70

Wells, Rosemary 1943-............ CLC 12
See also CLR 16; CA 85-88; SAAS 1;
SATA 18

Welty, Eudora (Alice)
1909- .... CLC 1, 2, 5, 14, 22, 33; SSC 1
See also CA 9-12R; CABS 1; DLB 2;
DLB-Y 87; CDALB 1941-1968

Wen I-to 1899-1946 .... TCLC 28

Werfel, Franz (V.) 1890-1945 ..... TCLC 8
See also CA 104; DLB 81

Wergeland, Henrik Arnold
1808-1845 .... NCLC 5

Wersba, Barbara 1932-............ CLC 30
See also CLR 3; CANR 16; CA 29-32R;
SAAS 2; SATA 1, 58; DLB 52

Wertmuller, Lina 1928- .... CLC 16
See also CA 97-100

Wescott, Glenway 1901-1987....... CLC 13
See also CANR 23; CA 13-16R;
obituary CA 121; DLB 4, 9

Wesker, Arnold 1932- .... CLC 3, 5, 42
See also CAAS 7; CANR 1; CA 1-4R;
DLB 13

Wesley, Richard (Errol) 1945-....... CLC 7
See also CA 57-60; DLB 38

Wessel, Johan Herman 1742-1785 .... LC 7

West, Anthony (Panther)
1914-1987 .... CLC 50
See also CANR 3, 19; CA 45-48; DLB 15

West, Jessamyn 1907-1984 ...... CLC 7, 17
See also CA 9-12R; obituary CA 112;
obituary SATA 37; DLB 6; DLB-Y 84

West, Morris L(anglo) 1916-..... CLC 6, 33
See also CA 5-8R; obituary CA 124

West, Nathanael 1903?-1940 .... TCLC 1, 14
See also Weinstein, Nathan Wallenstein
See also CA 125, 140; DLB 4, 9, 28

West, Paul 1930- .... CLC 7, 14
See also CAAS 7; CANR 22; CA 13-16R;
DLB 14

West, Rebecca 1892-1983 .. CLC 7, 9, 31, 50
See also CANR 19; CA 5-8R;
obituary CA 109; DLB 36; DLB-Y 83

Westall, Robert (Atkinson) 1929-... CLC 17
See also CLR 13; CANR 18; CA 69-72;
SAAS 2; SATA 23

Westlake, Donald E(dwin)
1933- .... CLC 7, 33
See also CANR 16; CA 17-20R

Westmacott, Mary 1890-1976
See Christie, (Dame) Agatha (Mary
Clarissa)

Whalen, Philip 1923- .... CLC 6, 29
See also CANR 5; CA 9-12R; DLB 16

Wharton, Edith (Newbold Jones)
1862-1937 .... TCLC 3, 9, 27; SSC 6
See also CA 104; DLB 4, 9, 12, 78;
CDALB 1865-1917

Wharton, William 1925-........ CLC 18, 37
See also CA 93-96; DLB-Y 80

Wheatley (Peters), Phillis
1753?-1784................. LC 3; PC 3
See also DLB 31, 50; CDALB 1640-1865

Wheelock, John Hall 1886-1978.... CLC 14
See also CANR 14; CA 13-16R;
obituary CA 77-80; DLB 45

Whelan, John 1900-
See O'Faolain, Sean

Whitaker, Rodney 1925-
See Trevanian

White, E(lwyn) B(rooks)
1899-1985 .... CLC 10, 34, 39
See also CLR 1; CANR 16; CA 13-16R;
obituary CA 116; SATA 2, 29, 44;
obituary SATA 44; DLB 11, 22

White, Edmund III 1940-.......... CLC 27
See also CANR 3, 19; CA 45-48

White, Patrick (Victor Martindale)
1912-1990 ..... CLC 3, 4, 5, 7, 9, 18, 65
See also CA 81-84; obituary CA 132

White, T(erence) H(anbury)
1906-1964 .... CLC 30
See also CA 73-76; SATA 12

White, Terence de Vere 1912-...... CLC 49
See also CANR 3; CA 49-52

White, Walter (Francis)
1893-1955 .... TCLC 15
See also CA 115, 124; DLB 51

White, William Hale 1831-1913
See Rutherford, Mark
See also CA 121

Whitehead, E(dward) A(nthony)
1933- .... CLC 5
See also CA 65-68

Whitemore, Hugh 1936-.......... CLC 37

Whitman, Sarah Helen
1803-1878 .... NCLC 19
See also DLB 1

Whitman, Walt
1819-1892 .... NCLC 4, 31; PC 3
See also SATA 20; DLB 3, 64;
CDALB 1640-1865

Whitney, Phyllis A(yame) 1903-.... CLC 42
See also CANR 3, 25; CA 1-4R; SATA 1,
30

Whittemore, (Edward) Reed (Jr.)
1919- .... CLC 4
See also CAAS 8; CANR 4; CA 9-12R;
DLB 5

Whittier, John Greenleaf
1807-1892 .... NCLC 8
See also DLB 1; CDALB 1640-1865

Wicker, Thomas Grey 1926-
See Wicker, Tom
See also CANR 21; CA 65-68

Wicker, Tom 1926-................ CLC 7
See also Wicker, Thomas Grey

Wideman, John Edgar
1941- .... CLC 5, 34, 36, 67
See also CANR 14; CA 85-88; DLB 33

Wiebe, Rudy (H.) 1934-...... CLC 6, 11, 14
See also CA 37-40R; DLB 60

Wieland, Christoph Martin
1733-1813 .... NCLC 17

Wieners, John 1934-............... CLC 7
See also CA 13-16R; DLB 16

Wiesel, Elie(zer) 1928-..... CLC 3, 5, 11, 37
See also CAAS 4; CANR 8; CA 5-8R;
SATA 56; DLB 83; DLB-Y 87

Wiggins, Marianne 1948-.......... CLC 57

Wight, James Alfred 1916-
See Herriot, James
See also CA 77-80; SATA 44

Wilbur, Richard (Purdy)
1921- .... CLC 3, 6, 9, 14, 53
See also CANR 2; CA 1-4R; CABS 2;
SATA 9; DLB 5

Wild, Peter 1940-................. CLC 14
See also CA 37-40R; DLB 5

Wilde, Oscar (Fingal O'Flahertie Wills)
1854-1900 .... TCLC 1, 8, 23, 41
See also CA 119; brief entry CA 104;
SATA 24; DLB 10, 19, 34, 57

Wilder, Billy 1906-............... CLC 20
See also Wilder, Samuel
See also DLB 26

Wilder, Samuel 1906-
See Wilder, Billy
See also CA 89-92

Wilder, Thornton (Niven)
    1897-1975 . . . . . **CLC 1, 5, 6, 10, 15, 35;**
                                                   DC 1
    See also CA 13-16R; obituary CA 61-64;
    DLB 4, 7, 9

Wiley, Richard 1944- . . . . **CLC 44**
    See also CA 121, 129

Wilhelm, Kate 1928- . . . . **CLC 7**
    See also CAAS 5; CANR 17; CA 37-40R;
    DLB 8

Willard, Nancy 1936- . . . . **CLC 7, 37**
    See also CLR 5; CANR 10; CA 89-92;
    SATA 30, 37; DLB 5, 52

Williams, C(harles) K(enneth)
    1936- . . . . **CLC 33, 56**
    See also CA 37-40R; DLB 5

Williams, Charles (Walter Stansby)
    1886-1945 . . . . **TCLC 1, 11**
    See also CA 104

Williams, Ella Gwendolen Rees 1890-1979
    See Rhys, Jean

Williams, (George) Emlyn
    1905-1987 . . . . **CLC 15**
    See also CA 104, 123; DLB 10, 77

Williams, Hugo 1942- . . . . **CLC 42**
    See also CA 17-20R; DLB 40

Williams, John A(lfred) 1925- . . . . **CLC 5, 13**
    See also CAAS 3; CANR 6, 26; CA 53-56;
    DLB 2, 33

Williams, Jonathan (Chamberlain)
    1929- . . . . **CLC 13**
    See also CANR 8; CA 9-12R; DLB 5

Williams, Joy 1944- . . . . **CLC 31**
    See also CANR 22; CA 41-44R

Williams, Norman 1952- . . . . **CLC 39**
    See also CA 118

Williams, Paulette 1948-
    See Shange, Ntozake

Williams, Tennessee
    1911-1983 . . . . **CLC 1, 2, 5, 7, 8, 11, 15,**
                                      19, 30, 39, 45
    See also CA 5-8R; obituary CA 108; DLB 7;
    DLB-Y 83; DLB-DS 4;
    CDALB 1941-1968

Williams, Thomas (Alonzo) 1926- . . . **CLC 14**
    See also CANR 2; CA 1-4R

Williams, Thomas Lanier 1911-1983
    See Williams, Tennessee

Williams, William Carlos
    1883-1963 . . . **CLC 1, 2, 5, 9, 13, 22, 42,**
                                                          67
    See also CA 89-92; DLB 4, 16, 54, 86;
    CDALB 1917-1929

Williamson, David 1932- . . . . **CLC 56**

Williamson, Jack 1908- . . . . **CLC 29**
    See also Williamson, John Stewart
    See also DLB 8

Williamson, John Stewart 1908-
    See Williamson, Jack
    See also CANR 123; CA 17-20R

Willingham, Calder (Baynard, Jr.)
    1922- . . . . **CLC 5, 51**
    See also CANR 3; CA 5-8R; DLB 2, 44

Wilson, A(ndrew) N(orman) 1950- . . **CLC 33**
    See also CA 112, 122; DLB 14

Wilson, Andrew 1948-
    See Wilson, Snoo

Wilson, Angus (Frank Johnstone)
    1913- . . . . **CLC 2, 3, 5, 25, 34**
    See also CANR 21; CA 5-8R; DLB 15

Wilson, August 1945- . . . . **CLC 39, 50, 63**
    See also CA 115, 122

Wilson, Brian 1942- . . . . **CLC 12**

Wilson, Colin 1931- . . . . **CLC 3, 14**
    See also CAAS 5; CANR 1, 122; CA 1-4R;
    DLB 14

Wilson, Edmund
    1895-1972 . . . . **CLC 1, 2, 3, 8, 24**
    See also CANR 1; CA 1-4R;
    obituary CA 37-40R; DLB 63

Wilson, Ethel Davis (Bryant)
    1888-1980 . . . . **CLC 13**
    See also CA 102; DLB 68

Wilson, John 1785-1854 . . . . **NCLC 5**

Wilson, John (Anthony) Burgess 1917-
    See Burgess, Anthony
    See also CANR 2; CA 1-4R

Wilson, Lanford 1937- . . . . **CLC 7, 14, 36**
    See also CA 17-20R; DLB 7

Wilson, Robert (M.) 1944- . . . . **CLC 7, 9**
    See also CANR 2; CA 49-52

Wilson, Sloan 1920- . . . . **CLC 32**
    See also CANR 1; CA 1-4R

Wilson, Snoo 1948- . . . . **CLC 33**
    See also CA 69-72

Wilson, William S(mith) 1932- . . . . . **CLC 49**
    See also CA 81-84

Winchilsea, Anne (Kingsmill) Finch, Countess
    of 1661-1720 . . . . **LC 3**

Winters, Janet Lewis 1899-
    See Lewis (Winters), Janet
    See also CAP 1; CA 9-10

Winters, (Arthur) Yvor
    1900-1968 . . . . **CLC 4, 8, 32**
    See also CAP 1; CA 11-12;
    obituary CA 25-28R; DLB 48

Winterson, Jeannette 1959- . . . . **CLC 64**

Wiseman, Frederick 1930- . . . . **CLC 20**

Wister, Owen 1860-1938 . . . . **TCLC 21**
    See also CA 108; DLB 9, 78

Witkiewicz, Stanislaw Ignacy
    1885-1939 . . . . **TCLC 8**
    See also CA 105; DLB 83

Wittig, Monique 1935?- . . . . **CLC 22**
    See also CA 116; DLB 83

Wittlin, Joseph 1896-1976 . . . . **CLC 25**
    See also Wittlin, Jozef

Wittlin, Jozef 1896-1976
    See Wittlin, Joseph
    See also CANR 3; CA 49-52;
    obituary CA 65-68

Wodehouse, (Sir) P(elham) G(renville)
    1881-1975 . . . **CLC 1, 2, 5, 10, 22; SSC 2**
    See also CANR 3; CA 45-48;
    obituary CA 57-60; SATA 22; DLB 34

Woiwode, Larry (Alfred) 1941- . . . **CLC 6, 10**
    See also CANR 16; CA 73-76; DLB 6

Wojciechowska, Maia (Teresa)
    1927- . . . . **CLC 26**
    See also CLR 1; CANR 4; CA 9-12R;
    SAAS 1; SATA 1, 28

Wolf, Christa 1929- . . . . **CLC 14, 29, 58**
    See also CA 85-88; DLB 75

Wolfe, Gene (Rodman) 1931- . . . . . . **CLC 25**
    See also CAAS 9; CANR 6; CA 57-60;
    DLB 8

Wolfe, George C. 1954- . . . . **CLC 49**

Wolfe, Thomas (Clayton)
    1900-1938 . . . . **TCLC 4, 13, 29**
    See also CA 104; DLB 9; DLB-Y 85;
    DLB-DS 2

Wolfe, Thomas Kennerly, Jr. 1931-
    See Wolfe, Tom
    See also CANR 9; CA 13-16R

Wolfe, Tom 1931- . . . **CLC 1, 2, 9, 15, 35, 51**
    See also Wolfe, Thomas Kennerly, Jr.

Wolff, Geoffrey (Ansell) 1937- . . . . . **CLC 41**
    See also CA 29-32R

Wolff, Tobias (Jonathan Ansell)
    1945- . . . . **CLC 39, 64**
    See also CA 114, 117

Wolfram von Eschenbach
    c. 1170-c. 1220 . . . . **CMLC 5**

Wolitzer, Hilma 1930- . . . . **CLC 17**
    See also CANR 18; CA 65-68; SATA 31

Wollstonecraft Godwin, Mary
    1759-1797 . . . . **LC 5**
    See also DLB 39

Wonder, Stevie 1950- . . . . **CLC 12**
    See also Morris, Steveland Judkins

Wong, Jade Snow 1922- . . . . **CLC 17**
    See also CA 109

Woodcott, Keith 1934-
    See Brunner, John (Kilian Houston)

Woolf, (Adeline) Virginia
    1882-1941 . . . . **TCLC 1, 5, 20; SSC 7**
    See also CA 130; brief entry CA 104;
    DLB 36

Woollcott, Alexander (Humphreys)
    1887-1943 . . . . **TCLC 5**
    See also CA 105; DLB 29

Wordsworth, Dorothy
    1771-1855 . . . . **NCLC 25**

Wordsworth, William 1770-1850 . . **NCLC 12**

Wouk, Herman 1915- . . . . **CLC 1, 9, 38**
    See also CANR 6; CA 5-8R; DLB-Y 82

Wright, Charles 1935- . . . . **CLC 6, 13, 28**
    See also CAAS 7; CA 29-32R; DLB-Y 82

Wright, Charles (Stevenson) 1932- . . **CLC 49**
    See also CA 9-12R; DLB 33

Wright, James (Arlington)
    1927-1980 . . . . **CLC 3, 5, 10, 28**
    See also CANR 4; CA 49-52;
    obituary CA 97-100; DLB 5

Wright, Judith 1915- . . . . **CLC 11, 53**
    See also CA 13-16R; SATA 14

Wright, L(aurali) R. 1939- . . . . **CLC 44**

Wright, Richard (Nathaniel)
    1908-1960 . . . **CLC 1, 3, 4, 9, 14, 21, 48;**
                                                       SSC 2
    See also CA 108; DLB 76; DLB-DS 2

Literary Criticism Series
Cumulative Topic Index

This index lists all topic entries in the Gale Literary Criticism Series *Contemporary Literary Criticism, Literature Criticism from 1400 to 1800, Nineteenth-Century Literature Criticism,* and *Twentieth-Century Literary Criticism.*

Topic Index

NCLC Cumulative Nationality Index

Nationality Index

NCLC Cumulative Title Index

Title Index

"Une charogne" ("A Carrion"; "A Rotting
  Corpse") (Baudelaire) 6:93, 115; 29:83-4,
  103
The Charterhouse of Parma (Stendhal)
  See *La chartreuse de Parme*
La chartreuse de Parme (*The Charterhouse of
  Parma*) (Stendhal) 23:345-56, 358-59, 361-
  63, 365, 368-71, 374, 376, 378, 383-85, 389,
  391, 393, 397, 400-02, 404-05, 408-17, 424-
  26
Charts de la patrie (Chateaubriand) 3:126
"La chasse" (Bertrand) 31:49
"La chasse au caribou" (Gobineau) 17:80,
  92-3, 103
"Le chasse de l'aigle" (Leconte de Lisle)
  29:216, 225
"La chasse spirituelle" (Rimbaud) 4:484
Le château de Combourg (Chateaubriand)
  3:133
Le château de la misère (Gautier) 1:346
"Le château de Robert le diable" (Nodier)
  19:378
*Chateaubriand et son groupe littéraire sous
  l'empire* (Sainte-Beuve) 5:338, 342, 349
De Chatillon (Hemans) 29:201
"Le châtiment de Tartufe" (Rimbaud) 4:471
Les châtiments (Hugo) 3:256, 262-64, 271,
  273; 21:214
Chatterton (Vigny) 7:471, 473-74, 479
"The Chaunt of Cholera" (Banim) 13:129
The Chaunt of the Cholera: Songs for Ireland
  (Banim) 13:129
"Che stai?" ("How Are You?") (Foscolo)
  8:278-79
Cheap Repository Tracts (More) 27:350-51
Checkmate (Le Fanu) 9:301, 304, 312, 317
Le chef-d'oeuvre inconnu (Balzac) 5:67, 79-80
"Le 'chêne" (Lamartine) 11:255, 270, 279
"Cheramour" (Leskov) 25:239
"Les chercheuses de poux" (Rimbaud) 4:454,
  458
Chérie (Goncourt) 7:173-74, 183, 188
Chester Rand (Alger) 8:44, 46
The Chestnut Tree (Tyler) 3:574
"Chesuncook" (Thoreau) 7:368
Le chevalier de maison-rouge (*Marie Antoinette;
  or, The Chevalier of the Red House: A Tale
  of the French Revolution*) (Dumas) 11:53,
  68, 76-77
Le chevalier des touches (Barbey D'Aurevilly)
  1:70-73
Le chevalier d'Harmental (Dumas) 11:51-52,
  60, 63, 68-69, 74
Les chevaliers (Lamartine) 11:289
"La chevelure" (Baudelaire) 6:79, 117-18,
  128; 29:73, 103, 109
"Chevelure" (Maupassant) 1:449
"Chevy Chase" (Maginn) 8:439
*Chidiock Tichbourne; or, The Catholic
  Conspiracy* (Clarke) 19:240
"The Child" (Kivi)
  See "Lapsi"
"Child and Hind" (Campbell) 19:190
"The Child Angel: A Dream" (Lamb)
  10:404, 435-36
Child from the Sea (Castro)
  See *La hija del mar*
"Child Harold" (Clare) 9:108, 112
The Child in the House (Pater)
  See *An Imaginary Portrait*
"Child Left in a Storm" (Sigourney) 21:293
The Child of Love (Kotzebue)

See *Das Kind der Liebe*
A Child of the Age (*Leicester, an
  Autobiography*) (Adams) 33:4, 10, 14, 16-
  17, 19-20
"The Child that Loved a Grave" (O'Brien)
  21:236
"Child Wife" (Verlaine) 2:632
Childe Harold's Pilgrimage: A Romaunt
  (Byron) 2:59, 62, 69, 71-72, 74-75, 81-82,
  85-86, 91-92, 94-95, 103; 12:73, 76, 88, 92,
  95, 102, 103, 104, 109, 112, 113, 114, 122,
  128, 129, 138, 143
Childe Harold's Pilgrimage: Canto the Second
  (Byron) 2:96, 99, 95
"'Childe Roland to the Dark Tower Came'"
  (Browning) 19:99, 106, 117, 141, 153-54
Childhood Years (Leskov)
  See *Detskie gody*
"The Children" (Very) 9:383
"Children of Adam" (Whitman) 4:551-52,
  557, 568-69, 577, 593, 599-601, 603-04
"The Children of Mount Ida" (Child) 6:201
"The Children of Venus" (Landor) 14:181
"The Children's Dance" (Wilson) 5:567
"The Children's Hour" (Longfellow) 2:490,
  499
"The Children's Joke" (Alcott) 6:16
"The Child's Answer" (Very) 9:387
A Child's Garden of Verses (Stevenson) 5:395-
  96, 402, 404, 413, 428
A Child's History of England (Dickens)
  18:117, 134
"Child's Play" (Stevenson) 5:389, 395
"The Child's Purchase" (Patmore) 9:352,
  357, 360
"A Child's Thought of God" (Browning)
  1:127
Les chimères (Nerval) 1:480, 483-88
"The Chimes" (Dickens) 3:145, 165
"The Chimney Sweeper" (Blake) 13:219-21,
  242
"Chione" (Lampman) 25:169
"Chiron" (Hölderlin) 16:191
"The Choice" (Allingham) 25:14
"The Choice" (Lazarus) 8:421
"The Choice" (Rossetti) 4:514, 529
The Choice: A Poem on Shelley's Death
  (Shelley) 14:272
Choses vues (*Things Seen*) (Hugo) 3:265
"Le Chretien Mourant" (Lamartine) 11:245
"Le Christ aux Oliviers" (Nerval) 1:478, 486
"Christ Stilling the Tempest" (Hemans)
  29:206
"Christabel" (Coleridge) 9:133-34, 138-40,
  142-44, 146, 148-50, 152, 156, 179-81, 183,
  187, 192-94
"Christabel" (Rossetti) 4:510
Christabel. Kubla Khan. The Pains of Sleep
  (Coleridge) 9:133-34
Die Christenheit oder Europa (*Christianity or
  Europe*) (Novalis) 13:386, 388, 402
*Christian Life: Its Course, Its Hindrances, and
  Its Helps* (Arnold) 18:7, 10, 15
*Christian Life: Its Hopes, Its Fears, and Its
  Close* (Arnold) 18:15
Christian Morals (More) 27:334
*The Christian Physiologist: Tales Illustrative of
  the Five Senses* (Griffin) 7:201, 204, 214,
  218
"The Christian Slave!" (Whittier) 8:489, 510
"Christian Worship" (Channing) 17:47
"Christianity and Progress" (Patmore) 9:342

Christianity or Europe (Novalis)
  See *Die Christenheit oder Europa*
Christianity Unveiled (Godwin) 14:56
Christie Johnstone (Reade) 2:532-34, 536,
  539-41, 543, 545, 548
"Christine" (Leconte de Lisle) 29:220
*Christine; ou, Stockholm, Fontainebleau, et
  Rome* (*Stockholm, Fontainebleau, et Rome*)
  (Dumas) 11:42, 47, 57, 63
"Christmas" (Irving) 19:351
"Christmas" (Timrod) 25:362, 364, 372, 382-
  83, 386, 388
"Christmas" (Very) 9:383
"The Christmas Banquet" (Hawthorne) 2:296
Christmas Books (Thackeray) 5:469
A Christmas Carol (Dickens) 3:144-45, 152,
  165, 173; 26:222
Christmas Chimes (Dickens) 3:149
"Christmas Creek" (Kendall) 12:194, 199
"Christmas Day" (Irving) 19:328
"Christmas Day" (Martineau) 26:313
"The Christmas Dinner" (Irving) 19:328
"Christmas Eve" (Browning) 19:132
"Christmas Eve" (Gogol) 5:217, 231
"Christmas Eve" (Wergeland) 5:537
Christmas-Eve and Easter-Day (Browning)
  19:130, 132
Christmas Stories (Leskov) 25:228
"Christopher at the Lakes" (Wilson) 5:568
"Christopher in His Aviary" (Wilson) 5:563
"Christopher North in His Sporting Jacket"
  (Wilson) 5:560
"Christopher on Colonsay" (Wilson) 5:568
"Christ's Hospital Five and Thirty Years Ago"
  (Lamb) 10:407-08, 435-36
"Christ's Night" (Saltykov) 16:369
Christus: A Mystery (Longfellow) 2:484, 495,
  497-98
"The Chronicle of Ladislas Kun" (Petőfi)
  See "Kun László Krónikája"
The Chronicle of the Conquest of Granada
  (Irving) 2:380, 384, 387
Chronicles of Carlingford (Oliphant) 11:429,
  432, 438-40, 445, 449, 453-54, 459
Chronicles of the Canongate (Scott) 15:269,
  277, 322
Chronicles of the Clovernook (Jerrold) 2:400,
  402, 404-05
Chronique du temps de Charles IX (*1572: A
  Chronicle of the Times of Charles the Ninth*)
  (Mérimée) 6:352-53, 356-58, 360, 362-63,
  365-66, 369
Chroniques italiennes (Stendhal) 23:381, 409
"Chrysaor" (Landor) 14:181, 183-84, 190
Chto delat'? (*What Is to Be Done? Tales about
  New People*) (Chernyshevsky) 1:159-68
"Church of Brou" (Arnold) 6:42, 44, 66-67,
  72; 29:36
La chute d'un ange (*The Fall of an Angel*)
  (Lamartine) 11:252-53, 255, 268, 271, 273-
  76, 278, 283-85, 287, 289
"Ciel brouillé" (Baudelaire) 6:80
"Le ciel ef Penfer" (Mérimée) 6:351, 362-63
La ciguë (Augier) 31:4, 8, 10-11, 14-15, 23,
  29, 34
El cinco de Agosto (*The Fifth of August*)
  (Tamayo y Baus) 1:565-66, 571
Cinderella (Grabbe)
  See *Aschenbrödel*
Cinq-Mars; ou, Une conjuration sous Louis XIII
  ("The Spider and the Fly") (Vigny) 7:467-
  71, 473, 477

Title Index

Title Index

Title Index

Title Index

Title Index

Title Index

Title Index

Title Index

Title Index

Title Index

"The Well at the World's End" (Morris)
4:424-36, 438

"Well! Dad's Dead" (Harris) 23:142, 146, 160

"The Well of Pen-Morfa" (Gaskell) 5:205

"Well! Thou Art Happy" (Byron) 2:77

"Welland River" (Morris) 4:431, 444

"Welldean Hall" (Hogg) 4:283

"Wellington's Funeral" (Rossetti) 4:518

Welsh Melodies (Hemans) 29:205

"The Welshmen of Tirawley" (Ferguson)
See "The Vengeance of the Welshmen of Tirawley"

Die Weltalter (*The Ages of the World*)
(Schelling) 30:141, 170

"Wen Gott betrügt, ist wohl betrogen" ("Is It True, Ye Gods, Who Treat Us") (Clough) 27:103, 107

"Wenn der lahme Weber träumt, er webe"
(Brentano) 1:105

"Wenn der Sturm das Meer umschlinget"
(Brentano) 1:104

The Wept of Wish-ton-Wish (*The Borderers; or, The Wept of Wish-ton-Wish*) (Cooper)
1:199, 221-22

"Wer ist der Verräter?" (Goethe) 4:194

"Die Werbung" (Lenau) 16:264, 285

"Das Werden im Vergehen" (Hölderlin)
16:178

"We're a Million in the Field" (Foster)
26:288

Werner (Byron) 2:67, 79-80, 90

West-Eastern Divan (Goethe)
See *West--östlicher Divan*

West--östlicher Divan (*West-Eastern Divan*)
(Goethe) 4:173, 193

"The West Wind" (Bryant) 6:176

The Western Journals of Washington Irving
(Irving) 2:382

"Westminster Abbey" (Irving) 2:381; 19:347

"Westminster Bridge" (Wordsworth) 12:431

Westward Ho! (Paulding) 2:527-30

"Wettgesang" (Schlegel) 15:229

"Weyla's Song" (Mörike)
See "Gesang Weylas"

The Whale (Melville) 3:329

"The Wharf Rat" (O'Brien) 21:234

"What Befell" (O'Brien) 21:245

"What Can an Old Man Do But Die?" (Hood)
16:219

"What Daddy Does Is Always Right"
(Andersen) 7:34

"What Do Poets Want with Gold?"
(Lampman) 25:160, 188, 200, 216

"What Does an Author Need?" (Karamzin)
3:289

"What for Us, My Heart, Are Pools of Blood"
(Rimbaud) 4:486

"What Had I Been If Thou Were Not?"
(Novalis)
See "Was wär' ich ohne dich gewesen?"

"What I Lived For" (Thoreau) 7:352, 381

"What Is a Classic" (Sainte-Beuve) 5:350

What Is Enlightenment? (Kant) 27:219, 231, 237

"What Is Heaven" (Dickinson)
See "What Is 'Paradise'"

"What Is Oblornovism?" (Dobrolyubov)
5:140-41, 145, 147, 149, 151

What Is Orientation in Thinking? (Kant)
27:220

"What Is 'Paradise'" ("What Is Heaven")
(Dickinson) 21:41

"What Is Poetry" (Mill) 11:384

"What is Poetry?" (Timrod) 25:380

"What Is" *Really*" My Belief" (Landor)
14:201

"What is the People?" (Hazlitt) 29:184

"What Is There in the Distant Hills" (Clare)
9:124

What Is to Be Done? Tales about New People
(Chernyshevsky)
See *Chto delat'?*

"What Must a Fairy's Dream Be" (Foster)
26:287

"What One Says to the Poet on the Subject of Flowers" (Rimbaud) 4:486

"What Santa Claus Brought Me" (O'Brien)
21:246

"What Shall I Call You" (Petőfi)
See "Minek nevezzelek"

"What Ship Puzzled at Sea" (Whitman)
31:388

"What the Birds Said" (Whittier) 8:517

"What the Black Man Wants" (Douglass)
7:130

"What the Lord Lyndhurst Really Was"
(Bagehot) 10:58

"What the Moon Saw" (Andersen) 7:29

"What the Voice Said" (Whittier) 8:530

"What Was It? A Mystery" (O'Brien)
21:235-36, 238, 240, 242, 245-46, 248-51, 253

What Will He Do with It? (Bulwer-Lytton)
1:151

"What Would I Give?" (Rossetti) 2:575

"What's This Uproar Again?" (Petőfi)
See "Mi lárma ez megént?"

"When Even the Voice of Thoughts Is Silent"
(Eminescu) 33:247

"When He Who Adores Thee" (Moore)
6:391

"When I Am Dead, My Dearest, Sing No Sad Songs for Me" (Rossetti) 2:563

"When I Saw You" (Eminescu) 33:265

"When in Death I Shall Calm Recline"
(Moore) 6:389

"When Israel Came Out of Egypt" (Clough)
27:41, 106

"When Lilacs Last in the Dooryard Bloom'd"
(Whitman) 4:544, 559, 561, 569, 571, 579-80, 582, 592, 595, 602; 31:368, 370, 385, 388-91, 404-05, 408, 432

"When Old Corruption First Begun" (Blake)
13:182

"When Panting Sighs the Bosom Fill"
(Clough) 27:52, 106

"When Soft September" (Clough) 27:104

"When the Kye Comes Home" (Hogg) 4:286

"When the Yellowing Fields Billow"
(Lermontov) 5:295

"When We Husked the Corn" (O'Brien)
21:245

"When Will the Day Come?" (Dobrolyubov)
5:140, 149

"When Youthful Hope Is Fled" (Lockhart)
6:296

"Where Be You Going, You Devon Maid?"
(Keats) 8:360

"Where Gleaming Fields of Haze" (Thoreau)
7:384

"Where I Have Lost, I Softer Tread"
(Dickinson) 21:55

Where It Is Thin, There It Breaks (Turgenev)
21:428, 432

"Wherefore" (Lazarus) 8:418

"Wherefore" (Lermontov) 5:299

"Wherever I Go and Look" (Eichendorff)
8:210

"Which is the True One?" (Baudelaire)
29:110

Whims and Oddities (Hood) 16:202, 205, 208, 213, 219

Whimsicalities (Hood) 16:217, 238

"A Whirl-Blast from behind the Hill"
(Wordsworth) 12:446

"Whisperings in the Wattle-Boughs" (Gordon)
21:154, 160-61, 173, 181

The White Doe of Rylstone; or, The Fate of the Nortons (Wordsworth) 12:400, 407-08, 422, 460, 466

"The White Eagle" (Leskov)
See "Belyj orel"

White-Jacket; or, The World in a Man-of-War
(Melville) 3:328, 332-34, 337, 339, 342, 345, 347-49, 359-61, 363, 365, 371, 373; 12:281; 29:318, 322, 325, 327-28, 331-34, 340-41, 345, 348, 350, 354, 358, 360-64, 367-69, 372, 374, 378

White Lies (Reade) 2:534, 536, 549

"White Margaret" (Lampman) 25:183, 220

"White Mountains" (Whittier) 8:485

"White Nights" (Dostoevsky) 33:201

"The White Old Maid" (Hawthorne) 2:292, 322

"The White Ship" (Rossetti) 4:499-500, 506-08, 518, 525-26, 532

Whitehall; or, The Days of George IV (Maginn)
8:432, 436, 441

Whiteladies (Oliphant) 11:441, 446

"Whitman" (Thomson) 18:407

"The Whitsuntide Fire" (Kivi)
See "Helavalkea"

"Who Can Be Happy and Free in Russia?"
(Nekrasov)
See "Komu na Rusi zhit khorosho"

"Who Hath Ears to Hear Let Him Hear"
(Very) 9:381

"Who Is This Woman...?" (De Quincey) 4:88

Who Is to Blame? (Herzen) 10:321-23, 326-27, 331, 333-34, 348

"Who Killed Zebedee?" (Collins) 1:188

"Who Learns My Lesson Complete"
(Whitman) 31:419, 425

"Who Shall Deliver Me?" (Rossetti) 2:572

"Whoever Wants to Wander to Foreign Lands" (Eichendorff) 8:210

Whom to Marry and How to Get Married! or, The Adventures of a Lady in Search of a Good Husband (Mayhew) 31:160-61, 178, 191

"Why--Do They Shut Me Out of Heaven"
(Dickinson) 21:53, 56

"Why Do Ye Call the Poet Lonely?"
(Lampman) 25:216

"Why I Am a Liberal" (Browning) 19:110

"Why Lombard Street Is Sometimes Highly Excited and Sometimes Very Dull"
(Bagehot) 10:22

"Why Mr. Disraeli Has Succeeded" (Bagehot)
10:31, 58

"Why Should We Hurry--Why Indeed?"
(Dickinson) 21:66

"Why the Heroes of Romances Are Insipid"
(Hazlitt) 29:148

ISBN 0-8103-5833-6

9 780810 358331

90000>